11. Format for Bank Reconciliation:

Cash balance according to bank statement		$xxx
Add: Additions by depositor not on bank statement	$xx	
Bank errors	xx	xx
		$xxx
Deduct: Deductions by depositor not on bank statement	$xx	
Bank errors	xx	xx
Adjusted balance		$xxx
Cash balance according to depositor's records		$xxx
Add: Additions by bank not recorded by depositor	$xx	
Depositor errors	xx	xx
		$xxx
Deduct: Deductions by bank not recorded by depositor	$xx	
Depositor errors	xx	xx
Adjusted balance		$xxx

12. Inventory Costing Methods:

1. First-in, First-out (fifo)
2. Last-in, First-out (lifo)
3. Average Cost

13. Interest Computations:

Interest = Face Amount (or Principal) × Rate × Time

14. Methods of Determining Annual Depreciation:

STRAIGHT-LINE: $\frac{\text{Cost} - \text{Estimated Residual Value}}{\text{Estimated Life}}$

DECLINING-BALANCE: Rate* × Book Value at Beginning of Period

*Rate is commonly twice the straight-line rate (1 ÷ Estimated Life).

15. Cash Provided by Operations on Statement of Cash Flows (indirect method):

Net income, per income statement		$xx
Add: Depreciation of fixed assets	$xx	
Amortization of bond payable discount and intangible assets	xx	
Decreases in current assets (receivables, inventories, prepaid expenses)	xx	
Increases in current liabilities (accounts and notes payable, accrued liabilities)	xx	
Losses on disposal of assets and retirement of debt	xx	xx
Deduct: Amortization of bond payable premium	$xx	
Increases in current assets (receivables, inventories, prepaid expenses)	xx	
Decreases in current liabilities (accounts and notes payable, accrued liabilities)	xx	
Gains on disposal of assets and retirement of debt	xx	xx
Net cash flow from operating activities		$xx

16. Contribution Margin

Unit Cont. margin = Sellin

17. Break-Even Sales (Units) = $\frac{\text{Fixed Costs}}{\text{Unit Contribution Margin}}$

18. Sales (Units) = $\frac{\text{Fixed Costs} + \text{Target Profit}}{\text{Unit Contribution Margin}}$

19. Margin of Safety = $\frac{\text{Sales} - \text{Sales at Break-Even Point}}{\text{Sales}}$

20. Operating Leverage = $\frac{\text{Contribution Margin}}{\text{Operating Income}}$

21. Variances

Direct Materials Price Variance = (Actual Price per Unit – Standard Price) × Actual Quantity Used

Direct Materials Quantity Variance = (Actual Quantity Used – Standard Quantity) × Standard Price per Unit

Direct Labor Rate Variance = (Actual Rate per Hour – Standard Rate) × Actual Hours Worked

Direct Labor Time Variance = (Actual Hours Worked – Standard Hours) × Standard Rate per Hour

Variable Factory Overhead Controllable Variance = Actual Variable Factory Overhead – Budgeted Variable Factory Overhead for Actual Amount Produced

Fixed Factory Overhead Volume Variance = (100% of Normal Capacity – Std. Capacity for Amount Produced) × Std. Fixed Factory Overhead Rate

22. Rate of Return on Investment (ROI) = $\frac{\text{Income from Operations}}{\text{Invested Assets}}$

Alternative ROI Computation:

$$\text{ROI} = \frac{\text{Income from Operations}}{\text{Sales}} \times \frac{\text{Sales}}{\text{Invested Assets}}$$

23. Capital Investment Analysis Methods:

1. Methods That Ignore Present Values:
   A. Average Rate of Return Method
   B. Cash Payback Method
2. Methods That Use Present Values:
   A. Net Present Value Method
   B. Internal Rate of Return Method

24. Average Rate of Return = $\frac{\text{Estimated Average Annual Income}}{\text{Average Investment}}$

25. Present Value Index = $\frac{\text{Total Present Value of Net Cash Flow}}{\text{Amount to Be Invested}}$

26. Present Value Factor for an Annuity of $1 = $\frac{\text{Amount to Be Invested}}{\text{Equal Annual Net Cash Flows}}$

Success Stories Start Here

Warren
Reeve
Fess

19TH EDITION

Leaders for the Long Run

Staying Power The ability to survive and thrive in any business climate. It's a special quality that only a select few corporations enjoy. On the cover of this 19th edition of *Accounting,* we pay tribute to a number of firms that have prospered not for a few years, but for many decades. These firms embody the rare ability to build upon a strong product or service and evolve with changing social and market conditions. For instance, AT&T, once strictly a telephone company, also brought us the transistor, the laser, and innumerable other technology innovations. Procter and Gamble, which posted $35.8 billion in sales in 1997, was once just a small soap manufacturer.

Accounting has rare staying power, as well. This marks its 19th edition, going to print 69 years since the first edition was published in 1929. A lot has happened in American business and in the field of accounting since *Accounting* was introduced. Innumerable accounting texts have come and gone since then. But this special text has kept pace with the students, instructors, and business world it serves. As a result of these efforts, over 10 million students have been introduced to accounting via this text.

Make that 10 million and counting.

Putting People First

It is a common practice for authors to conclude a text's preface with an acknowledgements section thanking colleagues who contributed ideas to or reviewed their work. It is an important tribute to the people who bring a text to life.

In the case of this text, however, a simple acknowledgements section alone is not enough. We must go against tradition and begin this preface by saluting the people who have secured this text's position as the most widely used textbook for accounting principles. Quite simply, *Accounting, 19e,* represents collaboration at its highest level. Users of the 18th edition provided valuable classroom feedback. Numerous focus groups and questionnaire respondents shared their personal insights. And dozens of reviewers kept us on track as we made many difficult choices during the revision of this edition. Reviewers offered many specific comments for improving the text; we took these comments very seriously and the text is stronger because of them.

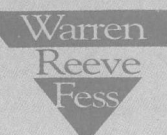

And while current *Accounting* users and reviewers made tremendous contributions, they represent only part of the reason that this text dominates the market. Hundreds of scholars, as users and reviewers, have helped to shape this text through its many editions. Just as Hershey, pictured on our cover and featured throughout the text, has grown and changed throughout this century through the efforts of many special individuals, so too has *Accounting* evolved through its long history. This evolution has been marshaled by a long list of authors, editors, and reviewers, all making unique and invaluable contributions.

A Tradition of Success

When the first edition was published in 1929, author James McKinsey could have only hoped for the kind of success and influence this text has enjoyed. Its dominance in the introductory accounting market has continued to grow for seven decades. As the current authors, we appreciate the responsibility to protect the spirit of McKinsey's vision, while continuing to shape the text to the evolving needs of students and instructors. We sincerely thank our many colleagues who have helped to make it happen.

"The teaching of accounting is no longer designed to train professional accountants only. With the growing complexity of business and the constantly increasing difficulty of the problems of management, it has become essential that everyone who aspires to a position of responsibility should have a knowledge of the fundamental principles of accounting."

—James O. McKinsey,
author, first edition, 1929

Warren Reeve Fess

Guided by the Experts: Content Changes

Extensive feedback from current users, independent reviews by educators, and market research ensures that the text balances the fundamentals of accounting with thorough coverage of today's important topics. As a result, *Accounting, 19e,* focuses squarely on the business of business–how accounting contributes to effective management while emphasizing the most important accounting procedures.

We recognize an important reality–80% of accounting courses are filled with non-accounting majors. *Accounting, 19e,* speaks to anyone who takes an introductory accounting course. Consider these changes in content and organization:

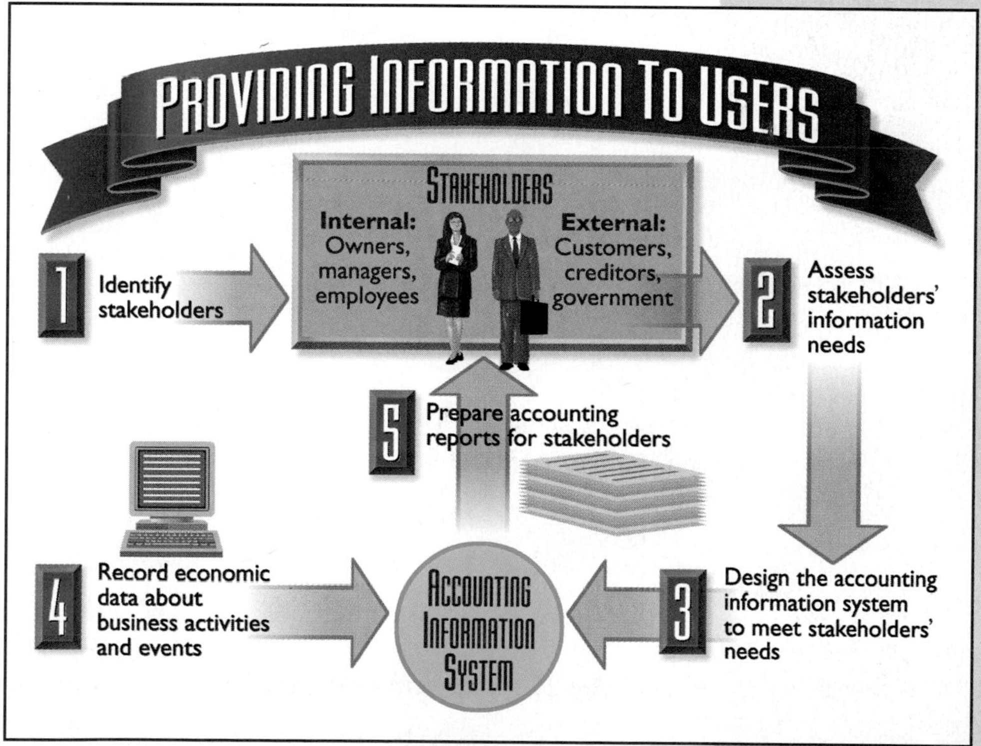

■ **Ch. 1 Introduction to Accounting and Business.** This chapter begins with a new section that defines business and describes common types of businesses, forms of organization, and the diverse interests of a business's stakeholders.

■ **Ch. 3 The Matching Concept and the Adjusting Process.** A new table summarizes each type of adjustment, adjusting entry, and the financial statement effect of omitting an adjusting entry. The discussion of adjustments ends with the adjusted trial balance, rather than a partial work sheet.

■ **Ch. 4 Completing the Accounting Cycle.** The work sheet is now introduced and completed in this chapter. Lines on the work sheet illustrations are numbered to assist you in your classroom presentation.

■ **Ch. 5 Accounting Systems and Internal Controls.** An illustration of the revenue and collection cycle in a computerized accounting system, using QuickBooks,® has been added.

NOITIDE 19TH

■ **Ch. 6 Accounting for Merchandising Businesses.** The discussion of perpetual inventory systems gives students a clear understanding of inventory accounting by drawing connections to buying groceries or fast food meals. Purchases are recorded at gross rather than net amounts. A new appendix describes a merchandiser's special journals in a manual system and electronic forms in a computerized system using QuickBooks.

■ **Ch. 8 Receivables.** The discussion of discounting notes receivable was moved to a chapter appendix. The discussion of temporary investments was moved to a later chapter and combined with the discussion of long-term investments.

■ **Ch. 9 Inventories.** A new section introduces the concept of inventory cost flows without reference to the perpetual or periodic systems. The journal entries in a perpetual system are presented alongside the inventory subsidiary ledger to illustrate the FIFO and LIFO flow of costs.

■ **Ch. 10 Fixed Assets and Intangible Assets.** Gains and losses on exchanges of fixed assets are discussed only from a GAAP viewpoint.

■ **Ch. 13 Corporations: Income and Taxes, Stockholders' Equity, and Investments in Stocks.** A new section on reporting stockholders' equity was added. The discussion of appropriated retained earnings and prior-period adjustments was significantly reduced. A new section covering short-term investments in stocks was added at the end of the chapter. The discussion of international transactions was moved to an appendix.

■ **Ch. 16 Financial Statement Analysis.** This is a new chapter, adapted from the appendix material included in the previous edition.

■ **Ch. 17 Introduction to Managerial Accounting and Job Order Cost Systems.** Two chapters from the previous edition have been combined into one new chapter. This combination is the result of moving the introduction of cost and manufacturing terms to other appropriate chapters.

■ NEW! **Appendixes on Foreign Currency Transactions** and **Partnerships** are at the end of the text.

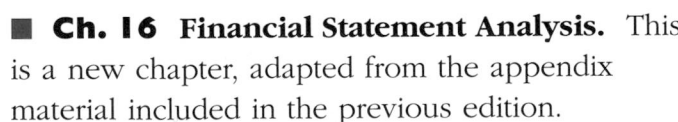

Leading by Listening: Special Features

The distinguished team of users and reviewers guided us to numerous format and feature changes for the 19th edition. Starting with a dynamic and colorful new design, the resulting text is perfect for a broad spectrum of students and classes. Among the feature changes that will help students make the connection between accounting and business are the following:

Setting the Stage. This feature (formerly You and Accounting) at the beginning of each chapter relates students' personal experiences to the chapter's topic. The immediate relevance of these passages provides excellent motivation to read on.

NEW! **Business on Stage.** This brief presentation of a business concept introduces students to the business context in which accounting functions.

Intermission. This feature (formerly Using Accounting To Understand Business) uses excerpts from current media coverage to demonstrate how managers and others use accounting information. Pieces from *The Wall Street Journal, Forbes, Business Week,* and other periodicals help students see the real world application of chapter subjects.

NEW! **Encore.** At the end of each chapter, the text presents a brief, interesting narrative about the success or failure of a real business.

Other features that will help students understand accounting as well as the way business works are:

NEW! **Questions & Answers.** At appropriate points in the margin of the text, questions with answers are provided to help students check their understanding of the material they have just read.

NEW! **Points of Interest.** These margin notes offer insight into subjects of special interest to students, such as careers and current events.

NEW! **Summaries.** Brief summary statements within each chapter bring special attention to important points.

NEW! **Business Transactions.** In Chapters 1 and 2, students are introduced to business transactions through non-business events that help them better understand the nature of transactions.

Accounting is an information system that provides reports to stakeholders about the economic activities and condition of a business.

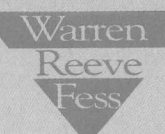

NEW! Real World Notes. J.C. Penney Co. and General Electric are just a couple of the familiar examples that provide a close-up look at how accounting operates in the marketplace. These examples are highlighted in the margin of the text:

- **AT&T**
- **Campbell Soup Company**
- **Coca-Cola Enterprises Inc.**
- **Delta Air Lines**
- **Ford Motor Co.**
- **Gillette**
- **Hewlett Packard**
- **Mercedes-Benz**
- **UPS**

NEW! Financial Analysis and Interpretation. At the end of each financial chapter, a section describing an important element of financial analysis helps students understand the information in financial statements and how that information is used.

Student Success Starts Here: End-of-Chapter Excellence

This edition takes students well beyond procedures into truly pertinent applications. Consider the following tools that will help students succeed in the business world:

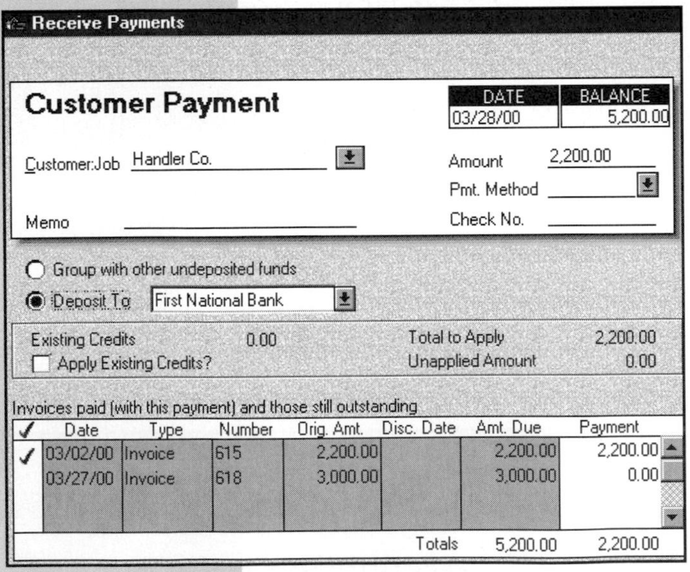

- **NEW! QuickBooks Problems** at the end of Chs. 5, 6, 8, 11, 17, and 20 can be solved using the invoice/billing features in QuickBooks.

- **Critical-Thinking and Decision-Making Activities.** Students need to develop analytical abilities, not just memorize rules. These activities focus on understanding and solving issues. Some are presented in dialogue format–a conversation in which students can "observe" and "participate" when they respond to the issue being discussed.

- **NEW! Group Learning Activities** let students learn accounting and business concepts while building teamwork skills at the same time.

■ NEW! **Internet Activities** launch students into accounting-related areas of the Worldwide Web's ever-expanding universe.

■ **"What Do You Think?"** These exercises and activities take students beyond the scope of the text to apply newly learned material.

■ **"What's Wrong With This?"** These innovative exercises challenge students to analyze and discover what is wrong with a financial statement, a report, or a management decision.

■ **Communications Items.** These activities help students develop communication skills that will be essential on the job, regardless of the fields they pursue.

Accounting, perhaps more than any other discipline, is a field that must be practiced to be understood and retained. The quantity and quality of the following end-of-chapter resources have always been distinguishing characteristics of *Accounting:*

■ **Continuing Problem** in Chs. 1-4. Here's a great opportunity for students to practice what they've learned. As they study each step of the accounting cycle, they can follow a single company–Music Today–from its transactions to the effect of those transactions on its financial statements.

■ **Illustrative Problem and Solution.** A solved problem models one or more of a chapter's assignment problems, helping students make the most of the chapter and end-of-chapter materials.

■ NEW! **Self-Examination Questions** now include a matching activity to help students review and retain terms and definitions.

■ **Exercises.** An average of 20 exercises at the end of each chapter–more than any other text on the market–can be assigned or used as examples in the classroom. Each exercise focuses on only one specific chapter objective.

■ **Problems.** Each chapter includes two full sets of problems for use as classroom illustrations, for assignments, for alternate assignments, or for independent studying. This edition features shortened problems to provide better focus on key chapter topics.

■ **Comprehensive Problems.** At the end of Chs. 4, 6, 11, and 14, cumulative learning applications integrate and summarize the concepts of several chapters to test students' comprehension. Two of these problems can be solved using the debit/credit features of QuickBooks.

A Collaborative Success: Comprehensive Resource Package

We've designed our entire supplement package around the comments instructors have provided about their courses and teaching needs. These comments have made this supplement package the best in the business.

Available to Students–Because every class, instructor, and student has different needs, *Accounting, 19e,* offers a broad range of supplements. Both print material and easy-to-use, affordable technologies help students succeed in the course and in the business world. Some of these supplements are:

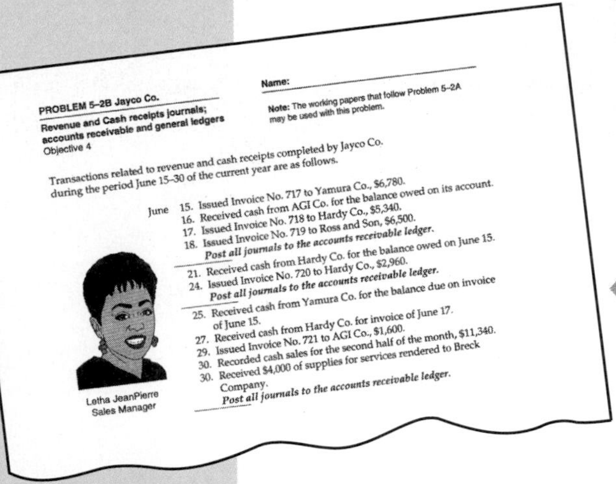

PROBLEM 5–2B Jayco Co.
Revenue and Cash receipts journals; accounts receivable and general ledgers
Objective 4

Name:

Note: The working papers that follow Problem 5–2A may be used with this problem.

Transactions related to revenue and cash receipts completed by Jayco Co. during the period June 15–30 of the current year are as follows.

June 15. Issued Invoice No. 717 to Yamura Co., $6,780.
16. Received cash from AGI Co. for the balance owed on its account.
17. Issued Invoice No. 718 to Hardy Co., $5,340.
18. Issued Invoice No. 719 to Ross and Son, $6,500.
Post all journals to the accounts receivable ledger.
21. Received cash from Hardy Co. for the balance owed on June 15.
24. Issued Invoice No. 720 to Hardy Co., $2,960.
Post all journals to the accounts receivable ledger.
25. Received cash from Yamura Co. for the balance due on invoice of June 15.
27. Received cash from Hardy Co. for invoice of June 17.
29. Issued Invoice No. 721 to AGI Co., $1,600.
30. Recorded cash sales for the second half of the month, $11,340.
30. Received $4,000 of supplies for services rendered to Breck Company.
Post all journals to the accounts receivable ledger.

Letha JeanPierre
Sales Manager

■ **Working Papers.** The traditional Working Papers are available both with and without problem-specific forms.

■ **Working Papers Plus,** prepared by John Wanlass of DeAnza College. This alternative to traditional working papers integrates the chapter learning objectives and glossary with forms for solving all textbook exercises and selected textbook problems.

■ **Study Guide,** prepared by James Heintz of the University of Connecticut and Carl Warren. The Study Guide includes quiz and test tips and multiple choice, fill-in-the-blank, and true-false questions with solutions. The Study Guide is packaged with a disk that allows students to score their own practice tests.

■ **PowerNotes,** prepared by John Wanlass. In a classroom where the PowerPoint™ transparencies are utilized, this workbook provides students with printed versions of the transparencies, along with critical-thinking activities and self-study review questions related to those slides.

■ **General Ledger Software,** prepared by Dale Klooster and Warren Allen. This best-selling educational general ledger package (formerly Solutions Software) is enhanced with planning tools, a Journal Wizard, more tool tips, a new color-coded system, and additional problems for the managerial

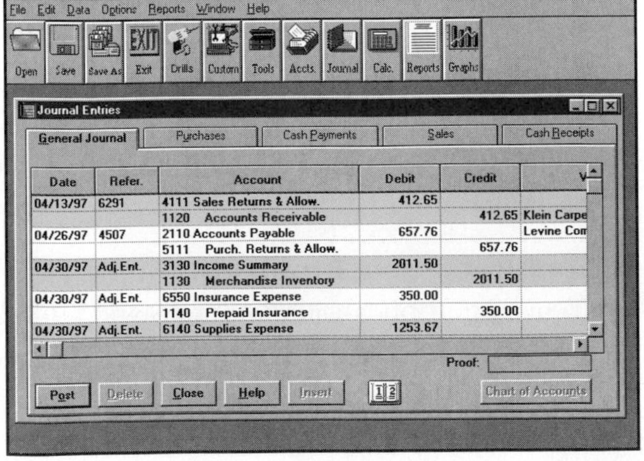

chapters. Solving end-of-chapter problems, comprehensive problems, as well as practice sets is as easy as clicking icons with a mouse.

■ **Homework Assistant and Tutor (HAT),** prepared by Ray Meservy of Brigham Young University. This user-friendly software for Windows visually teaches students the relationships between journals, ledgers, and financial statements as they solve selected end-of-chapter problems. A built-in tutor function includes numerous hints and help screens.

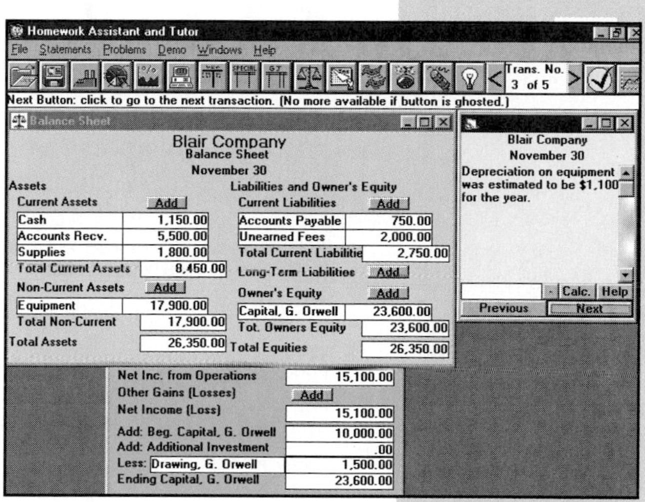

■ **Spreadsheet Applications Software.** Students can solve dozens of problems by using any of the standard spreadsheet packages, such as Lotus 1-2-3® and Excel® Alternative "what-if" scenarios are also presented and explored.

Available to Instructors–South-Western Publishing continues to lead the field in supplements for instructors, from traditional printed materials to the latest integrated classroom technology. Among these support tools are:

■ ***Virtual Community***–A variety of instructor resources are now available through South-Western's Web site. Organized by chapter and topic, this hyperlinked syllabus includes text-specific and other accounting-related resources.

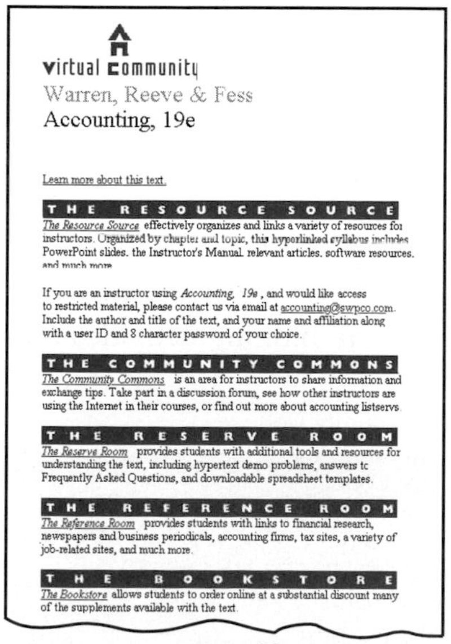

warren.swcollege.com

Many of these online resources are also available on CD-ROM. We invite you to be part of this community by sampling what we've provided and by sharing your own material, ideas, and comments with your colleagues and students. Visit our discussion forum and exchange information on current developments in the profession, and share ideas on the course and curriculum.

■ **PowerPoint™ Transparencies,** prepared by John Wanlass. PowerPoint Transparencies enhance lectures and simplify class preparation. You can also add your own custom slides, using this popular presentation package.

■ **Traditional Ancillaries.** The Instructor's Manual, Test Bank, and other traditional elements are available in separate bound volumes as well as on the instructor's CD-ROM. A wide range of writing exercises, group learning activities, demonstration problems, and accounting scenarios are included in the Instructor's Manual and the on-line Accounting Virtual Community.

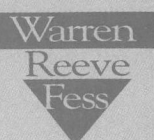

A Triumph of Teamwork: Acknowledgements

As we have described throughout this preface, this text is a tribute to the power of collaboration and collegial support. We thank the many people who have made the 19th edition a reality.

The following people kept diaries of their experience with the text:

Sam Allred
Forsyth Technical Community College

Thelma Bushong
Delta College

Patricia Conn
Atlantic Community College

Terry Elliott
Morehead State University

Richard Howden
Delta College

George Johnson
Norfolk State University

Ed Krohn
Miami-Dade Community College - South

Linda Kropp
Modesto Junior College

Michael Landers
Middlesex County College

Jim Lentz
Moraine Valley Community College

Larry Lofton
Hinds Community College

William Rencher
Seminole Community College

Ronald Richard
Westark Community College

John Teter
St. Petersburg Junior College

Henry Wilk, Jr.
Fisher College

The following people participated in focus groups:

William Allen
Camden County College

John Atella
Harrisburg Area Community College

Clarence Brown, Jr.
Harold Washington College

Yvonne Brown
University of Cincinnati

Donna Chadwick
Sinclair Community College

Robert Dan
San Antonio College

David Darst
Central Ohio Technical College

Sid Davidson
Foothill College

Carl Essig
Montgomery County Community College

Preston Ford
Malcolm X College

James Genseal
Joliet Junior College

Mary Govan
Sinclair Community College

Betty Habershon
Prince George's Community College

Ken Harper
DeAnza College

Paul Harris
Camden County College

George Heyman
Oakton Community College

Gloria Jackson
San Antonio College

Letha Jeanpierre
DeAnza College

Tom Joyce
Pasadena City College

Sanford Kahn
University of Cincinnati

Arthur Katz
Canada College
Sierra College

Hana Kovanic
Bergen Community College

Cathy Landers
San Antonio College

Jim Lentz
Moraine Valley Community College

Jane Loprest
Bucks County Community College

Florence McGovern
Bergen Community College

Hector Martinez
San Antonio College

Ken Miller
San Antonio College

Deborah Most
Dutchess Community College

Gene Pinchuk
Pasadena City College

Jim Puthoff
Sinclair Community College

Ed Riechman
Central State University

Jill Russell
Camden County College

Nancy Sheridan
Bucks County Community College

Barry Smith
DeAnza College

Doug Staley
Pasadena City College

Martin Stub
DeVry Institute of Technology

Larry Tartaglino
Cabrillo College

Russell Vermillion
Prince George's Community College

John Wanlass
DeAnza College

Tom Welsch
Harold Washington College

Phyllis Yasuda
DeAnza College

The following people reviewed manuscript for the text:

Sheryl J. Alley
Ball State University

Carl Ballard
Central Piedmont Community College

Frank R. Beigbeder
Santa Ana College

Clifford Bellers
Washtenaw Community College

John R. Blahnik
Lorain County Community College

Donna Chadwick
Sinclair Community College

Ken Coffey
Johnson County Community College

Ana Cruz
Miami-Dade Community College - Wolfson

Alan Davis
Community College of Philadelphia

Lyle Dehning
Metropolitan State College of Denver

Pamela Donahue
Northern Essex Community College

Estelle Faier
Metro Community College

Leonard Goldman
Kingsborough Community College

Debra Goorbin
Westchester Community College

Cynthia Greeson
Ivy Tech State College

Robert Gregrich
Brevard Community College

James L. Haydon
East Los Angeles Community College

Robert Held
Harper College

Tim Helton
Joliet Junior College

Brenda Hester
Volunteer State Community College

Margaret Hicks
Howard University

Bob Hildenbrand
Albuquerque T-VT Community College

Anita Hope
Tarrant County Junior College - Northeast

George Katz
St. Philip's College

Rebecca Kerr
Midlands Technical College

Jack Klett
Indian River Community College

Ed Krohn
Miami-Dade Community College - South

George Lazar
Owens Technical College

Jim Lentz
Moraine Valley Community College

Florence McGovern
Bergen Community College

Sal Marchionna
Triton College

S. A. Marino
Westchester Community College

Salah Negm
Prince George's Community College

Harris O'Brien
North Harris County College

Frank A. Paliotta
Berkeley College

Paige Paulsen
Salt Lake Community College

Loretta Burch Rojo
Central Piedmont Community College

Larry Roman
Cuyahoga Community College

Jill Russell
Camden County College

John J. Sabbagh
Northern Essex Community College

Richard Sarkisian
Camden County College

Lois Slutsky
Boward Community College - South

Steve Teeter
Utah Valley State College

Philip L. Trees
Broward Community College

Shafi Ullah
Broward Community College - South

Joan Weaver
Volunteer State Community College

Charles Wellens
Fitchburg State College

Thomas Welsch
Harold Washington College

Kathleen Wessman
Montgomery College

Preston Wilks
Big Bend Community College

Brief Contents

19TH EDITION

Accounting

Carl S. Warren, Ph.D., C.P.A., C.I.A.
Professor of Accounting
University of Georgia, Athens

James M. Reeve, Ph.D., C.P.A.
Professor of Accounting
University of Tennessee, Knoxville

Philip E. Fess, Ph.D., C.P.A.
Professor Emeritus of Accountancy
University of Illinois, Champaign-Urbana

Accounting Team Director: Richard Lindgren
Senior Acquisitions Editor: David L. Shaut
Senior Marketing Manager: Sharon Oblinger
Senior Developmental Editor: Ken Martin
Production Editor: Mark Sears
Production House: Litten Editing and Production with GGS Information Services
Cover and Internal Design: Lou Ann Thesing
Cover Illustration: © 1997 Rob Schuster, product photography by Joe Higgins
Internal Illustrations: Rob Schuster and GGS Information Services
Photo Editor: Cary Benbow
Photo Researchers: Feldman & Associates, Inc.
Media and Technology Editor: Diane M. Van Bakel
Media Production Editor: Lora Craver
Copy Writer, Preface: Steve Mott, Words & Occasional Wisdom
Cover Illustration Acknowledgments:
Ford Expedition used with permission of Ford Motor Company.
L.L. Bean catalog cover courtesy of L.L. Bean and Francis Golden.
Motorola logo and cellular phones courtesy of the Cellular Subscriber Sector of Motorola, Inc.
Tide detergent box © The Procter & Gamble Company. Reprinted with permission.
Wrigley's gum packages reprinted courtesy of the Wm. Wrigley Jr. Company.
Mattel logo © 1997 Mattel, Inc. All rights reserved. Used with permission.
McDonald's Golden Arches used with permission from McDonald's Corporation.
Levi's Jeans courtesy of Levi Strauss & Company.

I(T)P®

International Thomson Publishing
South-Western is an ITP Company. The ITP trademark is used under license.

Library of Congress Cataloging-in-Publication Data

Warren, Carl S.
Accounting / Carl S. Warren, James M. Reeve, Philip E. Fess. —
19th ed.
p. cm.
Includes index.
ISBN 0-538-86972-0 (alk. paper)
1. Accounting. I. Reeve, James M., II. Fess, Philip E. III. Title.
HF5635.F386 1998 98-18438
657—dc21 CIP

ISBN: 0-538-86972-0

1 2 3 4 5 6 7 VH 4 3 2 1 0 9 8

Printed in the United States of America

CARL S. WARREN

Dr. Carl S. Warren is the Arthur Andersen & Co. Alumni Professor of Accounting at the J.M. Tull School of Accounting at the University of Georgia, Athens. Professor Warren received his Ph.D. from Michigan State University in 1973. Dr. Warren's experience in listening to users of his texts sharpens his keen focus on helping students learn. When he is not teaching classes or writing textbooks, Dr. Warren enjoys golf, racquetball, and fishing.

JAMES M. REEVE

Dr. James M. Reeve is Professor of Accounting at the University of Tennessee, Knoxville. He received his Ph.D. from Oklahoma State University in 1980. Dr. Reeve is founder of the Cost Management Institute and a member of the Institute for Productivity Through Quality faculty at the University of Tennessee. In addition to his teaching experience, Dr. Reeve brings to this text a wealth of experience consulting on managerial accounting issues with numerous companies, including Procter & Gamble, AMOCO, Rockwell International, Harris Corporation, and Freddie Mac. Dr. Reeve's interests outside the classroom and the business world include golf, skiing, reading, and travel.

PHILIP E. FESS

Dr. Philip E. Fess is the Arthur Andersen & Co. Alumni Professor of Accountancy Emeritus at the University of Illinois, Champaign-Urbana. He received his Ph.D. from the University of Illinois. Dr. Fess has been involved in writing textbooks for over twenty-five years, and his knowledge of how to make texts user-friendly is reflected on the pages of this edition. Dr. Fess plays golf and tennis, and he has represented the United States in international tennis competition.

Contents

I

1

Introduction to Accounting and Business

Setting the STAGE

Do you use accounting? Yes, we all use accounting information in one form or another. For example, when you think about buying a car, you use accounting information to determine whether you can afford it. Similarly, when you decided to attend college, you considered the costs (the tuition, textbooks, and so on). Most likely, you also considered the benefits (the ability to obtain a higher-paying job or a more desirable job).

Is accounting important to you? Yes, accounting is important in your personal life as well as in your career, even though you may not become an accountant. For example, you may be the manager of a chain of pizza restaurants who is deciding on whether to buy new delivery cars. Accounting information about the restaurants will be a major factor in your decision to acquire the cars and the bank's decision to finance the purchase.

Our primary objective in this text is to illustrate basic accounting concepts that will help you to make good personal and business decisions. We begin by discussing what a business is, how it operates, and the role that accounting plays.

objectives

After studying this chapter, you should be able to:

1. Describe the nature of a business.
2. Describe the role of accounting in business.
3. Describe the importance of business ethics and the basic principles of proper ethical conduct.
4. Describe the profession of accounting.
5. Summarize the development of accounting principles and relate them to practice.
6. State the accounting equation and define each element of the equation.
7. Explain how business transactions can be stated in terms of the resulting changes in the three basic elements of the accounting equation.
8. Describe the financial statements of a proprietorship and explain how they interrelate.
9. Use the ratio of liabilities to owner's equity to analyze the ability of a business to withstand poor business conditions.

Nature of a Business

OBJECTIVE 1

Describe the nature of a business.

Name an example of a business. Your example might be a large company such as **General Motors**, **McDonald's**, or **AT&T**. It might be a local company, such as a gas station or a grocery store, or perhaps it might be your employer. It might be a restaurant, a law firm, or a medical office. These examples are all businesses, but what do they have in common that identifies them as businesses?

In general, a **business** is an organization in which basic resources (inputs), such as materials and labor, are assembled and processed to provide goods or services (outputs) to customers.[1] Businesses come in all sizes, from a local coffee house to a General Motors, which sells several billion dollars worth of cars and trucks each year. The customers of a business are individuals or other businesses who purchase goods or services in exchange for money or other items of value. In contrast, a church is not a business because those who receive its services are not obligated to pay for them.

The objective of most businesses is to maximize profits. **Profit** is the difference between the amounts received from customers for goods or services provided and the amounts paid for the inputs used to provide the goods or services. Some businesses operate with an objective other than to maximize profits. The objective of such nonprofit businesses is to provide some benefit to society, such as medical research or conservation of natural resources. In other cases, governmental units such as cities operate water works or sewage treatment plants on a nonprofit basis. Our focus in this text will be on businesses operated to earn a profit. However, many of the concepts and principles also apply to nonprofit businesses.

Types of Businesses

There are three different types of businesses that are operated for profit: manufacturing, merchandising, and service businesses. Each type of business has unique characteristics.

Manufacturing businesses change basic inputs into products that are sold to individual customers. Examples of manufacturing businesses and some of their products are shown below.

[1] A complete glossary of terms appears at the end of the text.

Manufacturing Business	Product
General Motors	Automobiles, trucks, vans
General Mills	Breakfast cereals
Boeing	Jet aircraft
Nike	Athletic shoes
Coca-Cola	Beverages
Sony	Stereos, televisions, radios

Merchandising businesses also sell products to customers. However, they do not make the products, but purchase them from other businesses (such as manufacturers). In this sense, merchandisers bring products and customers together. Examples of merchandising businesses and some of the products they sell are shown below.

Merchandising Business	Product
Wal-Mart	General merchandise
Barnes and Noble	Books
Toys "R" Us	Toys
Circuit City	Consumer electronics
Lands' End	Apparel

Service businesses provide services rather than products to customers. Examples of service businesses and the types of services they offer are shown below.

Service Business	Service
Disney	Entertainment
Delta Air Lines	Transportation
Marriott Hotels	Hospitality and lodging
Merrill Lynch	Financial
Sprint	Telecommunications

REAL WORLD

Roughly eight out of every ten workers in the United States are employed in providing services. In the past twenty years, 90 percent of the new jobs created in the United States have been in service businesses.

Source: Walter Kiechel III, "How We Will Work in the Year 2000," *Fortune*, May 17, 1993, p. 46.

Types of Business Organizations

A business is normally organized as one of three different forms: proprietorship, partnership, or corporation. In the following paragraphs, we briefly describe each form and discuss its advantages and disadvantages.

A **proprietorship** is owned by one individual. More than 70% of the businesses in the United States are organized as proprietorships. The popularity of this form is due to the ease and the low cost of organizing. The primary disadvantage of proprietorships is that the financial resources available to the business are limited to the individual owner's resources. Small local businesses such as hardware stores, repair shops, laundries, restaurants, and maid services are often organized as proprietorships.

As a business grows and more financial and managerial resources are needed, it may become a partnership. A **partnership** is owned by two or more individuals. Like proprietorships, small local businesses such as automotive repair shops, music stores, beauty shops, and men's and women's clothing stores may be organized as partnerships. Currently, about 10% of the businesses in the United States are organized as partnerships.

A **corporation** is organized under state or federal statutes as a separate legal entity. The ownership of a corporation is divided into shares of stock. A corpora-

BUSINESS ON STAGE

The Factors of Production

Businesses convert basic inputs into goods and services for customers. These inputs are known as *factors of production.* The factors of production common to all businesses are natural resources, labor, capital, and entrepreneurs. Natural resources are the basic raw materials, including farmland, forests, and mineral deposits. Labor is the employees who contribute their intellectual and physical efforts to a business. Capital represents the financial resources (money) invested in the business to purchase such items as machinery and buildings. Entrepreneurs are the people who combine natural resources, labor, and capital together to produce goods and services.

Let's examine a small pizza restaurant as an example of a business. The pizza ingredients of tomato sauce, dough, sausage, pepperoni, and cheese represent the natural resources that are derived from farming the land. The employees (labor) are the waitresses, the delivery person, the cash register clerk, and the baker. The money required to purchase the land, building, and equipment is the capital. The owner/manager who began the business and operates it on a daily basis is the entrepreneur. ■

tion issues the stock to individuals or other businesses, who then become owners or stockholders of the corporation.

A primary advantage of the corporate form is the ability to obtain large amounts of resources by issuing stock. For this reason, most companies that require large investments in equipment and facilities are organized as corporations. For example, **Toys "R" Us** has raised over $800 million by issuing shares of common stock to finance its operations. Other examples of corporations include **General Motors**, **Ford**, **International Business Machines (IBM)**, **Coca-Cola**, and **General Electric**.

About 20% of the businesses in the United States are organized as corporations. However, since most large companies are organized as corporations, over 90% of the total dollars of business receipts are received by corporations. Thus, corporations have a major influence on the economy.

The three types of businesses we discussed earlier—manufacturing, merchandising, and service—may be either proprietorships, partnerships, or corporations. However, because of the large amount of resources required to operate a manufacturing business, most manufacturing businesses are corporations. Likewise, most large retailers such as **Wal-Mart**, **Sears**, and **JC Penney** are corporations.

Manufacturing, merchandising, and service businesses are commonly organized as either proprietorships, partnerships, or corporations.

Business Stakeholders

A **business stakeholder** is a person or entity that has an interest in the economic performance of the business. These stakeholders normally include the owners, managers, employees, customers, creditors, and the government.

The **owners** who have invested resources in the business clearly have an interest in how well the business performs. Most owners want to get the most economic value for their investments. To the extent that the business is profitable, owners will expect to share in the business profits. Since owners may eventually decide to sell their business, they also have an interest in the total economic worth of the business. This economic worth may reflect results of past profits as well as prospects for future profits.

The **managers** are those individuals who the owners have authorized to operate the business. Managers are primarily evaluated on the economic performance of the business. The managers of businesses that perform poorly are often fired by the owners. Thus, managers have an incentive to maximize the economic value of the business. Owners may offer managers salary contracts that are tied directly to how well the business performs. For example, a manager might receive a percent of the profits or a percent of the increase in profits. Such contracts are often referred to as profit-sharing plans.

The **employees** provide services to the business in exchange for their pay. The employees have an interest in the economic performance of the business because their jobs depend upon it. During business downturns, it is not unusual for a business to lay off workers for

BUSINESS ON STAGE

Successful Entrepreneurs

What are the characteristics of entrepreneurs who start and manage a new business successfully?

It goes without saying that an entrepreneur must have a thorough technical knowledge of the business. For example, a successful computer consultant must have a thorough knowledge of computers. Entrepreneurs must also have basic management skills, such as the ability to organize and interact with others. Finally, entrepreneurs are often described using the following terms:

Vision	Need for achievement
Perseverance	Self-starter
Independent	Sense of commitment
Self-confident	Willingness to make personal sacrifices
Risk taker	Communication skills
High energy level	
Motivated	
Personal drive	
Spirit of adventure	

Examples of some well-known entrepreneurs and their companies are listed below.

Entrepreneur	Company
Henry Ford	Ford Motor Company
George Eastman	Kodak
King C. Gillette	Gillette Company
Steven Jobs	Apple Computer
Bill Gates	Microsoft
Frederick Smith	Federal Express
Sam Walton	Wal-Mart

Examples of entrepreneurs also include the owners of many small businesses in your community, from local restaurants to video rental stores. ■

extended periods of time. In the extreme, a business may fail and the employees lose their jobs permanently. Employee labor unions often use the good economic performance of a business to argue for wage increases. In contrast, businesses often use poor economic performance to argue for employee concessions such as wage decreases.

The **customers** may also have an interest in the continued success of a business. For example, if **Apple Computer** were to fail, customers might not be able to get hardware and software for their computers. Likewise, customers who purchase advance tickets on **Southwest Airlines** have an interest in whether Southwest will continue in business. Frequent flyers on **Eastern Airlines** lost their accumulated frequent-flyer points when Eastern went out of business.

Like the owners, the **creditors** invest resources in the business by extending credit. Therefore, the creditors of a business have an interest in how well the business performs. In order for the creditors to recover their investment, the business must generate enough cash to pay them. In addition, the business is the creditors' customer, and thus creditors have an interest in the continued success of the business.

REAL WORLD: The state of Alabama offered **Mercedes** millions of dollars in incentives to locate a Mercedes plant in Alabama.

Various **governments** have an interest in the economic performance of businesses. City, county, state, and federal governments collect taxes from businesses within their jurisdictions. The better a business does, the more taxes the government can collect. In addition, workers are taxed on their wages. In contrast, workers who are laid off and are unemployed can file claims for unemployment compensation, which results in a financial burden for the government. City and state governments often provide incentives for businesses to locate in their jurisdictions.

The Role of Accounting in Business

OBJECTIVE 2

Describe the role of accounting in business.

What is the role of accounting in business? The simplest answer to this question is that accounting provides information for managers to use in operating the business. In addition, accounting provides information to other stakeholders to use in assessing the economic performance and condition of the business.

In a general sense, **accounting** can be defined as an information system that provides reports to stakeholders about the economic activities and condition of a business. As we indicated earlier in this chapter, we will focus our discussions on accounting and its role in business. However, many of the concepts in this text also apply to individuals, governments, and other types of organizations. For example, individuals must account for activities such as hours worked, checks written, and bills due. Stakeholders for individuals include creditors, dependents, and the government. A main interest of the government is making sure that individuals pay the proper taxes.

Accounting is an information system that provides reports to stakeholders about the economic activities and condition of a business.

You may think of accounting as the "language of business." This is because accounting is the means by which business information is communicated to the stakeholders. For example, accounting reports summarizing the profitability of a new product help **Coca-Cola's** management decide whether to continue offering the new product for sale. Likewise, financial analysts use accounting reports in deciding whether to recommend the purchase of Coca-Cola's stock. Banks use accounting reports in deciding the amount of credit to extend to Coca-Cola. Suppliers use accounting reports in deciding whether to offer credit for Coca-Cola's purchases of supplies and raw materials. State and federal governments use accounting reports as a basis for assessing taxes on Coca-Cola.

The process by which accounting provides information to business stakeholders is illustrated in Exhibit 1. First, a business must identify its stakeholders. Then, it must assess their various information needs and design its accounting system to meet those needs. Finally, the accounting system records the economic data about business activities and events, which it reports to the stakeholders according to their information needs.

EXHIBIT 1
Accounting Information and the Stakeholders of a Business

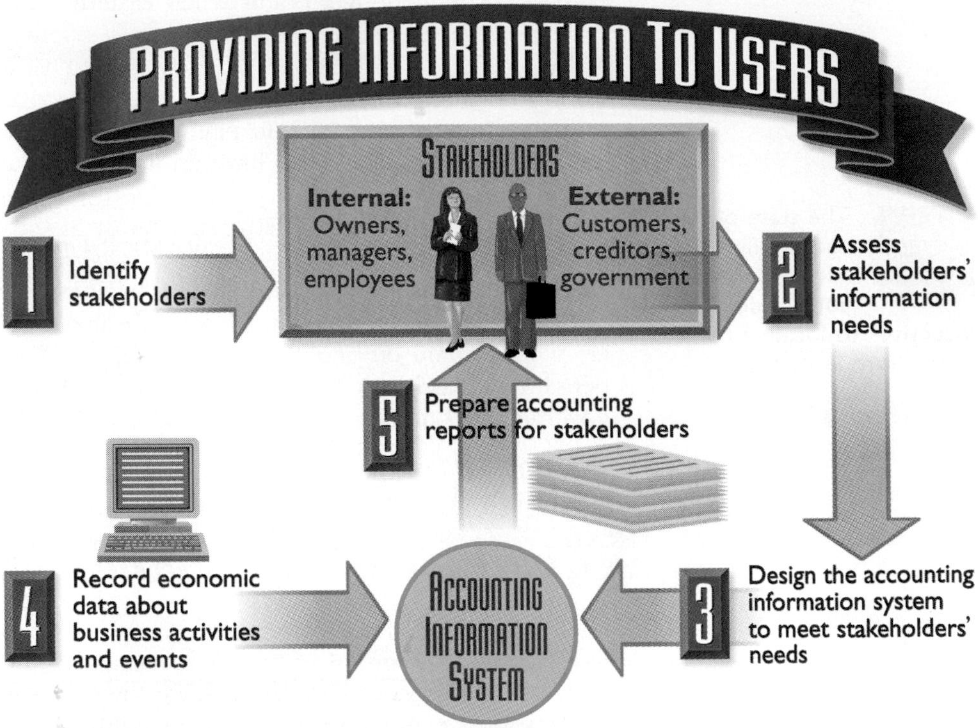

Stakeholders use accounting reports as a primary source of information on which they base their decisions. Stakeholders also use other information in making decisions about a business. For example, in deciding whether to extend credit to an appliance store, a banker might use economic forecasts to assess the future demand for the store's products. During periods of economic downturn, the demand for consumer appliances normally declines. The banker might inquire about the ability and reputation of the managers of the business. For small corporations, bankers may require major stockholders to personally guarantee the loans of the business. Finally, bankers might consult industry publications that rank similar businesses as to their quality of products, customer satisfaction, and future prospects for growth.

Business Ethics

OBJECTIVE 3

Describe the importance of business ethics and the basic principles of proper ethical conduct.

Individuals may differ as to what is "right" or "wrong" in a given situation. For example, you may believe it is wrong to copy another student's homework and hand it in as your own. Other students may feel that it is acceptable to copy homework if the instructor has no stated rule against it. Unfortunately, business managers are often in situations where they may feel pressure to violate personal ethics. For example, managers of **Sears** automotive service departments were accused of recommending unnecessary repairs and overcharging customers for actual repairs in order to meet company goals and earn bonuses.

Point of INTEREST

Most colleges and universities publish a Student Code of Conduct that sets forth the ethical conduct expected of students.

Ethics are the moral principles that guide the conduct of individuals. Regardless of differences among individuals, proper ethical conduct implies a behavior that considers the impact of one's actions on society and others. In other words, proper ethical conduct implies that you not only consider what's in your best interests, but also what's in the best interests of others.

Ethical conduct is good business. For example, an automobile manufacturer that fails to correct a safety defect to save costs may later lose sales from the loss of consumer confidence. Likewise, a business that pollutes the environment may find itself the focus of lawsuits and customer boycotts.

REAL WORLD

A survey of top managers by the accounting firm of **Deloitte & Touche** reports that "an enterprise actually strengthens its competitive position by maintaining high ethical standards." *Ethics in Business,* Deloitte & Touche, January 1988.

Businessmen and businesswomen should work within an ethical framework.[2] Although an ethical framework is based on individual experiences and training, there are a number of sound principles that form the foundation for ethical behavior:

1. *Avoid small ethical lapses.* Small ethical lapses may appear harmless in and of themselves. Unfortunately, such lapses can compromise your work. Small ethical lapses can build up and lead to larger consequences at a later point in time.
2. *Focus on your long-term reputation.* One characteristic of an ethical dilemma is that it places you under severe short-term pressure. The ethical dilemma is created by the stated or unstated threat that failure to "go along" may result in undesirable consequences. You should respond to ethical dilemmas by removing focus from the short-term pressures and instead focusing on long-term reputation. Your reputation is very valuable. You will lose your effectiveness if your reputation becomes tarnished.
3. *Expect to suffer adverse personal consequences for holding to an ethical position.* In some unethical organizations, managers have endured career setbacks for not budging from their ethical positions. Some managers have resigned their positions because they were unable to support management in what was perceived as unethical behavior. Thus, in the short term, ethical behavior can sometimes adversely affect your career.

REAL WORLD

Stanley James Cardiges, the top U.S. sales representative for **American Honda** from 1988 to 1992, admitted to receiving $2 million to $5 million in illegal kickbacks from dealers. After being sentenced to five years in prison, he admitted to "falling into a pattern [of unethical behavior] early in my career . . . and went along with the crowd."

Source: "Ex-Honda Executive Handed 5-Year Sentence," The Associated Press, *Knoxville News Sentinel,* August 26, 1995.

Profession of Accounting

OBJECTIVE 4

Describe the profession of accounting.

Accountants engage in either (1) private accounting or (2) public accounting. Accountants employed by a business firm or a not-for-profit organization are said to be engaged in **private accounting**. Accountants and their staff who provide services on a fee basis are said to be employed in **public accounting**.

Because all functions within a business use accounting information, experience in private or public accounting provides a solid foundation for a career. Many positions in industry and in government agencies are held by individuals with ac-

[2] An ethics discussion case is provided at the end of each chapter to focus attention on meaningful ethical situations that accountants often face in practice.

counting backgrounds. For example, in its 1990 Special Bonus Issue on "The Corporate Elite," *Business Week* reported the career paths for the chief executives of the 1,000 largest public corporations. These career paths are shown in Exhibit 2.

EXHIBIT 2
Career Paths of Corporate Executives

Private Accounting

The scope of activities and duties of private accountants varies widely. Private accountants are frequently called management accountants. If they are employed by a manufacturing concern, they may be called *industrial* or *cost accountants*. The chief accountant in a business may be called the **controller**. Various state and federal agencies and other not-for-profit agencies also employ accountants.

The Institute of Certified Management Accountants, an affiliate of the Institute of Management Accountants (IMA), sponsors the **Certified Management Accountant (CMA)** program. The CMA certificate is evidence of competence in management accounting. To become a CMA requires a college degree, two years of experience, and successful completion of a two-day examination. Continuing professional education is required for renewal of the CMA certificate. In addition, members of the IMA must adhere to standards of ethical conduct.

The Institute of Internal Auditors sponsors a similar program for internal auditors. Internal auditors are accountants who review the accounting and operating procedures prescribed by their firms. Accountants who specialize in internal auditing may be granted the **Certified Internal Auditor (CIA)** certificate.

Public Accounting

In public accounting, an accountant may practice as an individual or as a member of a public accounting firm. Public accountants who have met a state's education, experience, and examination requirements may become **Certified Public Accountants (CPAs)**.

Point of INTEREST

Information on a state's requirements for the CPA certification is available from that state's board of accountancy.

The requirements for obtaining a CPA certificate differ among the various states. All states require a college education in accounting, and most states require 150 semester hours of college credit. In addition, a candidate must pass a two-day examination prepared by the American Institute of Certified Public Accountants (AICPA).

Most states do not permit individuals to practice as CPAs until they have had from one to three years' experience in public accounting. Some states, however, accept similar employment in private accounting as equivalent experience. All states also require continuing professional education and adherence to standards of ethical conduct.[3]

Specialized Accounting Fields

You may think that all accounting is the same. However, you will find several specialized fields of accounting in practice. The two most common are financial accounting and managerial accounting. Other fields include cost accounting, environmental accounting, tax accounting, accounting systems, international accounting, not-for-profit accounting, and social accounting.

Financial accounting is primarily concerned with the recording and reporting of economic data and activities for a business. Although such reports provide useful information for managers, they are the primary reports for owners, creditors, governmental agencies, and the public. For example, if you wanted to own a portion of **PepsiCo**, **American Airlines**, or **McDonald's**, how would you know in which company to invest? One way is to review financial reports and compare the financial performance and condition of each company. The purpose of financial accounting is to provide such reports.

Managerial accounting, or **management accounting**, uses both financial accounting and estimated data to aid management in running day-to-day operations and in planning future operations. Management accountants gather and report information that is relevant and timely to the decision-making needs of management. For example, management might need information on alternative ways to finance the construction of a new building. Alternatively, management might need information on whether to expand its operations into a new product line. Thus, reports to management can differ widely in form and content.

Generally Accepted Accounting Principles

OBJECTIVE 5

Summarize the development of accounting principles and relate them to practice.

If the management of a company could record and report financial data as it saw fit, comparisons among companies would be difficult, if not impossible. Thus, financial accountants follow **generally accepted accounting principles (GAAP)** in preparing reports. These reports allow investors and other stakeholders to compare one company to another.

To illustrate the importance of generally accepted accounting principles, assume that each sports conference in college football used different rules for counting touchdowns. For example, assume that the Pacific Athletic Conference (PAC 10) counted a touchdown as six points and the Atlantic Coast Conference (ACC) counted a touchdown as two points. It would be difficult to evaluate the teams under such different scoring systems. A standard set of rules and a standard scoring system help fans compare teams across conferences. Likewise, a standard set of generally accepted accounting principles allows for the comparison of financial performance and condition across companies.

Accounting principles and concepts develop from research, accepted accounting practices, and pronouncements of authoritative bodies. Currently, the **Financial**

[3] The text of the *Code of Professional Conduct* (American Institute of Certified Public Accountants, New York, 1992) is reproduced in Appendix B.

INTERMISSION

Why Do We Need Accounting Principles?

In an editorial in *The Wall Street Journal,* Dennis R. Beresford, former Chairman of the Financial Accounting Standards Board, discussed the role of generally accepted accounting principles. He asserted that the primary role of accounting principles should be to truthfully portray the economic consequences of events on the financial statements of a business enterprise. In doing so, Mr. Beresford asserted, "... the truth will set investors free." Mr. Beresford goes on to state that "... Truth in accounting means telling it like it is, without bias or intent to encourage any particular mode of behavior by the user of the information." ■

Source: "In Accounting, Truth Above All," Letters to the Editor, *The Wall Street Journal,* March 21, 1994.

Accounting Standards Board (FASB) is the authoritative body that has the primary responsibility for developing accounting principles. The FASB publishes *Statements of Financial Accounting Standards* and *Interpretations* to these Standards.

REAL WORLD: The FASB is also developing a broad conceptual framework for financial accounting. Six *Statements of Financial Accounting Concepts* have been published to date.

Because generally accepted accounting principles impact how companies report and what they report, all stakeholders are interested in the setting of these principles. For example, the FASB proposed a standard on how to account for options granted employees and managers to purchase shares of ownership in the company. The proposal was opposed by managers because it would impact negatively the financial results of many companies. Managers and others, including the United States Senate, urged the FASB to revise or drop the proposal.[4] In response to these comments, the FASB significantly revised the proposed standard.

In this chapter and throughout this text, we emphasize accounting principles and concepts. It is through this emphasis on the "why" of accounting as well as the "how" that you will gain an understanding of the full significance of accounting. In the following paragraphs, we discuss the business entity concept and the cost principle.

Business Entity Concept

The individual business unit is the business entity for which economic data are needed. This entity could be an automobile dealer, a department store, or a grocery store. The business entity must be identified, so that the accountant can determine which economic data should be analyzed, recorded, and summarized in reports.

Under the business entity concept, the activities of a business are recorded separately from the activities of the stakeholders.

The **business entity concept** is important because it limits the economic data in the accounting system to data related directly to the activities of the business. In other words, the business is viewed as an entity separate from its owners, creditors, or other stakeholders. For example, the accountant for a business with one owner (a proprietorship) would record only activities of the business and not the personal activities, property, or debts of the owner.

The Cost Concept

If a building is bought for $150,000, that amount should be entered into the buyer's accounting records. The seller may have been asking $170,000 for the building up to the time of the sale. The buyer may have initially offered $130,000 for the building. The building may have been assessed at $125,000 for property tax purposes. The buyer may have received an offer of $175,000 for the building the day after it was acquired. These latter amounts have no effect on the accounting records because they did not result in an exchange of the building from the seller to the buyer. The **cost concept** is the basis for entering the *exchange price, or cost, of $150,000* into the accounting records for the building.

[4] Glenn Alan Cheney, "Senate Rips FASB on Stock Options," *Accounting Today,* May 23, 1994.

Continuing the illustration, the $175,000 offer received by the buyer the day after the building was acquired indicates that it was a bargain purchase at $150,000. To use $175,000 in the accounting records, however, would record an illusory or unrealized profit. If, after buying the building, the buyer accepts the offer and sells the building for $175,000, a profit of $25,000 is then realized and recorded. The new owner would record $175,000 as the cost of the building.

Using the cost concept involves two other important accounting concepts—objectivity and the unit of measure. The **objectivity concept** requires that the accounting records and reports be based upon objective evidence. In exchanges between a buyer and a seller, both try to get the best price. Only the final amount agreed upon is objective enough for accounting purposes. If the amounts for which properties were recorded were constantly revised upward and downward based on offers, appraisals, and opinions, accounting reports would soon become unstable and unreliable.

The **unit of measure concept** requires that economic data be recorded in dollars. Money is a common unit of measurement that allows for the reporting of uniform financial data and reports.

Assets, Liabilities, and Owner's Equity

OBJECTIVE 6

State the accounting equation and define each element of the equation.

The resources owned by a business are called **assets**. Examples of assets include cash, land, buildings, and equipment. The rights or claims to the properties are normally divided into two principal types: (1) the rights of creditors and (2) the rights of owners. The rights of creditors represent debts of the business and are called **liabilities**. The rights of the owners are called **owner's equity**. The relationship between the two may be stated in the form of an equation, as follows:

Assets = Liabilities + Owner's Equity

This equation is known as the **accounting equation**. It is usual to place liabilities before owner's equity in the accounting equation because creditors have first rights to the assets. The claim of the owners is sometimes given greater emphasis by transposing liabilities to the other side of the equation, which yields:

Assets − Liabilities = Owner's Equity

To illustrate, if the assets owned by a business amount to $100,000 and the liabilities amount to $30,000, the owner's equity is equal to $70,000, as shown below.

Assets	−	Liabilities	=	Owner's Equity
$100,000	−	$30,000	=	$70,000

Q&A

If a company's assets increase by $20,000 and its liabilities decrease by $5,000, how much did the owner's equity increase or decrease?

Change in assets	=	Change in liabilities	+	Change in owner's equity
+20,000	=	−5,000	+	X
+25,000	=			X

Business Transactions and the Accounting Equation

OBJECTIVE 7

Explain how business transactions can be stated in terms of the resulting changes in the three basic elements of the accounting equation.

Paying a monthly telephone bill of $68 affects a business's financial condition because it now has less cash on hand. Such an economic event or condition that directly changes an entity's financial condition or directly affects its results of operations is a **business transaction**. For example, purchasing land for $50,000 is a business transaction. In contrast, a change in a business's credit rating does not directly affect cash or any other element of its financial condition.

All business transactions can be stated in terms of changes in the three elements of the accounting equation.

All business transactions can be stated in terms of changes in the three elements of the accounting equation. You will see how business transactions affect the accounting equation by studying some typical transactions. For example, assume that on November 1, 1999, Pat King begins a business that will be known as Computer King. Using Pat's knowledge of microcomputers, the business will offer computer consulting services for a fee. Each transaction or group of similar transactions during the first month of operations is described in the following paragraphs. The effect of each transaction on the accounting equation is then shown.

COMPUTER KING

Transaction a. Pat King deposits $15,000 in a bank account in the name of Computer King. The effect of this transaction is to increase the asset (cash), on the left side of the equation, by $15,000. To balance the equation, the owner's equity, on the right side of the equation, is increased by the same amount. The equity of the owner is referred to by using the owner's name and "Capital," such as "Pat King, Capital." The effect of this transaction on Computer King's accounting equation is shown below.

	Assets	=	**Owner's Equity**	
	Cash	=	Pat King, Capital	
a.	15,000		15,000	Investment by Pat King

Note that since Pat King is the sole owner, Computer King is a proprietorship. In addition, note that the accounting equation shown above relates only to the business, Computer King. Under the business entity concept, Pat King's personal assets, such as a home or personal bank account, and personal liabilities are excluded from the equation.

Transaction b. If you purchased this textbook by paying cash, you entered into a transaction in which you exchanged one asset for another. That is, you exchanged cash for the textbook. Businesses often enter into similar transactions. Computer King, for example, exchanged $10,000 cash for land. The land is located near a shopping mall that contains three microcomputer stores. Pat King plans to rent office space and equipment for several months. If the business is a success, the company will build on the land.

The purchase of the land changes the makeup of the assets but does not change the total assets. The items in the equation prior to this transaction and the effect of the transaction are shown next. The new amounts or *balances* of the items are also shown.

	Assets			=	**Owner's Equity**
	Cash	+	Land	=	Pat King, Capital
Bal.	15,000				15,000
b.	−10,000		+10,000		
Bal.	5,000		10,000		15,000

Q&A

If Computer King had purchased a minivan for $18,000, paying $4,000 cash and signing a loan agreement (note payable) for $14,000, how would the transaction be recorded using the accounting equation?

Cash	+	**Truck**	=	**Notes Payable**
−4,000	+	18,000		+14,000

Transaction c. At one time or another, you have probably used a credit card to buy clothing or other merchandise. In this type of transaction, you received clothing for a promise to pay your credit card bill in the future. That is, you received an asset and incurred a liability to pay a future bill. During the month, Computer King entered into a similar transaction, buying supplies for $1,350 and agreeing to pay the supplier in the near future. This type of transaction is called a purchase *on ac-*

> Other examples of common prepaid expenses include insurance and rent. Businesses usually report these assets together as a single item, prepaid expenses.

count. The liability created is called an **account payable**. Items such as supplies that will be used in the business in the future are called **prepaid expenses**, which are assets. The effect of this transaction is to increase assets and liabilities by $1,350, as follows:

	Assets			=	Liabilities	+ Owner's Equity
	Cash +	Supplies +	Land	=	Accounts Payable +	Pat King, Capital
Bal.	5,000		10,000			15,000
c.		+1,350			+1,350	
Bal.	5,000	1,350	10,000		1,350	15,000

Transaction d. You may have earned money by mowing lawns. If so, you received money for rendering services to a customer. Likewise, a business earns money by selling goods or services to its customers. This amount is called **revenue**.

During its first month of operations, Computer King provided services to customers, earning fees of $7,500 and receiving the amount in cash. The receipt of cash increases Computer King's assets and also increases Pat King's equity in the business. Thus, this transaction increased cash and the owner's equity by $7,500, as shown here.

	Assets			=	Liabilities	+ Owner's Equity	
	Cash +	Supplies +	Land	=	Accounts Payable +	Pat King, Capital	
Bal.	5,000	1,350	10,000		1,350	15,000	
d.	+ 7,500					+ 7,500	Fees earned
Bal.	12,500	1,350	10,000		1,350	22,500	

Special terms may be used to describe certain kinds of revenue, such as **sales** for the sale of merchandise. Revenue from providing services is called **fees earned**. For example, a physician would record fees earned for services to patients. Other examples include **rent revenue** (money received for rent) and **interest revenue** (money received for interest).

Instead of requiring the payment of cash at the time services are provided or goods are sold, a business may accept payment at a later date. Such revenues are called *fees on account* or *sales on account.* In such cases, the firm has an **account receivable**, which is a claim against the customer. An account receivable is an asset, and the revenue is earned as if cash had been received. When customers pay their accounts, there is an exchange of one asset for another. Cash increases and accounts receivable decreases.

Transaction e. If you mowed lawns to earn money, you probably used your own lawn mower and bought your own gas. Computer King also spent cash or used up other assets in earning revenue. The amounts used in this process of earning revenue are called **expenses**. Expenses include supplies used, wages of employees, and other assets and services used in operating the business.

For Computer King, the expenses paid during the month were as follows: wages, $2,125; rent, $800; utilities, $450; and miscellaneous, $275. Miscellaneous expenses include small amounts paid for such items as postage due, coffee, and newspaper and magazine purchases. The effect of this group of transactions is the opposite of the effect of revenues. These transactions reduce cash and owner's equity, as shown at the top of the next page.

	Assets			=	Liabilities	+	Owner's Equity	
	Cash	Supplies	Land	=	Accounts Payable	+	Pat King, Capital	
Bal.	12,500	1,350	10,000		1,350		22,500	
e.	−3,650						−2,125	Wages expense
							− 800	Rent expense
							− 450	Utilities expense
							− 275	Misc. expense
	8,850	1,350	10,000		1,350		18,850	

Usually businesses record each revenue and expense transaction separately as it occurs. However, to simplify this illustration, we have summarized Computer King's revenues and expenses for the month in transactions (d) and (e).

Transaction f. When you pay your monthly credit card bill, you decrease the cash in your checking account and also decrease the amount you owe to the credit card company. Likewise, when Computer King pays $950 to creditors during the month, it reduces both assets and liabilities, as shown below.

	Assets			=	Liabilities	+	Owner's Equity
	Cash	Supplies	Land	=	Accounts Payable	+	Pat King, Capital
Bal.	8,850	1,350	10,000		1,350		18,850
f.	−950				−950		
Bal.	7,900	1,350	10,000		400		18,850

You should note that paying an amount on account is different from paying an amount for an expense. The payment of an expense reduces owner's equity, as illustrated in transaction (e). Paying an amount on account reduces the amount owed on a liability.

Transaction g. At the end of the month, the cost of the supplies on hand (not yet used) is $550. The remainder of the supplies ($1,350 − $550) was used in the operations of the business and is treated as an expense. This decrease of $800 in supplies and owner's equity is shown as follows:

If supplies of $2,500 were purchased during the month and supplies of $350 are on hand at the end of the month, how much is supplies expense for the month?

$2,150 ($2,500 supplies purchased − $350 on hand)

	Assets			=	Liabilities	+	Owner's Equity	
	Cash	Supplies	Land	=	Accounts Payable	+	Pat King, Capital	
Bal.	7,900	1,350	10,000		400		18,850	
g.		−800					− 800	Supplies expense
Bal.	7,900	550	10,000		400		18,050	

Transaction h. At the end of the month, Pat King withdraws $2,000 in cash from the business for personal use. This transaction is the exact opposite of an investment in the business by the owner. Cash and owner's equity are decreased. The cash payment is not a business expense but a withdrawal of a part of the owner's equity. The effect of the $2,000 withdrawal is shown as follows:

	Assets			=	Liabilities	+	Owner's Equity	
	Cash	Supplies	Land	=	Accounts Payable	+	Pat King, Capital	
Bal.	7,900	550	10,000		400		18,050	
h.	−2,000						−2,000	Withdrawal
Bal.	5,900	550	10,000		400		16,050	

You should be careful not to confuse withdrawals by the owner with expenses. Withdrawals *do not* represent assets or services used in the process of earning revenues. The owner's equity decrease from the withdrawals is listed in the equation under Capital. This is because withdrawals are considered a distribution of capital to the owner.

Summary. The transactions of Computer King are summarized as follows. They are identified by letter, and the balance of each item is shown after each transaction.

	Assets			= Liabilities +	Owner's Equity	
	Cash +	Supplies +	Land =	Accounts Payable +	Pat King, Capital	
a.	+15,000				+15,000	Investment by Pat King
b.	−10,000		+10,000			
Bal.	5,000		10,000		15,000	
c.		+1,350		+1,350		
Bal.	5,000	1,350	10,000	1,350	15,000	
d.	+ 7,500				+ 7,500	Fees earned
Bal.	12,500	1,350	10,000	1,350	22,500	
e.	− 3,650				− 2,125	Wages expense
					− 800	Rent expense
					− 450	Utilities expense
					− 275	Misc. expense
Bal.	8,850	1,350	10,000	1,350	18,850	
f.	− 950			− 950		
Bal.	7,900	1,350	10,000	400	18,850	
g.		− 800			− 800	Supplies expense
Bal.	7,900	550	10,000	400	18,050	
h.	− 2,000				− 2,000	Withdrawal
Bal.	5,900	550	10,000	400	16,050	

In reviewing the preceding summary, you should note the following, which apply to all types of businesses:

1. The effect of every transaction is *an increase or a decrease in one or more of the accounting equation elements.*
2. The two sides of the accounting equation are *always equal.*
3. The owner's equity is *increased by amounts invested by the owner* and is *decreased by withdrawals by the owner.* In addition, the owner's equity is *increased by revenues* and is *decreased by expenses.* The effects of these four types of transactions on owner's equity are illustrated in Exhibit 3.

EXHIBIT 3
Effects of Transactions on Owner's Equity

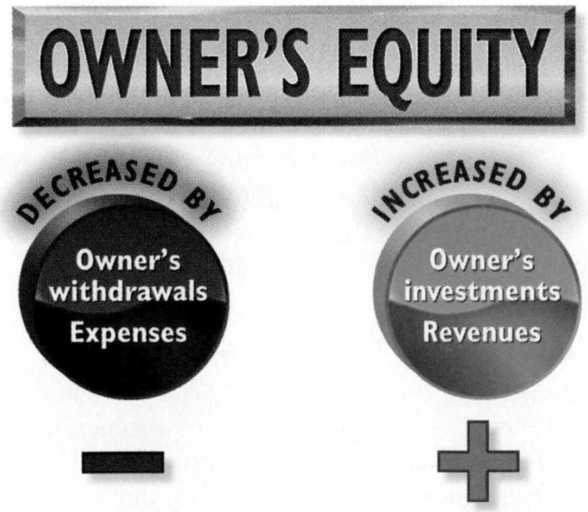

Financial Statements

OBJECTIVE 8

Describe the financial statements of a proprietorship and explain how they interrelate.

After transactions have been recorded and summarized, reports are prepared for users. The accounting reports that provide this information are called **financial statements**. The principal financial statements of a proprietorship are the income statement, the statement of owner's equity, the balance sheet, and the statement of cash flows. The order in which the statements are normally prepared and the nature of the data presented in each statement are as follows:

- **Income statement**—A summary of the revenue and expenses *for a specific period of time,* such as a month or a year.
- **Statement of owner's equity**—A summary of the changes in the owner's equity that have occurred *during a specific period of time,* such as a month or a year.
- **Balance sheet**—A list of the assets, liabilities, and owner's equity *as of a specific date,* usually at the close of the last day of a month or a year.
- **Statement of cash flows**—A summary of the cash receipts and cash payments *for a specific period of time,* such as a month or a year.

The basic features of the four statements and their interrelationships are illustrated in Exhibit 4. The data for the statements were taken from the summary of transactions of Computer King.

All financial statements should be identified by the name of the business, the title of the statement, and the *date* or *period of time*. The data presented in the income statement, the statement of owner's equity, and the statement of cash flows are for a period of time. The data presented in the balance sheet are for a specific date.

You should note the use of indents, captions, dollar signs, and rulings in the financial statements. They aid the reader by emphasizing the sections of the statements.

When you buy something at a store, you may *match* the cash register total with the amount you paid the cashier and with the amount of change, if any, you received.

Income Statement

The income statement reports the revenues and expenses for a period of time, based on the **matching concept**. This concept is applied by *matching* the expenses with the revenue generated during a period by those expenses. The income statement also reports the excess of the revenue over the expenses incurred. This excess of the revenue over the expenses is called **net income** or **net profit**. If the expenses exceed the revenue, the excess is a **net loss**.

Net income—the excess of revenue over expenses—increases owner's equity.

The effects of revenue earned and expenses incurred during the month for Computer King were shown in the equation as increases and decreases in owner's equity (capital). Net income for a period has the effect of increasing owner's equity (capital) for the period, whereas a net loss has the effect of decreasing owner's equity (capital) for the period.

The revenue, expenses, and the net income of $3,050 for Computer King are reported in the income statement in Exhibit 4. The order in which the expenses are listed in the income statement varies among businesses. One method is to list them in order of size, beginning with the larger items. Miscellaneous expense is usually shown as the last item, regardless of the amount.

Statement of Owner's Equity

The statement of owner's equity reports the changes in the owner's equity for a period of time. It is prepared *after* the income statement because the net income or net loss for the period must be reported in this statement. Similarly, it is prepared *before* the balance sheet, since the amount of owner's equity at the end of the pe-

EXHIBIT 4
Financial Statements

Computer King
Income Statement
For the Month Ended November 30, 1999

Fees earned		$7,500.00
Operating expenses:		
Wages expense	$2,125.00	
Rent expense	800.00	
Supplies expense	800.00	
Utilities expense	450.00	
Miscellaneous expense	275.00	
Total operating expenses		4,450.00
Net income		$3,050.00

Computer King
Statement of Owner's Equity
For the Month Ended November 30, 1999

Pat King, capital, November 1, 1999		$ 0
Investment on November 1, 1999	$15,000.00	
Net income for November	3,050.00	
	$18,050.00	
Less withdrawals	2,000.00	
Increase in owner's equity		16,050.00
Pat King, capital, November 30, 1999		$16,050.00

Computer King
Balance Sheet
November 30, 1999

Assets		Liabilities	
Cash	$ 5,900.00	Accounts payable	$ 400.00
Supplies	550.00	**Owner's Equity**	
Land	10,000.00	Pat King, capital	16,050.00
		Total liabilities and	
Total assets	$16,450.00	owner's equity	$16,450.00

Computer King
Statement of Cash Flows
For the Month Ended November 30, 1999

Cash flows from operating activities:		
Cash received from customers	$ 7,500.00	
Deduct cash payments for expenses and payments to creditors	4,600.00	
Net cash flow from operating activities		$ 2,900.00
Cash flows from investing activities:		
Cash payments for acquisition of land		(10,000.00)
Cash flows from financing activities:		
Cash received as owner's investment	$15,000.00	
Deduct cash withdrawal by owner	2,000.00	
Net cash flow from financing activities		13,000.00
Net cash flow and November 30, 1999 cash balance		$ 5,900.00

Financial statements are used to evaluate the current financial condition of a business and to predict its future operating results and cash flows. For example, bank loan officers use a business's financial statements in deciding whether to grant a loan to the business. Once the loan is granted, the borrower may be required to maintain a certain level of assets in excess of liabilities. The business's financial statements are used to monitor this level.

riod must be reported on the balance sheet. Because of this, the statement of owner's equity is often viewed as the connecting link between the income statement and balance sheet.

Three types of transactions affected owner's equity for Computer King during November: (1) the original investment of $15,000, (2) the revenue and expenses that resulted in net income of $3,050 for the month, and (3) a withdrawal of $2,000 by the owner. This information is summarized in the statement of owner's equity in Exhibit 4.

Balance Sheet

The balance sheet in Exhibit 4 reports the amounts of Computer King's assets, liabilities, and owner's equity at the end of November. These amounts are taken from the last line of the summary of transactions presented earlier. The form of balance sheet shown in Exhibit 4 is called the **account form** because it resembles the basic format of the accounting equation, with assets on the left side and the liabilities and owner's equity sections on the right side. An alternative form of balance sheet, called the **report form**, presents the liabilities and owner's equity sections below the assets section. We illustrate this form of balance sheet in a later chapter.

The assets section of the balance sheet normally presents assets in the order that they will be converted into cash or used in operations. Cash is presented first, followed by receivables, supplies, prepaid insurance, and other assets. Then, the assets of a more permanent nature are shown, such as land, buildings, and equipment.

In the liabilities section of the balance sheet in Exhibit 4, accounts payable is the only liability. When there are two or more categories of liabilities, each should be listed and the total amount of liabilities presented as shown below.

Liabilities		
Accounts payable	$12,900	
Wages payable	2,570	
Total liabilities		$15,470

Statement of Cash Flows

The statement of cash flows in Exhibit 4 consists of three sections: (1) operating activities, (2) investing activities, and (3) financing activities. Each of these sections is briefly described below.

Cash Flows from Operating Activities. This section reports a summary of cash receipts and cash payments from operations. The net cash flow from operating activities ($2,900 in Exhibit 4) will normally differ from the amount of net income for the period ($3,050 in Exhibit 4). This difference occurs because revenues and expenses may not be recorded at the same time that cash is received from customers and cash is paid to creditors.

Cash Flows from Investing Activities. This section reports the cash transactions for the acquisition and sale of relatively permanent assets.

Cash Flows from Financing Activities. This section reports the cash transactions related to cash investments by the owner, borrowings, and cash withdrawals by the owner.

Preparing the statement of cash flows requires an understanding of concepts that we have not discussed in this chapter. Therefore, we will illustrate the preparation of the statement of cash flows in a later chapter.

FINANCIAL ANALYSIS AND INTERPRETATION

OBJECTIVE 9

Use the ratio of liabilities to owner's equity to analyze the ability of a business to withstand poor business conditions.

As we discussed earlier in this chapter, financial statements are useful to bankers, creditors, owners, and other stakeholders in analyzing and interpreting the financial performance and condition of a business. Throughout this text, we will discuss various tools that are often used in practice to analyze and interpret the financial performance and condition of a business. The first such tool we will introduce is especially useful in analyzing the ability of a business to pay its creditors.

The relationship between liabilities and owner's equity, expressed as a ratio, is calculated as follows:

$$\textbf{Ratio of liabilities to owner's equity} = \frac{\textbf{Total liabilities}}{\textbf{Total owner's equity (or Total stockholders' equity)}}$$

COMPUTER KING

To illustrate, Computer King's ratio of liabilities to owner's equity at the end of 1999 is 0.025, as calculated below.

$$\textbf{Ratio of liabilities to owner's equity} = \frac{\$400}{\$16{,}050} = 0.025$$

For corporations, it is normal to refer to total owner's equity as total stockholders' equity. Thus, when computing this ratio for a corporation, you should substitute total stockholders' equity for total owner's equity.

The rights of creditors to a business's assets take precedence over the rights of the owners or stockholders. Thus, the lower the ratio of liabilities to owner's equity, the more able the business is to withstand poor business conditions and still fully meet its obligations to creditors.

To illustrate, a ratio of 1 indicates that the liabilities and owner's equity are equal. In other words, if the business suffers a loss equal to the total liabilities, the amount of total assets available to creditors will not drop below their claims on the assets. If this were to happen, the creditors could collect their claims and the owner would be left with nothing. In contrast, if the ratio were 3, a loss greater than one-third of the liabilities would drop the total assets below the creditors' claims.

ENCORE

Barbie and Ken

Many of today's large businesses began with an idea and a commitment of individuals to pursue that idea as far as possible.

In 1945, Elliott and Ruth Handler started a small toy company in their garage. The husband-and-wife team worked well together, with Elliott, an artist, focusing on the design of the toys and Ruth managing the business affairs and finding sales outlets for the toys. After struggling more than ten years to make the company a success, it was worth just over $500,000. In 1955, the Handlers decided to take a bold step to expand sales by advertising on a popular children's television program, The Mickey Mouse Club. The cost of the advertising campaign, if unsuccessful, would have potentially bankrupted the company. However, the campaign was successful and sales increased dramatically.

In 1959, the Handlers took another gamble by introducing a full-figured, teenage doll. The market experts predicted that such a doll

Barbie and Ken dolls

would not appeal to three- to eleven-year-old girls. The experts were wrong. The Barbie Doll, named after the Handlers' daughter Barbara, was a huge success. The Barbie Doll, which sold 350,000 its first year, has now sold over 500 billion. Later, the Handlers introduced a male doll, Ken, as a friend of Barbie. The Ken Doll was named after the Handlers' son.

Mattel Inc. has grown dramatically since its beginning in 1945. In 1996, Mattel reported revenues of over $3.7 billion and total assets of over $2.8 billion. ■

KEY POINTS

1 Describe the nature of a business.

A business is an organization in which basic resources (inputs), such as materials and labor, are assembled and processed to provide goods or services (outputs) to customers. The objective of most businesses is to maximize profits.

There are three different types of businesses that are operated for profit: manufacturing, merchandising, and service businesses. A business is normally organized in one of three different forms: proprietorship, partnership, or corporation. A business stakeholder is a person or entity (such as an owner, manager, employee, customer, creditor, or the government) that has an interest in the economic performance of the business.

2 Describe the role of accounting in business.

Accounting is an information system that provides reports to stakeholders about the economic activities and condition of a business. Accounting is the "language of business."

3 Describe the importance of business ethics and the basic principles of proper ethical conduct.

Ethics are moral principles that guide the conduct of individuals. Proper ethical conduct implies a behavior that considers the impact of one's actions on society and others. Sound ethical principles include (1) avoiding small ethical lapses, (2) focusing on your long-term reputation, and (3) being willing to suffer adverse personal consequences for holding to an ethical position.

4 Describe the profession of accounting.

Accountants are engaged in either private accounting or public accounting. The two most common specialized fields of accounting are financial accounting and managerial accounting. Other fields include cost accounting, environmental accounting, tax accounting, accounting systems, international accounting, not-for-profit accounting, and social accounting.

5 Summarize the development of accounting principles and relate them to practice.

Financial accountants follow generally accepted accounting principles (GAAP) in preparing reports so that stakeholders can compare one company to another. Accounting principles and concepts develop from research, accepted accounting practices, and pronouncements of authoritative bodies. Currently, the Financial Accounting Standards Board (FASB) is the authoritative body that has the primary responsibility for developing accounting principles.

The business entity concept views the business as an entity separate from its owners, creditors, or other stakeholders. The business entity limits the economic data in the accounting system to that related directly to the activities of the business. The cost concept requires that properties and services bought by a business be recorded in terms of actual cost. The objectivity concept requires that the accounting records and reports be based upon objective evidence. The unit of measure concept requires that economic data be recorded in dollars.

6 State the accounting equation and define each element of the equation.

The resources owned by a business and the rights or claims to these resources may be stated in the form of an equation, as follows:

Assets = Liabilities + Owner's Equity

7 Explain how business transactions can be stated in terms of the resulting changes in the three basic elements of the accounting equation.

All business transactions can be stated in terms of the change in one or more of the three elements of the accounting equation. That is, the effect of every transaction can be stated in terms of increases or decreases in one or more of these elements, while maintaining the equality between the two sides of the equation.

8 Describe the financial statements of a proprietorship and explain how they interrelate.
The principal financial statements of a proprietorship are the income statement, the statement of owner's equity, the balance sheet, and the statement of cash flows. The income statement reports a period's net income or net loss, which also appears on the statement of owner's equity. The ending owner's capital reported on the statement of owner's equity is also reported on the balance sheet. The ending cash balance is reported on the balance sheet and the statement of cash flows.

9 Use the ratio of liabilities to owner's equity to analyze the ability of a business to withstand poor business conditions.
The ratio of liabilities to owner's equity is useful in analyzing the ability of a business to pay its creditors. The lower the ratio, the more able the business is to withstand poor business conditions and still fully meet its obligations to creditors.

ILLUSTRATIVE PROBLEM

On July 1 of the current year, the assets and liabilities of Cecil Jameson, Attorney-at-Law, are as follows: cash, $1,000; accounts receivable, $3,200; supplies, $850; land, $10,000; accounts payable, $1,530. Cecil Jameson, Attorney-at-Law, is a proprietorship owned and operated by Cecil Jameson. Currently, office space and office equipment are being rented, pending the construction of an office complex on land purchased last year. Business transactions during July are summarized as follows:

a. Received cash from clients for services, $3,928.
b. Paid creditors on account, $1,055.
c. Received cash from Cecil Jameson as an additional investment, $3,700.
d. Paid office rent for the month, $1,200.
e. Charged clients for legal services on account, $2,025.
f. Purchased office supplies on account, $245.
g. Received cash from clients on account, $3,000.
h. Received invoice for paralegal services from Legal Aid Inc. for July (to be paid on August 10), $1,635.
i. Paid the following: wages expense, $850; answering service expense, $250; utilities expense, $325; and miscellaneous expense, $75.
j. Determined that the cost of office supplies on hand was $980; therefore, the cost of supplies used during the month was $115.
k. Jameson withdrew $1,000 in cash from the business for personal use.

Instructions

1. Determine the amount of owner's equity (Cecil Jameson's capital) as of July 1 of the current year.
2. State the assets, liabilities, and owner's equity as of July 1 in equation form similar to that shown in this chapter. In tabular form below the equation, indicate the increases and decreases resulting from each transaction and the new balances after each transaction. Explain the nature of each increase and decrease in owner's equity by an appropriate notation at the right of the amount.
3. Prepare an income statement for July, a statement of owner's equity for July, and a balance sheet as of July 31.

Solution

1. Assets − Liabilities = Owner's Equity (Cecil Jameson, capital)
$15,050 − $1,530 = Owner's Equity (Cecil Jameson, capital)
$13,520 = Owner's Equity (Cecil Jameson, capital)

2.

	Assets				= Liabilities	+ Owner's Equity	
	Cash	+ Accounts Receivable	+ Supplies	+ Land	= Accounts Payable	+ Cecil Jameson, Capital	
Bal.	1,000	3,200	850	10,000	1,530	13,520	
a.	+3,928					+ 3,928	Fees earned
Bal.	4,928	3,200	850	10,000	1,530	17,448	
b.	−1,055				−1,055		
Bal.	3,873	3,200	850	10,000	475	17,448	
c.	+3,700					+ 3,700	Investment
Bal.	7,573	3,200	850	10,000	475	21,148	
d.	−1,200					− 1,200	Rent expense
Bal.	6,373	3,200	850	10,000	475	19,948	
e.		+2,025				+ 2,025	Fees earned
Bal.	6,373	5,225	850	10,000	475	21,973	
f.			+ 245		+ 245		
Bal.	6,373	5,225	1,095	10,000	720	21,973	
g.	+3,000	−3,000					
Bal.	9,373	2,225	1,095	10,000	720	21,973	
h.					+1,635	− 1,635	Paralegal exp.
Bal.	9,373	2,225	1,095	10,000	2,355	20,338	
i.	−1,500					− 850	Wages exp.
						− 250	Answ. svc. exp.
						− 325	Utilities exp.
						− 75	Misc. exp.
Bal.	7,873	2,225	1,095	10,000	2,355	18,838	
j.			− 115			− 115	Supplies exp.
Bal.	7,873	2,225	980	10,000	2,355	18,723	
k.	−1,000					− 1,000	Withdrawal
	6,873	2,225	980	10,000	2,355	17,723	

3.

Cecil Jameson, Attorney-at-Law
Income Statement
For the Month Ended July 31, 20—

Fees earned		$5,953.00
Operating expenses:		
Paralegal expense	$1,635.00	
Rent expense	1,200.00	
Wages expense	850.00	
Utilities expense	325.00	
Answering service expense	250.00	
Supplies expense	115.00	
Miscellaneous expense	75.00	
Total operating expenses		4,450.00
Net income		$1,503.00

Cecil Jameson, Attorney-at-Law
Statement of Owner's Equity
For the Month Ended July 31, 20—

Cecil Jameson, capital, July 1, 20—		$13 520 00
Additional investment by owner	$3 700 00	
Net income for the month	1 503 00	
	$5 203 00	
Less withdrawals	1 000 00	
Increase in owner's equity		4 203 00
Cecil Jameson, capital, July 31, 20—		$17 723 00

Cecil Jameson, Attorney-at-Law
Balance Sheet
July 31, 20—

Assets		Liabilities	
Cash	$ 6 873 00	Accounts payable	$ 2 355 00
Accounts receivable	2 225 00	**Owner's Equity**	
Supplies	980 00	Cecil Jameson, capital	17 723 00
Land	10 000 00	Total liabilities and	
Total assets	$20 078 00	owner's equity	$20 078 00

SELF-EXAMINATION QUESTIONS

Answers at End of Chapter

Matching

Match each of the following statements with its proper term. Some terms may not be used.

- **A. Account form**
- **B. Account payable**
- **C. Account receivable**
- **D. Accounting**
- **E. Accounting equation**
- **F. Assets**
- **G. Balance sheet**
- **H. Business**
- **I. Business entity concept**
- **J. Business stakeholder**
- **K. Business transaction**
- **L. Corporation**
- **M. Cost concept**
- **N. Ethics**
- **O. Expenses**

H 1. An organization in which basic resources (inputs), such as materials and labor, are assembled and processed to provide goods or services (outputs) to customers.

W 2. A type of business that changes basic inputs into products that are sold to individual customers.

Y 3. A type of business that purchases products from other businesses and sells them to customers.

FF 4. A business owned by one individual.

DD 5. A business owned by two or more individuals.

L 6. A business organized under state or federal statutes as a separate legal entity.

J 7. A person or entity that has an interest in the economic performance of a business.

V 8. Individuals who the owners have authorized to operate the business.

D 9. An information system that provides reports to stakeholders about the economic activities and condition of a business.

N 10. Moral principles that guide the conduct of individuals.

P 11. A specialized field of accounting primarily concerned with the recording and reporting of economic data and activities to stakeholders outside the business.

(continues)

P. **Financial accounting**
Q. **Financial Accounting Standards Board (FASB)**
R. **Generally accepted accounting principles (GAAP)**
S. **Income statement**
T. **Liabilities**
U. **Managerial accounting**
V. **Managers**
W. **Manufacturing**
X. **Matching concept**
Y. **Merchandising**
Z. **Net income**
AA. **Net loss**
BB. **Objectivity concept**
CC. **Owner's equity**
DD. **Partnership**
EE. **Prepaid expenses**
FF. **Proprietorship**
GG. **Report form**
HH. **Revenue**
II. **Service**
JJ. **Statement of cash flows**
KK. **Statement of owner's equity**
LL. **Unit of measure concept**

U 12. A specialized field of accounting that uses estimated data to aid management in running day-to-day operations and in planning future operations.

Q 13. The authoritative body that has the primary responsibility for developing accounting principles.

I 14. A concept of accounting that limits the economic data in the accounting system to data related directly to the activities of the business.

LL 15. A concept of accounting that requires that economic data be recorded in dollars.

F 16. The resources owned by a business.

T 17. The rights of creditors represent debts of the business.

CC 18. The rights of the owners.

E 19. Assets = Liabilities + Owner's Equity

K 20. An economic event or condition that directly changes an entity's financial condition or directly affects its results of operations.

B 21. The liability created by a purchase on account.

EE 22. Items such as supplies that will be used in the business in the future.

C 23. A claim against the customer.

O 24. The amounts used in the process of earning revenue.

HH 25. The amount a business earns by selling goods or services to its customers.

S 26. A summary of the revenue and expenses *for a specific period of time,* such as a month or a year.

KK 27. A summary of the changes in the owner's equity that have occurred *during a specific period of time,* such as a month or a year.

G 28. A list of the assets, liabilities, and owner's equity *as of a specific date,* usually at the close of the last day of a month or a year.

JJ 29. A summary of the cash receipts and cash payments *for a specific period of time,* such as a month or a year.

X 30. A concept of accounting in which expenses are matched with the revenue generated during a period by those expenses.

A 31. The form of balance sheet that resembles the basic format of the accounting equation, with assets on the left side and the liabilities and owner's equity sections on the right side.

Multiple Choice

1. A profit-making business that is a separate legal entity and in which ownership is divided into shares of stock is known as a:
   A. proprietorship
   B. service business
   C. partnership
   D. corporation

2. The resources owned by a business are called:
   A. assets
   B. liabilities
   C. the accounting equation
   D. owner's equity

3. A list of assets, liabilities, and owner's equity of a business entity as of a specific date is:
   A. a balance sheet
   B. an income statement
   C. a statement of owner's equity
   D. a statement of cash flows

4. If total assets increased $20,000 during a period of time and total liabilities increased $12,000 during the same period, the amount and direction (increase or decrease) of the period's change in owner's equity is:
   A. $32,000 increase
   B. $32,000 decrease
   C. $8,000 increase
   D. $8,000 decrease

5. If revenue was $45,000, expenses were $37,500, and the owner's withdrawals were $10,000, the amount of net income or net loss would be:
   A. $45,000 net income
   B. $7,500 net income
   C. $37,500 net loss
   D. $2,500 net loss

CLASS DISCUSSION QUESTIONS

1. What is the objective of most businesses?
2. Who are normally included as the stakeholders of a business?
3. What is the role of accounting in business?
4. What are three sound principles that form the foundation for ethical behavior?
5. Distinguish between private accounting and public accounting.
6. Identify what the abbreviation FASB stands for and describe how the FASB sets generally accepted accounting principles.
7. Jamie Niles is the owner of Niles Delivery Service. Recently, Jamie paid interest of \$1,500 on a personal loan of \$50,000 that she used to begin the business. Should Niles Delivery Service record the interest payment? Explain.
8. On February 15, Adams Repair Service extended an offer of \$75,000 for land that had been priced for sale at \$100,000. On February 25, Adams Repair Service accepted the seller's counteroffer of \$80,000. Describe how Adams Repair Service should record the land.
9. a. Land with an assessed value of \$100,000 for property tax purposes is acquired by a business for \$125,000. Ten years later, the plot of land has an assessed value of \$210,000 and the business receives an offer of \$240,000 for it. Should the monetary amount assigned to the land in the business records now be increased?
   b. Assuming that the land acquired in (a) was sold for \$240,000, how would the various elements of the accounting equation be affected?
10. What are the two principal rights to the properties of a business?
11. Name the three elements of the accounting equation.
12. Describe the difference between an account receivable and an account payable.
13. A business had revenues of \$90,000 and operating expenses of \$120,000. Did the business (a) incur a net loss or (b) realize a net income?
14. A business had revenues of \$300,000 and operating expenses of \$270,000. Did the business (a) incur a net loss or (b) realize a net income?
15. Name the two types of transactions that increase the owner's equity of a proprietorship.
16. Briefly describe the nature of the information provided by each of the following financial statements:
    1. income statement
    2. statement of owner's equity
    3. balance sheet
    4. statement of cash flows
17. Indicate whether each of the financial statements in Question 16 (a) covers a period of time or (b) is for a specific date.
18. What particular item of financial or operating data appears on (a) both the income statement and the statement of owner's equity and (b) both the balance sheet and the statement of owner's equity?
19. Name the three types of activities reported in the statement of cash flows.

1 9 T H   E D I T I O N

Success Stories Start Here

Congratulations! You are using the most successful, most widely used accounting text of all time. More than 10 million students have started their own personal success stories with this very text.

Warren
Reeve
Fess

Everyone Wins

Accounting, by Warren, Reeve, and Fess, is designed to introduce accounting concepts in a practical and interesting way. Whether you're headed for a career as an entrepreneur, a manager of a business, or an accounting professional, here are some tips to get your success story started:

1. Read the chapter prior to your instructor's lecture.
2. Work the assigned problems.
3. Complete the Continuing Problem in Chapters 1-4 to learn one of the foundations of accounting - the accounting cycle.
4. Review the illustrative problems in each chapter as preparation for completing problems.
5. Attend class - there's no substitute for listening and note-taking to absorb accounting concepts.
6. Use the tools described on this page to make the most of your study time.

Resources for Your Success On-Line at warren.swcollege.com

This high impact site includes current articles on accounting and downloadable resources, organized by chapter for easy navigation. Visit the text's Web site now to check out the supplements listed below.

- **Study Guide.** The Study Guide provides ample opportunity for practice and study. It includes quiz and test tips and multiple choice, fill-in-the-blank, and true-false questions with solutions. The Study Guide is also packaged with a disk that allows you to score your own practice tests. (Chs. 1-16: ISBN 0-538-87421-X, Chs. 12-24: ISBN 0-538-87422-8)
- **Working Papers.** Working Papers guide you through solutions to selected end-of-chapter assignments. Included forms help you organize your calculations and see how it all fits together. (Chs. 1-16: ISBN 0-538-87415-5, Chs. 12-24: ISBN 0-538-87416-3)
- **Working Papers Plus.** This special edition of Working Papers integrates chapter learning objectives and glossary terms with forms for solving all textbook exercises and selected textbook problems. (Chs. 1-16: ISBN 0-538-87417-1, Chs. 12-24: ISBN 0-538-87418-X)
- **Blank Working Papers**. This set of blank forms allows you to work exercises and problems for Chapters 1-24. (ISBN 0-538-87414-7)
- **PowerNotes.** If your instructor utilizes PowerPoint™ transparencies, this workbook will significantly aid note-taking and comprehension. PowerNotes provide printed versions of the transparencies and room to take detailed notes, plus critical-thinking activities and self-study review questions related to the transparencies. (Chs. 1-16: ISBN 0-538-87419-8, Chs. 12-24: ISBN 0-538-87420-1)
- **General Ledger Software.** This educational general ledger package allows for point-and-click solutions to end-of-chapter problems, comprehensive problems, as well as practice sets. (ISBN 0-538-87423-6)
- **Homework Assistant and Tutor (HAT).** This user-friendly software for Windows visually demonstrates the relationships between journals, ledgers, and financial statements as you solve selected end-of-chapter problems. A built-in tutor function includes numerous hints and help screens. (ISBN 0-538-87431-7)
- **Spreadsheet Applications Software.** Use these spreadsheet templates to solve dozens of problems via popular spreadsheet packages, such as Lotus 1-2-3® and Excel® Alternative "what-if" scenarios are also presented and explored. (Chs. 1-16: ISBN 0-538-87437-6, Chs. 12-24: ISBN 0-538-87438-4)

Order Now!

To order any of these supplements, visit "The Bookstore" at
warren.swcollege.com
or call the ITP Academic Resource Center at **1-800-423-0563**

EXERCISES

Exercise 1–1
Professional ethics
Objective 3

A fertilizer manufacturing company wants to relocate to Collier County. A 13-year-old report from a fired researcher at the company says the company's product is releasing toxic by-products. The company has suppressed that report. A second report commissioned by the company shows there is no problem with the fertilizer.

Should the company's chief executive officer reveal the context of the unfavorable report in discussions with Collier County representatives? Discuss.

Source: "Business Leaders Ponder Ethical Questions," *Naples Daily News,* May 12, 1991, p. 1E.

Exercise 1–2
Accounting equation
Objective 6

✓ a. $62,000

Determine the missing amount for each of the following:

	Assets	=	Liabilities	+	Owner's Equity
a.	X	=	$20,500	+	$41,500
b.	$32,750	=	X	+	10,000
c.	57,000	=	18,000	+	X

Exercise 1–3
Accounting equation
Objectives 6, 8

✓ b. $303,000

David Plymouth is the owner and operator of Dyn-A-Go, a motivational consulting business. At the end of its accounting period, December 31, 1999, Dyn-A-Go has assets of $325,000 and liabilities of $85,000. Using the accounting equation and considering each case independently, determine the following amounts:

a. David Plymouth, capital, as of December 31, 1999.
b. David Plymouth, capital, as of December 31, 2000, assuming that during 2000, assets increased by $84,000 and liabilities increased by $21,000.
c. David Plymouth, capital, as of December 31, 2000, assuming that during 2000, assets decreased by $5,000 and liabilities increased by $17,000.
d. David Plymouth, capital, as of December 31, 2000, assuming that during 2000, assets increased by $75,000 and liabilities decreased by $35,000.
e. Net income (or net loss) during 2000, assuming that as of December 31, 2000, assets were $425,000, liabilities were $105,000, and there were no additional investments or withdrawals.

Exercise 1–4
Asset, liability, owner's equity items
Objective 7

Indicate whether each of the following is identified with (1) an asset, (2) a liability, or (3) owner's equity:

a. fees earned
b. supplies
c. wages expense
d. land
e. accounts payable
f. cash

Exercise 1–5
Effect of transactions on accounting equation
Objective 7

Describe how the following business transactions affect the three elements of the accounting equation.

a. Invested cash in business.
b. Received cash for services performed.
c. Purchased supplies for cash.
d. Paid for utilities used in the business.
e. Purchased supplies on account.

Exercise 1–6
Effect of transactions on accounting equation
Objective 7

✓ (a)(1) increase $70,000

a. A vacant lot acquired for $90,000, on which there is a balance owed of $30,000, is sold for $160,000 in cash. What is the effect of the sale on the total amount of the seller's (1) assets, (2) liabilities, and (3) owner's equity?
b. After receiving the $160,000 cash in (a), the seller pays the $30,000 owed. What is the effect of the payment on the total amount of the seller's (1) assets, (2) liabilities, and (3) owner's equity?

Exercise 1–7
Effect of transactions on owner's equity
Objective 7

Indicate whether each of the following types of transactions will (a) increase owner's equity or (b) decrease owner's equity:

1. owner's investments
2. revenues
3. expenses
4. owner's withdrawals

Exercise 1–8
Transactions
Objective 7

The following selected transactions were completed by On Time Delivery Service during May:

1. Received cash from cash customers, $6,250.
2. Paid creditors on account, $250.
3. Received cash from owner as additional investment, $25,000.
4. Paid advertising expense, $625.
5. Billed customers for delivery services on account, $2,900.
6. Purchased supplies for cash, $750.
7. Paid rent for July, $2,500.
8. Received cash from customers on account, $900.
9. Determined that the cost of supplies on hand was $180; therefore, $570 of supplies had been used during the month.
10. Paid cash to owner for personal use, $1,000.

Indicate the effect of each transaction on the accounting equation by listing the numbers identifying the transactions, (1) through (10), in a vertical column, and inserting at the right of each number the appropriate letter from the following list:

a. Increase in an asset, decrease in another asset.
b. Increase in an asset, increase in a liability.
c. Increase in an asset, increase in owner's equity.
d. Decrease in an asset, decrease in a liability.
e. Decrease in an asset, decrease in owner's equity.

Exercise 1–9
Nature of transactions
Objective 7

✓ d. $3,950

Joe Norwood operates his own catering service. Summary financial data for August are presented in equation form as follows. Each line designated by a number indicates the effect of a transaction on the equation. Each increase and decrease in owner's equity, except transaction (5), affects net income.

	Cash	+	Supplies	+	Land	=	Liabilities	+	Owner's Equity
Bal.	5,500		750		29,000		3,750		31,500
1.	+16,000								+16,000
2.	− 2,000				+ 2,000				
3.	−11,250								−11,250
4.			+600				+ 600		
5.	− 1,950								− 1,950
6.	− 2,300						−2,300		
7.			−800						− 800
Bal.	4,000		550		31,000		2,050		33,500

a. Describe each transaction.
b. What is the amount of net decrease in cash during the month?
c. What is the amount of net increase in owner's equity during the month?
d. What is the amount of the net income for the month?
e. How much of the net income for the month was retained in the business?

Exercise 1–10
Net income and owner's withdrawals
Objective 8

The income statement of a proprietorship for the month of February indicates a net income of $28,000. During the same period, the owner withdrew $35,000 in cash from the business for personal use.

Would it be correct to say that the business incurred a net loss of $7,000 during the month? Discuss.

Exercise 1–11
Net income and owner's equity for four businesses

Objective 8

✓ Company G: Net loss, $60,000

Four different proprietorships, E, F, G, and H, show the same balance sheet data at the beginning and end of a year. These data, exclusive of the amount of owner's equity, are summarized as follows:

	Total Assets	Total Liabilities
Beginning of the year	$325,000	$120,000
End of the year	570,000	325,000

On the basis of the above data and the following additional information for the year, determine the net income (or loss) of each company for the year. (Suggestion: First determine the amount of increase or decrease in owner's equity during the year.)

Company E: The owner had made no additional investments in the business and had made no withdrawals from the business.
Company F: The owner had made no additional investments in the business but had withdrawn $25,000.
Company G: The owner had made an additional investment of $100,000 but had made no withdrawals.
Company H: The owner had made an additional investment of $100,000 and had withdrawn $25,000.

Exercise 1–12
Balance sheet items

Objective 8

From the following list of selected items taken from the records of Reliable Appliance Service as of a specific date, identify those that would appear on the balance sheet:

1. Utilities Expense
2. Fees Earned
3. Supplies
4. Wages Expense
5. Accounts Payable
6. Cash
7. Supplies Expense
8. Land
9. Julie McCarthy, Capital
10. Wages Payable

Exercise 1–13
Income statement items

Objective 8

Based on the data presented in Exercise 1–12, identify those items that would appear on the income statement.

Exercise 1–14
Statement of owner's equity

Objective 8

✓ Meg Tewksbury, capital September 30, 2000: $350,250

Financial information related to Eldora Company, a proprietorship, for the month ended September 30, 2000, is as follows:

Net income for September	$ 91,250
Meg Tewksbury's withdrawals during September	12,000
Meg Tewksbury, capital, September 1, 2000	271,000

Prepare a statement of owner's equity for the month ended September 30, 2000.

Exercise 1–15
Income statement

Objective 8

✓ Net income: $19,700

Temporary Help Services was organized on November 1. A summary of the revenue and expense transactions for November are as follows:

Fees earned	$75,400
Wages expense	37,700
Miscellaneous expense	2,250
Rent expense	12,500
Supplies expense	3,250

Prepare an income statement for the month ended November 30.

Exercise 1–16
Missing amounts from balance sheet and income statement data
Objective 8

✓ (a) $211,000
✓ (d) $335,000

One item is omitted in each of the following summaries of balance sheet and income statement data for four different proprietorships, I, II, III, and IV.

	I	II	III	IV
Beginning of the year:				
Assets	$500,000	$ 95,000	$90,000	(d)
Liabilities	360,000	45,000	76,000	$150,000
End of the year:				
Assets	855,000	125,000	94,000	310,000
Liabilities	465,000	35,000	87,000	170,000
During the year:				
Additional investment in the business	(a)	22,000	5,000	50,000
Withdrawals from the business	46,750	8,000	(c)	75,000
Revenue	197,750	(b)	88,100	140,000
Expenses	112,000	52,000	89,600	160,000

Determine the amounts of the missing items, identifying them by letter. (Suggestion: First determine the amount of increase or decrease in owner's equity during the year.)

Exercise 1–17
Balance sheets, net income
Objective 8

✓ b. $10,170

Financial information related to the proprietorship of Lynch Interiors for May and June of the current year is as follows:

	May 31, 20—	June 30, 20—
Accounts payable	$ 5,720	$ 6,900
Accounts receivable	9,300	10,400
Kate Lynch, capital	?	?
Cash	15,000	25,500
Supplies	1,000	750

a. Prepare balance sheets for Lynch Interiors as of May 31 and as of June 30 of the current year.
b. Determine the amount of net income for June, assuming that the owner made no additional investments or withdrawals during the month.
c. Determine the amount of net income for June, assuming that the owner made no additional investments but withdrew $5,000 during the month.

Exercise 1–18
Financial statements
Objective 8

REAL WORLD

Each of the following items is shown in the financial statements of **Exxon Corporation**. Identify the financial statement (balance sheet or income statement) in which each item would appear.

a. Operating expenses
b. Crude oil inventory
c. Income taxes payable
d. Sales
e. Investments
f. Marketable securities
g. Exploration expenses
h. Notes and loans payable
i. Cash equivalents
j. Long-term debt
k. Selling expenses
l. Notes receivable
m. Equipment
n. Accounts payable
o. Prepaid taxes

Exercise 1–19
Statement of cash flows
Objective 8

Indicate whether each of the following activities would be reported on the statement of cash flows as (a) an operating activity, (b) an investing activity, or (c) a financing activity:

1. Cash received as owner's investment
2. Cash paid for land
3. Cash received from fees earned
4. Cash paid for expenses

Exercise 1–20
Financial statements
Objective 8

What's Wrong WITH THIS?

✓ Correct Amount of Total Assets is $13,875

Vineyard Realty, organized July 1, 2000, is owned and operated by Barbara Straud. How many errors can you find in the following financial statements for Vineyard Realty, prepared after its second month of operations?

Vineyard Realty
Income Statement
August 31, 2000

Sales commissions		$26,100.00
Operating expenses:		
Office salaries expense	$18,150.00	
Rent expense	2,800.00	
Automobile expense	1,750.00	
Miscellaneous expense	550.00	
Supplies expense	225.00	
Total operating expenses		23,475.00
Net income		$12,625.00

Barbara Straud
Statement of Owner's Equity
August 31, 1999

Barbara Straud, capital, August 1, 2000	$ 8,450.00
Less withdrawals during August	1,000.00
	$ 7,450.00
Additional investment during August	2,500.00
	$ 9,950.00
Net income for the month	12,625.00
Barbara Straud, capital, August 31, 2000	$22,575.00

Balance Sheet
For the Month Ended August 31, 2000

Assets		**Liabilities**	
Cash	$ 3,350.00	Accounts receivable	$ 9,200.00
Accounts payable	1,300.00	Supplies	1,325.00
		Owner's Equity	
		Barbara Straud, capital	22,575.00
Total assets	$ 4,650.00	Total liabilities and owner's equity	$33,100.00

Exercise 1–21
Ratio of liabilities to stockholders' equity
Objective 9

REAL WORLD

The financial statements for **Hershey Foods Corporation** are presented in Appendix G at the end of the text.

a. Determine the ratio of liabilities to stockholders' equity for Hershey Foods Corporation at the end of 1996 and 1995.
b. What conclusions regarding the margin of protection to the creditors can you draw from your analysis?

PROBLEMS SERIES A

Problem 1–1A
Transactions

Objective 7

✓ Cash Bal. at End of July: $23,895

Chris Oxnard established an insurance agency on July 1 of the current year and completed the following transactions during July:

a. Opened a business bank account with a deposit of $25,000.
b. Purchased supplies on account, $850.
c. Paid creditors on account, $625.
d. Received cash from fees earned, $4,250.
e. Paid rent on office and equipment for the month, $1,000.
f. Paid automobile expenses for month, $780, and miscellaneous expenses, $250.
g. Paid office salaries, $1,200.
h. Determined that the cost of supplies on hand was $275; therefore, the cost of supplies used was $575.
i. Billed insurance companies for sales commissions earned, $3,350.
j. Withdrew cash for personal use, $1,500.

Instructions

1. Indicate the effect of each transaction and the balances after each transaction, using the following tabular headings:

Assets	=	Liabilities	+	Owner's Equity
Cash + Accounts Receivable + Supplies	=	Accounts Payable	+	Chris Oxnard, Capital

   Explain the nature of each increase and decrease in owner's equity by an appropriate notation at the right of the amount.
2. Briefly explain why the owner's investment and revenues increased owner's equity, while withdrawals and expenses decreased owner's equity.

Problem 1–2A
Financial statements

Objective 8

✓ Net income: $26,300

Following are the amounts of the assets and liabilities of Las Posas Travel Service at June 30, 2000, the end of the current year, and its revenue and expenses for the year ended on that date. The capital of Gabriela Sanchez, owner, was $18,000 at July 1, 1999, the beginning of the current year, and the owner withdrew $15,000 during the current year.

Accounts payable	$ 6,100
Cash	33,725
Fees earned	108,775
Miscellaneous expense	1,825
Rent expense	18,900
Supplies	1,675
Supplies expense	3,550
Taxes expense	2,800
Utilities expense	10,500
Wages expense	44,900

Instructions

1. Prepare an income statement for the current year ended June 30, 2000.
2. Prepare a statement of owner's equity for the current year ended June 30, 2000.
3. Prepare a balance sheet as of June 30, 2000.

Problem 1–3A
Financial statements

Objective 8

✓ Net income: $4,770

Joe Oakley established Joe's Desktop Computer Services on August 1 of the current year. The effect of each transaction and the balances after each transaction for August are as follows:

	Assets			= Liabilities +	Owner's Equity	
	Cash +	Accounts Receivable +	Supplies =	Accounts Payable +	Joe Oakley, Capital	
a.	+10,000				+10,000	Investment
b.			+550	+550		
Bal.	10,000		550	550	10,000	
c.	+ 6,500				+ 6,500	Fees earned
Bal.	16,500		550	550	16,500	
d.	− 1,500				− 1,500	Rent expense
Bal.	15,000		550	550	15,000	
e.	− 250			−250		
Bal.	14,750		550	300	15,000	
f.		+3,750			+ 3,750	Fees earned
Bal.	14,750	3,750	550	300	18,750	
g.	− 1,155				− 780	Auto expense
					− 375	Misc. expense
Bal.	13,595	3,750	550	300	17,595	
h.	− 2,500				− 2,500	Salaries expense
Bal.	11,095	3,750	550	300	15,095	
i.			−325		− 325	Supplies expense
Bal.	11,095	3,750	225	300	14,770	
j.	− 1,000				− 1,000	Withdrawal
Bal.	10,095	3,750	225	300	13,770	

Instructions

1. Prepare an income statement for the month ended August 31.
2. Prepare a statement of owner's equity for the month ended August 31.
3. Prepare a balance sheet as of August 31.

Problem 1–4A

Transactions; financial statements

Objectives 7, 8

✓ Net income: $5,775

On May 1 of the current year, Tom O'Hare established Rabbit Realty. O'Hare completed the following transactions during the month of May:

a. Opened a business bank account with a deposit of $7,000.
b. Paid rent on office and equipment for the month, $4,600.
c. Paid automobile expenses (including rental charge) for month, $900, and miscellaneous expenses, $550.
d. Purchased supplies (pens, file folders, and copy paper) on account, $1,325.
e. Earned sales commissions, receiving cash, $16,500.
f. Paid creditor on account, $800.
g. Paid office salaries, $3,950.
h. Withdrew cash for personal use, $2,000.
i. Determined that the cost of supplies on hand was $600; therefore, the cost of supplies used was $725.

Instructions

1. Indicate the effect of each transaction and the balances after each transaction, using the following tabular headings:

Assets	=	Liabilities	+	Owner's Equity
Cash + Supplies	=	Accounts Payable	+	Tom O'Hare, Capital

   Explain the nature of each increase and decrease in owner's equity by an appropriate notation at the right of the amount.
2. Prepare an income statement for May, a statement of owner's equity for May, and a balance sheet as of May 31.

Problem 1–5A

Transactions; financial statements

Objectives 7, 8

HAT

✓ Net income: $7,625

Camarillo Dry Cleaners is owned and operated by Kelly Camarillo. Currently, a building and equipment are being rented, pending expansion to new facilities. The actual work of dry cleaning is done by another company at wholesale rates. The assets and the liabilities of the business on November 1 of the current year are as follows: Cash, $5,400; Accounts Receivable, $18,750; Supplies, $1,560; Land, $35,000; Accounts Payable, $5,880. Business transactions during November are summarized as follows:

a. Paid rent for the month, $2,450.
b. Charged customers for dry cleaning sales on account, $7,150.
c. Paid creditors on account, $1,680.
d. Purchased supplies on account, $840.
e. Received cash from cash customers for dry cleaning sales, $14,600.
f. Received cash from customers on account, $14,750.
g. Received monthly invoice for dry cleaning expense for November (to be paid on December 10), $7,400.
h. Paid the following: wages expense, $1,800; truck expense, $725; utilities expense, $510; miscellaneous expense, $190.
i. Determined that the cost of supplies on hand was $1,350; therefore, the cost of supplies used during the month was $1,050.

Instructions

1. Determine the amount of Kelly Camarillo's capital as of November 1 of the current year.
2. State the assets, liabilities, and owner's equity as of November 1 in equation form similar to that shown in this chapter. In tabular form below the equation, indicate increases and decreases resulting from each transaction and the new balances after each transaction. Explain the nature of each increase and decrease in owner's equity by an appropriate notation at the right of the amount.
3. Prepare an income statement for November, a statement of owner's equity for November, and a balance sheet as of November 30.

Problem 1–6A

Financial statements

Objective 8

HAT

✓ Net income: $122,375

Dreamaker Designs is an architectural firm. Following are the amounts of the assets and liabilities of Dreamaker Designs at March 31, 2000, the end of the current year, and its revenue and expenses for the year ended on that date. The capital of Cindy Lopez, owner, was $99,990 on April 1, 1999, the beginning of the current year. During the current year, the owner withdrew $35,000.

Accounts payable	$ 28,000
Accounts receivable	39,750
Advertising expense	20,000
Cash	24,515
Fees earned	527,500
Land	150,000
Miscellaneous expense	6,125
Rent expense	98,000
Supplies	4,250
Supplies expense	9,750
Taxes expense	23,500
Utilities expense	35,750
Wages expense	212,000
Wages payable	3,150

Instructions

1. Prepare an income statement for the current year ended March 31, 2000.
2. Prepare a statement of owner's equity for the current year ended March 31, 2000.
3. Prepare a balance sheet as of March 31, 2000.

PROBLEMS SERIES B

Problem 1–1B
Transactions
Objective 7

✓ Cash Bal. at End of Feb. $27,670

On February 1 of the current year, Diane Winn established a business to manage rental property. She completed the following transactions during February:

a. Opened a business bank account with a deposit of $30,000.
b. Purchased supplies (pens, file folders, and copy paper) on account, $1,250.
c. Received cash from fees earned, $5,500.
d. Paid rent on office and equipment for the month, $3,000.
e. Paid creditors on account, $575.
f. Billed customers for fees earned, $3,250.
g. Paid automobile expenses (including rental charges) for month, $980, and miscellaneous expenses, $775.
h. Paid office salaries, $1,500.
i. Determined that the cost of supplies on hand was $315; therefore, the cost of supplies used was $935.
j. Withdrew cash for personal use, $1,000.

Instructions

1. Indicate the effect of each transaction and the balances after each transaction, using the following tabular headings:

Assets	=	Liabilities	+	Owner's Equity
Cash + Accounts Receivable + Supplies	=	Accounts Payable	+	Diane Winn, Capital

   Explain the nature of each increase and decrease in owner's equity by an appropriate notation at the right of the amount.
2. Briefly explain why the owner's investment and revenues increased owner's equity, while withdrawals and expenses decreased owner's equity.

Problem 1–2B
Financial statements
Objective 8

✓ Net income: $46,655

Following are the amounts of the assets and liabilities of Seven Seas Travel Agency at December 31, 2000, the end of the current year, and its revenue and expenses for the year ended on that date. The capital of Trent Baker, owner, was $24,500 on January 1, 2000, the beginning of the current year. During the current year, Trent withdrew $30,000.

Accounts payable	$ 3,200
Cash	42,490
Fees earned	127,530
Miscellaneous expense	1,750
Rent expense	27,000
Supplies	1,865
Supplies expense	2,125
Utilities expense	4,500
Wages expense	45,500

Instructions

1. Prepare an income statement for the current year ended December 31, 2000.
2. Prepare a statement of owner's equity for the current year ended December 31, 2000.
3. Prepare a balance sheet as of December 31, 2000.

Problem 1–3B
Financial statements
Objective 8

✓ Net income: $4,950

Tanya Maguire established Five Star Services on March 1 of the current year. Five Star Services offers financial planning advice to its clients. The effect of each transaction and the balances after each transaction for March are as follows:

	Assets			=	Liabilities	+	Owner's Equity	
		Accounts			Accounts		Tanya Maguire,	
	Cash	+ Receivable	+ Supplies	=	Payable	+	Capital	
a.	+18,000						+18,000	Investment
b.			+1,725		+1,725			
Bal.	18,000		1,725		1,725		18,000	
c.	− 1,225				−1,225			
Bal.	16,775		1,725		500		18,000	
d.	+ 7,750						+ 7,750	Fees earned
Bal.	24,525		1,725		500		25,750	
e.	− 2,500						− 2,500	Rent expense
Bal.	22,025		1,725		500		23,250	
f.	− 1,600						− 1,250	Auto expense
							− 350	Misc. expense
Bal.	20,425		1,725		500		21,650	
g.	− 1,900						− 1,900	Salaries expense
Bal.	18,525		1,725		500		19,750	
h.			−1,150				− 1,150	Supplies expense
Bal.	18,525		575		500		18,600	
i.		+4,350					+ 4,350	Fees earned
Bal.	18,525	4,350	575		500		22,950	
j.	− 3,000						− 3,000	Withdrawal
Bal.	15,525	4,350	575		500		19,950	

Instructions

1. Prepare an income statement for the month ended March 31.
2. Prepare a statement of owner's equity for the month ended March 31.
3. Prepare a balance sheet as of March 31.

Problem 1–4B
Transactions; financial statements

Objectives 7, 8

✓ Net income: $9,250

On September 1 of the current year, Corean Pace established Rapid Realty. Pace completed the following transactions during the month of September:

a. Opened a business bank account with a deposit of $8,500.
b. Purchased supplies (pens, file folders, fax paper, etc.) on account, $1,250.
c. Paid creditor on account, $750.
d. Earned sales commissions, receiving cash, $18,200.
e. Paid rent on office and equipment for the month, $2,000.
f. Withdrew cash for personal use, $3,000.
g. Paid automobile expenses (including rental charge) for month, $1,900, and miscellaneous expenses, $350.
h. Paid office salaries, $4,150.
i. Determined that the cost of supplies on hand was $700; therefore, the cost of supplies used was $550.

Instructions

1. Indicate the effect of each transaction and the balances after each transaction, using the following tabular headings:

Assets	=	Liabilities	+	Owner's Equity
Cash + Supplies	=	Accounts Payable	+	Corean Pace, Capital

   Explain the nature of each increase and decrease in owner's equity by an appropriate notation at the right of the amount.
2. Prepare an income statement for September, a statement of owner's equity for September, and a balance sheet as of September 30.

Problem 1–5B

Transactions; financial statements

Objectives 7, 8

✓ Net income: $6,050

Magic Dry Cleaners is owned and operated by Gail Fox. Currently, a building and equipment are being rented, pending expansion to new facilities. The actual work of dry cleaning is done by another company at wholesale rates. The assets and the liabilities of the business on July 1 of the current year are as follows: Cash, $7,250; Accounts Receivable, $22,100; Supplies, $2,200; Land, $50,000; Accounts Payable, $6,800. Business transactions during July are summarized as follows:

a. Received cash from cash customers for dry cleaning sales, $17,750.
b. Paid rent for the month, $2,000.
c. Purchased supplies on account, $1,650.
d. Paid creditors on account, $6,800.
e. Charged customers for dry cleaning sales on account, $6,920.
f. Received monthly invoice for dry cleaning expense for July (to be paid on August 10), $9,700.
g. Paid the following: wages expense, $2,400; truck expense, $1,580; utilities expense, $960; miscellaneous expense, $630.
h. Received cash from customers on account, $12,100.
i. Determined that the cost of supplies on hand was $2,500; therefore, the cost of supplies used during the month was $1,350.

Instructions

1. Determine the amount of Gail Fox's capital as of July 1 of the current year.
2. State the assets, liabilities, and owner's equity as of July 1 in equation form similar to that shown in this chapter. In tabular form below the equation, indicate increases and decreases resulting from each transaction and the new balances after each transaction. Explain the nature of each increase and decrease in owner's equity by an appropriate notation at the right of the amount.
3. Prepare an income statement for July, a statement of owner's equity for July, and a balance sheet as of July 31.

Problem 1–6B

Financial statements

Objective 8

✓ Net income: $136,400

Design Services is an architectural firm. Following are the amounts of the assets and liabilities of Design Services at December 31, the end of the current year, and its revenue and expenses for the year ended on that date. The capital of Marc Conrad, owner, was $84,950 at January 1, the beginning of the current year, and the owner withdrew $50,000 during the current year.

Accounts payable	$ 13,100
Accounts receivable	52,000
Advertising expense	7,500
Cash	37,200
Fees earned	329,250
Land	90,000
Miscellaneous expense	1,250
Rent expense	42,000
Supplies	6,750
Supplies expense	13,800
Taxes expense	10,500
Utilities expense	18,100
Wages expense	99,700
Wages payable	1,500

Instructions

1. Prepare an income statement for the current year ended December 31.
2. Prepare a statement of owner's equity for the current year ended December 31.
3. Prepare a balance sheet as of December 31 of the current year.

CONTINUING PROBLEM

MUSIC TODAY

HAT

✓ 2. Net income: $305

Chris Stipe enjoys listening to all types of music and owns countless CDs and tapes. Over the years, Chris has gained a local reputation for knowledge of music from classical to rap and the ability to put together sets of recordings that appeal to all ages.

During the last several months, Chris served as a guest disc jockey on a local radio station. In addition, Chris has entertained at several friends' parties as the host deejay.

On November 1, 1999, Chris established a proprietorship known as Music Today. Using his extensive collection of CDs and tapes, Chris will serve as a disc jockey on a fee basis for weddings, college parties, and other events. During November, Chris entered into the following transactions:

Nov. 1. Deposited $1,500 in a checking account in the name of Music Today.
2. Received $500 from a local radio station to serve as the guest disc jockey for November.
2. Agreed to share office space with a local real estate agency, Picasso Realty. Music Today will pay ¼ of the rent. In addition, Music Today agreed to pay $110 a month toward the salary of the receptionist and to pay ¼ of the utilities. Paid $250 for the rent of the office.
3. Purchased supplies (blank cassette tapes, poster board, extension cords, etc.) from Ideal Office Supply Co. for $250. Agreed to pay $100 within 10 days and the remainder by December 3, 1999.
5. Paid $75 to a local radio station to advertise the services of Music Today twice daily for two weeks.
8. Paid $325 to a local electronics store for rent on two CD players, two cassette players, and eight speakers.
12. Paid $100 (music expense) to The Music Store for the use of its current demo CDs and tapes to make cassette tapes of various music sets.
13. Paid Ideal Office Supply Co. $100 on account.
16. Received $50 from a dentist for providing two music sets for the dentist to play for her patients.
22. Served as disc jockey for a wedding party. The father of the bride agreed to pay $400 the 1st of December.
25. Received $250 from a friend for serving as the disc jockey for a cancer charity ball hosted by the local hospital.
29. Paid $120 (music expense) to Crescendo Music for the use of its library of demo CDs and tapes.
30. Received $350 for serving as disc jockey for a local club's monthly dance.
30. Paid Picasso Realty $110 for Music Today's share of the receptionist's salary for November.
30. Paid Picasso Realty $100 for Music Today's share of the utilities for November.
30. Determined that the cost of supplies on hand is $160. Therefore, the cost of supplies used during the month was $90.
30. Paid for miscellaneous expenses, $75.
30. Withdrew $50 of cash from Music Today for personal use.

Instructions

1. Indicate the effect of each transaction and the balances after each transaction, using the following tabular headings:

Assets	=	Liabilities	+	Owner's Equity
Cash + Accounts Receivable + Supplies	=	Accounts Payable	+	Chris Stipe, Capital

Explain the nature of each increase and decrease in owner's equity by an appropriate notation at the right of the amount.

2. Prepare an income statement for Music Today for the month ended November 30, 1999.
3. Prepare a statement of owner's equity for Music Today for the month ended November 30, 1999.
4. Prepare a balance sheet for Music Today as of November 30, 1999.

SPECIAL ACTIVITIES

Activity 1–1 Gay Enterprises

Ethics and professional conduct in business

GROUP ACTIVITY

Nicole Gay, president of Gay Enterprises, applied for a $100,000 loan from Western National Bank. The bank requested financial statements from Gay Enterprises as a basis for granting the loan. Nicole has told her accountant to provide the bank with a balance sheet. Nicole has decided to omit the other financial statements because there was a net loss during the past year.

In groups of three or four, discuss the following questions:

1. Is Nicole behaving in a professional manner by omitting some of the financial statements?
2. a. What types of information about their businesses would owners be willing to provide bankers? What types of information would owners not be willing to provide?
   b. What types of information about a business would bankers want before extending a loan?
   c. What common interests are shared by bankers and the business owners?

Activity 1–2 Second Opinion

Net income

On January 3, 1999, Dr. Brittany Clark established Second Opinion, a medical practice organized as a proprietorship. The following conversation occurred the following August between Dr. Clark and a former medical school classmate, Dr. Herman Ryder, at an American Medical Association convention in Mexico City.

Dr. Ryder: Brittany, good to see you again. Why didn't you call when you were in Reno? We could have had dinner together.

Dr. Clark: Actually, I never made it to Reno this year. My husband and kids went up to our Lake Tahoe condo twice, but I got stuck in New York. I opened a new consulting practice this January and I haven't had any time for myself since.

Dr. Ryder: I heard about it . . . Second . . . something . . . right?

Dr. Clark: Yes, Second Opinion. My husband chose the name.

Dr. Ryder: I've thought about doing something like that. Are you making any money? I mean, is it worth your time?

Dr. Clark: You wouldn't believe it. I started by opening a bank account of $25,000, and my July bank statement has a balance of $225,000. Not bad for seven months—all pure profit.

Dr. Ryder: Maybe I'll try it in Reno. Let's have breakfast together tomorrow and you can fill me in on the details.

Comment on Dr. Clark's statement that the difference between the opening bank balance ($25,000) and the July statement balance ($225,000) is pure profit.

Activity 1–3 Match Point

Transactions and financial statements

HAT

Reva Inman, a junior in college, has been seeking ways to earn extra spending money. As an active sports enthusiast, Reva plays tennis regularly at the Racquet Club, where her family has a membership. The president of the club recently approached Reva with the proposal that she manage the club's tennis courts on weekends. Reva's primary duty would be to supervise the operation of the club's four indoor and six outdoor courts, including court reservations.

In return for her services, the club would pay Reva $75 per weekend, plus Reva could keep whatever she earned from lessons and the fees from the use of the ball machine. The club and Reva agreed to a one-month trial, after which both would consider an arrangement for the remaining two years of Reva's college career. On this basis, Reva organized Match Point. During September, Reva managed the tennis courts and entered into the following transactions:

a. Opened a business account by depositing $500.
b. Paid $180 for tennis supplies (practice tennis balls, etc.).
c. Paid $75 for the rental of videotape equipment to be used in offering lessons during September.

d. Arranged for the rental of two ball machines during September for $100. Paid $60 in advance, with the remaining $40 due October 1.
e. Received $875 for lessons given during September.
f. Received $120 in fees from the use of the ball machines during September.
g. Paid $300 for salaries of part-time employees who answered the telephone and took reservations while Reva was giving lessons.
h. Paid $90 for miscellaneous expenses.
i. Received $300 from the club for managing the tennis courts during September.
j. Determined that the cost of supplies on hand at the end of the month totaled $75; therefore, the cost of supplies used was $105.
k. Withdrew $500 for personal use on September 30.

As a friend and accounting student, you have been asked by Reva to aid her in assessing the venture.

1. Indicate the effect of each transaction and the balances after each transaction, using the following tabular headings:

Assets	=	Liabilities	+	Owner's Equity
Cash + Supplies	=	Accounts Payable	+	Reva Inman, Capital

   Explain the nature of each increase and decrease in owner's equity by an appropriate notation at the right of the amount.
2. Prepare an income statement for September.
3. Prepare a statement of owner's equity for September.
4. Prepare a balance sheet as of September 30.
5. a. Assume that Reva Inman could earn $7 per hour working 20 hours each of the four weekends as a waitress. Evaluate which of the two alternatives, working as a waitress or operating Match Point, would provide Reva with the most income per month.
   b. Discuss any other factors that you believe Reva should consider before discussing a long-term arrangement with the Racquet Club.

Activity 1–4 Into the Real World

Certification requirements for accountants

Internet ACTIVITY

By satisfying certain specific requirements, accountants may become certified as public accountants (CPAs), management accountants (CMAs), or internal auditors (CIAs). Find the certification requirements for *one* of these accounting groups by accessing the appropriate Internet site listed below.

Site	Description
www.ais-cpa.com	This site lists the address and/or Internet link for each state's board of accountancy. Find your state's requirements.
www.rutgers.edu/Accounting/raw/ima/icma.htm	This site lists the requirements for becoming a CMA.
www.rutgers.edu/Accounting/raw/iia	This site lists the requirements for becoming a CIA.

ANSWERS TO SELF-EXAMINATION QUESTIONS

Matching

1. H	5. DD	9. D	13. Q	17. T	21. B	25. HH	29. JJ
2. W	6. L	10. N	14. I	18. CC	22. EE	26. S	30. X
3. Y	7. J	11. P	15. LL	19. E	23. C	27. KK	31. A
4. FF	8. V	12. U	16. F	20. K	24. O	28. G	

Multiple Choice

1. **D** A corporation, organized in accordance with state or federal statutes, is a separate legal entity in which ownership is divided into shares of stock (answer D). A proprietorship (answer A) is an unincorporated business owned by one individual. A service business (answer B) provides services to its customers. It can be organized as a proprietorship, partnership, or corporation. A partnership (answer C) is an unincorporated business owned by two or more individuals.
2. **A** The resources owned by a business are called assets (answer A). The debts of the business are called liabilities (answer B), and the equity of the owners is called owner's equity (answer D). The relationship between assets, liabilities, and owner's equity is expressed as the accounting equation (answer C).
3. **A** The balance sheet is a listing of the assets, liabilities, and owner's equity of a business at a specific date (answer A). The income statement (answer B) is a summary of the revenue and expenses of a business for a specific period of time. The statement of owner's equity (answer C) summarizes the changes in owner's equity for a proprietorship or partnership during a specific period of time. The statement of cash flows (answer D) summarizes the cash receipts and cash payments for a specific period of time.
4. **C** The accounting equation is:

   Assets = Liabilities + Owner's Equity

   Therefore, if assets increased by $20,000 and liabilities increased by $12,000, owner's equity must have increased by $8,000 (answer C), as indicated in the following computation:

Assets	=	Liabilities	+	Owner's Equity
$20,000	=	$12,000	+	Owner's Equity
$20,000 − $12,000	=			Owner's Equity
$8,000	=			Owner's Equity

5. **B** Net income is the excess of revenue over expenses, or $7,500 (answer B). If expenses exceed revenue, the difference is a net loss. Withdrawals by the owner are the opposite of the owner's investing in the business and do not affect the amount of net income or net loss.

2

2

Analyzing Transactions

Setting the STAGE

Assume that you have been hired by a pizza restaurant to deliver pizzas, using your own car. You will be paid $5.00 per hour plus $0.20 per mile plus tips. What is the best way for you to determine how many miles you have driven each day in delivering pizzas?

One method would be to record the odometer mileage before work and then at quitting time. The difference would be the miles driven. For example, if the odometer read 56,743 at the start of work and 56,889 at the end of work, you would have driven 146 miles. However, this method is subject to error if you copy down the wrong reading or make a math error.

In the same way, managers of a business need information about the status of the business at different points in time. Such information is useful for analyzing the effects of transactions on the business and for making decisions. For example, the manager of your neighborhood dry cleaners needs to know how much cash is available, how much has been spent, and what services have been provided customers.

In Chapter 1, we analyzed and recorded this kind of information by using the accounting equation, Assets = Liabilities + Owner's Equity. Since such a format is not practical for most businesses, in Chapter 2 we will study more practical methods of recording transactions. We will conclude this chapter by discussing how accounting errors may occur and how they may be detected by the accounting process.

objectives

After studying this chapter, you should be able to:

1 Explain why accounts are used to record and summarize the effects of transactions on financial statements.

2 Explain the characteristics of an account.

3 List the rules of debit and credit and the normal balances of accounts.

4 Analyze and summarize the financial statement effects of transactions.

5 Prepare a trial balance and explain how it can be used to discover errors.

6 Discover errors in recording transactions and correct them.

7 Use horizontal analysis to compare financial statements from different periods.

Usefulness of an Account

OBJECTIVE 1

Explain why accounts are used to record and summarize the effects of transactions on financial statements.

Before making a major cash purchase, such as buying a CD player, you need to know the balance of your bank account. Likewise, managers need timely, useful information in order to make good decisions about their businesses.

How are accounting systems designed to provide this information? We illustrated a very simple design in Chapter 1, where transactions were recorded and summarized in the accounting equation format. However, this format is difficult to use when thousands of transactions must be recorded daily. Thus, accounting systems are designed to show the increases and decreases in each financial statement item in a separate record. This record is called an **account**. For example, since cash appears on the balance sheet, a separate record is kept of the increases and decreases in cash. Likewise, a separate record is kept of the increases and decreases for supplies, land, accounts payable, and the other balance sheet items. Similar records would be kept for income statement items, such as fees earned, wages expense, and rent expense.

The increases and decreases in each financial statement item are shown in an account.

A group of accounts for a business entity is called a **ledger**. A list of the accounts in the ledger is called a **chart of accounts**. The accounts are normally listed in the order in which they appear in the financial statements. The balance sheet accounts are usually listed first, in the order of assets, liabilities, and owner's equity. The income statement accounts are then listed in the order of revenues and expenses. Each of these major account classifications is briefly described below.

Assets are resources that are owned by the business entity. These resources are physical items or rights that have value. Examples of assets include cash, accounts receivable, supplies, prepaid expenses (such as insurance), buildings, equipment, land, and patent rights.

Liabilities are debts owed to outsiders (creditors). Liabilities are often identified on the balance sheet by titles that include the word *payable*. Examples of liabilities include accounts payable, notes payable, and wages payable. Cash received

INTERMISSION

The Telltale Chart of Accounts

What does a chart of accounts reveal about a business's operations? Look at the following revenue and expense accounts taken from the chart of accounts for a newspaper:

- Revenue accounts:
  - Circulation—carriers
  - Circulation—vending machines
  - Circulation—mail subscriptions
  - Advertising—commercial
  - Advertising—classified
- Expense accounts:
  - Newsprint
  - News ink
  - Wire services
  - Correspondent fees
  - Photography
  - Telephone
  - Postage
  - Delivery
  - Wages

These accounts tell us that the newspaper receives its primary revenues from circulation and advertising. In addition, the accounts reflect some of the decision-making needs of management. For example, matching the revenues from commercial and classified advertising with the related expenses helps management determine whether these services are profitable. This might lead management to consider expanding the paper's advertising space to take advantage of this profitability. ■

before services are delivered creates a liability to perform the services. These future service commitments are often called *unearned revenues.* Examples of unearned revenues are magazine subscriptions received by a publisher and tuition received by a college at the beginning of a term.

Owner's equity is the owner's right to the assets of the business. For a proprietorship, the owner's equity on the balance sheet is represented by the balance of the owner's *capital* account. A **drawing** account represents the amount of withdrawals made by the owner.

Revenues are increases in owner's equity as a result of selling services or products to customers. Examples of revenues include fees earned, fares earned, commissions revenue, and rent revenue.

Assets used up or services consumed in the process of generating revenues are **expenses**. Examples of typical expenses include wages expense, rent expense, utilities expense, supplies expense, and miscellaneous expense.

A chart of accounts is designed to meet the information needs of a company's managers and other users of its financial statements. Within the chart of accounts, the accounts are numbered for use as references. A flexible numbering system is normally used, so that new accounts can be added without affecting other account numbers.

Exhibit 1 is Computer King's chart of accounts that we will be using in this chapter. Additional accounts will be introduced in later chapters. In Exhibit 1, each account number has two digits. The first digit indicates the major classification of the ledger in which the account is located. Accounts beginning with 1 represent assets; 2, liabilities; 3, owner's equity; 4, revenue; and 5, expenses. The second digit indicates the location of the account within its class.

REAL WORLD **Procter & Gamble's** account numbers have over 30 digits to reflect P&G's many different operations and regions.

COMPUTER KING

EXHIBIT 1
Chart of Accounts for Computer King

Balance Sheet Accounts		Income Statement Accounts	
	1. Assets		4. Revenue
11	Cash	41	Fees Earned
12	Accounts Receivable		5. Expenses
14	Supplies	51	Wages Expense
15	Prepaid Insurance	52	Rent Expense
17	Land	54	Utilities Expense
18	Office Equipment	55	Supplies Expense
	2. Liabilities	59	Miscellaneous Expense
21	Accounts Payable		
23	Unearned Rent		
	3. Owner's Equity		
31	Pat King, Capital		
32	Pat King, Drawing		

Characteristics of an Account

OBJECTIVE 2

Explain the characteristics of an account.

The simplest form of an account has three parts. First, each account has a title, which is the name of the item recorded in the account. Second, each account has a space for recording increases in the amount of the item. Third, each account has a space for recording decreases in the amount of the item. The account form presented below is called a **T account** because it is similar to the letter T. The left side of the account is called the *debit* side, and the right side is called the *credit* side.[1]

Title	
Left side *debit*	Right side *credit*

Point of INTEREST

Many times when accountants analyze complex transactions, they use T accounts to simplify the thought process. In the same way, you will find T accounts a useful device in this and later accounting courses.

Amounts entered on the left side of an account, regardless of the account title, are called **debits** to the account. When debits are entered in an account, the account is said to be *debited* (or charged). Amounts entered on the right side of an account are called **credits**, and the account is said to be *credited*. Debits and credits are sometimes abbreviated as *Dr.* and *Cr.*

Amounts entered on the left side of an account are debits, and amounts entered on the right side of an account are credits.

In the cash account shown below, transactions involving receipts of cash are listed on the debit side of the account. The transactions involving cash payments are listed on the credit side. If at any time the total of the cash receipts is needed, the entries on the debit side of the account may be added and the total ($10,950) inserted below the last debit.[2] The total of the cash payments, $6,850 in the example, may be inserted on the credit side in a similar manner. Subtracting the smaller sum from the larger, $10,950 − $6,850, identifies the amount of cash on hand, $4,100. This amount is called the **balance of the account**. It may be inserted in the account, next to the total of the debit column. In this way, the balance is identified as a **debit balance**. If a balance sheet were to be prepared at this time, cash of $4,100 would be reported.

		Cash		
Debit side of account		3,750	850	Credit side of account
		4,300	1,400	
		2,900	700	
	4,100	*10,950*	2,900	
			1,000	
			6,850	
	Balance of account (Total debits − Total credits)	Total debits	Total credits	

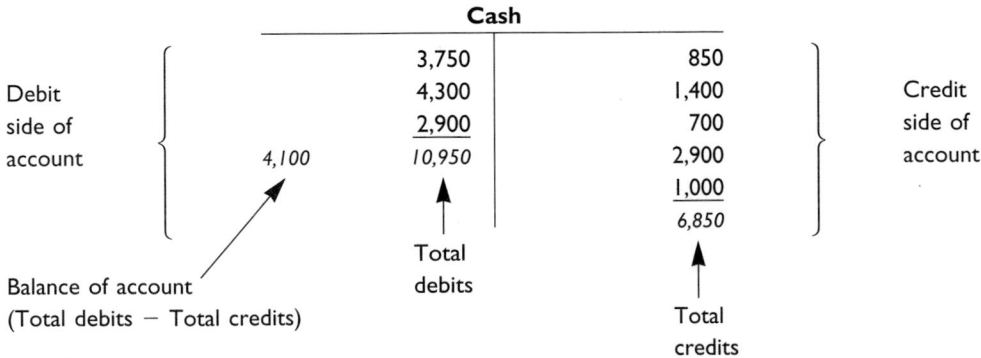

[1] The terms *debit* and *credit* are derived from the Latin *debere* and *credere*.

[2] This amount, called a *memorandum balance,* should be written in small figures or identified in some other way to avoid mistaking the amount for an additional debit.

Analyzing and Summarizing Transactions in Accounts

OBJECTIVE 3

List the rules of debit and credit and the normal balances of accounts.

COMPUTER KING

Every business transaction affects at least two accounts. To illustrate how transactions are analyzed and summarized in accounts, we will use the Computer King transactions from Chapter 1, with dates added. First, we illustrate how transactions (a), (b), (c), and (f) are analyzed and summarized in balance sheet accounts (assets, liabilities, and owner's equity). Next, we illustrate how transactions (d), (e), and (g) are analyzed and summarized in income statement accounts (revenues and expenses). Finally, we illustrate how the withdrawal of cash by Pat King, transaction (h), is analyzed and summarized in the accounts.

Every transaction affects at least two accounts.

Transactions and Balance Sheet Accounts

Pat King's first transaction, (a), was to deposit $15,000 in a bank account in the name of Computer King. The effect of this November 1 transaction on the balance sheet is to increase cash and increase the owner's equity, as shown below.

Computer King
Balance Sheet
November 1, 1999

Assets		Owner's Equity	
Cash	$15,000 00	Pat King, capital	$15,000 00

Point of INTEREST

A journal can be thought of as being similar to an individual's diary.

This transaction is initially entered in a record called a **journal**. The title of the account to be debited is listed first, followed by the amount to be debited. The title of the account to be credited is listed below and to the right of the debit, followed by the amount to be credited. This process of recording a transaction in the journal is called **journalizing**. This form of recording a transaction is called a **journal entry**. The journal entry for transaction (a) is shown below.

Entry A

JOURNAL **PAGE 1**

	Date		Description	Post. Ref.	Debit	Credit	
1	1999 Nov.	1	Cash		15,000 00		1
2			Pat King, Capital			15,000 00	2
3			Invested cash in Computer King.				3

The increase in the asset (Cash), which is reported on the left side of the balance sheet, is debited to the cash account. The increase in owner's equity, which is reported on the right side of the balance sheet, is credited to the Pat King, capital account. When other assets are acquired, the increases will also be recorded as debits to asset accounts. Likewise, other increases in owner's equity will be recorded as credits to owner's equity accounts.

The effects of this transaction are shown in the accounts by transferring the amount and the date of the journal entry to the left (debit) side of Cash and to the right (credit) side of Pat King, Capital, as follows:

Cash			Pat King, Capital		
Nov. 1	15,000			Nov. 1	15,000

On November 5 (transaction b), Computer King bought land for $10,000, paying cash. This transaction increases one asset account and decreases another. It is entered in the journal as a $10,000 increase (debit) to Land and a $10,000 decrease (credit) to Cash, as shown below.

Entry B

5	Land		10000 00	
	Cash			10000 00
	Purchased land for building site.			

The effect of this entry is shown in the accounts of Computer King as follows:

Cash		Land		Pat King, Capital	
Nov. 1 15,000	Nov. 5 10,000	Nov. 5 10,000			Nov. 1 15,000

On November 10 (transaction c), Computer King purchased supplies on account for $1,350. This transaction increases an asset account and increases a liability account. It is entered in the journal as a $1,350 increase (debit) to Supplies and a $1,350 increase (credit) to Accounts Payable, as shown below. To simplify the illustration, the effect of entry (c) and the remaining journal entries for Computer King will be shown in the accounts later.

Entry C

10	Supplies		1350 00	
	Accounts Payable			1350 00
	Purchased supplies on account.			

On November 30 (transaction f), Computer King paid creditors on account, $950. This transaction decreases a liability account and decreases an asset account. It is entered in the journal as a $950 decrease (debit) to Accounts Payable and a $950 decrease (credit) to Cash, as shown below.

Entry F

30	Accounts Payable		950 00	
	Cash			950 00
	Paid creditors on account.			

The left side of all accounts is the debit side, and the right side is the credit side.

In the preceding examples, you should observe that the left side of asset accounts is used for recording increases and the right side is used for recording decreases. Also, the right side of liability and owner's equity accounts is used to record increases, and the left side of such accounts is used to record decreases. The left side of all accounts, whether asset, liability, or owner's equity, is the debit side, and the right side is the credit side. Thus, a debit may be either an increase or a decrease, depending on the account affected. A credit likewise may be either an increase or a decrease, depending on the account. The general rules of debit and credit for balance sheet accounts therefore may be stated as follows:

BUSINESS ON STAGE

Most managers would probably agree that they spend a majority of their time communicating with peers, employees, suppliers, stockholders, customers, and various others. To be successful in business, you must be a good communicator. Some helpful rules of good communication include the following:

- Have a clear idea of what you hope to accomplish from the communication and know what you want to say before you say it.
- Remember that oral communication is more than just words. Your tone of voice, facial expressions, and gestures can say more than your words.
- Keep your audience in mind by considering their needs and interests.
- Always follow up to see that your message was understood.
- Be a good listener by not interrupting, avoiding hasty judgments, asking questions, and paying attention. ■

Source: Adapted from *The World of Business* by L. Gitman and C. McDaniel (2d Edition), p. 262.

	Debit		Credit	
Asset accounts	Increase	(+)	Decrease	(−)
Liability accounts	Decrease	(−)	Increase	(+)
Owner's equity (capital) accounts	Decrease	(−)	Increase	(+)

The rules of debit and credit may also be stated in relationship to the accounting equation, as shown below.

Balance Sheet Accounts

ASSETS Asset Accounts		LIABILITIES Liability Accounts	
Debit for increases (+)	Credit for decreases (−)	Debit for decreases (−)	Credit for increases (+)
		OWNER'S EQUITY Owner's Equity Accounts	
		Debit for decreases (−)	Credit for increases (+)

Income Statement Accounts

The analysis of business transactions affecting the income statement focuses on how each transaction affects owner's equity. Transactions that increase revenue will increase owner's equity. Just as increases in owner's equity are recorded as credits, so are increases in revenue accounts. Transactions that increase expense will decrease owner's equity. Just as decreases in owner's equity are recorded as debits, increases in expense accounts are recorded as debits.

We will use Computer King's transactions (d), (e), and (g) to illustrate the analysis of transactions and the rules of debit and credit for revenue and expense accounts. On November 18 (transaction d), Computer King received fees of $7,500 from customers for services. This transaction increases an asset account and increases a revenue account. It is entered in the journal as a $7,500 increase (debit) to Cash and a $7,500 increase (credit) to Fees Earned, as shown below.

Entry D

12							12
13		18	Cash		7,500 00		13
14			Fees Earned			7,500 00	14
15			Received fees from customers.				15

Throughout the month, Computer King incurred the following expenses: wages, $2,125; rent, $800; utilities, $450; and miscellaneous, $275. To simplify the illustration, the entry to journalize the payment of these expenses is recorded on November 30 (transaction e), as shown below. This transaction increases various expense accounts and decreases an asset account.

Entry E

Date	Description	Debit	Credit
30	Wages Expense	2 1 2 5 00	
	Rent Expense	8 0 0 00	
	Utilities Expense	4 5 0 00	
	Miscellaneous Expense	2 7 5 00	
	Cash		3 6 5 0 00
	Paid expenses.		

Point of INTEREST

In 1494, Luca Pacioli, a Franciscan monk, invented the double-entry accounting system that is still used today.

Regardless of the number of accounts, the sum of the debits is always equal to the sum of the credits in a journal entry. This equality of debit and credit for each transaction is built into the accounting equation: Assets = Liabilities + Owner's Equity. It is also because of this double equality that the system is known as **double-entry accounting**.

The sum of the debits must always equal the sum of the credits.

On November 30, Computer King recorded the amount of supplies used in the operations during the month (transaction g). This transaction increases an expense account and decreases an asset account. The journal entry for transaction (g) is shown below.

Entry G

Date	Description	Debit	Credit
30	Supplies Expense	8 0 0 00	
	Supplies		8 0 0 00
	Supplies used during November.		

The general rules of debit and credit for analyzing transactions affecting income statement accounts are stated below.

	Debit	Credit
Revenue accounts	Decrease (−)	Increase (+)
Expense accounts	Increase (+)	Decrease (−)

The rules of debit and credit for income statement accounts may also be summarized in relationship to the owner's equity in the accounting equation, as shown below.

Income Statement Accounts

Expense Accounts		Revenue Accounts	
Debit for increases (+)	Credit for decreases (−)	Debit for decreases (−)	Credit for increases (+)

Withdrawals by the Owner

The owner of a proprietorship may withdraw cash from the business for personal use. This practice is common if the owner devotes full time to the business. In this case, the business may be the owner's main source of income. Such withdrawals have the effect of decreasing owner's equity. Just as decreases in owner's equity are recorded as debits, increases in withdrawals are recorded as debits. Withdrawals are debited to an account with the owner's name followed by *Drawing* or *Personal.*

In transaction (h), Pat King withdrew $2,000 in cash from Computer King for personal use. The effect of this transaction is to increase the drawing account and decrease the cash account. The journal entry for transaction (h) is shown below.

Entry H

1	1999 Nov.	30	Pat King, Drawing	2 000 00		1
2			Cash		2 000 00	2
3			Pat King withdrew cash for			3
4			personal use.			4

Normal Balances of Accounts

The sum of the increases recorded in an account is usually equal to or greater than the sum of the decreases recorded in the account. For this reason, the normal balances of all accounts are positive rather than negative. For example, the total debits (increases) in an asset account will ordinarily be greater than the total credits (decreases). Thus, asset accounts normally have debit balances.

The rules of debit and credit and the normal balances of the various types of accounts are summarized as follows:

	Increase (Normal Balance)	Decrease
Balance sheet accounts:		
Asset	Debit	Credit
Liability	Credit	Debit
Owner's Equity:		
Capital	Credit	Debit
Drawing	Debit	Credit
Income statement accounts:		
Revenue	Credit	Debit
Expense	Debit	Credit

Q&A

A debit balance in which of the following accounts—Cash, Drawing, Wages Expense, Supplies, Fees Earned—would indicate that an error has occurred?

Fees Earned

When an account that normally has a debit balance actually has a credit balance, or vice versa, an error may have occurred or an unusual situation may exist. For example, a credit balance in the office equipment account could result only from an error. On the other hand, a debit balance in an accounts payable account could result from an overpayment.

Illustration of Analyzing and Summarizing Transactions

OBJECTIVE 4

Analyze and summarize the financial statement effects of transactions.

How does a transaction occur in a business? First, a manager or other employee authorizes the transaction. The transaction then occurs. The businesses involved in the transaction usually prepare documents that describe the details of the transaction. These documents then become the basis for analyzing and recording the transaction. For example, Pat King might authorize the purchase of supplies for Com-

Point of INTEREST

Business documents that you are likely to see often include checks, sales slips, deposit tickets, utility bills, and credit card receipts.

COMPUTER KING

puter King by telling an employee to buy computer paper at the local office supply store. The employee purchases the supplies for cash and receives a sales slip from the office supply store listing the details of the supplies bought. The employee then gives the sales slip to Pat King, who verifies and records the transaction.

As we discussed in the preceding section, a transaction is first recorded in a journal. Periodically, the journal entries are transferred to the accounts in the ledger. This process of transferring the debits and credits from the journal entries to the accounts is called **posting**. The flow of a transaction from its authorization to its posting in the accounts is shown in Exhibit 2.

Point of INTEREST

In computerized accounting systems, some transactions may be automatically authorized and recorded when certain events occur. For example, the salaries of managers may be paid automatically at the end of each pay period.

EXHIBIT 2
Flow of Business Transactions

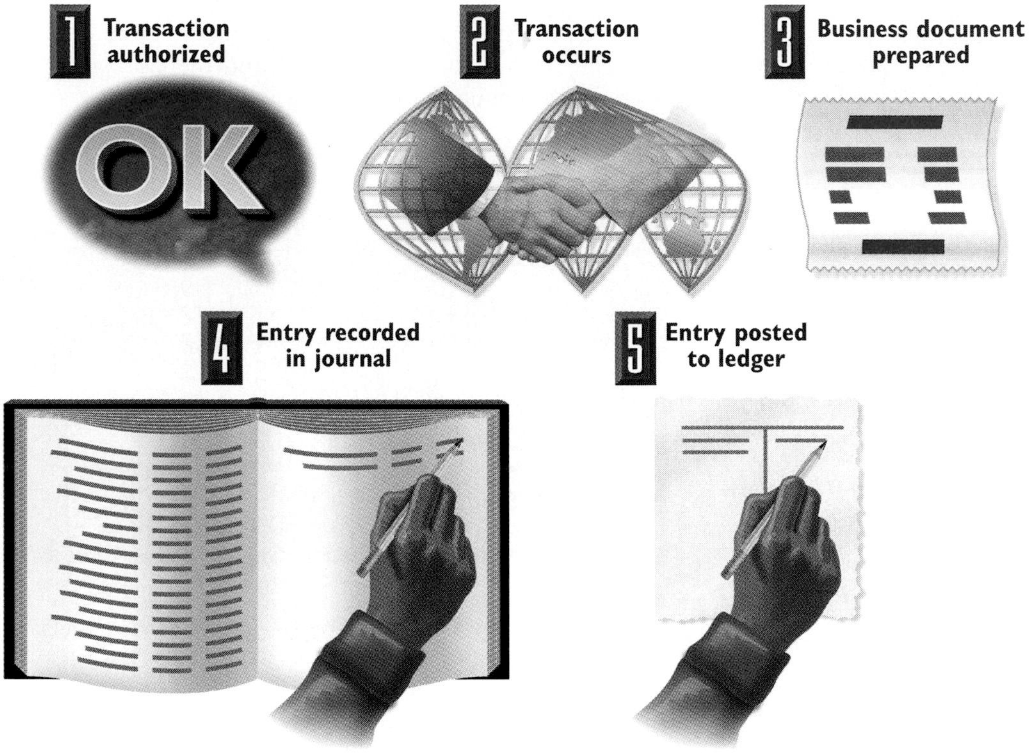

The double-entry accounting system is a very powerful tool in analyzing the effects of transactions. Using this system to analyze transactions is summarized as follows:

1. Determine whether an asset, a liability, owner's equity, revenue, or expense account is affected by the transaction.
2. For each account affected by the transaction, determine whether the account increases or decreases.
3. Determine whether each increase or decrease should be recorded as a debit or a credit.

In practice, businesses use a variety of formats for recording journal entries. A business may use one all-purpose journal, sometimes called a **two-column journal**, or it may use several journals. In the latter case, each journal is used to record different types of transactions, such as cash receipts or cash payments. The journals may be part of either a manual accounting system or a computerized accounting system.[3]

To illustrate recording a transaction in an all-purpose journal and posting in a manual accounting system, we will use the December transactions of Computer King. The first transaction in December occurred on December 1.

Dec. 1. Computer King paid a premium of $2,400 for a comprehensive insurance policy covering liability, theft, and fire. The policy covers a two-year period.

Analysis: When you purchased insurance for your automobile, you may have been required to pay the insurance premium in advance. In this case, your transaction was similar to Computer King's. Advance payments of expenses such as insurance are prepaid expenses, which are assets. For Computer King, the asset acquired for the cash payment is insurance protection for 24 months. The asset Prepaid Insurance increases and is debited for $2,400. The asset Cash decreases and is credited for $2,400.

The recording and posting of this transaction is shown in Exhibit 3.

EXHIBIT 3
Diagram of the Recording and Posting of a Debit and a Credit

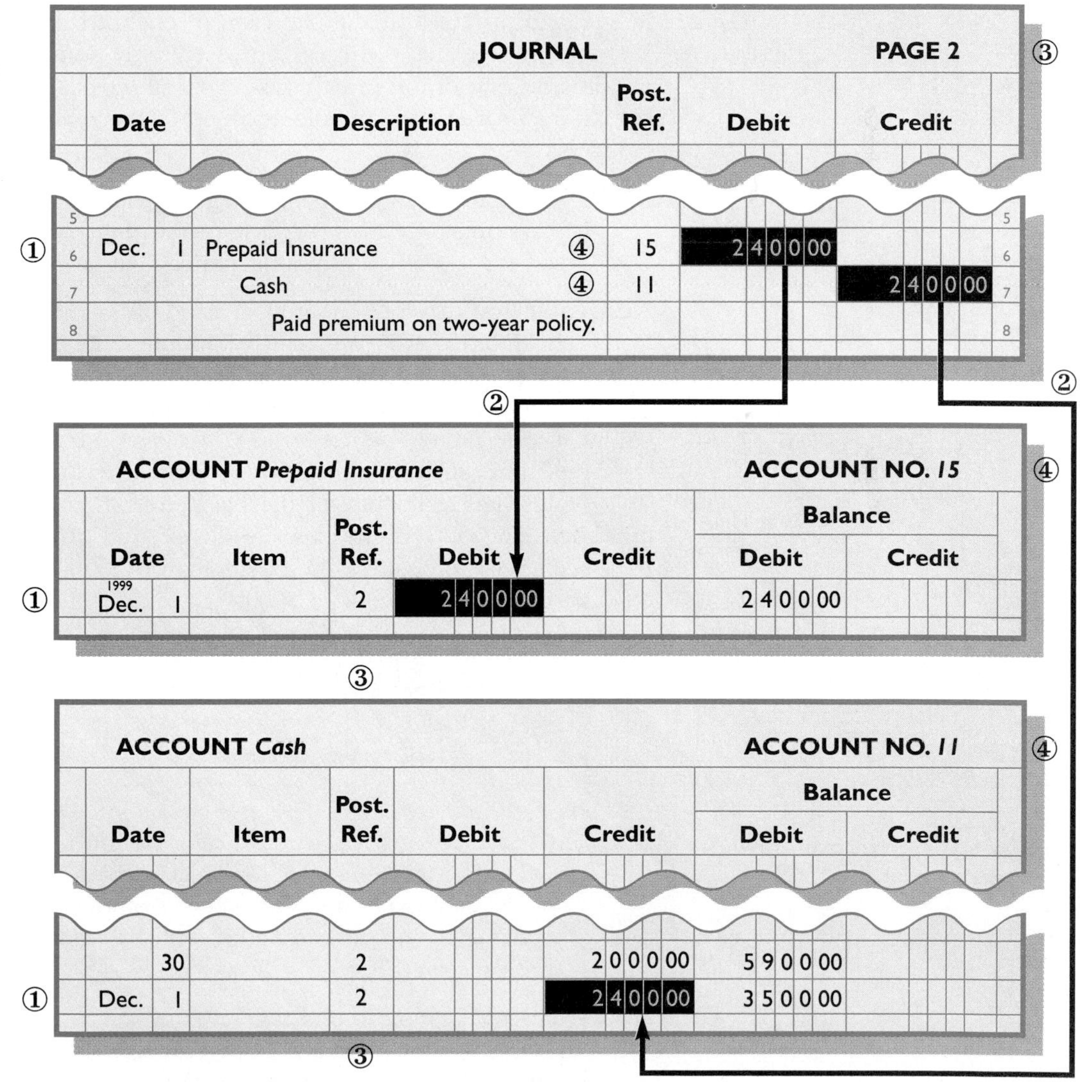

[3] The use of special journals and computerized accounting systems is discussed in later chapters, after the basics of accounting systems have been presented.

In the journal, you should note where the date of the transaction is recorded. Also note that the entry is explained as the payment of an insurance premium. Such explanations should be brief. For unusual and complex transactions, such as a long-term rental arrangement, the journal entry explanation may include a reference to the rental agreement or other business document.

You will note that the T account form is not used in this illustration. Although the T account clearly separates debit entries and credit entries, it is inefficient for summarizing a large quantity of transactions. In practice, the T account is usually replaced with the standard form shown in Exhibit 3.

The debits and credits for each journal entry are posted to the accounts in the order that they occur in the journal. In posting to the standard account, (1) the date is entered, and (2) the amount of the entry is entered. For future reference, (3) the journal page number is inserted in the Posting Reference column of the account, and (4) the account number is inserted in the Posting Reference column of the journal.

The remaining December transactions for Computer King are analyzed in the following paragraphs. These transactions are posted to the ledger in Exhibit 4, shown later. To simplify and reduce repetition, some of the December transactions are stated in summary form. For example, cash received for services is normally recorded on a daily basis. In this example, however, only summary totals are recorded at the middle and end of the month. Likewise, all fees earned on account during December are recorded at the middle and end of the month. In practice, each fee earned is recorded separately.

Dec. 1. Computer King paid rent for December, $800. The company from which Computer King is renting its store space now requires the payment of rent on the 1st of each month, rather than at the end of the month.

Analysis: You may pay monthly rent on an apartment on the first of each month. Your rent transaction is similar to Computer King's. The advance payment of rent is an asset, much like the advance payment of the insurance premium in the preceding transaction. However, unlike the insurance premium, this prepaid rent will expire in one month. When an asset that is purchased will be used up in a short period of time, such as a month, it is normal to debit an expense account initially. This avoids having to transfer the balance from an asset account (Prepaid Rent) to an expense account (Rent Expense) at the end of the month. Thus, when the rent for December is prepaid at the beginning of the month, Rent Expense is debited for $800 and Cash is credited for $800.

1	Rent Expense	52	800 00	
	Cash	11		800 00
	Paid rent for December.			

What would likely cause the cash account to have a credit balance?

An error or an overdrawn cash account.

Dec. 1. Computer King received an offer from a local retailer to rent the land purchased on November 5. The retailer plans to use the land as a parking lot for its employees and customers. Computer King agreed to rent the land to the retailer for three months, with the rent payable in advance. Computer King received $360 for three months' rent beginning December 1.

Analysis: By agreeing to rent the land and accepting the $360, Computer King has incurred an obligation (liability) to the retailer. This obligation is to make the land available for use for three months and not to interfere with its use. The liability created by receiving the cash in advance of providing the service is called **unearned revenue**. Thus, the $360 received is an increase in an asset and is debited to Cash. The liability account Unearned Rent increases and is credited for $360. As time passes, the unearned rent liability will decrease and will become revenue.

REAL WORLD

Magazines that receive subscriptions in advance must record the receipts as unearned revenues. Likewise, airlines that receive ticket payments in advance must record the receipts as unearned revenues until the passengers use the tickets.

14		1	Cash	11	360 00		14
15			Unearned Rent	23		360 00	15
16			Received advance payment for				16
17			three months' rent on land.				17

Dec. 4. Computer King purchased office equipment on account from Executive Supply Co. for $1,800.

Analysis: The asset account Office Equipment increases and is therefore debited for $1,800. The liability account Accounts Payable increases and is credited for $1,800.

19		4	Office Equipment	18	1 800 00		19
20			Accounts Payable	21		1 800 00	20
21			Purchased office equipment				21
22			on account.				22

Dec. 6. Computer King paid $180 for a newspaper advertisement.

Analysis: An expense increases and is debited for $180. The asset Cash decreases and is credited for $180. Expense items that are expected to be minor in amount are normally included as part of the miscellaneous expense. Thus, Miscellaneous Expense is debited for $180.

24		6	Miscellaneous Expense	59	180 00		24
25			Cash	11		180 00	25
26			Paid for newspaper ad.				26

Dec. 11. Computer King paid creditors $400.

Analysis: This payment decreases the liability account Accounts Payable, which is debited for $400. Cash also decreases and is credited for $400.

28		11	Accounts Payable	21	400 00		28
29			Cash	11		400 00	29
30			Paid creditors on account.				30

Dec. 13. Computer King paid a receptionist and a part-time assistant $950 for two weeks' wages.

Analysis: This transaction is similar to the December 6 transaction, where an expense account is increased and Cash is decreased. Thus, Wages Expense is debited for $950 and Cash is credited for $950.

JOURNAL **PAGE 3**

	Date		Description	Post. Ref.	Debit	Credit	
1	1999 Dec.	13	Wages Expense	51	950 00		1
2			Cash	11		950 00	2
3			Paid two weeks' wages.				3

Dec. 16. Computer King received $3,100 from fees earned for the first half of December.

Analysis: Cash increases and is debited for $3,100. The revenue account Fees Earned increases and is credited for $3,100.

16	Cash	11	3,100.00	
	Fees Earned	41		3,100.00
	Received fees from customers.			

Dec. 16. Fees earned on account totaled $1,750 for the first half of December.

Analysis: Assume that you have agreed to take care of a neighbor's dog for a week for $100. At the end of the week, you agree to wait until the first of the next month to receive the $100. Like Computer King, you have provided services on account and thus have a right to receive the payment from your neighbor. When a business agrees that payment for services provided or goods sold can be accepted at a later date, the firm has an **account receivable**, which is a claim against the customer. The account receivable is an asset, and the revenue is earned even though no cash has been received. Thus, Accounts Receivable increases and is debited for $1,750. The revenue account Fees Earned increases and is credited for $1,750.

16	Accounts Receivable	12	1,750.00	
	Fees Earned	41		1,750.00
	Fees earned on account.			

Dec. 20. Computer King paid $900 to Executive Supply Co. on the $1,800 debt owed from the December 4 transaction.

Analysis: This is similar to the transaction of December 11.

20	Accounts Payable	21	900.00	
	Cash	11		900.00
	Paid part of amount owed to			
	Executive Supply Co.			

Dec. 21. Computer King received $650 from customers in payment of their accounts.

Analysis: When customers pay amounts owed for services they have previously received, one asset increases and another asset decreases. Thus, Cash is debited for $650, and Accounts Receivable is credited for $650.

21	Cash	11	650.00	
	Accounts Receivable	12		650.00
	Received cash from customers			
	on account.			

Dec. 23. Computer King paid $1,450 for supplies.

Analysis: The asset account Supplies increases and is debited for $1,450. The asset account Cash decreases and is credited for $1,450.

	23	Supplies	14	1450 00	
		Cash	11		1450 00
		Purchased supplies.			

Dec. 27. Computer King paid the receptionist and the part-time assistant $1,200 for two weeks' wages.

Analysis: This is similar to the transaction of December 13.

	27	Wages Expense	51	1200 00	
		Cash	11		1200 00
		Paid two weeks' wages.			

Dec. 31. Computer King paid its $310 telephone bill for the month.

Analysis: Each month you pay a telephone bill. Businesses, such as Computer King, also must pay monthly utility bills. Such transactions are similar to the transaction of December 6. The expense account Utilities Expense is debited for $310, and Cash is credited for $310.

	31	Utilities Expense	54	310 00	
		Cash	11		310 00
		Paid telephone bill.			

Dec. 31. Computer King paid its $225 electric bill for the month.

Analysis: This is similar to the preceding transaction.

JOURNAL **PAGE 4**

Date		Description	Post. Ref.	Debit	Credit
1999 Dec.	31	Utilities Expense	54	225 00	
		Cash	11		225 00
		Paid electric bill.			

Dec. 31. Computer King received $2,870 from fees earned for the second half of December.

Analysis: This is similar to the transaction of December 16.

	31	Cash	11	2870 00	
		Fees Earned	41		2870 00
		Received fees from customers.			

Dec. 31. Fees earned on account totaled $1,120 for the second half of December.

Analysis: This is similar to the transaction of December 16.

Date	Description	Post. Ref.	Debit	Credit
31	Accounts Receivable	12	1120 00	
	Fees Earned	41		1120 00
	Fees earned on account.			

Dec. 31. Pat King withdrew $2,000 for personal use.

Analysis: This transaction resulted in an increase in the amount of withdrawals and is recorded by a $2,000 debit to Pat King, Drawing. The decrease in business cash is recorded by a $2,000 credit to Cash.

Date	Description	Post. Ref.	Debit	Credit
31	Pat King, Drawing	32	2000 00	
	Cash	11		2000 00
	Pat King withdrew cash for			
	personal use.			

The journal for Computer King since it was organized on November 1 is shown in Exhibit 4. Exhibit 4 also shows the ledger after the transactions for both November and December have been posted.

EXHIBIT 4
Journal and Ledger—Computer King

JOURNAL **PAGE 1**

Date		Description	Post. Ref.	Debit	Credit
1999 Nov.	1	Cash	11	15000 00	
		Pat King, Capital	31		15000 00
		Invested cash in Computer King.			
	5	Land	17	10000 00	
		Cash	11		10000 00
		Purchased land for building site.			
	10	Supplies	14	1350 00	
		Accounts Payable	21		1350 00
		Purchased supplies on account.			
	18	Cash	11	7500 00	
		Fees Earned	41		7500 00
		Received fees from customers.			
	30	Wages Expense	51	2125 00	
		Rent Expense	52	800 00	
		Utilities Expense	54	450 00	
		Miscellaneous Expense	59	275 00	
		Cash	11		3650 00
		Paid expenses.			
	30	Accounts Payable	21	950 00	
		Cash	11		950 00
		Paid creditors on account.			
	30	Supplies Expense	55	800 00	
		Supplies	14		800 00
		Supplies used during November.			

EXHIBIT 4 *(continued)*

JOURNAL **PAGE 2**

Date		Description	Post. Ref.	Debit	Credit
1999 Nov.	30	Pat King, Drawing	32	2000 00	
		Cash	11		2000 00
		Pat King withdrew cash for			
		personal use.			
Dec.	1	Prepaid Insurance	15	2400 00	
		Cash	11		2400 00
		Paid premium on two-year policy.			
	1	Rent Expense	52	800 00	
		Cash	11		800 00
		Paid rent for December.			
	1	Cash	11	360 00	
		Unearned Rent	23		360 00
		Received advance payment for			
		three months' rent on land.			
	4	Office Equipment	18	1800 00	
		Accounts Payable	21		1800 00
		Purchased office equipment			
		on account.			
	6	Miscellaneous Expense	59	180 00	
		Cash	11		180 00
		Paid for newspaper ad.			
	11	Accounts Payable	21	400 00	
		Cash	11		400 00
		Paid creditors on account.			

JOURNAL **PAGE 3**

Date		Description	Post. Ref.	Debit	Credit
1999 Dec.	13	Wages Expense	51	950 00	
		Cash	11		950 00
		Paid two weeks' wages.			
	16	Cash	11	3100 00	
		Fees Earned	41		3100 00
		Received fees from customers.			
	16	Accounts Receivable	12	1750 00	
		Fees Earned	41		1750 00
		Fees earned on account.			

EXHIBIT 4 *(continued)*

JOURNAL					PAGE 3
Date		**Description**	**Post. Ref.**	**Debit**	**Credit**
	20	Accounts Payable	21	900 00	
		Cash	11		900 00
		Paid part of amount owed to			
		Executive Supply Co.			
	21	Cash	11	650 00	
		Accounts Receivable	12		650 00
		Received cash from customers			
		on account.			
	23	Supplies	14	1 450 00	
		Cash	11		1 450 00
		Purchased supplies.			
	27	Wages Expense	51	1 200 00	
		Cash	11		1 200 00
		Paid two weeks' wages.			
	31	Utilities Expense	54	310 00	
		Cash	11		310 00
		Paid telephone bill.			

JOURNAL					PAGE 4
Date		**Description**	**Post. Ref.**	**Debit**	**Credit**
1999 Dec.	31	Utilities Expense	54	225 00	
		Cash	11		225 00
		Paid electric bill.			
	31	Cash	11	2 870 00	
		Fees Earned	41		2 870 00
		Received fees from customers.			
	31	Accounts Receivable	12	1 120 00	
		Fees Earned	41		1 120 00
		Fees earned on account.			
	31	Pat King, Drawing	32	2 000 00	
		Cash	11		2 000 00
		Pat King withdrew cash for			
		personal use.			

EXHIBIT 4 *(continued)*

LEDGER

ACCOUNT *Cash* **ACCOUNT NO.** *11*

Date		Item	Post. Ref.	Debit	Credit	Balance Debit	Balance Credit
1999 Nov.	1		1	15000 00		15000 00	
	5		1		10000 00	5000 00	
	18		1	7500 00		12500 00	
	30		1		3650 00	8850 00	
	30		1		950 00	7900 00	
	30		2		2000 00	5900 00	
Dec.	1		2		2400 00	3500 00	
	1		2		800 00	2700 00	
	1		2	360 00		3060 00	
	6		2		180 00	2880 00	
	11		2		400 00	2480 00	
	13		3		950 00	1530 00	
	16		3	3100 00		4630 00	
	20		3		900 00	3730 00	
	21		3	650 00		4380 00	
	23		3		1450 00	2930 00	
	27		3		1200 00	1730 00	
	31		3		310 00	1420 00	
	31		4		225 00	1195 00	
	31		4	2870 00		4065 00	
	31		4		2000 00	2065 00	

ACCOUNT *Accounts Receivable* **ACCOUNT NO.** *12*

Date		Item	Post. Ref.	Debit	Credit	Balance Debit	Balance Credit
1999 Dec.	16		3	1750 00		1750 00	
	21		3		650 00	1100 00	
	31		4	1120 00		2220 00	

ACCOUNT *Supplies* **ACCOUNT NO.** *14*

Date		Item	Post. Ref.	Debit	Credit	Balance Debit	Balance Credit
1999 Nov.	10		1	1350 00		1350 00	
	30		1		800 00	550 00	
Dec.	23		3	1450 00		2000 00	

EXHIBIT 4 *(continued)*

ACCOUNT ***Prepaid Insurance*** **ACCOUNT NO. *15***

Date		Item	Post. Ref.	Debit	Credit	Balance Debit	Balance Credit
1999 Dec.	1		2	2,400.00		2,400.00	

ACCOUNT ***Land*** **ACCOUNT NO. *17***

Date		Item	Post. Ref.	Debit	Credit	Balance Debit	Balance Credit
1999 Nov.	5		1	10,000.00		10,000.00	

ACCOUNT ***Office Equipment*** **ACCOUNT NO. *18***

Date		Item	Post. Ref.	Debit	Credit	Balance Debit	Balance Credit
1999 Dec.	4		2	1,800.00		1,800.00	

ACCOUNT ***Accounts Payable*** **ACCOUNT NO. *21***

Date		Item	Post. Ref.	Debit	Credit	Balance Debit	Balance Credit
1999 Nov.	10		1		1,350.00		1,350.00
	30		1	950.00			400.00
Dec.	4		2		1,800.00		2,200.00
	11		2	400.00			1,800.00
	20		3	900.00			900.00

ACCOUNT ***Unearned Rent*** **ACCOUNT NO. *23***

Date		Item	Post. Ref.	Debit	Credit	Balance Debit	Balance Credit
1999 Dec.	1		2		360.00		360.00

ACCOUNT ***Pat King, Capital*** **ACCOUNT NO. *31***

Date		Item	Post. Ref.	Debit	Credit	Balance Debit	Balance Credit
1999 Nov.	1		1		15,000.00		15,000.00

EXHIBIT 4 *(continued)*

ACCOUNT *Pat King, Drawing* **ACCOUNT NO.** *32*

Date		Item	Post. Ref.	Debit	Credit	Balance Debit	Balance Credit
1999 Nov.	30		2	2,000 00		2,000 00	
Dec.	31		4	2,000 00		4,000 00	

ACCOUNT *Fees Earned* **ACCOUNT NO.** *41*

Date		Item	Post. Ref.	Debit	Credit	Balance Debit	Balance Credit
1999 Nov.	18		1		7,500 00		7,500 00
Dec.	16		3		3,100 00		10,600 00
	16		3		1,750 00		12,350 00
	31		4		2,870 00		15,220 00
	31		4		1,120 00		16,340 00

ACCOUNT *Wages Expense* **ACCOUNT NO.** *51*

Date		Item	Post. Ref.	Debit	Credit	Balance Debit	Balance Credit
1999 Nov.	30		1	2,125 00		2,125 00	
Dec.	13		3	950 00		3,075 00	
	27		3	1,200 00		4,275 00	

ACCOUNT *Rent Expense* **ACCOUNT NO.** *52*

Date		Item	Post. Ref.	Debit	Credit	Balance Debit	Balance Credit
1999 Nov.	30		1	800 00		800 00	
Dec.	1		2	800 00		1,600 00	

ACCOUNT *Utilities Expense* **ACCOUNT NO.** *54*

Date		Item	Post. Ref.	Debit	Credit	Balance Debit	Balance Credit
1999 Nov.	30		1	450 00		450 00	
Dec.	31		3	310 00		760 00	
	31		4	225 00		985 00	

EXHIBIT 4 *(concluded)*

ACCOUNT *Supplies Expense*					ACCOUNT NO. *55*	
					Balance	
Date	Item	Post. Ref.	Debit	Credit	Debit	Credit
1999 Nov. 30		1	800 00		800 00	

ACCOUNT *Miscellaneous Expense*					ACCOUNT NO. *59*	
					Balance	
Date	Item	Post. Ref.	Debit	Credit	Debit	Credit
1999 Nov. 30		1	275 00		275 00	
Dec. 6		2	180 00		455 00	

Trial Balance

OBJECTIVE 5

Prepare a trial balance and explain how it can be used to discover errors.

How can you be sure that you have not made an error in posting the debits and credits to the ledger? One way is to determine the equality of the debits and credits in the ledger. This equality should be proved at the end of each accounting period, if not more often. Such a proof, called a **trial balance**, may be in the form of a computer printout or in the form shown in Exhibit 5.

Point of INTEREST

The proof of the equality of the debit and credit balances is called a trial balance because a "trial" is a process of proving or testing.

EXHIBIT 5
Trial Balance

Computer King
Trial Balance
December 31, 1999

Cash	2065 00	
Accounts Receivable	2220 00	
Supplies	2000 00	
Prepaid Insurance	2400 00	
Land	10000 00	
Office Equipment	1800 00	
Accounts Payable		900 00
Unearned Rent		360 00
Pat King, Capital		15000 00
Pat King, Drawing	4000 00	
Fees Earned		16340 00
Wages Expense	4275 00	
Rent Expense	1600 00	
Utilities Expense	985 00	
Supplies Expense	800 00	
Miscellaneous Expense	455 00	
	32600 00	32600 00

Q&A *If you incorrectly record $1,000 received on account as a debit to Cash and a credit to Accounts Payable, will the trial balance totals be equal?*

Yes.

The first step in preparing the trial balance is to determine the balance of each account in the ledger. When the standard account form is used, the balance of each account appears in the balance column on the same line as the last posting to the account.

The trial balance does not provide complete proof of the accuracy of the ledger. It indicates only that the debits and the credits are equal. This proof is of value, however, because errors often affect the equality of debits and credits. If the two totals of a trial balance are not equal, an error has occurred. In the remainder of this chapter, we will discuss procedures for discovering and correcting errors.

Discovery and Correction of Errors

OBJECTIVE 6

Discover errors in recording transactions and correct them.

Errors will sometimes occur in journalizing and posting transactions. In the following paragraphs, we describe and illustrate how errors may be discovered and corrected. In some cases, however, an error might not be significant enough to affect the decisions of management or others. In such cases, the **materiality concept** implies that the error may be treated in the easiest possible way. For example, an error of a few dollars in recording an asset as an expense for a business with millions of dollars in assets would be considered immaterial, and a correction would not be necessary. In the remaining paragraphs, we assume that errors discovered are material and should be corrected.

REAL WORLD Many large corporations such as **Microsoft** and **Quaker Oats** round their financial statements to millions of dollars.

Discovery of Errors

As mentioned previously, the trial balance is one of the primary ways for discovering errors in the ledger. However, it indicates only that the debits and credits are equal. If the two totals of the trial balance are not equal, it is probably due to one or more of the errors described in Exhibit 6.

EXHIBIT 6
Errors Causing Unequal Trial Balance

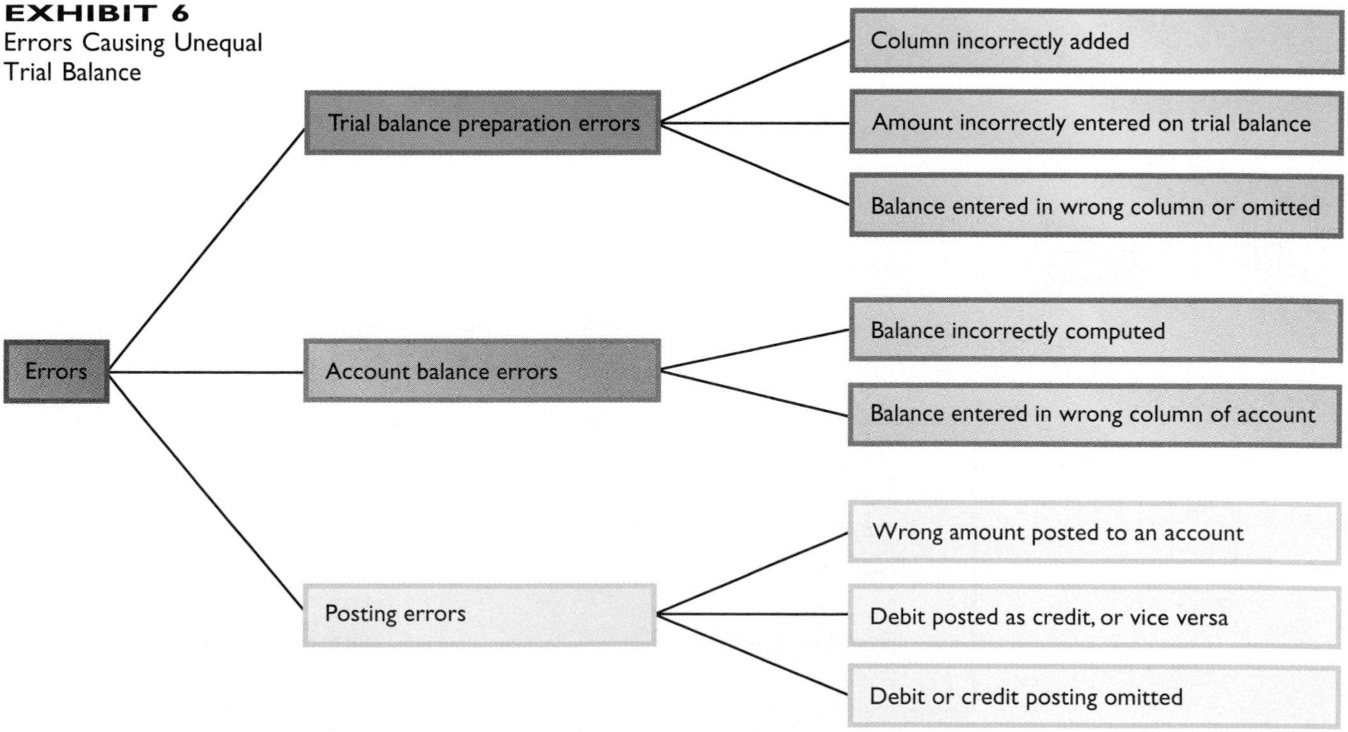

Among the types of errors that will not cause an inequality in the trial balance totals are the following:

1. Failure to record a transaction or to post a transaction.
2. Recording the same erroneous amount for both the debit and the credit parts of a transaction.
3. Recording the same transaction more than once.
4. Posting a part of a transaction correctly as a debit or credit but to the wrong account.

It is obvious that care should be used in recording transactions in the journal and in posting to the accounts. The need for accuracy in determining account balances and reporting them on the trial balance is also obvious.

Errors in the accounts may be discovered in various ways: (1) through audit procedures, (2) by chance, or (3) by looking at the trial balance. If the two trial balance totals are not equal, the amount of the difference between the totals should be determined before searching for the error.

The amount of the difference between the two totals of a trial balance sometimes gives a clue as to the nature of the error or where it occurred. For example, a difference of 10, 100, or 1,000 between two totals is often the result of an error in addition. A difference between totals can also be due to omitting a debit or a credit posting. If the difference can be evenly divided by 2, the error may be due to the posting of a debit as a credit, or vice versa. For example, if the debit total is $20,640 and the credit total is $20,236, the difference of $404 may indicate that a credit posting of $404 was omitted or that a credit of $202 was incorrectly posted as a debit.

Q&A *What type of error occurs when $14,500 is recorded as $15,400?*

A transposition.

Two other common types of errors are known as transpositions and slides. A **transposition** occurs when the order of the digits is changed mistakenly, such as writing $542 as $452 or $524. In a **slide**, the entire number is mistakenly moved one or more spaces to the right or the left, such as writing $542.00 as $54.20 or $5,420.00. If an error of either type has occurred and there are no other errors, the difference between the two trial balance totals can be evenly divided by 9.

If an error is not revealed by the trial balance, the steps in the accounting process must be retraced, beginning with the last step and working back to the entries in the journal. Usually, errors causing the trial balance totals to be unequal will be discovered before all of the steps are retraced.

Correction of Errors

The procedures used to correct an error in journalizing or posting vary according to the nature of the error and when the error is discovered. These procedures are summarized in Exhibit 7.

Correcting the first two types of errors shown in Exhibit 7 involves simply drawing a line through the error and inserting the correct title or amount. The person making corrections should normally initial the correction in case questions later arise.

EXHIBIT 7
Procedures for Correcting Errors

Error	Correction Procedure
1. Journal entry is incorrect but not posted.	Draw a line through the error and insert correct title or amount.
2. Journal entry is correct but posted incorrectly.	Draw a line through the error and post correctly.
3. Journal entry is incorrect and posted.	Journalize and post a correcting entry.

Correcting the third type of error in Exhibit 7 is more complex. To illustrate, assume that on May 5 a $12,500 purchase of office equipment on account was incorrectly journalized and posted as a debit to Supplies and a credit to Accounts Payable for $12,500. This posting of the incorrect entry is shown in the following T accounts.

Incorrect:

Supplies		Accounts Payable	
12,500			12,500

Before making a correcting entry, it is best to determine the debit(s) and credit(s) that should have been recorded. These are shown in the following T accounts.

Correct:

Office Equipment		Accounts Payable	
12,500			12,500

Comparing the two sets of T accounts shows that the incorrect debit of $12,500 to Supplies may be corrected by debiting Office Equipment for $12,500 and crediting Supplies for $12,500. The following correcting entry is then journalized and posted:

Entry to Correct Error:

18	May	31	Office Equipment	18	12 500 00		18
19			Supplies	14		12 500 00	19
20			To correct erroneous debit				20
21			to Supplies on May 5. See invoice				21
22			from Bell Office Equipment Co.				22

FINANCIAL ANALYSIS AND INTERPRETATION

OBJECTIVE 7

Use horizontal analysis to compare financial statements from different periods.

A single item appearing in a financial statement is often useful in interpreting the financial results of a business. However, comparing this item in a current statement with the same item in prior statements often makes the financial information more useful. **Horizontal analysis** is the term used to describe such comparisons.

In horizontal analysis, the amount of each item on the current financial statements is compared with the same item on one or more earlier statements. The increase or decrease in the *amount* of the item is computed, together with the *percent* of increase or decrease. When two statements are being compared, the earlier statement is used as the base for computing the amount and the percent of change.

To illustrate, the horizontal analysis of two income statements for J. Holmes, Attorney-at-Law, is shown in Exhibit 8.

EXHIBIT 8
Horizontal Analysis of Income Statement

J. Holmes, Attorney-at-Law
Income Statement
For the Years Ended December 31, 2000 and 2001

			Increase (Decrease)	
	2001	**2000**	**Amount**	**Percent**
Fees earned	$187,500	$150,000	$37,500	25.0%
Operating expenses:				
Wages expense	$ 60,000	$ 45,000	$15,000	33.3%
Rent expense	15,000	12,000	3,000	25.0%
Utilities expense	12,500	9,000	3,500	38.9%
Supplies expense	2,700	3,000	(300)	(10.0)%
Miscellaneous expense	2,300	1,800	500	27.8%
Total operating expenses	$ 92,500	$ 70,800	$21,700	30.6%
Net income	$ 95,000	$ 79,200	$15,800	19.9%

Exhibit 8 indicates both favorable and unfavorable trends affecting the income statement of J. Holmes, Attorney-at-Law. The increase in fees earned is a favorable trend, as is the decrease in supplies expense. Unfavorable trends include the increase in wages expense, utilities expense, and miscellaneous expense. These expenses increased faster than the increase in revenues, with total operating expenses increasing by 30.6%. Overall, net income increased by $15,800, or 19.9%, a favorable trend.

The significance of the various increases and decreases in the revenue and expense items in Exhibit 8 should be investigated to see if operations could be further improved. For example, the increase in utilities expense was the result of renting additional office space for use by a part-time law student in performing paralegal services. This explains the increase in rent expense of 25% and the increase in wages expense of 33.3%. Likewise, the increase in revenues reflects the fees generated by the new paralegal. Thus, it appears that hiring the paralegal was a good decision.

The preceding example illustrates how horizontal analysis can be useful in interpreting and analyzing financial statements. Horizontal analyses similar to that shown in Exhibit 8 can also be performed for the balance sheet, the statement of owner's equity, and the statement of cash flows.

ENCORE

The Hijacking Receivable

A company's chart of accounts should reflect the basic nature of its operations. Occasionally, however, transactions occur that give rise to unusual accounts. The following is a story of one such account.

During the early 1970s, before strict airport security was implemented across the United States, several airlines experienced hijacking incidents. One such incident occurred on November 10, 1972, when a Southern Airways DC-9 en route from Memphis to Miami was hijacked during a stopover in Birmingham, Alabama. The three hijackers boarded the plane in Birmingham armed with handguns and hand grenades. At gunpoint, the hijackers took the plane, the plane's crew of four, and 27 passengers to nine American cities, Toronto, and eventually to Havana, Cuba.

During the long flight, the hijackers threatened to crash the plane into the Oak Ridge, Tennessee nuclear facilities, demanded to talk with President Nixon, and demanded a ransom of $10 million. Southern Airways, however, was only able to come up with $2 million. Eventually, the pilot talked the hijackers into settling for the $2 million when the plane landed in Chattanooga for refueling.

Upon landing in Havana, the Cuban authorities arrested the hijackers and, after a brief delay, sent the plane, passengers, and crew back to the United States. The hijackers and $2 million stayed in Cuba.

How did Southern Airways account for and report the hijacking payment in its subsequent financial statements? As you might have analyzed, the initial entry credited Cash for $2 million. The debit was to an account entitled "Hijacking Payment." This account was reported as a type of receivable under "other assets" on Southern's balance sheet. The company maintained that it would be able to collect the cash from the Cuban government and that, therefore, a receivable existed. In fact, in August 1975, Southern Airways was repaid $2 million by the Cuban government, which was, at that time, attempting to improve relations with the United States. ■

KEY POINTS

1 Explain why accounts are used to record and summarize the effects of transactions on financial statements.

The record used for recording individual transactions is an account. A group of accounts is called a ledger. The system of accounts that make up a ledger is called a chart of accounts. The accounts are numbered and listed in the order in which they appear in the balance sheet and the income statement.

2 Explain the characteristics of an account.

The simplest form of an account, a T account, has three parts: (1) a title, which is the name of the item recorded in the account; (2) a left side, called the debit side; (3) a right side, called the credit side. Amounts entered on the left side of an account, regardless of the account title, are called debits to the account. Amounts entered on the right side of an account are called credits. Periodically, the debits in an account are added, the credits in the account are added, and the balance of the account is determined.

3 List the rules of debit and credit and the normal balances of accounts.

General rules of debit and credit have been established for recording increases or decreases in asset, liability, owner's equity, revenue, expense, and drawing accounts. Each transaction is recorded so that the sum of the debits is always equal to the sum of the credits. Transactions are initially entered in a record called a journal.

The sum of the increases recorded in an account is usually equal to or greater than the sum of the decreases recorded in the account. For this reason, the normal balance of an account is indicated by the side of the account (debit or credit) that receives the increases.

The rules of debit and credit and normal account balances are summarized in the following table:

	Increase (Normal Balance)	Decrease
Balance sheet accounts:		
Asset	Debit	Credit
Liability	Credit	Debit
Owner's Equity:		
Capital	Credit	Debit
Drawing	Debit	Credit
Income statement accounts:		
Revenue	Credit	Debit
Expense	Debit	Credit

4 Analyze and summarize the financial statement effects of transactions.

Transactions are analyzed by determining whether: (1) an asset, liability, owner's equity, revenue, or expense account is affected, (2) each account affected increases or decreases, and (3) each increase or decrease is recorded as a debit or a credit. A journal is used for recording the transaction initially. The journal entries are periodically posted to the accounts.

5 Prepare a trial balance and explain how it can be used to discover errors.

A trial balance is prepared by listing the accounts from the ledger and their balances. If the two totals of the trial balance are not equal, an error has occurred.

6 Discover errors in recording transactions and correct them.

Errors may be discovered (1) by audit procedures, (2) by chance, or (3) by looking at the trial balance. The procedures for correcting errors are summarized in Exhibit 7.

7 Use horizontal analysis to compare financial statements from different periods.

In horizontal analysis, the amount of each item on the current financial statements is compared with the same item on one or more earlier statements. The increase or decrease in the *amount* of the item is computed, together with the *percent* of increase or decrease.

ILLUSTRATIVE PROBLEM

J. F. Outz, M.D., has been practicing as a cardiologist for three years. During April, Outz completed the following transactions in her practice of cardiology.

April 1. Paid office rent for April, $800.
3. Purchased equipment on account, $2,100.
5. Received cash on account from patients, $3,150.
8. Purchased X-ray film and other supplies on account, $245.

April 9. One of the items of equipment purchased on April 3 was defective. It was returned with the permission of the supplier, who agreed to reduce the account for the amount charged for the item, $325.
12. Paid cash to creditors on account, $1,250.
17. Paid cash for renewal of a six-month property insurance policy, $370.
20. Discovered that the balance of the cash account and of the accounts payable account as of April 1 were overstated by $200. A payment of that amount to a creditor in March had not been recorded. Journalize the $200 payment as of April 20.
24. Paid cash for laboratory analysis, $545.
27. Paid cash from business bank account for personal and family expenses, $1,250.
30. Recorded the cash received in payment of services (on a cash basis) to patients during April, $1,720.
30. Paid salaries of receptionist and nurses, $1,725.
30. Paid various utility expenses, $360.
30. Recorded fees charged to patients on account for services performed in April, $5,145.
30. Paid miscellaneous expenses, $132.

Outz's account titles, numbers, and balances as of April 1 (all normal balances) are listed as follows: Cash, 11, $4,123; Accounts Receivable, 12, $6,725; Supplies, 13, $290; Prepaid Insurance, 14, $465; Equipment, 18, $19,745; Accounts Payable, 22, $765; J. F. Outz, Capital, 31, $30,583; J. F. Outz, Drawing, 32; Professional Fees, 41; Salary Expense, 51; Rent Expense, 53; Laboratory Expense, 55; Utilities Expense, 56; Miscellaneous Expense, 59.

Instructions

1. Open a ledger of standard four-column accounts for Dr. Outz as of April 1 of the current year. Enter the balances in the appropriate balance columns and place a check mark (✓) in the posting reference column. (It is advisable to verify the equality of the debit and credit balances in the ledger before proceeding with the next instruction.)
2. Journalize each transaction in a two-column journal.
3. Post the journal to the ledger, extending the month-end balances to the appropriate balance columns after each posting.
4. Prepare a trial balance as of April 30.

Solution

2. and **3.**

JOURNAL — **PAGE 27**

Date		Description	Post. Ref.	Debit	Credit
20— April	1	Rent Expense	53	800 00	
		Cash	11		800 00
		Paid office rent for April.			
	3	Equipment	18	2 100 00	
		Accounts Payable	22		2 100 00
		Purchased equipment on account.			
	5	Cash	11	3 150 00	
		Accounts Receivable	12		3 150 00
		Received cash on account.			
	8	Supplies	13	245 00	
		Accounts Payable	22		245 00
		Purchased supplies.			

JOURNAL — **PAGE 27**

Date		Description	Post. Ref.	Debit	Credit
	9	Accounts Payable	22	325 00	
		Equipment	18		325 00
		Returned defective equipment.			
	12	Accounts Payable	22	1250 00	
		Cash	11		1250 00
		Paid creditors on account.			
	17	Prepaid Insurance	14	370 00	
		Cash	11		370 00
		Renewed 6-month property policy.			
	20	Accounts Payable	22	200 00	
		Cash	11		200 00
		Recorded March payment			
		to creditor.			

JOURNAL — **PAGE 28**

Date		Description	Post. Ref.	Debit	Credit
20— April	24	Laboratory Expense	55	545 00	
		Cash	11		545 00
		Paid for laboratory analysis.			
	27	J. F. Outz, Drawing	32	1250 00	
		Cash	11		1250 00
		J. F. Outz withdrew cash for			
		personal use.			
	30	Cash	11	1720 00	
		Professional Fees	41		1720 00
		Received fees from patients.			
	30	Salary Expense	51	1725 00	
		Cash	11		1725 00
		Paid salaries.			
	30	Utilities Expense	56	360 00	
		Cash	11		360 00
		Paid utilities.			
	30	Accounts Receivable	12	5145 00	
		Professional Fees	41		5145 00
		Fees earned on account.			
	30	Miscellaneous Expense	59	132 00	
		Cash	11		132 00
		Paid expenses.			

1. and **3.**

ACCOUNT *Cash* **ACCOUNT NO.** *11*

Date		Item	Post. Ref.	Debit	Credit	Balance Debit	Balance Credit
20— April	1	Balance	✓			4,123.00	
	1		27		800.00	3,323.00	
	5		27	3,150.00		6,473.00	
	12		27		1,250.00	5,223.00	
	17		27		370.00	4,853.00	
	20		27		200.00	4,653.00	
	24		28		545.00	4,108.00	
	27		28		1,250.00	2,858.00	
	30		28	1,720.00		4,578.00	
	30		28		1,725.00	2,853.00	
	30		28		360.00	2,493.00	
	30		28		132.00	2,361.00	

ACCOUNT *Accounts Receivable* **ACCOUNT NO.** *12*

Date		Item	Post. Ref.	Debit	Credit	Balance Debit	Balance Credit
20— April	1	Balance	✓			6,725.00	
	5		27		3,150.00	3,575.00	
	30		28	5,145.00		8,720.00	

ACCOUNT *Supplies* **ACCOUNT NO.** *13*

Date		Item	Post. Ref.	Debit	Credit	Balance Debit	Balance Credit
20— April	1	Balance	✓			290.00	
	8		27	245.00		535.00	

ACCOUNT *Prepaid Insurance* **ACCOUNT NO.** *14*

Date		Item	Post. Ref.	Debit	Credit	Balance Debit	Balance Credit
20— April	1	Balance	✓			465.00	
	17		27	370.00		835.00	

ACCOUNT *Equipment* **ACCOUNT NO.** *18*

Date		Item	Post. Ref.	Debit	Credit	Balance Debit	Balance Credit
20— April	1	Balance	✓			19,745.00	
	3		27	2,100.00		21,845.00	
	9		27		325.00	21,520.00	

ACCOUNT *Accounts Payable* — **ACCOUNT NO. 22**

Date		Item	Post. Ref.	Debit	Credit	Balance Debit	Balance Credit
20— April	1	Balance	✓				765 00
	3		27		2,100 00		2,865 00
	8		27		245 00		3,110 00
	9		27	325 00			2,785 00
	12		27	1,250 00			1,535 00
	20		27	200 00			1,335 00

ACCOUNT *J. F. Outz, Capital* — **ACCOUNT NO. 31**

Date		Item	Post. Ref.	Debit	Credit	Balance Debit	Balance Credit
20— April	1	Balance	✓				30,583 00

ACCOUNT *J. F. Outz, Drawing* — **ACCOUNT NO. 32**

Date		Item	Post. Ref.	Debit	Credit	Balance Debit	Balance Credit
20— April	27		28	1,250 00		1,250 00	

ACCOUNT *Professional Fees* — **ACCOUNT NO. 41**

Date		Item	Post. Ref.	Debit	Credit	Balance Debit	Balance Credit
20— April	30		28		1,720 00		1,720 00
	30		28		5,145 00		6,865 00

ACCOUNT *Salary Expense* — **ACCOUNT NO. 51**

Date		Item	Post. Ref.	Debit	Credit	Balance Debit	Balance Credit
20— April	30		28	1,725 00		1,725 00	

ACCOUNT *Rent Expense* — **ACCOUNT NO. 53**

Date		Item	Post. Ref.	Debit	Credit	Balance Debit	Balance Credit
20— April	1		27	800 00		800 00	

ACCOUNT *Laboratory Expense* **ACCOUNT NO.** *55*

Date		Item	Post. Ref.	Debit	Credit	Balance Debit	Balance Credit
20— April	24		28	545 00		545 00	

ACCOUNT *Utilities Expense* **ACCOUNT NO.** *56*

Date		Item	Post. Ref.	Debit	Credit	Balance Debit	Balance Credit
20— April	30		28	360 00		360 00	

ACCOUNT *Miscellaneous Expense* **ACCOUNT NO.** *59*

Date		Item	Post. Ref.	Debit	Credit	Balance Debit	Balance Credit
20— April	30		28	132 00		132 00	

4.

J. F. Outz, M.D.
Trial Balance
April 30, 20—

Cash	2,361 00	
Accounts Receivable	872 00	
Supplies	535 00	
Prepaid Insurance	835 00	
Equipment	21,520 00	
Accounts Payable		1,335 00
J. F. Outz, Capital		30,583 00
J. F. Outz, Drawing	1,250 00	
Professional Fees		6,865 00
Salary Expense	1,725 00	
Rent Expense	800 00	
Laboratory Expense	545 00	
Utilities Expense	360 00	
Miscellaneous Expense	132 00	
	38,783 00	38,783 00

SELF-EXAMINATION QUESTIONS

Answers at End of Chapter

Matching

Match each of the following statements with its proper term. Some terms may not be used.

- **A.** **account**
- **B.** **assets**
- **C.** **balance of the account**
- **D.** **chart of accounts**
- **E.** **credits**
- **F.** **debits**
- **G.** **double-entry accounting**
- **H.** **drawing**
- **I.** **expenses**
- **J.** **horizontal analysis**
- **K.** **journal**
- **L.** **journal entry**
- **M.** **journalizing**
- **N.** **ledger**
- **O.** **liabilities**
- **P.** **materiality concept**
- **Q.** **objectivity concept**
- **R.** **owner's equity**
- **S.** **posting**
- **T.** **revenues**
- **U.** **slide**
- **V.** **T account**
- **W.** **transposition**
- **X.** **trial balance**
- **Y.** **two-column journal**
- **Z.** **unearned revenue**
- **AA.** **vertical analysis**

A 1. An accounting form that is used to record the increases and decreases in each financial statement item.

N 2. A group of accounts for a business.

D 3. A list of the accounts in the ledger.

B 4. Resources that are owned by the business.

O 5. Debts owed to outsiders (creditors).

R 6. The owner's right to the assets of the business.

T 7. Increases in owner's equity as a result of selling services or products to customers.

I 8. Assets used up or services consumed in the process of generating revenues.

V 9. The simplest form of an account.

F 10. Amounts entered on the left side of an account.

E 11. Amounts entered on the right side of an account.

C 12. The amount of the difference between the debits and the credits that have been entered into an account.

K 13. The initial record in which the effects of a transaction are recorded.

M 14. The process of recording a transaction in the journal.

L 15. The form of recording a transaction in a journal.

G 16. A system of accounting for recording transactions, based on recording increases and decreases in accounts so that debits equal credits.

H 17. The account used to record amounts withdrawn by an owner of a proprietorship.

S 18. The process of transferring the debits and credits from the journal entries to the accounts.

Y 19. An all-purpose journal.

Z 20. The liability created by receiving revenue in advance.

X 21. A summary listing of the titles and balances of accounts in the ledger.

P 22. A concept of accounting that implies that an error may be treated in the easiest possible way.

W 23. An error in which the order of the digits is changed, such as writing $542 as $452 or $524.

U 24. An error in which the entire number is moved one or more spaces to the right or the left, such as writing $542.00 as $54.20 or $5,420.00.

J 25. Financial analysis that compares an item in a current statement with the same item in prior statements.

Multiple Choice

1. A debit may signify:
   A. an increase in an asset account
   B. a decrease in an asset account
   C. an increase in a liability account
   D. an increase in the owner's capital account

2. The type of account with a normal credit balance is:
   A. an asset
   B. drawing
   C. a revenue
   D. an expense

3. A debit balance in which of the following accounts would indicate a likely error?
   A. Accounts Receivable
   B. Cash
   C. Fees Earned
   D. Miscellaneous Expense

4. The receipt of cash from customers in payment of their accounts would be recorded by a:
   A. debit to Cash; credit to Accounts Receivable
   B. debit to Accounts Receivable; credit to Cash
   C. debit to Cash; credit to Accounts Payable
   D. debit to Accounts Payable; credit to Cash

5. The form listing the titles and balances of the accounts in the ledger on a given date is the:
   A. income statement
   B. balance sheet
   C. statement of owner's equity
   D. trial balance

CLASS DISCUSSION QUESTIONS

1. What is the difference between an account and a ledger?
2. Describe in general terms the sequence of accounts in the ledger.
3. Do the terms *debit* and *credit* signify increase or decrease, or may they signify either? Explain.
4. Explain why the rules of debit and credit are the same for liability accounts and owner's equity accounts.
5. What is the effect (increase or decrease) of debits to expense accounts (a) in terms of owner's equity and (b) in terms of expense?
6. What is the effect (increase or decrease) of credits to revenue accounts (a) in terms of owner's equity and (b) in terms of revenue?
7. Activewear Company adheres to a policy of depositing all cash receipts in a bank account and making all payments by check. The cash account as of October 31 has a credit balance of $1,200, and there is no undeposited cash on hand. (a) Assuming that there were no errors in journalizing or posting, what caused this unusual balance? (b) Is the $1,200 credit balance in the cash account an asset, a liability, owner's equity, a revenue, or an expense?
8. Rearrange the following in proper sequence: (a) entry is posted to ledger, (b) business transaction occurs, (c) entry is recorded in journal, (d) business document is prepared, (e) business transaction is authorized.
9. Describe the three procedures required to post the credit portion of the following journal entry (Fees Earned is account no. 41):

JOURNAL **PAGE 32**

	Date		Description	Post. Ref.	Debit	Credit	
1	20— June	11	Accounts Receivable	12	875 00		1
2			Fees Earned			875 00	2

10. In the journal, what indicates that an entry has been posted to the accounts?
11. Lofton Company performed services in June for a specific customer, and the fee was $11,500. Payment was received the following July. (a) Was the revenue earned in June or July? (b) What accounts should be debited and credited in (1) June and (2) July?
12. What proof is provided by a trial balance?
13. If the two totals of a trial balance are equal, does it mean that there are no errors in the accounting records? Explain.
14. Assume that a trial balance is prepared with an account balance of $18,500 listed as $15,800 and an account balance of $8,000 listed as $800. Identify the transposition and the slide.
15. When a purchase of supplies of $580 for cash was recorded, both the debit and the credit were journalized and posted as $850. (a) Would this error cause the trial balance to be out of balance? (b) Would the answer be the same if the $580 entry had been journalized correctly, but the credit to Cash had been posted as $850?

16. How is a correction made when an error in an account title or amount in the journal is discovered before the entry is posted?
17. In journalizing and posting the entry to record the purchase of supplies on account, the accounts receivable account was credited in error. What is the preferred procedure to correct the error?
18. Banks rely heavily upon customers' deposits as a source of funds. Demand deposits normally pay interest to the customer, who is entitled to withdraw at any time without prior notice to the bank. Checking and NOW (negotiable order of withdrawal) accounts are the most common form of demand deposits for banks. Assume that The Package Company has a checking account at National Savings Bank. What type of account (asset, liability, owner's equity, revenue, expense, drawing) does the account balance of $21,500 represent from the viewpoint of (a) The Package Company and (b) National Savings Bank?

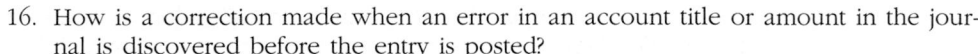

Resources for Your Success On-Line at warren.swcollege.com

Remember! If you need additional help, visit South-Western's Web site. See page 26 for a description of the online and printed materials that are available.

EXERCISES

Exercise 2–1
Chart of accounts
Objective 1

Adcock Interiors is owned and operated by Harold Adcock, an interior decorator. In the ledger of Adcock Interiors, the first digit of the account number indicates its major account classification (1—assets, 2—liabilities, 3—owner's equity, 4—revenues, 5—expenses). The second digit of the account number indicates the specific account within each of the preceding major account classifications.

Match each account number with its most likely account in the list below. The account numbers are 11, 12, 13, 21, 31, 32, 41, 51, 52, and 53.

Accounts:

Accounts Payable	Harold Adcock, Drawing
Accounts Receivable	Land
Cash	Miscellaneous Expense
Fees Earned	Supplies Expense
Harold Adcock, Capital	Wages Expense

Exercise 2–2
Chart of accounts
Objective 1

The Charm School is a newly organized business that teaches young people how to behave in a socially acceptable way. The list of accounts to be opened in the general ledger is as follows:

Accounts Payable	Heather Mock, Capital	Supplies
Accounts Receivable	Heather Mock, Drawing	Supplies Expense
Cash	Miscellaneous Expense	Unearned Rent
Equipment	Prepaid Insurance	Wages Expense
Fees Earned	Rent Expense	

List the accounts in the order in which they should appear in the ledger of The Charm School and assign account numbers. Each account number is to have two digits: the first digit is to indicate the major classification (*1* for assets, etc.), and the second digit is to identify the specific account within each major classification (1*1* for Cash, etc.).

Exercise 2–3
Identifying transactions
Objectives 2, 3

Sunrise Co. is a travel agency. The nine transactions recorded by Sunrise during June, its first month of operations, are indicated in the following T accounts:

Cash	
(1) 50,000	(2) 2,500
(7) 9,500	(3) 10,000
	(4) 6,050
	(6) 6,000
	(8) 2,500

Equipment	
(3) 30,000	

Cheng Sun, Drawing	
(8) 2,500	

Accounts Receivable	
(5) 12,500	(7) 9,500

Accounts Payable	
(6) 6,000	(3) 20,000

Service Revenue	
	(5) 12,500

Supplies	
(2) 2,500	(9) 1,450

Cheng Sun, Capital	
	(1) 50,000

Operating Expenses	
(4) 6,050	
(9) 1,450	

Indicate for each debit and each credit: (a) whether an asset, liability, owner's equity, drawing, revenue, or expense account was affected and (b) whether the account was increased (+) or decreased (−). Present your answers in the following form [transaction (1) is given as an example]:

	Account Debited		Account Credited	
Transaction	**Type**	**Effect**	**Type**	**Effect**
(1)	asset	+	owner's equity	+

Exercise 2–4
Journal entries
Objectives 3, 4

Based upon the T accounts in Exercise 2–3, prepare the nine journal entries from which the postings were made. Journal entry explanations may be omitted.

Exercise 2–5
Trial balance
Objective 5

✓ Total Debit Column: $76,500

Based upon the data presented in Exercise 2–3, prepare a trial balance, listing the accounts in their proper order.

Exercise 2–6
Normal entries for accounts
Objective 3

During the month, Dexter Labs Co. has a substantial number of transactions affecting each of the following accounts. State for each account whether it is likely to have (a) debit entries only, (b) credit entries only, or (c) both debit and credit entries.

1. Accounts Payable
2. Accounts Receivable
3. Cash
4. Fees Earned
5. Justin Sykes, Drawing
6. Miscellaneous Expense
7. Supplies Expense

Exercise 2–7
Normal balances of accounts
Objective 3

Identify each of the following accounts of Elrod Services Co. as asset, liability, owner's equity, revenue, or expense, and state in each case whether the normal balance is a debit or a credit.

a. Accounts Payable
b. Accounts Receivable
c. Cash
d. Chester Elrod, Capital
e. Chester Elrod, Drawing
f. Equipment
g. Fees Earned
h. Rent Expense
i. Salary Expense
j. Supplies

Exercise 2–8
Rules of debit and credit
Objective 3

The following table summarizes the rules of debit and credit. For each of the items (a) through (l), indicate whether the proper answer is a debit or a credit.

	Increase	Decrease	Normal Balance
Balance sheet accounts:			
Asset	(a)	Credit	Debit
Liability	(b)	(c)	(d)
Owner's Equity:			
Capital	(e)	(f)	Credit
Drawing	(g)	(h)	Debit
Income statement accounts:			
Revenue	Credit	(i)	(j)
Expense	(k)	Credit	(l)

Exercise 2–9
Capital account balance
Objective 2

✓ Negative $7,000

As of January 1, Wanda Deaton, Capital had a credit balance of $8,000. During the year, withdrawals totaled $10,000 and the business incurred a net loss of $5,000.

a. Calculate the balance of Wanda Deaton, Capital as of the end of the year.
b. Assuming that there have been no recording errors, will the balance sheet prepared at December 31 balance? Explain.

Exercise 2–10
Cash account balance
Objective 2

✓ b. $100,000

During the month, a business received $712,800 in cash and paid out $630,000 in cash.

a. Do the data indicate that the business earned $82,800 during the month? Explain.
b. If the balance of the cash account was $17,200 at the beginning of the month, what was the cash balance at the end of the month?

Exercise 2–11
Account balances
Objective 2

✓ c. $13,800

a. On April 1, the cash account balance was $11,250. During April, cash receipts totaled $31,800 and the April 30 balance was $12,500. Determine the cash payments made during April.
b. On June 1, the accounts receivable account balance was $23,900. During June, $21,000 was collected from customers on account. If the June 30 balance was $27,500, determine the fees billed to customers on account during June.
c. During August, $40,500 was paid to creditors on account and purchases on account were $77,700. If the August 31 balance of Accounts Payable was $51,000, determine the account balance on August 1.

Exercise 2–12
Transactions
Objectives 3, 4

The Wildlife Co. has the following accounts in its ledger: Cash; Accounts Receivable; Supplies; Office Equipment; Accounts Payable; Erin Fox, Capital; Erin Fox, Drawing; Fees Earned; Rent Expense; Advertising Expense; Utilities Expense; Miscellaneous Expense.

Journalize the following selected transactions in a two-column journal. Journal entry explanations may be omitted.

July 1. Paid rent for the month, $3,000.
2. Paid advertising expense, $500.
4. Paid cash for supplies, $770.
6. Purchased office equipment on account, $8,500.
8. Received cash from customers on account, $3,600.
12. Paid creditor on account, $2,150.
20. Withdrew cash for personal use, $1,500.
25. Paid cash for repairs to office equipment, $120.
30. Paid telephone bill for the month, $195.
31. Fees earned and billed to customers for the month, $11,150.
31. Paid electricity bill for the month, $430.

Exercise 2–13
Journalizing and posting

Objectives 3, 4

On April 8, 2000, Parshall Co. purchased $2,720 of supplies on account. In Parshall Co.'s chart of accounts, the supplies account is No. 15 and the accounts payable account is No. 21.

a. Journalize the April 8, 2000 transaction on page 12 of Parshall Co.'s two-column journal. Include an explanation of the entry.
b. Prepare a four-column account for Supplies. Enter a debit balance of $1,200 as of April 1, 2000. Place a check mark (✓) in the posting reference column.
c. Prepare a four-column account for Accounts Payable. Enter a credit balance of $11,734 as of April 1, 2000. Place a check mark (✓) in the posting reference column.
d. Post the April 8, 2000 transaction to the accounts.

Exercise 2–14
Transactions and T accounts

Objectives 2, 3, 4

The following selected transactions were completed during February of the current year:

1. Billed customers for fees earned, $5,210.
2. Purchased supplies on account, $520.
3. Received cash from customers on account, $3,200.
4. Paid creditors on account, $400.

a. Journalize the foregoing transactions in a two-column journal, using the appropriate number to identify the transactions. Journal entry explanations may be omitted.
b. Post the entries prepared in (a) to the following T accounts: Cash, Supplies, Accounts Receivable, Accounts Payable, Fees Earned. To the left of each amount posted in the accounts, place the appropriate number to identify the transactions.

Exercise 2–15
Trial balance

Objective 5

✓ Total Debit Column: $485,000

The accounts in the ledger of Asbury Park Co. as of August 31 of the current year are listed in alphabetical order as follows. All accounts have normal balances. The balance of the cash account has been intentionally omitted.

Accounts Payable	$ 18,710
Accounts Receivable	20,500
Cash	?
Dillon Garcia, Capital	110,290
Dillon Garcia, Drawing	20,000
Fees Earned	315,000
Insurance Expense	5,000
Land	125,000
Miscellaneous Expense	9,900
Notes Payable	35,000
Prepaid Insurance	3,150
Rent Expense	58,000
Supplies	4,100
Supplies Expense	5,900
Unearned Rent	6,000
Utilities Expense	41,500
Wages Expense	175,000

Prepare a trial balance, listing the accounts in their proper order and inserting the missing figure for cash.

Exercise 2–16
Effect of errors on trial balance

Objective 5

Indicate which of the following errors, each considered individually, would cause the trial balance totals to be unequal:

a. Payment of a cash withdrawal of $2,000 was journalized and posted as a debit of $200 to Salary Expense and a credit of $200 to Cash.

b. A payment of $5,000 for equipment purchased was posted as a debit of $5,000 to Equipment and a credit of $50,000 to Cash.
c. A fee of $3,100 earned and due from a client was not debited to Accounts Receivable or credited to a revenue account, because the cash had not been received.
d. A receipt of $500 from an account receivable was journalized and posted as a debit of $500 to Cash and a credit of $500 to Fees Earned.
e. A payment of $850 to a creditor was posted as a debit of $850 to Accounts Payable and a debit of $850 to Cash.

Exercise 2–17

Errors in trial balance

Objective 5

✓ Total of Credit Column: $143,280

The following preliminary trial balance of The Montana Co., a sports ticket agency, does not balance:

The Montana Co.
Trial Balance
December 31, 20—

Cash	83,000	
Accounts Receivable	23,600	
Prepaid Insurance		3,300
Equipment	4,500	
Accounts Payable		9,450
Unearned Rent		1,480
Ted Turner, Capital	68,550	
Ted Turner, Drawing	10,000	
Service Revenue		64,940
Wages Expense		33,400
Advertising Expense	5,200	
Miscellaneous Expense		1,380
	194,850	113,950

When the ledger and other records are reviewed, you discover the following: (1) the debits and credits in the cash account total $83,000 and $65,300, respectively; (2) a billing of $3,700 to a customer on account was not posted to the accounts receivable account; (3) a payment of $1,500 made to a creditor on account was not posted to the accounts payable account; (4) the balance of the unearned rent account is $1,840; (5) the correct balance of the equipment account is $45,000; and (6) each account has a normal balance.

Prepare a corrected trial balance.

Exercise 2–18

Effect of errors on trial balance

Objective 5

The following errors occurred in posting from a two-column journal:

1. A credit of $500 to Accounts Payable was posted as a debit.
2. An entry debiting Accounts Receivable and crediting Fees Earned for $4,500 was not posted.
3. A credit of $250 to Cash was posted as $520.
4. A debit of $750 to Cash was posted to Wages Expense.
5. A debit of $1,200 to Supplies was posted twice.
6. A debit of $1,575 to Wages Expense was posted as $1,755.
7. A credit of $1,830 to Accounts Receivable was not posted.

Considering each case individually (i.e., assuming that no other errors had occurred), indicate: (a) by "yes" or "no" whether the trial balance would be out of balance; (b) if answer to (a) is "yes," the amount by which the trial balance totals would differ; and (c) whether the debit or credit column of the trial balance would have the larger total. Answers should be presented in the following form [error (1) is given as an example]:

Error	(a) Out of Balance	(b) Difference	(c) Larger Total
1.	yes	$1,000	debit

Exercise 2–19

Errors in trial balance

Objective 5

✓ Total of Credit Column: $105,100

How many errors can you find in the following trial balance? All accounts have normal balances.

The Peasley Co.
Trial Balance
For the Month Ending March 31, 20—

Cash	3,010	
Accounts Receivable	16,400	
Prepaid Insurance		2,400
Equipment	41,200	
Accounts Payable	1,850	
Salaries Payable		750
Nikki Swoopes, Capital		34,600
Nikki Swoopes, Drawing		5,000
Service Revenue		67,900
Salary Expense		28,400
Advertising Expense	7,200	
Miscellaneous Expense	1,490	
	139,050	139,050

Exercise 2–20

Entries to correct errors

Objective 6

Errors in journalizing and posting transactions are described as follows:

a. A withdrawal of $15,000 by T. Woods, owner of the business, was recorded as a debit to Salary Expense and a credit to Cash.
b. Rent of $1,800 paid for the current month was recorded as a debit to Accounts Payable and a credit to cash.

Journalize the entries to correct the errors. Omit explanations.

Exercise 2–21

Entries to correct errors

Objective 6

Errors in journalizing and posting transactions are described as follows:

a. A $1,050 purchase of supplies on account was recorded as a debit to Cash and a credit to Accounts Payable.
b. Cash of $1,350 received on account was recorded as a debit to Accounts Payable and a credit to Cash.

Journalize the entries to correct the errors. Omit explanations.

Exercise 2–22

Horizontal analysis of income statement

Objective 7

The financial statements for **Hershey Foods Corporation** are presented in Appendix G at the end of the text.

a. For Hershey Foods Corporation, comparing 1996 with 1995, determine the amount of change and the percent of change for
   1. net sales (revenues) and
   2. selling, marketing, and administrative expenses.
b. What conclusions can you draw from your analysis of the net sales and the selling, marketing, and administrative expenses?

PROBLEMS SERIES A

Problem 2–1A
Entries into T accounts and trial balance

Objectives 2, 3, 4, 5

HAT

✓ 3. Total of Debit Column: $50,100

Robin Reich, an architect, opened an office on April 1 of the current year. During the month, he completed the following transactions connected with his professional practice:

a. Transferred cash from a personal bank account to an account to be used for the business, $30,000.
b. Purchased used automobile for $18,300, paying $6,000 cash and giving a non-interest-bearing note for the remainder.
c. Paid April rent for office and workroom, $2,200.
d. Paid cash for supplies, $300.
e. Purchased office and drafting room equipment on account, $4,200.
f. Paid cash for insurance policies on automobile and equipment, $810.
g. Received cash from a client for plans delivered, $2,725.
h. Paid cash to creditors on account, $2,100.
i. Paid cash for miscellaneous expenses, $120.
j. Received invoice for blueprint service, due in following month, $275.
k. Recorded fee earned on plans delivered, payment to be received in May, $3,500.
l. Paid salary of assistant, $1,500.
m. Paid cash for miscellaneous expenses, $60.
n. Paid installment due on note payable, $800.
o. Paid gas, oil, and repairs on automobile for April, $170.

Instructions

1. Record the foregoing transactions directly in the following T accounts, without journalizing: Cash; Accounts Receivable; Supplies; Prepaid Insurance; Automobiles; Equipment; Notes Payable; Accounts Payable; Robin Reich, Capital; Professional Fees; Rent Expense; Salary Expense; Automobile Expense; Blueprint Expense; Miscellaneous Expense. To the left of each amount entered in the accounts, place the appropriate letter to identify the transaction.
2. Determine the balances of the T accounts having two or more debits or credits. A memorandum balance should be inserted in accounts having both debits and credits, in the manner illustrated in the chapter. For accounts with entries on one side only (such as Professional Fees), there is no need to insert the memorandum balance in the item column. For accounts containing only a single debit and a single credit (such as Notes Payable), the memorandum balance should be inserted in the appropriate item column. Accounts containing a single entry only (such as Prepaid Insurance) do not need a memorandum balance.
3. Prepare a trial balance for Robin Reich, Architect, as of April 30 of the current year.

Problem 2–2A
Journal entries and trial balance

Objectives 2, 3, 4, 5

HAT
GENERAL LEDGER

✓ 4. a. $32,600
✓ b. $12,700

On October 1 of the current year, Clay Bryant established Northside Realty, which completed the following transactions during the month:

a. Clay Bryant transferred cash from a personal bank account to an account to be used for the business, $25,000.
b. Purchased supplies on account, $2,900.
c. Earned sales commissions, receiving cash, $32,600.
d. Paid rent on office and equipment for the month, $4,500.
e. Paid creditor on account, $1,000.
f. Withdrew cash for personal use, $2,000.
g. Paid automobile expenses (including rental charge) for month, $1,900, and miscellaneous expenses, $1,050.
h. Paid office salaries, $4,000.
i. Determined that the cost of supplies used was $1,250.

Instructions

1. Journalize entries for transactions (a) through (i), using the following account titles: Cash; Supplies; Accounts Payable; Clay Bryant, Capital; Clay Bryant, Drawing; Sales Commissions; Rent Expense; Office Salaries Expense; Automobile Expense; Supplies Expense; Miscellaneous Expense. Journal entry explanations may be omitted.
2. Prepare T accounts, using the account titles in (1). Post the journal entries to these accounts, placing the appropriate letter to the left of each amount to identify the transactions. Determine the account balances, after all posting is complete, for all accounts having two or more debits or credits. A memorandum balance should be inserted in accounts having both debits and credits, in the manner illustrated in the chapter. For accounts with entries on one side only, there is no need to insert a memorandum balance in the item column. For accounts containing only a single debit and a single credit, the memorandum balance should be inserted in the appropriate item column.
3. Prepare a trial balance as of October 31, 20—.
4. Determine the following:
   a. Amount of total revenue recorded in the ledger.
   b. Amount of total expenses recorded in the ledger.
   c. Amount of net income for October.

Problem 2–3A

Journal entries and trial balance

Objectives 2, 3, 4, 5

HAT
GENERAL LEDGER

✓ 3. Total of Credit Column: $36,425

On July 10 of the current year, Jong Woo established an interior decorating business, Asian Designs. During the remainder of the month, Jong Woo completed the following transactions related to the business:

July 10. Jong transferred cash from a personal bank account to an account to be used for the business, $20,000.
10. Paid rent for period of July 10 to end of month, $1,500.
11. Purchased a truck for $15,000, paying $5,000 cash and giving a note payable for the remainder.
12. Purchased equipment on account, $2,500.
14. Purchased supplies for cash, $1,050.
14. Paid premiums on property and casualty insurance, $750.
15. Received cash for job completed, $3,100.
21. Paid creditor for equipment purchased on July 12, $2,500.
24. Recorded jobs completed on account and sent invoices to customers, $3,100.
26. Received an invoice for truck expenses, to be paid in August, $225.
27. Paid utilities expense, $1,205.
27. Paid miscellaneous expenses, $173.
28. Received cash from customers on account, $1,420.
31. Paid wages of employees, $2,100.
31. Withdrew cash for personal use, $1,500.

Instructions

1. Journalize each transaction in a two-column journal, referring to the following chart of accounts in selecting the accounts to be debited and credited. (Do not insert the account numbers in the journal at this time.) Journal entry explanations may be omitted.

11	Cash	31	Jong Woo, Capital
12	Accounts Receivable	32	Jong Woo, Drawing
13	Supplies	41	Fees Earned
14	Prepaid Insurance	51	Wages Expense
16	Equipment	53	Rent Expense
18	Truck	54	Utilities Expense
21	Notes Payable	55	Truck Expense
22	Accounts Payable	59	Miscellaneous Expense

2. Post the journal to a ledger of four-column accounts, inserting appropriate posting references as each item is posted. Extend the balances to the appropriate balance columns after each transaction is posted.
3. Prepare a trial balance for Asian Designs as of July 31.

Problem 2–4A

Journal entries and trial balance

Objectives 2, 3, 4, 5

HAT

✓ 4. Total of Debit Column: $314,500

Cherokee Realty acts as an agent in buying, selling, renting, and managing real estate. The account balances at the end of April of the current year are as follows:

11	Cash	29,500	
12	Accounts Receivable	38,600	
13	Prepaid Insurance	750	
14	Office Supplies	625	
16	Land	0	
21	Accounts Payable		13,250
22	Notes Payable		0
31	Eva Wheless, Capital		63,025
32	Eva Wheless, Drawing	10,000	
41	Fees Earned		158,725
51	Salary and Commission Expense	123,075	
52	Rent Expense	19,000	
53	Advertising Expense	8,900	
54	Automobile Expense	3,950	
59	Miscellaneous Expense	600	
		235,000	235,000

The following business transactions were completed by Cherokee Realty during May of the current year:

May 1. Purchased office supplies on account, $1,100.
2. Paid rent on office for month, $2,500.
3. Received cash from clients on account, $34,200.
9. Paid insurance premiums, $1,925.
10. Returned a portion of the office supplies purchased on May 1, receiving full credit for their cost, $150.
15. Paid advertising expense, $2,150.
20. Paid creditors on account, $7,650.
29. Paid miscellaneous expenses, $215.
30. Paid automobile expense (including rental charges for an automobile), $850.
31. Discovered an error in computing a commission; received cash from the salesperson for the overpayment, $500.
31. Paid salaries and commissions for the month, $30,850.
31. Recorded revenue earned and billed to clients during the month, $46,200.
31. Purchased land for a future building site for $50,000, paying $10,000 in cash and giving a note payable for the remainder.
31. Withdrew cash for personal use, $2,500.

Instructions

1. Record the May 1 balance of each account in the appropriate balance column of a four-column account, write *Balance* in the item section, and place a check mark (✓) in the posting reference column.
2. Journalize the transactions for May in a two-column journal. Journal entry explanations may be omitted.
3. Post to the ledger, extending the account balance to the appropriate balance column after each posting.
4. Prepare a trial balance of the ledger as of May 31.

Problem 2–5A
Errors in trial balance

Objectives 5, 6

What's Wrong WITH THIS?

✓ 7. Total of Debit Column: $33,338.10

If the working papers correlating with this textbook are not used, omit Problem 2–5A. The following records of Couch TV Repair are presented in the working papers:

- Journal containing entries for the period March 1–31.
- Ledger to which the March entries have been posted.
- Preliminary trial balance as of March 31, which does not balance.

Locate the errors, supply the information requested, and prepare a corrected trial balance according to the following instructions. The balances recorded in the accounts as of March 1 and the entries in the journal are correctly stated. If it is necessary to correct any posted amounts in the ledger, a line should be drawn through the erroneous figure and the correct amount inserted above. Corrections or notations may be inserted on the preliminary trial balance in any manner desired. It is not necessary to complete all of the instructions if equal trial balance totals can be obtained earlier. However, the requirements of instructions (6) and (7) should be completed in any event.

Instructions

1. Verify the totals of the preliminary trial balance, inserting the correct amounts in the schedule provided in the working papers.
2. Compute the difference between the trial balance totals.
3. Compare the listings in the trial balance with the balances appearing in the ledger, and list the errors in the space provided in the working papers.
4. Verify the accuracy of the balance of each account in the ledger, and list the errors in the space provided in the working papers.
5. Trace the postings in the ledger back to the journal, using small check marks to identify items traced. Correct any amounts in the ledger that may be necessitated by errors in posting, and list the errors in the space provided in the working papers.
6. Journalize as of March 31 the payment of $113.40 for gas and electricity. The bill had been paid on March 31 but was inadvertently omitted from the journal. Post to the ledger. (Revise any amounts necessitated by posting this entry.)
7. Prepare a new trial balance.

Problem 2–6A
Corrected trial balance

Objectives 5, 6

SPREADSHEET

✓ 1. Total of Debit Column: $103,090

Newman Photography has the following trial balance as of December 31 of the current year:

Cash	4,025	
Accounts Receivable	9,350	
Supplies	1,277	
Prepaid Insurance	330	
Equipment	12,500	
Notes Payable		12,500
Accounts Payable		3,025
Jake Newman, Capital		13,240
Jake Newman, Drawing	6,000	
Fees Earned		80,750
Wages Expense	48,150	
Rent Expense	750	
Advertising Expense	5,250	
Gas, Electricity, and Water Expense	3,150	
	90,782	109,515

The debit and credit totals are not equal as a result of the following errors:

a. The balance of cash was overstated by $1,500.
b. A cash receipt of $1,200 was posted as a credit to Cash of $2,100.
c. A debit of $750 to Accounts Receivable was not posted.
d. A return of $252 of defective supplies was erroneously posted as a $225 credit to Supplies.
e. An insurance policy acquired at a cost of $310 was posted as a credit to Prepaid Insurance.

f. The balance of Notes Payable was overstated by $5,000.
g. A credit of $75 in Accounts Payable was overlooked when the balance of the account was determined.
h. A debit of $1,500 for a withdrawal by the owner was posted as a credit to Jake Newman, Capital.
i. The balance of $7,500 in Rent Expense was entered as $750 in the trial balance.
j. Miscellaneous Expense, with a balance of $915, was omitted from the trial balance.

Instructions

1. Prepare a corrected trial balance as of December 31 of the current year.
2. Does the fact that the trial balance in (1) is balanced mean that there are no errors in the accounts? Explain.

PROBLEMS SERIES B

Problem 2–1B

Entries into T accounts and trial balance

Objectives 2, 3, 4, 5

✓ 3. Total of Debit Column: $39,410

Veronica Mays, an architect, opened an office on January 1 of the current year. During the month, she completed the following transactions connected with her professional practice:

a. Transferred cash from a personal bank account to an account to be used for the business, $20,000.
b. Paid January rent for office and workroom, $2,500.
c. Purchased used automobile for $11,500, paying $2,500 cash and giving a non-interest-bearing note for the remainder.
d. Purchased office and drafting room equipment on account, $6,200.
e. Paid cash for supplies, $900.
f. Paid cash for insurance policies, $1,050.
g. Received cash from client for plans delivered, $3,100.
h. Paid cash for miscellaneous expenses, $75.
i. Paid cash to creditors on account, $2,950.
j. Paid installment due on note payable, $400.
k. Received invoice for blueprint service, due in February, $310.
l. Recorded fee earned on plans delivered, payment to be received in February, $4,150.
m. Paid salary of assistant, $1,150.
n. Paid gas, oil, and repairs on automobile for January, $175.

Instructions

1. Record the foregoing transactions directly in the following T accounts, without journalizing: Cash; Accounts Receivable; Supplies; Prepaid Insurance; Automobiles; Equipment; Notes Payable; Accounts Payable; Veronica Mays, Capital; Professional Fees; Rent Expense; Salary Expense; Automobile Expense; Blueprint Expense; Miscellaneous Expense. To the left of the amount entered in the accounts, place the appropriate letter to identify the transaction.
2. Determine the balances of the T accounts having two or more debits or credits. A memorandum balance should be inserted in accounts having both debits and credits, in the manner illustrated in the chapter. For accounts with entries on one side only (such as Professional Fees), there is no need to insert the memorandum balance in the item column. For accounts containing only a single debit and a single credit (such as Notes Payable), the memorandum balance should be inserted in the appropriate item column. Accounts containing a single entry only (such as Prepaid Insurance) do not need a memorandum balance.
3. Prepare a trial balance for Veronica Mays, Architect, as of January 31 of the current year.

Problem 2–2B

Journal entries and trial balance

Objectives 2, 3, 4, 5

GENERAL LEDGER

✓ 4. a. $20,750
✓ b. $11,200

On July 1 of the current year, Lamar Todd established Sky Realty, which completed the following transactions during the month:

a. Lamar Todd transferred cash from a personal bank account to an account to be used for the business, $15,000.
b. Paid rent on office and equipment for the month, $2,500.
c. Purchased supplies on account, $1,500.
d. Paid creditor on account, $900.
e. Earned sales commissions, receiving cash, $20,750.
f. Paid automobile expenses (including rental charge) for month, $2,400, and miscellaneous expenses, $1,250.
g. Paid office salaries, $4,000.
h. Determined that the cost of supplies used was $1,050.
i. Withdrew cash for personal use, $1,500.

Instructions

1. Journalize entries for transactions (a) through (i), using the following account titles: Cash; Supplies; Accounts Payable; Lamar Todd, Capital; Lamar Todd, Drawing; Sales Commissions; Office Salaries Expense; Rent Expense; Automobile Expense; Supplies Expense; Miscellaneous Expense. Explanations may be omitted.
2. Prepare T accounts, using the account titles in (1). Post the journal entries to these accounts, placing the appropriate letter to the left of each amount to identify the transactions. Determine the account balances, after all posting is complete, for all accounts having two or more debits or credits. A memorandum balance should also be inserted in accounts having both debits and credits, in the manner illustrated in the chapter. For accounts with entries on one side only, there is no need to insert a memorandum balance in the item column. For accounts containing only a single debit and a single credit, the memorandum balance should be inserted in the appropriate item column.
3. Prepare a trial balance as of July 31, 20—.
4. Determine the following:
   a. Amount of total revenue recorded in the ledger.
   b. Amount of total expenses recorded in the ledger.
   c. Amount of net income for July.

Problem 2–3B

Journal entries and trial balance

Objectives 2, 3, 4, 5

GENERAL LEDGER

✓ 3. Total of Credit Column: $46,040

On June 5 of the current year, Dave Chapman established an interior decorating business, Modern Designs. During the remainder of the month, Dave completed the following transactions related to the business:

June 5. Dave transferred cash from a personal bank account to an account to be used for the business, $25,000.
5. Paid rent for period of June 5 to end of month, $1,700.
7. Purchased office equipment on account, $10,500.
8. Purchased a used truck for $18,000, paying $10,000 cash and giving a note payable for the remainder.
10. Purchased supplies for cash, $1,315.
12. Received cash for job completed, $3,300.
20. Paid premiums on property and casualty insurance, $800.
22. Recorded jobs completed on account and sent invoices to customers, $1,950.
24. Received an invoice for truck expenses, to be paid in July, $290.
29. Paid utilities expense, $490.
29. Paid miscellaneous expenses, $195.
30. Received cash from customers on account, $1,200.
30. Paid wages of employees, $1,900.
30. Paid creditor a portion of the amount owed for equipment purchased on June 7, $3,000.
30. Withdrew cash for personal use, $2,500.

Instructions

1. Journalize each transaction in a two-column journal, referring to the following chart of accounts in selecting the accounts to be debited and credited. (Do not insert the account numbers in the journal at this time.) Explanations may be omitted.

11	Cash	31	Dave Chapman, Capital
12	Accounts Receivable	32	Dave Chapman, Drawing
13	Supplies	41	Fees Earned
14	Prepaid Insurance	51	Wages Expense
16	Equipment	53	Rent Expense
18	Truck	54	Utilities Expense
21	Notes Payable	55	Truck Expense
22	Accounts Payable	59	Miscellaneous Expense

2. Post the journal to a ledger of four-column accounts, inserting appropriate posting references as each item is posted. Extend the balances to the appropriate balance columns after each transaction is posted.
3. Prepare a trial balance for Modern Designs as of June 30.

Problem 2–4B

Journal entries and trial balance

Objectives 2, 3, 4, 5

✓ 4. Total of Debit Column: $260,200

Sycamore Realty acts as an agent in buying, selling, renting, and managing real estate. The account balances at the end of March of the current year are as follows:

11	Cash	28,150	
12	Accounts Receivable	38,750	
13	Prepaid Insurance	1,100	
14	Office Supplies	1,050	
16	Land	0	
21	Accounts Payable		11,510
22	Notes Payable		0
31	Shirley Collins, Capital		29,840
32	Shirley Collins, Drawing	1,000	
41	Fees Earned		126,500
51	Salary and Commission Expense	84,100	
52	Rent Expense	5,500	
53	Advertising Expense	3,900	
54	Automobile Expense	2,750	
59	Miscellaneous Expense	1,550	
		167,850	167,850

The following business transactions were completed by Sycamore Realty during April of the current year:

April 1. Paid rent on office for month, $2,500.
3. Purchased office supplies on account, $1,375.
5. Paid insurance premiums, $1,650.
7. Received cash from clients on account, $30,200.
15. Purchased land for a future building site for $75,000, paying $15,000 in cash and giving a note payable for the remainder.
18. Paid creditors on account, $7,150.
20. Returned a portion of the office supplies purchased on April 3, receiving full credit for their cost, $275.
24. Paid advertising expense, $1,550.
27. Discovered an error in computing a commission; received cash from the salesperson for the overpayment, $350.
28. Paid automobile expense (including rental charges for an automobile), $715.
29. Paid miscellaneous expenses, $215.
30. Recorded revenue earned and billed to clients during the month, $38,400.
30. Paid salaries and commissions for the month, $21,500.
30. Withdrew cash for personal use, $1,500.

Instructions

1. Record the April 1 balance of each account in the appropriate balance column of a four-column account, write *Balance* in the item section, and place a check mark (✓) in the posting reference column.

2. Journalize the transactions for April in a two-column journal. Journal entry explanations may be omitted.
3. Post to the ledger, extending the account balance to the appropriate balance column after each posting.
4. Prepare a trial balance of the ledger as of April 30.

Problem 2–5B
Errors in trial balance

Objectives 5, 6

What's Wrong WITH THIS?

✓ 7. Total of Debit Column: $33,338.10

If the working papers correlating with this textbook are not used, omit Problem 2–5B. The following records of Couch TV Repair are presented in the working papers:

- Journal containing entries for the period March 1–31.
- Ledger to which the March entries have been posted.
- Preliminary trial balance as of March 31, which does not balance.

Locate the errors, supply the information requested, and prepare a corrected trial balance according to the following instructions. The balances recorded in the accounts as of March 1 and the entries in the journal are correctly stated. If it is necessary to correct any posted amounts in the ledger, a line should be drawn through the erroneous figure and the correct amount inserted above. Corrections or notations may be inserted on the preliminary trial balance in any manner desired. It is not necessary to complete all of the instructions if equal trial balance totals can be obtained earlier. However, the requirements of instructions (6) and (7) should be completed in any event.

Instructions

1. Verify the totals of the preliminary trial balance, inserting the correct amounts in the schedule provided in the working papers.
2. Compute the difference between the trial balance totals.
3. Compare the listings in the trial balance with the balances appearing in the ledger, and list the errors in the space provided in the working papers.
4. Verify the accuracy of the balance of each account in the ledger, and list the errors in the space provided in the working papers.
5. Trace the postings in the ledger back to the journal, using small check marks to identify items traced. Correct any amounts in the ledger that may be necessitated by errors in posting, and list the errors in the space provided in the working papers.
6. Journalize as of March 31 the payment of $200 for advertising expense. The bill had been paid on March 31 but was inadvertently omitted from the journal. Post to the ledger. (Revise any amounts necessitated by posting this entry.)
7. Prepare a new trial balance.

Problem 2–6B
Corrected trial balance

Objectives 5, 6

SPREADSHEET

✓ 1. Total of Debit Column: $78,190

Doolittle Carpet has the following trial balance as of March 31 of the current year:

Cash	2,070	
Accounts Receivable	6,150	
Supplies	1,010	
Prepaid Insurance	250	
Equipment	15,500	
Notes Payable		15,000
Accounts Payable		4,810
Ellisa Doolittle, Capital		16,300
Ellisa Doolittle, Drawing	6,000	
Fees Earned		49,980
Wages Expense	28,500	
Rent Expense	6,400	
Advertising Expense	320	
Miscellaneous Expense	945	
	67,145	86,090

The debit and credit totals are not equal as a result of the following errors:

a. The balance of cash was understated by $750.
b. A cash receipt of $2,100 was posted as a debit to Cash of $1,200.
c. A debit of $2,000 for a withdrawal by the owner was posted as a credit to Ellisa Doolittle, Capital.

d. The balance of $3,200 in Advertising Expense was entered as $320 in the trial balance.
e. A debit of $975 to Accounts Receivable was not posted.
f. A return of $125 of defective supplies was erroneously posted as a $215 credit to Supplies.
g. The balance of Notes Payable was overstated by $5,000.
h. An insurance policy acquired at a cost of $150 was posted as a credit to Prepaid Insurance.
i. Gas, Electricity, and Water Expense, with a balance of $3,150, was omitted from the trial balance.
j. A debit of $900 in Accounts Payable was overlooked when determining the balance of the account.

Instructions

1. Prepare a corrected trial balance as of March 31 of the current year.
2. Does the fact that the trial balance in (1) is balanced mean that there are no errors in the accounts? Explain.

CONTINUING PROBLEM

MUSIC TODAY

HAT

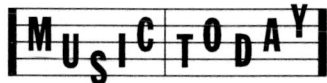

✓ 4. Total of Debit Column: $13,155

The transactions completed by Music Today during November 1999 were described at the end of Chapter 1. The following transactions were completed during December, the second month of the business's operations:

Dec. 1. Chris Stipe made an additional investment in Music Today by depositing $2,500 in Music Today's checking account.
1. Instead of continuing to share office space with a local real estate agency, Chris decided to rent office space near a local music store. Paid rent for December, $720.
1. Paid a premium of $1,680 for a comprehensive insurance policy covering liability, theft, and fire. The policy covers a two-year period.
2. Received $400 on account.
3. On behalf of Music Today, Chris signed a contract with a local radio station, KPRG, to provide guest spots for the next three months. The contract requires Music Today to provide a guest disc jockey for 40 hours per month for a monthly fee of $500. Any additional hours beyond 40 will be billed to KPRG at $15 per hour. In accordance with the contract, Chris received $1,500 from KPRG as an advance payment for the first three months.
3. Paid $150 on account.
4. Paid an attorney $75 for reviewing (on December 2) the contract with KPRG. (Record as Miscellaneous Expense.)
5. Purchased office equipment on account from One-Stop Office Mart, $2,500.
8. Paid for a newspaper advertisement, $100.
11. Received $300 for serving as a disc jockey for a college fraternity party.
13. Paid $250 to a local audio electronics store for rental of various equipment (speakers, CD players, etc.).
14. Paid wages of $400 to receptionist and part-time assistant.
16. Received $550 for serving as a disc jockey for a wedding reception.
18. Purchased supplies on account, $375.
21. Paid $120 to The Music Store for use of its current demo CDs and tapes in making cassettes of various music sets.
22. Paid $50 to a local radio station to advertise the services of Music Today twice daily for the remainder of December.
23. Served as disc jockey for an annual holiday party for $780. Received $200, with the remainder due January 6, 2000.
27. Paid electric bill, $280.
28. Paid wages of $400 to receptionist and part-time assistant.

Dec. 29. Paid miscellaneous expenses, $85.
30. Served as a disc jockey for a pre-New Year's Eve charity ball for $600. Received $300, with the remainder due on January 10, 2000.
31. Received $1,000 for serving as a disc jockey for a New Year's Eve party.
31. Withdrew $500 cash from Music Today for personal use.

Music Today's chart of accounts and the balance of accounts as of December 1, 1999 (all normal balances), are as follows:

11	Cash	$1,345
12	Accounts Receivable	400
14	Supplies	160
15	Prepaid Insurance	—
17	Office Equipment	—
21	Accounts Payable	150
23	Unearned Revenue	—
31	Chris Stipe, Capital	1,500
32	Chris Stipe, Drawing	50
41	Fees Earned	1,550
50	Wages Expense	110
51	Office Rent Expense	250
52	Equipment Rent Expense	325
53	Utilities Expense	100
54	Music Expense	220
55	Advertising Expense	75
56	Supplies Expense	90
59	Miscellaneous Expense	75

Instructions

1. Enter the December 1, 1999 account balances in the appropriate balance column of a four-column account. Write *Balance* in the Item column, and place a check mark (✓) in the Posting Reference column. (It is advisable to verify the equality of the debit and credit balances in the ledger before proceeding with the next instruction.)
2. Analyze and journalize each transaction in a two-column journal. Omit journal entry explanations.
3. Post the journal to the ledger, extending the account balance to the appropriate balance column after each posting.
4. Prepare a trial balance as of December 31, 1999.

SPECIAL ACTIVITIES

Activity 2–1
City Services Co.
Ethics and professional conduct in business

At the end of the current month, Oliva Ohl prepared a trial balance for City Services Co. The credit side of the trial balance exceeds the debit side by a significant amount. Oliva has decided to add the difference to the balance of the miscellaneous expense account in order to complete the preparation of the current month's financial statements by a 5 o'clock deadline. Oliva will look for the difference next week when there is more time. Discuss whether Oliva Ohl is behaving in a professional manner.

Activity 2–2
State College
Account for revenue

What do you THINK?

State College requires students to pay tuition each term before classes begin. Students who have not paid their tuition are not allowed to enroll or to attend classes.

What journal entry do you think would be used by State College to record the receipt of the students' tuition payments? Describe the nature of each account in the entry.

Activity 2–3
Aero Data Company
Record transactions

The following discussion took place between Anita Cain, the office manager of Aero Data Company, and a new accountant, Bob Nunez.

Bob: I've been thinking about our method of recording entries. It seems that it's inefficient.

Anita: In what way?

Bob: Well—correct me if I'm wrong—it seems like we have unnecessary steps in the process. We could very easily develop a trial balance by posting our transactions directly into the ledger and bypassing the journal altogether. In this way we could combine the recording and posting process into one step and save ourselves a lot of time. What do you think?

Anita: We need to have a talk.

What should Anita say to Bob?

Activity 2–4
Crestview Construction Co.
Debits and credits

GROUP ACTIVITY

The following is an excerpt from a conversation between Judy Parker, the president and chief operating officer of Crestview Construction Co., and her neighbor, Jack Vancel.

Jack: Judy, I'm taking a course in night school, "Intro to Accounting." I was wondering—could you answer a couple of questions for me?

Judy: Well, I will if I can.

Jack: Okay, our instructor says that it's critical that we understand the basic concepts of accounting, or we'll never get beyond the first test. My problem is with those rules of debit and credit . . . you know, assets increase with debits, decrease with credits, etc.

Judy: Yes, pretty basic stuff. You just have to memorize the rules. It shouldn't be too difficult.

Jack: Sure, I can memorize the rules, but my problem is I want to be sure I understand the basic concepts behind the rules.

For example, why can't assets be increased with credits and decreased with debits like revenue? As long as everyone did it that way, why not? It would seem easier if we had the same rules for all increases and decreases in accounts.

Also, why is the left side of an account called the debit side? Why couldn't it be called something simple . . . like the "LE" for Left Entry? The right side could be called just "RE" for Right Entry.

Finally, why are there just two sides to an entry? Why can't there be three or four sides to an entry?

In a group of four or five, select one person to play the role of "Judy" and one person to play the role of "Jack."

1. After listening to the conversation between Judy and Jack, help Judy answer Jack's questions.
2. What information (other than just debit and credit journal entries) could the accounting system gather that might be useful to Judy in managing Crestview Construction Co.?

Activity 2–5
Eagle Caddy Service
Transactions and income statement

HAT

During June through August, Dale Wells is planning to manage and operate Eagle Caddy Service at Cordele Golf and Country Club. Dale will rent a small maintenance building from the country club for $200 per month and will offer caddy services, including cart rentals, to golfers. Dale has had no formal training in record keeping. During June, he kept notes of all receipts and expenses in a shoe box.

An examination of Dale's shoe box records for June revealed the following:

June 1. Withdrew $2,000 from personal bank account to be used to operate the caddy service.
1. Paid rent to Cordele Golf and Country Club, $200.
2. Paid for golf supplies (practice balls, etc.), $200.
3. Arranged for the rental of forty regular (pulling) golf carts and ten gasoline-driven carts for $1,000 per month. Paid $750 in advance, with the remaining $250 due June 20.
7. Purchased supplies, including gasoline, for the golf carts on account, $325. Cordele Golf and Country Club has agreed to allow Dale to store the gasoline in one of its fuel tanks at no cost.

June 15. Received cash for services from June 1–15, $1,020.
17. Paid cash to creditors on account, $180.
20. Paid remaining rental on golf carts, $250.
22. Purchased supplies, including gasoline, on account, $280.
25. Accepted IOUs from customers on account, $410.
28. Paid miscellaneous expenses, $125.
30. Received cash for services from June 16–30, $1,475.
30. Paid telephone and electricity (utilities) expenses, $85.
30. Paid wages of part-time employees, $260.
30. Received cash in payment of IOUs on account, $150.
30. Supplies on hand at the end of June, $180.

Dale has asked you several questions concerning his financial affairs to date, and he has asked you to assist with his record keeping and reporting of financial data.

a. To assist Dale with his record keeping, prepare a chart of accounts that would be appropriate for Eagle Caddy Service.
b. Prepare an income statement for June in order to help Dale assess the profitability of Eagle Caddy Service. For this purpose, the use of T accounts may be helpful in analyzing the effects of each June transaction.
c. Based on Dale's records of receipts and payments, calculate the amount of cash on hand on June 30. For this purpose, a T account for cash may be useful.
d. A count of the cash on hand on June 30 totaled $2,135. Briefly discuss the possible causes of the difference between the amount of cash computed in (c) and the actual amount of cash on hand.

Activity 2–6
Into the Real World
Opportunities for accountants

Internet ACTIVITY

The increasing complexity of the current business and regulatory environment has created an increased demand for accountants who can analyze business transactions and interpret their effects on the financial statements. In addition, a basic ability to analyze the effects of transactions is necessary to be successful in all fields of business as well as in other disciplines, such as law. To better understand the importance of accounting in today's environment, search the Internet or your local newspaper for job opportunities. One possible Internet site is **www.jobweb.com**. Then do *one* of the following:

1. Print a listing of at least two ads for accounting jobs. Alternatively, bring to class at least two newspaper ads for accounting jobs.
2. Print a listing of at least two ads for nonaccounting jobs for which some knowledge of accounting is preferred or necessary. Alternatively, bring to class at least two newspaper ads for such jobs.

ANSWERS TO SELF-EXAMINATION QUESTIONS

Matching

1. A	5. O	8. I	11. E	14. M	17. H	20. Z	23. W
2. N	6. R	9. V	12. C	15. L	18. S	21. X	24. U
3. D	7. T	10. F	13. K	16. G	19. Y	22. P	25. J
4. B							

Multiple Choice

1. **A** A debit may signify an increase in an asset account (answer A) or a decrease in a liability or owner's capital account. A credit may signify a decrease in an asset account (answer B) or an increase in a liability or owner's capital account (answers C and D).
2. **C** Liability, capital, and revenue (answer C) accounts have normal credit balances. Asset (answer A), drawing (answer B), and expense (answer D) accounts have normal debit balances.
3. **C** Accounts Receivable (answer A), Cash (answer B),

and Miscellaneous Expense (answer D) would all normally have debit balances. Fees Earned should normally have a credit balance. Hence, a debit balance in Fees Earned (answer C) would indicate a likely error in the recording process.

4. **A** The receipt of cash from customers on account increases the asset Cash and decreases the asset Accounts Receivable, as indicated by answer A. Answer B has the debit and credit reversed, and answers C and D involve transactions with creditors (accounts payable) and not customers (accounts receivable).

5. **D** The trial balance (answer D) is a listing of the balances and the titles of the accounts in the ledger on a given date, so that the equality of the debits and credits in the ledger can be verified. The income statement (answer A) is a summary of revenue and expenses for a period of time. The balance sheet (answer B) is a presentation of the assets, liabilities, and owner's equity on a given date. The statement of owner's equity (answer C) is a summary of the changes in owner's equity for a period of time.

JANUARY
1
1999
DECEMBER
31
3
JANUARY
1
2000
DECEMBER
31

3

The Matching Concept and the Adjusting Process

Setting *the* STAGE

Assume that you rented an apartment last month and signed a nine-month lease. When you signed the lease agreement, you were required to pay the final month's rent of $500. This amount is not returnable to you.

You are now applying for a student loan at a local bank. The loan application requires a listing of all your assets. Should you list the $500 deposit as an asset?

The answer to this question is "yes." The deposit is an asset to you until you receive the use of the apartment in the ninth month.

A business faces similar accounting problems at the end of a period. A business must determine what assets, liabilities, and owner's equity should be reported on its balance sheet. It must also determine what revenues and expenses should be reported on its income statement.

As we illustrated in previous chapters, transactions are normally recorded as they occur. Periodically, financial statements are prepared, summarizing the effects of the transactions on the financial position and the operations of the business.

At any one point in time, however, the accounting records may not reflect all transactions. For example, most businesses do not record the daily use of supplies. Likewise, revenue may have been earned from providing services to customers yet the customers have not been billed by the time the accounting period ends. Thus, at the end of the period, the revenue and the receivable accounts must be updated.

In this chapter, we describe and illustrate this updating process. We will focus on accounts that normally require updating and the journal entries that update them.

objectives

After studying this chapter, you should be able to:

1. Explain how the matching concept relates to the accrual basis of accounting.
2. Explain why adjustments are necessary and list the characteristics of adjusting entries.
3. Journalize entries for accounts requiring adjustment.
4. Summarize the adjustment process and prepare an adjusted trial balance.
5. Use vertical analysis to compare financial statement items with each other and with industry averages.

The Matching Concept

OBJECTIVE 1

Explain how the matching concept relates to the accrual basis of accounting.

When accountants prepare financial statements, they are assuming that the economic life of the business can be divided into time periods. Using this **accounting period concept**, accountants must determine in which period the revenues and expenses of the business should be reported. To determine the appropriate period, accountants will use either (1) the cash basis of accounting or (2) the accrual basis of accounting.

Under the **cash basis**, revenues and expenses are reported in the income statement in the period in which cash is received or paid. For example, fees are recorded when cash is received from clients, and wages are recorded when cash is paid to employees. The net income (or net loss) is the difference between the cash receipts (revenues) and the cash payments (expenses).

Under the **accrual basis**, revenues are reported in the income statement in the period in which they are earned. For example, revenue is reported when the services are provided to customers. Cash may or may not be received from customers during this period. The concept that supports this reporting of revenues is called the **revenue recognition concept**.

Under the accrual basis, expenses are reported in the same period as the revenues to which they relate. For example, employee wages are reported as an expense in the period in which the employees provided services to customers and not necessarily when the wages are paid.

The accounting concept that supports reporting revenues and the related expenses in the same period is called the **matching concept** or **matching principle**. Under this concept, an income statement will report the resulting income or loss for the period.

Generally accepted accounting principles require the use of the accrual basis. However, small service businesses may use the cash basis because they have few receivables and payables. For example, attorneys, physicians, and real estate agents often use

REAL WORLD

American Airlines uses the accrual basis of accounting. Revenues are recognized when passengers take flights, not when the passenger makes the reservation or pays for the ticket.

REAL WORLD

A bank loan officer requires an individual, who normally keeps records on a cash basis, to list assets (automobiles, homes, investments, etc.) on an application for a loan or a line of credit. In addition, the application often asks for an estimate of the individual's liabilities, such as credit card amounts outstanding and balances of automobile loans. In a sense, the loan application converts the individual's cash-basis accounting system to an estimated accrual basis. The loan officer uses this information in assessing the individual's ability to repay the loan.

The matching concept supports reporting revenues and related expenses in the same period.

BUSINESS ON STAGE

Technology and Business

The business environment is a dynamic one in which there is constant change, with challenges and opportunities. The current technology revolution affects all businesses.

Computer and telecommunication technologies affect the production, storage, and use of information by business. Many businesses have developed Web sites for use in marketing products and services and for communicating with stakeholders. New software applications range from accounting software that provides updated accounting information to business simulation software capable of gauging the impact of alternative business decisions on operations.

The technological revolution challenges businesses to adapt quickly to software and hardware improvements. Such improvements offer opportunities for businesses to develop new products, reach more customers, develop new channels of product distribution, lower operating costs, improve product quality, obtain immediate customer feedback, and react quickly to market changes. Businesses unable to adapt quickly to the technological revolution may find themselves at a competitive disadvantage.

Technology also provides you with new and exciting opportunities. To the extent that you develop your computer and technological skills and talents, you will improve your chances of finding a job and advancing rapidly in your career. ■

---

the cash basis. For them, the cash basis will yield financial statements similar to those prepared under the accrual basis.

For most large businesses, the cash basis will not provide accurate financial statements for user needs. For this reason, we will emphasize the accrual basis in the remainder of this text. The accrual basis and its related matching concept require an analysis and updating of some accounts when financial statements are prepared. In the following paragraphs, we will describe and illustrate this process, called the **adjusting process**.

Nature of the Adjusting Process

OBJECTIVE 2

Explain why adjustments are necessary and list the characteristics of adjusting entries.

At the end of an accounting period, many of the balances of accounts in the ledger can be reported, without change, in the financial statements. For example, the balance of the cash account is normally the amount reported on the balance sheet.

Some accounts in the ledger, however, require updating. For example, the balances listed for prepaid expenses are normally overstated because the use of these assets is not recorded on a day-to-day basis. The balance of the supplies account usually represents the cost of supplies at the beginning of the period plus the cost of supplies acquired during the period. To record the daily use of supplies would require many entries with small amounts. In addition, the total amount of supplies is small relative to other assets, and managers usually do not require day-to-day information about supplies.

The journal entries that bring the accounts up to date at the end of the accounting period are called **adjusting entries**. All adjusting entries affect at least one income statement account and one balance sheet account. Thus, an adjusting entry will *always* involve a revenue or an expense account *and* an asset or a liability account.

> **All adjusting entries affect at least one income statement account and one balance sheet account.**

Is there an easy way to know when an adjusting entry is needed? Yes, four basic items require adjusting entries. The first two items are **deferrals**. Deferrals are created by recording a transaction in a way that *delays* or *defers* the recognition of an expense or a revenue, as described below.

- **Deferred expenses** or **prepaid expenses** are items that have been initially recorded as assets but are expected to become expenses over time or through the normal operations of the business. Supplies and prepaid insurance are two examples of prepaid expenses that may require adjustment at the end of an accounting period. Other examples include prepaid advertising and prepaid interest.

- **Deferred revenues** or **unearned revenues** are items that have been initially recorded as liabilities but are expected to become revenues over time or through the normal operations of the business. An example of deferred revenue is unearned rent. Other examples include tuition received in advance by a school, an annual retainer fee received by an attorney, premiums received in advance by an insurance company, and magazine subscriptions received in advance by a publisher.

The second two items that require adjusting entries are accruals. **Accruals** are created by an unrecorded expense that has been incurred or an unrecorded revenue that has been earned, as described below.

- **Accrued expenses** or **accrued liabilities** are expenses that have been incurred *but have not been recorded* in the accounts. An example of an accrued expense is accrued wages owed to employees at the end of a period. Other examples include accrued interest on notes payable and accrued taxes.
- **Accrued revenues** or **accrued assets** are revenues that have been earned *but have not been recorded* in the accounts. An example of an accrued revenue is fees for services that an attorney has provided but hasn't billed to the client at the end of the period. Other examples include unbilled commissions by a travel agent, accrued interest on notes receivable, and accrued rent on property rented to others.

How do you tell the difference between deferrals and accruals? Determine when cash is received or paid, as shown in Exhibit 1. If cash is received (for revenue) or if cash is paid (for expense) in the *current* period, but the revenue or expense relates to a future period, the revenue or expense is a deferred item. If cash will not be received or if cash will not be paid until a *future* period, but the revenue or expense relates to the current period, the revenue or expense is an accrued item.

EXHIBIT 1
Deferrals and Accruals

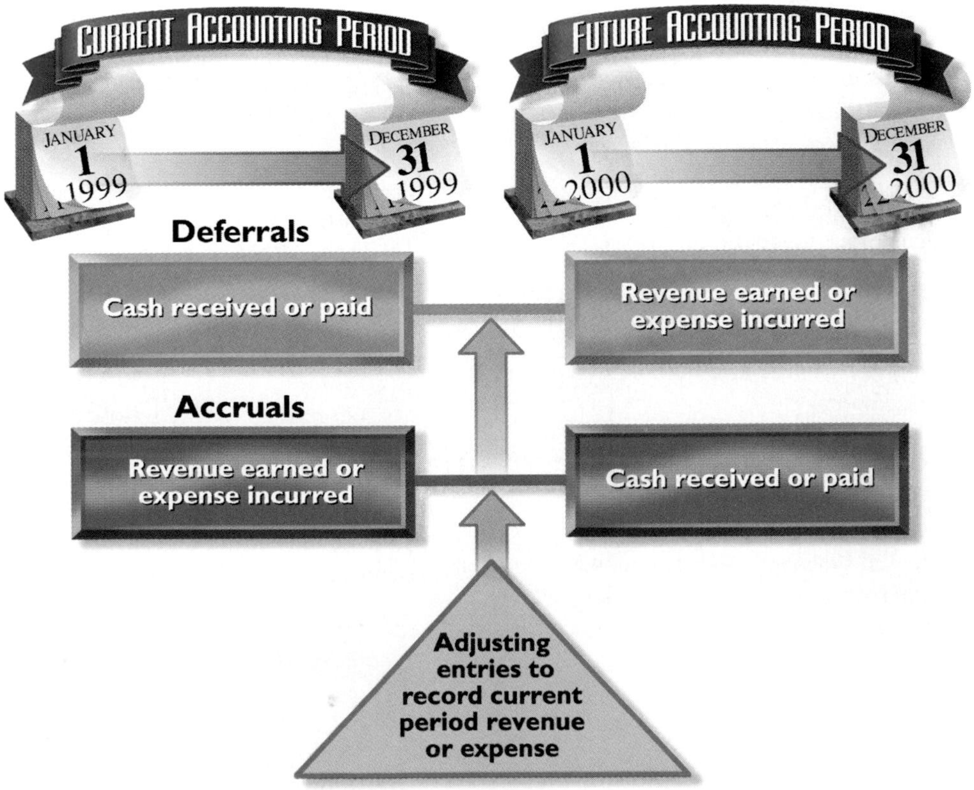

Recording Adjusting Entries

OBJECTIVE 3

Journalize entries for accounts requiring adjustment.

The examples of adjusting entries in the following paragraphs are based on the ledger of Computer King as reported in the December 31, 1999 trial balance in Exhibit 2. To simplify the examples, T accounts are used. The adjusting entries are shown in color in the accounts to separate them from other transactions.

EXHIBIT 2
Unadjusted Trial Balance for Computer King

Computer King
Trial Balance
December 31, 1999

Cash	2065 00	
Accounts Receivable	2220 00	
Supplies	2000 00	
Prepaid Insurance	2400 00	
Land	10000 00	
Office Equipment	1800 00	
Accounts Payable		900 00
Unearned Rent		360 00
Pat King, Capital		15000 00
Pat King, Drawing	4000 00	
Fees Earned		16340 00
Wages Expense	4275 00	
Rent Expense	1600 00	
Utilities Expense	985 00	
Supplies Expense	800 00	
Miscellaneous Expense	455 00	
	32600 00	32600 00

An expanded chart of accounts for Computer King is shown in Exhibit 3. The additional accounts that will be used in this chapter are shown in color.

EXHIBIT 3
Expanded Chart of Accounts for Computer King

Balance Sheet Accounts		Income Statement Accounts	
1. Assets		**4. Revenue**	
11	Cash	41	Fees Earned
12	Accounts Receivable	42	Rent Revenue
14	Supplies	**5. Expenses**	
15	Prepaid Insurance	51	Wages Expense
17	Land	52	Rent Expense
18	Office Equipment	53	Depreciation Expense
19	Accumulated Depreciation	54	Utilities Expense
2. Liabilities		55	Supplies Expense
21	Accounts Payable	56	Insurance Expense
22	Wages Payable	59	Miscellaneous Expense
23	Unearned Rent		
3. Owner's Equity			
31	Pat King, Capital		
32	Pat King, Drawing		

Deferred Expenses (Prepaid Expenses)

The concept of adjusting the accounting records was introduced in Chapters 1 and 2 in the illustration for Computer King. In that illustration, supplies were purchased on November 10 (transaction c). The supplies used during November were recorded on November 30 (transaction g).

The balance in Computer King's **supplies** account on December 31 is $2,000. Some of these supplies (computer diskettes, paper, envelopes, etc.) were used during December, and some are still on hand (not used). If either amount is known, the other can be determined. It is normally easier to determine the cost of the supplies on hand at the end of the month than it is to keep a daily record of those used. Assuming that on December 31 the amount of supplies on hand is $760, the amount to be transferred from the asset account to the expense account is $1,240, computed as follows:

Supplies available during December (balance of account)	$2,000
Supplies on hand, December 31	760
Supplies used (amount of adjustment)	$1,240

As we discussed in Chapter 2, increases in expense accounts are recorded as debits and decreases in asset accounts are recorded as credits. Hence, at the end of December, the supplies expense account should be debited for $1,240 and the supplies account should be credited for $1,240 to record the supplies used during December. The adjusting journal entry and T accounts for Supplies and Supplies Expense are as follows:

2	1999 Dec.	31	Supplies Expense	55	1 2 4 0 00		2
3			Supplies	14		1 2 4 0 00	3

Supplies

Bal.	2,000	Dec. 31	1,240
760			

Supplies Expense

Bal.	800		
Dec. 31	1,240		
	2,040		

After the adjustment has been recorded and posted, the supplies account has a debit balance of $760. This balance represents an asset that will become an expense in a future period.

The balance of a prepaid (deferred) expense is an asset that will become an expense in a future period.

The debit balance of $2,400 in Computer King's **prepaid insurance** account represents a December 1 prepayment of insurance for 24 months. At the end of December, the insurance expense account should be increased (debited) and the prepaid insurance account should be decreased (credited) by $100, the insurance for one month. The adjusting journal entry and the T accounts for Prepaid Insurance and Insurance Expense are as follows:

REAL WORLD **American Greetings Corporation**, which designs and distributes greeting cards, reported prepaid expenses for rent and insurance on its balance sheet.

5		31	Insurance Expense	56	1 0 0 00		5
6			Prepaid Insurance	15		1 0 0 00	6

Prepaid Insurance				Insurance Expense		
Bal.	2,400	Dec. 31	100	Dec. 31	100	
2,300						

Point of INTEREST

The tuition you pay at the beginning of each term is an example of a deferred expense to you, as a student.

After the adjustment has been recorded and posted, the prepaid insurance account has a debit balance of $2,300. This balance represents an asset that will become an expense in future periods. The insurance expense account has a debit balance of $100, which is an expense of the current period.

What is the effect of omitting adjusting entries? If the preceding adjustments for supplies ($1,240) and insurance ($100) are not recorded, the financial statements prepared as of December 31 will be misstated. On the income statement, Supplies Expense and Insurance Expense will be understated by a total of $1,340 and net income will be overstated by $1,340. On the balance sheet, Supplies and Prepaid Insurance will be overstated by a total of $1,340. Since net income increases owner's equity, Pat King, Capital will also be overstated by $1,340 on the balance sheet. The effects of omitting these adjusting entries on the income statement and balance sheet are shown below.

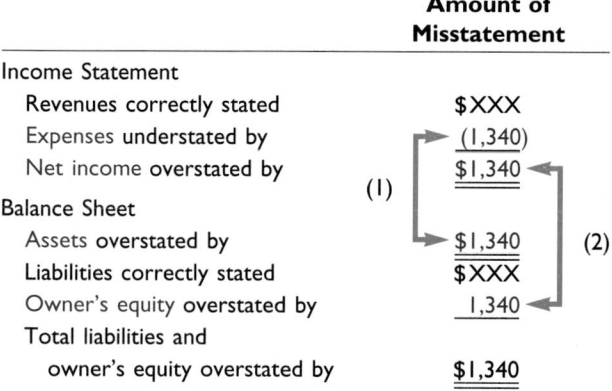

		Amount of Misstatement	
Income Statement			
Revenues correctly stated		$XXX	
Expenses understated by	(1)	(1,340)	
Net income overstated by		$1,340	(2)
Balance Sheet			
Assets overstated by	(1)	$1,340	
Liabilities correctly stated		$XXX	
Owner's equity overstated by		1,340	(2)
Total liabilities and owner's equity overstated by		$1,340	

Q&A

Supplies of $1,250 were on hand at the beginning of the period, supplies of $3,800 were purchased during the period, and supplies of $1,000 were on hand at the end of the period. What is the supplies expense for the period?

$4,050 ($1,250 + $3,800 − $1,000)

Arrow (1) indicates the effect of the understated expenses on assets. Arrow (2) indicates the effect of the overstated net income on owner's equity.

Prepayments of expenses are sometimes made at the beginning of the period in which they will be *entirely consumed.* On December 1, for example, Computer King paid rent of $800 for the month. On December 1, the rent payment represents the asset prepaid rent. The prepaid rent expires daily, and at the end of December, the entire amount has become an expense (rent expense). In cases such as this, the initial payment is recorded as an expense rather than as an asset. Thus, if the payment is recorded as a debit to Rent Expense, no adjusting entry is needed at the end of the period.[1]

Deferred Revenue (Unearned Revenue)

According to Computer King's trial balance on December 31, the balance in the **unearned rent** account is $360. This balance represents the receipt of three months' rent on December 1 for December, January, and February. At the end of December, the unearned rent account should be decreased (debited) by $120 and the rent revenue account should be increased (credited) by $120. The $120 represents the

[1] This alternative treatment of recording the cost of supplies, rent, and other prepayments of expenses is discussed in Appendix C.

rental revenue for one month ($360/3). The adjusting journal entry and T accounts are shown below.

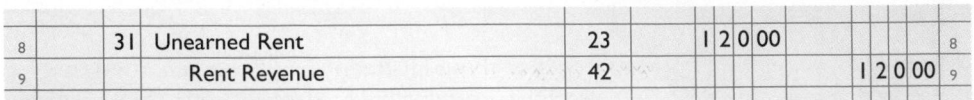

8	31	Unearned Rent	23	1 2 0 00		8
9		Rent Revenue	42		1 2 0 00	9

Unearned Rent				Rent Revenue			
Dec. 31	120	Bal.	360			Dec. 31	120
		240					

After the adjustment has been recorded and posted, the unearned rent account, which is a liability, has a credit balance of $240. This amount represents a deferral that will become revenue in a future period. The rent revenue account has a balance of $120, which is revenue of the current period.[2]

If the preceding adjustment of unearned rent and rent revenue is not recorded, the financial statements prepared on December 31 will be misstated. On the income statement, Rent Revenue and the net income will be understated by $120. On the balance sheet, Unearned Rent will be overstated by $120, and Pat King, Capital will be understated by $120. The effects of omitting this adjusting entry are shown below.

REAL WORLD **Sears, Roebuck and Co.** sells extended warranty contracts with terms between 12 and 36 months. The receipts from sales of these contracts are reported as unearned revenue (deferred revenue) on Sears's balance sheet. Revenue is recorded as the contracts expire.

Q&A *If Computer King's adjustment for unearned rent had been made incorrectly for $180 instead of $120, what would have been the effect on the financial statements?*

Revenues would have been overstated by $60; net income would have been overstated by $60; liabilities would have been understated by $60; and owner's equity would have been overstated by $60.

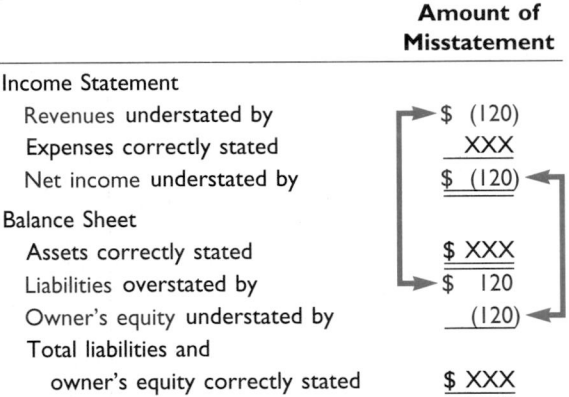

	Amount of Misstatement
Income Statement	
Revenues understated by	$ (120)
Expenses correctly stated	XXX
Net income understated by	$ (120)
Balance Sheet	
Assets correctly stated	$ XXX
Liabilities overstated by	$ 120
Owner's equity understated by	(120)
Total liabilities and owner's equity correctly stated	$ XXX

Accrued Expenses (Accrued Liabilities)

Some types of services, such as insurance, are normally paid for *before* they are used. These prepayments are deferrals. Other types of services are paid for *after* the service has been performed. For example, wages expense accumulates or *accrues* hour by hour and day by day, but payment may be made only weekly, biweekly, or monthly. The amount of such an accrued but unpaid item at the end of the accounting period is both an expense and a liability. In the case of wages expense, if the last day of a pay period is not the last day of the accounting period, the accrued wages expense and the related liability must be recorded in the accounts by an adjusting entry. This adjusting entry is necessary so that expenses are properly matched to the period in which they were incurred.

REAL WORLD **Callaway Golf Company**, a manufacturer of such innovative golf clubs as the "Big Bertha" driver, reports accrued warranty expense on its balance sheet.

[2] An alternative treatment of recording revenues received in advance of their being earned is discussed in Appendix C.

At the end of December, accrued wages for Computer King were $250. This amount is an additional expense of December and is debited to the **wages expense** account. It is also a liability as of December 31 and is credited to Wages Payable. The adjusting journal entry and T accounts are shown below.

11	31	Wages Expense	51	250 00		11
12		Wages Payable	22		250 00	12

Wages Expense

	Debit	Credit
Bal.	4,275	
Dec. 31	250	
	4,525	

Wages Payable

Debit		Credit
	Dec. 31	250

After the adjustment has been recorded and posted, the debit balance of the wages expense account is $4,525, which is the wages expense for the two months, November and December. The credit balance of $250 in Wages Payable is the amount of the liability for wages owed as of December 31.

The accrual of the wages expense for Computer King is summarized in Exhibit 4. You should note that Computer King paid wages of $950 on December 13 and $1,200 on December 27. These payments covered the biweekly pay periods that ended on those days. The wages of $250 incurred for Monday and Tuesday, December 30 and 31, are accrued at December 31. The wages paid on January 10 totaled $1,275, which included the $250 accrued wages of December 31.

EXHIBIT 4
Accrued Wages

1. Wages are paid on the second and fourth Fridays for the two-week periods ending on those Fridays. The payments were $950 on December 13 and $1,200 on December 27.
2. The wages accrued for Monday and Tuesday, December 30 and 31, are $250.
3. Wages paid on Friday, January 10, total $1,275.

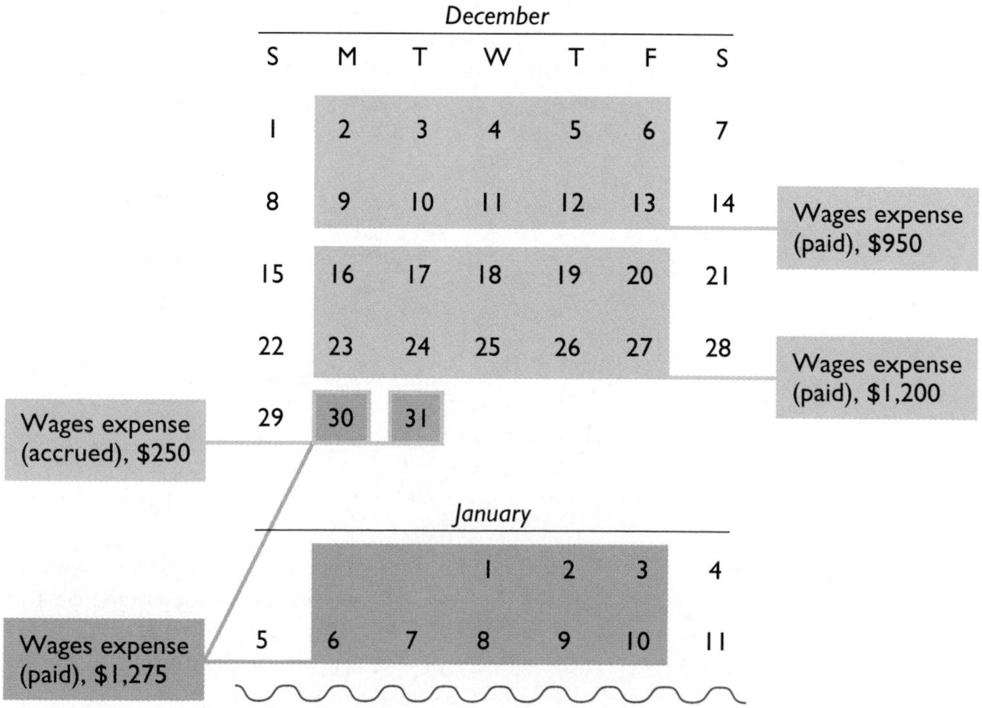

What would be the effect on the financial statements if the adjustment for wages ($250) is not recorded? On the income statement, Wages Expense will be understated by $250, and the net income will be overstated by $250. On the balance sheet, Wages Payable will be understated by $250, and Pat King, Capital will be overstated by $250. These effects of omitting the adjusting entry are shown below.

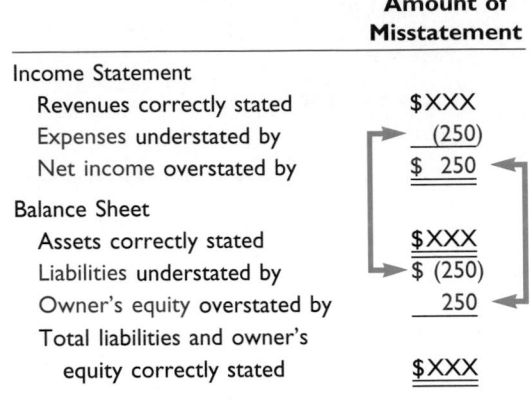

	Amount of Misstatement
Income Statement	
Revenues correctly stated	$XXX
Expenses understated by	(250)
Net income overstated by	$ 250
Balance Sheet	
Assets correctly stated	$XXX
Liabilities understated by	$ (250)
Owner's equity overstated by	250
Total liabilities and owner's equity correctly stated	$XXX

Q&A *Assume that weekly wages of $1,500 are paid on Fridays. If wages are incurred evenly throughout the week, what is the accrued wages payable if the accounting period ends on a Tuesday?*

$600 ($1,500/5 × 2 days)

Accrued Revenues (Accrued Assets)

During an accounting period, some revenues are recorded only when cash is received. Thus, at the end of an accounting period, there may be items of revenue that have been earned *but have not been recorded.* In such cases, the amount of the revenue should be recorded by debiting an asset account and crediting a revenue account.

To illustrate, assume that Computer King signed an agreement with Dankner Co. on December 15. The agreement provides that Computer King will be on call to answer computer questions and render assistance to Dankner Co.'s employees. The services provided will be billed to Dankner Co. on the fifteenth of each month at a rate of $20 per hour. As of December 31, Computer King had provided 25 hours of assistance to Dankner Co. Although the revenue of $500 (25 hours × $20) will be billed and collected in January, Computer King earned the revenue in December. The adjusting journal entry and T accounts to record the claim against the customer (an account receivable) and the **fees earned** in December are shown below.

REAL WORLD **Tandy Corporation and Subsidiaries** is engaged in consumer electronics retailing and owns **Radio Shack** and **Incredible Universe.** Tandy accrues receivables (accrued revenue) for finance charges, late charges, and returned check fees related to its credit operations.

31	Accounts Receivable	12	500 00	
	Fees Earned	41		500 00

Accounts Receivable

Bal.	2,220	
Dec. 31	500	
	2,720	

Fees Earned

	Bal.	16,340
	Dec. 31	500
		16,840

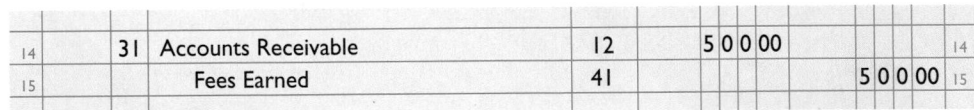

If the adjustment for the accrued asset ($500) is not recorded, Fees Earned and the net income will be understated by $500 on the income statement. On the balance sheet, Accounts Receivable and Pat King, Capital will be understated by $500. These effects of omitting the adjusting entry are shown below.

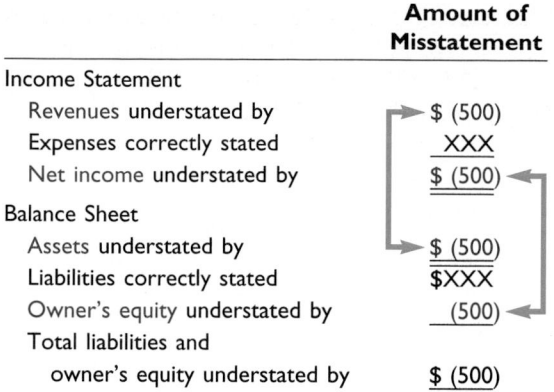

	Amount of Misstatement
Income Statement	
Revenues understated by	$ (500)
Expenses correctly stated	XXX
Net income understated by	$ (500)
Balance Sheet	
Assets understated by	$ (500)
Liabilities correctly stated	$XXX
Owner's equity understated by	(500)
Total liabilities and owner's equity understated by	$ (500)

Fixed Assets

Physical resources that are owned and used by a business and are permanent or have a long life are called **fixed assets** or **plant assets**. In a sense, fixed assets are a type of long-term deferred expense. However, because of their nature and long life, they are discussed separately from other deferred expenses, such as supplies and prepaid insurance.

Computer King's fixed assets include office equipment that is used much like the supplies are used to generate revenue. Unlike supplies, however, there is no visible reduction in the quantity of the equipment. Instead, as time passes, the equipment loses its ability to provide useful services. This decrease in usefulness is called **depreciation**.

All fixed assets, except land, lose their usefulness. Decreases in the usefulness of assets that are used in generating revenue are recorded as expenses. However, such decreases for fixed assets are difficult to measure. For this reason, a portion of the cost of a fixed asset is recorded as an expense each year of its useful life. This periodic expense is called **depreciation expense**. Methods of computing depreciation expense are discussed and illustrated in a later chapter.

The adjusting entry to record depreciation is similar to the adjusting entry for supplies used. The account debited is a depreciation expense account. However, the asset account Office Equipment is not credited because both the original cost of a fixed asset and the amount of depreciation recorded since its purchase are normally reported on the balance sheet. The account credited is an **accumulated depreciation** account. Accumulated depreciation accounts are called **contra accounts** or **contra asset accounts** because they are deducted from the related asset accounts on the balance sheet.

REAL WORLD **Lowe's Companies, Inc. and Subsidiaries** reported land, buildings, and store equipment at a cost of over $2.3 billion and accumulated depreciation of over $460 million.

Normal titles for fixed asset accounts and their related contra asset accounts are as follows:

Fixed Asset	Contra Asset
Land	None—Land is not depreciated.
Buildings	Accumulated Depreciation—Buildings
Store Equipment	Accumulated Depreciation—Store Equipment
Office Equipment	Accumulated Depreciation—Office Equipment

The adjusting entry to record depreciation for December for Computer King is illustrated in the following journal entry and T accounts. The estimated amount of depreciation for the month is assumed to be $50.

17	31	Depreciation Expense	53	50 00		17
18		Accumulated Depreciation—				18
19		Office Equipment	19		50 00	19

Office Equipment

Bal.	1,800	

Accumulated Depreciation

	Dec. 31	50

Depreciation Expense

Dec. 31	50	

Q&A *If equipment cost $5,000 and the related accumulated depreciation is $3,000, what is the book value?*

$2,000 ($5,000 − $3,000)

The $50 increase in the accumulated depreciation account is subtracted from the $1,800 cost recorded in the related fixed asset account. The difference between the two balances is the cost of $1,750 that has not yet been depreciated. This amount ($1,750) is called the **book value of the asset**, which may be presented on the balance sheet in the following manner:

Office equipment	$1,800	
Less accumulated depreciation	50	$1,750

You should note that the market value of a fixed asset normally differs from its book value. This is because depreciation is an *allocation* method, not a *valuation* method. That is, depreciation allocates the cost of a fixed asset to expense over its estimated life. Depreciation does not attempt to measure changes in market values, which may vary significantly from year to year.

If the previous adjustment for depreciation ($50) is not recorded, Depreciation Expense on the income statement will be understated by $50, and the net income will be overstated by $50. On the balance sheet, the book value of Office Equipment and Pat King, Capital will be overstated by $50. The effects of omitting the adjustment for depreciation are shown below.

	Amount of Misstatement
Income Statement	
Revenues correctly stated	$XX
Expenses understated by	(50)
Net income overstated by	$ 50
Balance Sheet	
Assets overstated by	$ 50
Liabilities correctly stated	$XX
Owner's equity overstated by	50
Total liabilities and owner's equity overstated by	$ 50

OBJECTIVE 4

Summarize the adjustment process and prepare an adjusted trial balance.

Summary of Adjustment Process

We have described and illustrated the basic types of adjusting entries in the preceding section. A summary of these basic adjustments, including the type of adjustment, the adjusting entry, and the effect of omitting an adjustment on the financial statements, is shown in Exhibit 5.

EXHIBIT 5 Summary of Basic Adjustments

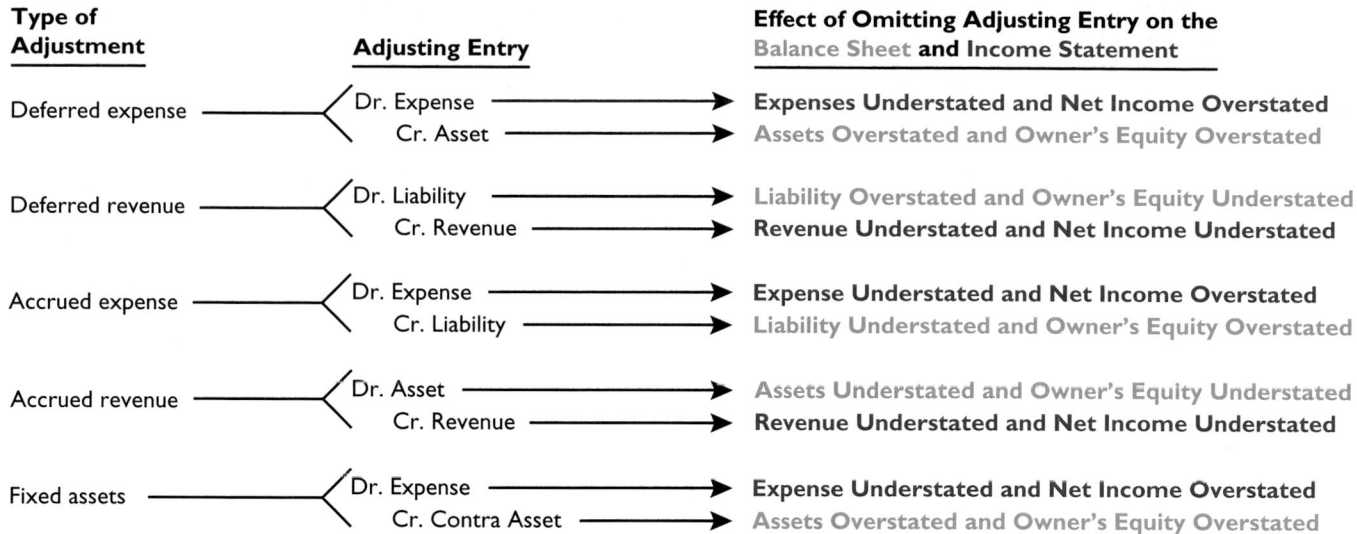

Type of Adjustment	Adjusting Entry	Effect of Omitting Adjusting Entry on the Balance Sheet and Income Statement
Deferred expense	Dr. Expense	Expenses Understated and Net Income Overstated
	Cr. Asset	Assets Overstated and Owner's Equity Overstated
Deferred revenue	Dr. Liability	Liability Overstated and Owner's Equity Understated
	Cr. Revenue	Revenue Understated and Net Income Understated
Accrued expense	Dr. Expense	Expense Understated and Net Income Overstated
	Cr. Liability	Liability Understated and Owner's Equity Overstated
Accrued revenue	Dr. Asset	Assets Understated and Owner's Equity Understated
	Cr. Revenue	Revenue Understated and Net Income Understated
Fixed assets	Dr. Expense	Expense Understated and Net Income Overstated
	Cr. Contra Asset	Assets Overstated and Owner's Equity Overstated

Which of the accounts—Fees Earned, Miscellaneous Expense, Cash, Wages Expense, Supplies, Accounts Receivable, Drawing, Equipment, Accumulated Depreciation—would normally require an adjusting entry?

Fees Earned; Wages Expense; Supplies; Accounts Receivable; Accumulated Depreciation.

The adjusting entries for Computer King that we illustrated in this chapter are shown in Exhibit 6. The adjusting entries are dated as of the last day of the period, even though they are usually recorded at a later date. Each entry may be supported by an explanation, but a caption above the first adjusting entry is acceptable.

These adjusting entries have been posted to the ledger for Computer King, and are shown in color in Exhibit 7. You should note that in the posting process the Post. Ref. column of the journal indicates the account number to which the entry was posted. The corresponding Post. Ref. column of the account indicates the journal page from which the entry was posted.

EXHIBIT 6 Adjusting Entries—Computer King

JOURNAL PAGE 5

Date		Description	Post. Ref.	Debit	Credit
		Adjusting Entries			
1999 Dec.	31	Supplies Expense	55	1 240 00	
		Supplies	14		1 240 00
	31	Insurance Expense	56	100 00	
		Prepaid Insurance	15		100 00
	31	Unearned Rent	23	120 00	
		Rent Revenue	42		120 00
	31	Wages Expense	51	250 00	
		Wages Payable	22		250 00
	31	Accounts Receivable	12	500 00	
		Fees Earned	41		500 00
	31	Depreciation Expense	53	50 00	
		Accumulated Depreciation—			
		Office Equipment	19		50 00

EXHIBIT 7
Ledger with Adjusting Entries—Computer King

ACCOUNT *Cash* — **ACCOUNT NO.** *11*

Date	Item	Post. Ref.	Debit	Credit	Balance Debit	Balance Credit
1999 Nov. 1		1	15,000		15,000	
5		1		10,000	5,000	
18		1	7,500		12,500	
30		1		3,650	8,850	
30		1		950	7,900	
30		2		2,000	5,900	
Dec. 1		2		2,400	3,500	
1		2		800	2,700	
1		2	360		3,060	
6		2		180	2,880	
11		2		400	2,480	
13		3		950	1,530	
16		3	3,100		4,630	
20		3		900	3,730	
21		3	650		4,380	
23		3		1,450	2,930	
27		3		1,200	1,730	
31		3		310	1,420	
31		4		225	1,195	
31		4	2,870		4,065	
31		4		2,000	2,065	

ACCOUNT *Accounts Receivable* — **ACCOUNT NO.** *12*

Date	Item	Post. Ref.	Debit	Credit	Balance Debit	Balance Credit
1999 Dec. 16		3	1,750		1,750	
21		3		650	1,100	
31		4	1,120		2,220	
31	**Adjusting**	**5**	**500**		**2,720**	

ACCOUNT *Supplies* — **ACCOUNT NO.** *14*

Date	Item	Post. Ref.	Debit	Credit	Balance Debit	Balance Credit
1999 Nov. 10		1	1,350		1,350	
30		1		800	550	
Dec. 23		3	1,450		2,000	
31	**Adjusting**	**5**		**1,240**	**760**	

ACCOUNT *Prepaid Insurance* — **ACCOUNT NO.** *15*

Date	Item	Post. Ref.	Debit	Credit	Balance Debit	Balance Credit
1999 Dec. 1		2	2,400		2,400	
31	**Adjusting**	**5**		**100**	**2,300**	

ACCOUNT *Land* — **ACCOUNT NO.** *17*

Date	Item	Post. Ref.	Debit	Credit	Balance Debit	Balance Credit
1999 Nov. 5		1	10,000		10,000	

ACCOUNT *Office Equipment* — **ACCOUNT NO.** *18*

Date	Item	Post. Ref.	Debit	Credit	Balance Debit	Balance Credit
1999 Dec. 4		2	1,800		1,800	

ACCOUNT *Accumulated Depreciation* — **ACCOUNT NO.** *19*

Date	Item	Post. Ref.	Debit	Credit	Balance Debit	Balance Credit
1999 Dec. 31	**Adjusting**	**5**		**50**		**50**

ACCOUNT *Accounts Payable* — **ACCOUNT NO.** *21*

Date	Item	Post. Ref.	Debit	Credit	Balance Debit	Balance Credit
1999 Nov. 10		1		1,350		1,350
30		1	950			400
Dec. 4		2		1,800		2,200
11		2	400			1,800
20		3	900			900

ACCOUNT *Wages Payable* — **ACCOUNT NO.** *22*

Date	Item	Post. Ref.	Debit	Credit	Balance Debit	Balance Credit
1999 Dec. 31	**Adjusting**	**5**		**250**		**250**

ACCOUNT *Unearned Rent* — **ACCOUNT NO.** *23*

Date	Item	Post. Ref.	Debit	Credit	Balance Debit	Balance Credit
1999 Dec. 1		2		360		360
31	**Adjusting**	**5**	**120**			**240**

ACCOUNT *Pat King, Capital* — **ACCOUNT NO.** *31*

Date	Item	Post. Ref.	Debit	Credit	Balance Debit	Balance Credit
1999 Nov. 1		1		15,000		15,000

ACCOUNT *Pat King, Drawing* **ACCOUNT NO. 32**

Date	Item	Post. Ref.	Debit	Credit	Balance Debit	Balance Credit
1999 Nov. 30		2	2,000		2,000	
Dec. 31		4	2,000		4,000	

ACCOUNT *Fees Earned* **ACCOUNT NO. 41**

Date	Item	Post. Ref.	Debit	Credit	Balance Debit	Balance Credit
1999 Nov. 18		1		7,500		7,500
Dec. 16		3		3,100		10,600
16		3		1,750		12,350
31		4		2,870		15,220
31		4		1,120		16,340
31	**Adjusting**	**5**		**500**		**16,840**

ACCOUNT *Rent Revenue* **ACCOUNT NO. 42**

Date	Item	Post. Ref.	Debit	Credit	Balance Debit	Balance Credit
1999 Dec. 31	**Adjusting**	**5**		**120**		**120**

ACCOUNT *Wages Expense* **ACCOUNT NO. 51**

Date	Item	Post. Ref.	Debit	Credit	Balance Debit	Balance Credit
1999 Nov. 30		1	2,125		2,125	
Dec. 13		3	950		3,075	
27		3	1,200		4,275	
31	**Adjusting**	**5**	**250**		**4,525**	

ACCOUNT *Rent Expense* **ACCOUNT NO. 52**

Date	Item	Post. Ref.	Debit	Credit	Balance Debit	Balance Credit
1999 Nov. 30		1	800		800	
Dec. 1		2	800		1,600	

ACCOUNT *Depreciation Expense* **ACCOUNT NO. 53**

Date	Item	Post. Ref.	Debit	Credit	Balance Debit	Balance Credit
1999 Dec. 31	**Adjusting**	**5**	**50**		**50**	

ACCOUNT *Utilities Expense* **ACCOUNT NO. 54**

Date	Item	Post. Ref.	Debit	Credit	Balance Debit	Balance Credit
1999 Nov. 30		1	450		450	
Dec. 31		3	310		760	
31		4	225		985	

ACCOUNT *Supplies Expense* **ACCOUNT NO. 55**

Date	Item	Post. Ref.	Debit	Credit	Balance Debit	Balance Credit
1999 Nov. 30		1	800		800	
Dec. 31	**Adjusting**	**5**	**1,240**		**2,040**	

ACCOUNT *Insurance Expense* **ACCOUNT NO. 56**

Date	Item	Post. Ref.	Debit	Credit	Balance Debit	Balance Credit
1999 Dec. 31	**Adjusting**	**5**	**100**		**100**	

ACCOUNT *Miscellaneous Expense* **ACCOUNT NO. 59**

Date	Item	Post. Ref.	Debit	Credit	Balance Debit	Balance Credit
1999 Nov. 30		1	275		275	
Dec. 6		2	180		455	

EXHIBIT 7
(concluded)

Point of INTEREST

One way for an accountant to check whether all adjustments have been made is to compare the current period's adjustments with those of the prior period.

After all the adjusting entries have been posted, another trial balance, called the **adjusted trial balance**, is prepared. The purpose of the adjusted trial balance is to verify the equality of the total debit balances and total credit balances before we prepare the financial statements. If the adjusted trial balance does not balance, an error has occurred. However, as we discussed in Chapter 2, errors may have occurred even though the adjusted trial balance totals agree. For example, the adjusted trial balance totals would agree if an adjusting entry has been omitted.

To highlight the effect of the adjustments on the accounts, Exhibit 8 shows the unadjusted trial balance, the accounts affected by the adjustments, and the adjusted trial balance. In Chapter 4, we discuss how financial statements, including a classified balance sheet, can be prepared from an adjusted trial balance. We also discuss

Computer King Unadjusted Trial Balance December 31, 1999			Effect of Adjusting Entry	Computer King Adjusted Trial Balance December 31, 1999		
Cash	2,065			Cash	2,065	
Accounts Receivable	2,220		+ 500	Accounts Receivable	**2,720**	
Supplies	2,000		−1,240	Supplies	**760**	
Prepaid Insurance	2,400		− 100	Prepaid Insurance	**2,300**	
Land	10,000			Land	10,000	
Office Equipment	1,800			Office Equipment	1,800	
Accumulated Depreciation			+ 50	Accumulated Depreciation		**50**
Accounts Payable		900		Accounts Payable		900
Wages Payable			+ 250	Wages Payable		**250**
Unearned Rent		360	− 120	Unearned Rent		**240**
Pat King, Capital		15,000		Pat King, Capital		15,000
Pat King, Drawing	4,000			Pat King, Drawing	4,000	
Fees Earned		16,340	+ 500	Fees Earned		**16,840**
Rent Revenue			+ 120	Rent Revenue		**120**
Wages Expense	4,275		+ 250	Wages Expense	**4,525**	
Rent Expense	1,600			Rent Expense	1,600	
Depreciation Expense			+ 50	Depreciation Expense	**50**	
Utilities Expense	985			Utilities Expense	985	
Supplies Expense	800		+1,240	Supplies Expense	**2,040**	
Insurance Expense			+ 100	Insurance Expense	**100**	
Miscellaneous Expense	455			Miscellaneous Expense	455	
	32,600	32,600			33,400	33,400

EXHIBIT 8
Trial Balances

the use of a work sheet as an aid to summarizing the data for preparing adjusting entries and financial statements.

FINANCIAL ANALYSIS AND INTERPRETATION

OBJECTIVE 5

Use vertical analysis to compare financial statement items with each other and with industry averages.

Comparing each item in a current statement with a total amount within that same statement can be useful in highlighting significant relationships within a financial statement. **Vertical analysis** is the term used to describe such comparisons.

In vertical analysis of a balance sheet, each asset item is stated as a percent of the total assets. Each liability and owner's equity item is stated as a percent of the total liabilities and owner's equity. In vertical analysis of an income statement, each item is stated as a percent of revenues or fees earned.

Vertical analysis may also be prepared for several periods to highlight changes in relationships over time. Vertical analysis of two years of income statements for J. Holmes, Attorney-at-Law, is shown in Exhibit 9.

Exhibit 9 indicates both favorable and unfavorable trends affecting the income statement of J. Holmes, Attorney-at-Law. The increase in wages expenses of 2% (32% − 30%) is an unfavorable trend, as is the increase in utilities expense of 0.7% (6.7% − 6.0%). A favorable trend is the decrease in supplies expense of 0.6% (2.0% − 1.4%). Rent expense and miscellaneous expense as a percent of fees earned were constant. The net result of these trends was that net income decreased as a percent of fees earned from 52.8% to 50.7%.

EXHIBIT 9
Vertical Analysis of Income Statements

J. Holmes, Attorney-at-Law
Income Statements
For the Years Ended December 31, 2000 and 2001

	2001		2000	
	Amount	**Percent**	**Amount**	**Percent**
Fees earned	$187,500	100.0%	$150,000	100.0%
Operating expenses:				
Wages expense	$60,000	32.0%	$45,000	30.0%
Rent expense	15,000	8.0%	12,000	8.0%
Utilities expense	12,500	6.7%	9,000	6.0%
Supplies expense	2,700	1.4%	3,000	2.0%
Miscellaneous expense	2,300	1.2%	1,800	1.2%
Total operating expenses	$92,500	49.3%	$70,800	47.2%
Net income	$95,000	50.7%	$79,200	52.8%

The analysis of the various percentages shown for J. Holmes, Attorney-at-Law, can be enhanced by comparisons with industry averages published by trade associations and financial information services. Any major differences between industry averages should be investigated.

ENCORE

Intel Corporation develops and produces microprocessors for personal computers. In the ten years ending in 1995, Intel's net revenues grew at an annual growth rate of 33%. Likewise, Intel's earnings have grown from a $195 million loss in 1986 to over $5 billion of operating income in 1995. Intel's success has been driven by its ability to design, develop, and produce newer and faster microprocessors. This ability has been a result of a strong research and development effort in which spending has increased at an annual rate of 21% over the past ten years. Intel's current microprocessor is so tiny that it would take 500 of them placed end to end to be as large as a human hair!

Intel's microprocessors have become well-known, beginning with the 8086 processor and continuing with the 286, 386, and 486 processors. Rather than name its next generation of microprocessor the 586, Intel named its new chip the "Pentium" and registered it as a trademark. This prevented Intel's competitors from selling their products as "Pentiums," which they had been able to do with the numbers 386 and 486. In addition, Intel began a promotional campaign to identify its microprocessor as unique. Intel did this by entering into a cooperative program with computer manufacturers and distributors to label personal computers with the slogan "Intel Inside" or "Pentium Inside."

Intel has been highly successful. However, technology companies such as Intel are subject to significant risks that their products will become out of date as technology changes. This is why Intel has invested so heavily in research and development over the years. In addition, Intel has the potential risk for faulty product designs or production of faulty processors due to poor quality control. For example, in 1994, Intel discovered an error related to the divide function in the floating point unit of its Pentium microprocessor. This error required an adjusting entry for replacement processors and inventory write-downs, which cost Intel approximately $475 million. ■

KEY POINTS

1 Explain how the matching concept relates to the accrual basis of accounting.

The accrual basis of accounting requires the use of an adjusting process at the end of the accounting period to match revenues and expenses properly. Revenues are reported in the period in which they are earned, and expenses are matched with the revenues they generate.

2 Explain why adjustments are necessary and list the characteristics of adjusting entries.

At the end of an accounting period, some of the amounts listed on the trial balance are not necessarily current balances. For example, amounts listed for prepaid expenses are normally overstated because the use of these assets has not been recorded on a daily basis. A delay in recognizing an expense already paid or a revenue already received is called a deferral.

Some revenues and expenses related to a period may not be recorded at the end of the period, since these items are normally recorded only when cash has been received or paid. A revenue or expense that has not been paid or recorded is called an accrual.

The entries required at the end of an accounting period to bring accounts up to date and to ensure the proper matching of revenues and expenses are called adjusting entries. Adjusting entries require a debit or a credit to a revenue or an expense account and an offsetting debit or credit to an asset or a liability account.

Adjusting entries affect amounts reported in the income statement and the balance sheet. Thus, if an adjusting entry is not recorded, these financial statements will be incorrect (misstated).

3 Journalize entries for accounts requiring adjustment.

Adjusting entries illustrated in this chapter include deferred (prepaid) expenses, deferred (unearned) revenues, accrued expenses (accrued liabilities), and accrued revenues (accrued assets). In addition, the adjusting entry necessary to record depreciation on fixed assets was illustrated.

4 Summarize the adjustment process and prepare an adjusted trial balance.

A summary of adjustments, including the type of adjustment, the adjusting entry, and the effect of omitting an adjustment on the financial statements, is shown in Exhibit 5. After all the adjusting entries have been posted, the equality of the total debit balances and total credit balances is verified by an adjusted trial balance.

5 Use vertical analysis to compare financial statement items with each other and with industry averages.

Comparing each item in a current statement with a total amount within the same statement is called vertical analysis. In vertical analysis of a balance sheet, each asset item is stated as a percent of the total assets. Each liability and owner's equity item is stated as a percent of the total liabilities and owner's equity. In vertical analysis of an income statement, each item is stated as a percent of revenues or fees earned.

ILLUSTRATIVE PROBLEM

Three years ago, T. Roderick organized Harbor Realty. At July 31, 2000, the end of the current year, the unadjusted trial balance of Harbor Realty appears as shown at the top of the following page. The data needed to determine year-end adjustments are as follows:

a. Supplies on hand at July 31, 2000, $380.
b. Insurance premiums expired during the year, $315.
c. Depreciation of equipment during the year, $4,950.
d. Wages accrued but not paid at July 31, 2000, $440.
e. Accrued fees earned but not recorded at July 31, 2000, $1,000.
f. Unearned fees on July 31, 2000, $750.

Harbor Realty
Trial Balance
July 31, 2000

Cash	3425 00	
Accounts Receivable	7000 00	
Supplies	1270 00	
Prepaid Insurance	620 00	
Office Equipment	51650 00	
Accumulated Depreciation		9700 00
Accounts Payable		925 00
Wages Payable		0 00
Unearned Fees		1250 00
T. Roderick, Capital		29000 00
T. Roderick, Drawing	5200 00	
Fees Earned		59125 00
Wages Expense	22415 00	
Depreciation Expense	0 00	
Rent Expense	4200 00	
Utilities Expense	2715 00	
Supplies Expense	0 00	
Insurance Expense	0 00	
Miscellaneous Expense	1505 00	
	100000 00	100000 00

Instructions

1. Prepare the necessary adjusting journal entries.
2. Determine the balance of the accounts affected by the adjusting entries and prepare an adjusted trial balance.

Solution

1.

JOURNAL

Date		Description	Post. Ref.	Debit	Credit
2000 July	31	Supplies Expense		890 00	
		Supplies			890 00
	31	Insurance Expense		315 00	
		Prepaid Insurance			315 00
	31	Depreciation Expense		4950 00	
		Accumulated Depreciation			4950 00
	31	Wages Expense		440 00	
		Wages Payable			440 00
	31	Accounts Receivable		1000 00	
		Fees Earned			1000 00
	31	Unearned Fees		500 00	
		Fees Earned			500 00

2.

Harbor Realty
Adjusted Trial Balance
July 31, 2000

Cash	3 425 00	
Accounts Receivable	8 000 00	
Supplies	380 00	
Prepaid Insurance	305 00	
Office Equipment	51 650 00	
Accumulated Depreciation		14 650 00
Accounts Payable		925 00
Wages Payable		440 00
Unearned Fees		750 00
T. Roderick, Capital		29 000 00
T. Roderick, Drawing	5 200 00	
Fees Earned		60 625 00
Wages Expense	22 855 00	
Depreciation Expense	4 950 00	
Rent Expense	4 200 00	
Utilities Expense	2 715 00	
Supplies Expense	890 00	
Insurance Expense	315 00	
Miscellaneous Expense	1 505 00	
	106 390 00	106 390 00

SELF-EXAMINATION QUESTIONS — Answers at End of Chapter

Matching

Match each of the following statements with its proper term. Some terms may not be used.

- **A. accounting period concept**
- **B. accrual basis**
- **C. accrued expenses**
- **D. accrued revenues**
- **E. accumulated depreciation**
- **F. adjusted trial balance**
- **G. adjusting entries**
- **H. adjusting process**
- **I. book value of the asset**
- **J. cash basis**
- **K. closing entries**
- **L. contra account**
- **M. deferred expenses**
- **N. deferred revenues**
- **O. depreciation**

A 1. The accounting concept that assumes that the economic life of the business can be divided into time periods.

J 2. Under this basis of accounting, revenues and expenses are reported in the income statement in the period in which cash is received or paid.

B 3. Under this basis of accounting, revenues are reported in the income statement in the period in which they are earned.

W 4. The accounting concept that supports reporting revenues when the services are provided to customers.

I 5. The accounting concept that supports reporting revenues and the related expenses in the same period.

H 6. An analysis and updating of the accounts when financial statements are prepared.

G 7. The journal entries that bring the accounts up to date at the end of the accounting period.

M 8. Items that have been initially recorded as assets but are expected to become expenses over time or through the normal operations of the business.

N 9. Items that have been initially recorded as liabilities but are expected to become revenues over time or through the normal operations of the business.

C 10. Expenses that have been incurred *but not recorded* in the accounts.

P. **depreciation expense**
Q. **final trial balance**
R. **fixed assets**
S. **horizontal analysis**
T. **matching concept**
U. **objectivity concept**
V. **post-closing trial balance**
W. **revenue recognition concept**
X. **vertical analysis**

D 11. Revenues that have been earned *but not recorded* in the accounts.
R 12. Physical resources that are owned and used by a business and are permanent or have a long life.
O 13. The decrease in the ability of a fixed asset to provide useful services.
P 14. The portion of the cost of a fixed asset that is recorded as an expense each year of its useful life.
E 15. The asset account credited when recording the depreciation of a fixed asset.
I 16. The difference between the cost of a fixed asset and its accumulated depreciation.
F 17. The trial balance prepared after all the adjusting entries have been posted.
X 18. An analysis that compares each item in a current statement with a total amount within the same statement.
L 19. An account offset against another account.

Multiple Choice

1. Which of the following items represents a deferral?
   A. Prepaid insurance
   B. Wages payable
   C. Fees earned
   D. Accumulated depreciation

2. If the supplies account, before adjustment on May 31, indicated a balance of $2,250, and supplies on hand at May 31 totaled $950, the adjusting entry would be:
   A. debit Supplies, $950; credit Supplies Expense, $950
   B. debit Supplies, $1,300; credit Supplies Expense, $1,300
   C. debit Supplies Expense, $950; credit Supplies, $950
   D. debit Supplies Expense, $1,300; credit Supplies, $1,300

3. The balance in the unearned rent account for Jones Co. as of December 31 is $1,200. If Jones Co. failed to record the adjusting entry for $600 of rent earned during December, the effect on the balance sheet and income statement for December is:
   A. assets understated $600; net income overstated $600
   B. liabilities understated $600; net income understated $600
   C. liabilities overstated $600; net income understated $600
   D. liabilities overstated $600; net income overstated $600

4. If the estimated amount of depreciation on equipment for a period is $2,000, the adjusting entry to record depreciation would be:
   A. debit Depreciation Expense, $2,000; credit Equipment, $2,000
   B. debit Equipment, $2,000; credit Depreciation Expense, $2,000
   C. debit Depreciation Expense, $2,000; credit Accumulated Depreciation, $2,000
   D. debit Accumulated Depreciation, $2,000; credit Depreciation Expense, $2,000

5. If the equipment account has a balance of $22,500 and its accumulated depreciation account has a balance of $14,000, the book value of the equipment is:
   A. $36,500
   B. $22,500
   C. $14,000
   D. $8,500

CLASS DISCUSSION QUESTIONS

1. How are revenues and expenses reported on the income statement under (a) the cash basis of accounting and (b) the accrual basis of accounting?
2. Fees for services provided are billed to a customer during 1999. The customer remits the amount owed in 2000. During which year would the revenues be reported on the income statement under (a) the cash basis? (b) the accrual basis?
3. Employees performed services in 1999, but the wages were not paid until 2000. During which year would the wages expense be reported on the income statement under (a) the cash basis? (b) the accrual basis?
4. Is the matching concept related to (a) the cash basis of accounting or (b) the accrual basis of accounting?
5. Is the balance listed for cash on the trial balance, before the accounts have been adjusted, the amount that should normally be reported on the balance sheet? Explain.

6. Is the balance listed for supplies on the trial balance, before the accounts have been adjusted, the amount that should normally be reported on the balance sheet? Explain.
7. Why are adjusting entries needed at the end of an accounting period?
8. Are adjusting entries in the journal dated as of the last day of the fiscal period or as of the day the entries are actually made? Explain.
9. What is the difference between *adjusting entries* and *correcting entries*?
10. Identify the five different categories of adjusting entries frequently required at the end of an accounting period.
11. If the effect of the credit portion of an adjusting entry is to increase the balance of a liability account, which of the following statements describes the effect of the debit portion of the entry?
    a. Increases the balance of a revenue account.
    b. Increases the balance of an expense account.
    c. Increases the balance of an asset account.
12. Does every adjusting entry have an effect on determining the amount of net income for a period? Explain.
13. What is the nature of the balance in the prepaid insurance account at the end of the accounting period (a) before adjustment? (b) after adjustment?
14. On May 1 of the current year, a business paid the May rent on the building that it occupies. (a) Do the rights acquired at May 1 represent an asset or an expense? (b) What is the justification for debiting Rent Expense at the time of payment?
15. In accounting for depreciation on equipment, what is the name of the contra asset account?
16. (a) Explain the purpose of the two accounts: Depreciation Expense and Accumulated Depreciation. (b) What is the normal balance of each account? (c) Is it customary for the balances of the two accounts to be equal in amount? (d) In what financial statements, if any, will each account appear?

Warren Reeve Fess

Resources for Your Success On-Line at warren.swcollege.com

Remember! If you need additional help, visit South-Western's Web site. See page 26 for a description of the online and printed materials that are available.

EXERCISES

Exercise 3–1
Classify accruals and deferrals
Objectives 2, 3

Classify the following items as (a) deferred expense (prepaid expense), (b) deferred revenue (unearned revenue), (c) accrued expense (accrued liability), or (d) accrued revenue (accrued asset).

1. Supplies on hand.
2. Fees received but not yet earned.
3. Utilities owed but not yet paid.
4. A two-year premium paid on a fire insurance policy.
5. Fees earned but not yet received.
6. Taxes owed but payable in the following period.
7. Salary owed but not yet paid.
8. Subscriptions received in advance by a magazine.

Exercise 3–2
Classify adjusting entries
Objectives 2, 3

The following accounts were taken from the unadjusted trial balance of O'Dell Co., a congressional lobbying firm. Indicate whether or not each account would normally require an adjusting entry. If the account normally requires an adjusting entry, use the following notation to indicate the type of adjustment:

AE—Accrued Expense
AR—Accrued Revenue
DR—Deferred Revenue
DE—Deferred Expense

To illustrate, the answers for the first two accounts are shown below:

Account	Answer
George Lee, Drawing	Does not normally require adjustment.
Accounts Receivable	Normally requires adjustment (AR).
Accumulated Depreciation	
Cash	
Interest Payable	
Interest Receivable	
Land	
Office Equipment	
Prepaid Insurance	
Supplies Expense	
Unearned Fees	
Wages Expense	

Exercise 3–3
Adjusting entry for supplies
Objective 3

✓ Amount of entry: $1,445

The balance in the supplies account, before adjustment at the end of the year, is $1,820. Journalize the adjusting entry required if the amount of supplies on hand at the end of the year is $375.

Exercise 3–4
Determine supplies purchased
Objective 3

✓ $1,300

The supplies and supplies expense accounts at December 31, after adjusting entries have been posted at the end of the first year of operations, are shown in the following T accounts:

Supplies			Supplies Expense		
Bal.	280		Bal.	1,020	

Determine the amount of supplies purchased during the year.

Exercise 3–5
Effect of omitting adjusting entry
Objective 3

At December 31, the end of the first month of operations, the usual adjusting entry transferring supplies used to an expense account is omitted. Which items will be incorrectly stated, because of the error, on (a) the income statement for December and (b) the balance sheet as of December 31? Also indicate whether the items in error will be overstated or understated.

Exercise 3–6
Adjusting entries for prepaid insurance
Objective 3

✓ Amount of entry: $1,140

The balance in the prepaid insurance account, before adjustment at the end of the year, is $3,780. Journalize the adjusting entry required under each of the following *alternatives* for determining the amount of the adjustment: (a) the amount of insurance expired during the year is $1,140; (b) the amount of unexpired insurance applicable to future periods is $2,640.

Exercise 3–7
Adjusting entries for prepaid insurance
Objective 3

✓ a. Amount of entry: $1,400

The prepaid insurance account had a balance of $2,400 at the beginning of the year. The account was debited for $1,800 for premiums on policies purchased during the year. Journalize the adjusting entry required at the end of the year for each of the following situations: (a) the amount of unexpired insurance applicable to future periods is $2,800; (b) the amount of insurance expired during the year is $1,650.

Exercise 3–8
Adjusting entries for unearned fees
Objective 3

✓ Amount of entry: $5,500

The balance in the unearned fees account, before adjustment at the end of the year, is $7,000. Journalize the adjusting entry required if the amount of unearned fees at the end of the year is $1,500.

Exercise 3–9
Effect of omitting adjusting entry
Objective 3

At the end of January, the first month of the year, the usual adjusting entry transferring rent earned to a revenue account from the unearned rent account was omitted. Indicate which items will be incorrectly stated, because of the error, on (a) the income statement for January and (b) the balance sheet as of January 31. Also indicate whether the items in error will be overstated or understated.

Exercise 3–10
Adjusting entries for accrued salaries
Objective 3

✓ a. $4,200

River Realty Co. pays weekly salaries of $10,500 on Friday for a five-day week ending on that day. Journalize the necessary adjusting entry at the end of the accounting period, assuming that the period ends (a) on Tuesday, (b) on Wednesday.

Exercise 3–11
Determine wages paid
Objective 3

✓ $52,520

The wages payable and wages expense accounts at December 31, after adjusting entries have been posted at the end of the first year of operations, are shown in the following T accounts:

Wages Payable			Wages Expense		
	Bal.	1,010	Bal.	53,530	

Determine the amount of wages paid during the year.

Exercise 3–12
Effect of omitting adjusting entry
Objective 3

Accrued salaries of $2,500 owed to employees for December 30 and 31 are not considered in preparing the financial statements for the year ended December 31. Indicate which items will be erroneously stated, because of the error, on (a) the income statement for the year and (b) the balance sheet as of December 31. Also indicate whether the items in error will be overstated or understated.

Exercise 3–13
Effect of omitting adjusting entry
Objective 3

Assume that the error in Exercise 3–12 was not corrected and that the $2,500 of accrued salaries was included in the first salary payment in January. Indicate which items will be erroneously stated, because of failure to correct the initial error, on (a) the income statement for the month of January and (b) the balance sheet as of January 31.

Exercise 3–14
Adjusting entries for prepaid and accrued taxes
Objective 3

✓ b. $8,572

Edwards Financial Planning Co. was organized on April 1 of the current year. On April 2, Edwards prepaid $1,296 to the city for taxes (license fees) for the *next* 12 months and debited the prepaid taxes account. Edwards is also required to pay in January an annual tax (on property) for the *previous* calendar year. The estimated amount of the property tax for the current year (April 1 to December 31) is $7,600. (a) Journalize the two adjusting entries required to bring the accounts affected by the two taxes up to date as of December 31, the end of the current year. (b) What is the amount of tax expense for the current year?

Exercise 3–15

Effects of errors on financial statements

Objective 3

REAL WORLD

✓ a. $534,000,000

The balance sheet for **The Quaker Oats Company** as of December 31, 1996, includes the following accrued expenses as liabilities:

Accrued payroll, benefits, bonus	$111,300,000
Accrued advertising and merchandising	130,200,000
Other accrued liabilities	292,500,000

The net income for The Quaker Oats Company for the year ended December 31, 1996, was $247,900,000. (a) If the accruals had not been recorded at December 31, 1996, by how much would net income have been misstated for the fiscal year ended December 31, 1996? (b) What is the percentage of the misstatement in (a) to the reported net income of $247,900,000?

Exercise 3–16

Effects of errors on financial statements

Objective 3

✓ 1. Revenue understated, $6,800

The accountant for Baskin Medical Co., a medical services consulting firm, mistakenly omitted adjusting entries for (a) unearned revenue ($6,800) and (b) accrued wages ($1,050). Indicate the effect of each error, considered individually, on the income statement for the current year ended December 31. Also indicate the effect of each error on the December 31 balance sheet. Set up a table similar to the following, and record your answers by inserting the dollar amount in the appropriate spaces. Insert a zero if the error does not affect the item.

	Error (a)		Error (b)	
	Over-stated	**Under-stated**	**Over-stated**	**Under-stated**
1. Revenue for the year would be	$	$	$	$
2. Expenses for the year would be	$	$	$	$
3. Net income for the year would be	$	$	$	$
4. Assets at December 31 would be	$	$	$	$
5. Liabilities at December 31 would be	$	$	$	$
6. Owner's equity at December 31 would be	$	$	$	$

Exercise 3–17

Effects of errors on financial statements

Objective 3

✓ $121,050

If the net income for the current year had been $115,300 in Exercise 3–16, what would be the correct net income if the proper adjusting entries had been made?

Exercise 3–18

Adjusting entry for accrued fees

Objective 3

At the end of the current year, $3,390 of fees have been earned but have not been billed to clients.

a. Journalize the adjusting entry to record the accrued fees.
b. If the cash basis rather than the accrual basis had been used, would an adjusting entry have been necessary? Explain.

Exercise 3–19

Adjusting entries for unearned and accrued fees

Objective 3

The balance in the unearned fees account, before adjustment at the end of the year, is $31,700. Of these fees, $21,500 have been earned. In addition, $9,100 of fees have been earned but have not been billed. Journalize the adjusting entries (a) to adjust the unearned fees account and (b) to record the accrued fees.

Exercise 3–20

Effect on financial statements of omitting adjusting entry

Objective 3

The adjusting entry for accrued fees was omitted at December 31, the end of the current year. Indicate which items will be in error, because of the omission, on (a) the income statement for the current year and (b) the balance sheet as of December 31. Also indicate whether the items in error will be overstated or understated.

Exercise 3–21
Adjusting entry for depreciation

Objective 3

The estimated amount of depreciation on equipment for the current year is $4,400. Journalize the adjusting entry to record the depreciation.

Exercise 3–22
Determine fixed asset's book value

Objective 3

✓ a. $263,800

The balance in the equipment account is $379,200, and the balance in the accumulated depreciation—equipment account is $115,400.

a. What is the book value of the equipment?

b. Does the balance in the accumulated depreciation account mean that the equipment's loss of value is $115,400? Explain.

Exercise 3–23
Book value of fixed assets

Objective 3

Microsoft Corporation reported *Property, Plant, and Equipment* of $2,777 million and *Accumulated Depreciation* of $1,312 million at June 30, 1997.

a. What was the book value of the fixed assets at June 30, 1997?

b. Would the book value of Microsoft Corporation's fixed assets normally approximate their fair market values?

Exercise 3–24
Adjusting entries for depreciation; effect of error

Objective 3

On December 31, a business estimates depreciation on equipment used during the first year of operations to be $4,300. (a) Journalize the adjusting entry required as of December 31. (b) If the adjusting entry in (a) were omitted, which items would be erroneously stated on (1) the income statement for the year and (2) the balance sheet as of December 31?

Exercise 3–25
Adjusting entries from trial balances

Objectives 3, 4

The unadjusted and adjusted trial balances for Surgical Services Co. on December 31, 1999, are shown below.

Surgical Services Co.
Trial Balance
December 31, 1999

	Unadjusted		Adjusted	
Cash	6		6	
Accounts Receivable	18		21	
Supplies	6		2	
Prepaid Insurance	10		6	
Land	12		12	
Equipment	20		20	
Accumulated Depr.—Equip.		3		5
Accounts Payable		13		13
Wages Payable		0		1
Randy Reese, Capital		44		44
Randy Reese, Drawing	4		4	
Fees Earned		36		39
Wages Expense	12		13	
Rent Expense	4		4	
Insurance Expense	0		4	
Utilities Expense	2		2	
Depreciation Expense	0		2	
Supplies Expense	0		4	
Miscellaneous Expense	2		2	
Totals	96	96	102	102

Journalize the five entries that adjusted the accounts at December 31, 1999. None of the accounts were affected by more than one adjusting entry.

Exercise 3–26
Adjusting entries from trial balances

Objective 3, 4

What's Wrong WITH THIS?

✓ Corrected trial balance totals, $177,520

The accountant for Homestead Laundry prepared the following unadjusted and adjusted trial balances. Assume that all balances in the unadjusted trial balance and the amounts of the adjustments are correct. How many errors can you find in the accountant's adjusting entries?

Homestead Laundry
Trial Balance
August 31, 1999

	Unadjusted		Adjusted	
Cash	7,790		7,790	
Accounts Receivable	10,000		12,500	
Laundry Supplies	4,750		8,660	
Prepaid Insurance*	2,825		1,325	
Laundry Equipment	85,600		79,880	
Accumulated Depreciation		55,700		55,700
Accounts Payable		4,950		5,800
Wages Payable				850
Kim Momin, Capital		30,900		30,900
Kim Momin, Drawing	8,000		8,000	
Laundry Revenue		76,900		76,900
Wages Expense	24,500		24,500	
Rent Expense	15,575		15,575	
Utilities Expense	8,500		8,500	
Depreciation Expense			5,720	
Laundry Supplies Expense			3,910	
Insurance Expense			500	
Miscellaneous Expense	910		910	
	168,450	168,450	177,770	170,150

*$1,500 of insurance expired during the year.

Exercise 3–27
Vertical analysis of income statement

Objective 5

REAL WORLD

The financial statements for **Hershey Foods Corporation** are presented in Appendix G at the end of the text.

a. Determine for Hershey Foods Corporation:
   1. The amount of the change and percent of change in net income for the year ended December 31, 1996.
   2. The percentage relationship between net income and net sales (net income divided by net sales) for the years ended December 31, 1996 and 1995.

b. What conclusions can you draw from your analysis?

PROBLEMS SERIES A

Problem 3–1A
Adjusting entries

Objective 3

HAT

On December 31, the end of the current year, the following data were accumulated to assist the accountant in preparing the adjusting entries for Lakeview Realty:

a. Fees accrued but unbilled at December 31 are $3,750.
b. The supplies account balance on December 31 is $3,100. The supplies on hand at December 31 are $720.
c. Wages accrued but not paid at December 31 are $1,100.
d. The unearned rent account balance at December 31 is $4,800, representing the receipt of an advance payment on December 1 of four months' rent from tenants.
e. Depreciation of office equipment for the year is $2,100.

Instructions

1. Journalize the adjusting entries required at December 31.
2. Briefly explain the difference between adjusting entries and entries that would be made to correct errors.

Problem 3–2A
Adjusting entries

Objective 3

HAT

Selected account balances before adjustment for Claremont Realty at October 31, the end of the current year, are as follows:

	Debits	Credits		Debits	Credits
Accounts Receivable	$ 9,250		Unearned Fees		$ 6,500
Supplies	2,700		Fees Earned		99,850
Prepaid Rent	21,000		Wages Expense	$40,750	
Equipment	50,500		Rent Expense	—	
Accumulated Depreciation		$16,900	Depreciation Expense	—	
Wages Payable		—	Supplies Expense	—	

Data needed for year-end adjustments are as follows:

a. Supplies on hand at Oct. 31, $1,030.
b. Depreciation of equipment during year, $1,800.
c. Rent expired during year, $18,000.
d. Wages accrued but not paid at Oct. 31, $990.
e. Unearned fees at Oct. 31, $2,500.
f. Unbilled fees at Oct. 31, $6,790.

Instructions

Journalize the six adjusting entries required at October 31, based upon the data presented.

Problem 3–3A
Adjusting entries

Objectives 3, 4

SPREADSHEET

Shelby Company specializes in the maintenance and repair of signs, such as billboards. On August 31, the end of the current year, the accountant for Shelby Company prepared a trial balance and an adjusted trial balance. The two trial balances are as follows:

Shelby Company
Trial Balance
August 31, 20—

	Unadjusted		Adjusted	
Cash	9,750		9,750	
Accounts Receivable	20,400		20,400	
Supplies	7,880		2,030	
Prepaid Insurance	2,700		1,100	
Land	47,500		47,500	
Buildings	107,480		107,480	
Accumulated Depreciation—Buildings		79,600		85,100
Trucks	72,000		72,000	
Accumulated Depreciation—Trucks		32,800		43,900
Accounts Payable		8,920		9,720
Salaries Payable		—		1,300
Unearned Service Fees		7,500		1,500
Angela Scanlon, Capital		93,890		93,890
Angela Scanlon, Drawing	8,000		8,000	
Service Fees Earned		152,680		158,680
Salary Expense	81,200		82,500	
Depreciation Expense—Trucks	—		11,100	
Rent Expense	9,600		9,600	
Supplies Expense	—		5,850	
Utilities Expense	6,200		7,000	
Depreciation Expense—Buildings	—		5,500	
Taxes Expense	1,720		1,720	
Insurance Expense	—		1,600	
Miscellaneous Expense	960		960	
	375,390	375,390	394,090	394,090

Instructions

Journalize the seven entries that adjusted the accounts at August 31. None of the accounts were affected by more than one adjusting entry.

Problem 3–4A
Adjusting entries

Objective 3

HAT
GENERAL LEDGER

Rainbow Trout Co., an outfitter store for fishing treks, prepared the following trial balance at the end of its first year of operations:

Rainbow Trout Co.
Trial Balance
April 30, 20—

Cash	1,150	
Accounts Receivable	3,500	
Supplies	1,300	
Equipment	9,900	
Accounts Payable		750
Unearned Fees		2,000
Lee Wulff, Capital		10,500
Lee Wulff, Drawing	1,000	
Fees Earned		36,750
Wages Expense	19,500	
Rent Expense	9,000	
Utilities Expense	3,750	
Miscellaneous Expense	900	
	50,000	50,000

For preparing the adjusting entries, the following data were assembled:

a. Supplies on hand on April 30 were $175.
b. Fees earned but unbilled on April 30 were $1,380.
c. Depreciation of equipment was estimated to be $800 for the year.
d. Unpaid wages accrued on April 30 were $450.
e. The balance in unearned fees represented the Jan. 1 receipt in advance for services to be provided. Only $750 of the services were provided between Jan. 1 and April 30.

Instructions

Journalize the adjusting entries necessary on April 30.

Problem 3–5A
Adjusting entries and adjusted trial balances

Objectives 3, 4

HAT
SPREADSHEET
GENERAL LEDGER

✓ 2. Total of Debit Column: $469,900

Atwater Service Co., which specializes in appliance repair services, is owned and operated by Carri Atwater. Atwater Service Co.'s accounting clerk prepared the following trial balance at December 31, the end of the current year:

Atwater Service Co.
Trial Balance
December 31, 20—

Cash	3,200	
Accounts Receivable	17,200	
Prepaid Insurance	3,900	
Supplies	2,450	
Land	50,000	
Building	141,500	
Accumulated Depreciation—Building		95,700
Equipment	90,100	
Accumulated Depreciation—Equipment		65,300
Accounts Payable		7,500
Unearned Rent		4,000
Carri Atwater, Capital		65,900
Carri Atwater, Drawing	5,000	
Fees Earned		218,400
Salaries and Wages Expense	78,700	
Utilities Expense	28,200	
Advertising Expense	19,000	
Repairs Expense	13,500	
Miscellaneous Expense	4,050	
	456,800	456,800

The data needed to determine year-end adjustments are as follows:

a. Depreciation of building for the year, $1,500.
b. Depreciation of equipment for the year, $5,500.
c. Accrued salaries and wages at December 31, $1,150.
d. Unexpired insurance at December 31, $1,100.
e. Fees earned but unbilled on December 31, $4,950.
f. Supplies on hand at December 31, $500.
g. Rent unearned at December 31, $1,500.

Instructions

1. Journalize the adjusting entries. Add additional accounts as needed.
2. Determine the balances of the accounts affected by the adjusting entries and prepare an adjusted trial balance.

Problem 3–6A

Adjusting entries and errors

Objective 3

✓ Corrected Net Income: $222,350

At the end of July, the first month of operations, the following selected data were taken from the financial statements of John Stuedemann, III, an attorney:

Net income for July	$213,500
Total assets at July 31	177,250
Total liabilities at July 31	36,500
Total owner's equity at July 31	140,750

In preparing the financial statements, adjustments for the following data were overlooked:

a. Unbilled fees earned at July 31, $16,900.
b. Depreciation of equipment for July, $4,000.
c. Accrued wages at July 31, $1,100.
d. Supplies used during July, $2,950.

Instructions

1. Journalize the entries to record the omitted adjustments.
2. Determine the correct amount of net income for July and the total assets, liabilities, and owner's equity at July 31. In addition to indicating the corrected amounts, indicate the effect of each omitted adjustment by setting up and completing a columnar table similar to the following. Adjustment (a) is presented as an example.

	Net Income	Total Assets	Total Liabilities	Total Owner's Equity
Reported amounts	$213,500	$177,250	$36,500	$140,750
Corrections:				
Adjustment (a)	+16,900	+16,900	0	+16,900
Adjustment (b)				
Adjustment (c)				
Adjustment (d)				
Corrected amounts				

PROBLEMS SERIES B

Problem 3–1B

Adjusting entries

Objective 3

On December 31, the end of the current year, the following data were accumulated to assist the accountant in preparing the adjusting entries for Simkin Realty:

a. The supplies account balance on December 31 is $1,450. The supplies on hand on December 31 are $315.
b. The unearned rent account balance on December 31 is $3,600, representing the receipt of an advance payment on December 1 of three months' rent from tenants.
c. Wages accrued but not paid at December 31 are $850.

d. Fees accrued but unbilled at December 31 are $11,500.
e. Depreciation of office equipment for the year is $1,500.

Instructions

1. Journalize the adjusting entries required at December 31.
2. Briefly explain the difference between adjusting entries and entries that would be made to correct errors.

Problem 3–2B

Adjusting entries

Objective 3

Selected account balances before adjustment for Ocean City Realty at December 31, the end of the current year, are as follows:

	Debits	Credits		Debits	Credits
Accounts Receivable	$11,250		Unearned Fees		$ 5,000
Supplies	4,750		Fees Earned		87,950
Prepaid Rent	27,000		Wages Expense	$29,400	
Equipment	42,500		Rent Expense	—	
Accumulated Depreciation		$10,900	Depreciation Expense	—	
Wages Payable		—	Supplies Expense	—	

Data needed for year-end adjustments are as follows:

a. Unbilled fees at December 31, $4,150.
b. Supplies on hand at December 31, $980.
c. Rent expired during year, $24,000.
d. Depreciation of equipment during year, $3,050.
e. Unearned fees at December 31, $3,750.
f. Wages accrued but not paid at December 31, $920.

Instructions

Journalize the six adjusting entries required at December 31, based upon the data presented.

Problem 3–3B

Adjusting entries

Objectives 3, 4

SPREADSHEET

Somerset Company specializes in the repair of music equipment and is owned and operated by Deana Perot. On April 30, 2000, the end of the current year, the accountant for Somerset Company prepared a trial balance and an adjusted trial balance. The two trial balances are as follows:

Somerset Company
Trial Balance
April 30, 2000

	Unadjusted		Adjusted	
Cash	11,825		11,825	
Accounts Receivable	29,500		29,500	
Supplies	6,950		1,340	
Prepaid Insurance	3,750		2,500	
Equipment	92,150		92,150	
Accumulated Depreciation—Equipment		53,480		61,270
Automobiles	36,500		36,500	
Accumulated Depreciation—Automobiles		18,250		22,900
Accounts Payable		8,310		9,890
Salaries Payable		—		1,800
Unearned Service Fees		5,000		2,500
Deana Perot, Capital		55,470		55,470
Deana Perot, Drawing	5,000		5,000	
Service Fees Earned		244,600		247,100
Salary Expense	172,300		174,100	
Rent Expense	18,000		18,000	
Supplies Expense	—		5,610	
Depreciation Expense—Equipment	—		7,790	
Depreciation Expense—Automobiles	—		4,650	
Utilities Expense	4,700		6,280	
Taxes Expense	2,725		2,725	
Insurance Expense	—		1,250	
Miscellaneous Expense	1,710		1,710	
	385,110	385,110	400,930	400,930

Instructions

Journalize the seven entries that adjusted the accounts at April 30. None of the accounts were affected by more than one adjusting entry.

Problem 3–4B

Adjusting entries

Objective 3

GENERAL LEDGER

Icarus Company, an electronics repair store, prepared the following trial balance at the end of its first year of operations:

Icarus Company
Trial Balance
June 30, 20—

Cash	1,150	
Accounts Receivable	5,500	
Supplies	1,800	
Equipment	17,900	
Accounts Payable		750
Unearned Fees		2,000
Sonja Ash, Capital		10,000
Sonja Ash, Drawing	1,500	
Fees Earned		35,250
Wages Expense	8,500	
Rent Expense	8,000	
Utilities Expense	2,750	
Miscellaneous Expense	900	
	48,000	48,000

For preparing the adjusting entries, the following data were assembled:

a. Fees earned but unbilled on June 30 were $1,200.
b. Supplies on hand on June 30 were $290.
c. Depreciation of equipment was estimated to be $1,000 for the year.
d. The balance in unearned fees represented the April 1 receipt in advance for services to be provided. Only $700 of the services was provided between April 1 and June 30.
e. Unpaid wages accrued on June 30 were $140.

Instructions

Journalize the adjusting entries necessary on June 30.

In Class Example

Problem 3–5B

Adjusting entries and adjusted trial balances

Objectives 3, 4

SPREADSHEET
GENERAL LEDGER

✓ 2. Total of Debit Column: $482,570

Zornes Company is a small editorial services company owned and operated by Valerie Spann. Zornes Company's accounting clerk prepared the trial balance shown at the top of the next page on December 31, the end of the current year.

The data needed to determine year-end adjustments are as follows:

a. Unexpired insurance at December 31, $1,200.
b. Supplies on hand at December 31, $500.
c. Depreciation of building for the year, $1,620.
d. Depreciation of equipment for the year, $5,500.
e. Rent unearned at December 31, $2,000.
f. Accrued salaries and wages at December 31, $1,300.
g. Fees earned but unbilled on December 31, $3,750.

Instructions

1. Journalize the adjusting entries. Add additional accounts as needed.
2. Determine the balances of the accounts affected by the adjusting entries and prepare an adjusted trial balance.

Zornes Company
Trial Balance
December 31, 20—

Cash	6,700	
Accounts Receivable	23,800	
Prepaid Insurance	3,400	
Supplies	1,950	
Land	50,000	
Building	141,500	
Accumulated Depreciation—Building		91,700
Equipment	90,100	
Accumulated Depreciation—Equipment		65,300
Accounts Payable		7,500
Unearned Rent		6,000
Valerie Spann, Capital		81,500
Valerie Spann, Drawing	10,000	
Fees Earned		218,400
Salaries and Wages Expense	80,200	
Utilities Expense	28,200	
Advertising Expense	19,000	
Repairs Expense	11,500	
Miscellaneous Expense	4,050	
	470,400	470,400

Problem 3–6B

Adjusting entries and errors

Objective 3

✓ Corrected Net Income: $133,700

At the end of June, the first month of operations, the following selected data were taken from the financial statements of E. Swindle, an attorney:

Net income for June	$132,750
Total assets at June 30	189,700
Total liabilities at June 30	20,200
Total owner's equity at June 30	169,500

In preparing the financial statements, adjustments for the following data were overlooked:

a. Supplies used during June, $1,600.
b. Unbilled fees earned at June 30, $5,000.
c. Depreciation of equipment for June, $1,500.
d. Accrued wages at June 30, $950.

Instructions

1. Journalize the entries to record the omitted adjustments.
2. Determine the correct amount of net income for June and the total assets, liabilities, and owner's equity at June 30. In addition to indicating the corrected amounts, indicate the effect of each omitted adjustment by setting up and completing a columnar table similar to the following. Adjustment (a) is presented as an example.

	Net Income	Total Assets	Total Liabilities	Total Owner's Equity
Reported amounts	$132,750	$189,700	$20,200	$169,500
Corrections:				
Adjustment (a)	−1,600	−1,600	0	−1,600
Adjustment (b)	______	______	______	______
Adjustment (c)	______	______	______	______
Adjustment (d)	______	______	______	______
Corrected amounts	______	______	______	______

CONTINUING PROBLEM

HAT

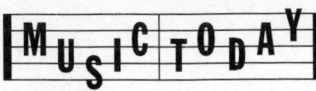

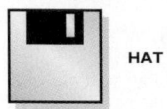

✓ 2. Total of Debit Column: $13,725

The trial balance that you prepared for Music Today at the end of Chapter 2 should appear as follows:

Music Today
Trial Balance
December 31, 1999

Cash	3,285	
Accounts Receivable	880	
Supplies	535	
Prepaid Insurance	1,680	
Office Equipment	2,500	
Accounts Payable		2,875
Unearned Revenue		1,500
Chris Stipe, Capital		4,000
Chris Stipe, Drawing	550	
Fees Earned		4,780
Wages Expense	910	
Office Rent Expense	970	
Equipment Rent Expense	575	
Utilities Expense	380	
Music Expense	340	
Advertising Expense	225	
Supplies Expense	90	
Miscellaneous Expense	235	
	13,155	13,155

The data needed to determine adjustments for the two-month period ending December 31, 1999, are as follows:

a. During December, Music Today provided guest disc jockeys for KPRG for a total of 70 hours. For information on the amount of the accrued revenue to be billed to KPRG, see the contract described in the December 3, 1999 transaction at the end of Chapter 2.
b. Supplies on hand at December 31, $340.
c. The balance of the prepaid insurance account relates to the December 1, 1999 transaction at the end of Chapter 2.
d. Depreciation of the office equipment is $45.
e. The balance of the unearned revenue account relates to the contract between Music Today and KPRG, described in the December 3, 1999 transaction at the end of Chapter 2.
f. Accrued wages as of December 31, 1999, were $75.

Instructions

1. Prepare adjusting journal entries. You will need the following additional accounts:

   18 Accumulated Depreciation—Office Equipment
   22 Wages Payable
   57 Insurance Expense
   58 Depreciation Expense

2. Post the adjusting entries, inserting balances in the accounts affected.
3. Prepare an adjusted trial balance.

SPECIAL ACTIVITIES

Activity 3–1
Flora Real Estate Co.
Ethics and professional conduct in business

Martha Clark opened Flora Real Estate Co. on January 1, 1998. At the end of the first year, the business needed additional capital. On behalf of Flora Real Estate, Martha applied to First City Bank for a loan of $30,000. Based on Flora Real Estate's financial statements, which had been prepared on a cash basis, the First City Bank loan officer rejected the loan as too risky.

After receiving the rejection notice, Martha instructed her accountant to prepare the financial statements on an accrual basis. These statements included $24,000 in accounts receivable and $3,000 in accounts payable. Martha then instructed her accountant to record an additional $12,000 of accounts receivable for commissions on property for which a contract had been signed on December 27, 1998, but which would not be formally "closed" and the title transferred until January 20, 1999.

Martha then applied for a $30,000 loan from Second City Bank, using the revised financial statements. On this application, Martha indicated that she had not previously been rejected for credit.

Discuss the ethical and professional conduct of Martha Clark in applying for the loan from Second City Bank.

Activity 3–2
Ford Motor Co.
Accrued expense

REAL WORLD

On December 30, 1999, you buy a Ford Expedition. It comes with a three-year, 36,000-mile warranty. On January 21, 2000, you return the Expedition to the dealership for some basic repairs covered under the warranty. The cost of the repairs to the dealership is $180. In what year, 1999 or 2000, should Ford Motor Co. recognize the cost of the warranty repairs as an expense?

Activity 3–3
United Airlines
Accrued revenue

REAL WORLD

What do you THINK?

The following is an excerpt from a conversation between Max Liu and Ethel Stern just before they boarded a flight to Puerto Rico on United Airlines. They are going to Puerto Rico to attend their company's annual sales conference.

Max: Ethel, aren't you taking an introductory accounting course at City College?

Ethel: Yes, I decided it's about time I learned something about accounting. You know, our annual bonuses are based upon the sales figures that come from the accounting department.

Max: I guess I never really thought about it.

Ethel: You should think about it! Last year, I placed a $100,000 order on December 21. But when I got my bonus, the $100,000 sale wasn't included. They said it hadn't been shipped until January 3, so it would have to count in next year's bonus.

Max: A real bummer!

Ethel: Right! I was counting on that bonus including the $100,000 sale.

Max: Did you complain?

Ethel: Yes, but it didn't do any good. Tracy, the head accountant, said something about matching revenues and expenses. Also, something about not recording revenues until the sale is final. I figure I'd take the accounting course and find out whether she's just jerking me around.

Max: I never really thought about it. When do you think United Airlines will record its revenues from this flight?

Ethel: Mmm . . . I guess it could record the revenue when it sells the ticket . . . or . . . when the boarding passes are taken at the door . . . or . . . when we get off the plane . . . or when our company pays for the tickets . . . or . . . I don't know. I'll ask my accounting instructor.

Discuss when United Airlines should recognize the revenue from ticket sales to properly match revenues and expenses.

Activity 3–4 Quick Television Repair

Adjustments and financial statements

Several years ago, your father opened Quick Television Repair. He made a small initial investment and added money from his personal bank account as needed. He withdrew money for living expenses at irregular intervals. As the business grew, he hired an assistant. He is now considering adding more employees, purchasing additional service trucks, and purchasing the building he now rents. To secure funds for the expansion, your father submitted a loan application to the bank and included the most recent financial statements (shown below) prepared from accounts maintained by a part-time bookkeeper.

Quick Television Repair
Income Statement
For the Year Ended December 31, 20—

Service revenue		$66,900
Less: Rent paid	$18,000	
Wages paid	16,500	
Supplies paid	7,000	
Utilities paid	3,100	
Insurance paid	3,000	
Miscellaneous payments	2,150	49,750
Net income		$17,150

Quick Television Repair
Balance Sheet
December 31, 20—

Assets	
Cash	$ 3,750
Amounts due from customers	2,100
Truck	25,000
Total assets	$30,850
Equities	
Owner's capital	$30,850

After reviewing the financial statements, the loan officer at the bank asked your father if he used the accrual basis of accounting for revenues and expenses. Your father responded that he did and that is why he included an account for "Amounts Due from Customers." The loan officer then asked whether or not the accounts were adjusted prior to the preparation of the statements. Your father answered that they had not been adjusted.

a. Why do you think the loan officer suspected that the accounts had not been adjusted prior to the preparation of the statements?
b. Indicate possible accounts that might need to be adjusted before an accurate set of financial statements could be prepared.

Activity 3–5 Into the Real World

Codes of ethics

GROUP ACTIVITY

Obtain a copy of your college or university's student code of conduct. In groups of three or four, answer the following questions.

1. Compare this code of conduct with the accountant's Codes of Professional Conduct in Appendix B at the end of this text. What are the similarities and differences between the two codes of conduct?
2. One of your classmates asks you for permission to copy your homework, which your instructor will be collecting and grading for part of your overall term grade. Although your instructor has not stated whether one student may or may not copy another student's homework, is it ethical for you to allow your classmate to copy your homework? Is it ethical for your classmate to copy your homework?

ANSWERS TO SELF-EXAMINATION QUESTIONS

Matching

1. A	4. W	7. G	10. C	12. R	14. P	16. I	18. X
2. J	5. T	8. M	11. D	13. O	15. E	17. F	19. L
3. B	6. H	9. N					

Multiple Choice

1. **A** A deferral is the delay in recording an expense already paid, such as prepaid insurance (answer A). Wages payable (answer B) is considered an accrued expense or accrued liability. Fees earned (answer C) is a revenue item. Accumulated depreciation (answer D) is a contra account to a fixed asset.
2. **D** The balance in the supplies account, before adjustment, represents the amount of supplies available. From this amount ($2,250) is subtracted the amount of supplies on hand ($950) to determine the supplies used ($1,300). Since increases in expense accounts are recorded by debits and decreases in asset accounts are recorded by credits, answer D is the correct entry.
3. **C** The failure to record the adjusting entry debiting unearned rent, $600, and crediting rent revenue, $600, would have the effect of overstating liabilities by $600 and understating net income by $600 (answer C).
4. **C** Since increases in expense accounts (such as depreciation expense) are recorded by debits and it is customary to record the decreases in usefulness of fixed assets as credits to accumulated depreciation accounts, answer C is the correct entry.
5. **D** The book value of a fixed asset is the difference between the balance in the asset account and the balance in the related accumulated depreciation account, or $22,500 − $14,000, as indicated by answer D ($8,500).

NER'S CAPITAL
4
INCOME
SUMMARY
DECEMBER
31
1999

4

Completing the Accounting Cycle

Setting *the* STAGE

Have you ever ridden in a taxicab? When you get in, you tell the driver where you want to go, and the driver lowers the meter lever (flag) to start the meter running. At the end of the trip, the driver stops the meter. You then pay the driver for the amount indicated on the meter. As the next passenger is picked up, the driver lowers the lever, and the cycle starts all over again.

Businesses also go through a cycle of activities. At the beginning of the cycle, management plans where it wants the business to go and begins the necessary actions to achieve its operating goals. Throughout the cycle, which is normally one year, the accountant records the operating activities (transactions) of the business. At the end of the cycle, the accountant prepares financial statements that summarize the operating activities for the year. The accountant then prepares the accounts for recording the operating activities in the next cycle.

As we saw in Chapter 1, the initial cycle for Computer King began with Pat King's investment in the business on November 1, 1999. The cycle continued with recording Computer King's transactions for November and December, as we discussed in Chapters 1 and 2. In Chapter 3, the cycle continued and we recorded the adjusting entries for the two months ending December 31, 1999. Now, in this chapter, we discuss the flow of the adjustment data into the accounts and into the financial statements. We show this process by using a work sheet. We conclude this chapter by discussing how the accounting records are prepared for the next period.

objectives

After studying this chapter, you should be able to:

1. Prepare a work sheet.
2. Prepare financial statements from a work sheet.
3. Prepare the adjusting and closing entries from a work sheet.
4. Explain what is meant by the fiscal year and the natural business year.
5. Review the seven basic steps of the accounting cycle.
6. Analyze and interpret the financial solvency of a business by computing the working capital and the current ratio.

Work Sheet

OBJECTIVE 1

Prepare a work sheet.

Accountants often use **working papers** for collecting and summarizing data they need for preparing various analyses and reports. Such working papers are useful tools, but they are not considered a part of the formal accounting records. This is in contrast to the chart of accounts, the journal, and the ledger, which are essential parts of the accounting system. Working papers are usually prepared by using a spreadsheet program on a computer.

REAL WORLD — Common spreadsheet programs used in business include Microsoft Excel® and Lotus 1-2-3®.

The **work sheet** is a working paper that accountants may use to summarize adjusting entries and the account balances for the financial statements. In small companies with few accounts and adjustments, a work sheet may not be necessary. For example, the financial statements for Computer King may be prepared directly from the adjusted trial balance illustrated in Chapter 3. In a computerized accounting system, a work sheet may not be necessary because the software program automatically posts entries to the accounts and prepares financial statements.

The work sheet is a useful device for understanding the flow of the accounting data from the unadjusted trial balance to the financial statements.

The work sheet is a useful device for understanding the flow of the accounting data from the unadjusted trial balance to the financial statements. This flow of data is the same in either a manual or a computerized accounting system. Because it is important that you understand this flow of data, we illustrate the preparation of the work sheet.

COMPUTER KING

Unadjusted Trial Balance Columns

To begin the work sheet, list at the top the name of the business, the type of working paper (work sheet), and the period of time, as shown in Exhibit 1. Next, enter the unadjusted trial balance directly on the work sheet. The work sheet in Exhibit 1 shows the unadjusted trial balance for Computer King at December 31, 1999.

Adjustments Columns

The adjustments that we explained and illustrated for Computer King in Chapter 3 are entered in the Adjustments columns as shown in Exhibit 2. Cross-referencing (by letters) the debit and credit of each adjustment is useful in reviewing the work sheet. It is also helpful for identifying the adjusting entries that need to be recorded in the journal.

The order in which the adjustments are entered on the work sheet is not important. Most accountants enter the adjustments in the order in which the data are assembled. If the titles of some of the accounts to be adjusted do not appear in the trial balance, they should be inserted in the Account Title column, below the trial balance totals, as needed.

To review, the entries in the Adjustments columns of the work sheet are:

(a) **Supplies.** The supplies account has a debit balance of $2,000. The cost of the supplies on hand at the end of the period is $760. Therefore, the supplies expense for December is the difference between the two amounts, or $1,240. Enter the adjustment by writing (1) $1,240 in the Adjustments Debit column on the same line as Supplies Expense and (2) $1,240 in the Adjustments Credit column on the same line as Supplies.

(b) **Prepaid Insurance.** The prepaid insurance account has a debit balance of $2,400, which represents the prepayment of insurance for 24 months beginning December 1. Thus, the insurance expense for December is $100 ($2,400/24). Enter the adjustment by writing (1) $100 in the Adjustments Debit column on the same line as Insurance Expense and (2) $100 in the Adjustments Credit column on the same line as Prepaid Insurance.

(c) **Unearned Rent.** The unearned rent account has a credit balance of $360, which represents the receipt of three months' rent, beginning with December. Thus, the rent revenue for December is $120. Enter the adjustment by writing (1) $120 in the Adjustments Debit column on the same line as Unearned Rent and (2) $120 in the Adjustments Credit column on the same line as Rent Revenue.

(d) **Wages.** Wages accrued but not paid at the end of December total $250. This amount is an increase in expenses and an increase in liabilities. Enter the adjustment by writing (1) $250 in the Adjustments Debit column on the same line as Wages Expense and (2) $250 in the Adjustments Credit column on the same line as Wages Payable.

(e) **Accrued Fees.** Fees accrued at the end of December but not recorded total $500. This amount is an increase in an asset and an increase in revenue. Enter the adjustment by writing (1) $500 in the Adjustments Debit column on the same line as Accounts Receivable and (2) $500 in the Adjustments Credit column on the same line as Fees Earned.

(f) **Depreciation.** Depreciation of the office equipment is $50 for December. Enter the adjustment by writing (1) $50 in the Adjustments Debit column on the same line as Depreciation Expense and (2) $50 in the Adjustments Credit column on the same line as Accumulated Depreciation.

Total the Adjustments columns to verify the mathematical accuracy of the adjustment data. The total of the Debit column must equal the total of the Credit column.

Adjusted Trial Balance Columns

The adjustment data are added to or subtracted from the amounts in the unadjusted Trial Balance columns. The adjusted amounts are then extended to (placed in) the Adjusted Trial Balance columns, as shown in Exhibit 2. For example, the cash amount of $2,065 is extended to the Adjusted Trial Balance Debit column, since no adjustments affected Cash. Accounts Receivable has an initial balance of $2,220 and a debit adjustment (increase) of $500. The amount to write in the Adjusted Trial Balance Debit column is the debit balance of $2,720. The same procedure continues until all account balances are extended to the Adjusted Trial Balance columns. Total the columns of the Adjusted Trial Balance to verify the equality of debits and credits.

Income Statement and Balance Sheet Columns

The work sheet is completed by extending the adjusted trial balance amounts to the Income Statement and Balance Sheet columns. The amounts for revenues and

EXHIBIT 1
Work Sheet with Unadjusted Trial Balance Entered

Computer King
Work Sheet
For the Two Months Ended December 31, 1999

	Trial Balance		Adjustments		Adjusted Trial Balance		Income Statement		Balance Sheet	
Account Title	**Dr.**	**Cr.**	**Dr.**	**Cr.**	**Dr.**	**Cr.**	**Dr.**	**Cr.**	**Dr.**	**Cr.**
Cash	2,065									
Accounts Receivable	2,220									
Supplies	2,000									
Prepaid Insurance	2,400									
Land	10,000									
Office Equipment	1,800									
Accounts Payable		900								
Unearned Rent		360								
Pat King, Capital		15,000								
Pat King, Drawing	4,000									
Fees Earned		16,340								
Wages Expense	4,275									
Rent Expense	1,600									
Utilities Expense	985									
Supplies Expense	800									
Miscellaneous Expense	455									
	32,600	32,600								

The work sheet is used for summarizing the effects of adjusting entries. It also aids in preparing financial statements.

EXHIBIT 2

Work Sheet with Unadjusted Trial Balance, Adjustments, and

The adjustments o
work sheet are us
preparing the adju
journal entries.

Accounts are added, as
needed, to complete the
adjustments.

EXHIBIT 2

Work Sheet with Unadjusted Trial Balance, Adjustments, and A

Accounts are added, as needed, to complete the adjustments.

The adjustments o
work sheet are us
preparing the adju
journal entries.

EXHIBIT 3
Work Sheet with Amounts Extended to Income Statement and Balance Sheet Columns

The reve
and expe
amounts
extendec
(placed i
the Inco
Statemer
columns.

The difference between the Income Statement column totals is the net income (or net loss) for the period. The difference between the Balance Sheet column totals is also the net income (or net loss) for the period.

EXHIBIT 5
Financial Statements Prepared from Work Sheet

Computer King
Income Statement
For the Two Months Ended December 31, 1999

Fees earned	$16,840.00	
Rent revenue	120.00	
Total revenues		$16,960.00
Expenses:		
Wages expense	$ 4,525.00	
Supplies expense	2,040.00	
Rent expense	1,600.00	
Utilities expense	985.00	
Insurance expense	100.00	
Depreciation expense	50.00	
Miscellaneous expense	455.00	
Total expenses		9,755.00
Net income		$ 7,205.00

Computer King
Statement of Owner's Equity
For the Two Months Ended December 31, 1999

Pat King, capital, November 1, 1999		$ 0
Investment on November 1, 1999	$15,000.00	
Net income for November and December	7,205.00	
	$22,205.00	
Less withdrawals	4,000.00	
Increase in owner's equity		18,205.00
Pat King, capital, December 31, 1999		$18,205.00

Computer King
Balance Sheet
December 31, 1999

Assets				**Liabilities**		
Current assets:				Current liabilities:		
Cash		$ 2,065.00		Accounts payable	$ 900.00	
Accounts receivable		2,720.00		Wages payable	250.00	
Supplies		760.00		Unearned rent	240.00	
Prepaid insurance		2,300.00		Total liabilities		$ 1,390.00
Total current assets			$ 7,845.00			
Property, plant, and equipment:						
Land		$10,000.00				
Office equipment	$1,800					
Less accum. depr.	50	1,750.00		**Owner's Equity**		
Total property, plant, and equipment			11,750.00	Pat King, capital		18,205.00
Total assets			$19,595.00	Total liabilities and owner's equity		$19,595.00

expenses are extended to the Income Statement columns. The amounts for assets, liabilities, owner's capital, and drawing are extended to the Balance Sheet columns.[1]

In the Computer King work sheet, the first account listed is Cash and the balance appearing in the Adjusted Trial Balance Debit column is $2,065. Cash is an asset, it is listed on the balance sheet, and it has a debit balance. Therefore, $2,065 is extended to the Balance Sheet Debit column. The balance of Fees Earned of $16,840 is extended to the Income Statement Credit column. The same procedure continues until all account balances have been extended to the proper columns, as shown in Exhibit 3.

After all of the balances have been extended to the four statement columns, total each of these columns, as shown in Exhibit 4. The difference between the two Income Statement column totals is the amount of the net income or the net loss for the period. Likewise, the difference between the two Balance Sheet column totals is also the amount of the net income or net loss for the period.

If the Income Statement Credit column total (representing total revenue) is greater than the Income Statement Debit column total (representing total expenses), the difference is the net income. If the Income Statement Debit column total is greater than the Income Statement Credit column total, the difference is a net loss. For Computer King, the computation of net income is as follows:

Total of Credit column (revenues)	$16,960
Total of Debit column (expenses)	9,755
Net income (excess of revenues over expenses)	$ 7,205

Q&A *If the total of the Balance Sheet Debit column of the work sheet is $350,000 and the total of the Balance Sheet Credit column is $400,000, what is the net income or net loss?*

$50,000 net loss ($350,000 − $400,000)

As shown in Exhibit 4, write the amount of the net income, $7,205, in the Income Statement Debit column and the Balance Sheet Credit column. Write the term *Net income* in the Account Title column. If there were a net loss instead of net income, you would write the amount in the Income Statement Credit column and the Balance Sheet Debit column and the term *Net loss* in the Account Title column. Inserting the net income or net loss in the statement columns on the work sheet shows the effect of transferring the net balance of the revenue and expense accounts to the owner's capital account. Later in this chapter, we explain how to journalize this transfer.

After the net income or net loss has been entered on the work sheet, again total each of the four statement columns. The totals of the two Income Statement columns must now be equal. The totals of the two Balance Sheet columns must also be equal.

Financial Statements

OBJECTIVE 2

Prepare financial statements from a work sheet.

The work sheet is an aid in preparing the income statement, the statement of owner's equity, and the balance sheet, which are presented in Exhibit 5. In the following paragraphs, we discuss these financial statements for Computer King, prepared from the completed work sheet in Exhibit 4. The statements are similar in form to those presented in Chapter 1.

Income Statement

The income statement is normally prepared directly from the work sheet. However, the order of the expenses may be changed. As we did in Chapter 1, we list the ex-

[1] The balances of the capital and drawing accounts are also extended to the Balance Sheet columns because this work sheet does not provide for separate Statement of Owner's Equity columns.

penses in the income statement in Exhibit 5 in order of size, beginning with the larger items. Miscellaneous expense is the last item, regardless of its amount.

Statement of Owner's Equity

The first item normally presented on the statement of owner's equity is the balance of the proprietor's capital account at the beginning of the period. On the work sheet, however, the amount listed as capital is not always the account balance at the beginning of the period. The proprietor may have invested additional assets in the business during the period. Hence, for the beginning balance and any additional investments, it is necessary to refer to the capital account in the ledger. These amounts, along with the net income (or net loss) and the drawing amount shown in the work sheet, are used to determine the ending capital account balance.

The basic form of the statement of owner's equity is shown in Exhibit 5. For Computer King, the amount of drawings by the owner was less than the net income. If the owner's withdrawals had exceeded the net income, the order of the net income and the withdrawals would have been reversed. The difference between the two items would then be deducted from the beginning capital account balance. Other factors, such as additional investments or a net loss, also require some change in the form, as shown in the following example:

Allan Johnson, capital, January 1, 20—	$39,000	
Additional investment during the year	6,000	
Total		$45,000
Net loss for the year	$ 5,600	
Withdrawals	9,500	
Decrease in owner's equity		15,100
Allan Johnson, capital, December 31, 20—		$29,900

Balance Sheet

The balance sheet in Exhibit 5 was expanded by adding subsections for current assets, property, plant, and equipment, and current liabilities. Such a balance sheet is a *classified* balance sheet. In the following paragraphs, we describe some of the sections and subsections that may be used in a balance sheet. We will introduce additional sections in later chapters.

Assets

Assets are commonly divided into classes for presentation on the balance sheet. Two of these classes are (1) current assets and (2) property, plant, and equipment.

Two common classes of assets are current assets and property, plant, and equipment.

Current Assets. Cash and other assets that are expected to be converted to cash or sold or used up usually within one year or less, through the normal operations of the business, are called **current assets**. In addition to cash, the current assets usually owned by a service business are notes receivable, accounts receivable, supplies, and other prepaid expenses.

Notes receivable are amounts customers owe. They are written promises to pay the amount of the note and possibly interest at an agreed rate. Accounts receivable are also amounts customers owe, but they are less formal than notes and do not provide for interest. Accounts receivable normally result from providing services or selling merchandise on account. Notes receivable and accounts receivable are current assets because they will usually be converted to cash within one year or less.

Business on Stage

The operations of a manufacturing business involve the purchase of raw materials (purchasing activity), the conversion of the raw materials into a product through the use of labor and machinery (production activity), the sale and distribution of the products to customers (sales activity), and the receipt of cash from customers (collection activity). This overall process is referred to as the *operating cycle*. Thus, the operating cycle begins with spending cash and it ends with receiving cash from customers. The operating cycle for a manufacturing business is shown below.

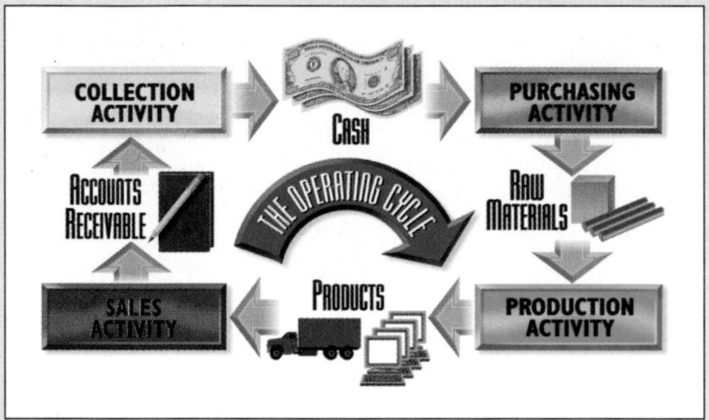

Operating cycles differ, depending upon the nature of the business and its operations. For example, the operating cycles for tobacco, distillery, and lumber industries are much longer than the operating cycles of the automobile, consumer electronics, and home furnishings industries. Likewise, the operating cycles for retailers are normally shorter than for manufacturers because retailers purchase goods in a form ready for sale to the customer. Of course, some retailers will have shorter operating cycles than others because of the nature of their products. For example, a jewelry store or an automobile dealer normally has a longer operating cycle than a consumer electronics store or a grocery store.

Businesses with longer operating cycles normally have higher profit margins on their products than businesses with shorter operating cycles. For example, it is not unusual for jewelry stores to price their jewelry at 30%–50% above cost. In contrast, grocery stores operate on very small profit margins, often below 5%. Grocery stores make up the difference by selling their products more quickly. ■

Property, Plant, and Equipment. The property, plant, and equipment section may also be described as **fixed assets** or **plant assets**. These assets include equipment, machinery, buildings, and land. With the exception of land, as we discussed in Chapter 3, fixed assets depreciate over a period of time. The cost, accumulated depreciation, and book value of each major type of fixed asset is normally reported on the balance sheet or in accompanying notes.

Liabilities

Liabilities are the amounts the business owes to creditors. The two most common classes of liabilities are (1) current liabilities and (2) long-term liabilities.

Two common classes of liabilities are current liabilities and long-term liabilities.

Current Liabilities. Liabilities that will be due within a short time (usually one year or less) and that are to be paid out of current assets are called **current liabilities**. The most common liabilities in this group are notes payable and accounts payable. Other current liability accounts commonly found in the ledger are Wages Payable, Interest Payable, Taxes Payable, and Unearned Fees.

Long-Term Liabilities. Liabilities that will not be due for a long time (usually more than one year) are called **long-term liabilities**. If Computer King had long-term liabilities, they would be reported below the current liabilities. As long-term liabilities come due and are to be paid within one year, they are classified as current liabilities. If they are to be renewed rather than paid, they would continue to be classified as long-term. When an asset is pledged as security for a liability, the obligation may be called a *mortgage note payable* or a *mortgage payable.*

Owner's Equity

The owner's right to the assets of the business is presented on the balance sheet below the liabilities section. The owner's equity is added to the total liabilities, and this total must be equal to the total assets.

Adjusting and Closing Entries

OBJECTIVE 3

Prepare the adjusting and closing entries from a work sheet.

As we discussed in Chapter 3, the adjusting entries are recorded in the journal at the end of the accounting period. If a work sheet has been prepared, the data for these entries are in the Adjustments columns. For Computer King, the adjusting entries prepared from the work sheet are shown in Exhibit 6.

EXHIBIT 6
Adjusting Entries for Computer King

JOURNAL **PAGE 5**

Date		Description	Post. Ref.	Debit	Credit
		Adjusting Entries			
1999 Dec.	31	Supplies Expense	55	1 2 4 0 00	
		Supplies	14		1 2 4 0 00
	31	Insurance Expense	56	1 0 0 00	
		Prepaid Insurance	15		1 0 0 00
	31	Unearned Rent	23	1 2 0 00	
		Rent Revenue	42		1 2 0 00
	31	Wages Expense	51	2 5 0 00	
		Wages Payable	22		2 5 0 00
	31	Accounts Receivable	12	5 0 0 00	
		Fees Earned	41		5 0 0 00
	31	Depreciation Expense	53	5 0 00	
		Accumulated Depreciation—			
		Office Equipment	19		5 0 00

After the adjusting entries have been posted to Computer King's ledger, shown in Exhibit 10, the ledger is in agreement with the data reported on the financial statements. The balances of the accounts reported on the balance sheet are carried forward from year to year. Because they are relatively permanent, these accounts are called **real accounts**. The balances of the accounts reported on the income statement are *not* carried forward from year to year. Likewise, the balance of the owner's withdrawal account, which is reported on the statement of owner's equity, is not carried forward. Because these accounts report amounts for only one period, they are called **temporary accounts** or **nominal accounts**.

To report amounts for only one period, temporary accounts should have zero balances at the beginning of a period. How are these balances converted to zero? The revenue and expense account balances are transferred to an account called **Income Summary**. The balance of Income Summary is then transferred to the owner's capital account. The balance of the owner's drawing account is also transferred to the owner's capital account. The entries that transfer these balances are called **closing entries**. The transfer process is called the **closing process**. Exhibit 7 is a diagram of this process.

Closing entries transfer the balances of temporary accounts to the owner's capital account.

EXHIBIT 7
The Closing Process

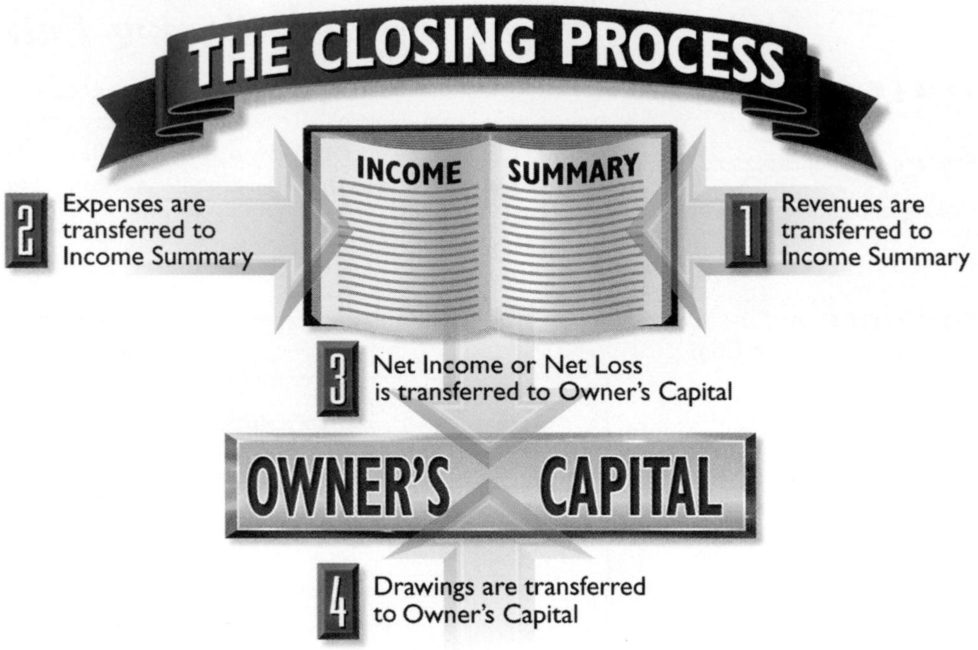
THE CLOSING PROCESS
INCOME SUMMARY
2 Expenses are transferred to Income Summary
1 Revenues are transferred to Income Summary
3 Net Income or Net Loss is transferred to Owner's Capital
OWNER'S CAPITAL
4 Drawings are transferred to Owner's Capital

The income summary account does *not* appear on the financial statements.

You should note that Income Summary is used only at the end of the period. At the beginning of the closing process, Income Summary has no balance. During the closing process, Income Summary will be debited and credited for various amounts. At the end of the closing process, Income Summary will again have no balance. Because Income Summary has the effect of clearing the revenue and expense accounts of their balances, it is sometimes called a **clearing account**. Other titles used for this account include Revenue and Expense Summary, Profit and Loss Summary, and Income and Expense Summary.

It is possible to close the temporary revenue and expense accounts without using a clearing account such as Income Summary. In this case, the balances of the revenue and expense accounts are closed directly to the owner's capital account. This process is automatic in a computerized accounting system. In a manual system, the use of an income summary account aids in detecting and correcting errors.

Journalizing and Posting Closing Entries

Four closing entries are required at the end of an accounting period, as outlined in Exhibit 7. The account titles and balances needed in preparing these entries may be obtained from the work sheet, the income statement and the statement of owner's equity, or the ledger. If a work sheet is used, the data for the first two entries appear in the Income Statement columns. The amount for the third entry is the net income or net loss appearing at the bottom of the work sheet. The amount for the fourth entry is the drawing account balance that appears in the Balance Sheet Debit column of the work sheet.

A flowchart of the closing entries for Computer King is shown in Exhibit 8. The balances in the accounts are those shown in the Adjusted Trial Balance columns of the work sheet in Exhibit 2.

The closing entries for Computer King are shown in Exhibit 9. After the closing entries have been posted to the ledger, as shown in Exhibit 10, the balance in the capital account will agree with the amount reported on the statement of owner's equity and the balance sheet. In addition, the revenue, expense, and drawing accounts will have zero balances.

EXHIBIT 8 Flowchart of Closing Entries for Computer King

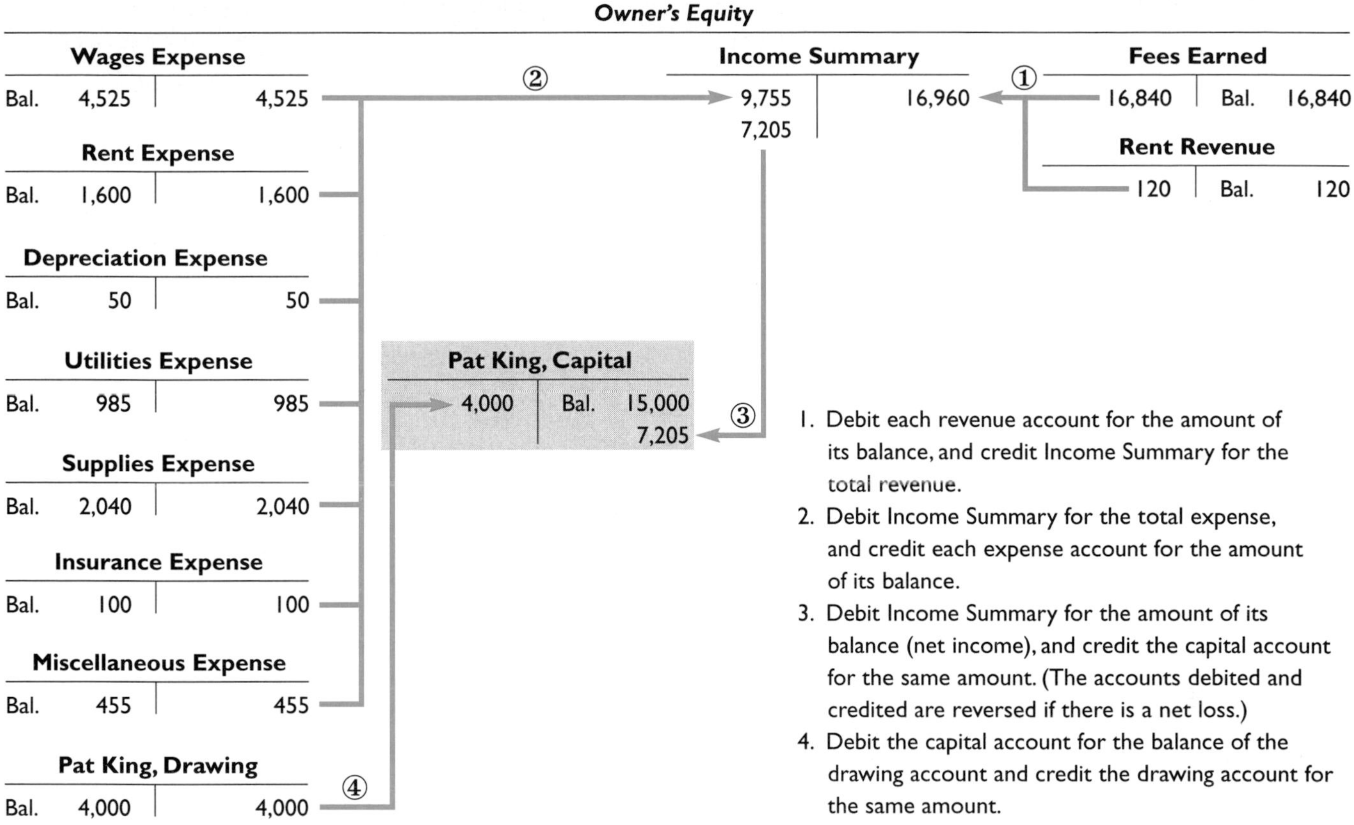

1. Debit each revenue account for the amount of its balance, and credit Income Summary for the total revenue.
2. Debit Income Summary for the total expense, and credit each expense account for the amount of its balance.
3. Debit Income Summary for the amount of its balance (net income), and credit the capital account for the same amount. (The accounts debited and credited are reversed if there is a net loss.)
4. Debit the capital account for the balance of the drawing account and credit the drawing account for the same amount.

EXHIBIT 9
Closing Entries for Computer King

JOURNAL — **PAGE 6**

Date		Description	Post. Ref.	Debit	Credit
		Closing Entries			
1999 Dec.	31	Fees Earned	41	16840 00	
		Rent Revenue	42	120 00	
		Income Summary	33		16960 00
	31	Income Summary	33	9755 00	
		Wages Expense	51		4525 00
		Rent Expense	52		1600 00
		Depreciation Expense	53		50 00
		Utilities Expense	54		985 00
		Supplies Expense	55		2040 00
		Insurance Expense	56		100 00
		Miscellaneous Expense	59		455 00
	31	Income Summary	33	7205 00	
		Pat King, Capital	31		7205 00
	31	Pat King, Capital	31	4000 00	
		Pat King, Drawing	32		4000 00

EXHIBIT 10
Ledger for Computer King

LEDGER

ACCOUNT *Cash* **ACCOUNT NO.** *11*

Date		Item	Post. Ref.	Debit	Credit	Balance Debit	Balance Credit
1999 Nov.	1		1	15,000.00		15,000.00	
	5		1		10,000.00	5,000.00	
	18		1	7,500.00		12,500.00	
	30		1		3,650.00	8,850.00	
	30		1		950.00	7,900.00	
	30		2		2,000.00	5,900.00	
Dec.	1		2		2,400.00	3,500.00	
	1		2		800.00	2,700.00	
	1		2	360.00		3,060.00	
	6		2		180.00	2,880.00	
	11		2		400.00	2,480.00	
	13		3		950.00	1,530.00	
	16		3	3,100.00		4,630.00	
	20		3		900.00	3,730.00	
	21		3	650.00		4,380.00	
	23		3		1,450.00	2,930.00	
	27		3		1,200.00	1,730.00	
	31		3		310.00	1,420.00	
	31		4		225.00	1,195.00	
	31		4	2,870.00		4,065.00	
	31		4		2,000.00	2,065.00	

ACCOUNT *Accounts Receivable* **ACCOUNT NO.** *12*

Date		Item	Post. Ref.	Debit	Credit	Balance Debit	Balance Credit
1999 Dec.	16		3	1,750.00		1,750.00	
	21		3		650.00	1,100.00	
	31		4	1,120.00		2,220.00	
	31	Adjusting	5	500.00		2,720.00	

ACCOUNT *Supplies* **ACCOUNT NO.** *14*

Date		Item	Post. Ref.	Debit	Credit	Balance Debit	Balance Credit
1999 Nov.	10		1	1,350.00		1,350.00	
	30		1		800.00	550.00	
Dec.	23		3	1,450.00		2,000.00	
	31	Adjusting	5		1,240.00	760.00	

ACCOUNT *Prepaid Insurance* **ACCOUNT NO.** *15*

Date		Item	Post. Ref.	Debit	Credit	Balance Debit	Balance Credit
1999 Dec.	1		2	2,400.00		2,400.00	
	31	Adjusting	5		100.00	2,300.00	

EXHIBIT 10
(continued)

ACCOUNT *Land* — **ACCOUNT NO.** *17*

Date		Item	Post. Ref.	Debit	Credit	Balance Debit	Balance Credit
1999 Nov.	5		1	10000 00		10000 00	

ACCOUNT *Office Equipment* — **ACCOUNT NO.** *18*

Date		Item	Post. Ref.	Debit	Credit	Balance Debit	Balance Credit
1999 Dec.	4		2	1800 00		1800 00	

ACCOUNT *Accumulated Depreciation* — **ACCOUNT NO.** *19*

Date		Item	Post. Ref.	Debit	Credit	Balance Debit	Balance Credit
1999 Dec.	31	Adjusting	5		50 00		50 00

ACCOUNT *Accounts Payable* — **ACCOUNT NO.** *21*

Date		Item	Post. Ref.	Debit	Credit	Balance Debit	Balance Credit
1999 Nov.	10		1		1350 00		1350 00
	30		1	950 00			400 00
Dec.	4		2		1800 00		2200 00
	11		2	400 00			1800 00
	20		3	900 00			900 00

ACCOUNT *Wages Payable* — **ACCOUNT NO.** *22*

Date		Item	Post. Ref.	Debit	Credit	Balance Debit	Balance Credit
1999 Dec.	31	Adjusting	5		250 00		250 00

ACCOUNT *Unearned Rent* — **ACCOUNT NO.** *23*

Date		Item	Post. Ref.	Debit	Credit	Balance Debit	Balance Credit
1999 Dec.	1		2		360 00		360 00
	31	Adjusting	5	120 00			240 00

ACCOUNT *Pat King, Capital* — **ACCOUNT NO.** *31*

Date		Item	Post. Ref.	Debit	Credit	Balance Debit	Balance Credit
1999 Nov.	1		1		15000 00		15000 00
Dec.	31	Closing	6		7205 00		22205 00
	31	Closing	6	4000 00			18205 00

EXHIBIT 10
(continued)

ACCOUNT *Pat King, Drawing* **ACCOUNT NO.** *32*

Date		Item	Post. Ref.	Debit	Credit	Balance Debit	Balance Credit
1999 Nov.	30		2	2000 00		2000 00	
Dec.	31		4	2000 00		4000 00	
	31	Closing	6		4000 00	—	—

ACCOUNT *Income Summary* **ACCOUNT NO.** *33*

Date		Item	Post. Ref.	Debit	Credit	Balance Debit	Balance Credit
1999 Dec.	31	Closing	6		16960 00		16960 00
	31	Closing	6	9755 00			7205 00
	31	Closing	6	7205 00		—	—

ACCOUNT *Fees Earned* **ACCOUNT NO.** *41*

Date		Item	Post. Ref.	Debit	Credit	Balance Debit	Balance Credit
1999 Nov.	18		1		7500 00		7500 00
Dec.	16		3		3100 00		10600 00
	16		3		1750 00		12350 00
	31		4		2870 00		15220 00
	31		4		1120 00		16340 00
	31	Adjusting	5		500 00		16840 00
	31	Closing	6	16840 00		—	—

ACCOUNT *Rent Revenue* **ACCOUNT NO.** *42*

Date		Item	Post. Ref.	Debit	Credit	Balance Debit	Balance Credit
1999 Dec.	31	Adjusting	5		120 00		120 00
	31	Closing	6	120 00		—	—

ACCOUNT *Wages Expense* **ACCOUNT NO.** *51*

Date		Item	Post. Ref.	Debit	Credit	Balance Debit	Balance Credit
1999 Nov.	30		1	2125 00		2125 00	
Dec.	13		3	950 00		3075 00	
	27		3	1200 00		4275 00	
	31	Adjusting	5	250 00		4525 00	
	31	Closing	6		4525 00	—	—

EXHIBIT 10
(concluded)

ACCOUNT *Rent Expense* — **ACCOUNT NO.** *52*

Date		Item	Post. Ref.	Debit	Credit	Balance Debit	Balance Credit
1999 Nov.	30		1	800 00		800 00	
Dec.	1		2	800 00		1 600 00	
	31	Closing	6		1 600 00	—	—

ACCOUNT *Depreciation Expense* — **ACCOUNT NO.** *53*

Date		Item	Post. Ref.	Debit	Credit	Balance Debit	Balance Credit
1999 Dec.	31	Adjusting	5	50 00		50 00	
	31	Closing	6		50 00	—	—

ACCOUNT *Utilities Expense* — **ACCOUNT NO.** *54*

Date		Item	Post. Ref.	Debit	Credit	Balance Debit	Balance Credit
1999 Nov.	30		1	450 00		450 00	
Dec.	31		3	310 00		760 00	
	31		4	225 00		985 00	
	31	Closing	6		985 00	—	—

ACCOUNT *Supplies Expense* — **ACCOUNT NO.** *55*

Date		Item	Post. Ref.	Debit	Credit	Balance Debit	Balance Credit
1999 Nov.	30		1	800 00		800 00	
Dec.	31	Adjusting	5	1 240 00		2 040 00	
	31	Closing	6		2 040 00	—	—

ACCOUNT *Insurance Expense* — **ACCOUNT NO.** *56*

Date		Item	Post. Ref.	Debit	Credit	Balance Debit	Balance Credit
1999 Dec.	31	Adjusting	5	100 00		100 00	
	31	Closing	6		100 00	—	—

ACCOUNT *Miscellaneous Expense* — **ACCOUNT NO.** *59*

Date		Item	Post. Ref.	Debit	Credit	Balance Debit	Balance Credit
1999 Nov.	30		1	275 00		275 00	
Dec.	6		2	180 00		455 00	
	31	Closing	6		455 00	—	—

After the entry to close an account has been posted, a line should be inserted in both balance columns opposite the final entry. The next period's transactions for the revenue, expense, and drawing accounts will be posted directly below the closing entry.

Post-Closing Trial Balance

The last accounting procedure for a period is to prepare a trial balance after the closing entries have been posted. The purpose of the **post-closing** (after closing) **trial balance** is to make sure that the ledger is in balance at the beginning of the next period. The accounts and amounts should agree exactly with the accounts and amounts listed on the balance sheet at the end of the period. The post-closing trial balance for Computer King is shown in Exhibit 11.

Q&A

If total revenues are $600,000, total expenses are $525,000, and drawing is $50,000, what is the balance of the income summary account that is closed to the owner's capital?

$75,000 ($600,000 − $525,000). The drawing account balance is closed directly to the owner's capital, rather than to Income Summary.

EXHIBIT 11
Post-Closing Trial Balance

Computer King
Post-Closing Trial Balance
December 31, 1999

Cash	2065 00	
Accounts Receivable	2720 00	
Supplies	760 00	
Prepaid Insurance	2300 00	
Land	10000 00	
Office Equipment	1800 00	
Accumulated Depreciation		50 00
Accounts Payable		900 00
Wages Payable		250 00
Unearned Rent		240 00
Pat King, Capital		18205 00
	19645 00	19645 00

Instead of preparing a formal post-closing trial balance, it is possible to list the accounts directly from the ledger, using a computer. The computer printout, in effect, becomes the post-closing trial balance. Without such a printout, there is no efficient means of determining the cause of unequal trial balance totals.

Fiscal Year

OBJECTIVE 4

Explain what is meant by the fiscal year and the natural business year.

In the Computer King illustration, operations began on November 1 and the accounting period was for two months, November and December. A proprietorship is required by the federal income tax law, except in rare cases, to maintain the same accounting period as its owner. Since Pat King maintains a calendar-year accounting period for tax purposes, Computer King must also close its accounts on December 31, 1999. In future years, the financial statements for Computer King will be prepared for twelve months ending on December 31 each year.

Circuit City's 1997 fiscal year-end was February 28, 1997. This should not surprise you, since you would expect that Circuit City experiences a high volume of sales around the December holiday season, followed by relatively low sales in January and February.

During its 1997 fiscal year, Circuit City reported the following net sales and operating revenues:

Net Sales and Operating Revenue (in thousands of dollars)

First quarter	$1,615,266
Second quarter	1,767,043
Third quarter	1,863,947
Fourth quarter	2,417,555

The annual accounting period adopted by a business is known as its **fiscal year**. Fiscal years begin with the first day of the month selected and end on the last day of the following twelfth month. The period most commonly used is the calendar year. Other periods are not unusual, especially for businesses organized as corporations. For example, a corporation may adopt a fiscal year that ends when business activities have reached the lowest point in its annual operating cycle. Such a fiscal year is called the **natural business year**. At the low point in its operating cycle, a business has more time to analyze the results of operations and to prepare financial statements.

Because companies with fiscal years often have highly seasonal operations, investors and others should be careful in interpreting partial-year reports for such companies. That is, you should expect the results of operations for these companies to vary significantly throughout the fiscal year.

The 1996 edition of *Accounting Trends & Techniques,* published by the American Institute of Certified Public Accountants, reported the following results of a survey concerning the month of the fiscal year-end of 600 industrial and merchandising companies:

Percentage of Companies with Fiscal Years Ending in the Month of:

January	4%	July	2%
February	2	August	2
March	2	September	6
April	1	October	4
May	3	November	3
June	10	December	61

The financial history of a business may be shown by a series of balance sheets and income statements for several fiscal years. If the life of a business is expressed by a line moving from left to right, the series of balance sheets and income statements may be graphed as follows:

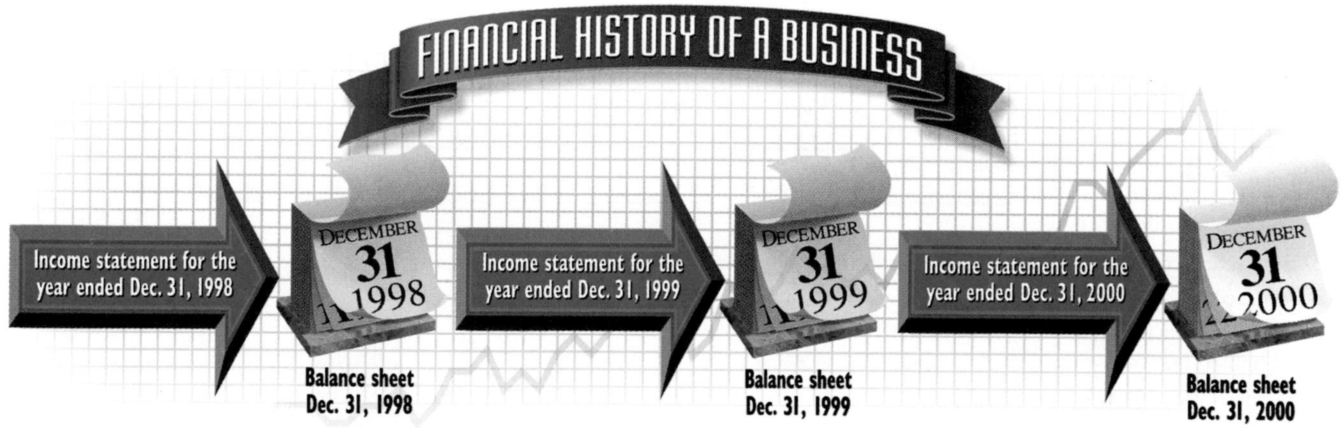

You may think of the income statements, balance sheets, and financial history of a business as similar to the record of a college football team. The final score of each football game is similar to the net income reported on the income statement of a business. The team's season record after each game is similar to the balance sheet. At the end of the season, the final record of the team measures its success or failure. Likewise, at the end of a life of a business, its final balance sheet is a measure of its financial success or failure.

OBJECTIVE 5

Review the seven basic steps of the accounting cycle.

Accounting Cycle

The process that begins with analyzing and journalizing transactions and ends with the post-closing trial balance is called the **accounting cycle**. The most important output of the accounting cycle is the financial statements.

Understanding the steps of the accounting cycle is essential for further study of accounting. The basic steps of the cycle are shown, by number, in the flowchart in Exhibit 12.

REAL WORLD In a computerized accounting system, the software automatically records and posts transactions. The ledger and supporting records are maintained in computerized master files. In addition, a work sheet is normally not prepared.

EXHIBIT 12 Accounting Cycle

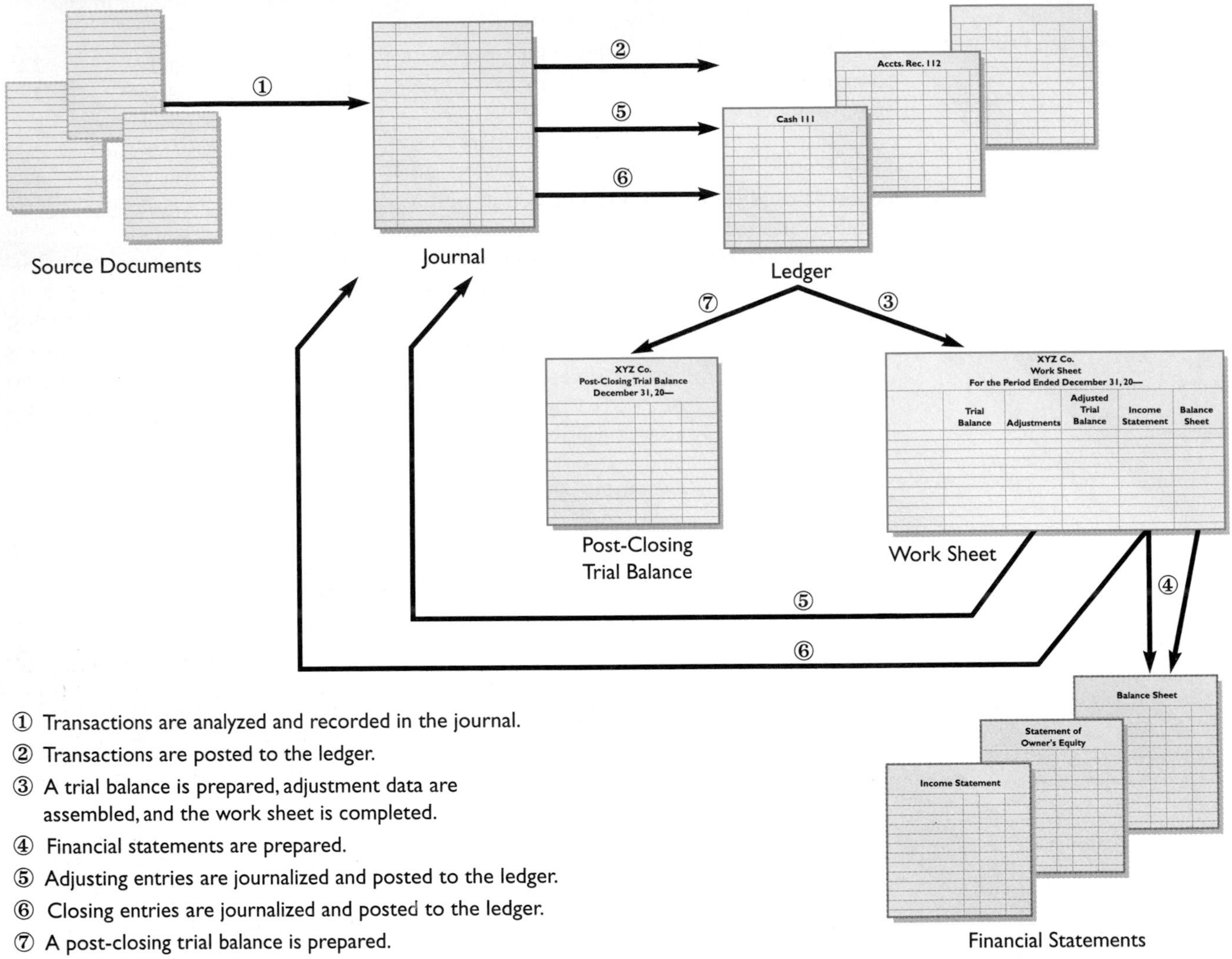

① Transactions are analyzed and recorded in the journal.
② Transactions are posted to the ledger.
③ A trial balance is prepared, adjustment data are assembled, and the work sheet is completed.
④ Financial statements are prepared.
⑤ Adjusting entries are journalized and posted to the ledger.
⑥ Closing entries are journalized and posted to the ledger.
⑦ A post-closing trial balance is prepared.

FINANCIAL ANALYSIS AND INTERPRETATION

OBJECTIVE 6

Analyze and interpret the financial solvency of a business by computing the working capital and the current ratio.

The ability of a business to pays its debts is called **solvency**. Two financial measures for evaluating a business's short-term solvency are working capital and the current ratio. **Working capital** is the excess of the current assets of a business over its current liabilities, as shown below.

Working capital = Current assets − Current liabilities

An excess of the current assets over the current liabilities implies that the business is able to pay its current liabilities. If the current liabilities are greater than the current assets, the business may not be able to pay its debts and continue in business.

To illustrate, Computer King's working capital at the end of 1999 is $6,455, as computed below. This amount of working capital implies that Computer King can pay its current liabilities.

Working capital = Current assets − Current liabilities
Working capital = $7,845 − $1,390
Working capital = $6,455

The **current ratio** is another means of expressing the relationship between current assets and current liabilities. The current ratio is computed by dividing current assets by current liabilities, as shown below.

Current ratio = Current assets/Current liabilities

To illustrate, the current ratio for Computer King at the end of 1999 is 5.6, computed as follows:

Current ratio = Current assets/Current liabilities
Current ratio = $7,845/$1,390 = 5.6

The current ratio is useful in making comparisons across companies and with industry averages. To illustrate, assume that as of December 31, 1999, the working capital of a company that competes with Computer King is much greater than $6,455, but its current ratio is only 1.3. Considering these facts alone, Computer King is in a more favorable position to obtain short-term credit, even though the competing company has a greater amount of working capital.

ENCORE

Financial statements prepared under accounting practices in other countries often differ from those prepared under generally accepted accounting principles found in the United States. This is to be expected, since cultures and market structures differ from country to country.

To illustrate, **Bayerische Motoren Werke Aktiengesellschaft** (better known as **BMW**!) prepares its financial statements under German law and German accounting principles. In doing so, BMW's balance sheet reports fixed assets first, followed by current assets. It also reports owner's equity before the liabilities. In contrast, balance sheets prepared under U.S. accounting principles report current assets followed by fixed assets and current liabilities followed by long-term liabilities and owner's equity. The U.S. form of balance sheet is organized to emphasize creditor interpretation and analysis. For example, current assets and current liabilities are presented first, so that working capital and the current ratio can be easily computed. Likewise, to emphasize their importance, liabilities are reported before owner's equity.

Regardless of these differences, the basic principles underlying the accounting equation and the double-entry accounting system are the same in Germany and the United States.

Even though differences in recording and reporting exist, the accounting equation holds true: the total assets still equal the total liabilities and owner's equity. ■

APPENDIX: REVERSING ENTRIES

Some of the adjusting entries recorded at the end of an accounting period have an important effect on otherwise routine transactions that occur in the following period. A typical example is accrued wages owed to employees at the end of a period. If there has been an adjusting entry for accrued wages expense, the first payment of wages in the following period will include the accrual. In the absence of some special provision, Wages Payable must be debited for the amount owed for the earlier period, and Wages Expense must be debited for the portion of the payroll that represents expense for the later period. However, an *optional* entry—the reversing entry—may be used to simplify the analysis and recording of this first payroll entry in a period. As the term implies, a **reversing entry** is the exact opposite of the adjusting entry to which it relates. The amounts and accounts are the same as the adjusting entry; the debits and credits are reversed.

COMPUTER KING

We will illustrate the use of reversing entries by using the data for Computer King's accrued wages, which were presented in Chapter 3. These data are summarized in Exhibit 13.

EXHIBIT 13
Accrued Wages

1. Wages are paid on the second and fourth Fridays for the two-week periods ending on those Fridays.
2. The wages accrued for Monday and Tuesday, December 30 and 31, are $250.
3. Wages paid on Friday, January 10, total $1,275.

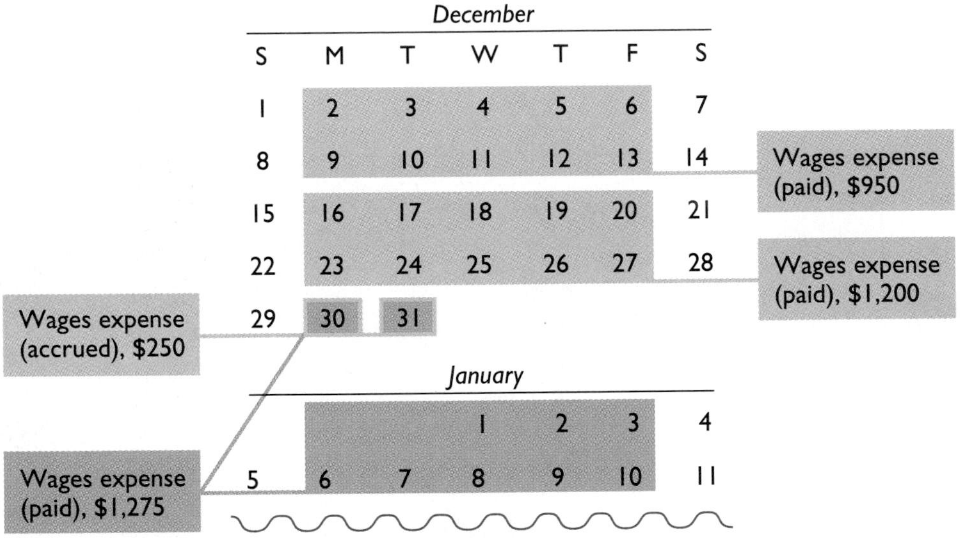

The adjusting entry for the accrued wages of December 30 and 31 is as follows:

Dec.	31	Wages Expense	51	250 00	
		Wages Payable	22		250 00

After the adjusting entry has been posted, Wages Expense will have a debit balance of $4,525 ($4,275 + $250), and Wages Payable will have a credit balance of $250. After the closing process is completed, Wages Expense will have a zero balance and will be ready for entries in the next period. Wages Payable, on the other hand, has a balance of $250. Without a reversing entry, it is necessary to record the $1,275 payroll on January 10 as follows:

Date		Description	Post. Ref.	Debit	Credit
2000 Jan.	10	Wages Payable	22	250 00	
		Wages Expense	51	1 025 00	
		Cash	11		1 275 00

The employee who records the January 10th entry must refer to the prior period's adjusting entry to determine the amount of the debits to Wages Payable and Wages Expense. Because the January 10th payroll is not recorded in the usual manner, there is a greater chance that an error may occur. This chance of error is reduced by recording a reversing entry as of the first day of the fiscal period. For example, the reversing entry for the accrued wages expense is as follows:

Date		Description	Post. Ref.	Debit	Credit
2000 Jan.	1	Wages Payable	22	250 00	
		Wages Expense	51		250 00

The reversing entry transfers the $250 liability from Wages Payable to the credit side of Wages Expense. The nature of the $250 is unchanged—it is still a liability. When the payroll is paid on January 10, the following entry is recorded:

Date		Description	Post. Ref.	Debit	Credit
Jan.	10	Wages Expense	51	1 275 00	
		Cash	11		1 275 00

After this entry is posted, Wages Expense has a debit balance of $1,025. This amount is the wages expense for the period January 1–10. The sequence of entries, including adjusting, closing, and reversing entries, is illustrated in the following accounts:

ACCOUNT ***Wages Payable*** **ACCOUNT NO. *22***

Date		Item	Post. Ref.	Debit	Credit	Balance Debit	Balance Credit
1999 Dec.	31	Adjusting	5		250 00		250 00
2000 Jan.	1	Reversing	7	250 00		—	—

ACCOUNT ***Wages Expense*** **ACCOUNT NO. *51***

Date		Item	Post. Ref.	Debit	Credit	Balance Debit	Balance Credit
1999 Nov.	30		1	2 125 00		2 125 00	
Dec.	13		3	950 00		3 075 00	
	27		3	1 200 00		4 275 00	
	31	Adjusting	5	250 00		4 525 00	
	31	Closing	6		4 525 00	—	—
2000 Jan.	1	Reversing	7		250 00		250 00
	10		7	1 275 00		1 025 00	

In addition to accrued expenses (accrued liabilities), reversing entries may be journalized for accrued revenues (accrued assets). For example, the following reversing entry could be recorded for Computer King's accrued fees earned:

Jan.	1	Fees Earned	41	500 00	
		Accounts Receivable	12		500 00

Reversing entries may also be journalized for prepaid expenses that are initially recorded as expenses and unearned revenues that are initially recorded as revenues. These situations are described and illustrated in Appendix C.

As we mentioned, the use of reversing entries is optional. However, with the increased use of computerized accounting systems, data entry personnel may be inputting routine accounting entries. In such an environment, reversing entries may be useful, since these individuals may not recognize the impact of adjusting entries on the related transactions in the following period.

KEY POINTS

1 Prepare a work sheet.

The work sheet is prepared by first entering a trial balance in the Trial Balance columns. The adjustments are then entered in the Adjustments Debit and Credit columns. The Trial Balance amounts plus or minus the adjustments are extended to the Adjusted Trial Balance columns. The work sheet is completed by extending the Adjusted Trial Balance amounts of assets, liabilities, owner's capital, and drawing to the Balance Sheet columns. The Adjusted Trial Balance amounts of revenues and expenses are extended to the Income Statement columns. The net income (or net loss) for the period is entered on the work sheet in the Income Statement Debit (or Credit) column and the Balance Sheet Credit (or Debit) column. Each of the four statement columns is then totaled.

2 Prepare financial statements from a work sheet.

The income statement is normally prepared directly from the work sheet. On the income statement, the expenses are normally presented in the order of size, from largest to smallest.

The basic form of the statement of owner's equity is prepared by listing the beginning balance of owner's equity, adding investments in the business and net income during the period, and deducting the owner's withdrawals. The amount listed on the work sheet as capital does not always represent the account balance at the beginning of the accounting period. The proprietor may have invested additional assets in the business during the period. Hence, for the beginning balance and any additional investments, it is necessary to refer to the capital account.

Various sections and subsections are often used in preparing a balance sheet. Two common classes of assets are current assets and fixed assets. Cash and other assets that are normally expected to be converted to cash or sold or used up within one year or less are called current assets. Property, plant, and equipment may also be called fixed assets or plant assets. The cost, accumulated depreciation, and book value of each major type of fixed asset are normally reported on the balance sheet.

Two common classes of liabilities are current liabilities and long-term liabilities. Liabilities that will be due within a short time (usually one year or less) and that are to be paid out of current assets are called current liabilities. Liabilities that will not be due for a long time (usually more than one year) are called long-term liabilities.

The owner's claim against the assets is presented below the liabilities section and added to the total liabilities. The total liabilities and total owner's equity must equal the total assets.

3 Prepare the adjusting and closing entries from a work sheet.

The data for journalizing the adjusting entries are in the Adjustments columns of the work sheet. The four entries required in closing the temporary accounts are:

1. Debit each revenue account for the amount of its balance, and credit Income Summary for the total revenue.
2. Debit Income Summary for the total expense, and credit each expense account for the amount of its balance.
3. Debit Income Summary for the amount of its balance (net income), and credit the capital account for the same amount. (Debit and credit are reversed if there is a net loss.)

4. Debit the capital account for the balance of the drawing account and credit the drawing account for the same amount.

After the closing entries have been posted to the ledger, the balance in the capital account will agree with the amount reported on the statement of owner's equity and balance sheet. In addition, the revenue, expense, and drawing accounts will have zero balances.

The last step of the accounting cycle is to prepare a post-closing trial balance. The purpose of the post-closing trial balance is to make sure that the ledger is in balance at the beginning of the next period.

4 Explain what is meant by the fiscal year and the natural business year.

The annual accounting period adopted by a business is known as its fiscal year. A corporation may adopt a fiscal year that ends when business activities have reached the lowest point in its annual operating cycle. Such a fiscal year is called the natural business year.

5 Review the seven basic steps of the accounting cycle.

The basic steps of the accounting cycle are:

1. Transactions are analyzed and recorded in a journal.
2. Transactions are posted to the ledger.
3. A trial balance is prepared, adjustment data are assembled, and the work sheet is completed.
4. Financial statements are prepared.
5. Adjusting entries are journalized and posted to the ledger.
6. Closing entries are journalized and posted to the ledger.
7. A post-closing trial balance is prepared.

6 Analyze and interpret the financial solvency of a business by computing the working capital and the current ratio.

The ability of a business to pay its debts is called solvency. Two financial measures for evaluating a business's short-term solvency are working capital and the current ratio. Working capital is the excess of the current assets of a business over its current liabilities. The current ratio is computed by dividing current assets by current liabilities.

ILLUSTRATIVE PROBLEM

Three years ago, T. Roderick organized Harbor Realty. At July 31, 2000, the end of the current fiscal year, the trial balance of Harbor Realty is as follows:

Harbor Realty
Trial Balance
July 31, 2000

Cash	3,425.00	
Accounts Receivable	7,000.00	
Supplies	1,270.00	
Prepaid Insurance	620.00	
Office Equipment	51,650.00	
Accumulated Depreciation		9,700.00
Accounts Payable		925.00
Unearned Fees		1,250.00
T. Roderick, Capital		29,000.00
T. Roderick, Drawing	5,200.00	
Fees Earned		59,125.00
Wages Expense	22,415.00	
Rent Expense	4,200.00	
Utilities Expense	2,715.00	
Miscellaneous Expense	1,505.00	
	100,000.00	100,000.00

The data needed to determine year-end adjustments are as follows:

a. Supplies on hand at July 31, 2000, are $380.
b. Insurance premiums expired during the year are $315.
c. Depreciation of equipment during the year is $4,950.
d. Wages accrued but not paid at July 31, 2000, are $440.
e. Accrued fees earned but not recorded at July 31, 2000, are $1,000.
f. Unearned fees on July 31, 2000, are $750.

Instructions

1. Enter the trial balance on a ten-column work sheet and complete the work sheet.
2. Prepare an income statement, a statement of owner's equity (no additional investments were made during the year), and a balance sheet.
3. On the basis of the data in the work sheet, journalize the closing entries.

Solution

1.

Harbor Realty
Work Sheet
For the Year Ended July 31, 2000

		Trial Balance		Adjustments		Adjusted Trial Balance		Income Statement		Balance Sheet		
	Account Title	Dr.	Cr.	Dr.	Cr.	Dr.	Cr.	Dr.	Cr.	Dr.	Cr.	
1	Cash	3425				3425				3425		1
2	Accounts Receivable	7000		(e)1000		8000				8000		2
3	Supplies	1270			(a) 890	380				380		3
4	Prepaid Insurance	620			(b) 315	305				305		4
5	Office Equipment	51650				51650				51650		5
6	Accum. Depreciation		9700		(c)4950		14650				14650	6
7	Accounts Payable		925				925				925	7
8	Unearned Fees		1250	(f) 500			750				750	8
9	T. Roderick, Capital		29000				29000				29000	9
10	T. Roderick, Drawing	5200				5200				5200		10
11	Fees Earned		59125		(e)1000		60625		60625			11
12					(f) 500							12
13	Wages Expense	22415		(d) 440		22855		22855				13
14	Rent Expense	4200				4200		4200				14
15	Utilities Expense	2715				2715		2715				15
16	Miscellaneous Expense	1505				1505		1505				16
17		100000	100000									17
18	Supplies Expense			(a) 890		890		890				18
19	Insurance Expense			(b) 315		315		315				19
20	Depreciation Expense			(c)4950		4950		4950				20
21	Wages Payable				(d) 440		440				440	21
22				8095	8095	106390	106390	37430	60625	68960	45765	22
23	Net income							23195			23195	23
24								60625	60625	68960	68960	24

2.

Harbor Realty
Income Statement
For the Year Ended July 31, 2000

Fees earned		$60,625.00
Operating expenses:		
Wages expense	$22,855.00	
Depreciation expense	4,950.00	
Rent expense	4,200.00	
Utilities expense	2,715.00	
Supplies expense	890.00	
Insurance expense	315.00	
Miscellaneous expense	1,505.00	
Total operating expenses		37,430.00
Net income		$23,195.00

Harbor Realty
Statement of Owner's Equity
For the Year Ended July 31, 2000

T. Roderick, capital, August 1, 1999		$29,000.00
Net income for the year	$23,195.00	
Less withdrawals	5,200.00	
Increase in owner's equity		17,995.00
T. Roderick, capital, July 31, 2000		$46,995.00

Harbor Realty
Balance Sheet
July 31, 2000

Assets			**Liabilities**		
Current assets:			Current liabilities:		
Cash	$ 3,425.00		Accounts payable	$925.00	
Accounts receivable	8,000.00		Unearned fees	750.00	
Supplies	380.00		Wages payable	440.00	
Prepaid insurance	305.00		Total liabilities		$ 2,115.00
Total current assets		$12,110.00			
Property, plant, and equipment:			**Owner's Equity**		
Office equipment	$51,650.00		T. Roderick, capital		46,995.00
Less accumulated depr.	14,650.00	37,000.00	Total liabilities and		
Total assets		$49,110.00	owner's equity		$49,110.00

3.

JOURNAL					PAGE
Date		**Description**	**Post. Ref.**	**Debit**	**Credit**
		Closing Entries			
2000 July	31	Fees Earned		60,625 00	
		Income Summary			60,625 00
	31	Income Summary		37,430 00	
		Wages Expense			22,855 00
		Rent Expense			4,200 00
		Utilities Expense			2,715 00
		Miscellaneous Expense			1,505 00
		Supplies Expense			890 00
		Insurance Expense			315 00
		Depreciation Expense			4,950 00
	31	Income Summary		23,195 00	
		T. Roderick, Capital			23,195 00
	31	T. Roderick, Capital		5,200 00	
		T. Roderick, Drawing			5,200 00

SELF-EXAMINATION QUESTIONS

Answers at End of Chapter

Matching

Match each of the following statements with its proper term. Some terms may not be used.

- **A.** accounting cycle
- **B.** adjusted trial balance
- **C.** adjusting entries
- **D.** closing entries
- **E.** current assets
- **F.** current liabilities
- **G.** current ratio
- **H.** fiscal year
- **I.** Income Summary
- **J.** long-term liabilities
- **K.** natural business year
- **L.** notes receivable
- **M.** owner's equity
- **N.** permanent assets
- **O.** post-closing trial balance

I 1. A working paper that accountants may use to summarize adjusting entries and the account balances for the financial statements.

E 2. Cash and other assets that are expected to be converted to cash or sold or used up, usually within one year or less, through the normal operations of the business.

L 3. A customer's written promise to pay an amount and possibly interest at an agreed rate.

F 4. Liabilities that will be due within a short time (usually one year or less) and that are to be paid out of current assets.

J 5. Liabilities that will not be due for usually more than one year.

I 6. An account to which the revenue and expense account balances are transferred at the end of a period.

O 7. The trial balance prepared after the closing entries have been posted.

H 8. The annual accounting period adopted by a business.

K 9. A fiscal year that ends when business activities have reached the lowest point in an annual operating cycle.

A 10. The process that begins with analyzing and journalizing transactions and ends with the post-closing trial balance.

P. **property, plant, and equipment**
Q. **real accounts**
R. **solvency**
S. **temporary accounts**
T. **work sheet**
U. **working capital**

R 11. The ability of a business to pays its debts.
U 12. The excess of the current assets of a business over its current liabilities.
G 13. A financial ratio that is computed by dividing current assets by current liabilities.
D 14. The entries that transfer the balances of the revenue, expense, and drawing accounts to the owner's capital account.
P 15. The section of the balance sheet that includes equipment, machinery, buildings, and land.
S 16. Accounts that report amounts for only one period.

Multiple Choice

1. Which of the following accounts in the Adjusted Trial Balance columns of the work sheet would be extended to the Balance Sheet columns?
   A. Utilities Expense
   B. Rent Revenue
   C. M. E. Jones, Drawing
   D. Miscellaneous Expense

2. Which of the following accounts would be classified as a current asset on the balance sheet?
   A. Office Equipment
   B. Land
   C. Accumulated Depreciation
   D. Accounts Receivable

3. Which of the following entries closes the owner's drawing account at the end of the period?
   A. Debit the drawing account, credit the income summary account.
   B. Debit the owner's capital account, credit the drawing account.
   C. Debit the income summary account, credit the drawing account.
   D. Debit the drawing account, credit the owner's capital account.

4. Which of the following accounts would not be closed to the income summary account at the end of a period?
   A. Fees Earned
   B. Wages Expense
   C. Rent Expense
   D. Accumulated Depreciation

5. Which of the following accounts would not be included in a post-closing trial balance?
   A. Cash
   B. Fees Earned
   C. Accumulated Depreciation
   D. J. C. Smith, Capital

CLASS DISCUSSION QUESTIONS

1. Is the work sheet a substitute for the financial statements? Discuss.
2. In the Income Statement columns of the work sheet, the Debit column total is greater than the Credit column total before the amount for the net income or net loss has been included. Would the income statement report a net income or a net loss? Explain.
3. In the Balance Sheet columns of the work sheet for Jones Co. for the current year, the Debit column total is $120,000 greater than the Credit column total before the amount for net income or net loss has been included. Would the income statement report a net income or a net loss? Explain.
4. Describe the nature of the assets that compose the following sections of a balance sheet: (a) current assets, (b) property, plant, and equipment.
5. What is the difference between a current liability and a long-term liability?
6. What types of accounts are referred to as temporary accounts?
7. Why are closing entries required at the end of an accounting period?
8. What is the difference between adjusting entries and closing entries?
9. Describe the four entries that close the temporary accounts.
10. What type of accounts are closed by transferring their balances (a) as a debit to Income Summary, (b) as a credit to Income Summary?
11. To what account is the income summary account closed?
12. To what account is the owner's drawing account closed?
13. What is the purpose of the post-closing trial balance?
14. What is the natural business year?

15. Why might a department store select a fiscal year ending January 31, rather than a fiscal year ending December 31?
16. The fiscal years for several well-known companies were as follows:

Company	Fiscal Year Ending
Kmart	January 30
J.C. Penney	January 26
Zayre Corp.	January 26
Toys "R" Us, Inc.	February 3
Federated Department Stores	February 3
The Limited, Inc.	February 2

What general characteristic shared by these companies explains why they do not have fiscal years ending December 31?

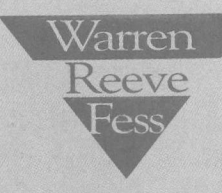

Resources for Your Success On-Line at warren.swcollege.com

Remember! If you need additional help, visit South-Western's Web site. See page 26 for a description of the online and printed materials that are available.

EXERCISES

Exercise 4–1
Place account balances in a work sheet

Objective 1

The balances for the accounts listed below appear in the Adjusted Trial Balance columns of the work sheet. Indicate whether each balance should be extended to (a) an Income Statement column or (b) a Balance Sheet column.

1. Accounts Payable
2. Wages Expense
3. Pete Parham, Capital
4. Fees Earned
5. Supplies
6. Unearned Fees
7. Utilities Expense
8. Pete Parham, Drawing
9. Wages Payable
10. Accounts Receivable

Exercise 4–2
Classify accounts

Objective 1

Balances for each of the following accounts appear in the Adjusted Trial Balance columns of the work sheet. Identify each as (a) asset, (b) liability, (c) revenue, or (d) expense.

1. Prepaid Advertising
2. Supplies
3. Unearned Rent
4. Rent Revenue
5. Salary Expense
6. Insurance Expense
7. Accounts Receivable
8. Land
9. Salary Payable
10. Fees Earned
11. Supplies Expense
12. Prepaid Insurance

Exercise 4–3
Steps in completing a work sheet

Objective 1

The steps performed in completing a work sheet are listed below in random order.

a. Add the Debit and Credit columns of the Balance Sheet and Income Statement columns of the work sheet to determine the amount of net income or net loss for the period.
b. Enter the unadjusted account balances from the general ledger into the unadjusted Trial Balance columns of the work sheet.
c. Enter the amount of net income or net loss for the period in the proper Income Statement column and Balance Sheet column.
d. Add the Debit and Credit columns of the Balance Sheet and Income Statement columns of the work sheet to verify that the totals are equal.
e. Extend the adjusted trial balance amounts to the Income Statement columns and the Balance Sheet columns.

f. Add the Debit and Credit columns of the Adjusted Trial Balance columns of the work sheet to verify that the totals are equal.
g. Add or deduct adjusting entry data to trial balance amounts and extend amounts to the Adjusted Trial Balance columns.
h. Add the Debit and Credit columns of the unadjusted Trial Balance columns of the work sheet to verify that the totals are equal.
i. Add the Debit and Credit columns of the Adjustments columns of the work sheet to verify that the totals are equal.
j. Enter the adjusting entries into the work sheet, based upon the adjustment data.

Indicate the order in which the preceding steps would be performed in preparing and completing a work sheet.

Exercise 4–4

Adjustments data on work sheet

Objective 1

✓ Total debits of Adjustments column: $14

Betty's Sanitize Services Co. offers cleaning services to business clients. The trial balance for Betty's Sanitize Services Co. has been prepared on the following work sheet for the year ended December 31, 1999:

Betty's Sanitize Services Co.
Work Sheet
For the Year Ended December 31, 1999

	Trial Balance		Adjustments		Adjusted Trial Balance	
Account Title	**Dr.**	**Cr.**	**Dr.**	**Cr.**	**Dr.**	**Cr.**
Cash	6					
Accounts Receivable	25					
Supplies	4					
Prepaid Insurance	6					
Land	10					
Equipment	14					
Accumulated Depr.—Equip.		1				
Accounts Payable		13				
Wages Payable		0				
Betty Ratcliff, Capital		41				
Betty Ratcliff, Drawing	4					
Fees Earned		30				
Wages Expense	8					
Rent Expense	4					
Insurance Expense	0					
Utilities Expense	2					
Depreciation Expense	0					
Supplies Expense	0					
Miscellaneous Expense	2					
Totals	85	85				

The data for year-end adjustments are as follows:

a. Fees earned, but not yet billed, $4.
b. Supplies on hand, $2.
c. Insurance premiums expired, $4.
d. Depreciation expense, $2.
e. Wages accrued, but not paid, $2.

Enter the adjustments data, and place the balances in the Adjusted Trial Balance columns.

Exercise 4–5

Complete a work sheet

Objective 1

✓ Net income: $8

Betty's Sanitize Services Co. offers cleaning services to business clients. The following is a partially completed work sheet for Betty's Sanitize Services Co.:

Betty's Sanitize Services Co.
Work Sheet
For the Year Ended December 31, 1999

Account Title	Adjusted Trial Balance Dr.	Adjusted Trial Balance Cr.	Income Statement Dr.	Income Statement Cr.	Balance Sheet Dr.	Balance Sheet Cr.
Cash	6					
Accounts Receivable	29					
Supplies	2					
Prepaid Insurance	2					
Land	10					
Equipment	14					
Accumulated Depr.—Equip.		3				
Accounts Payable		13				
Wages Payable		2				
Betty Ratcliff, Capital		41				
Betty Ratcliff, Drawing	4					
Fees Earned		34				
Wages Expense	10					
Rent Expense	4					
Insurance Expense	4					
Utilities Expense	2					
Depreciation Expense	2					
Supplies Expense	2					
Miscellaneous Expense	2					
Totals	93	93				
Net income (loss)						

Complete the work sheet.

Exercise 4–6
Financial statements
Objective 2

✓ Betty Ratcliff, capital, Dec. 31, 1999: $45

Based upon the data in Exercise 4–5, prepare an income statement, statement of owner's equity, and balance sheet for Betty's Sanitize Services Co.

Exercise 4–7
Adjusting entries
Objective 3

Based upon the data in Exercise 4–4, prepare the adjusting entries for Betty's Sanitize Services Co.

Exercise 4–8
Closing entries
Objective 3

Based upon the data in Exercise 4–5, prepare the closing entries for Betty's Sanitize Services Co.

Exercise 4–9
Income statement
Objective 2

✓ Net income: $99,950

The following account balances were taken from the Adjusted Trial Balance columns of the work sheet for The Messenger Co., a delivery service firm, for the current fiscal year ended June 30:

Fees Earned	$183,700
Salaries Expense	47,100
Rent Expense	18,000
Utilities Expense	7,500
Supplies Expense	3,100
Miscellaneous Expense	1,350
Insurance Expense	1,500
Depreciation Expense	5,200

Prepare an income statement.

Exercise 4–10
Income statement; net loss
Objective 2

✓ Net loss: $(4,150)

The following revenue and expense account balances were taken from the ledger of Reimer Services Co. after the accounts had been adjusted on March 31, the end of the current fiscal year:

Depreciation Expense	$ 7,500
Insurance Expense	3,900
Miscellaneous Expense	2,250
Rent Expense	36,000
Service Revenue	113,900
Supplies Expense	3,100
Utilities Expense	8,500
Wages Expense	56,800

Prepare an income statement.

Exercise 4–11
Statement of owner's equity
Objective 2

✓ Marion Weaver, capital, Dec. 31: $167,000

Neophyte Services Co. offers its services to new arrivals in the Evanston area. Selected accounts from the ledger of Neophyte Services Co. for the current fiscal year ended December 31 are as follows:

Marion Weaver, Capital

Dec. 31	10,000	Jan. 1	143,750
		Dec. 31	33,250

Marion Weaver, Drawing

Mar. 31	2,500	Dec. 31	10,000
June 30	2,500		
Sep. 30	2,500		
Dec. 31	2,500		

Income Summary

Dec. 31	578,150	Dec. 31	611,400
31	33,250		

Prepare a statement of owner's equity for the year.

Exercise 4–12
Statement of owner's equity; net loss
Objective 2

✓ Casey Martin, capital, July 31: $309,800

Selected accounts from the ledger of Casey Sports Services Co. for the current fiscal year ended July 31 are as follows:

Casey Martin, Capital

July 31	40,000	Aug. 1	410,300
31	60,500		

Casey Martin, Drawing

Oct. 31	10,000	July 31	40,000
Jan. 31	10,000		
Apr. 30	10,000		
July 31	10,000		

Income Summary

July 31	723,400	July 31	662,900
		31	60,500

Prepare a statement of owner's equity for the year.

Exercise 4–13
Classify assets
Objective 2

Identify each of the following as (a) a current asset or (b) property, plant, and equipment:

1. Accounts receivable
2. Building
3. Cash
4. Equipment
5. Land
6. Supplies

Exercise 4–14
Balance sheet classification
Objective 2

At the balance sheet date, a business owes a mortgage note payable of $450,000, the terms of which provide for monthly payments of $15,000.

Explain how the liability should be classified on the balance sheet.

Exercise 4–15
Balance sheet

Objective 2

✓ Total assets: $116,820

Looking Good Co. offers personal weight reduction consulting services to individuals. After all the accounts have been closed on April 30, the end of the current fiscal year, the balances of selected accounts from the ledger of Looking Good Co. are as follows:

Accounts Payable	$12,750	Prepaid Insurance	$4,100
Accounts Receivable	28,920	Prepaid Rent	2,400
Accumulated Depreciation—Equipment	21,100	Salaries Payable	3,750
Cash	7,150	Supplies	4,750
Equipment	90,600	Unearned Fees	2,500
M. Monroe, Capital	97,820		

Prepare a classified balance sheet.

Exercise 4–16
Balance sheet

Objective 2

What's Wrong WITH THIS?

✓ Corrected balance sheet, total assets: $132,500

List the errors you find in the following balance sheet. Prepare a corrected balance sheet.

SPA Services Co.
Balance Sheet
For the Year Ended August 31, 1999

Assets		
Current assets:		
Cash	$ 5,170	
Accounts payable	4,390	
Supplies	590	
Prepaid insurance	1,600	
Land	75,000	
Total current assets		$ 86,750
Property, plant, and equipment:		
Building		$ 55,500
Equipment		28,250
Total property, plant, and equipment		$101,250
Total assets		$188,000

Liabilities	
Current liabilities:	
Accounts receivable	$ 5,390
Accum. depr.—building	23,000
Accum. depr.—equipment	16,000
Net loss	15,500
Total liabilities	$ 59,890
Owner's Equity	
Wages payable	$ 975
S. Elby, capital	127,135
Total owner's equity	$128,110
Total liabilities and owner's equity	$188,000

Exercise 4–17
Adjusting entries from work sheet

Objective 3

Air Clean Purifier Co. is a consulting firm specializing in pollution control. The entries in the Adjustments columns of the work sheet for Air Clean Purifier Co. are shown below.

	Adjustments Dr.	Adjustments Cr.
Accounts Receivable	2,100	
Supplies		1,025
Prepaid Insurance		1,100
Accumulated Depreciation—Equipment		800
Wages Payable		636
Unearned Rent	3,500	
Fees Earned		2,100
Wages Expense	636	
Supplies Expense	1,025	
Rent Revenue		3,500
Insurance Expense	1,100	
Depreciation Expense	800	

Prepare the adjusting journal entries.

Exercise 4–18
Identify accounts to be closed

Objective 3

From the following list, identify the accounts that should be closed to Income Summary at the end of the fiscal year:

a. Accounts Payable
b. Accumulated Depreciation—Buildings
c. Depreciation Expense—Buildings
d. Donna Taff, Capital
e. Donna Taff, Drawing
f. Equipment
g. Fees Earned
h. Land
i. Salaries Expense
j. Salaries Payable
k. Supplies
l. Supplies Expense

Exercise 4–19
Closing entries
Objective 3

Prior to its closing, Income Summary had total debits of $417,500 and total credits of $520,000.

Briefly explain the purpose served by the income summary account and the nature of the entries that resulted in the $417,500 and the $520,000.

Exercise 4–20
Closing entries
Objective 3

✓ b. $438,000

After all revenue and expense accounts have been closed at the end of the fiscal year, Income Summary has a debit of $695,500 and a credit of $839,000. At the same date, Shawn Marsh, Capital has a credit balance of $319,500, and Shawn Marsh, Drawing has a balance of $25,000. (a) Journalize the entries required to complete the closing of the accounts. (b) Determine the amount of Shawn Marsh, Capital at the end of the period.

Exercise 4–21
Closing entries
Objective 3

Minish Services Co. offers its services to individuals desiring to improve their personal images. After the accounts have been adjusted at October 31, the end of the fiscal year, the following balances were taken from the ledger of Minish Services Co.

B. J. Galis, Capital	$298,500	Rent Expense	$74,000
B. J. Galis, Drawing	30,000	Supplies Expense	15,500
Fees Earned	355,000	Miscellaneous Expense	5,500
Wages Expense	197,300		

Journalize the four entries required to close the accounts.

Exercise 4–22
Identify permanent accounts
Objective 3

Which of the following accounts will usually appear in the post-closing trial balance?

a. Accounts Receivable
b. Accumulated Depreciation
c. Cash
d. Depreciation Expense
e. Equipment
f. Erik Geering, Capital
g. Erik Geering, Drawing
h. Fees Earned
i. Supplies
j. Wages Expense
k. Wages Payable

Exercise 4–23
Post-closing trial balance
Objective 3

What's Wrong WITH THIS?

✓ Correct column totals, $67,000

An accountant prepared the following post-closing trial balance:

Uptown Repairs Co.
Post-Closing Trial Balance
March 31, 20—

Cash	7,400	
Accounts Receivable	18,500	
Supplies		1,100
Equipment		40,000
Accumulated Depreciation—Equipment	11,100	
Accounts Payable	7,250	
Salaries Payable		1,500
Unearned Rent	4,000	
Lorraine Penn, Capital	43,150	
	91,400	42,600

Prepare a corrected post-closing trial balance. Assume that all accounts have normal balances and that the amounts shown are correct.

Exercise 4–24
Steps in the accounting cycle

Rearrange the following steps in the accounting cycle in proper sequence:

a. Adjusting entries are journalized and posted to the ledger.
b. Closing entries are journalized and posted to the ledger.
c. Financial statements are prepared.
d. A post-closing trial balance is prepared.
e. Transactions are analyzed and recorded in the journal.
f. Transactions are posted to the ledger.
g. A trial balance is prepared, adjustment data are assembled, and the work sheet is completed.

Exercise 4–25
Working capital and current ratio
Objective 6

REAL WORLD

The financial statements for Hershey Foods Corporation are presented in Appendix G at the end of the text.

a. Determine the working capital and the current ratio for Hershey Foods Corporation as of December 31, 1996 and 1995.
b. What conclusions concerning the company's ability to meets its financial obligations can you draw from these data?

Appendix Exercise 4–26
Adjusting and reversing entries

On the basis of the following data, (a) journalize the adjusting entries at December 31, 1999, the end of the current fiscal year, and (b) journalize the reversing entries on January 1, 2000, the first day of the following year.

1. Sales salaries are uniformly $7,500 for a five-day workweek, ending on Friday. The last payday of the year was Friday, December 26.
2. Accrued fees earned but not recorded at December 31, $13,200.

Appendix Exercise 4–27
Entries posted to the wages expense account

Portions of the wages expense account of a business are as follows:

ACCOUNT ***Wages Expense*** **ACCOUNT NO. 53**

Date		Item	Post. Ref.	Dr.	Cr.	Balance Dr.	Balance Cr.
1999							
Dec.	26	(1)	51	30,000		1,560,000	
	31	(2)	52	18,000		1,578,000	
	31	(3)	53		1,578,000	—	—
2000							
Jan.	1	(4)	54		18,000		18,000
	2	(5)	55	30,000		12,000	

a. Indicate the nature of the entry (payment, adjusting, closing, reversing) from which each numbered posting was made.
b. Journalize the complete entry from which each numbered posting was made.

PROBLEMS SERIES A

Problem 4–1A
Work sheet and related items
Objectives 1, 2, 3

HAT
SPREADSHEET
GENERAL LEDGER

✓ 2. Net income: $21,340

The trial balance of Wonder Wash Laundry at August 31, 2000, the end of the current fiscal year, and the data needed to determine year-end adjustments are as follows:

Wonder Wash Laundry
Trial Balance
August 31, 2000

Cash	13,100	
Laundry Supplies	6,560	
Prepaid Insurance	4,490	
Laundry Equipment	95,100	
Accumulated Depreciation		40,200
Accounts Payable		6,100
Louis Krupman, Capital		37,800
Louis Krupman, Drawing	2,000	
Laundry Revenue		140,900
Wages Expense	51,400	
Rent Expense	36,000	
Utilities Expense	13,650	
Miscellaneous Expense	2,700	
	225,000	225,000

a. Wages accrued but not paid at August 31 are $1,350.
b. Depreciation of equipment during the year is $6,600.
c. Laundry supplies on hand at August 31 are $1,500.
d. Insurance premiums expired during the year are $2,800.

Instructions

1. Enter the trial balance on a ten-column work sheet and complete the work sheet. Add accounts as needed.
2. Prepare an income statement, a statement of owner's equity (no additional investments were made during the year), and a balance sheet.
3. On the basis of the adjustment data in the work sheet, journalize the adjusting entries.
4. On the basis of the data in the work sheet, journalize the closing entries.

Problem 4–2A

Adjusting and closing entries; statement of owner's equity

Objectives 2, 3

HAT SPREADSHEET

✓ 2. K. Roemmich, capital, Dec. 31: $126,060

Roemmich Company is a financial planning services firm owned and operated by K. Roemmich. As of December 31, 1999, the end of the current fiscal year, the accountant for Roemmich Company prepared a work sheet, part of which is shown below.

Roemmich Company
Trial Balance
December 31, 1999

	Income Statement		Balance Sheet	
Cash			3,650	
Accounts Receivable			23,960	
Supplies			2,790	
Prepaid Insurance			1,000	
Land			42,500	
Buildings			116,000	
Accumulated Depreciation—Buildings				82,400
Equipment			82,000	
Accumulated Depreciation—Equipment				50,900
Accounts Payable				7,870
Salaries Payable				1,450
Taxes Payable				2,920
Unearned Rent				300
K. Roemmich, Capital				114,900
K. Roemmich, Drawing			10,000	
Service Fees Earned		144,260		
Rent Revenue		1,600		
Salary Expense	72,650			
Depreciation Expense—Equipment	18,100			
Rent Expense	9,000			
Supplies Expense	8,970			
Utilities Expense	5,300			
Depreciation Expense—Buildings	4,800			
Taxes Expense	3,520			
Insurance Expense	1,400			
Miscellaneous Expense	960			
	124,700	145,860	281,900	260,740
Net income	21,160			21,160
	145,860	145,860	281,900	281,900

Instructions

1. Journalize the entries that were required to close the accounts at December 31.
2. Prepare a statement of owner's equity for the fiscal year ended December 31. There were no additional investments during the year.
3. If the balance of K. Roemmich, Capital decreased $15,000 after the closing entries were posted, what was the amount of net income or net loss?

If the working papers correlating with this textbook are not used, omit Problem 4–3A.

Problem 4–3A
Ledger accounts and work sheet, and related items

Objectives 1, 2, 3

✓ 2. Net income: $4,033

The ledger and trial balance of Grisham Company as of January 31, 2000, the end of the first month of its current fiscal year, are presented in the working papers.

Instructions

1. Complete the ten-column work sheet. Data needed to determine the necessary adjusting entries are as follows:
   a. Service revenue accrued at January 31 is $750.
   b. Supplies on hand at January 31 are $500.
   c. Insurance premiums expired during January are $90.
   d. Depreciation of the building during January is $125.
   e. Depreciation of equipment during January is $95.
   f. Unearned rent at January 31 is $100.
   g. Wages accrued but not paid at January 31 are $600.
2. Prepare an income statement, a statement of owner's equity, and a balance sheet. (Note: The owner made an additional investment during the period.)
3. Journalize and post the adjusting entries, inserting balances in the accounts affected.
4. Journalize and post the closing entries. Indicate closed accounts by inserting a line in both Balance columns opposite the closing entry. Insert the new balance of the capital account.
5. Prepare a post-closing trial balance.

Problem 4–4A
Work sheet and financial statements

Objectives 1, 2

GENERAL LEDGER
HAT

✓ 2. Net income: $39,680

Last Chance Company offers legal consulting advice to death-row inmates. Last Chance Company prepared the following trial balance at April 30, 2000, the end of the current fiscal year:

Last Chance Company
Trial Balance
April 30, 2000

Cash	3,200	
Accounts Receivable	10,500	
Prepaid Insurance	3,800	
Supplies	1,950	
Land	50,000	
Building	137,500	
Accumulated Depreciation—Building		51,700
Equipment	90,100	
Accumulated Depreciation—Equipment		35,300
Accounts Payable		7,500
Unearned Rent		3,000
Jason Soroka, Capital		164,100
Jason Soroka, Drawing	10,000	
Fees Revenue		198,400
Salaries and Wages Expense	80,200	
Advertising Expense	38,200	
Utilities Expense	19,000	
Repairs Expense	11,500	
Miscellaneous Expense	4,050	
	460,000	460,000

The data needed to determine year-end adjustments are as follows:

a. Accrued fees revenue at April 30 are $3,800.
b. Insurance expired during the year is $2,900.
c. Supplies on hand at April 30 are $450.
d. Depreciation of building for the year is $1,620.
e. Depreciation of equipment for the year is $3,500.

f. Accrued salaries and wages at April 30 are $2,050.
g. Unearned rent at April 30 is $1,000.

Instructions

1. Enter the trial balance on a ten-column work sheet and complete the work sheet. Add accounts as needed.
2. Prepare an income statement for the year ended April 30.
3. Prepare a statement of owner's equity for the year ended April 30. No additional investments were made during the year.
4. Prepare a balance sheet as of April 30.
5. Compute the percent of net income to total revenue for the year.

Problem 4–5A

Ledger accounts, work sheet, and related items

Objectives 1, 2, 3

GENERAL LEDGER
HAT

✓ 2. Net income: $16,895

The trial balance of Avery Repairs at December 31, 2000, the end of the current year, and the data needed to determine year-end adjustments are as follows:

Avery Repairs
Trial Balance
December 31, 2000

11	Cash	6,825	
13	Supplies	4,820	
14	Prepaid Insurance	3,500	
16	Equipment	42,200	
17	Accumulated Depreciation—Equipment		9,050
18	Trucks	45,000	
19	Accumulated Depreciation—Trucks		27,100
21	Accounts Payable		4,015
31	Steve Galvine, Capital		29,885
32	Steve Galvine, Drawing	3,000	
41	Service Revenue		99,950
51	Wages Expense	42,010	
53	Rent Expense	10,100	
55	Truck Expense	9,350	
59	Miscellaneous Expense	3,195	
		170,000	170,000

a. Supplies on hand at December 31 are $1,100.
b. Insurance premiums expired during year are $2,500.
c. Depreciation of equipment during year is $6,080.
d. Depreciation of trucks during year is $5,500.
e. Wages accrued but not paid at December 31 are $600.

Instructions

1. For each account listed in the trial balance, enter the balance in the appropriate Balance column of a four-column account and place a check mark (✓) in the Posting Reference column.
2. Enter the trial balance on a ten-column work sheet and complete the work sheet. Add accounts as needed.
3. Prepare an income statement, a statement of owner's equity (no additional investments were made during the year), and a balance sheet.
4. Journalize and post the adjusting entries, inserting balances in the accounts affected. The following additional accounts from Avery's chart of accounts should be used: Wages Payable, 22; Supplies Expense, 52; Depreciation Expense—Equipment, 54; Depreciation Expense—Trucks, 56; Insurance Expense, 57.
5. Journalize and post the closing entries. (Income Summary is account #33 in the chart of accounts.) Indicate closed accounts by inserting a line in both Balance columns opposite the closing entry.
6. Prepare a post-closing trial balance.

PROBLEMS SERIES B

In Class

Problem 4–1B
Work sheet and related items

Objectives 1, 2, 3

SPREADSHEET
GENERAL LEDGER

✓ 2. Net income: $7,630

The trial balance of The Wash and Dry Laundromat at July 31, 2000, the end of the current fiscal year, and the data needed to determine year-end adjustments are as follows:

The Wash and Dry Laundromat
Trial Balance
July 31, 2000

Cash	6,290	
Laundry Supplies	5,850	
Prepaid Insurance	2,400	
Laundry Equipment	99,750	
Accumulated Depreciation		52,700
Accounts Payable		6,950
Nikki Weiss, Capital		37,450
Nikki Weiss, Drawing	4,000	
Laundry Revenue		67,900
Wages Expense	22,900	
Rent Expense	14,400	
Utilities Expense	8,500	
Miscellaneous Expense	910	
	165,000	165,000

a. Laundry supplies on hand at ~~March~~ July 31 are $1,240.
b. Insurance premiums expired during the year are $1,700.
c. Depreciation of equipment during the year is $6,200.
d. Wages accrued but not paid at ~~March~~ July 31 are $1,050.

Instructions

1. Enter the trial balance on a ten-column work sheet and complete the work sheet. Add accounts as needed.
2. Prepare an income statement, a statement of owner's equity (no additional investments were made during the year), and a balance sheet.
3. On the basis of the adjustment data in the work sheet, journalize the adjusting entries.
4. On the basis of the data in the work sheet, journalize the closing entries.

Problem 4–2B
Adjusting and closing entries; statement of owner's equity

Objectives 2, 3

SPREADSHEET

✓ 2. S. Holmes, capital, Nov. 30: $55,230

Holmes Company is an investigative services firm that is owned and operated by S. Holmes. On November 30, 1999, the end of the current fiscal year, the accountant for Holmes Company prepared a work sheet, a part of which is shown at the top of the next page.

Instructions

1. Journalize the entries that were required to close the accounts at November 30.
2. Prepare a statement of owner's equity for the fiscal year ended November 30, 1999. There were no additional investments during the year.
3. If S. Holmes, Capital decreased $10,000 after the closing entries were posted, what was the amount of net income or net loss?

Holmes Company
Work Sheet (Partial)
November 30, 1999

	Income Statement		Balance Sheet	
Cash			7,325	
Accounts Receivable			21,600	
Supplies			1,610	
Prepaid Insurance			1,350	
Equipment			69,750	
Accumulated Depreciation—Equipment				33,995
Accounts Payable				5,230
Salaries Payable				3,480
Taxes Payable				2,200
Unearned Rent				1,500
S. Holmes, Capital				31,345
S. Holmes, Drawing			7,500	
Service Fees Earned		185,900		
Rent Revenue		2,250		
Salary Expense	119,865			
Rent Expense	15,600			
Supplies Expense	5,310			
Depreciation Expense—Equipment	4,600			
Utilities Expense	3,640			
Taxes Expense	3,115			
Insurance Expense	2,925			
Miscellaneous Expense	1,710			
	156,765	188,150	109,135	77,750
Net income	31,385			31,385
	188,150	188,150	109,135	109,135

If the working papers correlating with this textbook are not used, omit Problem 4–3B.

Problem 4–3B
Ledger accounts, work sheet, and related items

Objectives 1, 2, 3

✓ 2. Net income: $4,617

The ledger and trial balance of Grisham Company as of January 31, 2000, the end of the first month of its current fiscal year, are presented in the working papers.

Instructions

1. Complete the ten-column work sheet. Data needed to determine the necessary adjusting entries are as follows:
   a. Service revenue accrued at January 31 is $1,100.
   b. Supplies on hand at January 31 are $449.
   c. Insurance premiums expired during January are $100.
   d. Depreciation of the building during January is $110.
   e. Depreciation of equipment during January is $115.
   f. Unearned rent at January 31 is $100.
   g. Wages accrued at January 31 are $300.
2. Prepare an income statement, a statement of owner's equity, and a balance sheet. (Note: The owner made an additional investment during the period.)
3. Journalize and post the adjusting entries, inserting balances in the accounts affected.
4. Journalize and post the closing entries. Indicate closed accounts by inserting a line in both Balance columns opposite the closing entry.
5. Prepare a post-closing trial balance.

Problem 4–4B
Work sheet and financial statements

Objectives 1, 2

GENERAL LEDGER

✓ 2. Net income: $46,670

Koontz Company maintains and repairs warning lights, such as those found on radio towers and lighthouses. Koontz Company prepared the following trial balance at May 31, 2000, the end of the current fiscal year:

Koontz Company
Trial Balance
May 31, 2000

Cash	7,500	
Accounts Receivable	16,500	
Prepaid Insurance	2,600	
Supplies	1,950	
Land	60,000	
Building	100,500	
Accumulated Depreciation—Building		81,700
Equipment	72,400	
Accumulated Depreciation—Equipment		63,800
Accounts Payable		6,100
Unearned Rent		1,500
Joe Carpenter, Capital		60,700
Joe Carpenter, Drawing	4,000	
Fees Revenue		161,200
Salaries and Wages Expense	60,200	
Advertising Expense	19,000	
Utilities Expense	18,200	
Repairs Expense	8,100	
Miscellaneous Expense	4,050	
	375,000	375,000

The data needed to determine year-end adjustments are as follows:

a. Fees revenue accrued at May 31 is $3,500.
b. Insurance expired during the year is $1,000.
c. Supplies on hand at May 31 are $450.
d. Depreciation of building for the year is $1,620.
e. Depreciation of equipment for the year is $3,160.
f. Accrued salaries and wages at May 31 are $1,700.
g. Unearned rent at May 31 is $1,000.

Instructions

1. Enter the trial balance on a ten-column work sheet and complete the work sheet. Add accounts as needed.
2. Prepare an income statement for the year ended May 31.
3. Prepare a statement of owner's equity for the year ended May 31. No additional investments were made during the year.
4. Prepare a balance sheet as of May 31.
5. Compute the percent of net income to total revenue for the year.

Problem 4–5B
Ledger accounts, work sheet, and related items

Objectives 1, 2, 3

GENERAL LEDGER

✓ 3. Net income: $23,275

The trial balance of Quick Repairs at March 31, 2000, the end of the current year, is shown at the top of the next page. The data needed to determine year-end adjustments are as follows:

a. Supplies on hand at March 31 are $1,205.
b. Insurance premiums expired during year are $935.
c. Depreciation of equipment during year is $3,380.
d. Depreciation of trucks during year is $4,400.
e. Wages accrued but not paid at March 31 are $800.

Quick Repairs
Trial Balance
March 31, 2000

11	Cash	6,950	
13	Supplies	4,295	
14	Prepaid Insurance	2,735	
16	Equipment	40,650	
17	Accumulated Depreciation—Equipment		11,209
18	Trucks	36,300	
19	Accumulated Depreciation—Trucks		6,400
21	Accounts Payable		2,015
31	Renee Dills, Capital		40,426
32	Renee Dills, Drawing	5,000	
41	Service Revenue		89,950
51	Wages Expense	33,925	
53	Rent Expense	9,600	
55	Truck Expense	8,350	
59	Miscellaneous Expense	2,195	
		150,000	150,000

Instructions

1. For each account listed in the trial balance, enter the balance in the appropriate Balance column of a four-column account and place a check mark (✓) in the Posting Reference column.
2. Enter the trial balance on a ten-column work sheet and complete the work sheet. Add accounts as needed.
3. Prepare an income statement, a statement of owner's equity (no additional investments were made during the year), and a balance sheet.
4. Journalize and post the adjusting entries, inserting balances in the accounts affected. The following additional accounts from Quick's chart of accounts should be used: Wages Payable, 22; Supplies Expense, 52; Depreciation Expense—Equipment, 54; Depreciation Expense—Trucks, 56; Insurance Expense, 57.
5. Journalize and post the closing entries. (Income Summary is account #33 in the chart of accounts.) Indicate closed accounts by inserting a line in both Balance columns opposite the closing entry.
6. Prepare a post-closing trial balance.

CONTINUING PROBLEM

MUSIC TODAY

HAT

✓ 2. Net income: $1,620

The unadjusted trial balance of Music Today as of December 31, 1999, along with the adjustment data for the two months ended December 31, 1999, are shown in Chapter 3.

Instructions

1. Prepare a ten-column work sheet.
2. Prepare an income statement, a statement of owner's equity, and a balance sheet. (Note: Chris Stipe made investments in Music Today on November 1 and December 1, 1999.)
3. Journalize and post the closing entries. The income summary account is #33 in the ledger of Music Today. Indicate closed accounts by inserting a line in both Balance columns opposite the closing entry.
4. Prepare a post-closing trial balance.

COMPREHENSIVE PROBLEM 1

GENERAL LEDGER
HAT
QUICKBOOKS

✓ 4. Net income: $6,775

For the past several years, Angie Mills has operated a part-time consulting business from her home. As of September 1, 2000, Angie decided to move to rented quarters and to operate the business, which was to be known as Interactive Consulting, on a full-time basis. Interactive Consulting entered into the following transactions during September:

Sept. 1. The following assets were received from Angie Mills: cash, $7,050; accounts receivable, $1,500; supplies, $1,250; and office equipment, $7,200. There were no liabilities received.
2. Paid three months' rent on a lease rental contract, $3,600.
2. Paid the premiums on property and casualty insurance policies, $1,500.
4. Received cash from clients as an advance payment for services to be provided and recorded it as unearned fees, $3,500.
5. Purchased additional office equipment on account from Payne Company, $1,800.
6. Received cash from clients on account, $800.
10. Paid cash for a newspaper advertisement, $120.
12. Paid Payne Company for part of the debt incurred on September 5, $800.
12. Recorded services provided on account for the period September 1–12, $1,200.
13. Paid part-time receptionist for two weeks' salary, $400.
17. Recorded cash from cash clients for fees earned during the first half of September, $2,100.
18. Paid cash for supplies, $750.
20. Recorded services provided on account for the period September 13–20, $1,100.
24. Recorded cash from cash clients for fees earned for the period September 17–24, $1,850.
25. Received cash from clients on account, $1,300.
27. Paid part-time receptionist for two weeks' salary, $400.
29. Paid telephone bill for September, $130.
30. Paid electricity bill for September, $200.
30. Recorded cash from cash clients for fees earned for the period September 25–30, $1,050.
30. Recorded services provided on account for the remainder of September, $500.
30. Angie withdrew $1,500 for personal use.

Instructions

1. Journalize each transaction in a two-column journal, referring to the following chart of accounts in selecting the accounts to be debited and credited. (Do not insert the account numbers in the journal at this time.)

11 Cash	31 Angie Mills, Capital
12 Accounts Receivable	32 Angie Mills, Drawing
14 Supplies	41 Fees Earned
15 Prepaid Rent	51 Salary Expense
16 Prepaid Insurance	52 Rent Expense
18 Office Equipment	53 Supplies Expense
19 Accumulated Depreciation	54 Depreciation Expense
21 Accounts Payable	55 Insurance Expense
22 Salaries Payable	59 Miscellaneous Expense
23 Unearned Fees	

2. Post the journal to a ledger of four-column accounts.
3. Prepare a trial balance as of September 30, 2000, on a ten-column work sheet, listing all the accounts in the order given in the ledger. Complete the work sheet, using the following adjustment data:
   a. Insurance expired during September is $125.
   b. Supplies on hand on September 30 are $1,220.

   c. Depreciation of office equipment for September is $250.
   d. Accrued receptionist salary on September 30 is $120.
   e. Rent expired during September is $800.
   f. Unearned fees on September 30 are $1,200.
4. Prepare an income statement, a statement of owner's equity, and a balance sheet.
5. Journalize and post the adjusting entries.
6. Journalize and post the closing entries. (Income Summary is account #33 in the chart of accounts.) Indicate closed accounts by inserting a line in both Balance columns opposite the closing entry.
7. Prepare a post-closing trial balance.

QuickBooks Instructions:

QuickBooks® is accounting software designed especially for small businesses. To launch the program, double click on the QuickBooks icon within the QuickBooks program group on your computer screen.

Select "New Company" from the File menu.

Note: When a window appears for which no specific instructions are given below, read the information in the window and then click "Next."

- *Welcome* window: After clicking on the "Next" button to begin the General section, click "No, I'm not upgrading." Then click "Next."
- *Your company name* window: Enter the company name as indicated in the problem. The legal name will be the same.
- *Your company address* window: Enter your address as the address of the company.
- *Other company information* window: Enter your I.D. number or Social Security number. Change the first month of the income tax year and the fiscal year from January if the company in your problem is just starting in business or is not on a calendar year.
- *Your company income tax form* window: Select <Other/None> for the Tax Form. In the message box that then appears, click "Do not display this message in the future." Then click OK."
- *Select your type of business* window: Select the type of business (e.g., service) as indicated in the problem.
- *Save As* window: Click "OK" when the file name is displayed (unless you want to change it). The file name displayed is based on the company name you entered.
- *Your income and expense accounts* window: Click "No, I'd like to create my own."
- *Sales tax* window: Click "No."
- *Your invoice format* window: Click "Service."
- *Employees* window: Enter "0" for zero.
- *Estimates* window: Click "No."
- *Time tracking* window: Click "No."
- *Tracking reimbursable expenses* window: Click "No."
- *Classifying transactions* window: Click "No."
- *Two ways to handle bills and payments* window: Click "Enter the bills first and then enter the payments later."
- *Reminders list* window: Click "When I ask for it."
- *Accrual- or cash-based reporting* window: Click "Accrual-based reports."
- *Choose your QuickBooks start date* window: Enter the date of the first transaction in the problem, in MM/DD/YY format.
- *Adding an income account* window: Enter the name of an income account shown in the problem chart of accounts.
- *Add another income account* window: Click "Yes" and continue to add necessary income accounts, or Click "No."
- *Expense accounts* window: Click "No thank you."
- *No accounts set up* window: Click "Yes."
- *Adding an expense account* window: Enter the name of an expense account shown in the problem chart of accounts.

- *Add another expense account* window: Click "Yes" and continue to add necessary expense accounts, or Click "No."
- *Receipt of payment* window: Click "Sometimes."
- *Statement charges* window: Click "No."
- *Service items* window: Click "No."
- *Non-inventory parts* window: Click "No."
- *Other charges* window: Click "No."
- *Income Details: Inventory* window: Click "Skip inventory items."
- *Enter customers* window: Click "No."
- *Adding vendors with open balances* window: Click "No."
- *Credit card accounts* window: Click "No."
- *Adding lines of credit* window: Click "No."
- *Loans and notes payable* window: Click "No."
- *Bank accounts* window: Click "Yes."
- *Adding a bank account* window: Enter "Cash" as the name of your bank account.
- *Last statement date and balance* window: Enter the date of the first transaction. Enter the opening balance (if any) of the cash account.
- *Adding another bank account* window: Click "No."
- *Asset accounts* window: Click "Yes."
- *Adding an asset account* window: Enter the name of an asset account (except for "Cash") shown in the problem chart of accounts. Identify the type of asset from the pull-down menu. Enter the opening balance (if any) of the asset account.
- *Adding another asset* window: Click "Yes" if other asset accounts need to be added. Otherwise, click "No." If the asset is a fixed asset, click "Yes" in response to the question: "Do you track depreciation for this fixed asset?" In the *Fixed asset cost and depreciation* window, enter "0."
- *Enabling payroll* window: Click "Skip payroll."
- *Employees* window: Click "No."
- *To Do List* window: Click "No."
- *Finance charges* window: Click "No."
- *Budgets* window: Click "No." Continue clicking the "Next" button to advance to the end of the EasyStep Interview. Then click the "Leave" button.

Before you begin recording transactions, you need to edit the chart of accounts to fit the form of business (proprietorship or corporation) in your problem. Select "Chart of Accounts" from the "Lists" pull-down menu. If you are working a proprietorship problem, select "Retained Earnings" from the Chart of Accounts window. From the pull-down "Edit" menu, choose "Delete Account." Click "OK" to confirm that you want to delete this account. Next, to add the problem's equity accounts, click "New" in the Account window. Choose the account type from the "Type" drop-down list. Enter the account's name. (The account description and bank number are optional.) Enter the account's opening balance (if any) and the start date in the "as of" field. If you need to add other asset or liability accounts, click "Next" to create another new account. When the chart of accounts for your problem is complete, click "OK" to close the window. Then click "X" to close the Chart of Accounts window.

You are now ready to begin recording your problem's first transaction. Click on the "Activities" pull-down menu. Then select the type of transaction you want to enter. For example, select "Make Journal Entry." Then, in the "General Journal Entry" window, change the date. Enter "1" as the Entry No., and Enter "Cash" in the Account column. Then press the Tab key and enter "7050" in the Debit column. Press the Tab key several times to move down to the next row and then enter "Accounts Receivable" in the Account column. Press the Tab key and enter "1500" in the Debit column. Press the Tab key several times to move down to the next row and then enter "Supplies" in the Account column. Press the Tab key and enter "1250" in the Debit column. Press the Tab key several times to move down to the next row and then enter "Office Equipment" in the Account column. Press the Tab key and enter "7200" in the debit column. Press the Tab key several times to move down to the next row and then enter "Angie Mills, Capital" in the Account column. The entry in the Credit column will display automatically. Click on "OK."

SPECIAL ACTIVITIES

Activity 4–1
VisCo Co.
Ethics and professional conduct in business

VisCo Co. is a graphics arts design consulting firm. Hugh Lowder, its treasurer and vice president of finance, has prepared a classified balance sheet as of March 31, 2000, the end of its fiscal year. This balance sheet will be submitted with VisCo's loan application to National Trust & Savings Bank.

In the Current Assets section of the balance sheet, Hugh reported a $40,000 receivable from Jill Reamy, the president of VisCo, as a trade account receivable. Jill borrowed the money from VisCo in February 1999 for a down payment on a new home. She has orally assured Hugh that she will pay off the account receivable within the next year. Hugh reported the $40,000 in the same manner on the preceding year's balance sheet.

Evaluate whether it is acceptable for Hugh Lowder to prepare the March 31, 2000 balance sheet in the manner indicated above.

Activity 4–2
Compadres Supplies Co.
Financial statements

The following is an excerpt from a telephone conversation between Janice Cato, president of Compadres Supplies Co., and Mike Metz, who is owner of Temp Employment Co.

Janice: Mike, you're going to have to do a better job of finding me a new computer programmer. That last guy was great at programming, but he didn't have any common sense.

Mike: What do you mean? The guy had a master's degree with straight A's.

Janice: Yes, well, last month he developed a new financial reporting system. He said we could do away with manually preparing a work sheet and financial statements. The computer would automatically generate our financial statements with "a push of a button."

Mike: So what's the big deal? Sounds to me like it would save you time and effort.

Janice: Right! The balance sheet showed a minus for supplies!

Mike: Minus supplies? How can that be?

Janice: That's what I asked.

Mike: So, what did he say?

Janice: Well, after he checked the program, he said that it must be right. The minuses were greater than the pluses . . .

Mike: Didn't he know that supplies can't have a credit balance—it must have a debit balance?

Janice: He asked me what a debit and credit were.

Mike: I see your point.

1. Comment on (a) the desirability of computerizing Compadres Supplies Co.'s financial reporting system, (b) the elimination of the work sheet in a computerized accounting system, and (c) the computer programmer's lack of accounting knowledge.
2. Explain to the programmer why supplies could not have a credit balance.

Activity 4–3
Bug Out
Financial statements

Assume that you recently accepted a position with the First National Bank as an assistant loan officer. As one of your first duties, you have been assigned the responsibility of evaluating a loan request for $60,000 from Bug Out, a small proprietorship. In support of the loan application, Linda Abney, owner, submitted a "Statement of Accounts" (trial balance) for the first year of operations ended December 31, 2000.

1. Explain to Linda Abney why a set of financial statements (income statement, statement of owner's equity, and balance sheet) would be useful to you in evaluating the loan request.
2. In discussing the "Statement of Accounts" with Linda Abney, you discovered that the accounts had not been adjusted at December 31. Analyze the "Statement of Accounts" (shown on the next page) and indicate possible adjusting entries that might be necessary before an accurate set of financial statements could be prepared.
3. Assuming that an accurate set of financial statements will be submitted by Linda Abney in a few days, what other considerations or information would you require before making a decision on the loan request?

Bug Out
Statement of Accounts
December 31, 2000

Cash	4,120	
Billings Due from Others	8,740	
Supplies (chemicals, etc.)	14,950	
Trucks	32,750	
Equipment	26,150	
Amounts Owed to Others		5,700
Investment in Business		47,500
Service Revenue		107,650
Wages Expense	60,100	
Utilities Expense	6,900	
Rent Expense	4,800	
Insurance Expense	1,400	
Other Expenses	940	
	160,850	160,850

Activity 4–4 Into the Real World
Compare balance sheets

GROUP ACTIVITY

Internet ACTIVITY

In groups of three or four, compare the balance sheets of two different companies, and present to the class a summary of the similarities and differences of the two companies. You may obtain the balance sheets you need from one of the following sources:

1. Your school or local library.
2. The investor relations department of each company.
3. The company's Web site on the Internet.
4. EDGAR (Electronic Data Gathering, Analysis, and Retrieval), the electronic archives of financial statements filed with the Securities and Exchange Commission. The EDGAR address is **www.sec.gov/edgarhp.htm**

   To obtain annual report information, type in a company name on the "Search EDGAR Archives" form. EDGAR will list the reports available for the selected company. A company's annual report (along with other information) is provided in its annual 10-K report to the SEC. Click on the 10-K (or 10-K405) report for the year you wish to download. If you wish, you can save the whole 10-K report to a file and then open it with your word processor.

ANSWERS TO SELF-EXAMINATION QUESTIONS

Matching

1. T	3. L	5. J	7. O	9. K	11. R	13. G	15. P
2. E	4. F	6. I	8. H	10. A	12. U	14. D	16. S

Multiple Choice

1. **C** The drawing account, M. E. Jones, Drawing (answer C), would be extended to the Balance Sheet columns of the work sheet. Utilities Expense (answer A), Rent Revenue (answer B), and Miscellaneous Expense (answer D) would all be extended to the Income Statement columns of the work sheet.
2. **D** Cash or other assets that are expected to be converted to cash or sold or used up within one year or less, through the normal operations of the business, are classified as current assets on the balance sheet. Accounts Receivable (answer D) is a current asset, since it will normally be converted to cash within one year. Office Equipment (answer A), Land (answer B), and Accumulated Depreciation (answer C) are all reported in the property, plant, and equipment section of the balance sheet.
3. **B** The entry to close the owner's drawing account is to debit the owner's capital account and credit the drawing account (answer B).
4. **D** Since all revenue and expense accounts are closed at the end of the period, Fees Earned (answer A), Wages Expense (answer B), and Rent Expense (answer C) would all be closed to Income Summary. Accumulated Depreciation (answer D) is a contra asset account that is not closed.
5. **B** Since the post-closing trial balance includes only balance sheet accounts (all of the revenue, expense, and drawing accounts are closed), Cash (answer A), Accumulated Depreciation (answer C), and J. C. Smith, Capital (answer D) would appear on the post-closing trial balance. Fees Earned (answer B) is a temporary account that is closed prior to preparing the post-closing trial balance.

5

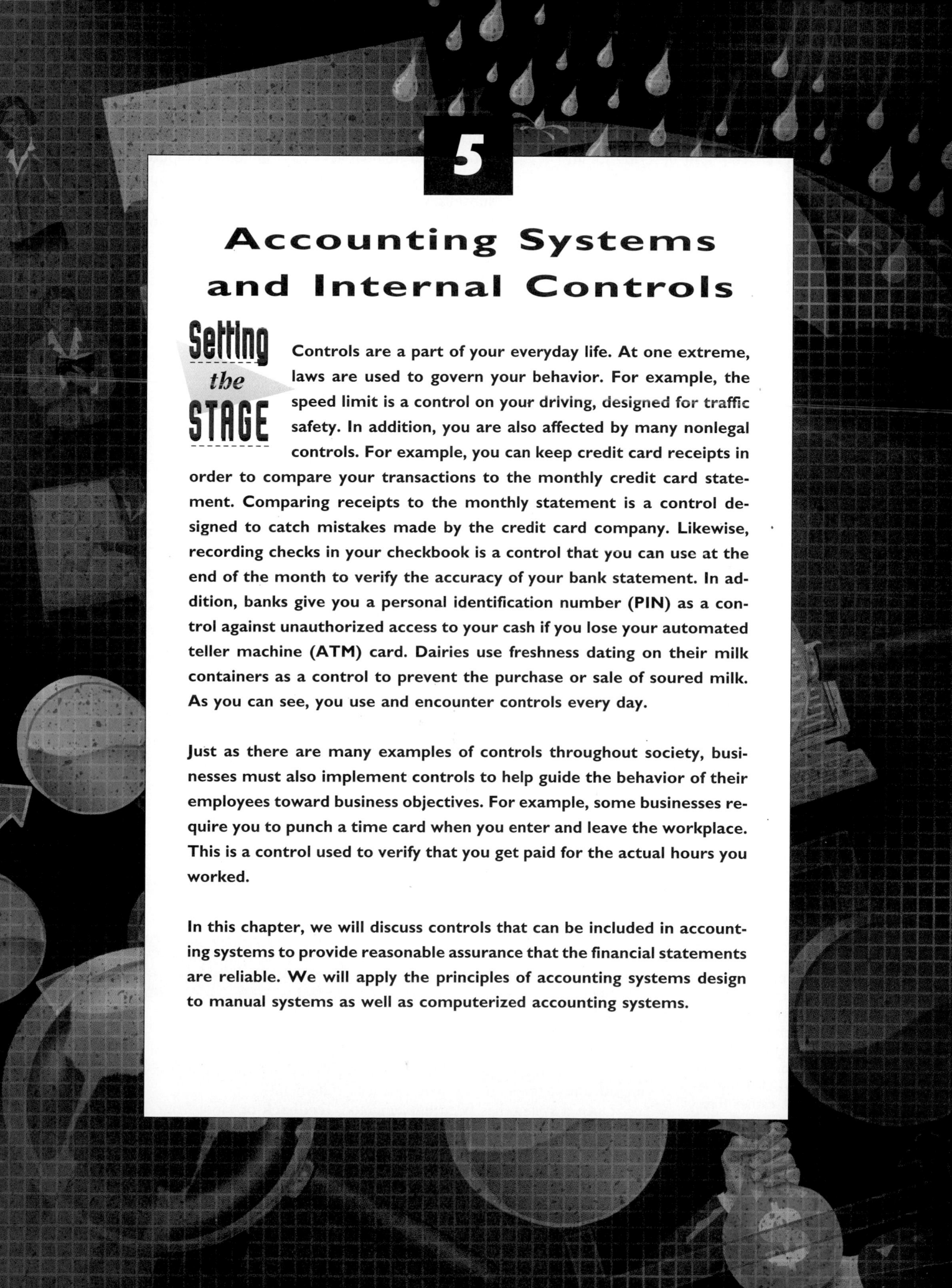

Accounting Systems and Internal Controls

Setting the STAGE

Controls are a part of your everyday life. At one extreme, laws are used to govern your behavior. For example, the speed limit is a control on your driving, designed for traffic safety. In addition, you are also affected by many nonlegal controls. For example, you can keep credit card receipts in order to compare your transactions to the monthly credit card statement. Comparing receipts to the monthly statement is a control designed to catch mistakes made by the credit card company. Likewise, recording checks in your checkbook is a control that you can use at the end of the month to verify the accuracy of your bank statement. In addition, banks give you a personal identification number (PIN) as a control against unauthorized access to your cash if you lose your automated teller machine (ATM) card. Dairies use freshness dating on their milk containers as a control to prevent the purchase or sale of soured milk. As you can see, you use and encounter controls every day.

Just as there are many examples of controls throughout society, businesses must also implement controls to help guide the behavior of their employees toward business objectives. For example, some businesses require you to punch a time card when you enter and leave the workplace. This is a control used to verify that you get paid for the actual hours you worked.

In this chapter, we will discuss controls that can be included in accounting systems to provide reasonable assurance that the financial statements are reliable. We will apply the principles of accounting systems design to manual systems as well as computerized accounting systems.

objectives

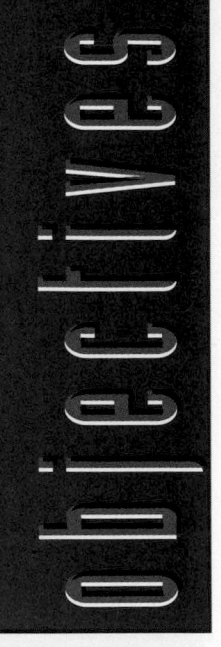

After studying this chapter, you should be able to:

1. Define an accounting system and describe its implementation.
2. List the three objectives of internal control and define and give examples of the five elements of internal control.
3. Journalize and post transactions in a manual accounting system that uses subsidiary ledgers and special journals.
4. Describe and give examples of additional subsidiary ledgers and modified special journals.
5. Describe the components of a computer system and apply computerized accounting to the revenue and collection cycle.

Basic Accounting Systems

OBJECTIVE 1

Define an accounting system and describe its implementation.

In the four previous chapters, we developed an accounting system for Computer King. An **accounting system** is the methods and procedures for collecting, classifying, summarizing, and reporting a business's financial and operating information. The accounting system for most businesses, however, is more complex than Computer King's. Accounting systems for large businesses must be able to collect, accumulate, and report many types of transactions. For example, **United Airlines**' accounting system collects and maintains information on ticket reservations, credit card collections, aircraft maintenance, employee hours, frequent-flier mileage balances, fuel consumption, and travel agent commissions, just to name a few. As you might expect, United Airlines' accounting system has evolved as the company has grown.

Accounting systems evolve through a three-step process as a business grows and changes. The first step in this process is **analysis**, which consists of (1) identifying the needs of those who use the business's financial information and (2) determining how the system should provide this information. For Computer King, we determined that Pat King would need financial statements for the new business. In the second step, the system is **designed** so that it will meet the users' needs. For Computer King, a very basic manual system was designed. This system included a chart of accounts, a two-column journal, and a general ledger. Finally, the system is **implemented** and used. For Computer King, the system was used to record transactions and prepare financial statements.

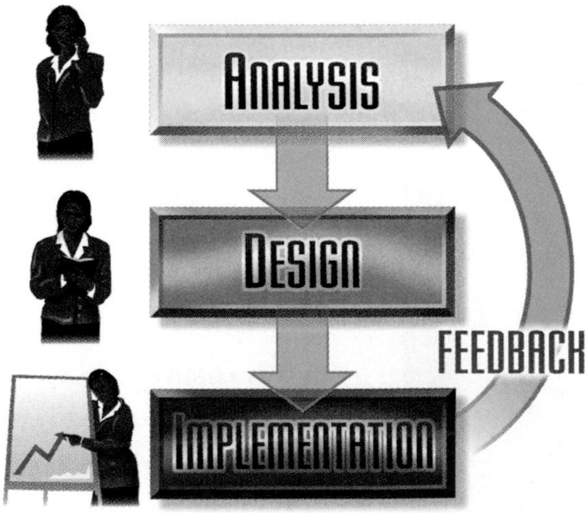

Once a system has been implemented, **feedback** or input from the users of the information can be used to analyze and improve the system. For example, in later chapters we will see that Computer King will expand its chart of accounts as it becomes a more complex business.

REAL WORLD

The **Internal Revenue Service (IRS)** learned the hard way that the *analysis* stage is very important. The IRS spent $3 billion on a widely criticized computer modernization program that had no clear outlines or goals. After spending this amount, the agency unveiled a blueprint for the project. Deputy Treasury Secretary Lawrence Summers declared that the IRS would begin more careful planning for the project. "We're [now] planning before we build, rather than building before we plan," he stated.

Internal controls protect assets, ensure that business information is accurate, and ensure that regulations are being followed.

Internal controls and information processing methods are essential in an accounting system. **Internal controls** are the policies and procedures that protect assets from misuse, ensure that business information is accurate, and ensure that laws and regulations are being followed. **Processing methods** are the means by which the system collects, summarizes, and reports accounting information. These methods may be either *manual* or *computerized.* In the following sections, we will discuss internal controls, manual accounting systems that use special journals, and computerized accounting systems.

Internal Control

OBJECTIVE 2

List the three objectives of internal control and define and give examples of the five elements of internal control.

Businesses use internal controls to guide their operations and prevent abuses of their systems. For example, assume that you own and manage a lawn care service. Your business uses several employee teams, and you provide each team with a vehicle and lawn equipment. What are some of the issues you would face as a manager in controlling the operations of this business? Below are some examples.

- Lawn care must be provided on time.
- The quality of lawn care services must meet customer expectations.
- Employees must provide work for the hours they are paid.
- Lawn care equipment should be used for business purposes only.
- Vehicles should be used for business purposes only.
- Customers must be billed and bills collected for services rendered.

How would you address some of these issues? You could, for example, develop a schedule at the beginning of each day and then inspect the work at the end of the day to verify that it was completed according to quality standards. You could have "surprise" inspections by arriving on site at random times to verify that the teams are working according to schedule. You could require employees to "clock in" at the beginning of the day and "clock out" at the end of the day, to make sure that they are paid for hours worked. You could require the work teams to return the vehicles and equipment to a central location to prevent unauthorized use. You could keep a log of odometer readings at the end of each day to verify that the vehicle has not been used for "joy riding." You could bill customers after you have inspected the work, and then you could monitor the collection of all receivables. All of these are examples of internal control.

REAL WORLD

A 1996 survey by **KPMG**, an international accounting firm, identified expense account manipulation, receiving payments from suppliers for favorable purchase treatment (kickbacks), purchases for personal use, and misappropriation of cash as the most typical methods of employee fraud. Based on a 1995 survey by the **Association of Fraud Examiners**, annual fraud losses are estimated to be $400 billion in the United States, which for the average organization would be 6% of revenues or $9 per day per employee.

Objectives of Internal Control

Internal control provides reasonable assurance that:

1. assets are safeguarded and used for business purposes.
2. business information is accurate.
3. employees comply with laws and regulations.

Internal control can safeguard assets by preventing theft, fraud, misuse, or misplacement. One of the most serious breaches of internal control is employee fraud. **Employee fraud** is the intentional act of deceiving an employer for personal gain. Such deception may range from purposely overstating expenses on a travel expense report in order to receive a higher reimbursement to embezzling millions of dollars through complex schemes.

Micky Monus, co-founder of the **Phar-Mor** drug store chain, overstated inventories by $9.4 million in order to finance the now defunct World Basketball League. The accounting records were falsified, which caused the chain to appear profitable when it was actually losing millions of dollars.

Accurate business information is necessary for operating a business successfully. The safeguarding of assets and accurate information often go hand-in-hand. The reason is that employees attempting to defraud a business will also need to adjust the accounting records in order to hide the fraud.

Businesses must comply with applicable laws and regulations and financial reporting standards. Examples of such standards and laws include environmental regulations, contract terms, safety regulations, and generally accepted accounting principles (GAAP).

Elements of Internal Control

How does management achieve its internal control objectives? Management is responsible for designing and applying five **elements of internal control** to meet the three internal control objectives. These elements are:[1]

1. the control environment
2. risk assessment
3. control procedures
4. monitoring
5. information and communication

The elements of internal control are illustrated in Exhibit 1. In this exhibit, the elements of internal control form an umbrella over the business to protect it from control threats. The business's control environment is represented by the size of the umbrella. Risk assessment, control procedures, and monitoring are the fabric that keeps the umbrella from leaking. Information and communication links the umbrella to management. In the following paragraphs, we discuss each of these elements.

Control Environment

A business's control environment is the overall attitude of management and employees about the importance of controls. One of the factors that influences the control environment is *management's philosophy and operating style.* A management that overemphasizes operating goals and deviates from control policies may indirectly encourage employees to ignore controls. For example, if management rou-

EXHIBIT 1
Elements of Internal Control

[1] *Internal Control—Integrated Framework by the Committee of Sponsoring Organizations* of the Treadway Commission (COSO), pp. 12–14. This document provides a professionally sponsored framework for internal control.

An employee of **J.C. Penney Co.** was convicted of taking $1 million in bribes and kickbacks from suppliers in exchange for information about competitors' bids. One of the prosecuting attorneys told the court, "This case will be discussed in corporate boardrooms. . . . The message ought to be sent out that there's a consequence to corporate fraud."

tinely ignores a policy requiring that safety glasses be worn in the plant, it may cause other employees to interpret the policy as "optional," thereby creating an unsafe work environment. On the other hand, a management that emphasizes the importance of controls and encourages adherence to control policies will create an effective control environment.

The business's *organizational structure,* which is the framework for planning and controlling operations, also influences the control environment. For example, a department store chain might organize each of its stores as separate business units. Each store manager has full authority over pricing and other operating activities. In such a structure, each store manager has the responsibility for establishing an effective control environment.

Personnel policies also affect the control environment. Personnel policies involve the hiring, training, evaluating, compensating, and promoting of employees. In addition, job descriptions, employee codes of ethics, and conflict-of-interest policies are part of the personnel policies. Such policies and procedures can enhance the internal control environment if they provide reasonable assurance that only competent, honest employees are hired and retained.

In the early 1990s, **Sears** had a policy of paying bonuses to its automobile department managers, based on the amount of service provided. This arrangement created incentives for managers to overstate the amount of work required by customers. Thus, customers were being charged for work that they did not need.

Allstate Corporation, an insurance company, used a risk-based internal control framework to develop its internal auditing process. The internal auditors looked for *potential* control weaknesses. They evaluated risk on the probability that it would occur and its significance if it should occur.

Risk Assessment

All organizations face risks. Examples of risk include changes in customer requirements, competitive threats, regulatory changes, changes in economic factors such as interest rates, and employee violations of company policies and procedures. Management should assess these risks and take necessary actions to control them, so that the objectives of internal control can be achieved.

Once risks are identified, they can be analyzed to estimate their significance, to assess their likelihood of occurring, and to determine actions that will minimize them. For example, the manager of a warehouse operation may analyze the risk of employee back injuries, which might give rise to lawsuits. If the manager determines that the risk is significant, the company may take action by purchasing back support braces for its warehouse employees and requiring them to wear the braces.

Control Procedures

Control procedures are established to provide reasonable assurance that business goals will be achieved, including the prevention of fraud. In the following paragraphs, we will briefly discuss control procedures that can be integrated throughout the accounting system. These procedures are listed in Exhibit 2.

An accounting clerk for the Grant County (Washington) Alcoholism Program was in charge of collecting money, making deposits, and keeping the records. While the clerk was away on maternity leave, the replacement clerk discovered a fraud: $17,800 in fees had been collected but had been hidden for personal gain.

Competent Personnel, Rotating Duties, and Mandatory Vacations. The successful operation of an accounting system requires procedures to ensure that people are able to perform the duties to which they are assigned. Hence, it is necessary that all accounting employees be adequately trained and supervised in performing their jobs. It may also be advisable to rotate duties of clerical personnel and mandate vacations for nonclerical personnel. These policies encourage employees to adhere to prescribed procedures. In addition, existing errors or fraud may be detected.

Separating Responsibilities for Related Operations. To decrease the possibility of inefficiency, errors, and fraud, the responsibility for related operations should be divided among two or more persons. For example, the responsibilities

EXHIBIT 2
Internal Control Procedures

for purchasing, receiving, and paying for computer supplies should be divided among three persons or departments. If the same person orders supplies, verifies the receipt of the supplies, and pays the supplier, the following abuses are possible:

1. Orders may be placed on the basis of friendship with a supplier, rather than on price, quality, and other objective factors.
2. The quantity and quality of supplies received may not be verified, thus causing payment for supplies not received or poor-quality supplies.
3. Supplies may be stolen by the employee.
4. The validity and accuracy of invoices may be verified carelessly, thus causing the payment of false or inaccurate invoices.

REAL WORLD

It has been estimated that the typical company pays one out of every one hundred invoices more than once.

Source: Checkers, Simon, and Rosner—*Client Report,* Spring 1994 (Issue 3).

The "checks and balances" provided by dividing responsibilities among various departments requires no duplication of effort. The business documents prepared by one department are designed to coordinate with and support those prepared by other departments.

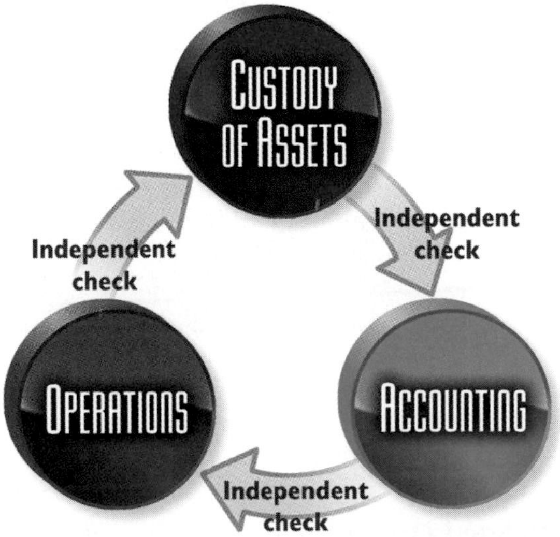

Separating Operations, Custody of Assets, and Accounting. Control policies should establish the responsibilities for various business activities. To reduce the possibility of errors and fraud, the responsibilities for operations, custody of assets, and accounting should be separated. The accounting records then serve as an independent check on the individuals who have custody of the assets and who engage in the business operations. For example, the employees entrusted with handling cash receipts from credit customers should not record cash receipts in the accounting records. To do so would allow employees to borrow or steal cash and hide the theft in the records. Likewise, if those engaged in operating activities also record the results of operations, they could distort the accounting reports to show favorable results. For example, a store manager whose year-end bonus is based upon operating profits might be tempted to record fictitious sales in order to receive a larger bonus.

One of the largest fraud losses in history involved a securities trader for the Singapore office of **Barings Bank**, a British merchant bank. The trader established an unauthorized account number that was used to hide $1.4 billion in losses. Even after Barings' internal auditors noted that the trader both executed trades and recorded them, management did not take action. As a result, a lone individual in a remote office, combined with weak controls, bankrupted an internationally recognized firm.

Proofs and Security Measures. Proofs and security measures should be used to safeguard assets and ensure reliable accounting data. This control procedure applies to many different techniques, such as authorization, approval, and reconciliation procedures. For example, employees who travel on company business may be required to obtain a department manager's approval on a travel request form.

Other examples of control procedures include the use of bank accounts and other measures to ensure the safety of cash and valuable documents. Using a cash register that displays the amount recorded for each sale and provides for the customer a printed receipt can be an effective part of the internal control structure. An all-night convenience store could use the following security measures to deter robberies:

1. Locating the cash register near the door, so that it is fully visible from outside the store; having two employees work late hours; employing a security guard.
2. Depositing cash in the bank daily, before 5 p.m.
3. Keeping only small amounts of cash on hand after 5 p.m. by depositing excess cash in a store safe that can't be opened by employees on duty.
4. Installing cameras and alarm systems.

Auditors for Bremerton, Washington, discovered a shortage of over $4,000 in traffic citation receipts collected as cash or checks by the municipal court cashier. The cashier was able to embezzle the cash because (1) there were no receipts issued for cash received, (2) bank deposits were not reconciled with total receipts, and (3) total tickets issued by the police were not reconciled with cash

Why is separation of duties considered a control procedure?

Internal control is enhanced by separating the control of a transaction from the record-keeping function. Fraud is more easily committed when a single individual controls both the transaction and the accounting for the transaction.

Monitoring

Monitoring the internal control system locates weaknesses and improves control effectiveness. The internal control system may be monitored through either ongoing efforts by management or by separate evaluations. Ongoing monitoring efforts may include observing both employee behavior and warning signs from the accounting system.[2] The indicators shown in Exhibit 3 may be clues to internal control problems.

Separate monitoring evaluations are generally performed when there are major changes in strategy, senior management, business structure, or operations. In large businesses, internal auditors who are independent of operations normally are responsible for monitoring the internal control system. In addition, external auditors also evaluate internal control as a normal part of their annual financial statement audit.

In one of the largest frauds ever committed against a university, a former financial aid officer for **New York University** was charged with stealing $4.1 million from the state of New York. The aid officer allegedly falsified over a thousand tuition assistance checks to students who were not entitled to receive aid and who did not know about the checks. The aid officer deposited the bogus checks for personal use. The initial evidence of the fraud was the officer's spending of $785,000 on expensive jewelry.

Information and Communication

Information and communication are essential elements of internal control. Information about the control environment, risk assessment, control procedures, and monitoring are needed by management to guide operations and ensure compliance with reporting, legal, and regulatory requirements.

[2] Edwin C. Bliss, "Employee Theft," *Boardroom Reports,* July 15, 1994, pp. 5–6.

EXHIBIT 3
Indicators of Internal Control Problems

Warning signs with regard to people

1. Abrupt change in lifestyle (without winning the lottery).
2. Close social relationships with suppliers.
3. Refusing to take a vacation.
4. Frequent borrowing from other employees.
5. Excessive use of alcohol or drugs.

Warning signs from the accounting system

1. Missing documents or gaps in transaction numbers (could mean documents are being used for fraudulent transactions).
2. An unusual increase in customer refunds (refunds may be phony).
3. Differences between daily cash receipts and bank deposits (could mean receipts are pocketed before being deposited).
4. Sudden increase in slow payments (employee may be pocketing the payment).
5. Backlog in recording transactions (possibly an attempt to delay detection of fraud).

Management can also use external information to assess events and conditions that impact decision making and external reporting. For example, management uses information from the Financial Accounting Standards Board (FASB) to assess the impact of possible changes in reporting standards.

Manual Accounting Systems

OBJECTIVE 3

Journalize and post transactions in a manual accounting system that uses subsidiary ledgers and special journals.

After the internal control procedures have been developed, the basic processing method must be selected. Accounting systems may be either manual or computerized. Since an understanding of manual accounting systems assists managers in recognizing the relationships that exist between accounting data and accounting reports, we illustrate manual systems first.

In preceding chapters, all transactions for Computer King were manually recorded in an all-purpose (two-column) journal. The journal entries were then posted individually to the accounts in the ledger. Such manual accounting systems are simple to use and easy to understand. Manually kept records may serve a business reasonably well when the amount of data collected, stored, and used is relatively small. For a large business with a large database, however, such manual processing is too costly and too time-consuming. For example, a large company such as **AT&T** has millions of long-distance telephone fees earned on account with millions of customers daily. Each telephone fee on account requires an entry debiting Accounts Receivable and crediting Fees Earned. In addition, a record of each customer's receivable must be kept. Clearly, a simple manual system would not serve the business needs of AT&T.

When a business has a large number of similar transactions, using an all-purpose journal is inefficient and impractical. In such cases, subsidiary ledgers and spe-

INTERMISSION

Accounting Systems and Profit Measurement

A Greek restaurant owner in Canada had his own system of accounting. He kept his accounts payable in a cigar box on the left-hand side of his cash register, his daily cash returns in the cash register, and his receipts for paid bills in another cigar box on the right. A truly "manual" system.

When his youngest son graduated as an accountant, he was appalled by his father's primitive methods. "I don't know how you can run a business that way," he said. "How do you know what your profits are?"

"Well, son," the father replied, "when I got off the boat from Greece, I had nothing but the pants I was wearing. Today, your brother is a doctor. You are an accountant. Your sister is a speech therapist. Your mother and I have a nice car, a city house, and a country home. We have a good business, and everything is paid for. . . ."

"So, you add all that together, subtract the pants, and there's your profit!" ■

cial journals are useful. In addition, the manual system can be supplemented or replaced by a computerized system. Although we will illustrate the manual use of subsidiary ledgers and special journals, the basic principles described in the following paragraphs also apply to a computerized accounting system.

Subsidiary Ledgers

An accounting system should be designed to provide information on the amounts due from various customers (accounts receivable) and amounts owed to various creditors (accounts payable). A separate account for each customer and creditor could be added to the ledger. However, as the number of customers and creditors increases, the ledger becomes awkward to use when it includes many customers and creditors.

A large number of individual accounts with a common characteristic can be grouped together in a separate ledger called a **subsidiary ledger**. The primary ledger, which contains all of the balance sheet and income statement accounts, is then called the **general ledger**. Each subsidiary ledger is represented in the general ledger by a summarizing account, called a **controlling account**. The sum of the balances of the accounts in a subsidiary ledger must equal the balance of the related controlling account. Thus, you may think of a subsidiary ledger as a secondary ledger that supports a controlling account in the general ledger.

The individual accounts with customers are arranged in alphabetical order in a subsidiary ledger called the **accounts receivable subsidiary ledger** or **customers ledger**. The controlling account in the general ledger that summarizes the debits and credits to the individual customer accounts is *Accounts Receivable*. The individual accounts with creditors are arranged in alphabetical order in a subsidiary ledger called the **accounts payable subsidiary ledger** or **creditors ledger**. The related controlling account in the general ledger is *Accounts Payable*. The relationship between the general ledger and these subsidiary ledgers is illustrated in Exhibit 4.

The sum of the balances of the subsidiary ledger accounts must equal the balance of the related controlling account.

Special Journals

One method of processing data more efficiently in a manual accounting system is to expand the all-purpose two-column journal to a multicolumn journal. Each column in a multicolumn journal is used only for recording transactions that affect a certain account. For example, a special column could be used only for recording debits to the cash account, and another special column could be used only for recording credits to the cash account. The addition of the two special columns would eliminate the writing of *Cash* in the journal for every receipt and every payment of cash. Also, there would be no need to post each individual debit and credit to the cash account. Instead, the *Cash Dr.* and *Cash Cr.* columns could be totaled periodically and only the totals posted. In a similar way, special columns could be added for recording credits to Fees Earned, debits and credits to Accounts Receivable and Accounts Payable, and for other entries that are often repeated.

EXHIBIT 4 General Ledger and Subsidiary Ledgers

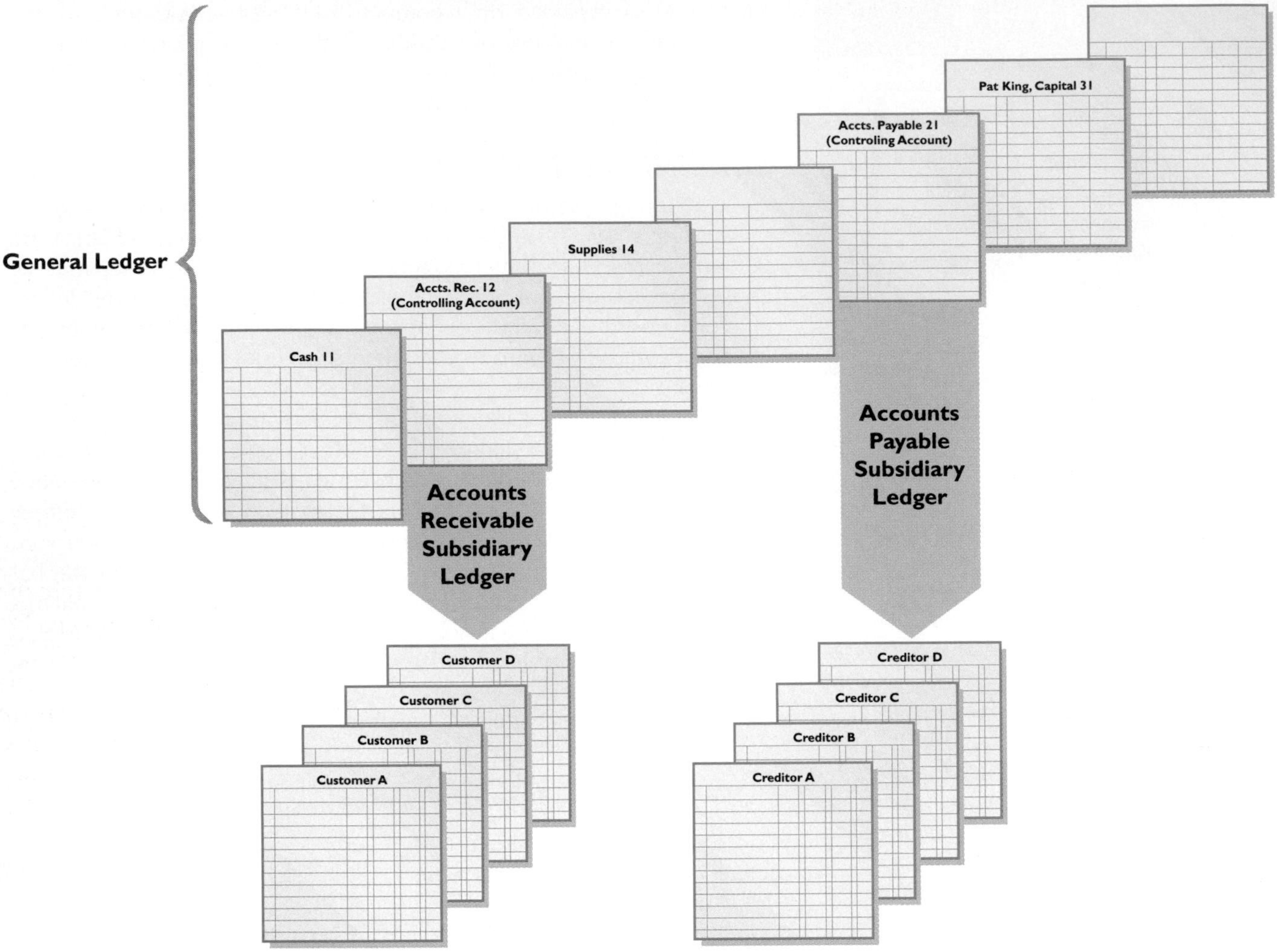

An all-purpose multicolumn journal may be adequate for a small business that has many transactions of a similar nature. However, a journal that has many columns for recording many different types of transactions is impractical for larger businesses.

The next logical extension of the accounting system is to replace the single multicolumn journal with several **special journals**. Each special journal is designed to be used for recording a single kind of transaction that occurs frequently. For example, since most businesses have many transactions in which cash is paid out, they will likely use a special journal for recording cash payments. Likewise, they will use another special journal for recording cash receipts. Special journals are a method of summarizing transactions, which is a basic feature of any accounting system.

Special journals are a method of summarizing transactions.

The format and number of special journals that a business uses depends upon the nature of the business. A business that gives credit might use a special journal designed for recording only revenue from services provided on credit. On the other hand, a business that does not give credit would have no need for such a journal. In other cases, record-keeping costs may be reduced by using supporting documents as special journals.

The transactions that occur most often in a small- to medium-size service business and the special journals in which they are recorded are as follows:

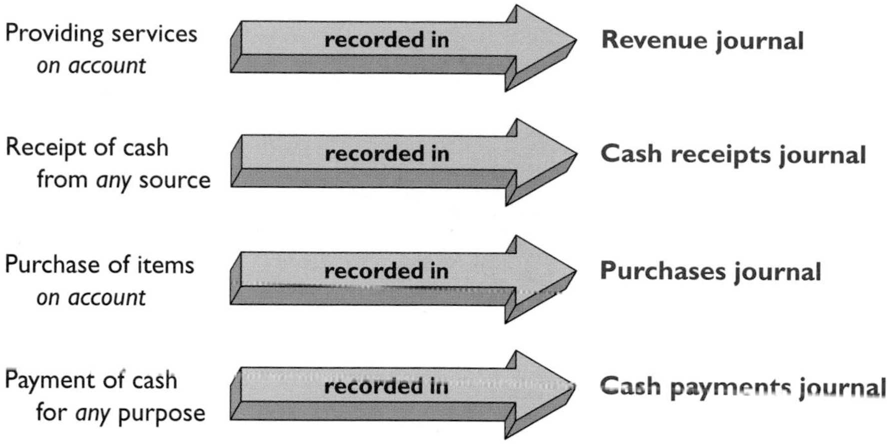

The all-purpose two-column journal, called the **general journal** or simply the **journal**, can be used for entries that do not fit into any of the special journals. For example, adjusting and closing entries are recorded in the general journal.

In the following paragraphs, we illustrate special journals and subsidiary ledgers in a manual accounting system for Computer King. To simplify the illustration, we will use a minimum number of transactions. We will focus our discussion on two common operating cycles: (1) the revenue and cash receipts cycle and (2) the purchase and payment cycle. We will assume that Computer King had the following selected general ledger balances on March 1, 2000:

Account Number	Account	Balance
11	Cash	$6,200
12	Accounts Receivable	3,400
14	Supplies	2,500
18	Office Equipment	2,500
21	Accounts Payable	1,230

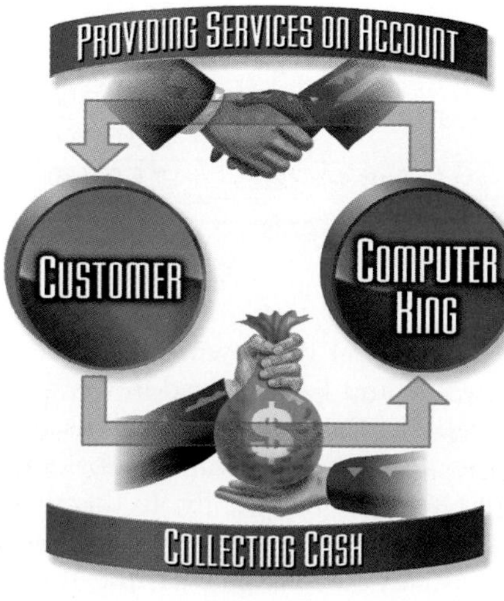

Manual Accounting System: The Revenue and Collection Cycle

The **revenue and collection cycle** for Computer King consists of providing services on account and collecting cash from customers. Revenues earned on account create a customer receivable and will be recorded in a revenue journal. Customers' accounts receivable are collected and will be recorded in a cash receipts journal.

Internal control is enhanced by separating the function of recording revenue transactions in the revenue journal from recording cash collections in the cash receipts journal. For example, if these duties are separated, it is more difficult for one person to steal cash collections and manipulate the accounting records.

Revenue Journal

The **revenue journal** is used only for recording **fees earned on account**. *Cash fees earned would be recorded in the cash receipts journal.* The sale of products is recorded in a **sales journal**, which is similar to the revenue journal. We will compare the efficiency of using a revenue journal with a general journal by assuming that Computer King recorded the following revenue transactions in a general journal:

2000 Mar.	2	Accounts Receivable—Handler Co.	12/✔	2 2 0 0 00	
		Fees Earned	41		2 2 0 0 00
	6	Accounts Receivable—Jordan Co.	12/✔	1 7 5 0 00	
		Fees Earned	41		1 7 5 0 00
	18	Accounts Receivable—Kenner Co.	12/✔	2 6 5 0 00	
		Fees Earned	41		2 6 5 0 00
	27	Accounts Receivable—Handler Co.	12/✔	3 0 0 0 00	
		Fees Earned	41		3 0 0 0 00

The general journal entry on March 2 is posted as a $2,200 debit to *Accounts Receivable* in the general ledger, a $2,200 debit to *Handler Co.* in the accounts receivable subsidiary ledger, and a $2,200 credit to *Fees Earned* in the general ledger.

For these four transactions, Computer King recorded eight account titles and eight amounts. In addition, Computer King made 12 postings to the ledgers—four to Accounts Receivable in the general ledger, four to the accounts receivable subsidiary ledger (indicated by each check mark), and four to Fees Earned in the general ledger. These transactions could be recorded more efficiently in a revenue journal, as shown in Exhibit 5. In each revenue transaction, the amount of the debit to Accounts Receivable is the same as the amount of the credit to Fees Earned. Therefore, only a single amount column is necessary. The date, invoice number, customer name, and amount are entered separately for each transaction.

EXHIBIT 5
Revenue Journal

REVENUE JOURNAL — **PAGE 35**

	Date		Invoice No.	Account Debited	Post. Ref.	Accts. Rec. Dr. Fees Earned Cr.	
1	2000 Mar.	2	615	Handler Co.		2 2 0 0 00	1
2		6	616	Jordan Co.		1 7 5 0 00	2
3		18	617	Kenner Co.		2 6 5 0 00	3
4		27	618	Handler Co.		3 0 0 0 00	4
5		31				9 6 0 0 00	5

The basic procedure of posting from a revenue journal is shown in Exhibit 6. A single monthly total is posted to Accounts Receivable and Fees Earned in the general ledger. Each transaction, such as the $2,200 debit to Handler Co., must also be posted individually to a customer account in the accounts receivable subsidiary ledger. These postings to customer accounts should be made frequently. In this way, management has information on the current balance of each customer's account. Since the balances in the customer accounts are usually debit balances, the three-column account form shown in the exhibit is often used.

EXHIBIT 6
Revenue Journal Postings to Ledgers

REVENUE JOURNAL **PAGE 35**

Date	Invoice No.	Account Debited	Post. Ref.	Accts. Rec. Dr. Fees Earned Cr.
2000				
March 2	615	Handler Co.	✓	2,200
6	616	Jordan Co.	✓	1,750
18	617	Kenner Co.	✓	2,650
27	618	Handler Co.	✓	3,000
31				9,600
				(12) (41)

GENERAL LEDGER

ACCOUNT **Accounts Receivable** **Account No. 12**

Date	Item	Post. Ref.	Dr.	Cr.	Balance Dr.	Balance Cr.
2000						
March 1	Balance	✓			3,400	
31		R35	9,600		13,000	

ACCOUNT **Fees Earned** **Account No. 41**

Date	Item	Post. Ref.	Dr.	Cr.	Balance Dr.	Balance Cr.
2000						
March 31		R35		9,600		9,600

ACCOUNTS RECEIVABLE SUBSIDIARY LEDGER

NAME: Handler Co.

Date	Item	Post. Ref.	Dr.	Cr.	Balance
2000					
March 2		R35	2,200		2,200
27		R35	3,000		5,200

NAME: Jordan Co.

Date	Item	Post. Ref.	Dr.	Cr.	Balance
2000					
March 6		R35	1,750		1,750

NAME: Kenner Co.

Date	Item	Post. Ref.	Dr.	Cr.	Balance
2000					
March 1	Balance	✓			3,400
18		R35	2,650		6,050

Q&A

What is the relationship between the revenue journal and the ledger accounts?

Revenue transactions are recorded and summarized in the revenue journal. Thus, the revenue journal is the source of postings to the subsidiary and general ledger accounts. The fees earned from services provided on account to individual customers are posted from the revenue journal to the customer subsidiary ledger accounts. At the end of the period, the total of the revenue journal column is then posted as a debit to the accounts receivable controlling account and a credit to the revenue account.

To provide a trail of the entries posted to the subsidiary ledger, the source of these entries is indicated in the *Posting Reference* column of each account by inserting the letter *R* (for revenue journal) and the page number of the revenue journal. A check mark (✓) instead of a number is then inserted in the *Posting Reference* column of the revenue journal, as shown in Exhibit 6.

If a customer's account has a credit balance, that fact should be indicated by an asterisk or parentheses in the *Balance* column. When an account's balance is zero, a line may be drawn in the *Balance* column.

At the end of each month, the amount column of the revenue journal is totaled. This total is equal to the sum of the month's debits to the individual accounts in the subsidiary ledger. It is posted in the general ledger as a debit to Accounts Receivable and a credit to Fees Earned, as shown in Exhibit 6. The respective account numbers (12 and 41) are then inserted below the total in the revenue journal to indicate that the posting is completed, as shown in Exhibit 6. In this way, all of the transactions for fees earned during the month are posted to the general ledger only once—at the end of the month—greatly simplifying the posting process.

Cash Receipts Journal

All transactions that involve the receipt of cash are recorded in a **cash receipts journal**. Thus, the cash receipts journal has a column entitled *Cash Dr.,* as shown in Exhibit 7. All transactions recorded in the cash receipts journal will involve an entry in the *Cash Dr.* column. For example, on March 28 Computer King received cash of $2,200 from Handler Co. and entered that amount in the *Cash Dr.* column.

The kinds of transactions in which cash is received and how often they occur determine the titles of the other columns. For Computer King, the most frequent source of cash is collections from customers. Thus, the cash receipts journal in Exhibit 7 has an *Accounts Receivable Cr.* column. On March 28, when Handler Co. made a payment on its account, Computer King entered *Handler Co.* in the *Account Credited* column and entered *2,200* in the *Accounts Receivable Cr.* column.

The *Other Accounts Cr.* column in Exhibit 7 is used for recording credits to any account for which there is no special credit column. For example, Computer King received cash on March 1 for rent. Since no special column exists for Rent Revenue, Computer King entered *Rent Revenue* in the *Account Credited* column and entered *400* in the *Other Accounts Cr.* column.

Postings from the cash receipts journal to the ledgers of Computer King are also shown in Exhibit 7. This posting process is similar to that of the revenue journal. At regular intervals, each amount in the *Other Accounts Cr.* column is posted to the proper account in the general ledger. The posting is indicated by inserting the account number in the *Posting Reference* column of the cash receipts journal. The posting reference *CR* (for cash receipts journal) and the proper page number are inserted in the *Posting Reference* columns of the accounts.

The amounts in the *Accounts Receivable Cr.* column are posted individually to the customer accounts in the accounts receivable subsidiary ledger. These postings should be made frequently. The posting reference *CR* and the proper page number are inserted in the *Posting Reference* column of each customer's account. A check mark is placed in the *Posting Reference* column of the cash receipts journal to show that each amount has been posted. None of the individual amounts in the *Cash Dr.* column is posted separately.

At the end of the month, all of the amount columns are totaled. The debits should equal the credits. Because each amount in the *Other Accounts Cr.* column has been posted individually to a general ledger account, a check mark is inserted below the column total to indicate that no further action is needed. The totals of the *Accounts Receivable Cr.* and *Cash Dr.* columns are posted to the proper accounts in the general ledger, and their account numbers are inserted below the totals to show that the postings have been completed.

Accounts Receivable Control and Subsidiary Ledger

After all posting has been completed for the month, the sum of the balances in the accounts receivable subsidiary ledger should be compared with the balance of the accounts receivable controlling account in the general ledger. If the controlling account and the subsidiary ledger do not agree, the error or errors must be located and corrected. The balances of the individual customer accounts may be summarized in a schedule. The total of Computer King's schedule of accounts receivable, $5,650, agrees with the balance of its accounts receivable controlling account on March 31, 2000, as shown below.

Accounts Receivable— (Controlling)	
Balance, March 31, 2000	$5,650

Computer King
Schedule of Accounts Receivable
March 31, 2000

Handler Co.	$3,000
Kenner Co.	2,650
Jordan Co.	0
Total accounts receivable	$5,650

EXHIBIT 7
Cash Receipts Journal and Postings

CASH RECEIPTS JOURNAL **PAGE 14**

Date	Account Credited	Post. Ref.	Other Accounts Cr.	Accounts Receivable Cr.	Cash Dr.
2000					
March 1	Rent Revenue	42	400		400
19	Kenner Co.	✔		3,400	3,400
28	Handler Co.	✔		2,200	2,200
30	Jordan Co.	✔		1,750	1,750
31			400	7,350	7,750
			(✔)	(12)	(11)

GENERAL LEDGER

ACCOUNT Rent Revenue — Account No. 42

Date	Item	Post. Ref.	Dr.	Cr.	Balance Dr.	Balance Cr.
2000						
March 1		CR14		400		400

ACCOUNT Accounts Receivable — Account No. 12

Date	Item	Post. Ref.	Dr.	Cr.	Balance Dr.	Balance Cr.
2000						
March 1	Balance	✔			3,400	
31		R35	9,600		13,000	
31		CR14		7,350	5,650	

ACCOUNT Cash — Account No. 11

Date	Item	Post. Ref.	Dr.	Cr.	Balance Dr.	Balance Cr.
2000						
March 1	Balance	✔			6,200	
31		CR14	7,750		13,950	

ACCOUNTS RECEIVABLE SUBSIDIARY LEDGER

NAME: Handler Co.

Date	Item	Post. Ref.	Dr.	Cr.	Balance
2000					
March 2		R35	2,200		2,200
27		R35	3,000		5,200
28		CR14		2,200	3,000

NAME: Jordan Co.

Date	Item	Post. Ref.	Dr.	Cr.	Balance
2000					
March 6		R35	1,750		1,750
30		CR14		1,750	—

NAME: Kenner Co.

Date	Item	Post. Ref.	Dr.	Cr.	Balance
2000					
March 1	Balance	✔			3,400
18		R35	2,650		6,050
19		CR14		3,400	2,650

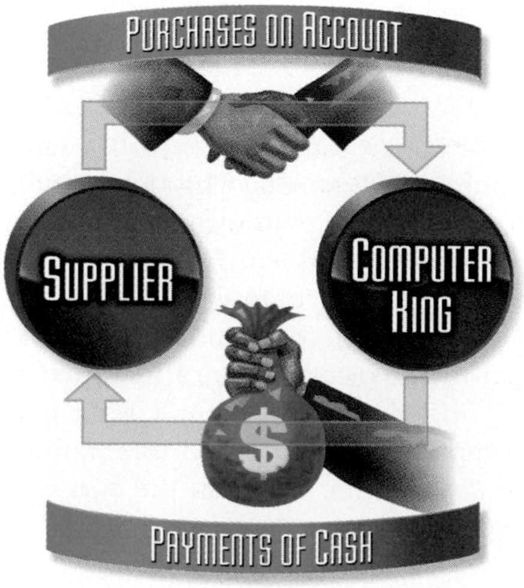

Manual Accounting System: The Purchase and Payment Cycle

The **purchase and payment cycle** for Computer King consists of purchases on account and payments of cash to suppliers. To make purchases of supplies and other items on account requires establishing a supplier account payable. These transactions will be recorded in a purchases journal. The payments of suppliers' accounts payable will be recorded in the cash payments journal.

Internal control is enhanced by separating the function of recording purchases in the purchases journal from recording cash payments in the cash payments journal. Separating duties in this way prevents an individual from establishing a fictitious supplier and then collecting payments for fictitious purchases from this supplier.

Purchases Journal

The **purchases journal** is designed for recording all **purchases on account**. *Cash purchases would be recorded in the cash payments journal.* The purchases journal has a column entitled *Accounts Payable Cr.* The purchases journal also has special columns for recording debits to the accounts most often affected. Since Computer King makes frequent debits to its supplies account, a *Supplies Dr.* column is included for these transactions. For example, as shown in Exhibit 8, Computer King recorded the purchase of supplies on March 3 by entering *600* in the *Supplies Dr.* column, *600* in the *Accounts Payable Cr.* column, and *Howard Supplies* in the *Account Credited* column.

The *Other Accounts Dr.* column in Exhibit 8 is used to record purchases, on account, of any item for which there is no special debit column. The title of the account to be debited is entered in the *Other Accounts* column, and the amount is entered in the *Amount* column. For example, Computer King recorded the purchase of office equipment on account on March 12 by entering *Office Equipment* in the *Other Accounts Dr.* column, *2,800* in the *Amount* column, *2,800* in the *Accounts Payable Cr.* column, and *Jewett Business Systems* in the *Account Credited* column.

Postings from the purchases journal to the ledgers of Computer King are also shown in Exhibit 8. The principles used in posting the purchases journal are similar to those used in posting the revenue and cash receipts journals. The source of the entries posted to the subsidiary and general ledgers is indicated in the *Posting Reference* column of each account by inserting the letter *P* (for purchases journal) and the page number of the purchases journal. A check mark (✓) is inserted in the *Posting Reference* column of the purchases journal after each credit is posted to a creditor's account in the accounts payable subsidiary ledger.

At regular intervals, the amounts in the *Other Accounts Dr.* column are posted to the accounts in the general ledger. As each amount is posted, the related general ledger account number is inserted in the *Posting Reference* column of the *Other Accounts* section.

At the end of each month, the amount columns in the purchases journal are totaled. The sum of the two debit column totals should equal the sum of the credit column.

The totals of the *Accounts Payable Cr.* and *Supplies Dr.* columns are posted to the appropriate general ledger accounts in the usual manner, with the related account numbers inserted below the column totals. Because each amount in the *Other Accounts Dr.* column was posted individually, a check mark is placed below the $2,800 total to show that no further action is needed.

Cash Payments Journal

The special columns for the **cash payments journal** are determined in the same manner as for the revenue, cash receipts, and purchases journals. The determining factors are the kinds of transactions to be recorded and how often they occur.

The cash payments journal has a *Cash Cr.* column, as shown in Exhibit 9. All transactions recorded in the cash payments journal will involve an entry in this column. Payments to creditors on account happen often enough to require an *Accounts Payable Dr.* column. Debits to creditor accounts for invoices paid are recorded in the *Accounts Payable Dr.* column. For example, on March 15 Computer King paid $1,230 on its account with Grayco Supplies. Computer King recorded this transaction by entering *1,230* in the *Accounts Payable Dr.* column, *1,230* in the *Cash Cr.* column, and *Grayco Supplies* in the *Account Debited* column.

EXHIBIT 8 Purchases Journal and Postings

PURCHASES JOURNAL — PAGE 11

Date		Account Credited	Post. Ref.	Accounts Payable Cr.	Supplies Dr.	Other Accounts Dr.	Post. Ref.	Amount
2000								
March	3	Howard Supplies	✔	600	600			
	7	Donnelly Supplies	✔	420	420			
	12	Jewett Business Systems	✔	2,800		Office Equipment	18	2,800
	19	Donnelly Supplies	✔	1,450	1,450			
	27	Howard Supplies	✔	960	960			
	31			6,230	3,430			2,800
				(21)	(14)			(✔)

GENERAL LEDGER

ACCOUNT Accounts Payable — Account No. 21

Date		Item	Post. Ref.	Dr.	Cr.	Balance
2000						
March	1	Balance	✔			1,230
	31		P11		6,230	7,460

ACCOUNT Supplies — Account No. 14

Date		Item	Post. Ref.	Dr.	Cr.	Balance
2000						
March	1	Balance	✔			2,500
	31		P11	3,430		5,930

ACCOUNT Office Equipment — Account No. 18

Date		Item	Post. Ref.	Dr.	Cr.	Balance
2000						
March	1	Balance	✔			2,500
	12		P11	2,800		5,300

ACCOUNTS PAYABLE SUBSIDIARY LEDGER

NAME: Donnelly Supplies

Date		Item	Post. Ref.	Dr.	Cr.	Balance
2000						
March	7		P11		420	420
	19		P11		1,450	1,870

NAME: Grayco Supplies

Date		Item	Post. Ref.	Dr.	Cr.	Balance
2000						
March	1	Balance	✔			1,230

NAME: Howard Supplies

Date		Item	Post. Ref.	Dr.	Cr.	Balance
2000						
March	3		P11		600	600
	27		P11		960	1,560

NAME: Jewett Business Systems

Date		Item	Post. Ref.	Dr.	Cr.	Balance
2000						
March	12		P11		2,800	2,800

Computer King makes all payments by check. As each transaction is recorded in the cash payments journal, the related check number is entered in the column at the right of the *Date* column. The check numbers are helpful in controlling cash payments, and they provide a useful cross-reference.

The *Other Accounts Dr.* column is used for recording debits to any account for which there is no special column. For example, Computer King paid $1,600 on March 2 for rent. The transaction was recorded by entering *Rent Expense* in the space provided and *1,600* in the *Other Accounts Dr.* and *Cash Cr.* columns.

Postings from the cash payments journal to the ledgers of Computer King are also shown in Exhibit 9. The amounts entered in the *Accounts Payable Dr.* column

EXHIBIT 9
Cash Payments Journal and Postings

CASH PAYMENTS JOURNAL — PAGE 7

	Date	Ck. No.	Account Debited	Post. Ref.	Other Accounts Dr.	Accounts Payable Dr.	Cash Cr.	
	2000							
1	March 2	150	Rent Expense	52	1,600		1,600	1
2	15	151	Grayco Supplies	✔		1,230	1,230	2
3	21	152	Jewett Business Systems	✔		2,800	2,800	3
4	22	153	Donnelly Supplies	✔		420	420	4
5	30	154	Utilities Expense	54	1,050		1,050	5
6	31	155	Howard Supplies	✔		600	600	6
7	31				2,650	5,050	7,700	7
8					(✔)	(21)	(11)	8

GENERAL LEDGER

ACCOUNT Accounts Payable — Account No. 21

Date	Item	Post. Ref.	Dr.	Cr.	Balance
2000					
March 1	Balance	✔			1,230
31		P11		6,230	7,460
31		CP7	5,050		2,410

ACCOUNT Cash — Account No. 11

Date	Item	Post. Ref.	Dr.	Cr.	Balance
2000					
March 1	Balance	✔			6,200
31		CR14	7,750		13,950
31		CP7		7,700	6,250

ACCOUNT Rent Expense — Account No. 52

Date	Item	Post. Ref.	Dr.	Cr.	Balance
2000					
March 2		CP7	1,600		1,600

ACCOUNT Utilities Expense — Account No. 54

Date	Item	Post. Ref.	Dr.	Cr.	Balance
2000					
March 30		CP7	1,050		1,050

ACCOUNTS PAYABLE SUBSIDIARY LEDGER

NAME: Donnelly Supplies

Date	Item	Post. Ref.	Dr.	Cr.	Balance
2000					
March 7		P11		420	420
19		P11		1,450	1,870
22		CP7	420		1,450

NAME: Grayco Supplies

Date	Item	Post. Ref.	Dr.	Cr.	Balance
2000					
March 1	Balance	✔			1,230
15		CP7	1,230		—

NAME: Howard Supplies

Date	Item	Post. Ref.	Dr.	Cr.	Balance
2000					
March 3		P11		600	600
27		P11		960	1,560
31		CP7	600		960

NAME: Jewett Business Systems

Date	Item	Post. Ref.	Dr.	Cr.	Balance
2000					
March 12		P11		2,800	2,800
21		CP7	2,800		—

are posted to the individual creditor accounts in the accounts payable subsidiary ledger. These postings should be made frequently. After each posting, *CP* (for cash payments journal) and the page number of the journal are inserted in the *Posting Reference* column of the account. A check mark is placed in the *Posting Reference* column of the cash payments journal to indicate that each amount has been posted.

At regular intervals, each item in the *Other Accounts Dr.* column is also posted individually to an account in the general ledger. The posting is indicated by writing the account number in the *Posting Reference* column of the cash payments journal.

At the end of the month, each of the amount columns in the cash payments journal is totaled. The sum of the two debit totals is compared with the credit total to determine their equality. A check mark is placed below the total of the *Other Accounts Dr.* column to indicate that no further action is needed. When each of the totals of the other two columns is posted to the general ledger, an account number is inserted below each column total.

Accounts Payable Control and Subsidiary Ledger

After all posting has been completed for the month, the sum of the balances in the accounts payable subsidiary ledger should be compared with the balance of the accounts payable controlling account in the general ledger. If the controlling account and the subsidiary ledger do not agree, the error or errors must be located and corrected. The balances of the individual supplier accounts may be summarized in a schedule. The total of Computer King's schedule of accounts payable, $2,410, agrees with the balance of the accounts payable controlling account on March 31, 2000, as shown below.

Accounts Payable—(Controlling)

Balance, March 31, 2000	$2,410

Computer King
Schedule of Accounts Payable
March 31, 2000

Donnelly Supplies	$1,450
Grayco Supplies	0
Howard Supplies	960
Jewett Business Systems	0
Total	$2,410

Adapting Manual Accounting Systems

OBJECTIVE 4

Describe and give examples of additional subsidiary ledgers and modified special journals.

The preceding sections of this chapter illustrate subsidiary ledgers and special journals that are common for a medium-size business. Many businesses use subsidiary ledgers for other accounts, in addition to Accounts Receivable and Accounts Payable. Also, special journals are often adapted or modified in practice to meet the specific needs of a business. In the following paragraphs, we describe other subsidiary ledgers and modified special journals.

Additional Subsidiary Ledgers

Generally, subsidiary ledgers are used for accounts that consist of a large number of individual items, each of which has unique characteristics. For example, businesses may use a subsidiary equipment ledger to keep track of each item of equipment purchased, its cost, location, and other data. Such ledgers are similar to the accounts receivable and accounts payable subsidiary ledgers that we illustrated in this chapter.

Modified Special Journals

A business may modify its special journals by adding one or more columns for recording transactions that occur frequently. For example, a business may collect sales taxes that must be remitted periodically to the taxing authorities. Thus, the business may add a special column for *Sales Taxes Payable* in its revenue journal, as shown below.

REVENUE JOURNAL **PAGE 40**

	Date		Invoice No.	Account Debited	Post. Ref.	Accts. Rec. Dr.	Fees Earned Cr.	Sales Taxes Payable Cr.	
1	2000 Nov.	2	842	Litten Co.	✔	4 770 00	4 500 00	270 00	1
2		3	843	Kauffman Supply Co.	✔	1 166 00	1 100 00	66 00	2

Some other examples of how special journals may be modified for a variety of different types of businesses are:

- **Farm**—The purchases journal may be modified to include columns for various types of seeds (corn, wheat), livestock (cows, hogs, sheep), fertilizer, and fuel.
- **Automobile Repair Shop**—The revenue journal may be modified to include columns for each major type of repair service. In addition, columns for warranty repairs, credit card charges, and sales taxes may be added.
- **Hospital**—The cash receipts journal may be modified to include columns for receipts from patients on account, from Blue Cross/Blue Shield or other major insurance reimbursers, and Medicare.
- **Movie Theater**—The cash receipts journal may be modified to include columns for revenues from admissions, gift certificates, and concession sales.
- **Restaurant**—The purchases journal may be modified to include columns for food, linen, silverware and glassware, and kitchen supplies.

Regardless of how a special journal is modified, the basic principles and procedures discussed in this chapter apply. For example, the columns in special journals are normally totaled at periodic intervals. The totals of the debit and credit columns are then compared to verify their equality before the totals are posted to the general ledger accounts.

Computerized Accounting Systems

OBJECTIVE 5

Describe the components of a computer system and apply computerized accounting to the revenue and collection cycle.

Computerized accounting systems have become more widely used as the cost of hardware and software has declined. We will begin with an introduction to basic computer terms and then illustrate the revenue and collection cycle in a computerized system.

Computer Hardware Basics

You may own a computer or be familiar with its basic elements. However, if you are not familiar with computer systems, we provide a brief overview in the following sections. A computerized accounting system requires **hardware**, which includes a computer, its components, and related equipment. The basic external hardware elements of a microcomputer are illustrated in Exhibit 10. These hardware elements provide for user input, data input, and data output.

The computer receives **user input** from the keyboard or the mouse. The computer receives **data input** from either a floppy disk or through a CD (compact disk) drive. Many computers have the floppy disk and CD drives built into the computer.

Data output from the computer may be displayed on the monitor or printed by a printer. Data input or output may also travel over a **network**, which is a method of connecting the computer to another user or data storage location. For example, telephone lines may serve as a data network.

EXHIBIT 10
External Hardware Elements of a Computer

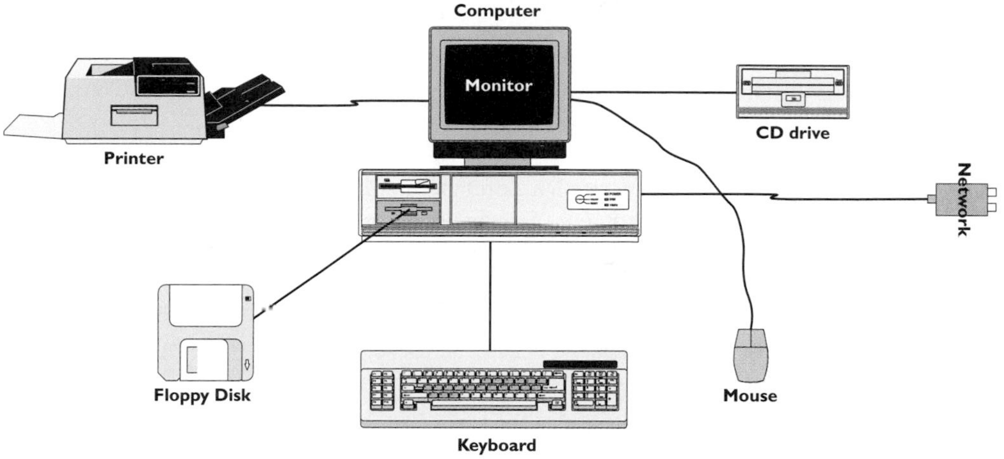

Computer Software Basics

The instructions used by the computer are provided by programs, or **software**. There are two major types of computer software: operating systems and applications. The **operating system** provides the instructions for the basic operations of the computer. The operating system also provides the underlying interface between the user and the computer. Every computer needs an operating system. An example of a popular operating system is Windows®. An **application** is software that performs a particular task. Examples of applications include word processing, spreadsheets, and accounting. There are thousands of applications available to perform many different tasks for users, from games to highly sophisticated mathematical analysis. Some common applications are listed below.

Applications

Type	Example
Word processing	Word, WordPerfect®
Spreadsheet	Excel, Lotus 1-2-3®
Presentation	PowerPoint®
Accounting	QuickBooks®, Peachtree®
Web browser	Netscape® Navigator

Point of INTEREST

Gordon Moore, chairman of **Intel**, once stated: "If the auto industry had moved at the same speed as our [computer] industry, your car today would cruise comfortably at a million miles an hour and probably get a half a million miles per gallon of gasoline. But it would be cheaper to throw your Rolls Royce away than to park it downtown for an evening."

Computerized System: An Illustration of the Revenue and Collection Cycle

Computerized accounting systems have three main advantages over manual systems. First, computerized systems simplify the record-keeping process. Transactions are recorded in electronic forms and, at the same time, posted electronically to general and subsidiary ledger accounts. Second, computerized systems are generally more accurate than manual systems. Third, computerized systems provide management current account balance information to support decision making, since account balances are posted as the transactions occur.

How do computerized accounting systems work? We will illustrate the revenue and collection cycle of Computer King by using a popular accounting application called

BUSINESS ON STAGE

Computers are being used today in virtually every area of business. In the not-too-distant future, it is difficult to imagine how any business could be successful without integrating computers into its operations and management.

What are some of the ways that computers are being used in manufacturing, management, marketing, accounting, and finance? Computer-aided design (CAD) and computer-aided manufacturing (CAM) are being used by manufacturing companies. CAD is used heavily by automobile companies to design and engineer new cars and trucks. The use of CAD speeds up the design process and allows manufacturers to deliver new products to the market sooner. CAM uses computers to control the production process and monitor the quality of the products. CAM is used heavily in chemical, oil refining, and other industries that involve volume processing of materials.

Many applications of computers exist in the management of businesses. For example, computers can facilitate training by providing an interactive medium that allows employees to obtain instant feedback on their performance and progress. One of the most exciting areas in which computers are affecting management is in communications. Electronic mail (e-mail) provides a very fast and inexpensive way of communicating written messages. In addition, the Internet and the World Wide Web allow rapid access to an almost infinite amount of information of potential usefulness to the managers of a business. Finally, teleconferencing and videoconferencing allow groups of managers to confer simultaneously over long distances, with significant savings in time, energy, and money.

Computers have allowed businesses to develop large databases from warranty cards, sweepstakes entries, coupons, promotions, and other sources. Such databases allow businesses insight into customer habits and preferences. This in turn allows businesses to target specific categories of customers for their marketing efforts. It also allows businesses to respond more quickly to changing customer preferences and needs.

In most businesses, the accounting area was the first to adopt computer technology for processing transactions and preparing management reports. Computers allow transactions to be processed almost instantaneously, with related reports available for immediate use by managers. In addition, computers can be used to plan for the future by modeling business operations and conducting "what if" analyses, using various assumptions and alternative decisions by management. ■

QuickBooks®. As shown in Exhibit 11, the first step is to enter information onto an electronic invoice form, as illustrated for the March 2 Handler Company invoice (No. 615). When the form is completed, it may be printed out and mailed to the customer. In addition, upon completing the invoice form the software automatically records the fees earned and posts the $2,200 to the Handler Co. account receivable.

In step two, the collection from the customer is received. Upon collection, the "receive payment" electronic form is opened and completed. In Exhibit 11, this form indicates that a $2,200 payment was collected from Handler Co. on March 28. This amount was applied to invoice 615, as shown by the check mark next to the March 2 date at the bottom of the form. The March 27 invoice of $3,000 remains uncollected, as shown at the bottom of the form. When this screen is completed, the cash account is automatically updated to reflect the increase in cash, and the Handler Company accounts receivable balance is automatically reduced from $5,200 to $3,000.

At any time, managers may request reports from the software. In step three, three such reports are illustrated in Exhibit 11: (1) the customer balance summary, (2) the income by customer summary, and (3) the check register. The reports are shown for March 31, 2000. Notice that the customer balance summary lists the outstanding accounts receivable balances by customer. This is essentially a report providing the details of the accounts receivable subsidiary ledger. It shows essentially the same information as Computer King's Schedule of Accounts Receivable on p. 190. The income by customer summary provides a listing of revenue by customer, which is similar to information provided by the revenue journal in a manual system. This listing is created from the electronic invoice form used in the first step of the cycle. The check register (First National Bank) lists the explanations for changes in the cash balance due to receipts and payments. Since receipts are only illustrated in this example, this report is similar to the cash receipts journal under the manual system. This listing is created from the "receive payment form" used in Step 2.

At the end of the month the manual system posted revenue journal and cash collection totals to the accounts receivable controlling ac-

EXHIBIT 11 The Revenue and Collection Cycle in QuickBooks®

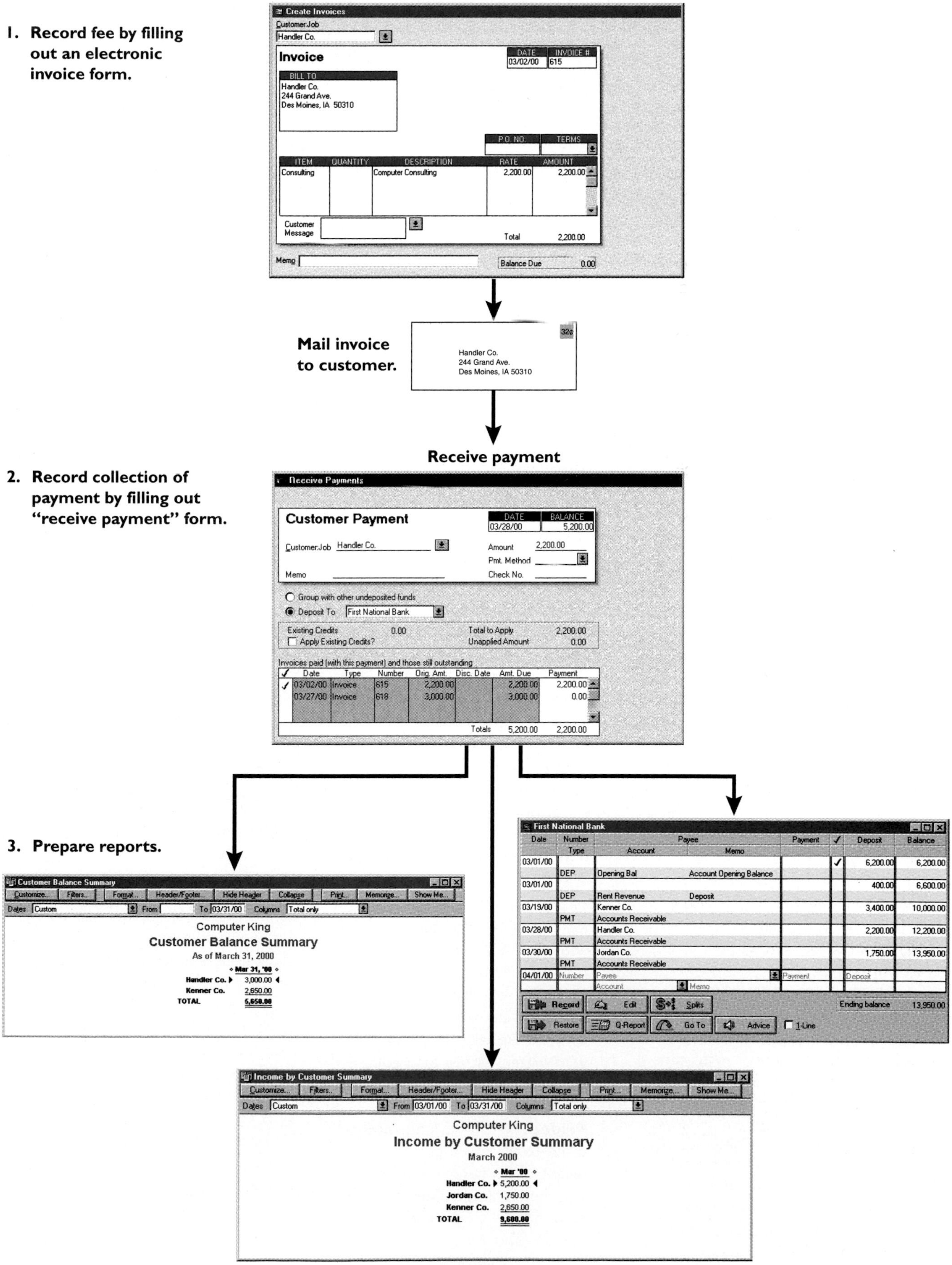

REAL WORLD

Most Windows-based accounting software uses electronic forms. An electronic form is a window that appears like a paper form. The form has spaces, or fields, in which to input information about a particular type of transaction. Many of the information spaces have pull-down lists for easy data entry. The most common electronic forms used by QuickBooks® are invoices, checks, bills, and receipts of payments.

count. In a computerized system, special journals typically are not used. Instead, transactions are recorded in electronic forms, which are automatically posted to affected accounts at the time the form is completed. In a manual system, the controlling account balance can be reconciled to the sum of the individual customer account balances to identify any posting and mathematical errors. The computer, however, does not make posting and mathematical errors. Thus, there are no month-end postings to controlling accounts. Controlling accounts are simply the sum of the balances of any individual subsidiary account balances.

We have illustrated the revenue and collection cycle to help you understand how a portion of a computerized accounting system works. A similar description could be provided for the purchases and payments cycle. A description of a complete computerized accounting system is beyond our scope. However, a thorough understanding of this chapter provides a solid foundation for applying the accounting system concepts in either a manual or a computerized system.

ENCORE

Lessons From ZZZZ Best

At the age of 16, Barry Minkow began a carpet cleaning company out of his parents' garage. Minkow aggressively promoted his company to Wall Street and attracted many outside investors. During this time, Minkow was considered a teenage tycoon. The story of his company, called **ZZZZ Best**, ended abruptly when Minkow, at the age of 21, was sentenced to 25 years for defrauding investors out of $26 million by falsely claiming his company was profitable and successful. Seven years later, upon his release from prison, Minkow claimed to be a changed man.

Minkow said his experience taught him the symptoms of personal corruption, and the lack of business controls.

- **Small compromises may lead to larger ones.** Minkow says for him it started with a $200 money order theft from a local liquor store. This escalated to overcharging customers' credit cards, and then eventually to investor fraud. Minkow says the fraudulent behavior becomes easy to rationalize: "If I can get away with it the first time, I can probably do it again with the same result."
- **An unhealthy obsession with what others think about you.** Minkow states that he felt insecure because he lived in an area where classmates were driven to school in Mercedes, and this led to an obsession for personal wealth and prestige.
- **Taking shortcuts, or the easy way out.** Minkow tells the story of completing a carpet cleaning job and selling the customer an additional $100 Scotchguard application. When returning to his truck, he found that there was no Scotchguard left. Minkow sprayed the customer's carpet with water, rather than going back to the shop and picking up more Scotchguard.
- **Pride.** Minkow says his mother came to his office during the height of his fame and asked whether he knew God. Minkow responded, "God. How much is He? I'll buy Him."

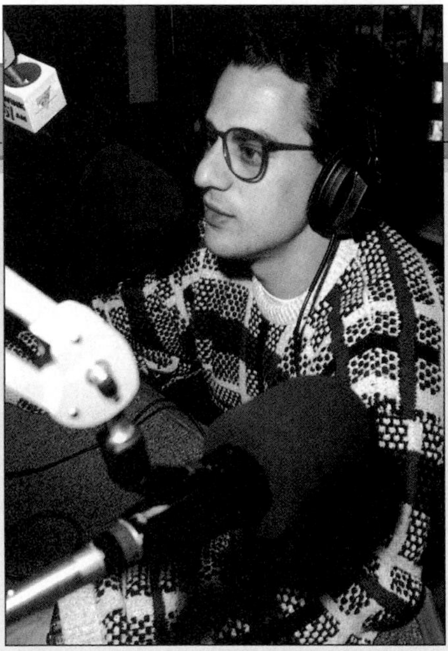

Minkow has written a book, is conducting Bible studies, has earned degrees in theology, is a radio talk-show host, and is providing lectures on his experiences. He states that any money from these efforts will go toward paying back the investors who lost their savings in ZZZZ Best. To those that say it's just another scam, his response is that "authenticity is confirmed by consistency." Minkow's defrauded investors will wait and see.

Sources: Los Angeles Times staff interview, March 31, 1995; Barry Minkow, "My Million-Dollar Lesson About Compromise," *New Man* (January–February 1996), pp. 34–37.

KEY POINTS

1 Define an accounting system and describe its implementation.

An accounting system is the methods and procedures for collecting, classifying, summarizing, and reporting a business's financial information. The three steps through which an accounting system evolves are (1) analysis of information needs, (2) design of the system, and (3) implementation of the systems design.

2 List the three objectives of internal control and define and give examples of the five elements of internal control.

Internal control provides reasonable assurance that (1) assets are safeguarded and used for business purposes, (2) business information is accurate, and (3) laws and regulations are complied with. The five elements of internal control are the control environment, risk assessment, control procedures, monitoring, and information and communication.

3 Journalize and post transactions in a manual accounting system that uses subsidiary ledgers and special journals.

Subsidiary ledgers may be used to maintain separate records for each customer (the accounts receivable subsidiary ledger) and creditor (the accounts payable subsidiary ledger). Each subsidiary ledger is represented in the general ledger by a summarizing account, called a controlling account. The sum of the balances of the accounts in a subsidiary ledger must agree with the balance of the related controlling account.

Special journals may be used to reduce the processing time and expense of recording a large number of similar transactions. The revenue journal is used to record the sale of services on account. The cash receipts journal is used to record all receipts of cash. The purchases journal is used to record purchases on account. The cash payments journal is used to record all payments of cash. The general journal is used for recording transactions that do not fit in any of the special journals. The use of each special journal and the accounts receivable and accounts payable subsidiary ledgers is illustrated in the chapter.

4 Describe and give examples of additional subsidiary ledgers and modified special journals.

Subsidiary ledgers may be maintained for a variety of accounts, such as fixed assets, as well as accounts receivable and accounts payable. Special journals may be modified by adding columns in which to record frequently occurring transactions. For example, an additional column is often added to the revenue journal for recording the collection of sales taxes payable.

5 Describe the components of a computer system and apply computerized accounting to the revenue and collection cycle.

Computers consist of both hardware and software. Hardware provides the data input/output functions as well as internal data management and processing. Software provides the instructions for the computer. The operating system provides the computer with basic instructions, while applications are software that perform a particular task. Computerized accounting systems are similar to manual accounting systems. The main advantages of a computerized accounting system are the simultaneous recording and posting of transactions, the high degree of accuracy, and the timeliness of reporting. An example of the revenue and collection cycle using QuickBooks® is provided in the chapter.

ILLUSTRATIVE PROBLEM

Selected transactions of O'Malley Co. for the month of May are as follows:

a. May 1 Issued Check No. 1001 in payment of rent for May, $1,200.
b. 2 Purchased office supplies on account from McMillan Co., $3,600.
c. 4 Issued Check No. 1003 in payment of transportation charges on the supplies purchased on May 2, $320.
d. 8 Rendered services on account to Waller Co., Invoice No. 51, $4,500.
e. 9 Issued Check No. 1005 for office supplies purchased, $450.
f. 10 Received cash for office supplies sold to employees at cost, $120.
g. 11 Purchased office equipment on account from Fender Office Products, $15,000.
h. 12 Issued Check No. 1010 in payment of the supplies purchased from McMillan Co. on May 2, $3,600.
i. 16 Rendered services on account to Riese Co., Invoice No. 58, $8,000.

j. May 18 Received $4,500 from Waller Co. in payment of May 8 invoice.
k. 20 Invested additional cash in the business, $10,000.
l. 25 Rendered services for cash, $15,900.
m. 30 Issued Check No. 1040 for withdrawal of cash for personal use, $1,000.
n. 30 Issued Check No. 1041 in payment of electricity and water bills, $690.
o. 30 Issued Check No. 1042 in payment of office and sales salaries for May, $15,800.
p. 31 Journalized adjusting entries from the work sheet prepared for the fiscal year ended May 31.

O'Malley Co. maintains a revenue journal, a cash receipts journal, a purchases journal, a cash payments journal, and a general journal. In addition, accounts receivable and accounts payable subsidiary ledgers are used.

Instructions

1. Indicate the journal in which each of the preceding transactions, (a) through (p), would be recorded.
2. Indicate whether an account in the accounts receivable or accounts payable subsidiary ledgers would be affected for each of the preceding transactions.
3. Journalize transactions (b), (c), (d), (h), and (j) in the appropriate journals.

Solution

	1. Journal	2. Subsidiary Ledger
a.	Cash payments journal	
b.	Purchases journal	Accounts payable ledger
c.	Cash payments journal	
d.	Revenue journal	Accounts receivable ledger
e.	Cash payments journal	
f.	Cash receipts journal	
g.	Purchases journal	Accounts payable ledger
h.	Cash payments journal	Accounts payable ledger
i.	Revenue journal	Accounts receivable ledger
j.	Cash receipts journal	Accounts receivable ledger
k.	Cash receipts journal	
l.	Cash receipts journal	
m.	Cash payments journal	
n.	Cash payments journal	
o.	Cash payments journal	
p.	General journal	

3.
Transaction (b):

PURCHASES JOURNAL

Date		Account Credited	Post. Ref.	Accounts Payable Cr.	Office Supplies Dr.	Other Accounts Dr.	Post. Ref.	Amount
May	2	McMillan Co.		3,600 00	3,600 00			

Transactions (c) and (h):

CASH PAYMENTS JOURNAL

Date		Ck. No.	Account Debited	Post. Ref.	Other Accounts Dr.	Accounts Payable Dr.	Cash Cr.
May	4	1003	Transportation In		320 00		320 00
	12	1010	McMillan Co.			3,600 00	3,600 00

Transaction (d):

REVENUE JOURNAL

Date		Invoice No.	Account Debited	Post. Ref.	Accts. Rec. Dr. Fees Earned Cr.
May	8	51	Waller Co.		4,500 00

Transaction (j):

CASH RECEIPTS JOURNAL

Date		Account Credited	Post. Ref.	Other Accounts Cr.	Accounts Receivable Cr.	Cash Dr.
May	18	Waller Co.			4,500 00	4,500 00

SELF-EXAMINATION QUESTIONS

Answers at End of Chapter

Matching

Match each of the following statements with its proper term. Some terms may not be used.

A. accounting system
B. accounts payable subsidiary ledger
C. accounts receivable subsidiary ledger

E 1. The journal in which all cash payments are recorded.
F 2. The journal in which all cash receipts are recorded.
I 3. The intentional act of deceiving an employer for personal gain.
C 4. The subsidiary ledger containing the individual accounts with customers (debtors).

D. application
E. cash payments journal
F. cash receipts journal
G. controlling account
H. elements of internal control
I. employee fraud
J. general journal
K. general ledger
L. hardware
M. internal controls
N. operating system
O. purchases journal
P. revenue journal
Q. software
R. special journals
S. subsidiary ledger

L 5. Computer equipment used for data input/output and internal data management and processing.

R 6. Journals designed to be used for recording a single type of transaction.

A 7. The methods and procedures used by a business to collect, classify, summarize, and report financial data for use by management and external users.

M 8. The policies and procedures used to safeguard assets, ensure accurate business information, and ensure compliance with laws and regulations.

B 9. The subsidiary ledger containing the individual accounts with suppliers (creditors).

D 10. Software that performs a specific task, such as word processing or spreadsheet.

H 11. The control environment, risk assessment, control activities, information and communication, and monitoring.

P 12. The journal in which all sales of services on account are recorded.

G 13. The account in the general ledger that summarizes the balances of the accounts in a subsidiary ledger.

O 14. The journal in which all items purchased on account are recorded.

N 15. Computer software that provides the basic instructions to the computer and serves as the interface between the user and the computer.

J 16. The two-column form used for entries that do not "fit" in any of the special journals.

K 17. The primary ledger, when used in conjunction with subsidiary ledgers, that contains all of the balance sheet and income statement accounts.

S 18. A ledger containing individual accounts with a common characteristic.

Multiple Choice

1. The initial step in the process of developing an accounting system is called:
   A. analysis
   B. design
   C. implementation
   D. feedback

2. The policies and procedures used by management to protect assets from misuse, ensure accurate business information, and assure compliance with laws and regulations are called:
   A. internal controls
   B. systems analysis
   C. systems design
   D. systems implementation

3. A payment of cash for the purchase of services should be recorded in the:
   A. purchases journal
   B. cash payments journal
   C. revenue journal
   D. cash receipts journal

4. When there are a large number of individual accounts with a common characteristic, it is common to place them in a separate ledger called:
   A. a subsidiary ledger
   B. a creditors ledger
   C. an accounts payable ledger
   D. an accounts receivable ledger

5. Which of the following would be used in a computerized accounting system?
   A. Revenue journal
   B. Cash receipts journal
   C. Electronic invoice form
   D. Month-end postings to the general ledger

CLASS DISCUSSION QUESTIONS

1. Why is the accounting system of a business an information system?
2. What is the three-step process of systems evolution?
3. What are the three objectives of internal control?
4. Name and describe the five elements of internal control.
5. How does a policy of rotating clerical employees from job to job aid in strengthening the control procedures within the control environment?
6. Why should the responsibility for a sequence of related operations be divided among different persons?

7. Why should the employee who handles cash receipts not have the responsibility for maintaining the accounts receivable records?
8. In an attempt to improve operating efficiency, one employee was made responsible for all purchasing, receiving, and storing of supplies. Is this organizational change wise from an internal control standpoint? Explain.
9. The ticket seller at a movie theater doubles as a ticket taker for a few minutes each day while the ticket taker is on a break. Which control procedure of a business's system of internal control is violated in this situation?
10. Why should the responsibility for maintaining the accounting records be separated from the responsibility for operations?
11. What is the term applied (a) to the ledger containing the individual customer accounts and (b) to the single account summarizing accounts receivable?
12. What are the major advantages of the use of special journals?
13. Environmental Services Co. uses the special journals described in this chapter. Which journal will be used to record fees earned (a) for cash, (b) on account?
14. In recording 250 fees earned on account during a single month, how many times will it be necessary to write Fees Earned (a) if each transaction, including fees earned, is recorded individually in a two-column general journal; (b) if each transaction for fees earned is recorded in a revenue journal?
15. How many individual postings to Fees Earned for the month would be needed in Question 14 if the procedure described in (a) had been used; if the procedure described in (b) had been used?
16. During the current month, the following errors occurred in recording transactions in the purchases journal or in posting from it.
    a. An invoice for $900 of supplies from Hoffman Co. was recorded as having been received from Hoffer Co., another supplier.
    b. A credit of $840 to JPC Company was posted as $480 in the subsidiary ledger.
    c. An invoice for equipment of $6,500 was recorded as $5,500.
    d. The Accounts Payable column of the purchases journal was overstated by $2,000.

    How will each error come to the bookkeeper's attention, other than by chance discovery?
17. The Accounts Payable and Cash columns in the cash payments journal were unknowingly overstated by $100 at the end of the month. (a) Assuming no other errors in recording or posting, will the error cause the trial balance totals to be unequal? (b) Will the creditors ledger agree with the accounts payable controlling account?
18. Assuming the use of a two-column general journal, a purchases journal, and a cash payments journal as illustrated in this chapter, indicate the journal in which each of the following transactions should be recorded:
    a. Purchase of supplies for cash.
    b. Purchase of office supplies on account.
    c. Payment of cash on account to creditor.
    d. Purchase of store equipment on account.
    e. Payment of cash for office supplies.
19. List five common computer hardware elements used for data input and output.
20. What is the difference between application software and the operating system?
21. What is an electronic form and how is it used in a computerized accounting system?
22. REAL WORLD In the **Equity Funding** fraud, approximately $2 billion of insurance policies that were claimed to have been sold by the company were bogus. The bogus policies, which were supported by falsified policy applications, were listed along with real policies on Equity Funding's computer tapes (records). Equity Funding personnel, including the computer programmers, kept these tapes in a separate room where they were easily accessible. In addition, computer programmers and other company personnel had access to the computer. What general weaknesses in Equity Funding's internal controls contributed to the occurrence and the size of the fraud?

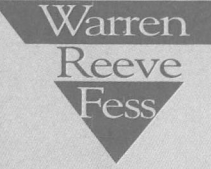

EXERCISES

Exercise 5–1
Internal controls
Objective 2

Debbie Byers has recently been hired as the manager of Long Island Deli. Long Island Deli is a national chain of franchised delicatessens. During her first month as store manager, Debbie encountered the following internal control situations:

a. Long Island Deli has one cash register. Prior to Debbie's joining the deli, each employee working on a shift would take a customer order, accept payment, and then prepare the order. Debbie made one employee on each shift responsible for taking orders and accepting the customer's payment. Other employees prepare the orders.
b. Since only one employee uses the cash register, that employee is responsible for counting the cash at the end of the shift and verifying that the cash in the drawer matches the amount of cash sales recorded by the cash register. Debbie expects each cashier to balance the drawer to the penny *every* time—no exceptions.
c. Debbie caught an employee putting a box of 100 single-serving bags of potato chips in his car. Not wanting to create a scene, Debbie smiled and said, "I don't think you're putting those chips on the right shelf. Don't they belong inside the deli?" The employee returned the chips to the stockroom.

State whether you agree or disagree with Debbie's method of handling each situation and explain your answer.

Exercise 5–2
Internal controls
Objective 2

Gypsy Fashions is a retail store specializing in women's clothing. The store has established a liberal return policy for the holiday season in order to encourage gift purchases. Any item purchased during November and December may be returned through January 31, with a receipt, for cash or exchange. If the customer does not have a receipt, cash will still be refunded for any item under $25. If the item is more than $25, a check is mailed to the customer.

Whenever an item is returned, a store clerk completes a return slip, which the customer signs. The return slip is placed in a special box. The store manager visits the return counter approximately once every two hours to authorize the return slips. Clerks are instructed to place the returned merchandise on the proper rack on the selling floor as soon as possible.

This year, returns at Gypsy Fashions have reached an all-time high. There are a large number of returns under $25 without receipts.

a. How can sales clerks employed at Gypsy Fashions use the store's return policy to steal money from the cash register?
b. 1. What internal control weaknesses do you see in the return policy that make cash thefts easier?
   2. Would issuing a store credit in place of a cash refund for all merchandise returned without a receipt reduce the possibility of theft? List some advantages and disadvantages of issuing a store credit in place of a cash refund.
   3. Assume that Gypsy Fashions is committed to the current policy of issuing cash refunds without a receipt. What changes could be made in the store's procedures regarding customer refunds in order to improve internal control?

Exercise 5–3
Internal controls for bank lending
Objective 2

Las Cruz Bank provides loans to businesses in the community through its Commercial Lending Department. Small loans (less than $100,000) may be approved by an individual loan officer, while larger loans (greater than $100,000) must be approved by a board of loan officers. Once a loan is approved, the funds are made available to the loan applicant under agreed terms. The president of Las Cruz Bank has instituted a policy whereby she has the individual authority to approve loans up to $5,000,000. The president believes that this policy will allow flexibility to approve loans to valued clients much quicker than under the previous policy.

As an internal auditor of Las Cruz Bank, how would you respond to this change in policy?

Exercise 5–4
Identify postings from revenue journal

Objective 3

Using the following revenue journal for J. A. Bach Co., identify each of the posting references, indicated by a letter, as representing (1) a posting to a general ledger account, (2) a posting to a subsidiary ledger account, or (3) a posting to two general ledger accounts.

REVENUE JOURNAL

Date	Invoice No.	Account Debited	Post. Ref.	
Nov. 1	772	Environmental Safety Co.	(a)	$2,465
10	773	Greenberg Co.	(b)	580
20	774	Smith and Smith	(c)	1,520
27	775	Envirolab	(d)	965
30				$5,530
				(e)

Exercise 5–5
Accounts receivable ledger

Objective 3

✓ d. Total accounts receivable, $5,965

Based upon the data presented in Exercise 5–4, assume that the beginning balances for the customer accounts were zero, except for Envirolab, which had a $435 beginning balance. In addition, there were no collections during the period.

a. Set up a T account for Accounts Receivable and T accounts for the four accounts needed in the customer ledger.
b. Post to the T accounts.
c. Determine the balance in the accounts, if necessary.
d. Prepare a schedule of accounts receivable at November 30.

Exercise 5–6
Identify journals

Objective 3

Assuming the use of a two-column (all-purpose) general journal, a revenue journal, and a cash receipts journal as illustrated in this chapter, indicate the journal in which each of the following transactions should be recorded:

a. Receipt of cash for rent.
b. Closing of drawing account at the end of the year.
c. Adjustment to record accrued salaries at the end of the year.
d. Sale of office supplies on account, at cost, to a neighboring business.
e. Receipt of cash on account from a customer.
f. Receipt of cash from sale of office equipment.
g. Providing services on account.
h. Providing services for cash.
i. Investment of additional cash in the business by the owner.
j. Receipt of cash refund from overpayment of taxes.

Exercise 5–7
Identify journals

Objective 3

Assuming the use of a two-column (all-purpose) general journal, a purchases journal, and a cash payments journal as illustrated in this chapter, indicate the journal in which each of the following transactions should be recorded:

a. Purchase of office equipment for cash.
b. Purchase of services on account.
c. Adjustment to prepaid insurance at the end of the month.
d. Adjustment to record depreciation at the end of the month.
e. Adjustment to prepaid rent at the end of the month.
f. Adjustment to record accrued salaries at the end of the period.
g. Purchase of office supplies for cash.
h. Advance payment of a one-year fire insurance policy on the office.
i. Purchase of office supplies on account.
j. Purchase of an office computer on account.
k. Payment of six months' rent in advance.

Exercise 5–8
Identify transactions in accounts receivable ledger

Objective 3

The debits and credits from three related transactions are presented in the following customer's account taken from the accounts receivable subsidiary ledger.

Describe each transaction, and identify the source of each posting.

NAME *Good Times Catering*
ADDRESS *1319 Maple Street*

Date	Item	Post. Ref.	Debit	Credit	Balance
2000					
Sep. 3		R50	450		450
9		J9		60	390
13		CR38		390	—

Exercise 5–9
Identify postings from purchases journal
Objective 3

Using the following purchases journal, identify each of the posting references, indicated by a letter, as representing (1) a posting to a general ledger account, (2) a posting to a subsidiary ledger account, or (3) that no posting is required.

PURCHASES JOURNAL **PAGE 49**

Date	Account Credited	Post. Ref.	Accounts Payable Cr.	Store Supplies Dr.	Office Supplies Dr.	Other Accounts Dr. Account	Other Accounts Dr. Post. Ref.	Other Accounts Dr. Amount
20—								
June 4	Coastal Insurance Co.	(a)	4,525			Prepaid Insurance	(b)	4,525
6	Porter Supply Co.	(c)	3,000			Office Equipment	(d)	3,000
11	Baker Products	(e)	1,950	1,500	450			
13	Wilson and Wilson	(f)	6,800		6,800			
20	Cowen Supply	(g)	3,775	3,775				
27	Porter Suppply Co.	(h)	9,100			Store Equipment	(i)	9,100
30			29,150	5,275	7,250			16,625
			(j)	(k)	(l)			(m)

Exercise 5–10
Identify postings from cash payments journal
Objective 3

Using the following cash payments journal, identify each of the posting references, indicated by a letter, as representing (1) a posting to a general ledger account, (2) a posting to a subsidiary ledger account, or (3) that no posting is required.

CASH PAYMENTS JOURNAL **PAGE 46**

Date	Ck. No.	Account Debited	Post. Ref.	Other Accounts Dr.	Accounts Payable Dr.	Cash Cr.
20—						
July 3	611	Aquatic Systems Co.	(a)		4,000	4,000
5	612	Utilities Expense	(b)	325		325
10	613	Prepaid Rent	(c)	3,200		3,200
17	614	Coe Bros.	(d)		2,500	2,500
20	615	Office Equipment	(e)	2,100		2,100
22	616	Advertising Expense	(f)	400		400
25	617	Office Supplies	(g)	250		250
27	618	Evans Co.	(h)		5,500	5,500
31	619	Salaries Expense	(i)	1,750		1,750
31				8,025	12,000	20,025
				(j)	(k)	(l)

Exercise 5–11
Identify transactions in accounts payable ledger account
Objective 3

The debits and credits from three related transactions are presented in the following creditor's account taken from the accounts payable ledger.

Describe each transaction, and identify the source of each posting.

NAME *Echo Co.*
ADDRESS *1717 Kirby Street*

Date	Item	Post. Ref.	Debit	Credit	Balance
2000					
July 6		P34		10,500	10,500
10		J10	500		10,000
16		CP37	10,000		—

Exercise 5–12
Error in accounts payable ledger and schedule of accounts payable
Objective 3

What's Wrong WITH THIS?

✓ b. Total accounts payable, $34,250

After Assurance Testing Services Inc. had completed all postings for October in the current year (2000), the sum of the balances in the following accounts payable ledger did not agree with the balance of the appropriate controlling account in the general ledger.

NAME *Martinez Mining Co.*
ADDRESS *1240 W. Main Street*

Date	Item	Post. Ref.	Debit	Credit	Balance
2000					
Oct. 1	Balance	(✓)			4,750
10		CP22	4,750		—
17		P30		4,400	4,400
25		J7	350		3,050

NAME *Cutler and Powell*
ADDRESS *717 Elm Street*

Date	Item	Post. Ref.	Debit	Credit	Balance
2000					
Oct. 1	Balance	(✓)			6,100
18		CP23	6,100		—
29		P31		7,500	7,500

NAME *C. D. Greer and Son*
ADDRESS *972 S. Tenth Street*

Date	Item	Post. Ref.	Debit	Credit	Balance
2000					
Oct. 17		P30		3,750	3,750
27		P31		9,000	12,750

NAME *Donnelly Minerals Inc.*
ADDRESS *1170 Mattis Avenue*

Date	Item	Post. Ref.	Debit	Credit	Balance
2000					
Oct. 1	Balance	(✓)			8,300
7		P30		4,900	13,300
12		J7	300		13,000
20		CP23	5,700		7,300

NAME *L. L. Weiss Co.*
ADDRESS *915 E. Walnut Street*

Date	Item	Post. Ref.	Debit	Credit	Balance
2000					
Oct. 5		P30		2,750	2,750

Assuming that the controlling account balance of $34,250 has been verified as correct, (a) determine the error(s) in the preceding accounts and (b) prepare a schedule of accounts payable from the corrected accounts payable subsidiary ledger.

Exercise 5–13
Identify postings from special journals
Objective 3

Albright Consulting Company makes most of its sales and purchases on credit. It uses the five journals described in this chapter (revenue, cash receipts, purchases, cash payments, and general journals). Identify the journal most likely used in recording the postings for selected transactions indicated by letter in the following T accounts:

Cash			
a.	10,000	b.	8,750

Prepaid Rent			
		f.	400

Accounts Receivable			
c.	10,950	d.	9,200

Accounts Payable			
g.	7,600	h.	7,790

Office Supplies			
e.	6,500		

Fees Earned			
		i.	10,950

Rent Expense			
j.	400		

Exercise 5–14
Cash receipts journal
Objective 3

What's Wrong WITH THIS?

The following cash receipts journal headings have been suggested for a small service firm. How many errors can you find in the headings?

CASH RECEIPTS JOURNAL PAGE

Date	Account Credited	Post. Ref.	Fees Earned Cr.	Accounts Rec. Cr.	Cash Cr.	Other Accounts Dr.

Exercise 5–15
Modified special journals
Objectives 3, 4

Wellguard Health Clinic was established on June 15 of the current year. The clients for whom Wellguard provided health services during the remainder of June are listed below. These clients pay Wellguard the amount indicated plus a 5% sales tax.

June 16. A. Sommerfeld on account, Invoice No. 1, $200 plus tax.
19. B. Lin, Invoice No. 2, $80 plus tax.
21. J. Koss, Invoice No. 3, $60 plus tax.
22. D. Jeffries, Invoice No. 4, $100 plus tax.
24. K. Sallinger, in exchange for medical supplies having a value of $160, plus tax.
26. J. Koss, Invoice No. 5, $120 plus tax.
28. B. Lin, Invoice No. 6, $40 plus tax.
30. D. Finnigan, Invoice No. 7, $260 plus tax.

a. Journalize the transactions for June, using a three-column revenue journal and a two-column general journal. Post the customer accounts in the accounts receivable subsidiary ledger and insert the balance immediately after recording each entry.
b. Post the general journal and the revenue journal to the following general ledger accounts, inserting account balances only after the last postings:

12 Accounts Receivable
14 Medical Supplies
22 Sales Tax Payable
41 Fees Earned

c. 1. What is the sum of the balances in the accounts receivable subsidiary ledger at June 30?
2. What is the balance of the controlling account at June 30?

Exercise 5–16
Computer components
Objective 5

Which of the following items are used for computer data input or output?

a. Keyboard
b. Monitor
c. Operating system
d. RAM
e. Modem
f. CD Drive
g. Hard Drive
h. Network
i. Application
j. Printer

Exercise 5–17
Computerized accounting systems
Objective 5

Most computerized accounting systems use electronic forms to record transaction information, as illustrated in Exhibit 11.

a. Identify the key input fields (spaces) to an electronic invoice form.
b. What accounts are posted from an electronic invoice form?
c. Why aren't special journal totals posted to control accounts at the end of the month in an electronic accounting system?

PROBLEMS SERIES A

Problem 5–1A
Revenue journal; accounts receivable and general ledgers
Objective 3

HAT

✓ 1. Revenue journal, total fees earned, $9,880

Worthy Accounting Services was established on May 15, 2000, to provide accounting and tax services. The clients for whom Worthy provided services during the remainder of May are listed below.

May 18. Jacob Co., Invoice No. 1, $970 on account.
20. Ro-Gain Co., Invoice No. 2, $650 on account.
22. Innis Co., Invoice No. 3, $2,600 on account.
27. D. L. Victor Co., Invoice No. 4, $1,870 on account.
28. Bower Co., Invoice No. 5, $1,200 on account.
28. Ro-Gain Co., $700 in exchange for supplies.
30. Ro-Gain Co., Invoice No. 6, $2,150 on account.
31. Innis Co., Invoice No. 7, $440 on account.

Instructions

1. Journalize the transactions for May, using a single-column revenue journal and a two-column general journal. Post to the following customer accounts in the accounts receivable ledger, and insert the balance immediately after recording each entry: Bower Co.; D. L. Victor Co.; Innis Co.; Jacob Co.; Ro-Gain Co.
2. Post the revenue journal to the following accounts in the general ledger, inserting the account balances only after the last postings:

   12 Accounts Receivable
   14 Supplies
   41 Fees Earned

3. a. What is the sum of the balances of the accounts in the subsidiary ledger at May 31?
   b. What is the balance of the controlling account at May 31?
4. Assume that on June 1, the state in which Worthy operates begins requiring that sales tax be collected on accounting services. Briefly explain how the revenue journal may be modified to accommodate sales of services on account requiring the collection of a state sales tax.

Problem 5–2A
Revenue and cash receipts journals; accounts receivable and general ledgers
Objective 3

Transactions related to revenue and cash receipts completed by Elite Engineering Services during the period November 15–30 of the current year are as follows:

Nov. 15. Issued Invoice No. 717 to Yamura Co., $9,450.
16. Received cash from AGI Co. for the balance owed on its account.
17. Issued Invoice No. 718 to Hardy Co., $2,400.
18. Issued Invoice No. 719 to Ross and Son, $9,600.
Post all journals to the accounts receivable ledger.

HAT

✓ 3. Total cash receipts, $98,880

Nov. 21. Received cash from Hardy Co. for the balance owed on November 15.
24. Issued Invoice No. 720 to Hardy Co., $11,400.
Post all journals to the accounts receivable ledger.
25. Received cash from Yamura Co. for the balance due on invoice of November 15.
26. Received cash from Hardy Co. for invoice of November 17.
27. Issued Invoice No. 721 to AGI Co., $9,540.
29. Recorded fees earned for the second half of the month, $14,300.
30. Received office equipment in settlement of balance due on the Ross and Son account.
Post all journals to the accounts receivable ledger.

Instructions

1. Insert the following balances in the general ledger as of November 1:

11	Cash	$ 9,450
12	Accounts Receivable	14,750
18	Office Equipment	4,500
41	Fees Earned	—

2. Insert the following balances in the accounts receivable subsidiary ledger as of November 15:

AGI Co.	$8,700
Hardy Co.	5,400
Ross and Son	—
Yamura Co.	—

3. In a single-column revenue journal and a cash receipts journal, insert *November 15 Total(s) Forwarded* on the left side of the first line of the journal. Use the following column headings for the cash receipts journal: Other Accounts, Fees Earned, Accounts Receivable, and Cash. The Fees Earned column is used to record cash fees. Insert a check mark (✓) in the Post. Ref. Column. The following dollar figures show the totals forwarded as of November 15 for their respective amount columns:

   Revenue journal: 38,750
   Cash receipts journal: 6,780; 12,450; 39,400; 58,630

   These amounts have not been posted, but represent the totals of the November 1–15 transactions.
4. Using the two special journals and the two-column general journal, journalize the transactions for the remainder of November. Post to the accounts receivable ledger, and insert the balances at the points indicated in the narrative of transactions. Determine the balance in the customer's account before recording a cash receipt.
5. Total each of the columns of the special journals, and post the individual entries and totals to the general ledger. Insert account balances after the last posting.
6. Determine that the subsidiary ledger agrees with the controlling account in the general ledger.

Problem 5–3A

Purchases, accounts payable account, and accounts payable ledger

Objective 3

HAT

Robbins Surveyors provides survey work for construction projects. The office staff use office supplies, while surveying crews use field supplies. Purchases on account completed by Robbins Surveyors during May 2000 are as follows:

May 1. Purchased field supplies on account from Wendell Co., $2,460.
3. Purchased office supplies on account from Lassiter Co., $1,670.
8. Purchased field supplies on account from Trent Supply, $950.
12. Purchased field supplies on account from Wendell Co., $1,050.
13. Purchased office equipment on account from Gore Computers Co., $8,600.
15. Purchased office supplies on account from J-Mart Co., $1,300.
19. Purchased office equipment on account from Eskew Co., $6,300.

✓ 3. Total accounts payable credit, $28,770

May 23. Purchased field supplies on account from Trent Supply, $1,400.
26. Purchased office supplies on account from J-Mart Co., $840.
30. Purchased field supplies on account from Trent Supply, $4,200.

Instructions

1. Insert the following balances in the general ledger as of May 1:

14	Field Supplies	$ 3,215
15	Office Supplies	1,400
18	Office Equipment	15,400
21	Accounts Payable	7,720

2. Insert the following balances in the accounts payable subsidiary ledger as of May 1:

Eskew Co.	$4,300
Gore Computers Co.	—
J-Mart Co.	970
Lassiter Co.	2,450
Trent Supply	—
Wendell Co.	—

3. Journalize the transactions for May, using a purchases journal similar to the one illustrated in this chapter. Prepare the purchases journal with columns for Accounts Payable, Field Supplies, Office Supplies, and Other Accounts. Post to the creditor accounts in the accounts payable ledger immediately after each entry.
4. Post the purchases journal to the accounts in the general ledger.
5. a. What is the sum of the balances in the subsidiary ledger at May 31?
   b. What is the balance of the controlling account at May 31?

Problem 5–4A

Purchases and cash payments journals; accounts payable and general ledgers

Objective 3

HAT SPREADSHEET

✓ 1. Total cash payments, $60,150

Black Gold Exploration Co. was established on March 15, 2000, to provide oil-drilling services. Black Gold uses field equipment (rigs and pipe) and field supplies (drill bits and lubricants) in its operations. Transactions related to purchases and cash payments during the remainder of March are as follows:

Mar. 16. Issued Check No. 1 in payment of rent for the remainder of March, $1,000.
16. Purchased field equipment on account from Harper Equipment Co., $20,000.
17. Purchased field supplies on account from Culver Supply Co., $6,200.
18. Issued Check No. 2 in payment of field supplies, $1,200, and office supplies, $120.
19. Purchased office equipment on account from Lacy Co., $12,400.
20. Purchased office supplies on account from Ange Supply Co., $230.
Post the journals to the accounts payable ledger.
24. Issued Check No. 3 to Harper Equipment Co. in payment of invoice, $20,000.
26. Issued Check No. 4 to Culver Supply Co. in payment of invoice, $6,200.
28. Issued Check No. 5 to purchase land from the owner, $10,000.
28. Issued Check No. 6 to Lacy Co. in payment of the balance owed.
28. Purchased office supplies on account from Ange Supply Co., $630.
Post the journals to the accounts payable ledger.
30. Purchased the following from Harper Equipment Co. on account: field supplies, $2,300, and office equipment, $4,400.
30. Issued Check No. 7 to Ange Supply Co. in payment of invoice, $230.
30. Purchased field supplies on account from Culver Supply Co., $1,900.
31. Issued Check No. 8 in payment of salaries, $9,000.
31. Acquired land in exchange for field equipment having a cost of $6,000.
Post the journals to the accounts payable ledger.

Instructions

1. Journalize the transactions for March. Use a purchases journal and a cash payments journal, similar to those illustrated in this chapter, and a two-column general journal. Refer to the following partial chart of accounts:

11	Cash	19	Land
14	Field Supplies	21	Accounts Payable
15	Office Supplies	61	Salary Expense
17	Field Equipment	71	Rent Expense
18	Office Equipment		

At the points indicated in the narrative of transactions, post to the following accounts in the accounts payable ledger:

Ange Supply Co.
Culver Supply Co.
Harper Equipment Co.
Lacy Co.

2. Post the individual entries (Other Accounts columns of the purchases journal and the cash payments journal; both columns of the general journal) to the appropriate general ledger accounts.
3. Total each of the columns of the purchases journal and the cash payments journal, and post the appropriate totals to the general ledger. (Because the problem does not include transactions related to cash receipts, the cash account in the ledger will have a credit balance.)
4. Prepare a schedule of accounts payable.

Problem 5–5A
All journals and general ledger; trial balance
Objective 3

GENERAL LEDGER

✓ 2. Total cash receipts, $50,250

The transactions completed by Same-Day Courier Company during May, the first month of the fiscal year, were as follows:

May 1. Issued Check No. 205 for May rent, $1,000.
2. Purchased a vehicle on account from Bunting Co., $24,500.
3. Purchased office equipment on account from Gill Computer Co., $4,600.
5. Issued Invoice No. 91 to Carlton Co., $1,600.
6. Received check for $4,200 from Pease Co. in payment of invoice.
6. Issued Check No. 206 for fuel expense, $800.
9. Issued Invoice No. 92 to Collins Co., $2,340.
10. Received check for $8,150 from Sing Co. in payment of invoice.
10. Issued Check No. 207 to Haber Enterprises in payment of $3,160 invoice.
10. Issued Check No. 208 to Bastille Co. in payment of $2,000 invoice.
11. Issued Invoice No. 93 to Joy Co., $950.
11. Issued Check No. 209 to Porter Co. in payment of $910 invoice.
12. Received check for $1,600 from Carlton Co. in payment of invoice.
13. Issued Check No. 210 to Bunting Co. in payment of $24,500 invoice.
16. Cash fees earned for May 1–16, $14,450.
16. Issued Check No. 211 for purchase of a vehicle, $12,000.
17. Purchased maintenance supplies on account from Bastille Co., $3,150.
18. Issued Check No. 212 for miscellaneous administrative expenses, $1,900.
18. Received check for rent revenue on office space, $1,100.
19. Purchased the following on account from Master Co.: maintenance supplies, $1,500, and office supplies, $2,500.
20. Issued Check No. 213 in payment of advertising expense, $1,350.
20. Used maintenance supplies with a cost of $3,900 to overhaul vehicle engines.
23. Issued Invoice No. 94 to Sing Co., $4,200.
24. Purchased office supplies on account from Haber Enterprises, $700.
25. Received check for $2,150 from Pease Co. in payment of invoice.
25. Issued Invoice No. 95 to Collins Co., $6,700.
26. Issued Check No. 214 to Gill Computer Co. in payment of $4,600 invoice.
27. Issued Check No. 215 to C. Davis as a personal withdrawal, $3,200.
30. Issued Check No. 216 in payment of driver salaries, $14,600.
31. Issued Check No. 217 in payment of office salaries, $6,700.
31. Issued Check No. 218 for office supplies, $720.
31. Cash fees earned for May 17–31, $18,600.

Instructions

1. Enter the following account balances in the general ledger as of May 1:

11	Cash	$ 28,400	32	C. Davis, Drawing	—
12	Accounts Receivable	14,500	41	Fees Earned	—
14	Maintenance Supplies	5,200	42	Rent Revenue	—
15	Office Supplies	3,400	51	Driver Salaries Expense	—
16	Office Equipment	16,800	52	Maintenance Supplies Expense	—
17	Accumulated Depreciation —Office Equipment	4,100	53	Fuel Expense	—
18	Vehicles	82,000	61	Office Salaries Expense	—
19	Accumulated Depreciation —Vehicles	16,300	62	Rent Expense	—
			63	Advertising Expense	—
21	Accounts Payable	6,070	64	Miscellaneous Administrative Expense	—
31	C. Davis, Capital	123,830			

2. Journalize the transactions for May 2000 using the following journals similar to those illustrated in this chapter: single-column revenue journal, cash receipts journal, purchases journal (with columns for Accounts Payable, Maintenance Supplies, Office Supplies, and Other Accounts), cash payments journal, and two-column general journal. You do not need to make daily postings to the individual accounts in the accounts payable ledger and the accounts receivable ledger.
3. Post the appropriate individual entries to the general ledger.
4. Total each of the columns of the special journals, and post the appropriate totals to the general ledger; insert the account balances.
5. Prepare a trial balance.
6. Verify the agreement of each subsidiary ledger with its controlling account. The sum of the balances of the accounts in the subsidiary ledgers as of May 31 are as follows:

Accounts receivable	$14,190
Accounts payable	7,850

PROBLEMS SERIES B

Problem 5–1B
Revenue journal; accounts receivable and general ledgers
Objective 3

✓ 1. Revenue journal, total fees earned, $950

Head Start Reading Labs was established on May 20, 2000, to provide educational services. The clients for whom Head Start provided services on account during the remainder of the month are as follows:

May 21. J. Dunlop, Invoice No. 1, $90 on account.
22. L. Stanley, Invoice No. 2, $140 on account.
24. T. Morris, Invoice No. 3, $65 on account.
25. L. Stanley, $140 in exchange for educational supplies.
27. F. Mintz, Invoice No. 4, $245 on account.
28. D. Bennett, Invoice No. 5, $120 on account.
30. L. Stanley, Invoice No. 6, $210 on account.
31. T. Morris, Invoice No. 7, $80 on account.

Instructions

1. Journalize the transactions for May, using a single-column revenue journal and a two-column general journal. Post to the following customer accounts in the accounts receivable ledger, and insert the balance immediately after recording each entry: D. Bennett; J. Dunlop; F. Mintz; T. Morris; L. Stanley.
2. Post the revenue journal and the general journal to the following accounts in the general ledger, inserting the account balances only after the last postings:

12	Accounts Receivable
13	Supplies
41	Fees Earned

3. a. What is the sum of the balances of the accounts in the subsidiary ledger at May 31?
   b. What is the balance of the controlling account at May 31?

4. Assume that on June 1, the state in which Head Start Reading Labs operates begins requiring that sales tax be collected on educational services. Briefly explain how the revenue journal may be modified to accommodate sales of services on account that require the collection of a state sales tax.

Problem 5–2B

Revenue and cash receipts journals; accounts receivable and general ledgers

Objective 3

✓ 3. Total cash receipts, $83,990

Transactions related to revenue and cash receipts completed by Continental Architects Co. during the period June 15–30, 2000, are as follows:

June 15. Issued Invoice No. 793 to Ping Co., $6,500.
16. Received cash from Morton Co. for the balance owed on its account.
19. Issued Invoice No. 794 to Quest Co., $5,570.
20. Issued Invoice No. 795 to Mendez Co., $6,780.
Post all journals to the accounts receivable ledger.
23. Received cash from Quest Co. for the balance owed on June 15.
24. Issued Invoice No. 796 to Quest Co., $2,430.
Post all journals to the accounts receivable ledger.
25. Received cash from Ping Co. for the balance due on invoice of June 15.
28. Received cash from Quest Co. for invoice of June 19.
28. Issued Invoice No. 797 to Morton Co., $3,460.
30. Received $6,780 notes receivable in settlement of the balance due on the Mendez Co. account.
30. Recorded cash fees received for the second half of the month, $8,500.
Post all journals to the accounts receivable ledger.

Instructions

1. Insert the following balances in the general ledger as of June 1:

11	Cash	$10,550
12	Accounts Receivable	12,650
14	Notes Receivable	4,000
41	Fees Earned	—

2. Insert the following balances in the accounts receivable ledger as of June 15:

Mendez Co.	—
Morton Co.	$14,500
Ping Co.	—
Quest Co.	8,350

3. In a single-column revenue journal and a cash receipts journal, insert *June 15 Total(s) Forwarded* on the left side of the first line of the journal. Use the following column headings for the cash receipts journal: Other Accounts, Fees Earned, Accounts Receivable, and Cash. The Fees Earned column is used to record cash fees. Insert a check mark (✓) in the Post. Ref. Column. The following dollar figures show the totals forwarded as of June 15 for their respective amount columns:

   Revenue journal: 32,650
   Cash receipts journal: 4,560; 13,560; 22,450; 40,570

   These amounts have not been posted, but represent the totals of the June 1–15 transactions.
4. Using the two special journals and the two-column general journal, journalize the transactions for the remainder of June. Post to the accounts receivable ledger, and insert the balances at the points indicated in the narrative of transactions. Determine the balance in the customer's account before recording a cash receipt.
5. Total each of the columns of the special journals, and post the individual entries and totals to the general ledger. Insert account balances after the last posting.
6. Determine that the subsidiary ledger agrees with the controlling account in the general ledger.

Problem 5–3B

Purchases, accounts payable account, and accounts payable ledger

Objective 3

✓ 3. Total accounts payable credit, $27,330

Lee Landscaping Services designs and installs landscaping. The landscape designers and office staff use office supplies, while field supplies (rock, bark, etc.) are used in the actual landscaping. Purchases on account completed by Lee Landscaping during July 2000 are as follows:

July 1. Purchased office equipment on account from Emerald Computers Co., $4,700.
5. Purchased office supplies on account from Lapp Co., $3,400.
9. Purchased office supplies on account from Lang Supplies Co., $2,400.
13. Purchased field supplies on account from Yin Co., $1,460.
14. Purchased field supplies on account from Yin Co., $2,340.
17. Purchased field supplies on account from Nelson Co., $950.
20. Purchased office equipment on account from Cencor Co., $7,530.
24. Purchased field supplies on account from Nelson Co., $3,210.
29. Purchased office supplies on account from Lang Supplies Co., $840.
31. Purchased field supplies on account from Nelson Co., $500.

Instructions

1. Insert the following balances in the general ledger as of July 1:

14	Field Supplies	$ 4,670
15	Office Supplies	850
18	Office Equipment	12,500
21	Accounts Payable	9,080

2. Insert the following balances in the accounts payable ledger as of July 1:

Cencor Co.	$5,670	Lapp Co.	$960
Emerald Computers Co.	—	Nelson Co.	—
Lang Supplies Co.	2,450	Yin Co.	—

3. Journalize the transactions for July, using a purchases journal similar to the one illustrated in this chapter. Prepare the purchases journal with columns for Accounts Payable, Field Supplies, Office Supplies, and Other Accounts. Post to the creditor accounts in the accounts payable ledger immediately after each entry.
4. Post the purchases journal to the accounts in the general ledger.
5. a. What is the sum of the balances in the subsidiary ledger at July 31?
   b. What is the balance of the controlling account at July 31?

Problem 5–4B

Purchases and cash payments journals; accounts payable and general ledgers

Objective 3

SPREADSHEET

✓ 1. Total cash payments, $57,030

Purity Water Testing Service was established on June 16, 2000. Purity uses field equipment and field supplies (chemicals and other supplies) to analyze water for unsafe contaminants in streams, lakes, and ponds. Transactions related to purchases and cash payments during the remainder of June are as follows:

June 16. Issued Check No. 1 in payment of rent for the remainder of June, $900.
16. Purchased field supplies on account from Heath Supply Co., $4,200.
16. Purchased field equipment on account from Juan Equipment Co., $13,000.
17. Purchased office supplies on account from Aztec Supply Co., $530.
18. Purchased office equipment on account from Chavez Co., $3,800.
19. Issued Check No. 2 in payment of field supplies, $2,200, and office supplies, $400.
Post the journals to the accounts payable ledger.
23. Purchased office supplies on account from Aztec Supply Co., $900.
23. Issued Check No. 3 to purchase land from the owner, $20,000.
24. Issued Check No. 4 to Heath Supply Co. in payment of invoice, $4,200.
25. Issued Check No. 5 to Chavez Co. in payment of the balance owed.
26. Issued Check No. 6 to Juan Equipment Co. in payment of invoice, $13,000.
Post the journals to the accounts payable ledger.
30. Acquired land in exchange for field equipment having a cost of $8,000.
30. Purchased field supplies on account from Heath Supply Co., $6,400.
30. Issued Check No. 7 to Aztec Supply Co. in payment of invoice, $530.

June 30. Purchased the following from Juan Equipment Co. on account: field supplies, $3,400, and field equipment, $5,000.

30. Issued Check No. 8 in payment of salaries, $12,000.

Post the journals to the accounts payable ledger.

Instructions

1. Journalize the transactions for June. Use a purchases journal and a cash payments journal, similar to those illustrated in this chapter, and a two-column general journal. Refer to the following partial chart of accounts:

11	Cash	19	Land
14	Field Supplies	21	Accounts Payable
15	Office Supplies	61	Salary Expense
17	Field Equipment	71	Rent Expense
18	Office Equipment		

At the points indicated in the narrative of transactions, post to the following accounts in the accounts payable ledger:

Aztec Supply Co.
Chavez Co.
Heath Supply Co.
Juan Equipment Co.

2. Post the individual entries (Other Accounts columns of the purchases journal and the cash payments journal and both columns of the general journal) to the appropriate general ledger accounts.
3. Total each of the columns of the purchases journal and the cash payments journal and post the appropriate totals to the general ledger. (Because the problem does not include transactions related to cash receipts, the cash account in the ledger will have a credit balance.)
4. Prepare a schedule of accounts payable.

Problem 5–5B

All journals and general ledger; trial balance

Objective 3

GENERAL LEDGER

✓ 2. Total cash receipts, $38,800

The transactions completed by Speedy Delivery Company during July, the first month of the fiscal year, were as follows:

July 1. Issued Check No. 610 for July rent, $1,000.
2. Issued Invoice No. 940 to Capps Co., $2,000.
3. Received check for $6,700 from Pease Co. in payment of invoice.
5. Purchased a vehicle on account from Browning Transportation, $21,300.
6. Purchased office equipment on account from Gunter Computer Co., $4,200.
6. Issued Invoice No. 941 to Collins Co., $3,500.
9. Issued Check No. 611 for fuel expense, $900.
10. Received check from Sokol Co. in payment of $4,400 invoice.
10. Issued Check No. 612 for $4,200 to Hoy Co. in payment of invoice.
10. Issued Invoice No. 942 to Joy Co., $6,600.
11. Issued Check No. 613 to Burks Co. in payment of $2,300 invoice.
11. Issued Check No. 614 for $1,500 to Porter Co. in payment of account.
12. Received check from Capps Co. in payment of $2,000 invoice.
13. Issued Check No. 615 to Browning Transportation in payment of $21,300 balance.
16. Issued Check No. 616 for $9,000 for cash purchase of a vehicle.
16. Cash fees earned for July 1–16, $10,600.
17. Issued Check No. 617 for miscellaneous administrative expense, $1,200.
18. Purchased maintenance supplies on account from Burks Co., $1,200.
19. Purchased the following on account from McClain Co.: maintenance supplies, $1,450; office supplies, $1,750.
20. Issued Check No. 618 in payment of advertising expense, $1,400.
20. Used $3,200 maintenance supplies to repair delivery vehicles.
23. Purchased office supplies on account from Hoy Co., $500.
24. Issued Invoice No. 943 to Sokol Co., $5,700.

July 24. Issued Check No. 619 to D. D. Miles as a personal withdrawal, $4,000.
25. Issued Invoice No. 944 to Collins Co., $9,300.
25. Received check for $7,200 from Pease Co. in payment of balance.
26. Issued Check No. 620 to Gunter Computer Co. in payment of $4,200 invoice of July 3.
30. Issued Check No. 621 for monthly salaries as follows: driver salaries, $12,000; office salaries, $8,000.
31. Cash fees earned for July 17–31, $7,400.
31. Issued Check No. 622 in payment for office supplies, $700.
31. Received check for rent revenue on office space, $500.

Instructions

1. Enter the following account balances in the general ledger as of July 1:

11	Cash	$ 36,800	32	D. D. Miles, Drawing	—
12	Accounts Receivable	18,300	41	Fees Earned	—
14	Maintenance Supplies	5,400	42	Rent Revenue	—
15	Office Supplies	3,600	51	Driver Salaries Expense	—
16	Office Equipment	18,900	52	Maintenance Supplies Expense	—
17	Accumulated Depreciation —Office Equipment	2,200	53	Fuel Expense	—
18	Vehicles	56,000	61	Office Salaries Expense	—
19	Accumulated Depreciation —Vehicles	8,800	62	Rent Expense	—
21	Accounts Payable	8,000	63	Advertising Expense	—
31	D. D. Miles, Capital	120,000	64	Miscellaneous Administrative Expense	—

2. Journalize the transactions for July 2000 using the following journals similar to those illustrated in this chapter: cash receipts journal, purchases journal (with columns for Accounts Payable, Maintenance Supplies, Office Supplies, and Other Accounts), single-column revenue journal, cash payments journal, and two-column general journal. You do not need to make daily postings to the individual accounts in the accounts payable ledger and the accounts receivable ledger.
3. Post the appropriate individual entries to the general ledger.
4. Total each of the columns of the special journals and post the appropriate totals to the general ledger; insert the account balances.
5. Prepare a trial balance.
6. Verify the agreement of each subsidiary ledger with its controlling account. The sum of the balances of the accounts in the subsidiary ledgers as of July 31 are:

Accounts receivable	$25,100
Accounts payable	4,900

QUICKBOOKS PROBLEM 1

The Revenue and Collection Cycle

This problem uses the Larry's Landscaping sample company provided with QuickBooks® 5.0. Begin by first copying *sample.qbw* into another file name, **revcol.qbw,** so that the original sample.qbw file will not be changed. You must copy the file using the copy and paste commands in your operating system. This is an important step, since we will be using the unchanged sample.qbw file later in the text. If you do not first copy sample.qbw into another file name, you will automatically change sample.qbw. We will be assuming that you have an unchanged version in future QuickBooks problems in this text.

Retrieve Larry's Landscaping by opening the file that you just created. The first time you open Larry's Landscaping you will be in QuickBooks Navigator®. You may wish to use the Navigator to review the forms used for "Sales and Customers." This problem will use these forms.

Larry's Landscaping has been in business since October of the current year. We will add some additional transactions to those that have already been recorded and saved in the company file. The following additional jobs were invoiced to customers:

Invoice No.	Customer	Class	Terms	Item(s)	Quantity	Rate	Amount	Sales Tax Rate
34	Desai, Ashmi	Design	Net 30	Custom design (nontaxable)	40 hrs.	$55	$2,200	San Dom. (7.75%)
35	Crenshaw, Bob	Land-scaping	Net 15	Rock fountain with $400 of concrete	Various	Various	960	San Thom. (8.25%)
36	Middlefield Elementary School	Land-scaping	Net 30	Gardening Plants/trees	 20 bushes	 $90	110 1,800	San Thom. (8.25%)
37	Paxton, Drew	Land-scaping	Net 30	Installation Garden rocks Garden lighting	50 hrs. 80 lbs. 1	$35 $9.75 $300	1,750 780 300	San Thom. (8.25%)

The following collections were made on account:

Customer	Amount	Applied to Invoice No.
Ecker Design	$4,107.22	28
Middlefield Elementary School	665.00	30
Benson Family Store	695.00	5

Instructions

1. Enter invoice nos. 34–37 on the electronic invoice forms in QuickBooks. To open the electronic invoice, click on the Invoice button or select the Invoice submenu item under "Activities."
2. Enter the three collections on the electronic "receive payment" forms of QuickBooks. To open the receive payment forms, select the submenu item under "Activities."
3. Print the following reports (submenu item under Reports in parentheses):
   a. Customer Balance Summary Report (A/R reports)
   b. Income by Customer Summary for December 1–15 (Sales reports)
   c. Income detail of Paxton Consulting for December 1–15. (Double-click on Paxton Consulting sales total on Customer Summary Report.)
   d. Deposit detail for December 1–15. (Other reports)

QUICKBOOKS PROBLEM 2

The Purchase and Payment Cycle

This problem uses the Larry's Landscaping sample company provided with QuickBooks® 5.0. Begin by first copying *sample.qbw* into another file name, **purpay.qbw,** so that the original sample.qbw file will not be changed. You must copy the file using the copy and paste commands in your operating system. This is an important step, since we will be using the unchanged sample.qbw file later in the text. If you do not first copy sample.qbw into another file name, you will automatically change sample.qbw. We will be assuming that you have an unchanged version in future QuickBooks problems in this text.

Retrieve Larry's Landscaping by opening the file that you just created. The first time you open Larry's Landscaping, you will be in QuickBooks Navigator. You may wish to use the Navigator to review the forms used for "Purchases and Vendors." This problem will use these forms.

Larry's Landscaping has been in business since October of the current year. We will add some additional transactions to those that have already been recorded and saved in the company file. The following bills were received from vendors:

Vendor	Amount	Expense Account	Amount	Customer: Job	Class
Denk's Nursery	$ 560	Job materials: fountain and garden lighting	$ 560	Wallace, Ralph	Landscaping
Doherty Patio & Deck Designs	2,500	Job expenses: subcontractor	2,500	Mills, Richard	Landscaping
Sena Lumber and Building Materials	550	Delivery fee	50	Hughes, David	Landscaping
		Materials: decks and patio	500		

The following payments were made to satisfy vendor accounts:

Conner Garden Supplies	$ 210
Middlefield Nursery	240
Sena Lumber and Building Materials	1,400

Instructions

1. Enter the three vendor bills into the electronic bills in QuickBooks. To open the electronic bill, click on the Bill button or select the Bill submenu item under "Activities."
2. Enter the three payments on the "pay bills" forms by checking the appropriate bill for payments. Deselect the "to be printed" option for checks. "Pay bills" is a submenu item under "Activities."
3. Print the following reports (submenu item under Reports in parentheses):
   a. Vendor Balance Summary. (A/P Reports)
   b. Vendor Balance Detail for Sena Lumber and Building Materials. (Double-click Sena Lumber and Building Materials balance on the summary report.)
   c. Expenses by Vendor Summary for Oct. 1–Dec. 15. (Profit & Loss)
   d. Expenses by Vendor Detail for Denk's Nursery for Oct. 1–Dec. 15. (Double-click Denk's Nursery expense balance on the Expenses by Vendor Summary Report.)

SPECIAL ACTIVITIES

Activity 5–1 Armor Security Co.

Ethics and professional conduct in business

Lee Baskin sells security systems for Armor Security Co. Baskin has a monthly sales quota of $40,000. If Baskin exceeds this quota, he is awarded a bonus. In measuring the quota, a sale is credited to the salesperson when a customer signs a contract for installation of a security system. Through the 25th of the current month, Baskin has sold $30,000 in security systems.

Vortex Co., a business rumored to be on the verge of bankruptcy, contacted Baskin on the 26th of the month about having a security system installed. Baskin estimates that the contract would yield about $14,000 worth of business for Armor Security Co. In addition, this contract would be large enough to put Baskin "over the top" for a bonus in the current month. However, Baskin is concerned that Vortex Co. will not be able to make the contract payment after the security system is installed. In fact, Baskin has heard rumors that a competing security services company refused to install a system for Vortex Co. because of these concerns.

Upon further consideration, Baskin concluded that his job is to sell security systems and that it's someone else's problem to collect the resulting accounts receivable. Thus, Baskin wrote the contract with Vortex Co. and received a bonus for the month.

Discuss whether Lee Baskin was acting in an ethical manner. How might Armor Security Co. use internal controls to prevent this scenario from occurring?

Activity 5–2 Blacktop Pavement Co.

Manual vs. computerized accounting systems

The following conversation took place between Blacktop Pavement Co.'s bookkeeper, Gerry Monroe, and the accounting supervisor, Lyn Hargrove.

Lyn: Gerry, I'm thinking about bringing in a new computerized accounting system to replace our manual system. I guess this will mean that you will need to learn how to do computerized accounting.

Gerry: What does computerized accounting mean?

Lyn: I'm not sure, but you'll need to prepare for this new way of doing business.

Gerry: I'm not so sure we need a computerized system. I've been looking at some of the sample reports from the software vendor. It looks to me like the computer will not add much to what we are already doing.

Lyn: What do you mean?

Gerry: Well, look at these reports. This Sales by Customer Report looks like our revenue journal, and the Deposit Detail Report looks like our cash receipts journal. Granted, the computer types them, so they look much neater than my special journals, but I don't see that we're gaining much from this change.

Lyn: Well, surely there's more to it than nice-looking reports. I've got to believe that a computerized system will save us time and effort someplace.

Gerry: I don't see how. We still need to key in transactions into the computer. If anything, there may be more work when it's all said and done.

Do you agree with Gerry? Why might a computerized environment be preferred over the manual system?

Activity 5–3
Windsor Company
Internal controls

What do you THINK?

Like most businesses, when Windsor Company renders services to another business, it is typical that the service is rendered "on account," rather than as a cash transaction. As a result, Windsor Company has an account receivable for the service provided. Likewise, the company receiving the service has an account payable for the amount owed for services received. At a later date, Windsor Company will receive cash from the customer to satisfy the accounts receivable balance. However, when individuals conduct transactions with each other, it is common for the transaction to be for cash. For example, when you buy a pizza, you often pay with cash.

Why is it unusual for businesses such as Windsor Company to engage in cash transactions, while for individuals it is more common?

Activity 5–4
Hershey Foods Corporation
Internal controls and the annual report

REAL WORLD

Corporations generally issue annual reports to their stockholders and other interested parties. These annual reports include a Management Responsibility (or Management Report) section as well as financial statements. The Management Responsibility section discusses responsibility for the financial statements and normally includes an assessment of the company's internal control system.

What does the annual report for **Hershey Foods Corporation** (in Appendix G) indicate about the internal control system?

Activity 5–5
Ragsdale Medical Group
Design of accounting systems

For the past few years, your client, Ragsdale Medical Group (RMG), has operated a small medical practice. RMG's current annual revenues are $420,000. Because the accountant has been spending more and more time each month recording all transactions in a two-column journal and preparing the financial statements, RMG is considering improving the accounting system by adding special journals and subsidiary ledgers. RMG has asked you to help with this project and has compiled the following information:

Type of Transaction	Estimated Frequency per Month
Fees earned on account	240
Purchase of medical supplies on account	190
Cash receipts from patients on account	175
Cash payments on account	160
Cash receipts from patients at time services provided	120
Purchase of office supplies on account	35
Purchase of magazine subscriptions on account	5
Purchase of medical equipment on account	4
Cash payments for office salaries	3
Cash payments for utilities expense	3

A local sales tax is collected on all patient bills, and monthly financial statements are prepared.

1. Briefly discuss the circumstances under which special journals would be used in place of a two-column (all-purpose) journal. Include in your answer your recommendations for RMG's medical practice.
2. Assume that RMG has decided to use a revenue journal and a purchases journal. Design the format for each journal, giving special consideration to the needs of the medical practice.
3. Which subsidiary ledgers would you recommend for the medical practice?

Activity 5–6 Into the Real World

Shopping for a microcomputer

INTERNET ACTIVITY GROUP ACTIVITY

Obtain a copy of a recent computer magazine (such as *PC Week*) from the library or magazine stand. In this magazine, select an ad by a company that offers a variety of microcomputer systems—from a basic system to a top-of-the-line system. Some good examples would be **Dell**, **Micron**, **Compaq**, or **Gateway 2000**. Alternatively, go to the web page of one of the computer companies to obtain product information. Divide responsibilities among your team so that you can accomplish the following tasks:

1. Bring to class one of the ads or a printout of web pages with product specifications. The Internet sites of the companies mentioned above are:

   www.dell.com
   www.micron.com
   www.compaq.com
   www.gateway.com

2. List and briefly explain each feature of the top-of-the-line computer identified in the ad or web page. Compare the features of the top-of-the-line system and the basic entry-level system. How do they differ? How do the prices differ?
3. Try to discover the purpose of the features that are not familiar to you by talking to others in your group or to friends.

ANSWERS TO SELF-EXAMINATION QUESTIONS

Matching

1. E	4. C	7. A	9. B	11. H	13. G	15. N	17. K
2. F	5. L	8. M	10. D	12. P	14. O	16. J	18. S
3. I	6. R						

Multiple Choice

1. **A** Analysis (answer A) is the initial step of determining the informational needs and how the system provides this information. Design (answer B) is the step in which proposals for changes are developed. Implementation (answer C) is the final step involving carrying out or implementing the proposals for changes. Feedback (answer D) is not a separate step but is considered part of the systems implementation.
2. **A** The policies and procedures that are established to safeguard assets, ensure accurate business information, and ensure compliance with laws and regulations are called internal controls (answer A). The three steps in setting up an accounting system are (1) analysis (answer B), (2) design (answer C), and (3) implementation (answer D).
3. **B** All payments of cash for any purpose are recorded in the cash payments journal (answer B). Only purchases of services or other items on account are recorded in the purchases journal (answer A). All sales of services on account are recorded in the revenue journal (answer C), and all receipts of cash are recorded in the cash receipts journal (answer D).
4. **A** The general term used to describe the type of separate ledger that contains a large number of individual accounts with a common characteristic is a subsidiary ledger (answer A). The creditors ledger (answer B), sometimes called the accounts payable ledger (answer C), is a specific subsidiary ledger containing only individual accounts with creditors. Likewise, the accounts receivable ledger (answer D), also called the customers ledger, is a specific subsidiary ledger containing only individual accounts with customers.
5. **C** Both the revenue journal (answer A) and the cash receipts journal (answer B) are generally not used in a computerized accounting system. Rather, electronic forms, such as an electronic invoice form (answer C), are used to record original transactions. The computer automatically posts transactions from electronic forms to the general ledger and individual accounts at the time the transactions are recorded. Therefore, month-end postings to the general ledger are not necessary (answer D) in a computerized accounting system.

6

Accounting for Merchandising Businesses

Setting the STAGE

Assume that you bought groceries at a store and received the receipt shown here. This receipt indicates that you purchased three items totaling $5.28, the sales tax was $.32 (6%), the total due was $5.60, you gave the clerk $10.00, and you received change of $4.40. The receipt also indicates that the sale was made by Store #426 of the Ingles chain, located in Athens, Georgia. The date and time of the sale and other data used internally by the store are also indicated.

INGLES #426
ATHENS GA

	10/02/99
GROCERY	2.99L
GROCERY	1.00L
FZ FOOD	1.29L
SUBTOTAL	5.28
TAX	.32
TOTAL	5.60
CASH	10.00
CHANGE	4.40
# ITEMS 3	

THANK YOU C123 R03 T12:38

When you buy groceries, textbooks, school supplies, or an automobile, you are doing business with a retail or merchandising business. The accounting for a merchandising business is more complex than for a service business. For example, the accounting system for a merchandiser must be designed to record the receipt of goods for resale, keep track of the goods available for sale, and record the sale and cost of the merchandise sold.

In this chapter, we will focus on the accounting principles and concepts for merchandising businesses. We begin our discussion by highlighting the basic differences in the activities of merchandise and service businesses. We then describe and illustrate purchases and sales transactions and financial statements for merchandising businesses.

objectives

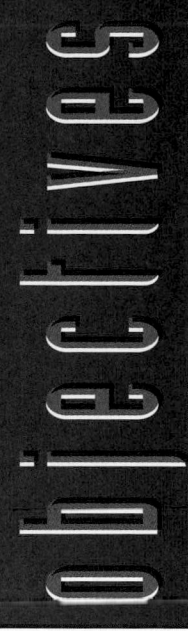

After studying this chapter, you should be able to:

1. Distinguish the activities of a service business from those of a merchandising business.
2. Journalize the entries for merchandise transactions, including:
   a. Merchandise purchases
   b. Merchandise sales
   c. Merchandise transportation costs
   d. Transactions for both the buyer and the seller
3. Prepare a chart of accounts for a merchandising business.
4. Prepare an income statement for a merchandising business.
5. Describe the accounting cycle for a merchandising business.
6. Compute the ratio of net sales to assets as a measure of how effectively a business is using its assets.

Nature of Merchandising Businesses

OBJECTIVE 1

Distinguish the activities of a service business from those of a merchandising business.

COMPUTER KING

How do the activities of Computer King, an attorney, and an architect, which are service businesses, differ from those of **Wal-Mart** or **Kmart**, which are merchandising businesses? These differences are best illustrated by focusing on the revenues and expenses in the following condensed income statements:

Service Business	
Fees earned	$XXX
Operating expenses	−XXX
Net income	$XXX

Merchandising Business	
Sales	$XXX
Cost of merchandise sold	−XXX
Gross profit	$XXX
Operating expenses	−XXX
Net income	$XXX

The revenue activities of a service business involve providing services to customers. On the income statement for a service business, the revenues from services are reported as *fees earned.* The operating expenses incurred in providing the services are subtracted from the fees earned to arrive at *net income.*

In contrast, the revenue activities of a merchandising business involve the buying and selling of merchandise. A merchandising business must first purchase merchandise to sell to its customers. When this merchandise is sold, the revenue is reported as sales, and its cost is recognized as an expense called the **cost of merchandise sold**. The cost of merchandise sold is subtracted from sales to arrive at gross profit. This amount is called **gross profit** because it is the profit *before* deducting operating expenses.

REAL WORLD

For many merchandising businesses, the cost of merchandise sold is usually the largest expense. For example, the approximate percentage of cost of merchandise sold to sales is 70% for **J.C. Penney Company** and 75% for **Lowe's Companies**.

Sales − Cost of Merchandise Sold = Gross Profit

Gross Profit − Operating Expenses = Net Income

Merchandise on hand (not sold) at the end of an accounting period is called **merchandise inventory**. Merchandise inventory is reported as a current asset on the balance sheet.

In the remainder of this chapter, we illustrate transactions that affect the income statement (sales, cost of merchandise sold, and gross profit) and the balance sheet (merchandise inventory). We will assume that Computer King opened a retail store in January 2001.

Merchandise transactions are recorded in the accounts, using the rules of debit and credit that we described and illustrated in earlier chapters. Special journals may be used, or transactions may be entered, recorded, and posted to the accounts electronically. Although journal entries may not be manually prepared, we will use a two-column general journal format in this chapter in order to simplify the discussion.[1]

Accounting for Purchases

OBJECTIVE 2a

Journalize the entries for merchandise purchases.

There are two systems for accounting for merchandise: perpetual and periodic. In the **perpetual inventory system**, each purchase and sale of merchandise is recorded in an inventory account. As a result, the amount of merchandise available for sale and the amount sold are continuously (perpetually) disclosed in the inventory records. In the **periodic inventory system**, the inventory records do not show the amount available for sale or sold during the period. Instead, a detailed listing of the merchandise for sale (called a **physical inventory**) at the end of the accounting period is prepared. This physical inventory is used to determine the cost of the merchandise on hand at the end of the period and the cost of the merchandise sold during the period.

In a perpetual inventory system, each purchase is debited to Merchandise Inventory, and the cost of each sale is credited to Merchandise Inventory.

REAL WORLD: Retailers, such as **Kmart**, **Sears**, and **Wal-Mart**, and grocery store chains, such as **Winn-Dixie** and **Kroger**, use bar codes and optical scanners as part of their computerized inventory systems.

Large retailers and many small merchandising businesses use computerized perpetual inventory systems. Such systems normally use bar codes, such as the one on the back of this textbook. An optical scanner reads the bar code to record merchandise purchased and sold.

Because the perpetual inventory system is widely used, we illustrate it in this chapter. We describe and illustrate the periodic inventory system in a later chapter and in an appendix at the end of the text.

Under the perpetual inventory system, cash purchases of merchandise are recorded as follows:

JOURNAL **PAGE 24**

	Date		Description	Post. Ref.	Debit	Credit	
1	20— Jan.	3	Merchandise Inventory		2,510 00		1
2			Cash			2,510 00	2
3			Purchased inventory from Bowen Co.				3

Purchases of merchandise on account are recorded as follows:

	Date		Description	Post. Ref.	Debit	Credit	
5	Jan.	4	Merchandise Inventory		9,250 00		5
6			Accounts Payable—Thomas Corporation			9,250 00	6
7			Purchased inventory on account.				7

[1] Special journals and computerized accounting systems for merchandising businesses are described in Appendix 1 at the end of this chapter.

Purchases Discounts

The terms of a purchase are normally indicated on the **invoice** or bill that the seller sends to the buyer. An example of such an invoice is shown in Exhibit 1.

EXHIBIT 1
Invoice

Wallace Electronics
3800 Mission Street
San Francisco, CA 94110-1732

Made in U.S.A.

SOLD TO Computer King 1000 Peachtree Street Atlanta, GA 30309-1000	**CUSTOMER'S ORDER NO. & DATE** 412 Jan. 10, 2001 **REFER TO INVOICE NO.** 106-8

DATE SHIPPED	**HOW SHIPPED AND ROUTE**	**TERMS**	**INVOICE DATE**
Jan. 12, 2001	Western Trucking Co.	2/10, n/30	Jan. 12, 2001
FROM	**F.O.B.**	**PREPAID OR COLLECT?**	
San Francisco	Atlanta	Prepaid	

QUANTITY	**DESCRIPTION**	**UNIT PRICE**	**AMOUNT**
20	392E Monitors	75.00	1,500.00

The terms for when payments for merchandise are to be made, agreed on by the buyer and the seller, are called the **credit terms**. If payment is required on delivery, the terms are *cash* or *net cash*. Otherwise, the buyer is allowed an amount of time, known as the **credit period**, in which to pay.

The credit period usually begins with the date of the sale as shown on the invoice. If payment is due within a stated number of days after the date of the invoice, such as 30 days, the terms are *net 30 days*. These terms may be written as *n/30*.[2] If payment is due by the end of the month in which the sale was made, the terms are written as *n/eom*.

As a means of encouraging the buyer to pay before the end of the credit period, the seller may offer a discount. For example, a seller may offer a 2% discount if the buyer pays within 10 days of the invoice date. If the buyer does not take the discount, the total amount is due within 30 days. These terms are expressed as *2/10, n/30* and are read as *2% discount if paid within 10 days, net amount due within 30 days*. The credit terms of 2/10, n/30 are summarized in Exhibit 2, using the information from the invoice in Exhibit 1.

Q&A *If an invoice dated August 13 has terms n/30, what is the due date of the invoice?*

September 12 [30 days = 18 days in August (31 days − 13 days) + 12 days in September]

EXHIBIT 2
Credit Terms

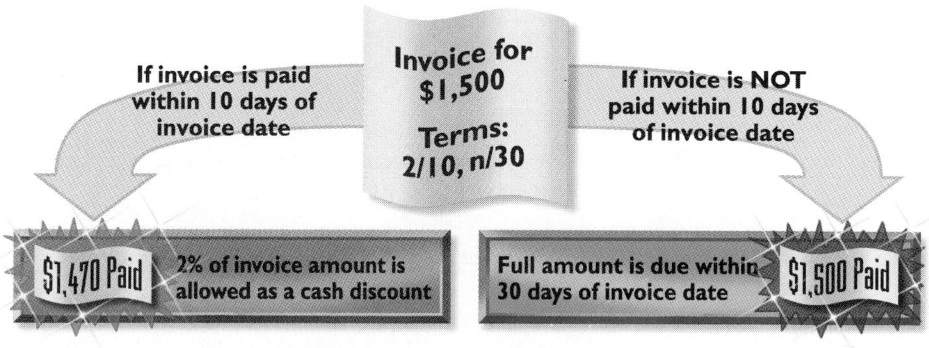

Invoice for $1,500
Terms: 2/10, n/30
If invoice is paid within 10 days of invoice date
If invoice is NOT paid within 10 days of invoice date
$1,470 Paid
2% of invoice amount is allowed as a cash discount
Full amount is due within 30 days of invoice date
$1,500 Paid

[2] The word *net* as used here does not have the usual meaning of a number after deductions have been subtracted, as in *net income*.

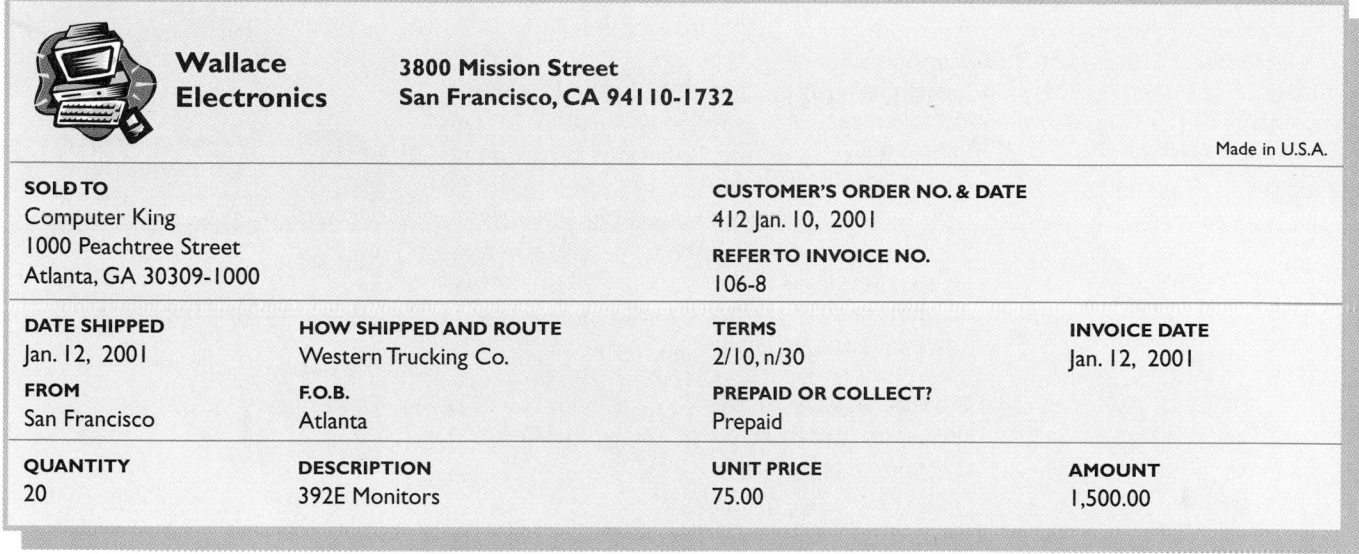

Q&A *If an invoice dated November 22 has credit terms 2/10, n/30, what is (a) the last day the invoice may be paid within the discount period and (b) the last day of the credit period if the discount is not taken?*

(a) December 2 [10 days = 8 days in November (30 days − 22 days) + 2 days in December]; (b) December 22 [30 days = 8 days in November (30 days − 22 days) + 22 days in December]

Discounts taken by the buyer for early payment of an invoice are called **purchases discounts**. These discounts reduce the cost of the merchandise purchased. Most businesses design their accounting systems so that all available discounts are taken. Even if the buyer has to borrow to make the payment within a discount period, it is normally to the buyer's advantage to do so. To illustrate, assume that Computer King borrows money to pay the invoice for $1,500, shown in Exhibit 1. The last day of the discount period in which the $30 discount can be taken is January 22, 2001. The money is borrowed for the remaining 20 days of the credit period. If we assume an annual interest rate of 12% and a 360-day year, the interest on the loan of $1,470 ($1,500 − $30) is $9.80 ($1,470 × 12% × 20/360). The net savings to Computer King is $20.20, computed as follows:

REAL WORLD Businesses often program their accounting systems to pay bills automatically at the right time.

Discount of 2% on $1,500	$30.00
Interest for 20 days at rate of 12% on $1,470	− 9.80
Savings from borrowing	$20.20

Point of INTEREST

Should you pay your bills, such as utility bills and credit card bills, as soon as they are received? Probably not. Most bills that you receive do not offer discounts for early payment. Rather, the bills normally indicate only a due date and perhaps a penalty for late payment. Many times you receive bills weeks before their due date. In such cases, it is to your advantage to file the bill by its due date in a folder or other organizer, such as a desk calendar, and mail the payment a few days before it is due. This way, you can use your money to earn interest in your checking or savings account.

The savings can also be seen by comparing the interest rate on the money saved by taking the discount and the interest rate on the money borrowed to take the discount. For Computer King, the interest rate on the money saved in this example is estimated by converting 2% for 20 days to a yearly rate, as follows:

$$2\% \times \frac{\textbf{360 days}}{\textbf{20 days}} = 2\% \times 18 = 36\%$$

If Computer King borrows the money to take the discount, it *pays* interest of 12%. If Computer King does not take the discount, it *pays* estimated interest of 36% for using the $30 for an additional 20 days.

Under the perpetual inventory system, the buyer initially debits the merchandise inventory account for the amount of the invoice. When paying the invoice, the buyer credits the merchandise inventory account for the amount of the discount. In this way, the merchandise inventory shows the *net* cost to the buyer. For example, Computer King would record the invoice in Exhibit 1 and its payment at the end of the discount period as follows:

Jan.	12	Merchandise Inventory		1 500 00	
		Accounts Payable—Wallace Electronics			1 500 00
		Invoice 106-8.			
	22	Accounts Payable—Wallace Electronics		1 500 00	
		Cash			1 470 00
		Merchandise Inventory			30 00
		Paid Invoice 106-8.			

If Computer King does not take the discount because it does not pay Invoice 106-8 until February 11, it would record the payment as follows:

Feb.	11	Accounts Payable—Wallace Electronics	1500 00	
		Cash		1500 00
		Paid Invoice 106-8 after discount period.		

Purchases Returns and Allowances

When merchandise is returned (**purchases return**) or a price adjustment is requested (**purchases allowance**), the buyer (debtor) usually sends the seller a letter or a debit memorandum. A **debit memorandum**, shown in Exhibit 3, informs the seller of the amount the buyer proposes to *debit* to the account payable due the seller. It also states the reasons for the return or the request for a price reduction.

EXHIBIT 3
Debit Memorandum

No. 18

COMPUTER KING
1000 Peachtree Street
Atlanta, GA 30309-1000

DEBIT MEMORANDUM

TO
Power Electronics
1614 LaSalle Street
Chicago, IL 60602-2391

DATE
March 7, 2001

WE DEBIT YOUR ACCOUNT AS FOLLOWS

5	No. 8241 Printer Covers, your Invoice No. 7291, are being returned via parcel post. Our order specified No. 825X.	@ 18.00	90.00

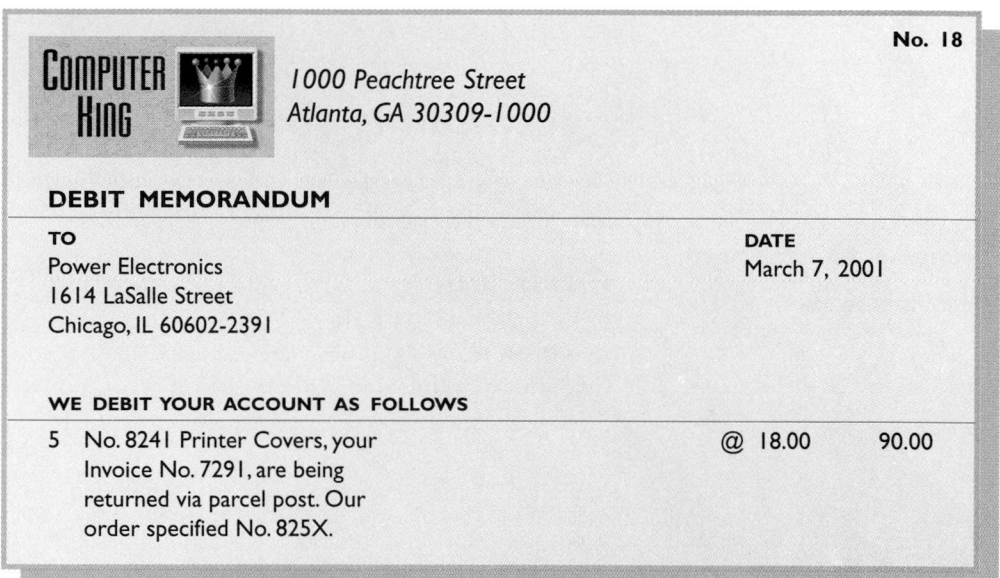

The buyer may use a copy of the debit memorandum as the basis for recording the return or allowance, or wait for approval from the seller (creditor). In either case, the buyer must debit Accounts Payable and credit Merchandise Inventory. To illustrate, Computer King records the return of the merchandise indicated in the debit memo in Exhibit 3 as follows:

Mar.	7	Accounts Payable—Power Electronics	90 00	
		Merchandise Inventory		90 00
		Debit Memo No. 18.		

When a buyer returns merchandise or has been granted an allowance prior to paying the invoice, the amount of the debit memorandum is deducted from the invoice amount. The amount is deducted before the purchase discount is computed. For example, assume that on May 2, Computer King purchases $5,000 of merchandise from Computer Maker, subject to terms 2/10, n/30. On May 4, Computer King returns $3,000 of the merchandise, and on May 12, Computer King pays the original invoice less the return. Computer King would record these transactions as follows:

May	2	Merchandise Inventory		5 0 0 0 00	
		Accounts Payable—Computer Maker			5 0 0 0 00
		Purchased merchandise.			
	4	Accounts Payable—Computer Maker		3 0 0 0 00	
		Merchandise Inventory			3 0 0 0 00
		Returned portion of merchandise purchased.			
	12	Accounts Payable—Computer Maker		2 0 0 0 00	
		Cash			1 9 6 0 00
		Merchandise Inventory			4 0 00
		Paid invoice [($5,000 – $3,000) × 2% = $40; $2,000 – $40 = $1,960].			

Q&A

Ennis Co. purchases merchandise of $8,000 on terms 2/10, n/30. Ennis pays the original invoice, less a return of $2,500, within the discount period. How much did Ennis Co. pay?

$5,390 [($8,000 – $2,500) × 2% = $110 discount; $8,000 – $2,500 – $110 = $5,390]

Accounting for Sales

OBJECTIVE 2b

Journalize the entries for merchandise sales.

Revenue from merchandise sales is usually identified in the ledger as *Sales*. Sometimes a business will use a more exact title, such as *Sales of Merchandise*.

Cash Sales

A business may sell merchandise for cash. Cash sales are normally rung up (entered) on a cash register and recorded in the accounts. To illustrate, if cash sales for January 3 are $1,800, they can be recorded as follows:

JOURNAL **PAGE 25**

	Date		Description	Post. Ref.	Debit	Credit	
1	20— Jan.	3	Cash		1 8 0 0 00		1
2			Sales			1 8 0 0 00	2
3			To record cash sales.				3

Under the perpetual inventory system, the cost of merchandise sold and the reduction in merchandise inventory should also be recorded. In this way, the merchandise inventory account will indicate the amount of merchandise on hand (not sold). On the income statement at the end of the period, the balance of the cost of merchandise sold account is subtracted from the related sales for the period in order to determine the gross profit. To illustrate, assume that the cost of merchandise sold on January 3 was $1,200. The entry to record the cost of merchandise sold and the reduction in the merchandise inventory is as follows:

Jan.	3	Cost of Merchandise Sold		1 2 0 0 00	
		Merchandise Inventory			1 2 0 0 00
		To record the cost of merchandise sold.			

How do retailers record sales made with the use of credit cards? Sales made to customers using credit cards issued by banks, such as **MasterCard** or **VISA**, are recorded as *cash sales.* The seller deposits the credit card receipts for these sales directly into its bank account.

Normally, banks charge service fees for handling credit card sales. The seller debits these service fees to an expense account. An entry at the end of a month to record the payment of service charges on bank credit card sales is shown below.

Jan.	31	Credit Card Expense	48 00	
		Cash		48 00
		To record service charges on credit card sales for the month.		

Sales on Account

A business may sell merchandise on account. The seller records such sales as a debit to Accounts Receivable and a credit to Sales. An example of an entry for a sale on account of $510 follows. The cost of merchandise sold was $280.

Jan.	12	Accounts Receivable—Sims Co.	510 00	
		Sales		510 00
		Invoice No. 7172.		
	12	Cost of Merchandise Sold	280 00	
		Merchandise Inventory		280 00
		Cost of merchandise sold on Invoice No. 7172.		

A retailer may accept **MasterCard** or **VISA** but not **American Express**. Why? The service fees that credit card companies charge retailers are the primary reason that some businesses do not accept all credit cards. For example, American Express Co.'s service fees are normally higher than MasterCard's or VISA's. As a result, some retailers choose not to accept American Express cards. The disadvantage of this practice is that the retailer may lose customers to competitors who do accept American Express cards.

Sales may also be made to customers using nonbank credit cards. An example of a nonbank credit card is the **American Express** card. Nonbank credit card sales must first be reported to the card company before cash is received. Therefore, such sales create a *receivable* with the card company. Before the card company pays cash, it normally deducts a service fee. For example, assume that American Express card sales of $1,000 are made and reported to the card company on January 20. The cost of the merchandise sold was $550. On January 27, the card company deducts a service fee of $50 and sends $950 to the seller. These transactions are recorded by the seller as follows:

Jan.	20	Accounts Receivable—American Express	1000 00	
		Sales		1000 00
		American Express (nonbank) credit card sales.		
	20	Cost of Merchandise Sold	550 00	
		Merchandise Inventory		550 00
		Cost of merchandise sold on American Express credit card sales.		
	27	Cash	950 00	
		Credit Card Expense	50 00	
		Accounts Receivable—American Express		1000 00
		Received cash from American Express for sales reported on January 20.		

Sales Discounts

As we mentioned in our discussion of purchase transactions, a seller may offer the buyer credit terms that include a discount for early payment. The seller refers to such discounts as **sales discounts**, which reduce sales revenue.

To reduce sales, the sales account could be debited. However, managers may want to know the amount of the sales discounts for a period in deciding whether to change credit terms. For this reason, the seller records the sales discounts in a separate account. The sales discounts account is a *contra* (or *offsetting*) account to Sales. To illustrate, assume that cash is received within the discount period (10 days) from the credit sale of $1,500, shown on the invoice in Exhibit 1. Wallace Electronics Supply would record the receipt of the cash as follows:

Jan.	22	Cash	1,470 00	
		Sales Discounts	30 00	
		Accounts Receivable—Computer King		1,500 00
		Collection on Invoice No. 106-8, less		
		2% discount.		

Sales Returns and Allowances

Merchandise sold may be returned to the seller (**sales return**). In addition, because of defects or for other reasons, the seller may reduce the initial price at which the goods were sold (**sales allowance**). If the return or allowance is for a sale on account, the seller usually issues the buyer a **credit memorandum**. This memorandum shows the amount of and the reason for the seller's credit to an account receivable. A credit memorandum is illustrated in Exhibit 4.

EXHIBIT 4
Credit Memorandum

No. 32

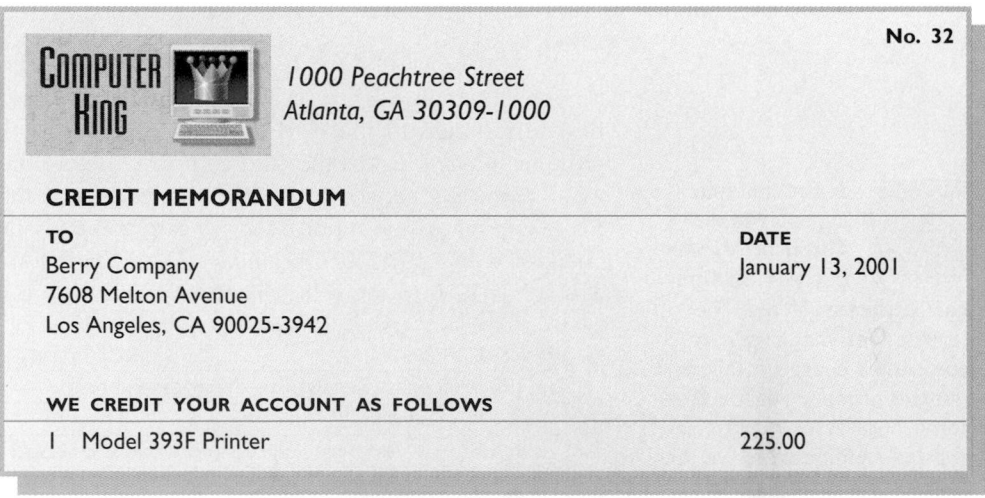

COMPUTER KING
1000 Peachtree Street
Atlanta, GA 30309-1000

CREDIT MEMORANDUM

TO
Berry Company
7608 Melton Avenue
Los Angeles, CA 90025-3942

DATE
January 13, 2001

WE CREDIT YOUR ACCOUNT AS FOLLOWS

1 Model 393F Printer 225.00

REAL WORLD Book publishers often experience large returns if a book is not immediately successful. For example, 35% of adult hardcover books shipped to retailers are returned to publishers, according to the Association of American Publishers.

Like sales discounts, sales returns and allowances reduce sales revenue. They also result in additional shipping and other expenses. Since managers often want to know the amount of returns and allowances for a period, the seller records sales returns and allowances in a separate account. Sales Returns and Allowances is a *contra* (or *offsetting*) account to Sales.

The seller debits Sales Returns and Allowances for the amount of the return or allowance. If the original sale was on account, the seller credits Accounts Receivable. Since the merchandise inventory is kept up to date in a perpetual system, the seller adds the cost of the returned merchandise to the merchandise inventory account. The seller must also credit the cost of returned merchandise to the cost of merchandise sold account, since this account was debited when the original sale was recorded. To illustrate, assume that the cost of the merchandise returned in Exhibit 4 was $140. Computer King records the credit memo in Exhibit 4 as follows:

Jan.	13	Sales Returns and Allowances		225 00	
		Accounts Receivable—Berry Company			225 00
		Credit Memo No. 32.			
	13	Merchandise Inventory		140 00	
		Cost of Merchandise Sold			140 00
		Cost of merchandise returned, Credit			
		Memo No. 32.			

What if the buyer pays for the merchandise and the merchandise is later returned? In this case, the seller may issue a credit and apply it against other accounts receivable owed by the buyer, or the cash may be refunded. If the credit is applied against the buyer's other receivables, the seller records entries similar to those preceding. If cash is refunded for merchandise returned or for an allowance, the seller debits Sales Returns and Allowances and credits Cash.

Sales Taxes

Almost all states and many other taxing units levy a tax on sales of merchandise.[3] The liability for the sales tax is incurred when the sale is made.

At the time of a cash sale, the seller collects the sales tax. When a sale is made on account, the seller charges the tax to the buyer by debiting Accounts Receivable. The seller credits the sales account for the amount of the sale and credits the tax to Sales Tax Payable. For example, the seller would record a sale of $100 on account, subject to a tax of 6%, as follows:

REAL WORLD The five states with the highest sales tax are Illinois, Minnesota, Nevada, Texas, and Washington. Some states have no sales tax, including Alaska, Delaware, Montana, New Hampshire, and Oregon.

Aug.	12	Accounts Receivable		106 00	
		Sales			100 00
		Sales Tax Payable			6 00
		Invoice No. 339.			

Normally on a regular basis, the seller pays to the taxing unit the amount of the sales tax collected. The seller records such a payment as follows:

Sept.	15	Sales Tax Payable		2,900 00	
		Cash			2,900 00
		Payment for sales taxes collected			
		during August.			

[3] Businesses that purchase merchandise for resale to others are normally exempt from paying sales taxes on their purchases. Only final buyers of merchandise normally pay sales taxes.

Q&A *A seller offered a 30% trade discount on an item listed in its catalog for $2,400. At what amount would the buyer record the purchase?*

$1,680 [$2,400 − ($2,400 × 30%), or $2,400 × 70%]

Trade Discounts

Wholesalers are businesses that sell merchandise to other businesses rather than to the general public. Many wholesalers publish catalogs. Rather than updating their catalogs frequently, wholesalers often publish price updates, which may involve large discounts from the list prices in their catalogs. In addition, wholesalers may offer special discounts to certain classes of buyers, such as government agencies or businesses that order large quantities. Such discounts are called **trade discounts**.

Sellers and buyers do not normally record the list prices of merchandise and the related trade discounts in their accounts. For example, assume that an item has a list price of $1,000 and a 40% trade discount. The seller records the sale of the item at $600 [$1,000 less the trade discount of $400 ($1,000 × 40%)]. Likewise, the buyer records the purchase at $600.

Transportation Costs

OBJECTIVE 2c

Journalize the entries for merchandise transportation costs.

The terms of a sale should indicate when the ownership (title) of the merchandise passes to the buyer. This point determines which party, the buyer or the seller, must pay the transportation costs.[4]

The buyer bears the transportation costs if the shipping terms are FOB shipping point.

The ownership of the merchandise may pass to the buyer when the seller delivers the merchandise to the transportation company or freight carrier. For example, **Chrysler Corp.** records the sale and the transfer of ownership of its vehicles to dealers when the vehicles are shipped. In this case, the terms are said to be **FOB (free on board) shipping point**. This term means that Chrysler is responsible for the transportation charges to the shipping point, which is where the shipment originates. The dealer then pays the transportation costs to the final destination. Such costs are part of the dealer's total cost of purchasing inventory and should be added to the cost of the inventory by debiting Merchandise Inventory.

COMPUTER KING

To illustrate, assume that on June 10, Computer King buys merchandise from Reese Company on account, $900, terms FOB shipping point, and pays the transportation cost of $50. Computer King records these two transactions as follows:

June	10	Merchandise Inventory		950 00	
		Accounts Payable—Reese Company			950 00
		Purchased merchandise, terms FOB shipping point.			
	10	Merchandise Inventory		50 00	
		Cash			50 00
		Paid shipping cost on merchandise purchased.			

The ownership of the merchandise may pass to the buyer when the buyer receives the merchandise. In this case, the terms are said to be **FOB (free on board)**

[4] The passage of title also determines whether the buyer or seller must pay other costs, such as the cost of insurance, while the merchandise is in transit.

destination. This term means that the seller delivers the merchandise to the buyer's final destination, free of transportation charges to the buyer. The seller thus pays the transportation costs to the final destination. The seller debits Transportation Out or Delivery Expense, which is reported on the seller's income statement as an expense.

The seller bears the transportation costs if the shipping terms are FOB destination.

To illustrate, assume that on June 15, Computer King sells merchandise to Kranz Company on account, $700, terms FOB destination. The cost of the merchandise sold is $480, and Computer King pays the transportation cost of $40. Computer King records the sale, the cost of the sale, and the transportation cost as follows:

REAL WORLD: Sometimes FOB shipping point and FOB destination are expressed in terms of the location at which the title to the merchandise passes to the buyer. For example, if **Toyota Motor Co.'s** assembly plant in Osaka, Japan, sells automobiles to a dealer in Chicago, FOB shipping point could be expressed as FOB Osaka. Likewise, FOB destination could be expressed as FOB Chicago.

June	15	Accounts Receivable—Kranz Company		700 00	
		Sales			700 00
		Sold merchandise, terms FOB destination.			
	15	Cost of Goods Sold		480 00	
		Merchandise Inventory			480 00
		Recorded cost of merchandise sold to Kranz Company.			
	15	Transportation Out		40 00	
		Cash			40 00
		Paid shipping cost on merchandise sold.			

Shipping terms, the passage of title, and whether the buyer or seller is to pay the transportation costs are summarized in Exhibit 5.

EXHIBIT 5 Transportation Terms

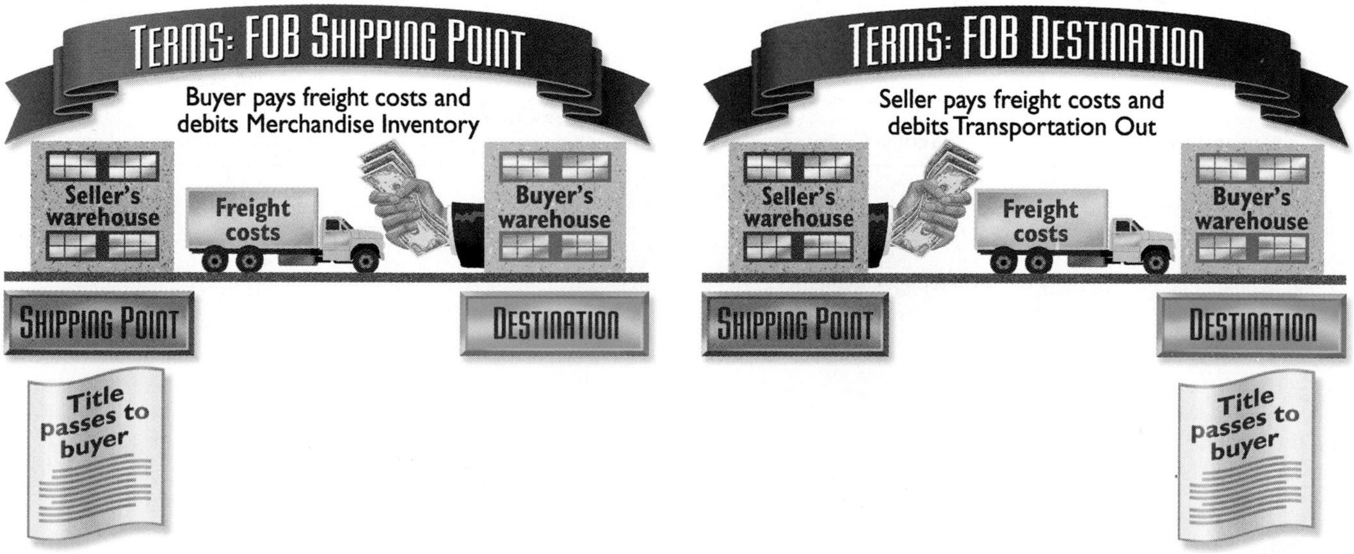

Q&A *Martin Co. sells $4,000 of merchandise to Oblinger Co. on account on terms 2/10, n/30, FOB shipping point. As a convenience to Oblinger, Martin Co. pays transportation costs of $250 and adds those costs to the invoice. (a) How much will Martin Co. bill Oblinger? (b) If Oblinger Co. pays within the discount period, what amount will Oblinger pay Martin?*

(a) $4,250 ($4,000 + $250); (b) $4,170 [$4,000 − ($4,000 × 2%) + $250]

As a convenience to the buyer, the seller may prepay the transportation costs, even though the terms are FOB shipping point. The seller will then add the transportation costs to the invoice. The buyer will debit Merchandise Inventory for the total amount of the invoice, including the transportation costs.

To illustrate, assume that on June 20, Computer King sells merchandise to Planter Company on account, $800, terms FOB shipping point. Computer King pays the transportation cost of $45 and adds it to the invoice. The cost of the merchandise sold is $360. Computer King records these transactions as follows:

June	20	Accounts Receivable—Planter Company		800 00	
		Sales			800 00
		Sold merchandise, terms FOB shipping point.			
	20	Cost of Merchandise Sold		360 00	
		Merchandise Inventory			360 00
		Recorded cost of merchandise sold to Planter Company.			
	20	Accounts Receivable—Planter Company		45 00	
		Cash			45 00
		Prepaid shipping cost on merchandise sold.			

Illustration of Accounting for Merchandise Transactions

OBJECTIVE 2d

Journalize the entries for merchandise transactions for both the buyer and the seller.

Each merchandising transaction affects a buyer and a seller. In the following illustration, we show how the same transactions would be recorded by both the seller and the buyer. In this example, the seller is Scully Company and the buyer is Burton Co.

Transaction	Scully Company (Seller)			Burton Co. (Buyer)		
July 1. Scully Company sold merchandise on account to Burton Co., $7,500, terms FOB shipping point, n/45. The cost of the merchandise sold was $4,500.	Accounts Receivable—Burton Co.	7,500		Merchandise Inventory	7,500	
	Sales		7,500	Accounts Payable—Scully Co.		7,500
	Cost of Merchandise Sold	4,500				
	Merchandise Inventory		4,500			
July 2. Burton Co. paid transportation charges of $150 on July 1 purchase from Scully Company.	No entry.			Merchandise Inventory	150	
				Cash		150

Transaction	Scully Company (Seller)			Burton Co. (Buyer)		
July 5. Scully Company sold merchandise on account to Burton Co., $5,000, terms FOB destination, n/30. The cost of the merchandise sold was $3,500.	Accounts Receivable—Burton Co.	5,000		Merchandise Inventory	5,000	
	Sales		5,000	Accounts Payable—Scully Co.		5,000
	Cost of Merchandise Sold	3,500				
	Merchandise Inventory		3,500			
July 7. Scully Company paid transportation costs of $250 for delivery of merchandise sold to Burton Co. on July 5.	Transportation Out	250		No entry.		
	Cash		250			
July 13. Scully Company issued Burton Co. a credit memorandum for merchandise returned, $1,000. The merchandise had been purchased by Burton Co. on account on July 5. The cost of the merchandise returned was $700.	Sales Returns & Allowances	1,000		Accounts Payable—Scully Co.	1,000	
	Accounts Receivable—Burton Co.		1,000	Merchandise Inventory		1,000
	Merchandise Inventory	700				
	Cost of Merchandise Sold		700			
July 15. Scully Company received payment from Burton Co. for purchase of July 5.	Cash	4,000		Accounts Payable—Scully Co.	4,000	
	Accounts Receivable—Burton Co.		4,000	Cash		4,000
July 18. Scully Company sold merchandise on account to Burton Co., $12,000, terms FOB shipping point, 2/10, n/eom. Scully Company prepaid transportation costs of $500, which were added to the invoice. The cost of the merchandise sold was $7,200.	Accounts Receivable—Burton Co.	12,000		Merchandise Inventory	12,500	
	Sales		12,000	Accounts Payable—Scully Co.		12,500
	Accounts Receivable—Burton Co.	500				
	Cash		500			
	Cost of Merchandise Sold	7,200				
	Merchandise Inventory		7,200			
July 28. Scully Company received payment from Burton Co. for purchase of July 18, less discount (2% × $12,000).	Cash	12,260		Accounts Payable—Scully Co.	12,500	
	Sales Discounts	240		Merchandise Inventory		240
	Accounts Receivable—Burton Co.		12,500	Cash		12,260

Chart of Accounts for a Merchandising Business

OBJECTIVE 3

Prepare a chart of accounts for a merchandising business.

The chart of accounts for a merchandising business should reflect the types of merchandising transactions we have described in this chapter. As a basis for illustration, we use Computer King.

On January 1, 2001, when Computer King opened a merchandising outlet selling microcomputers and software, it stopped providing consulting services. As a result, Computer King's chart of accounts changed from that of a service business to that of a merchandiser. A new chart of accounts for Computer King is shown in Exhibit 6. The accounts related to merchandising transactions are shown in color.

EXHIBIT 6
Chart of Accounts for Computer King, Merchandising Business

Balance Sheet Accounts		Income Statement Accounts	
	100 Assets		400 Revenues
110	Cash	410	Sales
111	Notes Receivable	411	Sales Returns and Allowances
112	Accounts Receivable	412	Sales Discounts
113	Interest Receivable		500 Costs and Expenses
115	Merchandise Inventory	510	Cost of Merchandise Sold
116	Office Supplies	520	Sales Salaries Expense
117	Prepaid Insurance	521	Advertising Expense
120	Land	522	Depreciation Expense—Store Equipment
123	Store Equipment	523	Transportation Out
124	Accumulated Depreciation—Store Equipment	529	Miscellaneous Selling Expense
125	Office Equipment	530	Office Salaries Expense
126	Accumulated Depreciation—Office Equipment	531	Rent Expense
	200 Liabilities	532	Depreciation Expense—Office Equipment
210	Accounts Payable	533	Insurance Expense
211	Salaries Payable	534	Office Supplies Expense
212	Unearned Rent	539	Misc. Administrative Expense
215	Notes Payable		600 Other Income
	300 Owner's Equity	610	Rent Revenue
310	Pat King, Capital	611	Interest Revenue
311	Pat King, Drawing		700 Other Expense
312	Income Summary	710	Interest Expense

Computer King is now using three-digit account numbers, which permits it to add new accounts as they are needed. The first digit indicates the major financial statement classification (1 for assets, 2 for liabilities, and so on). The second digit indicates the subclassification (e.g., 11 for current assets, 12 for noncurrent assets). The third digit identifies the specific account (e.g., 110 for Cash, 123 for Store Equipment).

Computer King is using a more complex numbering system because it has a greater variety of transactions. In addition, its growth creates a need for more detailed information for use in managing it. For example, a wages expense account was adequate for Computer King when it was a small service business with few employees. However, as a merchandising business, Computer King now uses two payroll accounts, one for Sales Salaries Expense and one for Office Salaries Expense.

Income Statement for a Merchandising Business

OBJECTIVE 4

Prepare an income statement for a merchandising business.

Although merchandising transactions affect the balance sheet in reporting inventory, they primarily affect the income statement. There are two widely used formats for preparing an income statement for a merchandising business: multiple step and single step.

The multiple-step form is used more often than the single-step form, as shown here.

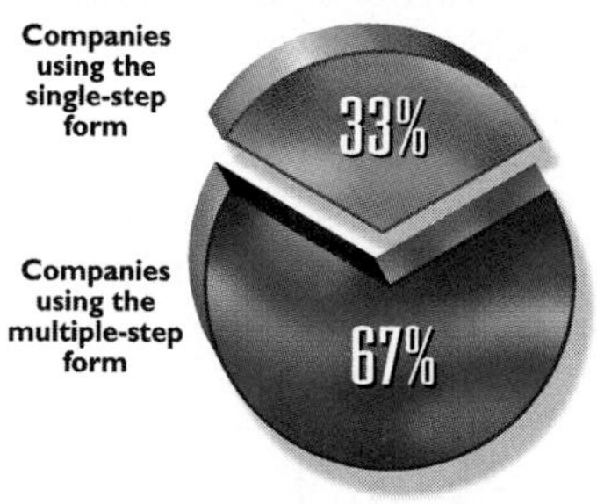

Source: 1996 edition of *Accounting Trends & Techniques.*

Multiple-Step Form

The **multiple-step income statement** contains several sections, subsections, and subtotals. We use Computer King's income statement, shown in Exhibit 7, as a basis for illustrating this form of statement.

EXHIBIT 7 Multiple-Step Income Statement

Computer King
Income Statement
For the Year Ended December 31, 2001

Revenue from sales:			
Sales		$720,185.00	
Less: Sales returns and allowances	$ 6,140.00		
Sales discounts	5,790.00	11,930.00	
Net sales			$708,255.00
Cost of merchandise sold			525,305.00
Gross profit			$182,950.00
Operating expenses:			
Selling expenses:			
Sales salaries expense	$60,030.00		
Advertising expense	10,860.00		
Depr. expense—store equipment	3,100.00		
Miscellaneous selling expense	630.00		
Total selling expense		$ 74,620.00	
Administrative expenses:			
Office salaries expense	$21,020.00		
Rent expense	8,100.00		
Depr. expense—office equipment	2,490.00		
Insurance expense	1,910.00		
Office supplies expense	610.00		
Misc. administrative expense	760.00		
Total administrative expenses		34,890.00	
Total operating expenses			109,510.00
Income from operations			$ 73,440.00
Other income:			
Interest revenue	$ 3,800.00		
Rent revenue	600.00		
Total other income		$ 4,400.00	
Other expense:			
Interest expense		2,440.00	1,960.00
Net income			$ 75,400.00

The amount of detail presented in the various sections varies from company to company. For example, instead of reporting gross sales, sales returns and allowances, and sales discounts, some companies just report net sales.

BUSINESS ON STAGE

Retailing

Retail operations can be classified as either (1) in-store retailing or (2) nonstore retailing. There are eleven general types of in-store retailing and three general types of nonstore retailing. Each type is briefly described below.

In-Store Retailing	Description	Examples
Department	Offers a variety of merchandise in many departments under one roof; each department is a separate buying and selling center	Sears, Rich's, J.C. Penney, Bloomingdale's
Specialty store	Offers a specific type of merchandise and carries a complete assortment	Toys R Us, Radio Shack, Zales Jewelers, Circuit City
Variety store	Offers a variety of inexpensive goods	Dollar General, Ben Franklin
Convenience store	Offers convenience goods, with long store hours	Circle K, 7 Eleven
Supermarket	Offers a wide variety of food, with self-service	Safeway, Kroger, Publix
Discount store	Offers low prices and high turnover of merchandise	Target, Kmart, Wal-Mart
Off-price retailer	Offers merchandise at prices 25% or more below normal prices with low service	T.J. Maxx, Ross
Factory outlet store	Offers close-outs and factory seconds; usually owned by the manufacturer	Levi Strauss, Bass, Polo, Lenox
Wholesale club	Offers food and general merchandise at deeply discounted prices to members	Sam's, Costco
Catalog store	Offers merchandise in showrooms where customers order from catalogs	Service Merchandise, Best, Lurias
Hypermart	Offers food and general merchandise at very low prices; sometimes called a "mall without a wall"	Hypermart USA, American Fare

Nonstore Retailing		
Vending machine	Offers merchandise for sale from machines	Canteen
Direct selling	Salesperson sells merchandise in customer's home	Avon, Amway
Direct response marketing	Offers merchandise for sale through catalogs, direct mail, and advertising	Lands' End, J. Crew, L.L. Bean ■

Revenue from Sales

The total amount charged customers for merchandise sold, for cash and on account, is reported in this section. Sales returns and allowances and sales discounts are deducted from this total to yield *net sales.*

Cost of Merchandise Sold

The cost of merchandise sold during the period may also be called the **cost of goods sold** or the **cost of sales**.

Gross Profit

The excess of net sales over the cost of merchandise sold is called the **gross profit**. It is sometimes called **gross profit on sales** or **gross margin**.

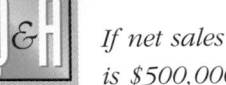

Q&A *If net sales is $500,000 and gross profit is $180,000, what is the cost of merchandise sold?*

$320,000

Operating Expenses

Most merchandising businesses classify operating expenses as either selling expenses or administrative expenses. Expenses that are incurred directly in the selling of merchandise are **selling expenses**. They include such expenses as salespersons' salaries, store supplies used, depreciation of store equipment, and advertising. Expenses incurred in the administration or general operations of the business are **administrative expenses** or **general expenses**. Examples of these expenses are office salaries, depreciation of office equipment, and office supplies used. Credit card expense is also normally classified as an administrative expense.

Expenses that are related to both selling and administration may be divided between the two classifications. In small businesses, however, such expenses as rent, insurance, and taxes are commonly reported as administrative expenses. Transactions for small, infrequent expenses are often reported as Miscellaneous Selling Expense or Miscellaneous Administrative Expense.

Income from Operations

The excess of gross profit over total operating expenses is called **income from operations** or **operating income**. The relationships of income from operations to total assets and to net sales are important factors in judging the efficiency and profitability of operations. If operating expenses are greater than the gross profit, the excess is called a **loss from operations**.

Other Income and Other Expense

Revenue from sources other than the primary operating activity of a business is classified as **other income**. In a merchandising business, these items include income from interest, rent, and gains resulting from the sale of fixed assets.

Expenses that cannot be traced directly to operations are identified as **other expense**. Interest expense that results from financing activities and losses incurred in the disposal of fixed assets are examples of these items.

Other income and other expense are offset against each other on the income statement. If the total of other income exceeds the total of other expense, the difference is added to income from operations. If the reverse is true, the difference is subtracted from income from operations.

Net Income

The final figure on the income statement is called **net income** (or **net loss**). It is the net increase (or net decrease) in the owner's equity as a result of the period's profit-making activities.

Single-Step Form

In the **single-step income statement**, the total of all expenses is deducted *in one step* from the total of all revenues. Such a statement is shown in Exhibit 8 for Computer King. The statement has been condensed to focus on its primary features.

EXHIBIT 8
Single-Step Income Statement

Computer King
Income Statement
For the Year Ended December 31, 2001

Revenues:		
Net sales		$708 255 00
Interest revenue		3 800 00
Rent revenue		600 00
Total revenues		$712 655 00
Expenses:		
Cost of merchandise sold	$525 305 00	
Selling expenses	74 620 00	
Administrative expenses	34 890 00	
Interest expense	2 440 00	
Total expenses		637 255 00
Net income		$ 75 400 00

The single-step form emphasizes total revenues and total expenses as the factors that determine net income. A criticism of the single-step form is that such amounts as gross profit and income from operations are not readily available for analysis.

OBJECTIVE 5

Describe the accounting cycle for a merchandising business.

The Accounting Cycle for a Merchandising Business

Earlier in this chapter, we described and illustrated the chart of accounts and the analysis and recording of transactions for a merchandising business. We also illustrated the preparation of an income statement for a merchandiser, Computer King, at the end of an accounting cycle. In the remainder of this chapter, we describe the other elements of the accounting cycle for a merchandising business. In this discussion, we will focus primarily on the elements of this cycle that are likely to differ from those of a service business.

Merchandise Inventory Shrinkage

Under the perpetual inventory system, a separate merchandise inventory account is maintained in the ledger. During the accounting period, this account shows the amount of merchandise for sale at any time. However, merchandising businesses may experience some loss of inventory due to shoplifting, employee theft, or errors in recording or counting inventory. As a result, the physical inventory taken at the end of the accounting period may differ from the amount of inventory shown in the inventory records. Normally, the amount of merchandise for sale, as indicated by the balance of the merchandise inventory account, is larger than the total amount of merchandise counted during the physical inventory. For this reason, the difference is often called **inventory shrinkage** or **inventory shortage**.

To illustrate, Computer King's inventory records indicate that $63,950 of merchandise should be available for sale on December 31, 2001. The physical inventory taken on December 31, 2001, however, indicates that only $62,150 of merchandise is actually available. Thus, the inventory shrinkage for the year ending December 31, 2001, is $1,800 ($63,950 − $62,150), as shown at the left. This amount is recorded by the following adjusting entry:

Q&A *If the inventory account has a balance of $280,000 and the physical inventory indicates merchandise on hand of $265,000, what is the amount of inventory shrinkage?*

$15,000 ($280,000 − $265,000)

		Adjusting Entry		
Dec.	31	Cost of Merchandise Sold	1 800 00	
		Merchandise Inventory		1 800 00

After this entry has been recorded, the accounting records agree with the actual physical inventory at the end of the period. Since no system of procedures and safeguards can totally eliminate it, inventory shrinkage is often considered a normal cost of operations. If the amount of the shrinkage is abnormally large, it may be disclosed separately on the income statement. In such cases, the shrinkage may be recorded in a separate account, such as Loss From Merchandise Inventory Shrinkage.

Work Sheet

Merchandising businesses that use a perpetual inventory system are also likely to use a computerized accounting system. In a computerized system, the adjusting entries are recorded and financial statements prepared without using a work sheet. For this reason, we illustrate the work sheet and the adjusting entries for Computer King in the appendix at the end of this chapter.

Statement of Owner's Equity

The statement of owner's equity for Computer King is shown in Exhibit 9. This statement is prepared in the same manner that we described previously for a service business.

EXHIBIT 9
Statement of Owner's Equity for Merchandising Business

Computer King
Statement of Owner's Equity
For the Year Ended December 31, 2001

Pat King, capital, January 1, 2001		$153 800 00
Net income for year	$75 400 00	
Less withdrawals	18 000 00	
Increase in owner's equity		57 400 00
Pat King, capital, December 31, 2001		$211 200 00

Balance Sheet

As we discussed and illustrated in previous chapters, the balance sheet may be presented with assets on the left-hand side and the liabilities and owner's equity on the right-hand side. This form of the balance sheet is called the **account form**. The balance sheet may also be presented in a downward sequence in three sections. This form of balance sheet is called the **report form**. The report form of balance sheet for Computer King is shown in Exhibit 10. In this balance sheet, note that

EXHIBIT 10
Report Form of Balance Sheet

Computer King
Balance Sheet
December 31, 2001

Assets			
Current assets:			
Cash		$52 950 00	
Notes receivable		40 000 00	
Accounts receivable		60 880 00	
Interest receivable		200 00	
Merchandise inventory		62 150 00	
Office supplies		480 00	
Prepaid insurance		2 650 00	
Total current assets			$219 310 00
Property, plant, and equipment:			
Land		$10 000 00	
Store equipment	$27 100 00		
Less accumulated depreciation	5 700 00	21 400 00	
Office equipment	$15 570 00		
Less accumulated depreciation	4 720 00	10 850 00	
Total property, plant, and equipment			42 250 00
Total assets			$261 560 00
Liabilities			
Current liabilities:			
Accounts payable		$22 420 00	
Note payable (current portion)		5 000 00	
Salaries payable		1 140 00	
Unearned rent		1 800 00	
Total current liabilities			$ 30 360 00
Long-term liabilities:			
Note payable (final payment due 2004)			20 000 00
Total liabilities			$ 50 360 00
Owner's Equity			
Pat King, capital			211 200 00
Total liabilities and owner's equity			$261 560 00

merchandise inventory at the end of the period is reported as a current asset and that the current portion of the note payable is $5,000.

Closing Entries

The closing entries for a merchandising business are similar to those for a service business. The first entry closes the temporary accounts with credit balances, such as Sales, to the income summary account. The second entry closes the temporary accounts with debit balances, including Sales Returns and Allowances, Sales Discounts, and Cost of Merchandise Sold, to the income summary account. The third entry closes the balance of the income summary account to the owner's capital account. The fourth entry closes the owner's drawing account to the owner's capital account.

In a computerized accounting system, the closing entries are prepared automatically. For this reason, we illustrate the closing entries for Computer King in the appendix at the end of this chapter.

FINANCIAL ANALYSIS AND INTERPRETATION

OBJECTIVE 6

Compute the ratio of net sales to assets as a measure of how effectively a business is using its assets.

The ratio of net sales to assets measures how effectively a business is using its assets to generate sales. A high ratio indicates an effective use of assets. The assets used in computing the ratio may be the total assets at the end of the year, the average of the total assets at the beginning and end of the year, or the average of the monthly assets. For our purposes, we will use the average of the total assets at the beginning and end of the year. The ratio is computed as follows:

$$\textbf{Ratio of net sales to assets} = \frac{\textbf{Net sales}}{\textbf{Average total assets}}$$

To illustrate the use of this ratio, the following data are taken from the 1996 annual reports of **Sears** and **J.C. Penney**:

	Sears	**J.C. Penney**
Net sales (in millions)	$38,236	$23,649
Total assets (in millions):		
Beginning of year	33,130	17,102
End of year	36,137	22,088

The ratio of net sales to assets for each company is as follows:

	Sears	**J.C. Penney**
Ratio of net sales to assets:	1.10*	1.21**

*$38,236/[($33,130 + $36,137)/2]
**$23,649/[($17,102 + $22,088)/2]

Based on these ratios, J.C. Penney appears better than Sears in utilizing its assets to generate sales. Comparing this ratio over time for both Sears and J.C. Penney, as well as comparing it with industry averages, would provide a better basis for interpreting the financial performance of each company.

ENCORE

As a young man just out of the Army, Sam Walton wanted to go into retailing and operate his own business. With $5,000 of his own money and a loan of $20,000 from his father-in-law, he opened his first store in Newport, Arkansas, on September 1, 1945. This first store was a Ben Franklin variety store. Within five years, this store was the No. 1 Ben Franklin store—for sales and profit—not only in Arkansas, but in a six-state region. Unfortunately, Sam forgot to include a renewal clause in the lease for his store building. His landlord decided not to renew Sam's lease, but instead offered to buy the business, including fixtures and inventory. The landlord wanted to purchase the profitable store for his son to own and operate. Without any other suitable location in town, Sam had to sell.

Unwilling to quit, Sam purchased a new store in Bentonville, Arkansas, and opened Walton's Five and Dime on August 1, 1951. By 1960, Sam had opened fifteen variety stores, with revenues of $1.4 million. Sam realized the potential of discounting when a regional discounter moved into Arkansas. So Sam opened his first Wal-Mart on July 2, 1962, choosing the name Wal-Mart because it didn't have many letters, which would make it cheaper to build and maintain the store signs. To avoid competing with Kmart, Sam initially expanded into small towns of less than 10,000 people.

Sam Walton

The rest of the story is history. Wal-Mart grew from 32 stores and $31 million in sales in 1970 to 276 stores and $1.2 billion in sales in 1980. Today it has over 2,000 stores and $70 billion in sales. During that time, Wal-Mart issued stock, opened Sam's Clubs, and Sam Walton became one of the richest men in America. ■

APPENDIX 1: ACCOUNTING SYSTEMS FOR MERCHANDISERS

Merchandising companies may use either manual or computerized accounting systems, similar to those used by service businesses. In this appendix, we describe and illustrate special journals and electronic forms that merchandise businesses may use in these systems.

Manual Accounting System

In a manual accounting system, a merchandise business normally uses four special journals: sales journal (for sales on account), purchases journal (for purchases on account), cash receipts journal, and cash payments journal. These journals can be adapted from the special journals that we illustrated earlier for a service business.

Exhibit 11 illustrates Computer King's sales journal, which is modified from a revenue journal. In a sales journal, each transaction is recorded by entering the sales amount in the *Accounts Receivable Dr./Sales Cr.* column and entering the cost of the merchandise sold amount in the *Cost of Merchandise Sold Dr./Merchandise Inventory Cr.* column. The totals of the two columns would be

COMPUTER KING

posted to the four general ledger accounts. The inventory and accounts receivable subsidiary ledgers would be updated when each transaction is recorded.

EXHIBIT 11
Sales Journal for a Merchandising Business

SALES JOURNAL **PAGE 35**

	Date		Invoice No.	Account Debited	Post. Ref.	Accts. Rec. Dr. Sales Cr.	Cost of Merchandise Sold Dr. Merchandise Inventory Cr.	
1	2001 Mar.	2	810	Berry Co.	✔	2750 00	2000 00	1
2		14	811	Handler Co.	✔	4260 00	3470 00	2
3		19	812	Jordan Co.	✔	5800 00	4650 00	3
4		26	813	Kenner Co.	✔	4500 00	3840 00	4
5						17310 00	13960 00	5
6						(112) (410)	(510) (115)	6

Exhibit 12 illustrates a purchases journal for Computer King's merchandising business. This journal is similar to the purchases journal for Computer King's service business that we illustrated previously. It includes an *Accounts Payable Cr.* column and a *Merchandise Inventory Dr.* column, rather than a *Supplies Dr.* column. At the end of the month, these two column totals would be posted to the general ledger controlling accounts, Accounts Payable and Merchandise Inventory. The amounts in *Other Amounts Dr.* would be posted individually. The inventory and accounts payable subsidiary ledgers would be updated when each transaction is recorded.

EXHIBIT 12 Purchases Journal for a Merchandising Business

PURCHASES JOURNAL **PAGE *11***

	Date		Account Credited	Post. Ref.	Accounts Payable Cr.	Merchandise Inventory Dr.	Other Accounts Dr.	Post. Ref.	Amount	
1	2001 Mar.	4	Compu-Tek	✔	13880 00	13880 00				1
2		7	Wallace Electronics Supply	✔	4650 00	4650 00				2
3		15	Dale Furniture Co.	✔	5700 00		Store Equipment	123	5700 00	3
4		22	Boss Computers	✔	3840 00	3840 00				4
5		29	Power Electronics	✔	3200 00	3200 00				5
6					31270 00	25570 00			5700 00	6
7					(210)	(115)			(✔)	7

Exhibit 13 illustrates a portion of Computer King's cash receipts journal. In this journal, cash sales are recorded in a *Sales Cr.* column rather than a *Fees Earned Cr.* column. In addition, the cost of merchandise sold for cash is recorded in a *Cost of Merchandise Sold Dr./Merchandise Inventory Cr.* column. Each entry in this column is posted to the inventory subsidiary ledger at the time the transaction is recorded. Sales discounts are recorded in a *Sales Discounts Dr.* column. At the end of the month, all the column totals except for *Other Accounts Cr.* are posted to the general ledger.

EXHIBIT 13 Cash Receipts Journal for Merchandising Business

CASH RECEIPTS JOURNAL **PAGE 14**

	Date		Account Credited	Post. Ref.	Other Accounts Cr.	Cost of Merchandise Sold Dr. Merchandise Inventory Cr.	Sales Cr.	Accounts Receivable Cr.	Sales Discounts Dr.	Cash Dr.	
1	2001 Mar.	3	Sales	✔		400 00	600 00			600 00	1
2		12	Berry Co.	✔				2 750 00	55 00	2 695 00	2

Exhibit 14 illustrates a portion of the cash payments journal for Computer King. This journal is modified for a merchandising business by adding a *Merchandise Inventory Cr.* column for recording discounts on purchases paid within the discount period. Each entry in this column is posted to the inventory subsidiary ledger at the time the transaction is recorded. At the end of the month, all the column totals except for *Other Accounts Dr.* are posted to the general ledger.

EXHIBIT 14 Cash Payments Journal for Merchandising Business

CASH PAYMENTS JOURNAL **PAGE 7**

	Date		Ck. No.	Account Debited	Post. Ref.	Other Accounts Dr.	Accounts Payable Dr.	Merchandise Inventory Cr.	Cash Cr.	
1	2001 Mar.	14	210	Compu-Tek	✔		13 880 00		13 880 00	1
2		17	211	Wallace Electronics Supply	✔		4 650 00	93 00	4 557 00	2

Computerized Accounting Systems

In a computerized accounting system, special journals may be replaced by electronic forms that capture the necessary information. The software then uses this information as the basis for making entries automatically. In QuickBooks, for example, the inventory items to be purchased and sold must first be identified, using an "Edit Item" form. The software will later record each item's purchase or sale, using information from this form. The Edit Item form in Exhibit 15 shows this information

EXHIBIT 15
Edit Item Form

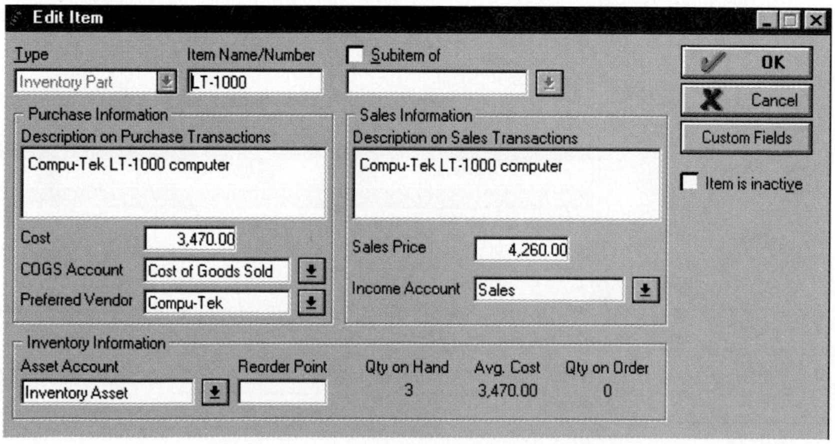

for Computer King's purchase of LT-1000 computers from Compu-Tek. Each computer cost $3,470 per unit and will be sold for $4,260 per unit.

After inventory items have been described inside QuickBooks, transaction data can be entered. We will begin with Computer King's March 4, 2001 purchase from Compu-Tek, which we illustrated previously in the purchases journal in Exhibit 12. We will use the "Enter Bills" form, shown in Exhibit 16, to record the purchase of four LT-1000's from Compu-Tek.

EXHIBIT 16
Enter Bills Form

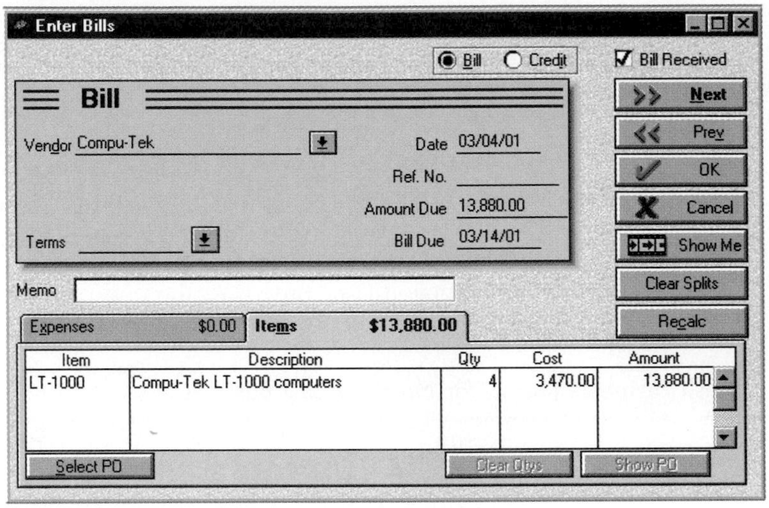
Enter Bills

Bill / Credit — Bill Received

Bill

Vendor: Compu-Tek
Date: 03/04/01
Ref. No.:
Amount Due: 13,880.00
Terms:
Bill Due: 03/14/01
Memo:

Expenses $0.00 | Items $13,880.00

Item	Description	Qty	Cost	Amount
LT-1000	Compu-Tek LT-1000 computers	4	3,470.00	13,880.00

Select PO | Clear Qtys | Show PO

Next | Prev | OK | Cancel | Show Me | Clear Splits | Recalc

After the Enter Bills form has been completed, the software adds the cost of four LT-1000s to Computer King's inventory. At the same time, it establishes an account payable to Compu-Tek for $13,880.

Now, assume that on March 14 Computer King bills Handler Co. for one of these computers, as illustrated in the sales journal in Exhibit 11. Using the "Create Invoices" form in QuickBooks, as shown in Exhibit 17, we enter the sale and the software establishes an account receivable for Handler Co. In addition, the software reduces the inventory stock level of the LT-1000 by $3,470 and records the cost of goods sold. This latter transaction is recorded automatically and is not shown on the Create Invoices form.

EXHIBIT 17
Create Invoices Form

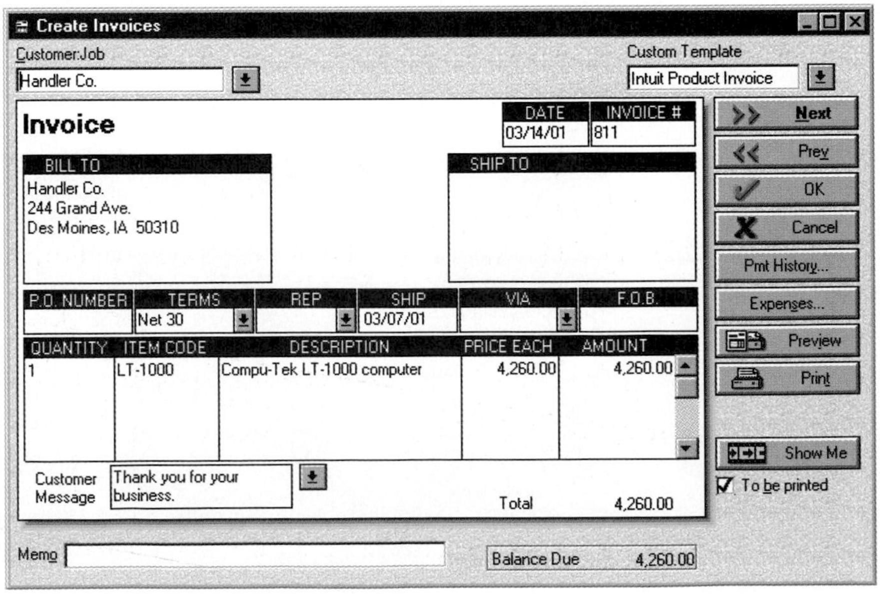
Create Invoices

Customer:Job: Handler Co.
Custom Template: Intuit Product Invoice

Invoice

DATE: 03/14/01 | INVOICE #: 811

BILL TO:
Handler Co.
244 Grand Ave.
Des Moines, IA 50310

SHIP TO:

P.O. NUMBER	TERMS	REP	SHIP	VIA	F.O.B.
	Net 30		03/07/01		

QUANTITY	ITEM CODE	DESCRIPTION	PRICE EACH	AMOUNT
1	LT-1000	Compu-Tek LT-1000 computer	4,260.00	4,260.00

Customer Message: Thank you for your business.
Total 4,260.00

Memo:
Balance Due 4,260.00

Next | Prev | OK | Cancel | Pmt History... | Expenses... | Preview | Print | Show Me | To be printed

An income statement prepared after these forms have been completed would show sales of $4,260, cost of goods sold of $3,470, and gross profit of $790. A balance sheet would show accounts receivable of $4,260, inventory of $10,410 (3 × $3,470), and accounts payable of $13,880.

APPENDIX 2: WORK SHEET AND ADJUSTING AND CLOSING ENTRIES FOR A MERCHANDISING BUSINESS

A merchandising business that does not use a computerized accounting system may use a work sheet in assembling the data for preparing financial statements and adjusting and closing entries. In this appendix, we illustrate such a work sheet, along with the adjusting and closing entries for a merchandising business.

The work sheet in Exhibit 18 is for Computer King on December 31, 2001, the end of its first year of operations as a merchandiser. In this work sheet, we list all of the accounts, including the accounts that have no balances, in the order that they appear in Computer King's ledger.

The data needed for adjusting the accounts of Computer King are as follows:

Interest accrued on notes receivable on December 31, 2001		$ 200
Physical merchandise inventory on December 31, 2001		62,150
Office supplies on hand on December 31, 2001		480
Insurance expired during 2001		1,910
Depreciation during 2001 on: Store equipment		3,100
Office equipment		2,490
Salaries accrued on December 31, 2001: Sales salaries	$780	
Office salaries	360	1,140
Rent earned during 2001		600

There is no specific order in which to analyze the accounts in the work sheet, assemble the adjustment data, and make the adjusting entries. However, you can normally save time by selecting the accounts in the order in which they appear on the trial balance. Using this approach, the adjustment for accrued interest is listed first {entry (a) on the work sheet}, followed by the adjustment for merchandise inventory shrinkage {entry (b) on the work sheet}, and so on.

After all the adjustments have been entered on the work sheet, the Adjustments columns are totaled to prove the equality of debits and credits. As we illustrated in previous chapters, the adjusted amounts of the balances in the Trial Balance columns are extended to the Adjusted Trial Balance columns.[5] The Adjusted Trial Balance columns are then totaled to prove the equality of debits and credits.

The balances, as adjusted, are then extended to the statement columns. The four statement columns are totaled, and the net income or net loss is determined. For Computer King, the difference between the credit and debit columns of the Income Statement section is $75,400, the amount of the net income. The difference between the debit and credit columns of the Balance Sheet section is also $75,400, which is the increase in owner's equity as a result of the net income. Agreement between the two balancing amounts is evidence of debit-credit equality and mathematical accuracy.

The income statement, statement of owner's equity, and balance sheet are prepared from the work sheet in a manner similar to that of a service business. The

[5] Some accountants prefer to eliminate the Adjusted Trial Balance columns and to extend the adjusted balances directly to the statement columns. Such a work sheet is often used if there are only a few adjustment items.

EXHIBIT 18 Work Sheet for Merchandising Business

Computer King
Work Sheet
For the Year Ended December 31, 2001

	Account Title	Trial Balance		Adjustments		Adjusted Trial Balance		Income Statement		Balance Sheet	
		Dr.	Cr.	Dr.	Cr.	Dr.	Cr.	Dr.	Cr.	Dr.	Cr.
1	Cash	52,950				52,950				52,950	
2	Notes Receivable	40,000				40,000				40,000	
3	Accounts Receivable	60,880				60,880				60,880	
4	Interest Receivable			(a) 200		200				200	
5	Merchandise Inventory	63,950			(b) 1,800	62,150				62,150	
6	Office Supplies	1,090			(c) 610	480				480	
7	Prepaid Insurance	4,560			(d) 1,910	2,650				2,650	
8	Land	10,000				10,000				10,000	
9	Store Equipment	27,100				27,100				27,100	
10	Accum. Depr.—Store Equip.		2,600		(e) 3,100		5,700				5,700
11	Office Equipment	15,570				15,570				15,570	
12	Accum. Depr.—Office Equip.		2,230		(f) 2,490		4,720				4,720
13	Accounts Payable		22,420				22,420				22,420
14	Salaries Payable				(g) 1,140		1,140				1,140
15	Unearned Rent		2,400	(h) 600			1,800				1,800
16	Notes Payable										
17	(final payment due 2008)		25,000				25,000				25,000
18	Pat King, Capital		153,800				153,800				153,800
19	Pat King, Drawing	18,000				18,000				18,000	
20	Sales		720,185				720,185		720,185		
21	Sales Returns and Allowances	6,140				6,140		6,140			
22	Sales Discounts	5,790				5,790		5,790			
23	Cost of Merchandise Sold	523,505		(b) 1,800		525,305		525,305			
24	Sales Salaries Expense	59,250		(g) 780		60,030		60,030			
25	Advertising Expense	10,860				10,860		10,860			
26	Depr. Exp.—Store Equip.			(e) 3,100		3,100		3,100			
27	Miscellaneous Selling Expense	630				630		630			
28	Office Salaries Expense	20,660		(g) 360		21,020		21,020			
29	Rent Expense	8,100				8,100		8,100			
30	Depr. Exp.—Office Equip.			(f) 2,490		2,490		2,490			
31	Insurance Expense			(d) 1,910		1,910		1,910			
32	Office Supplies Expense			(c) 610		610		610			
33	Misc. Administrative Expense	760				760		760			
34	Rent Revenue				(h) 600		600		600		
35	Interest Revenue		3,600		(a) 200		3,800		3,800		
36	Interest Expense	2,440				2,440		2,440			
37		932,235	932,235	11,850	11,850	939,165	939,165	649,185	724,585	289,980	214,580
38	Net income							75,400			75,400
39								724,585	724,585	289,980	289,980

(a) Interest earned but not received on notes receivable, $200.
(b) Merchandise inventory shrinkage for period, $1,800 ($63,950 − $62,150).
(c) Office supplies used, $610 ($1,090 − $480).
(d) Insurance expired, $1,910.
(e) Depreciation of store equipment, $3,100.
(f) Depreciation of office equipment, $2,490.
(g) Salaries accrued but not paid (sales salaries, $780; office salaries, $360), $1,140.
(h) Rent earned from amount received in advance, $600.

Adjustments columns in the work sheet provide the data for journalizing the adjusting entries. Computer King's adjusting entries at the end of 2001 are as follows:

JOURNAL **PAGE 28**

	Date		Description	Post. Ref.	Debit	Credit	
1	2001		Adjusting Entries				1
2	Dec.	31	Interest Receivable	113	200 00		2
3			Interest Revenue	611		200 00	3
4							4
5		31	Cost of Merchandise Sold	510	1 800 00		5
6			Merchandise Inventory	115		1 800 00	6
7							7
8		31	Office Supplies Expense	534	610 00		8
9			Office Supplies	116		610 00	9
10							10
11		31	Insurance Expense	533	1 910 00		11
12			Prepaid Insurance	117		1 910 00	12
13							13
14		31	Depreciation Expense—				14
15			Store Equipment	522	3 100 00		15
16			Accumulated Depreciation—				16
17			Store Equipment	124		3 100 00	17
18							18
19		31	Depreciation Expense—				19
20			Office Equipment	532	2 490 00		20
21			Accumulated Depreciation—				21
22			Office Equipment	126		2 490 00	22
23							23
24		31	Sales Salaries Expense	520	780 00		24
25			Office Salaries Expense	530	360 00		25
26			Salaries Payable	211		1 140 00	26
27							27
28		31	Unearned Rent	212	600 00		28
29			Rent Revenue	610		600 00	29

The Income Statement columns of the work sheet provide the data for preparing the closing entries. The closing entries for Computer King at the end of 2001 are as follows:

JOURNAL **PAGE 29**

	Date		Description	Post. Ref.	Debit	Credit	
1	2001		Closing Entries				1
2	Dec.	31	Sales	410	720 185 00		2
3			Rent Revenue	610	600 00		3
4			Interest Revenue	611	3 800 00		4
5			Income Summary	312		724 585 00	5

JOURNAL **PAGE 29**

Date		Description	Post. Ref.	Debit	Credit
Dec.	31	Income Summary	312	649 185 00	
		Sales Returns and Allowances	411		6 140 00
		Sales Discounts	412		5 790 00
		Cost of Merchandise Sold	510		525 305 00
		Sales Salaries Expense	520		60 030 00
		Advertising Expense	521		10 860 00
		Depr. Expense—Store Equipment	522		3 100 00
		Miscellaneous Selling Expense	529		630 00
		Office Salaries Expense	530		21 020 00
		Rent Expense	531		8 100 00
		Depr. Expense—Office Equipment	532		2 490 00
		Insurance Expense	533		1 910 00
		Office Supplies Expense	534		610 00
		Misc. Administrative Expense	539		760 00
		Interest Expense	710		2 440 00
	31	Income Summary	312	75 400 00	
		Pat King, Capital	310		75 400 00
	31	Pat King, Capital	310	18 000 00	
		Pat King, Drawing	311		18 000 00

The balance of Income Summary, after the first two closing entries have been posted, is the net income or net loss for the period. The third closing entry transfers this balance to the owner's capital account. Computer King's income summary account after the closing entries have been posted is as follows:

ACCOUNT ***Income Summary*** **ACCOUNT NO. 312**

Date		Item	Post. Ref.	Debit	Credit	Balance Debit	Balance Credit
2001 Dec.	31	Revenues	29		724 585 00		724 585 00
	31	Expenses	29	649 185 00			75 400 00
	31	Net income	29	75 400 00		—	—

After the closing entries have been prepared and posted to the accounts, a post-closing trial balance may be prepared to verify the debit-credit equality. The only accounts that should appear on the post-closing trial balance are the asset, contra asset, liability, and owner's capital accounts with balances. These are the same accounts that appear on the end-of-period balance sheet.

KEY POINTS

1 Distinguish the activities of a service business from those of a merchandising business.

The primary differences between a service business and a merchandising business relate to revenue activities. Merchandising businesses purchase merchandise for selling to customers.

On a merchandising business's income statement, revenue from selling merchandise is reported as sales. The cost of the merchandise sold is subtracted from sales to arrive at gross profit. The operating expenses are subtracted from gross profit to arrive at net income.

Merchandise inventory, which is merchandise not sold, is reported as a current asset on the balance sheet.

2a Journalize the entries for merchandise purchases.

Purchases of merchandise for cash or on account are recorded by debiting Merchandise Inventory. For purchases of merchandise on account, the credit terms may allow cash discounts for early payment. Such purchases discounts are viewed as a reduction in the cost of the merchandise purchased. When merchandise is returned or a price adjustment is granted, the buyer credits Merchandise Inventory.

2b Journalize the entries for merchandise sales.

Sales of merchandise for cash or on account are recorded by crediting Sales. The cost of merchandise sold and the reduction in merchandise inventory are also recorded for the sale.

For sales of merchandise on account, the credit terms may allow sales discounts for early payment. Such discounts are recorded by the seller as a debit to Sales Discounts. Sales discounts are reported as a deduction from the amount initially recorded in Sales. Likewise, when merchandise is returned or a price adjustment is granted, the seller debits Sales Returns and Allowances.

The liability for sales tax is incurred when the sale is made and is recorded by the seller as a credit to the sales tax payable account. When the amount of the sales tax is paid to the taxing unit, Sales Tax Payable is debited and Cash is credited.

Many wholesalers offer trade discounts, which are discounts off the list prices of merchandise. Normally, neither the seller or the buyer records the list price and the related trade discount in the accounts.

2c Journalize the entries for merchandise transportation costs.

When merchandise is shipped FOB shipping point, the buyer pays the transportation costs and debits Merchandise Inventory. When merchandise is shipped FOB destination, the seller pays the transportation costs and debits Transportation Out or Delivery Expense. If the seller prepays transportation costs as a convenience to the buyer, the seller debits Accounts Receivable for the costs.

2d Journalize the entries for merchandise transactions for both the buyer and the seller.

The illustration in this chapter summarizes the entries that the seller and the buyer of merchandise would record.

3 Prepare a chart of accounts for a merchandising business.

The chart of accounts for a merchandising business is more complex than that for a service business and normally includes accounts such as Sales, Sales Discounts, Sales Returns and Allowances, Cost of Merchandise Sold, and Merchandise Inventory.

4 Prepare an income statement for a merchandising business.

The income statement for a merchandising business reports sales, cost of merchandise sold, and gross profit. The income statement can be prepared in either the multiple-step form or the single-step form.

5 Describe the accounting cycle for a merchandising business.

The accounting cycle for a merchandising business is similar to that of a service business. However, a merchandiser is likely to experience inventory shrinkage, which must be recorded. The normal adjusting entry is to debit Cost of Merchandise Sold and credit Merchandise Inventory for the amount of the shrinkage.

The balance sheet may be prepared in either the account form or the report form. Merchandise inventory should be reported as a current asset.

6 Compute the ratio of net sales to assets as a measure of how effectively a business is using its assets.

The assets used in computing the ratio of net sales to assets may be total assets at the end of the year, the average of the total assets at the beginning and end of the year, or the average of the monthly assets. A high ratio of net sales to assets indicates an effective use of assets.

ILLUSTRATIVE PROBLEM

The following transactions were completed by Montrose Company during May of the current year. Montrose Company uses a perpetual inventory system.

May 3. Purchased merchandise on account from Floyd Co., $4,000, terms FOB shipping point, 2/10, n/30, with prepaid transportation costs of $120 added to the invoice.
5. Purchased merchandise on account from Kramer Co., $8,500, terms FOB destination, 1/10, n/30.
6. Sold merchandise on account to C. F. Howell Co., list price $4,000, trade discount 30%, terms 2/10, n/30. The cost of the merchandise sold was $1,125.
8. Purchased office supplies for cash, $150.
10. Returned merchandise purchased on May 5 from Kramer Co., $1,300.
13. Paid Floyd Co. on account for purchase of May 3, less discount.
14. Purchased merchandise for cash, $10,500.
15. Paid Kramer Co. on account for purchase of May 5, less return of May 10 and discount.
16. Received cash on account from sale of May 6 to C. F. Howell Co., less discount.
19. Sold merchandise on nonbank credit cards and reported accounts to the card company, American Express, $2,450. The cost of the merchandise sold was $980.
22. Sold merchandise on account to Comer Co., $3,480, terms 2/10, n/30. The cost of the merchandise sold was $1,400.
24. Sold merchandise for cash, $4,350. The cost of the merchandise sold was $1,750.
25. Received merchandise returned by Comer Co. from sale on May 22, $1,480. The cost of the returned merchandise was $600.
31. Received cash from card company for nonbank credit card sales of May 19, less $140 service fee.

Instructions

1. Journalize the preceding transactions.
2. Journalize the adjusting entry for merchandise inventory shrinkage, $3,750.

Solution

1.

May	3	Merchandise Inventory	4,120	
		Accounts Payable—Floyd Co.		4,120
	5	Merchandise Inventory	8,500	
		Accounts Payable—Kramer Co.		8,500
	6	Accounts Receivable—C. F. Howell Co.	2,800	
		Sales		2,800
		[$4,000 − (30% × $4,000)]		
	6	Cost of Merchandise Sold	1,125	
		Merchandise Inventory		1,125
	8	Office Supplies	150	
		Cash		150
	10	Accounts Payable—Kramer Co.	1,300	
		Merchandise Inventory		1,300
	13	Accounts Payable—Floyd Co.	4,120	
		Merchandise Inventory Discount		80
		Cash		4,040
		[$4,000 − (2% × $4,000) + $120]		

May 14	Merchandise Inventory	10,500	
	Cash		10,500
15	Accounts Payable—Kramer Co.	7,200	
	Merchandise Inventory		72
	Cash		7,128
	[($8,500 − $1,300) × 1% = $72; $8,500 − $1,300 − $72 = $7,128]		
16	Cash	2,744	
	Sales Discounts	56	
	Accounts Receivable—C. F. Howell Co.		2,800
19	Accounts Receivable—American Express	2,450	
	Sales		2,450
19	Cost of Merchandise Sold	980	
	Merchandise Inventory		980
22	Accounts Receivable—Comer Co.	3,480	
	Sales		3,480
22	Cost of Merchandise Sold	1,400	
	Merchandise Inventory		1,400
24	Cash	4,350	
	Sales		4,350
24	Cost of Merchandise Sold	1,750	
	Merchandise Inventory		1,750
25	Sales Returns and Allowances	1,480	
	Accounts Receivable—Comer Co.		1,480
25	Merchandise Inventory	600	
	Cost of Merchandise Sold		600
31	Cash	2,310	
	Credit Card Expense	140	
	Accounts Receivable—American Express		2,450

2.

May 31	Cost of Merchandise Sold	3,750	
	Merchandise Inventory		3,750

SELF-EXAMINATION QUESTIONS

Answers at End of Chapter

Matching

Match each of the following statements with its proper term. Some terms may not be used.

A. **account form**
B. **administrative expenses (general expenses)**
C. **cost of merchandise sold**
D. **credit memorandum**
E. **debit memorandum**

C 1. The cost that is reported as an expense when merchandise is sold.
H 2. Sales minus the cost of merchandise sold.
M 3. Merchandise on hand (not sold) at the end of an accounting period.
R 4. The inventory system in which each purchase and sale of merchandise is recorded in an inventory account.
Q 5. The inventory system in which the inventory records do not show the amount available for sale or sold during the period.
S 6. A detailed listing of the merchandise for sale at the end of an accounting period.

(continues)

F. **FOB (free on board) destination**
G. **FOB (free on board) shipping point**
H. **gross profit**
I. **income from operations (operating income)**
J. **inventory shrinkage**
K. **invoice**
L. **loss from operations**
M. **merchandise inventory**
N. **multiple-step income statement**
O. **other expense**
P. **other income**
Q. **periodic inventory system**
R. **perpetual inventory system**
S. **physical inventory**
T. **purchase return or allowance**
U. **purchases discounts**
V. **report form**
W. **sales discounts**
X. **sales return or allowance**
Y. **selling expenses**
Z. **single-step income statement**
AA. **trade discounts**

K 7. The bill that the seller sends to the buyer.

U 8. Discounts taken by the buyer for early payment of an invoice.

T 9. From the buyer's perspective, returned merchandise or an adjustment for defective merchandise.

E 10. A form used by a buyer to inform the seller of the amount the buyer proposes to debit to the account payable due the seller.

W 11. From the seller's perspective, discounts that a seller may offer the buyer for early payment.

X 12. From the seller's perspective, returned merchandise or an adjustment for defective merchandise.

D 13. A form used by a seller to inform the buyer of the amount the seller proposes to credit to the account receivable due from the buyer.

AA 14. Discounts from the list prices in published catalogs or special discounts offered to certain classes of buyers.

G 15. Freight terms in which the buyer pays the transportation costs from the shipping point to the final destination.

F 16. Freight terms in which the seller pays the transportation costs from the shipping point to the final destination.

N 17. A form of income statement that contains several sections, subsections, and subtotals.

Y 18. Expenses that are incurred directly in the selling of merchandise.

B 19. Expenses incurred in the administration or general operations of the business.

I 20. The excess of gross profit over total operating expenses.

L 21. The excess of operating expenses over gross profit.

P 22. Revenue from sources other than the primary operating activity of a business.

O 23. Expenses that cannot be traced directly to operations.

Z 24. A form of income statement in which the total of all expenses is deducted from the total of all revenues.

J 25. The amount by which the merchandise for sale, as indicated by the balance of the merchandise inventory account, is larger than the total amount of merchandise counted during the physical inventory.

A 26. The form of balance sheet in which assets are reported on the left-hand side and the liabilities and owner's equity on the right-hand side.

V 27. The form of balance sheet in which assets, liabilities, and owner's equity are reported in a downward sequence.

Multiple Choice

1. If merchandise purchased on account is returned, the buyer may inform the seller of the details by issuing:
   A. a debit memorandum
   B. a credit memorandum
   C. an invoice
   D. a bill

2. If merchandise is sold on account to a customer for $1,000, terms FOB shipping point, 1/10, n/30, and the seller prepays $50 in transportation costs, the amount of the discount for early payment would be:
   A. $0 C. $10.00
   B. $5.00 D. $10.50

3. The income statement in which the total of all expenses is deducted from the total of all revenues is termed:
   A. multiple-step form C. account form
   B. single-step form D. report form

4. On a multiple-step income statement, the excess of net sales over the cost of merchandise sold is called:
   A. operating income
   B. income from operations
   C. gross profit
   D. net income

5. Which of the following expenses would normally be classified as Other expense on a multiple-step income statement?
   A. Depreciation expense—office equipment
   B. Sales salaries expense
   C. Insurance expense
   D. Interest expense

CLASS DISCUSSION QUESTIONS

1. What distinguishes a merchandising business from a service business?
2. Can a business earn a gross profit but incur a net loss? Explain.
3. What is the name of the account in which purchases of merchandise are recorded in a perpetual inventory system?
4. What is the name of the account in which sales of merchandise are recorded?
5. How does the accounting for sales to customers using bank credit cards, such as MasterCard and VISA, differ from accounting for sales to customers using nonbank credit cards, such as American Express?
6. The credit period during which the buyer of merchandise is allowed to pay usually begins with what date?
7. What is the meaning of (a) 1/10, n/60; (b) n/30; (c) n/eom?
8. REAL WORLD It is not unusual for a customer to drive into some **Texaco**, **Mobil**, or **BP** gasoline stations and discover that the cash price per gallon is 3 or 4 cents less than the credit price per gallon. As a result, many customers pay cash rather than use their credit cards. Why would a gasoline station owner establish such a policy?
9. What is the nature of (a) a credit memorandum issued by the seller of merchandise, (b) a debit memorandum issued by the buyer of merchandise?
10. Who bears the transportation costs when the terms of sale are (a) FOB shipping point, (b) FOB destination?
11. Name at least three accounts that would normally appear in the chart of accounts of a merchandising business but would not appear in the chart of accounts of a service business.
12. Differentiate between the multiple-step and the single-step forms of the income statement.
13. What are the major advantages and disadvantages of the single-step form of income statement compared to the multiple-step statement?
14. What type of revenue is reported in the Other income section of the multiple-step income statement?
15. The Furniture Co., which uses a perpetual inventory system, experienced a normal inventory shrinkage of $32,000. What accounts would be debited and credited to record the adjustment for the inventory shrinkage at the end of the accounting period?
16. Assume that The Furniture Co. in Question 15 experienced an abnormal inventory shrinkage of $178,000. The Furniture Co. has decided to record the abnormal inventory shrinkage so that it would be separately disclosed on the income statement. What account would be debited for the abnormal inventory shrinkage?

Warren Reeve Fess

Resources for Your Success On-Line at warren.swcollege.com

Remember! If you need additional help, visit South-Western's Web site. See page 26 for a description of the online and printed materials that are available.

EXERCISES

Exercise 6–1
Determining gross profit

Objective 1

✓ a. $280,000

During the current year, merchandise is sold for $180,000 cash and for $520,000 on account. The cost of the merchandise sold is $420,000.

a. What is the amount of the gross profit?
b. Will the income statement necessarily report a net income? Explain.

Exercise 6–2
Determining cost of merchandise sold

Objective 1

✓ $330,000

Sales were $415,000, and the gross profit was $85,000. What was the amount of the cost of merchandise sold?

Exercise 6–3
Purchase-related transaction

Objective 2

✓ a. $2,940

Gupta Company purchased merchandise on account from a supplier for $4,000, terms 2/10, n/30. Gupta Company returned $1,000 of the merchandise and received full credit.

a. If Gupta Company pays the invoice within the discount period, what is the amount of cash required for the payment?
b. Under a perpetual inventory system, what account is credited by Gupta Company to record the return?

Exercise 6–4
Determining amounts to be paid on invoices

Objective 2

✓ a. $3,762

Determine the amount to be paid in full settlement of each of the following invoices, assuming that credit for returns and allowances was received prior to payment and that all invoices were paid within the discount period.

	Merchandise	Transportation Paid by Seller		Returns and Allowances
a.	$5,000	—	FOB shipping point, 1/10, n/30	$1,200
b.	1,000	$50	FOB shipping point, 2/10, n/30	600
c.	9,500	—	FOB destination, n/30	400
d.	3,000	75	FOB shipping point, 1/10, n/30	500
e.	5,000	—	FOB destination, 2/10, n/30	—

Exercise 6–5
Purchase-related transactions

Objective 2

✓ B: $7,227

A retailer is considering the purchase of ten units of a specific item from either of two suppliers. Their offers are as follows:

A: $700 a unit, total of $7,000, 2/10, n/30, plus transportation costs of $375.
B: $730 a unit, total of $7,300, 1/10, n/30, no charge for transportation.

Which of the two offers, A or B, yields the lower price?

Exercise 6–6
Purchase-related transactions

Objective 2

The debits and credits from four related transactions are presented in the following T accounts. Describe each transaction.

Cash

		(2)	150
		(4)	5,445

Accounts Payable

(3)	500	(1)	6,000
(4)	5,500		

Merchandise Inventory

(1)	6,000	(3)	500
(2)	150	(4)	55

Exercise 6–7
Purchase-related transactions

Objective 2

✓ (c) Cash, cr. $11,270

Elissa Co., a women's clothing store, purchased $14,000 of merchandise from a supplier on account, terms FOB destination, 2/10, n/30. Elissa Co. returned $2,500 of the merchandise, receiving a credit memorandum, and then paid the amount due within the discount period. Journalize Elissa Co.'s entries to record (a) the purchase, (b) the merchandise return, and (c) the payment.

Exercise 6–8
Purchase-related transactions

Objective 2

✓ (e) Cash, dr. $920

Journalize entries for the following related transactions of Restoration Company:

a. Purchased $10,000 of merchandise from Veneer Co. on account, terms 2/10, n/30.
b. Paid the amount owed on the invoice within the discount period.
c. Discovered that $4,000 of the merchandise was defective and returned items, receiving credit.
d. Purchased $3,000 of merchandise from Veneer Co. on account, terms n/30.
e. Received a check for the balance owed from the return in (c), after deducting for the purchase in (d).

Exercise 6–9
Sales-related transactions, including the use of credit cards

Objective 2

Journalize the entries for the following transactions:

a. Sold merchandise for cash, $12,800. The cost of the merchandise sold was $7,500.
b. Sold merchandise on account, $9,500. The cost of the merchandise sold was $6,000.
c. Sold merchandise to customers who used MasterCard and VISA, $6,750. The cost of the merchandise sold was $3,850.
d. Sold merchandise to customers who used American Express, $5,100. The cost of the merchandise sold was $2,860.
e. Paid an invoice from First National Bank for $350, representing a service fee for processing MasterCard and VISA sales.
f. Received $4,845 from American Express Company after a $255 collection fee had been deducted.

Exercise 6–10
Sales returns and allowances

Objective 2

What's Wrong WITH THIS?

During the year, sales returns and allowances totaled $212,150. The cost of the merchandise returned was $167,300. The accountant recorded all the returns and allowances by debiting the sales account and crediting Cost of Merchandise Sold for $212,150.

Was the accountant's method of recording returns acceptable? Explain. In your explanation, include the advantages of using a sales returns and allowances account.

Exercise 6–11
Sales-related transactions

Objective 2

✓ a. $7,350

After the amount due on a sale of $7,500, terms 2/10, n/eom, is received from a customer within the discount period, the seller consents to the return of the entire shipment. The cost of the merchandise returned was $4,380. (a) What is the amount of the refund owed to the customer? (b) Journalize the entries made by the seller to record the return and the refund.

Exercise 6–12
Sales-related transactions

Objective 2

The debits and credits for three related transactions are presented in the following T accounts. Describe each transaction.

Cash

(5)	7,920		

Sales

		(1)	9,000

Accounts Receivable

(1)	9,000	(3)	1,000
		(5)	8,000

Sales Discounts

(5)	80		

Merchandise Inventory

(4)	550	(2)	6,000

Sales Returns and Allowances

(3)	1,000		

Cost of Merchandise Sold

(2)	6,000	(4)	550

Exercise 6–13
Sales-related transactions
Objective 2

✓ d. $10,225

Merchandise is sold on account to a customer for $10,000, terms FOB shipping point, 3/10, n/30. The seller paid the transportation costs of $525. Determine the following: (a) amount of the sale, (b) amount debited to Accounts Receivable, (c) amount of the discount for early payment, and (d) amount due within the discount period.

Exercise 6–14
Sales tax
Objective 2

✓ c. $1,365

A sale of merchandise on account for $1,300 is subject to a 5% sales tax. (a) Should the sales tax be recorded at the time of sale or when payment is received? (b) What is the amount of the sale? (c) What is the amount debited to Accounts Receivable? (d) What is the title of the account to which the $65 is credited?

Exercise 6–15
Sales tax transactions
Objective 2

Journalize the entries to record the following selected transactions:

a. Sold $12,000 of merchandise on account, subject to a sales tax of 4%. The cost of the merchandise sold was $7,000.
b. Paid $2,380 to the state sales tax department for taxes collected.

Exercise 6–16
Sales-related transactions
Objective 2

Sauls Co., a furniture wholesaler, sells merchandise to Bayer Co. on account, $7,000, terms 2/15, n/30. The cost of the merchandise sold is $3,900. Sauls Co. issues a credit memorandum for $800 for merchandise returned and subsequently receives the amount due within the discount period. The cost of the merchandise returned is $410. Journalize Sauls Co.'s entries for (a) the sale, including the cost of the merchandise sold, (b) the credit memorandum, including the cost of the returned merchandise, and (c) the receipt of the check for the amount due from Bayer Co.

Exercise 6–17
Purchase-related transactions
Objective 2

Based on the data presented in Exercise 6–16, journalize Bayer Co.'s entries for (a) the purchase, (b) the return of the merchandise for credit, and (c) the payment of the invoice within the discount period.

Exercise 6–18
Normal balances of merchandise accounts
Objective 2

What is the normal balance of the following accounts: (a) Sales Returns and Allowances, (b) Merchandise Inventory, (c) Sales Discounts, (d) Transportation Out, (e) Sales, (f) Cost of Merchandise Sold?

Exercise 6–19
Chart of accounts
Objective 3

Hurley Co. is a newly organized business with the following list of accounts, arranged in alphabetical order:

Accounts Payable
Accounts Receivable
Accumulated Depreciation—Office Equipment
Accumulated Depreciation—Store Equipment
Advertising Expense
Cash
Cost of Merchandise Sold
Depreciation Expense—Office Equipment
Depreciation Expense—Store Equipment
Income Summary
Insurance Expense
Interest Expense
Interest Receivable
Interest Revenue
J. Hurley, Capital
J. Hurley, Drawing
Land
Merchandise Inventory
Miscellaneous Administrative Expense
Miscellaneous Selling Expense
Notes Payable (short-term)
Notes Receivable (short-term)
Office Equipment
Office Salaries Expense
Office Supplies
Office Supplies Expense
Prepaid Insurance
Rent Expense
Salaries Payable
Sales
Sales Discounts
Sales Returns and Allowances
Sales Salaries Expense
Store Equipment
Store Supplies
Store Supplies Expense
Transportation Out

Construct a chart of accounts, assigning account numbers and arranging the accounts in balance sheet and income statement order, as illustrated in Exhibit 6. Each account number is three digits: the first digit is to indicate the major classification ("1" for assets, and so on); the second digit is to indicate the subclassification ("11" for current assets, and so on); and the third digit is to identify the specific account ("110" for Cash, and so on).

Exercise 6–20
Income statement for merchandiser
Objective 4

✓ Gross profit: $1,130,000

For the fiscal year, sales were $3,230,000, sales discounts were $120,000, sales returns and allowances were $280,000, and the cost of merchandise sold was $1,700,000. What was the amount of net sales and gross profit?

Exercise 6–21
Income statement for merchandiser
Objective 4

The following expenses were incurred by a merchandising business during the year. In which expense section of the income statement should each be reported: (a) selling, (b) administrative, or (c) other?

1. Interest expense on notes payable.
2. Salaries of office personnel.
3. Advertising expense.
4. Insurance expense on store equipment.
5. Rent expense on office building.
6. Depreciation expense on office equipment.
7. Office supplies used.
8. Salary of sales manager.

Exercise 6–22
Determining amounts for items omitted from income statement
Objective 4

✓ a. $298,000
✓ h. $690,000

Two items are omitted in each of the following four lists of income statement data. Determine the amounts of the missing items, identifying them by letter.

Sales	$ (a)	$600,000	$800,000	$757,500
Sales returns and allowances	10,000	10,000	(e)	30,500
Sales discounts	8,000	5,000	10,000	(g)
Net sales	280,000	(c)	765,000	(h)
Cost of merchandise sold	150,000	345,000	(f)	540,000
Gross profit	(b)	(d)	300,000	150,000

Exercise 6–23
Multiple-step income statement
Objective 4

What's Wrong WITH THIS?

How many errors can you find in the following income statement?

The Platinum Company
Income Statement
For the Year Ended December 31, 20—

Revenue from sales:			
Sales		$1,000,000	
Add: Sales returns and allowances	$18,000		
Sales discounts	4,500	22,500	
Gross sales			$1,022,500
Cost of merchandise sold			495,000
Income from operations			$ 527,500
Operating expenses:			
Selling expenses		$ 145,000	
Transportation out		5,300	
Administrative expenses		87,200	
Total operating expenses			237,500
			$ 290,000
Other expense:			
Interest revenue			27,500
Gross profit			$ 262,500

Exercise 6–24
Single-step income statement
Objective 4

✓ Net income: $412,500

Summary operating data for McNeely Company during the current year ended June 30, 2000, are as follows: cost of merchandise sold, $900,000; administrative expenses, $125,000; interest expense, $17,500; rent revenue, $30,000; net sales, $1,600,000; and selling expenses, $175,000. Prepare a single-step income statement.

Exercise 6–25
Multiple-step income statement
Objective 4

SPREADSHEET

✓ Net income: $57,500

At the end of the year, the balances of the accounts appearing in the ledger of Satellite Company, a furniture wholesaler, are as follows:

Administrative Expenses	$ 70,000	Salaries Payable	$ 3,220
Building	512,500	Sales	975,000
Cash	48,500	Sales Discounts	10,000
Cost of Merchandise Sold	650,000	Sales Returns and Allowances	45,000
Interest Expense	7,500	Selling Expenses	135,000
Merchandise Inventory	130,000	Store Supplies	7,700
Notes Payable	25,000	T. Turner, Capital	638,580
Office Supplies	10,600	T. Turner, Drawing	15,000

a. Prepare a multiple-step income statement for the year ended December 31.
b. Compare the major advantages and disadvantages of the multiple-step and single-step forms of income statements.

Exercise 6–26
Adjusting entry for merchandise inventory shrinkage
Objective 5

Widmer Inc. perpetual inventory records indicate that $317,200 of merchandise should be on hand on December 31, 2000. The physical inventory indicates that $298,700 of merchandise is actually on hand. Journalize the adjusting entry for the inventory shrinkage for Widmer Inc. for the year ended December 31, 2000.

Exercise 6–27
Closing the accounts of a merchandiser
Objective 5

From the following list, identify the accounts that should be closed to Income Summary at the end of the fiscal year: (a) Accounts Receivable, (b) Cost of Merchandise Sold, (c) Merchandise Inventory, (d) Sales, (e) Sales Discounts, (f) Sales Returns and Allowances, (g) Supplies, (h) Supplies Expense, (i) Salaries Expense, (j) Salaries Payable.

Exercise 6–28
Ratio of net sales to total assets
Objective 6

REAL WORLD

HAT

The financial statements for **Hershey Foods Corporation** are presented in Appendix G at the end of the text.

a. Determine the ratio of net sales to average total assets for Hershey Foods Corporation for the years ended December 31, 1996 and 1995.
b. What conclusions can be drawn from these ratios concerning the trend in the ability of Hershey to effectively use its assets to generate sales?

Note: Hershey's total assets at the end of 1994 were $2,890,981,000.

Appendix 1
Exercise 6–29
Merchandising special journals

Castle Rug Company had the following credit sales transactions during May:

Date	Customer	Quantity	Rug Style	Sales
May 3	H. Harding	1	9 by 6 Chinese	$ 5,000
8	K. Thomas	1	8 by 10 Persian	8,000
19	L. Lao	1	8 by 10 Indian	9,000
26	F. Lopez	1	9 by 12 Persian	12,000

The May 1 inventory was $13,000, consisting of:

Quantity	Style	Cost per Rug	Total Cost
2	9 by 6 Chinese	$3,000	$6,000
2	8 by 10 Persian	3,500	7,000

During May, Castle Rug Company purchased the following rugs from Hadiz Rug Importers:

Date	Quantity	Rug Style	Cost per Rug	Amount
May 10	2	8 by 10 Indian	$4,000	$ 8,000
12	1	9 by 6 Chinese	3,500	3,500
21	3	9 by 12 Persian	6,000	18,000

The general ledger includes the following accounts:

Account Number	Account
11	Accounts Receivable
12	Merchandise Inventory
21	Accounts Payable
41	Sales
51	Cost of Merchandise Sold

a. Record the sales in a two-column sales journal. Use the sales journal form shown in the appendix at the end of this chapter. Begin with Invoice Number 60.
b. Record the purchases in a purchases journal. Use the purchases journal form shown in the appendix at the end of this chapter.
c. Assume that you have posted the journal entries to the appropriate ledgers. Insert the correct posting references in the sales and purchases journals.
d. Determine the May 31 balance of Merchandise Inventory.

Appendix 2
Exercise 6–30
Closing entries

Based on the data presented in Exercise 6–25, journalize the closing entries.

PROBLEMS SERIES A

Problem 6–1A
Purchase-related transactions
Objective 2

The following selected transactions were completed by Bartow Co. during August of the current year:

Aug. 1. Purchased merchandise from Jones Co., $8,000, terms FOB shipping point, 2/10, n/eom. Prepaid transportation costs of $250 were added to the invoice.
4. Purchased merchandise from Guthrie Co., $9,200, terms FOB destination, n/30.
10. Paid Jones Co. for invoice of August 1, less discount.
12. Purchased merchandise from Dobbs Co., $5,000, terms FOB destination, 1/10, n/30.
14. Issued debit memorandum to Dobbs Co. for $1,500 of merchandise returned from purchase on August 12.
18. Purchased merchandise from Aschor Company, $11,500, terms FOB shipping point, n/eom.
18. Paid transportation charges of $200 on August 18 purchase from Aschor Company.
19. Purchased merchandise from Hatcher Co., $7,500, terms FOB destination, 2/10, n/30.
22. Paid Dobbs Co. for invoice of August 12, less debit memorandum of August 14 and discount.
29. Paid Hatcher Co. for invoice of August 19, less discount.
31. Paid Aschor Company for invoice of August 18.
31. Paid Guthrie Co. for invoice of August 4.

Instructions

Journalize the entries to record the transactions of Bartow Co. for August.

Problem 6–2A
Sales-related transactions

Objective 2

The following selected transactions were completed by Cohen Supplies Co., which sells electrical supplies primarily to wholesalers and occasionally to retail customers.

May 1. Sold merchandise on account to Fox Co., $2,500, terms FOB shipping point, n/eom. The cost of merchandise sold was $1,300.
2. Sold merchandise for $3,000 plus 6% sales tax to cash customers. The cost of merchandise sold was $1,750.
5. Sold merchandise on account to Baldwin Company, $13,000, terms FOB destination, 1/10, n/30. The cost of merchandise sold was $9,200.
7. Sold merchandise for $2,150 plus 6% sales tax to customers who used VISA cards. Deposited credit card receipts into the bank. The cost of merchandise sold was $1,800.
13. Sold merchandise to customers who used American Express cards, $4,500. The cost of merchandise sold was $2,600.
14. Sold merchandise on account to Blech Co., $7,500, terms FOB shipping point, 1/10, n/30. The cost of merchandise sold was $4,000.
15. Received check for amount due from Baldwin Company for sale on May 5.
16. Issued credit memorandum for $800 to Blech Co. for merchandise returned from sale on May 14. The cost of the merchandise returned was $360.
18. Sold merchandise on account to Stockton Company, $9,000, terms FOB shipping point, 1/10, n/30. Paid $210 for transportation costs and added them to the invoice. The cost of merchandise sold was $5,000.
24. Received check for amount due from Blech Co. for sale on May 14 less credit memorandum of May 16 and discount.
27. Received $7,680 from American Express for $8,000 of sales reported during the week of May 12–18.
28. Received check for amount due from Stockton Company for sale of May 18.
31. Paid Anywhere Delivery Service $1,200 for merchandise delivered during May to customers under shipping terms of FOB destination.
31. Received check for amount due from Fox Co. for sale of May 1.

June 3. Paid First National Bank $325 for service fees for handling MasterCard sales during May.
10. Paid $1,100 to state sales tax division for taxes owed on May sales.

Instructions
Journalize the entries to record the transactions of Cohen Supplies Co.

Problem 6–3A
Sales-related and purchase-related transactions

Objective 2

GENERAL LEDGER

The following were selected from among the transactions completed by Taxel Company during March of the current year:

Mar. 2. Purchased merchandise on account from Queen Co., list price $25,000, trade discount 30%, terms FOB shipping point, 2/10, n/30, with prepaid transportation costs of $720 added to the invoice.
4. Purchased merchandise on account from Rossi Co., $6,000, terms FOB destination, 1/10, n/30.
6. Sold merchandise on account to C. F. Howell Co., list price $7,500, trade discount 40%, terms 2/10, n/30. The cost of the merchandise sold was $1,850.
9. Returned $1,300 of merchandise purchased on March 4 from Rossi Co.
12. Paid Queen Co. on account for purchase of March 2, less discount.
14. Paid Rossi Co. on account for purchase of March 4, less return of March 9 and discount.
16. Received cash on account from sale of March 6 to C. F. Howell Co., less discount.
19. Sold merchandise on nonbank credit cards and reported accounts to the card company, American Express, $4,450. The cost of the merchandise sold was $2,950.
22. Sold merchandise on account to Vantage Co., $3,480, terms 2/10, n/30. The cost of the merchandise sold was $1,400.
24. Sold merchandise for cash, $4,350. The cost of the merchandise sold was $1,750.
25. Received merchandise returned by Vantage Co. from sale on March 22, $1,480. The cost of the returned merchandise was $600.
31. Received cash from American Express for nonbank credit card sales of March 19, less $290 service fee.

Instructions

Journalize the transactions.

Problem 6–4A

Sales-related and purchase-related transactions for seller and buyer

Objective 2

The following selected transactions were completed during November between Singh Company and Bristol Company:

Nov. 3. Singh Company sold merchandise on account to Bristol Company, $11,200, terms FOB shipping point, 2/10, n/30. Singh Company paid transportation costs of $600, which were added to the invoice. The cost of the merchandise sold was $7,500.
8. Singh Company sold merchandise on account to Bristol Company, $13,500, terms FOB destination, 1/15, n/eom. The cost of the merchandise sold was $9,500.
8. Singh Company paid transportation costs of $750 for delivery of merchandise sold to Bristol Company on November 8.
12. Bristol Company returned $3,000 of merchandise purchased on account on November 8 from Singh Company. The cost of the merchandise returned was $1,600.
13. Bristol Company paid Singh Company for purchase of November 3, less discount.
23. Bristol Company paid Singh Company for purchase of November 8, less discount and less return of November 12.
24. Singh Company sold merchandise on account to Bristol Company, $7,100, terms FOB shipping point, n/eom. The cost of the merchandise sold was $4,000.
27. Bristol Company paid transportation charges of $150 on November 24 purchase from Singh Company.
30. Bristol Company paid Singh Company on account for purchase of November 24.

Instructions

Journalize the November transactions for (1) Singh Company and (2) Bristol Company.

Problem 6–5A

Multiple-step income statement and report form of balance sheet

Objective 5

✓ 1. Net income: $160,000

The following selected accounts and their normal balances appear in the ledger of Maxilla Co. for the fiscal year ended June 30, 2000:

Cash	$ 36,500	Sales Returns and Allowances	$ 19,000
Notes Receivable	50,000	Sales Discounts	11,000
Accounts Receivable	62,000	Cost of Merchandise Sold	870,000
Merchandise Inventory	100,000	Sales Salaries Expense	110,000
Office Supplies	1,600	Advertising Expense	28,300
Prepaid Insurance	6,800	Depreciation Expense—Store Equipment	4,600
Office Equipment	54,000	Miscellaneous Selling Expense	1,100
Accumulated Depreciation—Office Equipment	10,800	Office Salaries Expense	51,000
Store Equipment	107,500	Rent Expense	22,150
Accumulated Depreciation—Store Equipment	48,600	Insurance Expense	12,750
Accounts Payable	27,000	Depreciation Expense—Office Equipment	9,000
Salaries Payable	2,000	Office Supplies Expense	900
Note Payable (final payment due 2010)	30,000	Miscellaneous Administrative Expense	1,200
T. Zeller, Capital	200,000	Interest Revenue	5,000
T. Zeller, Drawing	60,000	Interest Expense	4,000
Sales	1,300,000		

Instructions

1. Prepare a multiple-step income statement.
2. Prepare a statement of owner's equity.
3. Prepare a report form of balance sheet, assuming that the current portion of the note payable is $5,000.

(*continues*)

4. Briefly explain (a) how multiple-step and single-step income statements differ and (b) how report-form and account-form balance sheets differ.

Problem 6–6A

Single-step income statement and account form of balance sheet

Objective 5

✓ 1. Net income: $160,000

Selected accounts and related amounts for Maxilla Co. for the fiscal year ended June 30, 2000, are presented in Problem 6–5A.

Instructions

1. Prepare a single-step income statement in the format shown in Exhibit 8.
2. Prepare a statement of owner's equity.
3. Prepare an account form of balance sheet, assuming that the current portion of the note payable is $5,000.

Appendix 2 Problem 6–7A

Work sheet, financial statements, and adjusting and closing entries

✓ 2. Net income: $153,865

The accounts and their balances in the ledger of The Wash Co. on December 31 of the current year are as follows:

Cash	$ 51,165	Sales	$1,007,500
Accounts Receivable	116,100	Sales Returns and Allowances	15,500
Merchandise Inventory	235,000	Sales Discounts	6,000
Prepaid Insurance	10,600	Cost of Merchandise Sold	571,200
Store Supplies	3,750	Sales Salaries Expense	86,400
Office Supplies	1,700	Advertising Expense	29,450
Store Equipment	125,000	Depreciation Expense— Store Equipment	—
Accumulated Depreciation— Store Equipment	40,300	Store Supplies Expense	—
Office Equipment	62,000	Miscellaneous Selling Expense	1,885
Accumulated Depreciation— Office Equipment	17,200	Office Salaries Expense	60,000
		Rent Expense	30,000
Accounts Payable	66,700	Insurance Expense	—
Salaries Payable	—	Depreciation Expense— Office Equipment	—
Unearned Rent	1,200	Office Supplies Expense	—
Note Payable (final payment due 2010)	105,000	Miscellaneous Administrative Expense	1,650
M. Tag, Capital	222,100		
M. Tag, Drawing	40,000	Rent Revenue	—
Income Summary	—	Interest Expense	12,600

The data needed for year-end adjustments on December 31 are as follows:

Physical merchandise inventory on December 31		$225,000
Insurance expired during the year		7,100
Supplies on hand on December 31:		
Store supplies		1,050
Office supplies		750
Depreciation for the year:		
Store equipment		8,500
Office equipment		4,500
Salaries payable on December 31:		
Sales salaries	$3,450	
Office salaries	2,550	6,000
Unearned rent on December 31		400

Instructions

1. Prepare a work sheet for the fiscal year ended December 31. List all accounts in the order given.
2. Prepare a multiple-step income statement.
3. Prepare a statement of owner's equity.

4. Prepare a report form of balance sheet, assuming that the current portion of the note payable is $15,000.
5. Journalize the adjusting entries.
6. Journalize the closing entries.

PROBLEMS SERIES B

Problem 6–1B
Purchase-related transactions
Objective 2

The following selected transactions were completed by Bolton Company during March of the current year:

Mar. 1. Purchased merchandise from Duke Co., $7,500, terms FOB destination, n/30.
4. Purchased merchandise from Laufer Co., $8,000, terms FOB shipping point, 2/10, n/eom. Prepaid transportation costs of $150 were added to the invoice.
5. Purchased merchandise from Harmon Co., $5,000, terms FOB destination, 2/10, n/30.
8. Issued debit memorandum to Harmon Co. for $1,000 of merchandise returned from purchase on March 5.
14. Paid Laufer Co. for invoice of March 4, less discount.
15. Paid Harmon Co. for invoice of March 5, less debit memorandum of March 8 and discount.
19. Purchased merchandise from Ivy Co., $5,000, terms FOB shipping point, n/eom.
19. Paid transportation charges of $120 on March 19 purchase from Ivy Co.
20. Purchased merchandise from Hatcher Co., $12,000, terms FOB destination, 1/10, n/30.
30. Paid Hatcher Co. for invoice of March 20, less discount.
31. Paid Duke Co. for invoice of March 1.
31. Paid Ivy Co. for invoice of March 19.

Instructions

Journalize the entries to record the transactions of Bolton Company for March.

Problem 6–2B
Sales-related transactions
Objective 2

The following selected transactions were completed by Greenley Supply Co., which sells office supplies primarily to wholesalers and occasionally to retail customers.

Oct. 1. Sold merchandise on account to Beck Co., $3,500, terms FOB destination, 2/10, n/30. The cost of the merchandise sold was $1,800.
2. Sold merchandise for $2,000 plus 5% sales tax to cash customers. The cost of merchandise sold was $1,100.
4. Sold merchandise on account to Atlas Co., $2,400, terms FOB shipping point, n/eom. The cost of merchandise sold was $1,800.
5. Sold merchandise for $1,400 plus 5% sales tax to customers who used MasterCard. Deposited credit card receipts into the bank. The cost of merchandise sold was $750.
11. Received check for amount due from Beck Co. for sale on October 1.
14. Sold merchandise to customers who used American Express cards, $6,600. The cost of merchandise sold was $4,200.
15. Sold merchandise on account to Monroe Co., $6,500, terms FOB shipping point, 1/10, n/30. The cost of merchandise sold was $3,900.
17. Issued credit memorandum for $1,500 to Monroe Co. for merchandise returned from sale on October 15. The cost of the merchandise returned was $650.
18. Sold merchandise on account to Hempel Co., $7,500, terms FOB shipping point, 1/10, n/30. Added $85 to the invoice for transportation costs prepaid. The cost of merchandise sold was $4,500.
25. Received check for amount due from Monroe Co. for sale on October 15 less credit memorandum of October 17 and discount.

Oct. 26. Received $9,410 from American Express for $10,000 of sales reported during the week of October 11–17.
28. Received check for amount due from Hempel Co. for sale of October 18.
31. Received check for amount due from Atlas Co. for sale of October 4.
31. Paid Fast Delivery Service $850 for merchandise delivered during October to customers under shipping terms of FOB destination.
Nov. 4. Paid First National Bank $390 for service fees for handling MasterCard sales during October.
10. Paid $1,050 to state sales tax division for taxes owed on October sales.

Instructions

Journalize the entries to record the transactions of Greenley Supply Co.

Problem 6–3B

Sales-related and purchase-related transactions

Objective 2

GENERAL LEDGER

The following were selected from among the transactions completed by The Document Company during April of the current year:

Apr. 4. Purchased merchandise on account from Vela Co., list price $20,000, trade discount 40%, terms FOB destination, 2/10, n/30.
5. Sold merchandise for cash, $4,100. The cost of the merchandise sold was $2,450.
7. Purchased merchandise on account from Summit Co., $7,500, terms FOB shipping point, 2/10, n/30, with prepaid transportation costs of $200 added to the invoice.
7. Returned $2,500 of merchandise purchased on April 4 from Vela Co.
11. Sold merchandise on account to Bowles Co., list price $2,250, trade discount 20%, terms 1/10, n/30. The cost of the merchandise sold was $1,050.
14. Paid Vela Co. on account for purchase of April 4, less return of April 7 and discount.
15. Sold merchandise on nonbank credit cards and reported accounts to the card company, American Express, $5,850. The cost of the merchandise sold was $3,900.
17. Paid Summit Co. on account for purchase of April 7, less discount.
21. Received cash on account from sale of April 11 to Bowles Co., less discount.
25. Sold merchandise on account to Clemons Co., $3,200, terms 1/10, n/30. The cost of the merchandise sold was $2,025.
28. Received cash from American Express for nonbank credit card sales of April 15, less $280 service fee.
30. Received merchandise returned by Clemons Co. from sale on April 25, $1,700. The cost of the returned merchandise was $810.

Instructions

Journalize the transactions.

Problem 6–4B

Sales-related and purchase-related transactions for seller and buyer

Objective 2

The following selected transactions were completed during July between Servco Company and Barkey Co.:

July 3. Servco Company sold merchandise on account to Barkey Co., $10,500, terms FOB destination, 2/15, n/eom. The cost of the merchandise sold was $6,000.
3. Servco Company paid transportation costs of $450 for delivery of merchandise sold to Barkey Co. on July 3.
10. Servco Company sold merchandise on account to Barkey Co., $12,000, terms FOB shipping point, n/eom. The cost of the merchandise sold was $9,000.
11. Barkey Co. returned $2,000 of merchandise purchased on account on July 3 from Servco Company. The cost of the merchandise returned was $1,200.
14. Barkey Co. paid transportation charges of $200 on July 10 purchase from Servco Company.
17. Servco Company sold merchandise on account to Barkey Co., $20,000, terms FOB shipping point, 1/10, n/30. Servco Company paid transportation costs of $1,750, which were added to the invoice. The cost of the merchandise sold was $12,000.

July 18. Barkey Co. paid Servco Company for purchase of July 3, less discount and less return of July 11.
27. Barkey Co. paid Servco Company on account for purchase of July 17, less discount.
31. Barkey Co. paid Servco Company on account for purchase of July 10.

Instructions

Journalize the July transactions for (1) Servco Company and (2) Barkey Co.

Problem 6–5B

Multiple-step income statement and report form of balance sheet

Objective 5

✓ 1. Net income: $230,000

The following selected accounts and their normal balances appear in the ledger of The Shirt Co. for the fiscal year ended March 31, 2000:

Cash	$ 23,000	Sales Returns and Allowances	$ 13,100
Notes Receivable	120,000	Sales Discounts	11,900
Accounts Receivable	141,000	Cost of Merchandise Sold	1,000,000
Merchandise Inventory	200,000	Sales Salaries Expense	113,200
Office Supplies	5,600	Advertising Expense	33,800
Prepaid Insurance	3,400	Depreciation Expense—Store Equipment	6,400
Office Equipment	85,000	Miscellaneous Selling Expense	1,600
Accumulated Depreciation—Office Equipment	12,800	Office Salaries Expense	54,150
Store Equipment	113,000	Rent Expense	21,350
Accumulated Depreciation—Store Equipment	24,200	Depreciation Expense—Office Equipment	12,700
Accounts Payable	45,600	Insurance Expense	3,900
Salaries Payable	2,400	Office Supplies Expense	1,300
Note Payable (final payment due 2010)	56,000	Miscellaneous Administrative Expense	1,600
J. Peterman, Capital	370,000	Interest Revenue	11,000
J. Peterman, Drawing	50,000	Interest Expense	6,000
Sales	1,500,000		

Instructions

1. Prepare a multiple-step income statement.
2. Prepare a statement of owner's equity.
3. Prepare a report form of balance sheet, assuming that the current portion of the note payable is $15,000.
4. Briefly explain (a) how multiple-step and single-step income statements differ and (b) how report-form and account-form balance sheets differ.

Problem 6–6B

Single-step income statement and account form of balance sheet

Objective 5

✓ 1. Net income: $230,000

Selected accounts and related amounts for The Shirt Co. for the fiscal year ended March 31, 2000, are presented in Problem 6–5B.

Instructions

1. Prepare a single-step income statement in the format shown in Exhibit 8.
2. Prepare a statement of owner's equity.
3. Prepare an account form of balance sheet, assuming that the current portion of the note payable is $15,000.

Appendix 2
Problem 6–7B

Work sheet, financial statements, and adjusting and closing entries

✓ 2. Net income: $169,250

The accounts and their balances in the ledger of The Shoe Co. on December 31 of the current year are as follows:

Cash	$ 38,000	Store Supplies	$ 4,250
Accounts Receivable	112,500	Office Supplies	2,100
Merchandise Inventory	230,000	Store Equipment	132,000
Prepaid Insurance	9,700		

Accumulated Depreciation— Store Equipment	$ 40,300	Sales Salaries Expense	$ 76,400
Office Equipment	50,000	Advertising Expense	25,000
Accumulated Depreciation— Office Equipment	17,200	Depreciation Expense— Store Equipment	—
Accounts Payable	66,700	Store Supplies Expense	—
Salaries Payable	—	Miscellaneous Selling Expense	1,600
Unearned Rent	1,200	Office Salaries Expense	44,000
Note Payable (final payment due 2010)	105,000	Rent Expense	26,000
J. Oxford, Capital	174,600	Insurance Expense	—
J. Oxford, Drawing	40,000	Depreciation Expense— Office Equipment	—
Income Summary	—	Office Supplies Expense	—
Sales	895,000	Miscellaneous Administrative Expense	1,650
Sales Returns and Allowances	11,900	Rent Revenue	—
Sales Discounts	7,100	Interest Expense	11,600
Cost of Merchandise Sold	476,200		

The data needed for year-end adjustments on December 31 are as follows:

Physical merchandise inventory on December 31		$212,000
Insurance expired during the year		6,500
Supplies on hand on December 31:		
Store supplies		1,300
Office supplies		750
Depreciation for the year:		
Store equipment		7,500
Office equipment		3,800
Salaries payable on December 31:		
Sales salaries	$3,850	
Office salaries	1,150	5,000
Unearned rent on December 31		400

Instructions

1. Prepare a work sheet for the fiscal year ended December 31. List all accounts in the order given.
2. Prepare a multiple-step income statement.
3. Prepare a statement of owner's equity.
4. Prepare a report form of balance sheet, assuming that the current portion of the note payable is $15,000.
5. Journalize the adjusting entries.
6. Journalize the closing entries.

QUICKBOOKS PROBLEM [APPENDIX 1]

Buying and Selling Inventory

This problem uses the Larry's Landscaping sample company provided with QuickBooks® 5.0. Begin by first copying *sample.qbw* into another file name, **invent.qbw**, so that the original sample.qbw file will not be changed. You must copy the file using the copy and paste commands in your operating system. This is an important step, since we will be using the unchanged sample.qbw file later in the text. If you do not first copy sample.qbw into another file name, you will automatically change sample.qbw. We will be assuming that you have an unchanged version in future QuickBooks problems in this text.

Retrieve Larry's Landscaping by opening the file that you just created. The first time you open Larry's Landscaping, you will be in QuickBooks Navigator®. You may wish to use the Navigator to review the forms used for "Purchases and Vendors." This problem will use these forms.

Begin by opening the "Item List" window and reviewing Larry's Landscaping's inventory items—pumps, lighting, soil, sprinkler pipes, and sprinkler heads, for example. There are currently seven fountain pumps in inventory.

Instructions

1. Enter a new item of inventory by selecting the "Edit Item" button at the bottom of the "Item List" window. The new item is an inventory part, "iron fountain." Its cost is $110, and its selling price is $150. The income account is "Fountains and Garden" (under job materials for landscaping services). The preferred vendor is Harper Metal Works. Set the descriptions as "Iron garden fountain" for both purchase and sale transactions.
2. Larry's Landscaping has received a bill from Harper Metal Works for the purchase of five iron fountains. Record this purchase, using the "Enter Bills" form. Use the "Items" tab to record the five fountains.
3. Prepare an invoice to Erica Pretell for landscaping services, using the "Create Invoices" form (invoice #34). The invoice should include three lines. The first line is for 40 hours of installation labor. The second line is for two iron fountains. The third line is for two fountain pumps.
4. Prepare a QuickBooks report showing the following:
   a. Inventory stock status by item.
   b. Summary sales by item for inventory items (showing sales, cost of goods sold, and gross margin) for December. Use the filter to report inventory items only.

COMPREHENSIVE PROBLEM 2

GENERAL LEDGER
QUICKBOOKS

✓ 5. Net income: $67,415

The Cycle Co. is a merchandising business. The account balances for The Cycle Co. as of May 1, 2000 (unless otherwise indicated) are as follows:

110	Cash	$ 29,160
111	Notes Receivable	—
112	Accounts Receivable	56,220
113	Interest Receivable	—
115	Merchandise Inventory	123,900
116	Prepaid Insurance	3,750
117	Store Supplies	2,550
123	Store Equipment	54,300
124	Accumulated Depreciation—Store Equipment	12,600
210	Accounts Payable	38,500
211	Salaries Payable	—
310	F. R. Schwinn, Capital, June 1, 1999	179,270
311	F. R. Schwinn, Drawing	25,000
312	Income Summary	—
410	Sales	731,600
411	Sales Returns and Allowances	13,600
412	Sales Discounts	5,200

510	Cost of Merchandise Sold	$497,540
520	Sales Salaries Expense	74,400
521	Advertising Expense	18,000
522	Depreciation Expense	—
523	Store Supplies Expense	—
529	Miscellaneous Selling Expense	2,800
530	Office Salaries Expense	29,400
531	Rent Expense	24,500
532	Insurance Expense	—
539	Miscellaneous Administrative Expense	1,650
611	Interest Revenue	—

During May, the last month of the fiscal year, the following transactions were completed:

May 1. Paid rent for May, $2,400.
1. Received a $7,500 note receivable from Holmes Co. on account.
2. Purchased merchandise on account from Lindsey Co., terms 2/10, n/30, FOB shipping point, $25,000.
3. Paid transportation charges on purchase of May 2, $750.
5. Sold merchandise on account to Richards Co., terms 2/10, n/30, FOB shipping point, $8,500. The cost of the merchandise sold was $5,000.
7. Received $16,900 cash from Vasquez Co. on account, no discount.
10. Sold merchandise for cash, $18,300. The cost of the merchandise sold was $11,000.
12. Paid for merchandise purchased on May 2, less discount.
13. Received merchandise returned on sale of May 5, $1,500. The cost of the merchandise returned was $900.
14. Paid advertising expense for last half of May, $2,500.
15. Received cash from sale of May 5, less return of May 13 and discount.
19. Purchased merchandise for cash, $7,400.
19. Paid $25,950 to Chang Co. on account, no discount.
20. Sold merchandise on account to Petroski Co., terms 1/10, n/30, FOB shipping point, $16,000. The cost of the merchandise sold was $9,600.
21. For the convenience of the customer, paid shipping charges on sale of May 20, $600.
21. Received $31,000 cash from Sinnett Co. on account, no discount.
21. Purchased merchandise on account from Hummer Co., terms 1/10, n/30, FOB destination, $15,000.
24. Returned $2,500 of damaged merchandise purchased on May 21, receiving credit from the seller.
25. Refunded cash on sales made for cash, $750. The cost of the merchandise returned was $480.
27. Paid sales salaries of $2,700 and office salaries of $900.
29. Purchased store supplies for cash, $350.
30. Sold merchandise on account to Brown Co., terms 2/10, n/30, FOB shipping point, $43,100. The cost of the merchandise sold was $25,000.
30. Received cash from sale of May 20, less discount, plus transportation paid on May 21.
31. Paid for purchase of May 21, less return of May 24 and discount.

Instructions

(*Note:* If the work sheet described in the appendix is used, follow the alternative instructions.)

1. Enter the balances of each of the accounts in the appropriate balance column of a four-column account. Write *Balance* in the item section, and place a check mark (✓) in the Posting Reference column.
2. Journalize the transactions for May.

3. Post the journal to the general ledger, extending the month-end balances to the appropriate balance columns after all posting is completed. In this problem, you are not required to update or post to the accounts receivable and accounts payable subsidiary ledgers.
4. Journalize and post the adjusting entries, using the following adjustment data:

a.	Interest accrued on notes receivable on May 31		$ 100
b.	Merchandise inventory on May 31		110,000
c.	Insurance expired during the year		1,250
d.	Store supplies on hand on May 31		1,050
e.	Depreciation for the current year		8,860
f.	Accrued salaries on May 31:		
	Sales salaries	$400	
	Office salaries	140	540

5. Prepare a multiple-step income statement, a statement of owner's equity, and a report form of balance sheet.
6. Journalize and post the closing entries. Indicate closed accounts by inserting a line in both balance columns opposite the closing entry. Insert the new balance in the owner's capital account.
7. Prepare a post-closing trial balance.

Alternative Instructions

1. Enter the balances of each of the accounts in the appropriate balance column of a four-column account. Write *Balance* in the item section, and place a check mark (✓) in the Posting Reference column.
2. Journalize the transactions for May.
3. Post the journal to the general ledger, extending the month-end balances to the appropriate balance columns after all posting is completed. In this problem, you are not required to update or post to the accounts receivable and accounts payable subsidiary ledgers.
4. Prepare a trial balance as of May 31 on a ten-column work sheet, listing all accounts in the order given in the ledger. Complete the work sheet for the fiscal year ended May 31, using the following adjustment data:

a.	Interest accrued on notes receivable on May 31		$ 100
b.	Merchandise inventory on May 31		110,000
c.	Insurance expired during the year		1,250
d.	Store supplies on hand on May 31		1,050
e.	Depreciation for the current year		8,860
f.	Accrued salaries on May 31:		
	Sales salaries	$400	
	Office salaries	140	540

5. Prepare a multiple-step income statement, a statement of owner's equity, and a report form of balance sheet.
6. Journalize and post the adjusting entries.
7. Journalize and post the closing entries. Indicate closed accounts by inserting a line in both balance columns opposite the closing entry. Insert the new balance in the owner's capital account.
8. Prepare a post-closing trial balance.

QuickBooks Instructions

To set up the company file, follow the QuickBooks instructions for Comprehensive Problem 1 at the end of Chapter 4.

SPECIAL ACTIVITIES

Activity 6–1 Druck Company

Ethics and professional conduct in business

On August 1, 2000, Druck Company, a garden retailer, purchased $10,000 of corn seed, terms 2/10, n/30, from Dynacorn Co. Even though the discount period had expired, Wing Yu subtracted the discount of $200 when he processed the documents for payment on August 15, 2000.

Discuss whether Wing Yu behaved in a professional manner by subtracting the discount, even though the discount period had expired.

Actvity 6–2 The Video Store Co.

Purchases discounts and accounts payable

The Video Store Co. is owned and operated by Gerry Crosby. The following is an excerpt from a conversation between Gerry Crosby and JoAnn Sims, the chief accountant for The Video Store.

Gerry: JoAnn, I've got a question about this recent balance sheet.
JoAnn: Sure, what's your question?
Gerry: Well, as you know, I'm applying for a bank loan to finance our new store in Albion, and I noticed that the accounts payable are listed as $150,000.
JoAnn: That's right. Approximately $120,000 of that represents amounts due our suppliers, and the remainder is miscellaneous payables to creditors for utilities, office equipment, supplies, etc.
Gerry: That's what I thought. But as you know, we normally receive a 2% discount from our suppliers for earlier payment, and we always try to take the discount.
JoAnn: That's right. I can't remember the last time we missed a discount.
Gerry: Well, in that case, it seems to me the accounts payable should be listed minus the 2% discount. Let's list the accounts payable due suppliers as $117,600, rather than $120,000. Every little bit helps. You never know. It might make the difference between getting the loan and not.

How would you respond to Gerry Crosby's request?

Activity 6–3 Mega Sound versus Ultra-Sound Electronics

Determining cost of purchase

The following is an excerpt from a conversation between Jill Mandel and Kim Kenwood. Jill is debating whether to buy a stereo system from Mega Sound, a locally owned electronics store, or Ultra-Sound Electronics, a mail-order electronics company.

Jill: Kim, I don't know what to do about buying my new stereo.
Kim: What's the problem?
Jill: Well, I can buy it locally at Mega Sound for $689.95. However, Ultra-Sound Electronics has the same system listed for $699.99.
Kim: So what's the big deal? Buy it from Mega Sound.
Jill: It's not quite that simple. Ultra-Sound said something about not having to pay sales tax, since I was out-of-state.
Kim: Yes, that's a good point. If you buy it at Mega Sound, they'll charge you 5% sales tax.
Jill: But Ultra-Sound Electronics charges $15 for shipping and handling. If I have them send it next-day air, it'll cost $35 for shipping and handling.
Kim: I guess it is a little confusing.
Jill: That's not all. Mega Sound will give an additional 1% discount if I pay cash. Otherwise, they will let me use my MasterCard, or I can pay it off in three monthly installments.
Kim: Anything else???
Jill: Well . . . Ultra-Sound says I have to charge it on my MasterCard. They don't accept checks.
Kim: I am not surprised. Many mail-order houses don't accept checks.
Jill: I give up. What would you do?

1. Assuming that Ultra-Sound Electronics doesn't charge sales tax on the sale to Jill, which company is offering the best buy?
2. What might be some considerations other than price that might influence Jill's decision on where to buy the stereo system?

Activity 6–4 Escapade Boat Company

Sales discounts

Your sister operates Escapade Boat Company, a mail-order boat parts distributorship that is in its third year of operation. The following income statement was recently prepared for the year ended October 31, 2000:

Escapade Boat Company
Income Statement
For the Year Ended October 31, 2000

Revenues:		
Net sales		$500,000
Interest revenue		2,500
Total revenues		$502,500
Expenses:		
Cost of merchandise sold	$350,000	
Selling expenses	46,000	
Administrative expenses	24,000	
Interest expense	5,000	
Total expenses		425,000
Net income		$ 77,500

Your sister is considering a proposal to increase net income by offering sales discounts of 2/15, n/30, and by shipping all merchandise FOB shipping point. Currently, no sales discounts are allowed and merchandise is shipped FOB destination. It is estimated that these credit terms will increase net sales by 10%. The ratio of the cost of merchandise sold to net sales is expected to be 70%. All selling and administrative expenses are expected to remain unchanged, except for store supplies, miscellaneous selling, office supplies, and miscellaneous administrative expenses, which are expected to increase proportionately with increased net sales. The amounts of these preceding items for the year ended October 31, 2000, were as follows:

Store supplies expense	$2,000
Miscellaneous selling expense	1,000
Office supplies expense	800
Miscellaneous administrative expense	1,500

The other income and other expense items will remain unchanged. The shipment of all merchandise FOB shipping point will eliminate all transportation-out expenses, which for the year ended October 31, 2000, were $18,000.

1. Prepare a projected single-step income statement for the year ending October 31, 2001, based on the proposal.
2. a. Based on the projected income statement in (1), would you recommend the implementation of the proposed changes?
   b. Describe any possible concerns you may have related to the proposed changes described in (1).

Activity 6–5 Into the Real World

Shopping for a television

GROUP ACTIVITY

Assume that you are planning to purchase a 32-inch Sony television. In groups of three or four, determine the lowest cost for the television, considering the available alternatives and the advantages and disadvantages of each alternative. For example, you could purchase locally, through mail order, or through an Internet shopping service. Consider such factors as delivery charges, interest-free financing, discounts, coupons, and availability of warranty services. Prepare a report for presentation to the class.

ANSWERS TO SELF-EXAMINATION QUESTIONS

Matching

1. C	5. Q	9. T	13. D	16. F	19. B	22. P	25. J
2. H	6. S	10. E	14. AA	17. N	20. I	23. O	26. A
3. M	7. K	11. W	15. G	18. Y	21. L	24. Z	27. V
4. R	8. U	12. X					

Multiple Choice

1. **A** A debit memorandum (answer A), issued by the buyer, indicates the amount the buyer proposes to debit to the accounts payable account. A credit memorandum (answer B), issued by the seller, indicates the amount the seller proposes to credit to the accounts receivable account. An invoice (answer C) or a bill (answer D), issued by the seller, indicates the amount and terms of the sale.
2. **C** The amount of discount for early payment is $10 (answer C), or 1% of $1,000. Although the $50 of transportation costs paid by the seller is debited to the customer's account, the customer is not entitled to a discount on that amount.
3. **B** The single-step form of income statement (answer B) is so named because the total of all expenses is deducted in one step from the total of all revenues. The multiple-step form (answer A) includes numerous sections and subsections with several subtotals. The account form (answer C) and the report form (answer D) are two common forms of the balance sheet.
4. **C** Gross profit (answer C) is the excess of net sales over the cost of merchandise sold. Operating income (answer A) or income from operations (answer B) is the excess of gross profit over operating expenses. Net income (answer D) is the final figure on the income statement after all revenues and expenses have been reported.
5. **D** Expenses such as interest expense (answer D) that cannot be associated directly with operations are identified as *Other expense* or *Nonoperating expense*. Depreciation expense—office equipment (answer A) is an administrative expense. Sales salaries expense (answer B) is a selling expense. Insurance expense (answer C) is a mixed expense with elements of both selling expense and administrative expense. For small businesses, insurance expense is usually reported as an administrative expense.

7

Cash

Setting the STAGE

If your bank returns checks it has paid from your account, along with your monthly bank statement, you may have noticed a magnetic coding in the bottom right-hand corner of each check. This coding indicates the amount of the check. In the past, you may have accepted this coding, as well as the bank statement, as correct. However, a clerk may have entered the magnetic coding incorrectly, which causes the check to be processed for the wrong amount. For example, the following check written for $25 was incorrectly processed as $250:

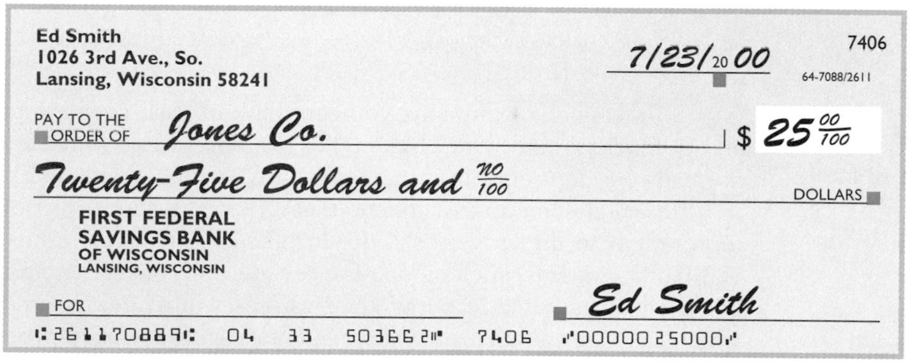
Ed Smith
1026 3rd Ave., So.
Lansing, Wisconsin 58241
7406
7/23/20 00
64-7088/2611
PAY TO THE ORDER OF Jones Co. $ 25 00/100
Twenty-Five Dollars and no/100 DOLLARS
FIRST FEDERAL SAVINGS BANK OF WISCONSIN
LANSING, WISCONSIN
FOR
Ed Smith
261170889 04 33 503662 7406 0000025000

We are all concerned about our cash. Likewise, businesses are concerned about safeguarding and controlling cash. Inadequate controls can and often do lead to theft, misuse of funds, or otherwise embarrassing situations. For example, in one of the biggest errors in banking history, Chemical Bank incorrectly deducted customer automated teller machine (ATM) withdrawals twice from each customer's account. For instance, if a customer withdrew $100 from an account, the customer actually had $200 deducted from the account balance. Before the error was discovered, Chemical Bank mistakenly deducted about $15 million from more than 100,000 customer accounts. The error was caused by inadequate controls over the changing of the bank's computer programs.[1]

To detect errors, control procedures should be used by both you and the bank. In this chapter, we will apply basic internal control concepts and procedures to the control of cash.

[1] Saul Hansell, "Cash Machines Getting Greedy At a Big Bank," *The Wall Street Journal,* February 18, 1994.

objectives

After studying this chapter, you should be able to:

1. Describe the nature of cash and the importance of internal control over cash.
2. Summarize basic procedures for achieving internal control over cash receipts.
3. Summarize basic procedures for achieving internal control over cash payments, including the use of a voucher system.
4. Describe the nature of a bank account and its use in controlling cash.
5. Prepare a bank reconciliation and journalize any necessary entries.
6. Account for small cash transactions, using a petty cash fund.
7. Summarize how cash is presented on the balance sheet.
8. Compute and interpret the ratio of cash to current liabilities.

Nature of Cash and the Importance of Controls Over Cash

OBJECTIVE 1

Describe the nature of cash and the importance of internal control over cash.

Cash includes coins, currency (paper money), checks, money orders, and money on deposit that is available for unrestricted withdrawal from banks and other financial institutions. Normally, you can think of cash as anything that a bank would accept for deposit in your account. For example, a check made payable to you could normally be deposited in a bank and thus is considered cash.

We will assume in this chapter that a business maintains only *one* bank account, represented in the ledger as *Cash*. In practice, however, a business may have several bank accounts, such as one for general cash payments and another for payroll. For each of its bank accounts, the business will maintain a ledger account, one of which may be called *Cash in Bank—First Bank,* for example. It will also maintain separate ledger accounts for cash that it does not keep in the bank, such as cash for small payments, and cash used for special purposes, such as travel reimbursements. We will introduce some of these other cash accounts in the chapter.

Because of the ease with which money can be transferred, cash is the asset most likely to be diverted and used improperly by employees. In addition, many transactions either directly or indirectly affect the receipt or the payment of cash. Businesses must therefore design and use controls that safeguard cash and control the authorization of cash transactions. In the following paragraphs, we will discuss these controls.

Control of Cash Receipts

OBJECTIVE 2

Summarize basic procedures for achieving internal control over cash receipts.

To protect cash from theft and misuse, a business must control cash from the time it is received until it is deposited in a bank. Such procedures are called **preventive controls**. Procedures that are designed to detect theft or misuse of cash are called **detective controls**. In a sense, detective controls are also preventive in nature, since employees are less likely to steal or misuse cash if they know there is a good chance they will be discovered.

Retail businesses normally receive cash from two main sources: (1) cash receipts from customers and (2) mail receipts from customers making payments on account. These two sources of cash are shown in Exhibit 1.

EXHIBIT 1 Retailers' Sources of Cash

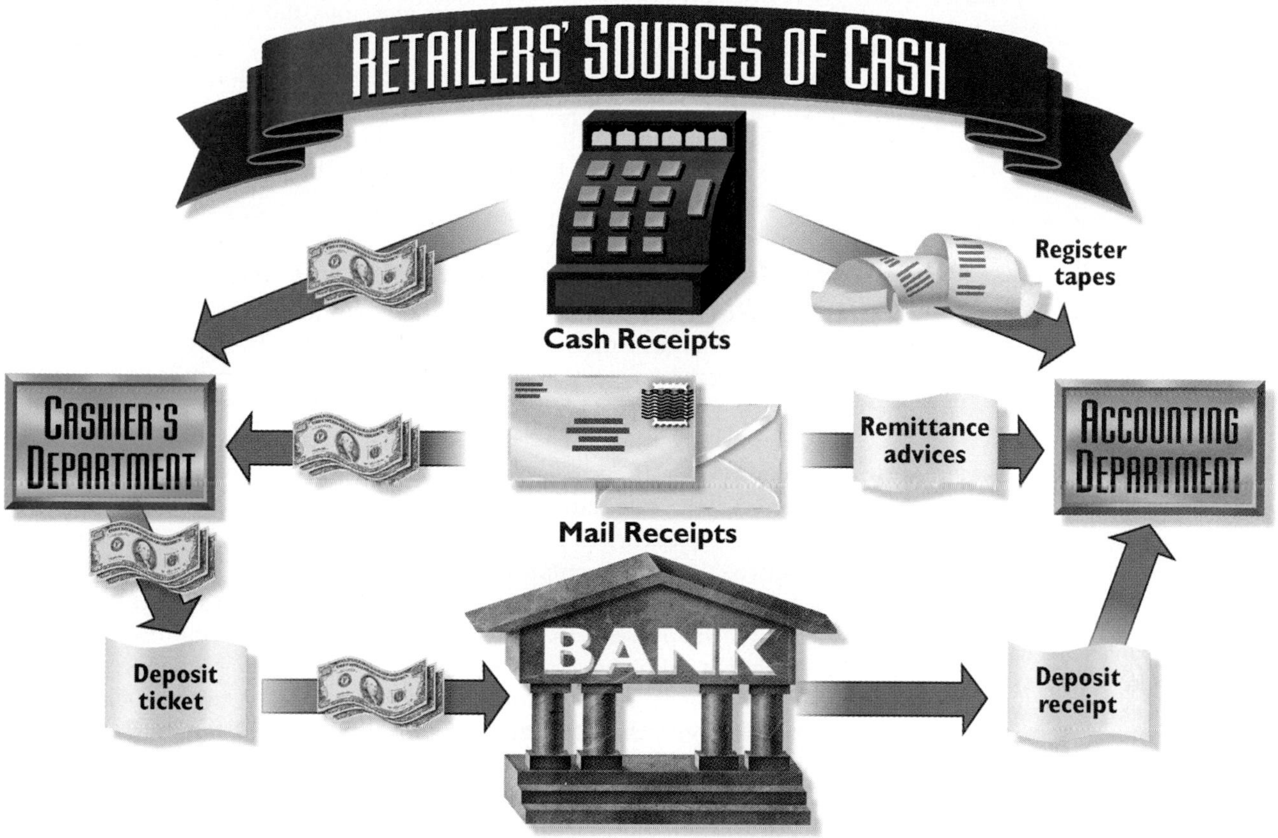

Fast-food restaurants, such as **McDonald's**, **Wendy's**, and **Burger King**, receive cash primarily from over-the-counter sales to customers. Mail-order retailers, such as **Lands' End**, **Orvis**, and **L.L. Bean**, receive cash primarily through the mail and from credit card companies.

Controlling Cash Received from Cash Sales

Regardless of the source of cash receipts, every business must properly safeguard and record its cash receipts. One of the most important controls to protect cash received in over-the-counter sales is a cash register. You may have noticed that when a clerk (cashier) enters the amount of a sale, the cash register normally displays the amount. This is a control to ensure that the clerk has charged you the correct amount. You also receive a receipt to verify the accuracy of the amount.

At the beginning of a work shift, each cash register clerk is given a cash drawer that contains a predetermined amount of cash for making change for customers. The amount in each drawer is sometimes called a **change fund**. At the end of the work shift, each clerk and the supervisor count the cash in the clerk's cash drawer. The amount of cash in each drawer should equal the beginning amount of cash plus the cash sales for the day. However, errors in recording cash sales or errors in making change cause the amount of actual cash on hand to differ from this amount. Such differences are recorded in a **cash short and over account**. For example, the following entry records a clerk's cash sales of $3,150 when the actual cash on hand is $3,142:

"Overs" are recorded as credits
"Shorts" as Debits

		Cash		3 1 4 2 00	
		Cash Short and Over		8 00	
		Sales			3 1 5 0 00
		To record cash sales and actual cash			
		on hand.			

At the end of the accounting period, a debit balance in the cash short and over account is included in Miscellaneous Administrative Expense in the income statement. A credit balance is included in the Other Income section. If a clerk consistently has significant cash short and over amounts, the supervisor may require the clerk to take additional training.

After a cash register clerk's cash has been counted and recorded on a memorandum form, the cash is then placed in a store safe in the Cashier's Department until it can be deposited in the bank. The supervisor forwards the clerk's cash register tapes to the Accounting Department, where they become the basis for recording the transactions for the day.

Controlling Cash Received in the Mail

Cash is received in the mail when customers pay their bills. This cash is usually in the form of checks and money orders. Most companies' invoices are designed so that customers return a portion of the invoice, called a **remittance advice**, with their payment. The employee who opens the incoming mail should initially compare the amount of cash received with the amount shown on the remittance advice. If a customer does not return a remittance advice, an employee prepares one. Like the cash register, the remittance advice serves as a record of cash initially received. It also helps ensure that the posting to the customer's account is accurate. Finally, as a preventive control, the employee opening the mail normally also stamps checks and money orders "For Deposit Only" in the bank account of the business.

Some retail companies are using debit card systems to transfer and record the receipt of cash. In a debit card system, a customer pays for goods at the time of purchase by presenting a plastic card. The card authorizes the electronic transfer of cash from the customer's checking account to the retailer's bank account at the time of the sale.

All cash received in the mail is sent to the Cashier's Department. An employee there combines it with the receipts from cash sales and prepares a bank deposit ticket. The remittance advices and their summary totals are delivered to the Accounting Department. An accounting clerk then prepares the records of the transactions and posts them to the customer accounts.

When cash is deposited in the bank, the bank normally stamps a duplicate copy of the deposit ticket with the amount received. This bank receipt is returned to the Accounting Department, where a clerk then compares the receipt with the total amount that should have been deposited. This control helps ensure that all the cash is deposited and that no cash is lost or stolen on the way to the bank. Any shortages are thus promptly detected.

The separation of the duties of the Cashier's Department, which handles cash, and the Accounting Department, which records cash, is a preventive control. If Accounting Department employees both handled and recorded cash, an employee could steal cash and change the accounting records to hide the theft.

Internal Control of Cash Payments

OBJECTIVE 3

Summarize basic procedures for achieving internal control over cash payments, including the use of a voucher system.

Internal control of cash payments should provide reasonable assurance that payments are made for only authorized transactions. In addition, controls should ensure that cash is used efficiently. For example, controls should ensure that all available discounts, such as purchase and trade discounts, are taken.

In a small business, an owner/manager may sign all checks, based upon personal knowledge of goods and services purchased. In a large business, however, checks are often prepared by employees who do not have such a complete knowledge of the transactions. In a large business, for example, the duties of pur-

Howard Schultz & Associates (HS&A) specializes in reviewing cash payments for its clients. HS&A searches for errors, such as duplicate payments, failures to take discounts, and inaccurate computations. The typical amount recovered for a client is about one-tenth of 1 percent (0.1%) of the total payments reviewed. This averages to about $300,000 per client. In one case, HS&A recovered over $4.5 million for a client.

Source: Thomas Buell, Jr., "Demand Grows for Auditor," *The Naples Daily News,* January 12, 1992, p. 14E.

chasing goods, inspecting the goods received, and verifying the invoices are usually performed by different employees. These duties must be coordinated to ensure that checks for proper amounts are issued to creditors. One system used for this purpose is the voucher system.

Basic Features of the Voucher System

A **voucher system** is a set of procedures for authorizing and recording liabilities and cash payments. A voucher system normally uses (1) vouchers, (2) a file for unpaid vouchers, and (3) a file for paid vouchers. Generally, a voucher is any document that serves as proof of authority to pay cash. For example, an invoice properly approved for payment could be considered a voucher. In many businesses, however, a **voucher** is a special form for recording relevant data about a liability and the details of its payment. An example of such a form is shown in Exhibit 2.

EXHIBIT 2 Voucher

(face)

COMPUTER KING — VOUCHER

① **Date** July 1, 2001 **Voucher No.** 451

② **Payee** Allied Manufacturing Company
683 Fairmont Road
Chicago, IL 60630-3168

Date	Details	Amount
③ June 28, 2001	Invoice No. 4693-C, $1,500.00, FOB Chicago, 2/10, n/30	1,500.00

Attach Supporting Documents

(back)

④ **ACCOUNT DISTRIBUTION**

DEBIT	AMOUNT	
MERCHANDISE INVENTORY	1500	00
SUPPLIES		
ADVERTISING EXPENSE		
DELIVERY EXPENSE		
MISC. SELLING EXPENSE		
MISC. ADMIN. EXPENSE		
CREDIT ACCOUNTS PAYABLE	1500	00

DISTRIBUTION APPROVED L. Donnelly

NO. 451

DATE 7/1/01 **DUE** 7/8/01

PAYEE
Allied Manufacturing Company
683 Fairmont Road
Chicago, IL 60630-3168

VOUCHER SUMMARY

AMOUNT	1500	00
ADJUSTMENT		
DISCOUNT	30	00
NET	1470	00

APPROVED M.C. Leshen **CONTROLLER**
RECORDED W.B.

PAYMENT SUMMARY ⑤

DATE 7/8/01
AMOUNT 1470.00
CHECK NO. 863
APPROVED Pat King
RECORDED L.K.R. A.S. ⑥

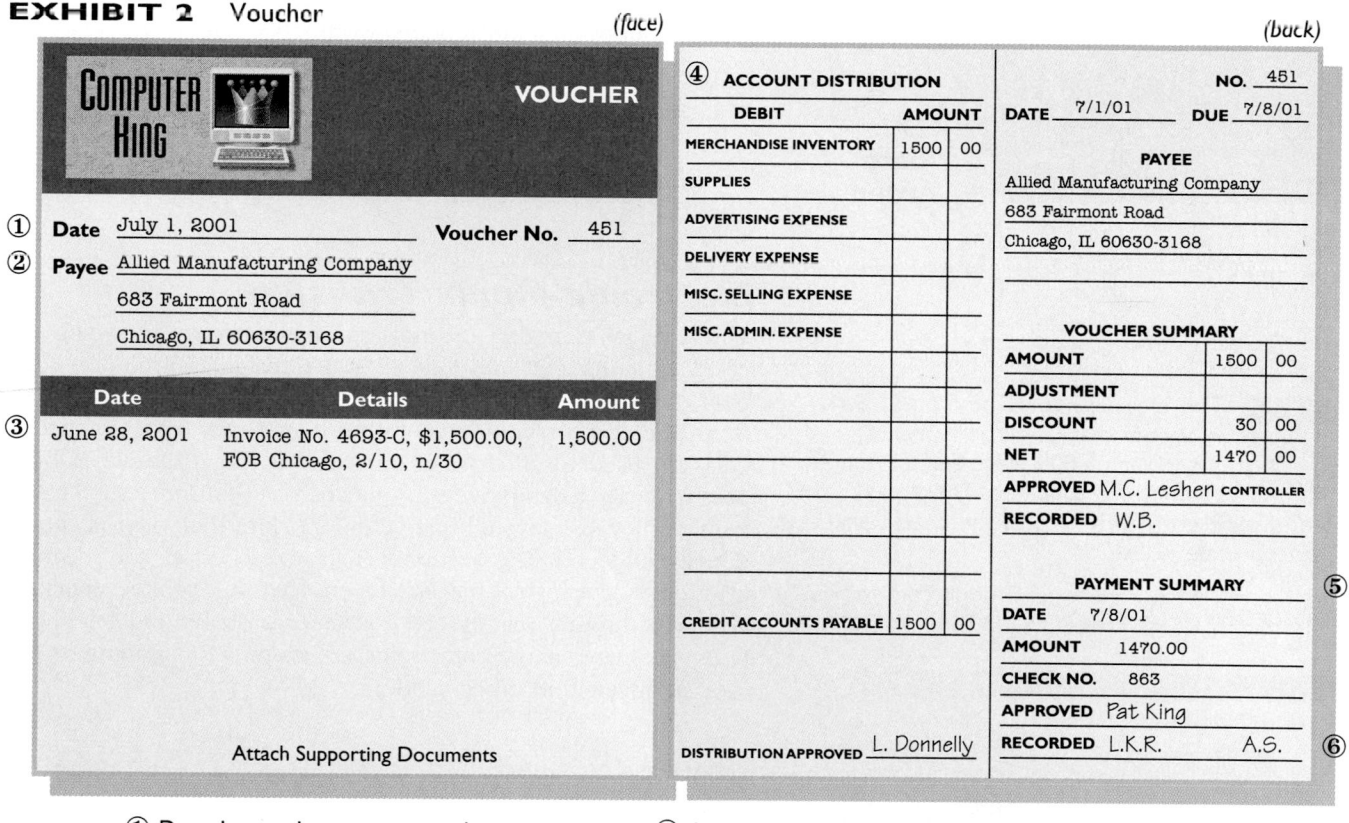

① Date the voucher was prepared
② Name and address of the creditor
③ Description of the supporting documents
④ Accounts used to record the payment
⑤ Details of payment
⑥ Spaces for signature or initials of approving employees

Each voucher includes the creditor's invoice number and the amount and terms of the invoice. The accounts used in recording the payment are listed in the *account distribution*.

A voucher is normally prepared in the Accounting Department, after all necessary supporting documents have been received. For example, when a voucher is prepared for the purchase of goods, the voucher should be supported by the supplier's invoice, a purchase order, and a receiving report. In preparing the voucher, an accounts payable clerk verifies the quantity, price, and mathematical accuracy of the supporting documents. This provides assurance that the payment is for goods that were properly ordered and received.

After a voucher is prepared, the voucher and its supporting documents are given to the proper official for approval. After it has been approved, the voucher is returned to the Accounting Department, where it is recorded in the accounts. It is then filed in an unpaid voucher file by its due date so that all available purchase discounts are taken.[2]

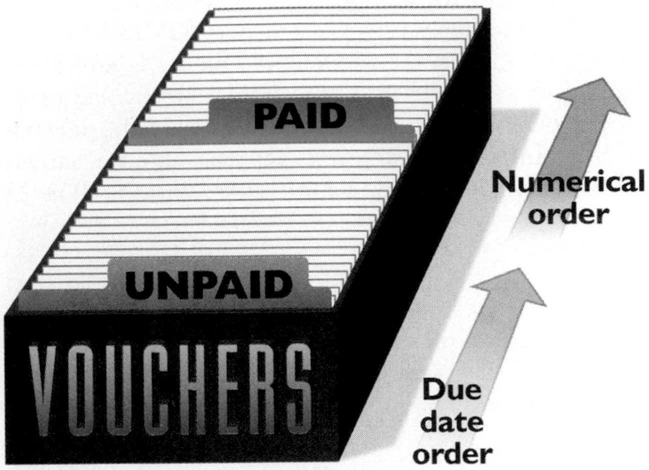

On its due date, the voucher is removed from the unpaid voucher file. The date, the number, and the amount of the check written in payment are listed on the back of the voucher. The payment of the voucher is recorded in the same manner as the payment of an account payable.

After payment, vouchers are marked "Paid" and are usually filed in numerical order in a paid voucher file. They are then readily available for examination by employees needing information about past payments.

A voucher system may be either manual or computerized. In a computerized system, properly approved supporting documents would be entered directly into computer files. At the due date, the checks would be automatically generated and mailed to creditors. At that time, the voucher would be automatically transferred to a paid voucher file. In some cases, payments may be made electronically rather than by check.

Electronic Funds Transfer

With rapidly changing technology, new systems are being devised to more efficiently record and transfer cash among companies. Such systems often use **electronic funds transfer (EFT)**. In an EFT system, computers rather than paper (money, checks, etc.) are used to effect cash transactions. For example, a business may pay its employees by means of EFT. Under such a system, employees may authorize the deposit of their payroll checks directly into checking accounts. Each pay period, the business electronically transfers the employees' net pay to their checking accounts through the use of computer systems and telephone lines. Likewise, many companies are using EFT systems to pay their suppliers and other vendors.

The treasurer for **Chevron U.S.A.** reported that Chevron is making more than 5,800 electronic payments a month to suppliers. These payments represent nearly 14% of the checks that Chevron once wrote.

Source: Fred R. Bleakley, "Fast Money: Electronic Payments Now Supplant Checks at More Large Firms," *The Wall Street Journal,* April 3, 1994.

Bank Accounts: Their Nature and Use as a Control Over Cash

OBJECTIVE 4

Describe the nature of a bank account and its use in controlling cash.

Most of you are already familiar with bank accounts. You have a checking account at a local bank, credit union, savings and loan association, or other financial institution. In this section, we discuss the nature of a bank account used by a business. The features of such accounts will be similar to your own bank account. We then discuss the use of bank accounts as an additional control over cash.

[2] Occasionally, a purchase discount is missed. Some companies record the amounts of missed discounts in an account titled Discounts Lost. Doing so allows managers to monitor the significance of discounts lost. Since most companies design controls to take all purchase discounts, we do not illustrate the use of a discounts lost account.

Business Bank Accounts

A business often maintains several bank accounts. The forms used with each bank account are a signature card, deposit ticket, check, and record of checks drawn.

When you open a checking account, you sign a **signature card**. This card is used by the bank to verify the signature on checks that are submitted for payment. Also, when you open an account, the bank assigns an identifying number to the account.

The details of a deposit are listed by the depositor on a printed **deposit ticket** supplied by the bank. These forms are often prepared in duplicate. The bank teller stamps or initials a copy of the deposit ticket and gives it to the depositor as a receipt. Other types of receipts may also be used to give the depositor written proof of the date and the total amount of the deposit.

A **check** is a written document signed by the depositor, ordering the bank to pay a sum of money to an individual or entity. There are three parties to a check—the drawer, the drawee, and the payee. The **drawer** is the one who signs the check, ordering payment by the bank. The **drawee** is the bank on which the check is drawn. The **payee** is the party to whom payment is to be made.

The name and address of the depositor are usually printed on each check. In addition, checks are prenumbered, so that they can easily be kept track of by both the issuer and the bank. Banks encode their identification number and the depositor's account number in magnetic ink on each check. These numbers make it possible for the bank to sort and post checks automatically. When a check is presented for payment, the amount for which it is drawn is inserted, next to the account number, in magnetic ink. The processed check shown at the beginning of this chapter illustrated these features.

Point of INTEREST

You may order checks from your bank, which will debit your account for a check printing charge. It is usually less costly, however, to order checks directly from a printer. If you use electronic banking services, you will use fewer checks, but you will probably pay a fee for each electronic transaction.

A record of each check should be prepared at the time a check is written. A small booklet called a **transactions register** is often used by both businesses and individuals for this purpose.

The purpose of a check may be written in space provided on the check or on an attachment to the check. Normally, checks issued to a creditor on account are sent with a form that identifies the specific invoice that is being paid. The purpose of this **remittance advice** is to make sure that proper credit is recorded in the accounts of the creditor. In this way, mistakes are less likely to occur. A check and remittance advice is shown in Exhibit 3.

EXHIBIT 3
Check and Remittance Advice

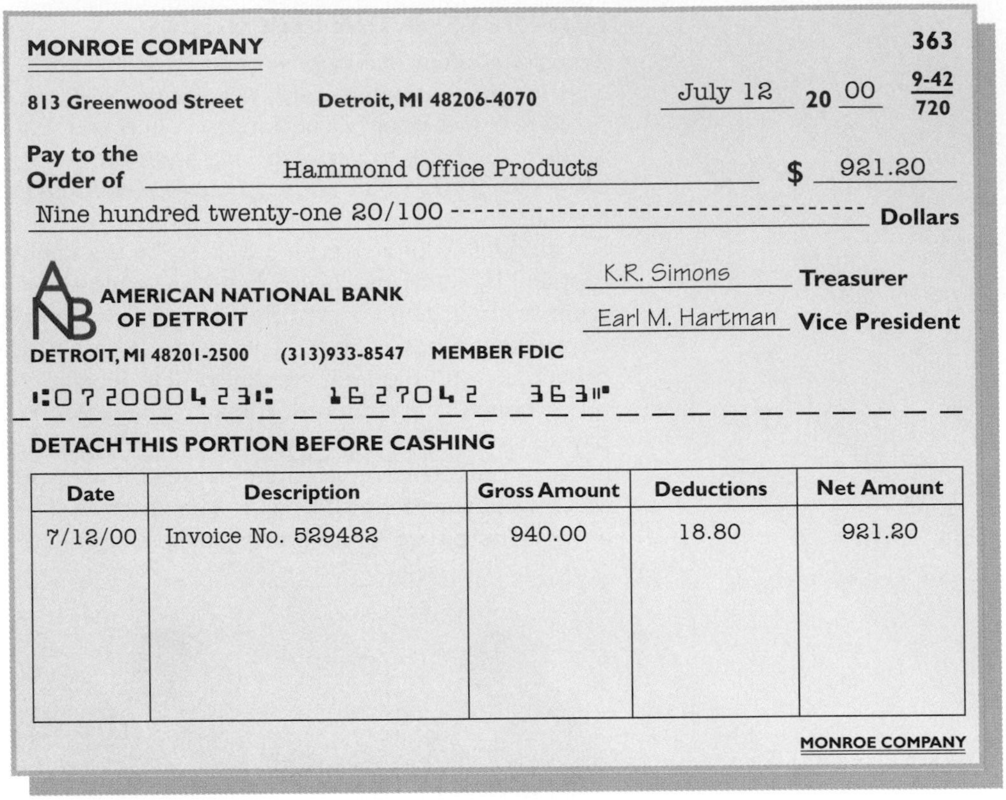

MONROE COMPANY
363

813 Greenwood Street   Detroit, MI 48206-4070   July 12 20 00   9-42/720

Pay to the Order of Hammond Office Products $ 921.20

Nine hundred twenty-one 20/100 ---------- Dollars

AMERICAN NATIONAL BANK OF DETROIT
DETROIT, MI 48201-2500   (313)933-8547   MEMBER FDIC

K.R. Simons   Treasurer
Earl M. Hartman   Vice President

⑆0720004231⑆ 1627042 363⑈

DETACH THIS PORTION BEFORE CASHING

Date	Description	Gross Amount	Deductions	Net Amount
7/12/00	Invoice No. 529482	940.00	18.80	921.20

MONROE COMPANY

Before depositing the check, the payee removes the remittance advice. The payee may then use the remittance advice as written proof of the details of the cash receipt.

Bank Statement

Banks usually maintain a record of all checking account transactions. A summary of all transactions, called a **statement of account**, is mailed to the depositor, usually each month. Like any account with a customer or a creditor, the bank statement shows the beginning balance, additions, deductions, and the balance at the end of the period. A typical bank statement is shown in Exhibit 4.

The depositor's checks received by the bank during the period may accompany the bank statement, arranged in the order of payment. The paid checks are stamped "Paid," together with the date of payment. Other entries that the bank has made in the depositor's account may be described in debit or credit memorandums enclosed with the statement.

You should note that a depositor's checking account balance *in the bank's records* is a liability with a credit balance. Debit memorandums issued by the bank on a depositor's account therefore decrease the depositor's balance. Likewise, credit memorandums increase the depositor's balance. A bank issues a debit memorandum to charge (decrease) a depositor's account for service charges or for deposited checks returned because of insufficient funds. Likewise, a bank issues a credit memorandum when it increases the depositor's account for collecting a note receivable for the depositor, making a loan to the depositor, or adding interest to the depositor's account.[3]

[3] Although interest-bearing checking accounts are common for individuals, Federal Reserve Regulation Q prohibits the paying of interest on corporate checking accounts.

EXHIBIT 4
Bank Statement

MEMBER FDIC

AMERICAN NATIONAL BANK OF DETROIT
DETROIT, MI 48201-2500 (313)933-8547

PAGE 1

	ACCOUNT NUMBER	1627042
	FROM 6/30/00	TO 7/31/00
	BALANCE	4,218.60
22	DEPOSITS	13,749.75
52	WITHDRAWALS	14,698.57
3	OTHER DEBITS AND CREDITS	90.00CR
	NEW BALANCE	3,359.78

MONROE COMPANY
813 GREENWOOD STREET
DETROIT, MI 48206-4070

CHECKS AND OTHER DEBITS			DEPOSITS	DATE	BALANCE
819.40	122.54		585.75	07/01	3,862.41
369.50	732.26	20.15	421.53	07/02	3,162.03
600.00	190.70	52.50	781.30	07/03	3,100.13
25.93	160.00		662.50	07/05	3,576.70
36.80	NSF 300.00		503.18	07/07	3,743.08
32.26	535.09		932.00	07/29	3,404.40
21.10	126.20		705.21	07/30	3,962.31
	SC 18.00		MS 408.00	07/30	4,352.31
26.12	1,615.13		648.72	07/31	3,359.78

EC — ERROR CORRECTION
MS — MISCELLANEOUS
NSF — NOT SUFFICIENT FUNDS
OD — OVERDRAFT
PS — PAYMENT STOPPED
SC — SERVICE CHARGE

* * *

THE RECONCILEMENT OF THIS STATEMENT WITH YOUR RECORDS IS ESSENTIAL.
ANY ERROR OR EXCEPTION SHOULD BE REPORTED IMMEDIATELY.

Bank Accounts as a Control Over Cash

A bank account is one of the primary tools a business uses to control cash. For example, businesses often require that all cash receipts be initially deposited in a bank account. Likewise, businesses usually use checks to make all cash payments, except for very small amounts. When such a system is used, there is a double record of cash transactions—one by the business and the other by the bank.

A bank account and a business's records provide a double record of cash transactions.

A business can use a bank statement to compare the cash transactions recorded in its accounting records to those recorded by the bank. The cash balance shown by a bank statement is usually different from the cash balance shown in the accounting records of the business, as shown in Exhibit 5.

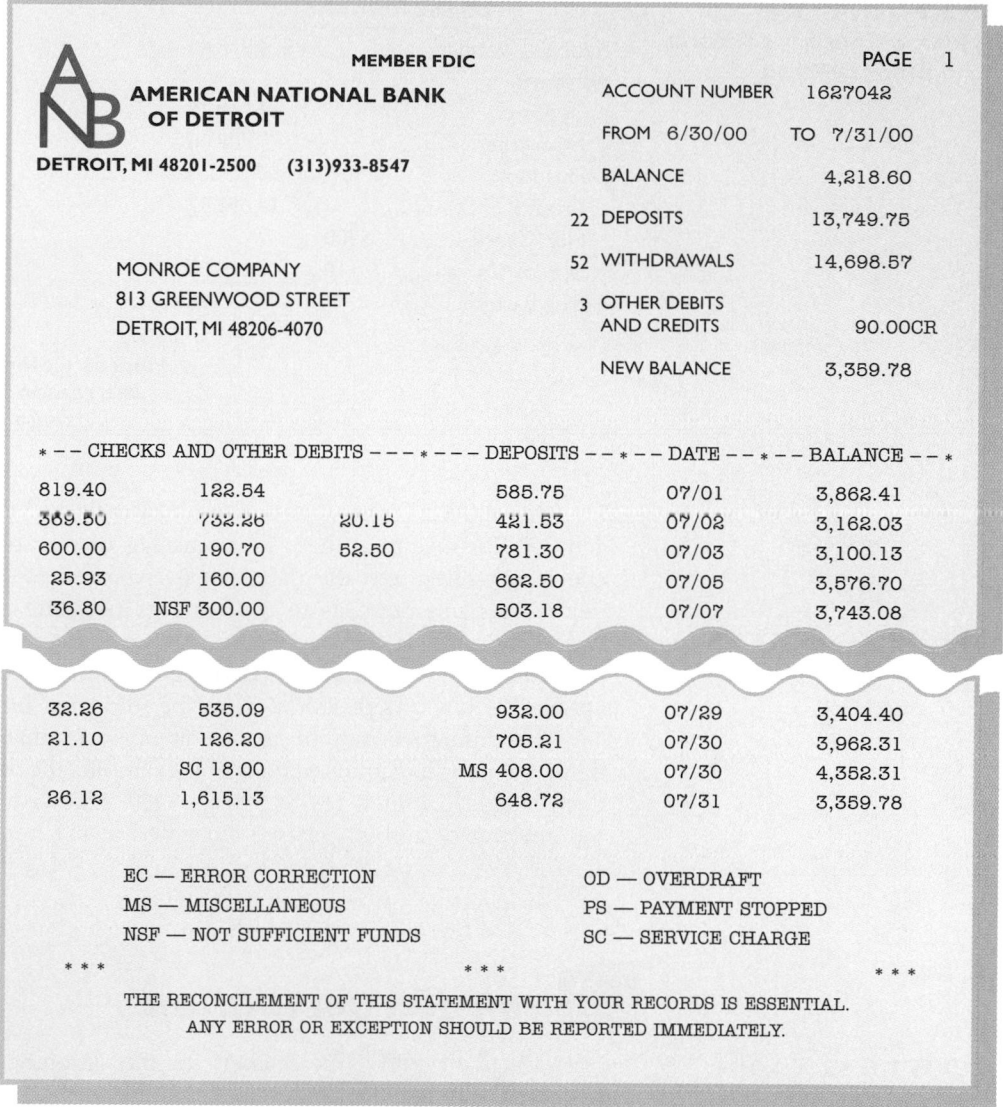

EXHIBIT 5
Monroe Company's Records and Bank Statement

Bank Statement			Monroe Company Records	
Beginning Balance . .		$ 4,218.60	Beginning Balance . .	$ 4,227.60
Additions:				
Deposits		13,749.75	Deposits	14,565.95
Miscellaneous . . .		408.00		
Deductions:				
Checks		14,698.57	Checks	16,243.56
NSF Check	$300			
Service Charge . .	18	318.00		
Ending Balance		$ 3,359.78	Ending Balance	$ 2,549.99

Monroe Company should determine the reason for the difference in these two amounts.

This difference may be the result of a delay by either party in recording transactions. For example, there is a time lag of one day or more between the date a check is written and the date that it is presented to the bank for payment. If the depositor mails deposits to the bank or uses the night depository, a time lag between the date of the deposit and the date that it is recorded by the bank is also probable. The bank may also debit or credit the depositor's account for transactions about which the depositor will not be informed until later.

The difference may be the result of errors made by either the business or the bank in recording transactions. For example, the business may incorrectly post to Cash a check written for $4,500 as $450. Likewise, a bank may incorrectly record the amount of a check, as we illustrated at the beginning of this chapter.

Bank Reconciliation

OBJECTIVE 5

Prepare a bank reconciliation and journalize any necessary entries.

For effective control, the reasons for the difference between the cash balance on the bank statement and the cash balance in the accounting records should be determined by preparing a bank reconciliation. A **bank reconciliation** is a listing of the items and amounts that cause the cash balance reported in the bank statement to differ from the balance of the cash account in the ledger.

A bank reconciliation is usually divided into two sections. The first section begins with the cash balance according to the bank statement and ends with the adjusted balance. The second section begins with the cash balance according to the depositor's records and ends with the adjusted balance. The two amounts designated as the adjusted balance must be equal. The content of the bank reconciliation is shown below.

Cash balance according to bank statement . . .		$XXX
Add: Additions by depositor not on bank statement	$XX	
Bank errors	XX	XX
		$XXX
Deduct: Deductions by depositor not on bank statement	$XX	
Bank errors	XX	XX
Adjusted balance		$XXX

Cash balance according to depositor's records		$XXX
Add: Additions by bank not recorded by depositor	$XX	
Depositor errors	XX	XX
		$XXX
Deduct: Deductions by bank not recorded by depositor	$XX	
Depositor errors	XX	XX
Adjusted balance		$XXX

must be equal

Business on Stage

The Federal Reserve System

One of the most powerful financial institutions in the United States is the *Federal Reserve System,* often referred to as the *Fed.* The Federal Reserve System consists of twelve district banks located in the following cities: Boston, New York, Philadelphia, Cleveland, Charlotte, Atlanta, St. Louis, Chicago, Minneapolis, Kansas City, Dallas, and San Francisco. The Fed's overall operations are coordinated by a seven-member Board of Governors headquartered in Washington, D.C. Four key activities of the Fed are (1) carrying out monetary policy, (2) setting rules on credit, (3) distributing currency, and (4) clearing checks.

The Fed carries out monetary policy in three ways. First, the Fed's open-market operations involve the purchase and sale of government securities. For example, when the Fed buys U.S. securities in the open market, it puts money into the economy. Second, the Fed sets the requirements for reserves that member banks must maintain on deposit. These reserves are unavailable for loans or other investments. Current reserve requirements range from 3% to 10% of a bank's deposits. Third, the Fed sets the discount rate. This rate is the interest rate that the Fed charges member banks for loans. The discount rate is often quoted in the financial press. It indirectly affects the interest rates that member banks charge customers on credit card balances, home mortgages, and other types of loans.

The Fed sets rules on credit in various ways. For example, the Fed sets minimum down payments and maximum repayment periods on consumer loans of member banks. The Fed also sets margin requirements for purchasing securities such as stocks. For example, if the margin requirement is 40%, then an investor who purchases stocks worth $20,000 must pay at least $8,000. The remaining $12,000 can be financed.

The Fed distributes to member banks the coins minted and the paper money printed by the U.S. Treasury. Almost all paper money is in the form of Federal Reserve Notes. For example, if you look at a dollar bill, you will see the words *Federal Reserve Note* above the picture of George Washington. The large letter in the seal to the left of the picture indicates which Federal Reserve Bank issued the Note.

Finally, the Fed helps banks clear checks. The Fed's check-clearing system lets banks quickly convert checks drawn on other banks into cash. ■

The following steps are useful in finding the reconciling items and determining the adjusted balance of Cash:

1. Compare each deposit listed on the bank statement with unrecorded deposits appearing in the preceding period's reconciliation and with deposit receipts or other records of deposits. *Add deposits not recorded by the bank to the balance according to the bank statement.*
2. Compare paid checks with outstanding checks appearing on the preceding period's reconciliation and with recorded checks. *Deduct checks outstanding that have not been paid by the bank from the balance according to the bank statement.*
3. Compare bank credit memorandums to entries in the journal. For example, a bank would issue a credit memorandum for a note receivable and interest that it collected for a depositor. *Add credit memorandums that have not been recorded to the balance according to the depositor's records.*
4. Compare bank debit memorandums to entries recording cash payments. For example, a bank normally issues debit memorandums for service charges and check printing charges. A bank also issues debit memorandums for not-sufficient-funds checks. A *not-sufficient-funds (NSF) check* is a customer's check that was recorded and deposited but was not paid when it was presented to the customer's bank for payment. NSF checks are normally charged back to the customer as an account receivable. *Deduct debit memorandums that have not been recorded from the balance according to the depositor's records.*
5. List any errors discovered during the preceding steps. For example, if an amount has been recorded incorrectly by the depositor, the amount of the error should be added to or deducted from the cash balance according to the depositor's records. Similarly, errors by the bank should be added to or deducted from the cash balance according to the bank statement.

To illustrate a bank reconciliation, we will use the bank statement for Monroe Company in Exhibit 4. This bank statement shows a balance of $3,359.78 as of July 31. The cash balance in Monroe Company's ledger as of the same date is $2,549.99. The following reconciling items are revealed by using the steps outlined above:

Deposit of July 31 not recorded on bank statement	$ 816.20
Checks outstanding: No. 812, $1,061.00; No. 878, $435.39; No. 883, $48.60	1,544.99
Note plus interest of $8 collected by bank (credit memorandum), not recorded in the journal	408.00
Check from customer (Thomas Ivey) returned by bank because of insufficient funds (NSF)	300.00
Bank service charges (debit memorandum) not recorded in the journal	18.00
Check No. 879 for $732.26 to Taylor Co. on account, recorded in the journal as $723.26	9.00

The bank reconciliation based on the bank statement and the reconciling items is shown in Exhibit 6.

EXHIBIT 6
Bank Reconciliation for Monroe Company

Monroe Company
Bank Reconciliation
July 31, 2000

Cash balance according to bank statement		$3,359.78	Cash balance according to depositor's records		$2,549.99
Add deposit of July 31, not recorded by bank		816.20	Add note and interest collected by bank		408.00
		$4,175.98			$2,957.99
			Deduct: Check returned because of insufficient funds	$ 300.00	
Deduct outstanding checks:					
No. 812	$1,061.00		Bank service charges	18.00	
No. 878	435.39		Error in recording		
No. 883	48.60	1,544.99	Check No. 879	9.00	327.00
Adjusted balance		$2,630.99	Adjusted balance		$2,630.99

Entries must be made in the depositor's accounts for any items that affect the business's record of cash.

No entries are necessary on the depositor's records as a result of the information included in the first section of the bank reconciliation. This section begins with the cash balance according to the bank statement. However, the bank should be notified of any errors that need to be corrected on its records.

Any items in the second section of the bank reconciliation must be recorded in the depositor's accounts. This section begins with the cash balance according to the depositor's records. For example, journal entries should be made for any unrecorded bank memorandums and any depositor's errors.

The journal entries for Monroe Company, based on the bank reconciliation above, are as follows:

1	July	31	Cash	408.00		1
2			Notes Receivable		400.00	2
3			Interest Revenue		8.00	3
4			Note collected by bank.			4
5						5
6		31	Accounts Receivable—Thomas Ivey	300.00		6
7			Miscellaneous Administrative Expense	18.00		7
8			Accounts Payable—Taylor Co.	9.00		8
9			Cash		327.00	9
10			NSF check, bank service charges, and error			10
11			in recording Check No. 879.			11

Assume that the bank recorded a deposit of $4,100 as $1,400. How would this bank error be shown on the bank reconciliation?

The error of $2,700 would be added to the cash balance according to the bank statement.

After these entries have been posted, the cash account will have a debit balance of $2,630.99. This balance agrees with the adjusted cash balance shown on the bank reconciliation. This is the amount of cash available as of July 31 and the amount that would be reported on Monroe Company's July 31 balance sheet.

Although businesses may reconcile their bank accounts in a slightly different format from what we described above, the objective is the same: to control cash by reconciling the company's records to the records of an independent outside source, the bank. In doing so, any errors or misuse of cash may be detected.

For effective control, the bank reconciliation should be prepared by an employee who does not take part in or record cash transactions. When these duties are not properly separated, mistakes are likely to occur, and it is more likely that cash will be stolen or otherwise misapplied. For example, an employee who takes part in all of these duties could prepare and cash an unauthorized check, omit it from the accounts, and omit it from the reconciliation.

Point of INTEREST

Many of you reconcile your bank account each month after you receive your bank statements. First you scan the bank statement for any bank entries that you have not yet recorded. Examples of such entries include service charges (a debit entry) and interest earned (a credit entry). You then enter these amounts in your checkbook (register) and determine the balance of your account. If you stop at this point, you are assuming that the bank hasn't made any errors. This may not be a good assumption.

If you fully reconcile your account, you should also scan your checkbook for items that the bank has not yet recorded: (1) deposits in transit and (2) outstanding checks. Deposits in transit should be added to the bank balance, and outstanding checks should be subtracted from the bank balance. The result is an adjusted bank balance which should agree with the balance of your checkbook. If the two are not equal, either you or the bank has made an error.

Petty Cash

OBJECTIVE 6

Account for small cash transactions, using a petty cash fund.

As in your own day-to-day life, it is usually not practical for a business to write checks to pay small amounts, such as postage. Yet, these small payments may occur often enough to add up to a significant total amount. Thus, it is desirable to control such payments. For this purpose, a special cash fund, called a **petty cash fund**, is used.

A petty cash fund is established by first estimating the amount of cash needed for payments from the fund during a period, such as a week or a month. After necessary approvals, a check is written and cashed for this amount. The money obtained from cashing the check is then given to an employee, called the petty cash custodian, who is authorized to disburse monies from the fund. For control purposes, the company may place restrictions on the maximum amount and the types of payments that may be made from the fund.

Each time monies are paid from petty cash, the custodian records the details of the payment on a petty cash receipt form. A typical petty cash receipt is illustrated in Exhibit 7.

REAL WORLD

Businesses often use other cash funds to meet their special needs, such as travel expenses for salespersons. For example, each salesperson might be given $1,000 for travel-related expenses. Periodically, the salesperson submits a detailed expense report and their travel funds are replenished.

EXHIBIT 7
Petty Cash Receipt

PETTY CASH RECEIPT

No. 121 **Date** August 1, 2001

Paid to Metropolitan Times **Amount** 3 00

For Daily newspaper

Charge to Miscellaneous Administrative Expense

Payment received:

S.O. Hall **Approved by** N.E.R.

The petty cash fund is normally replenished at periodic intervals or when it is depleted or reaches a minimum amount. When a petty cash fund is replenished, the accounts debited are determined by summarizing the petty cash receipts. A check is then written for this amount, payable to the petty cash custodian.

To illustrate normal petty cash fund entries, assume that a petty cash fund of $100 is established on August 1. The entry to record this transaction is as follows:

13	Aug.	1	Petty Cash	100 00		13
14			Cash		100 00	14
15			Established petty cash fund.			15

At the end of August, the petty cash receipts indicate expenditures for the following items: office supplies, $28; postage (office supplies), $22; store supplies, $35; and daily newspapers (miscellaneous administrative expense), $3. The entry to replenish the petty cash fund on August 31 is as follows:

17	Aug.	31	Office Supplies	50 00		17
18			Store Supplies	35 00		18
19			Miscellaneous Administrative Expense	3 00		19
20			Cash		88 00	20
21			Replenished petty cash fund.			21

Q&A

If the petty cash account has a balance of $200, the cash in the fund totals $20, and the petty cash receipts total $180 at the end of a period, what account is credited and what is the amount of the credit in the entry to replenish the fund?

Cash is credited for $180.

Replenishing the petty cash fund restores it to its original amount of $100. You should note that there is no entry in Petty Cash when the fund is replenished. Petty Cash is debited only when the fund is initially set up or when the amount of the fund is increased at a later time. Petty Cash is credited if it is being decreased.

Petty Cash is debited only when the fund is set up or the amount of the fund is increased.

Presentation of Cash on the Balance Sheet

OBJECTIVE 7

Summarize how cash is presented on the balance sheet.

Cash is the most liquid asset, and therefore it is listed as the first asset in the Current Assets section of the balance sheet. Most companies present only a single cash amount on the balance sheet by combining all their bank and cash fund accounts.

A company may have cash in excess of its operating needs. In such cases, the company normally invests in highly liquid investments in order to earn interest. These investments are called **cash equivalents**.[4] Examples of cash equivalents include U.S. Treasury Bills, notes issued by major corporations (referred to as commercial paper), and money market funds. Companies that have invested excess cash in cash equivalents usually report *Cash and cash equivalents* as one amount on the balance sheet.

Banks may require depositors to maintain minimum cash balances in their bank accounts. Such a balance is called a **compensating balance**. This requirement is often imposed by the bank as a part of a loan agreement or line of credit. A *line of credit* is a preapproved amount the bank is willing to lend to a customer upon request. Compensating balance requirements should be disclosed in notes to the financial statements.

REAL WORLD

The following note discloses compensating balance requirements for **Kmart Corporation**: . . . *In support of lines of credit, it is expected that compensating balances will be maintained on deposit with the banks, which will average 10% of the line to the extent that it is not in use and an additional 10% on the portion in use. . . .*

FINANCIAL ANALYSIS AND INTERPRETATION

OBJECTIVE 8

Compute and interpret the ratio of cash to current liabilities.

In an earlier chapter, we discussed the use of working capital and the current ratio in evaluating a company's ability to pay its current liabilities (short-term solvency). Both of these measures assume that the noncash current assets will be converted to cash in time to pay the current liabilities. For most companies, these measures are useful for assessing short-term solvency. However, a company that is in financial distress may have difficulty converting its receivables, inventory, and prepaid assets to cash on a timely basis. In these cases, the ratio of cash to current liabilities may be useful in assessing the ability of creditors to collect what they are owed. Because this ratio is most relevant for companies in financial distress, it is called the **doomsday ratio**.[5] Its name comes from the worst case assumption that the business ceases to exist and only the cash on hand is available to meet creditor obligations.

In computing the ratio of cash to current liabilities, cash and cash equivalents are used in the numerator, as shown below.

$$\textbf{Doomsday ratio} = \frac{\textbf{Cash and cash equivalents}}{\textbf{Current liabilities}}$$

To illustrate, assume the following data for Laettner Co. and Oakley Co. for the current year:

4 To be classified as a cash equivalent, according to *FASB Statement 95,* the investment is expected to be converted to cash within 90 days.

5 This ratio is discussed more fully in *101 Business Ratios* by Sheldon Gates, McLane Publications, Scottsdale, Arizona, 1993.

	Laettner Co.	Oakley Co.
Cash and cash equivalents	$100,000	$ 120,000
Current liabilities	400,000	1,500,000

The doomsday ratio for each company is computed as follows. In this case, Oakley Co. is more risky to creditors than is Laettner.

	Doomsday Ratio	
Laettner Co.	0.25	($100,000/$400,000)
Oakley Co.	0.08	($120,000/$1,500,000)

Because most businesses maintain cash and cash equivalents at amounts substantially less than their current liabilities, the doomsday ratio is almost always less than one. For example, the doomsday ratio for **Tandy Corporation** is 0.15. For **La-Z-Boy Chair Company**, it is 0.28.

Differences among companies will occur because of differences in management philosophy and operating styles. Nevertheless, a comparison over time that indicates a decreasing ratio generally indicates more risk for creditors.

ENCORE

The financial vice-president of **Perini Corporation** received a disturbing call from one of the company's banks. The bank reported that Perini's bank account was substantially overdrawn. Perini, a large construction company based near Boston, had never overdrawn any of its bank accounts in over twenty-five years. Shortly thereafter, another of Perini's banks called and reported that its Perini account was also overdrawn. A review of the recent bank statements, which had been lying around unreconciled for two weeks, revealed canceled checks of more than $1.1 million that had not been recorded.

Perini kept its unused checks in an unlocked room. Perini also kept its supply of coffee cups in the same room, where every clerk and secretary had access to them. A quick review revealed two missing boxes of checks.

Perini used a checkwriting machine that automatically signed the vice-president's name. Unfortunately, Perini didn't implement the controls suggested by its auditor. Instead, the machine-processed checks were placed in an unlocked box, there was no reconciliation of the counter on the machine with the number of checks that should have been written, and the keys to lock the machine were not carefully safeguarded. The vice-president said that such controls were "too much trouble."

The rest of the story involves a possible suspect who is killed in a lovers' feud involving a neurosurgeon; a bizarre arson in Perini's financial offices; a hit-and-run accident involving a boat; and a quiet, $22,000-a-year accountant who purchased a new Continental, moved to Las Vegas, bought an $85,000 house, and began running sex shows in casinos. Even though the FBI assigned one of its best agents to the case, the money was never recovered and the perpetrator of the theft remains a mystery. ■

KEY POINTS

1 Describe the nature of cash and the importance of internal control over cash.

Cash includes coins, currency (paper money), checks, money orders, and money on deposit that is available for unrestricted withdrawal from banks and other financial institutions. Because of the ease with which money can be transferred, businesses should design and use controls that safeguard cash and authorize cash transactions.

2 Summarize basic procedures for achieving internal control over cash receipts.

One of the most important controls to protect cash received in over-the-counter sales is a cash register. A remittance advice is a preventive control for cash received through the mail. Separating the duties of handling cash and recording cash is also a preventive control.

3 Summarize basic procedures for achieving internal control over cash payments, including the use of a voucher system.

A voucher system is a set of procedures for authorizing and recording liabilities and cash payments. A voucher system uses vouchers, a file for unpaid vouchers, and a file for paid vouchers.

4 Describe the nature of a bank account and its use in controlling cash.

The forms used with bank accounts are a signature card, deposit ticket, check, and record of checks drawn. Each month, the bank usually sends a bank statement to the depositor, summarizing all of the transactions for the month. The bank statement allows a business to compare the cash transactions recorded in the accounting records to those recorded by the bank.

5 Prepare a bank reconciliation and journalize any necessary entries.

The first section of the bank reconciliation begins with the cash balance according to the bank statement. This balance is adjusted for the depositor's changes in cash that do not appear on the bank statement and for any bank errors. The second section begins with the cash balance according to the depositor's records. This balance is adjusted for the bank's changes in cash that do not appear on the depositor's records and for any depositor errors. The adjusted balances for the two sections must be equal.

No entries are necessary on the depositor's records as a result of the information included in the first section of the bank reconciliation. However, the items in the second section must be journalized on the depositor's records.

6 Account for small cash transactions, using a petty cash fund.

A petty cash fund may be used by a business to make small payments that occur frequently. The money in a petty cash fund is placed in the custody of a specific employee, who authorizes payments from the fund. Periodically or when the amount of money in the fund is depleted or reduced to a minimum amount, the fund is replenished.

7 Summarize how cash is presented on the balance sheet.

Cash is listed as the first asset in the Current Assets section of the balance sheet. Companies that have invested excess cash in highly liquid investments usually report *Cash and cash equivalents* on the balance sheet.

8 Compute and interpret the ratio of cash to current liabilities.

A company that is in financial distress may have difficulty converting its receivables, inventory, and prepaid assets to cash on a timely basis. In these cases, the ratio of cash to current liabilities, called the doomsday ratio, may be useful in assessing the ability of creditors to collect what they are owed.

ILLUSTRATIVE PROBLEM

The bank statement for Urethane Company for June 30 indicates a balance of $9,143.11. All cash receipts are deposited each evening in a night depository, after banking hours. The accounting records indicate the following summary data for cash receipts and payments for June:

Cash balance as of June 1	$ 3,943.50
Total cash receipts for June	28,971.60
Total amount of checks issued in June	28,388.85

Comparing the bank statement and the accompanying canceled checks and memorandums with the records reveals the following reconciling items:

a. The bank had collected for Urethane Company $1,030 on a note left for collection. The face of the note was $1,000.
b. A deposit of $1,852.21, representing receipts of June 30, had been made too late to appear on the bank statement.
c. Checks outstanding totaled $5,265.27.
d. A check drawn for $139 had been incorrectly charged by the bank as $157.
e. A check for $30 returned with the statement had been recorded in the depositor's records as $240. The check was for the payment of an obligation to Avery Equipment Company for the purchase of office supplies on account.
f. Bank service charges for June amounted to $18.20.

Instructions

1. Prepare a bank reconciliation for June.
2. Journalize the entries that should be made by Urethane Company.

Solution

1.

Urethane Company
Bank Reconciliation
June 30, 20—

Cash balance according to bank statement		$ 9,143.11
Add: Deposit of June 30 not recorded by bank	$1,852.21	
Bank error in charging check as $157 instead of $139	18.00	1,870.21
		$11,013.32
Deduct: Outstanding checks		5,265.27
Adjusted balance		$ 5,748.05
Cash balance according to depositor's records		$ 4,526.25*
Add: Proceeds of note collected by bank, including $30 interest	$1,030.00	
Error in recording check	210.00	1,240.00
		$ 5,766.25
Deduct: Bank service charges		18.20
Adjusted balance		$ 5,748.05

*$3,943.50 + $28,971.60 − $28,388.85

2.

Cash	1,240.00	
Notes Receivable		1,000.00
Interest Revenue		30.00
Accounts Payable		210.00
Miscellaneous Administrative Expense	18.20	
Cash		18.20

SELF-EXAMINATION QUESTIONS

Answers at End of Chapter

Matching

Match each of the following statements with its proper term. Some terms may not be used.

A. bank reconciliation
B. bank statement
C. cash

____ 1. Coins, currency (paper money), checks, money orders, and money on deposit that is available for unrestricted withdrawal from banks and other financial institutions.

____ 2. A set of procedures for authorizing and recording liabilities and cash payments.

D. **cash equivalents**
E. **cash receipts journal**
F. **cash short and over**
G. **doomsday ratio**
H. **electronic funds transfer (EFT)**
I. **notes receivable**
J. **petty cash fund**
K. **voucher**
L. **voucher system**
M. **working capital ratio**

K 3. A special form for recording relevant data about a liability and the details of its payment.

H 4. A system in which computers rather than paper (money, checks, etc.) are used to effect cash transactions.

J 5. A special cash fund to pay relatively small amounts.

A 6. The analysis that details the items responsible for the difference between the cash balance reported in the bank statement and the balance of the cash account in the ledger.

D 7. Highly liquid investments that are usually reported with cash on the balance sheet.

G 8. The ratio of cash and cash equivalents to current liabilities.

If bank overcharges for check: add difference to bank statement
If bank undercharges for check: deduct difference from bank statement

Multiple Choice

1. The bank erroneously charged Tropical Services' account for $450.50 for a check that was correctly written and recorded by Tropical Services as $540.50. To reconcile the bank account of Tropical Services at the end of the month, you would:
   A. add $90 to the cash balance according to the bank statement.
   B. add $90 to the cash balance according to Tropical Services' records.
   C. deduct $90 from the cash balance according to the bank statement.
   D. deduct $90 from the cash balance according to Tropical Services' records.

2. In preparing a bank reconciliation, the amount of checks outstanding would be:
   A. added to the cash balance according to the bank statement.
   B. deducted from the cash balance according to the bank statement.
   C. added to the cash balance according to the depositor's records.
   D. deducted from the cash balance according to the depositor's records.

3. Journal entries based on the bank reconciliation are required for:
   A. additions to the cash balance according to the depositor's records.
   B. deductions from the cash balance according to the depositor's records.
   C. both A and B.
   D. neither A nor B.

4. A petty cash fund is:
   A. used to pay relatively small amounts.
   B. established by estimating the amount of cash needed for disbursements of relatively small amounts during a specified period.
   C. reimbursed when the amount of money in the fund is reduced to a predetermined minimum amount.
   D. all of the above.

5. Which of the following is the correct entry to replenish a petty cash fund?
   A. Debit Petty Cash; credit Cash
   B. Debit various expense accounts; credit Petty Cash
   C. Debit various expense accounts; credit Cash
   D. Debit Cash; credit Petty Cash

CLASS DISCUSSION QUESTIONS

1. Why is cash the asset that often warrants the most attention in the design of an effective internal control structure?
2. The combined cash count of all cash registers at the close of business is $14 less than the cash sales indicated by the cash register tapes. (a) In what account is the cash shortage recorded? (b) Are cash shortages debited or credited to this account?
3. In which section of the income statement would a credit balance in Cash Short and Over be reported?
4. Before a voucher for the purchase of merchandise is approved for payment, supporting documents should be compared to verify the accuracy of the liability. Name an example of a supporting document for the purchase of merchandise.
5. When is a voucher recorded?
6. The accounting clerk pays all obligations by prenumbered checks. What are the strengths and weaknesses in the internal control over cash payments in this situation?
7. In what order are vouchers ordinarily filed (a) in the unpaid voucher file and (b) in the paid voucher file? Give reasons for the answers.

8. The balance of Cash is likely to differ from the bank statement balance. What two factors are likely to be responsible for the difference?
9. What is the purpose of preparing a bank reconciliation?
10. Do items reported on the bank statement as credits represent (a) additions made by the bank to the depositor's balance, or (b) deductions made by the bank from the depositor's balance?
11. What entry should be made if a check received from a customer and deposited is returned by the bank for lack of sufficient funds (an NSF check)?
12. Explain why some cash payments are made in coins and currency from a petty cash fund.
13. What account or accounts are debited when (a) establishing a petty cash fund and (b) replenishing a petty cash fund?
14. The petty cash account has a debit balance of $500. At the end of the accounting period, there is $93 in the petty cash fund, along with petty cash receipts totaling $407. Should the fund be replenished as of the last day of the period? Discuss.
15. How are cash equivalents reported in the financial statements?
16. How is a compensating balance reported in the financial statements?

Warren Reeve Fess

Resources for Your Success On-Line at warren.swcollege.com

Remember! If you need additional help, visit South-Western's Web site. See page 26 for a description of the online and printed materials that are available.

EXERCISES

Exercise 7–1
Internal control of cash receipts
Objective 2

The procedures used for over-the-counter receipts are as follows. At the close of each day's business, the sales clerks count the cash in their respective cash drawers, after which they determine the amount recorded by the cash register and prepare the memorandum cash form, noting any discrepancies. An employee from the cashier's office counts the cash, compares the total with the memorandum, and takes the cash to the cashier's office.

a. Indicate the weak link in internal control.
b. How can the weakness be corrected?

Exercise 7–2
Internal control of cash receipts
Objective 2

Don Carey works at the drive-through window of Bob's Burgers. Occasionally, when a drive-through customer orders, Don fills the order and pockets the customer's money. He does not ring up the order on the cash register.

Identify the internal control weaknesses that exist at Bob's Burgers, and discuss what can be done to prevent this theft.

Exercise 7–3
Internal control of cash receipts
Objective 2

The mailroom employees send all remittances and remittance advices to the cashier. The cashier deposits the cash in the bank and forwards the remittance advices and duplicate deposit slips to the Accounting Department.

a. Indicate the weak link in internal control in the handling of cash receipts.
b. How can the weakness be corrected?

Exercise 7–4
Entry for cash sales; cash short

Objective 2

The actual cash received from cash sales was $11,940.50, and the amount indicated by the cash register total was $11,965.75. Journalize the entry to record the cash receipts and cash sales.

Exercise 7–5
Entry for cash sales; cash over

The actual cash received from cash sales was $13,189.20, and the amount indicated by the cash register total was $13,180.70. Journalize the entry to record the cash receipts and cash sales.

Exercise 7–6
Internal control of cash payments

Objective 3

Panatone Co. is a medium-size merchandising company. An investigation revealed that in spite of a sufficient bank balance, a significant amount of available cash discounts had been lost because of failure to make timely payments. In addition, it was discovered that several purchases invoices had been paid twice.

Outline procedures for the payment of vendors' invoices, so that the possibilities of losing available cash discounts and of paying an invoice a second time will be minimized.

Exercise 7–7
Internal control of cash payments

Objective 3

Comm3 Company, a communications equipment manufacturer, recently fell victim to an embezzlement scheme masterminded by one of its employees. To understand the scheme, it is necessary to review Comm3's procedures for the purchase of services.

The purchasing agent is responsible for ordering services (such as repairs to a photocopy machine or office cleaning) after receiving a service requisition from an authorized manager. However, since no tangible goods are delivered, a receiving report is not prepared. When the Accounting Department receives an invoice billing Comm3 for a service call, the accounts payable clerk calls the manager who requested the service in order to verify that it was performed.

The embezzlement scheme involves Kim Mira, the manager of plant and facilities. Kim arranged for her uncle's company, Gear Industrial Supply and Service, to be placed on Comm3's approved vendor list. Kim did not disclose the family relationship.

On several occasions, Kim would submit a requisition for services to be provided by Gear's Industrial Supply and Service. However, the service requested was really not needed, and it was never performed. Gear would bill Comm3 for the service and then split the cash payment with Kim.

Explain what changes should be made to Comm3's procedures for ordering and paying for services in order to prevent such occurrences in the future.

Exercise 7–8
Bank reconciliation

Objective 5

Identify each of the following reconciling items as: (a) an addition to the cash balance according to the bank statement, (b) a deduction from the cash balance according to the bank statement, (c) an addition to the cash balance according to the depositor's records, or (d) a deduction from the cash balance according to the depositor's records. (None of the transactions reported by bank debit and credit memorandums have been recorded by the depositor.)

1. Check for $37 charged by bank as $73.
2. Check drawn by depositor for $150 but recorded as $1,500.
3. Outstanding checks, $8,512.30.
4. Deposit in transit, $12,300.
5. Note collected by bank, $5,200.00.
6. Check of a customer returned by bank to depositor because of insufficient funds, $650.
7. Bank service charges, $30.

Exercise 7–9
Entries based on bank reconciliation

Objective 5

Which of the reconciling items listed in Exercise 7–8 require an entry in the depositor's accounts?

Exercise 7–10
Bank reconciliation
Objective 5

SPREADSHEET

✓ Adjusted balance: $12,604.70

The following data were accumulated for use in reconciling the bank account of The Skin Saver Co. for October:

a. Cash balance according to the depositor's records at October 31, $12,530.20.
b. Cash balance according to the bank statement at October 31, $11,100.50.
c. Checks outstanding, $3,276.20.
d. Deposit in transit, not recorded by bank, $4,780.40.
e. A check for $340 in payment of an account was erroneously recorded in the check register as $430.
f. Bank debit memorandum for service charges, $15.50.

Prepare a bank reconciliation, using the format shown in Exhibit 6.

Exercise 7–11
Entries for bank reconciliation
Objective 5

Using the data presented in Exercise 7–10, journalize the entry or entries that should be made by the depositor.

Exercise 7–12
Entries for note collected by bank
Objective 5

Accompanying a bank statement for Profumeria Company is a credit memorandum for $13,900, representing the principal ($13,000) and interest ($900) on a note that had been collected by the bank. The depositor had been notified by the bank at the time of the collection, but had made no entries. Journalize the entry that should be made by the depositor to bring the accounting records up to date.

Exercise 7–13
Bank reconciliation
Objective 5

✓ Adjusted balance: $13,055.15

An accounting clerk for The Zhanay Co. prepared the following bank reconciliation:

The Zhanay Co.
Bank Reconciliation
January 31, 2000

Cash balance according to depositor's records		$11,100.75
Add: Outstanding checks	$5,557.12	
Error by The Zhanay Co. in recording Check No. 345 as $2,510 instead of $2,150	360.00	
Note for $1,500 collected by bank, including interest	1,620.00	7,537.12
		$18,637.87
Deduct: Deposit in transit on January 31	$1,150.00	
Bank service charges	25.60	1,175.60
Cash balance according to bank statement		$17,462.27

a. From the data in the above bank reconciliation, prepare a new bank reconciliation for The Zhanay Co. using the format shown in the illustrative problem.
b. If a balance sheet were prepared for The Zhanay Co. on January 31, 2000, what amount should be reported for cash?

Exercise 7–14
Using bank reconciliation to determine cash receipts stolen
Objective 5

✓ a. $238.36

Monarch Co. records all cash receipts on the basis of its cash register tapes. Monarch Co. discovered during June 2000 that one of its sales clerks had stolen an undetermined amount of cash receipts when he took the daily deposits to the bank. The following data have been gathered for June:

Cash in bank according to the general ledger	$ 9,573.22
Cash according to the June 30, 2000 bank statement	12,271.14
Outstanding checks as of June 30, 2000	1,901.38
Bank service charge for June	25.10
Note receivable, including interest collected by bank in June	1,060.00

No deposits were in transit on June 30, which fell on a Sunday.

a. Determine the amount of cash receipts stolen by the sales clerk.
b. What accounting controls would have prevented or detected this theft?

Exercise 7–15
Bank reconciliation
Objective 5

What's Wrong WITH THIS?

✓ Corrected adjusted balance: $11,998.02

How many errors can you find in the following bank reconciliation prepared as of the end of the current month?

Enrico Co.
Bank Reconciliation
For the Month Ended June 30, 20—

Cash balance according to bank statement			$12,767.76
Add outstanding checks:			
No. 3721		$ 545.95	
3739		172.75	
3743		459.60	
3744		601.50	1,779.80
			$14,547.56
Deduct deposit of June 30, not recorded by bank			1,010.06
Adjusted balance			$12,537.50
Cash balance according to depositor's records			$ 9,048.72
Add: Proceeds of note collected by bank:			
Principal	$3,000.00		
Interest	150.00	$3,150.00	
Service charges		19.50	3,169.50
			$12,218.22
Deduct: Check returned because of insufficient funds		$ 451.20	
Error in recording May 15 deposit of $1,859 as $1,589		270.00	721.20
Adjusted balance			$11,497.02

Exercise 7–16
Petty cash fund entries
Objective 6

Journalize the entries to record the following:

a. Check No. 2511 is issued to establish a petty cash fund of $500.
b. The amount of cash in the petty cash fund is now $79.30. Check No. 2555 is issued to replenish the fund, based on the following summary of petty cash receipts: office supplies, $215.83; miscellaneous selling expense, $125.60; miscellaneous administrative expense, $68.10. (Since the amount of the check to replenish the fund plus the balance in the fund do not equal $500, record the discrepancy in the cash short and over account.)

Exercise 7–17
Doomsday ratio
Objective 8

REAL WORLD

HAT

The financial statements for **Hershey Foods Corporation** are presented in Appendix G at the end of the text.

a. Compute the doomsday ratio for Hershey Foods Corporation for 1996 and 1995.
b. What conclusions can be drawn from comparing the ratios for 1996 and 1995?

PROBLEMS SERIES A

Problem 7–1A
Evaluate internal control of cash
Objectives 1, 2, 3

The following procedures were recently installed by Sixto Company:

a. Each cashier is assigned a separate cash register drawer to which no other cashier has access.
b. All sales are rung up on the cash register, and a receipt is given to the customer. All sales are recorded on a tape locked inside the cash register.

c. At the end of a shift, each cashier counts the cash in his or her cash register, unlocks the tape, and compares the amount of cash with the amount on the tape to determine cash shortages and overages.
d. Checks received through the mail are given daily to the accounts receivable clerk for recording collections on account and for depositing in the bank.
e. The bank reconciliation is prepared by the accountant.
f. Disbursements are made from the petty cash fund only after a petty cash receipt has been completed and signed by the payee.
g. Vouchers and all supporting documents are perforated with a PAID designation after being paid by the treasurer.

Instructions

Indicate whether each of the procedures of internal control over cash represents (1) a strength or (2) a weakness. For each weakness, indicate why it exists.

Problem 7–2A

Transactions for petty cash, cash short and over

Objectives 2, 6

HAT

Levine Company completed the following selected transactions during April of the current year:

April 1. Established a petty cash fund of $1,000.

15. The cash sales for the day, according to the cash register tapes, totaled $9,995.60. The actual cash received from cash sales was $10,008.15.

26. Petty cash on hand was $342.15. Replenished the petty cash fund for the following disbursements, each evidenced by a petty cash receipt:

April 4. Store supplies, $210.75.
6. Express charges on merchandise purchased, $60.50 (Merchandise Inventory).
8. Office supplies, $94.30.
9. Office supplies, $35.20.
12. Postage stamps, $52.00 (Office Supplies).
16. Repair to adding machine, $39.50 (Miscellaneous Administrative Expense).
20. Repair to typewriter, $31.50 (Miscellaneous Administrative Expense).
22. Postage due on special delivery letter, $1.05 (Miscellaneous Administrative Expense).
24. Express charges on merchandise purchased, $115.60 (Merchandise Inventory).

30. The cash sales for the day, according to the cash register tapes, totaled $12,009.50. The actual cash received from cash sales was $11,998.90.

30. Decreased the petty cash fund by $250.

Instructions

Journalize the transactions.

Problem 7–3A

Bank reconciliation and entries

Objective 5

SPREADSHEET

✓ 1. Adjusted balance: $29,393.00

The cash account for Universal Systems at March 31 of the current year indicated a balance of $26,740.50. The bank statement indicated a balance of $33,391.40 on March 31. Comparing the bank statement and the accompanying canceled checks and memorandums with the records reveals the following reconciling items:

a. Checks outstanding totaled $4,943.90.
b. A deposit of $1,215.50, representing receipts of March 31, had been made too late to appear on the bank statement.
c. The bank had collected $2,600 on a note left for collection. The face of the note was $2,500.
d. A check for $675 returned with the statement had been incorrectly recorded by Universal Systems as $765. The check was for the payment of an obligation to Jones Co. for the purchase of office supplies on account.
e. A check drawn for $1,300 had been incorrectly charged by the bank as $1,030.
f. Bank service charges for March amounted to $37.50.

Instructions

1. Prepare a bank reconciliation.
2. Journalize the necessary entries. The accounts have not been closed.

Problem 7–4A

Bank reconciliation and entries

Objective 5

✓ 1. Adjusted balance: $10,131.88

The cash account for Etra Co. at June 1 of the current year indicated a balance of $5,911.95. During June, the total cash deposited was $40,500.40, and checks written totaled $38,850.47. The bank statement indicated a balance of $13,880.45 on June 30. Comparing the bank statement, the canceled checks, and the accompanying memorandums with the records revealed the following reconciling items:

a. Checks outstanding totaled $7,180.27.
b. A deposit of $3,481.70, representing receipts of June 30, had been made too late to appear on the bank statement.
c. A check for $450 had been incorrectly charged by the bank as $400.
d. A check for $136.75 returned with the statement had been recorded by Etra Co. as $316.75. The check was for the payment of an obligation to Scott and Son on account.
e. The bank had collected for Etra Co. $2,400 on a note left for collection. The face of the note was $2,000.
f. Bank service charges for June amounted to $10.

Instructions

1. Prepare a bank reconciliation as of June 30.
2. Journalize the necessary entries. The accounts have not been closed.

Problem 7–5A

Bank reconciliation and entries

Objective 5

✓ 1. Adjusted balance: $13,096.09

Elisha Interiors deposits all cash receipts each Wednesday and Friday in a night depository, after banking hours. The data required to reconcile the bank statement as of August 31 have been taken from various documents and records and are reproduced as follows. The sources of the data are printed in capital letters. All checks were written for payments on account.

CASH ACCOUNT:

Balance as of August 1	$10,578.00
CASH RECEIPTS FOR MONTH OF AUGUST	6,582.60

DUPLICATE DEPOSIT TICKETS:

Date and amount of each deposit in August:

Date	Amount	Date	Amount	Date	Amount
Aug. 2	$869.50	Aug. 12	$780.70	Aug. 23	$731.45
5	701.80	16	600.10	26	601.50
9	819.24	19	701.26	31	777.05

CHECKS WRITTEN:

Number and amount of each check issued in August:

Check No.	Amount	Check No.	Amount	Check No.	Amount
614	$243.50	621	$409.50	628	$ 737.70
615	650.10	622	Void	629	329.90
616	279.90	623	Void	630	882.80
617	395.50	624	770.01	631	1,081.56
618	535.40	625	658.63	632	62.40
619	320.10	626	550.03	633	310.08
620	238.87	627	318.73	634	203.30

Total amount of checks issued in August	$8,978.01

MEMBER FDIC

PAGE 1

AMERICAN NATIONAL BANK
OF DETROIT

DETROIT, MI 48201-2500 (313)933-8547

ELISHA INTERIORS

	ACCOUNT NUMBER	
	FROM 8/01/20–	TO 8/31/20–
	BALANCE	10,422.80
9	DEPOSITS	6,586.35
20	WITHDRAWALS	8,514.11
4	OTHER DEBITS AND CREDITS	4,850.50CR
	NEW BALANCE	13,345.54

CHECKS AND OTHER DEBITS					DEPOSITS	DATE	BALANCE
No.580	310.10	No.612	92.50		780.80	08/01	10,801.00
No.613	137.50	No.614	243.50		869.50	08/03	11,289.50
No.615	650.10	No.616	279.90		701.80	08/06	11,061.30
No.617	395.50	No.618	535.40		819.24	08/11	10,949.64
No.619	320.10	No.620	238.87		780.70	08/13	11,171.37
No.621	409.50	No.624	707.01		MS 5,000.00	08/14	15,054.86
No.625	658.63	No.626	550.03		MS 100.00	08/14	13,946.20
No.627	318.73	No.629	329.90		600.10	08/17	13,897.67
No.630	882.80	No.631	1,081.56	NSF 225.40		08/20	11,707.91
No.632	62.40	No.633	310.08		701.26	08/21	12,036.69
					731.45	08/24	12,768.14
					601.50	08/28	13,369.64
		SC	24.10			08/31	13,345.54

EC — ERROR CORRECTION
MS — MISCELLANEOUS
NSF — NOT SUFFICIENT FUNDS
OD — OVERDRAFT
PS — PAYMENT STOPPED
SC — SERVICE CHARGE

*** *** ***

THE RECONCILEMENT OF THIS STATEMENT WITH YOUR RECORDS IS ESSENTIAL.
ANY ERROR OR EXCEPTION SHOULD BE REPORTED IMMEDIATELY.

BANK RECONCILIATION FOR PRECEDING MONTH:

Elisha Interiors
Bank Reconciliation
July 31, 20—

Cash balance according to bank statement		$10,422.80
Add deposit of July 31, not recorded by bank		780.80
		$11,203.60
Deduct outstanding checks:		
No. 580	$310.10	
No. 602	85.50	
No. 612	92.50	
No. 613	137.50	625.60
Adjusted balance		$10,578.00
Cash balance according to depositor's records		$10,605.70
Deduct service charges		27.70
Adjusted balance		$10,578.00

Instructions

1. Prepare a bank reconciliation as of August 31. If errors in recording deposits or checks are discovered, assume that the errors were made by the company. Assume that all deposits are from cash sales. All checks are written to satisfy accounts payable.
2. Journalize the necessary entries. The accounts have not been closed.
3. What is the amount of Cash that should appear on the balance sheet as of August 31?
4. If in preparing the bank reconciliation you note that a canceled check for $180 has been incorrectly recorded by the bank as $810, briefly explain how the error would be included in the bank reconciliation and how it should be corrected.

PROBLEMS SERIES B

Problem 7–1B
Evaluating internal control of cash
Objectives 1, 2, 3

The following procedures were recently installed by Epic Company:

a. All mail is opened by the mail clerk, who forwards all cash remittances to the cashier. The cashier prepares a listing of the cash receipts and forwards a copy of the list to the accounts receivable clerk for recording in the accounts.
b. At the end of each day, an accounting clerk compares the duplicate copy of the daily cash deposit slip with the deposit receipt obtained from the bank.
c. The bank reconciliation is prepared by the cashier, who works under the supervision of the treasurer.
d. At the end of each day, any deposited cash receipts are placed in the bank's night depository.
e. At the end of the day, cash register clerks are required to use their own funds to make up any cash shortages in their registers.
f. The accounts payable clerk prepares a voucher for each disbursement. The voucher along with the supporting documentation is forwarded to the treasurer's office for approval.
g. After necessary approvals have been obtained for the payment of a voucher, the treasurer signs and mails the check. The treasurer then stamps the voucher and supporting documentation as paid and returns the voucher and supporting documentation to the accounts payable clerk for filing.
h. Along with petty cash expense receipts for postage, office supplies, etc., several post-dated employee checks are in the petty cash fund.

Instructions
Indicate whether each of the procedures of internal control over cash represents (1) a strength or (2) a weakness. For each weakness, indicate why it exists.

Problem 7–2B
Transactions for petty cash; cash short and over
Objectives 2, 6

Boron Company completed the following selected transactions during August of the current year:

Aug. 2. Established a petty cash fund of $600.
17. The cash sales for the day, according to the cash register tapes, totaled $3,970.60. The actual cash received from cash sales was $4,001.75.
29. Petty cash on hand was $73.80. Replenished the petty cash fund for the following disbursements, each evidenced by a petty cash receipt:
Aug. 3. Store supplies, $151.50.
5. Express charges on merchandise sold, $76 (Transportation Out).
8. Office supplies, $12.75.
11. Office supplies, $29.30.
17. Postage stamps, $52 (Office Supplies).
19. Repair to office calculator, $37.50 (Miscellaneous Administrative Expense).
22. Postage due on special delivery letter, $1.05 (Miscellaneous Administrative Expense).
23. Express charges on merchandise sold, $105 (Transportation Out).
27. Office supplies, $41.15.

Aug. 30. The cash sales for the day, according to the cash register tapes, totaled $3,055.50.
The actual cash received from cash sales was $3,049.10.
31. Increased the petty cash fund by $150.

Instructions

Journalize the transactions.

Problem 7–3B
Bank reconciliation and entries
Objective 5

SPREADSHEET

✓ 1. Adjusted balance: $27,854.30

The cash account for Astoria Carpets at November 30 of the current year indicated a balance of $25,640.30. The bank statement indicated a balance of $31,016.30 on November 30. Comparing the bank statement and the accompanying canceled checks and memorandums with the records revealed the following reconciling items:

a. Checks outstanding totaled $6,169.75.
b. A deposit of $2,917.75, representing receipts of November 30, had been made too late to appear on the bank statement.
c. The bank had collected $3,150 on a note left for collection. The face of the note was $3,000.
d. A check for $2,100 returned with the statement had been incorrectly recorded by Astoria Carpets as $1,200. The check was for the payment of an obligation to Ace Co. for the purchase of office equipment on account.
e. A check drawn for $1,780 had been erroneously charged by the bank as $1,870.
f. Bank service charges for November amounted to $36.00.

Instructions

1. Prepare a bank reconciliation.
2. Journalize the necessary entries. The accounts have not been closed.

Problem 7–4B
Bank reconciliation and entries
Objective 5

✓ 1. Adjusted balance: $15,119.87

The cash account for Ambos Co. at August 1 of the current year indicated a balance of $12,705.37. During August, the total cash deposited was $30,650.75, and checks written totaled $31,770.25. The bank statement indicated a balance of $16,465.50 on August 31. Comparing the bank statement, the canceled checks, and the accompanying memorandums with the records revealed the following reconciling items:

a. Checks outstanding totaled $8,003.84.
b. A deposit of $3,148.21, representing receipts of August 31, had been made too late to appear on the bank statement.
c. The bank had collected for Ambos Co. $3,650 on a note left for collection. The face of the note was $3,500.
d. A check for $390 returned with the statement had been incorrectly charged by the bank as $3,900.
e. A check for $210 returned with the statement had been recorded by Ambos Co. as $120. The check was for the payment of an obligation to Bartles Co. on account.
f. Bank service charges for August amounted to $26.

Instructions

1. Prepare a bank reconciliation as of August 31.
2. Journalize the necessary entries. The accounts have not been closed.

Problem 7–5B
Bank reconciliation and entries
Objective 5

✓ 1. Adjusted balance: $10,022.02

Merrick Company deposits all cash receipts each Wednesday and Friday in a night depository, after banking hours. The data required to reconcile the bank statement as of June 30 have been taken from various documents and records and are reproduced as follows. The sources of the data are printed in capital letters. All checks were written for payments on account.

CASH ACCOUNT:	
Balance as of June 1	$7,317.40
CASH RECEIPTS FOR MONTH OF JUNE	$8,151.58

DUPLICATE DEPOSIT TICKETS:

Date and amount of each deposit in June:

Date	Amount	Date	Amount	Date	Amount
June 1	$1,080.50	June 10	$ 896.61	June 22	$897.34
3	854.17	15	882.95	24	942.71
8	840.50	17	1,246.74	29	510.06

CHECKS WRITTEN:

Number and amount of each check issued in June:

Check No.	Amount	Check No.	Amount	Check No.	Amount
740	$237.50	747	Void	754	$249.75
741	495.15	748	$450.90	755	172.75
742	501.90	749	640.13	756	113.95
743	671.30	750	276.77	757	407.95
744	506.88	751	299.37	758	359.60
745	117.25	752	537.01	759	701.50
746	298.66	753	380.95	760	486.39

Total amount of checks issued in June $7,905.66

JUNE BANK STATEMENT:

MEMBER FDIC

PAGE 1

AMERICAN NATIONAL BANK OF DETROIT

DETROIT, MI 48201-2500 (313)933-8547

MERRICK COMPANY

	ACCOUNT NUMBER	
	FROM 6/01/20–	TO 6/30/20–
	BALANCE	7,447.20
9	DEPOSITS	8,691.77
20	WITHDRAWALS	7,345.91
4	OTHER DEBITS AND CREDITS	2,298.70CR
	NEW BALANCE	11,091.76

CHECKS AND OTHER DEBITS				DEPOSITS	DATE	BALANCE
No.731	162.15	No.738	251.40	690.25	06/01	7,723.90
No.739	60.55	No.740	237.50	1,080.50	06/02	8,506.35
No.741	495.15	No.742	501.90	854.17	06/04	8,363.47
No.743	671.30	No.744	506.88	840.50	06/09	8,025.79
No.745	117.25	No.746	298.66	MS 2,500.00	06/09	10,109.88
No.748	450.90	No.749	640.13	MS 125.00	06/09	9,143.85
No.750	276.77	No.751	299.37	896.61	06/11	9,464.32
No.752	537.01	No.753	380.95	882.95	06/16	9,429.31
No.754	449.75	No.756	113.95	1,606.74	06/18	10,472.35
No.757	407.95	No.760	486.39	897.34	06/23	10,475.35
				942.71	06/25	11,418.06
		NSF	291.90		06/28	11,126.16
		SC	34.40		06/30	11,091.76

EC — ERROR CORRECTION
MS — MISCELLANEOUS
NSF — NOT SUFFICIENT FUNDS
OD — OVERDRAFT
PS — PAYMENT STOPPED
SC — SERVICE CHARGE

* * * * * * * * *

THE RECONCILEMENT OF THIS STATEMENT WITH YOUR RECORDS IS ESSENTIAL.
ANY ERROR OR EXCEPTION SHOULD BE REPORTED IMMEDIATELY.

BANK RECONCILIATION FOR PRECEDING MONTH:

Merrick Company
Bank Reconciliation
May 31, 20—

Cash balance according to bank statement		$7,447.20
Add deposit for May 31, not recorded by bank		690.25
		$8,137.45
Deduct outstanding checks:		
No. 731	$162.15	
736	345.95	
738	251.40	
739	60.55	820.05
Adjusted balance		$7,317.40
Cash balance according to depositor's records		$7,352.50
Deduct service charges		35.10
Adjusted balance		$7,317.40

Instructions

1. Prepare a bank reconciliation as of June 30. If errors in recording deposits or checks are discovered, assume that the errors were made by the company. Assume that all deposits are from cash sales. All checks are written to satisfy accounts payable.
2. Journalize the necessary entries. The accounts have not been closed.
3. What is the amount of Cash that should appear on the balance sheet as of June 30?
4. If in preparing the bank reconciliation you note that a canceled check for $350 has been incorrectly recorded by the bank as $530, briefly explain how the error would be included in the bank reconciliation and how it should be corrected.

SPECIAL ACTIVITIES

Activity 7–1 The Beeper Co.
Ethics and professional conduct in business

During the preparation of the bank reconciliation for The Beeper Co., Bob Beck, the assistant controller, discovered that State National Bank incorrectly recorded a $1,350 check written by The Beeper Co. as $350. Bob has decided not to notify the bank, but to wait for the bank to detect the error. Bob plans to record the $1,000 error as Other Income if the bank fails to detect the error within the next three months.

Discuss whether Bob is behaving in a professional manner.

Activity 7–2 Up Down Electronics
Internal controls

The following is an excerpt from a conversation between two sales clerks, Carol Chern and Will Williams. Both Carol and Will are employed by Up Down Electronics, a locally owned and operated computer retail store.

Carol: Did you hear the news?
Will: What news?
Carol: Agatha and Bailey were both arrested this morning.
Will: What? Arrested? You're putting me on!
Carol: No, really! The police arrested them first thing this morning. Put them in handcuffs, read them their rights—the whole works. It was unreal!
Will: What did they do?
Carol: Well, apparently they were filling out merchandise refund forms for fictitious customers and then taking the cash.
Will: I guess I never thought of that. How did they catch them?
Carol: The store manager noticed that returns were twice that of last year and seemed to be increasing. When he confronted Agatha, she became flustered and admitted

to taking the cash, apparently over $4,000 in just three months. They're going over the last six months' transactions to try to determine how much Bailey stole. He apparently started stealing first.

Suggest appropriate control procedures that would have prevented or detected the theft of cash.

Activity 7–3
Healthy Grocery Stores
Internal controls

The following is an excerpt from a conversation between the store manager of Healthy Grocery Stores, Kim Hsu, and Myles Jacobson, president of Healthy Grocery Stores.

Myles: Kim, I'm concerned about this new scanning system.
Kim: What's the problem?
Myles: Well, how do we know the clerks are ringing up all the merchandise?
Kim: That's one of the strong points about the system. The scanner automatically rings up each item, based on its bar code. We update the prices daily, so we're sure that the sale is rung up for the right price.
Myles: That's not my concern. What keeps a clerk from pretending to scan items and then simply not charging his friends? If his friends were buying 10–15 items, it would be easy for the clerk to pass through several items with his finger over the bar code or just pass the merchandise through the scanner with the wrong side showing. It would look normal for anyone observing. In the old days, we at least could hear the cash register ringing up each sale.
Kim: I see your point.

Suggest ways that Healthy Grocery Stores could prevent or detect the theft of merchandise as described.

Activity 7–4
Two by Four Markets
Ethics and professional conduct in business

Leo Peltz and Deborah Ferris are both cash register clerks for Two by Four Markets. Jo Calloway is the store manager for Two by Four Markets. The following is an excerpt of a conversation between Leo and Deborah:

Leo: Debbie, how long have you been working for Two by Four Markets?
Deborah: Almost five years this October. You just started two weeks ago . . . right?
Leo: Yes. Do you mind if I ask you a question?
Deborah: No, go ahead.
Leo: What I want to know is, have they always had this rule that if your cash register is short at the end of the day you have to make up the shortage out of your own pocket?
Deborah: Yes, as long as I've been working here.
Leo: Well, it's the pits. Last week I had to pay in almost $30.
Deborah: It's not that big a deal. I just make sure that I'm not short at the end of the day.
Leo: How do you do that?
Deborah: I just short-change a few customers early in the day. There are a few jerks that deserve it anyway. Most of the time, their attention is elsewhere and they don't think to check their change.
Leo: What happens if you're over at the end of the day?
Deborah: Jo lets me keep it as long as it doesn't get to be too large. I've not been short in over a year. I usually clear about $10 to $20 extra per day.

Discuss this case from the viewpoint of proper controls and professional behavior.

Activity 7–5
Tofel Company
Bank reconciliation and internal control

The records of Tofel Company indicate an August 31 cash balance of $20,806.05, which includes undeposited receipts for August 30 and 31. The cash balance on the bank statement as of August 31 is $18,004.95. This balance includes a note of $3,000 plus $150 interest collected by the bank but not recorded in the journal. Checks outstanding on August 31 were as follows: No. 470, $1,050.20; No. 479, $510; No. 490, $616.50; No. 796, $127.40; No. 797, $520; and No. 799, $851.50.

On August 3, the cashier resigned, effective at the end of the month. Before leaving on August 31, the cashier prepared the following bank reconciliation:

Cash balance per books, August 31		$20,806.05
Add outstanding checks:		
No. 796	$127.40	
797	520.00	
799	851.50	1,198.90
		$22,004.95
Less undeposited receipts		4,000.00
Cash balance per bank, August 31		$18,004.95
Deduct unrecorded note with interest . .		3,150.00
True cash, August 31		$14,854.95

Calculator Tape of Outstanding Checks:

0.00 *
127.40 +
520.00 +
851.50 +
1,198.90 *

Subsequently, the owner of Tofel Company discovered that the cashier had stolen all undeposited receipts in excess of the $4,000 on hand on August 31. The owner, a close family friend, has asked your help in determining the amount that the former cashier has stolen.

1. Determine the amount the cashier stole from Tofel Company. Show your computations in good form.
2. How did the cashier attempt to conceal the theft?
3. a. Identify two major weaknesses in internal controls, which allowed the cashier to steal the undeposited cash receipts.
   b. Recommend improvements in internal controls, so that similar types of thefts of undeposited cash receipts can be prevented.

Activity 7–6
Into the Real World
Observe internal controls over cash

GROUP ACTIVITY

Select a business in your community and observe its internal controls over cash receipts and cash payments. The business could be a bank or a bookstore, restaurant, department store, or other retailer. In groups of three or four, identify and discuss the similarities and differences in each business's cash internal controls.

Activity 7–7
Into the Real World
Invest excess cash

Internet ACTIVITY

You have $10,000 cash. Go to the Web site of (or visit) a local bank and collect information about the savings and checking options that are available. Identify the option that is best for you and why it is best.

ANSWERS TO SELF-EXAMINATION QUESTIONS

Matching

1. C 2. L 3. K 4. H 5. J 6. A 7. D 8. G

Multiple Choice

1. **C** The error was made by the bank, so the cash balance according to the bank statement needs to be adjusted. Since the bank deducted $90 ($540.50 − $450.50) too little, the error of $90 should be deducted from the cash balance according to the bank statement (answer C).
2. **B** On any specific date, the cash account in a depositor's ledger may not agree with the account in the bank's ledger because of delays and/or errors by either party in recording transactions. The purpose of a bank reconciliation, therefore, is to determine the reasons for any differences between the two account balances. All errors should then be corrected by the depositor or the bank, as appropriate. In arriving at the adjusted (correct) cash balance according to the bank statement, outstanding checks must be deducted (answer B) to adjust for checks that have been written by the depositor but that have not yet been presented to the bank for payment.
3. **C** All reconciling items that are added to and deducted from the cash balance according to the depositor's records on the bank reconciliation (answer C) require that journal entries be made by the depositor to correct errors made in recording transactions or to bring the cash account up to date for delays in recording transactions.
4. **D** To avoid the delay, annoyance, and expense that is associated with paying all obligations by check, relatively small amounts (answer A) are paid from a petty cash fund. The fund is established by estimating the amount of cash needed to pay these small amounts during a specified period (answer B), and it is then reimbursed when the amount of money in the fund is reduced to a predetermined minimum amount (answer C).
5. **C** The journal entry to replenish the petty cash account debits the various expense accounts for which funds were disbursed and credits Cash (answer C). A petty cash account is established or increased by debiting Petty Cash and crediting Cash (answer A). A petty cash account is decreased or done away with by debiting Cash and crediting Petty Cash (answer D). Entry B is not a normal entry involving petty cash.

8

Receivables

Setting the STAGE

Assume that you have decided to sell your car to a neighbor for $7,500. Your neighbor agrees to pay you $1,500 immediately and the remaining $6,000 in a year. How much should you charge your neighbor for interest?

You could determine an appropriate interest rate by asking some financial institutions what they currently charge their customers. Using this information as a starting point, you could then negotiate with your neighbor and agree upon a rate. Assuming that the agreed-upon rate is 8%, you will receive interest totaling $480 for the one-year loan.

In this chapter, we will describe and illustrate how interest is computed. In addition, we will discuss the accounting for receivables, including uncollectible receivables. Most of these receivables result from a business rendering services or selling merchandise on account.

objectives

After studying this chapter, you should be able to:

1. List the common classifications of receivables.
2. Summarize and provide examples of internal control procedures that apply to receivables.
3. Describe the nature of and the accounting for uncollectible receivables.
4. Journalize the entries for the allowance method of accounting for uncollectibles, and estimate uncollectible receivables based on sales and on an analysis of receivables.
5. Journalize the entries for the direct write-off of uncollectible receivables.
6. Describe the nature and characteristics of promissory notes.
7. Journalize the entries for notes receivable transactions.
8. Prepare the Current Assets presentation of receivables on the balance sheet.
9. Compute and interpret the accounts receivable turnover and the number of days' sales in receivables.

Classification of Receivables

OBJECTIVE 1

List the common classifications of receivables.

Many companies sell on credit in order to sell more services or products. The receivables that result from such sales are normally classified as accounts receivable or notes receivable. The term **receivables** includes all money claims against other entities, including people, business firms, and other organizations. These receivables are usually a significant portion of the total current assets.

REAL WORLD

The 1996 annual report of **La-Z-Boy Chair Company** reported that receivables made up over 60% of La-Z-Boy's current assets.

Accounts Receivable

The most common transaction creating a receivable is selling merchandise or services on credit. The receivable is recorded as a debit to the accounts receivable account. Such **accounts receivable** are normally expected to be collected within a relatively short period, such as 30 or 60 days. They are classified on the balance sheet as a current asset.

Notes Receivable

As long as notes receivable are expected to be collected within a year, they are normally classified on the balance sheet as a current asset. **Notes receivable** are amounts that customers owe, for which a formal, written instrument of credit has been issued.

Notes are often used for credit periods of more than sixty days. For example, a dealer in automobiles or furniture may require a down payment at the time of sale and accept a note or a series of notes for the remainder. Such arrangements usually provide for monthly payments.

Notes may be used to settle a customer's account receivable. Notes and accounts receivable that result from sales transactions are sometimes called **trade receivables**. Unless we indicate otherwise, we will assume that all notes and accounts receivable in this chapter are from sales transactions.

Point of INTEREST

If you have purchased an automobile on credit, you probably signed a note. From your viewpoint, the note is a note payable. From the creditor's viewpoint, the note is a note receivable.

Other Receivables

Other receivables are normally listed separately on the balance sheet. If they are expected to be collected within one year, they are classified as a current asset. If collection is expected beyond one year, they are classified as a noncurrent asset and reported under the caption *Investments.* **Other receivables** include interest receivable, taxes receivable, and receivables from officers or employees.

OBJECTIVE 2

Summarize and provide examples of internal control procedures that apply to receivables.

Internal Control of Receivables

The principles of internal control that we discussed in prior chapters can be used to establish controls to safeguard receivables. For example, the four functions of credit approval, sales, accounting, and collections should be separated, as shown in Exhibit 1.

EXHIBIT 1
Separating the Receivable Functions

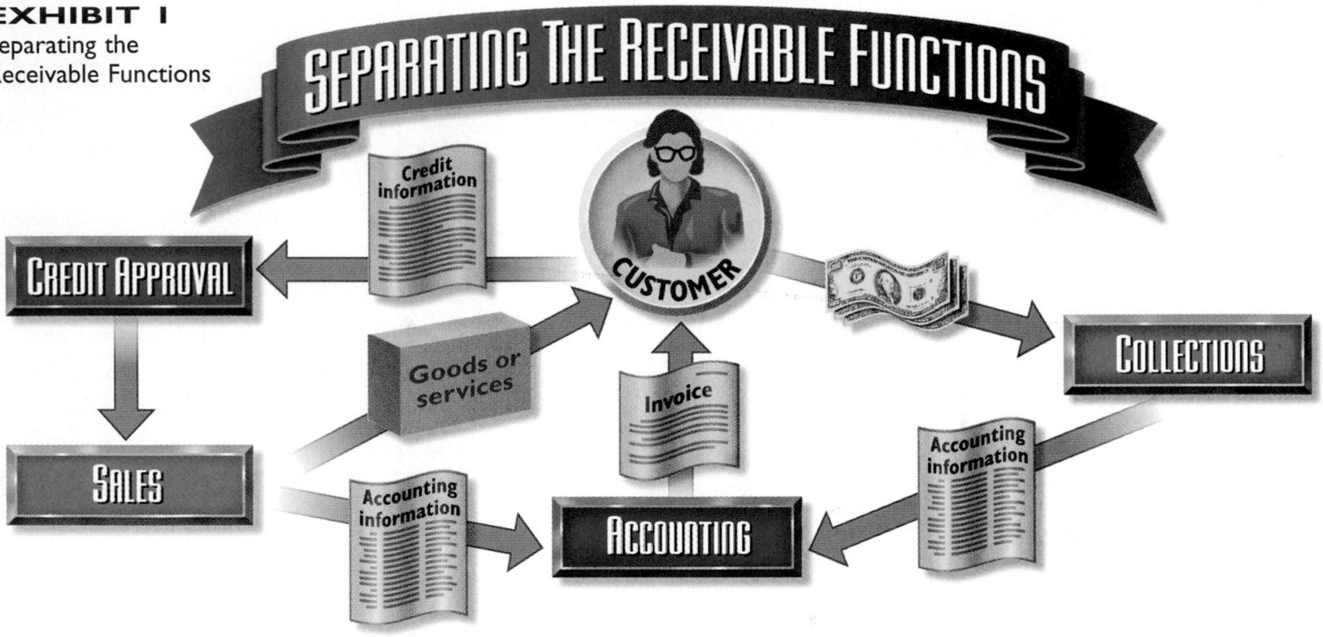

The individuals responsible for sales should be separate from the individuals accounting for the receivables and approving credit. By doing so, the accounting and credit approval functions serve as independent checks on sales. The employee who handles the accounting for receivables should not be involved with collecting receivables. Separating these functions reduces the possibility of errors and misuse of funds.

To illustrate the need to separate functions, assume that the accounts receivable billing clerk has access to cash receipts from customer collections. The clerk can steal a customer's cash payment and then alter the customer's monthly statement to indicate that the payment was received. The customer would not complain and the theft could go undetected.

To further illustrate the need for internal control of receivables, assume that salespersons have authority to approve credit. If the salespersons are paid commissions, say 10% of sales, they can increase their commissions by approving poor credit risks. Thus, the credit approval function is normally assigned to individuals outside the sales area.

BUSINESS ON STAGE

Credit standards are used by businesses to decide which customers should receive credit and how much credit they should receive. Setting credit standards requires businesses to assess the customer's "creditworthiness" or credit "quality." Traditionally, assessing creditworthiness involves considering the five Cs of credit. Each of these five Cs is briefly described below.

1. *Character* refers to the probability that the customer will honor an obligation. Many credit managers insist that this is the most important of the Cs. It reflects on the honesty of the customer and the customer's feeling of moral responsibility to honor debts. Credit managers often seek information on a customer's character by making inquiries within the business community. Such inquiries may be made with local bankers, attorneys, other creditors, and even competitors.
2. *Capacity* refers to a customer's ability to pay. Credit managers assess this factor by reviewing the customer's past payment history, a general knowledge of the customer's business, and perhaps even a physical observation of the customer's operations.
3. *Capital* refers to the general condition of the customer's business as assessed from the financial statements. Credit managers usually place special emphasis on solvency and liquidity measures and ratios such as working capital and the current ratio.
4. *Collateral* refers to assets that the customer may be willing to pledge as security for the credit. Financial institutions usually require collateral for major loans to businesses. The collateral may take the form of any asset, such as land, buildings, or inventory.
5. *Conditions* refers to the national and regional economic trends that may affect a customer's ability to pay. For example, during economic downturns credit managers usually tighten credit standards, with the anticipation that more customers will not be able to pay. ■

Uncollectible Receivables

OBJECTIVE 3

Describe the nature of and the accounting for uncollectible receivables.

In prior chapters, we described and illustrated the accounting for transactions involving sales of merchandise or services on credit. A major issue that we have not yet discussed is uncollectible receivables from these transactions.

Businesses attempt to limit the number and amount of uncollectible receivables by using various controls. The primary controls in this area involve the credit-granting function. These controls normally involve investigating customer creditworthiness, using references and background checks. For example, most of us have completed credit application forms requiring such information. Companies may also impose credit limits on new customers. For example, you may have been limited to a maximum of $500 or $1,000 when your credit card was first issued to you.

REAL WORLD: **In addition to their own credit departments, many businesses use external credit agencies, such as Dun and Bradstreet, to evaluate credit customers.**

Once a receivable is past due, companies should use procedures to maximize the collection of an account. After repeated attempts at collection, such procedures may include turning an account over to a collection agency.

Retail businesses often attempt to shift the risk of uncollectible receivables to other companies. For example, some retailers do not accept sales on account, but will only accept cash or credit cards. Such policies effectively shift the risk to the credit card companies. Other retailers, such as **Macy's**, **Sears**, and **J.C. Penney's**, have issued their own credit cards.

Companies often sell their receivables to other companies. This transaction is called **factoring** the receivables, and the buyer of the receivables is called a **factor**. An advantage of factoring is that the company selling its receivables receives immediate cash for operating and other needs. In addition, depending upon the factoring agreement, some of the risk of uncollectible accounts may be shifted to the factor.[1]

[1] The accounting for the factoring of accounts receivable is discussed in advanced accounting texts.

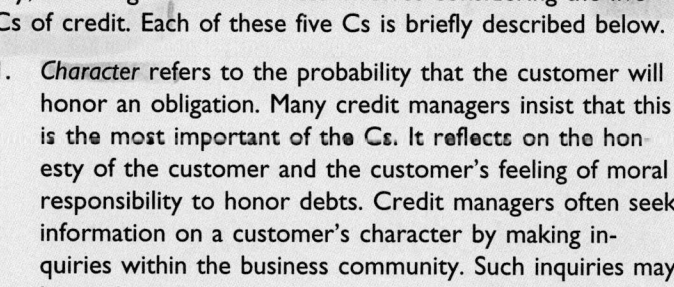

Regardless of the care used in granting credit and the collection procedures used, a part of the credit sales will not be collectible. The operating expense incurred because of the failure to collect receivables is called **uncollectible accounts expense**, **bad debts expense**, or **doubtful accounts expense**.[2]

When does an account or a note become uncollectible? There is no general rule for determining when an account becomes uncollectible. The fact that a debtor fails to pay an account according to a sales contract or fails to pay a note on the due date does not necessarily mean that the account will be uncollectible. The debtor's bankruptcy is one of the most significant indications of partial or complete uncollectibility. Other indications include the closing of the customer's business and the failure of repeated attempts to collect.

There are two methods of accounting for receivables that appear to be uncollectible. The **allowance method** provides an expense for uncollectible receivables in advance of their write-off.[3] The other procedure, called the **direct write-off method**, recognizes the expense only when accounts are judged to be worthless. We will discuss each of these methods next.

Allowance Method of Accounting for Uncollectibles

OBJECTIVE 4

Journalize the entries for the allowance method of accounting for uncollectibles, and estimate uncollectible receivables based on sales and on an analysis of receivables.

Most large businesses use the allowance method to estimate the uncollectible portion of their trade receivables. To illustrate this method, we will use assumed data for Richards Company. This new business began in August and chose to use the calendar year as its fiscal year. The accounts receivable account has a balance of $105,000 at the end of December.

The customer accounts making up the $105,000 balance in Accounts Receivable include some that are past due. However, Richards doesn't know which specific accounts will be uncollectible at this time. It is likely that some accounts will be collected only in part and that others will become worthless. Based on a careful study, Richards estimates that a total of $4,000 will eventually be uncollectible. The following adjusting entry at the end of the fiscal period records this estimate:

		Adjusting Entry			
Dec.	31	Uncollectible Accounts Expense		4 000 00	
		Allowance for Doubtful Accounts			4 000 00

The adjusting entry reduces receivables to their net realizable value and matches the uncollectible expense with revenues.

Because the $4,000 reduction in accounts receivable is an estimate, it cannot be credited to specific customer accounts or to the accounts receivable controlling account. Instead, a **contra asset** account entitled *Allowance for Doubtful Accounts* is credited.

As with all periodic adjustments, the entry above serves two purposes. First, it reduces the value of the receivables to the amount of cash expected to be realized in the future. This amount, which is $101,000 ($105,000 − $4,000), is called the **net realizable value** of the receivables. Second, the adjusting entry matches the $4,000 expense of uncollectible accounts with the related revenues of the period.

[2] If both notes and accounts are involved, both may be included in the expense account title, as in Uncollectible Notes and Accounts Expense, or Uncollectible Receivables Expense.

[3] The allowance method is not acceptable for determining the federal income tax of most taxpayers.

If the balance of accounts receivable is $380,000 and the balance of the allowance for doubtful accounts is $56,000, what is the net realizable value of the receivables?

$324,000 ($380,000 − $56,000)

After the adjusting entry has been posted, as shown in the following T accounts, Accounts Receivable still has a debit balance of $105,000. This balance is the amount of the total claims against customers on account. The credit balance of $4,000 in Allowance for Doubtful Accounts is the amount to be deducted from Accounts Receivable to determine the net realizable value. The balance of the Uncollectible Accounts Expense is reported in the current period income statement, normally as an administrative expense. This classification is used because the credit-granting and collection duties are the responsibilities of departments within the administrative area.

Accounts Receivable

Aug. 31	20,000	Sept. 30	15,000
Sept. 30	25,000	Oct. 31	25,000
Oct. 31	40,000	Nov. 30	23,000
Nov. 30	38,000	Dec. 31	30,000
Dec. 31	75,000		*93,000*
Bal. 105,000	*198,000*		

Allowance for Doubtful Accounts

		Dec. 31 Adj.	4,000

Uncollectible Accounts Expense

Dec. 31 Adj.	4,000		

Write-Offs to the Allowance Account

When a customer's account is identified as uncollectible, it is written off against the allowance account as follows:

Jan.	21	Allowance for Doubtful Accounts		610 00	
		Accounts Receivable—John Parker			610 00
		To write off the uncollectible			
		account.			

The authorization to support this entry should come from a designated manager. It should normally be in writing.

The total amount written off against the allowance account during a period will rarely be equal to the amount in the account at the beginning of the period. The allowance account will have a credit balance at the end of the period if the write-offs during the period are less than the beginning balance. It will have a debit balance if the write-offs exceed the beginning balance. However, after the year-end adjusting entry is recorded, the allowance account should have a credit balance. The flow into and out of the allowance account can be shown as in the illustration at the left.

An account receivable that has been written off against the allowance account may later be collected. In such cases, the account should be reinstated by an entry that reverses the write-off entry. The cash received in payment should then be recorded as a receipt on account. For example, assume that the account of $610 written off in the preceding entry is later collected on June 10. The entry to reinstate the account and the entry to record its collection are as follows:

June	10	Accounts Receivable—John Parker	610 00	
		Allowance for Doubtful Accounts		610 00
		To reinstate account written off earlier in the year.		
	10	Cash	610 00	
		Accounts Receivable—John Parker		610 00
		To record collection on account.		

The percentage of uncollectible accounts will vary across companies and industries. For example, in their annual reports, **J.C. Penney** reported 2.1% of its receivables as uncollectible, **Deere & Company** (manufacturer of John Deere tractors, etc.) reported only 1.2% of its dealer receivables as uncollectible, and **Columbia Healthcare Corporation** reported 31.6% of its receivables as uncollectible.

The two preceding entries can be combined. However, recording two separate entries in the customer's account, with proper notation of the write-off and reinstatement, provides useful credit information.

Estimating Uncollectibles

How is the amount of uncollectible accounts estimated? The estimate of uncollectibles at the end of a fiscal period is based on past experience and forecasts of the future. When the general economy is doing well, the amount of uncollectible expense is normally less than it would be when the economy is doing poorly. The estimate of uncollectibles is usually based on either (1) the amount of sales, as shown on the income statement for the period, or (2) the amount of the receivables, as shown on the balance sheet at the end of the period, and the age of the receivable accounts.

Estimate Based on Sales

The estimate based on sales is *added* to any balance in Allowance for Doubtful Accounts.

Accounts receivable are created by credit sales. The amount of credit sales during the period may therefore be used to estimate the amount of uncollectible accounts expense. The amount of this estimate is added to whatever balance exists in Allowance for Doubtful Accounts. For example, assume that the allowance account has a credit balance of $700 before adjustment. It is estimated from past experience that 1% of credit sales will be uncollectible. If credit sales for the period are $300,000, the adjusting entry for uncollectible accounts at the end of the period is as follows:

		Adjusting Entry		
Dec.	31	Uncollectible Accounts Expense	3 000 00	
		Allowance for Doubtful Accounts		3 000 00

Before the year-end adjustment, Allowance for Doubtful Accounts has a credit balance of $45,000. Uncollectible accounts are estimated as 2% of credit sales of $1,200,000. The accounts receivable balance before adjustment is $290,000. What are (1) the uncollectible expense for the period, (2) the balance of Allowance for Doubtful Accounts after adjustment, and (3) the net realizable value of the receivables after adjustment?

(1) $24,000 (2% × $1,200,000); (2) $69,000 ($24,000 + $45,000); and (3) $221,000 ($290,000 − $69,000)

After the adjusting entry has been posted, the balance of the allowance account is $3,700. If there had been a debit balance of $200 in the allowance account before the year-end adjustment, the amount of the adjustment would still have been $3,000. The balance in the allowance account would have been $2,800 ($3,000 − $200).

The estimate-based-on-sales method *emphasizes the matching of uncollectible accounts expense with the related sales of the period.* Thus, this method places more emphasis on the income statement than on the balance sheet.

Estimate Based on Analysis of Receivables

The longer an account receivable remains outstanding, the less likely that it will be collected. Thus, we can base the estimate of uncollectible accounts on how long the accounts have been outstanding. For this purpose, we can use a process called **aging the receivables**.

The *Annual Collectibility Survey* conducted by the Commercial Collection Agency Section of the Commercial Law League of America reported the following collection rates:

Source: Boardroom Reports, May 1994, p. 12.

The beginning point for determining the age of a receivable is its due date. Exhibit 2 shows an example of a typical aging of accounts receivable.

The estimate based on receivables is compared to the balance in the allowance account to determine the amount of the adjusting entry.

The aging schedule is completed by adding the columns to determine the total amount of receivables in each age group. A sliding scale of percentages, based on industry or company experience, is used to estimate the amount of uncollectibles in each group, as shown in Exhibit 3.

Based on Exhibit 3, the desired balance for the Allowance for Doubtful Accounts is estimated as $3,390. Comparing this estimate with the unadjusted balance of the allowance account determines the amount of the adjusting entry for uncollectible accounts expense. For example, assume that the unadjusted balance

EXHIBIT 2
Aging of Accounts Receivable

			Days Past Due					
Customer	Balance	Not Past Due	1–30	31–60	61–90	91–180	181–365	over 365
Ashby & Co.	$ 150			$ 150				
B.T. Barr	610					$ 350	$260	
Brock Co.	470	$ 470						
J. Zimmer Co.	160							160
Total	$86,300	$75,000	$4,000	$3,100	$1,900	$1,200	$800	$300

EXHIBIT 3
Estimate of Uncollectible Accounts

		Estimated Uncollectible Accounts	
Age Interval	Balance	Percent	Amount
Not past due	$75,000	2%	$1,500
1–30 days past due	4,000	5	200
31–60 days past due	3,100	10	310
61–90 days past due	1,900	20	380
91–180 days past due	1,200	30	360
181–365 days past due	800	50	400
Over 365 days past due	300	80	240
Total	$86,300		$3,390

of the allowance account is a credit balance of $510. The amount to be added to this balance is therefore $2,880 ($3,390 − $510). The adjusting entry is as follows:

		Adjusting Entry		
Dec.	31	Uncollectible Accounts Expense	2 8 8 0 00	
		Allowance for Doubtful Accounts		2 8 8 0 00

After the adjusting entry has been posted, the credit balance in the allowance account is $3,390, the desired amount. The net realizable value of the receivables is $82,910 ($86,300 − $3,390). If the unadjusted balance of the allowance account had been a debit balance of $300, the amount of the adjustment would have been $3,690 ($3,390 + $300).

Estimates of the uncollectible accounts expense based on the analysis of receivables *emphasizes the current net realizable value of the receivables.* Thus, this method places more emphasis on the balance sheet than on the income statement.

Q&A

Before the year-end adjustment, Allowance for Doubtful Accounts has a debit balance of $3,000. Using the aging of receivables method, the desired balance of the allowance for doubtful accounts is estimated as $55,000. The accounts receivable balance before adjustment is $290,000. What are (1) the uncollectible expense for the period, (2) the balance of Allowance for Doubtful Accounts after adjustment, and (3) the net realizable value of the receivables after adjustment?

(1) $58,000 ($3,000 + $55,000); (2) $55,000; and (3) $235,000 ($290,000 − $55,000)

Direct Write-Off Method of Accounting for Uncollectibles

OBJECTIVE 5

Journalize the entries for the direct write-off of uncollectible receivables.

The allowance method emphasizes reporting uncollectible accounts expense in the period in which the related sales occur. This emphasis on matching expenses with related revenue is the preferred method of accounting for uncollectible receivables.

There are situations, however, where it is impossible to estimate, with reasonable accuracy, the uncollectibles at the end of the period. Also, if a business sells most of its goods or services on a cash basis, the amount of its expense from uncollectible accounts is usually small. In such cases, the amount of receivables is also likely to represent a small part of the current assets. Examples of such a business are a physician's office, an attorney's office, and a small retail store such as a hardware store. In such cases, the direct write-off method of recording uncollectible expense may be used.

Under the direct write-off method, uncollectible accounts expense is not recorded until an account has been determined to be worthless. Thus, an allowance account and an adjusting entry are not needed at the end of the period. The entry to write off an account that has been determined to be uncollectible is as follows:

May	10	Uncollectible Accounts Expense	4 2 0 00	
		Accounts Receivable—D. L. Ross		4 2 0 00
		To write off uncollectible account.		

What if a customer later pays on an account that has been written off? If this happens, the account should be reinstated. The account is reinstated by reversing the earlier write-off entry. For example, assume that the account written off in the May 10 entry is collected in November of the same fiscal year.[4] The entry to reinstate the account is as follows:

Nov.	21	Accounts Receivable—D. L. Ross		420 00	
		Uncollectible Accounts Expense			420 00
		To reinstate account written off			
		earlier in the year.			

Cash received in payment of the reinstated amount is recorded in the usual manner. That is, Cash is debited and Accounts Receivable is credited for $420.

Characteristics of Notes Receivable

OBJECTIVE 6

Describe the nature and characteristics of promissory notes.

A claim supported by a note has some advantages over a claim in the form of an account receivable. By signing a note, the debtor recognizes the debt and agrees to pay it according to the terms listed. A note is therefore a stronger legal claim if there is a court action.

A **promissory note** is a written promise to pay a sum of money on demand or at a definite time. It is payable to the order of a person or firm or to the bearer or holder of the note. It is signed by the person or firm that makes the promise. The one to whose order the note is payable is called the **payee**, and the one making the promise is called the **maker**. In the example in Exhibit 4, Pearland Company is the payee and Selig Company is the maker.

EXHIBIT 4
Promissory Note

$ 2,500.00 Fresno, California March 16 20 00

Ninety days **AFTER DATE** We **PROMISE TO PAY TO**

THE ORDER OF Pearland Company

Two thousand five hundred 00/100 -------------------- **DOLLARS**

PAYABLE AT First National Bank

VALUE RECEIVED WITH INTEREST AT 10%

NO. 14 **DUE** June 14, 2000 H. B. Lane

TREASURER, *SELIG COMPANY*

Notes have several characteristics that affect how they are recorded and reported in the financial statements. We describe these characteristics next.

[4] As a practical matter, the entries to record the collection on an account previously written off are the same, regardless of whether the collection occurs in the current period or in a later fiscal period.

Due Date

The date a note is to be paid is called the **due date** or **maturity date**. The period of time between the issuance date and the due date of a short-term note may be stated in either days or months. When the term of a note is stated in days, the due date is the specified number of days after its issuance. To illustrate, the due date of the 90-day note in Exhibit 4 is determined as follows:

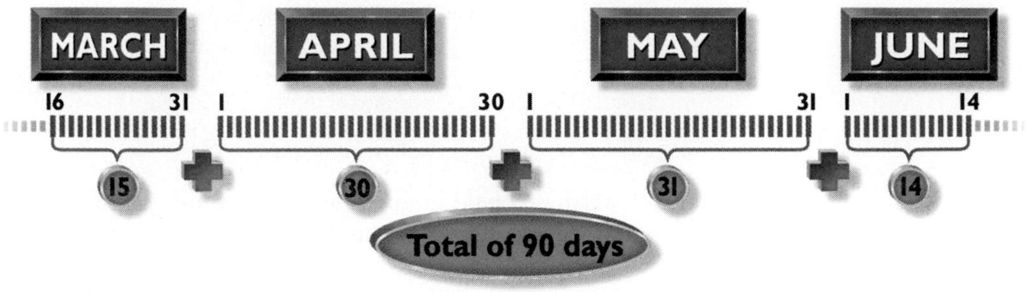

The term of a note may be stated as a certain number of months after the issuance date. In such cases, the due date is determined by counting the number of months from the issuance date. For example, a three-month note dated June 5 would be due on September 5. A two-month note dated July 31 would be due on September 30.

Q&A

What is the due date of a 120-day note receivable dated September 9?

January 7 [21 days in September (30 days − 9 days) + 31 days in October + 30 days in November + 31 days in December + 7 days in January = 120 days]

BUSINESS ON STAGE

Interest and the Length of a Year

Whenever a business borrows money or enters into a credit agreement that requires the payment of interest, it is important that the business understand how the interest will be computed. For example, the difference in 180 days' interest computed on the basis of a 365-day year versus a 360-day year is shown below for a loan of $40,000 at an interest rate of 12%.

$40,000 × 0.12 × 180/365 = $2,367.12
$40,000 × 0.12 × 180/360 = $2,400.00

The difference of $32.88 may seem small, but for a business that might enter into thousands of such transactions for millions of dollars, the difference between computing interest on a 360-day year versus a 365-day year can be significant. ■

Interest

A note normally specifies that interest be paid for the period between the issuance date and the due date.[5] Notes covering a period of time longer than one year normally provide that the interest be paid semiannually, quarterly, or at some other stated interval. When the term of the note is less than one year, the interest is usually payable at the time the note is paid.

The interest rate on notes is normally stated in terms of a year, regardless of the actual period of time involved. Thus, the interest on $2,000 for one year at 12% is $240 (12% of $2,000). The interest on $2,000 for one-fourth of one year at 12% is $60 (1/4 of $240).

Point of INTEREST

Your credit card balances that are not paid at the end of the month incur an interest charge expressed as a percent per month. Interest charges of 1½% per month are common. Such charges approximate an annual interest rate of 18% per year (1½% × 12). Thus, if you can borrow money at less than 18%, you are better off borrowing the money to pay off the credit card balance.

[5] You may occasionally see references to non-interest-bearing notes receivable. Such notes, which are not widely used, normally include an implicit interest rate.

The basic formula for computing interest is as follows:

Face Amount (or Principal) × Rate × Time = Interest

To illustrate the formula, the interest on the note in Exhibit 4 is computed as follows:

$$\$2{,}500 \times 0.10 \times \frac{90}{360} = \$62.50 \text{ interest}$$

In computing interest for a period of less than one year, agencies of the federal government and many financial institutions use the actual number of days in the year, 365. In the preceding computation, for example, the time would have been stated as 90/365 of one year. To simplify computations, however, we will use 360 days.

What is the maturity value of a $15,000, 90-day, 12% note?

$15,450 [$15,000 + ($15,000 × 0.12 × 90/360)]

Maturity Value

The amount that is due at the maturity or due date is called the **maturity value.** The maturity value of a note is the sum of the face amount and the interest. In the note in Exhibit 4, the maturity value is $2,562.50 ($2,500 face amount plus $62.50 interest).

Accounting for Notes Receivable

OBJECTIVE 7

Journalize the entries for notes receivable transactions.

As we mentioned earlier, a note may be received from a customer to replace an account receivable. To illustrate, assume that a 30-day, 12% note dated November 21, 2000, is accepted in settlement of the account of W. A. Bunn Co., which is past due and has a balance of $6,000. The entry to record the transaction is as follows:

Nov.	21	Notes Receivable	6,000.00	
		Accounts Receivable—W. A. Bunn Co.		6,000.00
		Received 30-day, 12% note dated		
		November 21, 2000.		

When the note matures, the entry to record the receipt of $6,060 ($6,000 principal plus $60 interest) is as follows:

Dec.	21	Cash	6,060.00	
		Notes Receivable		6,000.00
		Interest Revenue		60.00
		Received principal and interest on		
		matured note.		

If the maker of a note fails to pay the debt on the due date, the note is a **dishonored note receivable.** When a note is dishonored, the face value of the note plus any interest due is transferred to the accounts receivable account. For example, assume that the $6,000, 30-day, 12% note received from W. A. Bunn Co. and recorded on November 21 is dishonored at maturity. The entry to transfer the note and the interest back to the customer's account is as follows:

Dec.	21	Accounts Receivable—W. A. Bunn Co.	6,060 00	
		Notes Receivable		6,000 00
		Interest Revenue		60 00
		To record dishonored note and interest.		

The interest of $60 has been earned, even though the note has been dishonored. If the account receivable is uncollectible, the amount of $6,060 will be part of the uncollectible accounts expense.

If a note matures in a later fiscal period, the interest accrued in the period in which the note is received must be recorded by an adjusting entry. For example, assume that a 90-day, 12% note dated December 1, 2000, is received from Crawford Company to settle its account, which has a balance of $4,000. Assuming that the accounting period ends on December 31, the entries to record the receipt of the note, accrued interest, and payment of the note at maturity are shown below.

2000 Dec.	1	Notes Receivable	4,000 00	
		Accounts Receivable—Crawford Company		4,000 00
		Received note in settlement of account.		
	31	Interest Receivable	40 00	
		Interest Revenue		40 00
		Adjusting entry for accrued interest, $4,000 × 0.12 × 30/360.		
2001 Mar.	1	Cash	4,120 00	
		Notes Receivable		4,000 00
		Interest Receivable		40 00
		Interest Revenue		80 00
		Received payment of note and interest; maturity value, $4,000 × 0.12 × 90/360.		

The interest revenue account is closed at the end of each accounting period. The amount of interest revenue is normally reported in the Other Income section of the income statement.

OBJECTIVE 8

Prepare the Current Assets presentation of receivables on the balance sheet.

Receivables on the Balance Sheet

All receivables that are expected to be realized in cash within a year are presented in the Current Assets section of the balance sheet. It is normal to list the assets in the order of their liquidity. This is the order in which they are expected to be converted to cash during normal operations. An example of the presentation of receivables is shown in the partial balance sheet for Crabtree Co. in Exhibit 5.

EXHIBIT 5
Receivables in Balance Sheet

Crabtree Co.
Balance Sheet
December 31, 20—

Assets		
Current assets:		
Cash		$119,500.00
Notes receivable		250,000.00
Accounts receivable	$445,000.00	
Less allowance for doubtful accounts	15,000.00	430,000.00
Interest receivable		14,500.00

REAL WORLD

The following credit risk disclosure appeared in the financial statements of **Deere & Company**:

Credit receivables have significant concentrations of credit risk in the agricultural, industrial, lawn and grounds care, and recreational (non-Deere equipment) business sectors. . . . The portions of credit receivables related to the agricultural equipment business were 60 percent and 56 percent; those related to the industrial equipment business were 12 percent and 14 percent; those related to the lawn and grounds care equipment business were seven percent and eight percent; and those related to the recreational equipment business were 21 percent and 22 percent, respectively. On a geographic basis, there is not a disproportionate concentration of credit risk in any area. . . .

The balance of Crabtree's notes receivable, accounts receivable, and interest receivable accounts are reported in Exhibit 5. The allowance for doubtful accounts is subtracted from the accounts receivable. Alternatively, the accounts receivable may be listed on the balance sheet at its net realizable value of $430,000, with a note showing the amount of the allowance. If the allowance account includes provisions for doubtful notes as well as accounts, it should be deducted from the total of Notes Receivable and Accounts Receivable.

Other disclosures related to receivables are presented either on the face of the financial statements or in the accompanying notes. Such disclosures include the market (fair) value of the receivables.[6] In addition, if unusual credit risks exist within the receivables, the nature of the risks should be disclosed. For example, if the majority of the receivables are due from one customer or are due from customers located in one area of the country or one industry, these facts should be disclosed.[7]

FINANCIAL ANALYSIS AND INTERPRETATION

OBJECTIVE 9

Compute and interpret the accounts receivable turnover and the number of days' sales in receivables.

Businesses that grant long credit terms tend to have relatively greater amounts tied up in accounts receivable than those granting short credit terms. In either case, it is desirable to collect receivables as promptly as possible. The cash collected from receivables improves solvency and lessens the risk of loss from uncollectible accounts. Two financial measures that are especially useful in evaluating the efficiency in collecting receivables are (1) the accounts receivable turnover and (2) the number of days' sales in receivables.

The **accounts receivable turnover** measures how frequently during the year the accounts receivable are being converted to cash. For example, with credit terms of 2/10, n/30 days, the accounts receivable should turn over slightly more than twelve times per year. The accounts receivable turnover is computed as follows:

[6] *Statement of Financial Accounting Standards, No. 107,* "Disclosures about Fair Value of Financial Instruments," Financial Accounting Standards Board, Norwalk, 1991, pars. 10 and 19.

[7] *Statement of Financial Accounting Standards, No. 105,* "Disclosure of Information about Financial Instruments with Off-Balance Sheet Risk and Financial Instruments with Concentrations of Credit Risk," Financial Accounting Standards Board, Norwalk, 1990, par. 20, and *Statement of Financial Accounting Standards, No. 107, op.cit.,* par. 13.

$$\textbf{Accounts receivable turnover} = \frac{\textbf{Net sales on account}}{\textbf{Average accounts receivable}}$$

The average accounts receivable can be determined by using monthly data or by simply adding the beginning and ending accounts receivable balances and dividing by two. For example, assume that Sidner Company has net sales on account of \$36,000,000 and beginning and ending accounts receivable balances of \$1,080,000 and \$1,220,000. The accounts receivable turnover is 31.3, as shown below:

$$\textbf{Accounts receivable turnover} = \frac{\textbf{Net sales on account}}{\textbf{Average accounts receivable}}$$

$$= \frac{\$36{,}000{,}000}{(\$1{,}080{,}000 + \$1{,}220{,}000)/2} = 31.3$$

The **number of days' sales in receivables** is an estimate of the length of time the accounts receivable have been outstanding. With credit terms of 2/10, n/30 days, the number of days' sales in receivables should be less than 30 days. It is computed as follows:

$$\textbf{Number of days' sales in receivables} = \frac{\textbf{Accounts receivable, end of year}}{\textbf{Average daily sales on account}}$$

Average daily sales on account is determined by dividing net sales on account by 365 days. For example, using the preceding data for Sidner Company, the number of days' sales in receivables is 12.4, as shown below:

$$\textbf{Number of days' sales in receivables} = \frac{\textbf{Accounts receivable, end of year}}{\textbf{Average daily sales on account}}$$

$$= \frac{\$1{,}220{,}000}{(\$36{,}000{,}000/365\ \text{days})} = 12.4$$

For these measures to be meaningful, a company should compare its current measures with those from prior periods and with industry figures. An improvement in the efficiency in collecting accounts receivable is indicated when the accounts receivable turnover increases and the number of days' sales in receivables decreases.

ENCORE

Need a Friendly Loan?

If you are approached by a stranger and offered a quick loan to help you out of a financial bind, you should probably think twice. A young police officer in Hong Kong wishes he had.

Sergeant Li Chi-lok went to a local casino on a Friday night to play pai kau (Chinese dominoes). By 4 a.m. Saturday, he had lost his \$9,000 gambling stake. Tired and out of money, he watched other gamblers until a young man approached him. "Did you win or lose? If you need money, we have some," the loan shark said. Sergeant Li yielded to temptation and borrowed \$10,000, but was only given \$9,000—\$1,000 was taken as a service charge. When he stopped gambling, he had borrowed \$20,000 and owed \$25,000.

The loan sharks took Sergeant Li to an apartment, where he was told to call relatives to pay off his debt. However, the interest accumulated rapidly. By midday on Saturday, the amount owed had risen to $33,000. Twelve hours later, it rose to $44,000, and by lunchtime on Sunday it had risen to $60,000. Sergeant Li was allowed to go after his mother deposited $20,000 in a bank account and he signed an IOU for the remaining debt. During his ordeal, Sergeant Li was tied up and severely beaten. His injuries included a punctured lung and a broken leg, arm, and finger.

Loan sharks aren't confined to Hong Kong. In the United Kingdom, there are more than 27,000 legal moneylenders, who charge annual interest rates up to 500%. In the United States, most states have usury laws restricting the amount of interest that a creditor may charge. However, illegal loan sharking still exists. For example, a Boston loan shark and gambling bookie recently pleaded guilty to charging 100 customers interest rates ranging from 100% to 500%. In New York, a restaurant owner testified that he had paid $60,000 on a $20,000 loan, but that it was still not enough to satisfy a Buffalo loan shark. In another case, a woman embezzled more than $100,000 from a doctor she worked for in order to pay her husband's loan shark. She escaped prosecution by cooperating with the FBI's case against the loan shark. ■

APPENDIX: DISCOUNTING NOTES RECEIVABLE

Although it is not a common transaction, a company may endorse its notes receivable and transfer them to a bank. The bank transfers cash (the **proceeds**) to the company, after deducting a **discount** (interest) that is computed on the maturity value of the note for the discount period. The discount period is the time that the bank must hold the note before it becomes due.

To illustrate, assume that a 90-day, 12%, $1,800 note receivable from Pryor & Co., dated April 8, is discounted at the payee's bank on May 3 at the rate of 14%. The data used in determining the effect of the transaction are as follows:

Face value of note dated April 8	$1,800.00
Interest on note (90 days at 12%)	54.00
Maturity value of note due July 7	$1,854.00
Discount on maturity value (65 days from May 3 to July 7, at 14%)	46.87
Proceeds	$1,807.13

The endorser records as interest revenue the excess of the proceeds from discounting the note, $1,807.13, over its face value, $1,800, as follows:

May	3	Cash	1 8 0 7 13	
		Notes Receivable		1 8 0 0 00
		Interest Revenue		7 13
		Discounted $1,800, 90-day, 12% note at 14%.		

What if the proceeds from discounting a note receivable are less than the face value? When this situation occurs, the endorser records the excess of the face value over the proceeds as interest expense. The length of the discount period and the difference between the interest rate and the discount rate determine whether interest expense or interest revenue will result from discounting.

Without a statement limiting responsibility, the endorser of a note is committed to paying the note if the maker defaults. This potential liability is called a **contingent liability**. Thus, the endorser of a note that has been discounted has a contingent liability until the due date. If the maker pays the promised amount at maturity, the contingent liability is removed without any action on the part of the endorser. If, on the other hand, the maker dishonors the note and the endorser is notified according to legal requirements, the endorser's liability becomes an actual one.

When a discounted note receivable is dishonored, the bank notifies the endorser and asks for payment. In some cases, the bank may charge a **protest fee** for notifying the endorser that a note has been dishonored. The entire amount paid to the bank by the endorser, including the interest and protest fee, should be debited to the account receivable of the maker. For example, assume that the $1,800, 90-day, 12% note discounted on May 3 is dishonored at maturity by the maker, Pryor & Co. The bank charges a protest fee of $12. The endorser's entry to record the payment to the bank is as follows:

July	7	Accounts Receivable—Pryor & Co.		1 866 00	
		Cash			1 866 00
		Paid dishonored, discounted note (maturity value of $1,854 plus protest fee of $12).			

KEY POINTS

1 List the common classifications of receivables.

The term receivables includes all money claims against other entities, including people, business firms, and other organizations. They are normally classified as accounts receivable, notes receivable, or other receivables.

2 Summarize and provide examples of internal control procedures that apply to receivables.

The internal controls that apply to receivables include the separation of responsibilities for related functions. In this way, the work of one employee can serve as a check on the work of another employee.

3 Describe the nature of and the accounting for uncollectible receivables.

The two methods of accounting for uncollectible receivables are the allowance method and the direct write-off method. The allowance method provides in advance for uncollectible receivables. The direct write-off method recognizes the expense only when the account is judged to be uncollectible.

4 Journalize the entries for the allowance method of accounting for uncollectibles, and estimate uncollectible receivables based on sales and on an analysis of receivables.

A year-end adjusting entry provides for (1) the reduction of the value of the receivables to the amount of cash expected to be realized from them in the future and (2) the allocation to the current period of the expected expense resulting from such reduction. The adjusting entry debits Uncollectible Accounts Expense and credits Allowance for Doubtful Accounts. When an account is believed to be uncollectible, it is written off against the allowance account.

When the estimate of uncollectibles is based on the amount of sales for the fiscal period, the adjusting entry is made without regard to the balance of the allowance account. When the estimate of uncollectibles is based on the amount and the age of the receivable accounts at the end of the period, the adjusting entry is recorded so that the balance of the allowance account will equal the estimated uncollectibles at the end of the period.

The allowance account, which will have a credit balance after the adjusting entry has been posted, is a contra asset account. The uncollectible accounts expense is generally reported on the income statement as an administrative expense.

5 Journalize the entries for the direct write-off of uncollectible receivables.

Under the direct write-off method, the entry to write off an account debits Uncollectible Accounts Expense and credits Accounts Receivable. Neither an allowance account nor an adjusting entry is needed at the end of the period.

6 Describe the nature and characteristics of promissory notes.

A note is a written promise to pay a sum of money on demand or at a definite time. Characteristics of notes that affect how they are recorded and reported include the due date, interest rate, and maturity value. The basic formula for computing interest on a note is: Principal × Rate × Time = Interest. The due date is the date a note is to be paid, and the period of time between the issuance date and the due date is normally stated in either days or months. The maturity value of a note is the sum of the face amount and the interest.

7 Journalize the entries for notes receivable transactions.

A note received in settlement of an account receivable is recorded as a debit to Notes Receivable and a credit to Accounts Receivable. When a note matures, Cash is debited, Notes Receivable is credited, and Interest Revenue is credited. If the maker of a note fails to pay the debt on the due date, the note is said to be dishonored. When the holder of a dishonored note has been paid by the endorser, the amount of the endorser's claim against the maker of the note is debited to an accounts receivable account.

8 Prepare the Current Assets presentation of receivables on the balance sheet.

All receivables that are expected to be realized in cash within a year are presented in the Current Assets section of the balance sheet. It is normal to list the assets in the order of their liquidity, which is the order in which they can be converted to cash in normal operations.

9 Compute and interpret the accounts receivable turnover and the number of days' sales in receivables.

The accounts receivable turnover is net sales on account divided by average accounts receivable. It measures how frequently accounts receivable are being converted into cash. The number of days' sales in receivables is the end-of-year accounts receivable divided by the average daily sales on account. It measures the length of time the accounts receivable have been outstanding.

ILLUSTRATIVE PROBLEM

Ditzler Company, a construction supply company, uses the allowance method of accounting for uncollectible accounts receivable. Selected transactions completed by Ditzler Company are as follows:

Feb.	1.	Sold merchandise on account to Ames Co., $8,000. The cost of the merchandise sold was $4,500.
Mar.	15.	Accepted a 60-day, 12% note for $8,000 from Ames Co. on account.
Apr.	9.	Wrote off a $2,500 account from Dorset Co. as uncollectible.
	21.	Loaned $7,500 cash to Jill Klein, receiving a 90-day, 14% note.
May	14.	Received the interest due from Ames Co. and a new 90-day, 14% note as a renewal of the loan. (Record both the debit and the credit to the notes receivable account.)
June	13.	Reinstated the account of Dorset Co., written off on April 9, and received $2,500 in full payment.
July	20.	Jill Klein dishonored her note.
Aug.	12.	Received from Ames Co. the amount due on its note of May 14.
	19.	Received from Jill Klein the amount owed on the dishonored note, plus interest for 30 days at 15%, computed on the maturity value of the note.
Dec.	16.	Accepted a 60-day, 12% note for $12,000 from Global Company on account.
	31.	It is estimated that 3% of the credit sales of $1,375,000 for the year ended December 31 will be uncollectible.

Instructions

1. Journalize the transactions. Omit explanations.
2. Journalize the adjusting entry to record the accrued interest on December 31 on the Global Company note.

Solution

1.

Feb.	1	Accounts Receivable—Ames Co.	8,000.00	
		Sales		8,000.00
	1	Cost of Merchandise Sold	4,500.00	
		Merchandise Inventory		4,500.00
Mar.	15	Notes Receivable—Ames Co.	8,000.00	
		Accounts Receivable—Ames Co.		8,000.00
Apr.	9	Allowance for Doubtful Accounts	2,500.00	
		Accounts Receivable—Dorset Co.		2,500.00
	21	Notes Receivable—Jill Klein	7,500.00	
		Cash		7,500.00
May	14	Notes Receivable—Ames Co.	8,000.00	
		Cash	160.00	
		Notes Receivable—Ames Co.		8,000.00
		Interest Revenue		160.00
June	13	Accounts Receivable—Dorset Co.	2,500.00	
		Allowance for Doubtful Accounts		2,500.00
	13	Cash	2,500.00	
		Accounts Receivable—Dorset Co.		2,500.00
July	20	Accounts Receivable—Jill Klein	7,762.50	
		Notes Receivable—Jill Klein		500.00
		Interest Revenue		262.50
Aug.	12	Cash	8,280.00	
		Notes Receivable—Ames Co.		8,000.00
		Interest Revenue		280.00
	19	Cash	7,859.53	
		Accounts Receivable—Jill Klein		7,762.50
		Interest Revenue		97.03
		($7,762.50 × 15% × 30/360)		
Dec.	16	Notes Receivable—Global Company	12,000.00	
		Accounts Receivable—Global Company		12,000.00
	31	Uncollectible Accounts Expense	41,250.00	
		Allowance for Doubtful Accounts		41,250.00

2.

Dec.	31	Interest Receivable	60.00	
		Interest Revenue		60.00
		($12,000 × 12% × 15/360)		

SELF-EXAMINATION QUESTIONS

Answers at End of Chapter

Matching

Match each of the following statements with its proper term. Some terms may not be used.

- **A. accounts receivable**
- **B. accounts receivable turnover**
- **C. aging the receivables**
- **D. allowance method**
- **E. contra asset**
- **F. direct write-off method**
- **G. dishonored note receivable**
- **H. maturity value**
- **I. notes receivable**
- **J. number of days' sales in receivables**
- **K. promissory note**
- **L. receivables**
- **M. uncollectible accounts expense**

L 1. All money claims against other entities, including people, business firms, and other organizations.

A 2. A receivable created by selling merchandise or services on credit.

I 3. Amounts customers owe, for which a formal, written instrument of credit has been issued.

M 4. The operating expense incurred because of the failure to collect receivables.

D 5. The method of accounting for uncollectible accounts that provides an expense for uncollectible receivables in advance of their write-off.

F 6. The method of accounting for uncollectible accounts that recognizes the expense only when accounts are judged to be worthless.

C 7. The process of analyzing the accounts receivable and classifying them according to various age groupings, with the due date being the base point for determining age.

H 8. The amount that is due at the maturity or due date of a note.

G 9. A note that the maker fails to pay on the due date.

J 10. An estimate of the length of time the accounts receivable have been outstanding.

B 11. Measures how frequently during the year the accounts receivable are being converted to cash.

K 12. A written promise to pay a sum of money on demand or at a definite time.

Multiple Choice

1. At the end of the fiscal year, before the accounts are adjusted, Accounts Receivable has a balance of $200,000 and Allowance for Doubtful Accounts has a credit balance of $2,500. If the estimate of uncollectible accounts determined by aging the receivables is $8,500, the amount of uncollectible accounts expense is:
   A. $2,500 C. $8,500
   B. $6,000 D. $11,000

2. At the end of the fiscal year, Accounts Receivable has a balance of $100,000 and Allowance for Doubtful Accounts has a balance of $7,000. The expected net realizable value of the accounts receivable is:
   A. $7,000 C. $100,000
   B. $93,000 D. $107,000

3. What is the maturity value of a 90-day, 12% note for $10,000?
   A. $8,800 C. $10,300
   B. $10,000 D. $11,200

4. What is the due date of a $12,000, 90-day, 8% note receivable dated August 5?
   A. October 31 C. November 3
   B. November 2 D. November 4

5. When a note receivable is dishonored, Accounts Receivable is debited for what amount?
   A. The face value of the note
   B. The maturity value of the note
   C. The maturity value of the note less accrued interest
   D. The maturity value of the note plus accrued interest

CLASS DISCUSSION QUESTIONS

1. What are the three classifications of receivables?
2. What types of transactions give rise to accounts receivable?
3. In what section of the balance sheet should a note receivable be listed if its term is (a) 90 days, (b) 5 years?
4. Give two examples of other receivables.

5. The accounts receivable clerk is also responsible for handling cash receipts. Which principle of internal control is violated in this situation?
6. Which of the two methods of accounting for uncollectible accounts provides for the recognition of the expense at the earlier date?
7. What kind of an account (asset, liability, etc.) is Allowance for Doubtful Accounts, and is its normal balance a debit or a credit?
8. After the accounts are adjusted and closed at the end of the fiscal year, Accounts Receivable has a balance of $601,250 and Allowance for Doubtful Accounts has a balance of $32,250. Describe how the accounts receivable and the allowance for doubtful accounts are reported on the balance sheet.
9. A firm has consistently adjusted its allowance account at the end of the fiscal year by adding a fixed percent of the period's net sales on account. After five years, the balance in Allowance for Doubtful Accounts has become very large in relationship to the balance in Accounts Receivable. Give two possible explanations.
10. Which of the two methods of estimating uncollectibles provides for the most accurate estimate of the current net realizable value of the receivables?
11. For a business, what are the advantages of a note receivable in comparison to an account receivable?
12. Stamm Company issued a promissory note to Blair Company. (a) Who is the payee? (b) What is the title of the account used by Blair Company in recording the note?
13. If a note provides for payment of principal of $20,000 and interest at the rate of 10%, will the interest amount to $2,000? Explain.
14. The maker of a $6,000, 8%, 90-day note receivable failed to pay the note on the due date of June 30. What accounts should be debited and credited by the payee to record the dishonored note receivable?
15. The note receivable dishonored in Question 14 is paid on July 30 by the maker, plus interest for 30 days, 9%. What entry should be made to record the receipt of the payment?
16. Under what caption should accounts receivable be reported on the balance sheet?

Warren Reeve Fess

Resources for Your Success On-Line at warren.swcollege.com

Remember! If you need additional help, visit South-Western's Web site. See page 26 for a description of the online and printed materials that are available.

EXERCISES

Exercise 8–1
Internal control procedures
Objective 2

Cardinal Company sells carpeting. Over 75% of all carpet sales are on credit. The following procedures are used by Cardinal to process this large number of credit sales and the subsequent collections.

a. All credit sales to a first-time customer must be approved by the Credit Department. Salespersons will assist the customer in filling out a credit application, but an employee in the Credit Department is responsible for verifying employment and checking the customer's credit history before granting credit.
b. Cardinal's standard credit period is 45 days. The Credit Department may approve an extension of this repayment period of up to one year. Whenever an extension is

granted, the customer signs a promissory note. Up to 30% of the credit sales in any one year are for repayment periods exceeding 45 days.

c. A formal ledger is not maintained for customers who sign promissory notes. Cardinal simply keeps a copy of each signed note in a file cabinet. These unpaid notes are filed by due date.

d. Cardinal employs an accounts receivable clerk. The clerk is responsible for recording customer credit sales (based on sales tickets), receiving cash from customers, giving customers credit for their payments, and handling all customer billing complaints.

e. The general ledger control account for Accounts Receivable is maintained by the General Accounting Department at Cardinal. This department records total credit sales, based on credit sale information from the store's electronic cash register, and total customer receipts, based on the bank deposit slip.

State whether each of these procedures is appropriate or inappropriate, considering the principles of internal control. If inappropriate, state which internal control procedure is violated.

Exercise 8–2

Nature of uncollectible accounts

Objective 3

✓ a. 4.3%
✓ b. 25.3%

Hilton Hotels Corporation owns and operates casinos at several of its hotels, located primarily in Nevada. At the end of a recent fiscal year, the following accounts and notes receivable were reported (in thousands):

Hotel accounts and notes receivable	$75,796	
Less: Allowance for doubtful accounts	3,256	
		$72,540
Casino accounts receivable	$26,334	
Less: Allowance for doubtful accounts	6,654	
		19,680

a. Compute the percentage of allowance for doubtful accounts to the gross hotel accounts and notes receivable for the end of the fiscal year.

b. Compute the percentage of the allowance for doubtful accounts to the gross casino accounts receivable for the end of the fiscal year.

c. Discuss possible reasons for the difference in the two ratios computed in (a) and (b).

Exercise 8–3

Estimating doubtful accounts

Objective 4

✓ $20,685

Swenson Co. is a wholesaler of office supplies. An aging of the company's accounts receivable on December 31, 2000, and a historical analysis of the percentage of uncollectible accounts in each age category are as follows:

Age Interval	Balance	Percent Uncollectible
Not past due	$325,000	2%
1–30 days past due	86,000	4
31–60 days past due	17,000	9
61–90 days past due	12,000	15
91–180 days past due	7,400	60
Over 180 days past due	3,500	85
	$450,900	

Estimate what the proper balance of the allowance for doubtful accounts should be as of December 31, 2000.

Exercise 8–4

Entry for uncollectible accounts

Objective 4

Using the data in Exercise 8–3, assume that the allowance for doubtful accounts for Swenson Co. had a debit balance of $3,050 as of December 31, 2000.

Journalize the adjusting entry for uncollectible accounts as of December 31, 2000.

Exercise 8–5
Providing for doubtful accounts

Objective 4

✓ a. $10,000
✓ b. $35,600

At the end of the current year, the accounts receivable account has a debit balance of $575,000, and net sales for the year total $4,000,000. Determine the amount of the adjusting entry to provide for doubtful accounts under each of the following assumptions:

a. The allowance account before adjustment has a credit balance of $2,750. Uncollectible accounts expense is estimated at 1/4 of 1% of net sales.
b. The allowance account before adjustment has a credit balance of $2,750. Analysis of the accounts in the customer's ledger indicates doubtful accounts of $38,350.
c. The allowance account before adjustment has a debit balance of $1,050. Uncollectible accounts expense is estimated at 1/2 of 1% of net sales.
d. The allowance account before adjustment has a debit balance of $1,050. Analysis of the accounts in the customer's ledger indicates doubtful accounts of $31,400.

Exercise 8–6
Entries to write off accounts receivable

Objectives 4, 5

Aspen Company, a computer consulting firm, has decided to write off the $2,800 balance of an account owed by a customer. Journalize the entry to record the write-off, (a) assuming that the allowance method is used, and (b) assuming that the direct write-off method is used.

Exercise 8–7
Entries for uncollectible receivables, using allowance method

Objective 4

Journalize the following transactions in the accounts of Alpine Company, a restaurant supply company that uses the allowance method of accounting for uncollectible receivables:

Feb. 20. Sold merchandise on account to J. Renner, $5,500. The cost of the merchandise sold was $3,400.
May 19. Received $3,000 from J. Renner and wrote off the remainder owed on the sale of February 20 as uncollectible.
Sept. 30. Reinstated the account of J. Renner that had been written off on May 19 and received $2,500 cash in full payment.

Exercise 8–8
Entries for uncollectible accounts, using direct write-off method

Objective 5

Journalize the following transactions in the accounts of MedCo Co., a hospital supply company that uses the direct write-off method of accounting for uncollectible receivables:

Mar. 11. Sold merchandise on account to E. Hayes, $6,200. The cost of the merchandise sold was $4,250.
May 1. Received $1,800 from E. Hayes and wrote off the remainder owed on the sale of March 11 as uncollectible.
Aug. 15. Reinstated the account of E. Hayes that had been written off on May 1 and received $4,400 cash in full payment.

Exercise 8–9
Effect of doubtful accounts on net income

Objectives 4, 5

✓ $53,400

During its first year of operations, Klondike Automotive Supply Co. had net sales of $1,050,000, wrote off $32,800 of accounts as uncollectible, using the direct write-off method, and reported net income of $62,600. If the allowance method of accounting for uncollectibles had been used, 4% of net sales would have been estimated as uncollectible. Determine what the net income would have been if the allowance method had been used.

Exercise 8–10
Effect of doubtful accounts on net income

Objectives 4, 5

✓ a. $94,800
✓ b. $26,700

Using the data in Exercise 8–9, assume that during the second year of operations Klondike Automotive Supply Co. had net sales of $1,800,000, wrote off $54,500 of accounts as uncollectible, using the direct write-off method, and reported net income of $112,300.

a. Determine what net income would have been in the second year if the allowance method (using 4% of net sales) had been used in both the first and second years.
b. Determine what the balance of the allowance for doubtful accounts would have been at the end of the second year if the allowance method had been used in both the first and second years.

Exercise 8–11
Determine due date and interest on notes

Objective 6

Determine the due date and the amount of interest due at maturity on the following notes:

✓ a. May 18; $100

	Date of Note	Face Amount	Term of Note	Interest Rate
a.	April 3	$10,000	45 days	8%
b.	May 20	6,000	60 days	10%
c.	August 31	8,000	90 days	14%
d.	June 9	15,000	90 days	10%
e.	October 1	12,500	120 days	12%

Exercise 8–12
Entries for notes receivable
Objectives 6, 7

SPREADSHEET

✓ b. $15,450

Gier Interior Decorators issued a 120-day, 9% note for $15,000, dated March 3, to Everson Furniture Company on account.

a. Determine the due date of the note.
b. Determine the maturity value of the note.
c. Journalize the entries to record the following: (1) receipt of the note by the payee, and (2) receipt by the payee of payment of the note at maturity.

Exercise 8–13
Entries for notes receivable
Objective 7

The series of seven transactions recorded in the following T accounts were related to a sale to a customer on account and the receipt of the amount owed. Briefly describe each transaction.

Cash

(7)	28,300	(7)	28,000

Sales

		(1)	30,000

Notes Receivable

(5)	27,500	(6)	27,500

Sales Returns and Allowances

(3)	2,500		

Accounts Receivable

(1)	30,000	(3)	2,500
(6)	28,000	(5)	27,500
		(7)	28,000

Cost of Merchandise Sold

(2)	18,000	(4)	1,500

Merchandise Inventory

(4)	1,500	(2)	18,000

Interest Revenue

		(6)	500
		(7)	300

Exercise 8–14
Entries for notes receivable, including year-end entries
Objective 7

The following selected transactions were completed by Frith Co., a supplier of elastic bands for clothing:

1999
Dec. 15. Received from Acker Co., on account, a $27,000, 90-day, 10% note dated December 15.
31. Recorded an adjusting entry for accrued interest on the note of December 15.
31. Closed the interest revenue account. The only entry in this account originated from the December 31 adjustment.

2000
Mar. 14. Received payment of note and interest from Acker Co.

Journalize the transactions.

Exercise 8–15
Entries for receipt and dishonor of note receivable
Objective 7

Journalize the following transactions of Iris Theater Productions:

Aug. 1. Received a $60,000, 90-day, 10% note dated August 1 from Broadway Company on account.
Oct. 30. The note is dishonored by Broadway Company.
Nov. 29. Received the amount due on the dishonored note plus interest for 30 days at 15% on the total amount charged to Broadway Company on October 30.

Exercise 8–16
Entries for receipt and dishonor of notes receivable
Objectives 4, 7

Journalize the following transactions in the accounts of Clinton Co., which operates a riverboat casino:

Mar. 1. Received an $8,000, 30-day, 12% note dated March 1 from Adams Co. on account.
21. Received a $15,000, 60-day, 10% note dated March 21 from Murphy Co. on account.
31. The note dated March 1 from Adams Co. is dishonored, and the customer's account is charged for the note, including interest.
May 20. The note dated March 21 from Murphy Co. is dishonored, and the customer's account is charged for the note, including interest.
June 29. Cash is received for the amount due on the dishonored note dated March 1 plus interest for 90 days at 15% on the total amount debited to Adams Co. on March 31.
Aug. 31. Wrote off against the allowance account the amount charged to Murphy Co. on May 20 for the dishonored note dated March 21.

Exercise 8–17
Receivables in the balance sheet
Objective 8

What's Wrong WITH THIS?

List any errors you can find in the following partial balance sheet.

James Company
Balance Sheet
December 31, 20—

Assets		
Current assets:		
Cash		$ 95,000
Notes receivable	$250,000	
Less interest receivable	9,000	241,000
Accounts receivable	$445,000	
Plus allowance for doubtful accounts	15,000	460,000

Exercise 8–18
Accounts receivable turnover; number of days' sales in receivables
Objective 9

HAT

The financial statements for **Hershey Foods Corporation** are presented in Appendix G at the end of the text. Assume that all sales are credit sales and that the accounts receivable were $331,670,000 at December 31, 1994.

a. Compute the accounts receivable turnover for 1995 and 1996.
b. Compute the number of days' sales in receivables at December 31, 1995 and 1996.
c. What conclusions can be drawn from these analyses regarding Hershey's efficiency in collecting receivables?

Appendix Exercise 8–19
Discounting notes receivable

Hathaway Co., a building construction company, holds a 90-day, 8% note for $35,000, dated August 18, which was received from a customer on account. On September 17, the note is discounted at the bank at the rate of 12%.

a. Determine the maturity value of the note.
b. Determine the number of days in the discount period.
c. Determine the amount of the discount.
d. Determine the amount of the proceeds.
e. Journalize the entry to record the discounting of the note on September 17.

Appendix Exercise 8–20
Entries for receipt and discounting of note receivable and dishonored notes

Journalize the following transactions in the accounts of Big Time Theater Productions:

May. 1. Received a $100,000, 90-day, 10% note dated May 1 from Johns Company on account.
June 1. Discounted the note at City National Bank at 12%.
July 30. The note is dishonored by Johns Company; paid the bank the amount due on the note, plus a protest fee of $250.
Aug. 29. Received the amount due on the dishonored note plus interest for 30 days at 16% on the total amount charged to Johns Company on July 30.

PROBLEMS SERIES A

Problem 8–1A

Entries related to uncollectible accounts

Objective 4

✓ 3. $572,300

The following transactions, adjusting entries, and closing entries were completed by Runnels Contractors Co. during the current fiscal year ended December 31:

Feb. 10. Received 75% of the $18,000 balance owed by Sackett Co., a bankrupt business, and wrote off the remainder as uncollectible.

May 3. Reinstated the account of B. Pilon, which had been written off in the preceding year as uncollectible. Journalized the receipt of $2,050 cash in full payment of Pilon's account.

Sept. 19. Wrote off the $6,250 balance owed by Larkin Co., which has no assets.

Nov. 30. Reinstated the account of Giles Co., which had been written off in the preceding year as uncollectible. Journalized the receipt of $4,500 cash in full payment of the account.

Dec. 31. Wrote off the following accounts as uncollectible (compound entry): Huang Co., $2,950; Nance Co., $1,600; Powell Distributors, $6,500; J. J. Stevens, $3,200.

31. Based on an analysis of the $595,000 of accounts receivable, it was estimated that $22,700 will be uncollectible. Journalized the adjusting entry.

31. Journalized the entry to close the appropriate account to Income Summary.

Instructions

1. Record the January 1 credit balance of $20,050 in Allowance for Doubtful Accounts.
2. Journalize the transactions and the adjusting and closing entries. Post each entry that affects the following three selected accounts and determine the new balances:

   115 Allowance for Doubtful Accounts
   313 Income Summary
   718 Uncollectible Accounts Expense

3. Determine the expected net realizable value of the accounts receivable as of December 31.
4. Assuming that instead of basing the provision for uncollectible accounts on an analysis of receivables, the adjusting entry on December 31 had been based on an estimated expense of 3/4 of 1% of the net sales of $4,100,000 for the year, determine the following:
   a. Uncollectible accounts expense for the year.
   b. Balance in the allowance account after the adjustment of December 31.
   c. Expected net realizable value of the accounts receivable as of December 31.

Problem 8–2A

Compare two methods of accounting for uncollectible receivables

Objectives 4, 5

SPREADSHEET

✓ 1. Year 4: Balance of allowance account, end of year, $9,650.

Telco Company, a telephone service and supply company, has just completed its fourth year of operations. The direct write-off method of recording uncollectible accounts expense has been used during the entire period. Because of substantial increases in sales volume and amount of uncollectible accounts, the firm is considering changing to the allowance method. Information is requested as to the effect that an annual provision of 1% of sales would have had on the amount of uncollectible accounts expense reported for each of the past four years. It is also considered desirable to know what the balance of Allowance for Doubtful Accounts would have been at the end of each year. The following data have been obtained from the accounts:

			Year of Origin of Accounts Receivable Written Off as Uncollectible			
Year	Sales	Uncollectible Accounts Written Off	1st	2nd	3rd	4th
1st	$ 450,000	$2,500	$2,500			
2nd	660,000	3,950	1,900	$2,050		
3rd	850,000	6,700	700	2,600	$3,400	
4th	1,200,000	8,800		2,200	2,550	$4,050

Instructions

1. Assemble the desired data, using the following column headings:

	Uncollectible Accounts Expense			
Year	Expense Actually Reported	Expense Based on Estimate	Increase (Decrease) in Amount of Expense	Balance of Allowance Account, End of Year

2. Experience during the first four years of operations indicated that the receivables were either collected within two years or had to be written off as uncollectible. Does the estimate of 1% of sales appear to be reasonably close to the actual experience with uncollectible accounts originating during the first two years? Explain.

Problem 8–3A
Details of notes receivable and related entries

Objectives 6, 7

SPREADSHEET

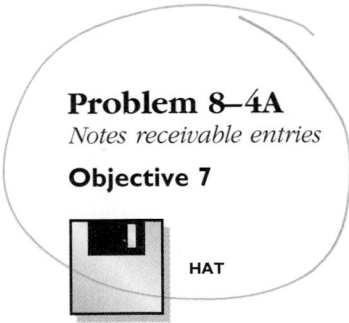

✓ 1. Note 2: Due date, July 11; Interest due at maturity, $150.

During the current fiscal year, Nehls Co. received the following notes. Nehls Co. wholesales bathroom fixtures.

	Date	Face Amount	Term	Interest Rate
1.	March 11	$24,000	60 days	8%
2.	June 11	15,000	30 days	12%
3.	Aug. 20	9,200	90 days	7%
4.	Oct. 31	12,000	60 days	9%
5.	Nov. 28	15,000	60 days	8%
6.	Dec. 26	18,000	30 days	12%

Instructions

1. Determine for each note (a) the due date and (b) the amount of interest due at maturity, identifying each note by number.
2. Journalize the entry to record the dishonor of Note (3) on its due date.
3. Journalize the adjusting entry to record the accrued interest on Notes (5) and (6) on December 31.
4. Journalize the entries to record the receipt of the amounts due on Notes (5) and (6) in January.

Problem 8–4A
Notes receivable entries

Objective 7

HAT

The following data relate to notes receivable and interest for Fiber Optic Co., a cable manufacturer and supplier. (All notes are dated as of the day they are received.)

July 1. Received a $12,000, 9%, 60-day note on account.
Aug. 16. Received a $30,000, 10%, 120-day note on account.
30. Received $12,180 on note of July 1.
Sept. 1. Received a $25,000, 9%, 60-day note on account.
Oct. 31. Received $25,375 on note of September 1.
Nov. 8. Received a $24,000, 7%, 30-day note on account.
30. Received a $15,000, 10%, 30-day note on account.
Dec. 8. Received $24,140 on note of November 8.
14. Received $31,000 on note of August 16.
30. Received $15,125 on note of November 30.

Instructions
Journalize entries to record the transactions.

Problem 8–5A
Sales and notes receivable transactions

Objective 7

The following were selected from among the transactions completed by Wurtz Co. during the current year. Wurtz Co. sells and installs home and business security systems.

Jan. 10. Loaned $25,000 cash to Joyce Yang, receiving a 90-day, 8% note.
Feb. 1. Sold merchandise on account to Spencer and Son, $12,000. The cost of the merchandise sold was $8,800.

GENERAL LEDGER
HAT

Feb. 10. Sold merchandise on account to Roper Co., $40,000. The cost of merchandise sold was $30,000.
Mar. 3. Accepted a 60-day, 10% note for $12,000 from Spencer and Son on account.
11. Accepted a 60-day, 12% note for $40,000 from Roper Co. on account.
Apr. 10. Received the interest due from Joyce Yang and a new 90-day, 12% note as a renewal of the loan of January 10. (Record both the debit and the credit to the notes receivable account.)
May 2. Received from Spencer and Son the amount due on the note of March 3.
10. Roper Co. dishonored its note dated March 11.
June 9. Received from Roper Co. the amount owed on the dishonored note, plus interest for 30 days at 15% computed on the maturity value of the note.
July 9. Received from Joyce Yang the amount due on her note of April 10.
Aug. 23. Sold merchandise on account to C. D. Connors Co., $8,000. The cost of the merchandise sold was $5,000.
Sep. 2. Received from C. D. Connors Co. the amount of the invoice of August 23, less 1% discount.

Instructions

Journalize the transactions.

PROBLEMS SERIES B

Problem 8–1B
Entries related to uncollectible accounts

Objective 4

✓ 3. $493,500

The following transactions, adjusting entries, and closing entries were completed by The Art Gallery during the current fiscal year ended December 31:

Jan. 21. Reinstated the account of Jill Luce, which had been written off in the preceding year as uncollectible. Journalized the receipt of $3,025 cash in full payment of Luce's account.
28. Wrote off the $7,500 balance owed by Oasis Co., which is bankrupt.
Mar. 7. Received 40% of the $8,000 balance owed by Primrose Co., a bankrupt business, and wrote off the remainder as uncollectible.
Aug. 29. Reinstated the account of Louis Sabo, which had been written off two years earlier as uncollectible. Recorded the receipt of $1,200 cash in full payment.
Dec. 30. Wrote off the following accounts as uncollectible (compound entry): Channel Co., $11,050; Engel Co., $6,260; Loach Furniture, $4,775; Briana Parker, $1,820.
31. Based on an analysis of the $535,500 of accounts receivable, it was estimated that $42,000 will be uncollectible. Journalized the adjusting entry.
31. Journalized the entry to close the appropriate account to Income Summary.

Instructions

1. Record the January 1 credit balance of $28,955 in Allowance for Doubtful Accounts.
2. Journalize the transactions and the adjusting and closing entries. Post each entry that affects the following three selected accounts and determine the new balances:

115	Allowance for Doubtful Accounts
313	Income Summary
718	Uncollectible Accounts Expense

3. Determine the expected net realizable value of the accounts receivable as of December 31.
4. Assuming that, instead of basing the provision for uncollectible accounts on an analysis of receivables, the adjusting entry on December 31 had been based on an estimated expense of 3/4 of 1% of the net sales of $5,500,000 for the year, determine the following:

a. Uncollectible accounts expense for the year.
b. Balance in the allowance account after the adjustment of December 31.
c. Expected net realizable value of the accounts receivable as of December 31.

Problem 8–2B

Compare two methods of accounting for uncollectible receivables

Objectives 4, 5

SPREADSHEET

✓ 1. Year 4: Balance of allowance account, end of year, $8,450

Baldwin Company, which operates a chain of 30 electronics supply stores, has just completed its fourth year of operations. The direct write-off method of recording uncollectible accounts expense has been used during the entire period. Because of substantial increases in sales volume and amount of uncollectible accounts, the firm is considering changing to the allowance method. Information is requested as to the effect that an annual provision of 1% of sales would have had on the amount of uncollectible accounts expense reported for each of the past four years. It is also considered desirable to know what the balance of Allowance for Doubtful Accounts would have been at the end of each year. The following data have been obtained from the accounts:

Year	Sales	Uncollectible Accounts Written Off	Year of Origin of Accounts Receivable Written Off as Uncollectible			
			1st	2nd	3rd	4th
1st	$ 650,000	$ 2,600	$2,600			
2nd	720,000	3,500	1,950	$1,550		
3rd	950,000	9,600	2,200	3,400	$4,000	
4th	1,250,000	11,550		2,300	2,950	$6,300

Instructions

1. Assemble the desired data, using the following column headings:

Year	Uncollectible Accounts Expense			Balance of Allowance Account, End of Year
	Expense Actually Reported	Expense Based on Estimate	Increase (Decrease) in Amount of Expense	

2. Experience during the first four years of operations indicated that the receivables were either collected within two years or had to be written off as uncollectible. Does the estimate of 1% of sales appear to be reasonably close to the actual experience with uncollectible accounts originating during the first two years? Explain.

Problem 8–3B

Details of notes receivable and related entries

Objectives 6, 7

SPREADSHEET

✓ 1. Note 2: Due date, Aug. 9; Interest due at maturity, $600

During the last six months of the current fiscal year, Norby Co. received the following notes. Norby Co. produces advertising videos.

	Date	Face Amount	Term	Interest Rate
1.	Apr. 1	$15,000	120 days	8%
2.	June 10	30,000	60 days	12%
3.	Aug. 11	18,000	90 days	8%
4.	Sept. 1	20,000	90 days	7%
5.	Nov. 1	24,000	90 days	9%
6.	Dec. 16	36,000	30 days	13%

Instructions

1. Determine for each note (a) the due date and (b) the amount of interest due at maturity, identifying each note by number.
2. Journalize the entry to record the dishonor of Note (3) on its due date.
3. Journalize the adjusting entry to record the accrued interest on Notes (5) and (6) on December 31.
4. Journalize the entries to record the receipt of the amounts due on Notes (5) and (6) in January.

Problem 8–4B

Notes receivable entries

Objective 7

The following data relate to notes receivable and interest for Robbins Co., a financial services company. (All notes are dated as of the day they are received.)

Mar. 1. Received a $30,000, 9%, 60-day note on account.
21. Received an $18,000, 9%, 90-day note on account.
Apr. 30. Received $30,450 on note of March 1.
May 16. Received a $48,000, 12%, 90-day note on account.
31. Received a $7,500, 8%, 30-day note on account.
June 19. Received $18,405 on note of March 21.
30. Received $7,550 on note of May 31.
July 1. Received a $5,000, 12%, 30-day note on account.
31. Received $5,050 on note of July 1.
Aug. 14. Received $49,440 on note of May 16.

Instructions

Journalize the entries to record the transactions.

Problem 8–5B

Sales and notes receivable transactions

Objective 7

GENERAL LEDGER

The following were selected from among the transactions completed during the current year by Cady Co., an appliance wholesale company:

Jan. 11. Sold merchandise on account to Hayden Co., $18,000. The cost of merchandise sold was $12,000.
Mar. 3. Accepted a 60-day, 10% note for $18,000 from Hayden Co. on account.
May 2. Received from Hayden Co. the amount due on the note of March 3.
June 1. Sold merchandise on account to Kohl's for $5,000. The cost of merchandise sold was $3,500.
5. Loaned $9,000 cash to Frank Scharf, receiving a 30-day, 12% note.
11. Received from Kohl's the amount due on the invoice of June 1, less 2% discount.
July 5. Received the interest due from Frank Scharf and a new 60-day, 14% note as a renewal of the loan of June 5. (Record both the debit and the credit to the notes receivable account.)
Sept. 3. Received from Frank Scharf the amount due on his note of July 5.
4. Sold merchandise on account to Nugent Co., $5,000. The cost of merchandise sold was $3,500.
Oct. 4. Accepted a 60-day, 12% note for $5,000 from Nugent Co. on account.
Dec. 3. Nugent Co. dishonored the note dated October 4.
23. Received from Nugent Co. the amount owed on the dishonored note, plus interest for 20 days at 12% computed on the maturity value of the note.

Instructions

Journalize the transactions.

QUICKBOOKS PROBLEM

Aging of Accounts Receivable

Open the *sample.qbw* file (Larry's Landscaping) in QuickBooks for this problem.

1. Print the "A/R Aging Summary" report for Larry's Landscaping.
2. Print the detailed invoices that are 1–30 days past due for Richard Mills. (Use the QuickZoom feature.)
3. Interpret the A/R Aging Summary report.

SPECIAL ACTIVITIES

Activity 8–1 Belgrade National Bank

Ethics and professional conduct in business

Kay Levitt, vice-president of operations for Belgrade National Bank, has instructed the bank's computer programmer to use a 365-day year to compute interest on depository accounts (payables). Kay also instructed the programmer to use a 360-day year to compute interest on loans (receivables).

Discuss whether Kay is behaving in a professional manner.

Activity 8–2 Itana Construction Supplies Co.

Collecting accounts receivable

The following is an excerpt from a conversation between the office manager, Jeremy Nevin, and the president of Itana Construction Supplies Co., Melinda Kirk. Itana sells building supplies to local contractors.

Jeremy: Melinda, we're going to have to do something about these overdue accounts receivable. One-third of our accounts are over 60 days past due, and I've had accounts that have stayed open for almost a year!

Melinda: I didn't realize it was that bad. Any ideas?

Jeremy: Well, we could stop giving credit. Make everyone pay with cash or a credit card. We accept MasterCard and Visa already, but only the walk-in customers use them. Almost all of the contractors put purchases on their bills.

Melinda: Yes, but we've been allowing credit for years. As far as I know, all of our competitors allow contractors credit. If we stopped giving credit, we'd lose many of our contractors. They'd just go elsewhere. You know, some of these guys run up bills as high as $40,000 or $50,000. There's no way they could put that kind of money on a credit card.

Jeremy: That's a good point. But we've got to do something.

Melinda: How many of the contractor accounts do you actually end up writing off as uncollectible?

Jeremy: Not many. Almost all eventually pay. It's just that they take so long!

Suggest one or more solutions to Itana Construction Supplies Co.'s problem concerning the collection of accounts receivable.

Activity 8–3 Costello Wholesale Co.

Value of receivables

The following is an excerpt from a conversation between Bryan Eastman, the president and owner of Costello Wholesale Co., and Michele Joiner, Costello's controller. The conversation took place on January 4, 2000, shortly after Michele began preparing the financial statements for the year ending December 31, 1999.

Michele: Bryan, I've completed my analysis of the collectibility of our accounts receivable. My staff and I estimate that the allowance for doubtful accounts should be somewhere between $50,000 and $80,000. Right now, the balance of the allowance account is $12,000.

Bryan: Oh, no! We are already below the estimated earnings projection I gave the bank last year. We used that as a basis for convincing the bank to loan us $100,000. They're going to be upset! Is there any way we can increase the allowance without the adjustment increasing expenses?

Michele: I'm afraid not. The allowance can only be increased by debiting the uncollectible accounts expense account.

Bryan: Well, I guess we're stuck. The bank will just have to live with it. But let's increase the allowance by only $38,000. That gets us into our range of estimates with the minimum expense increase.

Michele: Bryan, there is one more thing we need to discuss.

Bryan: What now?

Michele: Jim, my staff accountant, noticed that you haven't made any payments on your receivable for over a year. Also, it has increased from $25,000 last year to $75,000. Jim thinks we ought to reclassify it as a noncurrent asset and report it as an "other receivable."

Bryan: What's the problem? Didn't we just include it in accounts receivable last year?

Michele: Yes, but last year it was immaterial.

Bryan: Look, I'll make a $50,000 payment next week. So let's report it like we did last year.

If you were Michele, how would you address Bryan's suggestions?

Activity 8–4 Quick Rehab Co.
Estimate uncollectible accounts

For several years, sales have been on a "cash only" basis. On January 1, 1996, however, Quick Rehab Co. began offering credit on terms of n/30. The amount of the adjusting entry to record the estimated uncollectible receivables at the end of each year has been 1/2 of 1% of credit sales, which is the rate reported as the average for the industry. Credit sales and the year-end credit balances in Allowance for Doubtful Accounts for the past four years are as follows:

Year	Credit Sales	Allowance for Doubtful Accounts
1996	$5,800,000	$ 6,800
1997	6,000,000	7,200
1998	6,100,000	10,000
1999	6,250,000	13,000

LeRoy Tyson, president of Quick Rehab Co., is concerned that the method used to account for and write off uncollectible receivables is unsatisfactory. He has asked for your advice in the analysis of past operations in this area and for recommendations for change.

1. Determine the amount of (a) the addition to Allowance for Doubtful Accounts and (b) the accounts written off for each of the four years.
2. a. Advise LeRoy Tyson as to whether the estimate of 1/2 of 1% of credit sales appears reasonable.
   b. Assume that after discussing (a) with LeRoy Tyson, he asked you what action might be taken to determine what the balance of Allowance for Doubtful Accounts should be at December 31, 1999, and what possible changes, if any, you might recommend in accounting for uncollectible receivables. How would you respond?

Activity 8–5 Into the Real World
Granting credit

GROUP ACTIVITY

In groups of three or four, determine how credit is typically granted to customers. Interview an individual responsible for granting credit for a bank, a department store, an automobile dealer, or other business in your community. You should ask such questions as the following:

1. What procedures are used to decide whether to grant credit to a customer?
2. What procedures are used to try to collect from customers who are delinquent in their payments?
3. Approximately what percentage of customers' accounts are written off as uncollectible in a year?

Summarize your findings in a report to the class.

Activity 8–6 Into the Real World
Collection of receivables

Internet ACTIVITY

Go to the Web page of two department store chains, **Federated Department Stores Inc.** and **Mercantile Stores Co. Inc.** The Internet sites for these companies are:

www.federated-fds.com
www.rootsstore.com

Using the financial information provided at each site, calculate the most recent accounts receivable turnover for each company, and identify which company is collecting its receivables faster.

ANSWERS TO SELF-EXAMINATION QUESTIONS

Matching

1. L	3. I	5. D	7. C	9. G	11. B
2. A	4. M	6. F	8. H	10. J	12. K

Multiple Choice

1. **B** The estimate of uncollectible accounts, $8,500 (answer C), is the amount of the desired balance of Allowance for Doubtful Accounts after adjustment. The amount of the current provision to be made for uncollectible accounts expense is thus $6,000 (answer B), which is the amount that must be added to the Allowance for Doubtful Accounts credit balance of $2,500 (answer A), so that the account will have the desired balance of $8,500.
2. **B** The amount expected to be realized from accounts receivable is the balance of Accounts Receivable, $100,000, less the balance of Allowance for Doubtful Accounts, $7,000, or $93,000 (answer B).
3. **C** Maturity value is the amount that is due at the maturity or due date. The maturity value of $10,300 (answer C) is determined as follows:

Face amount of note	$10,000
Plus interest ($10,000 × 0.12 × 90/360)	300
Maturity value of note	$10,300

4. **C** November 3 is the due date of a $12,000, 90-day, 8% note receivable dated August 5 [26 days in August (31 days − 5 days) + 30 days in September + 31 days in October + 3 days in November].
5. **B** If a note is dishonored, Accounts Receivable is debited for the maturity value of the note (answer B). The maturity value of the note is its face value (answer A) plus the accrued interest. The maturity value of the note less accrued interest (answer C) is equal to the face value of the note. The maturity value of the note plus accrued interest (answer D) is incorrect, since the interest would be added twice.

9

Inventories

Setting the STAGE

Assume that you purchased a Compact Disc (CD)/Receiver in June. You planned on attaching pairs of speakers to the system. Initially, however, you could afford only one pair of speakers, which cost $160. In October, you purchased the second pair of speakers at a cost of $180.

Over the holidays, someone broke into your home and stole one pair of speakers. Luckily, your renters/homeowners insurance policy will cover the theft, but the insurance company needs to know the cost of the speakers that were stolen.

All of the speakers are identical. To respond to the insurance company, however, you will need to identify which pair of speakers was stolen. Was it the first pair, which cost $160? Or was it the second pair, which cost $180? Whichever assumption you make may determine the amount that you receive from the insurance company.

Merchandising businesses make similar assumptions when identical merchandise is purchased at different costs. At the end of a period, some of the merchandise will be in inventory and some will have been sold. But which costs relate to the sold merchandise and which costs relate to the merchandise in inventory? The company's assumption can involve large dollar amounts and thus can have a significant impact on the financial statements. For example, The Home Depot, Inc. has merchandise inventories that total over $2 billion, while Sears, Roebuck and Co.'s inventories total over $4 billion.

In this chapter, we will discuss such issues as how to determine the cost of merchandise in inventory and the cost of merchandise sold. However, we begin this chapter by discussing internal controls over merchandise inventory.

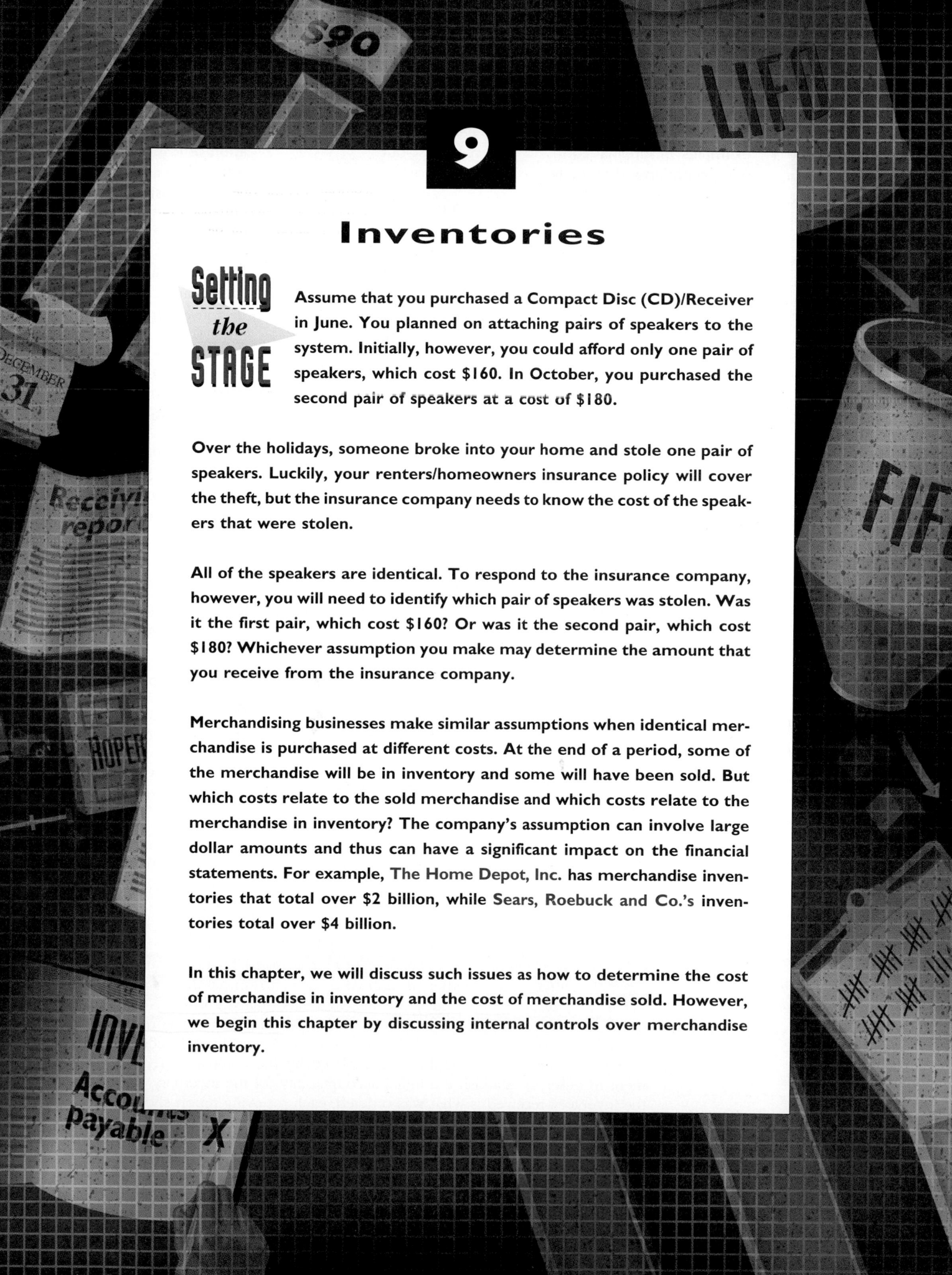

objectives

After studying this chapter, you should be able to:

1. Summarize and provide examples of internal control procedures that apply to inventories.
2. Describe the effect of inventory errors on the financial statements.
3. Describe three inventory cost flow assumptions and how they impact the income statement and balance sheet.
4. Compute the cost of inventory under the perpetual inventory system, using the following costing methods:
   First-in, first-out
   Last-in, first-out
   Average cost
5. Compute the cost of inventory under the periodic inventory system, using the following costing methods:
   First-in, first-out
   Last-in, first-out
   Average cost
6. Compare and contrast the use of the three inventory costing methods.
7. Compute the proper valuation of inventory at other than cost, using the lower-of-cost-or-market and net realizable value concepts.
8. Prepare a balance sheet presentation of merchandise inventory.
9. Estimate the cost of inventory, using the retail method and the gross profit method.
10. Compute and interpret the inventory turnover ratio and the number of days' sales in inventory.

Internal Control of Inventories

OBJECTIVE 1

Summarize and provide examples of internal control procedures that apply to inventories.

The cost of inventory is a significant item in many businesses' financial statements. What do we mean by the term inventory? **Inventory** is used to indicate (1) merchandise held for sale in the normal course of business and (2) materials in the process of production or held for production. In this chapter, we focus primarily on inventory of merchandise purchased for resale.

REAL WORLD

Circuit City's inventory represents over 75% of its current assets and over 50% of its total assets. Circuit City's cost of merchandise sold represents over 70% of its net sales.

What costs should be included in inventory? As we have illustrated in earlier chapters, the cost of merchandise is its purchase price, less any purchases discounts. These costs are usually the largest portion of the inventory cost. Merchandise inventory also includes other costs, such as transportation, import duties, and insurance against losses in transit.

For companies such as Circuit City, good internal control over inventory must be maintained. Two primary objectives of internal control over inventory are safeguarding the inventory and properly reporting it in the financial statements. These internal controls can be either preventive or detective in nature. A preventive control is designed to prevent errors or misstatements from occurring. A detective control is designed to detect an error or misstatement after it has occurred.

Q&A

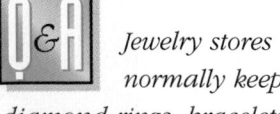

Jewelry stores normally keep diamond rings, bracelets, and other items in a locked glass case. Is this a preventive or a detective control?

This is a preventive control to protect against theft (shoplifting).

Control over inventory should begin as soon as the inventory is received. Prenumbered receiving reports should be completed by the company's receiving department in order to establish the initial accountability for the inventory. To make sure the inventory received is what was ordered, each receiving report should agree with the company's original purchase order for the merchandise. Likewise, the price at which the inventory was ordered, as shown on the purchase order, should be compared to the price at which the vendor billed the company, as shown on the vendor's invoice. After the receiving report, purchase order, and vendor's invoice have

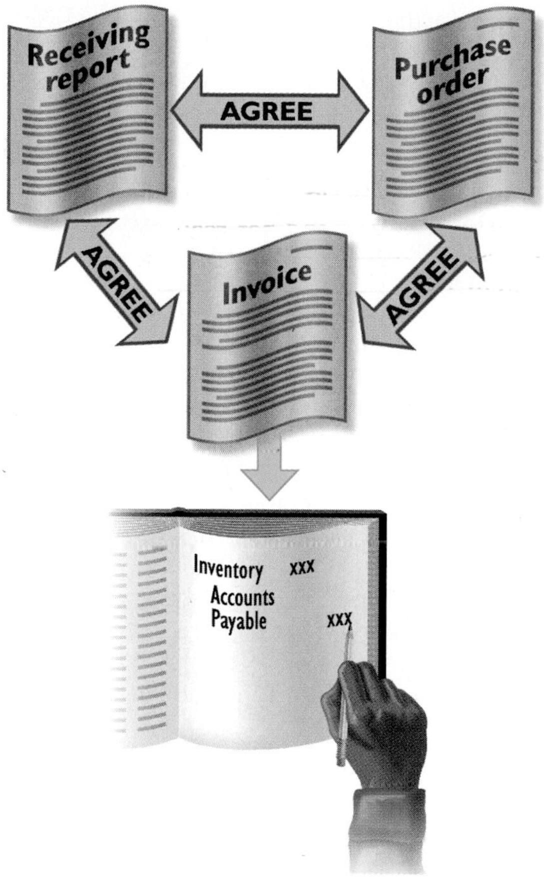

been reconciled, the company should record the inventory and related account payable in the accounting records.

Controls for safeguarding inventory include developing and using security measures to prevent inventory damage or employee theft. For example, inventory should be stored in a warehouse or other area to which access is restricted to authorized employees. The removal of merchandise from the warehouse should be controlled by using requisition forms, which should be properly authorized. The storage area should also be climate controlled to prevent damage from heat or cold. Further, when the business is not operating or is not open, the storage area should be locked.

When shopping, you may have noticed how retail stores protect inventory from customer theft. Retail stores often use such devices as two-way mirrors, cameras, and security guards. High-priced items are often displayed in locked cabinets. Retail clothing stores often place plastic alarm tags on valuable items such as leather coats. Sensors at the exit doors set off alarms if the tags have not been removed by the clerk. These controls are designed to prevent customers from shoplifting.

REAL WORLD **Sam's Club** and **Wal-Mart** stores use a greeter at the entry of each store to welcome customers. The greeter also serves as a preventive control by asking customers not to bring packages or other bags into the store, which could be used for shoplifting.

Using a perpetual inventory system for merchandise also provides an effective means of control over inventory. The amount of each type of merchandise is always readily available in a subsidiary **inventory ledger**. In addition, the subsidiary ledger can be an aid in maintaining inventory quantities at proper levels. Frequently comparing balances with predetermined maximum and minimum levels allows for the timely reordering of merchandise and prevents the ordering of excess inventory.

REAL WORLD Most companies take their physical inventories when their inventory levels are the lowest. For example, most retailers take their physical inventory in late January or early February, which is after the holiday selling season but before restocking for spring.

To ensure the accuracy of the amount of inventory reported in the financial statements, a merchandising business should take a **physical inventory** (i.e., count the merchandise). In a perpetual inventory system, the physical inventory is compared to the recorded inventory in order to determine the amount of shrinkage or shortage. If the inventory shrinkage is unusually large, management can investigate further and take any necessary corrective action. Knowledge that a physical inventory will be taken also helps prevent employee thefts or misuses of inventory.

How does a business "take" a physical inventory? The first step in this process is to determine the quantity of each kind of merchandise owned by the business. A common practice is to use teams of two persons. One person determines the quantity, and the other lists the quantity and description on inventory count sheets. Quantities of high-cost items are usually verified by supervisors or a second count team.

All merchandise *owned* by a business should be included in the business's inventory.

What merchandise should be included in inventory? All the merchandise *owned* by the business on the inventory date should be included. For merchandise in transit, the party (the seller or the buyer) who has title to the merchandise on the inventory date is the owner. To determine who has title, it may be necessary to examine purchases and sales invoices of the last few days of the current pe-

Business on Stage

What Does It Cost to Have an Inventory?

Inventories are essential for merchandising and manufacturing businesses. Inventories are necessary in order to generate sales, and sales are necessary in order to generate profits.

The primary benefit of carrying inventory is that it provides protection against unexpected events and disruptions in business operations. For example, an unexpected strike by a supplier's employees can halt production for a manufacturer or cause lost sales for a merchandiser. Businesses that rely upon foreign suppliers are particularly affected by disruptions caused by international crises and events. Carrying inventory also allows a business to meet unexpected increases in the demand for its product. Thus, you can think of inventories as a buffer or cushion against the unexpected.

Inventory is not free, however. The costs of carrying inventory are classified as (1) holding costs, (2) ordering costs, and (3) stockout costs. *Holding costs* include the costs of handling, storage, insurance, property taxes, and depreciation. In addition, holding costs for a merchandising business include losses that occur when customer preferences and tastes change unexpectedly and inventory is marked down. Finally, holding costs include the cost of funds that could be used for other purposes if they were not tied up in inventory. For example, if a business must borrow $100,000 at 10% to finance its inventories, then the interest of $10,000 per year is part of the cost of holding inventory.

Ordering costs are the costs of placing and processing orders with suppliers. Ordering costs also include the cost of investigating possible suppliers and negotiating contracts with suppliers.

Stockout costs include the costs of failing to meet customer demands—the cost of lost sales and lost profits, as well as lost customer goodwill. For a manufacturer, stockout costs include the costs of production delays and downtime, as well as the related costs of restarting production.

Inventory management involves the difficult task of balancing the benefits of carrying inventory against the related costs. In a merchandise business, inventory management is normally the responsibility of a merchandising manager or buyer. ■

riod and the first few days of the following period.

As we discussed in an earlier chapter, shipping terms determine when title passes. When goods are purchased or sold **FOB shipping point**, title passes to the buyer when the goods are shipped. When the terms are **FOB destination**, title passes to the buyer when the goods are delivered.

To illustrate, assume that Roper Co. orders $25,000 of merchandise on December 28, 2000. The merchandise is shipped FOB shipping point by the seller on December 30 and arrives at Roper Co.'s warehouse on January 4, 2001. As a result, the merchandise is not counted by the inventory crew on December 31, the end of Roper Co.'s fiscal year. However, the $25,000 of merchandise should be included in Roper's inventory because title has passed. Roper Co. should record the merchandise in transit on December 31, debiting Merchandise Inventory and crediting Accounts Payable for $25,000.

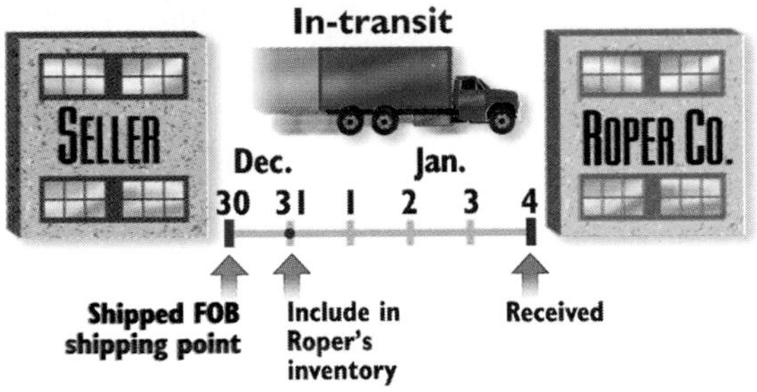

Manufacturers sometimes ship merchandise to retailers who act as the manufacturer's agent when selling the merchandise. The manufacturer retains title until the goods are sold. Such merchandise is said to be shipped *on consignment* to the retailers. The unsold merchandise is a part of the manufacturer's (consignor's) inventory, even though the merchandise is in the hands of the retailers. The consigned merchandise should not be included in the retailer's (consignee's) inventory.

OBJECTIVE 2

Describe the effect of inventory errors on the financial statements.

Effect of Inventory Errors on Financial Statements

Any errors in the inventory count will affect both the balance sheet and the income statement. For example, an error in the physical inventory will misstate the ending inventory, current assets, and total assets on the balance sheet. This is because the

Crazy Eddie Inc., which operated electronics stores, defrauded investors by misstating inventory. The company reported rapid gains in sales and earnings due to what the company said was store expansion, adept sales-floor techniques, and catchy commercials. However, Crazy Eddie had overstated inventory counts at one warehouse by $10 million, drafted phony inventory count sheets, and included in inventory $4 million of merchandise that, in fact, was being returned to suppliers. As a result, income was overstated. The apparent purpose of the scheme was to "artificially inflate the net worth of the company" and the value of stock owned by the store's founder, Eddie Antar, and others.

Source: Jeffrey A. Tannenbaum, "Filings by Crazy Eddie Suggest Founder Led Scheme to Inflate Company's Value," *The Wall Street Journal,* May 31, 1988, p. 28.

physical inventory is the basis for recording the adjusting entry for inventory shrinkage. Also, an error in taking the physical inventory misstates the cost of goods sold, gross profit, and net income on the income statement. In addition, because net income is closed to the owner's equity at the end of the period, owner's equity will also be misstated on the balance sheet. This misstatement of owner's equity will equal the misstatement of the ending inventory, current assets, and total assets.

To illustrate, assume that in taking the physical inventory on December 31, 2000, Sapra Company incorrectly recorded its physical inventory as $115,000 instead of the correct amount of $125,000. As a result, the merchandise inventory, current assets, and total assets reported on the December 31, 2000, balance sheet would be understated by $10,000 ($125,000 − $115,000). Because the ending physical inventory is understated, the inventory shrinkage and the cost of merchandise sold will be overstated by $10,000. Thus, the gross profit and the net income for the year will be understated by $10,000. Since the net income is closed to owner's equity at the end of the period, the owner's equity on the December 31, 2000 balance sheet will also be understated by $10,000. The effects on Sapra Company's financial statements are summarized as follows:

	Amount of Misstatement
Balance Sheet:	
Merchandise inventory understated	$(10,000)
Current assets understated	(10,000)
Total assets understated	(10,000)
Owner's equity understated	(10,000)
Income Statement:	
Cost of merchandise sold overstated	$ 10,000
Gross profit understated	(10,000)
Net income understated	(10,000)

At the end of 1999, the physical ending inventory of Melchor Co. was overstated by $25,000. What is the effect of this error on the financial statements (balance sheet and income statement) prepared at the end of 1999?

On the balance sheet, the merchandise inventory, current assets, total assets, and owner's equity are overstated by $25,000. On the income statement, the cost of merchandise sold is understated by $25,000, and the gross profit and net income are overstated by $25,000.

Now assume that in the preceding example the physical inventory had been *overstated* on December 31, 2000, by $10,000. That is, Sapra Company erroneously recorded its inventory as $135,000. In this case, the effects on the balance sheet and income statement would be just the *opposite* of those indicated above.

Errors in the physical inventory are normally detected in the period after they occur. In such cases, the financial statements of the prior year must be corrected. We will discuss such corrections in a later chapter.

OBJECTIVE 3

Describe three inventory cost flow assumptions and how they impact the income statement and balance sheet.

Inventory Cost Flow Assumptions

A major accounting issue arises when identical units of merchandise are acquired at different unit costs during a period. In such cases, when an item is sold, it is necessary to determine its unit cost so that the proper accounting entry can be recorded. To illustrate, assume that three identical units of Item X are purchased during May, as shown below.

	Item X	Units	Cost
May 10	Purchase	1	$ 9
18	Purchase	1	13
24	Purchase	1	14
Total		3	$36
Average cost per unit			$12

Assume that one unit is sold on May 30 for $20. If this unit can be identified with a specific purchase, the **specific identification method** can be used to determine the cost of the unit sold. For example, if the unit sold was purchased on May 18, the cost assigned to the unit is $13 and the gross profit is $7 ($20 − $13). If, however, the unit sold was purchased on May 10, the cost assigned to the unit is $9 and the gross profit is $11 ($20 − $9).

REAL WORLD The specific identification method is normally used by jewelry stores and art galleries.

The specific identification method is not practical unless each unit can be identified accurately. An automobile dealer, for example, may be able to use this method, since each automobile has a unique serial number. For many businesses, however, identical units cannot be separately identified, and a cost flow must be assumed. That is, which units have been sold and which units are still in inventory must be assumed.

There are three common cost flow assumptions used in business. Each of these assumptions is identified with an inventory costing method, as shown below.

Cost Flow Assumption	1. Cost flow is in the order in which the costs were incurred.	2. Cost flow is in the reverse order in which the costs were incurred.	3. Cost flow is an average of the costs.
Inventory Costing Method	First-in, first-out (fifo)	Last-in, first-out (lifo)	Average cost

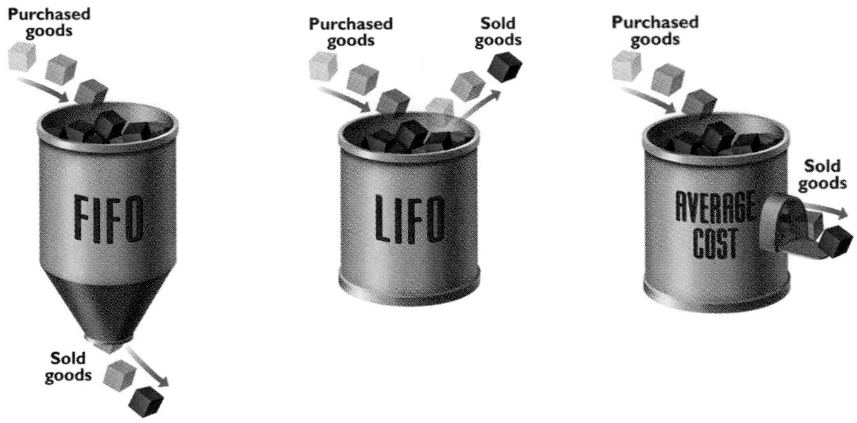

When the **first-in, first-out (fifo) method** is used, the ending inventory is made up of the most recent costs. When the **last-in, first-out (lifo) method** is used, the ending inventory is made up of the earliest costs. When the **average cost method** is used, the cost of the units in inventory is an average of the purchase costs.

To illustrate, we use the preceding example to prepare the income statement for May and the balance sheet as of May 31 for each of the cost flow methods. These financial statements are shown in Exhibit 1.

As you can see, the selection of an inventory costing method can have a significant impact on the financial statements. For this reason, the selection has important implications for managers and others in analyzing and interpreting the financial statements. The chart in Exhibit 2 shows the frequency with which fifo, lifo, and the average methods are used in practice.

EXHIBIT 1
Effect of Inventory Costing Methods on Financial Statements

Fifo Method

Income Statement	
Sales	$20
Cost of merchandise sold	9
Gross profit	$11

Balance Sheet	
Merchandise inventory	$27

Lifo Method

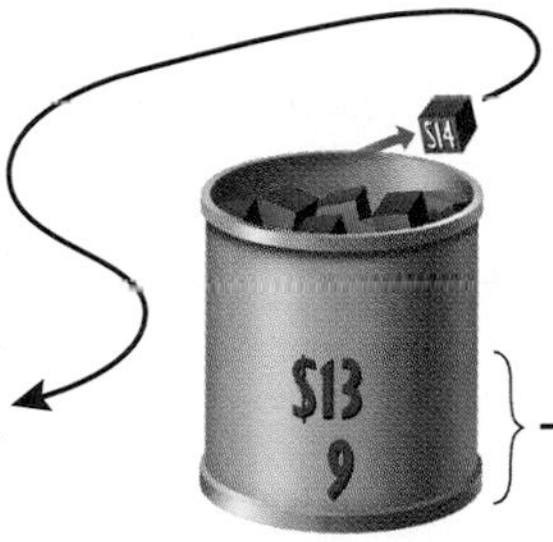

Income Statement	
Sales	$20
Cost of merchandise sold	14
Gross profit	$ 6

Balance Sheet	
Merchandise inventory	$22

Average Cost Method

Income Statement	
Sales	$20
Cost of merchandise sold	12
Gross profit	$ 8

Balance Sheet	
Merchandise inventory	$24

EXHIBIT 2
Inventory Costing Methods

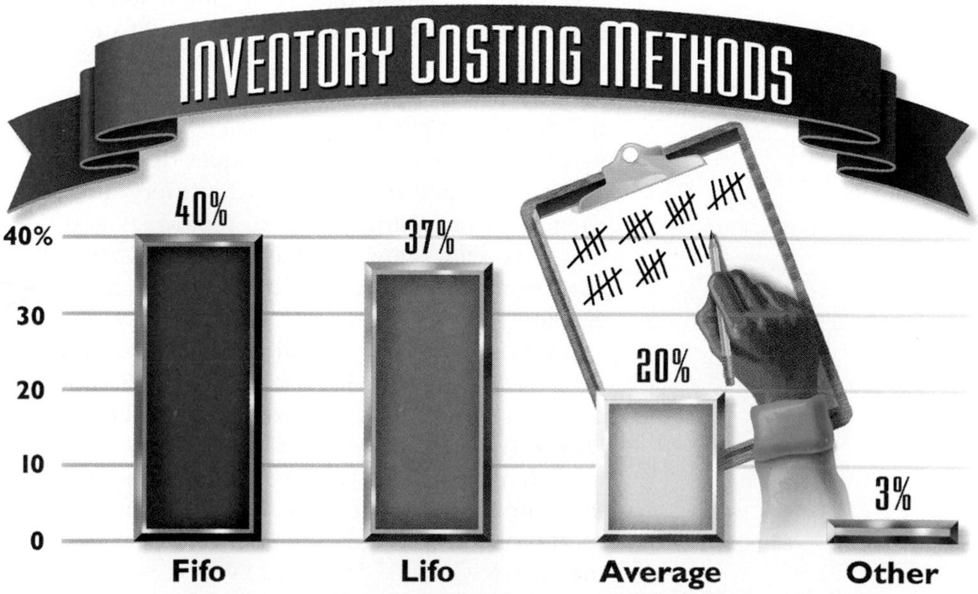

Source: Accounting Trends & Techniques, 50th ed., American Institute of Certified Public Accountants, New York, 1996.

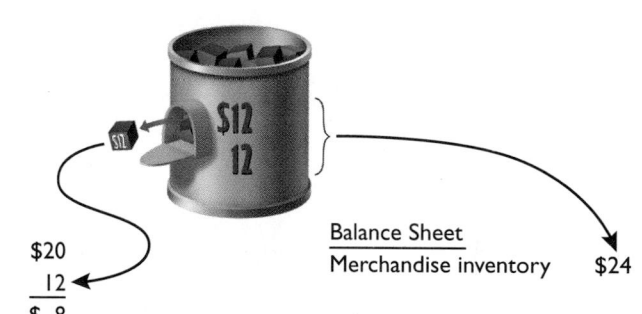

Inventory Costing Methods Under a Perpetual Inventory System

OBJECTIVE 4

Compute the cost of inventory under the perpetual inventory system, using the following costing methods:

First-in, first-out

Last-in, first-out

Average cost

In a perpetual inventory system, all merchandise increases and decreases are recorded in a manner similar to the recording of increases and decreases in cash. The merchandise inventory account at the beginning of an accounting period indicates the merchandise in stock on that date. Purchases are recorded by debiting *Merchandise Inventory* and crediting *Cash* or *Accounts Payable*. On the date of each sale, the cost of the merchandise sold is recorded by debiting *Cost of Merchandise Sold* and crediting *Merchandise Inventory*.

As we illustrated in the preceding section, when identical units of an item are purchased at different unit costs during a period, a cost flow must be assumed. In such cases, the fifo, lifo, or average cost method is used. We illustrate each of these methods, using the following data for Item 127B:

	Item 127B	Units	Cost
Jan. 1	Inventory	10	$20
4	Sale	7	
10	Purchase	8	21
22	Sale	4	
28	Sale	2	
30	Purchase	10	22

First-In, First-Out Method

Most businesses dispose of goods in the order in which the goods are purchased. This would be especially true of perishables and goods whose styles or models often change. For example, grocery stores shelve their milk products by expiration dates. Likewise, men's and women's clothing stores display clothes by season. At the end of a season, they often have sales to clear their stores of off-season or out-of-style clothing. Thus, the fifo method is often consistent with the *physical flow* or movement of merchandise. To the extent that this is the case, the fifo method provides results that are about the same as those obtained by identifying the specific costs of each item sold and in inventory.

When the fifo method of costing inventory is used, costs are included in the cost of merchandise sold in the order in which they were incurred. To illustrate, Exhibit 3 shows the journal entries for purchases and sales and the inventory subsidiary ledger account for Item 127B. The number of units in inventory after each transaction, together with total costs and unit costs, are shown in the account. We assume that the units are sold for $30 each on account.

Using fifo, costs are included in the merchandise sold in the order in which they were incurred.

You should note that after the 7 units were sold on January 4, there was an inventory of 3 units at $20 each. The 8 units purchased on January 10 were acquired at a unit cost of $21, instead of $20. Therefore, the inventory after the January 10 purchase is reported on two lines, 3 units at $20 each and 8 units at $21 each. Next, note that the $81 cost of the 4 units sold on January 22 is made up of the remaining 3 units at $20 each and 1 unit at $21. At this point, 7 units are in inventory at a cost of $21 per unit. The remainder of the illustration is explained in a similar manner.

EXHIBIT 3
Entries and Perpetual Inventory Account (Fifo)

Date	Account	Debit	Credit
Jan. 4	Accounts Receivable	210	
	Sales		210
4	Cost of Merchandise Sold	140	
	Merchandise Inventory		140
10	Merchandise Inventory	168	
	Accounts Payable		168
22	Accounts Receivable	120	
	Sales		120
22	Cost of Merchandise Sold	81	
	Merchandise Inventory		81
28	Accounts Receivable	60	
	Sales		60
28	Cost of Merchandise Sold	42	
	Merchandise Inventory		42
30	Merchandise Inventory	220	
	Accounts Payable		220

Item 127B

	Purchases			Cost of Merchandise Sold			Inventory		
Date	Quantity	Unit Cost	Total Cost	Quantity	Unit Cost	Total Cost	Quantity	Unit Cost	Total Cost
Jan. 1							10	20	200
4				7	20	140	3	20	60
10	8	21	168				3	20	60
							8	21	168
22				3	20	60			
				1	21	21	7	21	147
28				2	21	42	5	21	105
30	10	22	220				5	21	105
							10	22	220

Last-In, First-Out Method

When the lifo method is used in a perpetual inventory system, the cost of the units sold is the cost of the most recent purchases. To illustrate, Exhibit 4 shows the journal entries for purchases and sales and the subsidiary ledger account for Item 127B, prepared on a lifo basis.

Using lifo, the cost of units sold is the cost of the most recent purchases.

EXHIBIT 4
Entries and Perpetual Inventory Account (Lifo)

Date	Account	Debit	Credit
Jan. 4	Accounts Receivable	210	
	Sales		210
4	Cost of Merchandise Sold	140	
	Merchandise Inventory		140
10	Merchandise Inventory	168	
	Accounts Payable		168
22	Accounts Receivable	120	
	Sales		120
22	Cost of Merchandise Sold	84	
	Merchandise Inventory		84
28	Accounts Receivable	60	
	Sales		60
28	Cost of Merchandise Sold	42	
	Merchandise Inventory		42
30	Merchandise Inventory	220	
	Accounts Payable		220

Item 127B

	Purchases			Cost of Merchandise Sold			Inventory		
Date	Quantity	Unit Cost	Total Cost	Quantity	Unit Cost	Total Cost	Quantity	Unit Cost	Total Cost
Jan. 1							10	20	200
4				7	20	140	3	20	60
10	8	21	168				3	20	60
							8	21	168
22				4	21	84	3	20	60
							4	21	84
28				2	21	42	3	20	60
							2	21	42
30	10	22	220				3	20	60
							2	21	42
							10	22	220

If you compare the ledger accounts for the fifo perpetual system and the lifo perpetual system, you should discover that the accounts are the same through the January 10 purchase. Using lifo, however, the cost of the 4 units sold on January 22 is the cost of the units from the January 10 purchase ($21 per unit). The cost of the 7 units in inventory after the sale on January 22 is the cost of the 3 units remaining from the beginning inventory and the cost of the 4 units remaining from the January 10 purchase. The remainder of the lifo illustration is explained in a similar manner.

When the lifo method is used, the inventory ledger is sometimes maintained in units only. The units are converted to dollars when the financial statements are prepared at the end of the period.

The use of the lifo method was originally limited to rare situations in which the units sold were taken from the most recently acquired goods. For tax reasons, which we will discuss later, its use has greatly increased during the past few decades. Lifo is now often used even when it does not represent the physical flow of goods.

Average Cost Method

When the average cost method is used in a perpetual inventory system, an average unit cost for each type of item is computed each time a purchase is made. This unit cost is then used to determine the cost of each sale until another purchase is made and a new average is computed. This averaging technique is called a *moving average*. Since the average cost method is not often used in a perpetual inventory system, we do not illustrate it in this chapter.

Computerized Perpetual Inventory Systems

The records for a perpetual inventory system may be maintained manually. However, such a system is costly and time consuming for businesses with a large number of inventory items with many purchase and sales transactions. In most cases, the record keeping for perpetual inventory systems is computerized.

REAL WORLD: The fifo, lifo, and average cost flow assumptions also apply to other areas of business. For example, individuals and businesses often purchase marketable securities at different costs per share. When such investments are sold, the investor must either specifically identify which shares are sold or use the fifo cost flow assumption. To illustrate, assume that a business purchased 100 shares of **Microsoft Corporation** at $85 and 100 shares at $95. If the business later sells 100 shares for $100, which shares did it sell? The business must determine the cost of the shares sold so that it can report a gain or loss on the sale for tax purposes. In addition, it must report the gain or loss on its income statement.

An example of using computers in maintaining perpetual inventory records for retail stores is described below:

1. The relevant details for each inventory item, such as a description, quantity, and unit size, are stored in an inventory record. The individual inventory records make up the computerized inventory file, the total of which agrees with the balance of the inventory ledger account.
2. Each time an item is purchased or returned by a customer, the inventory data are entered into the computer's inventory records and files.
3. Each time an item is sold, a salesclerk scans the item's bar code with an optical scanner. The scanner reads the magnetic code and rings up the sale on the cash register. The inventory records and files are then updated.
4. After a physical inventory is taken, the inventory count data are entered into the computer. These data are compared with the current balances, and a listing of the overages and shortages is printed. The inventory balances are then adjusted to the quantities determined by the physical count.

REAL WORLD: **Wal-Mart, Kmart, Sears, and other retailers use bar code scanners as part of their perpetual inventory systems.**

Such systems can be extended to aid managers in controlling and managing inventory quantities. For example, items that are selling fast can be reordered before the stock is depleted. Past sales patterns can be analyzed to determine when to mark down merchandise for sales and when to restock seasonal merchandise. In addition, such systems can provide managers with data for developing and fine-tuning their marketing strategies. For example, such data can be used to evaluate the effectiveness of advertising campaigns and sales promotions.

Inventory Costing Methods Under a Periodic Inventory System

OBJECTIVE 5

Compute the cost of inventory under the periodic inventory system, using the following costing methods:

First-in, first-out

Last-in, first-out

Average cost

When the periodic inventory system is used, only revenue is recorded each time a sale is made. No entry is made at the time of the sale to record the cost of the merchandise sold. At the end of the accounting period, a physical inventory is taken to determine the cost of the inventory and the cost of the merchandise sold.

For merchandising businesses that use the periodic system, the cost of merchandise sold during a period is reported in a separate section in the income statement. To illustrate, assume that Computer King opened a merchandising outlet selling personal computers and software. During 2001, Computer King purchased $340,000 of merchandise. If the inventory at December 31, 2001, the end of the year, is $59,700, the cost of merchandise sold during 2001 would be reported as follows:

Cost of merchandise sold:		
Purchases	$340,000	
Less merchandise inventory, December 31, 2001	59,700	
Cost of merchandise sold		$280,300

To continue the illustration, assume that during 2002 Computer King purchased additional merchandise of $521,980. It received credit for purchases returns and allowances of $9,100, took purchases discounts of $2,525, and paid transportation costs of $17,400. The purchases returns and allowances and the purchases discounts are deducted from the total purchases to yield the *net purchases*. The transportation costs are added to the net purchases to yield the *cost of merchandise purchased*. These amounts would be reported in the cost of merchandise sold section of Computer King's income statement for 2002 as follows:

Purchases		$521,980	
Less: Purchases returns and allowances	$9,100		
Purchases discounts	2,525	11,625	
Net purchases		$510,355	
Add transportation in		17,400	
Cost of merchandise purchased			$527,755

The ending inventory of Computer King on December 31, 2001, $59,700, becomes the beginning inventory for 2002. In the cost of merchandise sold section of the income statement for 2002, this beginning inventory is added to the cost of merchandise purchased to yield the *merchandise available for sale*. The ending inventory, which is assumed to be $62,150, is then subtracted from the merchandise available for sale to yield the cost of merchandise sold. The cost of merchandise sold during 2002 would be reported as follows:

Cost of merchandise sold:			
Merchandise inventory, January 1, 2002			$ 59,700
Purchases		$521,980	
Less: Purchases returns and allowances	$9,100		
Purchases discounts	2,525	11,625	
Net purchases		$510,355	
Add transportation in		17,400	
Cost of merchandise purchased			527,755
Merchandise available for sale			$587,455
Less merchandise inventory, December 31, 2002			62,150
Cost of merchandise sold			$525,305

Q&A *What is the cost of merchandise sold if the beginning inventory is $50,000, the ending inventory is $65,000, the net purchases are $400,000, and the transportation in is $12,000?*

$397,000 ($50,000 + $400,000 + $12,000 − $65,000)

Like the perpetual inventory system, a cost flow assumption must be made when identical units are acquired at different unit costs during a period. In such cases, the fifo, lifo, or average cost method is used.

First-In, First-Out Method

To illustrate the use of the fifo method in a periodic inventory system, we assume the following data:

Jan. 1	Inventory:	200 units at	$ 9	$ 1,800
Mar. 10	Purchase:	300 units at	10	3,000
Sept. 21	Purchase:	400 units at	11	4,400
Nov. 18	Purchase:	100 units at	12	1,200
Available for sale during year		1,000		$10,400

The physical count on December 31 shows that 300 units have not been sold. Using the fifo method, the cost of the 700 units sold is determined as follows:

Earliest costs, Jan. 1:	200 units at	$ 9	$1,800
Next earliest costs, Mar. 10:	300 units at	10	3,000
Next earliest costs, Sept. 21:	200 units at	11	2,200
Cost of merchandise sold:	700		$7,000

Deducting the cost of merchandise sold of $7,000 from the $10,400 of merchandise available for sale yields $3,400 as the cost of the inventory at December 31. The $3,400 inventory is made up of the most recent costs incurred for this item. Exhibit 5 shows the relationship of the cost of merchandise sold during the year and the inventory at December 31.

EXHIBIT 5
First-In, First-Out Flow of Costs

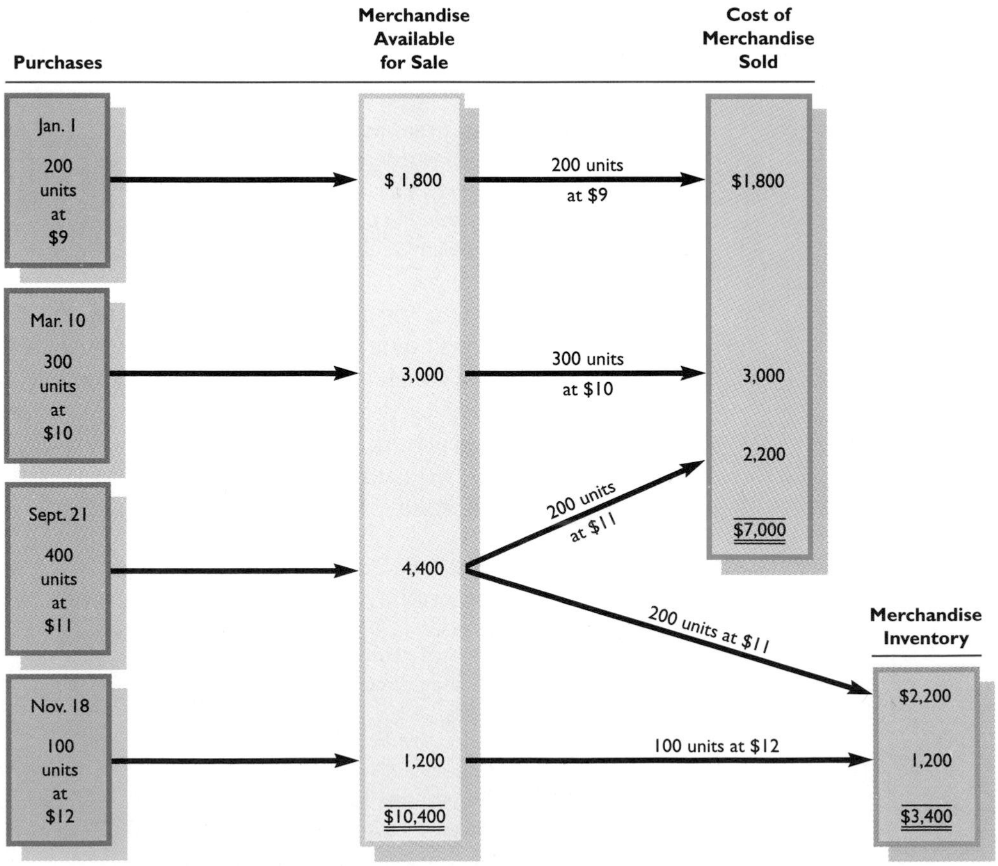

Last-In, First-Out Method

When the lifo method is used, the cost of merchandise sold is made up of the most recent costs. Based on the data in the fifo example, the cost of the 700 units of inventory is determined as follows:

Most recent costs, Nov. 18:	100 units at $12	$1,200
Next most recent costs, Sept. 21:	400 units at 11	4,400
Next most recent costs, Mar. 10:	200 units at 10	2,000
Cost of merchandise sold:	700	$7,600

Deducting the cost of merchandise sold of $7,600 from the $10,400 of merchandise available for sale yields $2,800 as the cost of the inventory at December 31. The $2,800 inventory is made up of the earliest costs incurred for this item. Exhibit 6 shows the relationship of the cost of merchandise sold during the year and the inventory at December 31.

EXHIBIT 6
Last-In, First-Out Flow of Costs

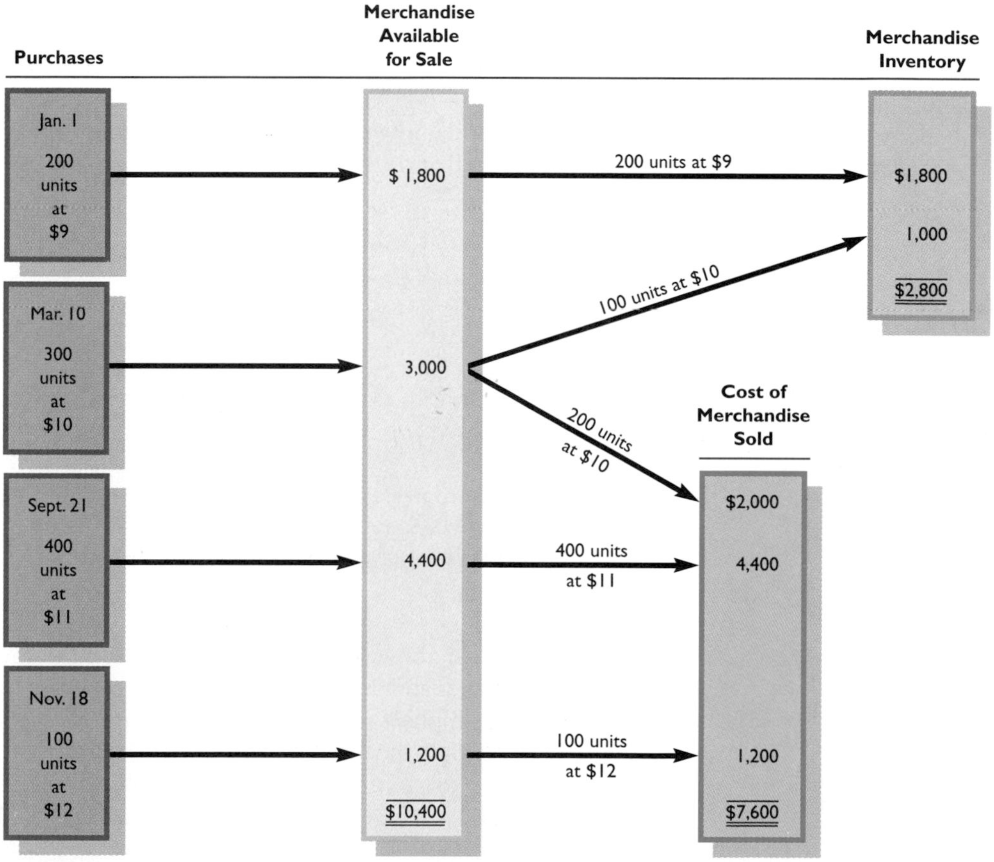

Average Cost Method

The average cost method is sometimes called the **weighted average method**. When this method is used, costs are matched against revenue according to an average of the unit costs of the goods sold. The same weighted average unit costs are used in determining the cost of the merchandise inventory at the end of the period. For businesses in which merchandise sales may be made up of various purchases of identical units, the average method approximates the physical flow of goods.

The weighted average unit cost is determined by dividing the total cost of the units of each item available for sale during the period by the related number of units of that item. Using the same cost data as in the fifo and lifo examples, the average cost of the 1,000 units, $10.40, and the cost of the 700 units, $7,280, are determined as follows:

Average unit cost: $10,400/1,000 units = $10.40
Cost of merchandise sold: 700 units at $10.40 = **$7,280**

Deducting the cost of merchandise sold of **$7,280** from the **$10,400** of merchandise available for sale yields **$3,120** as the cost of the inventory at December 31.

Comparing Inventory Costing Methods

OBJECTIVE 6

Compare and contrast the use of the three inventory costing methods.

As we have illustrated, a different cost flow is assumed for each of the three alternative methods of costing inventories. You should note that if the cost of units had remained stable, all three methods would have yielded the same results. Since prices do change, however, the three methods will normally yield different amounts for (1) the cost of the merchandise sold for the period, (2) the gross profit (and net income) for the period, and (3) the ending inventory. Using the preceding examples for the periodic inventory system and assuming that net sales were $15,000, the following partial income statements indicate the effects of each method when prices are rising:[1]

Partial Income Statements

	First-In, First-Out		Average Cost		Last-In, First-Out	
Net sales		$15,000		$15,000		$15,000
Cost of merchandise sold:						
Beginning inventory	$ 1,800		$ 1,800		$ 1,800	
Purchases	8,600		8,600		8,600	
Merchandise available for sale	$10,400		$10,400		$10,400	
Less ending inventory	3,400		3,120		2,800	
Cost of merchandise sold		7,000		7,280		7,600
Gross profit		$ 8,000		$ 7,720		$ 7,400

As shown above, the fifo method yielded the lowest amount for the cost of merchandise sold and the highest amount for gross profit (and net income). It also yielded the highest amount for the ending inventory. On the other hand, the lifo method yielded the highest amount for the cost of merchandise sold, the lowest amount for gross profit (and net income), and the lowest amount for ending inventory. The average cost method yielded results that were between those of fifo and lifo.

Use of the First-In, First-Out Method

When the fifo method is used during a period of inflation or rising prices, the earlier unit costs are lower than the more recent unit costs, as shown in the preceding fifo example. Much of the benefit of the larger amount of gross profit is lost, however, because the inventory must be replaced at ever higher prices. In fact, the

[1] Similar results would also occur when comparing inventory costing methods under a perpetual inventory system.

balance sheet will report the ending merchandise inventory at an amount that is about the same as its current replacement cost. When the rate of inflation reaches double digits, as it did during the 1970s, the larger gross profits that result from the fifo method are often called *inventory profits* or *illusory profits*. You should note that in a period of deflation or declining prices, the effect is just the opposite.

Use of the Last-In, First-Out Method

When the lifo method is used during a period of inflation or rising prices, the results are opposite those of the other two methods. As shown in the preceding example, the lifo method will yield a higher amount of cost of merchandise sold, a lower amount of gross profit, and a lower amount of inventory at the end of the period than the other two methods. The reason for these effects is that the cost of the most recently acquired units is about the same as the cost of their replacement. In a period of inflation, the more recent unit costs are higher than the earlier unit costs. Thus, it can be argued that the lifo method more nearly matches current costs with current revenues.

Chrysler Corporation's reason for changing from the fifo method to the lifo method was stated in the following footnote that accompanied its financial statements: *Chrysler changed its method of accounting from first-in, first-out (fifo) to last-in, first-out (lifo) for substantially all of its domestic productive inventories. The change to lifo was made to more accurately match current costs with current revenues.*

In the following note, **Sears, Roebuck and Co.** reported the difference in its inventory if fifo had been used instead of lifo: *Inventories would have been $730 million higher if valued on the first-in, first-out, or FIFO, method.*

During periods of rising prices, using lifo offers an income tax savings. The income tax savings results because lifo reports the lowest amount of net income of the three methods. During the double-digit inflationary period of the 1970s, many businesses changed from fifo to lifo for the tax savings. However, the ending inventory on the balance sheet may be quite different from its current replacement cost. In such cases, the financial statements normally include a note that states the estimated difference between the lifo inventory and the inventory if fifo had been used. Again, you should note that in a period of deflation or falling price levels, the effects are just the opposite.

Use of the Average Cost Method

As you might have already reasoned, the average cost method of inventory costing is, in a sense, a compromise between fifo and lifo. The effect of price trends is averaged in determining the cost of merchandise sold and the ending inventory. For a series of purchases, the average cost will be the same, regardless of the direction of price trends. For example, a complete reversal of the sequence of unit costs presented in the preceding illustration would not affect the reported cost of merchandise sold, gross profit, or ending inventory.

OBJECTIVE 7

Compute the proper valuation of inventory at other than cost, using the lower-of-cost-or-market and net realizable value concepts.

Valuation of Inventory at Other Than Cost

As we indicated earlier, cost is the primary basis for valuing inventories. In some cases, however, inventory is valued at other than cost. Two such cases arise when (1) the cost of replacing items in inventory is below the recorded cost and (2) the inventory is not salable at normal sales prices. This latter case may be due to imperfections, shop wear, style changes, or other causes.

Valuation at Lower of Cost or Market

If the cost of replacing an item in inventory is lower than the original purchase cost, the **lower-of-cost-or-market (LCM) method** is used to value the inventory. *Market,* as used in *lower of cost or market,* is the cost to replace the merchandise on the inventory date. This market value is based on quantities normally purchased from the usual source of supply. In businesses where inflation is the norm, market prices rarely decline. In businesses where technology changes rapidly (e.g., microcomputers and televisions), market declines are common. The primary advantage of the lower-of-cost-or-market method is that gross profit (and net income) is reduced in the period in which the market decline occurred.

During 1994, **Dell Computer Company** recorded over $39.3 million of charges (expenses) in writing down its inventory of computer notebooks. The remaining inventories of notebooks were then sold at significantly reduced prices.

If the cost of an item is $410, its current replacement cost is $400, and its selling price is $525, at what amount should the item be included in the inventory according to the LCM method?

$400

In applying the lower-of-cost-or-market method, the cost and replacement cost can be determined in one of three ways. Cost and replacement cost can be determined for (1) each item in the inventory, (2) major classes or categories of inventory, or (3) the inventory as a whole. In practice, the cost and replacement cost of each item are usually determined.

To illustrate, assume that there are 400 identical units of Item A in inventory, acquired at a unit cost of $10.25 each. If at the inventory date the item would cost $10.50 to replace, the cost price of $10.25 would be multiplied by 400 to determine the inventory value. On the other hand, if the item could be replaced at $9.50 a unit, the replacement cost of $9.50 would be used for valuation purposes.

Exhibit 7 illustrates a method of organizing inventory data and applying the lower-of-cost-or-market method to each inventory item. The amount of the market decline, $450 ($15,520 − $15,070), may be reported as a separate item on the income statement or included in the cost of merchandise sold. Regardless, net income will be reduced by the amount of the market decline.

EXHIBIT 7
Determining Inventory at Lower of Cost or Market

Commodity	Inventory Quantity	Unit Cost Price	Unit Market Price	Total Cost	Total Market	Total Lower of C or M
A	400	$10.25	$ 9.50	$ 4,100	$ 3,800	$ 3,800
B	120	22.50	24.10	2,700	2,892	2,700
C	600	8.00	7.75	4,800	4,650	4,650
D	280	14.00	14.75	3,920	4,130	3,920
Total				$15,520	$15,472	$15,070

Out-of-date merchandise is a major problem for many types of retailers. For example, you may have noticed the shelf-life dates of grocery products, such as milk, eggs, canned goods, and meat. Grocery stores often mark down the prices of products nearing the end of their shelf life to avoid having to dispose of the products as waste.

Valuation at Net Realizable Value

As you would expect, merchandise that is out of date, spoiled, or damaged or that can be sold only at prices below cost should be written down. Such merchandise should be valued at net realizable value. **Net realizable value** is the estimated selling price less any direct cost of disposal, such as sales commissions. For example, assume that damaged merchandise costing $1,000 can be sold for only $800, and direct selling expenses are estimated to be $150. This inventory should be valued at $650 ($800 − $150), which is its net realizable value.

Presentation of Merchandise Inventory on the Balance Sheet

OBJECTIVE 8

Prepare a balance sheet presentation of merchandise inventory.

Merchandise inventory is usually presented in the Current Assets section of the balance sheet, following receivables. Both the method of determining the cost of the inventory (fifo, lifo, or average) and the method of valuing the inventory (cost or the lower of cost or market) should be shown. It is not unusual for large businesses with varied activities to use different costing methods for different segments of their inventories. The details may be disclosed in parentheses on the balance sheet or in a footnote to the financial statements. Exhibit 8 shows how parentheses may be used.

REAL WORLD

The following note was taken from the financial statements of **Chrysler Corporation**: *Automotive inventories are valued at the lower of cost or market. The cost of substantially all domestic automotive inventories is recorded on a Last-In, First-Out (LIFO) basis. Aerospace inventories are stated at the lower of cost or market, with cost recognized on a First-In, First-Out (FIFO) basis.*

EXHIBIT 8
Merchandise Inventory on the Balance Sheet

Afro-Arts
Balance Sheet
December 31, 2001

Assets		
Current assets:		
Cash		$ 19 400 00
Accounts receivable	$80 000 00	
Less allowance for doubtful accounts	3 000 00	77 000 00
Merchandise inventory—at lower of cost (first-in, first-out method) or market		216 300 00

A company may change its inventory costing methods for a valid reason. In such cases, the effect of the change and the reason for the change should be disclosed in the financial statements for the period in which the change occurred.

Estimating Inventory Cost

OBJECTIVE 9

Estimate the cost of inventory, using the retail method and the gross profit method.

It may be necessary for a business to know the amount of inventory when perpetual inventory records are not maintained and it is impractical to take a physical inventory. For example, a business that uses a periodic inventory system may need monthly income statements, but taking a physical inventory each month may be too costly. Moreover, when a disaster such as a fire has destroyed the inventory, the amount of the loss must be determined. In this case, taking a physical inventory is impossible, and even if perpetual inventory records have been kept, the accounting records may also have been destroyed. In such cases, the inventory cost can be estimated by using (1) the retail method or (2) the gross profit method.

Retail Method of Inventory Costing

The **retail inventory method** of estimating inventory cost is based on the relationship of the cost of merchandise available for sale to the retail price of the same merchandise. To use this method, the retail prices of all merchandise are maintained and totaled. Next, the inventory at retail is determined by deducting sales for the period from the retail price of the goods that were available for sale during the period. The estimated inventory cost is then computed by multiplying the inventory at retail by the ratio of cost to selling (retail) price for the merchandise available for sale, as illustrated in Exhibit 9.

EXHIBIT 9
Determining Inventory by the Retail Method

	Cost	Retail
Merchandise inventory, January 1	$ 19,400	$ 36,000
Purchases in January (net)	42,600	64,000
Merchandise available for sale	$ 62,000	$100,000
Ratio of cost to retail price: $\frac{\$ 62,000}{\$100,000} = 62\%$		
Sales for January (net)		70,000
Merchandise inventory, January 31, at retail		$ 30,000
Merchandise inventory, January 31, at estimated cost ($30,000 × 62%)		$ 18,600

When estimating the percent of cost to selling price, we assume that the mix of the items in the ending inventory is the same as the entire stock of merchandise available for sale. In Exhibit 9, for example, it is unlikely that the retail price of every item was made up of exactly 62% cost and 38% gross profit. We assume, however, that the weighted average of the cost percentages of the merchandise in the inventory ($30,000) is the same as in the merchandise available for sale ($100,000). When the inventory is made up of different classes of merchandise with very different gross profit rates, the cost percentages and the inventory should be developed for each class of inventory.

One of the major advantages of the retail method is that it provides inventory figures for use in preparing monthly or quarterly statements when the periodic system is used. Department stores and similar merchandisers like to determine gross profit and operating income each month but may take a physical inventory only once a year. In addition, comparing the estimated ending inventory with the physical ending inventory, both at retail prices, will help identify inventory shortages resulting from shoplifting and other causes. Management can then take appropriate actions.

Q&A *If the ratio of cost to retail is 70% and the ending inventory at retail is $100,000, what is the estimated ending inventory at cost?*

$70,000 (70% × $100,000)

The retail method may also be used as an aid to taking a physical inventory. In this case, the items counted are recorded on the inventory sheets at their retail (selling) prices instead of their cost prices. The physical inventory at selling price is then converted to cost by applying the ratio of cost to selling (retail) price for the merchandise available for sale.

To illustrate, assume that the data in Exhibit 9 are for an entire fiscal year rather than for only January. If the physical inventory taken at the end of the year totaled $29,000, priced at retail, this amount rather than the $30,000 would be converted to cost. Thus, the inventory at cost would be $17,980 ($29,000 × 62%) instead of $18,600 ($30,000 × 62%). The $17,980 would be used for the year-end financial statements and for income tax purposes.

Gross Profit Method of Estimating Inventories

The **gross profit method** uses the estimated gross profit for the period to estimate the inventory at the end of the period. The gross profit is usually estimated from the actual rate for the preceding year, adjusted for any changes made in the cost and sales prices during the current period. By using the gross profit rate, the dollar amount of sales for a period can be divided into its two components: (1) gross profit and (2) cost of merchandise sold. The latter amount may then be deducted from the cost of merchandise available for sale to yield the estimated cost of the inventory.

Exhibit 10 illustrates the gross profit method for estimating a company's inventory on January 31. In this example, the inventory on January 1 is assumed to be $57,000, the net purchases during the month are $180,000, and the net sales during the month are $250,000. In addition, the historical gross profit was 30% of net sales.

EXHIBIT 10 Estimating Inventory by Gross Profit Method

Merchandise inventory, January 1		$ 57,000
Purchases in January (net)		180,000
Merchandise available for sale		$237,000
Sales in January (net)	$250,000	
Less estimated gross profit ($250,000 × 30%)	75,000	
Estimated cost of merchandise sold		175,000
Estimated merchandise inventory, January 31		$ 62,000

Q&A *What is the estimated cost of the ending inventory if the merchandise available for sale is $350,000, sales are $500,000, and the gross profit percentage is 40%?*

$50,000 [$350,000 − (60% × $500,000)]

The gross profit method is useful for estimating inventories for monthly or quarterly financial statements in a periodic inventory system. It is also useful in estimating the cost of merchandise destroyed by fire or other disasters.

FINANCIAL ANALYSIS AND INTERPRETATION

OBJECTIVE 10

Compute and interpret the inventory turnover ratio and the number of days' sales in inventory.

A merchandising business should keep enough inventory on hand to meet the needs of its customers. A failure to do so may result in lost sales. At the same time, too much inventory reduces solvency by tying up funds that could be better used to expand or improve operations. In addition, excess inventory increases expenses such as storage, insurance, and property taxes. Finally, excess inventory increases the risk of losses due to price declines, damage, or changes in customers' buying patterns.

As with many types of financial analyses, it is possible to use more than one measure to analyze the efficiency and effectiveness by which a business manages its inventory. Two such measures are the inventory turnover and the number of days' sales in inventory.

Inventory turnover measures the relationship between the volume of goods (merchandise) sold and the amount of inventory carried during the period. It is computed as follows:

$$\textbf{Inventory turnover} = \frac{\textbf{Cost of merchandise sold}}{\textbf{Average inventory}}$$

The average inventory can be computed using weekly, monthly, or yearly figures. To simplify, we determine the average inventory by dividing the sum of the inventories at the beginning and end of the year by 2. As long as the amount of inventory carried throughout the year remains stable, this average will be accurate enough for our analysis.

To illustrate, the following data have been taken from recent annual reports for **SUPERVALU INC.** and **La-Z-Boy Chair Company**:

	SUPERVALU	La-Z-Boy
Cost of merchandise sold	$15,040,117,000	$705,379,000
Inventories:		
Beginning of year	$1,113,937,000	$81,091,000
End of year	$1,109,791,000	$79,192,000
Average	$1,111,864,000	$80,141,500
Inventory turnover	13.5	8.8

The inventory turnover for SUPERVALU is 13.5 and 8.8 for La-Z-Boy. Generally, the larger the inventory turnover, the more efficient and effective the management of inventory. However, differences in companies and industries are too great to allow specific statements as to what is a good inventory turnover. For example, SUPERVALU is a leading food distributor and the twelfth largest food retailer in the United States. Because SUPERVALU's inventory is perishable, we would expect it to have a high inventory turnover. In contrast, La-Z-Boy is the largest reclining chair manufacturer in the United States. Thus, we would expect La-Z-Boy to have a lower inventory turnover than SUPERVALU. As with other financial measures we have discussed, a comparison of a company's inventory turnover over time and with industry averages will provide useful insights into the management of its inventory.

The **number of days' sales in inventory** is a rough measure of the length of time it takes to acquire, sell, and replace the inventory. It is computed as follows:

$$\textbf{Number of days' sales in inventory} = \frac{\textbf{Inventory, end of year}}{\textbf{Average daily cost of merchandise sold}}$$

The average daily cost of merchandise sold is determined by dividing the cost of merchandise sold by 365. The number of days' sales in inventory for SUPERVALU and La-Z-Boy is computed as shown below.

	SUPERVALU	La-Z-Boy
Average daily cost of merchandise sold:		
$15,040,117,000/365	$41,205,800	
$705,379,000/365		$1,932,545
Ending inventory	$1,109,791,000	$79,192,000
Number of days' sales in inventory	26.9 days	41 days

Generally, the lower the number of days' sales in inventory, the better. As with inventory turnover, we should expect differences among industries, such as those for SUPERVALU and La-Z-Boy.

ENCORE

Unusual Inventories— The Strange but True

We usually think of inventory in terms of retail stores such as grocery stores, department stores, and convenience stores. In the following paragraphs, however, we describe what you might think of as unusual inventories.

- **Studio Props.** Theaters periodically have sales to clear out items from past shows. The **Studio Theatre** in Washington, D.C., included the following items in one of its sales: patio furniture from "Together, Teeth Apart;" restaurant equipment from the ultra-real diner in "The Wash;" "Goblin Market's" giant rocking horse, doll house, quilt, and toy chest; an evening gown from "Death and the Maiden;" and

stuffed bunnies from "The Baltimore Waltz."

- **Movie Vehicles.** The mud-spattered 1930 Ford Model A pickup sat in a huge, heated garage. Although it looked like just an old truck, this Model A was a star of "The Untouchables." Pierre Laginess is the owner of **Antique and Classic Rental Service,** a Michigan-based business that provides used collector cars, trucks, and bicycles to film studios. The business began in the early 1970s when Laginess provided a stately, but menacing, 1928 Buick sedan for the original "Godfather." Since then, the business has provided vehicles for "Billy Bathgate," "Hoffa," "Lost in Yonkers," and the television series, "The Young Indiana Jones Chronicles." The business sells many of the cars that have been used in films. Laginess says producers shy away from a vehicle that has had too much exposure. Eagle-eyed fans recognize them, he said. So they go on sale.
- **Real Used Jeans.** While some jeans makers prewash, "stonewash," or even shotgun their garments to achieve the popular used look, at **Whiskey Dust** in New York City, you can get the sweaty cowboy finish the old-fashioned way: with real cowboy scent. Whiskey Dust's customers, which include rock stars Jon Bon Jovi and Eric Clapton, pay $65 for Montana Broke jeans that the store says were worn by genuine cowboys. Each well-used pair comes with a guarantee of authenticity and a "Montana Broke Tracking Guide," explaining the origin of each rip, splotch, and frayed hem. The store's customers enthusiastically embrace its unusual inventory. "It's wonderful value. You get a lot of history." Several thousand miles away, Judy McFarlane, a 55-year-old Montana homemaker and a used jeans supplier, has little problem getting her inventory. "I don't even bother to advertise. People call me all the time." The cowboys "think it's a riot," says Ms. McFarlane.
- **Unwanted Ashes.** The merger of two funeral homes has caused an unusual inventory problem: the unwanted, unclaimed ashes of 1,500 people who were cremated. The remains are those of eastern Washington residents who died between 1917 and 1972. A lot of remains come from the Great Depression era of the 1930s and include doctors, lawyers, and people from all walks of life. For various reasons, relatives didn't claim the ashes. The state law provides that a funeral home can dispose of unclaimed remains after a two-year holding period. The funeral home plans to pack the urns into caskets and bury them at a local cemetery. ■

KEY POINTS

1 **Summarize and provide examples of internal control procedures that apply to inventories.**

Internal control procedures for inventories include those developed to protect the inventories from damage, employee theft, and customer theft. In addition, a physical inventory count should be taken periodically to detect shortages as well as to deter employee thefts.

2 **Describe the effect of inventory errors on the financial statements.**

Any errors in reporting inventory based upon the physical inventory will misstate the ending inventory, current assets, total assets, and owner's equity on the balance sheet. In addition, the cost of goods sold, gross profit, and net income will be misstated on the income statement.

3 **Describe three inventory cost flow assumptions and how they impact the income statement and balance sheet.**

The three common cost flow assumptions used in business are the (1) first-in, first-out method, (2) last-in, first-out method, and (3) average cost method. Each method normally yields different amounts for the cost of merchandise sold and the ending merchandise inventory. Thus, the choice of a cost flow assumption directly affects the income statement and balance sheet.

4 **Compute the cost of inventory under the perpetual inventory system, using the following costing methods:**

First-in, first-out
Last-in, first-out
Average cost

In a perpetual inventory system, the number of units and the cost of each type of merchandise are recorded in a subsidiary inventory ledger, with a separate account for each type of merchandise. Inventory costs and the amounts charged against revenue are illustrated using the fifo and lifo methods.

5 **Compute the cost of inventory under the periodic inventory system, using the following costing methods:**

First-in, first-out
Last-in, first-out
Average cost

In a periodic inventory system, a physical inventory is taken to determine the cost of the inventory and the cost of merchandise sold. Inventory costs and the amounts charged against revenue are illustrated using fifo, lifo, and average cost methods.

6 Compare and contrast the use of the three inventory costing methods.
The three inventory costing methods will normally yield different amounts for (1) the ending inventory, (2) the cost of the merchandise sold for the period, and (3) the gross profit (and net income) for the period. During periods of inflation, the fifo method yields the lowest amount for the cost of merchandise sold, the highest amount for gross profit (and net income), and the highest amount for the ending inventory. The lifo method yields the opposite results. During periods of deflation, the preceding effects are reversed. The average cost method yields results that are between those of fifo and lifo.

7 Compute the proper valuation of inventory at other than cost, using the lower-of-cost-or-market and net realizable value concepts.
If the market price of an item of inventory is lower than its cost, the lower market price is used to compute the value of the item. Market price is the cost to replace the merchandise on the inventory date. It is possible to apply the lower of cost or market to each item in the inventory, to major classes or categories, or to the inventory as a whole.

Merchandise that can be sold only at prices below cost should be valued at net realizable value, which is the estimated selling price less any direct cost of disposal.

8 Prepare a balance sheet presentation of merchandise inventory.
Merchandise inventory is usually presented in the Current Assets section of the balance sheet, following receivables. Both the method of determining the cost of the inventory (fifo, lifo, or average) and the method of valuing the inventory (cost or the lower of cost or market) should be shown.

9 Estimate the cost of inventory, using the retail method and the gross profit method.
In using the retail method to estimate inventory, the retail prices of all merchandise acquired are accumulated. The inventory at retail is determined by deducting sales for the period from the retail price of the goods that were available for sale during the period. The inventory at retail is then converted to cost on the basis of the ratio of cost to selling (retail) price for the merchandise available for sale.

In using the gross profit method to estimate inventory, the estimated gross profit is deducted from the sales to determine the estimated cost of merchandise sold. This amount is then deducted from the cost of merchandise available for sale to determine the estimated ending inventory.

10 Compute and interpret the inventory turnover ratio and the number of days' sales in inventory.
The inventory turnover ratio, computed as the cost of merchandise sold divided by the average inventory, measures the relationship between the volume of goods (merchandise) sold and the amount of inventory carried during the period. The number of days' sales in inventory, computed as the ending inventory divided by the average daily cost of merchandise sold, measures the length of time it takes to acquire, sell, and replace the inventory.

ILLUSTRATIVE PROBLEM

Stewart Co.'s beginning inventory and purchases during the year ended December 31, 2001, were as follows:

		Units	Unit Cost	Total Cost
January 1	Inventory	1,000	$50.00	$ 50,000
March 10	Purchase	1,200	52.50	63,000
June 25	Sold 800 units			
August 30	Purchase	800	55.00	44,000
October 5	Sold 1,500 units			
November 26	Purchase	2,000	56.00	112,000
December 31	Sold 1,000 units			
Total		5,000		$269,000

Instructions

1. Determine the cost of inventory on December 31, 2001, using the perpetual inventory system and each of the following inventory costing methods:

a. first-in, first-out
b. last-in, first-out
2. Determine the cost of inventory on December 31, 2001, using the periodic inventory system and each of the following inventory costing methods:
a. first-in, first-out
b. last-in, first-out
c. average cost
3. Assume that during the fiscal year ended December 31, 2001, sales were $290,000 and the estimated gross profit rate was 40%. Estimate the ending inventory at December 31, 2001, using the gross profit method.

Solution

1. a. First-in, first-out method: $95,200

	Purchases			Cost of Merchandise Sold			Inventory		
Date	Quantity	Unit Cost	Total Cost	Quantity	Unit Cost	Total Cost	Quantity	Unit Cost	Total Cost
2001 Jan. 1							1,000	50.00	50,000
Mar. 10	1,200	52.50	63,000				1,000	50.00	50,000
							1,200	52.50	63,000
June 25				800	50.00	40,000	200	50.00	10,000
							1,200	52.50	63,000
Aug. 30	800	55.00	44,000				200	50.00	10,000
							1,200	52.50	63,000
							800	55.00	44,000
Oct. 5				200	50.00	10,000	700	55.00	38,500
				1,200	52.50	63,000			
				100	55.00	5,500			
Nov. 26	2,000	56.00	112,000				700	55.00	38,500
							2,000	56.00	112,000
Dec. 31				700	55.00	38,500	1,700	56.00	95,200
				300	56.00	16,800			

b. Last-in, first-out method: $91,000 ($35,000 + $56,000)

	Purchases			Cost of Merchandise Sold			Inventory		
Date	Quantity	Unit Cost	Total Cost	Quantity	Unit Cost	Total Cost	Quantity	Unit Cost	Total Cost
2001 Jan. 1							1,000	50.00	50,000
Mar. 10	1,200	52.50	63,000				1,000	50.00	50,000
							1,200	52.50	63,000
June 25				800	52.50	42,000	1,000	50.00	50,000
							400	52.50	21,000
Aug. 30	800	55.00	44,000				1,000	50.00	50,000
							400	52.50	21,000
							800	55.00	44,000
Oct. 5				800	55.00	44,000	700	50.00	35,000
				400	52.50	21,000			
				300	50.00	15,000			
Nov. 26	2,000	56.00	112,000				700	50.00	35,000
							2,000	56.00	112,000
Dec. 31				1,000	56.00	56,000	700	50.00	35,000
							1,000	56.00	56,000

2. a. First-in, first-out method:
1,700 units at \$56 = \$95,200

b. Last-in, first-out method:

1,000 units at \$50.00	\$50,000
700 units at \$52.50	36,750
1,700 units	\$86,750

c. Average cost method:

Average cost per unit: \$269,000 ÷ 5,000 units = \$53.80
Inventory, December 31, 2001: 1,700 units at \$53.80 = \$91,460

3.

Merchandise inventory, January 1, 2001		\$ 50,000
Purchases (net)		219,000
Merchandise available for sale		\$269,000
Sales (net)	\$290,000	
Less estimated gross profit (\$290,000 × 40%)	116,000	
Estimated cost of merchandise sold		174,000
Estimated merchandise inventory, December 31, 2001		\$ 95,000

SELF-EXAMINATION QUESTIONS

Answers at End of Chapter

Matching

Match each of the following statements with its proper term. Some terms may not be used.

- **A.** **average cost method**
- **B.** **first-in, first-out (fifo) method**
- **C.** **gross profit method**
- **D.** **inventory turnover**
- **E.** **last-in, first-out (lifo) method**
- **F.** **lower-of-cost-or-market (LCM) method**
- **G.** **net realizable value**
- **H.** **number of days' sales in inventory**
- **I.** **physical inventory**
- **J.** **retail inventory method**

I 1. A detailed listing of merchandise on hand.

B 2. A method of inventory costing based on the assumption that the costs of merchandise sold should be charged against revenue in the order in which the costs were incurred.

E 3. A method of inventory costing based on the assumption that the most recent merchandise inventory costs should be charged against revenue.

A 4. The method of inventory costing that is based upon the assumption that costs should be charged against revenue by using the weighted average unit cost of the items sold.

F 5. A method of valuing inventory that reports the inventory at the lower of its cost or current market value (replacement cost).

G 6. The estimated selling price of an item of inventory less any direct costs of disposal, such as sales commissions.

J 7. A method of estimating inventory cost that is based on the relationship of the cost of merchandise available for sale to the retail price of the same merchandise.

C 8. A method of estimating inventory cost that is based on the relationship of gross profit to sales.

H 9. A ratio that measures the relationship between the volume of goods (merchandise) sold and the amount of inventory carried during the period.

D 10. A measure of the length of time it takes to acquire, sell, and replace the inventory.

Multiple Choice

1. If the inventory shrinkage at the end of the year is overstated by \$7,500, the error will cause an:
   A. understatement of cost of merchandise sold for the year by \$7,500.
   B. overstatement of gross profit for the year by \$7,500.
   C. overstatement of merchandise inventory for the year by \$7,500.
   D. understatement of net income for the year by \$7,500.

2. The inventory costing method that is based on the assumption that costs should be charged against revenue in the order in which they were incurred is:
   A. fifo C. average cost
   B. lifo D. perpetual inventory

3. The following units of a particular item were purchased and sold during the period:

Beginning inventory	40 units at $20
First purchase	50 units at $21
Second purchase	50 units at $22
First sale	110 units
Third purchase	50 units at $23
Second sale	45 units

   What is the cost of the 35 units on hand at the end of the period as determined under the perpetual inventory system by the lifo costing method?
   A. $715 C. $700
   B. $705 D. $805

4. The following units of a particular item were available for sale during the period:

Beginning inventory	40 units at $20
First purchase	50 units at $21
Second purchase	50 units at $22
Third purchase	50 units at $23

   What is the unit cost of the 35 units on hand at the end of the period, as determined under the periodic inventory system by the fifo costing method?
   A. $20 C. $22
   B. $21 D. $23

5. If merchandise inventory is being valued at cost and the price level is steadily rising, the method of costing that will yield the highest net income is:
   A. lifo C. average
   B. fifo D. periodic

CLASS DISCUSSION QUESTIONS

1. What security measures may be used by retailers to protect merchandise inventory from customer theft?
2. Which inventory system provides the more effective means of controlling inventories (perpetual or periodic)? Why?
3. Before inventory purchases are recorded, the receiving report should be reconciled to what documents?
4. What document should be presented by an employee requesting inventory items to be released from the company's warehouse?
5. Why is it important to periodically take a physical inventory if the perpetual system is used?
6. The inventory shrinkage at the end of the year was understated by $10,000. (a) Did the error cause an overstatement or an understatement of the gross profit for the year? (b) Which items on the balance sheet at the end of the year were overstated or understated as a result of the error?
7. Ober Co. sold merchandise to Nunley Company on December 31, FOB shipping point. If the merchandise is in transit on December 31, the end of the fiscal year, which company would report it in its financial statements? Explain.
8. A manufacturer shipped merchandise to a retailer on a consignment basis. If the merchandise is unsold at the end of the period, in whose inventory should the merchandise be included?
9. Do the terms *fifo* and *lifo* refer to techniques used in determining quantities of the various classes of merchandise on hand? Explain.
10. Does the term *last-in* in the lifo method mean that the items in the inventory are assumed to be the most recent (last) acquisitions? Explain.
11. If merchandise inventory is being valued at cost and the price level is steadily rising, which of the three methods of costing—fifo, lifo, or average cost—will yield (a) the highest inventory cost, (b) the lowest inventory cost, (c) the highest gross profit, (d) the lowest gross profit?
12. Which of the three methods of inventory costing—fifo, lifo, or average cost—will in general yield an inventory cost most nearly approximating current replacement cost?
13. If inventory is being valued at cost and the price level is steadily rising, which of the three methods of costing—fifo, lifo, or average cost—will yield the lowest annual income tax expense? Explain.
14. Can a company change its method of costing inventory? Explain.

15. Because of imperfections, an item of merchandise cannot be sold at its normal selling price. How should this item be valued for financial statement purposes?
16. How is the method of determining the cost of the inventory and the method of valuing it disclosed in the financial statements?
17. What uses can be made of the estimate of the cost of inventory determined by the gross profit method?

Warren Reeve Fess

Resources for Your Success On-Line at warren.swcollege.com

Remember! If you need additional help, visit South-Western's Web site. See page 26 for a description of the online and printed materials that are available.

EXERCISES

Exercise 9–1
Internal control of inventories

Objective 1

Duce Hardware Store currently uses a periodic inventory system. Robin Templin, the owner, is considering the purchase of a computer system that would make it feasible to switch to a perpetual inventory system.

Robin is unhappy with the periodic inventory system because it does not provide timely information on inventory levels. Robin has noticed on several occasions that the store runs out of good-selling items, while too many poor-selling items are on hand.

Robin is also concerned about lost sales while a physical inventory is being taken. Duce Hardware currently takes a physical inventory twice a year. To minimize distractions, the store is closed on the day inventory is taken. Robin believes that closing the store is the only way to get an accurate inventory count.

Will switching to a perpetual inventory system strengthen Duce Hardware's control over inventory items? Will switching to a perpetual inventory system eliminate the need for a physical inventory count? Explain.

Exercise 9–2
Internal control of inventories

Objective 1

Bryers Luggage Shop is a small retail establishment located in a large shopping mall. This shop has implemented the following procedures regarding inventory items:

a. Whenever Bryers receives a shipment of new inventory, the items are taken directly to the stockroom. Bryers' accountant uses the vendor's invoice to record the amount of inventory received.
b. Since the display area of the store is limited, only a sample of each piece of luggage is kept on the selling floor. Whenever a customer selects a piece of luggage, the salesclerk gets the appropriate piece from the store's stockroom. Since all salesclerks need access to the stockroom, it is not locked. The stockroom is adjacent to the break room used by all mall employees.
c. Since the shop carries mostly high-quality, designer luggage, all inventory items are tagged with a control device that activates an alarm if a tagged item is removed from the store.

State whether each of these procedures is appropriate or inappropriate, considering the principles of internal control. If it is inappropriate, state which internal control procedure is violated.

Exercise 9–3
Identifying items to be included in inventory

Objective 1

Tobiason Co., which is located in Camanche, Iowa, has identified the following items for possible inclusion in its December 31, 1999 year-end inventory.

a. Tobiason has segregated $15,800 of merchandise ordered by one of its customers for shipment on January 3, 2000.

b. Tobiason has in its warehouse $21,000 of merchandise on consignment from Stovall Co.
c. Merchandise Tobiason shipped FOB shipping point on December 31, 1999, was picked up by the freight company at 11:50 p.m.
d. Merchandise Tobiason shipped to a customer FOB shipping point was picked up by the freight company on December 26, 1999, but had still not arrived at its destination as of December 31, 1999.
e. Tobiason has $35,000 of merchandise on hand, which was sold to customers earlier in the year, but which has been returned by customers to Tobiason for various warranty repairs.
f. Tobiason has sent $100,000 of merchandise to various retailers on a consignment basis.
g. On December 21, 1999, Tobiason ordered $85,000 of merchandise, FOB Camanche. The merchandise was shipped from the supplier on December 28, 1999, but had not been received by December 31, 1999.
h. On December 27, 1999, Tobiason ordered $15,000 of merchandise from a supplier in Des Moines. The merchandise was shipped FOB Des Moines on December 30, 1999, but had not been received by December 31, 1999.
i. On December 31, 1999, Tobiason received $28,000 of merchandise that had been returned by customers because the wrong merchandise had been shipped. The replacement order is to be shipped overnight on January 3, 2000.

Indicate which items should be included (I) and which should be excluded (E) from the inventory.

Exercise 9–4

Effect of errors in physical inventory

Objective 2

✓ a. Owner's equity, $13,800 understated

The River Bottom sells canoes, kayaks, whitewater rafts, and other boating supplies. During the taking of its physical inventory on December 31, 2000, The River Bottom incorrectly counted its inventory as $82,500 instead of the correct amount of $96,300.

a. State the effect of the error on the December 31, 2000 balance sheet of The River Bottom.
b. State the effect of the error on the income statement of The River Bottom for the year ended December 31, 2000.

Exercise 9–5

Effect of errors in physical inventory

Objective 2

✓ b. Net income, $6,100 overstated

Thema's Motorcycle Shop sells motorcycles, jet skis, and other related supplies and accessories. During the taking of its physical inventory on December 31, 2000, Thema's Motorcycle Shop incorrectly counted its inventory as $102,800 instead of the correct amount of $96,700.

a. State the effect of the error on the December 31, 2000 balance sheet of Thema's Motorcycle Shop.
b. State the effect of the error on the income statement of Thema's Motorcycle Shop for the year ended December 31, 2000.

Exercise 9–6

Error in inventory shrinkage

Objective 2

What's Wrong WITH THIS?

During 2000, the accountant discovered that the physical inventory at the end of 1999 had been understated by $45,000. Instead of correcting the error, however, the accountant assumed that a $45,000 overstatement of the physical inventory in 2000 would balance out the error.

Are there any flaws in the accountant's assumption? Explain.

Exercise 9–7

Perpetual inventory using fifo

Objectives 3, 4

✓ Inventory balance, April 30, $892

Beginning inventory, purchases, and sales data for Commodity MCX are as follows:

Apr.	1	Inventory	25 units at $40
	7	Sale	15 units
	12	Purchase	18 units at $42
	20	Sale	14 units
	22	Sale	3 units
	30	Purchase	10 units at $43

The business maintains a perpetual inventory system, costing by the first-in, first-out method. Determine the cost of the merchandise sold for each sale and the inventory balance after each sale, presenting the data in the form illustrated in Exhibit 3.

Exercise 9–8
Perpetual inventory using lifo
Objectives 3, 4

✓ Inventory balance, April 30, $872

Assume that the business in Exercise 9–7 maintains a perpetual inventory system, costing by the last-in, first-out method. Determine the cost of merchandise sold for each sale and the inventory balance after each sale, presenting the data in the form illustrated in Exhibit 4.

Exercise 9–9
Perpetual inventory using lifo
Objectives 3, 4

✓ Inventory balance, March 31, $238

Beginning inventory, purchases, and sales data for Commodity SKM for March are as follows:

Inventory		Purchases		Sales	
Mar. 1	30 units at $15	Mar. 8	10 units at $18	Mar. 11	9 units
		21	15 units at $19	17	24 units
				29	8 units

Assuming that the perpetual inventory system is used, costing by the lifo method, determine the cost of the inventory balance at March 31, presenting data in the form illustrated in Exhibit 4.

Exercise 9–10
Perpetual inventory using fifo
Objectives 3, 4

✓ Inventory balance, March 31, $266

Assume that the business in Exercise 9–9 maintains a perpetual inventory system, costing by the first-in, first-out method. Determine the cost of the inventory balance at March 31, presenting the data in the form illustrated in Exhibit 3.

Exercise 9–11
Fifo, lifo costs under perpetual inventory system
Objectives 3, 4

✓ a. $840

The following units of a particular item were available for sale during the year:

Beginning inventory	20 units at $45
Sale	15 units at $90
First purchase	30 units at $50
Sale	25 units at $90
Second purchase	40 units at $56
Sale	35 units at $90

The firm uses the perpetual inventory system, and there are 15 units of the item on hand at the end of the year. What is the total cost of the ending inventory according to (a) fifo, (b) lifo?

Exercise 9–12
Identify items missing in determining cost of merchandise sold
Objective 5

For (a) through (d), identify the items designated by "X."

a. Purchases − (X + X) = Net purchases.
b. Net purchases + X = Cost of merchandise purchased.
c. Merchandise inventory (beginning) + Cost of merchandise purchased = X.
d. Merchandise available for sale − X = Cost of merchandise sold.

Exercise 9–13
Cost of merchandise sold and related items
Objective 5

✓ a. Cost of merchandise sold, $536,500

The following data were extracted from the accounting records of C. L. Williams Company for the year ended April 30, 1999:

Merchandise Inventory, May 1, 1998 . . .	$115,000
Merchandise Inventory, April 30, 1999 . .	125,000
Purchases	550,000
Purchases Returns and Allowances	4,500
Purchases Discounts	2,950
Sales	670,625
Transportation In	3,950

a. Prepare the cost of merchandise sold section of the income statement for the year ended April 30, 1999.
b. Determine the gross profit to be reported on the income statement for the year ended April 30, 1999.

Exercise 9–14
Cost of merchandise sold
Objective 5

What's Wrong WITH THIS?

✓ Correct cost of merchandise sold, $489,700

How many errors can you find in the following schedule of cost of merchandise sold for the current year ended December 31?

Cost of merchandise sold:			
Merchandise inventory, December 31			$105,000
Purchases		$500,000	
Plus: Purchases returns and allowances	$12,500		
Purchases discounts	6,500	19,000	
Gross purchases		$519,000	
Less transportation in		2,400	
Cost of merchandise purchased			516,600
Merchandise available for sale			$621,600
Less merchandise inventory, January 1			111,300
Cost of merchandise sold			$510,300

Exercise 9–15
Periodic inventory by three methods
Objectives 3, 5

SPREADSHEET

✓ b. $1,055

The units of an item available for sale during the year were as follows:

Jan. 1	Inventory	35 units at $23
Mar. 4	Purchase	10 units at $25
Aug. 20	Purchase	30 units at $28
Nov. 30	Purchase	25 units at $30

There are 45 units of the item in the physical inventory at December 31. The periodic inventory system is used. Determine the inventory cost by (a) the first-in, first-out method, (b) the last-in, first-out method, and (c) the average cost method.

Exercise 9–16
Periodic inventory by three methods; cost of merchandise sold
Objectives 3, 5

SPREADSHEET

✓ a. Inventory, $1,390

The units of an item available for sale during the year were as follows:

Jan. 1	Inventory	25 units at $60
Mar. 4	Purchase	30 units at $65
Aug. 7	Purchase	10 units at $68
Nov. 15	Purchase	15 units at $70

There are 20 units of the item in the physical inventory at December 31. The periodic inventory system is used. Determine the inventory cost and the cost of merchandise sold by three methods, presenting your answers in the following form:

	Cost	
Inventory Method	**Merchandise Inventory**	**Merchandise Sold**
a. First-in, first-out	$	$
b. Last-in, first-out		
c. Average cost		

Exercise 9–17
Lower-of-cost-or-market inventory
Objective 7

✓ LCM: $11,715

On the basis of the following data, determine the value of the inventory at the lower of cost or market. Assemble the data in the form illustrated in Exhibit 7.

Commodity	Inventory Quantity	Unit Cost Price	Unit Market Price
4HU	10	$325	$320
153T	17	110	115
Z10	12	275	260
SAW1	15	51	45
SAW2	30	95	100

Exercise 9–18
Merchandise inventory on the balance sheet

Objective 8

Based on the data in Exercise 9–17 and assuming that cost was determined by the fifo method, show how the merchandise inventory would appear on the balance sheet.

Exercise 9–19
Retail inventory method

Objective 9

✓ Inventory: $228,000

A business using the retail method of inventory costing determines that merchandise inventory at retail is $380,000. If the ratio of cost to retail price is 60%, what is the amount of inventory to be reported on the financial statements?

Exercise 9–20
Retail inventory method

Objective 9

✓ Inventory, June 30: $307,200

On the basis of the following data, estimate the cost of the merchandise inventory at June 30 by the retail method:

		Cost	Retail
June 1	Merchandise inventory	$428,300	$ 670,500
June 1–30	Purchases (net)	608,500	949,500
June 1–30	Sales (net)		1,140,000

Exercise 9–21
Gross profit inventory method

Objective 9

✓ a. $318,800

The merchandise inventory was destroyed by fire on October 20. The following data were obtained from the accounting records:

Jan. 1	Merchandise inventory	$ 160,000
Jan. 1–Oct. 20	Purchases (net)	850,000
	Sales (net)	1,080,000
	Estimated gross profit rate	36%

a. Estimate the cost of the merchandise destroyed.
b. Briefly describe the situations in which the gross profit method is useful.

Exercise 9–22
Inventory turnover and number of days' sales in inventory

Objective 10

HAT

The financial statements for **Hershey Foods Corporation** are presented in Appendix G at the end of the text. Hershey Foods Corporation has inventories of $445,702,000 at December 31, 1994.

a. For the years ended December 31, 1996 and 1995, determine: (1) the inventory turnover, and (2) the number of days' sales in inventory.
b. What conclusions can be drawn from these analyses concerning Hershey's efficiency in managing inventory?

PROBLEMS SERIES A

Problem 9–1A
Fifo perpetual inventory

Objectives 3, 4

✓ 3. $6,500

The beginning inventory of Commodity PAC315 at Saunders Co. and data on purchases and sales for a three-month period are as follows:

Date	Transaction	Number of Units	Per Unit	Total
April 1	Inventory	15	$220	$3,300
7	Purchase	25	225	5,625
18	Sale	10	300	3,000
22	Sale	13	300	3,900
May 4	Purchase	15	230	3,450
10	Sale	10	310	3,100
21	Sale	5	310	1,550
31	Purchase	20	235	4,700
June 5	Sale	15	315	4,725
13	Sale	12	315	3,780
21	Purchase	20	240	4,800
28	Sale	14	320	4,480

Instructions

1. Record the inventory, purchases, and cost of merchandise sold data in a perpetual inventory record similar to the one illustrated in Exhibit 3, using the first-in, first-out method.
2. Determine the total sales and the total cost of Commodity PAC315 sold for the period. Journalize the entries in the sales and cost of merchandise sold accounts. Assume that all sales were on account.
3. Determine the gross profit from sales of Commodity PAC315 for the period.
4. Determine the ending inventory cost.

Problem 9–2A

Lifo perpetual inventory

Objectives 3, 4

✓ 2. Gross profit, $6,300

The beginning inventory of Commodity PAC315 and data on purchases and sales for a three-month period are shown in Problem 9–1A.

Instructions

1. Record the inventory, purchases, and cost of merchandise sold data in a perpetual inventory record similar to the one illustrated in Exhibit 4, using the last-in, first-out method.
2. Determine the total sales, the total cost of Commodity PAC315 sold, and the gross profit from sales for the period.
3. Determine the ending inventory cost.

Problem 9–3A

Periodic inventory by three methods

Objectives 3, 5

SPREADSHEET

✓ 1. $10,847

Three Rivers Television uses the periodic inventory system. Details regarding the inventory of television sets at January 1, purchases invoices during the year, and the inventory count at December 31 are summarized as follows:

		Purchases Invoices			
Model	Inventory, January 1	1st	2nd	3rd	Inventory Count, December 31
B91	4 at $149	6 at $151	8 at $157	7 at $156	6
F10	3 at 208	3 at 212	5 at 213	4 at 225	4
H21	2 at 520	2 at 527	2 at 530	2 at 535	3
J39	6 at 520	8 at 531	4 at 549	6 at 542	7
P80	9 at 213	7 at 215	6 at 222	6 at 225	8
T15	6 at 305	3 at 310	3 at 316	4 at 317	5
V11	—	4 at 222	4 at 232	—	1

Instructions

1. Determine the cost of the inventory on December 31 by the first-in, first-out method. Present data in columnar form, using the following headings:

Model	Quantity	Unit Cost	Total Cost

   If the inventory of a particular model comprises one entire purchase plus a portion of another purchase acquired at a different unit cost, use a separate line for each purchase.
2. Determine the cost of the inventory on December 31 by the last-in, first-out method, following the procedures indicated in (1).
3. Determine the cost of the inventory on December 31 by the average cost method, using the columnar headings indicated in (1).
4. Discuss which method (fifo or lifo) would be preferred for income tax purposes in periods of (a) rising prices and (b) declining prices.

Problem 9–4A

Lower-of-cost-or-market inventory

Objective 7

SPREADSHEET

✓ Total LCM, $54,272

If the working papers correlating with this textbook are not used, omit Problem 9–4A.

Data on the physical inventory of Tyner Co. as of December 31, the end of the current fiscal year, are presented in the working papers. The quantity of each commodity on hand has been determined and recorded on the inventory sheet. Unit market prices have also been determined as of December 31 and recorded on the sheet. The inventory is to be determined at cost and also at the lower of cost or market, using the first-in, first-out method. Quantity and cost data from the last purchases invoice of the year and the next-to-the-last purchases invoice are summarized as follows:

	Last Purchases Invoice		Next-to-the-Last Purchases Invoice	
Description	Quantity Purchased	Unit Cost	Quantity Purchased	Unit Cost
F71	30	$ 60	40	$ 58
C22	25	190	15	190
D82	18	143	15	142
E34	150	25	100	27
F17	6	550	15	540
J19	75	14	100	13
K41	8	400	5	398
M21	500	6	500	7
R72	70	17	50	16
T15	5	250	4	260
V55	500	9	500	8
AC2	100	45	100	46
BB7	5	410	5	400
BD1	120	19	100	17
DD1	50	15	40	16
EB2	50	28	50	27
FF7	55	28	50	28
GE4	6	701	5	699

Instructions

Record the appropriate unit costs on the inventory sheet, and complete the pricing of the inventory. When there are two different unit costs applicable to an item, proceed as follows:

1. Draw a line through the quantity, and insert the quantity and unit cost of the last purchase.
2. On the following line, insert the quantity and unit cost of the next-to-the-last purchase. The first item on the inventory sheet has been completed as an example.

Problem 9–5A

Retail method; gross profit method

Objective 9

SPREADSHEET

✓ 1. $98,800

✓ 2. a. $246,000

Selected data on merchandise inventory, purchases, and sales for Bozeman Co. and Gallatin Co. are as follows:

	Cost	Retail
Bozeman Co.		
Merchandise inventory, February 1	$ 177,100	$ 227,000
Transactions during February:		
Purchases (net)	903,200	1,435,000
Sales		1,550,000
Sales returns and allowances		40,000
Gallatin Co.		
Merchandise inventory, July 1	$ 317,900	
Transactions during July and August:		
Purchases (net)	1,432,100	
Sales	2,475,000	
Sales returns and allowances	125,000	
Estimated gross profit rate	36%	

Instructions

1. Determine the estimated cost of the merchandise inventory of Bozeman Co. on February 28 by the retail method, presenting details of the computations.
2. a. Estimate the cost of the merchandise inventory of Gallatin Co. on August 31 by the gross profit method, presenting details of the computations.
   b. Assume that Gallatin Co. took a physical inventory on August 31 and discovered that $212,900 of merchandise was on hand. What was the estimated loss of inventory due to theft or damage during July and August?

PROBLEMS SERIES B

Problem 9–1B
Fifo perpetual inventory

Objectives 3, 4

✓ 3. $214,750

In class example

The beginning inventory of ZIP910 at Marks Co. and data on purchases and sales for a three-month period are as follows:

Date	Transaction	Number of Units	Per Unit	Total
July 1	Inventory	25,000	$6.10	$152,500
8	Purchase	75,000	6.15	461,250
20	Sale	45,000	7.00	315,000
31	Sale	35,000	7.00	245,000
Aug. 8	Sale	5,000	7.10	35,500
10	Purchase	50,000	6.20	310,000
27	Sale	40,000	7.20	288,000
30	Sale	20,000	7.15	143,000
Sept. 5	Purchase	60,000	6.05	363,000
13	Sale	30,000	7.00	210,000
22	Purchase	35,000	6.00	210,000
30	Sale	55,000	7.00	385,000

Instructions

1. Record the inventory, purchases, and cost of merchandise sold data in a perpetual inventory record similar to the one illustrated in Exhibit 3, using the first-in, first-out method.
2. Determine the total sales and the total cost of Commodity ZIP910 sold for the period. Journalize the entries in the sales and cost of merchandise sold accounts. Assume that all sales were on account.
3. Determine the gross profit from sales for the period.
4. Determine the ending inventory cost.

Problem 9–2B
Lifo perpetual inventory

Objectives 3, 4

✓ 2. Gross profit, $215,750

The beginning inventory of ZIP910 at Marks Co. and data on purchases and sales for a three-month period are shown in Problem 9–1B.

Instructions

1. Record the inventory, purchases, and cost of merchandise sold data in a perpetual inventory record similar to the one illustrated in Exhibit 4, using the last-in, first-out method.
2. Determine the total sales, the total cost of Commodity ZIP910 sold, and the gross profit from sales for the period.
3. Determine the ending inventory cost.

Problem 9–3B
Periodic inventory by three methods

Objectives 3, 5

SPREADSHEET

✓ 1. $8,951

Martel Television uses the periodic inventory system. Details regarding the inventory of television sets at July 1, 1999, purchases invoices during the year, and the inventory count at June 30, 2000, are summarized as follows:

Model	Inventory, July 1	Purchases Invoices 1st	2nd	3rd	Inventory Count, June 30
A37	6 at $240	4 at $250	8 at $260	10 at $262	14
E15	6 at 80	5 at 82	8 at 89	8 at 90	8
L10	2 at 108	2 at 110	3 at 128	3 at 130	3
O18	8 at 88	4 at 79	3 at 85	6 at 92	8
K72	2 at 250	2 at 260	4 at 271	4 at 272	3
S91	5 at 160	4 at 170	4 at 175	7 at 180	8
V17	—	4 at 150	4 at 200	4 at 202	6

Instructions

1. Determine the cost of the inventory on June 30, 2000, by the first-in, first-out method. Present data in columnar form, using the following headings:

Model	Quantity	Unit Cost	Total Cost

   If the inventory of a particular model comprises one entire purchase plus a portion of another purchase acquired at a different unit cost, use a separate line for each purchase.
2. Determine the cost of the inventory on June 30, 2000, by the last-in, first-out method, following the procedures indicated in (1).
3. Determine the cost of the inventory on June 30, 2000, by the average cost method, using the columnar headings indicated in (1).
4. Discuss which method (fifo or lifo) would be preferred for income tax purposes in periods of (a) rising prices and (b) declining prices.

Problem 9–4B

Lower-of-cost-or-market inventory

Objective 7

SPREADSHEET

✓ Total LCM, $54,951

If the working papers correlating with this textbook are not used, omit Problem 9–4B.

Data on the physical inventory of Minish Company as of December 31, the end of the current fiscal year, are presented in the working papers. The quantity of each commodity on hand has been determined and recorded on the inventory sheet. Unit market prices have also been determined as of December 31 and recorded on the sheet. The inventory is to be determined at cost and also at the lower of cost or market, using the first-in, first-out method. Quantity and cost data from the last purchases invoice of the year and the next-to-the-last purchases invoice are summarized as follows:

	Last Purchases Invoice		Next-to-the-Last Purchases Invoice	
Description	**Quantity Purchased**	**Unit Cost**	**Quantity Purchased**	**Unit Cost**
F71	30	$ 60	30	$ 58
C22	25	208	20	205
D82	10	145	25	142
E34	150	25	100	24
F17	10	560	10	570
J19	100	15	100	14
K41	10	387	5	384
M21	500	6	500	6
R72	80	19	50	18
T15	5	255	4	260
V55	700	9	500	9
AC2	100	47	50	46
BB7	5	420	5	424
BD1	100	20	75	19
DD1	60	17	40	16
EB2	50	29	25	28
FF7	75	27	60	25
GE4	5	702	5	699

Instructions

Record the appropriate unit costs on the inventory sheet, and complete the pricing of the inventory. When there are two different unit costs applicable to an item, proceed as follows:

1. Draw a line through the quantity, and insert the quantity and unit cost of the last purchase.
2. On the following line, insert the quantity and unit cost of the next-to-the-last purchase. The first item on the inventory sheet has been completed as an example.

Problem 9–5B
Retail method; gross profit method

Objective 9

SPREADSHEET

✓ 1. $226,300
✓ 2. a. $128,440

Selected data on merchandise inventory, purchases, and sales for Hefron Co. and Cummins Co. are as follows:

	Cost	Retail
Hefron Co.		
Merchandise inventory, August 1	$ 137,980	$270,000
Transactions during August:		
Purchases (net)	658,450	821,000
Sales		790,000
Sales returns and allowances		9,000
Cummins Co.		
Merchandise inventory, April 1	$ 117,500	
Transactions during April and May:		
Purchases (net)	825,000	
Sales	1,325,000	
Sales returns and allowances	12,000	
Estimated gross profit rate	38%	

Instructions

1. Determine the estimated cost of the merchandise inventory of Hefron Co. on August 31 by the retail method, presenting details of the computations.
2. a. Estimate the cost of the merchandise inventory of Cummins Co. on May 31 by the gross profit method, presenting details of the computations.
   b. Assume that Cummins Co. took a physical inventory on May 31 and discovered that $118,000 of merchandise was on hand. What was the estimated loss of inventory due to theft or damage during April and May?

SPECIAL ACTIVITIES

Activity 9–1 Torres Co.
Ethics and professional conduct in business

Torres Co. is experiencing a decrease in sales and operating income for the fiscal year ending December 31, 2000. Jess Jaeger, controller of Torres Co., has suggested that all orders received before the end of the fiscal year be shipped by midnight, December 31, 2000, even if the shipping department must work overtime. Since Torres Co. ships all merchandise FOB shipping point, it would record all such shipments as sales for the year ending December 31, 2000, thereby offsetting some of the decreases in sales and operating income.

Discuss whether Jess Jaeger is behaving in a professional manner.

Activity 9–2 Walgreen Co.
Fifo vs. lifo

REAL WORLD

The following footnote was taken from the 1996 financial statements of **Walgreen Co.**:

Inventories are valued on a . . . last-in, first-out (LIFO) cost . . . basis. At August 31, 1996 and 1995, inventories would have been greater by $427,767,000 and $415,015,000 respectively, if they had been valued on a lower of first-in, first-out (FIFO) cost or market basis.

Additional data are as follows:

Earnings before income taxes, 1996	$ 606,937,000
Total lifo inventories, August 31, 1996	1,631,974,000

Based on the preceding data, determine (a) what the total inventories at August 31, 1996, would have been, using the fifo method, and (b) what the earnings before income taxes for the year ended August 31, 1996, would have been if fifo had been used instead of lifo.

Activity 9–3 Essex Wholesale Co.
Lifo and inventory flow

The following is an excerpt from a conversation between Jessica Erbert, the warehouse manager for Essex Wholesale Co., and its accountant, Tara Dowell. Essex Wholesale operates a large regional warehouse that supplies produce and other grocery products to grocery stores in smaller communities.

Jessica: Tara, can you explain what's going on here with these monthly statements?
Tara: Sure, Jessica. How can I help you?
Jessica: I don't understand this last-in, first-out inventory procedure. It just doesn't make sense.
Tara: Well, what it means is that we assume that the last goods we receive are the first ones sold. So the inventory is made up of the items we purchased first.
Jessica: Yes, but that's my problem. It doesn't work that way! We always distribute the oldest produce first. Some of that produce is perishable! We can't keep any of it very long or it'll spoil.
Tara: Jessica, you don't understand. We only *assume* that the products we distribute are the last ones received. We don't actually have to distribute the goods in this way.
Jessica: I always thought that accounting was supposed to show what really happened. It all sounds like "make believe" to me! Why not report what really happens?

Respond to Jessica's concerns.

Activity 9–4 Ritter Company
Costing inventory

Ritter Company began operations in 1999 by selling a single product. Data on purchases and sales for the year were as follows:

Purchases:

Date	Units Purchased	Unit Cost	Total Cost
April 8	4,875	$12.20	$ 59,475
May 10	5,125	13.00	66,625
June 4	5,000	13.20	66,000
July 10	5,000	14.00	70,000
August	3,400	14.25	48,450
October 5	1,600	14.50	23,200
November 1	1,000	14.75	14,750
December 10	1,000	16.00	16,000
	27,000		$364,500

Sales:

April	2,000 units
May	2,000
June	3,500
July	4,000
August	3,500
September	3,500
October	2,250
November	1,250
December	1,000
Total units	23,000
Total sales	$552,000

On January 3, 2000, the president of the company, Stuart Ritter, asked for your advice on costing the 4,000-unit physical inventory that was taken on December 31, 1999. Moreover, since the firm plans to expand its product line, he asked for your advice on the use of a perpetual inventory system in the future.

1. Determine the cost of the December 31, 1999 inventory under the periodic system, using the (a) first-in, first-out method, (b) last-in, first-out method, and (c) average cost method.
2. Determine the gross profit for the year under each of the three methods in (1).

3. a. Explain varying viewpoints why each of the three inventory costing methods may best reflect the results of operations for 1999.
   b. Which of the three inventory costing methods may best reflect the replacement cost of the inventory on the balance sheet as of December 31, 1999?
   c. Which inventory costing method would you choose to use for income tax purposes? Why?
   d. Discuss the advantages and disadvantages of using a perpetual inventory system. From the data presented in this case, is there any indication of the adequacy of inventory levels during the year?

Activity 9–5
Into the Real World
Observe internal controls over inventory

GROUP ACTIVITY

Select a business in your community and observe its internal controls over inventory. In groups of three or four, identify and discuss the similarities and differences in each business's inventory controls. Prepare a written summary of your findings.

Activity 9–6
Into the Real World
Compare inventory cost flow assumptions

GROUP ACTIVITY Internet ACTIVITY

In groups of three or four, examine the financial statements of a well-known retailing business. You may obtain the financial statements you need from one of the following sources:

1. Your school or local library.
2. The investor relations department of the company.
3. The company's Web site on the Internet.
4. EDGAR (Electronic Data Gathering, Analysis, and Retrieval), the electronic archives of financial statements filed with the Securities and Exchange Commission. The Edgar address is:

   www.sec.gov/edgarhp.htm

   To obtain annual report information, type in a company name on the "Search EDGAR Archives" form. EDGAR will list the reports available for the selected company. A company's annual report (along with other information) is provided in its annual 10-K report to the SEC. Click on the 10-K (or 10-K405) report for the year you wish to download. If you wish, you can save the whole 10-K report to a file, then open it with your word processor.

Determine the cost flow assumption(s) that the company is using for its inventory, and determine whether the company is using the lower-of-cost-or-market rule. Prepare a written summary of your findings.

ANSWERS TO SELF-EXAMINATION QUESTIONS

Matching

1. I	3. E	5. F	7. J	9. D
2. B	4. A	6. G	8. C	10. H

Multiple Choice

1. **D** The overstatement of inventory shrinkage by $7,500 at the end of the year will cause the cost of merchandise sold for the year to be overstated by $7,500, the gross profit for the year to be understated by $7,500, the merchandise inventory to be understated by $7,500, and the net income for the year to be understated by $7,500 (answer D).

2. **A** The fifo method (answer A) is based on the assumption that costs are charged against revenue in the order in which they were incurred. The lifo method (answer B) charges the most recent costs incurred against revenue, and the average cost method (answer C) charges a weighted average of unit costs of items sold against revenue. The perpetual inventory system (answer D) is a system and not a method of costing.

3. **A** The lifo method of costing is based on the assumption that costs should be charged against revenue in the reverse order in which costs were incurred. Thus, the oldest costs are assigned to inventory. Thirty of the 35 units would be assigned a unit cost of $20 (since 110 of the beginning inventory units were sold on the first sale), and the remaining 5 units would be assigned a cost of $23, for a total of $715 (answer A).
4. **D** The fifo method of costing is based on the assumption that costs should be charged against revenue in the order in which they were incurred (first-in, first-out). Thus, the most recent costs are assigned to inventory. The 35 units would be assigned a unit cost of $23 (answer D).
5. **B** When the price level is steadily rising, the earlier unit costs are lower than recent unit costs. Under the fifo method (answer B), these earlier costs are matched against revenue to yield the highest possible net income. The periodic inventory system (answer D) is a system and not a method of costing.

10

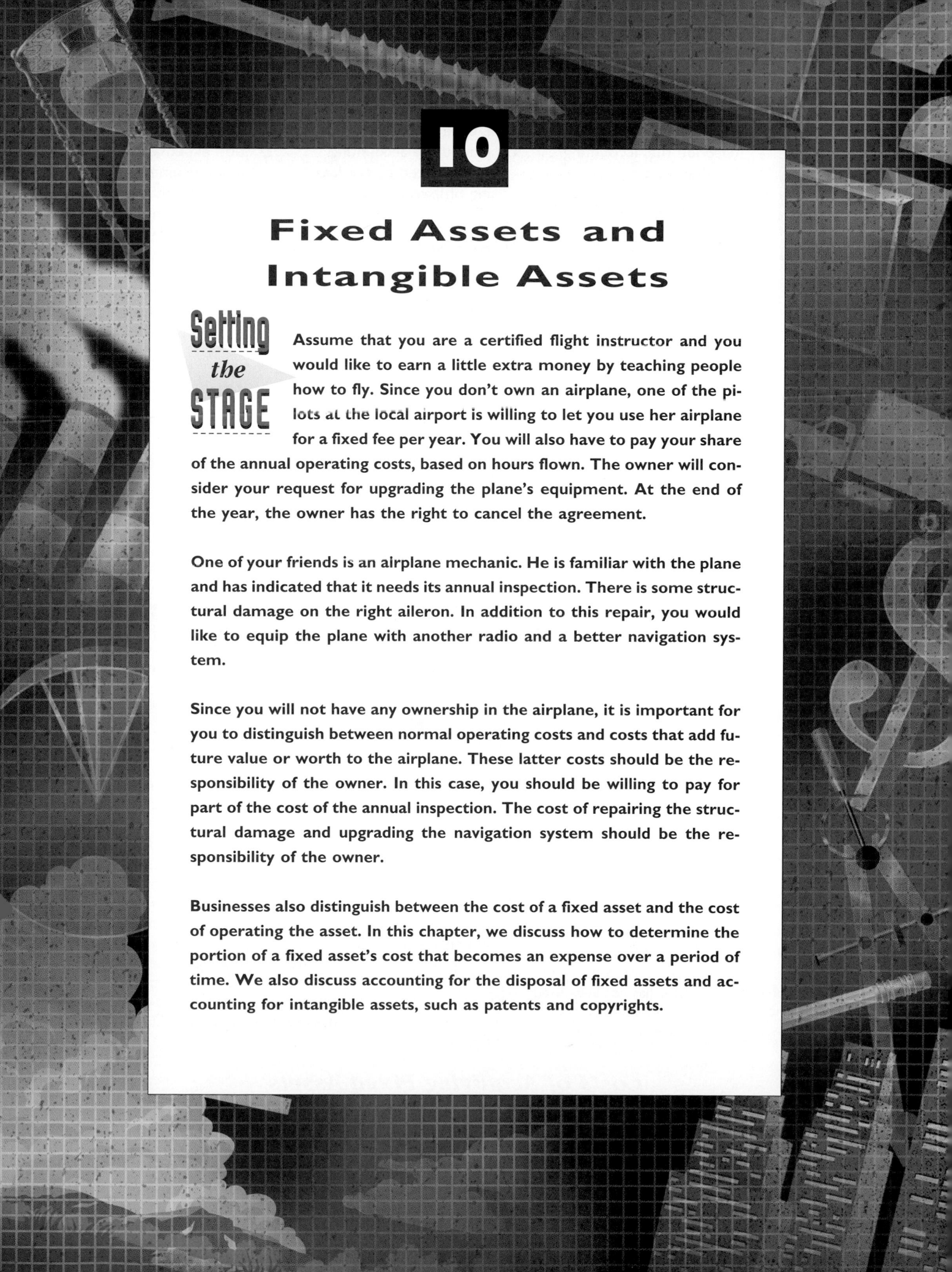

Fixed Assets and Intangible Assets

Setting *the* STAGE

Assume that you are a certified flight instructor and you would like to earn a little extra money by teaching people how to fly. Since you don't own an airplane, one of the pilots at the local airport is willing to let you use her airplane for a fixed fee per year. You will also have to pay your share of the annual operating costs, based on hours flown. The owner will consider your request for upgrading the plane's equipment. At the end of the year, the owner has the right to cancel the agreement.

One of your friends is an airplane mechanic. He is familiar with the plane and has indicated that it needs its annual inspection. There is some structural damage on the right aileron. In addition to this repair, you would like to equip the plane with another radio and a better navigation system.

Since you will not have any ownership in the airplane, it is important for you to distinguish between normal operating costs and costs that add future value or worth to the airplane. These latter costs should be the responsibility of the owner. In this case, you should be willing to pay for part of the cost of the annual inspection. The cost of repairing the structural damage and upgrading the navigation system should be the responsibility of the owner.

Businesses also distinguish between the cost of a fixed asset and the cost of operating the asset. In this chapter, we discuss how to determine the portion of a fixed asset's cost that becomes an expense over a period of time. We also discuss accounting for the disposal of fixed assets and accounting for intangible assets, such as patents and copyrights.

objectives

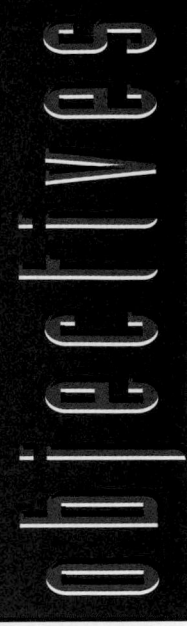

After studying this chapter, you should be able to:

1. Define fixed assets and describe the accounting for their cost.
2. Compute depreciation, using the following methods: straight-line method, units-of-production method, and declining-balance method.
3. Classify fixed asset costs as either capital expenditures or revenue expenditures.
4. Journalize entries for the disposal of fixed assets.
5. Define a lease and summarize the accounting rules related to the leasing of fixed assets.
6. Describe internal controls over fixed assets.
7. Compute depletion and journalize the entry for depletion.
8. Journalize the entries for acquiring and amortizing intangible assets, such as patents, copyrights, and goodwill.
9. Describe how depreciation expense is reported in an income statement and prepare a balance sheet that includes fixed assets and intangible assets.
10. Compute and interpret the ratio of fixed assets to long-term liabilities.

Nature of Fixed Assets

OBJECTIVE 1

Define fixed assets and describe the accounting for their cost.

Businesses use a variety of fixed assets, such as equipment, furniture, tools, machinery, buildings, and land. **Fixed assets** are long-term or relatively permanent assets. They are **tangible assets** because they exist physically. They are owned and used by the business and are not offered for sale as part of normal operations. Other descriptive titles for these assets are **plant assets** or **property, plant, and equipment**.

There is no standard rule for the minimum length of life necessary for an asset to be classified as a fixed asset. Such assets must be capable of providing repeated use or benefit and are normally expected to last more than a year. However, an asset need not actually be used on an ongoing basis or even often. For example, standby equipment for use in the event of a breakdown of regular equipment or for use only during peak periods is included in fixed assets.

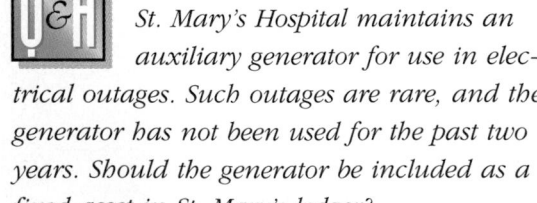

Q&A *St. Mary's Hospital maintains an auxiliary generator for use in electrical outages. Such outages are rare, and the generator has not been used for the past two years. Should the generator be included as a fixed asset in St. Mary's ledger?*

Yes. Even though the generator has not been used recently, it should be included as a fixed asset.

Long-term assets acquired for resale in the normal course of business are not classified as fixed assets, regardless of their permanent nature or the length of time they are held. For example, undeveloped land or other real estate acquired as an investment for resale should be listed on the balance sheet in the asset section entitled *Investments.*

The normal costs of using or operating a fixed asset are reported as expenses on a company's income statement. The costs of acquiring a fixed asset become expenses over a period of time. In the next section, we discuss these latter costs and their recognition as expenses.

Costs of Acquiring Fixed Assets

The cost of acquiring a fixed asset includes all amounts spent to get it in place and ready for use. For example, freight costs and the costs of installing equipment are included as part of the asset's total cost. Exhibit 1 summarizes some of the common costs of acquiring fixed assets. These costs should be recorded by debiting the re-

EXHIBIT 1
Costs of Acquiring Fixed Assets

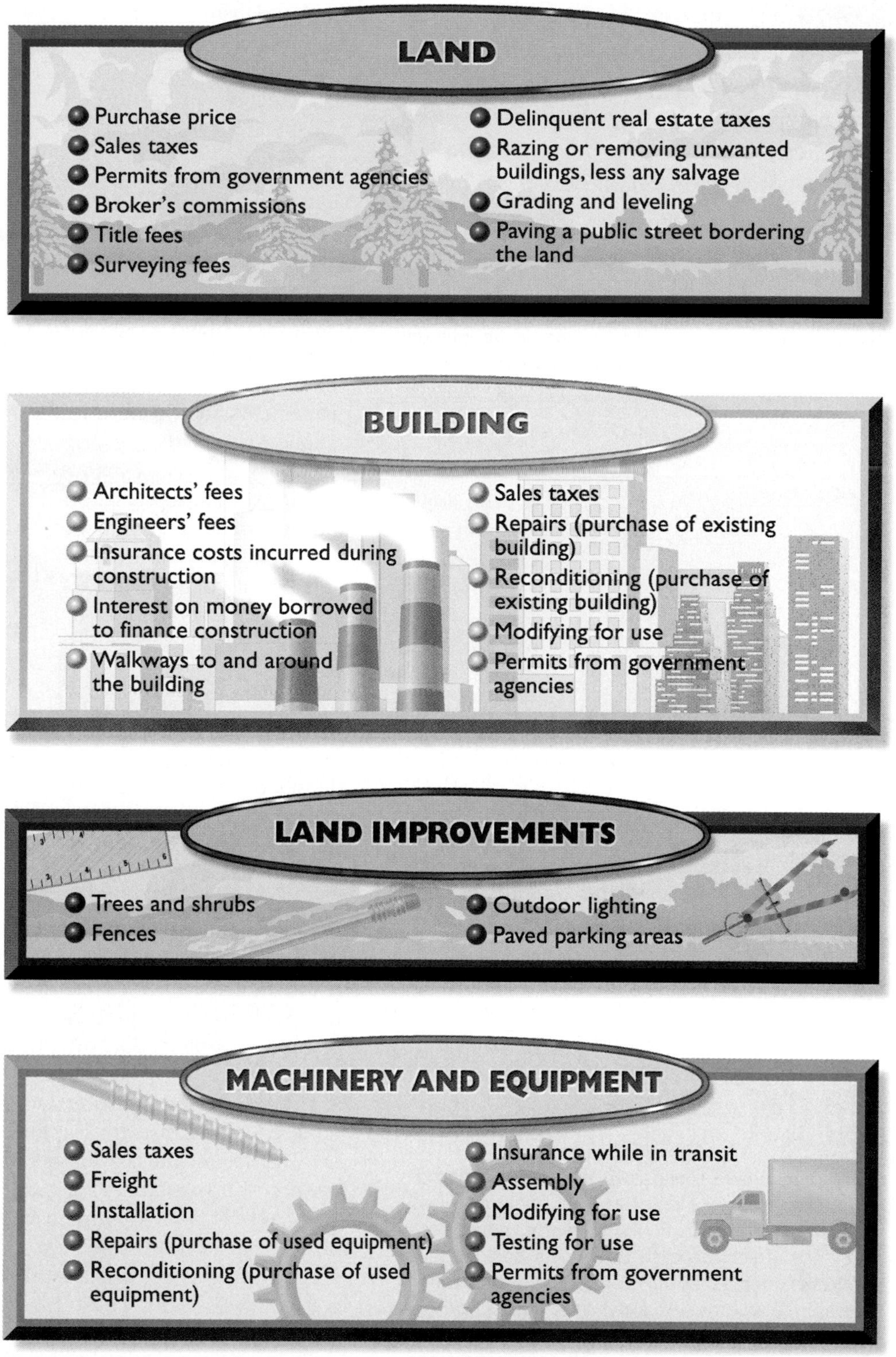

lated fixed asset account, such as Land,[1] Building, Land Improvements, or Machinery and Equipment.

LAND
Purchase price
Sales taxes
Permits from government agencies
Broker's commissions
Title fees
Surveying fees
Delinquent real estate taxes
Razing or removing unwanted buildings, less any salvage
Grading and leveling
Paving a public street bordering the land
BUILDING
Architects' fees
Engineers' fees
Insurance costs incurred during construction
Interest on money borrowed to finance construction
Walkways to and around the building
Sales taxes
Repairs (purchase of existing building)
Reconditioning (purchase of existing building)
Modifying for use
Permits from government agencies
LAND IMPROVEMENTS
Trees and shrubs
Fences
Outdoor lighting
Paved parking areas
MACHINERY AND EQUIPMENT
Sales taxes
Freight
Installation
Repairs (purchase of used equipment)
Reconditioning (purchase of used equipment)
Insurance while in transit
Assembly
Modifying for use
Testing for use
Permits from government agencies

Costs *not necessary* for getting a fixed asset ready for use do not increase the asset's usefulness. Such costs should not be included as part of the asset's total cost. For example, the following costs should be debited to an expense account:

[1] As discussed here, land is assumed to be used only as a location or site. Land acquired for its mineral deposits or other natural resources will be considered later in the chapter.

- Vandalism
- Mistakes in installation
- Uninsured theft
- Damage during unpacking and installing
- Fines for not obtaining proper permits from government agencies

Q&A

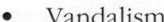

Glacier Co. is purchasing property (building and land) for use as a warehouse. In purchasing the land, Glacier has agreed to pay the prior owner's delinquent property taxes. Should the cost of paying the delinquent property taxes be included as part of the cost of the property?

Yes. All costs of acquiring the property, including the delinquent property taxes, should be included as part of the total cost of the property.

Nature of Depreciation

As we have discussed in earlier chapters, land has an unlimited life and therefore can provide unlimited services. On the other hand, other fixed assets such as equipment, buildings, and land improvements lose their ability, over time, to provide services. As a result, the costs of equipment, buildings, and land improvements should be transferred to expense accounts in a systematic manner during their expected useful lives. This periodic transfer of cost to expense is called **depreciation**.

The adjusting entry to record depreciation is usually made at the end of each month or at the end of the year. This entry debits *Depreciation Expense* and credits a *contra asset* account entitled *Accumulated Depreciation* or *Allowance for Depreciation*. The use of a contra asset account allows the original cost to remain unchanged in the fixed asset account.

The adjusting entry to record depreciation debits *Depreciation Expense* and credits *Accumulated Depreciation*.

Factors that cause a decline in the ability of a fixed asset to provide services may be identified as physical depreciation or functional depreciation. **Physical depreciation** occurs from wear and tear while in use and from the action of the weather. **Functional depreciation** occurs when a fixed asset is no longer able to provide services at the level for which it was intended. For example, a personal computer made in the 1980s would not be able to provide an Internet connection. Such advances in technology during this century have made functional depreciation an increasingly important cause of depreciation.

REAL WORLD

Companies often use different useful lives for similar assets. For example, **Sears, Roebuck and Co.** depreciates its equipment over 5 to 10 years, while **J.C. Penney Co.** depreciates its equipment over 10 to 20 years.

The term *depreciation* as used in accounting is often misunderstood because the same term is also used in business to mean a decline in the market value of an asset. However, the amount of a fixed asset's unexpired cost reported in the balance sheet usually does not agree with the amount that could be realized from its sale. Fixed assets are held for use in a business rather than for sale. It is assumed that the business will continue as a going concern. Thus, a decision to dispose of a fixed asset is based mainly on the usefulness of the asset to the business and not on its market value.

Another common misunderstanding is that accounting for depreciation provides cash needed to replace fixed assets as they wear out. This misunderstanding probably occurs because depreciation, unlike most expenses, does not require an outlay of cash in the period in which it is recorded. The cash account is neither increased nor decreased by the periodic entries that transfer the cost of fixed assets to depreciation expense accounts.

Point of INTEREST

Would you have more cash if you depreciated your car? The answer is no. Depreciation does not affect your cash flows. Likewise, depreciation does not affect the cash flows of a business. However, depreciation is subtracted in determining net income. As a result, analysts add depreciation back to a company's net income, so that they can estimate the cash generated from current operations. In the long run, however, fixed assets need to be replaced, and their replacement requires the outlay of cash. Thus, in considering the long-run, cash-generating ability of a business, the cash needed for replacement of fixed assets should be considered.

Accounting for Depreciation

OBJECTIVE 2

Compute depreciation, using the following methods: straight-line method, units-of-production method, and declining-balance method.

Three factors are considered in determining the amount of depreciation expense to be recognized each period. These three factors are (a) the fixed asset's initial cost, (b) its expected useful life, and (c) its estimated value at the end of its useful life. This third factor is called the **residual value**, **scrap value**, **salvage value**, or **trade-in value**. Exhibit 2 shows the relationship among the three factors and the periodic depreciation expense.

EXHIBIT 2 Factors that Determine Depreciation Expense

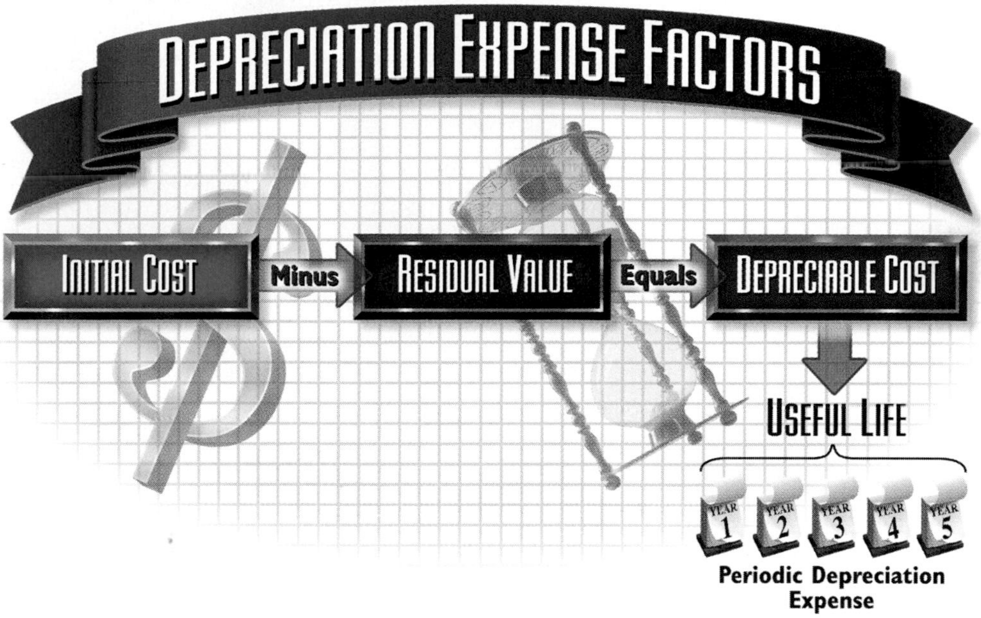

A fixed asset's **residual value** at the end of its expected useful life must be estimated at the time the asset is placed in service. If a fixed asset is expected to have little or no residual value when it is taken out of service, then its initial cost should be spread over its expected useful life as depreciation expense. If, however, a fixed asset is expected to have a significant residual value, the difference between its initial cost and its residual value, called the asset's **depreciable cost**, is the amount that is spread over the asset's useful life as depreciation expense.

A fixed asset's **expected useful life** must also be estimated at the time the asset is placed in service. Estimates of expected useful lives are available from various trade associations and other publications. For federal income tax purposes, the Internal Revenue Service has established guidelines for useful lives. These guidelines may also be helpful in determining depreciation for financial reporting purposes.

REAL WORLD: The Internal Revenue Service guideline for the useful life of automobiles and light-duty trucks is 5 years, while the designated life for most machinery and equipment is 7 years.

In practice, many businesses use the guideline that all assets placed in or taken out of service during the first half of a month are treated as if the event occurred on the first day of *that* month. That is, these businesses compute depreciation on these assets for the entire month. Likewise, all fixed asset additions and deductions during the second half of a month are treated as if the event occurred on the first day of the *next* month. We will follow this practice in this chapter.

It is not necessary that a business use a single method of computing depreciation for all its depreciable assets. The methods used in the accounts and financial statements may also differ from the methods used in determining income taxes and property taxes. The three methods used most often are (1) straight-line, (2) units-of-production, and (3) declining-balance.[2] Exhibit 3 shows the extent of the use of these methods in financial statements.

EXHIBIT 3
Use of Depreciation Methods

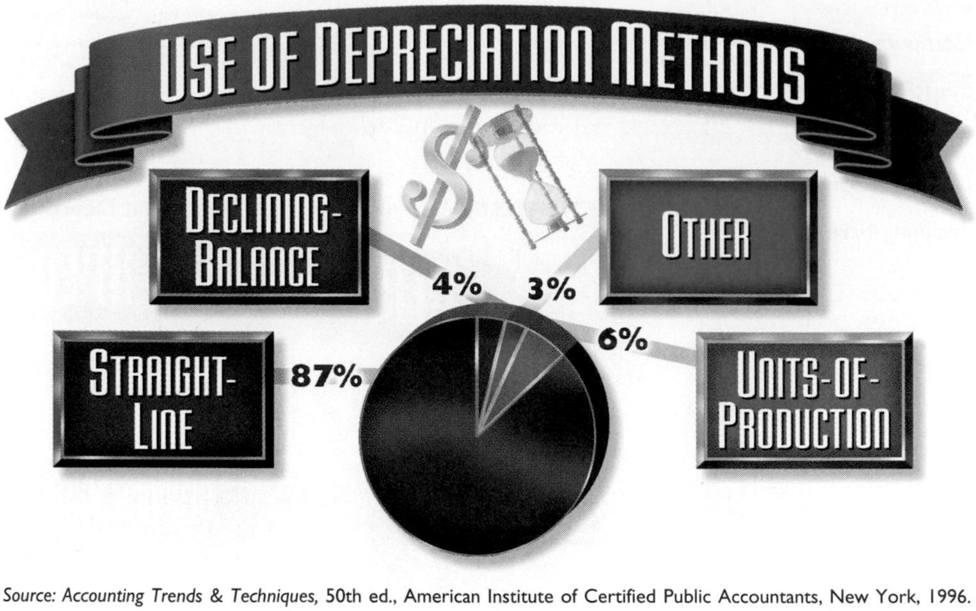

Source: Accounting Trends & Techniques, 50th ed., American Institute of Certified Public Accountants, New York, 1996.

Straight-Line Method

The **straight-line method** provides for the same amount of depreciation expense for each year of the asset's useful life. For example, assume that the cost of a depreciable asset is \$24,000, its estimated residual value is \$2,000, and its estimated life is 5 years. The annual depreciation is computed as follows:

$$\frac{\textbf{\$24,000 cost} - \textbf{\$2,000 estimated residual value}}{\textbf{5 years estimated life}} = \textbf{\$4,400 annual depreciation}$$

When an asset is used for only part of a year, the annual depreciation is prorated. For example, assume that the fiscal year ends on December 31 and that the asset in the above example is placed in service on October 1. The depreciation for the first fiscal year of use would be \$1,100 (\$4,400 × $^3/_{12}$).

For ease in applying the straight-line method, the annual depreciation may be converted to a percentage of the depreciable cost. This percentage is determined by dividing 100% by the number of years of useful life. For example, a useful life of 20 years converts to a 5% rate (100%/20), 8 years converts to a 12.5% rate (100%/8), and so on.[3] In the above example, the annual depreciation of \$4,400 can be computed by multiplying the depreciable cost of \$22,000 by 20% (100%/5).

The straight-line method is simple and is widely used. It provides a reasonable transfer of costs to periodic expense when the asset's use and the related revenues from its use are about the same from period to period.

Q&A

A truck that cost \$35,000 has a residual value of \$5,000 and a useful life of 12 years. What are (a) the depreciable cost, (b) the straight-line rate, and (c) the annual straight-line depreciation?

(a) \$30,000 (\$35,000 − \$5,000), (b) $8\frac{1}{3}$% ($^1/_{12}$), (c) \$2,500 (\$30,000 × $8\frac{1}{3}$%).

Units-of-Production Method

How would you depreciate a fixed asset when its service is related to use rather than time? When the amount of use of a fixed asset varies from year to year, the units-of-production method is more appropriate than the straight-line method. In

[2] Another method not often used today, called the *sum-of-the-years-digits method,* is described and illustrated in the appendix at the end of this chapter.

[3] The depreciation rate may also be expressed as a fraction. For example, the annual straight-line rate for an asset with a 3-year useful life is $^1/_3$.

Q&A *A truck that cost $35,000 has a residual value of $5,000 and a useful life of 125,000 miles. What are (a) the depreciation rate per mile and (b) the first year's depreciation if 18,000 miles were driven?*

(a) $0.24 per mile [($35,000 − $5,000)/125,000 miles], (b) $4,320 (18,000 miles × $0.24 per mile)

such cases, the units-of-production method better matches the depreciation expense with the related revenue.

The **units-of-production method** provides for the same amount of depreciation expense for each unit produced or each unit of capacity used by the asset. To apply this method, the useful life of the asset is expressed in terms of units of productive capacity such as hours or miles. The total depreciation expense for each accounting period is then determined by multiplying the unit depreciation by the number of units produced or used during the period. For example, assume that a machine with a cost of $24,000 and an estimated residual value of $2,000 is expected to have an estimated life of 10,000 operating hours. The depreciation for a unit of one hour is computed as follows:

$$\frac{\$24{,}000 \text{ cost} - \$2{,}000 \text{ estimated residual value}}{10{,}000 \text{ estimated hours}} = \$2.20 \text{ hourly depreciation}$$

Assuming that the machine was in operation for 2,100 hours during a year, the depreciation for that year would be $4,620 ($2.20 × 2,100 hours).

Declining-Balance Method

The **declining-balance method** provides for a declining periodic expense over the estimated useful life of the asset. To apply this method, the annual straight-line depreciation rate is doubled. For example, the declining-balance rate for an asset with an estimated life of 5 years is 40%, which is double the straight-line rate of 20% (100%/5).

For the first year of use, the cost of the asset is multiplied by the declining-balance rate. After the first year, the declining **book value** (cost minus accumulated depreciation) of the asset is multiplied by this rate. To illustrate, the annual declining-balance depreciation for an asset with an estimated 5-year life and a cost of $24,000 is shown below.

Year	Cost	Accum. Depr. at Beginning of Year	Book Value at Beginning of Year	Rate	Depreciation for Year	Book Value at End of Year
1	$24,000		$24,000.00	40%	$9,600.00	$14,400.00
2	24,000	$ 9,600.00	14,400.00	40%	5,760.00	8,640.00
3	24,000	15,360.00	8,640.00	40%	3,456.00	5,184.00
4	24,000	18,816.00	5,184.00	40%	2,073.60	3,110.40
5	24,000	20,889.60	3,110.40	—	1,110.40	2,000.00

You should note that when the declining-balance method is used, the estimated residual value is *not* considered in determining the depreciation rate. It is also ignored in computing the periodic depreciation. However, the asset should not be depreciated below its estimated residual value. In the above example the estimated residual value was $2,000. Therefore, the depreciation for the fifth year is $1,110.40 ($3,110.40 − $2,000.00) instead of $1,244.16 (40% × $3,110.40).

In the example above, we assumed that the first use of the asset occurred at the beginning of the fiscal year. This is normally not the case in practice, however, and depreciation for the first partial year of use must be computed. For example, assume that the asset above was in service at the end of the *third* month of the fiscal year. In this case, only a portion (9/12) of the first full year's depreciation of $9,600 is allocated to the first fiscal year. Thus, depreciation of $7,200 (9/12 × $9,600) is allocated to the first partial year of use. The depreciation for the second fiscal year would then be $6,720 [40% × ($24,000 − $7,200)].

Q&A *A truck that cost $35,000 has a residual value of $5,000 and a useful life of 12 years. What is the double-declining balance depreciation for the second full year of use?*

$4,861 {[$35,000 − ($35,000 × 16⅔%)] × 16⅔%}

Comparing Depreciation Methods

The straight-line method provides for the same periodic amounts of depreciation expense over the life of the asset. The units-of-production method provides for periodic amounts of depreciation expense that vary, depending upon the amount the asset is used.

The declining-balance method provides for a higher depreciation amount in the first year of the asset's use, followed by a gradually declining amount. For this reason, the declining-balance method is called an **accelerated depreciation method**. It is most appropriate when the decline in an asset's productivity or earning power is greater in the early years of its use than in later years. Further, using this method is often justified because repairs tend to increase with the age of an asset. The reduced amounts of depreciation in later years are thus offset to some extent by increased repair expenses.

The periodic depreciation amounts for the straight-line method and the declining-balance method are compared in Exhibit 4. This comparison is based on an asset cost of \$24,000, an estimated life of 5 years, and an estimated residual value of \$2,000.

EXHIBIT 4
Comparing Depreciation Methods

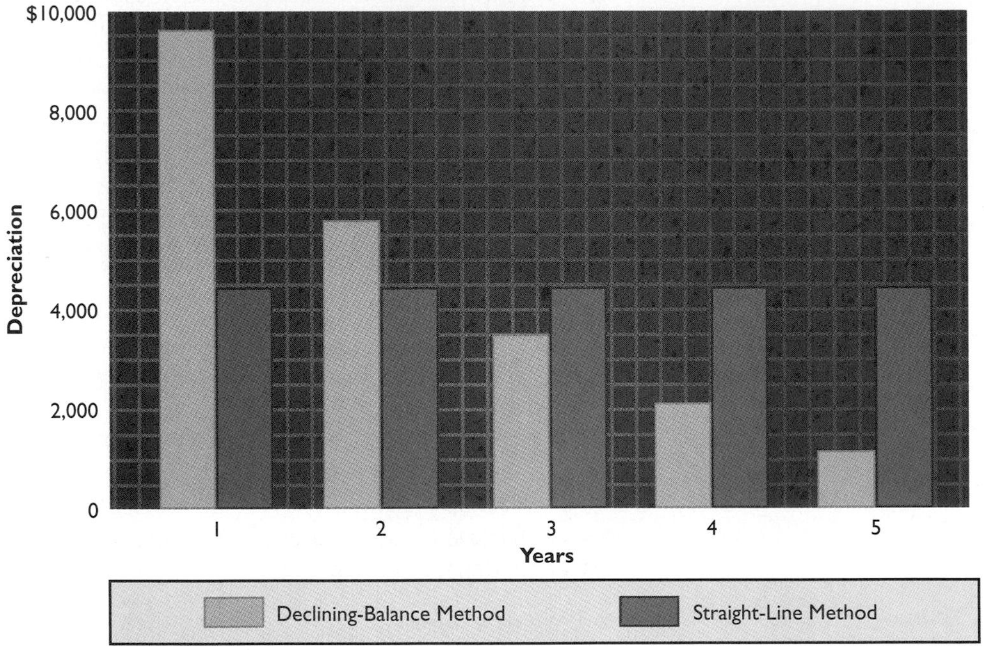

Depreciation for Federal Income Tax

The Internal Revenue Code specifies the *Modified Accelerated Cost Recovery System (MACRS)* for use by businesses in computing depreciation for tax purposes.[4] MACRS specifies eight classes of useful life and depreciation rates for each class. The two most common classes, other than real estate, are the 5-year class and the 7-year class.[5] The 5-year class includes automobiles and light-duty trucks, and the 7-year class includes most machinery and equipment. The depreciation deduction for these two classes is similar to that computed using the declining-balance method.

In using the MACRS rates, residual value is ignored, and all fixed assets are assumed to be put in and taken out of service in the middle of the year. For the

[4] Fixed assets that were acquired before 1987 are allowed to use depreciation methods other than MACRS. These are discussed in tax accounting texts.

[5] Real estate is in 27½-year classes and 31½-year classes and is depreciated by the straight-line method.

5-year-class assets, depreciation is spread over six years, as shown in the following MACRS schedule of depreciation rates:

Year	5-Year-Class Depreciation Rates
1	20.0%
2	32.0
3	19.2
4	11.5
5	11.5
6	5.8
	100.0%

To simplify its record keeping, a business will sometimes use the MACRS method for both financial statement and tax purposes. This is acceptable if MACRS does not result in significantly different amounts than would have been reported using one of the three depreciation methods discussed earlier in this chapter.

Using MACRS for both financial statement and tax purposes may, however, hurt a business. In one case, a business that had used MACRS depreciation for its financial statements lost a $1 million order because its fixed assets had low book values. The bank viewed these low book values as inadequate, so it would not loan the business the amount needed to produce the order.[6]

Q&A

What is the third year MACRS depreciation for an automobile that cost $26,000 and has a residual value of $6,500?

$4,992 ($26,000 × 19.2%)

Revising Depreciation Estimates

Revising the estimates of the residual value and the useful life is normal. When these estimates are revised, they are used to determine the depreciation expense in future periods. They do not affect the amounts of depreciation expense recorded in earlier years.

To illustrate, assume that a fixed asset purchased for $130,000 was originally estimated to have a useful life of 30 years and a residual value of $10,000. The asset has been depreciated for 10 years by the straight-line method. At the end of ten years, the asset's book value (undepreciated cost) is $90,000, determined as follows:

Asset cost	$130,000
Less accumulated depreciation ($4,000 per year × 10 years)	40,000
Book value (undepreciated cost), end of tenth year	$ 90,000

During the eleventh year, it is estimated that the remaining useful life is 25 years (instead of 20) and that the residual value is $5,000 (instead of $10,000). The depreciation expense for each of the remaining 25 years is $3,400, computed as follows:

Book value (undepreciated cost), end of tenth year	$90,000
Less revised estimated residual value	5,000
Revised remaining depreciable cost	$85,000
Revised annual depreciation expense ($85,000/25)	$ 3,400

Q&A

For the $130,000 asset in the example on this page, assume that after 10 more years (20 years in total) its remaining useful life is estimated at 5 years with no residual value. What is the revised depreciation for the twenty-first year?

$11,200 ($130,000 − $40,000 depreciation for years 1–10 = $90,000; $90,000 − $34,000 depreciation for years 11–20 = $56,000; $56,000 divided by 5 years = $11,200)

[6] Lee Berton, "Do's and Don'ts," *The Wall Street Journal,* June 10, 1988, p. 34R.

BUSINESS ON STAGE

Businesses that use equipment to provide goods or services must maintain that equipment. These businesses usually follow one of three maintenance philosophies: (1) corrective maintenance, (2) preventive maintenance, and (3) predictive maintenance.

- **Corrective maintenance.** Under this philosophy, equipment is fixed when the equipment breaks down. It would be similar to you changing the oil in your car when your engine freezes up. Companies that use corrective maintenance don't want to waste time performing maintenance until there is an actual failure. Unfortunately, an unplanned machine failure can cause significant disruptions. Such disruptions include unplanned stops in production, delays in waiting for replacement parts, and additional repair due to broken machine components. Because of this, many consider corrective maintenance a poor philosophy.
- **Preventive maintenance.** Under this philosophy, equipment is repaired under a planned schedule. It would be similar to you changing your car's oil every 6,000 miles. Preventive maintenance is considered superior to corrective maintenance because the maintenance is planned. Therefore, employees can be trained, multiple machines can be repaired, or housekeeping can be performed during the scheduled maintenance. In addition, replacement parts can be ordered ahead of time, minimizing delays caused by emergencies. Lastly, preventive maintenance may reduce the overall maintenance expenditures, because actual machine failures are minimized.
- **Predictive maintenance.** Under this new maintenance philosophy, equipment is repaired at the exact time it needs to be repaired prior to actual failure. It would be similar to you changing your car's oil when a sensor in the car indicated that the oil had reached a given level of impurity. Predictive maintenance is considered superior to preventive maintenance because maintenance is only performed when it is actually needed. This may reduce the total amount of time that equipment spends in maintenance during its life, compared to preventive maintenance. At the same time, however, predictive maintenance may still be planned, once it is indicated—so it has the same advantages as preventive maintenance. New sensors and computers are being developed to support predictive maintenance. Vibration sensors are one example. These sensors are placed on machines to measure vibration, which indicates bearing wear. When the vibration levels reach a certain point, bearings are replaced, which is just prior to their failing. ■

Composite-Rate Method

Assets may be grouped according to common traits, such as similar useful lives. For example, a group might include all delivery trucks with useful lives of less than 8 years. Likewise, a group might include all office equipment or all store fixtures. Depreciation may be determined for each group of assets, using a single *composite rate,* rather than a rate for each individual asset. The depreciation computations are similar for groups of assets as for individual assets.

Capital and Revenue Expenditures

OBJECTIVE 3

Classify fixed asset costs as either capital expenditures or revenue expenditures.

The costs of acquiring fixed assets, adding to a fixed asset, improving a fixed asset, or extending a fixed asset's useful life are called **capital expenditures**. Such expenditures are recorded by either debiting the asset account or its related accumulated depreciation account. Costs that benefit only the current period or costs incurred for normal maintenance and repairs are called **revenue expenditures**. Such expenditures are debited to expense accounts. For example, the cost of replacing spark plugs in an automobile or the cost of repainting a building should be debited to an expense account.

To properly match revenues and expenses, it is important to distinguish between capital and revenue expenditures. Capital expenditures will affect the depreciation expense of more than one period, while revenue expenditures will affect the expenses of only the current period.

Types of Capital Expenditures

We have discussed accounting for the initial costs of acquiring fixed assets. Capital expenditures on assets after they have been acquired may be either (a) additions, (b) betterments, or (c) extraordinary repairs.

Additions to Fixed Assets

The cost of an addition to a fixed asset should be debited to the related fixed asset account.

For example, the cost of adding a new wing to a building should be debited to the building account. This cost should then be depreciated over its estimated useful life or the remaining useful life of the building, whichever is shorter.

Betterments

An expenditure that improves a fixed asset's operating efficiency or capacity for its remaining useful life is called a **betterment**. Such expenditures should be debited to the related fixed asset account. For example, if the power unit attached to a machine is replaced by one of greater capacity, its cost should be debited to the machine account. Also, the cost and the accumulated depreciation related to the old power unit should be removed from the accounts. The cost of the new power unit should then be depreciated over its estimated useful life or the remaining useful life of the machine, whichever is shorter.

Extraordinary Repairs

An expenditure that increases the useful life of an asset beyond its original estimate is called an **extraordinary repair**. Such expenditures should be debited to the related accumulated depreciation account. In such cases, the repairs are said to *restore* or *make good* a portion of the depreciation recorded in prior years. The depreciation for future periods should be computed on the basis of the revised book value of the asset and the revised estimate of the remaining useful life.

To illustrate, assume that a machine costing $50,000 has no estimated residual value and an estimated useful life of 10 years. Assume also that the machine has been depreciated for 6 years by the straight-line method ($5,000 annual depreciation). At the beginning of the seventh year, an $11,500 extraordinary repair increases the remaining useful life of the machine to 7 years (instead of 4). The repair of $11,500 should be debited to Accumulated Depreciation. The annual depreciation for the remaining 7 years of use would be $4,500, computed as follows:

Q&A *Identify each of the items related to a truck as an addition, a betterment, or an extraordinary repair: (a) a snowplow attachment that allows the truck to be used for snow removal, (b) a new transmission, (c) a hydraulic hitch to replace a manual hitch.*

(a) addition, (b) extraordinary repair, (c) betterment.

Cost of machine		$50,000
Less Accumulated Depreciation balance:		
Depreciation for first 6 years ($5,000 × 6)	$30,000	
Deduct debit for extraordinary repairs	11,500	
Balance of Accumulated Depreciation		18,500
Revised book value of machine after extraordinary repair		$31,500
Annual depreciation ($31,500/7 years remaining useful life)		$ 4,500

Summary of Capital and Revenue Expenditures

Exhibit 5 summarizes the accounting for capital and revenue expenditures related to fixed assets.

EXHIBIT 5
Capital and Revenue Expenditures

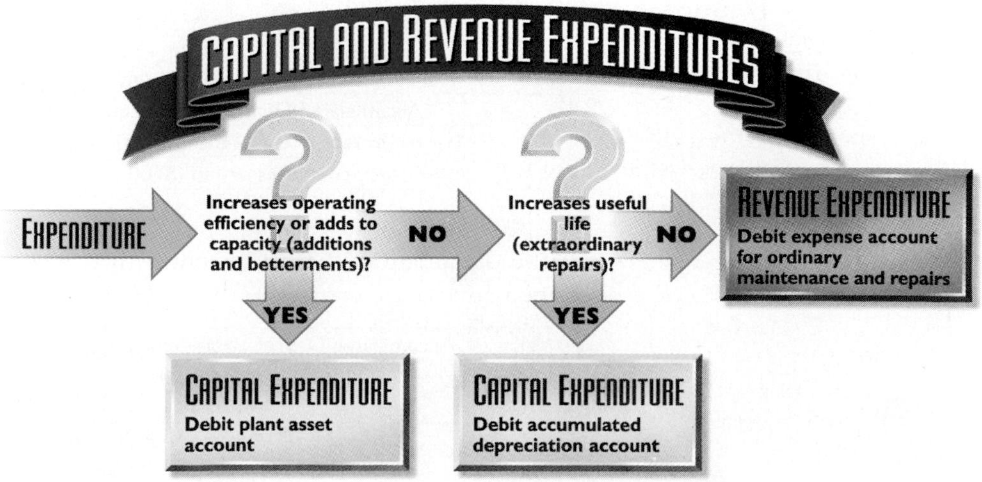

Disposal of Fixed Assets

OBJECTIVE 4

Journalize entries for the disposal of fixed assets.

Fixed assets that are no longer useful may be discarded, sold, or traded for other fixed assets. The details of the entry to record a disposal will vary. In all cases, however, the book value of the asset must be removed from the accounts. The entry for this purpose debits the asset's accumulated depreciation account for its balance on the date of disposal and credits the asset account for the cost of the asset.

The entry to record the disposal of a fixed asset removes the cost of the asset and its accumulated depreciation from the accounts.

A fixed asset should not be removed from the accounts only because it has been fully depreciated. If the asset is still used by the business, the cost and accumulated depreciation should remain in the ledger. This maintains accountability for the asset in the ledger. If the book value of the asset was removed from the ledger, the accounts would contain no evidence of the continued existence of the asset. In addition, the cost and the accumulated depreciation data on such assets are often needed for property tax and income tax reports.

Discarding Fixed Assets

When fixed assets are no longer useful to the business and have no residual or market value, they are discarded. To illustrate, assume that an item of equipment acquired at a cost of $25,000 is fully depreciated at December 31, the end of the preceding fiscal year. On February 14, the equipment is discarded. The entry to record this is as follows:

Feb.	14	Accumulated Depreciation—Equipment		25 000 00	
		Equipment			25 000 00
		To write off equipment discarded.			

If an asset has not been fully depreciated, depreciation should be recorded prior to removing it from service and from the accounting records. To illustrate, assume that equipment costing $6,000 is depreciated at an annual straight-line rate of 10%. In addition, assume that on December 31 of the preceding fiscal year, the accumulated depreciation balance, after adjusting entries, is $4,750. Finally, assume that the asset is removed from service on the following March 24. The entry to record the depreciation for the three months of the current period prior to the asset's removal from service is as follows:

Mar.	24	Depreciation Expense—Equipment		150 00	
		Accumulated Depreciation—Equipment			150 00
		To record current depreciation on			
		equipment discarded ($600 × $^3/_{12}$).			

The discarding of the equipment is then recorded by the following entry:

Mar.	24	Accumulated Depreciation—Equipment		4 900 00	
		Loss on Disposal of Fixed Assets		1 100 00	
		Equipment			6 000 00
		To write off equipment discarded.			

The loss of $1,100 is recorded because the balance of the accumulated depreciation account ($4,900) is less than the balance in the equipment account ($6,000). Losses on the discarding of fixed assets are nonoperating items and are normally reported in the Other Expense section of the income statement.

Selling Fixed Assets

The entry to record the sale of a fixed asset is similar to the entries illustrated above, except that the cash or other asset received must also be recorded. If the selling price is more than the book value of the asset, the transaction results in a gain. If the selling price is less than the book value, there is a loss.

To illustrate, assume that equipment is acquired at a cost of $10,000 and is depreciated at an annual straight-line rate of 10%. The equipment is sold for cash on October 12 of the eighth year of its use. The balance of the accumulated depreciation account as of the preceding December 31 is $7,000. The entry to update the depreciation for the nine months of the current year is as follows:

Oct.	12	Depreciation Expense—Equipment		750 00	
		Accumulated Depreciation—Equipment			750 00
		To record current depreciation on			
		equipment sold ($10,000 × 3/4 × 10%).			

After the current depreciation is recorded, the book value of the asset is $2,250 ($10,000 − $7,750). The entries to record the sale, assuming three different selling prices, are as follows:

Sold at book value, for $2,250. No gain or loss.

Oct.	12	Cash		2250 00	
		Accumulated Depreciation—Equipment		7750 00	
		Equipment			10000 00

Sold below book value, for $1,000. Loss of $1,250.

Oct.	12	Cash		1000 00	
		Accumulated Depreciation—Equipment		7750 00	
		Loss on Disposal of Fixed Assets		1250 00	
		Equipment			10000 00

Sold above book value, for $2,800. Gain of $550.

Oct.	12	Cash		2800 00	
		Accumulated Depreciation—Equipment		7750 00	
		Equipment			10000 00
		Gain on Disposal of Fixed Assets			550 00

Exchanging Similar Fixed Assets

Old equipment is often traded in for new equipment having a similar use. In such cases, the seller allows the buyer an amount for the old equipment traded in. This amount, called the **trade-in allowance**, may be either greater or less than the book value of the old equipment. The remaining balance—the amount owed—is either paid in cash or a liability is recorded. It is normally called **boot**, which is its tax name.

REAL WORLD Gains on exchanges of similar fixed assets are also not recognized for federal income tax purposes.

Gains on Exchanges

Gains on exchanges of similar fixed assets are not recognized for financial reporting purposes.[7] This is based on the theory that revenue occurs from the production and sale of goods produced by fixed assets and not from the exchange of similar fixed assets.

When the trade-in allowance exceeds the book value of an asset traded in and no gain is recognized, the cost recorded for the new asset can be determined in either of two ways:

1. Cost of new asset = List price of new asset − Unrecognized gain

or

2. Cost of new asset = Cash given (or liability assumed) + Book value of old asset

To illustrate, assume the following exchange:

Similar equipment acquired (new):		
List price of new equipment.		$5,000
Trade-in allowance on old equipment		1,100
Cash paid at June 19, date of exchange.		$3,900
Equipment traded in (old):		
Cost of old equipment.		$4,000
Accumulated depreciation at date of exchange		3,200
Book value at June 19, date of exchange.		$ 800
Recorded cost of new equipment:		
Method One:		
List price of new equipment.		$5,000
Trade-in allowance	$1,100	
Book value of old equipment	800	
Unrecognized gain on exchange		(300)
Cost of new equipment.		$4,700
Method Two:		
Book value of old equipment		$ 800
Cash paid at date of exchange		3,900
Cost of new equipment.		$4,700

Q&A *Equipment with a book value of $14,000 is traded in for similar equipment with a list price of $50,000. A trade-in allowance of $15,000 was allowed on the old equipment. What is the cost of the new equipment to be recorded in the accounts?*

$49,000 ($50,000 − $1,000 gain, or $14,000 + $35,000 boot)

The entry to record this exchange and the payment of cash is as follows:

June	19	Accumulated Depreciation—Equipment		3 200 00	
		Equipment (new equipment)		4 700 00	
		Equipment (old equipment)			4 000 00
		Cash			3 900 00
		To record exchange of equipment.			

Not recognizing the $300 gain ($1,100 trade-in allowance minus $800 book value) at the time of the exchange reduces future depreciation expense. That is, the depreciation expense for the new asset is based on a cost of $4,700 rather than on the list price of $5,000. In effect, the unrecognized gain of $300 reduces the total amount of depreciation taken during the life of the equipment by $300.

[7] Gains on exchanges of similar fixed assets are recognized if cash (boot) is received. This topic is discussed in advanced accounting texts.

Losses on exchanges of similar fixed assets are *not* recognized for federal income tax purposes.

Losses on Exchanges

For financial reporting purposes, losses are recognized on exchanges of similar fixed assets if the trade-in allowance is less than the book value of the old equipment. When there is a loss, the cost recorded for the new asset should be the market (list) price. To illustrate, assume the following exchange:

Similar equipment acquired (new):	
List price of new equipment	$10,000
Trade-in allowance on old equipment	2,000
Cash paid at September 7, date of exchange	$ 8,000
Equipment traded in (old):	
Cost of old equipment	$ 7,000
Accumulated depreciation at date of exchange	4,600
Book value at September 7, date of exchange	$ 2,400
Trade-in allowance on old equipment	2,000
Loss on exchange	$ 400

The entry to record the exchange is as follows:

Sept.	7	Accumulated Depreciation—Equipment		4600 00	
		Equipment		10000 00	
		Loss on Disposal of Fixed Assets		400 00	
		Equipment			7000 00
		Cash			8000 00
		To record exchange of equipment,			
		with loss.			

Review of Accounting for Exchanges of Similar Fixed Assets

Exhibit 6 reviews the accounting for exchanges of similar fixed assets, using the following data:

List price of new equipment acquired	$15,000
Cost of old equipment traded in	$12,500
Accumulated depreciation at date of exchange	10,100
Book value at date of exchange	$ 2,400

EXHIBIT 6
Summary Illustration—Accounting for Exchanges of Similar Fixed Assets

CASE ONE (GAIN): Trade-in allowance is more than book value of asset traded in.
Trade-in allowance, $3,000; cash paid, $12,000 ($15,000 − $3,000)

Cost of new asset	List price of new asset acquired, less unrecognized gain: $14,400 ($15,000 − $600) **or** Cash paid plus book value of asset traded in: $14,400 ($12,000 + $2,400)		
Gain recognized	None		
Entry	Equipment	14,400	
	Accumulated Depreciation	10,100	
	Equipment		12,500
	Cash		12,000

EXHIBIT 6 *(concluded)*

CASE TWO (LOSS): Trade-in allowance is less than book value of asset traded in.

Trade-in allowance, $2,000; cash paid, $13,000 ($15,000 − $2,000)

Cost of new asset	List price of new asset acquired: $15,000		
Loss recognized	$400		
Entry	Equipment	15,000	
	Accumulated Depreciation	10,100	
	Loss on Disposal of Fixed Assets	400	
	Equipment		12,500
	Cash		13,000

Leasing Fixed Assets

OBJECTIVE 5

Define a lease and summarize the accounting rules related to the leasing of fixed assets.

You are probably familiar with leases. A *lease* is a contract for the use of an asset for a stated period of time. Leases are frequently used in business. For example, automobiles, computers, medical equipment, buildings, and airplanes are often leased.

REAL WORLD: Of the companies surveyed in the 1996 edition of *Accounting Trends & Techniques,* 91% reported leases.

The two parties to a lease contract are the lessor and the lessee. The *lessor* is the party who owns the asset. The *lessee* is the party to whom the rights to use the asset are granted by the lessor. The lessee is obligated to make periodic rent payments for the lease term. All leases are classified by the lessee as either capital leases or operating leases.

A **capital lease** is accounted for as if the lessee has, in fact, purchased the asset. The lessee debits an asset account for the fair market value of the asset and credits a long-term lease liability account. The accounting for capital leases and the criteria that a capital lease must satisfy are discussed in more advanced accounting texts.

A lease that is not classified as a capital lease for accounting purposes is classified as an **operating lease**. The lessee records the payments under an operating lease by debiting *Rent Expense* and crediting *Cash*. Neither future lease obligations nor the future rights to use the leased asset are recognized in the accounts. However, the lessee must disclose future lease commitments in footnotes to the financial statements.

The asset rentals described in earlier chapters of this text were accounted for as operating leases. To simplify, we will continue to treat asset leases as operating leases.

Internal Control of Fixed Assets

OBJECTIVE 6

Describe internal controls over fixed assets.

Because of their dollar value and long-term nature, it is important to design and apply effective internal controls over fixed assets. Such controls should begin with authorization and approval procedures for the purchase of fixed assets. Controls should also exist to ensure that fixed assets are acquired at the lowest possible costs. One procedure to achieve this objective is to require competitive bids from preapproved vendors.

As soon as a fixed asset is received, it should be inspected and tagged for control purposes and recorded in a subsidiary ledger. This establishes the initial accountability for the asset. Subsidiary ledgers for fixed assets are also useful in determining depreciation expense and recording disposals. Operating data that may be recorded in the subsidiary ledger, such as number of breakdowns, length of time out of service, and cost of repairs, are useful in deciding whether to replace the asset. A company that maintains a computerized subsidiary ledger may use bar-coded tags, similar to the one on the back of this textbook, so that fixed asset data can be directly scanned into computer records.

Fixed assets should be insured against theft, fire, flooding, or other disasters. They should also be safeguarded from theft, misuse, or other damage. For example, fixed assets that are highly open to theft, such as computers, should be locked or otherwise protected when not in use. For computers, safeguarding also includes climate controls and special fire-extinguishing equipment. Procedures should also exist for training employees to properly operate fixed assets such as equipment and machinery.

A physical inventory of fixed assets should be taken periodically in order to verify the accuracy of the accounting records. Such an inventory would detect missing, obsolete, or idle fixed assets. In addition, fixed assets should be inspected periodically in order to determine their condition.

Careful control should also be exercised over the disposal of fixed assets. All disposals should be properly authorized and approved. Fully depreciated assets should be retained in the accounting records until disposal has been authorized and they are removed from service.

Natural Resources

OBJECTIVE 7

Compute depletion and journalize the entry for depletion.

Q&A *A business purchased mineral rights to 250,000 tons of ore for \$1,500,000. If 35,000 tons of ore were mined in the first year, what are (a) the depletion rate per ton and (2) the depletion expense for the first year?*

(a) \$6 per ton (\$1,500,000/250,000 tons); (b) \$210,000 (35,000 tons × \$6)

The fixed assets of some businesses include timber, metal ores, minerals, or other natural resources. As these businesses harvest or mine and then sell these resources, a portion of the cost of acquiring them must be debited to an expense account. This process of transferring the cost of natural resources to an expense account is called **depletion**. The amount of depletion is determined by multiplying the quantity extracted during the period by the depletion rate. This rate is computed by dividing the cost of the mineral deposit by its estimated size.

Computing depletion is similar to computing units-of-production depreciation. To illustrate, assume that a business paid \$400,000 for the mining rights to a mineral deposit estimated at 1,000,000 tons of ore. The depletion rate is \$0.40 per ton (\$400,000/1,000,000 tons). If 90,000 tons are mined during the year, the periodic depletion is \$36,000 (90,000 tons × \$0.40). The entry to record the depletion is shown below.

		Adjusting Entry			
Dec.	31	Depletion Expense		36 000 00	
		Accumulated Depletion			36 000 00

Like the accumulated depreciation account, Accumulated Depletion is a *contra asset* account. It is reported on the balance sheet as a deduction from the cost of the mineral deposit.

Intangible Assets

OBJECTIVE 8

Journalize the entries for acquiring and amortizing intangible assets, such as patents, copyrights, and goodwill.

Patents, copyrights, trademarks, and goodwill are long-term assets that are useful in the operations of a business and are not held for sale. These assets are called **intangible assets** because they do not exist physically.

The basic principles of accounting for intangible assets are like those described earlier for fixed assets. The major concerns are determining (1) the initial cost and (2) the **amortization**—the amount of cost to transfer to expense. Amortization results from the passage of time or a decline in the usefulness of the intangible asset.

Patents

Manufacturers may acquire exclusive rights to produce and sell goods with one or more unique features. Such rights are granted by **patents**, which the federal government issues to inventors. These rights continue in effect for 20 years. A business may purchase patent rights from others, or it may obtain patents developed by its own research and development efforts.

The initial cost of a purchased patent, including any related legal fees, should be debited to an asset account. This cost should be written off, or amortized, over the years of the patent's expected usefulness. This period of time may be less than the remaining legal life of the patent. The estimated useful life of the patent may also change as technology or consumer tastes change.

The straight-line method is normally used to determine the periodic amortization. When the amortization is recorded, it is debited to an expense account and credited directly to the patents account. Not using a separate contra asset account is common for all intangible assets.

To illustrate, assume that at the beginning of its fiscal year a business acquires patent rights for $100,000. The patent had been granted 6 years earlier by the Federal Patent Office. Although the patent will not expire for 14 years, its remaining useful life is estimated as 5 years. The entry to amortize the patent at the end of the fiscal year is as follows:

		Adjusting Entry		
Dec.	31	Amortization Expense—Patents	20 000 00	
		Patents		20 000 00

Rather than purchase patent rights, a business may incur significant costs in developing patents through its own research and development efforts. Such **research and development costs** are usually accounted for as current operating expenses in the period in which they are incurred.

Expensing research and development costs in the period they are incurred is justified for two reasons. First, the future benefits from research and development efforts are highly uncertain. In fact, most research and development efforts do not result in patents. Second, even if a patent is granted, it may be difficult to objectively estimate its cost. If many research projects are in process at the same time, for example, it is difficult to separate the costs of one project from another.

Copyrights and Trademarks

The exclusive right to publish and sell a literary, artistic, or musical composition is granted by a **copyright**. Copyrights are issued by the federal government and extend for 50 years beyond the author's death. The costs of a copyright include all costs of creating the work plus any administrative or legal costs of obtaining the copyright. A copyright that is purchased from another should be recorded at the

Coke® is one of the world's most recognizable trademarks. As stated in *LIFE*, "Two-thirds of the earth is covered by water; the rest is covered by Coke. If the French are known for wine and the Germans for beer, America achieved global beverage dominance with fizzy water and caramel color."

price paid for it. Because of the uncertainty regarding the useful life of a copyright, it is normally amortized over a short period of time. For example, the copyright costs of this text are amortized over 3 years.

A **trademark** is a name, term, or symbol used to identify a business and its products. For example, the distinctive red-and-white Coca Cola logo is an example of a trademark. Most businesses identify their trademarks with ® in their advertisements and on their products. Under federal law, businesses can protect against others using their trademarks by registering them for 10 years and renewing the registration for 10-year periods thereafter. Like a copyright, the legal costs of registering a trademark with the federal government should be recorded as an asset. Also, if a trademark is purchased from another business, the cost of its purchase would be recorded as an asset. The cost of a trademark should be amortized over its estimated useful life, but not more than 40 years.

Goodwill

In business, **goodwill** refers to an intangible asset of a business that is created from such favorable factors as location, product quality, reputation, and managerial skill. Goodwill allows a business to earn a rate of return on its investment that is often in excess of the normal rate for other firms in the same business.

Generally accepted accounting principles permit the recording of goodwill in the accounts only if it is objectively determined by a transaction. An example of a transaction that may justify recording goodwill is the purchase or sale of a business. Goodwill must be amortized over its estimated useful life, which cannot exceed 40 years.

In its 1996 annual report, **La-Z-Boy Chair Company** reported goodwill from acquired companies. La-Z-Boy amortizes this goodwill over a period of 30 years.

Financial Reporting for Fixed Assets and Intangible Assets

OBJECTIVE 9

Describe how depreciation expense is reported in an income statement and prepare a balance sheet that includes fixed assets and intangible assets.

How should fixed assets and intangible assets be reported in the financial statements? The amount of depreciation and amortization expense of a period should be reported separately in the income statement or disclosed in a footnote. A general description of the method or methods used in computing depreciation should also be reported.

The amount of each major class of fixed assets should be disclosed in the balance sheet or in footnotes. The related accumulated depreciation should also be disclosed, either by major class or in total. If there are too many classes of fixed assets, a single amount may be presented in the balance sheet, supported by a separate detailed listing. Fixed assets are normally presented under the more descriptive caption of **property, plant, and equipment**.

The cost of mineral rights or ore deposits is normally shown as part of the fixed assets section of the balance sheet. The related accumulated depletion should also be disclosed. In some cases, the mineral rights are shown net of depletion on the face of the balance sheet, accompanied by a footnote that discloses the amount of the accumulated depletion.

Intangible assets are usually reported in the balance sheet in a separate section immediately following fixed assets. The balance of each major class of intangible assets should be disclosed at an amount net of amortization taken to date. Exhibit 7 is a partial balance sheet that shows the reporting of fixed assets and intangible assets.

EXHIBIT 7
Fixed Assets and Intangible Assets in the Balance Sheet

Discovery Mining Co.
Balance Sheet
December 31, 20—

Assets

Total current assets					$ 462,500
		Accum.	Book		
Property, plant, and equipment:	Cost	Depr.	Value		
Land	$ 30,000	—	$ 30,000		
Buildings	110,000	$ 26,000	84,000		
Factory equipment	650,000	192,000	458,000		
Office equipment	120,000	13,000	107,000		
	$ 910,000	$ 231,000		$679,000	
		Accum.	Book		
Mineral deposits:	Cost	Depl.	Value		
Alaska deposit	$1,200,000	$ 800,000	$ 400,000		
Wyoming deposit	750,000	200,000	550,000		
	$1,950,000	$1,000,000		950,000	
Total property, plant, and equipment					1,629,000
Intangible assets:					
Patents				$ 75,000	
Goodwill				50,000	
Total intangible assets					125,000

FINANCIAL ANALYSIS AND INTERPRETATION

OBJECTIVE 10

Compute and interpret the ratio of fixed assets to long-term liabilities.

Long-term liabilities are often secured by fixed assets. The ratio of total fixed assets to long-term liabilities provides a solvency measure that indicates the margin of safety to creditors. It also gives an indication of the potential ability of the business to borrow additional funds on a long-term basis. The **ratio of fixed assets to long-term liabilities** is computed as follows:

$$\textbf{Ratio of fixed assets to long-term liabilities (debt)} = \frac{\textbf{Fixed assets (net)}}{\textbf{Long-term liabilities (debt)}}$$

To illustrate, the following data were taken from the 1996 and 1995 financial statements of **Procter & Gamble**:

	(in millions) 1996	1995
Property, plant, and equipment (net)	$11,118	$11,026
Long-term debt	4,670	5,161

The ratio of fixed assets to long-term liabilities (debt) is 2.4 ($11,118/$4,670) for 1996 and 2.1 ($11,026/$5,161) for 1995. The increase in the ratio from 1995 to 1996 indicates more of a margin of safety for creditors. As with other financial measures, the interpretation and analysis is enhanced by comparisons over time and with industry averages.

ENCORE

Would you like to become an inventor and own patents worth millions? Yoshiro Nakamatsu, who bills himself as the Thomas Edison of Japan, hopes to open a school that will teach people how to create new products. Yoshiro Nakamatsu is the president of Tokyo's **Hi-Tech Innovation Institute** and claims to have 3,042 patents over his inventing career. Nakamatsu's net worth from royalties from his inventions is estimated at $75 million.

At the age of 5, with encouragement from his grandfather, Nakamatsu invented a stabilizer to make planes fly better. He was granted his first patent at age 14. Since then, he has licensed 16 patents to **IBM**, including one for his 1952 invention of the floppy disk for personal computers. Some of Nakamatsu's other inventions and what he claims they do include the following:

- **Yummy TV.** A snack food designed to relieve eye strain caused by watching too much TV.
- **Enerex.** An engine that produces energy from water.
- **Cerebrex Chair.** A chair that uses electronic impulses to both sharpen the mind and rest the body.
- **Nakamatsu Golf Putter.** A putter that has an oversized vibrating handle to make putting 93 percent accurate within 10 feet.
- **Anti-Gravity Floating Vibrating Three-Dimensional Sonic System.** A speaker system for stereo compact disc players and other electronic products.
- **Magnetic Eyeglasses.** Eyeglasses that have magnets attached to them for improving the blood circulation of the eyes.
- **Dr. Nakamatsu's Yummi Nutri Brain Biscuits.** Food for your brain.
- **Nakamatsu's Engine.** An engine that is far more efficient than gasoline or electric engines because it runs on "cosmic" power.

In his lectures, Nakamatsu offers the following advice on how to become a genius and excel at inventing: (1) swim, (2) lift weights, (3) sleep less than six hours a night, (4) work between the hours of midnight and 4 a.m., and (5) never have sex before the age of 24. ■

Source: Dean Takahashi, "Japanese Inventor Nearly Triples Edison's Output," *The Austin American-Statesman,* May 17, 1996.

APPENDIX: SUM-OF-THE-YEARS-DIGITS DEPRECIATION

REAL WORLD

The 1996 edition of *Accounting Trends & Techniques* reported that only 1%–2% of the surveyed companies now use this method for financial reporting purposes.

At one time, the sum-of-the-years-digits method of depreciation was used by many businesses. However, the tax law changes of the 1980s limited its use for tax purposes.

Under the **sum-of-the-years-digits method**, depreciation expense is determined by multiplying the original cost of the asset less its estimated residual value by a smaller fraction each year. Thus, the sum-of-the-years-digits method is similar to the declining-balance method, in that the depreciation expense declines each year.

The denominator of the fraction used in determining the depreciation expense is the sum of the digits of the years of the asset's useful life. For example, an asset with a useful life of 5 years would have a denominator of 15 (5 + 4 + 3 + 2 + 1).[8] The numerator of the fraction is the number of years of useful life remaining at the beginning of each year for which depreciation is being computed. Thus, the numerator decreases each year by 1. For a useful life of 5 years, the numerator is 5 the first year, 4 the second year, 3 the third year, and so on.

The following depreciation schedule illustrates the sum-of-the-years-digits method for an asset with a cost of $24,000, an estimated residual value of $2,000, and an estimated useful life of 5 years:

Year	Cost Less Residual Value	Rate	Depreciation for Year	Accum. Depr. at End of Year	Book Value at End of Year
1	$22,000	5/15	$7,333.33	$ 7,333.33	$16,666.67
2	22,000	4/15	5,866.67	13,200.00	10,800.00
3	22,000	3/15	4,400.00	17,600.00	6,400.00
4	22,000	2/15	2,933.33	20,533.33	3,466.67
5	22,000	1/15	1,466.67	22,000.00	2,000.00

What if the fixed asset is not placed in service at the beginning of the year? When the date an asset is first put into service is not the beginning of a fiscal year, each full year's depreciation must be allocated between the two fiscal years benefited. To illustrate, assume that the asset in the above example was put into service at the beginning of the fourth month of the first fiscal year. The depreciation for that year would be $5,500 (9/12 × 5/15 × $22,000). The depreciation for the second year would be $6,233.33, computed as follows:

3/12 × 5/15 × $22,000	$1,833.33
9/12 × 4/15 × $22,000	4,400.00
Total depreciation for second fiscal year	$6,233.33

KEY POINTS

1 Define fixed assets and describe the accounting for their cost.

Fixed assets are long-term tangible assets that are owned by the business and are used in the normal operations of the business. Examples of fixed assets are equipment, buildings, and land. The initial cost of a fixed asset includes all amounts spent to get the asset in place and ready for use. For example, sales tax, freight, insurance in transit, and installation costs are all included in the cost of a fixed asset. As time passes, all fixed assets except land lose their ability to provide services. As a result, the cost of a fixed asset should be transferred to an expense account, in a systematic manner, during the asset's expected useful life. This periodic transfer of cost to expense is called depreciation.

2 Compute depreciation, using the following methods: straight-line method, units-of-production method, and declining-balance method.

In computing depreciation, three factors need to be considered: (1) the fixed asset's initial cost, (2) the useful life of the asset, and (3) the residual value of the asset.

The straight-line method spreads the initial cost less the residual value equally over the useful life. The units-of-production method spreads the initial cost less the residual value equally over the units expected to be produced by the asset during its useful life. The declining-balance method is applied by multiplying the declining book value of the asset by twice the straight-line rate.

3 Classify fixed asset costs as either capital expenditures or revenue expenditures.

Costs for additions to fixed assets and other costs related to improving efficiency or capacity are classified as capital expenditures. Costs for additions to an asset and costs that add to the usefulness of the asset for more than one period (called betterments) are also classified as capital ex-

[8] The denominator can also be determined from the following formula: $S = N[(N + 1)/2]$, where S = sum of the digits and N = number of years of estimated life.

penditures. Costs that increase the useful life of an asset beyond the original estimate are a capital expenditure and are called extraordinary repairs. Expenditures that benefit only the current period or that maintain normal operating efficiency are debited to expense accounts and are classified as revenue expenditures.

4 Journalize entries for the disposal of fixed assets.

The journal entries to record disposals of fixed assets will vary. In all cases, however, any depreciation for the current period should be recorded, and the book value of the asset is then removed from the accounts. The entry to remove the book value from the accounts is a debit to the asset's accumulated depreciation account and a credit to the asset account for the cost of the asset. For assets retired from service, a loss may be recorded for any remaining book value of the asset.

When a fixed asset is sold, the book value is removed and the cash or other asset received is also recorded. If the selling price is more than the book value of the asset, the transaction results in a gain. If the selling price is less than the book value, there is a loss.

When a fixed asset is exchanged for another of similar nature, no gain is recognized on the exchange. The acquired asset's cost is adjusted for any gains. A loss on an exchange of similar assets is recorded.

5 Define a lease and summarize the accounting rules related to the leasing of fixed assets.

A lease is a contract for the use of an asset for a period of time. A capital lease is accounted for as if the lessee has purchased the asset. The lease payments under an operating lease are accounted for as rent expense for the lessee.

6 Describe internal controls over fixed assets.

Internal controls over fixed assets should include procedures for authorizing the purchase of assets. Once acquired, fixed assets should be safeguarded from theft, misuse, or damage. A physical inventory of fixed assets should be taken periodically.

7 Compute depletion and journalize the entry for depletion.

The amount of periodic depletion is computed by multiplying the quantity of minerals extracted during the period by a depletion rate. The depletion rate is computed by dividing the cost of the mineral deposit by its estimated size. The entry to record depletion debits a depletion expense account and credits an accumulated depletion account.

8 Journalize the entries for acquiring and amortizing intangible assets, such as patents, copyrights, and goodwill.

Long-term assets that are without physical attributes but are used in the business are classified as intangible assets. Examples of intangible assets are patents, copyrights, trademarks, and goodwill. The initial cost of an intangible asset should be debited to an asset account. This cost should be written off, or amortized, over the years of the asset's expected usefulness by debiting an expense account and crediting the intangible asset account.

9 Describe how depreciation expense is reported in an income statement and prepare a balance sheet that includes fixed assets and intangible assets.

The amount of depreciation expense and the method or methods used in computing depreciation should be disclosed in the financial statements. In addition, each major class of fixed assets should be disclosed, along with the related accumulated depreciation. Intangible assets are usually presented in the balance sheet in a separate section immediately following fixed assets. Each major class of intangible assets should be disclosed at an amount net of the amortization recorded to date.

10 Compute and interpret the ratio of fixed assets to long-term liabilities.

The ratio of fixed assets to long-term liabilities is a solvency measure that indicates the margin of safety to creditors. It also provides an indication of the ability of a company to borrow additional funds on a long-term basis.

ILLUSTRATIVE PROBLEM

McCollum Company, a furniture wholesaler, acquired new equipment at a cost of $150,000 at the beginning of the fiscal year. The equipment has an estimated life of 5 years and an estimated residual value of $12,000. Ellen McCollum, the president, has requested information regarding alternative depreciation methods.

Instructions

1. Determine the annual depreciation for each of the five years of estimated useful life of the equipment, the accumulated depreciation at the end of each year, and the

book value of the equipment at the end of each year by (a) the straight-line method and (b) the declining-balance method (at twice the straight-line rate).

2. Assume that the equipment was depreciated under the declining-balance method. In the first week of the fifth year, the equipment was traded in for similar equipment priced at $175,000. The trade-in allowance on the old equipment was $10,000, and cash was paid for the balance. Journalize the entry to record the exchange.

Solution

1.

	Year	Depreciation Expense	Accumulated Depreciation, End of Year	Book Value, End of Year
a.	1	$27,600*	$ 27,600	$122,400
	2	27,600	55,200	94,800
	3	27,600	82,800	67,200
	4	27,600	110,400	39,600
	5	27,600	138,000	12,000

*$27,600 = ($150,000 − $12,000) ÷ 5

	Year	Depreciation Expense	Accumulated Depreciation, End of Year	Book Value, End of Year
b.	1	$60,000**	$ 60,000	$ 90,000
	2	36,000	96,000	54,000
	3	21,600	117,600	32,400
	4	12,960	130,560	19,440
	5	7,440***	138,000	12,000

**$60,000 = $150,000 × 40%

***The asset is not depreciated below the estimated residual value of $12,000.

2.

	Accumulated Depreciation—Equipment	130 560 00	
	Equipment	175 000 00	
	Loss on Disposal of Fixed Assets	9 440 00	
	Equipment		150 000 00
	Cash		165 000 00

SELF-EXAMINATION QUESTIONS

Answers at End of Chapter

Matching

Match each of the following statements with its proper term. Some terms may not be used.

A. accelerated depreciation method
B. amortization
C. betterment
D. book value
E. boot
F. capital expenditures
G. capital leases
H. copyright
I. declining-balance method
J. depletion

M 1. Long-term or relatively permanent tangible assets that are used in the normal business operations.

K 2. The systematic periodic transfer of the cost of a fixed asset to an expense account during its expected useful life.

I 3. The estimated value of a fixed asset at the end of its useful life.

V 4. A method of depreciation that provides for equal periodic depreciation expense over the estimated life of a fixed asset.

Y 5. A method of depreciation that provides for depreciation expense based on the expected productive capacity of a fixed asset.

I 6. A method of depreciation that provides declining periodic depreciation expense over the estimated life of a fixed asset.

D 7. The cost of a fixed asset minus accumulated depreciation on the asset.

A 8. A depreciation method that provides for a higher depreciation amount in the first year of the asset's use, followed by a gradually declining amount of depreciation.

K. depreciation
L. extraordinary repair
M. fixed assets
N. goodwill
O. intangible assets
P. operating leases
Q. patents
R. ratio of fixed assets to long-term liabilities
S. ratio of fixed assets to total assets
T. residual value
U. revenue expenditures
V. straight-line method
W. trade-in allowance
X. trademark
Y. units-of-production method

F 9. The costs of acquiring fixed assets, adding to a fixed asset, improving a fixed asset, or extending a fixed asset's useful life.

U 10. Costs that benefit only the current period or costs incurred for normal maintenance and repairs of fixed assets.

C 11. An expenditure that improves a fixed asset's operating efficiency or capacity for its remaining useful life.

L 12. An expenditure that increases the useful life of an asset beyond its original estimate.

W 13. The amount a seller allows a buyer for a fixed asset that is traded in for a similar asset.

E 14. The amount a buyer owes a seller when a fixed asset is traded in on a similar asset.

G 15. Leases that include one or more provisions that result in treating the leased assets as purchased assets in the accounts.

P 16. Leases that do not meet the criteria for capital leases and thus are accounted for as operating expenses.

J 17. The process of transferring the cost of natural resources to an expense account.

O 18. Long-term assets that are useful in the operations of a business, are not held for sale, and are without physical qualities.

B 19. The periodic transfer of the cost of an intangible asset to expense.

N 20. An intangible asset that is created from such favorable factors as location, product quality, reputation, and managerial skill.

Q 21. Exclusive rights to produce and sell goods with one or more unique features.

H 22. An exclusive right to publish and sell a literary, artistic, or musical composition.

X 23. A name, term, or symbol used to identify a business and its products.

R 24. A financial ratio that provides a measure indicating the margin of safety to creditors.

Multiple Choice

1. Which of the following expenditures incurred in connection with acquiring machinery is a proper charge to the asset account?
   A. Freight
   B. Installation costs
   C. Both A and B
   D. Neither A nor B

2. What is the amount of depreciation, using the declining-balance method (twice the straight-line rate) for the second year of use for equipment costing $9,000, with an estimated residual value of $600 and an estimated life of 3 years?
   A. $6,000
   B. $3,000
   C. $2,000
   D. $400

3. An example of an accelerated depreciation method is:
   A. Straight-line
   B. Declining-balance
   C. Units-of-production
   D. Depletion

4. A fixed asset priced at $100,000 is acquired by trading in a similar asset that has a book value of $25,000. Assuming that the trade-in allowance is $30,000 and that $70,000 cash is paid for the new asset, what is the cost of the new asset for financial reporting purposes?
   A. $100,000
   B. $95,000
   C. $70,000
   D. $30,000

5. Which of the following is an example of an intangible asset?
   A. Patents
   B. Goodwill
   C. Copyrights
   D. All of the above

CLASS DISCUSSION QUESTIONS

1. Which of the following qualities are characteristic of fixed assets? (a) tangible, (b) capable of repeated use in the operations of the business, (c) held for sale in the normal course of business, (d) used continuously in the operations of the business, (e) long-lived.

2. Gregg Office Equipment Co. has a fleet of automobiles and trucks for use by salespersons and for delivery of office supplies and equipment. Bridger Auto Sales Co. has automobiles and trucks for sale. Under what caption would the automobiles and trucks be reported on the balance sheet of (a) Gregg Office Equipment Co., (b) Bridger Auto Sales Co.?
3. Jolliff Co. acquired an adjacent vacant lot with the hope of selling it in the future at a gain. The lot is not intended to be used in Jolliff's business operations. Where should such real estate be listed in the balance sheet?
4. Parish Company solicited bids from several contractors to construct an addition to its office building. The lowest bid received was for $240,000. Parish Company decided to construct the addition itself at a cost of $225,000. What amount should be recorded in the building account?
5. Are the amounts at which fixed assets are reported in the balance sheet their approximate market values as of the balance sheet date? Discuss.
6. a. Does the recognition of depreciation in the accounts provide a special cash fund for the replacement of fixed assets? Explain.
   b. Describe the nature of depreciation as the term is used in accounting.
7. Name the three factors that need to be considered in determining the amount of periodic depreciation.
8. Wilkie Company purchased a machine that has a manufacturer's suggested life of 12 years. The company plans to use the machine on a special project that will last 8 years. At the completion of the project, the machine will be sold. Over how many years should the machine be depreciated?
9. Is it necessary for a business to use the same method of computing depreciation (a) for all classes of its depreciable assets, (b) in the financial statements and in determining income taxes?
10. Of the three common depreciation methods, which is most widely used?
11. a. Under what conditions is the use of an accelerated depreciation method most appropriate?
    b. Why is an accelerated depreciation method often used for income tax purposes?
    c. What is the Modified Accelerated Cost Recovery System (MACRS), and under what conditions is it used?
12. A revision of depreciable fixed asset lives resulted in an increase in the remaining lives of certain fixed assets. The company would like to include, as income of the current period, the cumulative effect of the changes, which reduces the depreciation expense of past periods. Is this in accordance with generally accepted accounting principles? Discuss.

    Source: "Q's and A's Technical Hotline," *Journal of Accountancy,* December 1991, p. 89.

13. Differentiate between capital expenditures and revenue expenditures.
14. Immediately after a used truck is acquired, a new motor is installed and the tires are replaced at a total cost of $2,750. Is this a capital expenditure or a revenue expenditure?
15. For some of the fixed assets of a business, the balance in Accumulated Depreciation is exactly equal to the cost of the asset. (a) Is it permissible to record additional depreciation on the assets if they are still useful to the business? Explain. (b) When should an entry be made to remove the cost and the accumulated depreciation from the accounts?
16. In what sections of the income statement are gains and losses from the disposal of fixed assets presented?
17. Differentiate between a capital lease and an operating lease.
18. The financial statements of **La-Z-Boy Chair Company** contain the following footnote:

    The Company has several long-term leases covering manufacturing facilities. The lease agreements require the Company to insure and maintain the facilities and provide for annual payments, which include interest. These leases give the Company the option to purchase the facilities for nominal amounts, or in some instances to renew the leases for extended periods at nominal annual rentals.

    Would these leases be classified as operating or capital leases? Discuss.
19. Describe the internal controls for acquiring fixed assets.

20. Why is a physical count of fixed assets necessary?
21. What is the term applied to the periodic charge for (a) ore removed from a mine, (b) the use of an intangible asset?
22. a. Over what period of time should the cost of a patent acquired by purchase be amortized?
    b. In general, what is the required treatment for research and development costs?
23. How should (a) fixed assets and (b) intangible assets be reported in the balance sheet?

Resources for Your Success On-Line at warren.swcollege.com

Remember! If you need additional help, visit South-Western's Web site. See page 26 for a description of the online and printed materials that are available.

EXERCISES

Exercise 10–1
Costs of acquiring fixed assets

Objective 1

Eileen Larkin owns and operates First Run Print Co. During July, First Run Print Co. incurred the following costs in acquiring two printing presses. One printing press was new, and the other was used by a business that recently filed for bankruptcy.

Costs related to new printing press:

1. Special foundation
2. Sales tax on purchase price
3. Insurance while in transit
4. Freight
5. New parts to replace those damaged in unloading
6. Fee paid to factory representative for installation

Costs related to secondhand printing press:

7. Freight
8. Installation
9. Repair of vandalism during installation
10. Replacement of worn-out parts
11. Repair of damage incurred in reconditioning the press
12. Fees paid to attorney to review purchase agreement

a. Indicate which costs incurred in acquiring the new printing press should be debited to the asset account.

b. Indicate which costs incurred in acquiring the secondhand printing press should be debited to the asset account.

Exercise 10–2
Determine cost of land

Objective 1

REAL WORLD

A company has developed a tract of land into a ski resort. The company has cut the trees, cleared and graded the land and hills, and constructed ski lifts. (a) Should the tree cutting, land clearing, and grading costs of constructing the ski slopes be debited to the land account? (b) If such costs are debited to Land, should they be depreciated?

Source: "Technical Issues Feature," *Journal of Accountancy,* December 1987, p. 82.

Exercise 10–3
Determine cost of land

Objective 1

✓ $136,200

Langley Delivery Company acquired an adjacent lot to construct a new warehouse, paying $30,000 and giving a short-term note for $90,000. Legal fees paid were $3,500, delinquent taxes assumed were $7,500, and fees paid to remove an old building from the land were $7,200. Materials salvaged from the demolition of the building were sold for $2,000. A contractor was paid $312,500 to construct a new warehouse. Determine the cost of the land to be reported on the balance sheet.

Exercise 10–4
Nature of depreciation

Objective 1

Sheehan Metal Casting Co. reported $625,000 for equipment and $310,000 for accumulated depreciation—equipment on its balance sheet.

Does this mean (a) that the replacement cost of the equipment is $625,000 and (b) that $310,000 is set aside in a special fund for the replacement of the equipment? Explain.

Exercise 10–5
Straight-line depreciation rates

Objective 2

✓ a. 25%

Convert each of the following estimates of useful life to a straight-line depreciation rate, stated as a percentage, assuming that the residual value of the fixed asset is to be ignored: (a) 4 years, (b) 5 years, (c) 10 years, (d) 20 years, (e) 25 years, (f) 40 years, (g) 50 years.

Exercise 10–6
Straight-line depreciation

Objective 2

✓ $12,800

A refrigerator used by a meat processor has a cost of $138,000, an estimated residual value of $10,000, and an estimated useful life of 10 years. What is the amount of the annual depreciation computed by the straight-line method?

Exercise 10–7
Depreciation by units-of-production method

Objective 2

✓ $54,750

A diesel-powered generator with a cost of $475,000 and estimated residual value of $25,000 is expected to have a useful operating life of 60,000 hours. During July, the generator was operated 7,300 hours. Determine the depreciation for the month.

Exercise 10–8
Depreciation by units-of-production method

Objective 2

✓ a. Truck #1, credit Accumulated Depreciation, $4,320

Prior to adjustment at the end of the year, the balance in Trucks is $150,000, and the balance in Accumulated Depreciation—Trucks is $62,800. Details of the subsidiary ledger are as follows:

Truck No.	Cost	Estimated Residual Value	Estimated Useful Life	Accumulated Depreciation at Beginning of Year	Miles Operated During Year
1	$65,000	$5,000	250,000 miles	$22,500	18,000 miles
2	38,600	3,600	200,000	32,000	20,000
3	28,000	3,000	100,000	9,300	34,500
4	18,400	1,000	120,000	—	12,000

a. Determine the depreciation rates per mile and the amount to be credited to the accumulated depreciation section of each of the subsidiary accounts for the miles operated during the current year.
b. Journalize the entry to record depreciation for the year.

Exercise 10–9
Depreciation by two methods

Objective 2

✓ a. $27,500

A backhoe acquired on January 2 at a cost of $220,000 has an estimated useful life of 8 years. Assuming that it will have no residual value, determine the depreciation for each of the first two years (a) by the straight-line method and (b) by the declining-balance method, using twice the straight-line rate.

Exercise 10–10
Depreciation by two methods
Objective 2

✓ a. $5,200

A dairy storage tank acquired at the beginning of the fiscal year at a cost of $60,000 has an estimated residual value of $8,000 and an estimated useful life of 10 years. Determine the following: (a) the amount of annual depreciation by the straight-line method and (b) the amount of depreciation for the first and second year computed by the declining-balance method (at twice the straight-line rate).

Exercise 10–11
Partial-year depreciation
Objective 2

✓ a. First year, $18,000
Second year, $24,000

Sandblasting equipment acquired at a cost of $125,000 has an estimated residual value of $5,000 and an estimated useful life of 5 years. It was placed in service on April 1 of the current fiscal year, which ends on December 31. Determine the depreciation for the current fiscal year and for the following fiscal year by (a) the straight-line method and (b) the declining-balance method, at twice the straight-line rate.

Exercise 10–12
Revision of depreciation
Objective 2

✓ a. $8,500

X-ray equipment with a cost of $360,000 has an estimated residual value of $20,000, an estimated useful life of 40 years, and is depreciated by the straight-line method. (a) What is the amount of the annual depreciation? (b) What is the book value at the end of the twentieth year of use? (c) If at the start of the twenty-first year it is estimated that the remaining life is 15 years and that the residual value is $10,000, what is the depreciation expense for each of the remaining 15 years?

Exercise 10–13
Revision of depreciation
Objective 2

✓ $10,000

Mobile communications equipment acquired on January 5, 1997, at a cost of $112,500, has an estimated residual value of $11,700 and an estimated useful life of 12 years. Depreciation has been recorded for the first four years ended December 31, 2000, by the straight-line method. Determine the amount of depreciation for the current year ended December 31, 2001, if the revised estimated residual value is $8,900 and the revised estimated remaining useful life (including the current year) is 7 years.

Exercise 10–14
Capital and revenue expenditures
Objective 3

Absaroka Co. incurred the following costs related to trucks and vans used in operating its delivery service:

1. Overhauled the engine on one of the trucks that had been purchased four years ago.
2. Removed a two-way radio from one of the trucks and installed a new radio with greater range of communication.
3. Installed a hydraulic lift to a van.
4. Changed the oil and greased the joints of all the trucks and vans.
5. Replaced two of the trucks' shock absorbers with new shock absorbers that allow for the delivery of heavier loads.
6. Replaced the brakes and alternator on a truck that had been in service for the past 5 years.
7. Installed security systems on three of the newer trucks.
8. Repaired a flat tire on one of the vans.
9. Rebuilt the transmission on one of the vans that had been driven only 25,000 miles. The van was no longer under warranty.
10. Tinted the back and side windows of one of the vans to discourage theft of contents.

Classify each of the costs as a capital expenditure or a revenue expenditure. For those costs identified as capital expenditures, classify each as an addition, a betterment, or an extraordinary repair.

Exercise 10–15
Capital and revenue expenditures
Objective 3

Mark Lemke Co. owns and operates Second to None Transport Co. During the past year, Mark incurred the following costs related to his 18-wheel truck.

1. Overhauled the engine.
2. Removed the old CB radio and replaced it with a newer model with greater range.
3. Replaced a headlight that had burned out.
4. Replaced the hydraulic brake system that had begun to fail during his latest trip through the Smoky Mountains.
5. Replaced a shock absorber that had worn out.
6. Installed fog lights.

7. Installed a wind deflector on top of the cab to increase fuel mileage.
8. Modified the factory-installed turbo charger with a special-order kit designed to add 30 more horsepower to the engine performance.
9. Replaced the old radar detector with a newer model that detects the KA frequencies now used by many of the state patrol radar guns. The detector is wired directly into the cab, so that it is partially hidden. In addition, Mark fastened the detector to the truck with a locking device that prevents its removal.
10. Installed a television in the sleeping compartment of the truck.

Classify each of the costs as a capital expenditure or a revenue expenditure. For those costs identified as capital expenditures, classify each as an addition, a betterment, or an extraordinary repair.

Exercise 10–16
Major repair to fixed asset
Objective 3

✓ a. $30,000
✓ d. $25,000

A number of major structural repairs on a building were completed at the beginning of the current fiscal year at a cost of $80,000. The repairs are expected to extend the life of the building 6 years beyond the original estimate. The original cost of the building was $750,000, and it is being depreciated by the straight-line method for 25 years. The residual value is expected to be negligible and has been ignored. The balance of the related accumulated depreciation account after the depreciation adjustment at the end of the preceding year is $330,000.

a. What has the amount of annual depreciation been in past years?
b. To what account should the cost of repairs ($80,000) be debited?
c. What is the book value of the building after the repairs have been recorded?
d. What is the amount of depreciation for the current year, using the straight-line method (assuming that the repairs were completed at the very beginning of the year)?

Exercise 10–17
Entries for sale of fixed asset
Objective 4

✓ a. $46,500

Metal recycling equipment acquired on January 3, 1997, at a cost of $87,500, has an estimated useful life of 8 years, an estimated residual value of $5,500, and is depreciated by the straight-line method.

a. What was the book value of the equipment at December 31, 2000, the end of the fiscal year?
b. Assuming that the equipment was sold on July 1, 2001, for $40,000, journalize the entries to record (1) depreciation for the six months of the current year ending December 31, 2001, and (2) the sale of the equipment.

Exercise 10–18
Disposal of fixed asset
Objective 4

✓ b. $15,500

Equipment acquired on January 3, 1997, at a cost of $51,500, has an estimated useful life of 4 years and an estimated residual value of $3,500.

a. What was the annual amount of depreciation for the years 1997, 1998, and 1999, using the straight-line method of depreciation?
b. What was the book value of the equipment on January 1, 2000?
c. Assuming that the equipment was sold on January 2, 2000, for $13,000, journalize the entry to record the sale.
d. Assuming that the equipment had been sold on January 2, 2000, for $17,000 instead of $13,000, journalize the entry to record the sale.

Exercise 10–19
Asset traded for similar asset
Objective 4

✓ a. $139,000

A printing press priced at $170,000 is acquired by trading in a similar press and paying cash for the difference between the trade-in allowance and the price of the new press. (a) Assuming that the trade-in allowance is $31,000, what is the amount of cash given? (b) Assuming that the book value of the press traded in is $23,800, what is the cost of the new press for financial reporting purposes?

Exercise 10–20
Asset traded for similar asset
Objective 4

✓ b. $170,000

Assume the same facts as in Exercise 10–19, except that the book value of the press traded in is $35,000. (a) What is the amount of cash given? (b) What is the cost of the new press for financial reporting purposes?

Exercise 10–21
Entries for trade of fixed asset
Objective 4

On April 1, Cougar Co., a water distiller, acquired new bottling equipment with a list price of $315,000. Cougar received a trade-in allowance of $50,000 on the old equipment of a similar type, paid cash of $30,000, and gave a series of five notes payable for the remainder. The following information about the old equipment is obtained from the account in the equipment ledger: cost, $212,500; accumulated depreciation on December 31, the end of the preceding fiscal year, $135,000; annual depreciation, $9,000. Journalize the entries to record (a) the current depreciation of the old equipment to the date of trade-in and (b) the transaction on April 1 for financial reporting purposes.

Exercise 10–22
Entries for trade of fixed asset
Objective 4

On October 1, Weissman Co. acquired a new truck with a list price of $125,000. Weissman received a trade-in allowance of $22,000 on an old truck of similar type, paid cash of $15,000, and gave a series of five notes payable for the remainder. The following information about the old truck is obtained from the account in the equipment ledger: cost, $82,500; accumulated depreciation on December 31, the end of the preceding fiscal year, $57,500; annual depreciation, $7,500. Journalize the entries to record (a) the current depreciation of the old truck to the date of trade-in and (b) the transaction on October 1 for financial reporting purposes.

Exercise 10–23
Depreciable cost of asset acquired by exchange
Objective 4

✓ a. $50,000

On the first day of the fiscal year, a delivery truck with a list price of $50,000 was acquired in exchange for an old delivery truck and $38,000 cash. The old truck had a book value of $14,000 at the date of the exchange.

a. Determine the depreciable cost for financial reporting purposes.
b. Assuming that the book value of the old delivery truck was $9,000, determine the depreciable cost for financial reporting purposes.

Exercise 10–24
Internal control of fixed assets
Objective 6

AllNet Co. is a computer software company marketing products in the United States and Canada. While AllNet Co. has over 90 sales offices, all accounting is handled at the company's headquarters in Cleveland, Ohio.

AllNet Co. keeps all its fixed asset records on a computerized system. The computer maintains a subsidiary ledger of all fixed assets owned by the company and calculates depreciation automatically. Whenever a manager at one of the ninety sales offices wants to purchase a fixed asset, a purchase request is submitted to headquarters for approval. Upon approval, the fixed asset is purchased and the invoice is sent back to headquarters so that the asset can be entered into the fixed asset system.

A manager who wants to dispose of a fixed asset simply sells or disposes of the asset and notifies headquarters to remove the asset from the system. Company cars and personal computers are frequently purchased by employees when they are disposed of. Most pieces of office equipment are traded in when new assets are acquired.

What internal control weakness exists in the procedures used to acquire and dispose of fixed assets at AllNet Co.?

Exercise 10–25
Depletion entries
Objective 7

✓ a. $5,100,000

Boxer Co. acquired mineral rights for $18,000,000. The mineral deposit is estimated at 30,000,000 tons. During the current year, 8,500,000 tons were mined and sold for $6,500,000.

a. Determine the amount of depletion expense for the current year.
b. Journalize the adjusting entry to recognize the expense.

Exercise 10–26
Amortization entries
Objective 8

✓ a. $56,750

Nitro Company acquired patent rights on January 3, 1997, for $935,000. The patent has a useful life equal to its legal life of 20 years. On January 5, 2000, Nitro successfully defended the patent in a lawsuit at a cost of $170,000.

a. Determine the patent amortization expense for the current year ended December 31, 2000.
b. Journalize the adjusting entry to recognize the amortization.

Exercise 10–27
Balance sheet presentation
Objective 9

What's Wrong WITH THIS?

How many errors can you find in the following partial balance sheet?

Gazette Company
Balance Sheet
December 31, 20—

Assets

	Replacement Cost	Accumulated Depreciation	Book Value	
Total current assets				$297,500
Property, plant, and equipment:				
Land	$ 65,000	$ 20,000	$ 45,000	
Buildings	160,000	76,000	84,000	
Factory equipment	450,000	192,000	258,000	
Office equipment	120,000	77,000	43,000	
Patents	60,000	—	60,000	
Goodwill	45,000	—	45,000	
Total property, plant, and equipment	$900,000	$365,000		535,000

Exercise 10–28
Ratio of fixed assets to long-term liabilities
Objective 10

HAT

The financial statements of **Hershey Foods Corporation** are presented in Appendix G at the end of the text.

a. Compute the ratio of fixed assets (property, plant, and equipment) to long-term liabilities (long-term debt) as of December 31, 1996 and 1995.

b. What conclusions can be drawn from these ratios concerning Hershey's ability to borrow additional funds on a long-term basis?

Appendix Exercise 10–29
Sum-of-the-years-digits depreciation

✓ First year: $48,889

Based on the data in Exercise 10–9, determine the depreciation for the backhoe for each of the first two years, using the sum-of-the-years-digits depreciation method.

Appendix Exercise 10–30
Sum-of-the-years-digits depreciation

✓ First year: $9,455

Based on the data in Exercise 10–10, determine the depreciation for the dairy storage tank for each of the first two years, using the sum-of-the-years-digits depreciation method.

Appendix Exercise 10–31
Partial-year depreciation

✓ First year: $30,000

Based on the data in Exercise 10–11, determine the depreciation for the sandblasting equipment for each of the first two years, using the sum-of-the-years-digits depreciation method.

PROBLEMS SERIES A

Problem 10–1A
Allocate payments and receipts to fixed asset accounts

Objective 1

SPREADSHEET

The following payments and receipts are related to land, land improvements, and buildings acquired for use in a wholesale apparel business. The receipts are identified by an asterisk.

a.	Finder's fee paid to real estate agency	$ 15,000
b.	Cost of real estate acquired as a plant site: Land	250,000
	Building	50,000
c.	Fee paid to attorney for title search	1,000
d.	Delinquent real estate taxes on property, assumed by purchaser	18,500
e.	Cost of razing and removing building	21,250
f.	Proceeds from sale of salvage materials from old building	3,500*
g.	Cost of filling and grading land	15,500
h.	Special assessment paid to city for extension of water main to the property	9,000
i.	Architect's and engineer's fees for plans and supervision	75,000
j.	Premium on 1-year insurance policy during construction	5,700
k.	Cost of repairing windstorm damage during construction	3,500
l.	Cost of repairing vandalism damage during construction	800
m.	Cost of paving parking lot to be used by customers	17,500
n.	Cost of trees and shrubbery planted	20,000
o.	Proceeds from insurance company for windstorm and vandalism damage	4,300*
p.	Interest incurred on building loan during construction	85,000
q.	Money borrowed to pay building contractor	1,000,000*
r.	Payment to building contractor for new building	1,250,000
s.	Refund of premium on insurance policy (j) canceled after 10 months	950*

Instructions

1. Assign each payment and receipt to Land (unlimited life), Land Improvements (limited life), Building, or Other Accounts. Indicate receipts by an asterisk. Identify each item by letter and list the amounts in columnar form, as follows:

Item	Land	Land Improvements	Building	Other Accounts

2. The costs assigned to the land, which is used as a plant site, will not be depreciated, while the costs assigned to land improvements will be depreciated. Explain this seemingly contradictory application of the concept of depreciation.

Problem 10–2A
Compare three depreciation methods

Objective 2

✓ 1999: straight-line depreciation, $45,000

Roche Company purchased waterproofing equipment on January 2, 1999, for $195,000. The equipment was expected to have a useful life of 4 years, or 45,000 operating hours, and a residual value of $15,000. The equipment was used for 8,900 hours during 1999, 13,100 hours in 2000, 14,500 hours in 2001, and 8,500 hours in 2002.

Instructions
Determine the amount of depreciation expense for the years ended December 31, 1999, 2000, 2001, and 2002, by (a) the straight-line method, (b) the units-of-production method, and (c) the declining-balance method, using twice the straight-line rate. Also determine the total depreciation expense for the four years by each method. The following columnar headings are suggested for recording the depreciation expense amounts:

	Depreciation Expense		
Year	Straight-Line Method	Units-of-Production Method	Declining-Balance Method

Problem 10–3A
Depreciation by three methods; partial years
Objective 2

✓ a. 1999, $20,400

Afco Company purchased tool sharpening equipment on July 1, 1999, for $129,600. The equipment was expected to have a useful life of 3 years, or 13,600 operating hours, and a residual value of $7,200. The equipment was used for 2,400 hours during 1999, 7,600 hours in 2000, 3,000 hours in 2001, and 600 hours in 2002.

Instructions

Determine the amount of depreciation expense for the years ended December 31, 1999, 2000, 2001, and 2002, by (a) the straight-line method, (b) the units-of-production method, and (c) the declining-balance method, using twice the straight-line rate.

Problem 10–4A
Depreciation by two methods; trade of fixed asset
Objectives 2, 4

SPREADSHEET

✓ 1. b. Year 1, $100,000 depreciation expense
✓ 2. $245,000

New tire retreading equipment, acquired at a cost of $200,000 at the beginning of a fiscal year, has an estimated useful life of 4 years and an estimated residual value of $15,000. The manager requested information regarding the effect of alternative methods on the amount of depreciation expense each year. On the basis of the data presented to the manager, the declining-balance method was selected.

In the first week of the fourth year, the equipment was traded in for similar equipment priced at $250,000. The trade-in allowance on the old equipment was $30,000, cash of $20,000 was paid, and a note payable was issued for the balance.

Instructions

1. Determine the annual depreciation expense for each of the estimated 4 years of use, the accumulated depreciation at the end of each year, and the book value of the equipment at the end of each year by (a) the straight-line method and (b) the declining-balance method (at twice the straight-line rate). The following columnar headings are suggested for each schedule:

Year	Depreciation Expense	Accumulated Depreciation, End of Year	Book Value, End of Year

2. For financial reporting purposes, determine the cost of the new equipment acquired in the exchange.
3. Journalize the entry to record the exchange.
4. Journalize the entry to record the exchange, assuming that the trade-in allowance was $18,000 instead of $30,000.

Problem 10–5A
Transactions for fixed assets, including trade
Objectives 1, 3, 4

HAT

The following transactions, adjusting entries, and closing entries were completed by New World Furniture Co. during a 3-year period. All are related to the use of delivery equipment. The declining-balance method (at twice the straight-line rate) of depreciation is used.

1998
Jan. 2. Purchased a used delivery truck for $15,000, paying cash.
5. Paid $3,000 to replace the automatic transmission and install new brakes on the truck. (Debit Delivery Equipment.)
June 7. Paid garage $125 for changing the oil, replacing the oil filter, and tuning the engine on the delivery truck.
Dec. 31. Recorded depreciation on the truck for the fiscal year. The estimated useful life of the truck is 8 years, with a residual value of $4,000.
31. Closed the appropriate accounts to the income summary account.

1999
Mar. 19. Paid garage $310 to tune the engine and make other minor repairs on the truck.
Apr. 30. Traded in the used truck for a new truck priced at $40,000, receiving a trade-in allowance of $13,375 and paying the balance in cash. (Record depreciation to date in 1999.)
Dec. 31. Recorded depreciation on the truck. It has an estimated trade-in value of $3,000 and an estimated life of 10 years.
31. Closed the appropriate accounts to the income summary account.

2000
Oct. 1. Purchased a new truck for $42,000, paying cash.
2. Sold the truck purchased April 30, 1999, for $30,000. (Record depreciation for the year.)
Dec. 31. Recorded depreciation on the remaining truck. It has an estimated residual value of $4,500 and an estimated useful life of 10 years.
31. Closed the appropriate accounts to the income summary account.

Instructions

Journalize the transactions and the adjusting and closing entries. Post to the following accounts in the ledger and determine the balances after each posting:

122	Delivery Equipment
123	Accumulated Depreciation—Delivery Equipment
616	Depreciation Expense—Delivery Equipment
617	Truck Repair Expense
812	Gain on Disposal of Fixed Assets

Problem 10–6A
Amortization and depletion entries

Objectives 7, 8

✓ a. $30,000

Data related to the acquisition of timber rights and intangible assets during the current year ended December 31 are as follows:

a. Goodwill in the amount of $1,200,000 was purchased on January 4. It is decided to amortize over the maximum period allowable.
b. Governmental and legal costs of $112,800 were incurred on July 3 in obtaining a patent with an estimated economic life of 8 years. Amortization is to be for one-half year.
c. Timber rights on a tract of land were purchased for $480,000 on July 3. The stand of timber is estimated at 1,600,000 board feet. During the current year, 350,000 board feet of timber were cut.

Instructions

1. Determine the amount of the amortization or depletion expense for the current year for each of the foregoing items.
2. Journalize the adjusting entries to record the amortization or depletion expense for each item.

PROBLEMS SERIES B

Problem 10–1B
Allocate payments and receipts to fixed asset accounts

Objective 1

SPREADSHEET

The following payments and receipts are related to land, land improvements, and buildings acquired for use in a wholesale ceramic business. The receipts are identified by an asterisk.

a.	Fee paid to attorney for title search	$ 1,500
b.	Cost of real estate acquired as a plant site: Land	300,000
	Building	125,000
c.	Delinquent real estate taxes on property, assumed by purchaser	18,750
d.	Cost of razing and removing building	5,800
e.	Proceeds from sale of salvage materials from old building	2,100*
f.	Special assessment paid to city for extension of water main to the property	5,000
g.	Premium on 1-year insurance policy during construction	6,600
h.	Cost of filling and grading land	29,700
i.	Cost of repairing windstorm damage during construction	1,500
j.	Cost of paving parking lot to be used by customers	12,500
k.	Cost of trees and shrubbery planted	15,000
l.	Architect's and engineer's fees for plans and supervision	60,000
m.	Cost of repairing vandalism damage during construction	500

n.	Interest incurred on building loan during construction	$ 48,000
o.	Cost of floodlights installed on parking lot	13,500
p.	Money borrowed to pay building contractor	600,000*
q.	Payment to building contractor for new building	850,000
r.	Proceeds from insurance company for windstorm and vandalism damage	2,000*
s.	Refund of premium on insurance policy (g) canceled after 11 months	550*

Instructions

1. Assign each payment and receipt to Land (unlimited life), Land Improvements (limited life), Building, or Other Accounts. Indicate receipts by an asterisk. Identify each item by letter and list the amounts in columnar form, as follows:

Item	Land	Land Improvements	Building	Other Accounts

2. The costs assigned to the land, which is used as a plant site, will not be depreciated, while the costs assigned to land improvements will be depreciated. Explain this seemingly contradictory application of the concept of depreciation.

Problem 10–2B

Compare three depreciation methods

Objective 2

✓ 1999: straight-line depreciation, $120,000

Westby Company purchased packaging equipment on January 3, 1999, for $375,000. The equipment was expected to have a useful life of 3 years, or 24,000 operating hours, and a residual value of $15,000. The equipment was used for 6,500 hours during 1999, 11,600 hours in 2000, and 5,900 hours in 2001.

Instructions

Determine the amount of depreciation expense for the years ended December 31, 1999, 2000, and 2001, by (a) the straight-line method, (b) the units-of-production method, and (c) the declining-balance method, using twice the straight-line rate. Also determine the total depreciation expense for the three years by each method. The following columnar headings are suggested for recording the depreciation expense amounts:

	Depreciation Expense		
Year	Straight-Line Method	Units-of-Production Method	Declining-Balance Method

Problem 10–3B

Depreciation by three methods; partial years

Objective 2

✓ a. 2002: $34,000

Newbauer Company purchased plastic laminating equipment on July 1, 1999, for $216,000. The equipment was expected to have a useful life of 3 years, or 34,000 operating hours, and a residual value of $12,000. The equipment was used for 4,800 hours during 1999, 15,200 hours in 2000, 9,600 hours in 2001, and 4,400 hours in 2002.

Instructions

Determine the amount of depreciation expense for the years ended December 31, 1999, 2000, 2001, and 2002, by (a) the straight-line method, (b) the units-of-production method, and (c) the declining-balance method, using twice the straight-line rate.

Problem 10–4B

Depreciation by two methods; trade of fixed asset

Objectives 2, 4

SPREADSHEET

✓ 1. b. Year 1: $100,000 depreciation expense

✓ 2. $292,400

New lithographic equipment, acquired at a cost of $250,000 at the beginning of a fiscal year, has an estimated useful life of 5 years and an estimated residual value of $20,000. The manager requested information regarding the effect of alternative methods on the amount of depreciation expense each year. On the basis of the data presented to the manager, the declining-balance method was selected.

In the first week of the fifth year, the equipment was traded in for similar equipment priced at $300,000. The trade-in allowance on the old equipment was $40,000, cash of $30,000 was paid, and a note payable was issued for the balance.

Instructions

1. Determine the annual depreciation expense for each of the estimated 5 years of use, the accumulated depreciation at the end of each year, and the book value of the

equipment at the end of each year by (a) the straight-line method and (b) the declining-balance method (at twice the straight-line rate). The following columnar headings are suggested for each schedule:

Year	Depreciation Expense	Accumulated Depreciation, End of Year	Book Value End of Year

2. For financial reporting purposes, determine the cost of the new equipment acquired in the exchange.
3. Journalize the entry to record the exchange.
4. Journalize the entry to record the exchange, assuming that the trade-in allowance was $25,000 instead of $40,000.

Problem 10–5B
Transactions for fixed assets, including trade
Objectives 1, 3, 4

The following transactions, adjusting entries, and closing entries were completed by Oak Furniture Co. during a 3-year period. All are related to the use of delivery equipment. The declining-balance method (at twice the straight-line rate) of depreciation is used.

1998
Jan. 3. Purchased a used delivery truck for $22,300, paying cash.
6. Paid $1,700 for a new transmission for the truck. (Debit Delivery Equipment.)
Sep. 17. Paid garage $415 for miscellaneous repairs to the truck.
Dec. 31. Recorded depreciation on the truck for the fiscal year. The estimated useful life of the truck is 4 years, with a residual value of $5,000.
31. Closed the appropriate accounts to the income summary account.

1999
June 30. Traded in the used truck for a new truck priced at $34,000, receiving a trade-in allowance of $11,000 and paying the balance in cash. (Record depreciation to date in 1999.)
Oct. 9. Paid garage $305 for miscellaneous repairs to the truck.
Dec. 31. Recorded depreciation on the truck. It has an estimated trade-in value of $8,000 and an estimated life of 5 years.
31. Closed the appropriate accounts to the income summary account.

2000
Oct. 1. Purchased a new truck for $40,000, paying cash.
2. Sold the truck purchased June 30, 1999, for $20,000. (Record depreciation for the year.)
Dec. 31. Recorded depreciation on the remaining truck. It has an estimated residual value of $5,000 and an estimated useful life of 8 years.
31. Closed the appropriate accounts to the income summary account.

Instructions

Journalize the transactions and the adjusting and closing entries. Post to the following accounts in the ledger and determine the balances after each posting:

122 Delivery Equipment
123 Accumulated Depreciation—Delivery Equipment
616 Depreciation Expense—Delivery Equipment
617 Truck Repair Expense
812 Gain on Disposal of Fixed Assets

Problem 10–6B
Amortization and depletion entries
Objectives 7, 8

✓ a. $108,000

Data related to the acquisition of timber rights and intangible assets during the current year ended December 31 are as follows:

a. Timber rights on a tract of land were purchased for $270,000 on May 5. The stand of timber is estimated at 1,500,000 board feet. During the current year, 600,000 board feet of timber were cut.
b. Goodwill in the amount of $3,000,000 was purchased on January 3. It is decided to amortize over the maximum period allowable.

c. Governmental and legal costs of $125,000 were incurred on July 1 in obtaining a patent with an estimated economic life of 10 years. Amortization is to be for one-half year.

Instructions

1. Determine the amount of the amortization or depletion expense for the current year for each of the foregoing items.
2. Journalize the adjusting entries required to record the amortization or depletion for each item.

SPECIAL ACTIVITIES

Activity 10–1
Fallon Co.
Ethics and professional conduct in business

Irene Stucky, CPA, is an assistant to the controller of Fallon Co. In her spare time, Irene also prepares tax returns and performs general accounting services for clients. Frequently, Irene performs these services after her normal working hours, using Fallon Co.'s computers and laser printers. Occasionally, Irene's clients will call her at the office during regular working hours.

Discuss whether Irene is performing in a professional manner.

Activity 10–2
Cascade Co.
Financial vs. tax depreciation

The following is an excerpt from a conversation between two employees of Cascade Co., Wendy Delaney and Alan Bentley. Wendy is the accounts payable clerk, and Alan is the cashier.

Wendy: Alan, could I get your opinion on something?
Alan: Sure, Wendy.
Wendy: Do you know Maggie, the fixed assets clerk?
Alan: I know who she is, but I don't know her real well. Why?
Wendy: Well, I was talking to her at lunch last Monday about how she liked her job, etc. You know, the usual . . . and she mentioned something about having to keep two sets of books . . . one for taxes and one for the financial statements. That can't be good accounting, can it? What do you think?
Alan: Two sets of books? It doesn't sound right.
Wendy: It doesn't seem right to me either. I was always taught that you had to use generally accepted accounting principles. How can there be two sets of books? What can be the difference between the two?

How would you respond to Alan and Wendy if you were Maggie?

Activity 10–3
Caddis Construction Co.
Effect of depreciation on net income

Caddis Construction Co. specializes in building replicas of historic houses. Jill Trout, president of Caddis, is considering the purchase of various items of equipment on July 1, 1997, for $300,000. The equipment would have a useful life of 5 years and no residual value. In the past, all equipment has been leased. For tax purposes, Jill is considering depreciating the equipment by the straight-line method. She discussed the matter with her CPA and learned that, although the straight-line method could be elected, it was to her advantage to use the modified accelerated cost recovery system (MACRS) for tax purposes. She asked for your advice as to which method to use for tax purposes.

1. Compute depreciation for each of the years (1997, 1998, 1999, 2000, 2001, and 2002) of useful life by (a) the straight-line method and (b) MACRS. In using the straight-line method, one-half year's depreciation should be computed for 1997 and 2002. Use the MACRS rates presented in the chapter.
2. Assuming that income before depreciation and income tax is estimated to be $300,000 uniformly per year and that the income tax rate is 30%, compute the net income for each of the years 1997, 1998, 1999, 2000, 2001, and 2002, if (a) the straight-line method is used and (b) MACRS is used.
3. What factors would you present for Jill's consideration in the selection of a depreciation method?

Activity 10–4
Into the Real World
Shopping for a delivery

GROUP ACTIVITY

You are planning to acquire a delivery truck for use in your business for three years. In groups of three or four, explore a local dealer's purchase and leasing options for the truck. Summarize the costs of purchasing versus leasing, and list other factors that might help you decide whether to buy or lease the truck.

Activity 10–5
Into the Real World
Applying for patents, copyrights, and trademarks

Internet ACTIVITY

Go to the Internet and review the procedures for applying for a patent, a copyright, and a trademark. One Internet site that is useful for this purpose is:

www.idresearch.com

Prepare a written summary of these procedures.

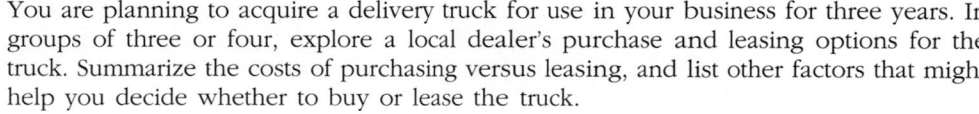

ANSWERS TO SELF-EXAMINATION QUESTIONS

Matching

1. M	4. V	7. D	10. U	13. W	16. P	19. B	22. H
2. K	5. Y	8. A	11. C	14. E	17. J	20. N	23. X
3. T	6. I	9. F	12. L	15. G	18. O	21. Q	24. R

Multiple Choice

1. **C** All amounts spent to get a fixed asset (such as machinery) in place and ready for use are proper charges to the asset account. In the case of machinery acquired, the freight (answer A) and the installation costs (answer B) are both (answer C) proper charges to the machinery account.
2. **C** The periodic charge for depreciation under the declining-balance method (twice the straight-line rate) for the second year is determined by first computing the depreciation charge for the first year. The depreciation for the first year of $6,000 (answer A) is computed by multiplying the cost of the equipment, $9,000, by $\frac{2}{3}$ (the straight-line rate of $\frac{1}{3}$ multiplied by 2). The depreciation for the second year of $2,000 (answer C) is then determined by multiplying the book value at the end of the first year, $3,000 (the cost of $9,000 minus the first-year depreciation of $6,000), by $\frac{2}{3}$. The third year's depreciation is $400 (answer D). It is determined by multiplying the book value at the end of the second year, $1,000, by $\frac{2}{3}$, thus yielding $667. However, the equipment cannot be depreciated below its residual value of $600; thus, the third-year depreciation is $400 ($1,000 − $600).
3. **B** A depreciation method that provides for a higher depreciation amount in the first year of the use of an asset and a gradually declining periodic amount thereafter is called an accelerated depreciation method. The declining-balance method (answer B) is an example of such a method.
4. **B** The acceptable method of accounting for an exchange of similar assets in which the trade-in allowance ($30,000) exceeds the book value of the old asset ($25,000) requires that the cost of the new asset be determined by adding the amount of cash given ($70,000) to the book value of the old asset ($25,000), which totals $95,000. Alternatively, the unrecognized gain ($5,000) can be subtracted from the list price ($100,000).
5. **D** Long-lived assets that are useful in operations, not held for sale, and without physical qualities are called intangible assets. Patents, goodwill, and copyrights are examples of intangible assets (answer D).

11

Current Liabilities

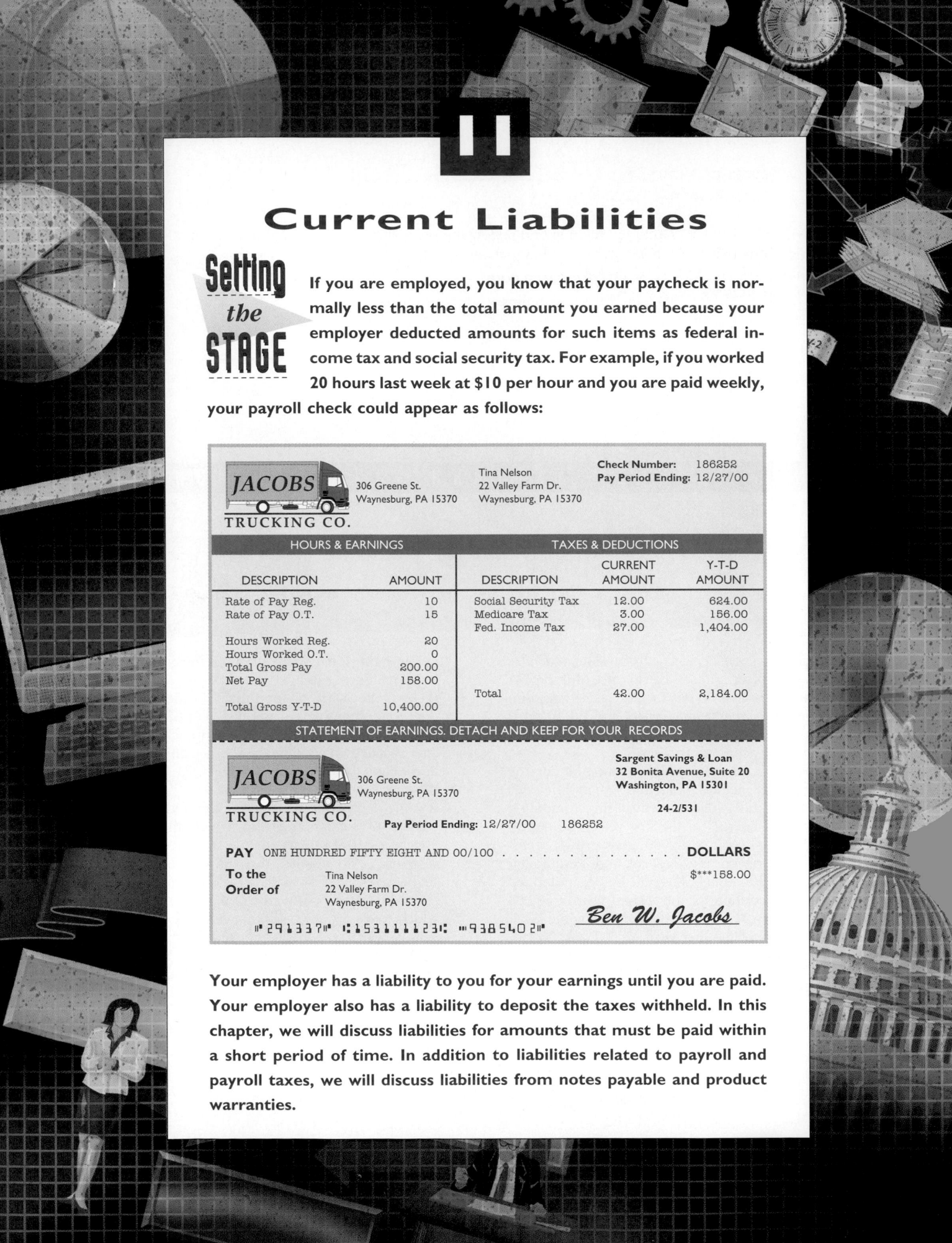

Setting the STAGE

If you are employed, you know that your paycheck is normally less than the total amount you earned because your employer deducted amounts for such items as federal income tax and social security tax. For example, if you worked 20 hours last week at $10 per hour and you are paid weekly, your payroll check could appear as follows:

JACOBS TRUCKING CO.
306 Greene St.
Waynesburg, PA 15370

Tina Nelson
22 Valley Farm Dr.
Waynesburg, PA 15370

Check Number: 186252
Pay Period Ending: 12/27/00

HOURS & EARNINGS		TAXES & DEDUCTIONS		
DESCRIPTION	AMOUNT	DESCRIPTION	CURRENT AMOUNT	Y-T-D AMOUNT
Rate of Pay Reg.	10	Social Security Tax	12.00	624.00
Rate of Pay O.T.	15	Medicare Tax	3.00	156.00
		Fed. Income Tax	27.00	1,404.00
Hours Worked Reg.	20			
Hours Worked O.T.	0			
Total Gross Pay	200.00			
Net Pay	158.00			
		Total	42.00	2,184.00
Total Gross Y-T-D	10,400.00			

STATEMENT OF EARNINGS. DETACH AND KEEP FOR YOUR RECORDS

JACOBS TRUCKING CO.
306 Greene St.
Waynesburg, PA 15370

Sargent Savings & Loan
32 Bonita Avenue, Suite 20
Washington, PA 15301

24-2/531

Pay Period Ending: 12/27/00 186252

PAY ONE HUNDRED FIFTY EIGHT AND 00/100 . . . . **DOLLARS**

$***158.00

To the Order of Tina Nelson
22 Valley Farm Dr.
Waynesburg, PA 15370

Ben W. Jacobs

⑈291337⑈ ⑆153111123⑆ ⑈9385402⑈

Your employer has a liability to you for your earnings until you are paid. Your employer also has a liability to deposit the taxes withheld. In this chapter, we will discuss liabilities for amounts that must be paid within a short period of time. In addition to liabilities related to payroll and payroll taxes, we will discuss liabilities from notes payable and product warranties.

objectives

After studying this chapter, you should be able to:

1 Define and give examples of current liabilities.

2 Journalize entries for short-term notes payable.

3 Describe the accounting treatment for contingent liabilities and journalize entries for product warranties.

4 Determine employer liabilities for payroll, including liabilities arising from employee earnings and deductions from earnings.

5 Describe payroll accounting systems that use a payroll register, employee earnings records, and a general journal.

6 Journalize entries for employee fringe benefits, including vacation pay and pensions.

7 Use the quick ratio to analyze the ability of a business to pay its current liabilities.

The Nature of Current Liabilities

OBJECTIVE 1

Define and give examples of current liabilities.

Your credit card balance is probably due within a short time, such as 30 days. Such liabilities that are to be paid out of current assets and are due within a short time, usually within one year, are called **current liabilities**. Most current liabilities arise from two basic transactions:

1. Receiving goods or services prior to making payment.
2. Receiving payment prior to delivering goods or services.

An example of the first type of transaction is **accounts payable** arising from purchases of merchandise for resale. An example of the second type of transaction is **unearned rent** arising from the receipt of rent in advance. Some additional examples of current liabilities that we discussed in previous chapters are:

- Taxes payable—the amount of taxes owed to governmental units
- Interest payable—the amount of interest owed on borrowed funds
- Wages payable—the amount owed to employees

In this chapter, we will introduce some other common current liabilities. These include short-term notes payable, contingencies, payroll liabilities, and employee fringe benefits.

Short-Term Notes Payable

OBJECTIVE 2

Journalize entries for short-term notes payable.

Notes may be issued when merchandise or other assets are purchased. They may also be issued to creditors to temporarily satisfy an account payable created earlier. For example, assume that a business issues a 90-day, 12% note for $1,000, dated August 1, 2000, to Murray Co. for a $1,000 overdue account. The entry to record the issuance of the note is as follows:

Aug.	1	Accounts Payable—Murray Co.	1 000 00	
		Notes Payable		1 000 00
		Issued a 90-day, 12% note on account.		

When the note matures, the entry to record the payment of $1,000 principal plus $30 interest ($1,000 × 12% × 90/360) is as follows:

Oct.	30	Notes Payable	1,000.00	
		Interest Expense	30.00	
		Cash		1,030.00
		Paid principal and interest due on note.		

The interest expense is reported in the Other Expense section of the income statement for the year ended December 31, 2000. The interest expense account is closed at December 31.

The preceding entries for notes payable are similar to those we discussed in an earlier chapter for notes receivable. Notes payable entries are presented from the viewpoint of the borrower, while notes receivable entries are presented from the viewpoint of the creditor or lender. To illustrate, the following entries are journalized for a borrower (Bowden Co.), who issues a note payable to a creditor (Coker Co.):

	Bowden Co. (Borrower)			**Coker Co. (Creditor)**		
May 1. Bowden Co. purchased merchandise on account from Coker Co., $10,000, 2/10, n/30. The merchandise cost Coker Co. $7,500.	Merchandise Inventory	10,000		Accounts Receivable	10,000	
	Accounts Payable		10,000	Sales		10,000
				Cost of Merchandise Sold	7,500	
				Merchandise Inventory		7,500
May 31. Bowden Co. issued a 60-day, 12% note for $10,000 to Coker Co. on account.	Accounts Payable	10,000		Notes Receivable	10,000	
	Notes Payable		10,000	Accounts Receivable		10,000
July 30. Bowden Co. paid Coker Co. the amount due on the note of May 31. Interest: $10,000 × 12% × 60/360.	Notes Payable	10,000		Cash	10,200	
	Interest Expense	200		Interest Revenue		200
	Cash		10,200	Notes Receivable		10,000

Notes may also be issued when money is borrowed from banks. Although the terms may vary, many banks would accept from the borrower an interest-bearing note for the amount of the loan. For example, assume that on September 19 a firm borrows $4,000 from First National Bank by giving the bank a 90-day, 15% note. The entry to record the receipt of cash and the issuance of the note is as follows:

Sep.	19	Cash	4,000.00	
		Notes Payable		4,000.00
		Issued a 90-day, 15% note to the bank.		

On the due date of the note (December 18), the borrower owes $4,000, the principal of the note, plus interest of $150 ($4,000 × 15% × 90/360). The entry to record the payment of the note is as follows:

Dec.	18	Notes Payable	4,000.00	
		Interest Expense	150.00	
		Cash		4,150.00
		Paid principal and interest due on note.		

The U.S. Treasury issues short-term treasury bills to investors at a discount.

Sometimes a borrower will issue to a creditor a discounted note rather than an interest-bearing note. Although such a note does not specify an interest rate, the creditor sets a rate of interest and deducts the interest from the face amount of the note. This interest is called the **discount**. The rate used in computing the discount is called the **discount rate**. The borrower is given the remainder, called the **proceeds**.

To illustrate, assume that on August 10, Cary Company issues a $20,000, 90-day note to Seinfeld Company in exchange for inventory. Seinfeld discounts the note at a rate of 15%. The amount of the discount, $750, is debited to *Interest Expense*. The proceeds, $19,250, are debited to *Merchandise Inventory*. *Notes Payable* is credited for the face amount of the note, which is also its maturity value. This entry is shown below.

In buying a used delivery truck, a business issues an $8,000, 60-day note dated July 15, which the truck's seller discounts at 12%. What is the cost of the truck (the proceeds)?

$7,840 [$8,000 − ($8,000 × 12% × 60/360)]

Aug.	10	Merchandise Inventory		19 250 00	
		Interest Expense		750 00	
		Notes Payable			20 000 00
		Issued a 90-day note to Seinfeld Co.,			
		discounted at 15%.			

When the note is paid, the following entry is recorded:[1]

Nov.	8	Notes Payable		20 000 00	
		Cash			20 000 00
		Paid note due.			

Contingent Liabilities

OBJECTIVE 3

Describe the accounting treatment for contingent liabilities and journalize entries for product warranties.

Some past transactions will result in liabilities if certain events occur in the future. These potential obligations are called **contingent liabilities**. For example, **Ford Motor Company** would have a contingent liability for the estimated costs associated with warranty work. The obligation is contingent upon a *future event,* namely, a customer requiring warranty work on a vehicle. The obligation is the result of a *past transaction,* which is the original sale of the vehicle.

If a contingent liability is *probable* and the amount of the liability can be *reasonably estimated,* it should be recorded in the accounts. **Ford Motor Company's** vehicle warranty costs are an example of a *recordable* contingent liability. The warranty costs are *probable*

Saturn Corporation has marketed itself as "A Different Kind of Car Company." One way Saturn acted "differently" was its response to a defective coolant placed in the radiators in some of its new cars. Instead of just replacing the coolant, Saturn replaced the cars! Saturn even gave customers a selection of free additional options on their replacement cars to compensate for the inconvenience. Saturn focuses on reducing warranty defects and has been consistently ranked in the top three of J.D. Power and Associates' customer satisfaction ratings.

[1] If the accounting period ends before a discounted note is paid, an adjusting entry should record the prepaid (deferred) interest that is not yet an expense. This deferred interest would be deducted from Notes Payable in the Current Liabilities section of the balance sheet.

because it is known that warranty repairs will be required on some vehicles. In addition, the costs can be *estimated* from past warranty experience.

To illustrate, assume that during June a company sells a product for $60,000 on which there is a 36-month warranty for repairing defects. Past experience indicates that the average cost to repair defects is 5% of the sales price. The entry to record the estimated product warranty expense for June is as follows:

A business sells to a customer $120,000 of commercial audio equipment with a one-year repair and replacement warranty. Historically, the average cost to repair or replace is 2% of sales. How is this contingent liability recorded?

Product Warranty Expense	2,400	
Product Warranty Payable		2,400

June	30	Product Warranty Expense	3000 00	
		Product Warranty Payable		3000 00
		Warranty expense for June, 5% × $60,000.		

This transaction matches revenues and expenses properly by recording warranty costs in the same period in which the sale is recorded. When the defective product is repaired, the repair costs are recorded by debiting *Product Warranty Payable* and crediting *Cash, Supplies,* or other appropriate accounts. Thus, if a customer required a $200 part replacement on August 16, the entry would be:

Aug.	16	Product Warranty Payable	200 00	
		Supplies		200 00
		Replaced defective part under warranty.		

If a contingent liability is probable but cannot be *reasonably estimated* or is only *possible,* then the nature of the contingent liability should be disclosed in the footnotes to the financial statements. Professional judgment is required in distinguishing between contingent liabilities that are probable versus those that are only possible.

The 1996 edition of *Accounting Trends & Techniques* indicates that 70% of the surveyed companies disclosed contingencies for litigation, 49% for environmental matters, 34% for guarantees, and 13% for sale of receivables.

Common examples of contingent liabilities disclosed in notes to the financial statements are litigation, environmental matters, guarantees, and sale of receivables. The following example of a contingency disclosure, related to tobacco litigation, was taken from an annual report of **Philip Morris Companies, Inc.**: *". . . Pending claims related to tobacco products generally fall within three categories: (i) smoking and health cases alleging personal injury brought on behalf of individual smokers, (ii) smoking and health cases alleging personal injury and purporting to be brought on behalf of a class of plaintiffs, and (iii) health care cost recovery actions brought primarily by states and local governments seeking reimbursement for Medicaid and other health care expenditures allegedly caused by cigarette smoking. . . ."*

The accounting treatment of contingent liabilities is summarized in Exhibit 1.

EXHIBIT 1
Accounting Treatment of Contingent Liabilities

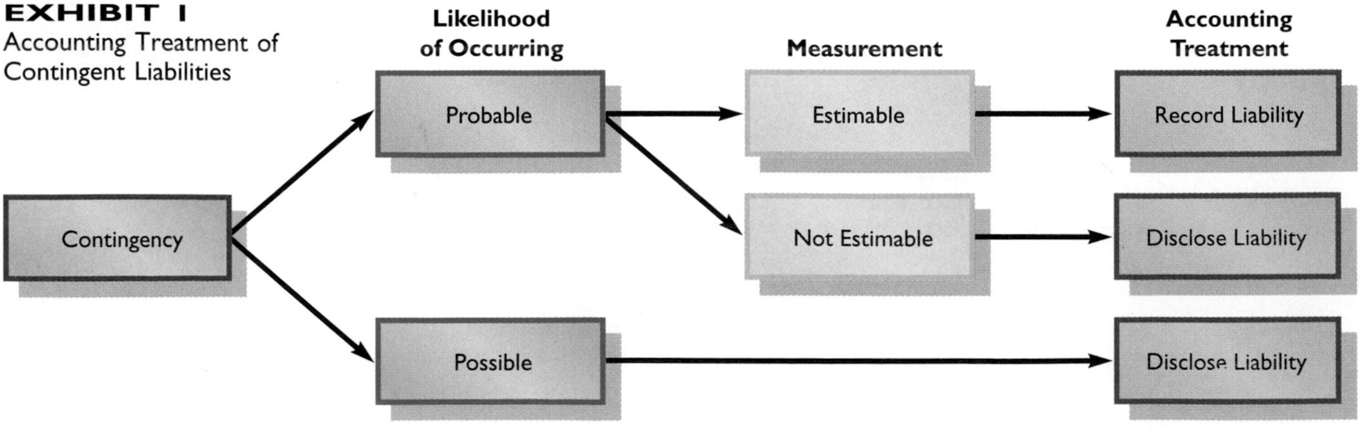

BUSINESS ON STAGE

Picture a factory in your mind. Do you see employees working alone, performing mind-numbing repetitive work? Fortunately, this picture is fast disappearing from the employment landscape. Many companies, such as **Procter & Gamble, Hewlett-Packard**, and **Federal Express**, are using teams. Teams typically consist of between 8 to 15 full-time employees. Often team members represent different functions, such as marketing, manufacturing, and finance.

Why are companies using teams? Teams have the following advantages over individual employees:

- Teams are able to put employees' skills together to solve problems, complete projects, and combine tasks that form a process.
- Teams perform the coordination and communication tasks formerly performed by middle management.
- Empowered teams are more creative and more satisfied in their work.
- Teams take on expanded responsibilities, such as ordering materials, conducting quality checks, making team hiring and firing decisions, developing work schedules, and jointly establishing performance targets with management.

One area of challenge is in the area of team compensation and rewards. Popular plans develop individual base pay rates on the basis of skills obtained, rather than just seniority. A recent survey noted that 85% of companies using teams set base pay rates above the industry average. Additional bonuses are available based on achieving team goals. The same survey noted such bonuses averaged around 10% of base pay.

Team-based management assigns responsibility and authority to the team members and provides rewards for this added work. As one team member put it, "It's a real mind shift. You're used to the expectation that it's your job to have the best idea. But no individual is going to have the best idea. That's not how it works—the best ideas come from the collective intelligence of the team. If you accept that, you're in for a big change in how you think about yourself." ■

Payroll and Payroll Taxes

OBJECTIVE 4

Determine employer liabilities for payroll, including liabilities arising from employee earnings and deductions from earnings.

We are all familiar with the term payroll. In accounting, the term **payroll** refers to the amount paid to employees for the services they provide during a period. A business's payroll is usually significant for several reasons. First, employees are sensitive to payroll errors and irregularities. Maintaining good employee morale requires that the payroll be paid on a timely, accurate basis. Second, the payroll is subject to various federal and state regulations. Finally, the payroll and related payroll taxes have a significant effect on the net income of most businesses. Although the amount of such expenses varies widely, it is not unusual for a business's payroll and payroll-related expenses to equal nearly one-third of its revenue.

Point of INTEREST

Information on average salaries for a variety of professions can be found at the *Economic Research Institute's* Web site at **www.erieri.com.**

Liability for Employee Earnings

Salaries and wages paid to employees are an employer's labor expenses. The term **salary** usually refers to payment for managerial, administrative, or similar services. The rate of salary is normally expressed in terms of a month or a year. The term **wages** usually refers to payment for manual labor, both skilled and unskilled. The rate of wages is normally stated on an hourly or weekly basis. In practice, the terms salary and wages are often used interchangeably.

Employee salaries and wages are expenses to an employer.

The basic salary or wage of an employee may be increased by commissions, profit sharing, or cost-of-living adjustments. Many businesses pay managers an annual bonus in addition to a basic salary. The amount of the bonus is often based on some measure of productivity, such as income or profit of the business. Although payment is usually made by check or in cash, it may be in the form of securities, notes, lodging, or other property or services. Generally, the form of

INTERMISSION

Your Social Security Taxes—Then and Now

In its 1936 publication, *Security in Your Old Age*, the Social Security Board set forth the following explanation of how the social security tax would affect a worker's paycheck:

The taxes called for in this law will be paid both by your employer and by you. For the next 3 years you will pay maybe 15 cents a week, maybe 25 cents a week, maybe 30 cents or more, according to what you earn. That is to say, during the next 3 years, beginning January 1, 1937, you will pay 1 cent for every dollar you earn, and at the same time your employer will pay 1 cent for every dollar you earn, up to $3,000 a year. Twenty-six million other workers and their employers will be paying at the same time.

After the first 3 years—that is to say, beginning in 1940—you will pay, and your employer will pay, $1\frac{1}{2}$ cents for each dollar you earn, up to $3,000 a year. This will be the tax for 3 years, and then beginning in 1943, you will pay 2 cents, and so will your employer, for every dollar you earn for the next three years. After that, you and your employer will each pay half a cent more for 3 years, and finally, beginning in 1949, twelve years from now, you and your employer will each pay 3 cents on each dollar you earn, up to $3,000 a year. That is the most you will ever pay.

The rate on January 1, 1998, was 7.65 cents per dollar earned (7.65%). The social security portion was 6.20% on the first $68,400 of earnings. The Medicare portion was 1.45% on all earnings. ■

Source: Arthur Lodge, "That Is the Most You Will Ever Pay," *Journal of Accountancy*, October 1985, p. 44.

payment has no effect on how salaries and wages are treated by either the employer or the employee.

Salary and wage rates are determined by agreement between the employer and the employees. Businesses engaged in interstate commerce must follow the requirements of the Fair Labor Standards Act. Employers covered by this legislation, which is commonly called the Federal Wage and Hour Law, are required to pay a minimum rate of $1\frac{1}{2}$ times the regular rate for all hours worked in excess of 40 hours per week. Exemptions are provided for executive, administrative, and certain supervisory positions. Premium rates for overtime or for working at night, holidays, or other less desirable times are fairly common, even when not required by law. In some cases, the premium rates may be as much as twice the base rate.

To illustrate computing an employee's earnings, assume that John T. McGrath is employed by McDermott Supply Co. at the rate of $25 per hour. Any hours in excess of 40 hours per week are paid at a rate of $1\frac{1}{2}$ times the normal rate, or $37.50 ($25 + $12.50) per hour. For the week ended December 27, McGrath's time card indicates that he worked 44 hours. His earnings for that week are computed as follows:

Earnings at base rate (40 × $25)	$1,000
Earnings at overtime rate (4 × $37.50)	150
Total earnings	$1,150

Deductions from Employee Earnings

The total earnings of an employee for a payroll period, including bonuses and overtime pay, are called **gross pay**. From this amount is subtracted one or more **deductions** to arrive at the net pay. **Net pay** is the amount the employer must pay the employee. The deductions for federal taxes are usually the largest deduction. Deductions may also be required for state or local income taxes. Other deductions may be made for medical insurance, contributions to pensions, and for items authorized by individual employees.

FICA Tax

Most of us have FICA tax withheld from our payroll checks by our employers. Employers are required by the Federal Insurance Contributions Act (FICA) to withhold a portion of the earnings of each of the employees. The amount of **FICA tax** withheld is the employees' contribution to two federal programs. Tax is withheld separately under each program. The first program, called **social security**, is for old age, survivors, and disability insurance (OASDI). The second program, called **Medicare**, is health insurance for senior citizens.

The amount of tax that employers are required to withhold from each employee is normally based on the amount of earnings paid in the *calendar* year. Although both the schedule of future tax rates and the maximum amount subject to tax are revised often by Congress, such changes have little effect on the basic payroll system. In this text, we will use a social security rate of 6% on the first $70,000 of annual earnings and a Medicare rate of 1.5% on all annual earnings.

REAL WORLD Tables are available from the Internal Revenue Service for determining social security and Medicare withholding.

To illustrate, assume that John T. McGrath's annual earnings prior to the

If an employee earns $6,000 per month and has been employed since January 1 of the current year, what is the total FICA tax deducted from the employee's December paycheck?

Social security tax ($4,000 × 6%)	$240
Medicare tax ($6,000 × 1.5%)	90
Total FICA tax	$330

current payroll period total $69,150. Assume also that the current period earnings are $1,150. The total FICA tax of $68.25 is determined as follows:

Earnings subject to 6% social security tax ($70,000 − $69,150)	$ 850	
Social security tax rate	× 6%	
Social security tax		$51.00
Earnings subject to 1.5% Medicare tax	$1,150	
Medicare tax rate	× 1.5%	
Medicare tax		17.25
Total FICA tax		$68.25

Income Taxes

Except for certain types of employment, all employers must withhold a portion of employee earnings for payment of the employees' federal income tax. As a basis for determining the amount to be withheld, each employee completes and submits to the employer an "Employee's Withholding Allowance Certificate," often called a W-4. Exhibit 2 is an example of a completed W-4 form.

EXHIBIT 2
Employee's Withholding Allowance Certificate (W-4 Form)

Cut here and give the certificate to your employer. Keep the top portion for your records.

Form **W-4** Department of the Treasury Internal Revenue Service

Employee's Withholding Allowance Certificate

▶ For Privacy Act and Paperwork Reduction Act Notice, see reverse.

OMB No. 1545-0010 **1999**

1 Type or print your first name and middle initial: John T. — Last name: McGrath

2 Your social security number: 381 48 9120

Home address (number and street or rural route): 1830 4th Street

3 ☒ Single ☐ Married ☐ Married, but withhold at higher Single rate.
Note: If married, but legally separated, or spouse is a nonresident alien, check the Single box.

City or town, state, and ZIP code: Clinton, Iowa 52732-6142

4 If your last name differs from that on your social security card, check here and call 1-800-772-1213 for a new card . . . . . ▶ ☐

5 Total number of allowances you are claiming (from line G above or from the worksheets on page 2 if they apply) . — 5: 1

6 Additional amount, if any, you want withheld from each paycheck . . . . — 6: $

7 I claim exemption from withholding for 1997, and I certify that I meet **BOTH** of the following conditions for exemption:
• Last year I had a right to a refund of **ALL** Federal income tax withheld because I had **NO** tax liability; **AND**
• This year I expect a refund of **ALL** Federal income tax withheld because I expect to have **NO** tax liability.
If you meet both conditions, enter "EXEMPT" here . . . . ▶ 7

Under penalties of perjury, I certify that I am entitled to the number of withholding allowances claimed on this certificate or entitled to claim exempt status.

Employee's signature ▶ John T. McGrath **Date ▶** June 2, 1999

8 Employer's name and address (Employer: Complete 8 and 10 only if sending to the IRS) | 9 Office code (optional) | 10 Employer identification number

You may recall filling out a W-4 form. On the W-4, an employee indicates marital status, the number of withholding allowances, and whether any additional withholdings are authorized. A single employee may claim one withholding allowance. A married employee may claim an additional allowance for a spouse. An employee may also claim an allowance for each dependent other than a spouse. Each allowance claimed reduces the amount of federal income tax withheld from the employee's check.

The amount that must be withheld for income tax differs, depending upon each employee's gross pay and completed W-4. Most employers use wage bracket withholding tables furnished by the Internal Revenue Service to determine the amount to be withheld.

REAL WORLD

Federal income tax withholding tables are available from the Internal Revenue Service as part of *Circular E*, "Employer's Tax Guide."

Exhibit 3 is an example of a wage bracket withholding table. This table is for a single employee who is paid weekly. Other tables are used for employees who are married or who are paid biweekly, semimonthly, monthly, or at other time periods. Unlike social security tax, there is no ceiling on the amount of employee earnings subject to federal income tax withholding.

EXHIBIT 3
Wage Bracket Withholding Table

SINGLE Persons—**WEEKLY** Payroll Period

If the wages are–		And the number of withholding allowances claimed is—										
At least	But less than	0	1	2	3	4	5	6	7	8	9	10
		The amount of income tax to be withheld is—										
900	910	180	166	152	138	123	109	95	80	67	59	52
910	920	183	169	155	140	126	112	98	83	69	61	53
920	930	186	172	157	143	129	115	100	86	72	62	55
930	940	189	175	160	146	132	117	103	89	75	64	56
940	950	192	177	163	149	135	120	106	92	77	65	58
950	960	194	180	166	152	137	123	109	94	80	67	59
960	970	197	183	169	154	140	126	112	97	83	69	61
970	980	200	186	171	157	143	129	114	100	86	72	62
980	990	203	189	174	160	146	131	117	103	89	74	64
990	1,000	206	191	177	163	149	134	120	106	91	77	65
1,000	1,010	208	194	180	166	151	137	123	108	94	80	67
1,010	1,020	211	197	183	168	154	140	126	111	97	83	68
1,020	1,030	214	200	185	171	157	143	128	114	100	86	71
1,030	1,040	217	203	188	174	160	145	131	117	103	88	74
1,040	1,050	220	205	191	177	163	148	134	120	105	91	77
1,050	1,060	222	208	194	180	165	151	137	122	108	94	80
1,060	1,070	225	211	197	182	168	154	140	125	111	97	82
1,070	1,080	228	214	199	185	171	157	142	128	114	100	85
1,080	1,090	231	217	202	188	174	159	145	131	117	102	88
1,090	1,100	235	219	205	191	177	162	148	134	119	105	91
1,100	1,110	238	222	208	194	179	165	151	136	122	108	94
1,110	1,120	241	225	211	196	182	168	154	139	125	111	96
1,120	1,130	244	228	213	199	185	171	156	142	128	114	99
1,130	1,140	247	231	216	202	188	173	159	145	131	116	102
1,140	1,150	250	234	219	205	191	176	162	148	133	119	105
1,150	1,160	253	237	222	208	193	179	165	150	136	122	108
1,160	1,170	256	240	225	210	196	182	168	153	139	125	110
1,170	1,180	259	244	228	213	199	185	170	156	142	128	113
1,180	1,190	262	247	231	216	202	187	173	159	145	130	116
1,190	1,200	266	250	234	219	205	190	176	162	147	133	119
1,200	1,210	269	253	237	222	207	193	179	164	150	136	122
1,210	1,220	272	256	240	224	210	196	182	167	153	139	124
1,220	1,230	275	259	243	227	213	199	184	170	156	142	127
1,230	1,240	278	262	246	231	216	201	187	173	159	144	130
1,240	1,250	281	265	249	234	219	204	190	176	161	147	133

In using the withholding table, the amount of federal income tax withheld each pay period is indicated where the row showing the employee's wage bracket intersects the column showing the employee's withholding allowances. For example, assume that John T. McGrath, who is single and has declared one withholding allowance, made $1,150 for the week ended December 27. Using the withholding table in Exhibit 3, the amount of federal income tax withheld is $237.

REAL WORLD

Professional athletes must pay local taxes in each location in which they play their sport.

In addition to the federal income tax, employees may also be required to pay a state income tax and a city income tax. State and city taxes are withheld from employees' earnings and paid to state and city governments.

Other Deductions

Neither the employer nor the employee has any choice in deducting taxes from gross earnings. However, employees may choose to have additional amounts deducted for other purposes. For example, you as an employee may authorize deductions for retirement savings, for contributions to charitable organizations, or for premiums on employee insurance. A union contract may also require the deduction of union dues.

Computing Employee Net Pay

Gross earnings less payroll deductions equals the amount to be paid to an employee for the payroll period. This amount is the *net pay,* which is often called the *take-home pay*. Assuming that John T. McGrath authorized deductions for retirement savings and for a United Way contribution, the amount to be paid McGrath for the week ended December 27 is $819.75, as shown below.

Gross earnings for the week		$1,150.00
Deductions:		
Social security tax	$ 51.00	
Medicare tax	17.25	
Federal income tax	237.00	
Retirement savings	20.00	
United Way	5.00	
Total deductions		330.25
Net pay		$ 819.75

Liability for Employer's Payroll Taxes

So far, we have discussed the payroll taxes that are withheld from the employees' earnings. Most employers are also subject to federal and state payroll taxes based on the amount paid their employees. Such taxes are an operating expense of the business. Exhibit 4 summarizes the responsibility for employee and employer payroll taxes.

EXHIBIT 4 Responsibility for Tax Payments

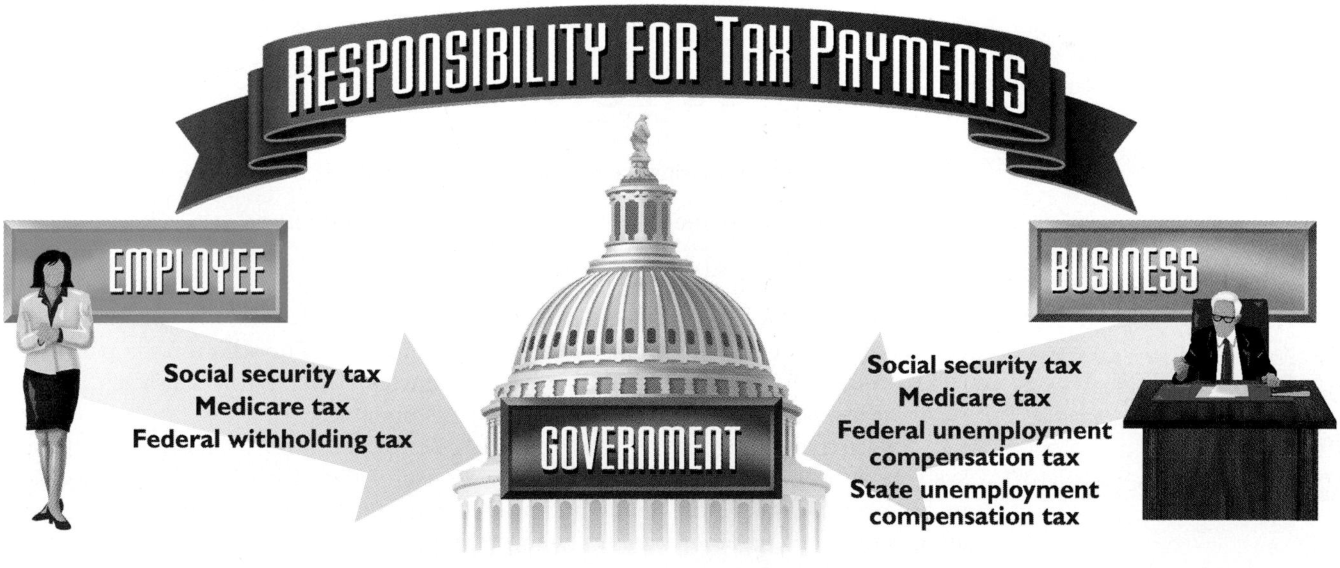

FICA Tax

Employers are required to contribute to the social security and Medicare programs for each employee. The employer must match the employee's contribution to each program.

The U.S. Government receives money from various taxes, fees, and borrowing. This money is spent on a variety of government services. The relative sizes of these sources and outlays for fiscal 1995 are shown below.

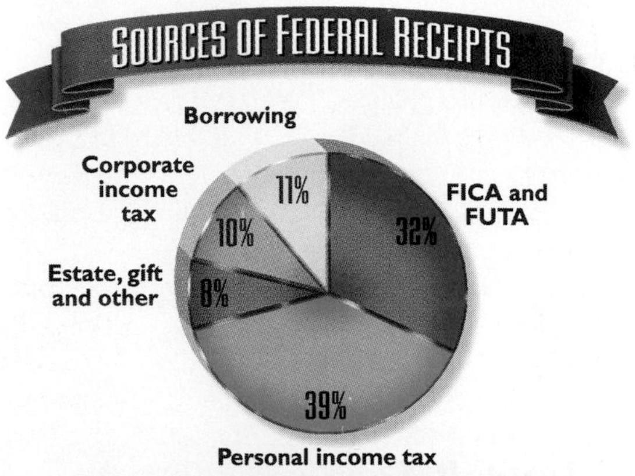

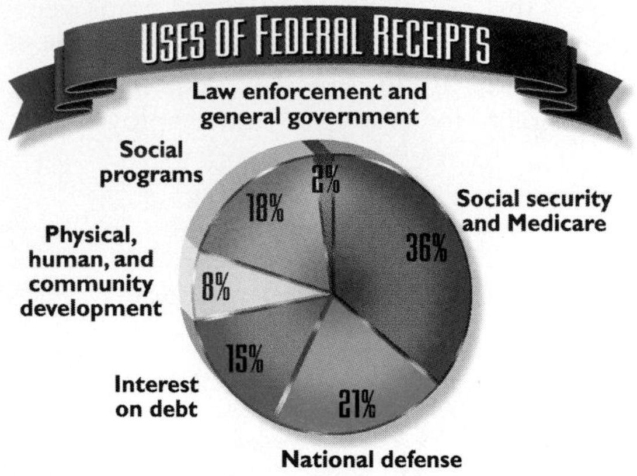

Source: Internal Revenue Service

Federal Unemployment Compensation Tax

The Federal Unemployment Tax Act (FUTA) provides for temporary payments to those who become unemployed as a result of layoffs due to economic causes beyond their control. Types of employment subject to this program are similar to those covered by FICA taxes. A tax of 6.2% is levied on employers only, rather than on both employers and employees.[2] It is applied to only the first $7,000 of the earnings of each covered employee during a calendar year. Congress often revises the rate and maximum earnings subject to federal unemployment compensation tax. The funds collected by the federal government are not paid directly to the unemployed, but are allocated among the states for use in state programs.

State Unemployment Compensation Tax

State Unemployment Tax Acts (SUTA) also provide for payments to unemployed workers. The amounts paid as benefits are obtained, for the most part, from a tax levied upon employers only. A few states require employee contributions also. The rates of tax and the tax bases vary. In most states, employers who provide stable employment for their employees are granted reduced rates. The employment experience and the status of each employer's tax account are reviewed annually, and the tax rates are adjusted accordingly.[3]

Accounting Systems for Payroll and Payroll Taxes

OBJECTIVE 5

Describe payroll accounting systems that use a payroll register, employee earnings records, and a general journal.

In designing payroll systems, the requirements of various federal, state, and local agencies for payroll data are considered. Payroll data must also be maintained accurately for each payroll period and for each employee. Periodic reports using payroll data must be submitted to government agencies. The payroll data itself must be retained for possible inspection by the various agencies.

Payroll systems must be designed to pay employees on a timely basis. Payroll systems should also be designed to provide useful data for management decision-making needs. Such needs might include settling employee grievances and negotiating retirement or other benefits with employees.

Although payroll systems differ among businesses, the major elements common to most payroll systems are the payroll register, employee's earnings record, and payroll checks. We discuss and illustrate each of these elements next. We have kept

[2] This rate may be reduced to 0.8% for credits for state unemployment compensation tax.
[3] As of January 1, 1998, the maximum state rate credited against the federal unemployment rate was 5.4% of the first $7,000 of each employee's earnings during a calendar year.

the illustrations relatively simple, and they may be modified in practice to meet the needs of each individual business.

Payroll Register

The **payroll register** is a multicolumn form used in assembling and summarizing the data needed for each payroll period. Its design varies according to the number and classes of employees and the extent to which computers are used. Exhibit 5 shows a form suitable for a small number of employees.

The nature of the data appearing in the payroll register is evident from the column headings. The number of hours worked and the earnings and deduction data are inserted in their proper columns. The sum of the deductions for each employee is then subtracted from the total earnings to yield the amount to be paid. The check numbers are recorded in the payroll register as evidence of payment.

The last two columns of the payroll register are used to accumulate the total wages or salaries to be debited to the various expense accounts. This process is usually called **payroll distribution**.

The format of the payroll register in Exhibit 5 aids in determining the mathematical accuracy of the payroll before checks are issued to employees. All column totals should be verified, as shown below.

Earnings:		
Regular	$13,328.00	
Overtime	574.00	
Total		$13,902.00
Deductions:		
Social security tax	$ 643.07	
Medicare tax	208.53	
Federal income tax	3,332.00	
Retirement savings	680.00	
United Way	470.00	
Accounts receivable	50.00	
Total		5,383.60
Paid—net amount		$ 8,518.40
Accounts debited:		
Sales Salaries Expense		$11,122.00
Office Salaries Expense		2,780.00
Total (as above)		$13,902.00

Recording Employees' Earnings

Amounts in the payroll register may be posted directly to the accounts. An alternative is to use the payroll register as a supporting record for a journal entry. The entry based on the payroll register in Exhibit 5 follows.

Dec.	27	Sales Salaries Expense		11 1 2 2 00	
		Office Salaries Expense		2 7 8 0 00	
		Social Security Tax Payable			6 4 3 07
		Medicare Tax Payable			2 0 8 53
		Employees Federal Income Tax Payable			3 3 3 2 00
		Retirement Savings Deductions Payable			6 8 0 00
		United Way Deductions Payable			4 7 0 00
		Accounts Receivable—Fred G. Elrod			5 0 00
		Salaries Payable			8 5 1 8 40
		Payroll for week ended December 27.			

EXHIBIT 5
Payroll Register

			Earnings			
	Employee Name	Total Hours	Regular	Overtime	Total	
1	Abrams, Julie S.	40	500.00		500.00	1
2	Elrod, Fred G.	44	392.00	58.80	450.80	2
3	Gomez, Jose C.	40	840.00		840.00	3
4	**McGrath, John T.**	**44**	**1,000.00**	**150.00**	**1,150.00**	4
25	Wilkes, Glenn K.	40	480.00		480.00	25
26	Zumpano, Michael W.	40	600.00		600.00	26
27	Total		13,328.00	574.00	13,902.00	27
28						28

Payroll taxes become a liability to the employer when the payroll is paid.

Recording and Paying Payroll Taxes

The employer's payroll taxes become liabilities when the related payroll is *paid* to employees. In addition, employers are required to compute and report payroll taxes on a *calendar-year* basis, even if a different fiscal year is used for financial reporting and income tax purposes.

To illustrate, assume that Everson Company's fiscal year ends on April 30. Also, assume that Everson Company owes its employees $26,000 of wages on December 31. The following portions of the $26,000 of wages are subject to payroll taxes on December 31:

	Earnings Subject to Payroll Taxes
Social Security Tax (6.0%)	$18,000
Medicare Tax (1.5%)	26,000
State and Federal Unemployment Compensation Tax	1,000

If the payroll is paid on December 31, the payroll taxes will be based on the preceding amounts. If the payroll is paid on January 2, however, the *entire* $26,000 will be subject to *all* payroll taxes.

The payroll register in Exhibit 5 indicates that the amount of social security tax withheld is $643.07 and Medicare tax withheld is $208.53. Since the employer must match the employees' FICA contributions, the employer's social security payroll tax will also be $643.07, and the Medicare tax will be $208.53. Further, assume that the earnings subject to state and federal unemployment compensation taxes are $2,710. Multiplying this amount by the state (5.4%) and federal (0.8%) rates yields the unemployment compensation taxes shown in the payroll tax computation on the next page.

REAL WORLD

Social security contributions (both the employees' and employer's amounts) and federal income taxes must be deposited quarterly in a federal depository bank. An "Employer's Quarterly Federal Tax Return" (Form 941) must also be filed. Unemployment compensation tax returns and payments are required annually by the federal government and most state governments.

	Deductions							Paid		Accounts Debited		
	Social Security Tax	Medicare Tax	Federal Income Tax	Retirement Savings	Misc.		Total	Net Amount	Check No.	Sales Salaries Expense	Office Salaries Expense	
1	30.00	7.50	74.00	20.00	UW	10.00	141.50	358.50	6857	500.00		1
2	27.05	6.76	62.00		AR	50.00	145.81	304.99	6858		450.80	2
3	50.40	12.60	173.00	25.00	UW	10.00	271.00	569.00	6859	840.00		3
4	**51.00**	**17.25**	**237.00**	**20.00**	**UW**	**5.00**	**330.25**	**819.75**	**6860**	**1,150.00**		4
25	28.80	7.20	69.00	10.00			115.00	365.00	6880	480.00		25
26	36.00	9.00	71.00	5.00	UW	2.00	123.00	477.00	6881		600.00	26
27	643.07	208.53	3,332.00	680.00	UW	470.00	5,383.60	8,518.40		11,122.00	2,780.00	27
28					AR	50.00						28

Miscellaneous Deductions: UW—United Way; AR—Accounts Receivable

EXHIBIT 5
(concluded)

Social security tax	$ 643.07
Medicare tax	208.53
State unemployment compensation tax (5.4% × $2,710)	146.34
Federal unemployment compensation tax (0.8% × $2,710)	21.68
Total payroll tax expense	$1,019.62

The entry to journalize the payroll tax expense for the week and the liability for the taxes accrued is shown below.

Dec.	27	Payroll Tax Expense	1 0 1 9 62	
		Social Security Tax Payable		6 4 3 07
		Medicare Tax Payable		2 0 8 53
		State Unemployment Tax Payable		1 4 6 34
		Federal Unemployment Tax Payable		2 1 68
		Payroll taxes for week ended		
		December 27.		

Employee's Earnings Record

The amount of each employee's earnings to date must be available at the end of each payroll period. This cumulative amount is required in order to compute each employee's social security and Medicare tax withholding and the employer's payroll taxes. It is essential, therefore, that a detailed payroll record be maintained for each employee. This record is called an **employee's earnings record**.

Exhibit 6 shows a portion of the employee's earnings record for John T. McGrath. The relationship between this record and the payroll register can be seen by tracing the amounts entered on McGrath's earnings record for December 27 back to its source—the fourth line of the payroll register in Exhibit 5.

In addition to spaces for recording data for each payroll period and the cumulative total of earnings, the employee's earnings record has spaces for quarterly totals and the yearly total. These totals are used in various reports for tax, insurance, and other purposes. One such report is the Wage and Tax Statement, commonly called a **Form W-2**. You may recall receiving a W-2 form for use in preparing your individual tax return. This form must be provided annually to each employee as well as to

EXHIBIT 6
Employee's Earnings Record

John T. McGrath
1830 4th Street
Clinton, IA 52732-6142 **PHONE: 555-3148**

MARRIED	NUMBER OF WITHHOLDING ALLOWANCES: 1		PAY RATE:	$1,000.00 Per Week			
OCCUPATION:	Salesperson		EQUIVALENT HOURLY RATE: $25				

			Earnings				
	Period Ending	Total Hours	Regular Earnings	Overtime Earnings	Total Earnings	Cumulative Total	
42	SEP. 27	51	1,000.00	412.50	1,412.50	52,800.00	42
43	THIRD QUARTER		13,000.00	4,800.00	17,800.00		43
44	OCT. 4	50	1,000.00	375.00	1,375.00	54,175.00	44
50	NOV. 15	48	1,000.00	300.00	1,300.00	62,200.00	50
51	NOV. 22	50	1,000.00	375.00	1,375.00	63,575.00	51
52	NOV. 29	52	1,000.00	450.00	1,450.00	65,025.00	52
53	DEC. 6	50	1,000.00	375.00	1,375.00	66,400.00	53
54	DEC. 13	48	1,000.00	300.00	1,300.00	67,700.00	54
55	DEC. 20	52	1,000.00	450.00	1,450.00	69,150.00	55
56	DEC. 27	44	1,000.00	150.00	1,150.00	70,300.00	56
57	FOURTH QUARTER		13,000.00	4,500.00	17,500.00		57
58	YEARLY TOTAL		52,000.00	18,300.00	70,300.00		58

the Social Security Administration. The amounts reported in the Form W-2 shown below were taken from McGrath's employee's earnings record.

a Control number 22222	Void ☐	For Official Use Only ▸ OMB No. 1545-0008
b Employer's identification number 61-8436524	1 Wages, tips, other compensation 70,300.00	2 Federal income tax withheld 16,772.00
c Employer's name, address, and ZIP code McDermott Supply Co. 415 5th Ave. So. Dubuque, IA 52736-0142	3 Social security wages 70,000.00	4 Social security tax withheld 4,200.00
	5 Medicare wages and tips 70,300.00	6 Medicare tax withheld 1,054.50
	7 Social security tips	8 Allocated tips
d Employee's social security number 381-48-9120	9 Advance EIC payment	10 Dependent care benefits
e Employee's name (first, middle initial, last) John T. McGrath 1830 4th St. Clinton, IA 52732-6142	11 Nonqualified plans	12 Benefits included in box 1
	13 See Instrs. for box 13	14 Other
f Employee's address and ZIP code	15 Statutory employee ☐ Deceased ☐ Pension plan ☐ Legal rep. ☐ Hshld. emp. ☐ Subtotal ☐ Deferred compensation ☐	

16 State	Employer's state I.D. No.	17 State wages, tips, etc.	18 State income tax	19 Locality name	20 Local wages, tips, etc.	21 Local income tax
IA				Dubuque		

Cat. No. 10134D

Department of the Treasury—Internal Revenue Service

Form **W-2** Wage and Tax Statement

For Paperwork Reduction Act Notice, see separate instructions.

Copy A For Social Security Administration

SOC. SEC. NO.: 381-48-9120 **EMPLOYEE NO.: 814**

DATE OF BIRTH: February 15, 1974

DATE EMPLOYMENT TERMINATED:

	Deductions						Paid		
	Social Security Tax	Medicare Tax	Federal Income Tax	Retirement Savings	Other	Total	Net Amount	Check No.	
42	84.75	21.19	339.00	20.00		464.94	947.56	6175	42
43	1,068.00	267.00	4,296.00	260.00	UW 40.00	5,931.00	11,869.00		43
44	82.50	20.63	330.00	20.00		453.13	921.87	6225	44
50	78.00	19.50	312.00	20.00		429.50	870.50	6530	50
51	82.50	20.63	330.00	20.00		453.13	921.87	6582	51
52	87.00	21.75	348.00	20.00		476.75	973.25	6640	52
53	82.50	20.63	330.00	20.00	UW 5.00	458.13	916.87	6688	53
54	78.00	19.50	312.00	20.00		429.50	870.50	6743	54
55	87.00	21.75	348.00	20.00		476.75	973.25	6801	55
56	51.00	17.25	237.00	20.00	UW 5.00	330.25	819.75	6860	56
57	1,032.00	262.50	4,100.00	260.00	UW 10.00	5,664.50	11,835.50		57
58	4,200.00	1,054.50	16,772.00	1,040.00	UW 100.00	23,166.50	47,133.50		58

EXHIBIT 6
(concluded)

Payroll Checks

At the end of each pay period, **payroll checks** are prepared. Each check includes a detachable statement showing the details of how the net pay was computed. Exhibit 7 is a payroll check for John T. McGrath.

The amount paid to employees is normally recorded as a single amount, regardless of the number of employees. There is no need to record each payroll check separately in the journal, since all of the details are available in the payroll register.

For paying their payroll, most employers use payroll checks drawn on a special bank account. After the data for the payroll period have been recorded and summarized in the payroll register, a single check for the total amount to be paid is written on the firm's regular bank account. This check is then deposited in the special payroll bank account. Individual payroll checks are written from the payroll account, and the numbers of the payroll checks are inserted in the payroll register.

An advantage of using a separate payroll bank account is that the task of reconciling the bank statements is simplified. In addition, a payroll bank account establishes control over payroll checks by preventing the theft or misuse of uncashed payroll checks.

EXHIBIT 7
Payroll Check

MS **McDermott Supply Co.**
415 5th Ave. So.
Dubuque, IA 52736-0142

John T. McGrath
1830 4th St.
Clinton, IA 52732-6142

Check Number: 6860
Pay Period Ending: 12/27/99

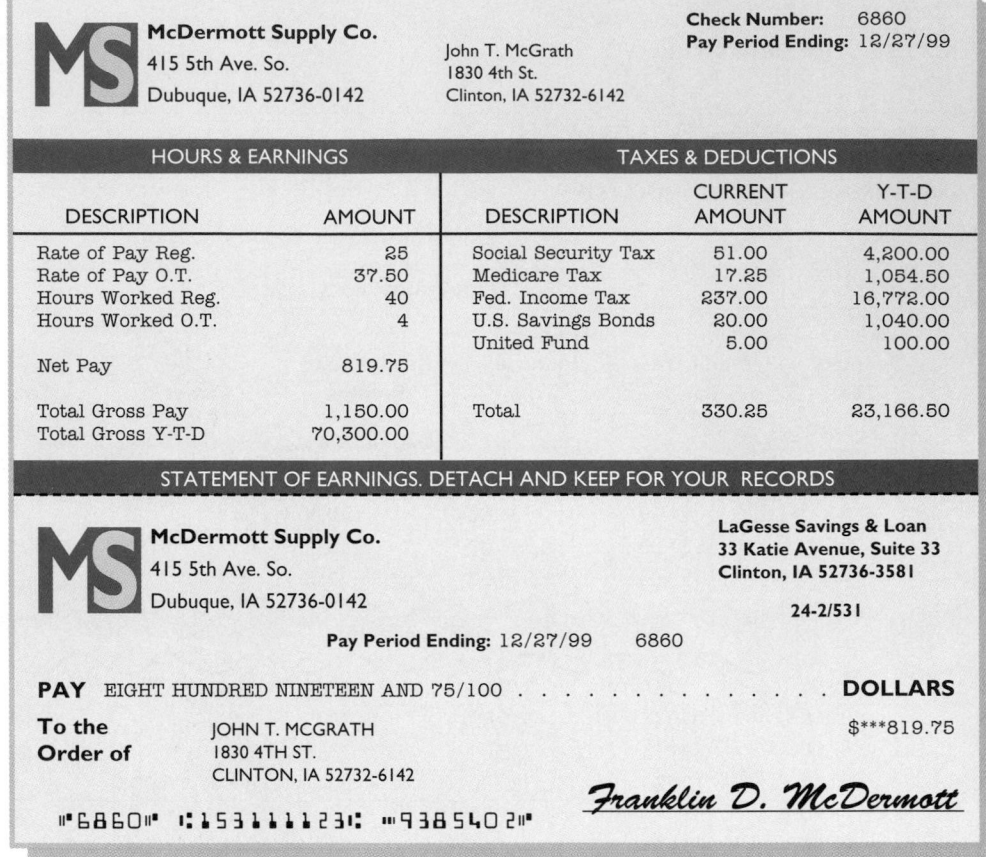

HOURS & EARNINGS		TAXES & DEDUCTIONS		
DESCRIPTION	AMOUNT	DESCRIPTION	CURRENT AMOUNT	Y-T-D AMOUNT
Rate of Pay Reg.	25	Social Security Tax	51.00	4,200.00
Rate of Pay O.T.	37.50	Medicare Tax	17.25	1,054.50
Hours Worked Reg.	40	Fed. Income Tax	237.00	16,772.00
Hours Worked O.T.	4	U.S. Savings Bonds	20.00	1,040.00
		United Fund	5.00	100.00
Net Pay	819.75			
Total Gross Pay	1,150.00	Total	330.25	23,166.50
Total Gross Y-T-D	70,300.00			

STATEMENT OF EARNINGS. DETACH AND KEEP FOR YOUR RECORDS

MS **McDermott Supply Co.**
415 5th Ave. So.
Dubuque, IA 52736-0142

LaGesse Savings & Loan
33 Katie Avenue, Suite 33
Clinton, IA 52736-3581

24-2/531

Pay Period Ending: 12/27/99 6860

PAY EIGHT HUNDRED NINETEEN AND 75/100 . . . . **DOLLARS**

To the Order of JOHN T. MCGRATH
1830 4TH ST.
CLINTON, IA 52732-6142

$***819.75

Franklin D. McDermott

⑈6860⑈ ⑆153111123⑆ ⑈9385402⑈

Currency may be used to pay payroll. However, many employees have their net pay deposited directly in a bank. In these cases, funds are transferred electronically.

Payroll System Diagram

You may find Exhibit 8 useful in following the flow of data within the payroll segment of an accounting system. The diagram indicates the relationships among the primary components of the payroll system we described in this chapter.

Our focus in the preceding discussion has been on the outputs of a payroll system: the payroll register, payroll checks, the employee's earnings record, and tax and other reports. As shown in the diagram in Exhibit 8, the inputs into a payroll system may be classified as either constants or variables.

Constants are data that remain unchanged from payroll to payroll and thus do not need to be entered into the system each pay period. Examples of constants include such data as each employee's name and social security number, marital status, number of income tax withholding allowances, rate of pay, payroll category (office, sales, etc.), and department where employed. The FICA tax rates and various tax tables are also constants that apply to all employees. In a computerized accounting system, constants are stored within a payroll file.

Variables are data that change from payroll to payroll and thus must be entered into the system each pay period. Examples of variables include such data as the number of hours or days worked for each employee during the payroll period, days of sick leave with pay, vacation credits, and cumulative earnings and taxes withheld. If salespersons are paid commissions, the amount of their sales would also vary from period to period.

EXHIBIT 8 Flow of Data in a Payroll System

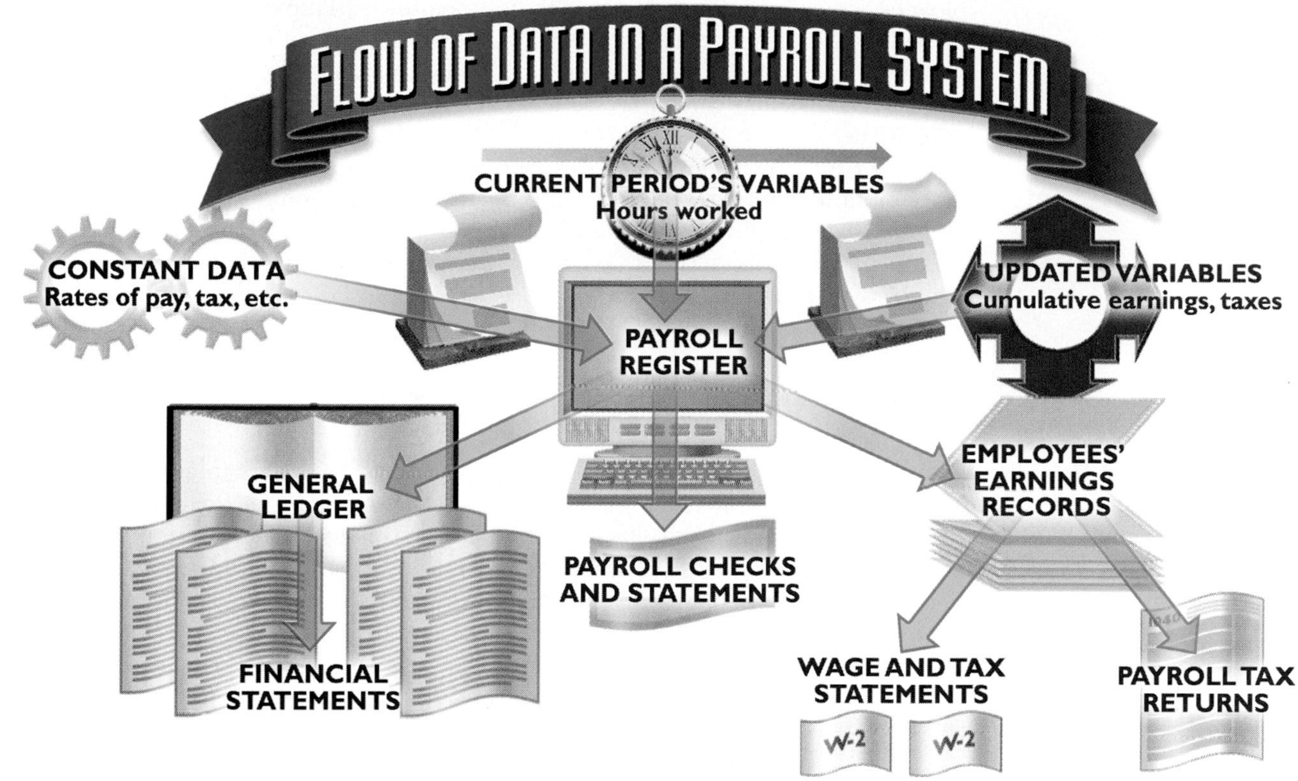

Internal Controls for Payroll Systems

Payroll processing, as we discussed above, requires the input of a large amount of data, along with numerous and sometimes complex computations. These factors, combined with the large dollar amounts involved, require controls to ensure that payroll payments are timely and accurate. In addition, the system must also provide adequate safeguards against theft or other misuse of funds.

The cash payment controls we discussed in the cash chapter also apply to payrolls. Thus, it is normally desirable to use a system that includes procedures for proper authorization and approval of payroll. When a check-signing machine is used, it is important that blank payroll checks and access to the machine be carefully controlled to prevent the theft or misuse of payroll funds.

It is especially important to authorize and approve in writing employee additions and deletions and changes in pay rates. For example, numerous payroll frauds have involved a supervisor adding fictitious employees to the payroll. The supervisor then cashes the fictitious employees' checks. Similar frauds have occurred where employees have been fired but the Payroll Department is not notified. As a result, payroll checks to the fired employees are prepared and cashed by a supervisor.

To prevent or detect frauds such as those we described above, employees' attendance records should be controlled. For example, you may have used an "In and Out" card on which your time of arrival to and departure from work was recorded when you inserted the card into a time clock. A Payroll Department employee may be stationed near

Point of INTEREST

In the movie *Superman III,* Gus Gorman embezzled payroll funds by programming the computer to round down each employee's payroll amount to the nearest penny. He then added the amount "rounded out" to his own payroll check. For example, if an employee's total pay was $458.533, the payroll program would pay the employee $458.53 and add the $.003 to a special account. The total in this special account would be transferred to Gus's paycheck at the end of the processing of the payroll. In this way, Gus's check increased from $143.80 to $85,000 in one pay period!

REAL WORLD

A Chicago politician, Ambrosio Medrano, was convicted of fraud involving fictitious employees (ghost employees). Medrano admitted placing two individuals, both supporters of his campaign, on the Cook County payroll. Neither of these people, also convicted of theft, was required to perform any services for their $48,000 in wages and benefits.

the time clock during normal arrival and departure times in order to verify that employees "clock in" only once and only for themselves. Employee identification cards or badges may also be used to verify that only authorized employees are clocking in and are permitted to enter work areas. When payroll checks are distributed, employee identification cards may be used to deter one employee from picking up another's check.

Other controls include verifying and approving all payroll rate changes. In addition, in a computerized system, all program changes should be properly approved and tested by employees who are independent of the payroll system. The use of a special payroll bank account, as we discussed earlier in the chapter, also enhances control over payroll.

Employees' Fringe Benefits

OBJECTIVE 6

Journalize entries for employee fringe benefits, including vacation pay and pensions.

Many companies provide their employees a variety of benefits in addition to salary and wages earned. Such **fringe benefits** may take many forms, including vacations, pension plans, and health, life, and disability insurance. When the employer pays part or all of the cost of the fringe benefits, these costs must be recognized as expenses. To properly match revenues and expenses, the estimated cost of these benefits should be recorded as an expense during the period in which the employee earns the benefit.

Exhibit 9 shows benefit dollars as a percent of total benefits for 864 companies surveyed by the U.S. Chamber of Commerce.

EXHIBIT 9
Benefit Dollars as a Percent of Total

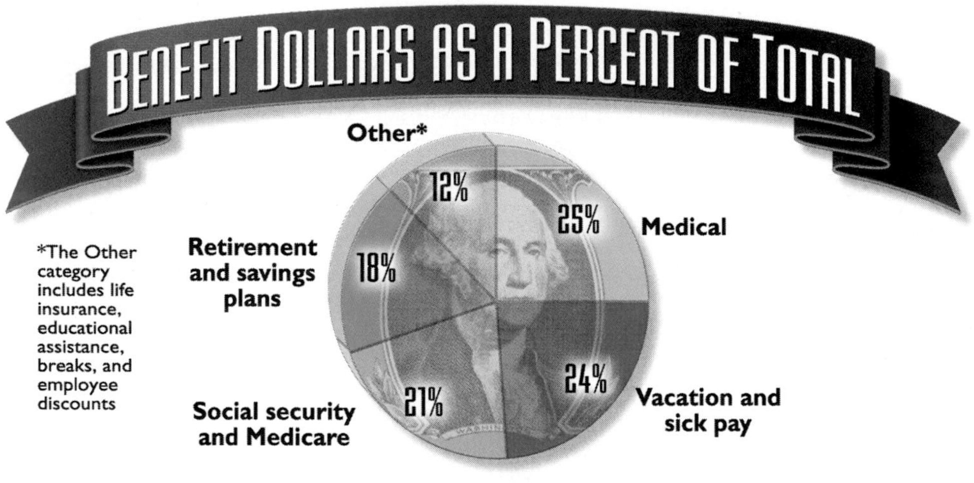

Source: U.S. Chamber of Commerce survey of employer benefits, 1996.

Vacation Pay

Most employers grant vacation rights, sometimes called **compensated absences**, to their employees. Such rights give rise to a recordable contingent liability. The liability for employees' vacation pay should be accrued as a liability as the vacation rights are earned. The entry to accrue vacation pay may be recorded in total at the end of each fiscal year, or it may be recorded at the end of each pay period. To illustrate this latter case, assume that employees earn one day of vacation for each month worked during the year. Assume also that the estimated vacation pay for the payroll period ending May 5 is $2,000. The entry to record the accrued vacation pay for this pay period is shown as follows.

Vacation pay becomes the employer's liability as the employee earns vacation rights.

May	5	Vacation Pay Expense	2,000 00	
		Vacation Pay Payable		2,000 00
		Vacation pay for week ended May 5.		

If employees are required to take all their vacation time within one year, the vacation pay payable is reported on the balance sheet as a current liability. If employees are allowed to accumulate their vacation time, the estimated vacation pay liability that is applicable to time that will *not* be taken within one year is a long-term liability.

When payroll is prepared for the period in which employees have taken vacations, the vacation pay payable is reduced. The entry debits *Vacation Pay Payable* and credits *Salaries Payable* and the other related accounts for taxes and withholdings.

Pensions

A **pension** represents a cash payment to retired employees. Rights to pension payments are earned by employees during their working years, based on the pension plan established by the employer. One of the fundamental characteristics of such a plan is whether it is a defined contribution plan or a defined benefit plan.

REAL WORLD Studies indicate that 57% of all civilian employees work for companies that sponsor pension plans. However, of this amount, only about 75% of the workers actually participate in these plans.

Defined Contribution Plan

A **defined contribution plan** requires that a fixed amount of money be invested for the employee's behalf during the employee's working years. In a defined contribution plan, the employer is required to make annual pension contributions. There is no promise of future pension payments, however, so the employee bears the investment risk in a defined contribution plan. The employer's cost is debited to *Pension Expense*. To illustrate, assume that the pension plan of Flossmoor Industries requires a contribution equal to 10% of employee annual salaries. The entry to record the transaction, assuming $500,000 of annual salaries, is as follows:

Dec.	31	Pension Expense	50,000 00	
		Cash		50,000 00
		Contributed 10% of annual salaries to pension plan.		

Once Flossmoor makes the annual contribution to the pension fund, its obligation is completed. The employee's final pension will depend on the investment results earned by the pension fund on the contributed balances.

REAL WORLD One of the more popular defined contribution pension plans is the *401K plan*. Under this plan, employees may contribute a limited part of their income to investments, such as mutual funds. A 401K plan offers employees two advantages: (1) the tax on the contribution is deferred (within limits), and (2) future investment earnings are tax deferred until withdrawn at retirement. In addition, for approximately 90% of the 401K plans, the employer matches some portion of the employee's contribution. For example, if the plan has a 50% matching feature, then each $1 contributed by the employee will be matched with a $0.50 contribution by the employer. Many financial planners advise employees to contribute to a 401K plan because of these benefits.

Defined Benefit Plan

Employers may choose to promise employees a fixed annual pension benefit at retirement, based on years of service and compensation levels. An example would be a promise to pay an annual pension based on a formula, such as the following:

1.5% × years of service × average salary for most recent 3 years prior to retirement

Pension benefits based on a formula are termed a **defined benefit plan**. Unlike a defined contribution plan, the employer bears the investment risk in funding a future retirement income benefit. As a result, many companies are replacing their defined benefit plans with defined contribution plans.

The number of defined contribution plans has been increasing, while defined benefit plans have been declining. In 1996, 83% of all plans were structured as defined contribution plans. This was up from 67% three years earlier.

The accounting for defined benefit plans is usually very complex due to the uncertainties of projecting future pension obligations. These obligations depend upon such factors as employee life expectancies, employee turnover, expected employee compensation levels, and investment income on pension contributions.

The pension cost of a defined benefit plan is debited to *Pension Expense*. The amount funded is credited to *Cash*. Any unfunded amount is credited to *Unfunded Pension Liability*. For example, assume that the pension plan of Hinkle Co. requires an annual pension cost of $80,000, based on an estimate of the future benefit obligation. Further assume that Hinkle Co. pays $60,000 to the pension fund. The entry to record this transaction is as follows:

Dec.	31	Pension Expense	80 000 00	
		Cash		60 000 00
		Unfunded Pension Liability		20 000 00
		To record annual pension cost and		
		contribution to pension plan.		

Many companies have underfunded defined benefit pension plans. The following companies have a large unfunded pension liability:

Company	Unfunded Pension Liability (in millions)
General Motors	$2,677
Bethlehem Steel	1,907
LTV Corporation	1,245
Navistar	960
Sears, Roebuck & Co.	446

Source: Pension Benefit Guarantee Corporation, 1996 Watch List.

If the unfunded pension liability is to be paid within one year, it will be classified as a current liability. That portion of the liability to be paid beyond one year is a long-term liability.

Postretirement Benefits Other than Pensions

In addition to the pension benefits described above, employees may earn rights to other **postretirement benefits** from their employer. Such benefits may include dental care, eye care, medical care, life insurance, tuition assistance, tax services, and legal services for employees or their dependents. The amount of the annual benefits expense is based upon health statistics of the workforce. This amount is recorded by debiting *Postretirement Benefits Expense*. *Cash* is credited for the same amount if the benefits are fully funded. If the benefits are not fully funded, a postretirement benefits plan liability account is credited. Thus, the accounting for postretirement health benefits is very similar to that of defined benefit pension plans.

A business's financial statements should fully disclose the nature of its postretirement benefit obligations. These disclosures are usually included as footnotes to the financial statements. The complex nature of accounting for postretirement benefits is described in more advanced accounting courses.

FINANCIAL ANALYSIS AND INTERPRETATION

OBJECTIVE 7

Use the quick ratio to analyze the ability of a business to pay its current liabilities.

A business must be able to pay its current liabilities within a short period of time, usually one year. One measure of its ability to make these payments is the **quick ratio** or **acid-test ratio**. The quick ratio is computed as follows:

$$\text{Quick Ratio} = \frac{\text{Quick Assets}}{\text{Current Liabilities}}$$

The quick ratio measures the "instant" debt-paying ability of a company, using quick assets. Quick assets are cash, cash equivalents, and receivables that can quickly be converted into cash. It is often considered desirable to have a quick ratio exceeding 1. A ratio less than 1 would indicate that current liabilities cannot be covered by cash and "near cash" assets.

To illustrate, assume that Noble Co. and Hart Co. have the following quick assets, current liabilities, and quick ratios:

	Noble Co.	Hart Co.
Quick assets:		
Cash	$100,000	$ 55,000
Cash equivalents	47,000	65,000
Accounts receivable (net)	84,000	472,000
Total	$231,000	$592,000
Current liabilities:		
Accounts payable	$125,000	$427,000
Wages payable	65,000	120,000
Employees federal income tax payable	18,000	36,000
Social security tax payable	3,025	7,200
Medicare tax payable	975	1,800
Notes payable	8,000	148,000
Total	$220,000	$740,000
Quick ratio	1.05	0.8

As you can see, Noble Co. has quick assets in excess of current liabilities, or a quick ratio of 1.05. The ratio exceeds 1, indicating that the quick assets should be sufficient to meet current liabilities. Hart Co., however, has a quick ratio of 0.8. Its quick assets will not be sufficient to cover the current liabilities. Hart could solve this problem by working with a bank to convert its short-term debt of $148,000 into a long-term obligation. This would remove the notes payable from current liabilities. If Hart did this, then its quick ratio would improve to 1 ($592,000 ÷ $592,000), which would be just sufficient for quick assets to cover current liabilities.

ENCORE

A recent survey found that 66% of individuals believe that their standard of living at retirement will be the same or higher than during their current working years. Yet, a third of these respondents don't have a formal savings plan for retirement. One-fourth of these respondents believe that they will need to save only $100,000 in order to maintain their lifestyle in retirement. However, experts believe that today's 25-year-old will need savings of $750,000 to $1 million to support a basic retirement, given increased life expectancies and inflation. How do you save this much money? The two keys to savings success are (1) save regularly, such as monthly or quarterly, even if it's a small amount, and (2) start early. For example, to have the same retirement income as a 25-year-old saving $100 per month, a 30-year-old would need to save $200 per month. Waiting until you are 35 years old would require saving $400 per month. Every five years of delay requires doubling the necessary contribution. This is the power of compound interest. Therefore, the worst strategy is to begin retirement saving at middle age. Unfortunately, according to one survey, 41% of workers age 25 to 34 who are eligible for defined contribution pension plans, such as a 401K, do not take advantage of them.

So how much would a 25-year-old need to save monthly to reach the $1 million mark? There are many assumptions that go into such a calculation. Let's assume that an individual begins saving $150 per month at the age of 25, earns 8% on these savings, increases the amount contributed by 5% per year (to match salary increases), and retires at the age of 65. Under these assumptions, the individual would accumulate $975,000 by age 65. What would be the retirement savings if the assumptions were changed so that the savings plan began at age 35, 45, or 55? The graph at the right shows what happens to the savings amount. As you can see, time is money. Beginning just 10 years later at age 35 reduces the accumulated savings by over 60%, to approximately $374,000.

Retirement planning work sheets are available from a number of mutual fund companies on the Internet. One easy-to-use work sheet is provided at the Web site of **T. Rowe Price, www.troweprice.com.** ■

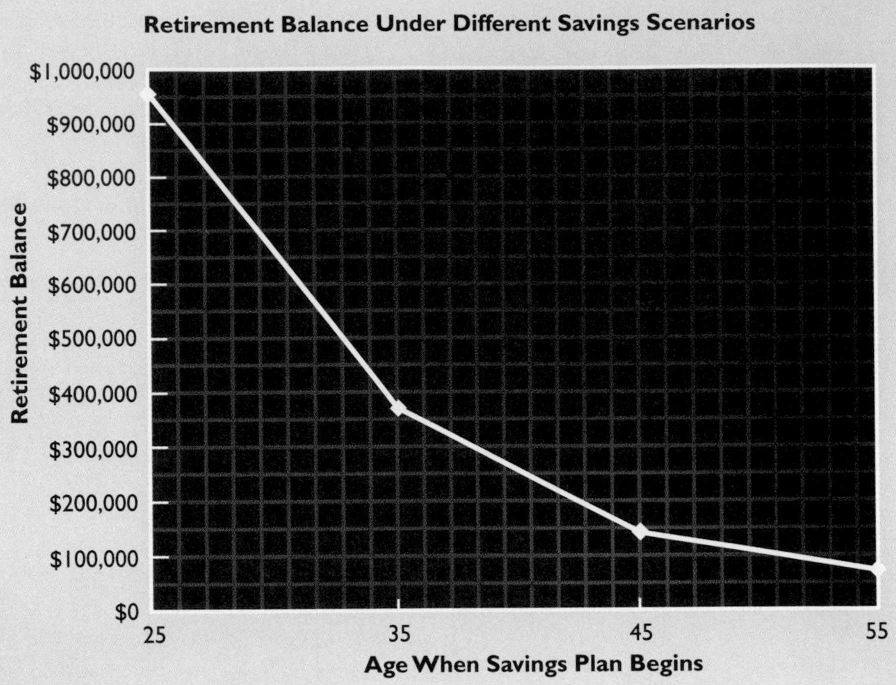

KEY POINTS

1 Define and give examples of current liabilities.

Current liabilities are obligations that are to be paid out of current assets and are due within a short time, usually within one year. Current liabilities arise from either (1) receiving goods or services prior to making payment or (2) receiving payment prior to delivering goods or services.

2 Journalize entries for short-term notes payable.

A note issued to a creditor to temporarily satisfy an account payable is recorded as a debit to *Accounts Payable* and a credit to *Notes Payable*. At the time the note is paid, *Notes Payable* and *Interest Expense* are debited and *Cash* is credited. Notes may also be issued to purchase merchandise or other assets or to borrow money from a bank. When a discounted note is issued, *Interest Expense* is debited for the interest deduction at the time of issuance, an asset account is debited for the proceeds, and *Notes Payable* is credited for the face value of the note. The face value and the maturity value of a discounted note are equal.

3 Describe the accounting treatment for contingent liabilities and journalize entries for product warranties.

A contingent liability is a potential obligation that results from a past transaction but depends on a future event. If the contingent liability is both probable and estimable, the liability should be recorded. If the contingent liability is reasonably possible or is not estimable, it should be disclosed in the footnotes to the financial statements. An example of a recordable contingent liability is product warranties. If a company grants a warranty on a product, an estimated warranty expense and liability should be recorded in the period of the sale. The expense and the liability are recorded by debiting *Product Warranty Expense* and crediting *Product Warranty Payable*.

4 Determine employer liabilities for payroll, including liabilities arising from employee earnings and deductions from earnings.

An employer's liability for payroll is calculated by determining employees' total earnings for a payroll period, including overtime pay. From this amount employee deductions are subtracted to arrive at the net pay to be paid each employee. The employer's liabilities for employee deductions are recognized at the time the payroll is recorded. Most employers also incur liabilities for payroll taxes, such as social security tax, Medicare tax, federal unemployment compensation tax, and state unemployment compensation tax.

5 Describe payroll accounting systems that use a payroll register, employee earnings records, and a general journal.
The payroll register is used in assembling and summarizing the data needed for each payroll period. The data recorded in the payroll register include the number of hours worked and the earnings and deduction data for each employee. The payroll register also includes columns for accumulating total wages or salaries to be debited to the various expense accounts. It is supported by a detailed payroll record for each employee, called an employee's earnings record.

6 Journalize entries for employee fringe benefits, including vacation pay and pensions.
Fringe benefits are expenses of the period in which the employees earn the benefits. Fringe benefits are recorded by debiting an expense account and crediting a liability account. For example, the entry to record accrued vacation pay debits *Vacation Pay Expense* and credits *Vacation Pay Payable.*

7 Use the quick ratio to analyze the ability of a business to pay its current liabilities.
The quick ratio or acid-test ratio is a measure of a business's ability to pay current liabilities within a short period of time. The quick ratio is quick assets divided by current liabilities. A quick ratio exceeding 1 is usually desirable.

ILLUSTRATIVE PROBLEM

Selected transactions of Taylor Company, completed during the fiscal year ended December 31, are as follows:

Mar. 1. Purchased merchandise on account from Kelvin Co., $20,000.
Apr. 10. Issued a 60-day, 12% note for $20,000 to Kelvin Co. on account.
June 9. Paid Kelvin Co. the amount owed on the note of April 10.
Aug. 1. Issued a $50,000, 90-day note to Harold Co. in exchange for a building. Harold Co. discounted the note at 15%.
Oct. 30. Paid Harold Co. the amount due on the note of August 1.
Dec. 27. Journalized the entry to record the biweekly payroll. A summary of the payroll record follows:

Salary distribution:		
Sales	$63,400	
Officers	36,600	
Office	10,000	$110,000
Deductions:		
Social security tax	$ 5,050	
Medicare tax	1,650	
Federal income tax withheld	17,600	
State income tax withheld	4,950	
Savings bond deductions	850	
Medical insurance deductions	1,120	31,220
Net amount		$ 78,780

30. Issued a check in payment of liabilities for employees' federal income tax of $17,600, social security tax of $10,100, and Medicare tax of $3,300.
31. Issued a check for $9,500 to the pension fund trustee to fully fund the pension cost for December.
31. Journalized an entry to record the employees' accrued vacation pay, $36,100.
31. Journalized an entry to record the estimated accrued product warranty liability, $37,240.

Instructions

Journalize the preceding transactions.

Solution

Mar.	1	Merchandise Inventory	20,000.00	
		Accounts Payable—Kelvin Co.		20,000.00
Apr.	10	Accounts Payable—Kelvin Co.	20,000.00	
		Notes Payable		20,000.00
June	9	Notes Payable	20,000.00	
		Interest Expense	400.00	
		Cash		20,400.00
Aug.	1	Building	48,125.00	
		Interest Expense	1,875.00	
		Notes Payable		50,000.00
Oct.	30	Notes Payable	50,000.00	
		Cash		50,000.00
Dec.	27	Sales Salaries Expense	63,400.00	
		Officers Salaries Expense	36,600.00	
		Office Salaries Expense	10,000.00	
		Social Security Tax Payable		5,050.00
		Medicare Tax Payable		1,650.00
		Employees Federal Income Tax Payable		17,600.00
		Employees State Income Tax Payable		4,950.00
		Bond Deductions Payable		850.00
		Medical Insurance Payable		1,120.00
		Salaries Payable		78,780.00
	30	Employees Federal Income Tax Payable	17,600.00	
		Social Security Income Payable	10,100.00	
		Medicare Tax Payable	3,300.00	
		Cash		31,000.00
	31	Pension Expense	9,500.00	
		Cash		9,500.00
	31	Vacation Pay Expense	36,100.00	
		Vacation Pay Payable		36,100.00
	31	Product Warranty Expense	37,240.00	
		Product Warranty Payable		37,240.00

SELF-EXAMINATION QUESTIONS

Answers at End of Chapter

Matching

Match each of the following statements with its proper term. Some terms may not be used.

A. defined benefit plan

B. defined contribution plan

E 1. A detailed record of each employee's earnings.

K 2. A multicolumn form used to assemble and summarize payroll data at the end of each payroll period.

C. **discount**
D. **discount rate**
E. **employee's earnings record**
F. **FICA tax**
G. **fringe benefit**
H. **gross pay**
I. **net pay**
J. **payroll**
K. **payroll register**
L. **postretirement benefits**
M. **proceeds**
N. **quick ratio**

A 3. A pension plan that promises employees a fixed annual pension benefit at retirement, based on years of service and compensation levels.
I 4. Gross pay less payroll deductions; the amount the employer is obligated to pay the employee.
M 5. The net amount available from discounting a note payable.
B 6. A pension plan that requires a fixed amount of money to be invested for the employee's behalf during the employee's working years.
G 7. Benefits provided to employees in addition to wages and salaries.
D 8. The rate used in computing the interest to be deducted from the maturity value of a note.
H 9. The total earnings of an employee for a payroll period.
L 10. Rights to benefits that employees earn during their term of employment, for themselves and their dependents, after they retire.
J 11. The total amount paid to employees for a certain period.
F 12. Federal Insurance Contributions Act tax used to finance federal programs for old-age and disability benefits (social security) and health insurance for the aged (Medicare).
N 13. A financial ratio that measures the ability to pay current liabilities within a short period of time.
C 14. The interest deducted from the maturity value of a note.

Multiple Choice

1. A business issued a $5,000, 60-day, 12% note to the bank. The amount due at maturity is:
   A. $4,900
   B. $5,000
   C. $5,100
   D. $5,600

2. A business issued a $5,000, 60-day note to a supplier, which discounted the note at 12%. The proceeds are:
   A. $4,400
   B. $4,900
   C. $5,000
   D. $5,100

3. An employee's rate of pay is $20 per hour, with time and a half for all hours worked in excess of 40 during a week. The social security rate is 6.0% on the first $70,000 of annual earnings, and the Medicare rate is 1.5% on all earnings. The following additional data are available:

Hours worked during current week	45
Year's cumulative earnings prior to current week	$69,400
Federal income tax withheld	$212

   Based on these data, the amount of the employee's net pay for the current week is:
   A. $620.50
   B. $641.50
   C. $666.75
   D. $687.75

4. Which of the following taxes are employers usually not required to withhold from employees?
   A. Federal income tax
   B. Federal unemployment compensation tax
   C. Medicare tax
   D. State and local income tax

5. Within limitations on the maximum earnings subject to the tax, employers do not incur operating costs for which of the following payroll taxes?
   A. Social security tax
   B. Federal unemployment compensation tax
   C. State unemployment compensation tax
   D. Employees' federal income tax

CLASS DISCUSSION QUESTIONS

1. What two types of transactions cause most current liabilities?
2. When are short-term notes payable issued?
3. When should the liability associated with a product warranty be recorded? Discuss.
4. **Compaq Computer Corporation** reported $469 million of product warranties in the current liabilities section of its December 31, 1996 balance sheet. How would costs of repairing a defective product be recorded?

5. The "Questions and Answers Technical Hotline" in the *Journal of Accountancy* included the following question:

   Several years ago, Company B instituted legal action against Company A. Under a memorandum of settlement and agreement, Company A agreed to pay Company B a total of $17,500 in three installments—$5,000 on March 1, $7,500 on July 1, and the remaining $5,000 on December 31. Company A paid the first two installments during its fiscal year ended September 30. Should the unpaid amount of $5,000 be presented as a current liability at September 30?

   How would you answer this question?
6. What programs are funded by the FICA (Federal Insurance Contributions Act) tax?
7. a. Identify the federal taxes that most employers are required to withhold from employees.
   b. Give the titles of the accounts to which the amounts withheld are credited.
8. For each of the following payroll-related taxes, indicate whether there is a ceiling on the annual earnings subject to the tax: (a) social security tax, (b) Medicare tax, (c) federal income tax, (d) federal unemployment compensation tax.
9. Why are deductions from employees' earnings classified as liabilities for the employer?
10. Do payroll taxes levied against employers become liabilities at the time the liabilities for wages are incurred or at the time the wages are paid?
11. Taylor Company, with 20 employees, is expanding operations. It is trying to decide whether to hire one employee full-time for $25,000 or two employees part-time for a total of $25,000. Would any of the employer's payroll taxes discussed in this chapter have a bearing on this decision? Explain.
12. For each of the following payroll-related taxes, indicate whether they generally apply to (a) employees only, (b) employers only, (c) both employees and employers:
    1. Social security tax
    2. Medicare tax
    3. Federal income tax
    4. Federal unemployment compensation tax
    5. State unemployment compensation tax
13. What are the principal reasons for using a special payroll checking account?
14. In a payroll system, what type of input data are referred to as (a) constants, (b) variables?
15. To strengthen internal controls, what department should provide written authorizations for the addition of names to the payroll?
16. Explain how a payroll system that is properly designed and operated tends to ensure that (a) wages paid are based on hours actually worked and (b) payroll checks are not issued to fictitious employees.
17. To match revenues and expenses properly, should the expense for employee vacation pay be recorded in the period during which the vacation privilege is earned or during the period in which the vacation is taken? Discuss.
18. Identify several factors that influence the future pension obligation of an employer under a defined benefit pension plan.
19. Where should the unfunded pension liability from a defined benefit pension plan be reported on the balance sheet?
20. What are some examples of postretirement benefits other than pensions that employees may earn for themselves and their dependents?

Warren Reeve Fess

Resources for Your Success On-Line at warren.swcollege.com

Remember! If you need additional help, visit South-Western's Web site. See page 26 for a description of the online and printed materials that are available.

EXERCISES

Exercise 11–1
Current liabilities
Objective 1

✓ Total current liabilities, $130,150

Tech World Magazine Inc. sold 3,200 annual subscriptions of *Tech World* for $36 during December 2000. These new subscribers will receive monthly issues, beginning in January 2001. In addition, the business had taxable income of $125,000 during the first calendar quarter of 2001. The federal tax rate is 35%. A quarterly tax payment will be made on April 7, 2001.

Prepare the current liabilities section of the balance sheet for Tech World Magazine Inc. on March 31, 2001.

Exercise 11–2
Entries for discounting notes payable
Objective 2

Star Bright Lighting Co. issues a 60-day note for $300,000 to Builtwell Wholesale Supply Co. for merchandise inventory. Builtwell discounts the note at 9%.

a. Journalize the borrower's entries to record:
   1. the issuance of the note.
   2. the payment of the note at maturity.
b. Journalize the creditor's entries to record:
   1. the receipt of the note.
   2. the receipt of the payment of the note at maturity.

Exercise 11–3
Evaluate alternative notes
Objective 2

✓ a. $2,000

A borrower has two alternatives for a loan: (1) issue an $80,000, 90-day, 10% note or (2) issue an $80,000, 90-day note that the creditor discounts at 10%.

a. Calculate the amount of the interest expense for each option.
b. Determine the proceeds received by the borrower in each situation.
c. Which alternative is more favorable to the borrower? Explain.

Exercise 11–4
Entries for notes payable
Objective 2

A business issued a 60-day, 12% note for $25,000 to a creditor on account. Journalize the entries to record (a) the issuance of the note and (b) the payment of the note at maturity, including interest.

Exercise 11–5
Fixed asset purchases with note
Objective 2

On June 30, Mario Game Company purchased land for $250,000 and a building for $730,000, paying $280,000 cash and issuing an 8% note for the balance, secured by a mortgage on the property. The terms of the note provide for 20 semiannual payments of $35,000 on the principal plus the interest accrued from the date of the preceding payment. Journalize the entry to record (a) the transaction on June 30, (b) the payment of the first installment on December 31, and (c) the payment of the second installment the following June 30.

Exercise 11–6
Accrued product warranty
Objective 3

Precision Audio Company warrants its products for one year. The estimated product warranty is 3% of sales. Assume that sales were $400,000 for January. In February, a customer received warranty repairs requiring $200 of parts and $600 of labor.

a. Journalize the adjusting entry required at January 31, the end of the first month of the current year, to record the accrued product warranty.
b. Journalize the entry to record the warranty work provided in February.

Exercise 11–7
Contingent liabilities
Objective 3

Several months ago, Endurance Battery Company experienced a hazardous materials spill at one of its plants. As a result, the Environmental Protection Agency (EPA) fined the company $150,000. The company is contesting the fine. In addition, an employee is seeking $600,000 damages related to the spill. Lastly, a homeowner has sued the company for $100,000. The homeowner lives 20 miles from the plant, but believes that the incident has reduced the home's resale value by $100,000.

Endurance Battery's legal counsel believes that it is probable that the EPA fine will stand. In addition, counsel indicates that an out-of-court settlement of $300,000 has recently been reached with the employee. The final papers will be signed next week. Counsel believes that the homeowner's case is much weaker and will be decided in favor of Endurance. Other litigation related to the spill is possible, but the damage amounts are uncertain.

a. Journalize the contingent liabilities associated with the hazardous materials spill.
b. Prepare a footnote disclosure relating to this incident.

Exercise 11–8
Calculate payroll

Objective 4

✓ b. Net pay, $786.50

An employee earns $20 per hour and 1½ times that rate for all hours in excess of 40 hours per week. Assume that the employee worked 50 hours during the week, and that the gross pay prior to the current week totaled $59,760. Assume further that the social security tax rate was 6.0% (on earnings up to $70,000), the Medicare tax rate was 1.5%, and federal income tax to be withheld was $231.

a. Determine the gross pay for the week.
b. Determine the net pay for the week.

Exercise 11–9
Calculate payroll

Objective 4

✓ Administrator net pay, $853.20

Prism Business Consultants has three employees—a consultant, a computer programmer, and an administrator. The following payroll information is available for each employee:

	Consultant	Computer Programmer	Administrator
Regular earnings rate	$3,000 per week	$28 per hour	$22 per hour
Overtime earnings rate	Not applicable	1½ times hourly rate	1½ times hourly rate
Gross pay prior to current pay period	$108,700	$69,100	$39,100
Number of withholding allowances	1	0	3

For the current pay period, the computer programmer worked 43 hours and the administrator worked 48 hours. For the current pay period, the federal income tax withheld for the consultant was $840. The federal income tax withheld for the computer programmer and the administrator can be determined from the wage bracket withholding table in Exhibit 3 in the chapter. Assume further that the social security tax rate was 6.0% on the first $70,000 of annual earnings, and the Medicare tax rate was 1.5%.

Determine the gross pay and the net pay for each of the three employees for the current pay period.

Exercise 11–10
Summary payroll data

Objectives 4, 5

✓ a. (3) Total earnings, $200,000

In the following summary of data for a payroll period, some amounts have been intentionally omitted:

Earnings:	
1. At regular rate	?
2. At overtime rate	$ 28,500
3. Total earnings	?
Deductions:	
4. Social security tax	11,500
5. Medicare tax	3,000
6. Income tax withheld	28,200
7. Medical insurance	1,050
8. Union dues	?
9. Total deductions	45,000
10. Net amount paid	155,000
Accounts debited:	
11. Factory Wages	124,300
12. Sales Salaries	?
13. Office Salaries	34,300

a. Calculate the amounts omitted in lines (1), (3), (8), and (12).
b. Journalize the entry to record the payroll accrual.
c. Journalize the entry to record the payment of the payroll.
d. From the data given in this exercise and your answer to (a), would you conclude that this payroll was paid sometime during the first few weeks of the calendar year? Explain.

Exercise 11–11
Payroll internal control procedures

Objective 5

Memphis Sounds is a retail store specializing in the sale of jazz compact discs and cassettes. The store employs 3 full-time and 10 part-time workers. The store's weekly payroll averages $1,800 for all 13 workers.

Memphis Sounds uses a personal computer to assist in preparing paychecks. Each week, the store's accountant collects employee time cards and enters the hours worked into the payroll program. The payroll program calculates each employee's pay and prints a paycheck. The accountant uses a check-signing machine to sign the paychecks. Next, the store's owner authorizes the transfer of funds from the store's regular bank account to the payroll account.

For the week of May 10, the accountant accidentally recorded 400 hours worked instead of 40 hours for one of the full-time employees.

Does Memphis Sounds have internal controls in place to catch this error? If so, how will this error be detected?

Exercise 11–12
Internal control procedures

Objective 5

Sure-Grip Tools is a small manufacturer of home workshop power tools. The company employs 30 production workers and 10 administrative persons. The following procedures are used to process the company's weekly payroll:

a. Whenever a salaried employee is terminated, Personnel authorizes Payroll to remove the employee from the payroll system. However, this procedure is not required when an hourly worker is terminated. Hourly employees only receive a paycheck if their time cards show hours worked. The computer automatically drops an employee from the payroll system when that employee has six consecutive weeks with no hours worked.
b. Whenever an employee receives a pay raise, the supervisor must fill out a wage adjustment form, which is signed by the company president. This form is used to change the employee's wage rate in the payroll system.
c. All employees are required to record their hours worked by clocking in and out on a time clock. Employees must clock out for lunch break. Due to congestion around the time clock area at lunch time, management has not objected to having one employee clock in and out for an entire department.
d. Paychecks are signed by using a check-signing machine. This machine is located in the main office, so that it can be easily accessed by anyone needing a check signed.
e. Sure-Grip maintains a separate checking account for payroll checks. Each week, the total net pay for all employees is transferred from the company's regular bank account to the payroll account.

State whether each of the procedures is appropriate or inappropriate after considering the principles of internal control. If a procedure is inappropriate, describe the appropriate procedure.

Exercise 11–13
Payroll tax entries

Objective 5

✓ a. $36,015

According to a summary of the payroll of Tender Heart Publishing Co., $460,000 was subject to the 6.0% social security tax and $510,000 was subject to the 1.5% Medicare tax. Also, $15,000 was subject to state and federal unemployment taxes.

a. Calculate the employer's payroll taxes, using the following rates: state unemployment, 4.3%; federal unemployment, 0.8%.
b. Journalize the entry to record the accrual of payroll taxes.

Exercise 11–14
Payroll procedures

Objective 5

What's Wrong WITH THIS?

The fiscal year for Homestead Stores Inc. ends on June 30. In addition, the company computes and reports payroll taxes on a fiscal-year basis. Thus, social security and FUTA maximum earnings limitations apply to the fiscal-year payroll.

What is wrong with these procedures for accounting for payroll taxes?

Exercise 11–15
Accrued vacation pay

Objective 6

A business provides its employees with varying amounts of vacation per year, depending on the length of employment. The estimated amount of the current year's vacation pay is $187,200. Journalize the adjusting entry required on January 31, the end of the first month of the current year, to record the accrued vacation pay.

Exercise 11–16
Pension plan entries
Objective 6

Forever Memories Inc. operates a chain of photography stores. The company maintains a defined contribution pension plan for its employees. The plan requires quarterly installments to be paid to the funding agent, Interstate Insurance Company, by the fifteenth of the month following the end of each quarter. Assuming that the pension cost is $175,000 for the quarter ended December 31, journalize entries to record (a) the accrued pension liability on December 31 and (b) the payment to the funding agent on January 15.

Exercise 11–17
Quick ratio
Objective 7

REAL WORLD

HAT

The financial statements for **Hershey Foods Corporation** are presented in Appendix G at the end of the text.

a. Compute the quick ratio as of December 31, 1995 and 1996.
b. What conclusions can be drawn from these data as to Hershey's ability to meet its current liabilities?

PROBLEMS SERIES A

Problem 11–1A
Liability transactions
Objectives 2, 3

HAT
GENERAL LEDGER

The following items were selected from among the transactions completed by Renaissance Products Co. during the current year:

Feb. 15. Purchased merchandise on account from Ranier Co., $14,000, terms n/30.
Mar. 17. Issued a 30-day, 9% note for $14,000 to Ranier Co., on account.
Apr. 16. Paid Ranier Co. the amount owed on the note of March 17.
July 15. Borrowed $20,000 from Security Bank, issuing a 90-day, 12% note.
25. Purchased tools by issuing a $60,000, 120-day note to Sun Supply Co., which discounted the note at the rate of 13%.
Oct. 13. Paid Security Bank the interest due on the note of July 15 and renewed the loan by issuing a new 30-day, 15% note for $20,000. (Journalize both the debit and credit to the notes payable account.)
Nov. 12. Paid Security Bank the amount due on the note of October 13.
22. Paid Sun Supply Co. the amount due on the note of July 25.
Dec. 1. Purchased office equipment from Valley Equipment Co. for $75,000, paying $15,000 and issuing a series of ten 12% notes for $6,000 each, coming due at 30-day intervals.
17. Settled a product liability lawsuit with a customer for $35,000, payable in January. Renaissance accrued the loss in a litigation claims payable account.
31. Paid the amount due Valley Equipment Co. on the first note in the series issued on December 1.

Instructions

1. Journalize the transactions.
2. Journalize the adjusting entry for each of the following accrued expenses at the end of the current year: (a) product warranty cost, $15,450; (b) interest on the nine remaining notes owed to Valley Equipment Co.

Problem 11–2A
Entries for payroll and payroll taxes
Objectives 4, 5

✓ 1. (b) Dr. Payroll Taxes Expense, $22,950

The following information about the payroll for the week ended December 30 was obtained from the records of Wallace Co.:

Salaries:		Deductions:	
Sales salaries	$185,000	Income tax withheld	$66,000
Warehouse salaries	36,800	Social security tax withheld	17,400
Office salaries	108,200	Medicare tax withheld	4,950
	$330,000	U.S. savings bonds	19,300
		Group insurance	28,700

Tax rates assumed:
Social security, 6% on first $70,000 of employee annual earnings
Medicare, 1.5%
State unemployment (employer only), 4.2%
Federal unemployment (employer only), 0.8%

Instructions

1. Assuming that the payroll for the last week of the year is to be paid on December 31, journalize the following entries:
   a. December 30, to record the payroll.
   b. December 30, to record the employer's payroll taxes on the payroll to be paid on December 31. Of the total payroll for the last week of the year, $12,000 is subject to unemployment compensation taxes.
2. Assuming that the payroll for the last week of the year is to be paid on January 5 of the following fiscal year, journalize the following entries:
   a. December 30, to record the payroll.
   b. January 5, to record the employer's payroll taxes on the payroll to be paid on January 5.

Problem 11–3A
Wage and tax statement data on employer FICA tax

Objectives 4, 5

SPREADSHEET

✓ 2. (e) $23,160

Sunrise Bread Company began business on January 2 of last year. Salaries were paid to employees on the last day of each month, and social security tax, Medicare tax, and federal income tax were withheld in the required amounts. An employee who is hired in the middle of the month receives half the monthly salary for that month. All required payroll tax reports were filed, and the correct amount of payroll taxes was remitted by the company for the calendar year. Before the Wage and Tax Statements (Form W-2) could be prepared for distribution to employees and for filing with the Social Security Administration, the employees' earnings records were inadvertently destroyed.

None of the employees resigned or were discharged during the year, and there were no changes in salary rates. The social security tax was withheld at the rate of 6.0% on the first $70,000 of salary and Medicare tax at the rate of 1.5% on salary. Data on dates of employment, salary rates, and employees' income taxes withheld, which are summarized as follows, were obtained from personnel records and payroll records.

Employee	Date First Employed	Monthly Salary	Monthly Income Tax Withheld
Alvarez	Jan. 16	$6,400	$1,376.00
Conrad	Nov. 1	3,000	544.20
Felix	Jan. 2	2,500	447.25
Lydall	July 16	4,200	783.30
Porter	Jan. 2	6,700	1,497.45
Soong	May 1	2,800	463.40
Walker	Feb. 16	5,000	1,027.00

Instructions

1. Calculate the amounts to be reported on each employee's Wage and Tax Statement (Form W-2) for the year, arranging the data in the following form:

Employee	Gross Earnings	Federal Income Tax Withheld	Social Security Tax Withheld	Medicare Tax Withheld

2. Calculate the following employer payroll taxes for the year: (a) social security; (b) Medicare; (c) state unemployment compensation at 4.2% on the first $7,000 of each employee's earnings; (d) federal unemployment compensation at 0.8% on the first $7,000 of each employee's earnings; (e) total.

If the working papers correlating with this textbook are not used, omit Problem 11–4A.

Problem 11–4A
Payroll register

Objectives 4, 5

✓ 3. Dr. Payroll Taxes Expense, $643.75

The payroll register for Argentina Leather Goods Co. for the week ended December 12, 2000, is presented in the working papers.

Instructions

1. Journalize the entry to record the payroll for the week.
2. Journalize the entry to record the issuance of the checks to employees.

3. Journalize the entry to record the employer's payroll taxes for the week. Assume the following tax rates: state unemployment, 3.6%; federal unemployment, 0.8%. Of the earnings, $1,250 is subject to unemployment taxes.
4. Journalize the entry to record a check issued on Dec. 15 to Second National Bank in payment of employees' income taxes, $1,422.18, social security taxes, $942.00, and Medicare taxes, $235.50.

Problem 11–5A
Payroll register

Objectives 4, 5

SPREADSHEET

✓ 1. Total net amount paid, $6,745.68

The following data for Grimsley Electrical Supplies Inc. relate to the payroll for the week ended December 7, 2000:

Employee	Hours Worked	Hourly Rate	Weekly Salary	Federal Income Tax	U.S. Savings Bonds	Accumulated Earnings, Nov. 30
M	48.00	$28.00		$321.00	$35.00	$61,100.00
N	20.00	21.00		65.00		12,600.00
O			$1,500.00	337.00	50.00	70,500.00
P	40.00	18.00		140.00	15.00	33,840.00
Q	42.00	20.00		112.00	10.00	37,600.00
R	45.00	19.50		168.00		42,300.00
S	40.00	16.00		110.00	15.00	30,080.00
T			1,000.00	217.00		47,000.00
U	50.00	32.00		401.00	40.00	73,100.00

Employees O and T are office staff, and all of the other employees are sales personnel. All sales personnel are paid $1\frac{1}{2}$ times the regular rate for all hours in excess of 40 hours per week. The social security tax rate is 6.0% on the first $70,000 of each employee's annual earnings, and Medicare tax is 1.5% of each employee's annual earnings. The next payroll check to be used is No. 818.

Instructions

1. Prepare a payroll register for Grimsley Electrical Supplies Inc. for the week ended December 7, 2000.
2. Journalize the entry to record the payroll for the week.

Problem 11–6A
Payroll accounts and year-end entries

Objectives 4, 5, 6

HAT
GENERAL LEDGER

The following accounts, with the balances indicated, appear in the ledger of Mid States CableView Co. on December 1 of the current year:

211	Salaries Payable	—
212	Social Security Tax Payable	$ 7,784
213	Medicare Tax Payable	2,048
214	Employees Federal Income Tax Payable	12,632
215	Employees State Income Tax Payable	12,291
216	State Unemployment Tax Payable	1,240
217	Federal Unemployment Tax Payable	325
218	Bond Deductions Payable	1,400
219	Medical Insurance Payable	4,500
611	Operations Salaries Expense	915,200
711	Officers Salaries Expense	365,300
712	Office Salaries Expense	221,700
719	Payroll Taxes Expense	119,566

The following transactions relating to payroll, payroll deductions, and payroll taxes occurred during December:

Dec. 2. Issued Check No. 728 for $1,400 to First National Bank to purchase U.S. savings bonds for employees.

3. Issued Check No. 729 to First National Bank for $22,464, in payment of $7,784 of social security tax, $2,048 of Medicare tax, and $12,632 of employees' federal income tax due.

Dec. 14. Journalized the entry to record the biweekly payroll. A summary of the payroll record follows:

Salary distribution:		
Operations	$42,400	
Officers	16,220	
Office	10,450	$69,070
Deductions:		
Social security tax	$ 3,799	
Medicare tax	1,036	
Federal income tax withheld	12,294	
State income tax withheld	3,108	
Savings bond deductions	700	
Medical insurance deductions	750	21,687
Net amount		$47,383

14. Issued Check No. 738 in payment of the net amount of the biweekly payroll.
14. Journalized the entry to record payroll taxes on employees' earnings of December 14: social security tax, $3,799; Medicare tax, $1,036; state unemployment tax, $286; federal unemployment tax, $77.
17. Issued Check No. 744 to First National Bank for $21,964, in payment of $7,598 of social security tax, $2,072 of Medicare tax, and $12,294 of employees' federal income tax due.
18. Issued Check No. 750 to Pico Insurance Company for $4,500, in payment of the semiannual premium on the group medical insurance policy.
28. Journalized the entry to record the biweekly payroll. A summary of the payroll record follows:

Salary distribution:		
Operations	$40,800	
Officers	16,350	
Office	10,580	$67,730
Deductions:		
Social security tax	$ 3,657	
Medicare tax	1,016	
Federal income tax withheld	12,056	
State income tax withheld	3,048	
Savings bond deduction	700	20,477
Net amount		$47,253

28. Issued Check No. 782 in payment of the net amount of the biweekly payroll.
28. Journalized the entry to record payroll taxes on employees' earnings of December 28: social security tax, $3,657; Medicare tax, $1,016; state unemployment tax, $174; federal unemployment tax, $38.
30. Issued Check No. 791 to First National Bank for $1,400 to purchase U.S. savings bonds for employees.
30. Issued Check No. 792 for $18,447 to First National Bank in payment of employees' state income tax due on December 31.
31. Paid $46,000 of the annual pension cost of $50,000. (Record both the payment and unfunded pension liability.)

Instructions

1. Journalize the transactions.
2. Journalize the following adjusting entries on December 31:
   a. Salaries accrued: operations salaries, $4,080; officers salaries, $1,635; office salaries, $1,058. The payroll taxes are immaterial and are not accrued.
   b. Vacation pay, $12,500.

PROBLEMS SERIES B

Problem 11–1B
Liability transactions

Objectives 2, 3

GENERAL LEDGER

The following items were selected from among the transactions completed by Pride Polymers during the current year:

Apr. 7. Borrowed $12,000 from First Financial Corporation, issuing a 60-day, 12% note for that amount.
May 10. Purchased equipment by issuing a $60,000, 120-day note to Milford Equipment Co., which discounted the note at the rate of 10%.
June 6. Paid First Financial Corporation the interest due on the note of April 7 and renewed the loan by issuing a new 30-day, 16% note for $12,000. (Record both the debit and credit to the notes payable account.)
July 6. Paid First Financial Corporation the amount due on the note of June 6.
Aug. 3. Purchased merchandise on account from Hamilton Co., $25,000, terms, n/30.
Sep. 2. Issued a 60-day, 15% note for $25,000 to Hamilton Co., on account.
7. Paid Milford Equipment Co. the amount due on the note of May 10.
Nov. 1. Paid Hamilton Co. the amount owed on the note of September 2.
15. Purchased store equipment from Shingo Equipment Co. for $80,000, paying $17,000 and issuing a series of seven 12% notes for $9,000 each, coming due at 30-day intervals.
Dec. 15. Paid the amount due Shingo Equipment Co. on the first note in the series issued on November 15.
21. Settled a product liability lawsuit with a customer for $50,000, to be paid in January. Pride Polymers accrued the loss in a litigation claims payable account.

Instructions

1. Journalize the transactions.
2. Journalize the adjusting entry for each of the following accrued expenses at the end of the current year:
   a. Product warranty cost, $9,500.
   b. Interest on the six remaining notes owed to Shingo Equipment Co.

Problem 11–2B
Entries for payroll and payroll taxes

Objectives 4, 5

✓ 1. (b) Dr. Payroll Taxes Expense, $32,280

The following information about the payroll for the week ended December 30 was obtained from the records of Hannah Co.:

Salaries:		Deductions:	
Sales salaries	$245,000	Income tax withheld	$104,500
Warehouse salaries	87,400	Social security tax withheld	24,120
Office salaries	165,600	Medicare tax withheld	7,470
	$498,000	U.S. savings bonds	24,400
		Group insurance	32,800

Tax rates assumed:
Social security, 6% on first $70,000 of employee annual earnings
Medicare, 1.5%
State unemployment (employer only), 3.8%
Federal unemployment (employer only), 0.8%

Instructions

1. Assuming that the payroll for the last week of the year is to be paid on December 31, journalize the following entries:
   a. December 30, to record the payroll.
   b. December 30, to record the employer's payroll taxes on the payroll to be paid on December 31. Of the total payroll for the last week of the year, $15,000 is subject to unemployment compensation taxes.
2. Assuming that the payroll for the last week of the year is to be paid on January 4 of the following fiscal year, journalize the following entries:

a. December 30, to record the payroll.
b. January 4, to record the employer's payroll taxes on the payroll to be paid on January 4.

Problem 11–3B

Wage and tax statement data and employer FICA tax

Objectives 4, 5

SPREADSHEET

✓ 2. (e) $24,701.70

Sanchez Company began business on January 2 of last year. Salaries were paid to employees on the last day of each month, and social security tax, Medicare tax, and federal income tax were withheld in the required amounts. An employee who is hired in the middle of the month receives half the monthly salary for that month. All required payroll tax reports were filed, and the correct amount of payroll taxes was remitted by the company for the calendar year. Before the Wage and Tax Statements (Form W-2) could be prepared for distribution to employees and for filing with the Social Security Administration, the employees' earnings records were inadvertently destroyed.

None of the employees resigned or were discharged during the year, and there were no changes in salary rates. The social security tax was withheld at the rate of 6.0% on the first $70,000 of salary and Medicare tax at the rate of 1.5% on salary. Data on dates of employment, salary rates, and employees' income taxes withheld, which are summarized as follows, were obtained from personnel records and payroll records.

Employee	Date First Employed	Monthly Salary	Monthly Income Tax Withheld
Albright	June 2	$5,400	$1,137.00
Charles	Jan. 2	6,500	1,426.25
Given	Mar. 1	3,700	686.35
Nelson	Jan. 2	4,200	783.30
Quinn	Nov. 15	3,800	722.00
Ramsey	Apr. 15	3,000	535.50
Wu	Jan. 16	7,000	1,564.50

Instructions

1. Calculate the amounts to be reported on each employee's Wage and Tax Statement (Form W-2) for the year, arranging the data in the following form:

Employee	Gross Earnings	Federal Income Tax Withheld	Social Security Tax Withheld	Medicare Tax Withheld

2. Calculate the following employer payroll taxes for the year: (a) social security; (b) Medicare; (c) state unemployment compensation at 3.8% on the first $7,000 of each employee's earnings; (d) federal unemployment compensation at 0.8% on the first $7,000 of each employee's earnings; (e) total.

If the working papers correlating with this textbook are not used, omit Problem 11–4B.

Problem 11–4B

Payroll register

Objectives 4, 5

✓ 3. Dr. Payroll Taxes Expense, $618.75

The payroll register for Chopin Piano Co. for the week ended December 12, 2000, is presented in the working papers.

Instructions

1. Journalize the entry to record the payroll for the week.
2. Journalize the entry to record the issuance of the checks to employees.
3. Journalize the entry to record the employer's payroll taxes for the week. Assume the following tax rates: state unemployment, 3.2%; federal unemployment, 0.8%. Of the earnings, $750 is subject to unemployment taxes.
4. Journalize the entry to record a check issued on Dec. 15 to Second National Bank in payment of employees' income taxes, $1,422.18, social security taxes, $942.00, and Medicare taxes, $235.50.

Problem 11–5B
Payroll register

Objectives 4, 5

SPREADSHEET

✓ 1. Total net amount paid, $5,545.09

The following data for Industrial Solvents Inc. relate to the payroll for the week ended December 7, 2000:

Employee	Hours Worked	Hourly Rate	Weekly Salary	Federal Income Tax	U.S. Savings Bonds	Accumulated Earnings, Nov. 30
A	46.00	$26.00		$247.00	$15.00	$51,640.00
B	40.00	18.00		136.00		38,880.00
C			$1,450.00	325.00	70.00	69,600.00
D	42.00	22.00		165.00	10.00	36,000.00
E	40.00	16.00		112.00		30,000.00
F	45.00	18.50		162.00	20.00	15,300.00
G	40.00	14.00		92.00	25.00	24,000.00
H			900.00	182.00		3,600.00
I	20.00	14.00		17.00	15.00	3,000.00

Employees C and H are office staff, and all of the other employees are sales personnel. All sales personnel are paid $1\frac{1}{2}$ times the regular rate for all hours in excess of 40 hours per week. The social security tax rate is 6.0% on the first $70,000 of each employee's annual earnings, and Medicare tax is 1.5% of each employee's annual earnings. The next payroll check to be used is No. 981.

Instructions

1. Prepare a payroll register for Industrial Solvents Inc. for the week ended December 7, 2000.
2. Journalize the entry to record the payroll for the week.

Problem 11–6B
Payroll accounts and year-end entries

Objectives 4, 5, 6

GENERAL LEDGER

The following accounts, with the balances indicated, appear in the ledger of Teton Outdoor Equipment Company on December 1 of the current year:

211	Salaries Payable	—
212	Social Security Tax Payable	$ 6,232
213	Medicare Tax Payable	1,640
214	Employees Federal Income Tax Payable	10,113
215	Employees State Income Tax Payable	9,839
216	State Unemployment Tax Payable	1,104
217	Federal Unemployment Tax Payable	288
218	Bond Deductions Payable	1,050
219	Medical Insurance Payable	3,800
611	Sales Salaries Expense	784,600
711	Officers Salaries Expense	296,700
712	Office Salaries Expense	121,300
719	Payroll Taxes Expense	96,343

The following transactions relating to payroll, payroll deductions, and payroll taxes occurred during December:

Dec. 1 Issued Check No. 728 to Pico Insurance Company for $3,800, in payment of the semiannual premium on the group medical insurance policy.

2. Issued Check No. 729 to First National Bank for $17,985, in payment for $6,232 of social security tax, $1,640 of Medicare tax, and $10,113 of employees' federal income tax due.

3. Issued Check No. 730 for $1,050 to First National Bank to purchase U.S. savings bonds for employees.

14. Journalized the entry to record the biweekly payroll. A summary of the payroll record follows:

Salary distribution:		
Sales	$36,110	
Officers	13,672	
Office	5,675	$55,457
Deductions:		
Social security tax	$ 3,050	
Medicare tax	832	
Federal income tax withheld	9,871	
State income tax withheld	2,496	
Savings bond deductions	525	
Medical insurance deductions	633	17,407
Net amount		$38,050

Dec. 14. Issued Check No. 738 in payment of the net amount of the biweekly payroll.

14. Journalized the entry to record payroll taxes on employees' earnings of December 14: social security tax, $3,050; Medicare tax, $832; state unemployment tax, $242; federal unemployment tax, $65.

17. Issued Check No. 744 to First National Bank for $17,635, in payment for $6,100 of social security tax, $1,664 of Medicare tax, and $9,871 of employees' federal income tax due.

28. Journalized the entry to record the biweekly payroll. A summary of the payroll record follows:

Salary distribution:		
Sales	$37,450	
Officers	13,600	
Office	5,820	$56,870
Deductions:		
Social security tax	$ 3,071	
Medicare tax	853	
Federal income tax withheld	10,123	
State income tax withheld	2,559	
Savings bond deduction	525	17,131
Net amount		$39,739

28. Issued Check No. 782 for the net amount of the biweekly payroll.

28. Journalized the entry to record payroll taxes on employees' earnings of December 28: social security tax, $3,071; Medicare tax, $853; state unemployment tax, $196; federal unemployment tax, $44.

30. Issued Check No. 791 for $14,894 to First National Bank, in payment of employees' state income tax due on December 31.

30. Issued Check No. 792 to First National Bank for $1,050 to purchase U.S. savings bonds for employees.

31. Paid $57,700 of the annual pension cost of $65,000. (Record both the payment and the unfunded pension liability.)

Instructions

1. Journalize the transactions.
2. Journalize the following adjusting entries on December 31:
   a. Salaries accrued: sales salaries, $3,745; officers salaries, $1,360; office salaries, $582. The payroll taxes are immaterial and are not accrued.
   b. Vacation pay, $14,200.

QUICKBOOKS PROBLEM

Payroll

This problem uses the Larry's Landscaping sample company provided with QuickBooks® 5.0. Begin by first copying *sample.qbw* into another file name, **payroll.qbw,** so that the original sample.qbw file will not be changed. You can copy the file using the copy and paste commands in your operating system. This is an important step, since we will be using the unchanged sample.qbw file later in the text.

Retrieve Larry's Landscaping by opening the file that you just created. The first time you open Larry's Landscaping, you will be in QuickBooks Navigator®. You may wish to use the Navigator to review the forms used for "Payroll and Employees." This problem will use some of these forms.

Larry's Landscaping has been in business since October of the current year. We will add some payroll transactions to those that have already been recorded and saved in the company file.

We will begin by adding a new employee. Under the "lists" menu item, select "employees." This window displays the list of present employees. Use the "employee" drop-down list in the list window to add a "new" employee. A form for employee information is opened. Fill in the form with the following information:

Address Information:

Mr. Tyrone K. Highwater
216 Bridge Road
Bayshore, CA 94326
(415) 555-2335
SS #: 432-56-1234

Payroll Information:

Regular pay, $10 per hour; overtime pay, $15 per hour (enter as two separate lines under "earnings").

Set "class" at "landscaping" from the drop-down list. Set the "pay period" to weekly from the drop-down list. Mr. Highwater is single and claims one deduction for federal and state tax purposes.

Vacation and sick pay are set at default values. Health insurance is $25 per pay period (−25 in the amount column) up to a limit of $600 for the calendar year (−600 in the limit column), and there is no employer training tax (delete line by using edit menu).

Create Payroll Check:

We will now create a payroll check for Mr. Highwater. Begin by selecting the activity "payroll," then "pay employees" (or clicking the "payroll" button on the menu bar). Deselect the "to be printed" check box. Select Tyrone K. Highwater by clicking a check mark next to his name. Change the payroll period ending and check date to December 20. Select the button "enter hours and preview check before creating." We are now ready to create the payroll check. Select "create."

The "create" window collects the payroll information needed for Mr. Highwater. Enter 40 hours of regular pay and 8 hours for overtime pay. All hours were for work performed for David Hughes (from drop-down list). The health insurance rate of $25 per pay period is automatically inserted from the payroll information entered previously. Notice how the software automatically calculates federal withholding tax, California withholding tax, social security tax, and Medicare tax.

Instructions

Open the payroll report "payroll summary by employee" from the "reports" menu item. Change the beginning and ending dates for the report from December 15 to December 20. Print the report for Tyrone Highwater. Notice that QuickBooks automatically calculates a summary of Highwater's gross pay, deductions, and net pay. In addition, all the employer payroll taxes, including social security tax (employer's portion), Medicare tax (employer's portion), FUTA, and SUTA are shown on the report. QuickBooks uses this information to prepare a check to satisfy federal payroll tax liabilities, along with automatically filling out Form 941.

COMPREHENSIVE PROBLEM 3

GENERAL LEDGER

Selected transactions completed by Wacker Co. during its first fiscal year ending December 31 were as follows:

Jan. 2. Issued a check to establish a petty cash fund of $400.
Mar. 1. Replenished the petty cash fund, based on the following summary of petty cash receipts: office supplies, $144; miscellaneous selling expense, $97; miscellaneous administrative expense, $138.
Apr. 5. Purchased $8,000 of merchandise on account, terms 1/10, n/30. The perpetual inventory system is used to account for inventory.
May 5. Paid the invoice of April 5 after the discount period had passed.
10. Received cash from daily cash sales for $8,710. The amount indicated by the cash register was $8,750.
June 2. Received a 60-day, 12% note for $40,000 on account.
Aug. 1. Received amount owed on June 2 note, plus interest at the maturity date.
3. Received $700 on account and wrote off the remainder owed on a $1,000 accounts receivable balance. (The allowance method is used in accounting for uncollectible receivables.)
28. Reinstated the account written off on August 3 and received $300 cash in full payment.
Sep. 2. Purchased land by issuing a $30,000, 90-day note to Ace Development Co., which discounted it at 12%.
Oct. 1. Traded office equipment for new equipment with a list price of $140,000. A trade-in allowance of $25,000 was received on the old equipment that had cost $80,000 and had accumulated depreciation of $50,000 as of October 1. A 120-day, 12% note was issued for the balance owed.
Nov. 30. Journalized the monthly payroll for November, based on the following data:

Salaries:		**Deductions:**	
Sales salaries	$15,500	Income tax withheld	$3,885
Office salaries	5,500	Social security tax withheld	1,260
	$21,000	Medicare tax withheld	315

Unemployment tax rates:	
State unemployment	3.8%
Federal unemployment	0.8%
Amount subject to unemployment taxes:	
State unemployment	$500
Federal unemployment	500

30. Journalized the employer's payroll taxes on the payroll.
Dec. 1. Journalized the payment of the September 2 note at maturity.
30. The pension cost for the year was $40,000, of which $36,000 was paid to the pension plan trustee.

Instructions

1. Journalize the selected transactions.
2. Based on the following data, prepare a bank reconciliation for December of the current year:
   a. Balance according to the bank statement at December 31, $89,560.
   b. Balance according to the ledger at December 31, $69,685.
   c. Checks outstanding at December 31, $34,310.
   d. Deposit in transit, not recorded by bank, $14,200.
   e. Bank debit memorandum for service charges, $55.
   f. A check for $200 in payment of an invoice was incorrectly recorded in the accounts as $20.
3. Based on the bank reconciliation prepared in (2), journalize the entry or entries to be made by Wacker Co.
4. Based on the following selected data, journalize the adjusting entries as of December 31 of the current year:
   a. Estimated uncollectible accounts at December 31, $4,220. The balance of Allowance for Doubtful Accounts at December 31 was $800 (debit).
   b. The physical inventory on December 31 indicated an inventory shrinkage of $2,600.

c. Prepaid insurance expired during the year, $14,400.
d. Office supplies used during the year, $3,900.
e. Depreciation is computed as follows:

Asset	Cost	Residual Value	Acquisition Date	Useful Life in Years	Depreciation Method Used
Buildings	$290,000	$ 0	January 2	50	Straight-line
Office Equip.	140,000	12,000	July 1	5	Straight-line
Store Equip.	90,000	10,000	January 3	8	Declining-balance (at twice the straight-line rate)

f. A patent costing $36,000 when acquired on January 2 has a remaining legal life of 9 years and is expected to have value for 6 years.
g. The cost of mineral rights was $80,000. Of the estimated deposit of 25,000 tons of ore, 4,000 tons were mined during the year.
h. Total vacation pay expense for the year, $6,000.
i. A product warranty was granted beginning December 1 and covering a one-year period. The estimated cost is 3% of sales, which totaled $390,000 in December.

5. Based on the following post-closing trial balance and other data, prepare a balance sheet in report form at December 31 of the current year.

Wacker Co.
Post-Closing Trial Balance
December 31, 2000

Petty Cash	400	
Cash	69,450	
Notes Receivable	50,000	
Accounts Receivable	194,300	
Allowance for Doubtful Accounts		4,220
Merchandise Inventory	40,250	
Prepaid Insurance	28,800	
Office Supplies	6,300	
Land	50,000	
Buildings	290,000	
Accumulated Depreciation—Buildings		5,800
Office Equipment	140,000	
Accumulated Depreciation—Office Equipment		12,800
Store Equipment	90,000	
Accumulated Depreciation—Store Equipment		22,500
Mineral Rights	80,000	
Accumulated Depletion		12,800
Patents	30,000	
Social Security Tax Payable		2,640
Medicare Tax Payable		660
Employees Federal Income Tax Payable		4,100
State Unemployment Tax Payable		45
Federal Unemployment Tax Payable		20
Salaries Payable		16,000
Accounts Payable		94,000
Product Warranty Payable		11,700
Vacation Pay Payable		6,000
Unfunded Pension Liability		4,000
Notes Payable		450,000
B. Wacker, Capital		422,215
	1,069,500	1,069,500

The following information relating to the balance sheet accounts at December 31 is obtained from supplementary records:

Notes receivable is a current asset.
The merchandise inventory is stated at cost by the LIFO method.
The product warranty payable is a current liability.
Vacation pay payable:

Current liability	$ 5,000
Long-term liability	1,000

The unfunded pension liability is a long-term liability.
Notes payable:

Current liability	$115,000
Long-term liability	335,000

6. On February 7 of the following year, the merchandise inventory was destroyed by fire. Based on the following data obtained from the accounting records, estimate the cost of the merchandise destroyed:

Jan. 1 Merchandise inventory	$ 40,250
Jan. 1–Feb. 7 Purchases (net)	235,250
Jan. 1–Feb. 7 Sales (net)	420,000
Estimated gross profit rate	40%

SPECIAL ACTIVITIES

Activity 11–1 Bennett and Barns, CPAs

Ethics and professional conduct in business

Ellen Thomson is a certified public accountant (CPA) and staff assistant for Bennett and Barns, a local CPA firm. It had been the policy of the firm to provide a holiday bonus equal to two weeks' salary to all employees. The firm's new management team announced on November 25 that a bonus equal to only one week's salary would be made available to employees this year. Ellen thought that this policy was unfair because she and her co-workers planned on the full two-week bonus. The two-week bonus had been given for ten straight years, so it seemed as though the firm had breached an implied commitment. Thus, Ellen decided that she would make up the lost bonus week by working an extra six hours of overtime per week over the next five weeks until the end of the year. Bennett and Barns' policy is to pay overtime at 150% of straight time.

Ellen's supervisor was surprised to see overtime being reported, since there is generally very little additional or unusual client service demands at the end of the calendar year. However, the overtime was not questioned, since firm employees are on the "honor system" in reporting their overtime.

Discuss whether the firm is acting in an ethical manner by changing the bonus. Is Ellen behaving in an ethical manner?

Activity 11–2 Tri-America Company

Recognizing pension expense

What do you THINK?

The annual examination of Tri-America Company's financial statements by its external public accounting firm (auditors) is nearing completion. The following conversation took place between the controller of Tri-America Company (Donald) and the audit manager from the public accounting firm (Cathy).

Cathy: You know, Donald, we are about to wrap up our audit for this fiscal year. Yet, there is one item still to be resolved.

Donald: What's that?

Cathy: Well, as you know, at the beginning of the year, Tri-America began a defined benefit pension plan. This plan promises your employees an annual payment when they retire, using a formula based on their salaries at retirement and their years of service. I believe that a pension expense should be recognized this year, equal to the amount of pension earned by your employees.

Donald: Wait a minute. I think you have it all wrong. The company doesn't have a pension expense until it actually pays the pension in cash when the employee retires. After all, some of these employees may not reach retirement, and if they don't, the company doesn't owe them anything.

Cathy: You're not really seeing this the right way. The pension is earned by your employees during their working years. You actually make the payment much later—when they retire. It's like one long accrual—much like incurring wages in one period and paying them in the next. Thus, I think that you should recognize the expense in the period the pension is earned by the employees.

Donald: Let me see if I've got this straight. I should recognize an expense this period for something that may or may not be paid to the employees in 20 or 30 years, when they finally retire. How am I supposed to determine what the expense is for the current year? The amount of the final retirement depends on many uncertainties: salary levels, employee longevity, mortality rates, and interest earned on investments to fund the pension. I don't think that an amount can be determined, even if I accepted your arguments.

Evaluate Cathy's position. Is she right or is Donald correct?

Activity 11–3 Bolton's Trucking Company

Executive bonuses and accounting methods

Chris Bolton, the owner of Bolton Trucking Company, initiated an executive bonus plan for his chief executive officer (CEO). The new plan provides a bonus to the CEO equal to 3% of the income before taxes. Upon learning of the new bonus arrangement, the CEO issued instructions to change the company's accounting for trucks. The CEO has asked the controller to make the following two changes:

a. Change from the double-declining-balance method to the straight-line method of depreciation.
b. Add 50% to the useful lives of all trucks.

Why did the CEO ask for these changes? How would you respond to the CEO's request?

Activity 11–4 Into the Real World

Salary survey

Several Internet services provide career guidance, classified employment ads, placement services, resumé posting, career questionnaires, and salary surveys. Select one of the following Internet sites to determine current average salary levels for one of your career options:

www.cfstaffing.com/salary.html	Accounting salary information
www.tripod.com/work	General career guidance, career profiles, and salary information
www.espan.com/salary	Computer, engineering, finance, and accounting salary information
www.occ.com	Online Career Center

Activity 11–5 Into the Real World

Payroll forms

Payroll accounting involves the use of government-supplied forms to account for payroll taxes. Three common forms are the W-2, Form 940, and Form 941. Form a team with several of your classmates and retrieve copies of each of these forms. They may be obtained from a local IRS office, a library, or downloaded from the Internet at **www.irs.treas.gov** (go to forms and publications). Alternatively, these forms can also be retrieved from QuickBooks® accounting software.

a. Briefly describe the purpose of each of the three forms.
b. Fill in the forms using the information provided (leaving blanks where there is no information provided). Assume that your group began a business, called Audit-Proof Tax Service, on November 1 of the current year. Each of you makes a salary of $2,000 per month and claims a single exemption. Salaries were paid on November 30 and December 31. Assume that the withholding tax was $234 per month for each person in the group.

ANSWERS TO SELF-EXAMINATION QUESTIONS

Matching

1. E	3. A	5. M	7. G	9. H	11. J	13. N	14. C
2. K	4. I	6. B	8. D	10. L	12. F		

Multiple Choice

1. **C** The maturity value is $5,100, determined as follows:

Face amount of note	$5,000
Plus interest ($5,000 × 12% × 60/360)	100
Maturity value	$5,100

2. **B** The net amount available to a borrower from discounting a note payable is called the proceeds. The proceeds of $4,900 (answer B) is determined as follows:

Face amount of note	$5,000
Less discount ($5,000 × 12% × 60/360)	100
Proceeds	$4,900

3. **D** The amount of net pay of $687.75 (answer D) is determined as follows:

Gross pay:			
40 hours at $20.		$800.00	
5 hours at $30.		150.00	$950.00
Deductions:			
Federal income tax withheld.		$212.00	
FICA:			
Social security tax ($600 × .06)	$36.00		
Medicare tax ($950 × .015)	14.25	50.25	262.25
			$687.75

4. **B** Employers are usually required to withhold a portion of their employees' earnings for payment of federal income taxes (answer A), Medicare tax (answer C), and state and local income taxes (answer D). Generally, federal unemployment compensation taxes (answer B) are levied against the employer only and thus are not deducted from employee earnings.

5. **D** The employer incurs operating costs for social security tax (answer A), federal unemployment compensation tax (answer B), and state unemployment compensation tax (answer C). The employees' federal income tax (answer D) is not an operating cost of the employer. It is withheld from the employees' earnings.

12

Corporations: Organization, Capital Stock Transactions, and Dividends

Setting *the* STAGE

If you own stock in a corporation, you are interested in how the stock is doing in the market. If you are considering buying stocks, you are interested in your rights as a stockholder and returns that you can expect from the stock. In either case, you should be able to interpret stock market quotations, such as the following:

39 1/2	22	WalMart	WMT	.27	.7	25	24165	36 1/8	35 3/8	36 1/16	+	5/8
29 15/16	18 1/8	Walgreen	WAG	.24	.9	32	6482	28 1/8	27 3/8	28 1/16	+	9/16
39 1/2	25 5/8	WallaceCS	WCS	.621	1.6	20	1808	38 3/16	37	38 1/16	+	5/8
35 9/16	22	Warnaco	WAC	.32	1.0	26	1017	30 3/4	30 11/16	30 11/16		...
147 1/4	61 7/8	WarnerLamb	WLA	1.52	1.0	53	11305	147 13/16	145 1/2	147 1/8	+	2 1/16
27 1/16	20 7/8	WashGasLt	WGL	1.18	4.5	15	689	26 3/8	25 7/8	26 1/8	−	1/16
5	3 5/8	WashHomes	WHI	.15	3.3	dd	53	4 1/2	4 7/16	4 1/2	+	1/16

Although you may not own any stocks, you probably buy services or products from corporations, and you may work for a corporation. Understanding the corporate form of organization will help you in your role as a stockholder, a consumer, or an employee. In this chapter, we discuss the characteristics of corporations, as well as how corporations account for stocks.

objectives

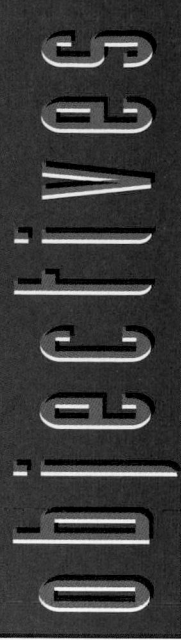

After studying this chapter, you should be able to:

1. Describe the nature of the corporate form of organization.
2. List the two main sources of stockholders' equity.
3. List the major sources of paid-in capital, including the various classes of stock.
4. Journalize the entries for issuing stock.
5. Journalize the entries for treasury stock transactions.
6. State the effect of stock splits on corporate financial statements.
7. Journalize the entries for cash dividends and stock dividends.
8. Compute and interpret the dividend yield on common stock.

Nature of a Corporation

OBJECTIVE 1

Describe the nature of the corporate form of organization.

In the preceding chapters, we used the proprietorship in illustrations. As we mentioned in a previous chapter, more than 70% of all businesses are proprietorships and 10% are partnerships. Most of these businesses are small businesses. The remaining 20% of businesses are corporations. Many corporations are large and, as a result, they generate more than 90% of the total business dollars in the United States.

Characteristics of a Corporation

A **corporation** is a legal entity, distinct and separate from the individuals who create and operate it. As a legal entity, a corporation may acquire, own, and dispose of property in its own name. It may also incur liabilities and enter into contracts.

A corporation was defined in the Dartmouth College case of 1819, in which Chief Justice Marshall of the United States Supreme Court stated: "A corporation is an artificial being, invisible, intangible, and existing only in contemplation of the law."

Because a corporation is a legal entity, it can sell shares of ownership, called **stock**, without affecting its operations or continued existence. The **stockholders** or **shareholders** who own the stock own the corporation. Corporations whose shares of stock are traded in public markets are called **public corporations**. Corporations whose shares are not traded publicly are usually owned by a small group of investors and are called **nonpublic** or **private corporations**.

The **Coca-Cola Corporation** is a well-known public corporation. The **Mars Candy Company**, which is owned by family members, is a well-known private corporation.

Corporations can be large because they have the ability to raise large amounts of capital by selling stock. In contrast, a proprietorship's ability to raise capital is limited because it has only one owner. A **partnership** is similar to a proprietorship, except that it has more than one owner. Like a proprietorship, a partnership's ability to raise capital is limited because ownership is not easily transferred.[1]

Stockholders can buy and sell stock without affecting the corporation. In contrast, a proprietorship or a partnership ceases to exist whenever the owner or a partner leaves the business. Likewise, if a new partner is admitted, a new partnership must be formed.

Point of INTEREST

If you invest in a public corporation, the most you can lose is the amount of your investment, regardless of actions of the corporation.

The stockholders of a corporation have **limited liability**. This means that a corporation's creditors usually may not go beyond the assets of the corporation to satisfy their claims. Thus, the financial loss that a stockholder may suffer is limited to the amount invested. This feature has contributed to the rapid growth of the corporate form of business.

[1] The accounting for partnerships is discussed in Appendix F.

Point of INTEREST

If you start a business as a proprietorship or as a partnership with others, your personal assets are at risk for any debts incurred by the business. For example, you could be personally liable for damages awarded in a lawsuit against the business.

In contrast, the owner of a proprietorship and the partners of a partnership have **unlimited liability**. They are individually liable to creditors for debts incurred by the business. Thus, if a proprietorship or a partnership is not able to pay its debts, the owner or the partners must contribute personal assets to settle the business debts. This characteristic is significant for partnerships because partners are **mutual agents**, which means that the actions of one partner bind the entire partnership.[2]

A proprietorship is controlled directly by its owner. A partnership is controlled by the partners according to a contract, called the *articles of partnership* or *partnership agreement.* In contrast, the stockholders control a corporation by electing a **board of directors**. This board meets periodically to establish corporate policies. It also selects the chief executive officer (CEO) and other major officers to manage the corporation's day-to-day affairs. Exhibit 1 shows the organizational structure of a corporation.

EXHIBIT 1
Organizational Structure of a Corporation

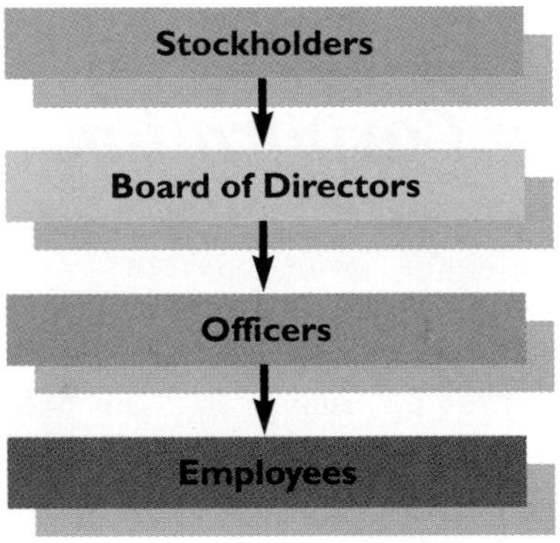

Corporations have a separate legal existence, transferable units of ownership, and limited stockholder liability.

As a separate entity, a corporation is subject to taxes. For example, corporations must pay federal income taxes on their income.[3] Thus, corporate income that is distributed to stockholders in the form of **dividends** has already been taxed. In turn, stockholders must pay income taxes on the dividends they receive. This *double taxation* of corporate earnings is a major disadvantage of the corporate form.[4] In contrast, proprietorships and partnerships are not required to pay federal income taxes. Instead, the owner or partners report their share of the business's income on their personal tax returns.

Forming a Corporation

The first step in forming a corporation is to file an **application of incorporation** with the state. State incorporation laws differ, and corporations often organize in those states with the more favorable laws. For example, more than half of the largest companies are incorporated in Delaware. Exhibit 2 lists some corporations that you may be familiar with, their states of incorporation, and the location of their headquarters.

After the application of incorporation has been approved, the state grants a **charter** or **articles of incorporation**. The articles

REAL WORLD Corporations may be organized for nonprofit reasons, such as recreational, educational, charitable, or humanitarian purposes. Such corporations are not required to pay federal taxes. Examples of nonprofit corporations include the **Sierra Club** and the **National Audubon Society**. However, most corporations are organized to earn a profit and a fair rate of return for their stockholders. Examples of for-profit corporations include **PepsiCo**, **General Motors**, and **Microsoft**.

[2] Some states permit limited partnerships, in which the liability of some partners is limited to the amount of their capital investment. However, a limited partnership must have at least one partner who has unlimited liability.

[3] Some states also require corporations to pay income taxes.

[4] Under the *Internal Revenue Code,* a corporation with a few stockholders may elect to be treated like a partnership for income tax purposes. Such corporations are known as Subchapter S corporations.

EXHIBIT 2
Examples of Corporations and Their States of Incorporation

Corporation	State of Incorporation	Headquarters
Borden, Inc.	New Jersey	New York, N.Y.
Caterpillar, Inc.	Delaware	Peoria, Ill.
Delta Air Lines, Inc.	Delaware	Atlanta, Ga.
Dow Chemical Company	Delaware	Midland, Mich.
General Electric Company	New York	Fairfield, Conn.
The Home Depot	Delaware	Atlanta, Ga.
Kellogg Company	Delaware	Battle Creek, Mich.
3M	Delaware	St. Paul, Minn.
May Department Stores	New York	St. Louis, Mo.
RJR Nabisco	Delaware	New York, N.Y.
Tandy Corporation	Delaware	Ft. Worth, Tex.
The Washington Post Company	Delaware	Washington, D.C.
Whirlpool Corporation	Delaware	Benton Harbor, Mich.

of incorporation formally create the corporation.[5] The corporate management and board of directors then prepare a set of **bylaws**, which are the rules and procedures for conducting the corporation's affairs.

Significant costs may be incurred in organizing a corporation. These costs include legal fees, taxes, state incorporation fees, license fees, and promotional costs. Such costs are debited to an intangible asset account entitled *Organization Costs* and are normally amortized over a five-year period.

The following entries illustrate the recording of a corporation's organization costs of $8,500 on January 5 and the amortization of those costs on December 31, the end of the first year of operations:

Jan.	5	Organization Costs	8 500 00	
		Cash		8 500 00
		Paid costs of organizing the corporation.		
Dec.	31	Amortization Expense—Organization Costs	1 700 00	
		Organization Costs		1 700 00
		Amortized organization costs at end of		
		first year ($8,500/5 years = $1,700).		

Stockholders' Equity

OBJECTIVE 2

List the two main sources of stockholders' equity.

The owners' equity in a corporation is commonly called **stockholders' equity**, **shareholders' equity**, **shareholders' investment**, or **capital**. In a corporation balance sheet, the Stockholders' Equity section reports the amount of each of the two main sources of stockholders' equity. The first source is capital contributed to the corporation by the stockholders and others, called **paid-in capital** or **contributed capital**. The second source is net income retained in the business, called **retained earnings**.

An example of a Stockholders' Equity section of a corporation balance sheet is shown below.

[5] The articles of incorporation may also restrict a corporation's activities in certain areas, such as owning certain types of real estate, conducting certain types of business activities, or purchasing its own stock.

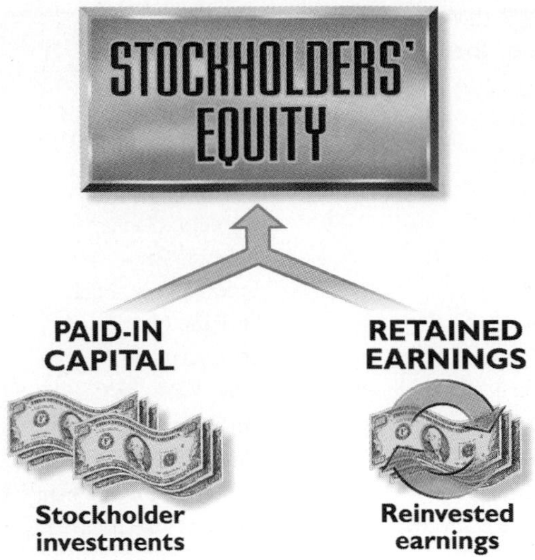

Stockholders' Equity		
Paid-in capital:		
Common stock	$330,000	
Retained earnings	80,000	
Total stockholders' equity		$410,000

The paid-in capital contributed by the stockholders is recorded in separate accounts for each class of stock. If there is only one class of stock, the account is entitled *Common Stock* or *Capital Stock.*

Retained earnings are generated from operations. Net income increases retained earnings while dividends decrease retained earnings. Thus, retained earnings represents a corporation's accumulated net income that has not been distributed to stockholders as dividends.

The two main sources of stockholders' equity are paid-in capital and retained earnings.

The balance of the retained earnings account at the end of the fiscal year is created by closing entries. First, the balance in the income summary account (the net income or net loss) is transferred to Retained Earnings. Second, the balance of the dividends account, which is similar to the drawing account for a proprietorship, is transferred to Retained Earnings.

Other terms that may be used to identify retained earnings in the financial statements include *earnings retained for use in the business* and *earnings reinvested in the business*. A debit balance in Retained Earnings is called a **deficit**. Such a balance results from accumulated net losses. In the Stockholders' Equity section, a deficit is deducted from paid-in capital in determining total stockholders' equity.

The balance of retained earnings should not be interpreted as representing surplus cash or cash left over for dividends. The reason for this is that earnings retained in the business and the related cash generated from these earnings are normally used by management to improve or expand operations. As cash is used to expand or improve operations, its balance decreases. However, the balance of the retained earnings account is unaffected. As a result, over time the balance of the retained earnings account normally becomes less and less related to the balance of the cash account.

Sources of Paid-In Capital

OBJECTIVE 3

List the major sources of paid-in capital, including the various classes of stock.

As we mentioned in the preceding section, the two main sources of stockholders' equity are paid-in capital (or contributed capital) and retained earnings. The main source of paid-in capital is from issuing stock. In the following paragraphs, we discuss the characteristics of the various classes of stock. We conclude this section with a brief discussion of other sources of paid-in capital.

Stock

The number of shares of stock that a corporation is *authorized* to issue is stated in its charter. The term *issued* refers to the shares issued to the stockholders. A corporation may, under circumstances we discuss later in this chapter, reacquire some of the stock that it has issued. The stock remaining in the hands of stockholders is then called **outstanding stock**. The relationship between authorized, issued, and outstanding stock is shown in the graphic at the top of the next page.

Shares of stock are often assigned a monetary amount, called **par**. Corporations may issue **stock certificates** to stockholders to document their ownership. Printed

Number of shares authorized, issued, and outstanding

on a stock certificate is the par value of the stock, the name of the stockholder, and the number of shares owned. Stock may also be issued without par, in which case it is called **no-par stock**. Some states require the board of directors to assign a **stated value** to no-par stock.

REAL WORLD Some corporations have stopped issuing stock certificates except on special request. In these cases, the corporation maintains records of ownership by using electronic media.

Because corporations have limited liability, creditors have no claim against the personal assets of stockholders. However, some state laws require that corporations maintain a minimum **stockholder** contribution to protect creditors. This minimum amount is called *legal capital*. The amount of required legal capital varies among the states, but it usually includes the amount of par or stated value of the shares of stock issued.

The major rights that accompany ownership of a share of stock are as follows:

1. The right to vote in matters concerning the corporation.
2. The right to share in distributions of earnings.
3. The right to share in assets on liquidation.

Q&A *On its balance sheet, a corporation reports the following three numbers related to its common stock: 200,000 shares; 150,000 shares; and 138,000 shares. What is the number of shares authorized, issued, outstanding, and reacquired?*

200,000 shares authorized; 150,000 shares issued; 138,000 shares outstanding; 12,000 (150,000 − 138,000) shares reacquired.

When only one class of stock is issued, it is called **common stock**. In this case, each share of common stock has equal rights. To appeal to a broader investment market, a corporation may issue one or more classes of stock with various preference rights. A common example of such a right is the preference to dividends. Such a stock is generally called a **preferred stock**.

The two primary classes of paid-in capital are common stock and preferred stock.

The dividend rights of preferred stock are usually stated in monetary terms or as a percent of par. For example, *$4 preferred stock* has a right to an annual $4 per share dividend. If the par value of the preferred stock were $50, the same right to dividends could be stated as *8%* ($4/$50) *preferred stock*.

The board of directors of a corporation has the sole authority to distribute dividends to the stockholders. When such action is taken, the directors are said to *declare* a dividend. Since dividends are normally based on earnings, a corporation cannot guarantee dividends even to preferred stockholders. However, because they have first rights to any dividends, the preferred stockholders have a greater chance of receiving regular dividends than do the common stockholders.

Nonparticipating Preferred Stock

Preferred stockholders' dividend rights are usually limited to a certain amount. Such stock is said to be **nonparticipating preferred stock**.[6] To continue our preced-

[6] In some cases, preferred stock may receive additional dividends if certain conditions are met. Such stock is called *participating preferred stock*. It is rarely used in today's financial markets.

ing example, assume that a corporation has 1,000 shares of $4 nonparticipating preferred stock and 4,000 shares of common stock outstanding. Also assume that the net income, amount of earnings retained, and the amount of earnings distributed by the board of directors for the first three years of operations are as follows:

	1999	2000	2001
Net income	$20,000	$55,000	$62,000
Amount retained	10,000	20,000	40,000
Amount distributed	$10,000	$35,000	$22,000

Exhibit 3 shows the earnings distributed each year to the preferred stock and the common stock. In this example, the preferred stockholders received an annual dividend of $4 per share, compared to the common stockholders' dividends of $1.50, $7.75, and $4.50 per share. You should note that although preferred stockholders have a greater chance of receiving a regular dividend, common stockholders have a greater chance of receiving larger dividends than do the preferred stockholders.

EXHIBIT 3
Dividends to Nonparticipating Preferred Stock

	1999	2000	2001
Amount distributed	$10,000	$35,000	$22,000
Preferred dividend (1,000 shares)	4,000	4,000	4,000
Common dividend (4,000 shares)	$ 6,000	$31,000	$18,000
Dividends per share:			
Preferred	$ 4.00	$ 4.00	$ 4.00
Common	$ 1.50	$ 7.75	$ 4.50

Cumulative Preferred Stock

Cumulative preferred stock has a right to receive regular dividends that have been passed (not declared) before any common stock dividends are paid. Noncumulative preferred stock does not have this right.

Dividends that have been passed are said to be **in arrears**. Such dividends should be disclosed, normally in a footnote to the financial statements.

To illustrate how dividends on cumulative preferred stock are calculated, assume that the preferred stock in Exhibit 3 is cumulative, and that no dividends were paid in 1999 and 2000. In 2001, the board of directors declares dividends of $22,000. Exhibit 4 shows how the dividends paid in 2001 are distributed between the preferred and common stockholders.

Point of INTEREST

With an investment objective of earning dividends, cumulative preferred stock is a safer investment than noncumulative preferred stock, and both types of preferred stock are a safer investment than common stock.

Q&A

Romer Corporation has 50,000 shares of $2, $100 par cumulative preferred stock outstanding. Preferred dividends are three years in arrears (not including the current year). What amount of preferred dividends must be paid before any dividends on common shares can be paid?

$400,000 [3 years in arrears (50,000 × $2 × 3) plus the current year's dividend of $100,000]

Other Preferential Rights

In addition to dividend preference, preferred stock may be given preferences to assets if the corporation goes out of business and is liquidated. However, claims of creditors must be satisfied first. Preferred stockholders are next in line to receive any remaining assets, followed by the common stockholders.

EXHIBIT 4
Dividends to Cumulative Preferred Stock

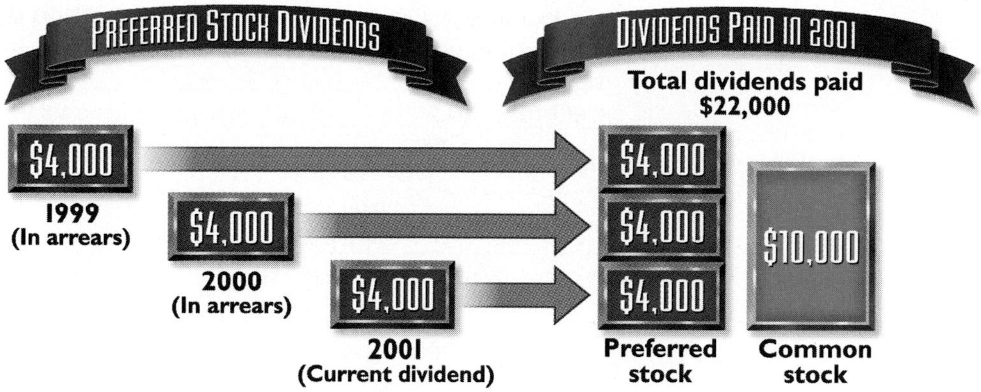

Amount distributed		$22,000
Preferred dividend (1,000 shares):		
1999 dividend in arrears	$4,000	
2000 dividend in arrears	4,000	
2001 dividend	4,000	12,000
Common dividend (4,000 shares)		$10,000
Dividends per share:		
Preferred		$ 12.00
Common		$ 2.50

Other Sources of Paid-In Capital

In addition to arising from the issuance of stock, paid-in capital may arise from receiving donations of real estate or other assets. Civic groups and municipalities sometimes give land or buildings to a corporation as an incentive to locate or remain in a community. In such cases, the corporation debits the assets for their fair market value and credits *Donated Capital.*

To illustrate, assume that on April 20 the city of Moraine donated land to Merrick Corporation as an incentive for it to relocate its headquarters to Moraine. The land was valued at $500,000. Merrick Corporation would record the land as follows:

Apr.	20	Land	500 0 0 0 00	
		Donated Capital		500 0 0 0 00
		Recorded land donated by the city		
		of Moraine.		

Paid-in capital may also arise when a corporation buys and sells its own stock in the marketplace. Later in this chapter, we will discuss the recording of such transactions.

OBJECTIVE 4

Journalize the entries for issuing stock.

Issuing Stock

A separate account is used for recording the amount of each class of stock issued to investors in a corporation. For example, assume that a corporation is authorized to issue 10,000 shares of preferred stock, $100 par, and 100,000 shares of common stock, $20 par. One-half of each class of authorized shares is issued at par for cash. The corporation's entry to record the stock issue is as follows:[7]

		Cash	1,500 0 0 0 00	
		Preferred Stock		500 0 0 0 00
		Common Stock		1,000 0 0 0 00
		Issued preferred stock and common stock at par for cash.		

INTERMISSION

Preferred stocks shield shareholders somewhat from the lows of corporate fortunes. If dividend payments must be reduced, preferred stockholders receive dividends before common shareholders. However, preferred stockholders often miss out on the highs of corporate fortunes. Because preferred shareholders receive a fixed dividend, and the bulk of any large dividends goes to common shareholders, most preferred stock is nonparticipating. These "safe-but-stodgy" equities can offer dramatic profits, however, as described in the following excerpt from an article in *Business Week*:

... In times of grave financial trouble, dividends on preferreds are often suspended and placed in arrears.... If and when the company reinstates dividends, current shareholders are entitled to all the back payments, whether or not they owned stock during the arrearage period—if the preferred is cumulative....

The gains [from purchasing preferred stock with dividends in arrears] can be impressive. ***Bethlehem Steel*** *announced in April that it would pay $22.5 million in arrears and resume the regular quarterly dividend on its two classes of preferred stock. Because Bethlehem had missed four payments, investors receive an extra year's worth of dividends: One class that usually pays $1.25 quarterly will return $6.25—not bad on a stock that traded in the low 30s just a few months ago.*

Playing preferreds in arrears requires patience. ***Long Island Lighting,*** *for instance, recently announced that it would try to resume paying dividends next year after a four-year hiatus. But the larger concern lies in the fact that you're betting on a turnaround. And all bets are off if the company goes bankrupt: You not only lose arrearages but you're also sure to see the share price plummet. On the repayment totem pole, preferreds occupy the second-lowest notch—before the common shareholders but after the creditors and bondholders....* ■

Source: Troy Segal, "Preferred Stock: The Risky Hunt for Hidden Rewards," *Business Week,* June 13, 1988, p. 114.

Stock is often issued by a corporation at a price other than its par. This is because the par value of a stock is simply its legal capital. The price at which stock can be sold by a corporation depends on a variety of factors, such as:

1. The financial condition, earnings record, and dividend record of the corporation.
2. Investor expectations of the corporation's potential earning power.
3. General business and economic conditions and prospects.

When stock is issued for a price that is more than its par, the stock has sold at a **premium**. When stock is issued for a price that is less than its par, the stock has sold at a **discount**. Thus, if stock with a par of $50 is issued for a price of $60, the stock has sold at a premium of $10. If the same stock is issued for a price of $45, the stock has sold at a discount of $5. Many states do not permit stock to be issued at a discount. In others, it may be done only under unusual conditions. Since issuing stock at a discount is rare, we will not illustrate it.

A corporation issuing stock must maintain records of the stockholders in order to issue dividend checks and distribute financial statements and other reports. Large public corporations normally use a financial institution, such as a bank, for this purpose.[8] In such cases, the financial institution is referred to as a *transfer agent* or *registrar*. For example, the transfer agent and registrar for **Coca-Cola Enterprises** is **First Chicago Trust Company of New York**.

[7] The accounting for investments in stocks from the point of view of the investor is discussed in a later chapter.

[8] Small corporations may use a subsidiary ledger, called a *stockholders ledger*. In this case, the stock accounts (Preferred Stock and Common Stock) are controlling accounts for the subsidiary ledger.

REAL WORLD

The following stock quotation for **Wal-Mart Corporation** is taken from *The Wall Street Journal*:

NEW YORK STOCK EXCHANGE

52 Weeks Hi	52 Weeks Lo	Stock	Sym	Div	Yld %	PE	Vol 100s	Hi	Lo	Close	Net Chg
$39\frac{1}{2}$	22	WalMart	WMT	.27	.7	25	24165	$36\frac{1}{8}$	$35\frac{3}{8}$	$36\frac{1}{16}$	$+\frac{5}{6}$

The preceding quotation is interpreted as follows:

Hi	Highest price during the past 52 weeks
Lo	Lowest price during the past 52 weeks
Stock	Name of the company
Sym	Stock exchange symbol (WMT for Wal-Mart)
Div	Dividends paid per share during the past year
Yld %	Annual dividend yield per share based on the closing price (Wal-Mart's 0.7% yield on common stock is computed as $0.27/$$36\frac{1}{16}$)
PE	Price-earnings ratio on common stock (price ÷ earnings per share)
Vol	The volume of stock traded in 100s
Hi	Highest price for the day
Lo	Lowest price for the day
Close	Closing price for the day
Net Chg	The net change in price from the previous day

Premium on Stock

When stock is issued at a premium, Cash or other asset accounts are debited for the amount received. Common Stock or Preferred Stock is then credited for the par amount. The excess of the amount paid over par is a part of the total investment of the stockholders in the corporation. Therefore, such an amount in excess of par should be classified as a part of the paid-in capital. An account entitled *Paid-In Capital in Excess of Par* is usually credited for this amount.

To illustrate, assume that Caldwell Company issues 2,000 shares of $50 par preferred stock for cash at $55. The entry to record this transaction is as follows:

Cash	110 0 0 0 00	
Preferred Stock		100 0 0 0 00
Paid-In Capital in Excess of		
Par—Preferred Stock		10 0 0 0 00
Issued $50 par preferred stock at $55.		

When stock is issued in exchange for assets other than cash, such as land, buildings, and equipment, the assets acquired should be recorded at their fair market value. If this value cannot be objectively determined, the fair market price of the stock issued may be used.

To illustrate, assume that a corporation acquired land for which the fair market value cannot be determined. In exchange, the corporation issued 10,000 shares of its $10 par common. Assuming that the stock has a current market price of $12 per share, this transaction is recorded as follows:

Land	120 0 0 0 00	
Common Stock		100 0 0 0 00
Paid-In Capital in Excess of Par		20 0 0 0 00
Issued $10 par common stock, valued at		
$12 per share, for land.		

No-Par Stock

In most states, both preferred and common stock may be issued without a par value. When no-par stock is issued, the entire proceeds are credited to the stock account. This is true even though the issue price varies from time to time. For example, assume that a corporation issues 10,000 shares of no-par common stock at $40 a share and at a later date issues 1,000 additional shares at $36. The entries to record the no-par stock are as follows:

Cash	400 0 0 0 00	
Common Stock		400 0 0 0 00
Issued 10,000 shares of no-par		
common at $40.		
Cash	36 0 0 0 00	
Common Stock		36 0 0 0 00
Issued 1,000 shares of no-par		
common at $36.		

Some states require that the entire proceeds from the issue of no-par stock be recorded as legal capital. In this case, the preceding entries would be proper. In other states, no-par stock may be assigned a *stated value per share*. The stated value is recorded like a par value, and the excess of the proceeds over the stated value is recorded as follows:

Cash	400,000 00	
Common Stock		250,000 00
Paid-In Capital in Excess of Stated Value		150,000 00
Issued 10,000 shares of no-par common		
at $40; stated value, $25.		
Cash	36,000 00	
Common Stock		25,000 00
Paid-In Capital in Excess of Stated Value		11,000 00
Issued 1,000 shares of no-par common		
at $36; stated value, $25.		

Treasury Stock Transactions

OBJECTIVE 5

Journalize the entries for treasury stock transactions.

The 1996 edition of *Accounting Trends & Techniques* indicated that over 64% of the companies surveyed reported treasury stock.

A corporation may buy its own stock to provide shares for resale to employees, for reissuing as a bonus to employees, or for supporting the market price of the stock. For example, **General Motors** bought back its common stock and stated that two primary uses of this stock would be for incentive compensation plans and employee savings plans. Such stock that a corporation has once issued and then reacquires is called **treasury stock**.

A commonly used method of accounting for the purchase and resale of treasury stock is the **cost method**.[9] When the stock is purchased by the corporation, the account *Treasury Stock* is debited for its cost (the price paid for it). The par value and the price at which the stock was originally issued are ignored. When the stock is resold, Treasury Stock is credited for its cost, and any difference between the cost and the selling price is normally debited or credited to *Paid-In Capital from Sale of Treasury Stock*.

To illustrate, assume that the paid-in capital of a corporation is as follows:

Common stock, $25 par (20,000 shares authorized and issued)	$500,000	
Excess of issue price over par	150,000	$650,000

The purchase and sale of the treasury stock are recorded as follows:

Treasury Stock	45,000 00	
Cash		45,000 00
Purchased 1,000 shares of treasury		
stock at $45.		

[9] Another method that is infrequently used, called the *par value method*, is discussed in advanced accounting texts.

Cash	12,000.00	
Treasury Stock		9,000.00
Paid-In Capital from Sale of Treasury Stock		3,000.00
Sold 200 shares of treasury stock at $60.		
Cash	8,000.00	
Paid-In Capital from Sale of Treasury Stock	1,000.00	
Treasury Stock		9,000.00
Sold 200 shares of treasury stock at $40.		

As shown above, a sale of treasury stock may result in a decrease in paid-in capital. To the extent that Paid-In Capital from Sale of Treasury Stock has a credit balance, it should be debited for any decrease. Any remaining decrease should then be debited to the retained earnings account.

At the end of the period, the balance in the treasury stock account is reported as a deduction from the total of the paid-in capital and retained earnings. The balance of Paid-In Capital from Sale of Treasury Stock is reported as part of the paid-in capital, as shown in Exhibit 5.

EXHIBIT 5
Stockholders' Equity Section with Treasury Stock

Stockholders' Equity

Paid-in capital:			
Common stock, $25 par (20,000 shares authorized and issued)	$500,000		
Excess of issue price over par	150,000		
From sale of treasury stock	2,000		
Total paid-in capital		$652,000	
Retained earnings		130,000	
Total		$782,000	
Deduct treasury stock (600 shares at cost)		27,000	
Total stockholders' equity			$755,000

Stock Splits

OBJECTIVE 6

State the effect of stock splits on corporate financial statements.

Corporations sometimes reduce the par or stated value of their common stock and issue a proportionate number of additional shares. When this is done, a corporation is said to have *split* its stock, and the process is called a **stock split**.

When stock is split, the reduction in par or stated value applies to all shares, including the unissued, issued, and treasury shares. A major objective of a stock split is to reduce the market price per share of the stock. This, in turn, should attract more investors to enter the market for the stock and broaden the types and numbers of stockholders.

REAL WORLD

When **Nature's Sunshine Products Inc.** declared a two-for-one stock split, the company president said:

We believe the split will place our stock price in a range attractive to both individual and institutional investors, broadening the market for the stock.

To illustrate a stock split, assume that Rojek Corporation has 10,000 shares of $100 par common stock outstanding with a current market price of $150 per share. The board of directors declares a 5-for-1 stock split, reduces the par to $20, and increases the number of shares to 50,000. The amount of common stock outstanding is $1,000,000

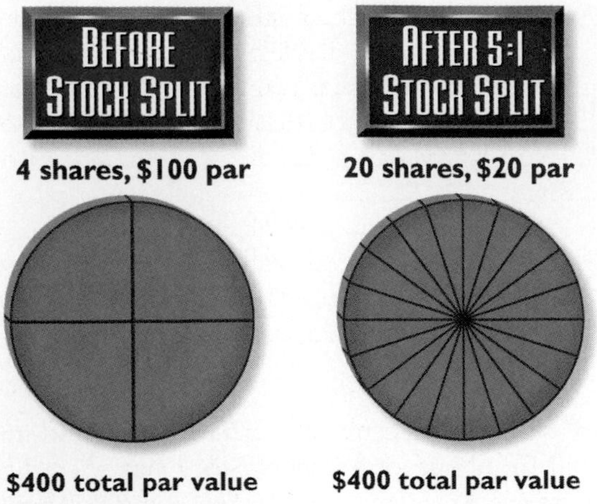

both before and after the stock split. Only the number of shares and the par per share are changed. Each Rojek Corporation shareholder owns the same total par amount of stock before and after the stock split. For example, a stockholder who owned 4 shares of $100 par stock before the split (total par of $400) would own 20 shares of $20 par stock after the split (total par of $400).

Since there are more shares outstanding after the stock split, we would expect that the market price of the stock would fall. For example, in the preceding example, there would be 5 times as many shares outstanding after the split. Thus, we would expect the market price of the stock to fall from $150 to approximately $30 ($150/5).

Since a stock split changes only the par or stated value and the number of shares outstanding, it is not recorded by a journal entry. Although the accounts are not affected, the details of stock splits are normally disclosed in the notes to the financial statements.

Q&A *LTM Corporation announced a 4-for-1 stock split of its $50 par value common stock, which is currently trading for $120 per share. What is the new par value and the estimated market price of the stock after the split?*

$12.50 ($50/4) par value; $30 ($120/4) estimated market price.

A stock split does not change the balance of any corporation accounts.

Accounting for Dividends

OBJECTIVE 7

Journalize the entries for cash dividends and stock dividends.

When a board of directors declares a cash dividend, it authorizes the distribution of a portion of the corporation's cash to stockholders. When a board of directors declares a stock dividend, it authorizes the distribution of a portion of its stock. In both cases, the declaration of a dividend reduces the retained earnings of the corporation.[10]

Cash Dividends

A cash distribution of earnings by a corporation to its shareholders is called a **cash dividend**. Although dividends may be paid in the form of other assets, cash dividends are the most common form.

There are usually three conditions that a corporation must meet to pay a cash dividend:

1. Sufficient retained earnings
2. Sufficient cash
3. Formal action by the board of directors

A large amount of retained earnings does not always mean that a corporation is able to pay dividends. As we indicated earlier in the chapter, the balance of the cash and retained earnings account are often unrelated. Thus, a large retained earnings account does not mean that there is cash available to pay dividends.

A corporation's board of directors is not required by law to declare dividends. This is true even if both retained earnings and cash are large enough to justify a dividend. However, most corporations try to maintain a stable dividend record in

[10] In rare cases, when a corporation is reducing its operations or going out of business, a dividend may be a distribution of paid-in capital. Such a dividend is called a *liquidating dividend*.

BUSINESS ON STAGE

Stocks are bought and sold through stock exchanges. The New York Stock Exchange and the American Stock Exchange are the two national exchanges. In addition, regional exchanges and the over-the-counter market serve important roles in the trading of stocks.

New York Stock Exchange. This exchange, founded in 1792, is located on Wall Street in New York City. It consists of over 1,366 members who own "seats" on the exchange and who are allowed to trade securities. Only stocks listed on the exchange (the "Big Board") can be traded. Currently, stocks of over 3,000 generally older, well-established, larger companies are listed. To qualify for listing, a company must have over 1 million shares outstanding and $2.5 million of pretax profits. Examples of such companies include **General Motors** and **Conrail**.

American Stock Exchange. This exchange is similar to the New York Stock Exchange, except that the companies are generally small to medium-size companies. To qualify for listing, a company must have over 500,000 shares outstanding and $750,000 of pretax profits. Currently, about 800 stocks are listed on the American Stock Exchange. As a company grows, it may move from the American Stock Exchange to the New York Stock Exchange. Examples of American Stock Exchange companies include **El Paso Electric** and **Amdahl**.

Regional Exchanges. There are several regional exchanges, including Chicago, Boston, Cincinnati, Philadelphia, and San Francisco. Initially, such exchanges traded mostly in stocks of local firms. Today, many firms, such as **Sears**, are traded on both regional and national exchanges.

Over-the-Counter Market. This market refers to a network of brokers who communicate with each other to set prices and trade securities. This system is referred to as the *National Association of Securities Dealers Automated Quotation* system, or more simply by its abbreviation, *Nasdaq*. Larger, actively traded issues are referred to as Nasdaq National Market issues, while less active issues are referred to as Nasdaq Small-Cap issues. Approximately, 30,000 stocks are traded on Nasdaq. Examples of Nasdaq companies include **Apple Computer**, **Intel**, and **Microsoft**. ■

order to make their stock attractive to investors. Although dividends may be paid once a year or semiannually, most corporations pay dividends quarterly. In years of high profits, a corporation may declare a *special* or *extra* dividend.

You may have seen announcements of dividend declarations in financial newspapers or investor services. An example of such an announcement is shown below.

On June 26, the board of directors of ***Campbell Soup Co.*** *declared a quarterly cash dividend of $0.33 per common share to stockholders of record as of the close of business on July 8, payable on July 31.*

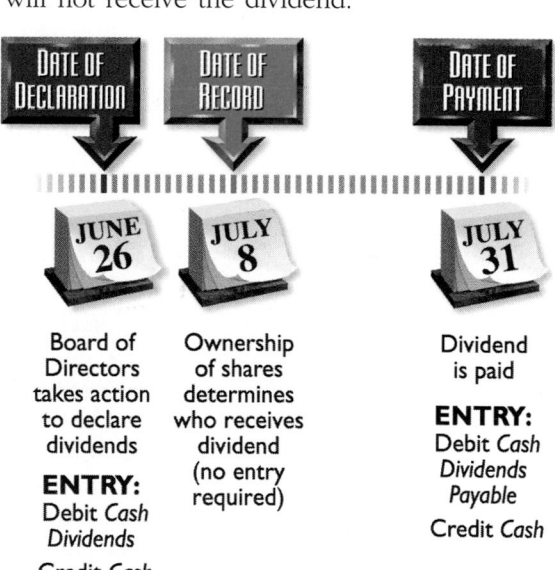

This announcement includes three important dates: the *date of declaration* (June 26), the *date of record* (July 8), and the *date of payment* (July 31). During the period of time between the record date and the payment date, the stock price is usually quoted as selling *ex-dividends*. This means that since the date of record has passed, a new investor will not receive the dividend.

Board of Directors takes action to declare dividends

ENTRY:
Debit *Cash Dividends*
Credit *Cash Dividends Payable*

Ownership of shares determines who receives dividend (no entry required)

Dividend is paid

ENTRY:
Debit *Cash Dividends Payable*
Credit *Cash*

To illustrate, assume that on *December 1* the board of directors of Hiber Corporation declares the following quarterly cash dividends. The date of record is *December 10,* and the date of payment is *January 2.*

	Dividend per Share	Total Dividends
Preferred stock, $100 par, 5,000 shares outstanding	$2.50	$12,500
Common stock, $10 par, 100,000 shares outstanding	$0.30	30,000
Total		$42,500

Hiber Corporation records the $42,500 liability for the dividends on December 1, the declaration date, as follows:

Dec.	1	Cash Dividends	42 500 00	
		Cash Dividends Payable		42 500 00
		Declared cash dividend.		

No entry is required on the date of record, December 10, since this date merely determines which stockholders will receive the dividend. On the date of payment, January 2, the corporation records the $42,500 payment of the dividends as follows:

Jan.	2	Cash Dividends Payable	42 500 00	
		Cash		42 500 00
		Paid cash dividend.		

If Hiber Corporation's fiscal year ends December 31, the balance in Cash Dividends will be transferred to Retained Earnings as a part of the closing process by debiting Retained Earnings and crediting Cash Dividends. Cash Dividends Payable will be listed on the December 31 balance sheet as a current liability.

If a corporation that holds treasury stock declares a cash dividend, the dividends are not paid on the treasury shares. To do so would place the corporation in the position of earning income through dealing with itself. For example, if Hiber Corporation in the preceding illustration had held 5,000 shares of its own common stock, the cash dividends on the common stock would have been $28,500 [(100,000 − 5,000) × $0.30] instead of $30,000.

Stock Dividends

A distribution of shares of stock to stockholders is called a **stock dividend**. Usually, such distributions are in common stock and are issued to holders of common stock. Stock dividends are different from cash dividends in that there is no distribution of cash or other assets to stockholders.

The effect of a stock dividend on the stockholders' equity of the issuing corporation is to transfer retained earnings to paid-in capital. For public corporations, the amount transferred from retained earnings to paid-in capital is normally the *fair value* (market price) of the shares issued in the stock dividend.[11] To illustrate, assume that the stockholders' equity accounts of Hendrix Corporation as of December 15 are as follows:

Common Stock, $20 par (2,000,000 shares issued)	$40,000,000
Paid-In Capital in Excess of Par—Common Stock	9,000,000
Retained Earnings	26,600,000

On December 15, the board of directors declares a stock dividend of 5% or 100,000 shares (2,000,000 shares × 5%) to be issued on January 10 to stockholders of record on December 31. The market price of the stock on the declaration date is $31 a share. The entry to record the declaration is as follows:

[11] The use of fair market value is justified as long as the number of shares issued for the stock dividend is small (less than 25% of the shares outstanding).

Dec.	15	Stock Dividends (100,000 × $31 market price)	3,100,000.00	
		Stock Dividends Distributable		
		(100,000 × $20 Par)		2,000,000.00
		Paid-In Capital in Excess of		
		Par—Common Stock		1,100,000.00
		Declared stock dividend.		

The $3,100,000 balance in Stock Dividends is closed to Retained Earnings on December 31. The stock dividends distributable account is listed in the Paid-In Capital section of the balance sheet. Thus, the effect of the stock dividend is to transfer $3,100,000 of retained earnings to paid-in capital.

On January 10, the number of shares outstanding is increased by 100,000 by the following entry to record the issue of the stock:

Jan.	10	Stock Dividends Distributable	2,000,000.00	
		Common Stock		2,000,000.00
		Issued stock for the stock dividend.		

A stock dividend does not change the assets, liabilities, or total stockholders' equity of the corporation. Likewise, it does not change a stockholder's proportionate interest (equity) in the corporation. For example, if a stockholder owned 1,000 of a corporation's 10,000 shares outstanding, the stockholder owns 10% (1,000/10,000) of the corporation. After declaring a 6% stock dividend, the corporation will issue 600 additional shares (10,000 shares × 6%), and the total shares outstanding will be 10,600. The stockholder of 1,000 shares will receive 60 additional shares and will now own 1,060 shares, which is still a 10% equity.

FINANCIAL ANALYSIS AND INTERPRETATION

OBJECTIVE 8

Compute and interpret the dividend yield on common stock.

The **dividend yield** indicates the rate of return to stockholders in terms of cash dividend distributions. Although the dividend yield can be computed for both preferred and common stock, it is most often computed for common stock. This is because most preferred stock has a stated dividend rate or amount. In contrast, the amount of common stock dividends normally varies with the profitability of the corporation.

The dividend yield is computed by dividing the annual dividends paid per share of common stock by the market price per share at a specific date, as shown below:

$$\textbf{Dividend Yield} = \frac{\textbf{Dividends per Share of Common Stock}}{\textbf{Market Price per Share of Common Stock}}$$

To illustrate, the market price of **Coca-Cola's** common stock was $61 as of the close of business, February 14, 1997. During the past year, Coca-Cola had paid dividends of $0.50 per share. Thus, the dividend yield of Coca-Cola's common stock is 0.8% ($0.50/$61). Because the market price of a corporation's stock will vary from day to day, its dividend yield will also vary from day to day.

The dividend yield on common stock is of special interest to investors whose main objective is to receive a current dividend return on their investment. This is in contrast to investors whose main objective is a rapid increase in the market price of their investments. For example, technology companies often do not pay dividends, but reinvest their earnings in research and development. The main attraction of such stocks, such as **Microsoft's** common stock, is the expectation of the market price of the stock rising. Since many factors affect stock prices, an investment strategy relying solely on market price increases is more risky than a strategy based on dividend yields.

ENCORE

Would You Like to Own a Sports Team?

The **Florida Panthers**, a National League Hockey team based in Fort Lauderdale, sold its common stock to the public. At an initial offering price of $10 per share, the stock appeared to be a bargain compared to some of the Panthers' official merchandise. For example, a Panthers' playoff cap is $19, a replica air-knit jersey is $79, and a hockey stick puck holder is $29.

Like many sports teams, the Panthers are facing some difficult financial issues. For example, the team's margins are being squeezed by players' salaries, which have more than doubled in two years. In addition, the Panthers must share the Miami Arena and some of its revenues with the **Miami Heat** basketball team. Until the Panthers move into a new arena for the 1998–99 season, they expect net losses of up to $20 million a year. The prospectus distributed to potential investors indicates that the Panthers have no plans to pay a dividend "in the foreseeable future."

But what about the thrill of owning a team and voting on draft picks, hiring and firing coaches, and attending games in the owner's box? Not likely. The stock offering is structured so that the current owner, H. Wayne Huizenga, will receive 250,000 shares of Class B common stock. While 7.3 million shares of Class A common stock will be issued to the public, each share of Class B stock has 10,000 times more voting power than 1 share of Class A stock.

So, are you interested? With no dividend, projected losses for the next two years, and no voting power, do you think that buying a share of Panthers stock would be a good investment or just end up being a piece of sports memorabilia? In November 1996 the Panthers did issue their stock at $10 per share. The stock is traded on the NYSE under the symbol *PAW*. At the end of trading on December 26, 1997, it was at $18.125 per share. ■

Source: Tim Carvell, "So You Want to Own a Team?" *Fortune,* November 11, 1996, pp. 46–48.

KEY POINTS

1 Describe the nature of the corporate form of organization.

Corporations have a separate legal existence, transferable units of stock, and limited stockholders' liability. Corporations may be either public or private corporations, and they are subject to federal income taxes.

The documents included in forming a corporation include an application of incorporation, articles of incorporation, and bylaws. Costs often incurred in organizing a corporation include legal fees, taxes, state incorporation fees, and promotional costs. Such costs are debited to an intangible asset account entitled Organization Costs. They are normally amortized to expense over five years.

2 List the two main sources of stockholders' equity.

The two main sources of stockholders' equity are (1) capital contributed by the stockholders and others, called paid-in capital, and (2) net income retained in the business, called retained earnings. Stockholders' equity is reported in a corporation balance sheet according to these two sources.

3 List the major sources of paid-in capital, including the various classes of stock.
The main source of paid-in capital is from issuing stock. The two primary classes of stock are common stock and preferred stock. Preferred stock is normally nonparticipating and may be cumulative or noncumulative. In addition to the issuance of stock, paid-in capital may arise from donations of assets and from treasury stock transactions.

4 Journalize the entries for issuing stock.
When a corporation issues stock at par for cash, the cash account is debited and the class of stock issued is credited for its par amount. When a corporation issues stock at more than par, Paid-In Capital in Excess of Par is credited for the difference between the cash received and the par value of the stock. When stock is issued in exchange for assets other than cash, the assets acquired should be recorded at their fair market value.

When no-par stock is issued, the entire proceeds are credited to the stock account. No-par stock may be assigned a stated value per share, and the excess of the proceeds over the stated value may be credited to Paid-In Capital in Excess of Stated Value.

5 Journalize the entries for treasury stock transactions.
When a corporation buys its own stock, the cost method of accounting is normally used. Treasury Stock is debited for its cost, and Cash is credited. If the stock is resold, Treasury Stock is credited for its cost and any difference between the cost and the selling price is normally debited or credited to Paid-In Capital from Sale of Treasury Stock.

6 State the effect of stock splits on corporate financial statements.
When a corporation reduces the par or stated value of its common stock and issues a proportionate number of additional shares, a stock split has occurred. There are no changes in the balances of any corporation accounts, and no entry is required for a stock split.

7 Journalize the entries for cash dividends and stock dividends.
The entry to record a declaration of cash dividends debits Dividends and credits Dividends Payable for each class of stock. The payment of dividends is recorded in the normal manner. When a stock dividend is declared, Stock Dividends is debited for the fair value of the stock to be issued. Stock Dividends Distributable is credited for the par or stated value of the common stock to be issued. The difference between the fair value of the stock and its par or stated value is credited to Paid-In Capital in Excess of Par—Common Stock. When the stock is issued on the date of payment, Stock Dividends Distributable is debited and Common Stock is credited for the par or stated value of the stock issued.

8 Compute and interpret the dividend yield on common stock.
The dividend yield indicates the rate of return to stockholders in terms of cash dividend distributions. It is computed by dividing the annual dividends paid per share of common stock by the market price per share at a specific date. This ratio is of special interest to investors whose main objective is to receive a current dividend return on their investment.

ILLUSTRATIVE PROBLEM

Altenburg Inc. is a lighting fixture wholesaler located in Arizona. During its current fiscal year, ended December 31, 2000, Altenburg Inc. completed the following selected transactions:

Feb. 3. Purchased 2,500 shares of its own common stock at $26, recording the stock at cost. (Prior to the purchase, there were 40,000 shares of $20 par common stock outstanding.)
May 1. Declared a semiannual dividend of $1 on the 10,000 shares of preferred stock and a 30¢ dividend on the common stock to stockholders of record on May 31, payable on June 15.
June 15. Paid the cash dividends.
Sep. 23. Sold 1,000 shares of treasury stock at $28, receiving cash.
Nov. 1. Declared semiannual dividends of $1 on the preferred stock and 30¢ on the common stock. In addition, a 5% common stock dividend was declared on

the common stock outstanding, to be capitalized at the fair market value of the common stock, which is estimated at $30.

Dec. 1. Paid the cash dividends and issued the certificates for the common stock dividend.

Instructions

Journalize the entries to record the transactions for Altenburg Inc.

Solution

2000 Feb.	3	Treasury Stock	65 000 00	
		Cash		65 000 00
May	1	Cash Dividends	21 250 00	
		Cash Dividends Payable		21 250 00*
		*(10,000 × $1) + [(40,000 − 2,500) × $0.30]		
June	15	Cash Dividends Payable	21 250 00	
		Cash		21 250 00
Sep.	23	Cash	28 000 00	
		Treasury Stock		26 000 00
		Paid-In Capital from Sale of Treasury Stock		2 000 00
Nov.	1	Cash Dividends	21 550 00*	
		Cash Dividends Payable		21 550 00
		*(10,000 × $1) + [(40,000 − 1,500) × $0.30]		
	1	Stock Dividends	57 750 00*	
		Stock Dividends Distributable		38 500 00
		Paid-In Capital in Excess of Par—Common Stock		19 250 00
		*(40,000 − 1,500) × 5% × $30		
Dec.	1	Cash Dividends Payable	21 550 00	
		Stock Dividends Distributable	38 500 00	
		Cash		21 550 00
		Common Stock		38 500 00

SELF-EXAMINATION QUESTIONS

Answers at End of Chapter

Matching

Match each of the following statements with its proper term. Some terms may not be used.

A. cash dividend
B. common stock
C. cumulative preferred stock
D. deficit

O 1. Shares of ownership of a corporation.
R 2. The owners of a corporation.
S 3. The owners' equity in a corporation.
I 4. Capital contributed to a corporation by the stockholders and others.
M 5. Net income retained in a corporation.
D 6. A debit balance in the retained earnings account.

E. **discount**
F. **dividend yield**
G. **nonparticipating preferred stock**
H. **outstanding stock**
I. **paid-in capital**
J. **par**
K. **preferred stock**
L. **premium**
M. **retained earnings**
N. **stated value**
O. **stock**
P. **stock dividend**
Q. **stock split**
R. **stockholders**
S. **stockholders' equity**
T. **treasury stock**

H 7. The stock in the hands of stockholders.

N 8. A value, similar to par value, approved by the board of directors of a corporation for no-par stock.

B 9. The stock outstanding when a corporation has issued only one class of stock.

K 10. A class of stock with preferential rights over common stock.

G 11. A class of preferred stock whose dividend rights are usually limited to a certain amount.

C 12. A class of preferred stock that has a right to receive regular dividends that have been passed (not declared) before any common stock dividends are paid.

L 13. The excess of the issue price of a stock over its par value.

E 14. The excess of the par value of a stock over its issue price.

T 15. Stock that a corporation has once issued and then reacquires.

Q 16. A reduction in the par or stated value of a common stock and the issuance of a proportionate number of additional shares.

A 17. A cash distribution of earnings by a corporation to its shareholders.

P 18. A distribution of shares of stock to its stockholders.

F 19. A ratio, computed by dividing the annual dividends paid per share of common stock by the market price per share at a specific date, that indicates the rate of return to stockholders in terms of cash dividend distributions.

J 20. The monetary amount printed on a stock certificate.

Multiple Choice

1. If a corporation has outstanding 1,000 shares of $9 cumulative preferred stock of $100 par and dividends have been passed for the preceding three years, what is the amount of preferred dividends that must be declared in the current year before a dividend can be declared on common stock?
   A. $ 9,000 C. $36,000
   B. $27,000 D. $45,000

2. Paid-in capital for a corporation may arise from which of the following sources?
   A. Issuing cumulative preferred stock
   B. Receiving donations of real estate
   C. Selling the corporation's treasury stock
   D. All of the above

3. The Stockholders' Equity section of the balance sheet may include:
   A. Common Stock C. Preferred Stock
   B. Donated Capital D. All of the above

4. If a corporation reacquires its own stock, the stock is listed on the balance sheet in the:
   A. Current Assets section.
   B. Long-Term Liabilities section.
   C. Stockholders' Equity section.
   D. Investments section.

5. A corporation has issued 25,000 shares of $100 par common stock and holds 3,000 of these shares as treasury stock. If the corporation declares a $2 per share cash dividend, what amount will be recorded as cash dividends?
   A. $22,000 C. $44,000
   B. $25,000 D. $50,000

CLASS DISCUSSION QUESTIONS

1. Contrast the owners' liability to creditors of (a) a partnership (partners) and (b) a corporation (stockholders).
2. Why is it said that the earnings of a corporation are subject to *double taxation*? Discuss.
3. Why are most large businesses organized as corporations?
4. a. What type of expenditure is charged to the organization costs account?
   b. Give examples of such expenditures.
   c. In what section of the balance sheet is the balance of Organization Costs listed?
5. Distinguish between paid-in capital and retained earnings of a corporation.
6. The retained earnings account of a corporation at the beginning of the year had a

credit balance of $175,000. The only other entry in the account during the year was a debit of $200,000 transferred from the income summary account at the end of the year. (a) What is the term applied to the $200,000 debit? (b) What is the term applied to the debit balance of retained earnings at the end of the year, after all closing entries have been posted?

7. Of two corporations organized at approximately the same time and engaged in competing businesses, one issued $100 par common stock, and the other issued $25 par common stock. Do the par designations provide any indication as to which stock is preferable as an investment? Explain.
8. What are the three basic rights that accompany ownership of a share of common stock?
9. a. Differentiate between common stock and preferred stock.
   b. Describe briefly (1) nonparticipating preferred stock and (2) cumulative preferred stock.
10. A stockbroker advises a client to "buy cumulative preferred stock. . . . With that type of stock, . . .[you] will never have to worry about losing the dividends." Is the broker right?
11. What are some sources of paid-in capital other than the issuance of stock?
12. If a corporation is given land as an inducement to locate in a particular community, (a) how should the amount of the debit to the land account be determined, and (b) what is the title of the account that should be credited for the same amount?
13. If common stock of $50 par is sold for $70, what is the $20 difference between the issue price and par called?
14. What are some of the factors that influence the market price of a corporation's stock?
15. When a corporation issues stock at a premium, is the premium income? Explain.
16. Land is acquired by a corporation for 5,000 shares of its $50 par common stock, which is currently selling for $65 per share on a national stock exchange. What accounts should be credited to record the transaction?
17. Indicate which of the following accounts would be reported as part of paid-in capital on the balance sheet:
    a. Retained Earnings
    b. Common Stock
    c. Donated Capital
    d. Preferred Stock
18. a. In what respect does treasury stock differ from unissued stock?
    b. How should treasury stock be presented on the balance sheet?
19. A corporation reacquires 7,500 shares of its own $25 par common stock for $225,000, recording it at cost. (a) What effect does this transaction have on revenue or expense of the period? (b) What effect does it have on stockholders' equity?
20. The treasury stock in Question 19 is resold for $280,000. (a) What is the effect on the corporation's revenue of the period? (b) What is the effect on stockholders' equity?
21. What is the primary purpose of a stock split?
22. What are the three conditions for the declaration and the payment of a cash dividend?
23. The dates in connection with the declaration of a cash dividend are April 1, May 15, and May 30. Identify each date.
24. A corporation with both cumulative preferred stock and common stock outstanding has a substantial credit balance in its retained earnings account at the beginning of the current fiscal year. Although net income for the current year is sufficient to pay the preferred dividend of $50,000 each quarter and a common dividend of $200,000 each quarter, the board of directors declares dividends only on the preferred stock. Suggest possible reasons for passing the dividends on the common stock.
25. An owner of 200 shares of Dunston Company common stock receives a stock dividend of 4 shares. (a) What is the effect of the stock dividend on the stockholder's proportionate interest (equity) in the corporation? (b) How does the total equity of 204 shares compare with the total equity of 200 shares before the stock dividend?
26. a. Where should a declared but unpaid cash dividend be reported on the balance sheet?
    b. Where should a declared but unissued stock dividend be reported on the balance sheet?

Warren Reeve Fess

Resources for Your Success On-Line at warren.swcollege.com

Remember! If you need additional help, visit South-Western's Web site. See page 26 for a description of the online and printed materials that are available.

EXERCISES

Exercise 12–1
Dividends per share
Objective 3

✓ Preferred stock, 3rd year: $4.00

Davenport Inc., a developer of radiology equipment, has stock outstanding as follows: 15,000 shares of $4 (4%) nonparticipating, noncumulative preferred stock of $100 par, and 250,000 shares of $75 par common. During its first five years of operations, the following amounts were distributed as dividends: first year, none; second year, $45,000; third year, $90,000; fourth year, $200,000; fifth year, $240,000. Calculate the dividends per share on each class of stock for each of the five years.

Exercise 12–2
Dividends per share
Objective 3

✓ Preferred stock, 4th year: $8.00

Taft Inc., a computer software development firm, has stock outstanding as follows: 25,000 shares of $3 (3%) cumulative, nonparticipating preferred stock of $100 par, and 100,000 shares of $50 par common. During its first five years of operations, the following amounts were distributed as dividends: first year, none; second year, $20,000; third year, $80,000; fourth year, $220,000; fifth year, $180,000. Calculate the dividends per share on each class of stock for each of the five years.

Exercise 12–3
Entries for issuing par stock
Objective 4

✓ b. $420,000

On June 5, Szabo Inc., a marble contractor, issued for cash 15,000 shares of $18 par common stock at $24, and on August 7, it issued for cash 5,000 shares of $10 par preferred stock at $12.

a. Journalize the entries for June 5 and August 7.
b. What is the total amount invested (total paid-in capital) by all stockholders as of August 7?

Exercise 12–4
Entries for issuing no-par stock
Objective 4

✓ b. $175,500

On January 3, Elco Corp., a carpet wholesaler, issued for cash 2,500 shares of no-par common stock (with a stated value of $50) at $65, and on May 15, it issued for cash 1,000 shares of $10 par preferred stock at $13.

a. Journalize the entries for January 3 and May 15, assuming that the common stock is to be credited with the stated value.
b. What is the total amount invested (total paid-in capital) by all stockholders as of May 15?

Exercise 12–5
Issuing stock for assets other than cash
Objective 4

On April 10, Morriss Corporation, a wholesaler of hydraulic lifts, acquired land in exchange for 1,500 shares of $50 par common stock with a current market price of $82. Journalize the entry to record the transaction.

Exercise 12–6
Selected stock transactions
Objective 4

The Guitar Corp., an electric guitar retailer, was organized by Patty Hilderbrand, Ed Petty, and Kathy Yan. The charter authorized 50,000 shares of common stock with a par of $10. The following transactions affecting stockholders' equity were completed during the first year of operations:

a. Issued 800 shares of stock at par to Petty for cash.
b. Issued 100 shares of stock at par to Hilderbrand for promotional services rendered in connection with the organization of the corporation, and issued 900 shares of stock at par to Hilderbrand for cash.

c. Purchased land and a building from Yan. The building is mortgaged for $25,000 for 22 years at 9%, and there is accrued interest of $500 on the mortgage note at the time of the purchase. It is agreed that the land is to be priced at $30,000 and the building at $40,000, and that Yan's equity will be exchanged for stock at par. The corporation agreed to assume responsibility for paying the mortgage note and the accrued interest.

Journalize the entries to record the transactions.

Exercise 12–7
Issuing stock
Objective 4

Biomed Inc., with an authorization of 20,000 shares of preferred stock and 100,000 shares of common stock, completed several transactions involving its stock on July 1, the first day of operations. The trial balance at the close of the day follows:

Cash	450,000	
Land	90,000	
Buildings	60,000	
Preferred $5 Stock, $100 par		100,000
Paid-In Capital in Excess of Par—Preferred Stock		50,000
Common Stock, $50 par		320,000
Paid-In Capital in Excess of Par—Common Stock		130,000
	600,000	600,000

All shares within each class of stock were sold at the same price. The preferred stock was issued in exchange for the land and buildings.

Journalize the two entries to record the transactions summarized in the trial balance.

Exercise 12–8
Issuing stock
Objective 4

Office Products Inc., a wholesaler of office products, was organized on January 7 of the current year, with an authorization of 50,000 shares of $3 noncumulative preferred stock, $100 par and 250,000 shares of $20 par common stock. The following selected transactions were completed during the first year of operations:

Jan. 7. Issued 30,000 shares of common stock at par for cash.
9. Issued 900 shares of common stock at par to an attorney in payment of legal fees for organizing the corporation.
Feb. 4. Issued 8,500 shares of common stock in exchange for land, buildings, and equipment with fair market prices of $60,000, $120,000, and $12,000, respectively.
Mar. 15. Issued 5,000 shares of preferred stock at $101 for cash.

Journalize the transactions.

Exercise 12–9
Treasury stock transactions
Objective 5

✓ b. $3,000 credit

Heavenly Inc. bottles and distributes spring water. On July 1 of the current year, Heavenly Inc. reacquired 3,000 shares of its common stock at $40 per share. On August 10, Heavenly Inc. sold 1,500 of the reacquired shares at $43 per share. The remaining 1,500 shares were sold at $39 per share on December 19.

a. Journalize the transactions of July 1, August 10, and December 19.
b. What is the balance in Paid-In Capital from Sale of Treasury Stock on December 31 of the current year?
c. Where will the balance in Paid-In Capital from Sale of Treasury Stock be reported on the balance sheet?
d. For what reasons might Heavenly Inc. have purchased the treasury stock?

Exercise 12–10
Treasury stock transactions
Objective 5

✓ b. $44,000 credit

Spray Inc. develops and produces spraying equipment for lawn maintenance and industrial uses. On October 1 of the current year, Spray Inc. reacquired 7,500 shares of its common stock at $89 per share. On November 15, 2,000 of the reacquired shares were sold at $93 per share, and on December 28, 4,000 of the reacquired shares were sold at $98.

a. Journalize the transactions of October 1, November 15, and December 28.
b. What is the balance in Paid-In Capital from Sale of Treasury Stock on December 31 of the current year?

c. What is the balance in Treasury Stock on December 31 of the current year?
d. How will the balance in Treasury Stock be reported on the balance sheet?

Exercise 12–11
Effect of stock split
Objective 6

✓ a. 75,000 shares

Flanagan Corporation wholesales ovens and ranges to restaurants throughout the Northeast. Flanagan Corporation, which had 15,000 shares of common stock outstanding, declared a 5-for-1 stock split (4 additional shares for each share issued).

a. What will be the number of shares outstanding after the split?
b. If the common stock had a market price of $175 per share before the stock split, what would be an approximate market price per share after the split?

Exercise 12–12
Effect of cash dividend and stock split
Objectives 6, 7

Indicate whether the following actions would (+) increase, (−) decrease, or (0) not affect Collier Inc.'s total assets, liabilities, and stockholders' equity:

	Assets	Liabilities	Stockholders' Equity
(1) Declaring a cash dividend	_______	_______	_______
(2) Paying the cash dividend declared in (1)	_______	_______	_______
(3) Declaring a stock dividend	_______	_______	_______
(4) Issuing stock certificates for the stock dividend declared in (3)	_______	_______	_______
(5) Authorizing and issuing stock certificates in a stock split	_______	_______	_______

Exercise 12–13
Entries for cash dividends
Objective 7

The dates of importance in connection with a cash dividend of $60,000 on a corporation's common stock are January 3, January 27, and February 15. Journalize the entries required on each date.

Exercise 12–14
Entries for stock dividends
Objective 7

✓ b. (1) $342,500
(3) $642,000

Quick-Fix Inc. is an HMO for twelve businesses in the Cincinnati area. The following account balances appear on the balance sheet of Quick-Fix Inc.: Common stock (50,000 shares authorized), $10 par, $300,000; Paid-in capital in excess of par—common stock, $42,500; and Retained earnings, $299,500. The board of directors declared a 2% stock dividend when the market price of the stock was $16 a share. Quick-Fix Inc. reported no income or loss for the current year.

a. Journalize the entries to record (1) the declaration of the dividend, capitalizing an amount equal to market value, and (2) the issuance of the stock certificates.
b. Determine the following amounts before the stock dividend was declared: (1) total paid-in capital, (2) total retained earnings, and (3) total stockholders' equity.
c. Determine the following amounts after the stock dividend was declared and closing entries were recorded at the end of the year: (1) total paid-in capital, (2) total retained earnings, and (3) total stockholders' equity.

Exercise 12–15
Selected stock and dividend transactions
Objectives 4, 6, 7

Selected transactions completed by SWAT Boating Supply Corporation during the current fiscal year are as follows:

Jan. 9. Split the common stock 3 for 1 and reduced the par from $75 to $25 per share. After the split, there were 150,000 common shares outstanding.
Mar. 1. Declared semiannual dividends of $2 on 5,000 shares of preferred stock and $0.50 on the common stock to stockholders of record on March 25, payable on April 15.
Apr. 15. Paid the cash dividends.
Nov. 30. Declared semiannual dividends of $2 on the preferred stock and $0.80 on the common stock (before the stock dividend). In addition, a 2% common stock dividend was declared on the common stock outstanding. The fair market value of the common stock is estimated at $51.
Dec. 30. Paid the cash dividends and issued the certificates for the common stock dividend.

Journalize the transactions.

Exercise 12–16
Dividend yield
Objective 8

HAT

The finanical statements for **Hershey Foods Corporation** are presented in Appendix G at the end of this text.

a. Determine Hershey's dividend yield as of December 31, 1996 and 1995 on common stock (exclude Class B Common Stock).
Note: Hershey's common stock price was $43.75 and $32.50 on December 31, 1996 and 1995, respectively.
b. What conclusions can you reach from an analysis of these data?

PROBLEMS SERIES A

Problem 12–1A
Dividends on preferred and common stock
Objective 3

SPREADSHEET

✓ 1. Common dividends in 1996: $5,000

Gallatin Corp. manufactures mountain bikes and distributes them through retail outlets in Colorado and Montana. Gallatin Corp. has declared the following annual dividends over a six-year period: 1996, $25,000; 1997, $8,000; 1998, $10,000; 1999, $4,000; 2000, $50,000; and 2001, $75,500. During the entire period, the outstanding stock of the company was composed of 10,000 shares of cumulative, nonparticipating, $2 preferred stock, $50 par, and 25,000 shares of common stock, $10 par.

Instructions

1. Calculate the total dividends and the per-share dividends declared on each class of stock for each of the six years. There were no dividends in arrears on January 1, 1996. Summarize the data in tabular form, using the following column headings:

	Total	Preferred Dividends		Common Dividends	
Year	**Dividends**	**Total**	**Per Share**	**Total**	**Per Share**
1996	$25,000				
1997	8,000				
1998	10,000				
1999	4,000				
2000	50,000				
2001	75,500				

2. Calculate the average annual dividend per share for each class of stock for the six-year period.
3. Assuming that the preferred stock was sold at par and common stock was sold at $10 at the beginning of the six-year period, calculate the percentage return on initial shareholders' investment, based on the average annual dividend per share (a) for preferred stock and (b) for common stock.

Problem 12–2A
Stock transaction for corporate expansion
Objective 4

VXT Corp. produces medical lasers for use in hospitals. The following accounts and their balances appear in the ledger of VXT Corp. on April 30 of the current year:

Preferred $9 Stock, $100 par (20,000 shares authorized, 8,000 shares issued)	$ 800,000
Paid-In Capital in Excess of Par—Preferred Stock	86,000
Common Stock, $20 par (100,000 shares authorized, 75,000 shares issued)	1,500,000
Paid-In Capital in Excess of Par—Common Stock	210,000
Retained Earnings	715,000

At the annual stockholders' meeting on May 12, the board of directors presented a plan for modernizing and expanding plant operations at a cost of approximately $1,000,000. The plan provided (a) that the corporation borrow $220,000, (b) that 3,000 shares of the unissued preferred stock be issued through an underwriter, and (c) that a building, valued at $355,000, and the land on which it is located, valued at $100,000, be acquired in accordance with preliminary negotiations by the issuance of 16,000 shares of common stock. The plan was approved by the stockholders and accomplished by the following transactions:

June 2. Borrowed $220,000 from Palmer National Bank, giving a 10% mortgage note.
10. Issued 3,000 shares of preferred stock, receiving $108 per share in cash from the underwriter.
30. Issued 16,000 shares of common stock in exchange for land and a building, according to the plan.

No other transactions occurred during June.

Instructions

Journalize the entries to record the foregoing transactions.

Problem 12–3A

Selected stock transactions

Objectives 4, 5, 7

GENERAL LEDGER
HAT

Robin Corporation sells and services pipe welding equipment in Texas. The following selected accounts appear in the ledger of Robin Corporation on January 1, 2000, the beginning of the current fiscal year:

Preferred 3% Stock, $100 par (20,000 shares authorized, 12,500 shares issued)	$1,250,000
Paid-In Capital in Excess of Par—Preferred Stock	112,500
Common Stock, $10 par (600,000 shares authorized, 400,000 shares issued)	4,000,000
Paid-In Capital in Excess of Par—Common Stock	600,000
Retained Earnings	1,450,000

During the year, the corporation completed a number of transactions affecting the stockholders' equity. They are summarized as follows:

a. Purchased 20,000 shares of treasury common for $380,000.
b. Sold 5,000 shares of treasury common for $135,000.
c. Sold 3,000 shares of preferred 3% stock at $110.
d. Issued 50,000 shares of common stock at $32, receiving cash.
e. Sold 10,000 shares of treasury common for $170,000.
f. Declared cash dividends of $3 per share on preferred stock and $0.25 per share on common stock.
g. Paid the cash dividends.

Instructions

Journalize the entries to record the transactions. Identify each entry by letter.

Problem 12–4A

Entries for selected corporate transactions

Objectives 4, 5, 7

GENERAL LEDGER
HAT

✓ 3. $1,850,470

GPS Enterprises Inc. produces aeronautical navigation equipment. The stockholders' equity accounts of GPS Enterprises Inc., with balances on January 1 of the current fiscal year, are as follows:

Common Stock, $10 stated value (100,000 shares authorized, 80,000 shares issued)	$800,000
Paid-In Capital in Excess of Stated Value	180,000
Retained Earnings	497,750
Treasury Stock (4,000 shares, at cost)	60,000

The following selected transactions occurred during the year:

Jan. 31. Paid cash dividends of $1 per share on the common stock. The dividend had been properly recorded when declared on December 28 of the preceding fiscal year for $76,000.
Mar. 7. Sold all of the treasury stock for $81,000.
May 5. Issued 10,000 shares of common stock for $210,000.
June 11. Received land from the Olinville City Council as a donation. The land had an estimated fair market value of $75,000.
July 30. Declared a 4% stock dividend on common stock, to be capitalized at the market price of the stock, which is $22 a share.

Aug. 27. Issued the certificates for the dividend declared on July 30.
Oct. 8. Purchased 2,000 shares of treasury stock for $42,500.
Dec. 20. Declared an $0.80-per-share dividend on common stock.
31. Closed the credit balance of the income summary account, $182,500.
31. Closed the two dividends accounts to Retained Earnings.

Instructions

1. Enter the January 1 balances in T accounts for the stockholders' equity accounts listed. Also prepare T accounts for the following: Paid-In Capital from Sale of Treasury Stock; Donated Capital; Stock Dividends Distributable; Stock Dividends; Cash Dividends.
2. Journalize the entries to record the transactions, and post to the nine selected accounts.
3. Determine the total stockholders' equity on December 31.

Problem 12–5A

Entries for selected corporate transactions

Objectives 4, 5, 6, 7

GENERAL LEDGER
HAT

Ocean Pacific Corporation manufactures and distributes leisure clothing. Selected transactions completed by Ocean Pacific during the current fiscal year are as follows:

Jan. 2. Split the common stock 5 for 1 and reduced the par from $50 to $10 per share. After the split, there were 75,000 common shares outstanding.
Mar. 3. Declared semiannual dividends of $4 on 10,000 shares of preferred stock and $0.60 on the 75,000 shares of $10 par common stock to stockholders of record on March 28, payable on April 15.
Apr. 15. Paid the cash dividends.
30. Purchased 8,000 shares of the corporation's own common stock at $17, recording the stock at cost.
July 10. Sold 3,000 shares of treasury stock at $20, receiving cash.
23. Declared semiannual dividends of $4 on the preferred stock and $0.75 on the common stock (before the stock dividend). In addition, a 2% common stock dividend was declared on the common stock outstanding, to be capitalized at the fair market value of the common stock, which is estimated at $21.
Aug. 25. Paid the cash dividends and issued the certificates for the common stock dividend.

Instructions

Journalize the transactions.

PROBLEMS SERIES B

Problem 12–1B

Dividends on preferred and common stock

Objective 3

SPREADSHEET

✓ 1. Common dividends in 1998: $31,000

TCX Inc. owns and operates movie theaters throughout Georgia and Alabama. TCX Inc. has declared the following annual dividends over a six-year period: 1996, $32,000; 1997, $65,000; 1998, $84,000; 1999, $60,000; 2000, $72,000; and 2001, $95,000. During the entire period, the outstanding stock of the company was composed of 5,000 shares of cumulative, nonparticipating, $10 preferred stock, $100 par, and 20,000 shares of common stock, $10 par.

Instructions

1. Calculate the total dividends and the per-share dividends declared on each class of stock for each of the six years. There were no dividends in arrears on January 1, 1996. Summarize the data in tabular form, using the following column headings:

	Total	Preferred Dividends		Common Dividends	
Year	**Dividends**	**Total**	**Per Share**	**Total**	**Per Share**
1996	$32,000				
1997	65,000				
1998	84,000				
1999	60,000				
2000	72,000				
2001	95,000				

2. Calculate the average annual dividend per share for each class of stock for the six-year period.
3. Assuming that the preferred stock was sold at par and common stock was sold at $15 at the beginning of the six-year period, calculate the percentage return on initial shareholders' investment, based on the average annual dividend per share (a) for preferred stock and (b) for common stock.

Problem 12–2B

Stock transactions for corporate expansion

Objective 4

On January 1 of the current year, the following accounts and their balances appear in the ledger of Teca Corp., a meat processor:

Preferred $9 Stock, $100 par (10,000 shares authorized, 5,000 shares issued)	$ 500,000
Paid-In Capital in Excess of Par—Preferred Stock	80,000
Common Stock, $20 par (100,000 shares authorized, 75,000 shares issued)	1,500,000
Paid-In Capital in Excess of Par—Common Stock	125,000
Retained Earnings	505,000

At the annual stockholders' meeting on February 11, the board of directors presented a plan for modernizing and expanding plant operations at a cost of approximately $800,000. The plan provided (a) that a building, valued at $280,000, and the land on which it is located, valued at $50,000, be acquired in accordance with preliminary negotiations by the issuance of 12,000 shares of common stock, (b) that 2,500 shares of the unissued preferred stock be issued through an underwriter, and (c) that the corporation borrow $200,000. The plan was approved by the stockholders and accomplished by the following transactions:

Mar. 3. Issued 12,000 shares of common stock in exchange for land and a building, according to the plan.
15. Issued 2,500 shares of preferred stock, receiving $104 per share in cash from the underwriter.
31. Borrowed $200,000 from Highland National Bank, giving a 9% mortgage note.

No other transactions occurred during March.

Instructions

Journalize the entries to record the foregoing transactions.

Problem 12–3B

Selected stock transactions

Objectives 4, 5, 7

GENERAL LEDGER

The following selected accounts appear in the ledger of KWR Environmental Corporation on July 1, 1999, the beginning of the current fiscal year:

Preferred 4% Stock, $50 par (10,000 shares authorized, 7,000 shares issued)	$350,000
Paid-In Capital in Excess of Par—Preferred Stock	28,000
Common Stock, $20 par (50,000 shares authorized, 25,000 shares issued)	500,000
Paid-In Capital in Excess of Par—Common Stock	90,000
Retained Earnings	537,000

During the year, the corporation completed a number of transactions affecting the stockholders' equity. They are summarized as follows:

a. Issued 5,000 shares of common stock at $30, receiving cash.
b. Sold 1,000 shares of preferred 4% stock at $53.
c. Purchased 2,500 shares of treasury common for $60,000.
d. Sold 1,500 shares of treasury common for $45,000.
e. Sold 500 shares of treasury common for $11,500.
f. Declared cash dividends of $2 per share on preferred stock and $1 per share on common stock.
g. Paid the cash dividends.

Instructions

Journalize the entries to record the transactions. Identify each entry by letter.

Problem 12–4B

Entries for selected corporate transactions

Objectives 4, 5, 7

GENERAL LEDGER

✓ 3. $2,692,090

Pittard Enterprises Inc. manufactures bathroom fixtures. The stockholders' equity accounts of Pittard Enterprises Inc., with balances on January 1 of the current fiscal year, are as follows:

Common Stock, $25 stated value (100,000 shares authorized, 50,000 shares issued)	$1,250,000
Paid-In Capital in Excess of Stated Value	250,000
Retained Earnings	725,000
Treasury Stock (2,500 shares, at cost)	80,000

The following selected transactions occurred during the year:

Jan. 20. Received land from the city as a donation. The land had an estimated fair market value of $150,000.
29. Paid cash dividends of $1 per share on the common stock. The dividend had been properly recorded when declared on December 30 of the preceding fiscal year for $47,500.
Mar. 3. Issued 6,000 shares of common stock for $240,000.
Apr. 1. Sold all of the treasury stock for $105,000.
July 1. Declared a 2% stock dividend on common stock, to be capitalized at the market price of the stock, which is $42 a share.
Aug. 11. Issued the certificates for the dividend declared on July 1.
Nov. 20. Purchased 2,500 shares of treasury stock for $90,000.
Dec. 21. Declared a $0.50-per-share dividend on common stock.
31. Closed the credit balance of the income summary account, $169,400.
31. Closed the two dividends accounts to Retained Earnings.

Instructions

1. Enter the January 1 balances in T accounts for the stockholders' equity accounts listed. Also prepare T accounts for the following: Paid-In Capital from Sale of Treasury Stock; Donated Capital; Stock Dividends Distributable; Stock Dividends; Cash Dividends.
2. Journalize the entries to record the transactions, and post to the nine selected accounts.
3. Determine the total stockholders' equity on December 31.

Problem 12–5B

Entries for selected corporate transactions

Objectives 4, 5, 6, 7

GENERAL LEDGER

Selected transactions completed by CSB Boating Supply Corporation during the current fiscal year are as follows:

Jan. 9. Split the common stock 4 for 1 and reduced the par from $100 to $25 per share. After the split, there were 100,000 common shares outstanding.
Feb. 10. Purchased 5,000 shares of the corporation's own common stock at $38, recording the stock at cost.
May 1. Declared semiannual dividends of $3 on 5,000 shares of preferred stock and $0.80 on the common stock to stockholders of record on May 20, payable on July 15.
July 15. Paid the cash dividends.
Aug. 22. Sold 2,500 shares of treasury stock at $44, receiving cash.
Nov. 30. Declared semiannual dividends of $3 on the preferred stock and $0.90 on the common stock (before the stock dividend). In addition, a 2% common stock dividend was declared on the common stock outstanding. The fair market value of the common stock is estimated at $51.
Dec. 30. Paid the cash dividends and issued the certificates for the common stock dividend.

Instructions

Journalize the transactions.

SPECIAL ACTIVITIES

Activity 12–1
Resources Unlimited Inc.
Ethics and professional conduct in business

Aubrey Stone and Karl Murray are organizing Resources Unlimited Inc. to undertake a high-risk gold-mining venture in Mexico. Aubrey and Karl tentatively plan to request authorization for 100,000,000 shares of common stock to be sold to the general public. Aubrey and Karl have decided to establish par of $0.10 per share in order to appeal to a wide variety of potential investors. Aubrey and Karl feel that investors would be more willing to invest in the company if they received a large quantity of shares for what might appear to be a "bargain" price.

Discuss whether Aubrey and Karl are behaving in a professional manner.

Activity 12–2
Wellness Inc.
Issuing stock

What do you THINK?

Wellness Inc. began operations on January 3, 2000, with the issuance of 50,000 shares of $100 par common stock. The sole stockholders of Wellness Inc. are Neal Barnes and Dr. Donna Elfand, who organized Wellness Inc. with the objective of developing a new flu vaccine. Dr. Elfand claims that the flu vaccine, which is nearing the final development stage, will protect individuals against 98% of the flu types that have been medically identified. To complete the project, Wellness Inc. needs $3,000,000 of additional funds. The local banks have been unwilling to loan the funds because of the lack of sufficient collateral and the riskiness of the business.

The following is a conversation between Neal Barnes, the chief executive officer of Wellness Inc., and Dr. Donna Elfand, the leading researcher.

Barnes: What are we going to do? The banks won't loan us any more money, and we've got to have $3 million to complete the project. We are so close! It would be a disaster to quit now. The only thing I can think of is to issue additional stock. Do you have any suggestions?

Elfand: I guess you're right. But if the banks won't loan us any more money, how do you think we can find any investors to buy stock?

Barnes: I've been thinking about that. What if we promise the investors that we will pay them 2% of net sales until they have received an amount equal to what they paid for the stock?

Elfand: What happens when we pay back the $3 million? Do the investors get to keep the stock? If they do, it'll dilute our ownership.

Barnes: How about, if after we pay back the $3 million, we make them turn in their stock for $200 per share? That's twice what they paid for it, plus they would have already gotten all their money back. That's a $200 profit per share for the investors.

Elfand: It could work. We get our money, but don't have to pay any interest, dividends, or the $200 until we start generating net sales. At the same time, the investors could get their money back plus $200 per share.

Barnes: We'll need current financial statements for the new investors. I'll get our accountant working on them and contact our attorney to draw up a legally binding contract for the new investors. Yes, this could work.

In late 2000, the attorney and the various regulatory authorities approved the new stock offering, and 30,000 shares of common stock were privately sold to new investors at the stock's par of $100.

In preparing financial statements for 2000, Neal Barnes and Chris Thaxton, the controller for Wellness Inc., have the following conversation.

Thaxton: Neal, I've got a problem.

Barnes: What's that, Chris?

Thaxton: Issuing common stock to raise that additional $3 million was a great idea. But . . .

Barnes: But what?

Thaxton: I've got to prepare the 2000 annual financial statements, and I am not sure how to classify the common stock.

Barnes: What do you mean? It's common stock.

Thaxton: I'm not so sure. I called the auditor and explained how we are contractually obligated to pay the new stockholders 2% of net sales until $100 per share is paid. Then, we may be obligated to pay them $200 per share.

Barnes: So . . .

Thaxton: So the auditor thinks that we should classify the additional issuance of $3 million as debt, not stock! And, if we put the $3 million on the balance sheet as debt, we will violate our other loan agreements with the banks. And, if these agreements are violated, the banks may call in all our debt immediately. If they do that, we are in deep trouble. We'll probably have to file for bankruptcy. We just don't have the cash to pay off the banks.

1. Discuss the arguments for and against classifying the issuance of the $3 million of stock as debt.
2. What do you think might be a practical solution to this classification problem?

Activity 12–3 Tidmore Inc.

Dividends

Tidmore Inc. has paid quarterly cash dividends since 1990. These dividends have steadily increased from $0.20 per share to the latest dividend declaration of $0.50 per share. The board of directors would like to continue this trend and is hesitant to suspend or decrease the amount of quarterly dividends. Unfortunately, sales dropped sharply in the fourth quarter of 2000 because of worsening economic conditions and increased competition. As a result, the board is uncertain as to whether it should declare a dividend for the last quarter of 2000.

On November 1, 2000, Tidmore Inc. borrowed $500,000 from Second National Bank to use in modernizing its retail stores and to expand its product line in reaction to its competition. The terms of the 10-year, 12% loan require Tidmore Inc. to:

a. Pay monthly interest on last day of month.
b. Pay $50,000 of the principal each November 1, beginning in 2001.
c. Maintain a current ratio (current assets ÷ current liabilities) of 2.
d. Maintain a minimum balance (a compensating balance) of $25,000 in its Second National Bank account.

On December 31, 2000, the $500,000 loan had been disbursed in modernization of the retail stores and in expansion of the product line. Tidmore Inc.'s balance sheet as of December 31, 2000, is as follows:

Tidmore Inc.
Balance Sheet
December 31, 2000

Assets

Current assets:			
Cash		$ 40,000	
Accounts receivable	$ 91,500		
Less allowance for doubtful accounts	6,500	85,000	
Merchandise inventory		500,000	
Prepaid expenses		4,500	
Total current assets			$ 629,500
Property, plant, and equipment:			
Land		$150,000	
Buildings	$950,000		
Less accumulated depreciation	215,000	735,000	
Equipment	$460,000		
Less accumulated depreciation	110,000	350,000	
Total property, plant, and equipment			1,235,000
Total assets			$1,864,500

(continues)

Liabilities			
Current liabilities:			
Accounts payable	$ 71,800		
Notes payable (Second National Bank)	50,000		
Salaries payable	3,200		
Total current liabilities		$125,000	
Long-term liabilities:			
Notes payable (Second National Bank)		450,000	
Total liabilities			$ 575,000
Stockholders' Equity			
Paid-in capital:			
Common stock, $20 par (50,000 shares authorized, 25,000 shares issued)	$500,000		
Excess of issue price over par	40,000		
Total paid-in capital		$540,000	
Retained earnings		749,500	
Total stockholders' equity			1,289,500
Total liabilities and stockholders' equity			$1,864,500

The board of directors is scheduled to meet January 10, 2001, to discuss the results of operations for 2000 and to consider the declaration of dividends for the fourth quarter of 2000. The chairman of the board has asked for your advice on the declaration of dividends.

1. What factors should the board consider in deciding whether to declare a cash dividend?
2. The board is considering the declaration of a stock dividend instead of a cash dividend. Discuss the issuance of a stock dividend from the point of view of (a) a stockholder and (b) the board of directors.

Activity 12–4
Into the Real World
Profiling a corporation

GROUP ACTIVITY

Internet ACTIVITY

Select a public corporation you are familiar with or which interests you. Using the Internet, your school library, and other sources, develop a short (2 to 5 pages) profile of the corporation. Include in your profile the following information:

1. Name of the corporation.
2. State of incorporation.
3. Nature of its operations.
4. Total assets for the most recent balance sheet.
5. Total revenues for the most recent income statement.
6. Net income for the most recent income statement.
7. Classes of stock outstanding.
8. Market price of the stock outstanding.
9. High and low price of the stock for the past year.
10. Dividends paid for each share of stock during the past year.

In groups of three or four, discuss each corporate profile. Select one of the corporations, assuming that your group has $100,000 to invest in its stock. Summarize why your group selected the corporation it did and how financial accounting information may have affected your decision. Keep track of the performance of your corporation's stock for the remainder of the term.

Note: Most major corporations maintain "home pages" on the Internet. This home page provides a variety of information on the corporation and often includes the corporation's financial statements. In addition, the New York Stock Exchange Web site (**www.nyse.com**) includes links to the home pages of many listed companies. Financial statements can also be accessed using EDGAR, the electronic archives of financial statements filed with the Securities and Exchange Commission (SEC). The EDGAR Internet address is **www.sec.gov/edgarhp.htm.**

To obtain annual report information, type in a company name on the "Search EDGAR Archives" form. EDGAR will list the reports available for the selected company. A company's annual report (along with other information) is provided in its annual 10-K report to the SEC. Click on the 10-K (or 10-K405) report for the year you wish to download. If you wish, you can save the whole 10-K report to a file, then open it with your word processor.

ANSWERS TO SELF-EXAMINATION QUESTIONS

Matching

1. O	4. I	7. H	10. K	13. L	15. T	17. A	19. F
2. R	5. M	8. N	11. G	14. E	16. Q	18. P	20. J
3. S	6. D	9. B	12. C				

Multiple Choice

1. **C** If a corporation has cumulative preferred stock outstanding, dividends that have been passed for prior years plus the dividend for the current year must be paid before dividends may be declared on common stock. In this case, dividends of \$27,000 (\$9,000 × 3) have been passed for the preceding three years, and the current year's dividends are \$9,000, making a total of \$36,000 (answer C) that must be paid to preferred stockholders before dividends can be declared on common stock.
2. **D** Paid-in capital is one of the two major subdivisions of the stockholders' equity of a corporation. It may result from many sources, including the issuance of cumulative preferred stock (answer A), the receipt of donated real estate (answer B), or the sale of a corporation's treasury stock (answer C).
3. **D** The Stockholders' Equity section of corporate balance sheets is divided into two principal subsections: (1) investments contributed by the stockholders and others and (2) net income retained in the business. Included as part of the investments by stockholders and others is the par of common stock (answer A), donated capital (answer B), and the par of preferred stock (answer C).
4. **C** Reacquired stock, known as treasury stock, should be listed in the Stockholders' Equity section (answer C) of the balance sheet. The price paid for the treasury stock is deducted from the total of all the stockholders' equity accounts.
5. **C** If a corporation that holds treasury stock declares a cash dividend, the dividends are not paid on the treasury shares. To do so would place the corporation in the position of earning income through dealing with itself. Thus, the corporation will record \$44,000 (answer C) as cash dividends [(25,000 shares issued less 3,000 shares held as treasury stock) × \$2 per share dividend].

13

Corporations: Income and Taxes, Stockholders' Equity, and Investments in Stocks

Setting the STAGE

If you apply for a bank loan, you will be required to list your assets and liabilities on a loan application. In addition, you will be asked to indicate your monthly income. Assume that the day you were filling out the application, you won $3,000 in the state lottery. The $3,000 lottery winnings increase your assets by $3,000. Should you also show your lottery winnings as part of your monthly income?

The answer, of course, is no. Winning the lottery is an unusual event and, for most of us, a nonrecurring event. In determining whether to grant the loan, the bank is interested in your ability to make monthly loan payments. Such payments depend upon your recurring monthly income.

Businesses also experience unusual and nonrecurring events that affect their financial statements. Such events should be clearly disclosed in the financial statements so that stakeholders in the business will not misinterpret the financial effects of the events. In this chapter, we discuss unusual items that affect corporate income statements and illustrate how such items should be reported.

objectives

After studying this chapter, you should be able to:

1. Journalize the entries for corporate income taxes, including deferred income taxes.
2. Prepare an income statement reporting the following unusual items: discontinued operations, extraordinary items, and changes in accounting principles.
3. Prepare an income statement reporting earnings per share data.
4. Prepare financial statement presentations of stockholders' equity.
5. Describe the concept and the reporting of comprehensive income.
6. Describe the accounting for investments in stocks.
7. Describe alternative methods of combining businesses and how consolidated financial statements are prepared.
8. Compute and interpret the price-earnings ratio.

Corporate Income Taxes

OBJECTIVE 1

Journalize the entries for corporate income taxes, including deferred income taxes.

Under the United States tax code, corporations are taxable entities that must pay federal income taxes. Depending upon where it is located, a corporation may also be required to pay state and local income taxes. Although we limit our discussion to federal income taxes, the basic concepts also apply to other income taxes.

Point of INTEREST

Individuals must pay estimated taxes (on the 15th of January, April, June, and September) if the amount of tax withholding is not sufficient to pay their taxes at the end of the year. This usually occurs when a significant portion of an individual's income is from rent, dividends, or interest.

Payment of Income Taxes

Most corporations are required to pay estimated federal income taxes in four installments throughout the year. For example, assume that a corporation with a calendar-year accounting period estimates its income tax expense for the year as $84,000. The entry to record the first of the four estimated tax payments of $21,000 (1/4 of $84,000) is as follows:

April	15	Income Tax Expense	21 000 00	
		Cash		21 000 00
		To record quarterly payment of		
		estimated income tax.		

At year end, the actual taxable income and the related tax are determined.[1] If additional taxes are owed, the additional liability is recorded. If the total estimated tax payments are greater than the tax liability based on actual taxable income, the overpayment should be debited to a receivable account and credited to *Income Tax Expense*.

[1] A corporation's income tax returns and supporting records are subject to audits by taxing authorities, who may assess additional taxes. Because of this possibility, the liability for income taxes is sometimes described in the balance sheet as *Estimated income tax payable*.

Because income taxes are often a significant amount, they are normally reported on the income statement as a special deduction, as shown below in an excerpt from an income statement for **The Procter & Gamble Company**.

Years Ended June 30	1997
Net Sales	**$35,764**
Cost of products sold	**20,316**
Marketing, research, and administrative expenses	**9,960**
Operating Income	**5,488**
Interest expense	**457**
Other income, net	**218**
Earnings Before Income Taxes	**5,249**
Income taxes	**1,834**
Net Earnings	**$ 3,415**

Allocation of Income Taxes

The **taxable income** of a corporation is determined according to the tax laws. It is often different from the income before income taxes reported in the income statement according to generally accepted accounting principles. As a result, the *income tax based on taxable income* usually differs from the *income tax based on income before taxes.* This difference may need to be allocated between various financial statement periods, depending on the nature of the items causing the differences.

Some differences between taxable income and income before income taxes are created because items are recognized in one period for tax purposes and in another period for income statement purposes. Such differences, called **temporary differences**, reverse or turn around in later years. Some examples of items that create temporary differences are listed below.

1. *Revenues or gains are taxed* **after** *they are reported in the income statement.* Example: In some cases, companies who make sales under an installment plan recognize revenue for financial reporting purposes when a sale is made, but defer recognizing revenue for tax purposes until cash is collected.
2. *Expenses or losses are deducted in determining taxable income* **after** *they are reported in the income statement.* Example: Product warranty expense estimated and reported in the year of the sale for financial statement reporting is deducted for tax reporting when paid.
3. *Revenues or gains are taxed* **before** *they are reported in the income statement.* Example: Cash received in advance for magazine subscriptions is included in taxable income when received, but included in the income statement only when earned in a future period.
4. *Expenses or losses are deducted in determining taxable income* **before** *they are reported in the income statement.* Example: MACRS depreciation is used for tax purposes, and the straight-line method is used for financial reporting purposes.

Since temporary differences reverse in later years, they do not change or reduce the total amount of taxable income over the life of a business. Exhibit 1 illustrates the reversing nature of temporary differences in which a business uses MACRS depreciation for tax purposes and straight-line depreciation for financial statement purposes. MACRS recognizes more depreciation in the early years, but less depreciation in the later years. The total depreciation expense is the same for both methods over the life of the asset.

EXHIBIT 1
Temporary Differences

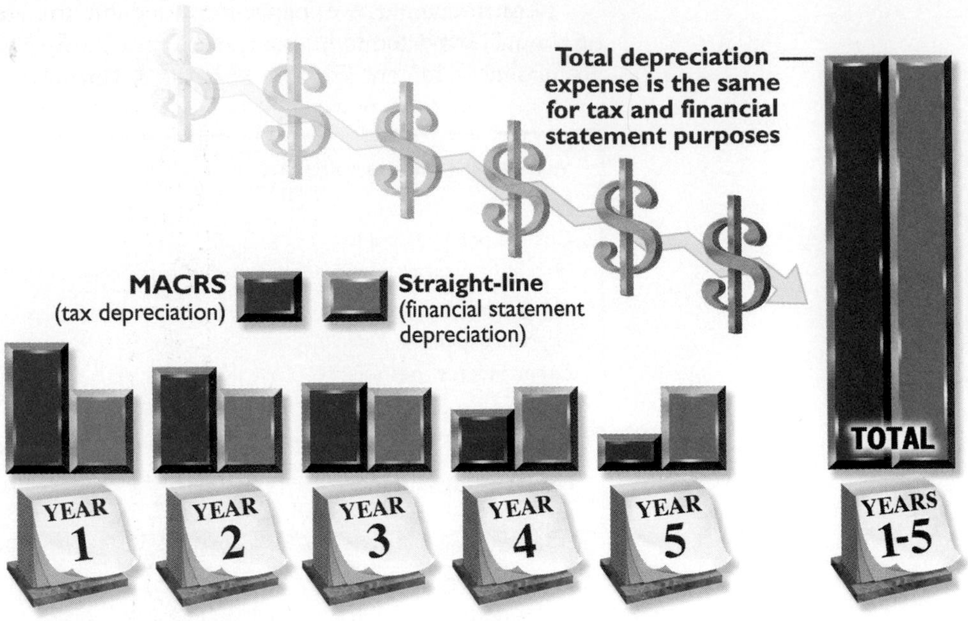

As Exhibit 1 illustrates, temporary differences affect only the timing of when revenues and expenses are recognized for tax purposes. As a result, the total amount of taxes paid does not change. Only the timing of the payment of taxes is affected. In most cases, managers use tax-planning techniques so that temporary differences delay or defer the payment of taxes to later years. As a result, at the end of each year, the amount of the current tax liability and the postponed (deferred) liability must be recorded.

To illustrate, assume that at the end of the first year of operations a corporation reports $300,000 income before income taxes on its income statement. If we assume an income tax rate of 40%, the income tax expense reported on the income statement is $120,000 ($300,000 × 40%).[2] However, to reduce the amount owed for current income taxes, the corporation uses tax planning to reduce the taxable income to $100,000. Thus, the income tax actually due for the year is only $40,000 ($100,000 × 40%). The $80,000 ($120,000 − $40,000) difference between the two tax amounts is created by timing differences in recognizing revenue. This amount is deferred to future years. The example is summarized below.

Income tax based on $300,000 reported income at 40%	$120,000
Income tax based on $100,000 taxable income at 40%	40,000
Income tax deferred to future years	$ 80,000

Q&A *A corporation has $300,000 income before income taxes and $130,000 taxable income. What is the amount of deferred income tax?*

$68,000 [($300,000 × 40%) − ($130,000 × 40%)]

To match the current year's expenses (including income tax) against the current year's revenue on the income statement, income tax is allocated between periods, using the following journal entry:

		Income Tax Expense	120 000 00	
		Income Tax Payable		40 000 00
		Deferred Income Tax Payable		80 000 00
		To record income tax for the year.		

[2] For purposes of illustration, the 40% rate is assumed to include all federal, state, and local income taxes.

The income tax expense reported on the income statement is the total tax, $120,000, expected to be paid on the income for the year. In future years, the $80,000 in *Deferred Income Tax Payable* will be transferred to *Income Tax Payable* as the timing differences reverse and the taxes become due. For example, if $48,000 of the deferred tax reverses and becomes due in the second year, the following journal entry would be made in the second year:

	Deferred Income Tax Payable	48 000 00	
	Income Tax Payable		48 000 00
	To record current liability for		
	deferred tax.		

The balance of *Deferred Income Tax Payable* at the end of a year is reported as a liability. The amount due within one year is classified as a current liability. The remainder is classified as a long-term liability or reported in a Deferred Credits section following the Long-Term Liabilities section.[3]

Differences between taxable income and income (before taxes) reported on the income statement may also arise because certain revenues are exempt from tax and certain expenses are not deductible in determining taxable income.[4] For example, interest income on municipal bonds may be exempt from taxation. Such differences create no special financial reporting problems, since the amount of income tax determined according to the tax laws is the *same* amount reported on the income statement.

Point of INTEREST

Interest from investments in municipal bonds is also tax exempt for individual tax purposes.

Unusual Items that Affect the Income Statement

OBJECTIVE 2

Prepare an income statement reporting the following unusual items: discontinued operations, extraordinary items, and changes in accounting principles.

Three types of unusual items that may affect the current year's net income are:

1. The results of discontinued operations.
2. Extraordinary items that result in a gain or loss.
3. A change from one generally accepted accounting principle to another.

These items are reported separately in the income statement, as shown in the income statement for Jones Corporation in Exhibit 2. Many different terms and formats may be used. For example, the related tax effects of unusual items may be reported with the item with which they are associated or in the notes to the statement.

In the following paragraphs, we briefly discuss each of the three types of unusual items. We assume that these items are material to the financial statements. Immaterial items would not affect the normal financial statement presentation.

[3] In some cases, a deferred tax asset may arise for tax benefits to be received in the future. Such deferred tax assets are reported as either a current or a long-term asset, depending on when the benefits are expected to be realized.

[4] Such differences, which will not reverse with the passage of time, are sometimes called *permanent differences*.

EXHIBIT 2
Unusual Items in Income Statement

Jones Corporation
Income Statement
For the Year Ended December 31, 2000

Net sales	$9,600,000
Cost of merchandise sold	5,800,000
Gross profit	$3,800,000
Operating expenses	2,490,000
Income from continuing operations before income tax	$1,310,000
Income tax expense	620,000
Income from continuing operations	$ 690,000
Loss on discontinued operations (Note A)	100,000
Income before extraordinary items and cumulative effect of a change in accounting principle	$ 590,000
Extraordinary item:	
Gain on condemnation of land, net of applicable income tax of $65,000	150,000
Cumulative effect on prior years of changing to a different depreciation method (Note B)	92,000
Net income	$ 832,000

Note A.

On July 1 of the current year, the electrical products division of the corporation was sold at a loss of $100,000, net of applicable income tax of $50,000. The net sales of the division for the current year were $2,900,000. The assets sold were composed of inventories, equipment, and plant totaling $2,100,000. The purchaser assumed liabilities of $600,000.

Note B.

Depreciation of all property, plant, and equipment has been computed by the straight-line method in 2000. Prior to 2000, depreciation of equipment for one of the divisions had been computed on the double-declining-balance method. In 2000, the straight-line method was adopted for this division in order to achieve uniformity and to better match depreciation charges with the estimated economic utility of such assets. Consistent with APB Opinion No. 20, this change in depreciation has been applied to prior years. The effect of the change was to increase income by $30,000 before extraordinary items for 2000. The adjustment of $92,000 (after reduction for income tax of $88,000) to apply the new method to prior years is also included in income for 2000.

Discontinued Operations

A gain or loss from disposing of a business segment is reported on the income statement as a gain or loss from **discontinued operations**. The term **business segment** refers to a major line of business for a company, such as a division or a department or a certain class of customer. For example, assume that Jones Corporation has separate divisions that produce electrical products, hardware supplies, and lawn equipment. Jones sells its electrical products division at a loss. As shown in Exhibit 2, this loss is deducted from Jones's income from continuing operations (income from its hardware and lawn equipment divisions). In addition, Note A discloses the identity of the segment sold, the disposal date, a description of the segment's assets and liabilities, and the manner of disposal.

REAL WORLD Events that are both unusual and infrequent are uncommon. For example, the 1996 edition of *Accounting Trends & Techniques* indicated that only 81 of 600 companies surveyed reported extraordinary items.

Extraordinary Items

Extraordinary items result from events and transactions that (1) are significantly different (unusual) from the typical or the normal operating activities of the business and (2) occur infrequently. The gains and losses that result from natural disasters which occur infrequently, such as floods, earthquakes, and fires, are extraordinary items. Gains or losses from condemning land or buildings for public use are also extraordinary. Such gains and losses, other than those from disposing of a business segment, should be reported in the income statement as extraordinary items, as shown in Exhibit 2.

Sometimes extraordinary items result in unusual financial results. For example, **Delta Air Lines** once reported an extraordinary gain of over $5.5 million as the result of the crash of one of its 727s. The plane that crashed was insured for $6.5 million, but its book value in Delta's accounting records was $962,000.

Gains and losses on the disposal of fixed assets are *not* extraordinary items. This is because (1) they are not unusual and (2) they recur from time to time in the normal operations of a business. Likewise, gains and losses from the sale of investments are usual and recurring for most businesses.

Changes in Accounting Principles

Businesses are often required to change their accounting principles when the Financial Accounting Standards Board (FASB) issues a new accounting standard. In addition, a business may voluntarily change from one generally accepted accounting principle to another. For example, a corporation may change from the fifo to the lifo method of costing inventory to better match revenues and expenses. Changes in generally accepted accounting principles should be disclosed in the financial statements (or in notes to the statements) of the period in which they occur. This disclosure should include the following:

1. The nature of the change.
2. The justification for the change.
3. The effect on the current year's net income.
4. The cumulative effect of the change on the net income of prior periods.

To illustrate, assume that one of Jones Corporation's divisions changes from the double-declining-balance method to the straight-line method of depreciation. As shown in Exhibit 2, the cumulative effect of this change is reported after the extraordinary items. The effect on the prior period is explained in Note B. If financial statements for prior periods are also presented, they should be restated as if the change had been made in the prior periods, and the effect of the restatement should be reported either on the face of the statements or in a note.

REAL WORLD: The 1996 edition of *Accounting Trends & Techniques* indicated that the majority of accounting changes were due to adopting a new accounting standard issued by the Financial Accounting Standards Board.

REAL WORLD: **Sears, Roebuck and Co.** reported net income of $1,801 million in 1995, $1,454 million in 1994, and $2,374 million in 1993. However, Sears also reported gains from discontinued operations of $776 million in 1995, $402 million in 1994, and $1,960 million in 1993. These gains reflect Sears' decision to refocus its efforts on its retail operations. So, for example, Sears spun off (discontinued) its **Allstate** insurance operations in 1995 at a gain of $776 million. Thus, the income from continuing operations for 1995 was $1,025 ($1,801 − $776) million. Without adequate disclosure and reporting of such unusual items, a reasonable prediction of future earnings and cash flows would be impaired.

Reporting unusual items separately on the income statement allows investors to isolate the effects of these items on income and cash flows. By reporting such items, investors and other users of the financial statements can consider such factors in assessing a business's future income and cash flows.

Earnings per Common Share

OBJECTIVE 3

Prepare an income statement reporting earnings per share data.

The amount of net income is often used by investors and creditors in evaluating a company's profitability. However, net income by itself is difficult to use in comparing companies of different sizes. Also, trends in net income may be difficult to evaluate, using only net income, if there have been significant changes in a company's stockholders' equity. Thus, the profitability of companies is often expressed as earnings per share. **Earnings per common share (EPS)**, sometimes called **basic earnings per share**, is the net income per share of common stock outstanding during a period.

Because of its importance, earnings per share is reported in the financial press and by various investor services, such as **Moody's** and **Standard & Poor's**. Changes in earnings per share can lead to significant changes in the price of a corporation's stock in the marketplace. For example, **Ben & Jerry's Homemade Inc.** stock dropped to its lowest point in three years ($13.375 per share) after the company announced earnings per share of 10 cents. The premium ice cream company had earned 34 cents per share a year earlier, and Wall Street analysts had been expecting earnings of 27 cents per share. In contrast, during the same time, the stock of **Scientific-Atlanta Inc.** surged by over 13 percent to $39 per share, after the company announced earnings per share of 53 cents as compared to 25 cents per share a year earlier. Wall Street analysts had been expecting earnings per share of 41 cents.

Corporations whose stock is traded in a public market must report earnings per common share on their income statements.[5] If no preferred stock is outstanding, the earnings per common share is calculated as follows:

$$\text{Earnings per common share} = \frac{\text{Net income}}{\text{Number of common shares outstanding}}$$

When the number of common shares outstanding has changed during the period, a weighted average number of shares outstanding is used. If a company has preferred stock outstanding, the net income must be reduced by the amount of any preferred dividends, as shown below.

$$\text{Earnings per common share} = \frac{\text{Net income} - \text{Preferred stock dividends}}{\text{Number of common shares outstanding}}$$

Comparing the earnings per share of two or more years, based on only the net incomes of those years, could be misleading. For example, assume that Jones Corporation, whose partial income statement was presented in Exhibit 2, reported $700,000 net income for 1999. Also assume that no extraordinary or other unusual items were reported in 1999. Jones has no preferred stock outstanding and has 200,000 common shares outstanding in 1999 and 2000. The earnings per common share is $3.50 ($700,000/200,000 shares) for 1999 and $4.16 ($832,000/200,000 shares) for 2000. Comparing the two earnings per share amounts suggests that operations have improved. However, the 2000 earnings per share comparable to the $3.50 is $3.45, which is the income from continuing operations of $690,000 divided by 200,000 shares. The latter amount indicates a slight downturn in normal earnings.

When unusual items exist, earnings per common share should be reported for those items. To illustrate, a partial income statement for Jones Corporation, showing earnings per common share, is shown in Exhibit 3. In this income statement, Jones reports all the earnings per common share amounts on the face of the income statement. However, only earnings per share amounts for income from continuing opera-

EXHIBIT 3
Income Statement with Earnings per Share

Jones Corporation
Income Statement
For the Year Ended December 31, 2000

Earnings per common share:	
Income from continuing operations	$3.45
Loss on discontinued operations (Note A)	0.50
Income before extraordinary items and cumulative effect of a change in accounting principle	$2.95
Extraordinary item:	
Gain on condemnation of land, net of applicable income tax of $65,000	0.75
Cumulative effect on prior years of changing to a different depreciation method (Note B)	0.46
Net income	$4.16

[5] *Statement of Financial Accounting Standards No. 128,* "Earnings per Share," Financial Accounting Standards Board (Norwalk, Connecticut: 1997).

tions and net income are required to be presented on the face of the statement. The other per share amounts may be presented in the notes to the financial statements.[6]

In the preceding paragraphs, we have assumed a simple capital structure with only common stock or common stock and preferred stock outstanding. Often, however, corporations have complex capital structures with various types of securities outstanding, such as convertible preferred stock, options, warrants, and contingently issuable shares. In such cases, the possible effects of converting such securities to common stock must be calculated and reported in the financial statements.[7] Such effects are often reported as *earnings per common share assuming dilution* or *diluted earnings per share*. Considering the effect of such securities on earnings per share is discussed in advanced accounting texts.

Reporting Stockholders' Equity

OBJECTIVE 4

Prepare financial statement presentations of stockholders' equity.

As with other sections of the balance sheet, alternative terms and formats may be used in reporting stockholders' equity. In addition, the significant changes in the sources of stockholders' equity—paid-in capital and retained earnings—may be reported in separate statements or notes that support the balance sheet presentation.

Reporting Paid-In Capital

Two alternatives for reporting paid-in capital in the balance sheet are shown in Exhibit 4. In the first example, each class of stock is listed first, followed by its related paid-in capital accounts. In the second example, the stock accounts are listed first. The other paid-in capital accounts are listed as a single item described as *Addi-*

EXHIBIT 4
Paid-In Capital Section of Stockholders' Equity

Stockholders' Equity

Paid-in capital:			
Preferred $5 stock, cumulative, $50 par (2,000 shares authorized and issued)	$100,000		
Excess of issue price over par . .	10,000	$ 110,000	
Common stock, $20 par (50,000 shares authorized, 45,000 shares issued)	$900,000		
Excess of issue price over par . .	132,000	1,032,000	
From donated land		60,000	
Total paid-in capital			$1,202,000

Shareholders' Equity

Contributed capital:		
Preferred 10% stock, cumulative, $50 par (2,000 shares authorized and issued)	$100,000	
Common stock, $20 par (50,000 shares authorized, 45,000 shares issued)	900,000	
Additional paid-in capital	202,000	
Total contributed capital		$1,202,000

[6] Ibid., pars. 36 & 37.
[7] Ibid., pars. 11–39.

tional paid-in capital. These combined accounts could also be described as *Capital in excess of par (or stated value) of shares* or a similar title.

Significant changes in paid-in capital during a period may be presented either in a *statement of stockholders' equity* or in notes to the financial statements. We describe and illustrate the statement of stockholders' equity later in this section. In addition, relevant rights and privileges of the various classes of stock outstanding must be disclosed.[8] Examples of types of information that must be disclosed include dividend and liquidation preferences, rights to participate in earnings, conversion rights, and redemption rights. Such information may be disclosed on the face of the balance sheet or in the accompanying notes.

REAL WORLD: The 1996 edition of *Accounting Trends & Techniques* reported that over 80% of the companies surveyed presented a statement of stockholders' equity.

Reporting Retained Earnings

REAL WORLD: The 1996 edition of *Accounting Trends & Techniques* indicated that 6% of the companies surveyed presented a separate statement of retained earnings, 3% presented a combined income and retained earnings statement, and 9% presented changes in retained earnings in the notes to the financial statements. The other 82% of the companies presented changes in retained earnings in a statement of stockholders' equity.

A corporation may report changes in retained earnings by preparing a separate retained earnings statement, a combined income and retained earnings statement, or a statement of stockholders' equity.

When a separate retained earnings statement is prepared, the beginning balance of retained earnings is reported. The net income is then added (or net loss is subtracted) and any dividends are subtracted to arrive at the ending retained earnings for the period. An example of a such a statement for Adang Corporation is shown in Exhibit 5.

EXHIBIT 5
Retained Earnings Statement

Adang Corporation
Retained Earnings Statement
For the Year Ended June 30, 2000

Retained earnings, July 1, 1999		$350,000
Net income	$280,000	
Less dividends declared	75,000	
Increase in retained earnings		205,000
Retained earnings, June 30, 2000		$555,000

An alternative format for presenting the retained earnings statement is to combine it with the income statement. An advantage of the combined format is that it emphasizes net income as the connecting link between the income statement and the retained earnings portion of stockholders' equity. Since the combined form is not often used, we do not illustrate it.

Appropriations

REAL WORLD: The 1996 edition of *Accounting Trends & Techniques* reported that 356 of the 600 companies surveyed disclosed dividend restrictions in notes to their financial statements.

The retained earnings available for use as dividends may be restricted by action of a corporation's board of directors. The amount restricted, called an **appropriation**, remains part of the retained earnings. However, it must be disclosed, usually in the notes to the financial statements.

Appropriations may be classified as either legal, contractual, or discretionary. The board of directors may be legally required to restrict retained earnings because

[8] *Statement of Financial Accounting Standards No. 129,* "Disclosure Information about Capital Structure," Financial Accounting Standards Board (Norwalk, Connecticut: 1997).

of state laws. For example, some state laws require that retained earnings be restricted by the amount of treasury stock purchased, so that legal capital will not be used for dividends. The board may also be required to restrict retained earnings because of contractual requirements. For example, the terms of a bank loan may require restrictions, so that money for repaying the loan will not be used for dividends. Finally, the board may restrict retained earnings voluntarily. For example, the board may limit dividend distributions so that more money is available for expanding the business.

Prior Period Adjustments

Material errors in a prior period's net income may arise from mathematical mistakes and from mistakes in applying accounting principles. The effect of material errors that are not discovered within the same fiscal period in which they occurred should not be included in determining net income for the current period. Instead, corrections of such errors, called **prior period adjustments**, are reported in the retained earnings statement. These adjustments are reported as an adjustment to the retained earnings balance at the beginning of the period in which the error is discovered and corrected. Because prior period adjustments are rare, we do not illustrate their reporting.

Statement of Stockholders' Equity

Significant changes in stockholders' equity should be reported for the period in which they occur. These changes may be reported in a **statement of stockholders' equity**. This statement is often prepared in a columnar format, where each column represents a major stockholders' equity classification. Changes in each classification are then described in the left-hand column. Exhibit 6 is a statement of stockholders' equity for Telex Inc.

EXHIBIT 6 Statement of Stockholders' Equity

Telex Inc.
Statement of Stockholders' Equity
For the Year Ended December 31, 2000

	Preferred Stock	Common Stock	Paid-In Capital in Excess of Par—Common Stock	Retained Earnings	Treasury (Common) Stock	Total
Balance, January 1	$5,000,000	$10,000,000	$3,000,000	$2,000,000	$(500,000)	$19,500,000
Net income				850,000		850,000
Dividends on preferred stock				(250,000)		(250,000)
Dividends on common stock				(400,000)		(400,000)
Issuance of additional common stock		500,000	50,000			550,000
Purchase of treasury stock					(30,000)	(30,000)
Balance, December 31	$5,000,000	$10,500,000	$3,050,000	$2,200,000	$(530,000)	$20,220,000

OBJECTIVE 5

Describe the concept and the reporting of comprehensive income.

Comprehensive Income

In 1997, the Financial Accounting Standards Board issued an accounting standard that required the reporting concept referred to as *comprehensive income*.[9] This new standard defines **comprehensive income** as all changes in stockholders' equity

[9] *Statement of Financial Accounting Standards No. 130,* "Reporting Comprehensive Income," Financial Accounting Standards Board (Norwalk, Connecticut: 1997).

during a period except those resulting from dividends and stockholders' investments. Under this standard, companies must report traditional net income plus or minus other comprehensive income items to arrive at comprehensive income. *Other comprehensive income items* include foreign currency items, pension liability adjustments, and unrealized gains and losses on investments.

To the extent that other comprehensive income items give rise to tax effects, the taxes should be allocated to these items as we illustrated earlier in this chapter. The cumulative effects of other comprehensive income items must be reported separately from retained earnings and paid-in capital on the balance sheet. When other comprehensive income items are not present, the income statement and balance sheet formats are similar to those we have illustrated in this and preceding chapters.

Companies may report comprehensive income on the income statement, in a separate statement of comprehensive income, or in the statement of stockholders' equity. In addition, companies may use terms other than comprehensive income, such as *total nonowner changes in equity*.

You should note that comprehensive income does not affect the determination of net income or retained earnings as we have discussed and illustrated. In the next section, we will illustrate the reporting of unrealized gains and losses on investments as part of other comprehensive income.

Accounting for Investments in Stocks

OBJECTIVE 6

Describe the accounting for investments in stocks.

Corporations not only issue stock, but they also purchase stocks of other companies for investment purposes. Like individuals, businesses have a variety of reasons for investing in stocks, called **equity securities**. A business may purchase stocks as a means of earning a return (income) on excess cash that it does not need for its normal operations. Such investments are usually for a short period of time. In other cases, a business may purchase the stock of another company as a means of developing or maintaining business relationships with the other company. A business may also purchase common stock as a means of gaining control of another company's operations. In these two latter cases, the business usually intends to hold the investment for a long period of time.

REAL WORLD

Warren Buffett became one of the wealthiest men in the world through wise and patient investing. Buffett invests through a public company called **Berkshire Hathaway Inc.**, of which he owns 40%. Berkshire Hathaway started as an old-line textile company. Today, however, it has over $27 billion of equity investment holdings, listed on its balance sheet as "available-for-sale" securities. Some of these investments include **Coca-Cola Company**, **Gillette Company**, and **McDonald's Corporation**.

The equity securities in which a business invests may be classified as trading securities or available-for-sale securities. **Trading securities** are securities that management intends to actively trade for profit. Businesses holding trading securities are those whose normal operations involve buying and selling securities. Examples of such businesses include banks and insurance companies. **Available-for-sale securities** are securities that management expects to sell in the future, but which are not actively traded for profit. In this section, we describe and illustrate the accounting for available-for-sale equity securities. The accounting for trading securities is described and illustrated in advanced accounting texts.

Short-Term Investments in Stocks

Rather than allow excess cash to be idle until it is needed, a business may invest all or part of it in income-yielding securities. Since these investments can be quickly sold and converted to cash as needed, they are called **temporary investments** or

marketable securities. Although such investments may be retained for several years, they continue to be classified as temporary, provided they meet two conditions. First, the securities are readily marketable and can be sold for cash at any time. Second, management intends to sell the securities when the business needs cash for operations.

Temporary investments are recorded in a current asset account, *Marketable Securities,* at their cost. This cost includes all amounts spent to acquire the securities, such as broker's commissions. Any dividends received on the investment are recorded as a debit to *Cash* and a credit to *Dividend Revenue.*

To illustrate, assume that on June 1 Crabtree Co. purchased 2,000 shares of Inis Corporation common stock at $89.75 per share plus a brokerage fee of $500. On October 1, Inis declared a $0.90 per share cash dividend payable on November 30. Crabtree's entries to record the stock purchase and the receipt of the dividend are as follows:

June	1	Marketable Securities	180 000 00	
		Cash		180 000 00
		Purchased 2,000 shares of Inis		
		Corporation common stock		
		($89.75 × 2,000 shares = $179,500;		
		$179,500 + $500 = $180,000).		
Nov.	30	Cash	1 800 00	
		Dividend Revenue		1 800 00
		Received dividend on Inis Corporation		
		common stock		
		(2,000 shares × $0.90 = $1,800).		

Point of INTEREST

You may monitor market values of stocks on a continuous basis throughout the day through brokers or the major stock exchanges, such as **www.NYSE.com** or **www.Nasdaq.com.**

On the balance sheet, temporary investments are reported at their fair market value. Market values are normally available from stock quotations in financial newspapers, such as *The Wall Street Journal.* Any difference between the fair market values of the securities and their cost is an **unrealized holding gain or loss**. This gain or loss is termed "unrealized" because a transaction (the sale of the securities) is necessary before a gain or loss becomes real (realized).

To illustrate, assume that Crabtree Co.'s portfolio of temporary investments has the following fair market values and unrealized gains and losses on December 31, 2000:

Common Stock	Cost	Market	Unrealized Gain (Loss)
Edwards Inc.	$150,000	$190,000	$40,000
SWS Corp.	200,000	200,000	—
Inis Corporation	180,000	210,000	30,000
Bass Co.	160,000	150,000	(10,000)
Total	$690,000	$750,000	$60,000

If income taxes of $18,000 are allocated to the unrealized gain, Crabtree's temporary investments should be reported at their total cost of $690,000, plus the unrealized gain (net of applicable income tax) of $42,000 ($60,000 − $18,000), as shown in Exhibit 7.

EXHIBIT 7
Temporary Investments on the Balance Sheet

Crabtree Co. Balance Sheet December 31, 2000		
Assets		
Current assets:		
Cash		$119,500
Temporary investments in marketable securities at cost	$690,000	
Plus unrealized gain (net of applicable income tax of $18,000)	42,000	732,000

The unrealized gain (net of applicable taxes) of $42,000 should also be reported as an *other comprehensive income* item, as we mentioned in the preceding section. For example, assume that Crabtree Co. has net income of $720,000 for the year ended December 31, 2000. Crabtree elects to report net income and comprehensive income on one financial statement, *Statement of Income and Comprehensive Income,* as shown in Exhibit 8.

EXHIBIT 8
Statement of Income and Comprehensive Income

Crabtree Co. Statement of Income and Comprehensive Income For the Year Ended December 31, 2000	
Net income	$720,000
Other comprehensive income:	
Unrealized gain on temporary investments in marketable securities (net of applicable income tax of $18,000)	42,000
Comprehensive income	$762,000

Unrealized losses are reported in a similar manner. Unrealized gains and losses are reported as other comprehensive income items until the related securities are sold. When temporary securities are sold, the unrealized gains or losses become realized and are included in determining net income.[10]

Long-Term Investments in Stocks

Long-term investments in stocks are not intended as a source of cash in the normal operations of the business. They are reported in the balance sheet under the caption **Investments**, which usually follows the Current Assets section.

There are two methods of accounting for long-term investments in stock: (1) the cost method and (2) the equity method. The method used depends on whether the investor (the buyer of the stock) has a significant influence over the operating and financing activities of the company (the investee) whose stock is owned. If the investor does not have a significant influence, the cost method is used. If the investor has a significant influence, the equity method is used. Evidence of such in-

[10]To avoid double-counting, realized gains and losses must be removed from comprehensive income. These adjustments are discussed in advanced accounting texts.

fluence includes the percentage of ownership, the existence of intercompany transactions, and the interchange of managerial personnel. Generally, if the investor owns 20% or more of the voting stock of the investee, it is assumed that the investor has significant influence over the investee.

Cost Method

Under the **cost method**, the accounting for long-term investments in stocks is similar to that for short-term investments in stocks, which we illustrated in the preceding section. The cost of the stocks is debited to an investment (asset) account. Cash dividends received on the stock are recorded as a debit to *Cash* and a credit to *Dividend Revenue.* On the balance sheet, the stocks are reported at their fair market value net of any applicable income tax effects. In addition, the unrealized gains and losses are reported as part of the comprehensive income.[11]

To illustrate the purchase of stock and the receipt of dividends under the cost method, assume that on March 1, Makowski Corporation purchases 100 shares of Compton Corporation common stock at 59 plus a brokerage fee of $40. On April 30, Compton Corporation declares a $2-per-share dividend, payable on June 15. Makowski's entries to record the investment and the dividend are as follows:

Mar.	1	Investment in Compton Corp. Stock		5,940 00	
		Cash			5,940 00
		Purchased 100 shares of Compton Corp. common stock at 59 plus brokerage fee of $40.			
June	15	Cash		200 00	
		Dividend Revenue			200 00
		Received dividend of $2 per share on Compton Corp. common stock.			

REAL WORLD The 1996 edition of *Accounting Trends & Techniques* indicated that 17% of the companies surveyed used the cost method to account for investments.

Equity Method

Under the **equity method**, a stock purchase is recorded in the same manner as if the cost method were used. The equity method, however, is different from the cost method in the way in which net income and cash dividends of the investee are recorded. The equity method of recording these items is summarized as follows:

1. The investor's share of the periodic net income of the investee is recorded as an *increase in the investment account* and as *revenue for the period.* Likewise, the investor's share of an investee's net loss is recorded as a *decrease in the investment account* and as a *loss for the period.*
2. The investor's share of cash dividends from the investee is recorded as an *increase in the cash account* and a *decrease in the investment account.*

REAL WORLD The 1996 edition of *Accounting Trends & Techniques* indicated that over 40% of the companies surveyed used the equity method to account for investments.

To illustrate, assume that on January 2, Hally Inc. pays cash of $350,000 for 40% of the common stock and net assets of Brock Corporation. Assume also that, for the year ending December 31, Brock Corporation reports net income of $105,000 and

[11] An exception to reporting unrealized gains and losses as part of comprehensive income is made if the decrease in the market value for a stock is considered permanent. In this case, the cost of the individual stock is written down (decreased), and the amount of the write-down is included in net income.

declares and pays $45,000 in dividends. Using the equity method, Hally Inc. (the investor) records these transactions as follows:

Jan.	2	Investment in Brock Corp. Stock	350 000 00	
		Cash		350 000 00
		Purchased 40% of Brock Corp.		
		common stock.		
Dec.	31	Investment in Brock Corp. Stock	42 000 00	
		Income of Brock Corp.		42 000 00
		Recorded share (40%) of Brock Corp.		
		net income of $105,000.		
Dec.	31	Cash	18 000 00	
		Investment in Brock Corp. Stock		18 000 00
		Recorded share (40%) of dividends of		
		$45,000 paid by Brock Corp.		

The combined effect of recording 40% of Brock Corporation's net income and dividends is to increase Hally's interest in the net assets of Brock by $24,000 ($42,000 − $18,000), as shown below.

Q&A *Assume that Hally Inc. increased its ownership in Brock Corporation to 60% at the beginning of the next year. If Brock Corporation reported net income of $80,000 and declared dividends of $50,000, how much would Hally Inc. debit Investment in Brock Corp. Stock?*

$18,000 [($80,000 × 60%) − ($50,000 × 60%)]

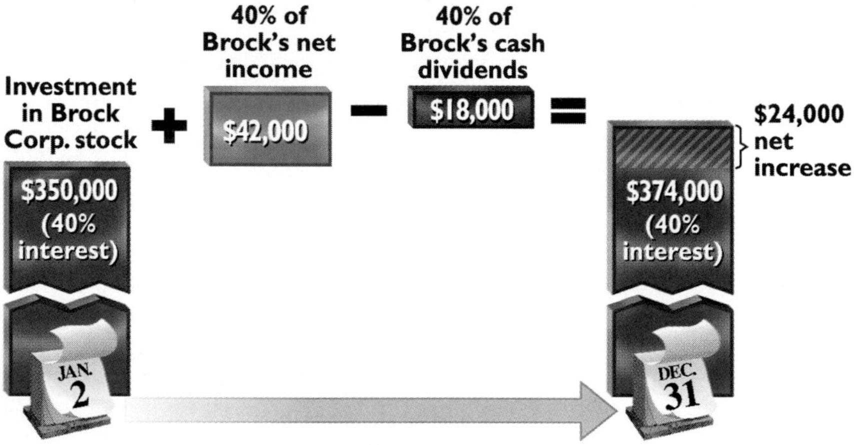

Sale of Investments in Stocks

The accounting for the sale of stock is the same for both short-term and long-term investments. When shares of stock are sold, the investment account is credited for the carrying amount (book value) of the shares sold. The cash or receivables account is debited for the proceeds (sales price less commission and other selling costs). Any difference between the proceeds and the carrying amount is recorded as a gain or loss on the sale and is included in the determination of net income.

To illustrate, assume that an investment in Drey Inc. stock has a carrying amount of $15,700 when it is sold on March 1. If the proceeds from the sale of the stock are $17,500, the entry to record the transaction is as follows:

Mar.	1	Cash	17 500 00	
		Investment in Drey Inc. Stock		15 700 00
		Gain on Sale of Investments		1 800 00
		Sold investment in Drey Inc. stock.		

Business Combinations

OBJECTIVE 7

Describe alternative methods of combining businesses and how consolidated financial statements are prepared.

Each year, many businesses combine in order to produce more efficiently or to diversify product lines. Business combinations often involve complex accounting principles and terminology. Our objective in this section is to introduce you to some of the unique terminology and concepts related to business combinations. We also briefly describe the use and preparation of consolidated financial statements.

Mergers and Consolidations

One corporation may acquire all the assets and liabilities of another corporation, which is then dissolved. This joining of two corporations is called a **merger**. The acquiring company may use cash, debt, or its own stock as the payment. Whatever the form of payment, the amount received by the dissolving corporation is distributed to its stockholders in final liquidation.

REAL WORLD: **Boeing Co.** acquired **McDonnell Douglas Corporation** for $15 billion in mid-1997. The merged company will become the United States' biggest aerospace company, with projected sales of more than $38 billion. Under the merger, McDonnell Douglas will no longer exist as a separate company.

A new corporation may be created, and the assets and liabilities of two or more existing corporations transferred to it. This type of combination is called a **consolidation**. The new corporation usually issues its own stock in exchange for the net assets acquired. The original corporations are then dissolved.

Parent and Subsidiary Corporations

Business combinations may also occur when one corporation buys a controlling share of the outstanding voting stock of one or more other corporations. In this case, none of the corporations dissolve. The corporations continue as separate legal entities in a parent-subsidiary relationship. The corporation owning all or a majority of the voting stock of the other corporation is called the **parent company**. The corporation that is controlled is called the **subsidiary company**. Two or more corporations closely related through stock ownership are sometimes called **affiliated** companies. An example of an affiliated company is **Waldenbooks**, a subsidiary of **Kmart**.

A corporation may acquire the controlling share of the voting common stock of another corporation by paying cash, exchanging other assets, issuing debt, or using some combination of these methods. The stockholders of the acquired company, in turn, transfer their stock to the parent corporation. In such cases, the transaction is recorded like a normal purchase of assets, and the combination is accounted for by the **purchase method**.

A parent-subsidiary relationship may be created by exchanging the voting common stock of the acquiring corporation (the parent) for the common stock of the acquired corporation (the subsidiary). If at least 90% of the stock of the subsidiary is acquired in this way, the transaction is a pooling of interests, and the combination is accounted for by the **pooling-of-interests method**. In a pooling of interests, the stockholders of the acquired company (the subsidiary) become stockholders of the acquiring company (the parent).

The accounting for a purchase and a pooling of interests are significantly different. A purchase is accounted for as a *sale-purchase transaction,* whereas a pooling of interests is accounted for as a *joining of ownership interests.* Because businesses must meet very strict criteria to use the pooling-of-interests method, the vast majority of business combinations are accounted for by using the purchase method.

REAL WORLD: The 1996 edition of *Accounting Trends & Techniques* reported that 88% of the business combinations surveyed were accounted for by the purchase method.

Consolidated Financial Statements

Although parent and subsidiary corporations may operate as a single economic unit, they continue to maintain separate accounting records and prepare their own periodic financial statements. At the end of the year, the financial statements of the parent and subsidiary are combined and reported as a single company. These combined financial statements are called **consolidated financial statements**. Such statements are usually identified by adding "and subsidiary(ies)" to the name of the parent corporation or by adding "consolidated" to the statement title.

To the stockholders of the parent company, consolidated financial statements are more meaningful than separate statements for each corporation. This is because the parent company, in substance, controls the subsidiaries, even though the parent and its subsidiaries are separate entities.

When a business combination is accounted for as a purchase, the subsidiary's net assets are reported in the consolidated balance sheet at their fair market value at the time of the purchase. In some cases, a parent may pay more than the fair market value of a subsidiary's net assets because the subsidiary has prospects for high future earnings. The difference between the amount paid by the parent and the fair market value of the subsidiary's net assets is reported on the consolidated balance sheet as an intangible asset. This asset is identified as **Goodwill** or **Excess of cost of business acquired over related net assets.**

When a consolidated balance sheet is prepared, the ownership interest of the parent in the subsidiary's stock, which is the balance in the parent's investment in subsidiary account, must be eliminated. This is done by eliminating the parent's investment in subsidiary account against the balances of the subsidiary's stockholders' equity accounts.

If the parent owns less than 100% of the subsidiary stock, the subsidiary stock owned by outsiders is *not* eliminated but is normally reported immediately preceding the consolidated stockholders' equity. This amount is described as the **minority interest**.

When the data on the financial statements of the parent and its subsidiaries are combined to form the consolidated statements, intercompany transactions are given special attention. An example of such a transaction is the parent purchasing goods from the subsidiary or the subsidiary loaning money to the parent.

BUSINESS ON STAGE

Buying and Selling Stocks

After you have evaluated a business and identified companies in which you would like to make an investment, how would you go about making the purchase? The most common method is to purchase common stock through a stockbroker, or account representative. A *stockbroker* is a person who executes trades on the major stock exchanges on your behalf. Stockbrokers can be associated with large "full-service" firms, such as **Merrill Lynch**; "discount" brokerage firms, such as **OLDE Discount Brokers**; or regional and local firms.

Once you've selected your stockbroker, you begin by opening an account. This usually involves placing money in the account. After your account is opened, you can place an order for the purchase of your selected stocks. There are two basic types of purchase orders—a market order and a limit order.

A *market order* instructs the broker to buy the stock at the best possible price. If the stock is actively traded, the buy price will usually be close to the last traded price prior to the order. Stockbrokers usually execute trades within minutes of taking an order. A *limit order* instructs the broker to buy the stock at a specified price or lower. An example of a limit order would be to buy 50 shares of **Coca-Cola** common stock at $60 or lower. The limit order prohibits the broker from purchasing the stock at a price higher than $60.

When you decide to sell, you can place a stop-loss order. With a *stop-loss order,* you set a selling market price below the current price. If the market price drops to your limit, then the sale is executed, thus limiting your loss. After your trade is executed, you will receive a statement confirming your trade, which shows your investment, the number of shares bought or sold, the dollar value, and the stockbroker's commission. These statements should be kept for tax purposes.

Recently, an alternative method of trading stocks has emerged on the Internet. Internet trading is just beginning, but it appears to be a promising alternative to using a stockbroker. For more information, see E*TRADE's home page at **www.etrade.com.** ■

REAL WORLD

The 1996 edition of *Accounting Trends & Techniques* indicates that most of the companies surveyed reported minority interest in the long-term liabilities (noncurrent) section of the consolidated balance sheet.

These transactions affect the individual accounts of the parent and subsidiary and thus the financial statements of both companies.[12] To illustrate, assume that P Inc. (the parent) sold merchandise to S Inc. (the subsidiary) for $90,000. The merchandise cost P $50,000. In turn, S Inc. sold the merchandise to a customer for $120,000.

The individual income statements for P Inc. and S Inc. are shown in Exhibit 9. The consolidated (combined) income statement is shown in Exhibit 10. The consolidated income statement presents the income statements for P Inc. and S Inc. as if they were one operating entity. Thus, the $90,000 sale and the $90,000 cost of merchandise sold are eliminated. This is because the consolidated entity cannot sell to itself or buy from itself.

EXHIBIT 9
Income Statements for P Inc. and S Inc.

	P Inc.		S Inc.	
Sales		$950,000		$400,000
Cost of merchandise sold		625,000		240,000
Gross profit		$325,000		$160,000
Operating expenses:				
Selling expenses	$155,000		$55,000	
Administrative expenses	85,000	240,000	35,000	90,000
Net income		$ 85,000		$ 70,000

EXHIBIT 10
Consolidated Income Statement for P Inc. and S Inc.

Sales		$1,260,000*
Cost of merchandise sold		775,000**
Gross profit		$ 485,000
Operating expenses:		
Selling expenses	$210,000	
Administrative expenses	120,000	330,000
Net income		$ 155,000

*$950,000 − $90,000 + $400,000

**$625,000 + $240,000 − $90,000

General Motors Corporation is a multinational company that consolidates its foreign subsidiaries, such as the European *Opel* division, into U.S. dollars.

Many U.S. corporations own subsidiaries in foreign countries. Such corporations are often called *multinational corporations*. The financial statements of the foreign subsidiary are usually prepared in the foreign currency. Before the financial statements of foreign subsidiaries are consolidated with their domestic parent's financial statements, the amounts shown on the statements for the foreign companies must be converted to U.S. dollars.

FINANCIAL ANALYSIS AND INTERPRETATION

OBJECTIVE 8

Compute and interpret the price-earnings ratio.

The assessment of a firm's growth potential and future earnings prospects is indicated by how much the market is willing to pay per dollar of a company's earnings. This ratio, called the **price-earnings ratio**, or **P/E ratio**, is commonly included

[12] Examples of accounts often affected by intercompany transactions include *Accounts Receivable* and *Accounts Payable*, *Interest Receivable* and *Interest Payable*, and *Interest Expense* and *Interest Revenue*.

in stock market quotations reported by the financial press. A high P/E ratio indicates that the market expects high growth and earnings in the future. Likewise, a low P/E ratio indicates lower growth and earnings expectations.

The price-earnings ratio on common stock is computed by dividing the stock's market price per share at a specific date by the company's annual earnings per share, as shown below:

$$\textbf{Price-earnings ratio} = \frac{\textbf{Market price per share of common stock}}{\textbf{Earnings per share of common stock}}$$

To illustrate, assume that Harper Inc. reported earnings per share of $1.64 in 2000 and $1.35 in 1999. The market prices per common share are $20.50 at the end of 2000 and $13.50 at the end of 1999. The price-earnings ratio on this stock is computed as follows:

	Price-Earnings Ratio
Year 2000	12.5 ($20.50/$1.64)
Year 1999	10.0 ($13.50/$1.35)

The price-earnings ratio indicates that a share of Harper Inc.'s common stock was selling for 10 times the amount of earnings per share at the end of 1999. At the end of 2000, the common stock was selling for 12.5 times the amount of earnings per share. These results would indicate a generally improving expectation of growth and earnings for Harper Inc. However, a prospective investor should also consider the price-earnings ratios for competing firms in the same industry.

ENCORE

Monster Eats into Mattell's Profits

Mattell Inc., one of the largest toy makers in the world, is best known for its Barbie dolls, Fisher-Price infant and preschool toys, Hot Wheels die-cast cars, and its Cabbage Patch dolls. It is estimated that over 80 million Cabbage Patch dolls have been sold since they were introduced in 1983.

In the fall of 1996, Mattell decided to introduce a new version of the Cabbage Patch dolls, called Snacktime Kids. The Snacktime Kids come with pieces of plastic shaped carrots, pretzels, biscuits, and licorice that can be put into the doll's mechanical mouth. Once in the doll's mouth, a battery-driven motor "chews" them and ejects them into a pack on the doll's back.

Unfortunately, the dolls cannot discern between the plastic snacks and other small objects provided by its owner, such as hair and fingers. One young father demonstrated how he was forced to decapitate a Snacktime Kid after it "attacked" his daughter. Evidently, the doll began devouring the little girl's hair as if it were spaghetti. Fearing the worst, the father terminated the ravenous toy *with extreme prejudice.* Similar hair-gobbling incidents were reported across the country.

In early January 1997, Mattell announced a refund program for the dolls, offering to buy back Snacktime Kids from parents for $40 a doll. Mattell estimated that 500,000 Snacktime Kids had been sold and another 200,000 dolls were still on the shelves. The buyback of the monster dolls cost Mattell $10 million in sales and $8 million in after-tax earnings. In addition, at least one lawsuit claiming grievous psychological trauma was filed against Mattell. The lawsuit asked for $25 million in punitive damages.

Although Mattell hopes that the buyback program will have a nonrecurring impact on its profits, it isn't the first time that Mattell has had to pull a toy from the market. In 1992, Mattell pulled Teacher Barbie from stores after the talking doll was criticized by educators, who said it set a bad example with comments like, "Math class is tough." Teacher Barbie was "reeducated," however, and put back on the market. ■

KEY POINTS

1 Journalize the entries for corporate income taxes, including deferred income taxes.

Corporations are subject to federal income tax and are required to make estimated payments throughout the year. To record the payment of estimated tax, Income Tax is debited and Cash is credited. If additional taxes are owed at the end of the year, Income Tax is debited and Income Tax Payable is credited for the amount owed. If the estimated tax payments are greater than the actual tax liability, a receivable account is debited and Income Tax is credited.

The tax effects of temporary differences between taxable income and income before income taxes must be allocated between periods. The journal entry for such allocations normally debits Income Tax and credits Income Tax Payable and Deferred Income Tax Payable.

2 Prepare an income statement reporting the following unusual items: discontinued operations, extraordinary items, and changes in accounting principles.

A gain or loss resulting from the disposal of a business segment should be identified on the income statement, net of related income tax. The results of continuing operations should also be identified.

Gains and losses may result from events and transactions that are unusual and occur infrequently. Such extraordinary items, net of related income tax, should be identified on the income statement.

A change in an accounting principle results from the adoption of a generally accepted accounting principle different from the one used previously for reporting purposes. The effect of the change in principle on net income in the current period, as well as the cumulative effect on income of prior periods, should be disclosed in the financial statements. The effects of a change in an accounting principle should be reported net of related income tax.

3 Prepare an income statement reporting earnings per share data.

Earnings per share is reported on the income statements of public corporations. If there are unusual items on the income statement, the per share amount should be presented for each of these items as well as net income.

4 Prepare financial statement presentations of stockholders' equity.

Significant changes in the sources of stockholders' equity—paid-in capital and retained earnings—may be reported in separate statements or notes that support the balance sheet presentation.

Changes in retained earnings may be reported by preparing a separate retained earnings statement, a combined income and retained earnings statement, or a statement of stockholders' equity. Restrictions to retained earnings, called appropriations, must be disclosed, usually in the notes to the financial statements. Material errors in a prior period's net income, called prior-period adjustments, are reported in the retained earnings statement. Significant changes in stockholders' equity may also be reported in a statement of stockholders' equity.

5 Describe the concept and the reporting of comprehensive income.

Comprehensive income is all changes in stockholders' equity during a period except those resulting from dividends and stockholders' investments. Companies must report traditional net income plus or minus other comprehensive income items to arrive at comprehensive income. Other comprehensive income items include transactions and events that are excluded from net income, such as unrealized gains and losses on certain investments in debt and equity securities.

6 Describe the accounting for investments in stocks.

A business may purchase stocks as a means of earning a return (income) on excess cash that it does not need for its normal operations. Such investments are recorded in a marketable securities account. Their cost includes all amounts spent to acquire the securities. Any dividends received on an investment are recorded as a debit to Cash and a credit to Dividend Revenue. On the balance sheet, temporary investments are reported at their fair market values. Any difference between the fair market values of the securities and their cost is an unrealized holding gain or loss (net of applicable taxes) that is reported as an other comprehensive income item.

Long-term investments in stocks are not intended as a source of cash in the normal operations of the business. They are reported in the balance sheet under the caption Investments. Two methods of accounting for long-term investments in stock are (1) the cost method and (2) the equity method.

The accounting for the sale of stock is the same for both short-term and long-term investments. The investment account is credited for the carrying amount (book value) of the shares sold, the cash or receivables account is debited for the proceeds, and any difference between the proceeds and the carrying amount is recorded as a gain or loss on the sale.

7 Describe alternative methods of combining businesses and how consolidated financial statements are prepared.

Businesses may combine in a merger or a consolidation. Business combinations may also occur when one corporation acquires a controlling share of the outstanding voting stock of another corporation. In this case, a parent-subsidiary relationship exists, and the companies are called affiliated or associated companies.

Although the corporations that make up a parent-subsidiary affiliation may operate as a single economic unit, they usually continue to maintain separate accounting records and prepare their own periodic financial statements. The financial statements prepared by combining the parent and subsidiary statements are called consolidated financial statements.

When a parent corporation purchases less than 100% of the subsidiary's stock, the remaining stockholders' equity is identified as minority interest. The minority interest is reported on the consolidated balance sheet, usually preceding stockholders' equity.

In preparing consolidated income statements for a parent and its subsidiary, all amounts from intercompany transactions, such as intercompany sales of merchandise and cost of merchandise sold, are eliminated.

8 Compute and interpret the price-earnings ratio.

The assessment of a firm's growth potential and future earnings prospects is indicated by the price-earnings ratio, or P/E ratio. It is computed by dividing the stock's market price per share at a specific date by the company's annual earnings per share.

ILLUSTRATIVE PROBLEM

The following data were selected from the records of Botanica Greenhouses Inc. for the current fiscal year ended August 31:

Administrative expenses	$ 82,200
Cost of merchandise sold	750,000
Gain on condemnation of land	25,000
Income tax:	
Applicable to continuing operations	27,200
Applicable to gain on condemnation of land	10,000
Applicable to loss from disposal of a segment of the business (reduction)	24,000
Interest expense	15,200
Loss from disposal of a segment of the business	60,200
Sales	1,097,500
Selling expenses	182,100

Instructions

Prepare a multiple-step income statement, concluding with a section for earnings per share in the form illustrated in this chapter. There were 10,000 shares of common stock (no preferred) outstanding throughout the year. Assume that the gain on condemnation of land is an extraordinary item.

Solution

Botanica Greenhouses Inc.
Income Statement
For the Year Ended August 31, 20—

Sales		$1,097,500
Cost of merchandise sold		750,000
Gross profit		$ 347,500
Operating expenses:		
Selling expenses	$182,100	
Administrative expenses	82,200	
Total operating expenses		264,300
Income from operations		$ 83,200
Other expense:		
Interest expense		15,200
Income from continuing operations before income tax		$ 68,000
Income tax expense		27,200
Income from continuing operations		$ 40,800
Loss from disposal of a segment of the business	$ 60,200	
Less applicable income tax	24,000	36,200
Income before extraordinary item		$ 4,600
Extraordinary item:		
Gain on condemnation of land	$ 25,000	
Less applicable income tax	10,000	15,000
Net income		$ 19,600
Earnings per share:		
Income from continuing operations		$4.08
Loss on discontinued operations		3.62
Income before extraordinary item		$0.46
Extraordinary item		1.50
Net income		$1.96

SELF-EXAMINATION QUESTIONS

Answers at End of Chapter

Matching

Match each of the following statements with its proper term. Some terms may not be used.

A. appropriation
B. available-for-sale securities
C. balance sheet
D. comprehensive income
E. consolidated financial statements
F. consolidation

Z 1. The income according to the tax laws that is used as a base for determining the amount of taxes owed.

AA 2. Differences between taxable income and income before income taxes, created because items are recognized in one period for tax purposes and in another period for income statement purposes. Such differences reverse or turn around in later years.

H 3. Operations of a major line of business for a company, such as a division, a department, or a certain class of customer, that have been disposed of.

M 4. Events and transactions that (1) are significantly different (unusual) from the typical or the normal operating activities of a business and (2) occur infrequently.

I 5. Net income per share of common stock outstanding during a period.

(continues)

G. **cost method**
H. **discontinued operations**
I. **earnings per common share (EPS)**
J. **equity method**
K. **equity per share**
L. **equity security**
M. **extraordinary items**
N. **investments**
O. **merger**
P. **minority interest**
Q. **parent company**
R. **permanent differences**
S. **pooling-of-interests method**
T. **price-earnings ratio**
U. **prior period adjustments**
V. **purchase method**
W. **statement of cash flows**
X. **statement of stockholders' equity**
Y. **subsidiary company**
Z. **taxable income**
AA. **temporary differences**
BB. **temporary investments**
CC. **trading securities**
DD. **unrealized holding gain or loss**

___ 6. The amount of retained earnings that has been restricted and therefore is unavailable for use as dividends.

___ 7. Errors in a prior period's net income that arise from mathematical mistakes or from mistakes in applying accounting principles.

___ 8. A statement summarizing significant changes in stockholders' equity that have occured during a period.

___ 9. All changes in stockholders' equity during a period, except those resulting from dividends and stockholders' investments.

___ 10. Preferred or common stock.

___ 11. Securities that management intends to actively trade for profit.

___ 12. Securities that management expects to sell in the future but which are not actively traded for profit.

___ 13. The balance sheet caption used to report investments in income-yielding securities that can be quickly sold and converted to cash as needed.

___ 14. The difference between the fair market values of the securities and their cost.

___ 15. The balance sheet caption used to report long-term investments in stocks not intended as a source of cash in the normal operations of the business.

___ 16. A method of accounting for an investment in common stock by which the investor recognizes as income its share of cash dividends of the investee.

___ 17. A method of accounting for an investment in common stock by which the investment account is adjusted for the investor's share of periodic net income and cash dividends of the investee.

___ 18. The joining of two corporations in which one company acquires all the assets and liabilities of another corporation, which is then dissolved.

___ 19. The creation of a new corporation by the transfer of assets and liabilities of two or more existing corporations, which are then dissolved.

___ 20. The corporation owning all or a majority of the voting stock of the other corporation.

___ 21. The corporation that is controlled by a parent company.

___ 22. The accounting method used when a corporation acquires the controlling share of the voting common stock of another corporation by paying cash, exchanging other assets, issuing debt, or some combination of these methods.

___ 23. The accounting method used when a corporation acquires the controlling share of the voting common stock of another corporation by exchanging the voting common stock of the acquiring corporation for the common stock of the acquired corporation.

___ 24. Financial statements resulting from combining parent and subsidiary statements.

___ 25. The portion of a subsidiary corporation's stock owned by outsiders.

___ 26. The ratio computed by dividing a corporation's stock market price per share at a specific date by the company's annual earnings per share.

Multiple Choice

1. During its first year of operations, a corporation elected to use the straight-line method of depreciation for financial reporting purposes and MACRS in determining taxable income. If the income tax is 40% and the amount of depreciation expense is $60,000 under the straight-line method and $100,000 under MACRS, what is the amount of income tax deferred to future years?
   A. $16,000   C. $40,000
   B. $24,000   D. $60,000

2. A material gain resulting from condemning land for public use would be reported on the income statement as:
   A. an extraordinary item
   B. an other income item
   C. revenue from sales
   D. a change in estimate

3. An appropriation for plant expansion would normally be reported in the financial statements in the:

A. Property, plant, and equipment section
B. Long-term liabilities section
C. Stockholders' equity section
D. Notes to the statements

4. An item treated as a prior period adjustment should be reported in the financial statements as:
A. an extraordinary item
B. an other expense item
C. an adjustment of the beginning balance of Retained Earnings
D. a change in estimate

5. Cisneros Corporation owns 75% of Harrell Inc. During the current year, Harrell Inc. reported net income of $150,000 and declared dividends of $40,000. How much would Cisneros Corporation increase Investment in Harrell Inc. Stock for the current year?
A. $0
B. $30,000
C. $82,500
D. $112,500

CLASS DISCUSSION QUESTIONS

1. A corporation has paid estimated federal income tax during the year on the basis of its estimated income. Indicate the accounts that would be debited and credited at the end of the year if the corporation (a) owes an additional tax; (b) overpaid its tax.
2. How would the amount of deferred income tax payable be reported in the balance sheet if (a) it is payable within one year and (b) it is payable beyond one year?
3. What two criteria must be met to classify an item as an extraordinary item on the income statement?
4. During the current year, 20 acres of land that cost $150,000 were condemned for construction of an interstate highway. Assuming that an award of $180,000 in cash was received and that the applicable income tax on this transaction is 30%, how would this information be presented in the income statement?
5. Corporation X realized a material gain when its facilities at a designated floodway were acquired by the urban renewal agency. How should the gain be reported in the income statement?

Source: "Technical Hotline," *Journal of Accountancy,* June 1989, p. 32.

6. The annual report of **Sears, Roebuck and Co.** disclosed the discontinuance of several business segments, including **Coldwell Banker Residential Services**. The estimated loss on disposal of these operations was $64 million, including $22 million of tax expense. Indicate how the loss from discontinued operations should be reported by Sears, Roebuck and Co. on its income statement.
7. If significant changes are made in the accounting principles applied from one period to the next, why should the effect of these changes be disclosed in the financial statements?
8. A corporation reports earnings per share of $1.12 for the most recent year and $1.00 for the preceding year. The $1.12 includes a $0.17-per-share gain from a sale of the only investment owned since the business was organized in 1940. (a) Should the composition of the $1.12 be disclosed in the financial reports? (b) On the basis of the limited information presented, would you conclude that operations had improved or declined?
9. What is the primary advantage of combining the retained earnings statement with the income statement?
10. What are the three classifications of appropriations and how are appropriations normally reported in the financial statements?
11. Indicate how prior period adjustments would be reported on the financial statements presented only for the current period.
12. Describe the format of the statement of stockholders' equity.
13. How is comprehensive income determined?
14. a. List some examples of other comprehensive income items.
    b. Does the reporting of comprehensive income affect the determination of net income and retained earnings?

15. Why might a business invest in another company's stock?
16. How are temporary investments in marketable securities reported on the balance sheet?
17. How are unrealized gains and losses on temporary investments in marketable securities reported on the statement of income and comprehensive income?
18. a. What are two methods of accounting for long-term investments in stock?
    b. Under what caption are long-term investments in stock reported on the balance sheet?
19. Rosetta Inc. received a $0.25-per-share cash dividend on 40,000 shares of MGS Corporation common stock, which Rosetta Inc. carries as a long-term investment. (a) Assuming that Rosetta Inc. uses the cost method of accounting for its investment in MGS Corporation, what account would be credited for the receipt of the $10,000 dividend? (b) Assuming that Rosetta Inc. uses the equity method of accounting for its investment in MGS Corporation, what account would be credited for the receipt of the $10,000 dividend?
20. Which method of accounting for long-term investments in stock (cost or equity) should be used by the parent company in accounting for its investments in stock of subsidiaries?
21. What are the two methods of accounting for the creation of a parent-subsidiary relationship?
22. P Company purchases the entire common stock of S Corporation for $18,000,000. What accounts on S's balance sheet are represented in the investment account on P's balance sheet?
23. Parent Corporation owns 85% of the outstanding common stock of Subsidiary Corporation, which has no preferred stock. (a) What is the term applied to the remaining 15% interest? (b) On the consolidated balance sheet, where is the amount of Subsidiary's book equity allocable to outsiders reported?
24. REAL WORLD An annual report of **The Campbell Soup Company** reported on its income statement $2.4 million as "equity in earnings of affiliates." Journalize the entry that Campbell would have made to record this equity in earnings of affiliates.

Warren Reeve Fess

Resources for Your Success On-Line at warren.swcollege.com

Remember! If you need additional help, visit South-Western's Web site. See page 26 for a description of the online and printed materials that are available.

EXERCISES

Exercise 13–1
Income tax entries
Objective 1

Journalize the entries to record the following selected transactions of Masters Grave Markers Inc.:

Apr. 15. Paid the first installment of the estimated income tax for the current fiscal year ending December 31, $60,000. No entry had been made to record the liability.
June 15. Paid the second installment of $60,000.
Sep. 15. Paid the third installment of $60,000.
Dec. 31. Recorded the estimated income tax liability for the year just ended and the deferred income tax liability, based on the transactions above and the following data:

Income tax rate	40%
Income before income tax	$850,000
Taxable income according to tax return	700,000

Jan. 15. Paid the fourth installment of $100,000.

Exercise 13–2
Extraordinary item
Objective 2

A company received life insurance proceeds on the death of its president before the end of its fiscal year. It intends to report the amount in its income statement as an extraordinary item.

Would this be in conformity with generally accepted accounting principles? Discuss.

Source: "Technical Hotline," *Journal of Accountancy,* June 1989, p. 31.

Exercise 13–3
Extraordinary item
Objective 2

REAL WORLD

On May 11, 1996, **ValuJet** tragically lost its Flight 592 en route from Miami to Atlanta. One hundred and ten people lost their lives. The crash cost ValuJet millions of dollars, including $2 million the company paid to the Federal Aviation Administration (FAA) to compensate it for the costs of the special inspections that were conducted. Do you believe that the costs related to this crash should be reported as an extraordinary item on the 1996 income statement of ValuJet?

Exercise 13–4
Identifying extraordinary items
Objective 2

Assume that the amount of each of the following items is material to the financial statements. Classify each item as either normally recurring (NR) or extraordinary (E).

a. Salaries of corporate officers.
b. Gain on sale of land condemned for public use.
c. Uncollectible accounts expense.
d. Interest revenue on notes receivable.
e. Uninsured flood loss. (Flood insurance is unavailable because of periodic flooding in the area.)
f. Loss on sale of fixed assets.
g. Uninsured loss on building due to hurricane damage. The firm was organized in 1920 and had not previously incurred hurricane damage.
h. Loss on disposal of equipment considered to be obsolete because of development of new technology.

Exercise 13–5
Income statement
Objectives 2, 3

✓ Net income, $87,000

Ocean-Way Inc. produces and distributes equipment for sailboats. On the basis of the following data for the current fiscal year ended April 30, prepare a multiple-step income statement for Ocean-Way Inc., including an analysis of earnings per share in the form illustrated in this chapter. There were 20,000 shares of $100 par common stock outstanding throughout the year.

Administrative expenses	$ 36,750
Cost of merchandise sold	620,000
Cumulative effect on prior years of changing to a different depreciation method (decrease in income)	50,000
Gain on condemnation of land (extraordinary item)	37,750
Income tax reduction applicable to change in depreciation method	18,200
Income tax applicable to gain on condemnation of land	7,750
Income tax reduction applicable to loss from discontinued operations	45,500
Income tax applicable to ordinary income	105,200
Loss on discontinued operations	114,500
Sales	985,500
Selling expenses	65,750

Exercise 13–6

Income statement

Objectives 2, 3

What's Wrong WITH THIS?

✓ Correct EPS for net income, $13.55

Ultra Sound Inc. sells automotive and home stereo equipment. It has 50,000 shares of $100 par common stock and 10,000 shares of $2, $100 par cumulative preferred stock outstanding as of December 31, 2000. It also holds 10,000 shares of common stock as treasury stock as of December 31, 2000. How many errors can you find in the following income statement for the year ended December 31, 2000?

Ultra Sound Inc.
Income Statement
For the Year Ended December 31, 2000

Net sales		$8,450,000
Cost of merchandise sold		6,100,000
Gross profit		$2,350,000
Operating expenses:		
Selling expenses	$1,020,000	
Administrative expenses	280,000	1,300,000
Income from continuing operations before income tax		$1,050,000
Income tax expense		420,000
Income from continuing operations		$ 530,000
Cumulative effect on prior years' income (decrease) of changing to a different depreciation method (net of applicable income tax of $36,000)		(92,000)
Correction of error (understatement) in December 31, 1999 physical inventory (net of applicable income tax of $20,000)		30,000
Income before condemnation of land and discontinued operations		$ 468,000
Extraordinary item:		
Gain on condemnation of land, net of applicable income tax of $80,000		120,000
Loss on discontinued operations (net of applicable income tax of $64,000)		(96,000)
Net income		$ 492,000
Earnings per common share:		
Income from continuing operations		$10.60
Cumulative effect on prior years' income (decrease) of changing to a different depreciation method		(1.84)
Correction of error (understatement) in December 31, 1999 physical inventory		0.60
Income before extraordinary item and discontinued operations		$ 9.36
Extraordinary item		2.40
Loss on discontinued operations		(1.92)
Net income		$ 9.84

Exercise 13–7

Reporting paid-in capital

Objective 4

✓ Total paid-in capital, $1,628,000

The following accounts and their balances were selected from the unadjusted trial balance of FastCo Inc., a freight forwarder, at December 31, the end of the current fiscal year:

Preferred $1 Stock, $50 par	$ 500,000
Paid-In Capital in Excess of Par—Preferred Stock	75,000
Common Stock, no par, $10 stated value	750,000
Paid-In Capital in Excess of Par—Common Stock	140,000
Paid-In Capital from Sale of Treasury Stock	13,000
Donated Capital	150,000
Retained Earnings	1,230,000

Prepare the Paid-In Capital portion of the Stockholders' Equity section of the balance sheet. There are 100,000 shares of common stock authorized and 50,000 shares of preferred stock authorized.

Exercise 13–8
Stockholders' equity section of balance sheet

Objective 4

✓ Total stockholders' equity, $582,000

The following accounts and their balances appear in the ledger of McCopy Inc. on September 30 of the current year:

Common Stock, $10 par	$250,000
Paid-In Capital in Excess of Par	40,000
Paid-In Capital from Sale of Treasury Stock	7,000
Retained Earnings	310,000
Treasury Stock	25,000

Prepare the Stockholders' Equity section of the balance sheet as of September 30. Thirty thousand shares of common stock are authorized, and 2,500 shares have been reacquired.

Exercise 13–9
Stockholders' equity section of balance sheet

Objective 4

✓ Total stockholders' equity, $2,637,500

Le'Car Inc. retails racing products for BMWs, Porsches, and Ferraris. The following accounts and their balances appear in the ledger of Le'Car Inc. on December 31, the end of the current year:

Common Stock, $10 par	$ 800,000
Paid-In Capital in Excess of Par—Common Stock	127,500
Paid-In Capital in Excess of Par—Preferred Stock	37,500
Paid-In Capital from Sale of Treasury Stock—Common	15,000
Preferred $2 Stock, $100 par	500,000
Retained Earnings	1,252,500
Treasury Stock—Common	95,000

Ten thousand shares of preferred and 150,000 shares of common stock are authorized. There are 5,000 shares of common stock held as treasury stock.

Prepare the Stockholders' Equity section of the balance sheet as of December 31, the end of the current year.

Exercise 13–10
Retained earnings statement

Objective 4

McArthur Corporation, a manufacturer of industrial pumps, reports the following results for the year ending August 31, 2000:

Retained earnings, September 1, 1999	$1,356,800
Net income	472,000
Cash dividends declared	100,000
Stock dividends declared	85,000

Prepare a retained earnings statement for the fiscal year ended August 31, 2000.

Exercise 13–11
Stockholders' equity section of balance sheet

Objective 4

What's Wrong WITH THIS?

✓ Corrected total stockholders' equity, $1,435,000

How many errors can you find in the following Stockholders' Equity section of the balance sheet prepared as of the end of the current year?

Stockholders' Equity

Paid-in capital:		
Preferred $2 stock, cumulative, $100 par (2,500 shares authorized and issued)	$250,000	
Excess of issue price over par	60,000	$ 310,000
Retained earnings		340,000
Treasury stock (4,000 shares at cost)		75,000
Dividends payable		60,000
Total paid-in capital		$ 785,000
Common stock, $15 par (50,000 shares authorized, 40,000 shares issued)	$810,000	
Donated capital	50,000	
Organization costs	120,000	980,000
Total stockholders' equity		$1,765,000

Exercise 13–12

Statement of stockholders' equity

Objective 4

✓ Total stockholders' equity, Dec. 31, $1,787,000

The stockholders' equity accounts of Monique Corporation for the current fiscal year ended December 31 are as follows:

ACCOUNT ***Common Stock, $1 Par***

Date		Item	Debit	Credit	Balance Debit	Balance Credit
20—						
Jan.	1	Balance				100,000
May	20	Issued 40,000 shares		40,000		140,000

ACCOUNT ***Paid-In Capital in Excess of Par***

Date		Item	Debit	Credit	Balance Debit	Balance Credit
20—						
Jan.	1	Balance				400,000
May	20	Issued 40,000 shares		24,000		424,000

ACCOUNT ***Treasury Stock***

Date		Item	Debit	Credit	Balance Debit	Balance Credit
20—						
Nov.	30	Purchased 5,000 shares	7,000		7,000	

ACCOUNT ***Retained Earnings***

Date		Item	Debit	Credit	Balance Debit	Balance Credit
20—						
Jan.	1	Balance				925,000
Dec.	31	Income summary		320,000		1,245,000
	31	Cash dividends	15,000			1,230,000

ACCOUNT ***Cash Dividends***

Date		Item	Debit	Credit	Balance Debit	Balance Credit
20—						
Mar.	12		10,000		10,000	
June	17		5,000		15,000	
Dec.	31	Closing		15,000	—	—

Prepare a statement of stockholders' equity for the fiscal year ended December 31.

Exercise 13–13

Temporary investments in marketable securities

Objective 6

During its first year of operations, Loran Corporation purchased the following securities as a temporary investment:

Security	Shares Purchased	Cost	Cash Dividends Received
Geer Inc.	5,000	$18,000	$1,500
Jones Corp.	3,000	24,000	600

a. Journalize the purchase of the temporary investments for cash.
b. Journalize the receipt of the dividends.

Exercise 13–14

Financial statement reporting of temporary investments

Objectives 5, 6

✓ b. Comprehensive income, $127,800

Using the data for Loran Corporation in Exercise 13–13, assume that as of December 31, 2000, the Geer Inc. stock had a market value of $5 per share and the Jones Corp. stock had a market value of $10 per share. For the year ending December 31, 2000, Loran Corporation had net income of $120,000. Its tax rate is 40%.

a. Prepare the balance sheet presentation for the temporary investments.
b. Prepare a statement of income and comprehensive income presentation for the temporary investments.

Exercise 13–15

Entries for investment in stock, receipt of dividends, and sale of shares

Objective 6

On February 3, Adair Corporation acquired 1,500 shares of the 40,000 outstanding shares of TZ Co. common stock at 60½ plus commission charges of $510. On August 13, a cash dividend of $1 per share and a 4% stock dividend were received. On November 15, 500 shares were sold at 62, less commission charges of $275. Journalize the entries to record (a) the purchase of the stock, (b) the receipt of dividends, and (c) the sale of the 500 shares.

Exercise 13–16

Equity method

Objective 6

The following note to the consolidated financial statements for **The Goodyear Tire and Rubber Co.** relates to the principles of consolidation used in preparing the financial statements:

The Company's investments in 20% to 50% owned companies in which it has the ability to exercise significant influence over operating and financial policies are accounted for by the equity method. Accordingly, the Company's share of the earnings of these companies is included in consolidated net income.

Is it a requirement that Goodyear use the equity method in this situation? Explain.

Exercise 13–17

Entries using equity method for stock investment

Objective 6

At a total cost of $9,000,000, Eastern Corporation acquired 75,000 shares of Southern Corp. common stock as a long-term investment. Eastern Corporation uses the equity method of accounting for this investment. Southern Corp. has 250,000 shares of common stock outstanding, including the shares acquired by Eastern Corporation. Journalize the entries by Eastern Corporation to record the following information:

a. Southern Corp. reports net income of $500,000 for the current period.
b. A cash dividend of $1.20 per common share is paid by Southern Corp. during the current period.

Exercise 13–18

Eliminations for consolidated income statement

Objective 7

✓ a. (1) $100,000
✓ b. $1,285,000

For the current year ended June 30, the results of operations of Montana Corporation and its wholly owned subsidiary, Blue Sky Enterprises, are as follows:

	Montana Corporation		Blue Sky Enterprises	
Sales		$2,150,000		$650,000
Cost of merchandise sold	$725,000		$340,000	
Selling expenses	255,000		75,000	
Administrative expenses	85,000		35,000	
Interest expense (revenue)	(12,000)	1,053,000	12,000	462,000
Net income		$1,097,000		$188,000

During the year, Montana sold merchandise to Blue Sky for $100,000. The merchandise was sold by Blue Sky to nonaffiliated companies for $150,000. Montana's interest revenue was realized from a long-term loan to Blue Sky.

a. Determine the amounts to be eliminated from the following items in preparing a consolidated income statement for the current year: (1) sales and (2) cost of merchandise sold.
b. Determine the consolidated net income.

Exercise 13–19
Price-earnings ratio
Objective 8

HAT

The financial statements for **Hershey Foods Corporation** are presented in Appendix G at the end of the text.

a. Determine the price-earnings ratio for Hershey Foods Corporation for 1996 and 1995. The market price of Hershey Foods common stock was $43\frac{3}{4}$ and $32\frac{1}{2}$ on December 31, 1996 and 1995, respectively. (Use only the Class A common stock.)
b. What conclusions can you reach by considering the price-earnings ratio?

PROBLEMS SERIES A

Problem 13–1A
Income tax allocation
Objective 1

SPREADSHEET

✓ 1. Year-end balance, 3rd year, $51,500

Differences between the accounting methods applied to accounts and financial reports and those used in determining taxable income yielded the following amounts for the first four years of a corporation's operations:

	First Year	Second Year	Third Year	Fourth Year
Income before income taxes	$250,000	$340,000	$420,000	$495,000
Taxable income	170,000	282,500	428,750	510,000

The income tax rate for each of the four years was 40% of taxable income, and each year's taxes were promptly paid.

Instructions

1. Determine for each year the amounts described by the following captions, presenting the information in the form indicated:

			Deferred Income Tax Payable	
Year	Income Tax Deducted on Income Statement	Income Tax Payments for the Year	Year's Addition (Deduction)	Year-End Balance

2. Total the first three amount columns.

Problem 13–2A
Income tax; income statement
Objectives 1, 2

SPREADSHEET

✓ Net income, $98,800

Off-Road Inc. produces and sells off-road motorcycles and jeeps. The following data were selected from the records of Off-Road Inc. for the current fiscal year ended March 31:

Advertising expense	$ 42,900
Cost of merchandise sold	395,000
Depreciation expense—office equipment	6,000
Depreciation expense—store equipment	21,500
Gain on condemnation of land	40,000
Income tax:	
Applicable to continuing operations	63,200
Applicable to loss from disposal of a segment of the business (reduction)	5,000
Applicable to gain on condemnation of land	16,000
Interest revenue	13,200
Loss from disposal of a segment of the business	26,000
Miscellaneous administrative expense	9,900
Miscellaneous selling expense	3,500
Office salaries expense	68,000

Rent expense	$ 20,000
Sales	835,000
Sales salaries expense	119,800
Store supplies expense	2,600

Instructions

Prepare a multiple-step income statement, concluding with a section for earnings per share (rounded to the nearest cent) in the form illustrated in this chapter. There were 30,000 shares of common stock (no preferred) outstanding throughout the year. Assume that the gain on condemnation of land is an extraordinary item.

Problem 13–3A

Income statement, retained earnings statement, balance sheet

Objectives 1, 2, 3, 4

✓ Net income, $400,950

The following data were taken from the records of Masuda Corporation for the year ended March 31, 2000:

Income statement data:	
Administrative expenses	$ 130,000
Cost of merchandise sold	4,000,000
Gain on condemnation of land	6,100
Income tax:	
Applicable to continuing operations	308,975
Applicable to loss from disposal of a segment of the business	21,100
Applicable to gain on condemnation of land	1,150
Interest expense	68,500
Interest revenue	675
Loss from disposal of a segment of the business	80,500
Sales	5,500,000
Selling expenses	537,800
Retained earnings and balance sheet data:	
Accounts payable	$ 149,500
Accounts receivable	329,050
Accumulated depreciation	3,050,000
Allowance for doubtful accounts	11,500
Cash	125,500
Common stock, $25 par (400,000 shares authorized; 104,900 shares issued)	2,622,500
Deferred income taxes payable (current portion, $4,700)	25,700
Dividends:	
Cash dividends for common stock	100,000
Cash dividends for preferred stock	110,000
Stock dividends for common stock	150,900
Dividends payable	25,000
Equipment	11,064,050
Income tax payable	55,900
Interest receivable	2,500
Merchandise inventory (March 31, 2000), at lower of cost (fifo) or market	522,500
Organization costs	55,000
Paid-in capital from sale of treasury stock	5,000
Paid-in capital in excess of par—common stock	325,000
Paid-in capital in excess of par—preferred stock	240,000
Preferred 8% stock, $100 par (30,000 shares authorized; 15,000 shares issued)	1,500,000
Prepaid expenses	15,900
Retained earnings, April 1, 1999	4,104,350
Treasury stock (1,000 shares of common stock at cost of $40 per share)	40,000

Instructions

1. Prepare a multiple-step income statement for the year ended March 31, 2000, concluding with earnings per share. In computing earnings per share, assume that the average number of common shares outstanding was 100,000 and preferred dividends were $110,000. Round to nearest cent. Assume that the gain on condemnation of land is an extraordinary item.
2. Prepare a retained earnings statement for the year ended March 31, 2000.
3. Prepare a balance sheet in report form as of March 31, 2000.

Problem 13–4A

Entries for investments in stock

Objective 6

HAT

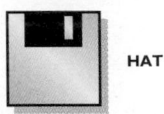

Vaughn Company produces and sells theater costumes. The following transactions relate to certain securities acquired by Vaughn Company, whose fiscal year ends on December 31:

1997

Mar. 20. Purchased 3,000 shares of the 40,000 outstanding common shares of Cruise Corporation at 27½ plus commission and other costs of $975.

June 15. Received the regular cash dividend of $1 a share on Cruise Corporation stock.

Dec. 15. Received the regular cash dividend of $1 a share plus an extra dividend of $0.20 a share on Cruise Corporation stock.

(Assume that all intervening transactions have been recorded properly and that the number of shares of stock owned have not changed from December 31, 1997, to December 31, 2000.)

2001

Jan. 3. Purchased controlling interest in Minish Inc. for $350,000 by purchasing 40,000 shares directly from the estate of the founder of Minish. There are 60,000 shares of Minish Inc. stock outstanding.

Mar. 20. Received the regular cash dividend of $1 a share and a 5% stock dividend on the Cruise Corporation stock.

July 20. Sold 750 shares of Cruise Corporation stock at 30. The broker deducted commission and other costs of $200, remitting the balance.

Dec. 18. Received a cash dividend at the new rate of $1.08 a share on the Cruise Corporation stock.

31. Received $48,000 of cash dividends on Minish Inc. stock. Minish Inc. reported net income of $120,000 in 2001. Vaughn uses the equity method of accounting for its investment in Minish Inc.

Instructions

Journalize the entries for the preceding transactions.

PROBLEMS SERIES B

Problem 13–1B

Income tax allocation

Objective 1

SPREADSHEET

✓ 1. Year-end balance, 3rd year, $70,500

Differences between the accounting methods applied to accounts and financial reports and those used in determining taxable income yielded the following amounts for the first four years of a corporation's operations:

	First Year	Second Year	Third Year	Fourth Year
Income before income taxes	$320,000	$450,000	$400,000	$649,000
Taxable income	250,000	360,000	383,750	678,750

The income tax rate for each of the four years was 40% of taxable income, and each year's taxes were promptly paid.

Instructions

1. Determine for each year the amounts described by the following captions, presenting the information in the form indicated:

			Deferred Income Tax Payable	
Year	Income Tax Deducted on Income Statement	Income Tax Payments for the Year	Year's Addition (Deduction)	Year-End Balance

2. Total the first three amount columns.

Problem 13–2B

Income tax; income statement

Objectives 1, 2

SPREADSHEET

✓ Net income, $33,500

The following data were selected from the records of Sunny Greenhouses Inc. for the current fiscal year ended July 31:

Advertising expense	$ 47,000
Cost of merchandise sold	750,000
Depreciation expense—office equipment	5,200
Depreciation expense—store equipment	29,000
Gain from disposal of a segment of the business	60,200
Income tax:	
Applicable to continuing operations	8,200
Applicable to gain from disposal of a segment of the business	24,000
Applicable to loss on condemnation of land (reduction)	10,000
Insurance expense	8,000
Interest expense	15,200
Loss on condemnation of land	25,000
Miscellaneous administrative expense	5,250
Miscellaneous selling expense	10,100
Office salaries expense	42,750
Rent expense	21,000
Sales	1,100,000
Sales commissions expense	146,000

Instructions

Prepare a multiple-step income statement, concluding with a section for earnings per share in the form illustrated in this chapter. There were 5,000 shares of common stock (no preferred) outstanding throughout the year. Assume that the loss on condemnation of land is an extraordinary item.

Problem 13–3B

Income statement, retained earnings statement, balance sheet

Objectives 1, 2, 3, 4

✓ Net income, $314,600

The following data were taken from the records of Aarstol Corporation for the year ended July 31, 2000:

Income statement data:	
Administrative expenses	$ 130,000
Cost of merchandise sold	3,850,000
Gain on condemnation of land	1,900
Income tax:	
Applicable to continuing operations	254,775
Applicable to loss from disposal of a segment of the business	21,100
Applicable to gain on condemnation of land	500
Interest expense	68,500
Interest revenue	3,675
Loss from disposal of a segment of the business	80,500
Sales	5,100,000
Selling expenses	427,800
Retained earnings and balance sheet data:	
Accounts payable	$ 149,500
Accounts receivable	309,050

Accumulated depreciation	$ 3,050,000
Allowance for doubtful accounts	21,500
Cash	145,500
Common stock, $25 par (400,000 shares authorized; 104,850 shares issued)	2,621,250
Deferred income taxes payable (current portion, $4,700)	25,700
Dividends:	
Cash dividends for common stock	120,000
Cash dividends for preferred stock	105,000
Stock dividends for common stock	198,850
Dividends payable	30,000
Equipment	11,014,050
Income tax payable	55,900
Interest receivable	2,500
Merchandise inventory (July 31, 2000), at lower of cost (fifo) or market	425,000
Notes receivable	77,500
Organization costs	55,000
Paid-in capital from sale of treasury stock	16,000
Paid-in capital in excess of par—common stock	325,000
Paid-in capital in excess of par—preferred stock	240,000
Preferred 8% stock, $100 par (30,000 shares authorized; 15,000 shares issued)	1,500,000
Prepaid expenses	15,900
Retained earnings, August 1, 1999	4,158,900
Treasury stock (1,000 shares of common stock at cost of $40 per share)	40,000

Instructions

1. Prepare a multiple-step income statement for the year ended July 31, 2000, concluding with earnings per share. In computing earnings per share, assume that the average number of common shares outstanding was 100,000 and preferred dividends were $105,000. Round to nearest cent. Assume that the gain on condemnation of land is an extraordinary item.
2. Prepare a retained earnings statement for the year ended July 31, 2000.
3. Prepare a balance sheet in report form as of July 31, 2000.

Problem 13–4B

Entries for investments in stock

Objective 6

Killian Company is a wholesaler of men's hair products. The following transactions relate to certain securities acquired by Killian Company, whose fiscal year ends on December 31:

1997

Jan. 11. Purchased 2,500 shares of the 40,000 outstanding common shares of Burnell Corporation at 23¼ plus commission and other costs of $375.

July 5. Received the regular cash dividend of $1 a share on Burnell Corporation stock.

Dec. 5. Received the regular cash dividend of $1 a share plus an extra dividend of $0.15 a share on Burnell Corporation stock.
(Assume that all intervening transactions have been recorded properly and that the number of shares of stock owned have not changed from December 31, 1997, to December 31, 2000.)

2001

Jan. 2. Purchased controlling interest in Nelda Inc. for $500,000 by purchasing 30,000 shares directly from the estate of the founder of Nelda. There are 50,000 shares of Nelda Inc. stock outstanding.

July 7. Received the regular cash dividend of $1 a share and a 4% stock dividend on the Burnell Corporation stock.

Aug. 20. Sold 500 shares of Burnell Corporation stock at 24. The broker deducted commission and other costs of $125, remitting the balance.

Dec. 9. Received a cash dividend at the new rate of $1.10 a share on the Burnell Corporation stock.

31. Received $36,000 of cash dividends on Nelda Inc. stock. Nelda Inc. reported net income of $90,000 in 2001. Killian uses the equity method of accounting for its investment in Nelda Inc.

Instructions

Journalize the entries for the preceding transactions.

SPECIAL ACTIVITIES

Activity 13–1
Lindquest Inc.
Ethics and professional conduct in business

At a recent dinner party, you met Fred Proctor, the controller for Lindquest Inc. Fred has worked for Lindquest for the past six years. During your conversation, you complained about having to pay your third-quarter estimated taxes on Monday, September 15. In response, Fred indicated that he always *underpays* his estimated taxes. That way, he can use his money as long as possible. Is it appropriate to deliberately underpay your estimated taxes?

Activity 13–2
Wasley Corporation
Ethics and professional conduct in business

Joel Wasley is the president and chief operating officer of Wasley Corporation, a developer of personal financial planning software. During the past year, Wasley Corporation was forced to sell three acres of land to the city of Dallas for expansion of a freeway exit. The corporation fought the sale, but after condemnation hearings, a judge ordered it to sell the land. Because of the location of the land and the fact that Wasley Corporation had purchased the land over 15 years ago, the corporation recorded a $0.75-per-share gain on the sale. Always looking to turn a negative into a positive, Joel Wasley has decided to announce the corporation's earnings per share of $2.20, without identifying the $0.75 impact of selling the land. Although he will retain majority ownership, Joel plans on selling 10,000 of his shares in the corporation sometime within the next month. Are Joel's plans to announce earnings per share of $2.20 without mentioning the $0.75 impact of selling the land ethical and professional?

Activity 13–3
Oranges Inc.
Reporting extraordinary item

Oranges Inc. is in the process of preparing its annual financial statements. Oranges Inc. is a large citrus grower located in central Florida. The following is a discussion between Gene Pierno, the controller, and Judith Reimers, the chief executive officer and president of Oranges Inc.

Judith: Gene, I've got a question about your rough draft of this year's income statement.

Gene: Sure, Judith. What's your question?

Judith: Well, your draft shows a net loss of $1.5 million.

Gene: That's right. We'd have had a profit, except for this year's frost damage. I figured that the frost destroyed over 25 percent of our crop. We had a good year otherwise.

Judith: That's my concern. I estimated that if we eliminate the frost damage, we'd show a profit of . . . let's see . . . about $500,000.

Gene: That sounds about right.

Judith: This income statement seems misleading. Why can't we show the loss on the frost damage separately? That way the bank and our outside investors will be able to see that this year's loss is just temporary. I'd hate to get them upset over nothing.

Gene: Maybe we can do something. I recall from my accounting courses something about showing unusual items separately. Let's see . . . yes, I remember. They're called extraordinary items.

Judith: Well, we haven't had any frost damage in over five years. This year's damage is certainly extraordinary. Let's do it!

Discuss the appropriateness of revising Oranges Inc.'s income statement to report the frost damage separately as an extraordinary item.

Activity 13–4 Geraldine Icerman

Consolidated financial statements

Your grandmother recently retired, sold her home in Boston, and moved to a retirement community in Arizona. With some of the proceeds from the sale of her home, she is considering investing $350,000 in the stock market.

In the process of selecting among alternative stock investments, your grandmother collected annual reports from twenty different companies. In reviewing these reports, however, she has become confused and has questions concerning several items that appear in the financial reports. She has asked for your help and has written down the following questions for you to answer:

a. *In reviewing the annual reports, I noticed many references to "consolidated financial statements." What are consolidated financial statements?*

b. *"Excess of cost of business acquired over related net assets" appears on the consolidated balance sheets in several annual reports. What does this mean? Is it an asset (it appears with other assets)?*

c. *What is minority interest?*

d. *A footnote to one of the consolidated statements indicated interest and the amount of a loan from one company to another had been eliminated. Is this good accounting? A loan is a loan. How can a company just eliminate a loan that hasn't been paid off?*

e. *How can financial statements for an American company (in dollars) be combined with a British subsidiary (in pounds)?*

1. Briefly respond to each of your grandmother's questions.
2. While discussing the items in (1) with your grandmother, she asked for your advice on whether she should limit her investment to one stock. What would you advise?

Activity 13–5 Into the Real World

Extraordinary items and discontinued operations

GROUP ACTIVITY Internet ACTIVITY

In groups of three or four students, search company annual reports, news releases, or the Internet for extraordinary items and announcements of discontinued operations. Identify the most unusual extraordinary item in your group. Also, select a discontinued operation of a well-known company that might be familiar to other students or might interest them.

Prepare a brief analysis of the earnings per share impact of both the extraordinary item and the discontinued operation. Estimate the *potential* impact on the company's market price by multiplying the current price-earnings ratio by the earnings per share amount of each item.

One Internet site that has annual reports is EDGAR (Electronic Data Gathering, Analysis, and Retrieval), the electronic archives of financial statements filed with the Securities and Exchange Commission. The EDGAR address is:

www.sec.gov/edgarhp.htm

To obtain annual report information, type in a company name on the "Search EDGAR Archives" form. EDGAR will list the reports available for the selected company. A company's annual report (along with other information) is provided in its annual 10-K report to the SEC. Click on the 10-K (or 10-K405) report for the year you wish to download. If you wish, you can save the whole 10-K report to a file and then open it with your word processor.

ANSWERS TO SELF-EXAMINATION QUESTIONS

Matching

1. Z	5. I	9. D	12. B	15. N	18. O	21. Y	24. E
2. AA	6. A	10. L	13. BB	16. G	19. F	22. V	25. P
3. H	7. U	11. CC	14. DD	17. J	20. Q	23. S	26. T
4. M	8. X						

Multiple Choice

1. **A** The amount of income tax deferred to future years is $16,000 (answer A), determined as follows:

Depreciation expense, MACRS	$100,000
Depreciation expense, straight-line method . . .	60,000
Excess expense in determining taxable income	$ 40,000
Income tax rate	× 40%
Income tax deferred to future years	$ 16,000

2. **A** Events and transactions that are distinguished by their unusual nature and by the infrequency of their occurrence, such as a gain on condemning land for public use, are reported in the income statement as extraordinary items (answer A).
3. **D** Appropriations are normally reported in the notes to the financial statements.
4. **C** The correction of a material error related to a prior period should be excluded from the determination of net income of the current period and reported as an adjustment of the balance of retained earnings at the beginning of the current period (answer C).
5. **C** Under the equity method of accounting for investments in stocks, Cisneros Corporation records its share of both net income and dividends of Harrell Inc. in Investment in Harrell Inc. Stock. Thus, Investment in Harrell Inc. Stock would increase by $82,500 [($150,000 × 75%) – ($40,000 × 75%)] for the current year. $30,000 (answer B) is only Cisneros Corporation's share of Harrell's dividends for the current year. $112,500 (answer D) is only Cisneros Corporation's share of Harrell's net income for the year.

14

Bonds Payable and Investments in Bonds

Setting the STAGE

You have just inherited $50,000 from a distant relative, and you are considering some options for investing the money. Some of your friends have suggested that you invest it in long-term bonds. As a result, you have scanned *The Wall Street Journal's* March 3, 1997 listing of New York Exchange Bonds. You've identified the following two listings as possible bond investments, both of which mature in the year 2007:

- **ATT (American Telephone & Telegraph) 7³/₄% Bonds**
- **OffDep (Office Depot) Zero**

The AT&T bonds are selling for 105³/₄, while the Office Depot bonds are selling for only 63¹/₂. The AT&T bonds are selling for over one and one-half times the price of the Office Depot bonds. Does this mean that the Office Depot bonds are a better buy? Does the 7³/₄% mean that if you buy the AT&T bonds you can actually earn 7³/₄% interest? What does the "zero" mean? Does it have anything to do with the fact that the Office Depot bonds are only selling for 63¹/₂?

In this chapter, we will answer each of these questions. We first discuss the advantages and disadvantages of financing a corporation's operations by issuing debt rather than equity. We then discuss the accounting principles related to issuing long-term debt. Finally, we discuss the accounting for investments in bonds.

objectives

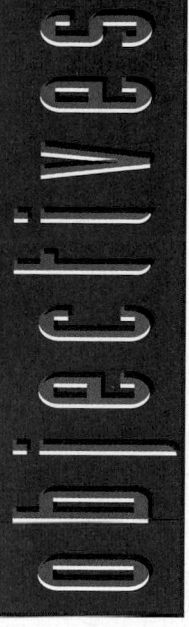

After studying this chapter, you should be able to:

1 Compute the potential impact of long-term borrowing on the earnings per share of a corporation.

2 Describe the characteristics of bonds.

3 Compute the present value of bonds payable.

4 Journalize entries for bonds payable.

5 Describe bond sinking funds.

6 Journalize entries for bond redemptions.

7 Journalize entries for the purchase, interest, discount and premium amortization, and sale of bond investments.

8 Prepare a corporation balance sheet.

9 Compute and interpret the number of times interest charges earned.

Financing Corporations

OBJECTIVE 1

Compute the potential impact of long-term borrowing on the earnings per share of a corporation.

Most of you have financed (purchased on credit) an automobile, a home, or a computer. Similarly, corporations often finance their operations by purchasing on credit and issuing notes or bonds. We have discussed accounts payable and notes payable in earlier chapters. A **bond** is simply a form of an interest-bearing note. Like a note, a bond requires periodic interest payments, and the face amount must be repaid at the maturity date. Bondholders are creditors of the issuing corporation, and their claims on the assets of the corporation rank ahead of stockholders.

Point of INTEREST

Bonds of major corporations are actively traded on bond exchanges. You can purchase bonds through a financial services firm, such as **Merrill Lynch** or **A. G. Edwards & Sons**.

One of the many factors that influence the decision to issue debt or equity is the effect of each alternative on earnings per share. To illustrate the possible effects, assume that a corporation's board of directors is considering the following alternative plans for financing a $4,000,000 company:

Plan 1: 100% financing from issuing common stock, $10 par

Plan 2: 50% financing from issuing preferred 9% stock, $50 par
50% financing from issuing common stock, $10 par

Plan 3: 50% financing from issuing 12% bonds
25% financing from issuing preferred 9% stock, $50 par
25% financing from issuing common stock, $10 par

In each case, we assume that the stocks or bonds are issued at their par or face amount. The corporation is expecting to earn $800,000 annually, before deducting interest on the bonds and income taxes estimated at 40% of income. Exhibit 1 shows the effect of the three plans on the income of the corporation and the earnings per share on common stock.

Exhibit 1 indicates that Plan 3 yields the highest earnings per share on common stock and is thus the most attractive for common stockholders. If the estimated earnings are more than $800,000, the difference between the earnings per share to

EXHIBIT 1
Effect of Alternative Financing Plans—$800,000 Earnings

	Plan 1	Plan 2	Plan 3
12% bonds	—	—	$2,000,000
Preferred 9% stock, $50 par	—	$2,000,000	1,000,000
Common stock, $10 par	$4,000,000	2,000,000	1,000,000
Total	$4,000,000	$4,000,000	$4,000,000
Earnings before interest and income tax	$ 800,000	$ 800,000	$ 800,000
Deduct interest on bonds	—	—	240,000
Income before income tax	$ 800,000	$ 800,000	$ 560,000
Deduct income tax	320,000	320,000	224,000
Net income	$ 480,000	$ 480,000	$ 336,000
Dividends on preferred stock	—	180,000	90,000
Available for dividends on common stock	$ 480,000	$ 300,000	$ 246,000
Shares of common stock outstanding	÷ 400,000	÷ 200,000	÷ 100,000
Earnings per share on common stock	$ 1.20	$ 1.50	$ 2.46

common stockholders under Plan 1 and Plan 3 is even greater.[1] However, if smaller earnings occur, Plans 2 and 3 become less attractive to common stockholders. To illustrate, the effect of earnings of $440,000 rather than $800,000 is shown in Exhibit 2.

EXHIBIT 2
Effect of Alternative Financing Plans—$440,000 Earnings

	Plan 1	Plan 2	Plan 3
12% bonds	—	—	$2,000,000
Preferred 9% stock, $50 par	—	$2,000,000	1,000,000
Common stock, $10 par	$4,000,000	2,000,000	1,000,000
Total	$4,000,000	$4,000,000	$4,000,000
Earnings before interest and income tax	$ 440,000	$ 440,000	$ 440,000
Deduct interest on bonds	—	—	240,000
Income before income tax	$ 440,000	$ 440,000	$ 200,000
Deduct income tax	176,000	176,000	80,000
Net income	$ 264,000	$ 264,000	$ 120,000
Dividends on preferred stock	—	180,000	90,000
Available for dividends on common stock	$ 264,000	$ 84,000	$ 30,000
Shares of common stock outstanding	÷ 400,000	÷ 200,000	÷ 100,000
Earnings per share on common stock	$ 0.66	$ 0.42	$ 0.30

In addition to the effect on earnings per share, the board of directors should consider other factors in deciding whether to issue debt or equity. For example, once bonds are issued, periodic interest payments and repayment of the face value of the bonds are beyond the control of the corporation. That is, if these payments are not made, the bondholders could seek court action and could force the company into bankruptcy. In contrast, a corporation is not legally obligated to pay dividends.

REAL WORLD

When interest rates are low, corporations usually finance their operations with debt. For example, as interest rates fell in the early 1990s, corporations rushed to issue new debt. In one day alone, more than $4.5 billion of debt was issued.

[1] The higher earnings per share under Plan 1 is due to a finance concept known as **leverage**. This concept is discussed further in a later chapter.

Characteristics of Bonds Payable

OBJECTIVE 2

Describe the characteristics of bonds.

A corporation that issues bonds enters into a contract, called a **bond indenture** or **trust indenture**, with the bondholders. A bond issue is normally divided into a number of individual bonds. Usually the face value of each bond, called the **principal**, is $1,000 or a multiple of $1,000. The interest on bonds may be payable annually, semiannually, or quarterly. Most bonds pay interest semiannually.

The prices of bonds are quoted as a percentage of the bonds' face value. Thus, investors could purchase or sell **Whirlpool** bonds quoted at 106¼ for $1,062.50. Likewise, bonds quoted at 109 could be purchased or sold for $1,090.

REAL WORLD: **AT&T** 7½% bonds maturing in 2006 were listed as selling for 106⅞ on October 7, 1997.

When all bonds of an issue mature at the same time, they are called **term bonds**. If the maturities are spread over several dates, they are called **serial bonds**. For example, one-tenth of an issue of $1,000,000 bonds, or $100,000, may mature 16 years from the issue date, another $100,000 in the 17th year, and so on until the final $100,000 matures in the 25th year.

Bonds that may be exchanged for other securities, such as common stock, are called **convertible bonds**. Bonds that a corporation reserves the right to redeem before their maturity are called **callable bonds**. Bonds issued on the basis of the general credit of the corporation are called **debenture bonds**.

INTERMISSION

Some of the same factors that influence a corporation's decision on financing are also considered when a company refinances, or changes the structure of its debt and stockholders' equity. These concerns are described in the following excerpt from an article in *USA TODAY*.

When a major company like **Allegis Corp.** *announces that it is "recapitalizing" [refinancing], many shareholders may be baffled. . . . Recapitalization plans aren't as complicated as they seem, however. . . . How companies balance equity and debt is up to them. At* **IBM Corp.**, *only 11% of total capital is debt.* **Sears, Roebuck and Co.** *has 46% debt. The level of debt a company keeps depends on the risk its managers are willing to assume.*

What does risk have to do with it?

It's no different for a company than for an individual. The more debt you have, the greater the risk. Reason: Any profit you earn first must go to meet interest payments. If earnings aren't sufficient to cover the interest owed, you'll have to deplete your savings—or sell something—to raise the needed cash.

What happens in a recapitalization?

A company decides to borrow heavily to raise cash for a large, one-time cash . . . payment to shareholders. . . . [In addition,] . . . shareholders also receive new shares to replace their old shares in the company. . . . [In] the process, the company generally [reduces its equity]. It's replaced with debt.

How can the company afford the debt load?

The company is forced to operate more efficiently than ever. It will have to slash expenses to keep earnings up in the face of higher interest expenses. **Owens-Corning Fiberglas Corp.**, *for example, pared its research costs significantly after its recapitalization last year. . . .*

Is there any advantage in being so heavily in debt?

Debt does have a good side. By borrowing, you gain "leverage"—the ability to control more assets by using someone else's money. That can magnify the return to shareholders, if business is good and the firm operates efficiently. . . . ■

Source: Neil Budde, "How Company Recapitalization Plans Work," *USA TODAY*, June 8, 1987.

The Present-Value Concept and Bonds Payable

OBJECTIVE 3

Compute the present value of bonds payable.

When a corporation issues bonds, the price that buyers are willing to pay for the bonds depends upon the following three factors:

1. The face amount of the bonds, which is the amount due at the maturity date.
2. The periodic interest to be paid on the bonds.
3. The market rate of interest.

The face amount and the periodic interest to be paid on the bonds is identified in the bond indenture. The periodic interest is expressed as a percentage of the face amount of the bond. This percentage or rate of interest is called the **contract rate** or **coupon rate**.

The **market** or **effective rate of interest** is determined by transactions between buyers and sellers of similar bonds. The market rate of interest is affected by a variety of factors, including investors' assessment of current economic conditions as well as future expectations.

If the contract rate of interest equals the market rate of interest, the bonds will sell at their face amount. If the market rate is higher than the contract rate, the bonds will sell at a **discount**, or less than their face amount. Why is this the case? Buyers are not willing to pay the face amount for bonds whose contract rate is lower than the market rate. The discount, in effect, represents the amount necessary to make up for the difference in the market and the contract interest rates. In contrast, if the market rate is lower than the contract rate, the bonds will sell at a **premium**, or more than their face amount. In this case, buyers are willing to pay more than the face amount for bonds whose contract rate is higher than the market rate.

Q&A

If IBM $7\frac{1}{4}\%$ bonds maturing in 2002 are listed as selling for $104\frac{3}{8}$, is the market rate of interest higher or lower than that for similar bonds?

Lower

The face amount of the bonds and the periodic interest on the bonds represent cash to be received by the buyer in the future. The buyer determines how much to pay for the bonds by computing the present value of these future cash receipts, using the market rate of interest. The concept of present value is based on the time value of money.

What is the time value of money? An amount of cash to be received at some date in the future is worth less than the same amount of cash held today. For example, what would you rather have: $100 today or $100 one year from now? You would rather have the $100 today because it could be invested to earn income. For example, if the $100 could be invested to earn 10% per year, the $100 will accumulate to $110 ($100 plus $10 earnings) in one year. In this sense, you can think of the $100 in hand today as the **present value** of $110 to be received a year from today. This present value is illustrated in the following time line:

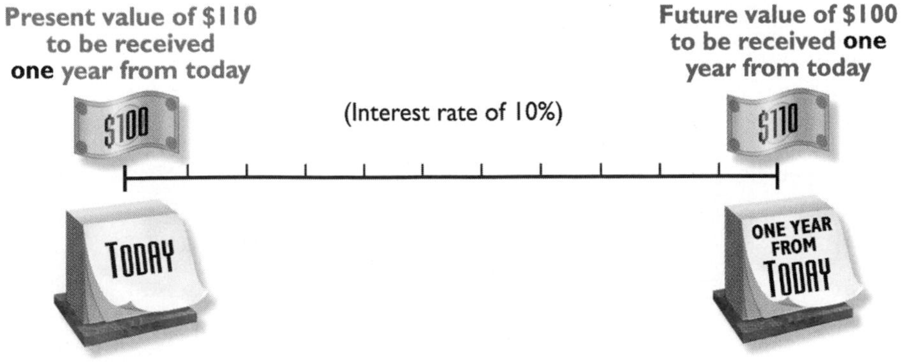

Q&A *What is the future value of $100 to be received in two years, assuming an interest rate of 10%?*

$121 ($100 × 1.10 × 1.10)

A related concept to present value is **future value**. In the preceding illustration, the $110 to be received a year from today is the future value of $100 today, assuming an interest rate of 10%.

Present Value of the Face Amount of Bonds

The present value of the face amount of bonds is the value today of the amount to be received at a future maturity date. For example, assume that you are to receive the face value of a $1,000 bond in one year. If the market rate of interest is 10%, the present value of the face value of the $1,000 bond is $909.09 ($1,000/1.10). This present value is illustrated in the following time line:

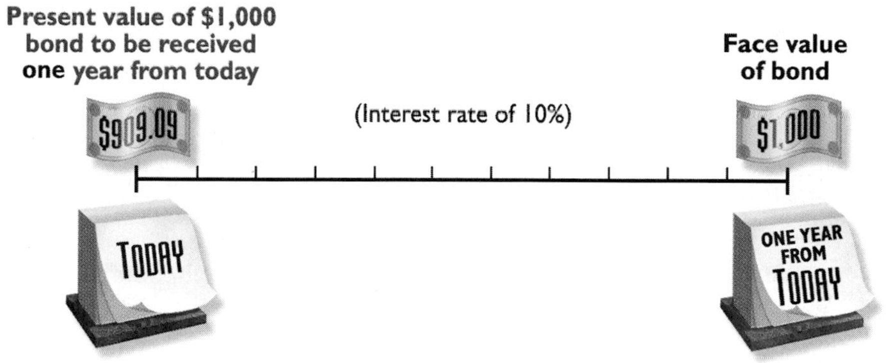

If you are to receive the face value of a $1,000 bond in two years, with interest of 10% compounded at the end of the first year, the present value is $826.45 ($909.09/1.10).[2] We illustrate this present value in the following time line:

Q&A *What is the present value of $1,000 to be received in three years, assuming an interest rate of 10%?*

$751.32 ($826.45/1.10)

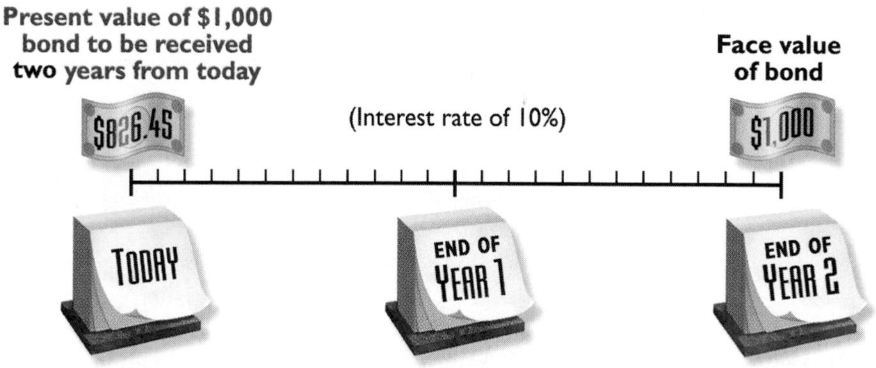

Point of INTEREST

Spreadsheet software with built-in present value functions can be used to calculate present values.

You can determine the present value of the face amount of bonds to be received in the future by a time line and a series of divisions. In practice, however, it is easier to use a table of present values. The *present value of $1 table* can be used to find the present-value factor for $1 to be received after a number of periods in the future. The face amount of the bonds is then multiplied by this factor to determine its present value. Exhibit 3 is a partial table of the present value of $1.[3]

[2] Note that the future value of $826.45 in two years, at an interest rate of 10% compounded annually, is $1,000.

[3] To simplify the illustrations and homework assignments, the tables presented in this chapter are limited to 10 periods for a small number of interest rates, and the amounts are carried to only five decimal places. Computer programs are available for determining present value factors for any number of interest rates, decimal places, or periods. More complete interest tables, including future value tables, are presented in Appendix A.

EXHIBIT 3 Present Value of $1 at Compound Interest

Periods	5%	5½%	6%	6½%	7%	10%	11%	12%	13%	14%
1	0.95238	0.94787	0.94340	0.93897	0.93458	0.90909	0.90090	0.89286	0.88496	0.87719
2	0.90703	0.89845	0.89000	0.88166	0.87344	0.82645	0.81162	0.79719	0.78315	0.76947
3	0.86384	0.85161	0.83962	0.82785	0.81630	0.75132	0.73119	0.71178	0.69305	0.67497
4	0.82270	0.80722	0.79209	0.77732	0.76290	0.68301	0.65873	0.63552	0.61332	0.59208
5	0.78353	0.76513	0.74726	0.72988	0.71299	0.62092	0.59345	0.56743	0.54276	0.51937
6	0.74622	0.72525	0.70496	0.68533	0.66634	0.56447	0.53464	0.50663	0.48032	0.45559
7	0.71068	0.68744	0.66506	0.64351	0.62275	0.51316	0.48166	0.45235	0.42506	0.39964
8	0.67684	0.65160	0.62741	0.60423	0.58201	0.46651	0.43393	0.40388	0.37616	0.35056
9	0.64461	0.61763	0.59190	0.56735	0.54393	0.42410	0.39092	0.36061	0.33288	0.30751
10	0.61391	0.58543	0.55840	0.53273	0.50835	0.38554	0.35218	0.32197	0.29459	0.26974

What is the present value of $3,000 to be received in 5 years at a market rate of interest of 14% compounded annually?

$1,558.11 ($3,000 × 0.51937)

Exhibit 3 indicates that the present value of $1 to be received in two years with a market rate of interest of 10% a year is 0.82645. Multiplying the $1,000 face amount of the bond in the preceding example by 0.82645 yields $826.45.

In Exhibit 3, the Periods column represents the number of compounding periods, and the percentage columns represent the compound interest rate per period. For example, 10% for two years compounded *annually,* as in the preceding example, is 10% for two periods. Likewise, 10% for two years compounded *semiannually* would be 5% (10% per year/2 semiannual periods) for four periods (2 years × 2 semiannual periods). Similarly, 10% for three years compounded semiannually would be 5% (10%/2) for six periods (3 years × 2 semiannual periods).

Present Value of the Periodic Bond Interest Payments

The present value of the periodic bond interest payments is the value today of the amount of interest to be received at the end of each interest period. Such a series of equal cash payments at fixed intervals is called an **annuity**.

The **present value of an annuity** is the sum of the present values of each cash flow. To illustrate, assume that the $1,000 bond in the preceding example pays interest of 10% annually and that the market rate of interest is also 10%. In addition, assume that the bond matures at the end of two years. The present value of the two interest payments of $100 ($1,000 × 10%) is $173.56, as shown in the time line at the left. It can be determined by using the present value table shown in Exhibit 3.

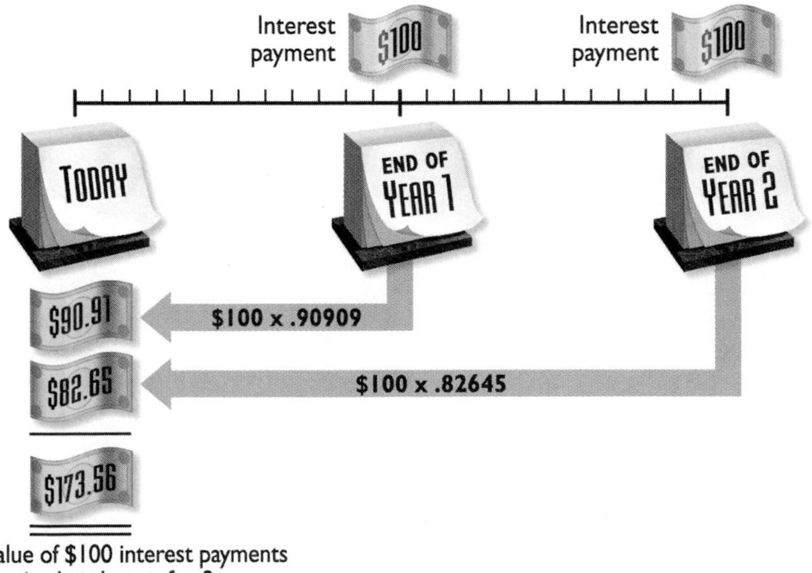

Present value of $100 interest payments to be received each year for 2 years (rounded to the nearest cent)

Instead of using present value of amount tables, such as Exhibit 3, separate present value tables are normally used for annuities. Exhibit 4 is a partial table of the *present value of an annuity of $1* at compound interest. It shows the present value of $1 to be received at the end of each period for various compound rates of interest. For example, the present value of $100 to be received at the end of each of the next two years at 10% compound interest per period is $173.55 ($100 × 1.73554). This amount is the same amount that we computed previously, except for rounding.

EXHIBIT 4 Present Value of Annuity of $1 at Compound Interest

Periods	5%	5½%	6%	6½%	7%	10%	11%	12%	13%	14%
1	0.95238	0.94787	0.94340	0.93897	0.93458	0.90909	0.90090	0.89286	0.88496	0.87719
2	1.85941	1.84632	1.83339	1.82063	1.80802	1.73554	1.71252	1.69015	1.66810	1.64666
3	2.72325	2.69793	2.67301	2.64848	2.62432	2.48685	2.44371	2.40183	2.36115	2.32163
4	3.54595	3.50515	3.46511	3.42580	3.38721	3.16987	3.10245	3.03735	2.97447	2.91371
5	4.32948	4.27028	4.21236	4.15568	4.10020	3.79079	3.69590	3.60478	3.51723	3.43308
6	5.07569	4.99553	4.91732	4.84101	4.76654	4.35526	4.23054	4.11141	3.99755	3.88867
7	5.78637	5.68297	5.58238	5.48452	5.38929	4.86842	4.71220	4.56376	4.42261	4.28830
8	6.46321	6.33457	6.20979	6.08875	5.97130	5.33493	5.14612	4.96764	4.79677	4.63886
9	7.10782	6.95220	6.80169	6.65610	6.51523	5.75902	5.53705	5.32825	5.13166	4.94637
10	7.72174	7.53763	7.36009	7.18883	7.02358	6.14457	5.88923	5.65022	5.42624	5.21612

Q&A *What is the present value of a $10,000, 7%, 5-year bond that pays interest annually, assuming a market rate of interest of 7%?*

$10,000 [($10,000 × 0.71299) + ($700 × 4.10020)]

As we stated earlier, the amount buyers are willing to pay for a bond is the sum of the present value of the face value and the periodic interest payments, calculated by using the market rate of interest. In our example, this calculation is as follows:

Present value of face value of $1,000 due in 2 years at 10% compounded annually: $1,000 × 0.82645 (present value factor of $1 for 2 periods at 10%)	$ 826.45
Present value of 2 annual interest payments of $100 at 10% compounded annually: $100 × 1.73554 (present value of annuity of $1 for 2 periods at 10%)	173.55
Total present value of bonds	$1,000.00

In this example, the market rate and the contract rate of interest are the same. Thus, the present value is the same as the face value.

Accounting for Bonds Payable

OBJECTIVE 4

Journalize entries for bonds payable.

In the preceding section, we described and illustrated how present value concepts are used in determining how much buyers are willing to pay for bonds. In this section, we describe and illustrate how corporations record the issuance of bonds and the payment of bond interest.

Bonds Issued at Face Amount

To illustrate the journal entries for issuing bonds, assume that on January 1, 1999, a corporation issues for cash $100,000 of 12%, five-year bonds, with interest of $6,000 payable *semiannually*. The market rate of interest at the time the bonds are issued is 12%. Since the contract rate and the market rate of interest are the same, the bonds will sell at their face amount. This amount is the sum of (1) the present value of the face amount of $100,000 to be repaid in five years and (2) the present value of ten *semiannual* interest payments of $6,000 each. This computation and a time line are shown below.

Present value of face amount of $100,000 due in 5 years, at 12% compounded semiannually: $100,000 × 0.55840 (present value of $1 for 10 periods at 6%)	$ 55,840
Present value of 10 semiannual interest payments of $6,000, at 12% compounded semiannually: $6,000 × 7.36009 (present value of annuity of $1 for 10 periods at 6%)	44,160*
Total present value of bonds	$100,000

* Because the present-value tables are rounded to five decimal places, minor rounding differences may appear in the illustrations.

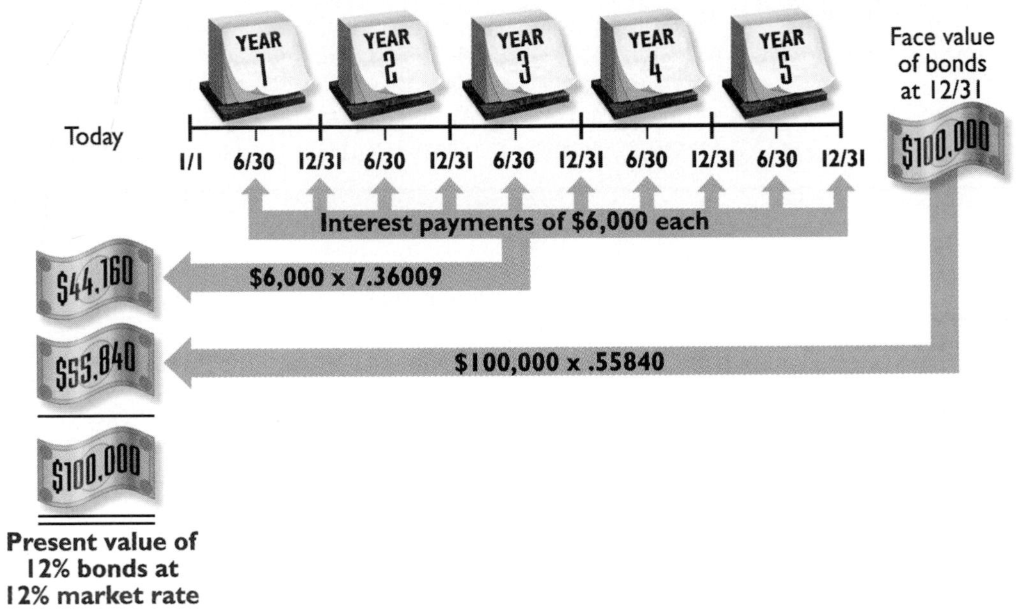

The following entry records the issuing of the $100,000 bonds at their face amount:

1999 Jan.	1	Cash	100 000 00	
		Bonds Payable		100 000 00
		Issued $100,000 bonds payable at face amount.		

Every six months after the bonds have been issued, interest payments of $6,000 are made. The first interest payment is recorded as shown below.

June	30	Interest Expense	6 000 00	
		Cash		6 000 00
		Paid six months' interest on bonds.		

At the maturity date, the payment of the principal of $100,000 is recorded as follows:

2003 Dec.	31	Bonds Payable	100 0 0 0 00	
		Cash		100 0 0 0 00
		Paid bond principal at maturity date.		

Bonds Issued at a Discount

Bonds will sell at a discount when the market rate of interest is higher than the contract rate.

What if the market rate of interest is higher than the contract rate of interest? If the market rate of interest is 13% and the contract rate is 12% on the five-year, $100,000 bonds, the bonds will sell at a discount. The present value of these bonds is calculated as follows:

Present value of face amount of $100,000 due in 5 years, at 13% compounded semiannually: $100,000 × 0.53273 (present value of $1 for 10 periods at 6½%)	$53,273
Present value of 10 semiannual interest payments of $6,000, at 13% compounded semiannually: $6,000 × 7.18883 (present value of an annuity of $1 for 10 periods at 6½%)	43,133
Total present value of bonds	$96,406

The two present values that make up the total are both less than the related amounts in the preceding example. This is because the market rate of interest was 12% in the first example, while the market rate of interest is 13% in this example. The present value of a future amount becomes less and less as the interest rate used to compute the present value increases.

The entry to record the issuing of the $100,000 bonds at a discount is shown below.

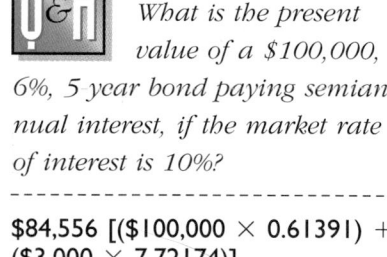

Q&A *What is the present value of a $100,000, 6%, 5 year bond paying semiannual interest, if the market rate of interest is 10%?*

$84,556 [($100,000 × 0.61391) + ($3,000 × 7.72174)]

1999 Jan.	1	Cash	96 4 0 6 00	
		Discount on Bonds Payable	3 5 9 4 00	
		Bonds Payable		100 0 0 0 00
		Issued $100,000 bonds at discount.		

The $3,594 discount may be viewed as the amount that is needed to entice investors to accept a contract rate of interest that is below the market rate. You may think of the discount as the market's way of adjusting a bond's contract rate of interest to the higher market rate of interest. Using this logic, generally accepted accounting principles require that bond discounts be amortized as interest expense over the life of the bond.

Amortizing a Bond Discount

There are two methods of amortizing a bond discount: (1) the **straight-line method** and (2) the **effective interest rate method**, often called the **interest method**. Both methods amortize the same total amount of discount over the life of the bonds. The interest method is required by generally accepted accounting principles. However, the straight-line method is acceptable if the results obtained do not materially differ from the results that would be obtained by using the interest method. Because the straight-line method illustrates the basic concept of amortizing discounts and is sim-

Q&A *If the amount of a bond discount on a newly issued 6%, 5-year, $100,000 bond is $28,092, what are (a) the semiannual straight-line amortization of the discount and (b) the annual interest expense?*

(a) $2,809.20, (b) $11,618.40 ($2,809.20 + $2,809.20 + $6,000)

pler, we will use it in this chapter. We illustrate the interest method in an appendix to this chapter.

The straight-line method of amortizing a bond discount provides for amortization in equal periodic amounts. Applying this method to the preceding example yields amortization of 1/10 of $3,594, or $359.40, each half year. The amount of the interest expense on the bonds is the same, $6,359.40 ($6,000 + $359.40) for each half year. The entry to record the first interest payment and the amortization of the related discount is shown below.

1999 June	30	Interest Expense	6,359.40	
		Discount on Bonds Payable		359.40
		Cash		6,000.00
		Paid semiannual interest and amortized 1/10 of bond discount.		

Bonds will sell at a premium when the market rate of interest is less than the contract rate.

Bonds Issued at a Premium

If the market rate of interest is 11% and the contract rate is 12% on the five-year, $100,000 bonds, the bonds will sell at a premium. The present value of these bonds is computed as follows:

Present value of face amount of $100,000 due in 5 years, at 11% compounded semiannually: $100,000 × 0.58543 (present value of $1 for 10 periods at 5½%)	$ 58,543
Present value of 10 semiannual interest payments of $6,000, at 11% compounded semiannually: $6,000 × 7.53763 (present value of an annuity of $1 for 10 periods at 5½%)	45,226
Total present value of bonds	$103,769

The entry to record the issuing of the bonds is as follows:

1999 Jan.	1	Cash	103,769.00	
		Bonds Payable		100,000.00
		Premium on Bonds Payable		3,769.00
		Issued $100,000 bonds at a premium.		

Q&A *If the amount of a bond premium on a newly issued 13%, 5-year, $100,000 bond is $11,581, what are (a) the semiannual straight-line amortization of the premium and (b) the annual interest expense?*

(a) $1,158.10, (b) $10,683.80 ($13,000 − $1,158.10 − $1,158.10)

Amortizing a Bond Premium

The amortization of bond premiums is basically the same as that for bond discounts, except that interest expense is decreased. In the above example, the straight-line method yields amortization of 1/10 of $3,769, or $376.90, each half year. The entry to record the first interest payment and the amortization of the related premium is as follows:

1999 June	30	Interest Expense	5,623.10	
		Premium on Bonds Payable	376.90	
		Cash		6,000.00
		Paid semiannual interest and amortized 1/10 of bond premium.		

Zero-Coupon Bonds

Some corporations issue bonds that provide for only the payment of the face amount at the maturity date. Such bonds are called **zero-coupon bonds**. Because they do not provide for interest payments, these bonds sell at a large discount. For example, **Office Depot's** zero-coupon bonds maturing in 2007 were selling for 63½ on March 3, 1997.

Some bonds with high contract rates, as well as some zero-coupon bonds, are issued by weak companies. Because such bonds are high-risk bonds, they are called **junk bonds.**

The issuing price of zero-coupon bonds is the present value of their face amount. To illustrate, if the market rate of interest is 13%, the present value of $100,000 zero-coupon, five-year bonds is calculated as follows:

Present value of $100,000 due in 5 years, at 13% compounded semiannually: $100,000 × 0.53273 (present value of $1 for 10 periods at 6½%)	$53,273

The accounting for zero-coupon bonds is similar to that for interest-bearing bonds that have been sold at a discount. The discount is amortized as interest expense over the life of the bonds. The entry to record the issuing of the bonds is as follows:

1999 Jan.	1	Cash		53,273 00	
		Discount on Bonds Payable		46,727 00	
		Bonds Payable			100,000 00
		Issued $100,000 zero-coupon bonds.			

Bond Sinking Funds

OBJECTIVE 5

Describe bond sinking funds.

A bond indenture may restrict dividend payments to stockholders as a means of increasing the likelihood that the bonds will be paid at maturity. In addition to or instead of this restriction, the bond indenture may require that funds for the payment of the face value of the bonds at maturity be set aside over the life of the bond issue. The amounts set aside are kept separate from other assets in a special fund called a **sinking fund**.

When cash is transferred to the sinking fund, it is recorded in an account called *Sinking Fund Cash*. When investments are purchased with the sinking fund cash, they are recorded in an account called *Sinking Fund Investments*. As income (interest or dividends) is received, it is recorded in an account called *Sinking Fund Revenue*.

Sinking fund revenue represents earnings of the corporation and is reported in the income statement as Other Income. The cash and the securities making up the sinking fund are reported in the balance sheet as Investments, immediately below the Current Assets section.

BUSINESS ON STAGE

Bonds are rated as to their riskiness as investments by such independent financial reporting services as **Moody's** and **Standard and Poor's**. These services rely heavily on analysis of the financial statements and the terms of the bond indenture in setting the credit rating. This credit rating, in turn, influences how much the bonds will sell for in the marketplace. Moody's and Standard and Poor's rate bonds slightly differently. The following table shows each rating and its accompanying interpretation.

Moody's Rating	Standard and Poor's Rating	Interpretation
AAA	Aaa	Highest rating; ability to pay interest and principal is very secure.
AA	Aa	High quality; differs from highest-rated bonds only to a small degree.
A	A	Upper-medium quality; interest and principal may be in jeopardy if a long, deep economic downturn (recession) occurs.
BBB	Baa	Medium grade; adequate ability to pay interest and principal in normal economic conditions.
BB	Ba	Quite risky; modest ability to pay interest and principal.
B	B	Poor investment; highly speculative; ability to pay interest and principal over a long period is small.
CCC	Caa	Poor standing; may be in default; purchase for speculative purposes only.
CC	Ca	Highly speculative; often in default on current payments.
C	C	Very poor prospects for ever being a good investment.
D	—	In default; little chance of ever receiving interest or principal.

Moody's classifies bonds of BBB or greater as "Investment Grade" bonds. In addition, Moody's will use a "+" sign or "−" sign to indicate the relative strength of a bond within a general rating category. For example, AAA+ indicates that a bond is at the high end of the AAA category.

Standard & Poor's classifies bonds of Baa or greater as "Investment Grade." Instead of using a "+" or "−" sign to indicate relative strength within a rating category, Standard & Poor's uses 1, 2, and 3. For example, Aaa1 indicates that a bond is in the upper third of the Aaa category, while Aaa3 indicates that a bond is in the bottom third. ■

Bond Redemption

OBJECTIVE 6

Journalize entries for bond redemptions.

A corporation may call or redeem bonds before they mature. This is often done if the market rate of interest declines significantly after the bonds have been issued. In this situation, the corporation may sell new bonds at a lower interest rate and use the funds to redeem the original bond issue. The corporation can thus save on future interest expenses.

A corporation often issues callable bonds to protect itself against significant declines in future interest rates. However, callable bonds are more risky for investors, who may not be able to replace the called bonds with investments paying an equal amount of interest.

Callable bonds can be redeemed by the issuing corporation within the period of time and at the price stated in the bond indenture. Normally, the call price is above the face value. A corporation may also redeem its bonds by purchasing them on the open market.

REAL WORLD **Indo Rayon** issued 5-year, 10% bonds, callable after 3 years.

A corporation usually redeems its bonds at a price different from that of the carrying amount (or book value) of the bonds. The **carrying amount** of bonds payable is the balance of the bonds payable account (face amount of the bonds) less any unamortized discount or plus any unamortized premium. If the price paid for redemption is below the bond carrying amount, the difference in these two amounts is recorded as a gain. If the price paid for the redemption is above the carrying amount, a loss is recorded. Gains and losses on the redemption of bonds are reported as an extraordinary item on the income statement.

To illustrate, assume that on June 30 a corporation has a bond issue of $100,000 outstanding, on which there is an unamortized premium of $4,000. Assuming that the corporation purchases one-fourth ($25,000) of the bonds for $24,000 on June 30, the entry to record the redemption is as follows:

1999 June	30	Bonds Payable		25 000 00	
		Premium on Bonds Payable		1 000 00	
		Cash			24 000 00
		Gain on Redemption of Bonds			2 000 00
		Redeemed $25,000 bonds for $24,000.			

Q&A

A $250,000 bond issue on which there is an unamortized discount of $20,000 is redeemed for $235,000. What is the gain or loss on the redemption of the bonds?

$5,000 loss ($250,000 − $20,000 − $235,000)

In the preceding entry, only a portion of the premium relating to the redeemed bonds is written off. The difference between the carrying amount of the bonds purchased, $26,000 ($25,000 + $1,000), and the price paid for the redemption, $24,000, is recorded as a gain.

If the corporation calls the entire bond issue for $105,000 on June 30, the entry to record the redemption is as follows:

1999 June	30	Bonds Payable		100 000 00	
		Premium on Bonds Payable		4 000 00	
		Loss on Redemption of Bonds		1 000 00	
		Cash			105 000 00
		Redeemed $100,000 bonds for $105,000.			

Investments in Bonds

OBJECTIVE 7

Journalize entries for the purchase, interest, discount and premium amortization, and sale of bond investments.

Throughout this chapter, we have discussed bonds and the related transactions of the issuing corporation (the debtor). However, these transactions also affect investors. In this section, we discuss the accounting for bonds from the point of view of investors.

Accounting for Bond Investments—Purchase, Interest, and Amortization

Bonds may be purchased either directly from the issuing corporation or through an organized bond exchange. Bond exchanges publish daily bond quotations. These quotations normally include the bond interest rate, maturity date, volume of sales, and the high, low, and closing prices for each corporation's bonds traded during the day. Prices for bonds are quoted as a percentage of the face amount. Thus, the price of a $1,000 bond quoted at $99\frac{1}{2}$ would be $995, while the price of a bond quoted at $104\frac{1}{4}$ would be $1,042.50.

REAL WORLD

IBM's $7\frac{1}{8}$% bonds maturing in 2096 were listed as selling for $98\frac{1}{8}$ on October 8, 1997.

As with other assets, the cost of a bond investment includes all costs related to the purchase. For example, for bonds purchased through an exchange, the amount paid as a broker's commission should be included as part of the cost of the investment.

When bonds are purchased between interest dates, the buyer normally pays the seller the interest accrued from the last interest payment date to the date of purchase. The amount of the interest paid is normally debited to *Interest Revenue,* since it is an offset against the amount that will be received at the next interest date.

To illustrate, assume that an investor purchases a $1,000 bond at 102 plus a brokerage fee of $5.30 and accrued interest of $10.20. The investor records the transaction as follows:

1999 Apr.	2	Investment in Lewis Co. Bonds	1 025 30	
		Interest Revenue	10 20	
		Cash		1 035 50

The cost of the bond is recorded in a single investment account. The face amount of the bond and the premium (or discount) are normally not recorded in separate accounts. This is different from the accounting for bonds payable. Separate premium and discount accounts are usually not used by investors, because they usually do not hold bond investments until the bonds mature.

A premium or discount on a bond investment is recorded in the investment account and is amortized over the remaining life of the bonds.

When bonds held as long-term investments are purchased at a price other than the face amount, the premium or discount should be amortized over the remaining life of the bonds. The amortization of premiums and discounts affects the investment and interest accounts as shown below.

Premium Amortization:			*Discount Amortization:*		
Interest Revenue	XXX		Investment in Bonds	XXX	
Investment in Bonds		XXX	Interest Revenue		XXX

The amount of the amortization can be determined by using either the straight-line or interest methods. Unlike bonds payable, the amortization of premiums and discounts on bond investments is usually recorded at the end of the period, rather than when interest is received.

To illustrate the accounting for bond investments, assume that on July 1, 1999, Crenshaw Inc. purchases $50,000 of 8% bonds of Deitz Corporation, due in $8\frac{3}{4}$ years. Crenshaw Inc. purchases the bonds directly from Deitz Corporation to yield an effective interest rate of 11%. The purchase price is $41,706 plus interest of $1,000 ($50,000 × 8% × $\frac{3}{12}$) accrued from April 1, 1999, the date of the last semiannual interest payment. Entries in the accounts of Crenshaw Inc. at the time of purchase and for the remainder of the fiscal period ending December 31, 1999, are as follows:

1999 July	1	Investment in Deitz Corp. Bonds		41 706 00	
		Interest Revenue		1 000 00	
		Cash			42 706 00
		Purchased investment in bonds,			
		plus accrued interest:			
		Cost of $50,000 of Deitz			
		Corp. bonds	$41,706		
		Interest accrued ($50,000			
		× 8% × $\frac{3}{12}$)	1,000		
		Total	$42,706		

Oct.	1	Cash	2,000.00	
		Interest Revenue		2,000.00
		Received semiannual interest for April 1 to October 1 ($50,000 × 8% × 6/12).		
Dec.	31	Interest Receivable	1,000.00	
		Interest Revenue		1,000.00
		Adjusting entry for interest accrued from October 1 to December 31 ($50,000 × 8% × 3/12).		
	31	Investment in Deitz Corp. Bonds	474.00	
		Interest Revenue		474.00
		Adjusting entry for amortization of discount for July 1 to December 31: Face value of bonds $50,000 Cost of bond investment 41,706 Discount on bond investment $ 8,294 Number of months to maturity (8 3/4 years × 12) 105 months Monthly amortization ($8,294/105 months, rounded to nearest dollar) $79 per mo. Amortization for 6 months ($79 × 6) $474		

The effect of these entries on the interest revenue account is shown below.

Interest Revenue

July 1	1,000	Oct. 1	2,000
		Dec. 31	1,000
		31	474
		Bal. 2,474	*3,474*

Accounting for Bond Investments—Sale

Many long-term investments in bonds are sold before their maturity date. When this occurs, the seller receives the sales price (less commissions and other selling costs) plus any accrued interest since the last interest payment date. Before recording the cash proceeds, the seller should amortize any discount or premium for the current period up to the date of sale. Any gain or loss on the sale is then recorded when the cash proceeds are recorded. Such gains and losses are normally reported in the Other Income section of the income statement.

To illustrate, assume that the Deitz Corporation bonds in the above example are sold for $47,350 plus accrued interest on June 30, 2006. The *carrying amount* of the bonds (cost plus amortized discount) as of January 1, 2006 (78 months after their purchase) is $47,868 [$41,706 + ($79 per mo. × 78 months)]. The entries to amortize the discount for the current year and to record the sale of the bonds are as follows:

Date		Description		Debit	Credit
2006 June	30	Investment in Deitz Corp. Bonds		474 00	
		Interest Revenue			474 00
		Amortized discount for current year ($79 × 6 months).			
	30	Cash		48,350 00	
		Loss on Sale of Investments		992 00	
		Interest Revenue			1,000 00
		Investment in Deitz Corp. Bonds			48,342 00
		Received interest and proceeds from sale of bonds.			
		Interest for April 1 to June 30 = $50,000 × 8% × 3/12 = $1,000			
		Carrying amount of bonds on Jan. 1, 2006	$47,868		
		Discount amortized, Jan. 1 to June 30, 2006	474		
		Carrying amount of bonds on June 30, 2006	$48,342		
		Proceeds of sale	47,350		
		Loss on sale	$ 992		

Q&A

If the Deitz Corporation bonds had been sold on September 30 instead of June 30, what would have been the amount of the loss?

$1,229 {$47,350 − [$48,342 + ($79 × 3 months)]}

Corporation Balance Sheet

OBJECTIVE 8

Prepare a corporation balance sheet.

In previous chapters, we illustrated the income statement and retained earnings statement for a corporation. The consolidated balance sheet in Exhibit 5 illustrates the presentation of many of the items discussed in this and preceding chapters. These items include bond sinking funds, investments in bonds, goodwill, deferred income taxes, bonds payable and unamortized discount, and minority interest in subsidiaries.

Balance Sheet Presentation of Bonds Payable

In Exhibit 5, Escoe Corporation's bonds payable are reported as long-term liabilities. If there were two or more bond issues, the details of each would be reported on the balance sheet or in a supporting schedule or note. Separate accounts are normally maintained for each bond issue.

When the balance sheet date is within one year of the maturity date of the bonds, the bonds may be classified as a current liability. This would be the case if the bonds are to be paid out of current assets. If the bonds are to be paid from a sinking fund or if they are to be refinanced with another bond issue, they should remain in the noncurrent category. In this case, the details of the retirement of the bonds are normally disclosed in a note to the financial statements.

The balance in Escoe's discount on bonds payable account is reported as a *deduction* from the bonds payable. Conversely, the balance in a bond premium ac-

EXHIBIT 5 Balance Sheet of a Corporation

Escoe Corporation and Subsidiaries
Consolidated Balance Sheet
December 31, 2000

Assets				
Current assets:				
Cash			$ 255,000	
Marketable securities		$ 160,000		
Less unrealized loss		7,500	152,500	
Accounts and notes receivable		$ 722,000		
Less allowance for doubtful receivables		37,000	685,000	
Inventories, at lower of cost (first-in, first-out) or market			917,500	
Prepaid expenses			70,000	
Total current assets				$2,080,000
Investments:				
Bond sinking fund (market value, $473,000)			$ 422,500	
Investment in bonds of Dalton Company (market value, $231,000)			240,000	
Total investments				662,500
	Cost	**Accumulated Depreciation**	**Book Value**	
Property, plant, and equipment (depreciated by the straight-line method):				
Land	$ 250,000	—	$ 250,000	
Buildings	920,000	$ 379,955	540,045	
Machinery and equipment	2,764,400	766,200	1,998,200	
Total property, plant, and equipment	$3,934,400	$1,146,155		2,788,245
Intangible assets:				
Goodwill			$ 300,000	
Organization costs			50,000	
Total intangible assets				350,000
Total assets				$5,880,745
Liabilities				
Current liabilities:				
Accounts payable			$ 508,810	
Income tax payable			120,500	
Dividends payable			94,000	
Accrued liabilities			81,400	
Deferred income tax payable			10,000	
Total current liabilities				$ 814,710
Long-term liabilities:				
Debenture 8% bonds payable, due December 31, 2015 (market value, $950,000)		$1,000,000		
Less unamortized discount		60,000	$ 940,000	
Minority interest in subsidiaries			115,000	
Total long-term liabilities				1,055,000
Deferred credits:				
Deferred income tax payable				85,500
Total liabilities				$1,955,210
Stockholders' Equity				
Paid-in capital:				
Common stock, $20 par (250,000 shares authorized, 100,000 shares issued)		$2,000,000		
Excess of issue price over par		320,000		
Total paid-in capital			$2,320,000	
Retained earnings			1,605,535	
Total stockholders' equity				3,925,535
Total liabilities and stockholders' equity				$5,880,745

count would be reported as an *addition* to the related bonds payable. Either on the face of the financial statements or in accompanying notes, a description of the bonds (terms, due date, and effective interest rate) and other relevant information such as sinking fund requirements should be disclosed.[4] Finally, the market (fair) value of the bonds payable should also be disclosed.

Balance Sheet Presentation of Bond Investments

Investments in bonds or other debt securities that management intends to hold to their maturity are called **held-to-maturity securities.** Such securities are classified as long-term investments under the caption Investments. These investments are reported at their cost less any amortized premium or plus any amortized discount. In addition, the market (fair) value of the bond investments should be disclosed, either on the face of the balance sheet or in an accompanying note.

FINANCIAL ANALYSIS AND INTERPRETATION

OBJECTIVE 9

Compute and interpret the number of times interest charges earned.

Some corporations, such as railroads and public utilities, have a high ratio of debt to stockholders' equity. For such corporations, analysts often assess the relative risk of the debtholders in terms of the **number of times the interest charges are earned** during the year. The higher the ratio, the greater the chance that interest payments will continue to be made if earnings decrease.[5]

The amount available to make interest payments is not affected by taxes on income. This is because interest is deductible in determining taxable income. To illustrate, the following data were taken from the 1996 annual report of **Briggs & Stratton Corporation**:

Interest expense	$10,060,000
Income before income tax	$149,052,000

The number of times interest charges are earned, 15.8, is calculated below.

$$\textbf{Number of times interest charges earned} = \frac{\textbf{Income before income tax + Interest expense}}{\textbf{Interest expense}}$$

$$\textbf{Number of times interest charges earned} = \frac{\$149{,}052{,}000 + \$10{,}060{,}000}{\$10{,}060{,}000} = 15.8$$

The number of times interest charges are earned indicates that the debtholders of Briggs & Stratton have adequate protection against a potential drop in earnings jeopardizing their receipt of interest payments. However, a final assessment should include a review of trends of past years and a comparison with industry averages.

4 *Statement of Financial Accounting Standards No. 129,* "Disclosure Information About Capital Structure," Financial Accounting Standards Board (Norwalk, Connecticut: 1997).

5 A similar analysis can also be applied to dividends on preferred stock. In such cases, net income would be divided by the amount of preferred dividends to yield the number of times preferred dividends were earned. This measure gives an indication of the relative assurance of continued dividend payments to preferred stockholders.

ENCORE

Let's Dance—A Bond with a Tune

How would you like to tune into some of the royalties from David Bowie's hit song, *Let's Dance*? Recently, the British rock star offered bonds backed by future royalties from his hit songs and albums recorded prior to 1990. In addition to *Let's Dance*, other songs include *Jean Genie, A Space Oddity, Changes, Diamond Dogs,* and *Rebel.*

Bowie's bonds, which have an average maturity of 10 years, pay 7.9% annual interest. Such asset-backed bonds have grown in popularity. However, this is the first time that a popular artist has made use of future royalties as asset backing. The Bowie Bonds, which are officially called Class-A royalty-backed securities, were rated AAA—the highest rating—by **Moody's Investors Service.**

The 50-year-old Bowie is one of the most financially savvy rock stars in the world, with a well-chosen art collection and an appreciation for market trends. Bowie's principal residence is a $3.4 million, 640-acre estate in County Wicklow, Ireland, a noted tax haven. He lives there with his second wife, the supermodel and actress Iman. Still, Bowie's business manager said that when he approached him with the bond idea, "he [Bowie] kind of looked at me cross-eyed and said, 'What?'"

Potential investors were reassured by the fact that Bowie never sells fewer than a million albums a year. At the time of the offering, Bowie's latest album, "Earthling," was near the top of the European charts. In addition, the month before the offering, he performed for a sold-out concert at New York's Madison Square Garden.

Prudential Insurance Co. isn't kidding when it says you can own a piece of the *rock*. In a private placement in early 1997, Prudential purchased all of David Bowie's $55 million bonds for its general investment fund, where the money of life insurance policyholders is invested. ■

APPENDIX—EFFECTIVE INTEREST RATE METHOD OF AMORTIZATION

The effective interest rate method of amortizing discounts and premiums provides for a constant rate of interest on the carrying amount of the bonds at the beginning of each period. This is in contrast to the straight-line method, which provides for a constant amount of interest expense.

The interest rate used in the interest method of amortization is the market rate on the date the bonds are issued. The carrying amount of the bonds to which the interest rate is applied is the face amount of the bonds minus any unamortized discount or plus any unamortized premium. Under the interest method, the interest expense to be reported on the income statement is computed by multiplying the effective interest rate by the carrying amount of the bonds. The difference between the interest expense computed in this way and the periodic interest payment is the amount of discount or premium to be amortized for the period.

Amortization of Discount by the Interest Method

To illustrate the interest method for amortizing bond discounts, we assume the following data from the chapter illustration of issuing $100,000 bonds at a discount:

Face value of 12%, 5-year bonds, interest compounded semiannually	$100,000
Present value of bonds at effective (market) rate of interest of 13%	96,406
Discount on bonds payable	$ 3,594

Applying the interest method to these data yields the amortization table in Exhibit 6. You should note the following items in this table:

1. The interest paid (Column A) remains constant at 6% of $100,000, the face amount of the bonds.
2. The interest expense (Column B) is computed at 6½% of the bond carrying amount at the beginning of each period. This results in an increasing interest expense each period.
3. The excess of the interest expense over the interest payment of $6,000 is the amount of discount to be amortized (Column C).
4. The unamortized discount (Column D) decreases from the initial balance, $3,594, to a zero balance at the maturity date of the bonds.
5. The carrying amount (Column E) increases from $96,406, the amount received for the bonds, to $100,000 at maturity.

EXHIBIT 6 Amortization of Discount on Bonds Payable

Interest Payment	A Interest Paid (6% of Face Amount)	B Interest Expense (6½% of Bond Carrying Amount)	C Discount Amortization (B − A)	D Unamortized Discount (D − C)	E Bond Carrying Amount ($100,000 − D)
				$3,594	$ 96,406
1	$6,000	$6,266 (6½% of $96,406)	$266	3,328	96,672
2	6,000	6,284 (6½% of $96,672)	284	3,044	96,956
3	6,000	6,302 (6½% of $96,956)	302	2,742	97,258
4	6,000	6,322 (6½% of $97,258)	322	2,420	97,580
5	6,000	6,343 (6½% of $97,580)	343	2,077	97,923
6	6,000	6,365 (6½% of $97,923)	365	1,712	98,288
7	6,000	6,389 (6½% of $98,288)	389	1,323	98,677
8	6,000	6,414 (6½% of $98,677)	414	909	99,091
9	6,000	6,441 (6½% of $99,091)	441	468	99,532
10	6,000	6,470 (6½% of $99,532)	468*	—	100,000

*Cannot exceed unamortized discount.

The entry to record the first interest payment on June 30, 1999, and the related discount amortization is as follows:

1999 June	30	Interest Expense	6 2 6 6 00	
		Discount on Bonds Payable		2 6 6 00
		Cash		6 0 0 0 00
		Paid semiannual interest and amortized bond discount for one-half year.		

If the amortization is recorded only at the end of the year, the amount of the discount amortized on December 31 would be $550. This is the sum of the first two semiannual amortization amounts ($266 and $284) from Exhibit 6.

Amortization of Premium by the Interest Method

To illustrate the interest method for amortizing bond premiums, we assume the following data from the chapter illustration of issuing $100,000 bonds at a premium:

Present value of bonds at effective (market) rate of interest of 11%	$103,769
Face value of 12%, 5-year bonds, interest compounded semiannually	100,000
Premium on bonds payable	$ 3,769

Using the interest method to amortize the above premium yields the amortization table in Exhibit 7. You should note the following items in this table:

1. The interest paid (Column A) remains constant at 6% of $100,000, the face amount of the bonds.
2. The interest expense (Column B) is computed at 5½% of the bond carrying amount at the beginning of each period. This results in a decreasing interest expense each period.
3. The excess of the periodic interest payment of $6,000 over the interest expense is the amount of premium to be amortized (Column C).
4. The unamortized premium (Column D) decreases from the initial balance, $3,769, to a zero balance at the maturity date of the bonds.
5. The carrying amount (Column E) decreases from $103,769, the amount received for the bonds, to $100,000 at maturity.

EXHIBIT 7 Amortization of Premium on Bonds Payable

Interest Payment	A Interest Paid (6% of Face Amount)	B Interest Expense (5½% of Bond Carrying Amount)	C Premium Amortization (A − B)	D Unamortized Premium (D − C)	E Bond Carrying Amount ($100,000 + D)
				$3,769	$103,769
1	$6,000	$5,707 (5½% of $103,769)	$293	3,476	103,476
2	6,000	5,691 (5½% of $103,476)	309	3,167	103,167
3	6,000	5,674 (5½% of $103,167)	326	2,841	102,841
4	6,000	5,656 (5½% of $102,841)	344	2,497	102,497
5	6,000	5,637 (5½% of $102,497)	363	2,134	102,134
6	6,000	5,617 (5½% of $102,134)	383	1,751	101,751
7	6,000	5,596 (5½% of $101,751)	404	1,347	101,347
8	6,000	5,574 (5½% of $101,347)	426	921	100,921
9	6,000	5,551 (5½% of $100,921)	449	472	100,472
10	6,000	5,526 (5½% of $100,472)	472*	—	100,000

*Cannot exceed unamortized premium.

The entry to record the first interest payment on June 30, 1999, and the related premium amortization is as follows:

1999 June	30	Interest Expense	5 707 00	
		Premium on Bonds Payable	293 00	
		Cash		6 000 00
		Paid semiannual interest and amortized bond premium for one-half year.		

If the amortization is recorded only at the end of the year, the amount of the premium amortized on December 31, 1999, would be $602. This is the sum of the first two semiannual amortization amounts ($293 and $309) from Exhibit 7.

KEY POINTS

1 Compute the potential impact of long-term borrowing on the earnings per share of a corporation.

Three alternative plans for financing a corporation by issuing common stock, preferred stock, or bonds are illustrated in Exhibits 1 and 2. The effects of alternative financing on the earnings per share vary significantly, depending upon the level of earnings.

2 Describe the characteristics of bonds.

The characteristics of bonds depend upon the type of bonds issued by a corporation. Bonds that may be issued include term bonds, serial bonds, convertible bonds, callable bonds, and debenture bonds.

3 Compute the present value of bonds payable.

The concept of present value is based on the time value of money. That is, an amount of cash to be received at some date in the future is worth less than the same amount of cash held today. For example, if $100 cash today can be invested to earn 10% per year, the $100 today is referred to as the present value amount that is equal to $110 to be received a year from today.

A price that a buyer is willing to pay for a bond is the sum of (1) the present value of the face amount of the bonds at the maturity date and (2) the present value of the periodic interest payments.

4 Journalize entries for bonds payable.

The journal entry for issuing bonds payable debits Cash for the proceeds received and credits Bonds Payable for the face amount of the bonds. Any difference between the face amount of the bonds and the proceeds is debited to Discount on Bonds Payable or credited to Premium on Bonds Payable.

A discount or premium on bonds payable is amortized to interest expense over the life of the bonds. The entry to amortize a discount debits Interest Expense and credits Discount on Bonds Payable. The entry to amortize a premium debits Premium on Bonds Payable and credits Interest Expense.

5 Describe bond sinking funds.

A bond indenture may require that funds for the payment of the bonds at maturity be set aside over the life of the bonds. The amounts set aside are kept separate from other assets in a special fund called a sinking fund. A sinking fund is reported as an Investment on the balance sheet. Income from a sinking fund is reported as Other Income on the income statement.

6 Journalize entries for bond redemptions.

When a corporation redeems bonds, Bonds Payable is debited for the face amount of the bonds, the premium (discount) on bonds account is debited (credited) for its balance, Cash is credited, and any gain or loss on the redemption is recorded.

7 Journalize entries for the purchase, interest, discount and premium amortization, and sale of bond investments.

A long-term investment in bonds is recorded by debiting Investment in Bonds. When bonds are purchased between interest dates, the amount of the interest paid should be debited to Interest Revenue. Any discount or premium on bond investments should be amortized, using the straight-line or effective interest rate methods. The amortization of a discount is recorded by debiting Investment in Bonds and crediting Interest Revenue. The amortization of a premium is recorded by debiting Interest Revenue and crediting Investment in Bonds.

When bonds held as long-term investments are sold, any

discount or premium for the current period should first be amortized. Cash is then debited for the proceeds of the sale, Investment in Bonds is credited for its balance, and any gain or loss is recorded.

8 Prepare a corporation balance sheet.

The corporation balance sheet may include bond sinking funds, investments in bonds, goodwill, deferred income taxes, bonds payable and unamortized premium or discount, and minority interest in subsidiaries.

Bonds payable are usually reported as long-term liabilities. A discount on bonds should be reported as a deduction from the related bonds payable. A premium on bonds should be reported as an addition to the related bonds payable. Investments in bonds that are held-to-maturity securities are reported as Investments at cost less any amortized premium or plus any amortized discount.

9 Compute and interpret the number of times interest charges earned.

The number of times interest charges are earned during the year is a measure of the risk that interest payments to debtholders will continue to be made if earnings decrease. It is computed by dividing income before income tax plus interest expense by interest expense.

ILLUSTRATIVE PROBLEM

The fiscal year of Russell Inc., a manufacturer of acoustical supplies, ends December 31. Selected transactions for the period 1999 through 2006, involving bonds payable issued by Russell Inc., are as follows:

1999
June 30. Issued $2,000,000 of 25-year, 7% callable bonds dated June 30, 1999, for cash of $1,920,000. Interest is payable semiannually on June 30 and December 31.
Dec. 31. Paid the semiannual interest on the bonds.
31. Recorded straight-line amortization of $1,600 of discount on the bonds.
31. Closed the interest expense account.

2000
June 30. Paid the semiannual interest on the bonds.
Dec. 31. Paid the semiannual interest on the bonds.
31. Recorded straight-line amortization of $3,200 of discount on the bonds.
31. Closed the interest expense account.

2006
June 30. Recorded the redemption of the bonds, which were called at 101½. The balance in the bond discount account is $57,600 after the payment of interest and amortization of discount have been recorded. (Record the redemption only.)

Instructions

1. Journalize entries to record the preceding transactions.
2. Determine the amount of interest expense for 1999 and 2000.
3. Estimate the effective annual interest rate by dividing the interest expense for 1999 by the bond carrying amount at the time of issuance and multiplying by 2.
4. Determine the carrying amount of the bonds as of December 31, 2000.

Solution

1.

1999 June	30	Cash		1,920,000 00	
		Discount on Bonds Payable		80,000 00	
		Bonds Payable			2,000,000 00
Dec.	31	Interest Expense		70,000 00	
		Cash			70,000 00
	31	Interest Expense		1,600 00	
		Discount on Bonds Payable			1,600 00

Dec.	31	Income Summary	71,600 00	
		Interest Expense		71,600 00
2000 June	30	Interest Expense	70,000 00	
		Cash		70,000 00
Dec.	31	Interest Expense	70,000 00	
		Cash		70,000 00
	31	Interest Expense	3,200 00	
		Discount on Bonds Payable		3,200 00
	31	Income Summary	143,200 00	
		Interest Expense		143,200 00
2006 June	30	Bonds Payable	2,000,000 00	
		Loss on Redemption of Bonds Payable	87,600 00	
		Discount on Bonds Payable		57,600 00
		Cash		2,030,000 00

2. a. 1999—$71,600
b. 2000—$143,200

3. $71,600 ÷ $1,920,000 = 3.73% rate for six months of a year
3.73% × 2 = 7.46% annual rate

4.

Initial carrying amount of bonds	$1,920,000
Discount amortized on December 31, 1999	1,600
Discount amortized on December 31, 2000	3,200
Carrying amount of bonds, December 31, 2000	$1,924,800

SELF-EXAMINATION QUESTIONS

Answers at End of Chapter

Matching

Match each of the following statements with its proper term. Some terms may not be used.

A. annuity
B. available-for-sale securities
C. bond
D. bond fund
E. bond indenture
F. carrying amount
G. contract rate
H. discount
I. dividend yield
J. effective interest rate method
K. effective rate of interest
L. future value
M. held-to-maturity securities

C 1. A form of an interest-bearing note used by corporations to borrow on a long-term basis.
E 2. The contract between a corporation issuing bonds and the bondholders.
G 3. The periodic interest to be paid on the bonds that is identified in the bond indenture; expressed as a percentage of the face amount of the bond.
A 4. A series of equal cash flows at fixed intervals.
Q 5. The sum of the present values of a series of equal cash flows to be received at fixed intervals.
P 6. The estimated worth today of an amount of cash to be received (or paid) in the future.
L 7. The estimated worth in the future of an amount of cash on hand today invested at a fixed rate of interest.
H 8. The excess of the face amount of bonds over their issue price.
O 9. The excess of the issue price of bonds over their face amount.
R 10. A fund in which cash or assets are set aside for the purpose of paying the face amount of the bonds at maturity.

N. **number of times interest charges earned**
O. **premium**
P. **present value**
Q. **present value of an annuity**
R. **sinking fund**

F 11. The balance of the bonds payable account (face amount of the bonds) less any unamortized discount or plus any unamortized premium.

M 12. Investments in bonds or other debt securities that management intends to hold to their maturity.

N 13. A ratio that measures the risk that interest payments to debtholders will continue to be made if earnings decrease.

K 14. The market rate of interest at the time bonds are issued.

Multiple Choice

1. If a corporation plans to issue $1,000,000 of 12% bonds at a time when the market rate for similar bonds is 10%, the bonds can be expected to sell at:
   A. their face amount
   B. a premium
   C. a discount
   D. a price below their face amount

2. If the bonds payable account has a balance of $500,000 and the discount on bonds payable account has a balance of $40,000, what is the carrying amount of the bonds?
   A. $460,000
   B. $500,000
   C. $540,000
   D. $580,000

3. The cash and securities that make up the sinking fund established for the payment of bonds at maturity are classified on the balance sheet as:
   A. current assets
   B. investments
   C. long-term liabilities
   D. current liabilities

4. If a firm purchases $100,000 of bonds of X Company at 101 plus accrued interest of $2,000 and pays broker's commissions of $50, the amount debited to Investment in X Company Bonds would be:
   A. $100,000
   B. $101,050
   C. $103,000
   D. $103,050

5. The balance in the discount on bonds payable account would usually be reported in the balance sheet in the:
   A. Current Assets section
   B. Current Liabilities section
   C. Long-Term Liabilities section
   D. Investments section

CLASS DISCUSSION QUESTIONS

1. Describe the two distinct obligations incurred by a corporation when issuing bonds.
2. Explain the meaning of each of the following terms as they relate to a bond issue: (a) convertible, (b) callable, and (c) debenture.
3. What is meant by the "time value of money?"
4. What has the higher present value: (a) $3,000 to be received at the end of two years, or (b) $1,500 to be received at the end of each of the next two years?
5. If you asked your broker to purchase for you an 8% bond when the market interest rate for such bonds was 9%, would you expect to pay more or less than the face amount for the bond? Explain.
6. A corporation issues $7,500,000 of 7% bonds to yield interest at the rate of 6%. (a) Was the amount of cash received from the sale of the bonds greater or less than $7,500,000? (b) Identify the following terms related to the bond issue: (1) face amount, (2) market or effective rate of interest, (3) contract rate of interest, and (4) maturity amount.
7. If bonds issued by a corporation are sold at a premium, is the market rate of interest greater or less than the contract rate?
8. The following data relate to a $500,000, 8% bond issue for a selected semiannual interest period:

Bond carrying amount at beginning of period	$525,000
Interest paid at end of period	20,000
Interest expense allocable to the period	18,750

   (a) Were the bonds issued at a discount or at a premium? (b) What is the unamortized amount of the discount or premium account at the beginning of the period? (c) What account was debited to amortize the discount or premium?

9. Assume that Koffee Co. amortizes premiums and discounts on bonds payable at the end of the year rather than when interest is paid. What accounts would be debited and credited to record (a) the amortization of a discount on bonds payable and (b) the amortization of a premium on bonds payable?
10. Would a zero-coupon bond ever sell for its face amount?
11. What is the purpose of a bond sinking fund?
12. How are earnings from investments in a sinking fund reported on the income statement?
13. How are cash and securities comprising a sinking fund classified on the balance sheet?
14. Assume that two 10-year, 8% bond issues are identical, except that one bond issue is callable at its face amount at the end of 6 years. Which of the two bond issues do you think will sell for a higher value?
15. Bonds Payable has a balance of $800,000, and Premium on Bonds Payable has a balance of $15,000. If the issuing corporation redeems the bonds at 102, is there a gain or loss on the bond redemption?
16. How are gains or losses on bond redemptions reported on the income statement?
17. Assume that a company purchases bonds between interest dates. What accounts would normally be debited?
18. Indicate how the following accounts should be reported on the balance sheet: (a) Premium on Bonds Payable and (b) Discount on Bonds Payable.
19. Where are investments in bonds that are classified as held-to-maturity securities reported on the balance sheet?
20. At what amount are held-to-maturity investments in bonds reported on the balance sheet?

Resources for Your Success On-Line at warren.swcollege.com

Remember! If you need additional help, visit South-Western's Web site. See page 26 for a description of the online and printed materials that are available.

EXERCISES

Exercise 14–1
Effect of financing on earnings per share
Objective 1

SPREADSHEET

✓ a. $0.30

Nevin Co., which produces and sells skiing equipment, is financed as follows:

Bonds payable, 10% (issued at face amount)	$2,000,000
Preferred $9 stock (nonparticipating), $100 par	2,000,000
Common stock, $10 par	2,000,000

Income tax is estimated at 40% of income.

Determine the earnings per share of common stock, assuming that the income before bond interest and income tax is (a) $600,000, (b) $1,000,000, and (c) $2,500,000.

Exercise 14–2
Evaluate alternative financing plans
Objective 1

Based upon the data in Exercise 14–1, discuss factors other than earnings per share that should be considered in evaluating such financing plans.

Exercise 14–3
Present value of amounts due
Objective 3

✓ a. $8,164

Determine the present value of $10,000 to be received in three years, using an interest rate of 7%, compounded annually, as follows:

a. By successive divisions. (Round to the nearest dollar.)
b. By using the present value table in Exhibit 3.

Exercise 14–4
Present value of annuity
Objective 3

✓ a. $17,129

Determine the present value of $5,000 to be received at the end of each of four years, using an interest rate of $6\frac{1}{2}\%$, compounded annually, as follows:

a. By successive computations, using the present value table in Exhibit 3.
b. By using the present value table in Exhibit 4.

Exercise 14–5
Present value of an annuity
Objective 3

✓ $511,334.40

On January 1, 2000, you win $1,000,000 in the state lottery. The $1,000,000 prize will be paid in equal installments of $40,000 over 25 years. The payments will be made on December 31 of each year, beginning on December 31, 2000. If the current interest rate is 6%, determine the present value of your winnings. Use the present value tables in Appendix A.

Exercise 14–6
Present value of an annuity
Objective 3

Assume the same data as in Exercise 14–5, except that the current interest rate is 12%. Will the present value of your winnings using an interest rate of 12% be one-half the present value of your winnings using an interest rate of 6%? Why or why not?

Exercise 14–7
Present value of bonds payable; discount
Objectives 3, 4

✓ $9,227,796

Beall Co. produces and sells bottle capping equipment for soft drink and spring water bottlers. To finance its operations, Beall Co. issued $10,000,000 of five-year, 8% bonds with interest payable semiannually at an effective interest rate of 10%. Determine the present value of the bonds payable, using the present value tables in Exhibits 3 and 4.

Exercise 14–8
Present value of bonds payable; premium
Objectives 3, 4

✓ $5,188,439

Whitsell Automotive Alarms Co. issued $5,000,000 of five-year, 12% bonds with interest payable semiannually, at an effective interest rate of 11%. Determine the present value of the bonds payable, using the present value tables in Exhibits 3 and 4.

Exercise 14–9
Bond price
Objectives 3, 4

REAL WORLD

IBM Corporation $8\frac{3}{8}\%$ bonds due in 2019 were reported in *The Wall Street Journal* as selling for 115 on October 7, 1997.

Were the bonds selling at a premium or at a discount on October 7, 1997? Explain.

Exercise 14–10
Entries for issuing bonds
Objective 4

Wilmer Co. produces and distributes fiber optic cable for use by telecommunications companies. Wilmer Co. issued $7,500,000 of 20-year, 8% bonds on April 1 of the current year, with interest payable on April 1 and October 1. The fiscal year of the company is the calendar year. Journalize the entries to record the following selected transactions for the current year:

Apr. 1. Issued the bonds for cash at their face amount.
Oct. 1. Paid the interest on the bonds.
Dec. 31. Recorded accrued interest for three months.

Exercise 14–11
Entries for issuing bonds and amortizing discount by straight-line method
Objective 4

✓ b. $917,753

On the first day of its fiscal year, Ryland Company issued $8,000,000 of five-year, 10% bonds to finance its operations of producing and selling home electronics equipment. Interest is payable semiannually. The bonds were issued at an effective interest rate of 12%, resulting in Ryland Company receiving cash of $7,411,236.

a. Journalize the entries to record the following:
   1. Sale of the bonds.
   2. First semiannual interest payment. (Amortization of discount is to be recorded annually.)
   3. Second semiannual interest payment.
   4. Amortization of discount at the end of the first year, using the straight-line method. (Round to the nearest dollar.)
b. Determine the amount of the bond interest expense for the first year.

Exercise 14–12
Computing bond proceeds, entries for bond issuing, and amortizing premium by straight-line method
Objectives 3, 4

Markle Corporation wholesales oil and grease products to equipment manufacturers. On March 1, 2000, Markle Corporation issued $5,000,000 of five-year, 12% bonds at an effective interest rate of 10%. Interest is payable semiannually on March 1 and September 1. Journalize the entries to record the following:

a. Sale of bonds on March 1, 2000. (Use the tables of present values in Exhibits 3 and 4 to determine the bond proceeds.)
b. First interest payment on September 1, 2000, and amortization of bond premium for six months, using the straight-line method. (Round to the nearest dollar.)

Exercise 14–13
Entries for issuing and calling bonds; loss
Objectives 4, 6

Gier Corp., a wholesaler of office furniture, issued $9,000,000 of 20-year, 8% callable bonds on March 1, 2000, with interest payable on March 1 and September 1. The fiscal year of the company is the calendar year. Journalize the entries to record the following selected transactions:

2000
Mar. 1. Issued the bonds for cash at their face amount.
Sep. 1. Paid the interest on the bonds.
2004
Sep. 1. Called the bond issue at 101½, the rate provided in the bond indenture. (Omit entry for payment of interest.)

Exercise 14–14
Entries for issuing and calling bonds; gain
Objectives 4, 6

Mosser Corp. produces and sells automotive and aircraft safety belts. To finance its operations, Mosser Corp. issued $12,000,000 of 30-year, 7% callable bonds on June 1, 1999, with interest payable on June 1 and December 1. The fiscal year of the company is the calendar year. Journalize the entries to record the following selected transactions:

1999
June 1. Issued the bonds for cash at their face amount.
Dec. 1. Paid the interest on the bonds.
2005
Dec. 1. Called the bond issue at 99, the rate provided in the bond indenture. (Omit entry for payment of interest.)

Exercise 14–15
Reporting bonds
Objectives 5, 6, 8

What's Wrong WITH THIS?

At the beginning of the current year, two bond issues (MM and QQ) were outstanding. During the year, bond issue MM was redeemed and a significant loss on the redemption of bonds was reported as Other Expense on the income statement. At the end of the year, bond issue QQ was reported as a current liability because its maturity date was early in the following year. A sinking fund of cash and securities sufficient to pay the series QQ bonds was reported in the balance sheet as *Investments*.

Can you find any flaws in the reporting practices related to the two bond issues?

Exercise 14–16
Amortizing discount on bond investment
Objective 7

A company purchased a $1,000, 20-year zero-coupon bond for $189 to yield 8.5% to maturity. How is the interest revenue computed?

Source: "Technical Hotline," *Journal of Accountancy,* January 1989, p. 100.

Exercise 14–17
Entries for purchase and sale of investment in bonds; loss
Objective 7

Crone Co. sells optical supplies to opticians and ophthalmologists. Journalize the entries to record the following selected transactions of Crone Co.:

a. Purchased for cash $200,000 of Lambert Co. 6% bonds at 103 plus accrued interest of $2,000.
b. Received first semiannual interest.
c. At the end of the first year, amortized $250 of the bond premium.
d. Sold the bonds at 99 plus accrued interest of $4,000. The bonds were carried at $203,500 at the time of the sale.

Exercise 14–18
Entries for purchase and sale of investment in bonds; gain
Objective 7

Rockne Company develops and sells graphics software for use by architects. Journalize the entries to record the following selected transactions of Rockne Company:

a. Purchased for cash $150,000 of Culp Co. 6% bonds at 97 plus accrued interest of $1,500.
b. Received first semiannual interest.
c. Amortized $200 on the bond investment at the end of the first year.
d. Sold the bonds at 99 plus accrued interest of $3,000. The bonds were carried at $148,000 at the time of the sale.

Exercise 14–19
Number of times interest charges earned
Objective 9

REAL WORLD HAT

The financial statements for **Hershey Foods Corporation** are presented in Appendix G at the end of the text.

a. Determine the number of times interest charges were earned for the years ended December 31, 1996 and 1995. (The makeup of "interest expense, net" as reported on the income statement is described in Note 6 to the statements. Use only the interest on long-term and lease obligations and short-term debt in your computation.)
b. What conclusions can be drawn from the data concerning the risk of the debtholders for the interest payments and the general financial strength of Hershey?

Appendix Exercise 14–20
Amortize discount by interest method

✓ b. $892,029

On the first day of its fiscal year, Ryland Company issued $8,000,000 of five-year, 10% bonds to finance its operations of producing and selling home electronics equipment. Interest is payable semiannually. The bonds were issued at an effective interest rate of 12%, resulting in Ryland Company receiving cash of $7,411,236.

a. Journalize the entries to record the following:
   1. Sale of the bonds.
   2. First semiannual interest payment. (Amortization of discount is to be recorded annually.)
   3. Second semiannual interest payment.
   4. Amortization of discount at the end of the first year, using the interest method. (Round to the nearest dollar.)
b. Compute the amount of the bond interest expense for the first year.

Appendix Exercise 14–21
Amortize premium by interest method

✓ b. $537,073

Markle Corporation wholesales oil and grease products to equipment manufacturers. On March 1, 2000, Markle Corporation issued $5,000,000 of five-year, 12% bonds at an effective interest rate of 10%, receiving cash of $5,386,072. Interest is payable semiannually on March 1 and September 1. Markle Corporation's fiscal year begins on March 1.

a. Journalize the entries to record the following:
   1. First interest payment on September 1, 2000. (Amortization of premium is to be recorded annually.)
   2. Second interest payment on March 1, 2001.
   3. Amortization of premium at the end of the first year, using the interest method. (Round to the nearest dollar.)
b. Determine the bond interest expense for the first year.

Appendix Exercise 14–22
Compute bond proceeds, amortizing premium by interest method, and interest expense

Fabian Co. produces and sells spray painting equipment for construction contractors. On the first day of its fiscal year, Fabian Co. issued $10,000,000 of five-year, 11% bonds at an effective interest rate of 10%, with interest payable semiannually. Compute the following, presenting figures used in your computations.

✓ a. $10,386,057
✓ b. $30,697

a. The amount of cash proceeds from the sale of the bonds. (Use the tables of present values in Exhibits 3 and 4.)
b. The amount of premium to be amortized for the first semiannual interest payment period, using the interest method. (Round to the nearest dollar.)
c. The amount of premium to be amortized for the second semiannual interest payment period, using the interest method. (Round to the nearest dollar.)
d. The amount of the bond interest expense for the first year.

Appendix Exercise 14–23

Compute bond proceeds, amortizing discount by interest method, and interest expense

✓ a. $3,705,618
✓ b. $22,337

Leland Co. produces and sells concrete mixing equipment. On the first day of its fiscal year, Leland Co. issued $4,000,000 of five-year, 10% bonds at an effective interest rate of 12%, with interest payable semiannually. Compute the following, presenting figures used in your computations.

a. The amount of cash proceeds from the sale of the bonds. (Use the tables of present values in Exhibits 3 and 4.)
b. The amount of discount to be amortized for the first semiannual interest payment period, using the interest method. (Round to the nearest dollar.)
c. The amount of discount to be amortized for the second semiannual interest payment period, using the interest method. (Round to the nearest dollar.)
d. The amount of the bond interest expense for the first year.

PROBLEMS SERIES A

Problem 14–1A

Effect of financing on earnings per share

Objective 1

SPREADSHEET

✓ 1. Plan 3: $7.36

Three different plans for financing a $10,000,000 corporation are under consideration by its organizers. Under each of the following plans, the securities will be issued at their par or face amount, and the income tax rate is estimated at 40% of income.

	Plan 1	Plan 2	Plan 3
12% bonds			$ 5,000,000
Preferred 8% stock, $100 par		$ 5,000,000	2,500,000
Common stock, $10 par	$10,000,000	5,000,000	2,500,000
Total	$10,000,000	$10,000,000	$10,000,000

Instructions

1. Determine for each plan the earnings per share of common stock, assuming that the income before bond interest and income tax is $4,000,000.
2. Determine for each plan the earnings per share of common stock, assuming that the income before bond interest and income tax is $1,000,000.
3. Discuss the advantages and disadvantages of each plan.

Problem 14–2A

Present value; bond premium; entries for bonds payable transactions

Objectives 3, 4

✓ 3. $268,844

Willard Corporation produces and sells burial vaults. On July 1, 2000, Willard Corporation issued $5,000,000 of ten-year, 12% bonds at an effective interest rate of 10%. Interest on the bonds is payable semiannually on December 31 and June 30. The fiscal year of the company is the calendar year.

Instructions

1. Journalize the entry to record the amount of the cash proceeds from the sale of the bonds. Use the tables of present values in Appendix A to compute the cash proceeds, rounding to the nearest dollar.
2. Journalize the entries to record the following:
   a. The first semiannual interest payment on December 31, 2000, and the amortization of the bond premium, using the straight-line method. (Round to the nearest dollar.)
   b. The interest payment on June 30, 2001, and the amortization of the bond premium, using the straight-line method.
3. Determine the total interest expense for 2000.

4. Will the bond proceeds always be greater than the face amount of the bonds when the contract rate is greater than the market rate of interest? Explain.

Problem 14–3A

Present value; bond discount; entries for bonds payable transactions

Objectives 3, 4

✓ 3. $694,407

On July 1, 1999, Geyser Corporation, a wholesaler of used robotic equipment, issued $12,000,000 of ten-year, 11% bonds at an effective interest rate of 12%. Interest on the bonds is payable semiannually on December 31 and June 30. The fiscal year of the company is the calendar year.

Instructions

1. Journalize the entry to record the amount of the cash proceeds from the sale of the bonds. Use the tables of present values in Appendix A to compute the cash proceeds, rounding to the nearest dollar.
2. Journalize the entries to record the following:
   a. The first semiannual interest payment on December 31, 1999, and the amortization of the bond discount, using the straight-line method. (Round to the nearest dollar.)
   b. The interest payment on June 30, 2000, and the amortization of the bond discount, using the straight-line method.
3. Determine the total interest expense for 1999.
4. Will the bond proceeds always be less than the face amount of the bonds when the contract rate is less than the market rate of interest? Explain.

Problem 14–4A

Entries for bonds payable transactions

Objectives 4, 6

HAT

✓ 2. a. $240,578

The following transactions were completed by Stucco Inc., whose fiscal year is the calendar year:

1999

July 1. Issued $5,000,000 of 10-year, 9% callable bonds dated July 1, 1999, at an effective rate of 10%, receiving cash of $4,688,442. Interest is payable semiannually on December 31 and June 30.

Dec. 31. Paid the semiannual interest on the bonds.

31. Recorded bond discount amortization of $15,578, which was determined by using the straight-line method.

31. Closed the interest expense account.

2000

June 30. Paid the semiannual interest on the bonds.

Dec. 31. Paid the semiannual interest on the bonds.

31. Recorded bond discount amortization of $31,156, which was determined by using the straight-line method.

31. Closed the interest expense account.

2007

June 30. Recorded the redemption of the bonds, which were called at 99. The balance in the bond discount account is $62,310 after payment of interest and amortization of discount have been recorded. (Record the redemption only.)

Instructions

1. Journalize the entries to record the foregoing transactions.
2. Indicate the amount of the interest expense in (a) 1999 and (b) 2000.
3. Determine the carrying amount of the bonds as of December 31, 2000.

Problem 14–5A

Entries for bond investments

Objective 7

HAT

Finney Inc. develops and leases databases of publicly available information. The following selected transactions relate to certain securities acquired as a long-term investment by Finney Inc., whose fiscal year ends on December 31:

1999

Sep. 1. Purchased $300,000 of Miller Company 10-year, 10% bonds dated July 1, 1999, directly from the issuing company, for $308,850 plus accrued interest of $5,000.

Dec. 31. Received the semiannual interest on the Miller Company bonds.

31. Recorded bond premium amortization of $300 on the Miller Company bonds. The amortization amount was determined by using the straight-line method.

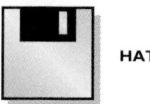

(Assume that all intervening transactions and adjustments have been properly recorded and that the number of bonds owned has not changed from Dec. 31, 1999, to Dec. 31, 2004.)

2005
June 30. Received the semiannual interest on the Miller Company bonds.
Aug. 31. Sold one-half of the Miller Company bonds at 102 plus accrued interest. The broker deducted $700 for commission, etc., remitting the balance. Prior to the sale, $300 of premium on one-half of the bonds is to be amortized, reducing the carrying amount of those bonds to $151,725.
Dec. 31. Received the semiannual interest on the Miller Company bonds.
31. Recorded bond premium amortization of $450 on the Miller Company bonds.

Instructions

Journalize the entries to record the foregoing transactions.

Appendix Problem 14–6A

Entries for bonds payable transactions; interest method of amortizing bond premium

✓ 2. $281,156

Willard Corporation produces and sells burial vaults. On July 1, 2000, Willard Corporation issued $5,000,000 of ten-year, 12% bonds at an effective interest rate of 10%, receiving proceeds of $5,623,113. Interest on the bonds is payable semiannually on December 31 and June 30. The fiscal year of the company is the calendar year.

Instructions

1. Journalize the entries to record the following:
   a. The first semiannual interest payment on December 31, 2000, and the amortization of the bond premium, using the interest method. (Round to nearest dollar.)
   b. The interest payment on June 30, 2001, and the amortization of the bond premium, using the interest method. (Round to nearest dollar.)
2. Determine the total interest expense for 2000.

Appendix Problem 14–7A

Entries for bonds payable transactions; interest method of amortizing bond discount

✓ 2. $678,712

On July 1, 1999, Geyser Corporation, a wholesaler of used robotic equipment, issued $12,000,000 of ten-year, 11% bonds at an effective interest rate of 12%, receiving proceeds of $11,311,867. Interest on the bonds is payable semiannually on December 31 and June 30. The fiscal year of the company is the calendar year.

Instructions

1. Journalize the entries to record the following:
   a. The first semiannual interest payment on December 31, 1999, and the amortization of the bond discount, using the interest method. (Round to nearest dollar.)
   b. The interest payment on June 30, 2000, and the amortization of the bond discount, using the interest method. (Round to nearest dollar.)
2. Determine the total interest expense for 1999.

PROBLEMS SERIES B

Problem 14–1B

Effect of financing on earnings per share

Objective 1

SPREADSHEET

✓ 1. Plan 3: $7.60

Three different plans for financing a $15,000,000 corporation are under consideration by its organizers. Under each of the following plans, the securities will be issued at their par or face amount, and the income tax rate is estimated at 40% of income.

	Plan 1	Plan 2	Plan 3
12% bonds			$ 6,250,000
Preferred $4 stock, $50 par		$ 7,500,000	5,000,000
Common stock, $30 par	$15,000,000	7,500,000	3,750,000
Total	$15,000,000	$15,000,000	$15,000,000

Instructions

1. Determine for each plan the earnings per share of common stock, assuming that the income before bond interest and income tax is $3,000,000.
2. Determine for each plan the earnings per share of common stock, assuming that the income before bond interest and income tax is $1,450,000.
3. Discuss the advantages and disadvantages of each plan.

Problem 14–2B

Present value; bond premium; entries for bonds payable transactions

Objectives 3, 4

✓ 3. $509,422

Leibee Inc. produces and sells voltage regulators. On July 1, 1999, Leibee Inc. issued $10,000,000 of ten-year, $10\frac{1}{2}\%$ bonds at an effective interest rate of 10%. Interest on the bonds is payable semiannually on December 31 and June 30. The fiscal year of the company is the calendar year.

Instructions

1. Journalize the entry to record the amount of the cash proceeds from the sale of the bonds. Use the tables of present values in Appendix A to compute the cash proceeds, rounding to the nearest dollar.
2. Journalize the entries to record the following:
   a. The first semiannual interest payment on December 31, 1999, including the amortization of the bond premium, using the straight-line method.
   b. The interest payment on June 30, 2000, and the amortization of the bond premium, using the straight-line method.
3. Determine the total interest expense for 1999.
4. Will the bond proceeds always be greater than the face amount of the bonds when the contract rate is greater than the market rate of interest? Explain.

Problem 14–3B

Present value; bond discount; entries for bonds payable transactions

Objectives 3, 4

✓ 3. $346,733

On July 1, 1999, Cyrano Communications Equipment Inc. issued $7,500,000 of ten-year, 8% bonds at an effective interest rate of 10%. Interest on the bonds is payable semiannually on December 31 and June 30. The fiscal year of the company is the calendar year.

Instructions

1. Journalize the entry to record the amount of the cash proceeds from the sale of the bonds. Use the tables of present values in Appendix A to compute the cash proceeds, rounding to the nearest dollar.
2. Journalize the entries to record the following:
   a. The first semiannual interest payment on December 31, 1999, and the amortization of the bond discount, using the straight-line method. (Round to the nearest dollar.)
   b. The interest payment on June 30, 2000, and the amortization of the bond discount, using the straight-line method.
3. Determine the total interest expense for 1999.
4. Will the bond proceeds always be less than the face amount of the bonds when the contract rate is less than the market rate of interest? Explain.

Problem 14–4B

Entries for bonds payable transactions

Objectives 4, 6

✓ 2. a. $621,325

Coquette Co. produces and sells synthetic string for tennis rackets. The following transactions were completed by Coquette Co., whose fiscal year is the calendar year:

1999

July 1. Issued $10,000,000 of 10-year, 13% callable bonds dated July 1, 1999, at an effective rate of 12%, receiving cash of $10,573,500. Interest is payable semiannually on December 31 and June 30.

Dec. 31. Paid the semiannual interest on the bonds.

31. Recorded bond premium amortization of $28,675, which was determined by using the straight-line method.

31. Closed the interest expense account.

2000

June 30. Paid the semiannual interest on the bonds.

Dec. 31. Paid the semiannual interest on the bonds.

31. Recorded bond premium amortization of $57,350, which was determined by using the straight-line method.

31. Closed the interest expense account.

2005
July 1. Recorded the redemption of the bonds, which were called at 101. The balance in the bond premium account is $229,400 after the payment of interest and amortization of premium have been recorded. (Record the redemption only.)

Instructions

1. Journalize the entries to record the foregoing transactions.
2. Indicate the amount of the interest expense in (a) 1999 and (b) 2000.
3. Determine the carrying amount of the bonds as of December 31, 2000.

Problem 14–5B
Entries for bond investments
Objective 7

The following selected transactions relate to certain securities acquired by McFeters Blueprints Inc., whose fiscal year ends on December 31:

1999
Sep. 1. Purchased $1,000,000 of Buday Company 20-year, 9% bonds dated July 1, 1999, directly from the issuing company, for $964,300 plus accrued interest of $15,000.
Dec. 31. Received the semiannual interest on the Buday Company bonds.
31. Recorded bond discount amortization of $600 on the Buday Company bonds. The amortization amount was determined by using the straight-line method.

(Assume that all intervening transactions and adjustments have been properly recorded and that the number of bonds owned has not changed from December 31, 1999, to December 31, 2003.)

2004
June 30. Received the semiannual interest on the Buday Company bonds.
Oct. 31. Sold one-half of the Buday Company bonds at 97 plus accrued interest. The broker deducted $850 for commission, etc., remitting the balance. Prior to the sale, $750 of discount on one-half of the bonds was amortized, reducing the carrying amount of those bonds to $486,800.
Dec. 31. Received the semiannual interest on the Buday Company bonds.
31. Recorded bond discount amortization of $900 on the Buday Company bonds.

Instructions
Journalize the entries to record the foregoing transactions.

Appendix Problem 14–6B
Entries for bonds payable transactions; interest method of amortizing bond premium

✓ 2. $515,578

Leibee Inc. produces and sells voltage regulators. On July 1, 1999, Leibee Inc. issued $10,000,000 of ten-year, 10½% bonds at an effective interest rate of 10%, receiving proceeds of $10,311,560. Interest on the bonds is payable semiannually on December 31 and June 30. The fiscal year of the company is the calendar year.

Instructions

1. Journalize the entries to record the following:
   a. The first semiannual interest payment on December 31, 1999, and the amortization of the bond premium, using the interest method. (Round to nearest dollar.)
   b. The interest payment on June 30, 2000, and the amortization of the bond premium, using the interest method. (Round to nearest dollar.)
2. Determine the total interest expense for 1999.

Appendix Problem 14–7B
Entries for bonds payable transactions; interest method of amortizing bond discount

✓ 2. $328,267

On July 1, 1999, Cyrano Communications Equipment Inc. issued $7,500,000 of ten-year, 8% bonds at an effective interest rate of 10%, receiving proceeds of $6,565,338. Interest on the bonds is payable semiannually on December 31 and June 30. The fiscal year of the company is the calendar year.

Instructions

1. Journalize the entries to record the following:
   a. The first semiannual interest payment on December 31, 1999, and the amortization of the bond discount, using the interest method.

   b. The interest payment on June 30, 2000, and the amortization of the bond discount, using the interest method.
2. Determine the total interest expense for 1999.

COMPREHENSIVE PROBLEM 4

GENERAL LEDGER

Selected transactions completed by Stryker Products Inc. during the fiscal year ending July 31, 2000, were as follows:

a. Issued 10,000 shares of $25 par common stock at $45, receiving cash.
b. Issued 7,500 shares of $100 par preferred 8% stock at $120, receiving cash.
c. Issued $2,000,000 of 10-year, 10½% bonds at an effective interest rate of 10%, with interest payable semiannually. Use the present value tables in Appendix A to determine the bond proceeds. Round to the nearest dollar.
d. Declared a dividend of $0.40 per share on common stock and $2 per share on preferred stock. On the date of record, 100,000 shares of common stock were outstanding, no treasury shares were held, and 15,000 shares of preferred stock were outstanding.
e. Paid the cash dividends declared in (d).
f. Redeemed $300,000 of 8-year, 12% bonds at 101. The balance in the bond premium account is $7,900 after the payment of interest and amortization of premium have been recorded. (Record only the redemption of the bonds payable.)
g. Purchased 3,000 shares of treasury common stock at $42 per share.
h. Declared a 5% stock dividend on common stock and a $2 cash dividend per share on preferred stock. On the date of declaration, the market value of the common stock was $41 per share. On the date of record, 100,000 shares of common stock had been issued, 3,000 shares of treasury common stock were held, and 15,000 shares of preferred stock had been issued.
i. Issued the stock certificates for the stock dividends declared in (h) and paid the cash dividends to the preferred stockholders.
j. Purchased $100,000 of Dilmore Inc. 10-year, 15% bonds, directly from the issuing company, for $97,000 plus accrued interest of $3,750.
k. Sold, at $48 per share, 2,000 shares of treasury common stock purchased in (g).
l. Recorded the payment of semiannual interest on the bonds issued in (c) and the amortization of the premium for six months. The amortization was determined using the straight-line method. (Round the amortization to the nearest dollar.)
m. Accrued interest for four months on the Dilmore Inc. bonds purchased in (j). Also recorded amortization of $100.

Instructions

1. Journalize the selected transactions.
2. After all of the transactions for the year ended July 31, 2000, had been posted (including the transactions recorded in (1) and all adjusting entries), the following data were taken from the records of Stryker Products Inc.:

Income statement data:	
Advertising expense	$ 75,000
Cost of merchandise sold	3,850,000
Delivery expense	17,000
Depreciation expense—office equipment	13,100
Depreciation expense—store equipment	45,000
Gain on redemption of bonds	4,900
Income tax:	
Applicable to continuing operations	254,775
Applicable to loss from disposal of a segment of the business	21,100
Applicable to gain from redemption of bonds	1,000

Interest expense	$ 101,884
Interest revenue	1,350
Loss from disposal of a segment of the business	80,500
Miscellaneous administrative expenses	1,600
Miscellaneous selling expenses	6,300
Office rent expense	25,000
Office salaries expense	85,000
Office supplies expense	5,300
Sales	5,100,000
Sales commissions	95,000
Sales salaries expense	180,000
Store supplies expense	9,500

Retained earnings and balance sheet data:

Accounts payable	$ 149,500
Accounts receivable	280,500
Accumulated depreciation—office equipment	835,250
Accumulated depreciation—store equipment	2,214,750
Allowance for doubtful accounts	21,500
Bonds payable, $10\frac{1}{2}$%, due 2010	2,000,000
Cash	125,500
Common stock, $25 par (400,000 shares authorized; 104,850 shares outstanding)	2,621,250
Deferred income tax payable (current portion, $4,700)	25,700
Dividends:	
Cash dividends for common stock	120,000
Cash dividends for preferred stock	105,000
Stock dividends for common stock	198,850
Dividends payable	30,000
Income tax payable	55,900
Interest receivable	5,000
Investment in Dilmore Inc. bonds (long-term)	97,100
Merchandise inventory (July 31, 2000), at lower of cost (fifo) or market	425,000
Notes receivable	77,500
Office equipment	2,410,100
Organization costs	55,000
Paid-in capital from sale of treasury stock	12,000
Paid-in capital in excess of par—common stock	325,000
Paid-in capital in excess of par—preferred stock	240,000
Preferred 8% stock, $100 par (30,000 shares authorized; 15,000 shares issued)	1,500,000
Premium on bonds payable	59,196
Prepaid expenses	15,900
Retained earnings, August 1, 1999	2,868,684
Store equipment	9,282,671
Treasury stock (1,000 shares of common stock at cost of $42 per share)	42,000

a. Prepare a multiple-step income statement for the year ended July 31, 2000, concluding with earnings per share. In computing earnings per share, assume that the average number of common shares outstanding was 100,000 and preferred dividends were $105,000. Round to nearest cent.
b. Prepare a retained earnings statement for the year ended July 31, 2000.
c. Prepare a balance sheet in report form as of July 31, 2000.

SPECIAL ACTIVITIES

Activity 14–1 SlideCo
Ethics and professional conduct in business

SlideCo produces and sells water slides for theme parks. SlideCo has outstanding a $40,000,000, 25-year, 10% debenture bond issue dated July 1, 1991. The bond issue is due June 30, 2016. The bond indenture requires a sinking fund, which has a balance of $10,000,000 as of July 1, 2000. SlideCo is currently experiencing a shortage of funds due to a recent plant expansion. Eli Cronin, treasurer of SlideCo, has suggested using the sinking fund cash to temporarily relieve the shortage of funds. Cronin's brother-in-law, who is trustee of the sinking fund, is willing to loan SlideCo the necessary funds from the sinking fund.

Discuss whether Eli Cronin is behaving in a professional manner.

Activity 14–2 Ludwig Distributors Inc.
Present values

Ludwig Distributors Inc. is a wholesaler of oriental rugs. The following is a luncheon conversation between Jennifer Sabel, the assistant controller, and Clancy Bishop, an assistant financial analyst for Ludwig.

Clancy: Jenny, do you mind if I spoil your lunch and ask you an accounting question?

Jennifer: No, go ahead. This chicken salad sandwich is pretty bad. It smells like it's three days old, and I've already picked three bones out of it.

Clancy: Well, as you know, in finance we use present values for capital budgeting analysis, assessing financing alternatives, etc. It's probably the most important concept that I learned in school that I actually use.

Jennifer: So . . . ?

Clancy: I was just wondering why accountants don't use present values more.

Jennifer: What do you mean?

Clancy: Well, it seems to me that you ought to value all the balance sheet liabilities at their present values.

How would you respond if you were Jennifer?

Activity 14–3 Playmill Inc.
Preferred stock vs. bonds

Playmill Inc. has decided to expand its operations to owning and operating theme parks. The following is an excerpt from a conversation between the chief executive officer, JoAnn Robison, and the vice-president of finance, Pat Coffey.

JoAnn: Pat, have you given any thought to how we're going to finance the acquisition of WaterWave Corporation?

Pat: Well, the two basic options, as I see it, are to issue either preferred stock or bonds. The equity market is a little depressed right now. The rumor is that the Federal Reserve Bank's going to increase the interest rates either this month or next.

JoAnn: Yes, I've heard the rumor. The problem is that we can't wait around to see what's going to happen. We'll have to move on this next week if we want any chance to complete the acquisition of WaterWave.

Pat: Well, the bond market is strong right now. Maybe we should issue debt this time around.

JoAnn: That's what I would have guessed as well. WaterWave's financial statements look pretty good, except for the volatility of their income and cash flows. But that's characteristic of their industry.

Discuss the advantages and disadvantages of issuing preferred stock versus bonds.

Activity 14–4 Shea Bottling Co.
Financing business expansion

You hold a 25% common stock interest in the family-owned business, a soft drink bottling distributorship. Your sister, who is the manager, has proposed an expansion of plant facilities at an expected cost of $2,500,000. Two alternative plans have been suggested as methods of financing the expansion. Each plan is briefly described as follows:

Plan 1. Issue $2,500,000 of 20-year, 8% notes at face amount.

Plan 2. Issue an additional 35,000 shares of $20 par common stock at $25 per share, and $1,625,000 of 20-year, 8% notes at face amount.

The balance sheet as of the end of the previous fiscal year is as follows:

Shea Bottling Co.
Balance Sheet
December 31, 20—

Assets	
Current assets	$2,350,000
Property, plant, and equipment	5,150,000
Total assets	$7,500,000
Liabilities and Stockholders' Equity	
Liabilities	$2,000,000
Common stock, $20	800,000
Paid-in capital in excess of par	80,000
Retained earnings	4,620,000
Total liabilities and stockholders' equity	$7,500,000

Net income has remained relatively constant over the past several years. The expansion program is expected to increase yearly income before bond interest and income tax from $500,000 in the previous year to $600,000 for this year. Your sister has asked you, as the company treasurer, to prepare an analysis of each financing plan.

1. Prepare a table indicating the expected earnings per share on the common stock under each plan. Assume an income tax rate of 40%.
2. a. Discuss the factors that should be considered in evaluating the two plans.
   b. Which plan offers the greater benefit to the present stockholders? Give reasons for your opinion.

Activity 14–5
Into the Real World
Investing in bonds

Select a bond from listings that appear daily in *The Wall Street Journal,* and summarize the information related to the bond you select. Include the following information in your summary:

1. Contract rate of interest
2. Year when the bond matures
3. Current yield (effective rate of interest)
4. Closing price of bond (indicate date)
5. Other information noted about the bond, such as whether it is a zero-coupon bond (see the Explanatory Notes to the listings)

In groups of three or four, share the information you developed about the bond you selected. As a group, select one bond to invest $100,000 in and prepare a justification for your choice for presentation to the class. For example, your justification should include a consideration of risk and return.

Activity 14–6
Into the Real World
Bond ratings

Moody's Investors Service maintains a Web site at **www.Moodys.com.** One of the services offered at this site is a listing of announcements of recent bond rating changes. Visit this site and read over some of these announcements. Write down several of the reasons provided for rating downgrades and upgrades. If you were a bond investor or bond issuer, would you care if Moody's changed the rating on your bonds? Why or why not?

ANSWERS TO SELF-EXAMINATION QUESTIONS

Matching

1. C	3. G	5. Q	7. L	9. O	11. F	13. N	14. K
2. E	4. A	6. P	8. H	10. R	12. M		

Multiple Choice

1. **B** Since the contract rate on the bonds is higher than the prevailing market rate, a rational investor would be willing to pay more than the face amount, or a premium (answer B), for the bonds. If the contract rate and the market rate were equal, the bonds could be expected to sell at their face amount (answer A). Likewise, if the market rate is higher than the contract rate, the bonds would sell at a price below their face amount (answer D) or at a discount (answer C).
2. **A** The bond carrying amount is the face amount plus unamortized premium or less unamortized discount. For this question, the carrying amount is $500,000 less $40,000, or $460,000 (answer A).
3. **B** Although the sinking fund may consist of cash as well as securities, the fund is listed on the balance sheet as an investment (answer B) because it is to be used to pay the long-term liability at maturity.
4. **B** The amount debited to the investment account is the cost of the bonds, which includes the amount paid to the seller for the bonds (101% × $100,000) plus broker's commissions ($50), or $101,050 (answer B). The $2,000 of accrued interest that is paid to the seller should be debited to Interest Revenue, since it is an offset against the amount that will be received as interest at the next interest date.
5. **C** The balance of Discount on Bonds Payable is usually reported as a deduction from Bonds Payable in the Long-Term Liabilities section (answer C) of the balance sheet. Likewise, a balance in a premium on bonds payable account would usually be reported as an addition to Bonds Payable in the Long-Term Liabilities section of the balance sheet.

15

Statement of Cash Flows

Setting the STAGE

How much cash do you have in the bank or in your wallet or purse? How much cash did you have at the beginning of the month? The difference between these two amounts is the net change in your cash during the month. Knowing the reasons for the change in cash may be useful in evaluating whether your financial position has improved and whether you will be able to pay your bills in the future.

For example, assume that you had $200 at the beginning of the month and $550 at the end of the month. The net change in cash is $350. Based on this net change, it appears that your financial position has improved. However, this conclusion may or may not be valid, depending upon how the change of $350 was created. If you borrowed $1,000 during the month and spent $650 on living expenses, your cash would have increased by $350 by living off of borrowed funds. On the other hand, if you earned $1,000 and spent $650 on living expenses, your cash would have also increased by $350, but your financial position is improved compared to the first scenario.

In previous chapters, we have used the income statement, balance sheet, and retained earnings statement and other information to analyze the effects of management decisions on a business's financial position and operating performance. In this chapter, we present how to prepare and use the statement of cash flows.

objectives

After studying this chapter, you should be able to:

1. Explain why the statement of cash flows is one of the basic financial statements.
2. Summarize the types of cash flow activities reported in the statement of cash flows.
3. Prepare a statement of cash flows, using the indirect method.
4. Prepare a statement of cash flows, using the direct method.
5. Calculate and interpret the free cash flow.

Purpose of the Statement of Cash Flows

OBJECTIVE 1

Explain why the statement of cash flows is one of the basic financial statements.

The **statement of cash flows** reports a firm's major cash inflows and outflows for a period.[1] It provides useful information about a firm's ability to generate cash from operations, maintain and expand its operating capacity, meet its financial obligations, and pay dividends.

The statement of cash flows is one of the basic financial statements. It is useful to managers in evaluating past operations and in planning future investing and financing activities. It is useful to investors, creditors, and others in assessing a firm's profit potential. In addition, it provides a basis for assessing the ability of a firm to pay its maturing debt.

The statement of cash flows is one of the basic financial statements.

Reporting Cash Flows

OBJECTIVE 2

Summarize the types of cash flow activities reported in the statement of cash flows.

The statement of cash flows reports cash flows by three types of activities:

1. **Cash flows from operating activities** are cash flows from transactions that affect net income. Examples of such transactions include the purchase and sale of merchandise by a retailer.
2. **Cash flows from investing activities** are cash flows from transactions that affect the investments in noncurrent assets. Examples of such transactions include the sale and purchase of fixed assets, such as equipment and buildings.
3. **Cash flows from financing activities** are cash flows from transactions that affect the equity and debt of the business. Examples of such transactions include issuing or retiring equity and debt securities.

The statement of cash flows reports cash flows from operating, investing, and financing activities.

The cash flows from operating activities is normally presented first, followed by the cash flows from investing activities and financing activities. The total of the net cash flow from these activities is the net increase or decrease in cash for the period. The cash balance at the beginning of the period is added to the net

[1] As used in this chapter, cash refers to cash and cash equivalents. Examples of cash equivalents include marketable securities, certificates of deposit, U.S. Treasury bills, and money market funds.

INTERMISSION

In the past, investors and creditors have relied heavily on a company's earnings information in judging the company's performance. Now, more and more investors and creditors are also focusing on cash flows for providing additional information, as described below.

As the term suggests, cash flow is basically a measure of the money flowing into—or out of—a business. If large companies were run, like lemonade stands, on a cash basis, earnings and cash flow would be identical.

Every major corporation, however, keeps its books on an accrual basis. . . . [This] can give a truer picture of corporate profitability, but sometimes it obscures important developments.

Take a company that spent $140 million on new machinery last year. If it depreciates the equipment over a seven-year period, it will be subtracting $20 million from reported profits each year.

But if the machines will stay up to date and useful for 25 years, the company's reported earnings may understate its true strength. . . .

Sometimes the reverse is true. If a company has been neglecting capital spending, its earnings may look good. But on a cash-flow basis, it will look no better . . . than its competitors. ■

Source: John R. Dorfman, "Stock Analysts Increase Focus on Cash Flow," *The Wall Street Journal*, February 17, 1987, Section 2, p. 1.

increase or decrease in cash, and the cash balance at the end of the period is reported. The ending cash balance on the statement of cash flows equals the cash reported on the balance sheet.

Exhibit 1 shows common cash flow transactions reported in each of the three sections of the statement of cash flows. By reporting cash flows by operating, investing, and financing activities, significant relationships within and among the activities can be evaluated. For example, the cash receipts from issuing bonds can be related to repayments of borrowings when both are reported as financing activities. Also, the impact of each of the three activities (operating, investing, and financing) on cash flows can be identified. This allows investors and creditors to evaluate the effects of cash flows on a firm's profits and ability to pay debt.

EXHIBIT 1 Cash Flows

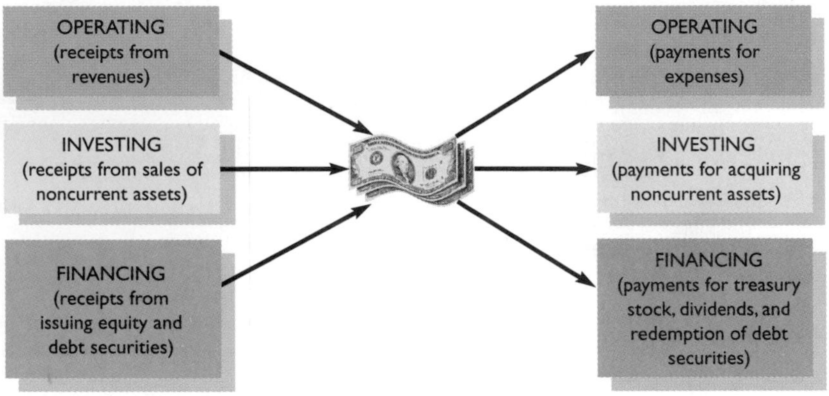

Cash Flows from Operating Activities

The most frequent and often the most important cash flows of a business relate to operating activities. There are two alternative methods for reporting cash flows from operating activities in the statement of cash flows. These methods are (1) the direct method and (2) the indirect method.

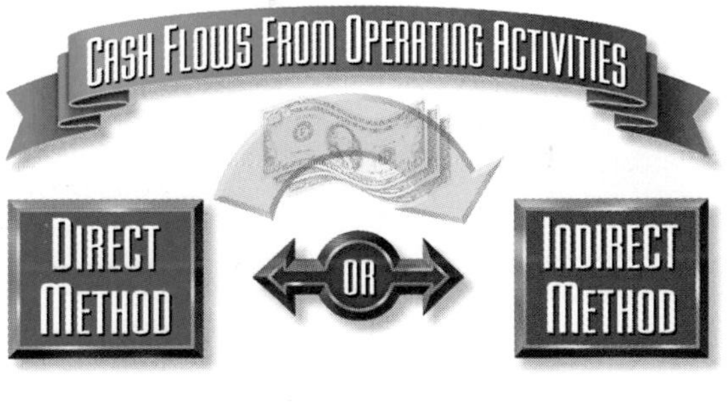

The **direct method** reports the sources of operating cash and the uses of operating cash. The major source of operating cash is cash received from customers. The major uses of operating cash include cash paid to suppliers for merchandise and services and cash paid to employees for wages. The difference between these operating cash receipts and cash payments is the net cash flow from operating activities.

Which U.S. manufacturing companies have the largest cash balances? The list from 1996 fiscal year-end balance sheets is as follows:

	In millions
General Motors	$14,063
IBM	7,687
Microsoft	6,940
Chrysler	5,158
Boeing	4,375
General Electric	4,191
Intel	4,165

These companies have had substantial cash flows from operations over the past 3–5 years, and as a result, have been able to build large cash balances (in the billions!). These balances can be used to cushion future business downturns, as would be the case for businesses subject to boom and bust cycles, such as GM, Chrysler, and Boeing. Alternatively, the cash can be used to expand the business or move into new markets, as would be the case for technology companies, such as Microsoft, Intel, IBM, and GE.

The primary advantage of the direct method is that it reports the sources and uses of cash in the statement of cash flows. Its primary disadvantage is that the necessary data may not be readily available and may be costly to gather.

The **indirect method** reports the operating cash flows by beginning with net income and adjusting it for revenues and expenses that do not involve the receipt or payment of cash. In other words, accrual net income is adjusted to determine the net amount of cash flows from operating activities.

A major advantage of the indirect method is that it focuses on the differences between net income and cash flows from operations. In this sense, it shows the relationship between the income statement, the balance sheet, and the statement of cash flows. Because the data are readily available, the indirect method is normally less costly to use than the direct method.

Exhibit 2 illustrates the cash flow from operating activities section of the statement of cash flows under the direct and indirect methods. Both statements are for Computer King for the month ended November 1999. Both methods show the same amount of net cash flow from operating activities, regardless of the method. We will illustrate both methods in detail later in this chapter.

EXHIBIT 2 Cash Flow from Operations: Direct and Indirect Methods

Direct Method	
Cash flows from operating activities:	
Cash received from customers	$7,500
Deduct cash payments for expenses and payments to creditors	4,600
Net cash flow from operating activities	$2,900

Indirect Method	
Cash flows from operating activities:	
Net income, per income statement	$3,050
Add increase in accounts payable	400
	$3,450
Deduct increase in supplies	550
Net cash flow from operating activities	$2,900

Over the next five years, **Chrysler** plans to spend $23 billion in new product development, while **General Motors** plans to invest $3 billion overseas.

Cash Flows from Investing Activities

Cash inflows from investing activities normally arise from selling fixed assets, investments, and intangible assets. Cash outflows normally include payments to acquire fixed assets, investments, and intangible assets.

Cash flows from investing activities are reported on the statement of cash flows by first listing the cash inflows. The cash outflows are then presented. If the inflows are greater than the outflows, **net cash flow provided by investing activities** is reported. If the cash inflows are less than the cash outflows, **net cash flow used for investing activities** is reported.

The cash flows from investing activities section in the statement of cash flows for Computer King is shown below.

Cash flows from investing activities:	
Cash payments for acquiring land	$(10,000)

BUSINESS ON STAGE

A business must manage its cash position so that there is enough cash on hand to pay bills and other liabilities. Cash management is particularly important for seasonal businesses, which use cash in one part of the year and generate it in another. For example, consider this assumed cash position from operations for Smart Toys, Inc., a toy retailer:

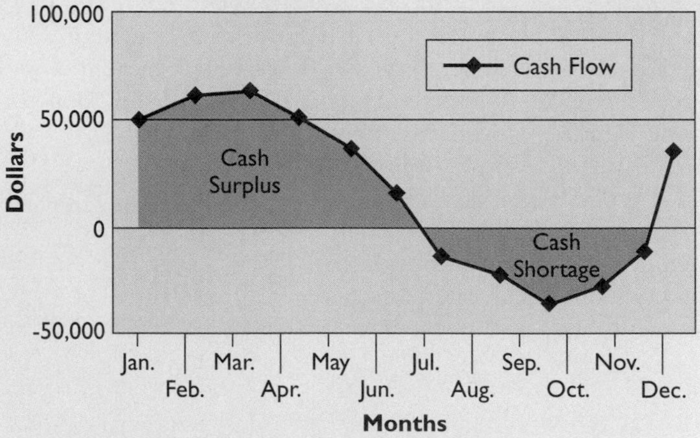

Smart Toys uses cash to purchase inventory prior to the winter holiday season. It is able to generate surplus cash by selling its inventory throughout the holiday season and into the early part of the calendar year.

If the cash required to purchase inventory exceeds Smart Toys' ability to generate operating cash flow, it may experience a cash shortage. In such a case, it must obtain short-term credit, which may be structured as a line of credit from a bank. A line of credit is an agreement that allows the business to borrow an unsecured amount of money up to some stated limit. For example, Smart Toys has a line of credit of $60,000, of which $40,000 was used during the year. Amounts drawn on a line of credit must usually be paid back within a year.

Seasonal businesses must be careful to avoid overextending their cash position during the "down cycle." For example, if Smart Toys purchases items that do not sell, a cash surplus will not be generated during the selling season. ■

Cash Flows from Financing Activities

Cash inflows from financing activities normally arise from issuing debt or equity securities. Examples of such inflows include issuing bonds, notes payable, and preferred and common stocks. Cash outflows from financing activities include paying cash dividends, repaying debt, and acquiring treasury stock.

REAL WORLD **Intel Corp.** plans to keep enough cash on hand to build two computer chip factories. What happens when you have twice that amount on hand? Intel used its excess cash in 1996 ($1.3 billion) to repurchase common stock (treasury stock).

Cash flows from financing activities are reported on the statement of cash flows by first listing the cash inflows. The cash outflows are then presented. If the inflows are greater than the outflows, **net cash flow provided by financing activities** is reported. If the cash inflows are less than the cash outflows, **net cash flow used for financing activities** is reported.

The cash flows from financing activities section in the statement of cash flows for Computer King is shown below.

Cash flows from financing activities:	
Cash received as owner's investment . .	$15,000
Deduct cash withdrawal by owner	2,000
Net cash flow from financing activities . .	$13,000

Noncash Investing and Financing Activities

A business may enter into investing and financing activities that do not directly involve cash. For example, it may issue common stock to retire long-term debt. Such a transaction does not have a direct effect on cash. However, the transaction does eliminate the need for future cash payments to pay interest and retire the bonds. Thus, because of their future effect on cash flows, such transactions should be reported to readers of the financial statements.

When noncash investing and financing transactions occur during a period, their effect is reported in a separate schedule. This schedule usually appears at the bottom of the statement of cash flows. Other examples of noncash investing and financing transactions include acquiring fixed assets by issuing bonds or capital stock and issuing common stock in exchange for convertible preferred stock.

No Cash Flow per Share

The term *cash flow per share* is sometimes reported in the financial press. Often, the term is used to mean "cash flow from operations per share." Such reporting may be misleading to users of the financial statements. For example, users might interpret cash flow per share as the amount available for dividends. This would not be the case if most of the cash generated by operations is required for repaying loans or for reinvesting in the business. Users might also think that cash flow per share is equivalent or perhaps superior to earnings per share. For these reasons, the financial statements, including the statement of cash flows, should not report cash flow per share.

Statement of Cash Flows— The Indirect Method

OBJECTIVE 3

Prepare a statement of cash flows, using the indirect method.

The indirect method of reporting cash flows from operating activities is normally less costly and more efficient than the direct method. In addition, when the direct method is used, the indirect method must also be used in preparing a supplemental reconciliation of net income with cash flows from operations. The 1996 edition of *Accounting Trends & Techniques* reported that 98% of the companies surveyed used the indirect method. For these reasons, we will discuss first the indirect method of preparing the statement of cash flows.

To collect the data for the statement of cash flows, all the cash receipts and cash payments for a period could be analyzed. However, this procedure is expensive and time-consuming. A more efficient approach is to analyze the changes in the noncash balance sheet accounts. The logic of this approach is that a change in any balance sheet account (including cash) can be analyzed in terms of changes in the other balance sheet accounts. To illustrate, the accounting equation is rewritten below to focus on the cash account:

Assets = Liabilities + Stockholders' Equity
Cash + Noncash Assets = Liabilities + Stockholders' Equity
Cash = Liabilities + Stockholders' Equity − Noncash Assets

Any change in the cash account results in a change in one or more noncash balance sheet accounts. That is, if the cash account changes, then a liability, stockholders' equity, or noncash asset account must also change.

Additional data are also obtained by analyzing the income statement accounts and supporting records. For example, since the net income or net loss for the period is closed to *Retained Earnings,* a change in the retained earnings account can be partially explained by the net income or net loss reported on the income statement.

There is no order in which the noncash balance sheet accounts must be analyzed. However, it is usually more efficient to analyze the accounts in the reverse order in which they appear on the balance sheet. Thus, the analysis of retained earnings provides the starting point for determining the cash flows from operating activities, which is the first section of the statement of cash flows.

The comparative balance sheet for Rundell Inc. on December 31, 2000 and 1999, is used to illustrate the indirect method. This balance sheet is shown in Exhibit 3. Selected ledger accounts and other data are presented as needed.[2]

[2] An appendix that discusses using a work sheet as an aid in assembling data for the statement of cash flows is presented at the end of this chapter. This appendix illustrates a work sheet that can be used with the indirect method and a work sheet that can be used with the direct method of reporting cash flows from operating activities.

EXHIBIT 3
Comparative Balance Sheet

Rundell Inc.
Comparative Balance Sheet
December 31, 2000 and 1999

Assets	2000	1999	Increase Decrease*
Cash	$ 97,500	$ 26,000	$71,500
Accounts receivable (net)	74,000	65,000	9,000
Inventories	172,000	180,000	8,000*
Land	80,000	125,000	45,000*
Building	260,000	200,000	60,000
Accumulated depreciation—building	(65,300)	(58,300)	(7,000)
Total assets	$618,200	$537,700	$80,500
Liabilities			
Accounts payable (merchandise creditors)	$ 43,500	$ 46,700	$ 3,200*
Accrued expenses payable (operating expenses)	26,500	24,300	2,200
Income taxes payable	7,900	8,400	500*
Dividends payable	14,000	10,000	4,000
Bonds payable	100,000	150,000	50,000*
Total liabilities	$191,900	$239,400	$47,500*
Stockholders' Equity			
Common stock ($2 par)	$ 24,000	$ 16,000	$ 8,000
Paid-in capital in excess of par	120,000	80,000	40,000
Retained earnings	282,300	202,300	80,000
Total stockholders' equity	$426,300	$298,300	$128,000
Total liabilities and stockholders' equity	$618,200	$537,700	$ 80,500

Retained Earnings

The comparative balance sheet for Rundell Inc. shows that retained earnings increased $80,000 during the year. Analyzing the entries posted to the retained earnings account indicates how this change occurred. The retained earnings account for Rundell Inc. is shown below.

ACCOUNT ***Retained Earnings*** **ACCOUNT NO.**

Date		Item	Debit	Credit	Balance Debit	Balance Credit
2000 Jan.	1	Balance				202,300
Dec.	31	Net income		108,000		310,300
	31	Cash dividends	28,000			282,300

The retained earnings account must be carefully analyzed because some of the entries to retained earnings may not affect cash. For example, a decrease in retained earnings resulting from issuing a stock dividend does not affect cash. Such transactions are not reported on the statement of cash flows.

For Rundell Inc., the retained earnings account indicates that the $80,000 change resulted from net income of $108,000 and cash dividends declared of $28,000. The effect of each of these items on cash flows is discussed below.

Cash Flows from Operating Activities

The net income of $108,000 reported by Rundell Inc. normally is not equal to the amount of cash generated from operations during the period. This is because net income is determined using the accrual method of accounting.

Under the accrual method of accounting, the time when revenues and expenses are recorded often differs from when cash is received or paid. For example, merchandise may be sold on account and the cash received at a later date.

Likewise, insurance expense represents the amount of insurance expired during the period. The premiums for the insurance may have been paid in a prior period. Thus, the net income reported on the income statement must be adjusted in determining cash flows from operating activities. The typical adjustments to net income are summarized in Exhibit 4.[3]

EXHIBIT 4
Adjustments to Net Income—Indirect Method

Net income, per income statement		$XX	
Add: Depreciation of fixed assets and amortization of intangible assets	$XX		
Decreases in current assets (receivables, inventories, prepaid expenses)	XX		
Increases in current liabilities (accounts and notes payable, accrued liabilities)	XX		
Losses on disposal of assets	XX	XX	
Deduct: Increases in current assets (receivables, inventories, prepaid expenses)	$XX		
Decreases in current liabilities (accounts and notes payable, accrued liabilities)	XX		
Gains on disposal of assets	XX	XX	
Net cash flow from operating activities			$XX

Some of the adjustment items in Exhibit 4 are for expenses that affect noncurrent accounts but not cash. For example, depreciation of fixed assets and amortization of intangible assets are deducted from revenue but do not affect cash.

Some of the adjustment items in Exhibit 4 are for revenues and expenses that affect current assets and current liabilities but not cash flows. For example, a sale of $10,000 on account increases accounts receivable by $10,000. However, cash is not affected. Thus, the increase in accounts receivable of $10,000 between two balance sheet dates is deducted from net income in arriving at cash flows from operating activities.

Cash flows from operating activities should not include investing or financing transactions. For example, assume that land costing $50,000 was sold for $90,000 (a gain of $40,000). The sale should be reported as an investing activity: "Cash receipts from the sale of land, $90,000." However, the $40,000 gain on the sale of the land is included in net income on the income statement. Thus, the $40,000 gain is deducted from net income in determining cash flows from operations in order to avoid "double counting" the cash flow from the gain. Losses from the sale of fixed assets are added to net income in determining cash flows from operations.

The effect of dividends payable on cash flows from operating activities is omitted from Exhibit 4. Dividends payable is omitted because dividends do not affect net income. Later in the chapter, we will discuss the reporting of dividends in the statement of cash flows. In the following paragraphs, we will discuss the adjustment of Rundell Inc.'s net income to "Cash flows from operating activities."

[3] Other items that also require adjustments to net income to obtain cash flow from operating activities include amortization of bonds payable discounts (add), losses on debt retirement (add), amortization of bonds payable premium (deduct), and gains on retirement of debt (deduct).

Depreciation

The comparative balance sheet in Exhibit 3 indicates that Accumulated Depreciation—Building increased by $7,000. As shown below, this account indicates that depreciation for the year was $7,000 for the building.

ACCOUNT ***Accumulated Depreciation—Building*** **ACCOUNT NO.**

Date		Item	Debit	Credit	Balance Debit	Balance Credit
2000 Jan.	1	Balance				58,300
Dec.	31	Depreciation for year		7,000		65,300

Net income was $45,000 for the year. The accumulated depreciation balance increased by $15,000 over the year. There were no sales of fixed assets or changes in noncash current assets or liabilities. What is the cash flow from operations?

$60,000 ($45,000 + $15,000)

The $7,000 of depreciation expense reduced net income but did not require an outflow of cash. Thus, the $7,000 is added to net income in determining cash flows from operating activities, as follows:

Cash flows from operating activities:		
Net income	$108,000	
Add depreciation	7,000	$115,000

Current Assets and Current Liabilities

As shown in Exhibit 4, decreases in noncash current assets and increases in current liabilities are added to net income. In contrast, increases in noncash current assets and decreases in current liabilities are deducted from net income. The current asset and current liability accounts of Rundell Inc. are as follows:

Accounts	December 31 2000	December 31 1999	Increase Decrease*
Accounts receivable (net)	$ 74,000	$ 65,000	$9,000
Inventories	172,000	180,000	8,000*
Accounts payable (merchandise creditors)	43,500	46,700	3,200*
Accrued expenses payable (operating expenses)	26,500	24,300	2,200
Income taxes payable	7,900	8,400	500*

The $9,000 increase in **accounts receivable** indicates that the sales on account during the year are $9,000 more than collections from customers on account. The amount reported as sales on the income statement therefore includes $9,000 that did not result in a cash inflow during the year. Thus, $9,000 is deducted from net income.

The $8,000 decrease in **inventories** indicates that the merchandise sold exceeds the cost of the merchandise purchased by $8,000. The amount deducted as cost of merchandise sold on the income statement therefore includes $8,000 that did not require a cash outflow during the year. Thus, $8,000 is added to net income.

The $3,200 decrease in **accounts payable** indicates that the amount of cash payments for merchandise exceeds the merchandise purchased on account by $3,200. The amount reported on the income statement for cost of mer-

Apple Computer had a loss of $816 million in 1996, but a positive cash flow from operations of $519 million. This is a difference of approximately $1.3 billion. Most of this difference was explained by a $1.1 billion reduction in inventory balances.

REAL WORLD The Chief Financial Officer (CFO) of **Honeywell Corporation** put all managers through a financial training course. The CFO wanted the managers to understand how cash can be tied up in such things as receivables and inventory and that growth can be achieved without significant working capital requirements. As a result, Honeywell generated cash by reducing its working capital needs from $2.2 billion to $1.6 billion.

chandise sold therefore excludes $3,200 that required a cash outflow during the year. Thus, $3,200 is deducted from net income.

The $2,200 increase in **accrued expenses payable** indicates that the amount incurred during the year for operating expenses exceeds the cash payments by $2,200. The amount reported on the income statement for operating expenses therefore includes $2,200 that did not require a cash outflow during the year. Thus, $2,200 is added to net income.

The $500 decrease in **income taxes payable** indicates that the amount paid for taxes exceeds the amount incurred during the year by $500. The amount reported on the income statement for income tax therefore is less than the amount paid by $500. Thus, $500 is deducted from net income.

Q&A *Net income was $36,000 for the year. Accounts receivable increased $3,000 and accounts payable increased $5,000. What is the cash flow from operations?*

$38,000 ($36,000 − $3,000 + $5,000)

Gain on Sale of Land

The ledger or income statement of Rundell Inc. indicates that the sale of land resulted in a gain of $12,000. As we discussed previously, the sale proceeds, which include the gain and the carrying value of the land, are included in cash flows from investing activities.[4] The gain is also included in net income. Thus, to avoid double reporting, the gain of $12,000 is deducted from net income in determining cash flows from operating activities, as shown below.

Cash flows from operating activities:	
Net income	$108,000
Deduct gain on sale of land	12,000

Reporting Cash Flows from Operating Activities

We have now presented all the necessary adjustments to convert the net income to cash flows from operating activities for Rundell Inc. These adjustments are summarized in Exhibit 5 in a format suitable for the statement of cash flows.

EXHIBIT 5
Cash Flows from Operating Activities—Indirect Method

Cash flows from operating activities:			
Net income		$108,000	
Add: Depreciation	$ 7,000		
Decrease in inventories	8,000		
Increase in accrued expenses	2,200	17,200	
		$125,200	
Deduct: Increase in accounts receivable	$ 9,000		
Decrease in accounts payable	3,200		
Decrease in income taxes payable	500		
Gain on sale of land	12,000	24,700	
Net cash flow from operating activities			$100,500

Cash Flows Used for Payment of Dividends

According to the retained earnings account of Rundell Inc., shown earlier in the chapter, cash dividends of $28,000 were declared during the year. However, the dividends payable account, shown below, indicates that dividends of only $24,000 were paid during the year.

[4] The reporting of the proceeds (cash flows) from the sale of land as part of investing activities is discussed later in this chapter.

ACCOUNT *Dividends Payable*					ACCOUNT NO.	
					Balance	
Date		Item	Debit	Credit	Debit	Credit
2000 Jan.	1	Balance				10,000
	10	Cash paid	10,000		—	—
June	20	Dividends declared		14,000		14,000
July	10	Cash paid	14,000		—	—
Dec.	20	Dividends declared		14,000		14,000

The $24,000 of dividend payments represents a cash outflow that is reported in the financing activities section as follows:

Cash flows from financing activities:
Cash paid for dividends $24,000

Common Stock

The common stock account increased by $8,000, and the paid-in capital in excess of par—common stock account increased by $40,000, as shown below. These increases result from issuing 4,000 shares of common stock for $12 per share.

ACCOUNT *Common Stock*					ACCOUNT NO.	
					Balance	
Date		Item	Debit	Credit	Debit	Credit
2000 Jan.	1	Balance				16,000
Nov.	1	4,000 shares issued for cash		8,000		24,000

ACCOUNT *Paid-In Capital in Excess of Par—Common Stock*					ACCOUNT NO.	
					Balance	
Date		Item	Debit	Credit	Debit	Credit
2000 Jan.	1	Balance				80,000
Nov.	1	4,000 shares issued for cash		40,000		120,000

This cash inflow is reported in the financing activities section as follows:

Cash flows from financing activities:
Cash received from sale of common stock $48,000

Bonds Payable

The bonds payable account decreased by $50,000, as shown below. This decrease results from retiring the bonds by a cash payment for their face amount.

ACCOUNT *Bonds Payable*					ACCOUNT NO.	
					Balance	
Date		Item	Debit	Credit	Debit	Credit
2000 Jan.	1	Balance				150,000
June	30	Retired by payment of cash at face amount	50,000			100,000

This cash outflow is reported in the financing activities section as follows:

Cash flows from financing activities:
Cash paid to retire bonds payable $50,000

Building

The building account increased by $60,000, and the accumulated depreciation—building account increased by $7,000, as shown below.

ACCOUNT *Building*					ACCOUNT NO.	
					Balance	
Date		Item	Debit	Credit	Debit	Credit
2000 Jan.	1	Balance			200,000	
Dec.	27	Purchased for cash	60,000		260,000	

ACCOUNT *Accumulated Depreciation—Building*					ACCOUNT NO.	
					Balance	
Date		Item	Debit	Credit	Debit	Credit
2000 Jan.	1	Balance				58,300
Dec.	31	Depreciation for the year		7,000		65,300

The purchase of a building for cash of $60,000 is reported as an outflow of cash in the investing activities section, as follows:

Cash flows from investing activities:
Cash paid for purchase of building $60,000

The credit in the accumulated depreciation—building account, shown earlier, represents depreciation expense for the year. This depreciation expense of $7,000 on the building has already been considered as an addition to net income in determining cash flows from operating activities, as reported in Exhibit 5.

Q&A *A building with a cost of $145,000 and accumulated depreciation of $35,000 was sold for a $10,000 gain. How much cash was generated from this investing activity?*

$120,000 ($145,000 − $35,000 + $10,000)

Land

The $45,000 decline in the land account resulted from two separate transactions, as shown below.

ACCOUNT *Land*					ACCOUNT NO.	
					Balance	
Date		Item	Debit	Credit	Debit	Credit
2000 Jan.	1	Balance			125,000	
June	8	Sold for $72,000 cash		60,000	65,000	
Oct.	12	Purchased for $15,000 cash	15,000		80,000	

A negative cash flow from operations would normally be considered a cause for concern. Such a condition could not be sustained indefinitely. However, in the short term, a firm could seek cash through additional financing or liquidating assets. For example, **America Online** (AOL) has had a negative cumulative cash flow from operations from its inception until 1996. However, AOL has been able to grow by obtaining cash from the sale of common stock. Investors are willing to purchase the common stock on the belief that AOL will have a very profitable future as the Internet online market matures.

The first transaction is the sale of land with a cost of $60,000 for $72,000 in cash. The $72,000 proceeds from the sale are reported in the investing activities section, as follows:

Cash flows from investing activities:	
Cash received from sale of land (includes $12,000 gain reported in net income)	$72,000

The proceeds of $72,000 include the $12,000 gain on the sale of land and the $60,000 cost (book value) of the land. As shown in Exhibit 5, the $12,000 gain is also deducted from net income in the cash flows from operating activities section. This is necessary so that the $12,000 cash inflow related to the gain is not included twice as a cash inflow.

The second transaction is the purchase of land for cash of $15,000. This transaction is reported as an outflow of cash in the investing activities section, as follows:

Cash flows from investing activities:	
Cash paid for purchase of land	$15,000

Preparing the Statement of Cash Flows

The statement of cash flows for Rundell Inc. is prepared from the data assembled and analyzed above, using the indirect method. Exhibit 6 shows the statement of cash flows prepared by Rundell Inc. The statement indicates that the cash position

EXHIBIT 6
Statement of Cash Flows—Indirect Method

Rundell Inc.
Statement of Cash Flows
For the Year Ended December 31, 2000

Cash flows from operating activities:			
Net income		$108,000	
Add: Depreciation	$ 7,000		
Decrease in inventories	8,000		
Increase in accrued expenses	2,200	17,200	
		$125,200	
Deduct: Increase in accounts receivable	$ 9,000		
Decrease in accounts payable	3,200		
Decrease in income taxes payable	500		
Gain on sale of land	12,000	24,700	
Net cash flow from operating activities			$100,500
Cash flows from investing activities:			
Cash from sale of land		$ 72,000	
Less: Cash paid to purchase land	$15,000		
Cash paid for purchase of building	60,000	75,000	
Net cash flow used for investing activities			(3,000)
Cash flows from financing activities:			
Cash received from sale of common stock		$ 48,000	
Less: Cash paid to retire bonds payable	$50,000		
Cash paid for dividends	24,000	74,000	
Net cash flow used for financing activities			(26,000)
Increase in cash			$ 71,500
Cash at the beginning of the year			26,000
Cash at the end of the year			$ 97,500

Cash management is not only important for businesses, but also for governmental units. The city of Miami faced a cash squeeze, due to an excessive public payroll, graft, and inefficiency. For example, the Miami police were allowed to take their police cruisers home with them, which effectively doubled the number of police cars needed by the city. The cash shortfall was so severe that the city considered merging with Dade County.

Source: Peter Katel, "Miami Goes to the Dogs," *Newsweek,* December 16, 1996.

increased by $71,500 during the year. The most significant increase in net cash flows, $100,500, was from operating activities. The most significant use of cash, $26,000, was for financing activities.

Statement of Cash Flows—The Direct Method

OBJECTIVE 4

Prepare a statement of cash flows, using the direct method.

As we discussed previously, the manner of reporting cash flows from investing and financing activities is the same under the direct and indirect methods. In addition, the direct method and the indirect method will report the same amount of cash flows from operating activities. However, the methods differ in how the cash flows from operating activities data are obtained, analyzed, and reported.

To illustrate the direct method, we will use the comparative balance sheet and the income statement for Rundell Inc. In this way, we can compare the statement of cash flows under the direct method and the indirect method.

Exhibit 7 shows the changes in the current asset and liability account balances for Rundell Inc. The income statement in Exhibit 7 shows additional data for Rundell Inc.

EXHIBIT 7
Balance Sheet and Income Statement Data for Direct Method

Rundell Inc.
Schedule of Changes in Current Accounts

Accounts	December 31 2000	December 31 1999	Increase Decrease*
Cash	$ 97,500	$ 26,000	$71,500
Accounts receivable (net)	74,000	65,000	9,000
Inventories	172,000	180,000	8,000*
Accounts payable (merchandise creditors)	43,500	46,700	3,200*
Accrued expenses payable (operating expenses)	26,500	24,300	2,200
Income taxes payable	7,900	8,400	500*
Dividends payable	14,000	10,000	4,000

Rundell Inc.
Income Statement
For the Year Ended December 31, 2000

Sales		$1,180,000
Cost of merchandise sold		790,000
Gross profit		$ 390,000
Operating expenses:		
Depreciation expense	$ 7,000	
Other operating expenses	196,000	
Total operating expenses		203,000
Income from operations		$ 187,000
Other income:		
Gain on sale of land	$ 12,000	
Other expense:		
Interest expense	8,000	4,000
Income before income tax		$ 191,000
Income tax expense		83,000
Net income		$ 108,000

The direct method reports cash flows from operating activities by major classes of operating cash receipts and operating cash payments. The difference between the major classes of total operating cash receipts and total operating cash payments is the net cash flow from operating activities.

Cash Received from Customers

The $1,180,000 of sales for Rundell Inc. is reported by using the accrual method. To determine the cash received from sales to customers, the $1,180,000 must be adjusted. The adjustments necessary to convert the sales reported on the income statement to the cash received from customers is summarized below.

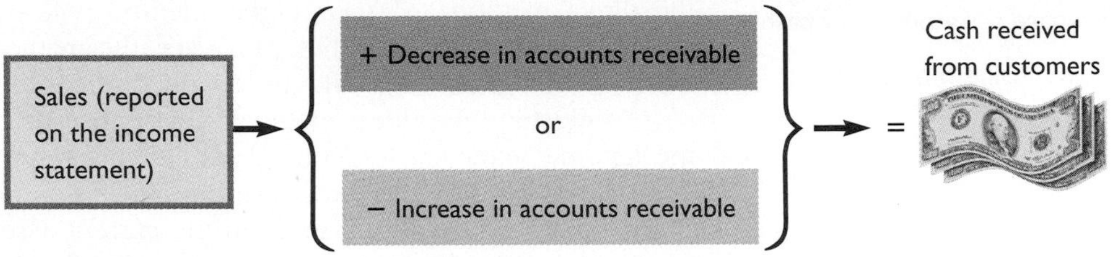

Sales reported on the income statement were $350,000. The accounts receivable balance declined $8,000 over the year. What was the amount of cash received from customers?

$358,000 ($350,000 + $8,000)

For Rundell Inc., the cash received from customers is $1,171,000, as shown below.

Sales	$1,180,000
Less increase in accounts receivable	9,000
Cash received from customers	$1,171,000

The additions to **accounts receivable** for sales on account during the year were $9,000 more than the amounts collected from customers on account. Sales reported on the income statement therefore included $9,000 that did not result in a cash inflow during the year. In other words, the increase of $9,000 in accounts receivable during 2000 indicates that sales on account exceeded cash received from customers by $9,000. Thus, $9,000 is deducted from sales to determine the cash received from customers. The $1,171,000 of cash received from customers is reported in the cash flows from operating activities section of the cash flow statement.

Cash Payments for Merchandise

The $790,000 of cost of merchandise sold is reported on the income statement for Rundell Inc., using the accrual method. The adjustments necessary to convert the cost of merchandise sold to cash payments for merchandise during 2000 are summarized below.

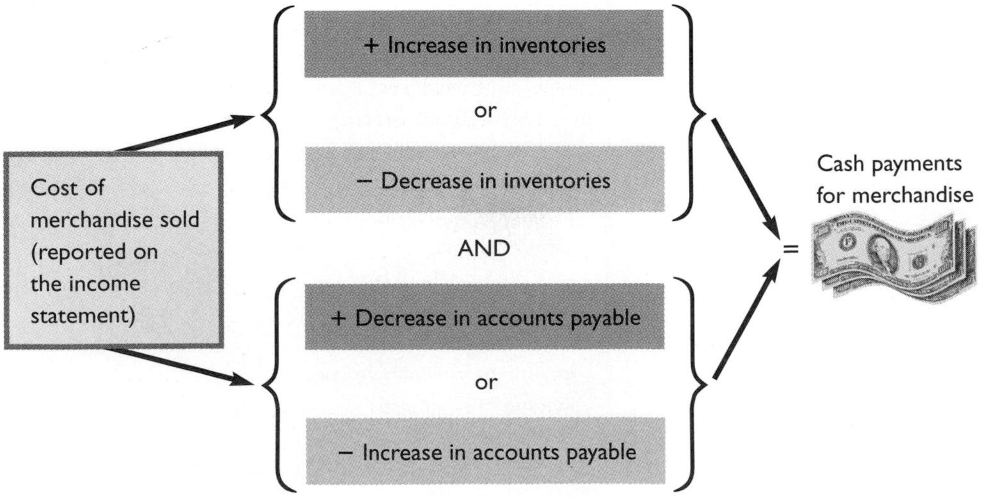

For Rundell Inc., the amount of cash payments for merchandise is $785,200, as determined below.

Cost of merchandise sold	$790,000
Deduct decrease in inventories	(8,000)
Add decrease in accounts payable	3,200
Cash payments for merchandise	$785,200

The $8,000 decrease in **inventories** indicates that the merchandise sold exceeded the cost of the merchandise purchased by $8,000. The amount reported on the income statement for cost of merchandise sold therefore includes $8,000 that did not require a cash outflow during the year. Thus, $8,000 is deducted from the cost of merchandise sold in determining the cash payments for merchandise.

The $3,200 decrease in **accounts payable** (merchandise creditors) indicates a cash outflow that is excluded from cost of merchandise sold. In other words, the decrease in accounts payable indicates that cash payments for merchandise were $3,200 more than the purchases on account during 2000. Thus, $3,200 is added to the cost of merchandise sold in determining the cash payments for merchandise.

Cash Payments for Operating Expenses

The $7,000 of depreciation expense reported on the income statement did not require a cash outflow. Thus, under the direct method, it is not reported on the statement of cash flows. The $196,000 reported for other operating expenses is adjusted to reflect the cash payments for operating expenses, as summarized below.

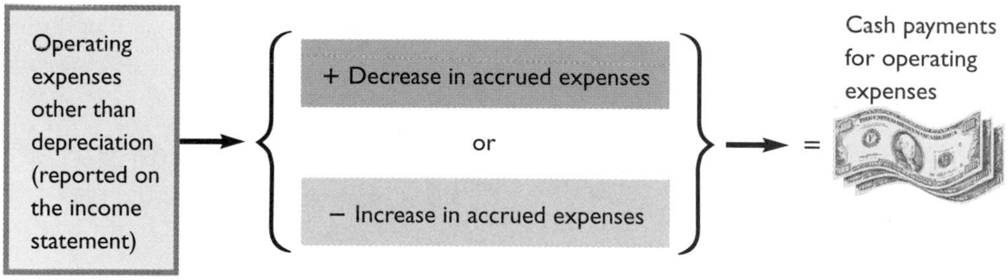

For Rundell Inc., the amount of cash payments for operating expenses is $193,800, determined as follows:

Operating expenses other than depreciation	$196,000
Deduct increase in accrued expenses	2,200
Cash payments for operating expenses	$193,800

The increase in **accrued expenses** (operating expenses) indicates that operating expenses include $2,200 for which there was no cash outflow (payment) during the year. In other words, the increase in accrued expenses indicates that the cash payments for operating expenses were $2,200 less than the amount reported as an expense during the year. Thus, $2,200 is deducted from the operating expenses on the income statement in determining the cash payments for operating expenses.

Gain on Sale of Land

The income statement for Rundell Inc. in Exhibit 7 reports a gain of $12,000 on the sale of land. As we discussed previously, the gain is included in the proceeds from the sale of land, which is reported as part of the cash flows from investing activities.

Interest Expense

The income statement for Rundell Inc. in Exhibit 7 reports interest expense of $8,000. The interest expense is related to the bonds payable that were outstanding during the year. We assume that interest on the bonds is paid on June 30 and December 31. Thus, $8,000 cash outflow for interest expense is reported on the statement of cash flows as an operating activity.

If interest payable had existed at the end of the year, the interest expense would be adjusted for any increase or decrease in interest payable from the beginning to the end of the year. That is, a decrease in interest payable would be added to interest expense and an increase in interest payable would be subtracted from interest expense. This is similar to the adjustment for changes in income taxes payable, which we will illustrate in the following paragraphs.

Cash Payments for Income Taxes

The adjustment to convert the income tax reported on the income statement to the cash basis is summarized below.

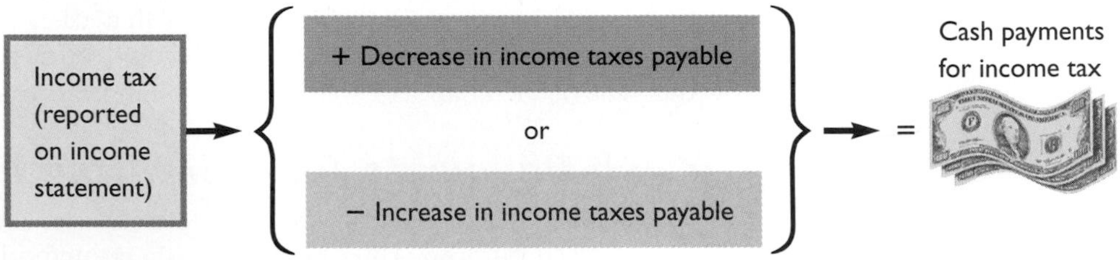

For Rundell Inc., cash payments for income tax are $83,500, determined as follows:

Income tax	$83,000
Add decrease in income taxes payable	500
Cash payments for income tax	$83,500

The cash outflow for income taxes exceeded the income tax deducted as an expense during the period by $500. Thus, $500 is added to the amount of income tax reported on the income statement in determining the cash payments for income tax.

Reporting Cash Flows from Operating Activities—Direct Method

Exhibit 8 is a complete statement of cash flows for Rundell Inc., using the direct method for reporting cash flows from operating activities. The portions of this statement that differ from the indirect method are highlighted in color. Exhibit 8 also includes the separate schedule reconciling net income and net cash flow from operating activities. This schedule must accompany the statement of cash flows when the direct method is used. This schedule is similar to the cash flows from operating activities section of the statement of cash flows prepared using the indirect method.

INTERMISSION

Ameritech's chairman and CEO (chief executive officer), Richard Notebaert, has stated recently, "We are emphasizing cash-flow management as never before. We're counting on it to provide flexibility in meeting the needs of our customers and business. Cash flow management simply is an aspect of business operations that no company can afford to ignore." Some of Ameritech's cash flow management techniques include:

a. Analyze customer credit and sort into risk groups. This allows Ameritech to avoid poor credit risks and respond to collection problems quickly.
b. Consolidate collection from multiple sites into a single site and adopt better collection procedures. This reduces collection cycle time and improves cash flow.
c. Negotiate extended payment terms with suppliers. This increases the payment cycle time and slows cash outflows.

These new procedures have resulted in an increase of $200–$300 million in annual cash flow from operations, which can now be invested in the business. ■

Source: Steve Bergsman, "Ameritech's Excellent Adventure," *Chief Executive*, June 1996.

EXHIBIT 8
Statement of Cash Flows—Direct Method

Rundell Inc.
Statement of Cash Flows
For the Year Ended December 31, 2000

Cash flows from operating activities:			
Cash received from customers		$1,171,000	
Deduct: Cash payments for merchandise	$785,200		
Cash payments for operating expense	193,800		
Cash payments for interest	8,000		
Cash payments for income taxes	83,500	1,070,500	
Net cash flow from operating activities			$100,500
Cash flows from investing activities:			
Cash from sale of land		$ 72,000	
Less: Cash paid to purchase land	$ 15,000		
Cash paid for purchase of building	60,000	75,000	
Net cash flow used for investing activities			(3,000)
Cash flows from financing activities:			
Cash received from sale of common stock		$ 48,000	
Less: Cash paid to retire bonds payable	$ 50,000		
Cash paid for dividends	24,000	74,000	
Net cash flow used for financing activities			(26,000)
Increase in cash			$ 71,500
Cash at the beginning of the year			26,000
Cash at the end of the year			$ 97,500

Schedule Reconciling Net Income with Cash Flows from Operating Activities:

Net income, per income statement		$108,000
Add: Depreciation	$ 7,000	
Decrease in inventories	8,000	
Increase in accrued expenses	2,200	17,200
		$125,200
Deduct: Increase in accounts receivable	$ 9,000	
Decrease in accounts payable	3,200	
Decrease in income taxes payable	500	
Gain on sale of land	12,000	24,700
Net cash flow from operating activities		$100,500

FINANCIAL ANALYSIS AND INTERPRETATION

OBJECTIVE 5

Calculate and interpret the free cash flow.

A valuable tool for evaluating the cash position of a business is free cash flow. **Free cash flow** is a measure of operating cash flow available for corporate purposes after providing sufficient fixed asset additions to maintain current productive capacity and dividends. Thus, free cash flow can be calculated as follows:

	Cash flow from operations
Less:	Cash used to purchase fixed assets to maintain productive capacity used up in producing income during the period
Less:	Cash used for dividends
	Free cash flow

REAL WORLD

Many high technology firms must aggressively reinvest in new technology to remain competitive. This can reduce free cash flow. For example, **Motorola's** free cash flow is less than 10% of the cash flow from operating activities. In contrast, **Coca-Cola's** free cash flow is approximately 75% of the cash flow from operating activities.

To illustrate, assume that O'Brien Company had cash flow from operations of $1,400,000. O'Brien Company invested $450,000 in fixed assets to maintain productive capacity, and another $300,000 to expand capacity. Dividends were $100,000. Thus, free cash flow is as follows:

Cash flow from operations		$1,400,000
Less: Cash invested in fixed assets to maintain productive capacity	$450,000	
Cash for dividends	100,000	550,000
Free cash flow		$ 850,000

A company that has free cash flow is able to fund internal growth, retire debt, and enjoy financial flexibility. A company with no free cash flow is unable to maintain current productive capacity or dividend payouts to stockholders. Lack of free cash flow can be an early indicator of liquidity problems. Indeed, all three of the major credit rating agencies use a form of free cash flow in evaluating the creditworthiness of businesses.[5]

ENCORE

"The Pack's" Cash Flow

The **Green Bay Packers** NFL football franchise recorded record earnings of $5.4 million for fiscal year 1995. The increased earnings were caused by a strong 13% increase in revenues, combined with a more modest increase in operating costs, thanks to the NFL salary cap. Even so, the Packers ranked only 22nd in total revenues out of 30 NFL clubs. In addition, the record earnings weren't enough to prevent cash from declining by $3.6 million. Why did cash decline in the face of such strong earnings? The answer is simple. The Packers have spent $43.2 million on facilities over the last dozen years, which has caused a negative cash flow for the last three seasons. John Underwood, treasurer, stated to stockholders, "In spite of the record year, we really need to focus our attention on generating higher levels of cash. The reasons are pretty obvious. In the business we're in, cash is king. And every dollar we make in this franchise goes to only one of two purposes: the football team or the facilities. With the reality of the competition, particularly regarding signing bonuses, it's really critical that our strategy now is to build and replenish cash so that we do have the funds to compete." How could the Green Bay Packers increase cash flow? Some ideas might include:

1. Increase ticket prices. (The Packers presently rank 29th in average ticket prices.)
2. Expand private box revenue and corporate sponsorships.
3. Expand the team's pro shop.
4. Rent Lambeau Field for concerts or festivals during the off-season.
5. Distribute pay-for-view games over direct TV. ■

Source: Tom Mulhern, "Packer Finances Bittersweet," *Post-Crescent* (Appleton, Wisconsin), May 30, 1996.

[5] Jeff Ryser, "Cash Flow and the Single A," *CFO: The Magazine for Senior Financial Executives* (October 1995), pp. 87–89. The three major credit-rating agencies that rate the bonds (debt) sold to outside investors are **Fitch Investor Services**, **Standard and Poor's**, and **Moody's**. The ratings are used by investors in evaluating the risk of bond default.

APPENDIX: WORK SHEET FOR STATEMENT OF CASH FLOWS

A work sheet may be useful in assembling data for the statement of cash flows. Whether or not a work sheet is used, the concepts of cash flow and the statements of cash flows presented in this chapter are not affected. In this appendix, we will describe and illustrate the use of work sheets for the indirect method and the direct method.

Work Sheet—Indirect Method

We will use the data for Rundell Inc., presented in Exhibit 3, as a basis for illustrating the work sheet for the indirect method. The procedures used in preparing this work sheet, shown in Exhibit 9, are outlined at the top of the next page.

EXHIBIT 9 Work Sheet for Statement of Cash Flows—Indirect Method

Rundell Inc.
Work Sheet for Statement of Cash Flows
For the Year Ended December 31, 2000

Accounts	Balance Dec. 31, 1999	Transactions Debit	Transactions Credit	Balance Dec. 31, 2000
Cash	26,000	(o) 71,500		97,500
Accounts receivable (net)	65,000	(n) 9,000		74,000
Inventories	180,000		(m) 8,000	172,000
Land	125,000	(k) 15,000	(l) 60,000	80,000
Building	200,000	(j) 60,000		260,000
Accumulated depreciation—building	(58,300)		(i) 7,000	(65,300)
Accounts payable (merchandise creditors)	(46,700)	(h) 3,200		(43,500)
Accrued expenses payable (operating expenses)	(24,300)		(g) 2,200	(26,500)
Income taxes payable	(8,400)	(f) 500		(7,900)
Dividends payable	(10,000)		(e) 4,000	(14,000)
Bonds payable	(150,000)	(d) 50,000		(100,000)
Common stock	(16,000)		(c) 8,000	(24,000)
Paid-in capital in excess of par	(80,000)		(c) 40,000	(120,000)
Retained earnings	(202,300)	(b) 28,000	(a) 108,000	(282,300)
Totals	0	237,200	237,200	0
Operating activities:				
Net income		(a) 108,000		
Depreciation of building		(i) 7,000		
Decrease in inventories		(m) 8,000		
Increase in accrued expenses		(g) 2,200		
Increase in accounts receivable			(n) 9,000	
Decrease in accounts payable			(h) 3,200	
Decrease in income taxes payable			(f) 500	
Gain on sale of land			(l) 12,000	
Investing activities:				
Sale of land		(l) 72,000		
Purchase of land			(k) 15,000	
Purchase of building			(j) 60,000	
Financing activities:				
Issued common stock		(c) 48,000		
Retired bonds payable			(d) 50,000	
Declared cash dividends			(b) 28,000	
Increase in dividends payable		(e) 4,000		
Net increase in cash			(o) 71,500	
Totals		249,200	249,200	

1. List the title of each balance sheet account in the Accounts column. For each account, enter its balance as of December 31, 1999, in the first column and its balance as of December 31, 2000, in the last column. Place the credit balances in parentheses. The column totals should equal zero, since the total of the debits in a column should equal the total of the credits in a column.
2. Analyze the change during the year in each account to determine the net increase (decrease) in cash and the cash flows from operating activities, investing activities, financing activities, and the noncash investing and financing activities. Show the effect of the change on cash flows by making entries in the Transactions columns.

Analyzing Accounts

An efficient method of analyzing cash flows is to determine the type of cash flow activity that led to changes in balance sheet accounts during the period. As we analyze each noncash account, we will make entries on the work sheet for specific types of cash flow activities related to the noncash accounts. After we have analyzed all the noncash accounts, we will make an entry for the increase (decrease) in cash during the period. These entries, however, are not posted to the ledger. They only aid in assembling the data on the work sheet.

The order in which the accounts are analyzed is unimportant. However, it is more efficient to begin with the retained earnings account and proceed upward in the account listing.

Retained Earnings. The work sheet shows a Retained Earnings balance of $202,300 at December 31, 1999, and $282,300 at December 31, 2000. Thus, Retained Earnings increased $80,000 during the year. This increase resulted from two factors: (1) net income of $108,000 and (2) declaring cash dividends of $28,000. To identify the cash flows by activity, we will make two entries on the work sheet. These entries also serve to account for or explain, in terms of cash flows, the increase of $80,000.

In closing the accounts at the end of the year, the retained earnings account was credited for the net income of $108,000. The $108,000 is reported on the statement of cash flows as "cash flows from operating activities." The following entry is made in the Transactions columns on the work sheet. This entry (1) accounts for the credit portion of the closing entry (to Retained Earnings) and (2) identifies the cash flow in the bottom portion of the work sheet.

(a)	Operating Activities—Net Income	108,000	
	Retained Earnings		108,000

In closing the accounts at the end of the year, the retained earnings account was debited for dividends declared of $28,000. The $28,000 is reported as a financing activity on the statement of cash flows. The following entry on the work sheet (1) accounts for the debit portion of the closing entry (to Retained Earnings) and (2) identifies the cash flow in the bottom portion of the work sheet.

(b)	Retained Earnings	28,000	
	Financing Activities—Declared Cash Dividends		28,000

The $28,000 of declared dividends will be adjusted later for the actual amount of cash dividends paid during the year.

Other Accounts. The entries for the other accounts are made in the work sheet in a manner similar to entries (a) and (b). A summary of these entries is as follows:

(c)	Financing Activities—Issued Common Stock	48,000	
	Common Stock		8,000
	Paid-In Capital in Excess of Par—Common Stock		40,000

(d)	Bonds Payable	50,000	
	Financing Activities—Retired Bonds Payable		50,000
(e)	Financing Activities—Increase in Dividends Payable	4,000	
	Dividends Payable		4,000
(f)	Income Taxes Payable	500	
	Operating Activities—Decrease in Income Taxes Payable		500
(g)	Operating Activities—Increase in Accrued Expenses	2,200	
	Accrued Expenses		2,200
(h)	Accounts Payable	3,200	
	Operating Activities—Decrease in Accounts Payable		3,200
(i)	Operating Activities—Depreciation of Building	7,000	
	Accumulated Depreciation—Building		7,000
(j)	Building	60,000	
	Investing Activities—Purchase of Building		60,000
(k)	Land	15,000	
	Investing Activities—Purchase of Land		15,000
(l)	Investing Activities—Sale of Land	72,000	
	Operating Activities—Gain on Sale of Land		12,000
	Land		60,000
(m)	Operating Activities—Decrease in Inventories	8,000	
	Inventories		8,000
(n)	Accounts Receivable	9,000	
	Operating Activities—Increase in Accounts Receivable		9,000
(o)	Cash	71,500	
	Net Increase in Cash		71,500

Completing the Work Sheet

After we have analyzed all the balance sheet accounts and made the entries on the work sheet, all the operating, investing, and financing activities are identified in the bottom portion of the work sheet. The accuracy of the work sheet entries is verified by the equality of each pair of the totals of the debit and credit Transactions columns.

Preparing the Statement of Cash Flows

The statement of cash flows prepared from the work sheet is identical to the statement in Exhibit 6. The data for the three sections of the statement are obtained from the bottom portion of the work sheet.

In the cash flows from operating activities section, the effect of depreciation is normally presented first. The effects of increases and decreases in current assets and current liabilities are then presented. The effects of any gains and losses on operating activities are normally reported last. The cash paid for dividends is reported as \$24,000 instead of the amount of dividends declared (\$28,000) less the increase in dividends payable (\$4,000). Any noncash investing and financing activities are usually reported in a separate schedule at the bottom of the statement.

Work Sheet—Direct Method

As a basis for illustrating the direct method work sheet, we will use the balance sheet data for Rundell Inc. in Exhibit 3 and the income statement data in Exhibit 7. The procedures used in preparing the work sheet are outlined following Exhibit 10.

EXHIBIT 10 Work Sheet for Statement of Cash Flows—Direct Method

Rundell Inc.
Work Sheet for Statement of Cash Flows
For the Year Ended December 31, 2000

Accounts	Balance Dec. 31, 1999	Transactions Debit	Transactions Credit	Balance Dec. 31, 2000
Balance Sheet				
Cash	26,000	(t) 71,500		97,500
Accounts receivable (net)	65,000	(s) 9,000		74,000
Inventories	180,000		(r) 8,000	172,000
Land	125,000	(q) 15,000	(e) 60,000	80,000
Building	200,000	(p) 60,000		260,000
Accumulated depreciation—building	(58,300)		(c) 7,000	(65,300)
Accounts payable (merchandise creditors)	(46,700)	(o) 3,200		(43,500)
Accrued expenses payable (operating expenses)	(24,300)		(n) 2,200	(26,500)
Income taxes payable	(8,400)	(m) 500		(7,900)
Dividends payable	(10,000)		(l) 4,000	(14,000)
Bonds payable	(150,000)	(k) 50,000		(100,000)
Common stock	(16,000)		(j) 8,000	(24,000)
Paid-in capital in excess of par	(80,000)		(j) 40,000	(120,000)
Retained earnings	(202,300)	(i) 28,000	(h) 108,000	(282,300)
Totals	0	237,200	237,200	0
Income Statement				
Sales			(a) 1,180,000	
Cost of merchandise sold		(b) 790,000		
Depreciation expense		(c) 7,000		
Other operating expenses		(d) 196,000		
Gain on sale of land			(e) 12,000	
Interest expense		(f) 8,000		
Income taxes		(g) 83,000		
Net income		(h) 108,000		
Cash Flows				
Operating activities:				
Cash received from customers		(a) 1,180,000	(s) 9,000	
Cash payments:				
Merchandise		(r) 8,000	(b) 790,000	
			(o) 3,200	
Operating expense		(n) 2,200	(d) 196,000	
Interest			(f) 8,000	
Income taxes			(g) 83,000	
			(m) 500	
Investing activities:				
Sale of land		(e) 72,000		
Purchase of land			(q) 15,000	
Purchase of building			(p) 60,000	
Financing activities:				
Issued common stock		(j) 48,000		
Retired bonds payable			(k) 50,000	
Declared cash dividends			(i) 28,000	
Increase in dividends payable		(l) 4,000		
Net increase in cash			(t) 71,500	
Totals		2,506,200	2,506,200	

1. List the title of each balance sheet account in the Accounts column. For each account, enter its balance as of December 31, 1999, in the first column and its balance as of December 31, 2000, in the last column. Place the credit balances in parentheses. The column totals should equal zero, since the total of the debits in a column should equal the total of the credits in a column.
2. List the title of each income statement account and "Net Income" on the work sheet.
3. Analyze the effect of each income statement item on cash flows from operating activities. Beginning with sales, enter the balance of each item in the proper Transactions column. Complete the entry in the Transactions columns to show the effect on cash flows.
4. Analyze the change during the year in each balance sheet account to determine the net increase (decrease) in cash and the cash flows from operating activities, investing activities, financing activities, and the noncash investing and financing activities. Show the effect of the change on cash flows by making entries in the Transactions columns.

Analyzing Accounts

Under the direct method of reporting cash flows from operating activities, analyzing accounts begins with the income statement. As we analyze each income statement account, we will make entries on the work sheet that show the effect on cash flows from operating activities. After we have analyzed the income statement accounts, we will analyze changes in the balance sheet accounts.

The order in which the balance sheet accounts are analyzed is unimportant. However, it is more efficient to begin with the retained earnings account and proceed upward in the account listing. As each noncash balance sheet account is analyzed, we will make entries on the work sheet for the related cash flow activities. After we have analyzed all the noncash accounts, we will make an entry for the increase (decrease) in cash during the period.

Sales. The income statement for Rundell Inc. shows sales of $1,180,000 for the year. Sales for cash provide cash when the sale is made. Sales on account provide cash when customers pay their bills. The entry on the work sheet is as follows:

(a)	Operating Activities—Receipts from Customers	1,180,000	
	Sales		1,180,000

Cost of Merchandise Sold. The income statement for Rundell Inc. shows cost of merchandise sold of $790,000 for the year. The cost of merchandise sold requires cash payments for cash purchases of merchandise. For purchases on account, cash payments are made when the invoices are due. The entry on the work sheet is as follows:

(b)	Cost of Merchandise Sold	790,000	
	Operating Activities—Payments for Merchandise		790,000

Depreciation Expense. The income statement for Rundell Inc. shows depreciation expense of $7,000. Depreciation expense does not require a cash outflow and thus is not reported on the statement of cash flows. The entry on the work sheet to fully account for the depreciation expense is as follows:

(c)	Depreciation Expense	7,000	
	Accumulated Depreciation—Building		7,000

Other Accounts. The entries for the other accounts are made on the work sheet in a manner similar to entries (a), (b), and (c). A summary of these entries is as follows:

(d)	Other Operating Expenses	196,000	
	Operating Activities—Paid Operating Expenses		196,000
(e)	Investing Activities—Sale of Land	72,000	
	Land		60,000
	Gain on Sale of Land		12,000
(f)	Interest Expense	8,000	
	Operating Activities—Paid Interest		8,000
(g)	Income Taxes	83,000	
	Operating Activities—Paid Income Taxes		83,000
(h)	Net Income	108,000	
	Retained Earnings		108,000
(i)	Retained Earnings	28,000	
	Financing Activities—Declared Cash Dividends		28,000
(j)	Financing Activities—Issued Common Stock	48,000	
	Common Stock		8,000
	Paid-In Capital in Excess of Par—Common Stock		40,000
(k)	Bonds Payable	50,000	
	Financing Activities—Retired Bonds Payable		50,000
(l)	Financing Activities—Increase in Dividends Payable	4,000	
	Dividends Payable		4,000
(m)	Income Taxes Payable	500	
	Operating Activities—Cash Paid for Income Taxes		500
(n)	Operating Activities—Cash Paid for Operating Expenses	2,200	
	Accrued Expenses		2,200
(o)	Accounts Payable	3,200	
	Operating Activities—Cash Paid for Merchandise		3,200
(p)	Building	60,000	
	Investing Activities—Purchase of Building		60,000
(q)	Land	15,000	
	Investing Activities—Purchase of Land		15,000
(r)	Operating Activities—Cash Paid for Merchandise	8,000	
	Inventories		8,000
(s)	Accounts Receivable	9,000	
	Operating Activities—Cash Received from Customers		9,000
(t)	Cash	71,500	
	Net Increase in Cash		71,500

Completing the Work Sheet

After we have analyzed all the income statement and balance sheet accounts and have made the entries on the work sheet, all the operating, investing, and financing activities are identified in the bottom portion of the work sheet. The mathematical accuracy of the work sheet entries is verified by the equality of each pair of the totals of the debit and credit Transactions columns.

Preparing the Statement of Cash Flows

The statement of cash flows prepared from the work sheet is identical to the statement in Exhibit 8. The data for the three sections of the statement are obtained from the bottom portion of the work sheet. Some of these data may not be reported exactly as they appear on the work sheet. The cash paid for dividends is reported as

$24,000 instead of the amount of dividends declared ($28,000) less the increase in the dividends payable ($4,000).

KEY POINTS

1 Explain why the statement of cash flows is one of the basic financial statements.

The statement of cash flows reports useful information about a firm's ability to generate cash from operations, maintain and expand its operating capacity, meet its financial obligations, and pay dividends. This information assists investors, creditors, and others in assessing the firm's profit potential and its ability to pay its maturing debt. The statement of cash flows is also useful to managers in evaluating past operations and in planning future operating, investing, and financing activities.

2 Summarize the types of cash flow activities reported in the statement of cash flows.

The statement of cash flows reports cash receipts and cash payments by three types of activities: operating activities, investing activities, and financing activities.

Cash flows from operating activities are cash flows from transactions that affect net income. There are two methods of reporting cash flows from operating activities: (1) the direct method and (2) the indirect method.

Cash inflows from investing activities are cash flows from the sale of investments, fixed assets, and intangible assets. Cash outflows generally include payments to acquire investments, fixed assets, and intangible assets.

Cash inflows from financing activities include proceeds from issuing equity securities, such as preferred and common stock. Cash inflows also arise from issuing bonds, mortgage notes payable, and other long-term debt. Cash outflows from financing activities arise from paying cash dividends, purchasing treasury stock, and repaying amounts borrowed.

Investing and financing for a business may be affected by transactions that do not involve cash. The effect of such transactions should be reported in a separate schedule accompanying the statement of cash flows.

Because it may be misleading, cash flow per share is not reported in the statement of cash flows.

3 Prepare a statement of cash flows, using the indirect method.

To prepare the statement of cash flows, changes in the noncash balance sheet accounts are analyzed. This logic relies on the fact that a change in any balance sheet account can be analyzed in terms of changes in the other balance sheet accounts. Thus, by analyzing the noncash balance sheet accounts, those activities that resulted in cash flows can be identified. Although the noncash balance sheet accounts may be analyzed in any order, it is usually more efficient to begin with retained earnings. Additional data are obtained by analyzing the income statement accounts and supporting records.

4 Prepare a statement of cash flows, using the direct method.

The direct method and the indirect method will report the same amount of cash flows from operating activities. Also, the manner of reporting cash flows from investing and financing activities is the same under both methods. The methods differ in how the cash flows from operating activities data are obtained, analyzed, and reported. The direct method reports cash flows from operating activities by major classes of operating cash receipts and cash payments. The difference between the major classes of total operating cash receipts and total operating cash payments is the net cash flow from operating activities.

The data for reporting cash flows from operating activities by the direct method can be obtained by analyzing the cash flows related to the revenues and expenses reported on the income statement. The revenues and expenses are adjusted from the accrual basis of accounting to the cash basis for purposes of preparing the statement of cash flows.

When the direct method is used, a reconciliation of net income and net cash flow from operating activities is reported in a separate schedule. This schedule is similar to the cash flows from the operating activities section of the statement of cash flows prepared using the indirect method.

5 Calculate and interpret the free cash flow.

Free cash flow is the amount of operating cash flow remaining after replacing current productive capacity and maintaining current dividends. Free cash flow is the amount of cash available to reduce debt, grow the business, or return to shareholders through increased dividends or treasury stock purchases.

ILLUSTRATIVE PROBLEM

The comparative balance sheet of Dowling Company for December 31, 2001 and 2000, is as follows:

Dowling Company
Comparative Balance Sheet
December 31, 2001 and 2000

	2001	2000
Assets		
Cash	$ 140,350	$ 95,900
Accounts receivable (net)	95,300	102,300
Inventories	165,200	157,900
Prepaid expenses	6,240	5,860
Investments (long-term)	35,700	84,700
Land	75,000	90,000
Buildings	375,000	260,000
Accumulated depreciation—buildings	(71,300)	(58,300)
Machinery and equipment	428,300	428,300
Accumulated depreciation—machinery and equipment	(148,500)	(138,000)
Patents	58,000	65,000
Total assets	$1,159,290	$1,093,660
Liabilities and Stockholders' Equity		
Accounts payable (merchandise creditors)	$ 43,500	$ 46,700
Accrued expenses (operating expenses)	14,000	12,500
Income taxes payable	7,900	8,400
Dividends payable	14,000	10,000
Mortgage note payable, due 2001	40,000	0
Bonds payable	150,000	250,000
Common stock, $30 par	450,000	375,000
Excess of issue price over par—common stock	66,250	41,250
Retained earnings	373,640	349,810
Total liabilities and stockholders' equity	$1,159,290	$1,093,660

The income statement for Dowling Company is shown below.

Dowling Company
Income Statement
For the Year Ended December 31, 2001

Sales		$1,100,000
Cost of merchandise sold		710,000
Gross profit		$ 390,000
Operating expenses:		
Depreciation expense	$ 23,500	
Patent amortization	7,000	
Other operating expenses	196,000	
Total operating expenses		226,500
Income from operations		$ 163,500
Other income:		
Gain on sale of investments	$ 11,000	
Other expense:		
Interest expense	26,000	(15,000)
Income before income tax		$ 148,500
Income tax expense		50,000
Net income		$ 98,500

An examination of the accounting records revealed the following additional information applicable to 2001:

a. Land costing $15,000 was sold for $15,000.
b. A mortgage note was issued for $40,000.
c. A building costing $115,000 was constructed.
d. 2,500 shares of common stock were issued at 40 in exchange for the bonds payable.
e. Cash dividends declared were $74,670.

Instructions

1. Prepare a statement of cash flows, using the indirect method of reporting cash flows from operating activities.
2. Prepare a statement of cash flows, using the direct method of reporting cash flows from operating activities.

Solution

1.

Dowling Company
Statement of Cash Flows—Indirect Method
For the Year Ended December 31, 2001

Cash flows from operating activities:			
Net income, per income statement		$ 98,500	
Add: Depreciation	$ 23,500		
Amortization of patents	7,000		
Decrease in accounts receivable	7,000		
Increase in accrued expenses	1,500	39,000	
		$137,500	
Deduct: Increase in inventories	$ 7,300		
Increase in prepaid expenses	380		
Decrease in accounts payable	3,200		
Decrease in income taxes payable	500		
Gain on sale of investments	11,000	22,380	
Net cash flow from operating activities			$115,120
Cash flows from investing activities:			
Cash received from sale of:			
Investments	$ 60,000		
Land	15,000	$ 75,000	
Less: Cash paid for construction of building		115,000	
Net cash flow used for investing activities			(40,000)
Cash flows from financing activities:			
Cash received from issuing mortgage note payable		$ 40,000	
Less: Cash paid for dividends		70,670	
Net cash flow used for financing activities			(30,670)
Increase in cash			$ 44,450
Cash at the beginning of the year			95,900
Cash at the end of the year			$140,350

Schedule of Noncash Investing and Financing Activities:

Issued common stock to retire bonds payable	$100,000

2.

Dowling Company
Statement of Cash Flows—Direct Method
For the Year Ended December 31, 2001

Cash flows from operating activities:			
Cash received from customers[1]		$1,107,000	
Deduct: Cash paid for merchandise[2]	$720,500		
Cash paid for operating expenses[3]	194,880		
Cash paid for interest expense	26,000		
Cash paid for income tax[4]	50,500	991,880	
Net cash flow from operating activities			$115,120
Cash flows from investing activities:			
Cash received from sale of:			
Investments	$ 60,000		
Land	15,000	$ 75,000	
Less: Cash paid for construction of building		115,000	
Net cash flow used for investing activities			(40,000)
Cash flows from financing activities:			
Cash received from issuing mortgage note payable		$ 40,000	
Less: Cash paid for dividends[5]		70,670	
Net cash flow used for financing activities			(30,670)
Increase in cash			$ 44,450
Cash at the beginning of the year			95,900
Cash at the end of the year			$140,350

Schedule of Noncash Investing and Financing Activities:

Issued common stock to retire bonds payable	$100,000

Computations:

[1]$1,100,000 + $7,000 = $1,107,000
[2]$710,000 + $3,200 + $7,300 = $720,500
[3]$196,000 + $380 − $1,500 = $194,880
[4]$50,000 + $500 = $50,500
[5]$74,670 + $10,000 − $14,000 = $70,670

SELF-EXAMINATION QUESTIONS

Answers at End of Chapter

Matching

Match each of the following statements with its proper term. Some terms may not be used.

A. cash flows from financing activities
B. cash flows from investing activities
C. cash flows from operating activities
D. decrease in accounts payable
E. decrease in accounts receivable
F. direct method

E 1. An addition to sales under the direct method for determining cash flows from operating activities.
L 2. A statement of cash flows disclosure item.
A 3. The section of the statement of cash flows that reports cash flows from transactions affecting the equity and debt of the business.
K 4. A financing activity that increases cash.
I 5. An addition to net income under the indirect method for determining cash flows from operating activities.
B 6. The section of the statement of cash flows that reports cash flows from transactions affecting investments in noncurrent assets.
N 7. A summary of the major cash receipts and cash payments for a period.

G. dividends declared
H. free cash flow
I. loss on sale of land
J. indirect method
K. issuance of common stock
L. purchase of land with common stock
M. sale of land
N. statement of cash flows

___ 8. A deduction from net income under the indirect method for determining cash flows from operating activities.

___ 9. A method of reporting the cash flows from operating activities as the difference between the operating cash receipts and the operating cash payments.

___ 10. The section of the statement of cash flows that reports the cash transactions affecting the determination of net income.

___ 11. A method of reporting the cash flows from operating activities as the net income from operations adjusted for all deferrals of past cash receipts and payments and all accruals of expected future cash receipts and payments.

___ 12. An investing activity.

___ 13. The amount of operating cash flow remaining after replacing current productive capacity and maintaining current dividends.

Multiple Choice

1. An example of a cash flow from an operating activity is:
   A. receipt of cash from the sale of stock
   B. receipt of cash from the sale of bonds
   C. payment of cash for dividends
   D. receipt of cash from customers on account

2. An example of a cash flow from an investing activity is:
   A. receipt of cash from the sale of equipment
   B. receipt of cash from the sale of stock
   C. payment of cash for dividends
   D. payment of cash to acquire treasury stock

3. An example of a cash flow from a financing activity is:
   A. receipt of cash from customers on account
   B. receipt of cash from the sale of equipment
   C. payment of cash for dividends
   D. payment of cash to acquire marketable securities

4. Which of the following methods of reporting cash flows from operating activities adjusts net income for revenues and expenses not involving the receipt or payment of cash?
   A. Direct method
   B. Purchase method
   C. Reciprocal method
   D. Indirect method

5. The net income reported on the income statement for the year was $55,000, and depreciation of fixed assets for the year was $22,000. The balances of the current asset and current liability accounts at the beginning and end of the year are as follows:

	End	Beginning
Cash	$ 65,000	$ 70,000
Accounts receivable	100,000	90,000
Inventories	145,000	150,000
Prepaid expenses	7,500	8,000
Accounts payable (merchandise creditors)	51,000	58,000

The total amount reported for cash flows from operating activities in the statement of cash flows, using the indirect method, is:
   A. $33,000
   B. $55,000
   C. $65,500
   D. $77,000

CLASS DISCUSSION QUESTIONS

1. What is the principal disadvantage of the direct method of reporting cash flows from operating activities?
2. What are the major advantages of the indirect method of reporting cash flows from operating activities?
3. A corporation issued $200,000 of common stock in exchange for $200,000 of fixed assets. Where would this transaction be reported on the statement of cash flows?
4. a. What is the effect on cash flows of declaring and issuing a stock dividend?
   b. Is the stock dividend reported on the statement of cash flows?
5. A retail business, using the accrual method of accounting, owed merchandise creditors (accounts payable) $290,000 at the beginning of the year and $315,000 at the end of the year. How would the $25,000 increase be used to adjust net income in determining the amount of cash flows from operating activities by the indirect method? Explain.

6. If salaries payable was $75,000 at the beginning of the year and $65,000 at the end of the year, should $10,000 be added to or deducted from income to determine the amount of cash flows from operating activities by the indirect method? Explain.
7. A long-term investment in bonds with a cost of $75,000 was sold for $80,000 cash. (a) What was the gain or loss on the sale? (b) What was the effect of the transaction on cash flows? (c) How should the transaction be reported in the statement of cash flows if cash flows from operating activities are reported by the indirect method?
8. A corporation issued $5,000,000 of 20-year bonds for cash at 105. How would the transaction be reported on the statement of cash flows?
9. Fully depreciated equipment costing $55,000 was discarded. What was the effect of the transaction on cash flows if (a) $5,000 cash is received, (b) there is no salvage value?
10. For the current year, Accord Company decided to switch from the indirect method to the direct method for reporting cash flows from operating activities on the statement of cash flows. Will the change cause the amount of net cash flow from operating activities to be (a) larger, (b) smaller, or (c) the same as if the indirect method had been used? Explain.
11. Name five common major classes of operating cash receipts or operating cash payments presented on the statement of cash flows when the cash flows from operating activities are reported by the direct method.
12. In a recent annual report, **PepsiCo, Inc.**, reported that during the year it issued treasury stock and debt of $162.7 million for acquisitions. How would this be reported on the statement of cash flows?

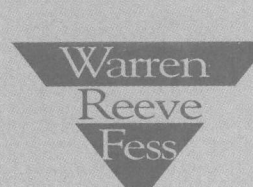

Resources for Your Success On-Line at warren.swcollege.com

Remember! If you need additional help, visit South-Western's Web site. See page 26 for a description of the online and printed materials that are available.

EXERCISES

Exercise 15–1

Cash flows from operating activities—net loss

Objective 2

On its income statement for the current year, Marconi Company reported a net loss of $65,000 from operations. On its statement of cash flows, it reported $20,000 of cash flows from operating activities.

Explain this apparent contradiction between the loss and the positive cash flows.

Exercise 15–2

Effect of transactions on cash flows

Objective 2

✓ c. Cash payment, $501,000

State the effect (cash receipt or payment and amount) of each of the following transactions, considered individually, on cash flows:

a. Paid dividends of $1.50 per share. There were 30,000 shares issued and 5,000 shares of treasury stock.
b. Purchased a building by paying $30,000 cash and issuing a $90,000 mortgage note payable.
c. Retired $500,000 of bonds, on which there was $2,500 of unamortized discount, for $501,000.
d. Purchased land for $120,000 cash.
e. Sold a new issue of $100,000 of bonds at 101.
f. Purchased 5,000 shares of $30 par common stock as treasury stock at $50 per share.
g. Sold 5,000 shares of $30 par common stock for $45 per share.
h. Sold equipment with a book value of $42,500 for $41,000.

Exercise 15–3
Classifying cash flows

Objective 2

Identify the type of cash flow activity for each of the following events (operating, investing, or financing):

a. Paid cash dividends.
b. Sold long-term investments.
c. Issued bonds.
d. Issued common stock.
e. Sold equipment.
f. Net income.
g. Issued preferred stock.
h. Redeemed bonds.
i. Purchased patents.
j. Purchased treasury stock.
k. Purchased buildings.

Exercise 15–4
Cash flows from operating activities—indirect method

Objective 3

Indicate whether each of the following would be added to or deducted from net income in determining net cash flow from operating activities by the indirect method:

a. Decrease in accounts receivable
b. Amortization of patent
c. Depreciation of fixed assets
d. Decrease in salaries payable
e. Decrease in accounts payable
f. Loss on disposal of fixed assets
g. Increase in notes payable due in 90 days
h. Amortization of goodwill
i. Increase in notes receivable due in 90 days
j. Decrease in prepaid expenses
k. Increase in merchandise inventory
l. Gain on retirement of long-term debt

Exercise 15–5
Cash flows from operating activities—indirect method

Objectives 2, 3

✓ a. Cash flows from operating activities, $153,850

The net income reported on the income statement for the current year was $134,800. Depreciation recorded on equipment and a building amounted to $27,400 for the year. Balances of the current asset and current liability accounts at the beginning and end of the year are as follows:

	End of Year	Beginning of Year
Cash	$ 23,500	$37,400
Accounts receivable (net)	84,500	80,350
Inventories	100,200	94,300
Prepaid expenses	4,970	5,300
Accounts payable (merchandise creditors)	71,400	68,900
Salaries payable	5,320	6,450

a. Prepare the cash flows from operating activities section of the statement of cash flows, using the indirect method.
b. If the direct method had been used, would the net cash flow from operating activities have been the same? Explain.

Exercise 15–6
Cash flows from operating activities—indirect method

Objective 3

SPREADSHEET

✓ Cash flows from operating activities, $537,800

The net income reported on the income statement for the current year was $465,000. Depreciation recorded on store equipment for the year amounted to $96,800. Balances of the current asset and current liability accounts at the beginning and end of the year are as follows:

	End of Year	Beginning of Year
Cash	$345,000	$386,000
Accounts receivable (net)	554,300	567,800
Merchandise inventory	693,000	672,400
Prepaid expenses	27,000	24,000
Accounts payable (merchandise creditors)	510,000	527,400
Wages payable	39,500	36,000

Prepare the cash flows from operating activities section of a statement of cash flows, using the indirect method.

Exercise 15–7
Determining cash payments to stockholders
Objective 3

The board of directors declared cash dividends totaling $240,000 during the current year. The comparative balance sheet indicates dividends payable of $50,000 at the beginning of the year and $60,000 at the end of the year. What was the amount of cash payments to stockholders during the year?

Exercise 15–8
Reporting changes in equipment on statement of cash flows
Objective 3

An analysis of the general ledger accounts indicates that office equipment, which had cost $245,000 and on which accumulated depreciation totaled $95,000 on the date of sale, was sold for $130,000 during the year. Using this information, indicate the items to be reported on the statement of cash flows.

Exercise 15–9
Reporting changes in equipment on statement of cash flows
Objective 3

An analysis of the general ledger accounts indicates that delivery equipment, which had cost $39,000 and on which accumulated depreciation totaled $23,000 on the date of sale, was sold for $20,000 during the year. Using this information, indicate the items to be reported on the statement of cash flows.

Exercise 15–10
Reporting land transactions on statement of cash flows
Objective 3

On the basis of the details of the following fixed asset account, indicate the items to be reported on the statement of cash flows:

ACCOUNT *Land* **ACCOUNT NO.**

Date		Item	Debit	Credit	Balance Debit	Balance Credit
2000						
Jan.	1	Balance			400,000	
Feb.	5	Purchased for cash	250,000		650,000	
Oct.	30	Sold for $95,000		80,000	570,000	

Exercise 15–11
Reporting stockholders' equity items on statement of cash flows
Objective 3

On the basis of the following stockholders' equity accounts, indicate the items, exclusive of net income, to be reported on the statement of cash flows. There were no unpaid dividends at either the beginning or the end of the year.

ACCOUNT *Common Stock, $10 Par* **ACCOUNT NO.**

Date		Item	Debit	Credit	Balance Debit	Balance Credit
2000						
Jan.	1	Balance, 50,000 shares				500,000
Feb.	11	5,000 shares issued for cash		50,000		550,000
June	30	2,750-share stock dividend		27,500		577,500

ACCOUNT *Paid-In Capital in Excess of Par—Common Stock* **ACCOUNT NO.**

Date		Item	Debit	Credit	Balance Debit	Balance Credit
2000						
Jan.	1	Balance				90,000
Feb.	11	5,000 shares issued for cash		200,000		290,000
June	30	Stock dividend		137,500		427,500

ACCOUNT *Retained Earnings* **ACCOUNT NO.**

Date		Item	Debit	Credit	Balance Debit	Balance Credit
2000						
Jan.	1	Balance				475,000
June	30	Stock dividend	165,000			310,000
Dec.	30	Cash dividend	200,000			110,000
	31	Net income		500,000		610,000

Exercise 15–12
Reporting land acquisition for cash and mortgage note on statement of cash flows

Objective 3

On the basis of the details of the following fixed asset account, indicate the items to be reported on the statement of cash flows:

ACCOUNT *Land* **ACCOUNT NO.**

Date		Item	Debit	Credit	Balance	
					Debit	Credit
2000						
Jan.	1	Balance			450,000	
Feb.	10	Purchased for cash	125,000		575,000	
Nov.	20	Purchased with long-term mortgage note	200,000		775,000	

Exercise 15–13
Determining net income from net cash flow from operating activities

Objective 3

✓ Net income, $89,150

Tiger Golf Inc. reported a net cash flow from operating activities of $102,500 on its statement of cash flows for the year ended December 31, 2000. The following information was reported in the cash flows from operating activities section of the statement of cash flows, using the indirect method:

Decrease in income taxes payable	$ 1,400
Decrease in inventories	6,200
Depreciation	15,400
Gain on sale of investments	9,450
Increase in accounts payable	9,100
Increase in prepaid expenses	1,000
Increase in accounts receivable	5,500

Determine the net income reported by Tiger Golf Inc. for the year ended December 31, 2000.

Exercise 15–14
Cash flows from operating activities

Objective 3

REAL WORLD

✓ Cash flows from operating activities, $743,400

Selected data from the income statement and statement of cash flows of **Toys "R" Us, Inc.**, for the year ending February 1, 1997, are as follows:

Income Statement Data (dollars in thousands)

Net earnings	$427,400
Depreciation and amortization	206,400
Deferred portion of current period tax expense (noncash expense)	23,400

Statement of Cash Flows Data (dollars in thousands)

Increase in accounts receivable	$ 14,300
Increase in merchandise inventories	194,600
Increase in prepaid expenses and other operating assets	10,100
Increase in accounts payable, accrued expenses, and taxes	261,400
Increase in income tax payable	43,800

Prepare the cash flows from operating activities section of the statement of cash flows (using the indirect method) for Toys "R" Us, Inc., for the year ending February 1, 1997.

Exercise 15–15
Cash flows from operating activities—direct method

Objective 4

✓ a. $865,000

The cash flows from operating activities are reported by the direct method on the statement of cash flows. Determine the following:

a. If sales for the current year were $820,000 and accounts receivable decreased by $45,000 during the year, what was the amount of cash received from customers?

b. If income tax expense for the current year was $64,000 and income tax payable decreased by $6,000 during the year, what was the amount of cash payments for income tax?

Exercise 15–16

Determining selected amounts for cash flows from operating activities—direct method

Objective 4

✓ b. $311,700

Selected data taken from the accounting records of Hi Gain Electronics Company for the current year ended December 31 are as follows:

	Balance January 1	Balance December 31
Accrued expenses (operating expenses)	$ 14,300	$11,100
Accounts payable (merchandise creditors)	112,000	90,000
Inventories	83,400	76,500
Prepaid expenses	21,000	19,500

During the current year, the cost of merchandise sold was $870,000 and the operating expenses other than depreciation were $310,000. The direct method is used for presenting the cash flows from operating activities on the statement of cash flows.

Determine the amount reported on the statement of cash flows for (a) cash payments for merchandise and (b) cash payments for operating expenses.

Exercise 15–17

Cash flows from operating activities—direct method

Objective 4

✓ Cash flows from operating activities, $101,800

The income statement of Tru-Blu Greeting Card Company for the current year ended June 30 is as follows:

Sales		$865,000
Cost of merchandise sold		525,000
Gross profit		$340,000
Operating expenses:		
Depreciation expense	$ 45,000	
Other operating expenses	210,400	
Total operating expenses		255,400
Income before income tax		$ 84,600
Income tax expense		35,000
Net income		$ 49,600

Changes in the balances of selected accounts from the beginning to the end of the current year are as follows:

	Increase Decrease*
Accounts receivable (net)	$27,000*
Inventories	11,200
Prepaid expenses	2,400*
Accounts payable (merchandise creditors)	18,300*
Accrued expenses (operating expenses)	10,700
Income tax payable	3,400*

Prepare the cash flows from operating activities section of the statement of cash flows, using the direct method.

Exercise 15–18

Cash flows from operating activities—direct method

Objective 4

✓ Cash flows from operating activities, $75,450

The income statement for Wholly Donut Company for the current year ended June 30 and balances of selected accounts at the beginning and the end of the year are as follows:

Sales		$683,000
Cost of merchandise sold		395,700
Gross profit		$287,300
Operating expenses:		
Depreciation expense	$ 49,500	
Other operating expenses	172,600	
Total operating expenses		222,100
Income before income tax		$ 65,200
Income tax expense		28,600
Net income		$ 36,600

	End of Year	Beginning of Year
Accounts receivable (net)	$85,000	$82,000
Inventories	98,600	85,000
Prepaid expenses	6,100	8,150
Accounts payable (merchandise creditors)	76,600	71,100
Accrued expenses (operating expenses)	4,250	5,850
Income tax payable	1,600	1,600

Prepare the cash flows from operating activities section of the statement of cash flows, using the direct method.

Exercise 15–19
Statement of cash flows
Objective 3

What's Wrong WITH THIS?

List the errors you find in the following statement of cash flows. The cash balance at the beginning of the year was $70,700. All other figures are correct.

Monarch Games Inc.
Statement of Cash Flows
For the Year Ended December 31, 2000

Cash flows from operating activities:			
Net income, per income statement		$100,500	
Add: Depreciation	$ 49,000		
Increase in accounts receivable	9,500		
Gain on sale of investments	5,000	63,500	
		$164,000	
Deduct: Increase in accounts payable	$ 4,400		
Increase in inventories	18,300		
Decrease in accrued expenses	1,600	24,300	
Net cash flow from operating activities			$139,700
Cash flows from investing activities:			
Cash received from sale of investments		$ 85,000	
Less: Cash paid for purchase of land	$ 90,000		
Cash paid for purchase of equipment	150,100	240,100	
Net cash flow used for investing activities			(155,100)
Cash flows from financing activities:			
Cash received from sale of common stock		$107,000	
Cash paid for dividends		36,800	
Net cash flow provided by financing activities			143,800
Increase in cash			$128,400
Cash at the end of the year			105,300
Cash at the beginning of the year			$233,700

Exercise 15–20
Free cash flow
Objective 5

REAL WORLD

The financial statements for **Hershey Foods Corporation** are presented in Appendix G at the end of the text.

a. Determine the free cash flow for 1995 and 1996 from the statements of cash flows. Assume that 80% of the capital additions for each year are used to maintain productive capacity and that the remaining 20% adds to productive capacity.
b. What conclusions can you draw from your analysis?

PROBLEMS SERIES A

Problem 15–1A
Statement of cash flows—indirect method
Objective 3

The comparative balance sheet of Idaho Al's Golf Shops Co. for December 31, 2000 and 1999, is as follows:

HAT

✓ Net cash flow from operating activities, $72,800

	Dec. 31, 2000	Dec. 31, 1999
Assets		
Cash	$ 86,400	$ 51,600
Accounts receivable (net)	132,400	112,600
Inventories	153,400	141,300
Investments	0	115,000
Land	85,000	0
Equipment	785,000	635,000
Accumulated depreciation—equipment	(265,000)	(211,500)
	$977,200	$844,000
Liabilities and Stockholders' Equity		
Accounts payable (merchandise creditors)	$ 85,000	$ 70,600
Accrued expenses (operating expenses)	4,700	6,700
Dividends payable	20,000	15,000
Common stock, $10 par	60,000	40,000
Paid-in capital in excess of par—common stock	220,000	100,000
Retained earnings	587,500	611,700
	$977,200	$844,000

The following additional information was taken from the records:

a. The investments were sold for $132,000 cash.
b. Equipment and land were acquired for cash.
c. There were no disposals of equipment during the year.
d. The common stock was issued for cash.
e. There was a $55,800 credit to Retained Earnings for net income.
f. There was an $80,000 debit to Retained Earnings for cash dividends declared.

Instructions

Prepare a statement of cash flows, using the indirect method of presenting cash flows from operating activities.

Problem 15–2A

Statement of cash flows—indirect method

Objective 3

SPREADSHEET

✓ Net cash flow from operating activities, $315,400

The comparative balance sheet of Endless Summer Apparel Inc. at December 31, 2000 and 1999, is as follows:

	Dec. 31, 2000	Dec. 31, 1999
Assets		
Cash	$ 209,500	$ 290,500
Accounts receivable (net)	687,200	765,300
Merchandise inventory	604,100	587,900
Prepaid expenses	14,500	12,000
Equipment	990,000	900,000
Accumulated depreciation—equipment	(315,400)	(365,800)
	$2,189,900	$2,189,900
Liabilities and Stockholders' Equity		
Accounts payable (merchandise creditors)	$ 514,500	$ 465,800
Mortgage note payable	0	220,000
Common stock, $10 par	100,000	70,000
Paid-in capital in excess of par—common stock	810,000	720,000
Retained earnings	765,400	714,100
	$2,189,900	$2,189,900

Additional data obtained from the income statement and from an examination of the accounts in the ledger are as follows:

a. Net income, $111,300.
b. Depreciation reported on the income statement, $96,000.

c. Equipment was purchased at a cost of $236,400, and fully depreciated equipment costing $146,400 was discarded, with no salvage realized.
d. The mortgage note payable was not due until 2003, but the terms permitted earlier payment without penalty.
e. 3,000 shares of common stock were issued at $40 for cash.
f. Cash dividends declared and paid, $60,000.

Instructions

Prepare a statement of cash flows, using the indirect method of presenting cash flows from operating activities.

Problem 15–3A

Statement of cash flows—indirect method

Objective 3

HAT

✓ Net cash flow from operating activities, ($166,000)

The comparative balance sheet of Gates Lumber Company at December 31, 2000 and 1999, is as follows:

	Dec. 31, 2000	Dec. 31, 1999
Assets		
Cash	$ 194,700	$ 211,600
Accounts receivable (net)	347,800	325,700
Inventories	402,100	387,500
Prepaid expenses	6,200	8,000
Land	70,000	100,000
Buildings	525,000	400,000
Accumulated depreciation—buildings	(172,500)	(150,000)
Equipment	167,900	157,000
Accumulated depreciation—equipment	(39,000)	(42,000)
	$1,502,200	$1,397,800
Liabilities and Stockholders' Equity		
Accounts payable (merchandise creditors)	$ 347,900	$ 356,800
Income tax payable	12,400	6,800
Bonds payable	90,000	0
Common stock, $1 par	60,000	50,000
Paid-in capital in excess of par—common stock	400,000	200,000
Retained earnings	591,900	784,200
	$1,502,200	$1,397,800

The noncurrent asset, the noncurrent liability, and the stockholders' equity accounts for 2000 are as follows:

ACCOUNT *Land* **ACCOUNT NO.**

Date		Item	Debit	Credit	Balance Debit	Balance Credit
2000						
Jan.	1	Balance			100,000	
April	20	Realized $45,000 cash from sale		30,000	70,000	

ACCOUNT *Buildings* **ACCOUNT NO.**

Date		Item	Debit	Credit	Balance Debit	Balance Credit
2000						
Jan.	1	Balance			400,000	
April	20	Acquired for cash	125,000		525,000	

ACCOUNT *Accumulated Depreciation—Buildings* **ACCOUNT NO.**

Date		Item	Debit	Credit	Balance Debit	Balance Credit
2000						
Jan.	1	Balance				150,000
Dec.	31	Depreciation for year		22,500		172,500

ACCOUNT ***Equipment*** **ACCOUNT NO.**

Date		Item	Debit	Credit	Balance Debit	Balance Credit
2000						
Jan.	1	Balance			157,000	
	26	Discarded, no salvage		40,000	117,000	
Aug.	11	Purchased for cash	50,900		167,900	

ACCOUNT ***Accumulated Depreciation—Equipment*** **ACCOUNT NO.**

Date		Item	Debit	Credit	Balance Debit	Balance Credit
2000						
Jan.	1	Balance				42,000
	26	Equipment discarded	40,000			2,000
Dec.	31	Depreciation for year		37,000		39,000

ACCOUNT ***Bonds Payable*** **ACCOUNT NO.**

Date		Item	Debit	Credit	Balance Debit	Balance Credit
2000						
May	1	Issued 20-year bonds		90,000		90,000

ACCOUNT ***Common Stock, $1 Par*** **ACCOUNT NO.**

Date		Item	Debit	Credit	Balance Debit	Balance Credit
2000						
Jan.	1	Balance				50,000
Dec.	7	Issued 10,000 shares of common stock for $21 per share		10,000		60,000

ACCOUNT ***Paid-In Capital in Excess of Par—Common Stock*** **ACCOUNT NO.**

Date		Item	Debit	Credit	Balance Debit	Balance Credit
2000						
Jan.	1	Balance				200,000
Dec.	7	Issued 10,000 shares of common stock for $21 per share		200,000		400,000

ACCOUNT ***Retained Earnings*** **ACCOUNT NO.**

Date		Item	Debit	Credit	Balance Debit	Balance Credit
2000						
Jan.	1	Balance				784,200
Dec.	31	Net loss	172,300			611,900
	31	Cash dividends	20,000			591,900

Instructions

Prepare a statement of cash flows, using the indirect method of presenting cash flows from operating activities.

Problem 15–4A

Statement of cash flows—direct method

Objective 4

SPREADSHEET GENERAL LEDGER

✓ Net cash flow from operating activities, $67,800

The comparative balance sheet of Corning Plumbing Supply Company for December 31, 2001 and 2000, is as follows:

	Dec. 31, 2001	Dec. 31, 2000
Assets		
Cash	$ 69,200	$ 76,500
Accounts receivable (net)	135,700	132,400
Inventories	223,800	201,400
Investments	—	45,000
Land	74,000	—
Equipment	340,000	250,000
Accumulated depreciation	(79,300)	(66,800)
	$763,400	$638,500

Liabilities and Stockholders' Equity		
Accounts payable (merchandise creditors)	$194,300	$187,400
Accrued expenses (operating expenses)	5,000	6,400
Dividends payable	3,800	3,000
Common stock, $1 par	14,000	10,000
Paid-in capital in excess of par—common stock	138,000	90,000
Retained earnings	408,300	341,700
	$763,400	$638,500

The income statement for the year ended December 31, 2001, is as follows:

Sales		$867,000
Cost of merchandise sold		553,000
Gross profit		$314,000
Operating expenses:		
Depreciation expense	$ 12,500	
Other operating expenses	198,000	
Total operating expenses		210,500
Operating income		$103,500
Other income:		
Gain on sale of investments		9,000
Income before income tax		$112,500
Income tax expense		28,000
Net income		$ 84,500

The following additional information was taken from the records:

a. Equipment and land were acquired for cash.
b. There were no disposals of equipment during the year.
c. The investments were sold for $54,000 cash.
d. The common stock was issued for cash.
e. There was a $17,900 debit to Retained Earnings for cash dividends declared.

Instructions

Prepare a statement of cash flows, using the direct method of presenting cash flows from operating activities.

Problem 15–5A

Statement of cash flows—direct method applied to Problem 15–1A

Objective 4

HAT

✓ Net cash flow from operating activities, $72,800

The comparative balance sheet of Idaho Al's Golf Shops Co. for December 31, 2000 and 1999, is as follows:

	Dec. 31, 2000	Dec. 31, 1999
Assets		
Cash	$ 86,400	$ 51,600
Accounts receivable (net)	132,400	112,600
Inventories	153,400	141,300
Investments	0	115,000
Land	85,000	0
Equipment	785,000	635,000
Accumulated depreciation—equipment	(265,000)	(211,500)
	$977,200	$844,000
Liabilities and Stockholders' Equity		
Accounts payable (merchandise creditors)	$ 85,000	$ 70,600
Accrued expenses (operating expenses)	4,700	6,700
Dividends payable	20,000	15,000
Common stock, $10 par	60,000	40,000
Paid-in capital in excess of par—common stock	220,000	100,000
Retained earnings	587,500	611,700
	$977,200	$844,000

The income statement for the year ended December 31, 2000, is as follows:

Sales		$693,200
Cost of merchandise sold		394,500
Gross profit		$298,700
Operating expenses:		
Depreciation expense	$ 53,500	
Other operating expenses	172,900	
Total operating expenses		226,400
Operating income		$ 72,300
Other income:		
Gain on sale of investments		17,000
Income before income tax		$ 89,300
Income tax expense		33,500
Net income		$ 55,800

The following additional information was taken from the records:

a. The investments were sold for $132,000 cash.
b. Equipment and land were acquired for cash.
c. There were no disposals of equipment during the year.
d. The common stock was issued for cash.
e. There was an $80,000 debit to Retained Earnings for cash dividends declared.

Instructions

Prepare a statement of cash flows, using the direct method of presenting cash flows from operating activities.

PROBLEMS SERIES B

Problem 15–1B

Statement of cash flows—indirect method

Objective 3

✓ Net cash flow from operating activities, $95,500

The comparative balance sheet of Mother Nature Health Foods Inc. for June 30, 2000 and 1999, is as follows:

	June 30, 2000	June 30, 1999
Assets		
Cash	$ 93,400	$ 57,800
Accounts receivable (net)	125,000	123,500
Inventories	146,500	108,900
Investments	0	65,000
Land	145,000	0
Equipment	367,600	278,600
Accumulated depreciation	(110,900)	(87,400)
	$766,600	$546,400
Liabilities and Stockholders' Equity		
Accounts payable (merchandise creditors)	$ 82,400	$ 74,000
Accrued expenses (operating expenses)	6,700	6,000
Dividends payable	18,400	15,700
Common stock, $10 par	100,000	70,000
Paid-in capital in excess of par—common stock	320,000	200,000
Retained earnings	239,100	180,700
	$766,600	$546,400

The following additional information was taken from the records of Mother Nature Health Foods Inc.:

a. Equipment and land were acquired for cash.
b. There were no disposals of equipment during the year.
c. The investments were sold for $95,000 cash.
d. The common stock was issued for cash.
e. There was a $132,000 credit to Retained Earnings for net income.
f. There was a $73,600 debit to Retained Earnings for cash dividends declared.

Instructions

Prepare a statement of cash flows, using the indirect method of presenting cash flows from operating activities.

Problem 15–2B

Statement of cash flows—indirect method

Objective 3

SPREADSHEET

✓ Net cash flow from operating activities, $129,600

The comparative balance sheet of Bon Voyage Luggage Company at December 31, 2000 and 1999, is as follows:

	Dec. 31, 2000	Dec. 31, 1999
Assets		
Cash	$ 184,200	$ 124,600
Accounts receivable (net)	202,800	148,700
Inventories	250,500	275,000
Prepaid expenses	5,400	4,500
Land	85,000	85,000
Buildings	575,000	465,000
Accumulated depreciation—buildings	(192,000)	(168,000)
Machinery and equipment	345,800	345,800
Accumulated depreciation—machinery & equipment	(134,000)	(99,000)
Patents	39,500	45,000
	$1,362,200	$1,226,600
Liabilities and Stockholders' Equity		
Accounts payable (merchandise creditors)	$ 114,500	$ 132,400
Dividends payable	14,500	12,000
Salaries payable	8,900	10,900
Mortgage note payable, due 2001	65,000	—
Bonds payable	—	105,000
Common stock, $1 par	25,000	20,000
Paid-in capital in excess of par—common stock	150,000	50,000
Retained earnings	984,300	896,300
	$1,362,200	$1,226,600

An examination of the income statement and the accounting records revealed the following additional information applicable to 2000:

a. Net income, $115,500.
b. Depreciation expense reported on the income statement: buildings, $24,000; machinery and equipment, $35,000.
c. Patent amortization reported on the income statement, $5,500.
d. A building was constructed for $110,000.
e. A mortgage note for $65,000 was issued for cash.
f. 5,000 shares of common stock were issued at $21 in exchange for the bonds payable.
g. Cash dividends declared, $27,500.

Instructions

Prepare a statement of cash flows, using the indirect method of presenting cash flows from operating activities.

Problem 15–3B

Statement of cash flows—indirect method

Objective 3

The comparative balance sheet of Apple Supply Inc. at December 31, 2000 and 1999, is as follows:

✓ Net cash flow from operating activities, ($41,600)

	Dec. 31, 2000	Dec. 31, 1999
Assets		
Cash	$ 74,800	$ 99,400
Accounts receivable (net)	136,700	125,300
Inventories	301,200	267,800
Prepaid expenses	5,000	5,500
Land	50,000	75,000
Buildings	285,000	175,000
Accumulated depreciation—buildings	(74,700)	(65,200)
Equipment	259,500	239,500
Accumulated depreciation—equipment	(100,100)	(105,700)
	$937,400	$816,600
Liabilities and Stockholders' Equity		
Accounts payable (merchandise creditors)	$174,800	$185,400
Income tax payable	5,800	4,500
Bonds payable	40,000	—
Common stock, $1 par	35,000	30,000
Paid-in capital in excess of par—common stock	400,000	300,000
Retained earnings	281,800	296,700
	$937,400	$816,600

The noncurrent asset, the noncurrent liability, and the stockholders' equity accounts for 2000 are as follows:

ACCOUNT *Land* **ACCOUNT NO.**

Date		Item	Debit	Credit	Balance Debit	Balance Credit
2000						
Jan.	1	Balance			75,000	
April	20	Realized $32,000 cash from sale		25,000	50,000	

ACCOUNT *Buildings* **ACCOUNT NO.**

Date		Item	Debit	Credit	Balance Debit	Balance Credit
2000						
Jan.	1	Balance			175,000	
April	20	Acquired for cash	110,000		285,000	

ACCOUNT *Accumulated Depreciation—Buildings* **ACCOUNT NO.**

Date		Item	Debit	Credit	Balance Debit	Balance Credit
2000						
Jan.	1	Balance				65,200
Dec.	31	Depreciation for year		9,500		74,700

ACCOUNT *Equipment* **ACCOUNT NO.**

Date		Item	Debit	Credit	Balance Debit	Balance Credit
2000						
Jan.	1	Balance			239,500	
	26	Discarded, no salvage		25,000	214,500	
Aug.	11	Purchased for cash	45,000		259,500	

ACCOUNT *Accumulated Depreciation—Equipment* **ACCOUNT NO.**

Date		Item	Debit	Credit	Balance Debit	Balance Credit
2000						
Jan.	1	Balance				105,700
	26	Equipment discarded	25,000			80,700
Dec.	31	Depreciation for year		19,400		100,100

ACCOUNT *Bonds Payable* **ACCOUNT NO.**

Date		Item	Debit	Credit	Balance Debit	Balance Credit
2000						
May	1	Issued 20-year bonds		40,000		40,000

ACCOUNT ***Common Stock, $1 Par*** **ACCOUNT NO.**

Date		Item	Debit	Credit	Balance Debit	Balance Credit
2000						
Jan.	1	Balance				30,000
Dec.	7	Issued 5000 shares of common stock for $21 per share		5,000		35,000

ACCOUNT ***Paid-In Capital in Excess of Par—Common Stock*** **ACCOUNT NO.**

Date		Item	Debit	Credit	Balance Debit	Balance Credit
2000						
Jan.	1	Balance				300,000
Dec.	7	Issued 5000 shares of common stock for $21 per share		100,000		400,000

ACCOUNT ***Retained Earnings*** **ACCOUNT NO.**

Date		Item	Debit	Credit	Balance Debit	Balance Credit
2000						
Jan.	1	Balance				296,700
Dec.	31	Net loss	9,900			286,800
	31	Cash dividends	5,000			281,800

Instructions

Prepare a statement of cash flows, using the indirect method of presenting cash flows from operating activities.

Problem 15–4B

Statement of cash flows—direct method

Objective 4

GENERAL LEDGER SPREADSHEET

✓ Net cash flow from operating activities, $127,500

The comparative balance sheet of Green Thumb Nursery Inc. for December 31, 2000 and 2001, is as follows:

	Dec. 31, 2001	Dec. 31, 2000
Assets		
Cash	$ 136,700	$147,300
Accounts receivable (net)	220,000	210,500
Inventories	276,200	254,700
Investments	—	60,000
Land	95,000	—
Equipment	575,000	450,000
Accumulated depreciation	(176,500)	(134,000)
	$1,126,400	$988,500
Liabilities and Stockholders' Equity		
Accounts payable (merchandise creditors)	$ 58,400	$ 55,000
Accrued expenses (operating expenses)	7,100	8,000
Dividends payable	16,000	14,500
Common stock, $1 par	30,000	25,000
Paid-in capital in excess of par—common stock	510,000	400,000
Retained earnings	504,900	486,000
	$1,126,400	$988,500

The income statement for the year ended December 31, 2001, is as follows:

Sales		$1,430,000
Cost of merchandise sold		845,000
Gross profit		$ 585,000
Operating expenses:		
Depreciation expense	$ 42,500	
Other operating expenses	345,000	
Total operating expenses		387,500
Operating income		$ 197,500
Other income:		
Gain on sale of investments		15,000
Income before income tax		$ 212,500
Income tax expense		84,000
Net income		$ 128,500

The following additional information was taken from the records:

a. Equipment and land were acquired for cash.
b. There were no disposals of equipment during the year.
c. The investments were sold for $75,000 cash.
d. The common stock was issued for cash.
e. There was a $109,600 debit to Retained Earnings for cash dividends declared.

Instructions
Prepare a statement of cash flows, using the direct method of presenting cash flows from operating activities.

Problem 15–5B
Statement of cash flows—direct method applied to Problem 15–1B
Objective 4

✓ Net cash flow from operating activities, $95,500

The comparative balance sheet of Mother Nature Health Foods Inc. for June 30, 2000 and 1999, is as follows:

	June 30, 2000	June 30, 1999
Assets		
Cash	$ 93,400	$ 57,800
Accounts receivable (net)	125,000	123,500
Inventories	146,500	108,900
Investments	0	65,000
Land	145,000	0
Equipment	367,600	278,600
Accumulated depreciation	(110,900)	(87,400)
	$766,600	$546,400
Liabilities and Stockholders' Equity		
Accounts payable (merchandise creditors)	$ 82,400	$ 74,000
Accrued expenses (operating expenses)	6,700	6,000
Dividends payable	18,400	15,700
Common stock, $10 par	100,000	70,000
Paid-in capital in excess of par—common stock	320,000	200,000
Retained earnings	239,100	180,700
	$766,600	$546,400

The income statement for the year ended June 30, 2000, is as follows:

Sales		$724,700
Cost of merchandise sold		423,100
Gross profit		$301,600
Operating expenses:		
Depreciation expense	$ 23,500	
Other operating expenses	102,900	
Total operating expenses		126,400
Operating income		$175,200
Other income:		
Gain on sale of investments		30,000
Income before income tax		$205,200
Income tax expense		73,200
Net income		$132,000

The following additional information was taken from the records:

a. Equipment and land were acquired for cash.
b. There were no disposals of equipment during the year.
c. The investments were sold for $95,000 cash.
d. The common stock was issued for cash.
e. There was a $73,600 debit to Retained Earnings for cash dividends declared.

Instructions
Prepare a statement of cash flows, using the direct method of presenting cash flows from operating activities.

SPECIAL ACTIVITIES

Activity 15–1 Elite Fashions Inc.
Ethics and professional conduct in business

Carl Allsop, president of Elite Fashions Inc., believes that reporting operating cash flow per share on the income statement would be a useful addition to the company's just completed financial statements. The following discussion took place between Carl Allsop and Elite Fashion's controller, Kim Lee, in January, after the close of the fiscal year.

Carl: I have been reviewing our financial statements for the last year. I am disappointed that our net income per share has dropped by 10% from last year. This is not going to look good to our shareholders. Isn't there anything we can do about this?

Kim: What do you mean? The past is the past, and the numbers are in. There isn't much that can be done about it. Our financial statements were prepared according to generally accepted accounting principles, and I don't see much leeway for significant change at this point.

Carl: No, no. I'm not suggesting that we "cook the books." But look at the cash flow from operations on the statement of cash flows. The cash flow from operations has increased by 20%. This is very good news—and, I might add, useful information. The higher cash flow from operations will give our creditors comfort.

Kim: Well, the cash flow from operations is on the statement of cash flows, so I guess users will be able to see the improved cash flow figures there.

Carl: This is true, but somehow I feel that this information should be given a much higher profile. I don't like this information being "buried" in the statement of cash flows. You know as well as I do that many users will focus on the income statement. Therefore, I think we ought to include an operating cash flow per share number on the face of the income statement—someplace under the earnings per share number. In this way users will get the complete picture of our operating performance. Yes, our earnings per share dropped this year, but our cash flow from operations improved! And all the information is in one place where users can see and compare the figures. What do you think?

Kim: I've never really thought about it like that before. I guess we could put the operating cash flow per share on the income statement, under the earnings per share. Users would really benefit from this disclosure. Thanks for the idea—I'll start working on it.

Carl: Glad to be of service.

How would you interpret this situation? Is Kim behaving in an ethical and professional manner?

Activity 15–2 DiscArcade Inc.
Using the statement of cash flows

What do you THINK?

You are considering an investment in a new start-up software company, DiscArcade Inc. A review of the company's financial statements reveals a negative retained earnings. In addition, it appears as though the company has been running a negative cash flow from operations since the company's inception.

How is the company staying in business under these circumstances? Could this be a good investment?

Activity 15–3 Books and More Company
Analysis of cash flow from operations

The Retailing Division of Books and More Company provided the following information on its cash flow from operations:

Net income	$ 450,000
Increase in accounts receivable	(340,000)
Increase in inventory	(300,000)
Decrease in accounts payable	(90,000)
Depreciation	100,000
Cash flow from operations	$(180,000)

The manager of the Retailing Division provided the accompanying memo with this report:

From: Senior Vice President, Retailing Division

I am pleased to report that we had earnings of $450,000 over the last period. This resulted in a return on invested capital of 10%, which is near our targets for this division. I have been aggressive in building the revenue volume in the division. As a result, I am happy to report that we have increased the number of new credit card customers as a result of an aggressive marketing campaign. In addition, we have found some excellent merchandise opportunities. Some of our suppliers have made some of their apparel merchandise available at a deep discount. We have purchased as much of these goods as possible in order to improve profitability. I'm also happy to report that our vendor payment problems have improved. We are nearly caught up on our overdue payables balances.

Comment on the senior vice president's memo in light of the cash flow information.

Activity 15–4 Into the Real World

Statement of cash flows

The activity will require two teams to retrieve statement of cash flow information from the Internet. One team is to obtain the the most recent year's statement of cash flows for **Intel Corporation**, and the other team the most recent year's statement of cash flows for **America Online (AOL)**.

The statement of cash flows is part of the annual report information that is a required disclosure to the Securities Exchange Commission (SEC). The SEC, in turn, provides this information on the Internet through its EDGAR (Electronic Data Gathering, Analysis, and Retrieval) service. The Edgar address is **www.sec.gov/edgarhp.htm.**

To obtain annual report information, type in a company name on the "Search EDGAR archives" form. EDGAR will list the reports available for the selected company. A company's annual report (along with much more information) is provided in its annual 10-K report to the SEC. Click on the 10-K (or 10-K405) report for the year you wish to download. If you wish, you can save the whole 10-K report to a file, then open it with your word processor.

As a group, compare the two statements of cash flows. How are Intel and America Online similar or different regarding cash flows?

Activity 15–5 Chrysler Corporation

Analysis of statement of cash flows

The following is the statement of cash flows for **Chrysler Corporation** for the years ended December 31, 1996, 1995, and 1994.

Chrysler Corporation
Statement of Cash Flows (000s)
For the Years Ended December 31, 1996, 1995, and 1994

	1996	1995	1994
Operations:			
Net income	3,529	2,025	3,713
Depreciation	2,312	2,220	1,955
Other adjustments	1,460	2,709	1,125
Cash flows from operations	7,301	6,954	6,793
Investing activities:			
Purchases of marketable securities	(4,346)	(5,160)	(5,425)
Sales and maturities of marketable securities	5,294	6,122	3,519
Finance receivables acquired	(19,906)	(24,437)	(20,149)
Finance receivables collected	3,062	3,795	5,772
Proceeds from sales of finance receivables	16,809	17,602	13,138
Expenditures for property, equipment, and tools	(4,635)	(3,646)	(3,843)
Other	155	(187)	30
Total	(3,567)	(5,911)	(6,958)
Financing activities:			
Change in short-term debt	410	(1,971)	1,348
Proceeds under long-term borrowings and revolving lines of credit	1,390	4,731	1,305
Payments on long-term borrowings and revolving lines of credit	(2,167)	(1,687)	(1,011)
Payment for early extinguishment of debt	(853)	—	—
Repurchases of common stock	(2,041)	(1,047)	—
Dividends paid	(963)	(710)	(399)
Other	105	39	27
Total financing activities	(4,119)	(645)	1,270
Net change in cash	(385)	398	1,105

a. In 1995 cash increased by $398 million, then decreased by $385 million in 1996. Was 1996 a "bad year" for Chrysler because the cash declined?
b. Provide an analysis of Chrysler's cash flow performance for the three years.
c. Within the investing section there are three lines associated with finance receivables. Interpret these lines.

Activity 15–6 Stainless Kitchens, Inc.

Analysis of statement of cash flows

Alan Hoyt is the president and majority shareholder of Stainless Kitchens, Inc., a small retail store chain. Recently, Hoyt submitted a loan application for Stainless Kitchens, Inc. to Montvale National Bank. It called for a $200,000, 11%, ten-year loan to help finance the construction of a building and the purchase of store equipment, costing a total of $250,000, to enable Stainless Kitchens, Inc. to open a store in Montvale. Land for this purpose was acquired last year. The bank's loan officer requested a statement of cash flows in addition to the most recent income statement, balance sheet, and retained earnings statement that Hoyt had submitted with the loan application.

As a close family friend, Hoyt asked you to prepare a statement of cash flows. From the records provided, you prepared the following statement.

Stainless Kitchens, Inc.
Statement of Cash Flows
For the Year Ended December 31, 2000

Cash flows from operating activities:			
Net income, per income statement		$ 86,400	
Add: Depreciation	$31,000		
Decrease in accounts receivable	11,500	42,500	
		$128,900	
Deduct: Increase in inventory	$12,000		
Increase in prepaid expenses	1,500		
Decrease in accounts payable	3,000		
Gain on sale of investments	7,500	24,000	
Net cash flow from operating activities			$104,900
Cash flows from investing activities:			
Cash received from investments sold		$ 42,500	
Less: Cash paid for purchase of store equipment		31,000	
Net cash flow from investing activities			11,500
Cash flows from financing activities:			
Cash paid for dividends		$ 40,000	
Net cash flow used for financing activities			(40,000)
Increase in cash			$ 76,400
Cash at the beginning of the year			27,500
Cash at the end of the year			$103,900
Schedule of Noncash Financing and Investing Activities:			
Issued common stock at par for land			$ 40,000

After reviewing the statement, Hoyt telephoned you and commented, "Are you sure this statement is right?" Hoyt then raised the following questions:

1. "How can depreciation be a cash flow?"
2. "Issuing common stock for the land is listed in a separate schedule. This transaction has nothing to do with cash! Shouldn't this transaction be eliminated from the statement?"
3. "How can the gain on sale of investments be a deduction from net income in determining the cash flow from operating activities?"
4. "Why does the bank need this statement anyway? They can compute the increase in cash from the balance sheets for the last two years."

After jotting down Hoyt's questions, you assured him that this statement was "right." However, to alleviate Hoyt's concern, you arranged a meeting for the following day.

a. How would you respond to each of Hoyt's questions?
b. Do you think that the statement of cash flows enhances the chances of Stainless Kitchens, Inc. receiving the loan? Discuss.

ANSWERS TO SELF-EXAMINATION QUESTIONS

Matching

1. E	3. A	5. I	7. N	9. F	11. J	12. M	13. H
2. L	4. K	6. B	8. D	10. C			

Multiple Choice

1. **D** Cash flows from operating activities affect transactions that enter into the determination of net income, such as the receipt of cash from customers on account (answer D). Receipts of cash from the sale of stock (answer A) and the sale of bonds (answer B) and payments of cash for dividends (answer C) are cash flows from financing activities.
2. **A** Cash flows from investing activities include receipts from the sale of noncurrent assets, such as equipment (answer A), and payments to acquire noncurrent assets. Receipts of cash from the sale of stock (answer B) and payments of cash for dividends (answer C) and to acquire treasury stock (answer D) are cash flows from financing activities.
3. **C** Payment of cash dividends (answer C) is an example of a financing activity. The receipt of cash from customers on account (answer A) is an operating activity. The receipt of cash from the sale of equipment (answer B) is an investing activity. The payment of cash to acquire marketable securities (answer D) is an example of an investing activity.
4. **D** The indirect method (answer D) reports cash flows from operating activities by beginning with net income and adjusting it for revenues and expenses not involving the receipt or payment of cash.
5. **C** The cash flows from operating activities section of the statement of cash flows would report net cash flow from operating activities of $65,500, determined as follows:

Net income		$55,000
Add: Depreciation	$22,000	
Decrease in inventories	5,000	
Decrease in prepaid expenses	500	27,500
		$82,500
Deduct: Increase in accounts receivable	$10,000	
Decrease in accounts payable	7,000	17,000
Net cash flow from operating activities		$65,500

16

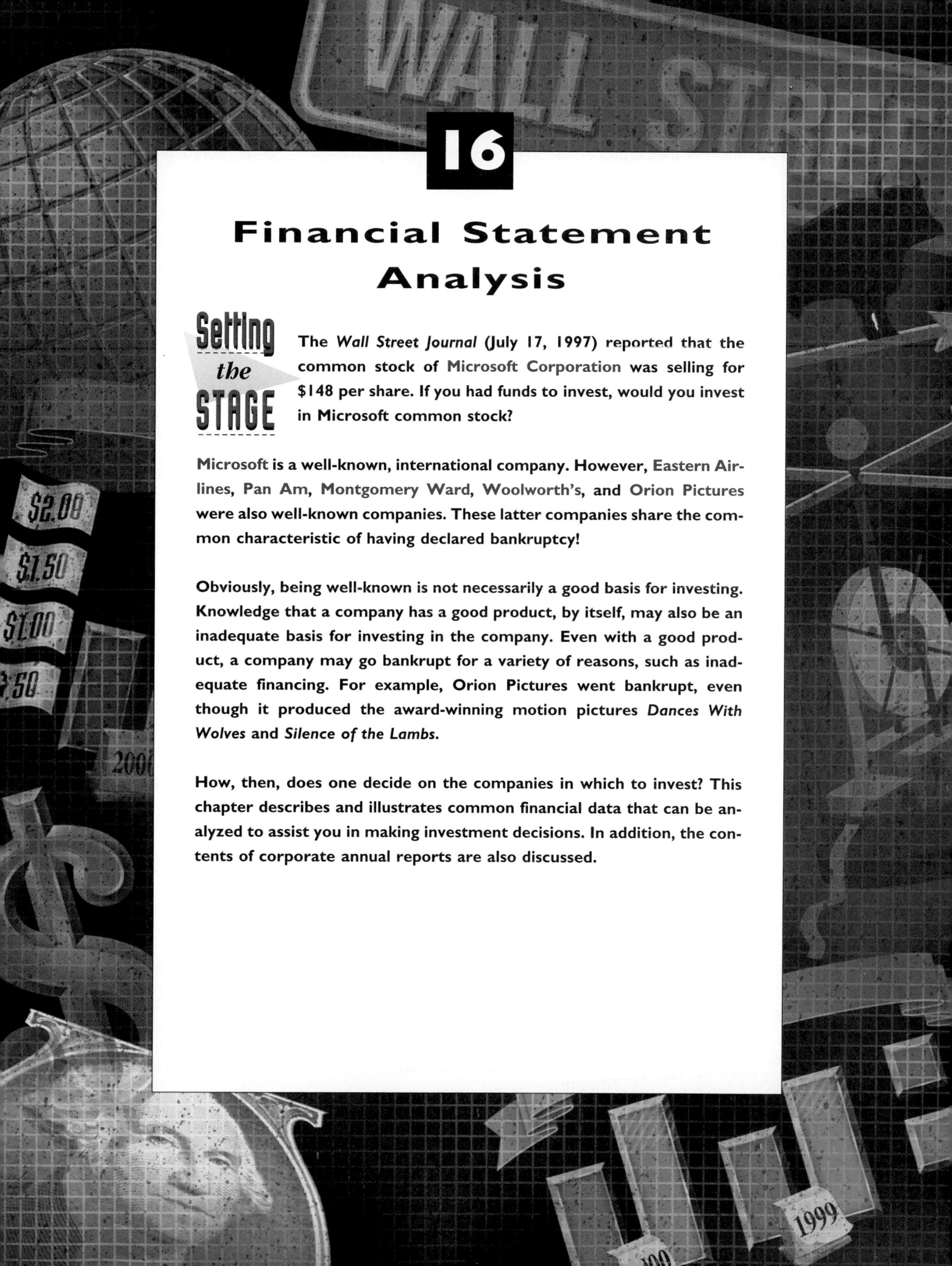

Financial Statement Analysis

Setting the STAGE

The *Wall Street Journal* (July 17, 1997) reported that the common stock of Microsoft Corporation was selling for $148 per share. If you had funds to invest, would you invest in Microsoft common stock?

Microsoft is a well-known, international company. However, Eastern Airlines, Pan Am, Montgomery Ward, Woolworth's, and Orion Pictures were also well-known companies. These latter companies share the common characteristic of having declared bankruptcy!

Obviously, being well-known is not necessarily a good basis for investing. Knowledge that a company has a good product, by itself, may also be an inadequate basis for investing in the company. Even with a good product, a company may go bankrupt for a variety of reasons, such as inadequate financing. For example, Orion Pictures went bankrupt, even though it produced the award-winning motion pictures *Dances With Wolves* and *Silence of the Lambs.*

How, then, does one decide on the companies in which to invest? This chapter describes and illustrates common financial data that can be analyzed to assist you in making investment decisions. In addition, the contents of corporate annual reports are also discussed.

objectives

After studying this chapter, you should be able to:

1 List basic financial statement analytical procedures.

2 Apply financial statement analysis to assess the solvency of a business.

3 Apply financial statement analysis to assess the profitability of a business.

4 Summarize the uses and limitations of analytical measures.

5 Describe the contents of corporate annual reports.

Basic Analytical Procedures

OBJECTIVE 1

List basic financial statement analytical procedures.

The basic financial statements provide much of the information users need to make economic decisions about businesses. In this chapter, we illustrate how to perform a complete analysis of these statements by integrating individual analytical measures.

Analytical procedures may be used to compare items on a current statement with related items on earlier statements. For example, cash of $150,000 on the current balance sheet may be compared with cash of $100,000 on the balance sheet of a year earlier. The current year's cash may be expressed as 1.5 or 150% of the earlier amount or as an increase of 50% or $50,000.

Analytical procedures are also widely used to examine relationships within a financial statement. To illustrate, assume that cash of $50,000 and inventories of $250,000 are included in the total assets of $1,000,000 on a balance sheet. In relative terms, the cash balance is 5% of the total assets, and the inventories are 25% of the total assets.

In the following discussion, we emphasize the importance of each of the various analytical measures illustrated. The measures are not ends in themselves. They are only guides in evaluating financial and operating data. Many other factors, such as trends in the industry and general economic conditions, should also be considered.

Q&A *Accounts Payable was $600,000 in the current year and $500,000 in the preceding year. What is the amount and the percentage of increase or decrease that would be shown in a balance sheet with horizontal analysis?*

$100,000 or 20% ($100,000/$500,000) increase

Horizontal Analysis

The percentage analysis of increases and decreases in related items in comparative financial statements is called **horizontal analysis**. The amount of each item on the most recent statement is compared with the related item on one or more earlier statements. The amount of increase or decrease in the item is listed, along with the percent of increase or decrease.

Horizontal analysis may include a comparison between two statements. In this case, the earlier statement is used as the base. Horizontal analysis may also include three or more comparative statements. In this case, the earliest date or period may be used as the base for comparing all later dates or periods. Alternatively, each statement may be compared to the immediately preceding statement. Exhibit 1 is a condensed comparative balance sheet for two years for Lincoln Company, with horizontal analysis.

We cannot fully evaluate the significance of the various increases and decreases in the items shown in Exhibit 1 without additional information. Although total assets at the end of 2000 were $91,000 (7.4%) less than at the beginning of the year, liabilities were reduced by $133,000 (30%), and stockholders' equity increased $42,000

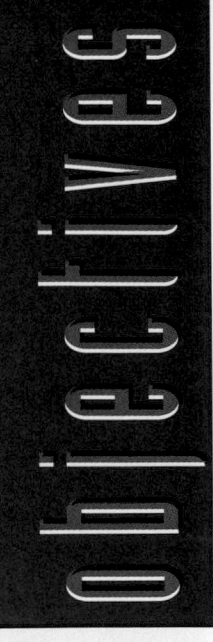

EXHIBIT 1
Comparative Balance Sheet—Horizontal Analysis

Lincoln Company
Comparative Balance Sheet
December 31, 2000 and 1999

	2000	1999	Increase (Decrease) Amount	Increase (Decrease) Percent
Assets				
Current assets	$ 550,000	$ 533,000	$ 17,000	3.2%
Long-term investments	95,000	177,500	(82,500)	(46.5%)
Property, plant, and equipment (net)	444,500	470,000	(25,500)	(5.4%)
Intangible assets	50,000	50,000	—	
Total assets	$1,139,500	$1,230,500	$ (91,000)	(7.4%)
Liabilities				
Current liabilities	$ 210,000	$ 243,000	$ (33,000)	(13.6%)
Long-term liabilities	100,000	200,000	(100,000)	(50.0%)
Total liabilities	$ 310,000	$ 443,000	$(133,000)	(30.0%)
Stockholders' Equity				
Preferred 6% stock, $100 par	$ 150,000	$ 150,000	—	—
Common stock, $10 par	500,000	500,000	—	—
Retained earnings	179,500	137,500	$ 42,000	30.5%
Total stockholders' equity	$ 829,500	$ 787,500	$ 42,000	5.3%
Total liabilities and stockholders' equity	$1,139,500	$1,230,500	$ (91,000)	(7.4%)

(5.3%). It appears that the reduction of $100,000 in long-term liabilities was achieved mostly through the sale of long-term investments.

The balance sheet in Exhibit 1 may be expanded to include the details of the various categories of assets and liabilities. An alternative is to present the details in separate schedules. Exhibit 2 is a supporting schedule with horizontal analysis.

EXHIBIT 2
Comparative Schedule of Current Assets—Horizontal Analysis

Lincoln Company
Comparative Schedule of Current Assets
December 31, 2000 and 1999

	2000	1999	Increase (Decrease) Amount	Increase (Decrease) Percent
Cash	$ 90,500	$ 64,700	$ 25,800	39.9%
Marketable securities	75,000	60,000	15,000	25.0%
Accounts receivable (net)	115,000	120,000	(5,000)	(4.2%)
Inventories	264,000	283,000	(19,000)	(6.7%)
Prepaid expenses	5,500	5,300	200	3.8%
Total current assets	$550,000	$533,000	$ 17,000	3.2%

The decrease in accounts receivable may be due to changes in credit terms or improved collection policies. Likewise, a decrease in inventories during a period of increased sales may indicate an improvement in the management of inventories.

The changes in the current assets in Exhibit 2 appear favorable. This assessment is supported by the 24.8% increase in net sales shown in Exhibit 3.

EXHIBIT 3
Comparative Income Statement—Horizontal Analysis

Lincoln Company
Comparative Income Statement
For the Years Ended December 31, 2000 and 1999

			Increase (Decrease)	
	2000	1999	Amount	Percent
Sales	$1,530,500	$1,234,000	$296,500	24.0%
Sales returns and allowances	32,500	34,000	(1,500)	(4.4%)
Net sales	$1,498,000	$1,200,000	$298,000	24.8%
Cost of goods sold	1,043,000	820,000	223,000	27.2%
Gross profit	$ 455,000	$ 380,000	$ 75,000	19.7%
Selling expenses	$ 191,000	$ 147,000	$ 44,000	29.9%
Administrative expenses	104,000	97,400	6,600	6.8%
Total operating expenses	$ 295,000	$ 244,400	$ 50,600	20.7%
Income from operations	$ 160,000	$ 135,600	$ 24,400	18.0%
Other income	8,500	11,000	(2,500)	(22.7%)
	$ 168,500	$ 146,600	$ 21,900	14.9%
Other expense	6,000	12,000	(6,000)	(50.0%)
Income before income tax	$ 162,500	$ 134,600	$ 27,900	20.7%
Income tax expense	71,500	58,100	13,400	23.1%
Net income	$ 91,000	$ 76,500	$ 14,500	19.0%

An increase in net sales may not have a favorable effect on operating performance. The percentage increase in Lincoln Company's net sales is accompanied by a greater percentage increase in the cost of goods (merchandise) sold.[1] This has the effect of reducing gross profit. Selling expenses increased significantly, and administrative expenses increased slightly. Overall, operating expenses increased by 20.7%, whereas gross profit increased by only 19.7%.

The increase in income from operations and in net income is favorable. However, a study of the expenses and additional analyses and comparisons should be made before reaching a conclusion.

Exhibit 4 illustrates a comparative retained earnings statement with horizontal analysis. It reveals an increase of 30.5% in retained earnings for the year. The increase is due to net income of $91,000 for the year, less dividends of $49,000.

EXHIBIT 4
Comparative Retained Earnings Statement—Horizontal Analysis

Lincoln Company
Comparative Retained Earnings Statement
December 31, 2000 and 1999

			Increase (Decrease)	
	2000	1999	Amount	Percent
Retained earnings, January 1	$137,500	$100,000	$37,500	37.5%
Net income for the year	91,000	76,500	14,500	19.0%
Total	$228,500	$176,500	$52,000	29.5%
Dividends:				
On preferred stock	$ 9,000	$ 9,000	—	—
On common stock	40,000	30,000	$10,000	33.3%
Total	$ 49,000	$ 39,000	$10,000	25.6%
Retained earnings, December 31	$179,500	$137,500	$42,000	30.5%

[1] The term *cost of goods sold* is often used in practice in place of *cost of merchandise sold*. Such usage is followed in this chapter.

Vertical Analysis

A percentage analysis may also be used to show the relationship of each component to the total within a single statement. This type of analysis is called **vertical analysis**. Like horizontal analysis, the statements may be prepared in either detailed or condensed form. In the latter case, additional details of the changes in individual items may be presented in supporting schedules. In such schedules, the percentage analysis may be based on either the total of the schedule or the statement total. Although vertical analysis is limited to an individual statement, its significance may be improved by preparing comparative statements.

In vertical analysis of the balance sheet, each asset item is stated as a percent of the total assets. Each liability and stockholders' equity item is stated as a percent of the total liabilities and stockholders' equity. Exhibit 5 is a condensed comparative balance sheet with vertical analysis for Lincoln Company.

EXHIBIT 5
Comparative Balance Sheet—Vertical Analysis

Lincoln Company
Comparative Balance Sheet
December 31, 2000 and 1999

	2000		1999	
	Amount	**Percent**	**Amount**	**Percent**
Assets				
Current assets	$ 550,000	48.3%	$ 533,000	43.3%
Long-term investments	95,000	8.3	177,500	14.4
Property, plant, and equipment (net)	444,500	39.0	470,000	38.2
Intangible assets	50,000	4.4	50,000	4.1
Total assets	$1,139,500	100.0%	$1,230,500	100.0%
Liabilities				
Current liabilities	$ 210,000	18.4%	$ 243,000	19.7%
Long-term liabilities	100,000	8.8	200,000	16.3
Total liabilities	$ 310,000	27.2%	$ 443,000	36.0%
Stockholders' Equity				
Preferred 6% stock, $100 par	$ 150,000	13.2%	$ 150,000	12.2%
Common stock, $10 par	500,000	43.9	500,000	40.6
Retained earnings	179,500	15.7	137,500	11.2
Total stockholders' equity	$ 829,500	72.8%	$ 787,500	64.0%
Total liabilities and stockholders' equity	$1,139,500	100.0%	$1,230,500	100.0%

The major percentage changes in Lincoln Company's assets are in the current asset and long-term investment categories. In the Liabilities and Stockholders' Equity sections of the balance sheet, the greatest percentage changes are in long-term liabilities and retained earnings. Stockholders' equity increased from 64% to 72.8% of total liabilities and stockholders' equity in 2000. There is a comparable decrease in liabilities.

In a vertical analysis of the income statement, each item is stated as a percent of net sales. Exhibit 6 is a condensed comparative income statement with vertical analysis for Lincoln Company.

Q&A

At the end of the current year, Accounts Payable was $600,000 and total liabilities and stockholders' equity was $1,200,000. What percent would be shown for Accounts Payable in a balance sheet with vertical analysis?

50% ($600,000/$1,200,000)

EXHIBIT 6
Comparative Income Statement—Vertical Analysis

Lincoln Company
Comparative Income Statement
For the Years Ended December 31, 2000 and 1999

	2000		1999	
	Amount	**Percent**	**Amount**	**Percent**
Sales	$1,530,500	102.2%	$1,234,000	102.8%
Sales returns and allowances	32,500	2.2	34,000	2.8
Net sales	$1,498,000	100.0%	$1,200,000	100.0%
Cost of goods sold	1,043,000	69.6	820,000	68.3
Gross profit	$ 455,000	30.4%	$ 380,000	31.7%
Selling expenses	$ 191,000	12.8%	$ 147,000	12.3%
Administrative expenses	104,000	6.9	97,400	8.1
Total operating expenses	$ 295,000	19.7%	$ 244,400	20.4%
Income from operations	$ 160,000	10.7%	$ 135,600	11.3%
Other income	8,500	0.6	11,000	0.9
	$ 168,500	11.3%	$ 146,600	12.2%
Other expense	6,000	0.4	12,000	1.0
Income before income tax	$ 162,500	10.9%	$ 134,600	11.2%
Income tax expense	71,500	4.8	58,100	4.8
Net income	$ 91,000	6.1%	$ 76,500	6.4%

We must be careful when judging the significance of differences between percentages for the two years. For example, the decline of the gross profit rate from 31.7% in 1999 to 30.4% in 2000 is only 1.3 percentage points. In terms of dollars of potential gross profit, however, it represents a decline of approximately $19,500 (1.3% × $1,498,000).

Common-Size Statements

Horizontal and vertical analyses with both dollar and percentage amounts are useful in assessing relationships and trends in financial conditions and operations of a business. Vertical analysis with both dollar and percentage amounts is also useful in comparing one company with another or with industry averages. Such comparisons are easier to make with the use of common-size statements. In a **common-size statement**, all items are expressed in percentages.

Common-size statements are useful in comparing the current period with prior periods, individual businesses, or one business with industry percentages. Industry data are often available from trade associations and financial information services. Exhibit 7 is a comparative common-size income statement for two businesses.

Exhibit 7 indicates that Lincoln Company has a slightly higher rate of gross profit than Madison Corporation. However, this advantage is more than offset by Lincoln Company's higher percentage of selling and administrative expenses. As a result, the operating income of Lincoln Company is 10.7% of net sales, compared with 14.4% for Madison Corporation—an unfavorable difference of 3.7 percentage points.

REAL WORLD

The percentages of gross profit and net income to sales for fiscal year-end 1996 for **Kmart Corp.** and **Wal-Mart Stores Inc.** are shown below.

	Kmart Corp.	Wal-Mart Stores Inc.
Gross profit to sales	22.4%	20.2%
Net income to sales	0.7%	2.9%

Wal-Mart has a lower gross profit margin than Kmart, which is likely due to lower prices. However, Wal-Mart has a much leaner operating expense structure, so is able to earn an overall higher percentage of net income to sales.

Other Analytical Measures

In addition to the preceding analyses, other relationships may be expressed in ratios and percentages. Often, these items are taken

EXHIBIT 7
Common-Size Income Statement

Lincoln Company and Madison Corporation
Condensed Common-Size Income Statement
For the Year Ended December 31, 2000

	Lincoln Company	Madison Corporation
Sales	102.2%	102.3%
Sales returns and allowances	2.2	2.3
Net sales	100.0%	100.0%
Cost of goods sold	69.6	70.0
Gross profit	30.4%	30.0%
Selling expenses	12.8%	11.5%
Administrative expenses	6.9	4.1
Total operating expenses	19.7%	15.6%
Income from operations	10.7%	14.4%
Other income	0.6	0.6
	11.3%	15.0%
Other expense	0.4	0.5
Income before income tax	10.9%	14.5%
Income tax expense	4.8	5.5
Net income	6.1%	9.0%

from the financial statements and thus are a type of vertical analysis. Comparison of these items with items from earlier periods is a type of horizontal analysis.

Solvency Analysis

OBJECTIVE 2

Apply financial statement analysis to assess the solvency of a business.

Some aspects of a business's financial condition and operations are of greater importance to some users than others. However, all users are interested in the ability of a business to pay its debts as they are due and to earn income. The ability of a business to meet its financial obligations (debts) is called **solvency**. The ability of a business to earn income is called **profitability**.

The factors of solvency and profitability are interrelated. A business that cannot pay its debts on a timely basis may experience difficulty in obtaining credit. A lack of available credit may, in turn, lead to a decline in the business's profitability. Eventually, the business may be forced into bankruptcy. Likewise, a business that is less profitable than its competitors is likely to be at a disadvantage in obtaining credit or new capital from stockholders.

In the following paragraphs, we discuss various types of financial analyses that are useful in evaluating the solvency of a business. In the next section, we discuss various types of profitability analyses. The examples in both sections are based on Lincoln Company's financial statements presented earlier. In some cases, data from Lincoln Company's financial statements of the preceding year and from other sources are also used. These historical data are useful in assessing the past performance of a business and in forecasting its future performance. The results of financial analyses may be

REAL WORLD

Two popular printed sources for industry ratios are available in *Annual Statement Studies* from **Robert Morris Associates** and *Industry Norms & Key Business Ratios* from **Dun's Analytical Services**. Additional sources are available on the Internet at **www.sunsite.unc.edu/reference/rita/ratios.html**

even more useful when they are compared with those of competing businesses and with industry averages.

Solvency analysis focuses on the ability of a business to pay or otherwise satisfy its current and noncurrent liabilities. It is normally assessed by examining balance sheet relationships, using the following major analyses:

Solvency analysis focuses on the ability of a business to pay or otherwise satisfy its current and noncurrent liabilities.

1. Current position analysis
2. Accounts receivable analysis
3. Inventory analysis
4. The ratio of fixed assets to long-term liabilities
5. The ratio of liabilities to stockholders' equity
6. The number of times interest charges are earned

Current Position Analysis

To be useful in assessing solvency, a ratio or other financial measure must relate to a business's ability to pay or otherwise satisfy its liabilities. The use of such measures to assess the ability of a business to pay its current liabilities is called **current position analysis**. Such analysis is of special interest to short-term creditors.

An analysis of a firm's current position normally includes determining the working capital, the current ratio, and the acid-test ratio. The current and acid-test ratios are most useful when analyzed together and compared to previous periods and other firms in the industry.

Working Capital

The excess of the current assets of a business over its current liabilities is called **working capital**. The working capital is often used in evaluating a company's ability to meet currently maturing debts. It is especially useful in making monthly or other period-to-period comparisons for a company. However, amounts of working capital are difficult to assess when comparing companies of different sizes or in comparing such amounts with industry figures. For example, working capital of $250,000 may be adequate for a small residential contractor, but it may be inadequate for a large commercial contractor.

Current Ratio

Another means of expressing the relationship between current assets and current liabilities is the **current ratio**. This ratio is sometimes called the **working capital ratio** or **bankers' ratio**. The ratio is computed by dividing the total current assets by the total current liabilities. For Lincoln Company, working capital and the current ratio for 2000 and 1999 are as follows:

	2000	1999
Current assets	$550,000	$533,000
Current liabilities	210,000	243,000
Working capital	$340,000	$290,000
Current ratio	2.6	2.2

The current ratio is a more reliable indicator of solvency than is working capital. To illustrate, assume that as of December 31, 2000, the working capital of a competitor is much greater than $340,000, but its current ratio is only 1.3. Considering these facts alone, Lincoln Company, with its current ratio of 2.6, is in a more favorable position to obtain short-term credit than the competitor, which has the greater amount of working capital.

REAL WORLD

The current ratio for a **Microsoft Corporation** balance sheet (dated June 30, 1996) was 4.17. The explanation for this high current ratio was Microsoft's cash hoard of $4.75 billion. Microsoft essentially generated cash faster than it could profitably invest it.

Acid-Test Ratio

The working capital and the current ratio do not consider the makeup of the current assets. To illustrate the importance of this consideration, the current position data for Lincoln Company and Jefferson Corporation as of December 31, 2000, are as follows:

	Lincoln Company	Jefferson Corporation
Current assets:		
Cash	$ 90,500	$ 45,500
Marketable securities	75,000	25,000
Accounts receivable (net)	115,000	90,000
Inventories	264,000	380,000
Prepaid expenses	5,500	9,500
Total current assets	$550,000	$550,000
Current liabilities	210,000	210,000
Working capital	$340,000	$340,000
Current ratio	2.6	2.6

Both companies have a working capital of $340,000 and a current ratio of 2.6. But the ability of each company to pay its current debts is significantly different. Jefferson Corporation has more of its current assets in inventories. Some of these inventories must be sold and the receivables collected before the current liabilities can be paid in full. Thus, a large amount of time may be necessary to convert these inventories into cash. Declines in market prices and a reduction in demand could also impair its ability to pay current liabilities. In contrast, Lincoln Company has cash and current assets (marketable securities and accounts receivable) that can generally be converted to cash rather quickly to meet its current liabilities.

Q&A *A balance sheet shows $300,000 of cash, marketable securities, and receivables, and $250,000 of inventories. Current liabilities are $200,000. What are (a) the current ratio and (b) the acid-test ratio?*

(a) 2.75 ($550,000/$200,000); (b) 1.5 ($300,000/$200,000)

A ratio that measures the "instant" debt-paying ability of a company is called the **acid-test ratio** or **quick ratio**. It is the ratio of the total quick assets to the total current liabilities. **Quick assets** are cash and other current assets that can be quickly converted to cash. Quick assets normally include cash, marketable securities, and receivables. The acid-test ratio data for Lincoln Company are as follows:

	2000	1999
Quick assets:		
Cash	$ 90,500	$ 64,700
Marketable equity securities	75,000	60,000
Accounts receivable (net)	115,000	120,000
Total quick assets	$280,500	$244,700
Current liabilities	$210,000	$243,000
Acid-test ratio	1.3	1.0

Accounts Receivable Analysis

The size and makeup of accounts receivable change constantly during business operations. Sales on account increase accounts receivable, whereas collections from customers decrease accounts receivable. Firms that grant long credit terms usually have larger accounts receivable balances than those granting short credit terms. Increases or decreases in the volume of sales also affect the balance of accounts receivable.

It is desirable to collect receivables as promptly as possible. The cash collected from receivables improves solvency. In addition, the cash generated by prompt collections from customers may be used in operations for such purposes as purchasing merchandise in large quantities at lower prices. The cash may also be used for payment of dividends to stockholders or for other investing or financing purposes. Prompt collection also lessens the risk of loss from uncollectible accounts.

Accounts Receivable Turnover

The relationship between credit sales and accounts receivable may be stated as the **accounts receivable turnover**. This ratio is computed by dividing net sales on account by the average net accounts receivable. It is desirable to base the average on monthly balances, which allows for seasonal changes in sales. When such data are not available, it may be necessary to use the average of the accounts receivable balance at the beginning and the end of the year. If there are trade notes receivable as well as accounts, the two may be combined. The accounts receivable turnover data for Lincoln Company are as follows. All sales were made on account.

	2000	1999
Net sales on account	$1,498,000	$1,200,000
Accounts receivable (net):		
Beginning of year	$ 120,000	$ 140,000
End of year	115,000	120,000
Total	$ 235,000	$ 260,000
Average (Total ÷ 2)	$ 117,500	$ 130,000
Accounts receivable turnover	12.7	9.2

The increase in the accounts receivable turnover for 2000 indicates that there has been an improvement in the collection of receivables. This may be due to a change in the granting of credit or in collection practices or both.

Number of Days' Sales in Receivables

Another measure of the relationship between credit sales and accounts receivable is the **number of days' sales in receivables**. This ratio is computed by dividing the net accounts receivable at the end of the year by the average daily sales on account. Average daily sales on account is determined by dividing net sales on account by 365 days. The number of days' sales in receivables is computed for Lincoln Company as follows:

	2000	1999
Accounts receivable (net), end of year	$ 115,000	$ 120,000
Net sales on account	$1,498,000	$1,200,000
Average daily sales on account (sales ÷ 365)	$ 4,104	$ 3,288
Number of days' sales in receivables	28.0*	36.5*

*Accounts receivable ÷ Average daily sales on account

Q&A *Sales were $1,200,000, of which 80% were on account. The accounts receivable balance at the beginning of the year was $56,000, and at the end of the year it was $40,000. What are (a) the accounts receivable turnover and (b) the number of days' sales in receivables?*

(a) 20 [(0.80 × $1,200,000)/($56,000 + $40,000)/2];
(b) 15.2 days [$40,000/($960,000/365)]

The number of days' sales in receivables is an estimate of the length of time the accounts receivable have been outstanding. Comparing this measure with the credit terms provides information on the efficiency in collecting receivables. For example, assume that the number of days' sales in receivables for Grant Inc. is 40. If Grant Inc.'s credit terms are n/45, then its collection process appears to be efficient. On the other hand, if Grant Inc.'s credit terms are n/30, its collection process does not appear to be efficient. A comparison with other firms in the same industry and with prior years also provides useful information. Such comparisons may indicate efficiency of collection procedures and trends in credit management.

Inventory Analysis

A business should keep enough inventory on hand to meet the needs of its customers and its operations. At the same time, however, an excessive amount of inventory reduces solvency by tying up funds. Excess inventories also increase insurance expense, property taxes, storage costs, and other related expenses. These expenses further reduce funds that could be used elsewhere to improve operations. Finally, excess inventory also increases the risk of losses because of price declines or obsolescence of the inventory. Two measures that are useful for evaluating the management of inventory are the inventory turnover and the number of days' sales in inventory.

Inventory Turnover

The relationship between the volume of goods (merchandise) sold and inventory may be stated as the **inventory turnover**. It is computed by dividing the cost of goods sold by the average inventory. If monthly data are not available, the average of the inventories at the beginning and the end of the year may be used. The inventory turnover for Lincoln Company is computed as follows:

	2000	1999
Cost of goods sold	$1,043,000	$820,000
Inventories:		
Beginning of year	$ 283,000	$311,000
End of year	264,000	283,000
Total	$ 547,000	$594,000
Average (Total ÷ 2)	$ 273,500	$297,000
Inventory turnover	3.8	2.8

The inventory turnover of **McDonald's Corporation** for a recent year was 40, while for **Toys "R" Us Inc.**, it was 3.27. McDonald's inventory turnover is higher because it sells perishable food products, while toys can sit on the shelf longer without "spoiling."

The inventory turnover improved for Lincoln Company because of an increase in the cost of goods sold and a decrease in the average inventories. Differences across inventories, companies, and industries are too great to allow a general statement on what is a good inventory turnover. For example, a firm selling food should have a higher turnover than a firm selling furniture or jewelry. Likewise, the perishable foods department of a supermarket should have a higher turnover than the soaps and cleansers department. However, for each business or each department within a business, there is a reasonable turnover rate. A turnover lower than this rate could mean that inventory is not being managed properly.

Number of Days' Sales in Inventory

Another measure of the relationship between the cost of goods sold and inventory is the **number of days' sales in inventory**. This measure is computed by dividing the inventory at the end of the year by the average daily cost of goods sold (cost of goods sold divided by 365). The number of days' sales in inventory for Lincoln Company is computed as follows:

	2000	1999
Inventories, end of year	$ 264,000	$283,000
Cost of goods sold	$1,043,000	$820,000
Average daily cost of goods sold (COGS ÷ 365 days)	$ 2,858	$ 2,247
Number of days' sales in inventory	92.4	125.9

The number of days' sales in inventory is a rough measure of the length of time it takes to acquire, sell, and replace the inventory. For Lincoln Company, there is a major improvement in the number of days' sales in inventory during 2000. However, a comparison with earlier years and similar firms would be useful in assessing Lincoln Company's overall inventory management.

Ratio of Fixed Assets to Long-Term Liabilities

Long-term notes and bonds are often secured by mortgages on fixed assets. The **ratio of fixed assets to long-term liabilities** is a solvency measure that indicates the margin of safety of the noteholders or bondholders. It also indicates the ability of the business to borrow additional funds on a long-term basis. The ratio of fixed assets to long-term liabilities for Lincoln Company is as follows:

	2000	1999
Fixed assets (net)	$444,500	$470,000
Long-term liabilities	$100,000	$200,000
Ratio of fixed assets to long-term liabilities	4.4	2.4

The major increase in this ratio at the end of 2000 is mainly due to liquidating one-half of Lincoln Company's long-term liabilities. If the company needs to borrow additional funds on a long-term basis in the future, it is in a strong position to do so.

Ratio of Liabilities to Stockholders' Equity

Claims against the total assets of a business are divided into two groups: (1) claims of creditors and (2) claims of owners. The relationship between the total claims of the creditors and owners—the **ratio of liabilities to stockholders' equity**—is a solvency measure that indicates the margin of safety for creditors. It also indicates the ability of the business to withstand adverse business conditions. When the claims of creditors are large in relation to the equity of the stockholders, there are usually significant interest payments. If earnings decline to the point where the company is unable to meet its interest payments, the business may be taken over by the creditors.

The relationship between creditor and stockholder equity is shown in the vertical analysis of the balance sheet. For example, the balance sheet of Lincoln Company in Exhibit 5 indicates that on December 31, 2000, liabilities represented 27.2% and stockholders' equity represented 72.8% of the total liabilities and stockholders' equity (100.0%). Instead of expressing each item as a percent of the total, this relationship may be expressed as a ratio of one to the other, as follows:

	2000	1999
Total liabilities	$310,000	$443,000
Total stockholders' equity	$829,500	$787,500
Ratio of liabilities to stockholders' equity	0.37	0.56

The balance sheet of Lincoln Company shows that the major factor affecting the change in the ratio was the $100,000 decrease in long-term liabilities during 2000. The ratio at the end of both years shows a large margin of safety for the creditors.

REAL WORLD

The ratio of liabilities to stockholders' equity varies across industries. For example, recent annual reports of some selected companies showed the following ratio of liabilities to stockholders' equity:

Delta Air Lines	3.81
Procter & Gamble	1.36
Bell South	0.36

The airline industry generally uses more debt financing than the consumer product or utility industries. Thus, the airline industry is generally considered more risky.

Number of Times Interest Charges Earned

Corporations in some industries, such as airlines, normally have high ratios of debt to stockholders' equity. For such corporations, the relative risk of the debtholders is normally measured as the **number of times interest charges are earned** during the year. The higher the ratio, the lower the risk that interest payments will not be made if earnings decrease. In other words, the higher the ratio, the greater the assurance that interest payments will be made on a continuing basis. This measure also indicates the general financial strength of the business, which is of interest to stockholders and employees as well as creditors.

The amount available to meet interest charges is not affected by taxes on income. This is because interest is deductible in determining taxable income. Thus, the number of times interest charges are earned is computed as shown below.

Q&A

What would be the number of times interest charges are earned for a company with $1,500,000, 10% debt; net income of $120,000; and a corporate tax rate of 40%?

$$\frac{[\$120{,}000/(1.0 - 0.4)] + \$150{,}000}{\$150{,}000} = 2.33$$

	2000	1999
Income before income tax	$ 900,000	$ 800,000
Add interest expense	300,000	250,000
Amount available to meet interest charges	$1,200,000	$1,050,000
Number of times interest charges earned	4	4.2

Analysis such as this can also be applied to dividends on preferred stock. In such a case, net income is divided by the amount of preferred dividends to yield the **number of times preferred dividends are earned.** This measure indicates the risk that dividends to preferred stockholders may not be paid.

Profitability Analysis

OBJECTIVE 3

Apply financial statement analysis to assess the profitability of a business.

The ability of a business to earn profits depends on the effectiveness and efficiency of its operations as well as the resources available to it. Profitability analysis, therefore, focuses primarily on the relationship between operating results as reported in the income statement and resources available to the business as reported in the balance sheet. Major analyses used in assessing profitability include the following:

1. Ratio of net sales to assets
2. Rate earned on total assets
3. Rate earned on stockholders' equity
4. Rate earned on common stockholders' equity
5. Earnings per share on common stock
6. Price-earnings ratio
7. Dividends per share
8. Dividend yield

Profitability analysis focuses on the relationship between operating results and the resources available to a business.

Ratio of Net Sales to Assets

The **ratio of net sales to assets** is a profitability measure that shows how effectively a firm utilizes its assets. For example, two competing businesses have equal amounts of assets. If the sales of one are twice the sales of the other, the business with the higher sales is making better use of its assets.

In computing the ratio of net sales to assets, any long-term investments are excluded from total assets. This is because such investments are unrelated to normal operations involving the sale of goods or services. Assets may be measured as the total at the end of the year, the average at the beginning and end of the year, or the average of monthly totals. The basic data and the computation of this ratio for Lincoln Company are as follows:

	2000	1999
Net sales	$1,498,000	$1,200,000
Total assets (excluding long-term investments):		
Beginning of year	$1,053,000	$1,010,000
End of year	1,044,500	1,053,000
Total	$2,097,500	$2,063,000
Average (Total ÷ 2)	$1,048,750	$1,031,500
Ratio of net sales to assets	1.4	1.2

There was an improvement in this ratio during 2000. This was primarily due to an increase in sales volume. A comparison with similar companies or industry averages would be helpful in assessing the effectiveness of Lincoln Company's use of its assets.

Rate Earned on Total Assets

The **rate earned on total assets** measures the profitability of total assets, without considering how the assets are financed. This rate is therefore not affected by whether the assets are financed primarily by creditors or stockholders.

The rate earned on total assets is computed by adding interest expense to net income and dividing this sum by the average total assets. The addition of interest expense to net income eliminates the effect of whether the assets are financed by debt or equity. The rate earned by Lincoln Company on total assets is computed as follows:

	2000	1999
Net income	$ 91,000	$ 76,500
Plus interest expense	6,000	12,000
Total	$ 97,000	$ 88,500
Total assets:		
Beginning of year	$1,230,500	$1,187,500
End of year	1,139,500	1,230,500
Total	$2,370,000	$2,418,000
Average (Total ÷ 2)	$1,185,000	$1,209,000
Rate earned on total assets	8.2%	7.3%

The rate earned on total assets of Lincoln Company during 2000 improved over that of 1999. A comparison with similar companies and industry averages would be useful in evaluating Lincoln Company's profitability on total assets.

Sometimes it may be desirable to compute the **rate of income from operations to total assets**. This is especially true if significant amounts of nonoperating income and expense are reported on the income statement. In this case, any assets related to the nonoperating income and expense items should be excluded from total assets in computing the rate. In addition, using income from operations (which is before tax) has the advantage of eliminating the effects of any changes in the tax structure on the rate of earnings. When evaluating published data on rates earned on assets, you should be careful to determine the exact nature of the measure that is reported.

Rate Earned on Stockholders' Equity

Another measure of profitability is the **rate earned on stockholders' equity**. It is computed by dividing net income by average total stockholders' equity. In contrast to the rate earned on total assets, this measure emphasizes the rate of income earned on the amount invested by the stockholders.

The total stockholders' equity may vary throughout a period. For example, a business may issue or retire stock, pay dividends, and earn net income. If monthly amounts are not available, the average of the stockholders' equity at the beginning and the end of the year is normally used to compute this rate. For Lincoln Company, the rate earned on stockholders' equity is computed as follows:

	2000	1999
Net income	$ 91,000	$ 76,500
Stockholders' equity:		
Beginning of year	$ 787,500	$ 750,000
End of year	829,500	787,500
Total	$1,617,000	$1,537,500
Average (Total ÷ 2)	$ 808,500	$ 768,750
Rate earned on stockholders' equity	11.3%	10.0%

The rate earned by a business on the equity of its stockholders is usually higher than the rate earned on total assets. This occurs when the amount earned on assets acquired with creditors' funds is more than the interest paid to creditors. This difference in the rate on stockholders' equity and the rate on total assets is called **leverage**.

Lincoln Company's rate earned on stockholders' equity for 2000, 11.3%, is greater than the rate of 8.2% earned on total assets. The leverage of 3.1% (11.3% − 8.2%) for 2000 compares favorably with the 2.7% (10.0% − 7.3%) leverage for 1999. Exhibit 8 shows the 2000 and 1999 leverages for Lincoln Company.

EXHIBIT 8
Leverage

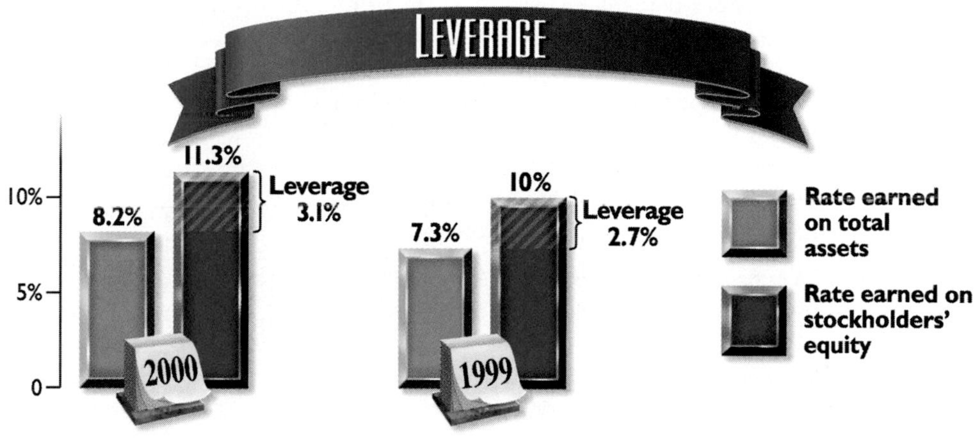

The approximate rates earned on assets and stockholders' equity for **Adolph Coors Company** and **Anheuser-Busch Companies** for a recent fiscal year are shown below.

	Adolph Coors	Anheuser-Busch
Rate earned on assets	3%	11%
Rate earned on stockholders' equity	6%	28%

Anheuser-Busch has been more profitable and has benefited from a greater use of leverage than has Adolph Coors.

Rate Earned on Common Stockholders' Equity

A corporation may have both preferred and common stock outstanding. In this case, the common stockholders have the residual claim on earnings. The **rate earned on common stockholders' equity** focuses only on the rate of profits earned on the amount invested by the common stockholders. It is computed by subtracting preferred dividend requirements from the net income and dividing by the average common stockholders' equity.

Lincoln Company has \$150,000 of 6% nonparticipating preferred stock outstanding on December 31, 2000 and 1999. Thus, the annual preferred dividend requirement is \$9,000 (\$150,000 × 6%). The common stockholders' equity equals the total stockholders' equity, including retained earnings, less the par of the preferred stock (\$150,000). The basic data and the rate earned on common stockholders' equity for Lincoln Company are as follows:

	2000	1999
Net income	\$ 91,000	\$ 76,500
Preferred dividends	9,000	9,000
Remainder—identified with common stock	\$ 82,000	\$ 67,500
Common stockholders' equity:		
Beginning of year	\$ 637,500	\$ 600,000
End of year	679,500	637,500
Total	\$1,317,000	\$1,237,500
Average (Total ÷ 2)	\$ 658,500	\$ 618,750
Rate earned on common stockholders' equity	12.5%	10.9%

BUSINESS ON STAGE

Analysis and Red Flags

An additional source of information about a corporation is the independent auditor's report, which must accompany the financial statements of a public corporation. The purpose of this report is to provide assurance to investors that the financial statements are fairly presented in conformity with generally accepted accounting principles.

The auditor's report may raise "red flags" indicating that profitability and solvency measures should be analyzed further. In such cases, an investor should read the auditor's report carefully to see if the "reliability" of these measures has been affected by one or more of the following factors:

1. There may be substantial doubt as to the ability of the company to continue as a going concern beyond one year.
2. An unusual accounting practice is being followed.
3. The company changed accounting principles from prior years.
4. The auditor wants to call your attention to a specific matter of importance.
5. The financial statements do not conform to generally accepted accounting principles.

The date of the auditor's report is also significant. It represents the last date that the auditor searched for events occurring subsequent to the date of the financial statements—events that might be significant to the interpretation of those statements. For example, the company may have sold a subsidiary after year-end or suffered a substantial loss as a result of some disaster. Such events should be disclosed in notes to the financial statements. ■

The rate earned on common stockholders' equity differs from the rates earned by Lincoln Company on total assets and total stockholders' equity. This occurs if there are borrowed funds and also preferred stock outstanding, which rank ahead of the common shares in their claim on earnings. Thus, the concept of leverage, as we discussed in the preceding section, can also be applied to the use of funds from the sale of preferred stock as well as borrowing. Funds from both sources can be used in an attempt to increase the return on common stockholders' equity.

Earnings per Share on Common Stock

One of the profitability measures often quoted by the financial press is **earnings per share (EPS) on common stock**. It is also normally reported in the income statement in corporate annual reports. If a company has issued only one class of stock, the earnings per share is computed by dividing net income by the number of shares of stock outstanding. If preferred and common stock are outstanding, the net income is first reduced by the amount of preferred dividend requirements.[2]

The data on the earnings per share of common stock for Lincoln Company are as follows:

	2000	1999
Net income	$91,000	$76,500
Preferred dividends	9,000	9,000
Remainder—identified with common stock	$82,000	$67,500
Shares of common stock outstanding	50,000	50,000
Earnings per share on common stock	$1.64	$1.35

Price-Earnings Ratio

Another profitability measure quoted by the financial press is the **price-earnings (P/E) ratio** on common stock. The price-earnings ratio is an indicator of a firm's future earnings prospects. It is computed by dividing the market price per share of common stock at a specific date by the annual earnings per share. To illustrate, assume that the market prices per common share are $20\frac{1}{2}$ at the end of 2000 and $13\frac{1}{2}$ at the end of 1999. The price-earnings ratio on common stock of Lincoln Company is computed as follows:

	2000	1999
Market price per share of common stock	$20.50	$13.50
Earnings per share on common stock	÷ 1.64	÷ 1.35
Price-earnings ratio on common stock	12.5	10.0

[2] Additional details related to earnings per share were discussed in a previous chapter.

The price-earnings ratio indicates that a share of common stock of Lincoln Company was selling for 10 times the amount of earnings per share at the end of 1999. At the end of 2000, the common stock was selling for 12.5 times the amount of earnings per share.

P/E ratios that are much higher than the market averages are generally associated with companies with fast-growing profits. P/E ratios that are much lower than the market averages are generally associated with "out of favor" or declining profit companies.

Dividends per Share and Dividend Yield

Since the primary basis for dividends is earnings, **dividends per share** and earnings per share on common stock are commonly used by investors in assessing alternative stock investments. The dividends per share for Lincoln Company were $0.80 ($40,000 ÷ 50,000 shares) for 2000 and $0.60 ($30,000 ÷ 50,000 shares) for 1999.

Dividends per share can be reported with earnings per share to indicate the relationship between dividends and earnings. A comparison of these two per share amounts indicates the extent to which the corporation is retaining its earnings for use in operations. Exhibit 9 shows these relationships for Lincoln Company:

EXHIBIT 9
Dividends and Earnings per Share of Common Stock

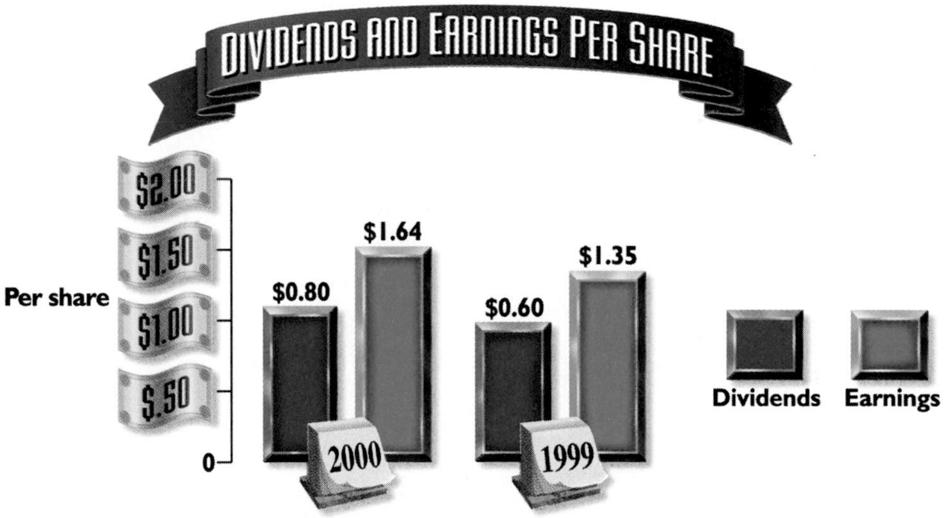

The **dividend yield** on common stock is a profitability measure that shows the rate of return to common stockholders in terms of cash dividends. It is of special interest to investors whose main investment objective is to receive current returns (dividends) on an investment rather than an increase in the market price of the investment. The dividend yield is computed by dividing the annual dividends paid per share of common stock by the market price per share on a specific date. To illustrate, assume that the market price was 20½ at the end of 2000 and 13½ at the end of 1999. The dividend yield on common stock of Lincoln Company is as follows:

	2000	1999
Dividends per share of common stock	$ 0.80	$ 0.60
Market price per share of common stock	÷ 20.50	÷ 13.50
Dividend yield on common stock	3.9%	4.4%

The earnings per share and dividend yield of a common stock are normally quoted on the daily listing of stock prices in the *Wall Street Journal* and other financial publications.

Summary of Analytical Measures

OBJECTIVE 4

Summarize the uses and limitations of analytical measures.

Exhibit 10 presents a summary of the analytical measures that we have discussed. These measures can be computed for most medium-size businesses. Depending on the specific business being analyzed, some measures might be omitted or additional measures could be developed. The type of industry, the capital structure, and the diversity of the business's operations usually affect the measures used. For example, analysis for an airline might include revenue per passenger mile and cost per available seat as measures. Likewise, analysis for a hotel might focus on occupancy rates.

Percentage analyses, ratios, turnovers, and other measures of financial position and operating results are useful analytical measures. They are helpful in assessing a business's past performance and predicting its future. They are not, however, a substitute for sound judgment. In selecting and interpreting analytical measures, conditions peculiar to a business or its industry should be considered. In addition, the influence of the general economic and business environment should be considered.

In determining trends, the interrelationship of the measures used in assessing a business should be carefully studied. Comparable indexes of earlier periods should also be studied. Data from competing businesses may be useful in assessing the efficiency of operations for the firm under analysis. In making such comparisons, however, the effects of differences in the accounting methods used by the businesses should be considered.

EXHIBIT 10
Summary of Analytical Measures

	Method of Computation	Use
Solvency measures:		
Working capital	Current assets − Current liabilities	To indicate the ability to meet currently maturing obligations (working capital and current ratio)
Current ratio	Current assets / Current liabilities	
Acid-test ratio	Quick assets / Current liabilities	To indicate instant debt-paying ability
Accounts receivable turnover	Net sales on account / Average accounts receivable	To assess the efficiency in collecting receivables and in the management of credit (accounts receivable turnover and number of days' sales in receivables)
Numbers of days' sales in receivables	Accounts receivable, end of year / Average daily sales on account	
Inventory turnover	Cost of goods sold / Average inventory	To assess the efficiency in the management of inventory (inventory turnover and number of days' sales in inventory)
Number of days' sales in inventory	Inventory, end of year / Average daily cost of goods sold	
Ratio of fixed assets to long-term liabilities	Fixed assets (net) / Long-term liabilities	To indicate the margin of safety to long-term creditors
Ratio of liabilities to stockholders' equity	Total liabilities / Total stockholders' equity	To indicate the margin of safety to creditors
Number of times interest charges earned	Income before income tax + Interest expense / Interest expense	To assess the risk to debtholders in terms of number of times interest charges were earned

EXHIBIT 10
(concluded)

	Method of Computation	Use
Profitability measures:		
Ratio of net sales to assets	Net sales / Average total assets (excluding long-term investments)	To assess the effectiveness in the use of assets
Rate earned on total assets	(Net income + Interest expense) / Average total assets	To assess the profitability of the assets
Rate earned on stockholders' equity	Net income / Average total stockholders' equity	To assess the profitability of the investment by stockholders
Rate earned on common stockholders' equity	(Net Income − Preferred dividends) / Average common stockholders' equity	To assess the profitability of the investment by common stockholders
Earnings per share on common stock	(Net income − Preferred dividends) / Shares of common stock outstanding	To assess the profitability of the investment by common stockholders
Price-earnings ratio	Market price per share of common stock / Earnings per share of common stock	To indicate future earnings prospects, based on the relationship between market value of common stock and earnings
Dividends per share of common stock	Dividends / Shares of common stock outstanding	To indicate the extent to which earnings are being distributed to common stockholders
Dividend yield	Dividends per share of common stock / Market price per share of common stock	To indicate the rate of return to common stockholders in terms of dividends

Corporate Annual Reports

OBJECTIVE 5

Describe the contents of corporate annual reports.

Corporations normally issue annual reports to their stockholders and other interested parties. Such reports summarize the corporation's operating activities for the past year and plans for the future. There are many variations in the order and form for presenting the major sections of annual reports. However, one section of the annual report is devoted to the financial statements, including the accompanying notes. In addition, annual reports usually include the following sections:

1. Financial Highlights
2. President's Letter to the Stockholders
3. Management Report
4. Independent Auditors' Report
5. Historical Summary

In the following paragraphs, we describe these sections. Each section, as well as the financial statements, is illustrated in the 1996 annual report for **Hershey Foods Corporation** in Appendix G.

Financial Highlights

The Financial Highlights section summarizes the operating results for the last year or two. It is sometimes called *Results in Brief*. It is usually presented on the first one or two pages of the annual report.

There are many variations in the format and content of the Financial Highlights section. Such items as sales, net income, net income per common share, cash dividends paid, cash dividends per common share, and the amount of capital expenditures are typically presented. In addition to these data, information about the financial position at the end of the year may be presented. The Financial Highlights section for Hershey Foods Corporation includes the year-end amounts of stockholders' equity, common shares outstanding, book value per share, and the price per share.

President's Letter to the Stockholders

A letter from the company president to the stockholders is also presented in most annual reports. These letters usually discuss such items as reasons for an increase or decrease in net income, changes in existing plants, purchase or construction of new plants, significant new financing commitments, social responsibility issues, and future plans.

Management Report

The management of the corporation is responsible for the corporation's accounting system and financial statements. In the Management Report section, the chief financial officer or other corporate officer normally includes the following:

1. A statement that the financial statements are management's responsibility and that they have been prepared according to generally accepted accounting principles.
2. Management's assessment of the company's internal accounting control system.
3. Comments on any other relevant matters related to the accounting system, the financial statements, and the examination by the independent auditor.

Independent Auditors' Report

Before issuing annual statements, all publicly held corporations are required to have an independent audit (examination) of their financial statements. For the financial statements of most companies, the CPAs who conduct the audit render an opinion on the fairness of the statements, as shown in the Independent Auditors' Report for Hershey Foods Corporation.

REAL WORLD

During the mid-1990s, the largest companies in the U.S. and in most parts of the world were audited by six large international accounting firms: **Arthur Andersen, Coopers & Lybrand, Deloitte & Touche, Ernst & Young, KPMG Peat Marwick,** and **Price Waterhouse.** In 1997, Coopers & Lybrand and Price Waterhouse announced their intention to merge, as did Ernst & Young and KPMG Peat Marwick. These mergers were motivated by the firms' desires to grow their consulting practices. However, the business community has expressed the concern that these mergers may jeopardize the competition among auditors, resulting in higher audit fees. In addition, regulators (such as the SEC) are concerned that it will be more difficult for auditors to maintain their independence from clients for whom they also perform consulting services.

Historical Summary

The Historical Summary section reports selected financial and operating data of past periods, usually for five or ten years. It is usually presented near the financial statements for the current year. There are wide variations in the types of data reported and the title of this section. In the annual report for Hershey Foods Corporation, this section is called the "Eleven-Year Consolidated Financial Summary."

Other Information

Some annual reports may include other financial information. For example, some reports may include forecasts that indicate financial plans and expectations for the year ahead and other supplemental data.

ENCORE

A Tale of Two Retailers

Two of the oldest and most venerable names in U.S. retailing are **Sears** and **Montgomery Ward**. These two companies virtually defined the "mall-based" retail concept. However, beginning in the mid-1980s, their stories could not be more different. The charts below show the ratio of net income to sales, ratio of liabilities to stockholders' equity, and the rate earned on stockholders' equity for 1992–1996 for the two retailers. As can be seen, their fortunes have diverged significantly over the time period. What happened?

Both companies faced daunting challenges during the mid-80s. First, consumers were becoming very value-conscious. Second, "category killers", such as **Home Depot** and **Circuit City**, began their move on U.S. retailing. Third, **Wal-Mart** began to dominate the price-conscious end of the market. This left both Sears and Montgomery Ward caught in a retailing squeeze. How did these two companies respond to these common threats?

Montgomery Ward failed to find its niche. It reduced prices below other mall-based retailers, but not enough to compete with Wal-Mart. However, at the same time, it failed to modernize its stores or freshen up its brands. Also, it moved away from apparel toward favoring electronics and thus went head to head against Circuit City. Price-conscious retailers shopped at Wal-Mart or Circuit City, while the mall-based shopper chose **J.C. Penney** or Sears for a more pleasant shopping experience.

Sears, on the other hand, identified its key customer group as the 30- to 50-year-old woman shopping for herself or her family. Then, it launched a $4 billion renovation project to create an appealing atmosphere for women. In addition, it expanded space and launched new brand items for women's apparel. All of this was combined with a new advertising campaign stressing "the softer side of Sears." Lastly, Sears focused on its core merchandising business by eliminating the catalog business and distributing **Allstate Insurance** back to the shareholders via a special dividend (which is why

the ratio of liabilities to stockholders' equity doubled between 1994 and 1995).

How does the story end? It's not over yet, but Montgomery Ward entered Chapter 11 bankruptcy in the summer of 1997, shed 3,900 workers, and put its **Lechmere** and **Electric Avenue & More** units up for sale. Some analysts believe Montgomery Ward may eventually be liquidated. What can be said for Sears? It still faces significant competition, but it's fair to say that Montgomery Ward's pain becomes Sears' gain. ■

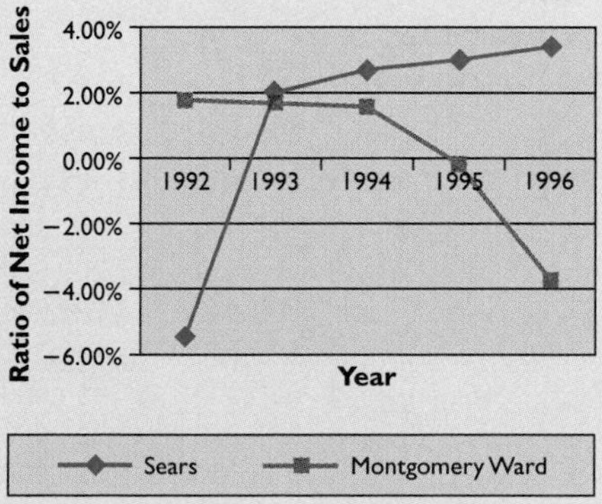

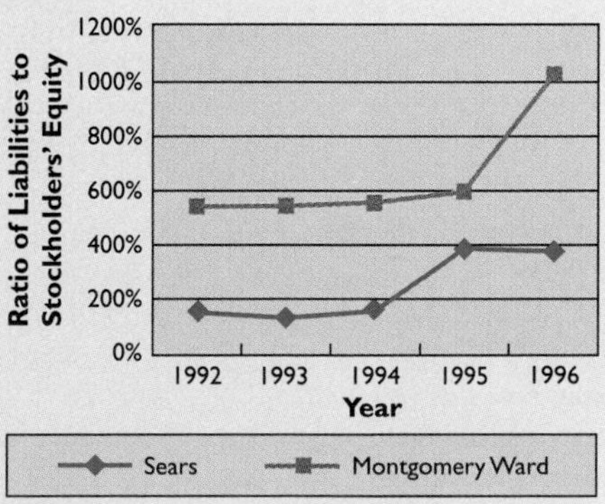

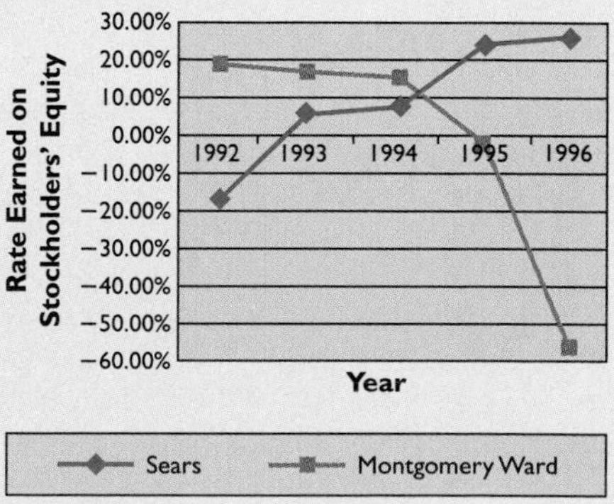

KEY POINTS

1 List basic financial statement analytical procedures.

The analysis of percentage increases and decreases in related items in comparative financial statements is called horizontal analysis. The analysis of percentages of component parts to the total in a single statement is called vertical analysis. Financial statements in which all amounts are expressed in percentages for purposes of analysis are called common-size statements.

2 Apply financial statement analysis to assess the solvency of a business.

The primay focus of financial statement analysis is the assessment of solvency and profitability. All users are interested in the ability of a business to pay its debts as they come due (solvency) and to earn income (profitability). Solvency analysis is normally assessed by examining the following balance sheet relationships: (1) current position analysis, (2) accounts receivable analysis, (3) inventory analysis, (4) the ratio of fixed assets to long-term liabilities, (5) the ratio of liabilities to stockholders' equity, and (6) the number of times interest charges are earned.

3 Apply financial statement analysis to assess the profitability of a business.

Profitability analysis focuses mainly on the relationship between operating results (income statement) and resources available (balance sheet). Major analyses used in assessing profitability include (1) the ratio of net sales to assets, (2) the rate earned on total assets, (3) the rate earned on stockholders' equity, (4) the rate earned on common stockholders' equity, (5) earnings per share on common stock, (6) the price-earnings ratio, (7) dividends per share, and (8) dividend yield.

4 Summarize the uses and limitations of analytical measures.

In selecting and interpreting analytical measures, conditions peculiar to a business or its industry should be considered. For example, the type of industry, capital structure, and diversity of the business's operations affect the measures used. In addition, the influence of the general economic and business environment should be considered.

5 Describe the contents of corporate annual reports.

Corporate annual reports normally include financial statements and the following sections: Financial Highlights, President's Letter to the Stockholders, Management Report, Independent Auditors' Report, and Historical Summary.

ILLUSTRATIVE PROBLEM

Rainbow Paint Co.'s comparative financial statements for the years ending December 31, 2000 and 1999, are as follows. The market price of Rainbow Paint Co.'s common stock was $30 on December 31, 1999, and $25 on December 31, 2000.

Rainbow Paint Co.
Comparative Income Statement
For the Years Ended December 31, 2000 and 1999

	2000	1999
Sales (all on account)	$5,125,000	$3,257,600
Sales returns and allowances	125,000	57,600
Net sales	$5,000,000	$3,200,000
Cost of goods sold	3,400,000	2,080,000
Gross profit	$1,600,000	$1,120,000
Selling expenses	$ 650,000	$ 464,000
Administrative expenses	325,000	224,000
Total operating expenses	$ 975,000	$ 688,000
Income from operations	$ 625,000	$ 432,000
Other income	25,000	19,200
	$ 650,000	$ 451,200
Other expense (interest)	105,000	64,000
Income before income tax	$ 545,000	$ 387,200
Income tax expense	300,000	176,000
Net income	$ 245,000	$ 211,200

Rainbow Paint Co.
Comparative Retained Earnings Statement
For the Years Ended December 31, 2000 and 1999

	2000	1999
Retained earnings, January 1	$723,000	$581,800
Add net income for year	245,000	211,200
Total	$968,000	$793,000
Deduct dividends:		
On preferred stock	$ 40,000	$ 40,000
On common stock	45,000	30,000
Total	$ 85,000	$ 70,000
Retained earnings, December 31	$883,000	$723,000

Rainbow Paint Co.
Comparative Balance Sheet
December 31, 2000 and 1999

	2000	1999
Assets		
Current assets:		
Cash	$ 175,000	$ 125,000
Marketable securities	150,000	50,000
Accounts receivable (net)	425,000	325,000
Inventories	720,000	480,000
Prepaid expenses	30,000	20,000
Total current assets	$1,500,000	$1,000,000
Long-term investments	250,000	225,000
Property, plant, and equipment (net)	2,093,000	1,948,000
Total assets	$3,843,000	$3,173,000
Liabilities		
Current liabilities	$ 750,000	$ 650,000
Long-term liabilities:		
Mortgage note payable, 10%, due 2003	$ 410,000	—
Bonds payable, 8%, due 2006	800,000	$ 800,000
Total long-term liabilities	$1,210,000	$ 800,000
Total liabilities	$1,960,000	$1,450,000
Stockholders' Equity		
Preferred 8% stock, $100 par	$ 500,000	$ 500,000
Common stock, $10 par	500,000	500,000
Retained earnings	883,000	723,000
Total stockholders' equity	$1,883,000	$1,723,000
Total liabilities and stockholders' equity	$3,843,000	$3,173,000

Instructions

Determine the following measures for 2000:

1. Working capital
2. Current ratio
3. Acid-test ratio
4. Accounts receivable turnover
5. Number of days' sales in receivables
6. Inventory turnover
7. Number of days' sales in inventory
8. Ratio of fixed assets to long-term liabilities
9. Ratio of liabilities to stockholders' equity
10. Number of times interest charges earned
11. Number of times preferred dividends earned
12. Ratio of net sales to assets
13. Rate earned on total assets
14. Rate earned on stockholders' equity
15. Rate earned on common stockholders' equity
16. Earnings per share on common stock

17. Price-earnings ratio
18. Dividends per share of common stock
19. Dividend yield

Solution

(Ratios are rounded to the nearest single digit after the decimal point.)

1. Working capital: $750,000
   $1,500,000 − $750,000
2. Current ratio: 2.0
   $1,500,000 ÷ $750,000
3. Acid-test ratio: 1.0
   $750,000 ÷ $750,000
4. Accounts receivable turnover: 13.3
   $5,000,000 ÷ [($425,000 + $325,000) ÷ 2]
5. Number of days' sales in receivables: 31 days
   $5,000,000 ÷ 365 = $13,699
   $425,000 ÷ $13,699
6. Inventory turnover: 5.7
   $3,400,000 ÷ [($720,000 + $480,000) ÷ 2]
7. Number of days' sales in inventory: 77.3 days
   $3,400,000 ÷ 365 = $9,315
   $720,000 ÷ $9,315
8. Ratio of fixed assets to long-term liabilities: 1.7
   $2,093,000 ÷ $1,210,000
9. Ratio of liabilities to stockholders' equity: 1.0
   $1,960,000 ÷ $1,883,000
10. Number of times interest charges earned: 6.2
    ($545,000 + $105,000) ÷ $105,000
11. Number of times preferred dividends earned: 6.1
    $245,000 ÷ $40,000
12. Ratio of net sales to assets: 1.5
    $5,000,000 ÷ [($3,593,000 + $2,948,000) ÷ 2]
13. Rate earned on total assets: 10.0%
    ($245,000 + $105,000) ÷ [($3,843,000 + $3,173,000) ÷ 2]
14. Rate earned on stockholders' equity: 13.6%
    $245,000 ÷ [($1,883,000 + $1,723,000) ÷ 2]
15. Rate earned on common stockholders' equity: 15.7%
    ($245,000 − $40,000) ÷ [($1,383,000 + $1,223,000) ÷ 2]
16. Earnings per share on common stock: $4.10
    ($245,000 − $40,000) ÷ 50,000
17. Price-earnings ratio: 6.1
    $25 ÷ $4.10
18. Dividends per share of common stock: $0.90
    $45,000 ÷ 50,000 shares
19. Dividend yield: 3.6%
    $0.90 ÷ $25

SELF-EXAMINATION QUESTIONS

Answers at End of Chapter

Matching

Match each of the following statements with its proper term. Some terms may not be used.

A. accounts receivable turnover
B. acid-test ratio

H 1. The percentage of increases and decreases in corresponding items in comparative financial statements.

P 2. The sum of cash, receivables, and marketable securities.

C. **common-size statement**
D. **current ratio**
E. **dividends per share**
F. **dividend yield**
G. **earnings per share (EPS) on common stock**
H. **horizontal analysis**
I. **inventory turnover**
J. **leverage**
K. **number of days' sales in inventory**
L. **number of days' sales in receivables**
M. **number of times interest charges earned**
N. **price-earnings (P/E) ratio**
O. **profitability**
P. **quick assets**
Q. **rate earned on common stockholders' equity**
R. **rate earned on stockholders' equity**
S. **rate earned on total assets**
T. **ratio of fixed assets to long-term liabilities**
U. **ratio of liabilities to stockholders' equity**
V. **ratio of net sales to assets**
W. **solvency**
X. **vertical analysis**
Y. **working capital**

K 3. The relationship between the volume of sales and inventory, computed by dividing the inventory at the end of the year by the average daily cost of goods sold.

W 4. The ability of a firm to pay its debts as they come due.

L 5. The relationship between credit sales and accounts receivable, computed by dividing the net accounts receivable at the end of the year by the average daily sales on account.

A 6. The relationship between credit sales and accounts receivable, computed by dividing net sales on account by the average net accounts receivable.

J 7. The tendency of the rate earned on stockholders' equity to vary from the rate earned on total assets because the amount earned on assets acquired through the use of funds provided by creditors varies from the interest paid to these creditors.

C 8. A financial statement in which all items are expressed only in relative terms.

R 9. A measure of profitability computed by dividing net income by total stockholders' equity.

Y 10. The excess of total current assets over total current liabilities at some point in time.

N 11. The ratio of the market price per share of common stock, at a specific date, to the annual earnings per share.

S 12. A measure of the profitability of assets, without regard to the equity of creditors and stockholders in the assets.

G 13. The profitability ratio of net income available to common shareholders to the number of common shares outstanding.

B 14. The ratio of the sum of cash, receivables, and marketable securities to current liabilities.

X 15. The percentage analysis of component parts in relation to the total of the parts in a single financial statement.

Q 16. A measure of profitability computed by dividing net income, reduced by preferred dividend requirements, by common stockholders' equity.

D 17. The ratio of current assets to current liabilities.

I 18. The relationship between the volume of goods sold and inventory, computed by dividing the cost of goods sold by the average inventory.

O 19. The ability of a firm to earn income.

Multiple Choice

1. What type of analysis is indicated by the following?

	Amount	**Percent**
Current assets	$100,000	20%
Property, plant, and equipment	400,000	80
Total assets	$500,000	100%

A. Vertical analysis
B. Horizontal analysis
C. Profitability analysis
D. Contribution margin analysis

2. Which of the following measures is useful as an indication of the ability of a firm to pay its current liabilities?

A. Working capital
B. Current ratio
C. Acid-test ratio
D. All of the above

3. The ratio determined by dividing total current assets by total current liabilities is:

A. current ratio
B. working capital ratio
C. bankers' ratio
D. all of the above

4. The ratio of the quick assets to current liabilities, which indicates the "instant" debt-paying ability of a firm, is:

A. current ratio
B. working capital ratio
C. acid-test ratio
D. bankers' ratio

5. A measure useful in evaluating the efficiency in the management of inventories is:

A. working capital ratio
B. acid-test ratio
C. number of days' sales in inventory
D. ratio of fixed assets to long-term liabilities

CLASS DISCUSSION QUESTIONS

1. What is the difference between horizontal and vertical analysis of financial statements?
2. What is the advantage of using comparative statements for financial analysis rather than statements for a single date or period?
3. The current year's amount of net income (after income tax) is 15% larger than that of the preceding year. Does this indicate an improved operating performance? Discuss.
4. How would you respond to a horizontal analysis that showed an expense increasing by over 100%?
5. a. Name the major ratios useful in assessing solvency and profitability.
   b. Why is it important not to rely on only one ratio or measure in assessing the solvency or profitability of a business?
6. How would the current and acid-test ratios of a service business compare?
7. For Lindsay Corporation, the working capital at the end of the current year is $50,000 greater than the working capital at the end of the preceding year, reported as follows:

	Current Year	Preceding Year
Current assets:		
Cash, marketable securities, and receivables	$340,000	$300,000
Inventories	510,000	325,000
Total current assets	$850,000	$625,000
Current liabilities	425,000	250,000
Working capital	$425,000	$375,000

   Has the current position improved? Explain.
8. A company that grants terms of n/30 on all sales has a yearly accounts receivable turnover, based on monthly averages, of 6. Is this a satisfactory turnover? Discuss.
9. What does an increase in the number of days' sales in receivables ordinarily indicate about the credit and collection policy of the firm?
10. a. Why is it advantageous to have a high inventory turnover?
    b. Is it possible for the inventory turnover to be too high? Discuss.
    c. Is it possible to have a high inventory turnover and a high number of days' sales in inventory? Discuss.
11. What do the following data taken from a comparative balance sheet indicate about the company's ability to borrow additional funds on a long-term basis in the current year as compared to the preceding year?

	Current Year	Preceding Year
Fixed assets (net)	$1,750,000	$1,700,000
Total long-term liabilities	700,000	850,000

12. What does a decrease in the ratio of liabilities to stockholders' equity indicate about the margin of safety for a firm's creditors and the ability of the firm to withstand adverse business conditions?
13. In computing the ratio of net sales to assets, why are long-term investments excluded in determining the amount of the total assets?
14. In determining the number of times interest charges are earned, why are interest charges added to income before income tax?
15. In determining the rate earned on total assets, why is interest expense added to net income before dividing by total assets?
16. a. Why is the rate earned on stockholders' equity by a thriving business ordinarily higher than the rate earned on total assets?
    b. Should the rate earned on common stockholders' equity normally be higher or lower than the rate earned on total stockholders' equity? Explain.

17. The net income (after income tax) of A. L. Gibson Inc. was $25 per common share in the latest year and $40 per common share for the preceding year. At the beginning of the latest year, the number of shares outstanding was doubled by a stock split. There were no other changes in the amount of stock outstanding. What were the earnings per share in the preceding year, adjusted for comparison with the latest year?
18. The price-earnings ratio for the common stock of Essian Company was 10 at December 31, the end of the current fiscal year. What does the ratio indicate about the selling price of the common stock in relation to current earnings?
19. Why would the dividend yield differ significantly from the rate earned on common stockholders' equity?
20. Favorable business conditions may bring about certain seemingly unfavorable ratios, and unfavorable business operations may result in apparently favorable ratios. For example, Sanchez Company increased its sales and net income substantially for the current year, yet the current ratio at the end of the year is lower than at the beginning of the year. Discuss some possible causes of the apparent weakening of the current position, while sales and net income have increased substantially.
21. a. What are the major components of an annual report?
    b. Indicate the purpose of the Financial Highlights section and the President's Letter.

Resources for Your Success On-Line at warren.swcollege.com

Remember! If you need additional help, visit South-Western's Web site. See page 26 for a description of the online and printed materials that are available.

EXERCISES

Exercise 16–1
Vertical analysis of income statement

Objective 1

✓ 2000 net income: $52,800; 8% of sales

Revenue and expense data for Cabot Cabinet Co. are as follows:

	2000	1999
Sales	$660,000	$600,000
Cost of goods sold	389,400	384,000
Selling expenses	105,600	84,000
Administrative expenses	66,000	54,000
Income tax expense	46,200	42,000

a. Prepare an income statement in comparative form, stating each item for both 2000 and 1999 as a percent of sales.
b. Comment on the significant changes disclosed by the comparative income statement.

Exercise 16–2
Vertical analysis of income statement

Objective 1

REAL WORLD

✓ a. 1997 operating income, 9.2% of revenues

The following comparative income statement (in thousands of dollars) for the years ending February 2, 1997, and January 31, 1996, was adapted from the 1997 annual report of **Dell Computer Corporation**:

	1997	1996
Revenues	$7,759,000	$5,296,000
Costs and expenses:		
Cost of sales	6,093,000	4,229,000
Gross profit	$1,666,000	$1,067,000
Selling, distribution, and administrative expenses	952,000	690,000
Operating income	$ 714,000	$ 377,000

a. Prepare a comparative income statement for 1997 and 1996 in vertical form, stating each item as a percent of revenues. Round to one digit after the decimal place.
b. Based upon the 1996 income statement, comment on the significant changes.

Exercise 16–3
Common-size income statement

Objective 1

✓ a. Keystone net income: $642,000; 9.2% of sales

Revenue and expense data for the current calendar year for Keystone Publishing Company and for the publishing industry are as follows. The Keystone Publishing Company data are expressed in dollars. The publishing industry averages are expressed in percentages.

	Keystone Publishing Company	Publishing Industry Average
Sales	$7,070,000	100.5%
Sales returns and allowances	70,000	0.5
Cost of goods sold	4,900,000	69.0
Selling expenses	560,000	9.0
Administrative expenses	490,000	8.2
Other income	42,000	0.6
Other expense	100,000	1.4
Income tax expense	350,000	5.0

a. Prepare a common-size income statement comparing the results of operations for Keystone Publishing Company with the industry average. Round to one digit after the decimal place.
b. As far as the data permit, comment on significant relationships revealed by the comparisons.

Exercise 16–4
Vertical analysis of balance sheet

Objective 1

✓ Retained earnings, Dec. 31, 2000, 33.75%

Balance sheet data for Fisher Fabrics Company on December 31, the end of the fiscal year, are as follows:

	2000	1999
Current assets	$280,000	$260,000
Property, plant, and equipment	480,000	400,000
Intangible assets	40,000	41,000
Current liabilities	100,000	71,000
Long-term liabilities	180,000	220,000
Common stock	250,000	200,000
Retained earnings	270,000	210,000

Prepare a comparative balance sheet for 2000 and 1999, stating each asset as a percent of total assets and each liability and stockholders' equity item as a percent of the total liabilities and stockholders' equity. Round to two digits after the decimal place.

Exercise 16–5
Horizontal analysis of the income statement

Objective 1

✓ a. Net income increase, 73.9%

Income statement data for Neon Flashlight Company for the year ended December 31, 2000 and 1999, are as follows:

	2000	1999
Sales	$940,000	$850,000
Cost of goods sold	610,000	580,000
Gross profit	$330,000	$270,000
Selling expenses	$126,000	$137,000
Administrative expenses	44,000	53,500
Total operating expenses	$170,000	$190,500
Income before income tax	$160,000	$ 79,500
Income tax expense	60,000	22,000
Net income	$100,000	$ 57,500

a. Prepare a comparative income statement with horizontal analysis, indicating the increase (decrease) for 2000 when compared with 1999. Round to one digit after the decimal place.
b. What conclusions can be drawn from the horizontal analysis?

Exercise 16–6
Current position analysis
Objective 2

✓ Current year working capital, $360,000

The following data were taken from the balance sheet of Precision Engine Company:

	Current Year	Preceding Year
Cash	$ 89,500	$139,000
Marketable securities	110,000	98,000
Accounts and notes receivable (net)	190,500	153,000
Inventories	250,500	222,000
Prepaid expenses	19,500	38,000
Accounts and notes payable (short-term)	245,000	203,500
Accrued liabilities	55,000	56,500

a. Determine for each year (1) the working capital, (2) the current ratio, and (3) the acid-test ratio.
b. What conclusions can be drawn from these data as to the company's ability to meet its currently maturing debts?

Exercise 16–7
Current position analysis
Objective 2

What's Wrong WITH THIS?

The bond indenture for the 10-year, 9½% debenture bonds dated January 2, 1999, required working capital of $350,000, a current ratio of 1.5, and an acid-test ratio of 1 at the end of each calendar year until the bonds mature. At December 31, 2000, the three measures were computed as follows:

1.

Current assets:		
Cash	$295,000	
Marketable securities	148,000	
Accounts and notes receivable (net)	172,000	
Inventories	300,000	
Prepaid expenses	135,000	
Goodwill	150,000	
Total current assets		$1,200,000
Current liabilities:		
Accounts and short-term notes payable	$500,000	
Accrued liabilities	250,000	
Total current liabilities		750,000
Working capital		$ 450,000

2. Current ratio = 1.6 ($1,200,000 ÷ $750,000)
3. Acid-test ratio = 1.2 ($615,000 ÷ $500,000)

a. Can you find any errors in the determination of the three measures of current position analysis?
b. Is the company satisfying the terms of the bond indenture?

Exercise 16–8
Accounts receivable analysis
Objective 2

HAT

✓ a. Accounts receivable turnover, current year, 6.0

The following data are taken from the financial statements of North Company. Terms of all sales are 1/10, n/60.

	Current Year	Preceding Year
Accounts receivable, end of year	$ 572,000	$ 408,333
Monthly average accounts receivable (net)	476,667	350,000
Net sales on account	2,860,000	2,450,000

a. Determine for each year (1) the accounts receivable turnover and (2) the number of days' sales in receivables. Round to one digit after the decimal place.
b. What conclusions can be drawn from these data concerning accounts receivable and credit policies?

Exercise 16–9
Inventory analysis

Objective 2

HAT

✓ a. Inventory turnover, current year, 8.0

The following data were extracted from the income statement of Cascade Instruments Inc.:

	Current Year	Preceding Year
Sales	$7,400,000	$5,200,000
Beginning inventories	642,500	607,500
Cost of goods sold	5,280,000	3,750,000
Ending inventories	677,500	642,500

a. Determine for each year (1) the inventory turnover and (2) the number of days' sales in inventory. Round to one digit after the decimal place.
b. What conclusions can be drawn from these data concerning the inventories?

Exercise 16–10
Ratio of liabilities to stockholders' equity and number of times interest charges earned

Objective 2

✓ a. Ratio of liabilities to stockholders' equity, Dec. 31, 2000, 0.56

The following data were taken from the financial statements of Mountain Spring Water Co. for December 31, 2000 and 1999:

	December 31, 2000	December 31, 1999
Accounts payable	$ 200,000	$ 400,000
Current maturities of serial bonds payable	400,000	400,000
Serial bonds payable, 12%, issued 1995, due 2004	1,600,000	2,000,000
Common stock, $1 par value	100,000	100,000
Paid-in capital in excess of par	1,000,000	1,000,000
Retained earnings	2,860,000	2,400,000

The income before income tax was $780,000 and $216,000 for the years 2000 and 1999, respectively.

a. Determine the ratio of liabilities to stockholders' equity at the end of each year. Round to two digits after the decimal place.
b. Determine the number of times the bond interest charges are earned during the year for both years.
c. What conclusions can be drawn from these data as to the company's ability to meet its currently maturing debts?

Exercise 16–11
Profitability ratios

Objective 3

HAT

✓ a. Rate earned on total assets, 2001, 14%

The following selected data were taken from the financial statements of Ohio Cement Co. for December 31, 2001, 2000, and 1999:

	December 31, 2001	December 31, 2000	December 31, 1999
Total assets	$3,200,000	$2,800,000	$2,000,000
Notes payable (8% interest)	500,000	500,000	500,000
Common stock	900,000	900,000	900,000
Preferred $10 stock, $100 par, cumulative, nonparticipating (no change during year)	300,000	300,000	300,000
Retained earnings	1,430,000	1,050,000	250,000

The 2001 net income was $380,000, and the 2000 net income was $800,000. No dividends on common stock were declared between 1999 and 2001.

a. Determine the rate earned on total assets, the rate earned on stockholders' equity, and the rate earned on common stockholders' equity for the years 2000 and 2001. Round to one digit after the decimal place.
b. What conclusions can be drawn from these data as to the company's profitability?

Exercise 16–12
Six measures of solvency or profitability

Objectives 2, 3

HAT

✓ c. Ratio of net sales to assets, 1.44

The following data were taken from the financial statements of Premium Printers Inc. for the current fiscal year:

Property, plant, and equipment (net)			$1,000,000
Liabilities:			
Current liabilities		$400,000	
Mortgage note payable, 10%, issued 1990, due 2005		800,000	
Total liabilities			$1,200,000
Stockholders' equity:			
Preferred $4 stock, $80 par, cumulative, nonparticipating (no change during year)			$ 400,000
Common stock, $10 par (no change during year)			1,200,000
Retained earnings:			
Balance, beginning of year	$600,000		
Net income	300,000	$900,000	
Preferred dividends	$ 20,000		
Common dividends	80,000	100,000	
Balance, end of year			800,000
Total stockholders' equity			$2,400,000
Net sales			$4,500,000
Interest expense			$ 80,000

Assuming that long-term investments totaled $175,000 throughout the year and that total assets were $3,000,000 at the beginning of the year, determine the following: (a) ratio of fixed assets to long-term liabilities, (b) ratio of liabilities to stockholders' equity, (c) ratio of net sales to assets, (d) rate earned on total assets, (e) rate earned on stockholders' equity, and (f) rate earned on common stockholders' equity. Round to two digits after the decimal place.

Exercise 16–13
Five measures of solvency or profitability

Objectives 2, 3

HAT

✓ d. Price-earnings ratio, 24

The balance sheet for Aspen Avionics Corporation at the end of the current fiscal year indicated the following:

Bonds payable, 10% (issued in 1990, due in 2010)	$4,000,000
Preferred $10 stock, $100 par	1,000,000
Common stock, $20 par	8,000,000

Income before income tax was $1,000,000, and income taxes were $300,000 for the current year. Cash dividends paid on common stock during the current year totaled $288,000. The common stock was selling for $36 per share at the end of the year. Determine each of the following: (a) number of times bond interest charges were earned, (b) number of times preferred dividends were earned, (c) earnings per share on common stock, (d) price-earnings ratio, (e) dividends per share of common stock, and (f) dividend yield.

Exercise 16–14
Earnings per share, price-earnings ratio, dividend yield

Objective 3

✓ b. Price-earnings ratio, 15

The following information was taken from the financial statements of Cool Breeze Air Conditioners Inc. for December 31 of the current fiscal year:

Common stock, $15 par value (no change during the year)	$4,500,000
Preferred $8 stock, $100 par, cumulative, nonparticipating (no change during year)	800,000

The net income was $574,000 and the declared dividends on the common stock were $225,000 for the current year. The market price of the common stock is $25.50 per share.

For the common stock, determine the (a) earnings per share, (b) price-earnings ratio, (c) dividends per share, and (d) dividend yield.

Exercise 16–15
Earnings per share

Objective 3

✓ b. Earnings per share on common stock, $6.50

The net income reported on the income statement of United Fruit Co. was $4,200,000. There were 400,000 shares of $20 par common stock and 200,000 shares of $8 cumulative preferred stock outstanding throughout the current year. The income statement included two extraordinary items: a $1,250,000 gain from condemnation of land and a $250,000 loss arising from flood damage, both after applicable income tax. Determine the per share figures for common stock for (a) income before extraordinary items and (b) net income.

PROBLEMS SERIES A

Problem 16–1A
Horizontal analysis for income statement

Objective 1

GENERAL LEDGER

✓ 1. Sales, 10% increase

For 2000, Wang Company reported its most significant decline in net income in years. At the end of the year, Hai Wang, the president, is presented with the following condensed comparative income statement:

Wang Company
Comparative Income Statement
For the Years Ended December 31, 2000 and 1999

	2000	1999
Sales	$495,000	$450,000
Sales returns and allowances	5,000	2,000
Net sales	$490,000	$448,000
Cost of goods sold	312,000	260,000
Gross profit	$178,000	$188,000
Selling expenses	$ 84,000	$ 70,000
Administrative expenses	38,500	35,000
Total operating expenses	$122,500	$105,000
Income from operations	$ 55,500	$ 83,000
Other income	2,500	2,000
Income before income tax	$ 58,000	$ 85,000
Income tax expense	20,000	28,000
Net income	$ 38,000	$ 57,000

Instructions

1. Prepare a comparative income statement with horizontal analysis for the two-year period, using 1999 as the base year. Round to one digit after the decimal place.
2. To the extent the data permit, comment on the significant relationships revealed by the horizontal analysis prepared in (1).

Problem 16–2A
Vertical analysis for income statement

Objective 1

GENERAL LEDGER
SPREADSHEET

✓ 1. Net income, 2000, 8.6%

For 2000, Kasouski Company initiated a sales promotion campaign that included the expenditure of an additional $10,000 for advertising. At the end of the year, Leszek Kasouski, the president, is presented with the following condensed comparative income statement:

Kasouski Company
Comparative Income Statement
For the Years Ended December 31, 2000 and 1999

	2000	1999
Sales	$720,000	$650,000
Sales returns and allowances	20,000	15,000
Net sales	$700,000	$635,000
Cost of goods sold	290,000	270,000
Gross profit	$410,000	$365,000
Selling expenses	200,000	190,000
Administrative expenses	125,000	115,000
Total operating expenses	$325,000	$305,000
Income from operations	$ 85,000	$ 60,000
Other income	10,000	9,000
Income before income tax	$ 95,000	$ 69,000
Income tax expense	35,000	26,000
Net income	$ 60,000	$ 43,000

Instructions

1. Prepare a comparative income statement for the two-year period, presenting an analysis of each item in relationship to net sales for each of the years. Round to one digit after the decimal place.

2. To the extent the data permit, comment on the significant relationships revealed by the vertical analysis prepared in (1).

Problem 16–3A

Effect of transactions on current position analysis

Objective 2

✓ 1. Current ratio, 2.5

Data pertaining to the current position of Clarity Glass Company are as follows:

Cash	$256,000
Marketable securities	84,000
Accounts and notes receivable (net)	360,000
Inventories	532,000
Prepaid expenses	18,000
Accounts payable	380,000
Notes payable (short-term)	80,000
Accrued expenses	40,000

Instructions

1. Compute (a) the working capital, (b) the current ratio, and (c) the acid-test ratio.
2. List the following captions on a sheet of paper:

Transaction	Working Capital	Current Ratio	Acid-Test Ratio

Compute the working capital, the current ratio, and the acid-test ratio after each of the following transactions, and record the results in the appropriate columns. Consider each transaction separately and assume that only that transaction affects the data given above. Round to two digits after the decimal point.

a. Sold marketable securities at no gain or loss, $56,000.
b. Paid accounts payable, $40,000.
c. Purchased goods on account, $80,000.
d. Paid notes payable, $30,000.
e. Declared a cash dividend, $25,000.
f. Declared a common stock dividend on common stock, $28,500.
g. Borrowed cash from bank on a long-term note, $140,000.
h. Received cash on account, $164,000.
i. Issued additional shares of stock for cash, $200,000.
j. Paid cash for prepaid expenses, $10,000.

Problem 16–4A

Eighteen measures of solvency and profitability

Objectives 2, 3

HAT SPREADSHEET

✓ 5. Number of days' sales in receivables, 39.7

The comparative financial statements of Boston Bagel Company are as follows. The market price of Boston Bagel Company common stock was $36 on December 31, 2000.

Boston Bagel Company
Comparative Income Statement
For the Years Ended December 31, 2000 and 1999

	2000	1999
Sales (all on account)	$2,450,000	$2,100,000
Sales returns and allowances	50,000	40,000
Net sales	$2,400,000	$2,060,000
Cost of goods sold	1,100,000	960,000
Gross profit	$1,300,000	$1,100,000
Selling expenses	$ 426,000	$ 395,000
Administrative expenses	354,000	345,000
Total operating expenses	$ 780,000	$ 740,000
Income from operations	$ 520,000	$ 360,000
Other income	80,000	30,000
	$ 600,000	$ 390,000
Other expense (interest)	130,000	90,000
Income before income tax	$ 470,000	$ 300,000
Income tax expense	140,000	100,000
Net income	$ 330,000	$ 200,000

Boston Bagel Company
Comparative Retained Earnings Statement
For the Years Ended December 31, 2000 and 1999

	Dec. 31, 2000	Dec. 31, 1999
Retained earnings, January 1	$275,000	$113,000
Add net income for year	330,000	200,000
Total	$605,000	$313,000
Deduct dividends:		
On preferred stock	$ 30,000	$ 18,000
On common stock	20,000	20,000
Total	$ 50,000	$ 38,000
Retained earnings, December 31	$555,000	$275,000

Boston Bagel Company
Comparative Balance Sheet
December 31, 2000 and 1999

	Dec. 31, 2000	Dec. 31, 1999
Assets		
Current assets:		
Cash	$ 67,000	$ 84,000
Marketable securities	152,000	161,000
Accounts receivable (net)	261,000	295,000
Inventories	325,000	348,000
Prepaid expenses	25,000	22,000
Total current assets	$ 830,000	$ 910,000
Long-term investments	1,000,000	300,000
Property, plant, and equipment (net)	1,675,000	1,290,000
Total assets	$3,505,000	$2,500,000
Liabilities		
Current liabilities	$ 450,000	$ 325,000
Long-term liabilities:		
Mortgage note payable, 10%, due 2005	$ 400,000	—
Bonds payable, 15%, due 2009	600,000	$ 600,000
Total long-term liabilities	$1,000,000	$ 600,000
Total liabilities	$1,450,000	$ 925,000
Stockholders' Equity		
Preferred $6 stock, $100 par	$ 500,000	$ 300,000
Common stock, $10 par	1,000,000	1,000,000
Retained earnings	555,000	275,000
Total stockholders' equity	$2,055,000	$1,575,000
Total liabilities and stockholders' equity	$3,505,000	$2,500,000

Instructions

Determine the following measures for 2000, rounding to the nearest single digit after the decimal point:

1. Working capital
2. Current ratio
3. Acid-test ratio
4. Accounts receivable turnover
5. Number of days' sales in receivables
6. Inventory turnover
7. Number of days' sales in inventory
8. Ratio of fixed assets to long-term liabilities
9. Ratio of liabilities to stockholders' equity
10. Number of times interest charges earned
11. Number of times preferred dividends earned
12. Ratio of net sales to assets
13. Rate earned on total assets
14. Rate earned on stockholders' equity
15. Rate earned on common stockholders' equity
16. Earnings per share on common stock

17. Price-earnings ratio
18. Dividends per share of common stock
19. Dividend yield

Problem 16–5A

Solvency and profitability trend analysis

Objectives 2, 3

Song Shoe Company has provided the following comparative information:

	2000	1999	1998	1997	1996
Net income	$ 600,000	$ 300,000	$ 200,000	$ 100,000	$ 50,000
Income tax expense	150,000	75,000	50,000	25,000	12,500
Interest	140,000	100,000	30,000	20,000	20,000
Average total assets	3,800,000	2,800,000	1,800,000	1,500,000	1,400,000
Average total stockholders' equity	2,400,000	1,800,000	1,500,000	1,300,000	1,200,000

You have been asked to evaluate the historical performance of the company over the last five years. Selected industry ratios have remained relatively steady for the last five years at the following levels:

	1996–2000
Rate earned on total assets	14%
Rate earned on stockholders' equity	18%
Number of times interest charges earned	6.0
Ratio of liabilities to stockholders' equity	0.6

Instructions

1. Prepare four line graphs, with ratio on the vertical axis and years on the horizontal axis for the following four ratios (rounded to two digits after the decimal place):
   a. Rate earned on total assets
   b. Rate earned on stockholders' equity
   c. Number of times interest charges earned
   d. Ratio of liabilities to stockholders' equity (using average balances)
   Display both the company ratio and the industry benchmark on each graph (each graph should have two lines).
2. Prepare an analysis of the graphs in (1).

PROBLEMS SERIES B

Problem 16–1B

Horizontal analysis for income statement

Objective 1

GENERAL LEDGER

✓ 1. Sales, 20% increase

For 1999, Better Biscuit Company reported its most significant increase in net income in years. At the end of the year, John Newton, the president, is presented with the following condensed comparative income statement:

Better Biscuit Company
Comparative Income Statement
For the Years Ended December 31, 2000 and 1999

	2000	1999
Sales	$840,000	$700,000
Sales returns and allowances	5,000	5,000
Net sales	$835,000	$695,000
Cost of goods sold	450,000	400,000
Gross profit	$385,000	$295,000
Selling expenses	$115,000	$100,000
Administrative expenses	49,500	45,000
Total operating expenses	$164,500	$145,000
Income from operations	$220,500	$150,000
Other income	4,500	6,000
Income before income tax	$225,000	$156,000
Income tax expense	70,000	50,000
Net income	$155,000	$106,000

Instructions

1. Prepare a comparative income statement with horizontal analysis for the two-year period, using 1999 as the base year. Round to one digit after the decimal place.
2. To the extent the data permit, comment on the significant relationships revealed by the horizontal analysis prepared in (1).

Problem 16–2B

Vertical analysis for income statement

Objective 1

GENERAL LEDGER
SPREADSHEET

✓ 1. Net income, 2000, 5.4%

For 2000, Stainless Exhaust Systems Inc. initiated a sales promotion campaign that included the expenditure of an additional $50,000 for advertising. At the end of the year, Edmundo Gonzalez, the president, is presented with the following condensed comparative income statement:

Stainless Exhaust Systems Inc.
Comparative Income Statement
For the Years Ended December 31, 2000 and 1999

	2000	1999
Sales	$490,000	$460,000
Sales returns and allowances	10,000	10,000
Net sales	$480,000	$450,000
Cost of goods sold	215,000	200,000
Gross profit	$265,000	$250,000
Selling expenses	$150,000	$100,000
Administrative expenses	85,000	80,000
Total operating expenses	$235,000	$180,000
Income from operations	$ 30,000	$ 70,000
Other income	10,000	9,000
Income before income tax	$ 40,000	$ 79,000
Income tax expense	14,000	30,000
Net income	$ 26,000	$ 49,000

Instructions

1. Prepare a comparative income statement for the two-year period, presenting an analysis of each item in relationship to net sales for each of the years. Round to one digit after the decimal place.
2. To the extent the data permit, comment on the significant relationships revealed by the vertical analysis prepared in (1).

Problem 16–3B

Effect of transactions on current position analysis

Objective 2

✓ 1. Acid-test ratio, 1.8

Data pertaining to the current position of Granular Aggregates Inc. are as follows:

Cash	$143,000
Marketable securities	57,000
Accounts and notes receivable (net)	250,000
Inventories	266,000
Prepaid expenses	9,000
Accounts payable	190,000
Notes payable (short-term)	40,000
Accrued expenses	20,000

Instructions

1. Compute (a) the working capital, (b) the current ratio, and (c) the acid-test ratio.
2. List the following captions on a sheet of paper:

Transaction	Working Capital	Current Ratio	Acid-Test Ratio

Compute the working capital, the current ratio, and the acid-test ratio after each of the following transactions, and record the results in the appropriate columns. Consider each transaction separately and assume that only that transaction affects the data given above. Round to two digits after the decimal point.

a. Sold marketable securities at no gain or loss, $34,000.
b. Paid accounts payable, $60,000.
c. Purchased goods on account, $50,000.
d. Paid notes payable, $20,000.
e. Declared a cash dividend, $15,000.
f. Declared a common stock dividend on common stock, $16,500.
g. Borrowed cash from bank on a long-term note, $120,000.
h. Received cash on account, $86,000.
i. Issued additional shares of stock for cash, $160,000.
j. Paid cash for prepaid expenses, $12,000.

Problem 16–4B
Eighteen measures of solvency and profitability

Objectives 2, 3

HAT SPREADSHEET

✓ 9. Ratio of liabilities to stockholders' equity, 0.7

The comparative financial statements of General Grains Company are as follows. The market price of General Grains Company common stock was $18 on December 31, 2000.

General Grains Company
Comparative Income Statement
For the Years Ended December 31, 2000 and 1999

	2000	1999
Sales (all on account)	$5,000,000	$4,200,000
Sales returns and allowances	50,000	50,000
Net sales	$4,950,000	$4,150,000
Cost of goods sold	2,350,000	1,950,000
Gross profit	$2,600,000	$2,200,000
Selling expenses	$1,000,000	$ 950,000
Administrative expenses	700,000	650,000
Total operating expenses	$1,700,000	$1,600,000
Income from operations	$ 900,000	$ 600,000
Other income	80,000	40,000
	$ 980,000	$ 640,000
Other expense (interest)	200,000	120,000
Income before income tax	$ 780,000	$ 520,000
Income tax expense	300,000	200,000
Net income	$ 480,000	$ 320,000

General Grains Company
Comparative Retained Earnings Statement
For the Years Ended December 31, 2000 and 1999

	Dec. 31, 2000	Dec. 31, 1999
Retained earnings, January 1	$350,000	$102,000
Add net income for year	480,000	320,000
Total	$830,000	$422,000
Deduct dividends:		
On preferred stock	$ 48,000	$ 32,000
On common stock	40,000	40,000
Total	$ 88,000	$ 72,000
Retained earnings, December 31	$742,000	$350,000

General Grains Company
Comparative Balance Sheet
December 31, 2000 and 1999

Assets	Dec. 31, 2000	Dec. 31, 1999
Current assets:		
Cash	$ 264,000	$ 124,000
Marketable securities	202,000	182,000
Accounts receivable (net)	364,000	344,000
Inventories	469,000	422,000
Prepaid expenses	31,000	28,000
Total current assets	$1,330,000	$1,100,000
Long-term investments	1,200,000	400,000
Property, plant, and equipment (net)	3,212,000	2,700,000
Total assets	$5,742,000	$4,200,000
Liabilities		
Current liabilities	$ 600,000	$ 450,000
Long-term liabilities:		
Mortgage note payable, 10%, due 2005	$ 800,000	—
Bonds payable, 12%, due 2009	1,000,000	$1,000,000
Total long-term liabilities	$1,800,000	$1,000,000
Total liabilities	$2,400,000	$1,450,000
Stockholders' Equity		
Preferred $8 stock, $100 par	$ 600,000	$ 400,000
Common stock, $10 par	2,000,000	2,000,000
Retained earnings	742,000	350,000
Total stockholders' equity	$3,342,000	$2,750,000
Total liabilities and stockholders' equity	$5,742,000	$4,200,000

Instructions

Determine the following measures for 2000, rounding to nearest single digit after the decimal point:

1. Working capital
2. Current ratio
3. Acid-test ratio
4. Accounts receivable turnover
5. Number of days' sales in receivables
6. Inventory turnover
7. Number of days' sales in inventory
8. Ratio of fixed assets to long-term liabilities
9. Ratio of liabilities to stockholders' equity
10. Number of times interest charges earned
11. Number of times preferred dividends earned
12. Ratio of net sales to assets
13. Rate earned on total assets
14. Rate earned on stockholders' equity
15. Rate earned on common stockholders' equity
16. Earnings per share on common stock
17. Price-earnings ratio
18. Dividends per share of common stock
19. Dividend yield

Problem 16–5B
Solvency and profitability trend analysis

Objectives 2, 3

Asian Arts Company has provided the following comparative information:

	2000	1999	1998	1997	1996
Net income	$ 300,000	$ 500,000	$1,000,000	$ 800,000	$ 500,000
Income tax expense	90,000	150,000	300,000	240,000	150,000
Interest	300,000	200,000	170,000	100,000	50,000
Average total assets	8,600,000	7,300,000	6,500,000	4,800,000	3,500,000
Average total stockholders' equity	5,600,000	5,300,000	4,800,000	3,800,000	3,000,000

You have been asked to evaluate the historical performance of the company over the last five years.

Selected industry ratios have remained relatively steady for the last five years at the following levels:

	1996–2000
Rate earned on total assets	12%
Rate earned on stockholders' equity	15%
Number of times interest charges earned	9.0
Ratio of liabilities to stockholders' equity	0.40

Instructions

1. Prepare four line graphs, with the ratio on the vertical axis and the years on the horizontal axis for the following four ratios (round to two digits after the decimal place):
   a. Rate earned on total assets
   b. Rate earned on stockholders' equity
   c. Number of times interest charges earned
   d. Ratio of liabilities to stockholders' equity (using average balances)
   Display both the company ratio and the industry benchmark on each graph (each graph should have two lines).
2. Prepare an analysis of the graphs in (1).

HERSHEY FOODS CORPORATION PROBLEM

Financial Statement Analysis

HAT

The financial statements for **Hershey Foods Corporation** are presented in Appendix G at the end of the text. The following additional information is available:

Accounts receivable at December 31, 1994	$ 331,670,000
Inventories at December 31, 1994	445,702,000
Total assets at December 31, 1994	2,890,981,000
Stockholders' equity at December 31, 1994	1,441,100,000

Assume that all sales are credit sales.

The makeup of "interest expense, net" is described in Note 6 to the statements. Use only the interest on long-term debt and lease obligations and short-term debt in your computations.

Instructions

1. Determine the following measures for 1996 and 1995:
   a. Working capital
   b. Current ratio
   c. Acid-test ratio
   d. Accounts receivable turnover
   e. Number of days' sales in receivables
   f. Inventory turnover
   g. Number of days' sales in inventory
   h. Ratio of fixed assets (property, plant, and equipment) to long-term liabilities (debt)
   i. Ratio of liabilities to stockholders' equity
   j. Number of times interest charges earned
   k. Ratio of net sales to average total assets
   l. Rate earned on average total assets
   m. Rate earned on average common stockholders' equity
   n. Price-earnings ratio
   o. Dividend yield (on common stock only)
   p. Percentage relationship of net income and net sales

q. Amount of change and percent of change in (1) net sales (revenue for 1996) and (2) selling, marketing, and administrative expense (for 1996)

r. Amount of change and percent of change in net income (for 1996)

2. What conclusions can be drawn from these analyses?

QUICKBOOKS PROBLEM

Vertical Analysis

Use QuickBooks to open the *sample.qbw* file (Larry's Landscaping) for this problem.

1. Use the report feature to print a standard profit and loss report for December 1 to December 15 to your screen. Use the "customize" button to provide a vertical analysis, as a percent of sales, of the standard report.
2. Interpret the vertical analysis.

SPECIAL ACTIVITIES

Activity 16–1
Taylor Equipment Co.
Ethics and professional conduct in business

Lee Taylor, president of Taylor Equipment Co., prepared a draft of the President's Letter to be included with Taylor Equipment Co.'s 2000 annual report. The letter mentions a 10% increase in sales and a recent expansion of plant facilities, but fails to mention the net loss of $175,000 for the year. You have been asked to review the letter for inclusion in the annual report.

How would you respond to the omission of the net loss of $175,000? Specifically, is such an action ethical?

Activity 16–2
Cascade Brewery
Analysis of financing corporate growth

What do you THINK?

Assume that the president of Cascade Brewery made the following statement in the President's Letter to Shareholders:

"The founding family, and majority shareholders, of the company do not believe in using debt to finance future growth. The founding family learned from hard experience during Prohibition and the Great Depression that debt can cause loss of flexibility and eventual loss of corporate control. The company will not place itself at such risk. As such, all future growth will be financed either by stock sales to the public or by internally generated resources."

As a public shareholder of this company, how would you respond to this policy?

Activity 16–3
Pinnacle Computer Company
Receivables and inventory turnover

Pinnacle Computer Company has completed its fiscal year on December 31, 2000. The auditor, Carol Blake, has approached the CFO, Chase Williams, regarding the year-end receivables and inventory levels of Pinnacle. The following conversation takes place:

Carol: We are beginning our audit of Pinnacle and have prepared ratio analyses to determine if there have been significant changes in operations or financial position. This helps us guide the audit process. This analysis indicates that the inventory turnover has decreased from 5 to 2.8, while the accounts receivable turnover has decreased from 12 to 8. I was wondering if you could explain this change in operations.

Chase: There is little need for concern. The inventory represents computers that we were unable to sell during the holiday buying season. We are confident, however, that we will be able to sell these computers as we move into the next fiscal year.

Carol: What gives you this confidence?

Chase: We will increase our advertising and provide some very attractive price concessions to move these machines. We have no choice. Newer technology is already out there, and we have to unload this inventory.

Carol: . . . and the receivables?

Chase: As you may be aware, the company is under tremendous pressure to expand sales and profits. As a result, we lowered our credit standards to our commercial customers so that we would be able to sell products to a broader customer base. As a result of this policy change, we have been able to expand sales by 35%.

Carol: Your responses have not been reassuring to me.

Chase: I'm a little confused. Assets are good, right? Why don't you look at our current ratio? It has improved, hasn't it? I would think that you would view that very favorably.

Why is Carol concerned about the inventory and accounts receivable turnover ratios and Chase's responses to them? What action may Carol need to take? How would you respond to Chase's last comment?

Activity 16–4 Apple Computer and Dell Computer

Vertical analysis

The condensed income statements for **Apple Computer Co.** and **Dell Computer Co.** are reproduced below for recent fiscal years:

	Dell Computer Co. For the Year Ended February 2, 1997	Apple Computer Co. For the Year Ended September 27, 1996
Sales (net)	$7,759	$ 9,833
Cost of sales	6,093	8,865
Gross profit	$1,666	$ 968
Selling, general, and administrative expense	826	1,568
Research and development	126	604
Operating income	$ 714	$ (1,204)
Other income and expenses	33	(91)
Income before taxes	$ 747	$ (1,295)
Income tax expense (benefit)	216	(479)
Income before extraordinary items	$ 531	$ (816)

Prepare comparative vertical analyses, rounding to two digits after the decimal point. Interpret the analyses.

Activity 16–5 Into the Real World

Horizontal analysis and profitability analysis

Go to the **Microsoft** Web site at **www.microsoft.com** and download Microsoft's comparative income statements for the last three fiscal years as an Excel® file. Next, go to the *Wall Street Journal* and look up Microsoft in the NASDAQ National Market pages. Under this listing, report the price-earnings ratio and dividend yield for Microsoft.

Use the comparative income statement Excel® file to prepare a horizontal analysis for the last two fiscal years (delete the oldest year from the analysis). Use Microsoft's balance sheet and income statement information to determine the rate earned on stockholders' equity for the latest fiscal year. How do these analyses reconcile with Microsoft's price-earnings ratio and dividend yield?

Activity 16–6 Into the Real World

Solvency and profitability analysis

One team should obtain the latest annual report for **Wal-Mart Stores Inc.**, and the other team should obtain the latest **Kmart Corp.** annual report. These annual reports can be obtained from a library or the company's 10-K filing with the Securities and Exchange Commission at **www.sec.gov/edgarhp.htm.**

To obtain annual report information, type in the company name on the "Search EDGAR Archives" form. EDGAR will list the reports available for the company. Click on the 10-K (or 10-K405) report for the year you wish to download. If you wish, you can save the whole 10-K report to a file and then open it with your word processor.

Each team should compute the following for their company:

a. Current ratio
b. Inventory turnover
c. Rate earned on stockholders' equity
d. Rate earned on total assets
e. Net income as a percentage of sales
f. Ratio of liabilities to stockholders' equity

As a class, prepare a report comparing the two companies for the latest fiscal period.

ANSWERS TO SELF-EXAMINATION QUESTIONS

Matching

1. H	4. W	7. J	10. Y	13. G	16. Q	18. I
2. P	5. L	8. C	11. N	14. B	17. D	19. O
3. K	6. A	9. R	12. S	15. X		

Multiple Choice

1. **A** Percentage analysis indicating the relationship of the component parts to the total in a financial statement, such as the relationship of current assets to total assets (20% to 100%) in the question, is called vertical analysis (answer A). Percentage analysis of increases and decreases in corresponding items in comparative financial statements is called horizontal analysis (answer B). An example of horizontal analysis would be the presentation of the amount of current assets in the preceding balance sheet, along with the amount of current assets at the end of the current year, with the increase or decrease in current assets between the periods expressed as a percentage. Profitability analysis (answer C) is the analysis of a firm's ability to earn income. Contribution margin analysis (answer D) is discussed in a later managerial accounting chapter.
2. **D** Various solvency measures, categorized as current position analysis, indicate a firm's ability to meet currently maturing obligations. Each measure contributes in the analysis of a firm's current position and is most useful when viewed with other measures and when compared with similar measures for other periods and for other firms. Working capital (answer A) is the excess of current assets over current liabilities; the current ratio (answer B) is the ratio of current assets to current liabilities; and the acid-test ratio (answer C) is the ratio of the sum of cash, receivables, and marketable securities to current liabilities.
3. **D** The ratio of current assets to current liabilities is usually called the current ratio (answer A). It is sometimes called the working capital ratio (answer B) or bankers' ratio (answer C).
4. **C** The ratio of the sum of cash, receivables, and marketable securities (sometimes called quick assets) to current liabilities is called the acid-test ratio (answer C) or quick ratio. The current ratio (answer A), working capital ratio (answer B), and bankers' ratio (answer D) are terms that describe the ratio of current assets to current liabilities.
5. **C** The number of days' sales in inventory (answer C), which is determined by dividing the inventories at the end of the year by the average daily cost of goods sold, expresses the relationship between the cost of goods sold and inventory. It indicates the efficiency in the management of inventory. The working capital ratio (answer A) indicates the ability of the business to meet currently maturing obligations (debt). The acid-test ratio (answer B) indicates the "instant" debt-paying ability of the business. The ratio of fixed assets to long-term liabilities (answer D) indicates the margin of safety for long-term creditors.

17

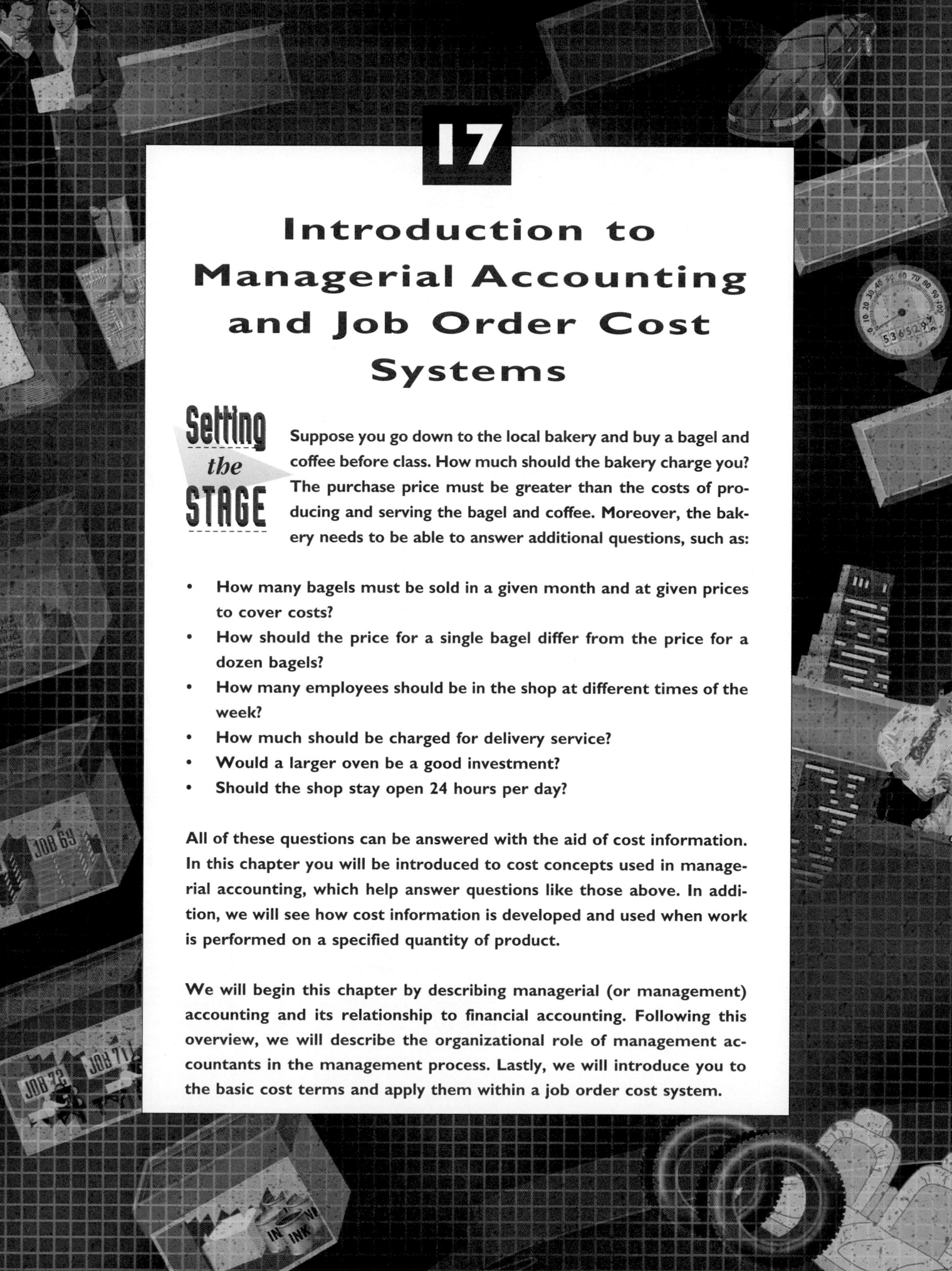

Introduction to Managerial Accounting and Job Order Cost Systems

Setting the STAGE

Suppose you go down to the local bakery and buy a bagel and coffee before class. How much should the bakery charge you? The purchase price must be greater than the costs of producing and serving the bagel and coffee. Moreover, the bakery needs to be able to answer additional questions, such as:

- How many bagels must be sold in a given month and at given prices to cover costs?
- How should the price for a single bagel differ from the price for a dozen bagels?
- How many employees should be in the shop at different times of the week?
- How much should be charged for delivery service?
- Would a larger oven be a good investment?
- Should the shop stay open 24 hours per day?

All of these questions can be answered with the aid of cost information. In this chapter you will be introduced to cost concepts used in managerial accounting, which help answer questions like those above. In addition, we will see how cost information is developed and used when work is performed on a specified quantity of product.

We will begin this chapter by describing managerial (or management) accounting and its relationship to financial accounting. Following this overview, we will describe the organizational role of management accountants in the management process. Lastly, we will introduce you to the basic cost terms and apply them within a job order cost system.

objectives

After studying this chapter, you should be able to:

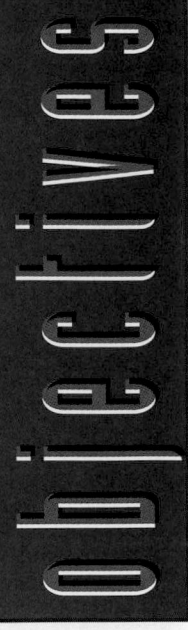

1. Describe the differences between managerial and financial accounting.
2. Evaluate the organizational role of management accountants.
3. Define and illustrate materials, factory labor, and factory overhead costs.
4. Describe accounting systems used by manufacturing businesses.
5. Describe and prepare summary journal entries for a job order cost accounting system.
6. Use job order cost information for decision making.
7. Diagram the flow of costs for a service business that uses a job order cost accounting system.

The Differences Between Managerial and Financial Accounting

OBJECTIVE 1

Describe the differences between managerial and financial accounting.

Although economic information can be classified in many ways, accountants often divide accounting information into two types: financial and managerial. The diagram in Exhibit 1 illustrates the relationship between financial accounting and managerial accounting. Understanding this relationship is useful in understanding the information needs of management.

EXHIBIT 1
Financial Accounting and Managerial Accounting

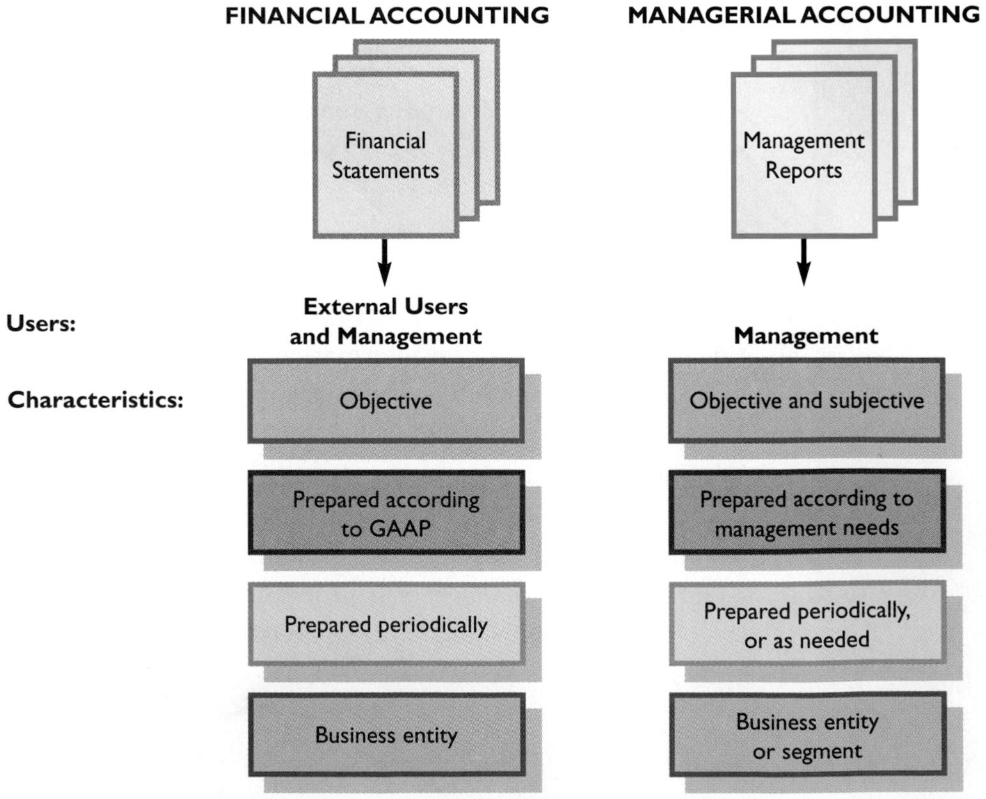

BUSINESS ON STAGE

The management process consists of planning, directing, controlling, and improving. *Planning* is used by management to develop the organization's objectives (goals) and to translate those objectives into courses of action. *Strategic planning* is developing long-range courses of action, called *strategies*, to achieve goals. For example, **Toyota Motor Company** has established an assembly facility in the United States as a strategy to capture a greater North American market share (the goal) by avoiding import controls and currency fluctuations. *Operational planning*, sometimes called *tactical planning*, is the short-term planning used for achieving operational goals. For example, Toyota's operational plans for its Georgetown, Kentucky assembly plant are to hire and train employees to support an operational goal of increasing the annual production target.

Directing is the process by which managers, given their assigned level of responsibilities, run day-to-day operations. Examples of directing include a production supervisor's efforts to keep the production line moving smoothly throughout a work shift and the credit manager's efforts to assess the credit standing of potential customers.

Once managers have planned the goals and directed the action, there comes the need to assess how well the plan is working. *Controlling* consists of monitoring the operating results of implemented plans and comparing the actual results with the expected results. This feedback allows management to isolate significant departures from plan for further investigation and possible corrective action. It may also lead to revising future plans.

Feedback can also be used by managers to support improvement in business processes. *Continuous process improvement* is the business philosophy of continually improving employees, business processes, and products by using process information to eliminate the source of process problems. This philosophy requires managers to be responsible for permanent process improvement, rather than temporary solutions that fail to address the root cause of a problem. ■

Financial accounting information is reported in statements that are useful for persons or institutions who are "outside" or external to the organization. Examples of such users include shareholders, creditors, government agencies, and the general public. To the extent that management uses the financial statements in directing current operations and planning future operations, the two areas of accounting overlap. For example, in planning future operations, management often begins by evaluating the results of past activities as reported in the financial statements. The financial statements objectively and periodically report the results of past operations and the financial condition of the business according to generally accepted accounting principles (GAAP).

Managerial accounting information includes both historical and estimated data used by management in conducting daily operations, planning future operations, and developing overall business strategies. The characteristics of managerial accounting are influenced by the varying needs of management. First, managerial accounting reports provide both objective measures of past operations and subjective estimates about future decisions. Using subjective estimates in managerial accounting reports assists management in responding to business opportunities. Second, managerial reports need not be prepared according to generally accepted accounting principles. Since only management uses managerial accounting information, the accountant can provide the information according to management's needs. Third, managerial accounting reports may be provided periodically, as with financial accounting, or at any time management needs information. For example, if senior management is deciding on a geographical expansion, a managerial accounting report can be developed in a format and within a time frame to assist management in the decision. Lastly, managerial accounting reports can be prepared to report information for the business entity or a segment of the entity, such as a division, product, project, or territory.

The Management Accountant in the Organization

OBJECTIVE 2

Evaluate the organizational role of management accountants.

In most large organizations, departments or similar units are assigned responsibilities for specific functions or activities. This operating structure of an organization can be diagrammed in an organization chart. Exhibit 2 is a condensed organization chart for **Callaway Golf Company,** the manufacturer and distributor of Big Bertha® woods and irons.

EXHIBIT 2 Condensed Organization Chart for Callaway Golf Company

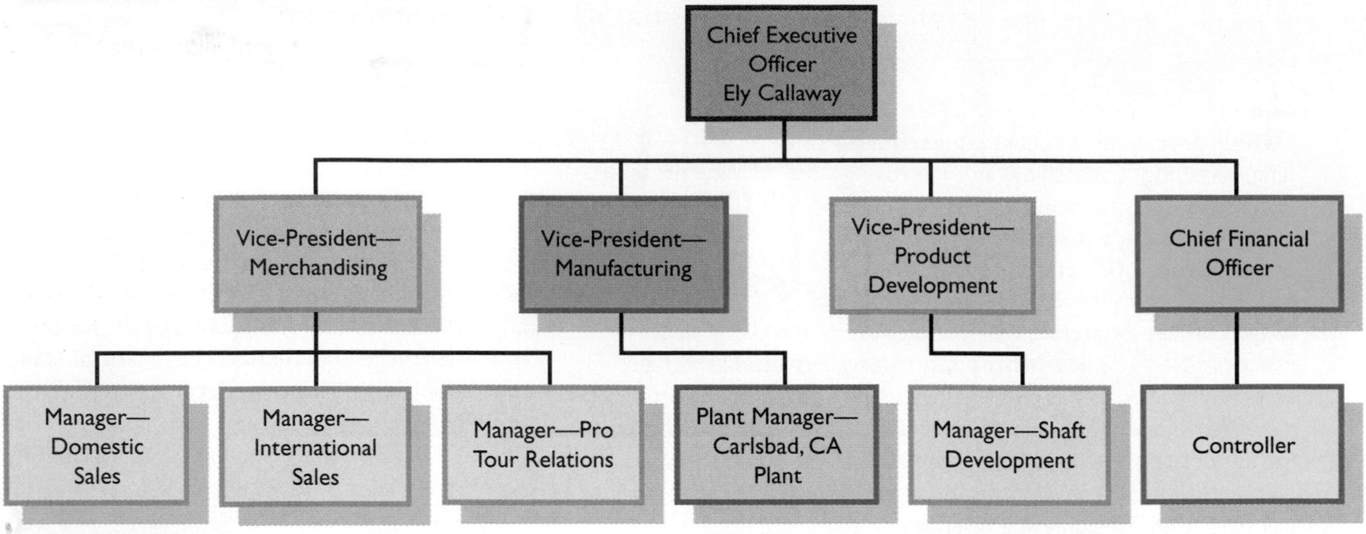

The individual reporting units in an organization can be viewed as having either (1) line responsibilities or (2) staff responsibilities. A **line** department or unit is one directly involved in the basic objectives of the organization. For Callaway Golf, the vice-president of manufacturing and the manager of the Carlsbad plant occupy line positions because they are responsible for manufacturing Callaway's products. Likewise, the vice-president of merchandising (sales) and the regional sales managers are in line positions because they are directly responsible for generating revenues.

A **staff** department or unit is one that provides services, assistance, and advice to the departments with line or other staff responsibilities. A staff department has no direct authority over a line department. For example, the manager of pro tour relations is a staff position supporting the sales organization. In addition, the vice-president of product development occupies a staff position because new products are developed to support sales and manufacturing. Likewise, the vice-president of finance (sometimes called the chief financial officer) occupies a staff position, to which the controller reports. In most business organizations, the **controller** is the chief management accountant.

REAL WORLD **In many organizations, plant controllers report to both the plant manager and the company controller, which is termed *matrix* reporting. This is done to enhance the controller's independence of the plant manager.**

The controller's staff often consists of several management accountants. Each accountant is responsible for a specialized accounting function, such as systems and procedures, general accounting, budgets and budget analysis, special reports and analysis, taxes, and cost accounting.

Experience in managerial accounting is often an excellent training ground for senior management positions. One poll indicated that over 21% of the chief executive officers (CEOs) of the largest 1,000 companies in the United States have career paths that began with accounting or finance. More CEOs started out in these areas than in any

INTERMISSION

Line and Staff in Service Industries

The terms *line* and *staff* may be applied to service organizations, such as banks, hospitals, hotels, or public accounting firms. For example, the line positions in a hospital would be the nurses, doctors, and other caregivers. Staff positions would include admissions and records. What would be the line and staff positions for a professional basketball team, such as the **Boston Celtics**? The basketball players and coaches would be the "line" positions, since they are directly involved in the basic objectives of the organization—playing professional basketball. Staff positions would include public relations, player development and recruiting, legal staff, and accounting. These positions serve and advise the players and coaches. ■

other functional business area.[1] This is not surprising, since accounting and finance bring an individual into contact with all phases of operations.

OBJECTIVE 3

Define and illustrate materials, factory labor, and factory overhead costs.

Manufacturing Cost Terms

Managers rely on managerial accountants to provide useful *cost* information to support decision making. What is a cost? A **cost** is a payment of cash or its equivalent or the commitment to pay cash in the future for the purpose of generating revenues.

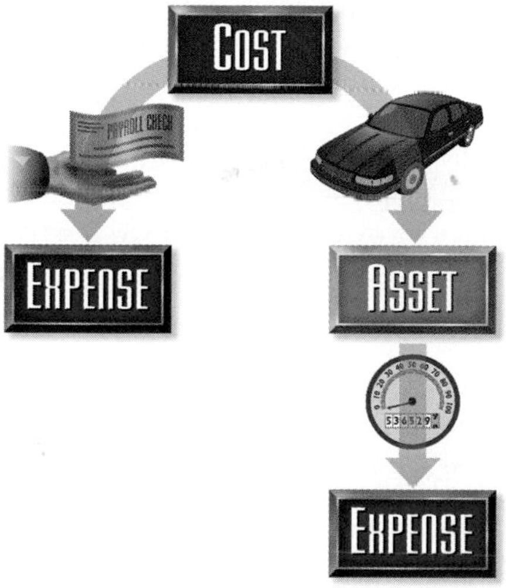

A cost represents either a benefit that is used immediately or deferred to a future period of time. If the benefit is used immediately, then the cost is an expense, such as salary expense. If the benefit is deferred, then the cost is an asset, such as equipment. As the asset is used, an expense, such as depreciation expense, is recognized.

In this section, we will illustrate manufacturing costs for Goodwell Printers, a manufacturing firm. A **manufacturing business** converts materials into a finished product through the use of machinery and labor. Goodwell Printers prints textbooks, like the one you are using now. Exhibit 3 provides an overview of Goodwell Printers' textbook printing operations. The Printing Department feeds large rolls of paper into printing presses. The printing presses use electricity and ink. From the Printing Department, the printed pages are stacked and moved to the Binding Department. In the Binding Department, the pages are cut, separated, stacked, and bound to book covers. A finished book is the final output of the Binding Department.

EXHIBIT 3 Textbook Printing Operations of Goodwell Printers

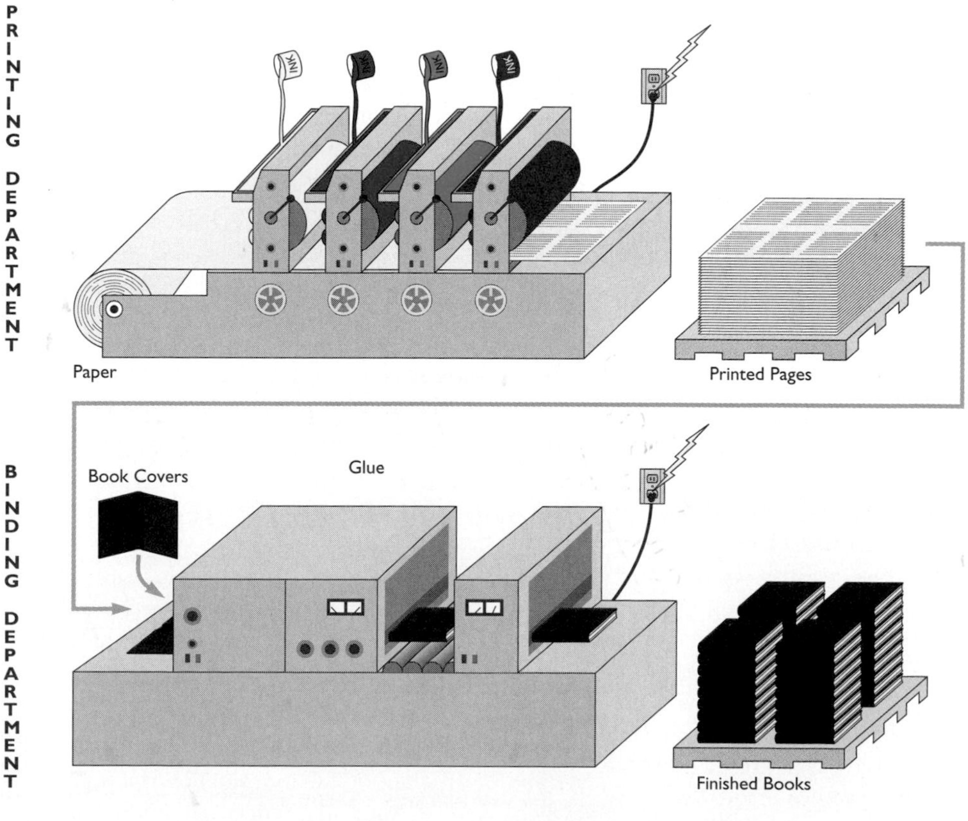

[1] "Corporate Elite Career Path," *Business Week*, October 11, 1993, p. 65.

Materials

The cost of materials that are an integral part of the product is classified as **direct materials cost**. For example, the direct materials cost for Goodwell Printers would include paper and book covers.

As a practical matter, a direct materials cost must not only be an integral part of the finished product, but it must also be a significant portion of the total cost of the product. Other examples of direct materials costs are the cost of electronic components for a TV manufacturer and tires for an automobile manufacturer.

The costs of materials that are not a significant portion of the total product cost are termed **indirect materials.** Indirect materials are considered a part of factory overhead, which we discuss later. For Goodwell Printers, the costs of ink and binding glue are classified as indirect materials.

REAL WORLD: Some service companies also have direct materials costs. For example, fuel is a direct materials cost to a flight for an airline, while medicines are a direct materials cost to a patient in a hospital.

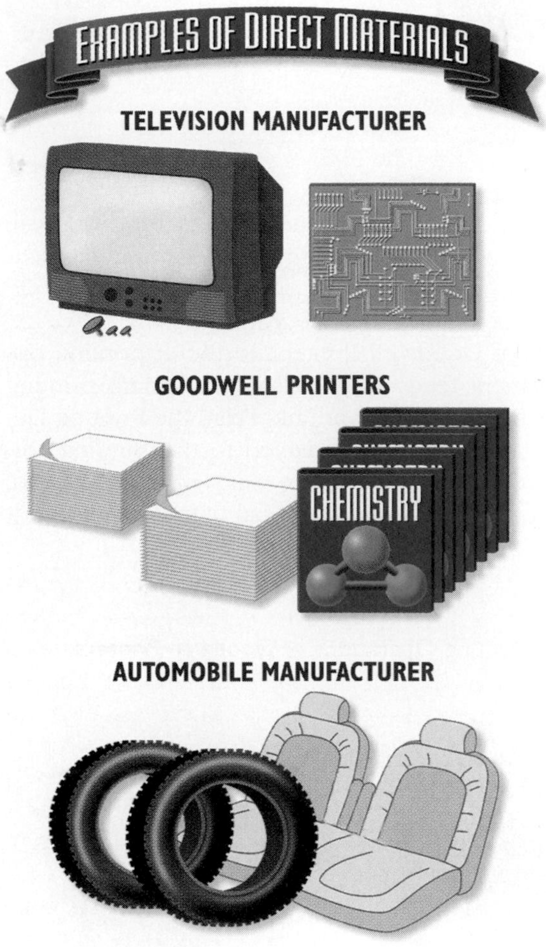

Factory Labor

The cost of wages of employees who are directly involved in converting materials into the manufactured product is classified as **direct labor cost**. The direct labor cost of Goodwell Printers includes the wages of the employees who operate the printing presses. Other examples of direct labor costs are carpenters' wages for a construction contractor, mechanics' wages in an automotive repair shop, machine operators' wages in a tool manufacturing plant, and assemblers' wages in a microcomputer assembly plant.

As a practical matter, a direct labor cost must not only be an integral part of the finished product, but it must also be a significant portion of the total cost of the product. For Goodwell Printers, the printing press operators' wages are a significant portion of the total cost of each book. Labor costs that do not enter directly into the manufacture of a product are termed **indirect labor** and are recorded as factory overhead. Indirect labor for Goodwell Printers might include the salaries of maintenance, plant management, and quality control personnel.

Q&A: *Identify whether the following costs are direct materials, direct labor, or factory overhead for an automobile assembler: tires, quality engineering salaries, assembly wages, coil steel, painter wages, plant manager salary, cleaning fluids.*

Tires and coil steel—direct materials; assembly wages, painter wages—direct labor; quality engineering salaries, plant manager's salary, cleaning fluids—factory overhead.

Factory Overhead Cost

Costs other than direct materials cost and direct labor cost incurred in the manufacturing process are classified as **factory overhead cost**. Factory overhead is sometimes called **manufacturing overhead** or **factory burden**. Examples of factory overhead costs, in addition to indirect materials and indirect labor, are machine depreciation, factory utilities, factory supplies, and factory insurance. In addition, payments to employees for overtime and nonproductive time (such as idle time) are considered factory overhead. For many industries, factory overhead costs are becoming a larger portion of the costs of a product as manufacturing processes become more automated.

The direct materials, direct labor, and factory overhead costs are considered **product costs**, because they are associated with making a product. The costs of converting the materials into finished products consist of direct labor and factory overhead costs, which are commonly called **conversion costs**.

Direct materials, direct labor, and factory overhead costs are product costs.

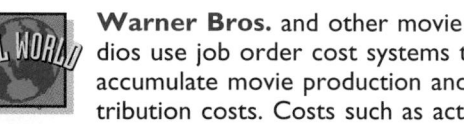

Cost Accounting System Overview

OBJECTIVE 4

Describe accounting systems used by manufacturing businesses.

An objective of a **cost accounting system** is to accumulate product costs. Product cost information is used by managers to establish product prices, control operations, and develop financial statements. In addition, the cost accounting system improves control by supplying data on the costs incurred by each manufacturing department or process.

There are two main types of cost accounting systems for manufacturing operations: job order cost systems and process cost systems. Each of the two systems is widely used, and any one manufacturer may use more than one type. In this chapter, we will illustrate the job order cost system. In the next chapter, we will illustrate the process cost system.

A **job order cost system** provides a separate record for the cost of each quantity of product that passes through the factory. A particular quantity of product is termed a *job*. A job order cost system is best suited to industries that manufacture custom goods to fill special orders from customers or that produce a high variety of products for stock. Manufacturers that use a job order cost system are sometimes called **job shops**. An example of a job shop would be an apparel manufacturer, such as **Levi Strauss**.

Many service firms also use job order cost systems to accumulate the costs associated with providing client services. For example, an accounting firm will accumulate all of the costs associated with a particular client engagement, such as accountant time, copying charges, and travel costs. Recording costs in this manner helps the accounting firm control costs during a client engagement and determines client billing and profitability.

REAL WORLD

Warner Bros. and other movie studios use job order cost systems to accumulate movie production and distribution costs. Costs such as actor salaries, production costs, movie print costs, and marketing costs are accumulated in a job account for a particular movie. Cost information from the job cost report can be used to control the costs of the movie while it is being produced and to determine the profitability of the movie after it has been exhibited.

Under a **process cost system**, costs are accumulated for each of the departments or processes within the factory. A process system is best suited for manufacturers of units of product that are not distinguishable from each other during a continuous production process. An example would be an oil refinery.

Exhibit 4 summarizes a survey of manufacturers, showing the breakdown between the use of job order and process costing. Exhibit 4 indicates that over 50% of the respondents use some other type of cost system. Although not indicated in this survey, these other respondents probably use a hybrid system that combines features of a job order and a process cost system.

Q&A

Name two types of cost systems and a typical user of each system.

Job order cost system: cabinet manufacturer, law practice, apparel manufacturing, movie studio. Process cost system: food processing, paper processing, metal processing, petroleum refining.

EXHIBIT 4
Cost Accounting Practices by Major Industries

Industry Group	% Using Job Order Costing	% Using Process Costing
Metal, chemical, oil, gas, paper	21	41
Machinery	35	15
Automobile	11	8
Aerospace	45	10
Electronics	24	15
High technology	33	43
Other industrial products	13	23
Consumer products	2	33
Diverse products	50	31
Average of all respondents	20%	23%

Source: R. A. Howell, J. D. Brown, S. R. Soucy, and A. H. Seed, *Management Accounting in the New Manufacturing Environment,* IMA/CAM-I, 1987, p. 36.

Job Order Cost Systems for Manufacturing Businesses

OBJECTIVE 5

Describe and prepare summary journal entries for a job order cost accounting system.

In this section, we will illustrate the job order cost system for a manufacturing firm, Goodwell Printers. The job order system accumulates manufacturing costs by job, as shown in Exhibit 5. The **materials inventory**, sometimes called **raw materials inventory**, consists of the costs of the direct and indirect materials that have not yet entered the manufacturing process. For Goodwell Printers, the materials inventory would consist of paper, ink, glue, and book covers. The **work in process inventory** consists of direct materials costs, direct labor costs, and factory overhead costs that have entered the manufacturing process but are associated with products that have not been completed. Examples are the costs of Jobs 71 and 72 that are still in the printing process in Exhibit 5. Completed jobs that have not been sold are termed **finished goods inventory**. Examples are completed printed books from

EXHIBIT 5 Manufacturing Costs and Jobs

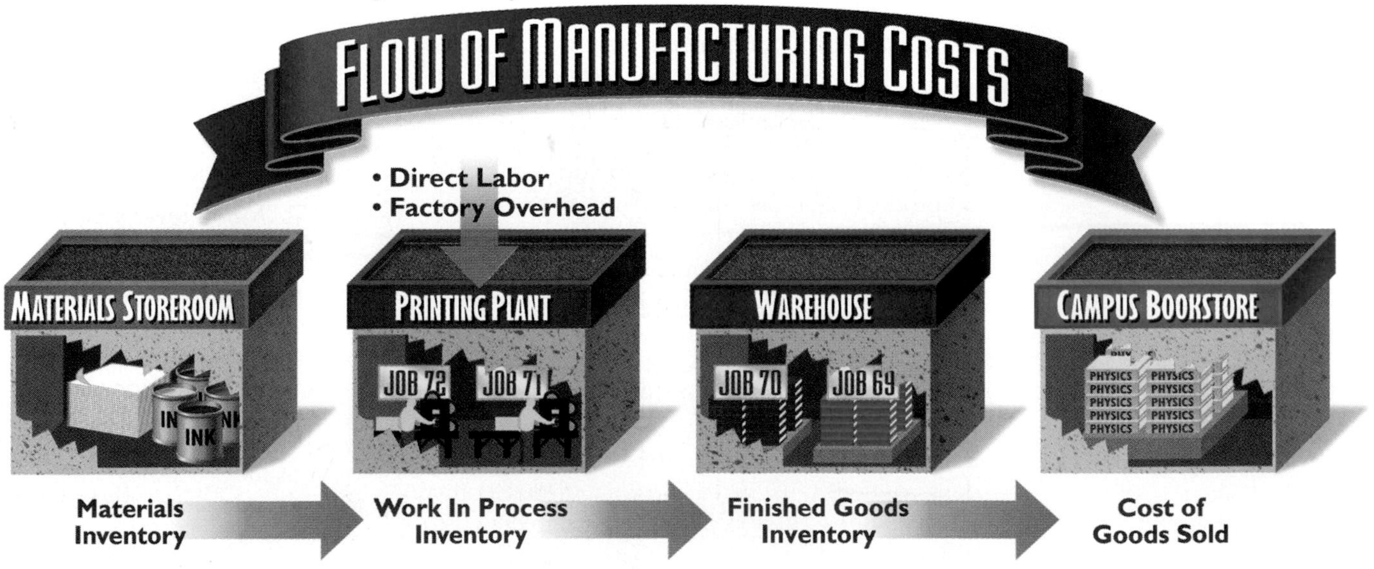

Jobs 69 and 70 shown in Exhibit 5. Upon sale, a manufacturer will record the cost of the sale as **cost of goods sold**. An example is the case of *Physics* books sold to the bookstore in Exhibit 5. The *cost of goods sold* for a manufacturer is comparable to the *cost of merchandise sold* for a merchandising business.

In a job order cost accounting system, perpetual inventory controlling accounts and subsidiary ledgers are maintained for materials, work in process, and finished goods inventories. Each inventory account is debited for all additions and is credited for all deductions. The balance of each account thus represents the balance on hand.

The work in process inventory consists of direct materials, direct labor, and factory overhead costs of products not yet completed.

Materials

The procedures used to purchase, store, and issue materials to production often differ among manufacturers. Exhibit 6 shows the basic information and cost flows for the paper received and issued to production by Goodwell Printers.

EXHIBIT 6
Materials Information and Cost Flows

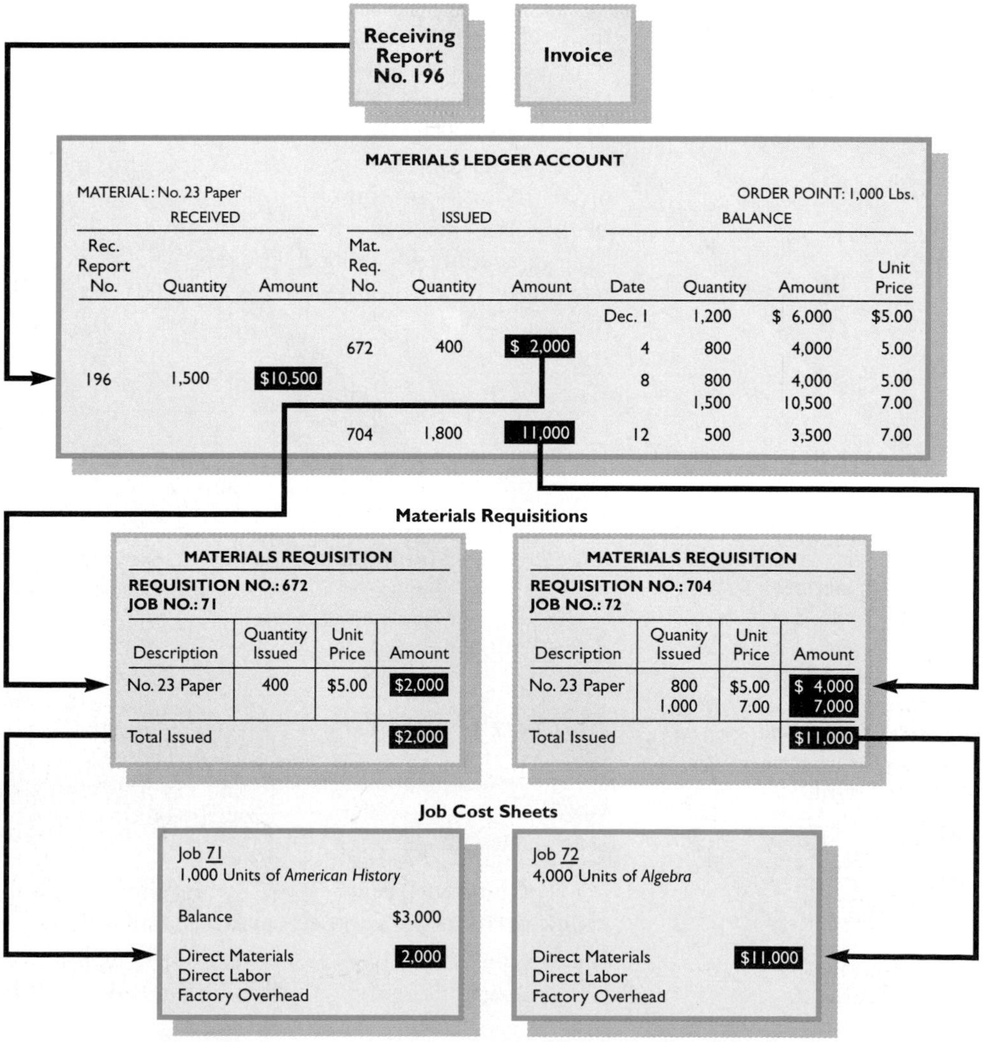

RECEIVED			ISSUED			BALANCE			
Rec. Report No.	Quantity	Amount	Mat. Req. No.	Quantity	Amount	Date	Quantity	Amount	Unit Price
						Dec. 1	1,200	$ 6,000	$5.00
			672	400	$ 2,000	4	800	4,000	5.00
196	1,500	$10,500				8	800 1,500	4,000 10,500	5.00 7.00
			704	1,800	11,000	12	500	3,500	7.00

Materials Requisitions

MATERIALS REQUISITION
REQUISITION NO.: 672
JOB NO.: 71

Description	Quantity Issued	Unit Price	Amount
No. 23 Paper	400	$5.00	$2,000
Total Issued			$2,000

MATERIALS REQUISITION
REQUISITION NO.: 704
JOB NO.: 72

Description	Quanity Issued	Unit Price	Amount
No. 23 Paper	800 1,000	$5.00 7.00	$ 4,000 7,000
Total Issued			$11,000

Job Cost Sheets

Job 71
1,000 Units of *American History*

Balance	$3,000
Direct Materials	2,000
Direct Labor	
Factory Overhead	

Job 72
4,000 Units of *Algebra*

Direct Materials	$11,000
Direct Labor	
Factory Overhead	

Purchased materials are first received and inspected by the Receiving Department. The Receiving Department personnel prepare a **receiving report**, showing the quantity received and its condition. Some organizations now use bar code scanning devices in place of receiving reports to record and electronically transmit incoming materials data. The receiving information and invoice are used to record the receipt and control the payment for purchased items. The journal entry to record Receiving Report No. 196 in Exhibit 6 is:

a.	Materials	10500 00	
	Accounts Payable		10500 00
	Materials purchased during		
	December.		

The materials account in the general ledger is a controlling account. A separate account for each type of material is maintained in a subsidiary **materials ledger**. Details as to the quantity and cost of materials received are recorded in the materials ledger on the basis of the receiving reports. A typical form of a materials ledger account is illustrated in Exhibit 6.

Materials are released from the storeroom to the factory in response to **materials requisitions** from the Production Department. An illustration of a materials requisition is in Exhibit 6. The completed requisition for each job serves as the basis for posting quantities and dollar data to the job cost sheets in the case of direct materials or to factory overhead in the case of indirect materials. **Job cost sheets**, which are illustrated in Exhibit 6, are the work in process subsidiary ledger. For Goodwell Printers, Job 71 is for 1,000 textbooks titled *American History,* while Job 72 is for 4,000 textbooks titled *Algebra.*

In Exhibit 6, the first-in, first-out costing method is used. A summary of the materials requisitions completed during the month is the basis for transferring the cost of the direct materials from the materials account in the general ledger to the controlling account for work in process. The flow of materials from the materials storeroom into production ($2,000 + $11,000) is recorded by the following entry:

b.	Work in Process	13000 00	
	Materials		13000 00
	Materials requisitioned to jobs.		

REAL WORLD For many manufacturing firms, the direct materials cost can be greater than 50% of the total cost to manufacture a product. This is why controlling materials costs is very important.

Many organizations are using computerized information processes that account for the flow of materials. In a computerized setting, the storeroom manager would record the release of materials into a computer, which would automatically update the subsidiary materials records.

Factory Labor

There are two primary objectives in accounting for factory labor. One objective is to determine the correct amount to be paid each employee for each payroll period. A second objective is to properly allocate factory labor costs to factory overhead and individual job orders.

The amount of time spent by an employee in the factory is usually recorded on **clock cards** or **in-and-out cards**. The amount of time spent by each employee and the labor cost incurred for each individual job are recorded on **time tickets**. Exhibit 7 shows typical time ticket forms and cost flows for direct labor for Goodwell Printers.

EXHIBIT 7
Labor Information and Cost Flows

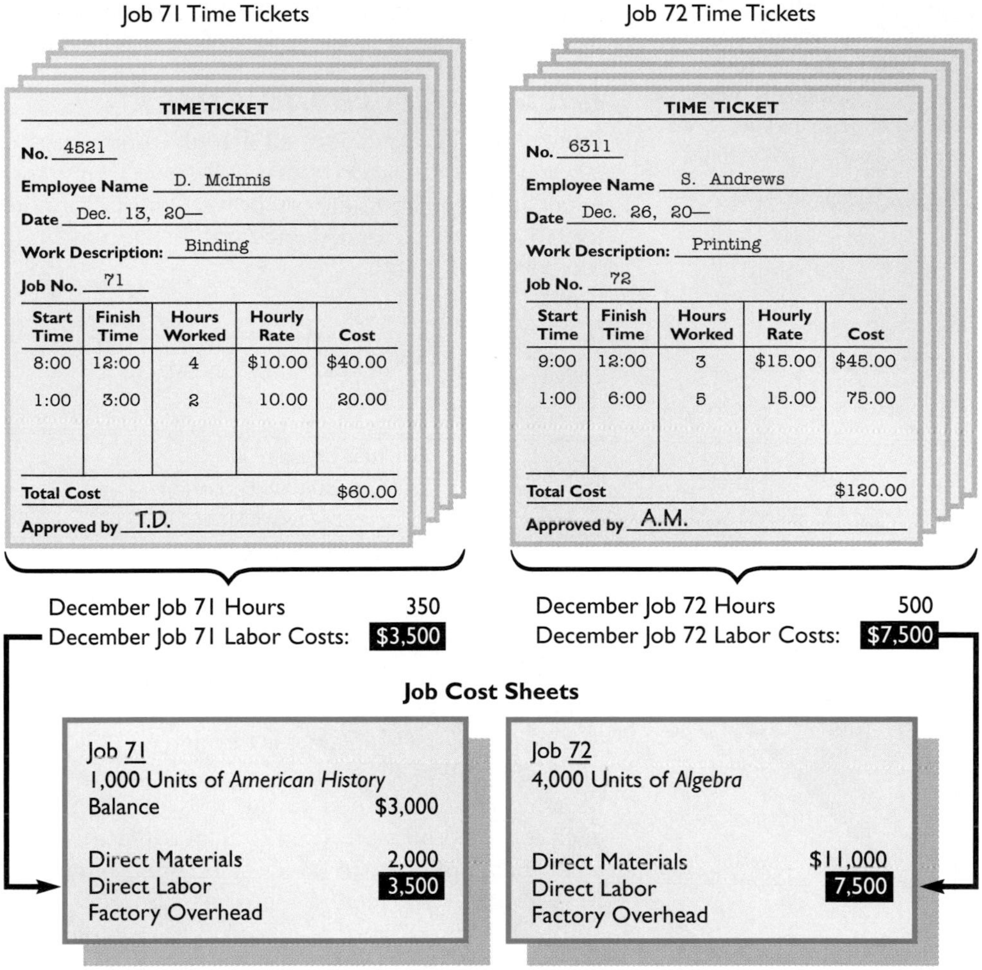
Job 71 Time Tickets
TIME TICKET
No. 4521
Employee Name D. McInnis
Date Dec. 13, 20—
Work Description: Binding
Job No. 71
Start Time | Finish Time | Hours Worked | Hourly Rate | Cost
8:00 | 12:00 | 4 | $10.00 | $40.00
1:00 | 3:00 | 2 | 10.00 | 20.00
Total Cost $60.00
Approved by T.D.
Job 72 Time Tickets
TIME TICKET
No. 6311
Employee Name S. Andrews
Date Dec. 26, 20—
Work Description: Printing
Job No. 72
Start Time | Finish Time | Hours Worked | Hourly Rate | Cost
9:00 | 12:00 | 3 | $15.00 | $45.00
1:00 | 6:00 | 5 | 15.00 | 75.00
Total Cost $120.00
Approved by A.M.
December Job 71 Hours 350
December Job 71 Labor Costs: $3,500
December Job 72 Hours 500
December Job 72 Labor Costs: $7,500
Job Cost Sheets
Job 71
1,000 Units of American History
Balance $3,000
Direct Materials 2,000
Direct Labor 3,500
Factory Overhead
Job 72
4,000 Units of Algebra
Direct Materials $11,000
Direct Labor 7,500
Factory Overhead

A summary of the time tickets at the end of each month is the basis for recording the direct and indirect labor costs incurred in production. Direct labor is posted to each job cost sheet, while indirect labor is debited to Factory Overhead.[2] Goodwell Printers incurred 850 direct labor hours on Jobs 71 and 72 during December. The total direct labor costs were $11,000, divided into $3,500 for Job 71 and $7,500 for Job 72. The labor costs that flow into production are recorded by the following summary entry to the work in process controlling account:

	c.	Work in Process	11,000.00	
		Wages Payable		11,000.00
		Factory labor used in production		
		of jobs.		

As with recording materials, many organizations are automating the labor recording process. For example, in companies that build very large products, such as submarines, jet aircraft, or space vehicles, direct labor employees can be given magnetic cards, much like credit cards. These cards can be used to log in and log out

[2] There are a variety of methods for recording direct labor costs. In the approach illustrated in this chapter, we assume that labor costs are automatically recorded to jobs or factory overhead when incurred. Alternatively, wages could first be debited to Factory Labor when incurred and then later distributed to jobs and factory overhead.

Shell Oil Company uses a magnetic system to track the work of maintenance crews in its refineries.

of particular work assignments on particular jobs by running the card through a magnetic reader at any number of remote computer terminals.

Factory Overhead Cost

Factory overhead includes all manufacturing costs except direct materials and direct labor. Debits to Factory Overhead come from various sources, such as indirect materials, indirect labor, factory power, and factory depreciation. For example, the factory overhead of $4,600 incurred in December for Goodwell Printers would be recorded as follows:

d.	Factory Overhead		4 6 0 0 00	
	Materials			5 0 0 00
	Wages Payable			2 0 0 0 00
	Utilities Payable			9 0 0 00
	Accumulated Depreciation			1 2 0 0 00
	Factory overhead incurred in production.			

Allocating Factory Overhead

Factory overhead is much different from direct labor and direct materials because it is indirectly related to the jobs. How, then, do the jobs get assigned a portion of overhead costs? The answer is through cost allocation. **Cost allocation** is the process of assigning factory overhead costs to a cost object, such as a job. The factory overhead costs are assigned to the jobs on the basis of some known measure about each job. The measure used to allocate factory overhead is frequently called an **activity base**, **allocation base**, or **activity driver**. The estimated activity base should be a measure that reflects the consumption or use of factory overhead cost. For example, the direct labor is recorded for each job, using time tickets. Thus, direct labor could be used to allocate production-related factory overhead costs to each job. Likewise, direct materials costs are known about each job through the materials requisitions. Thus, materials-related factory overhead, such as Purchasing Department salaries, could logically be allocated to the job on the basis of materials cost.

Predetermined Factory Overhead Rate

In order that job costs may be currently available, factory overhead may be allocated or applied to production using a **predetermined factory overhead rate**. The predetermined factory overhead rate is calculated by dividing the estimated amount of factory overhead for the forthcoming year by the estimated activity base, such as machine hours, direct materials costs, direct labor costs, or direct labor hours.

To illustrate calculating a predetermined overhead rate, assume that Goodwell Printers estimates the total factory overhead cost to be $50,000 for the year and the activity base to be 10,000 direct labor hours. The predetermined factory overhead rate would be calculated as $5 per direct labor hour, as follows:

$$\textbf{Predetermined factory overhead rate} = \frac{\textbf{Estimated total factory overhead costs}}{\textbf{Estimated activity base}}$$

$$\text{Predetermined factory overhead rate} = \frac{\$50{,}000}{10{,}000 \text{ direct labor hours}} = \$5 \text{ per direct labor hour}$$

Why is the predetermined overhead rate calculated from estimated numbers at the beginning of the period? The answer is to ensure timely information. If a company waited until the end of an accounting period, when all overhead costs are known, the allocated factory overhead would be accurate but not timely. If the cost system is to have maximum usefulness, cost data should be available as each job is completed, even though there may be a small sacrifice in accuracy. Only through timely reporting

A variety of activity bases may be used to allocate factory overhead to jobs. One survey reported the following activity bases used by manufacturers:

Description of Activity Base (Driver)	Percentage of Survey Respondents Indicating Usage*
Direct labor hours	61%
Direct labor dollars	54
Machine hours	54
Direct material dollars	26
Other	25

*Note: The percentages total more than 100% because many firms use more than one activity base in different parts of their operations.

Source: James A. Hendricks, "Applying Cost Accounting to Factory Automation," *Management Accounting,* December 1988, pp. 24–30.

can management make needed adjustments in pricing or in manufacturing methods and achieve the best possible combination of revenue and cost on future jobs.

A number of companies are using a new product-costing approach called activity-based costing. **Activity-based costing** is a method of accumulating and allocating factory overhead costs to products, using many overhead rates. Each rate is related to separate factory activities, such as inspecting, moving, and machining. Activity-based costing is discussed and illustrated in the appendix to Chapter 23.

A recent survey conducted by the Cost Management Group of the Institute for Management Accountants found that 43% of survey respondents have adopted activity-based costing and 39% are considering it.

Applying Factory Overhead to Work in Process

As factory overhead costs are incurred, they are debited to the factory overhead account, as shown previously in transaction (d). For Goodwell Printers, factory overhead costs are applied to production at the rate of $5 per direct labor hour. The amount of factory overhead applied to each job would be recorded in the job cost sheets as shown in Exhibit 8. For example, the 850 di-

EXHIBIT 8
Assigning Factory Overhead to Jobs

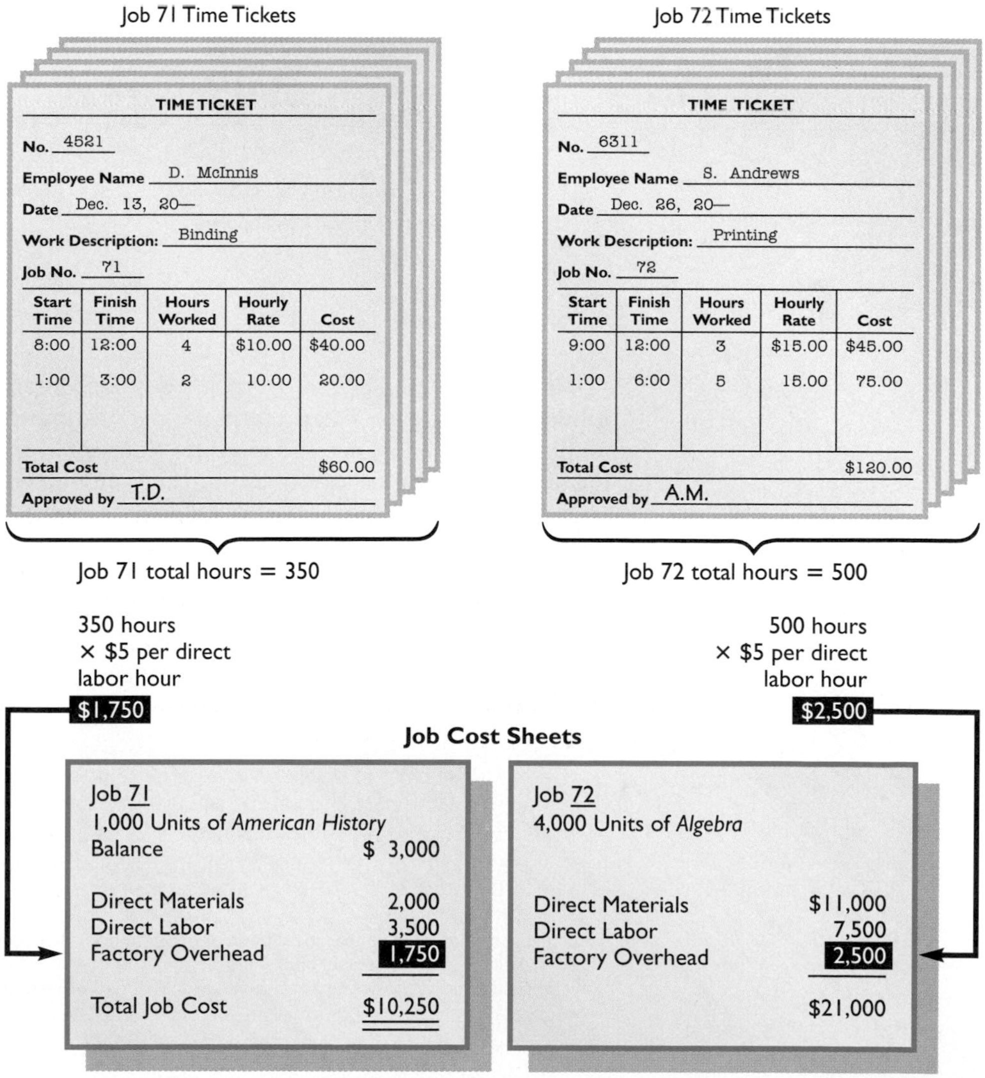

rect labor hours used in Goodwell's December operations would all be traced to individual jobs. Job 71 used 350 labor hours, so $1,750 (350 × $5) of factory overhead would be applied to Job 71. Similarly, $2,500 (500 × $5) of factory overhead would be applied to Job 72.

The factory overhead costs applied to production are periodically debited to the work in process account and credited to the factory overhead account. The summary entry to apply the $4,250 ($1,750 + $2,500) of factory overhead is as follows:

e.	Work in Process	4,250 00	
	Factory Overhead		4,250 00
	Factory overhead applied to jobs according to the predetermined overhead rate.		

Q&A *Factory overhead costs are estimated to be $120,000. Direct labor hours are estimated to be 20,000 hours. Determine (a) the predetermined factory overhead rate and (b) the amount of factory overhead applied to a job with 30 direct labor hours.*

(a) $6 per hour ($120,000/20,000); (b) $180 ($6 × 30 hours)

The factory overhead costs applied and the actual factory overhead costs incurred during a period will usually differ. If the amount applied exceeds the actual costs incurred, the factory overhead account will have a credit balance. This credit is described as **overapplied** or **overabsorbed factory overhead**. If the amount applied is less than the actual costs incurred, the account will have a debit balance. This debit is described as **underapplied** or **underabsorbed factory overhead**. Both cases are illustrated in the following account for Goodwell Printers:

ACCOUNT *Factory Overhead* **ACCOUNT NO.**

Date		Item	Post. Ref.	Debit	Credit	Balance Debit	Balance Credit
Dec.	1	Balance					200
	31	Factory overhead cost incurred		4,600		4,400	
	31	Factory overhead cost applied			4,250	150	

Underapplied balance (150)
Overapplied balance (200)

If the underapplied or overapplied balance increases in only one direction and it becomes large, the balance and the overhead rate should be investigated. For example, if a large balance is caused by changes in manufacturing methods or in production goals, the factory overhead rate should be revised. On the other hand, a large underapplied balance may indicate a serious control problem caused by inefficiencies in production methods, excessive costs, or a combination of factors.

Disposal of Factory Overhead Balance

The balance in the factory overhead account is carried forward from month to month. It is reported on interim balance sheets as a deferred debit or credit. This balance, should not be carried over to the next year, however, since it applies to the operations of the year just ended.

One approach for disposing of the balance of factory overhead at the end of the year is to transfer the entire balance to the cost of goods sold account.[3] To illustrate, the journal entry to eliminate Goodwell Printers' underapplied overhead balance of $150 at the end of the calendar year would be:

[3] Alternatively, the balance may be allocated among the work in process, finished goods, and cost of goods sold balances. This approach brings the accounts into agreement with the costs actually incurred. Since this approach is a more complex calculation that adds little additional accuracy, it will not be used in this text.

f.	Cost of Goods Sold		150 00	
	Factory Overhead			150 00
	Closed underapplied factory overhead to cost of goods sold.			

Work in Process

Costs incurred for the various jobs are debited to Work in Process. Goodwell Printers' job costs described in the preceding sections may be summarized as follows:

- **Direct materials, $13,000**—Work in Process debited and Materials credited; data obtained from summary of materials requisitions.
- **Direct labor, $11,000**—Work in Process debited and Wages Payable credited; data obtained from summary of time tickets.
- **Factory overhead, $4,250**—Work in Process debited and Factory Overhead credited; data obtained from summary of time tickets.

The details concerning the costs incurred on each job order are accumulated in the job cost sheets. Exhibit 9 illustrates the relationship between the job cost sheets and the work in process controlling account.

EXHIBIT 9
Job Cost Sheets and the Work in Process Controlling Account

Job Cost Sheets

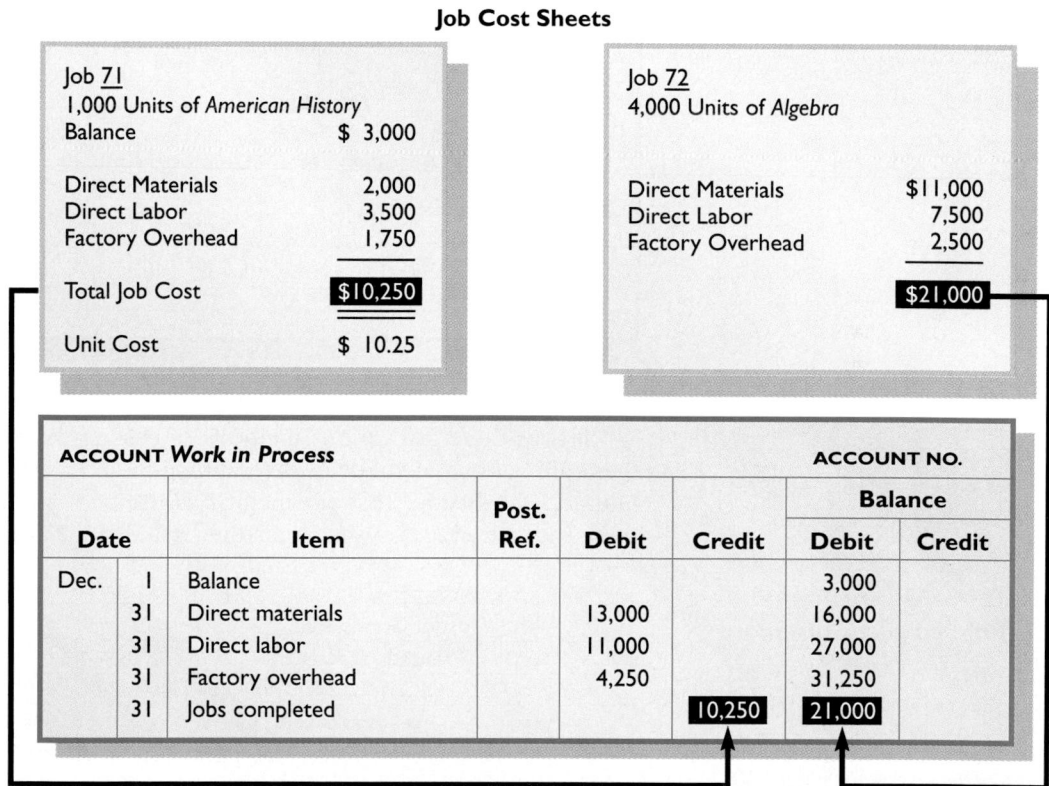

Job 71	
1,000 Units of *American History*	
Balance	$ 3,000
Direct Materials	2,000
Direct Labor	3,500
Factory Overhead	1,750
Total Job Cost	$10,250
Unit Cost	$ 10.25

Job 72	
4,000 Units of *Algebra*	
Direct Materials	$11,000
Direct Labor	7,500
Factory Overhead	2,500
	$21,000

ACCOUNT *Work in Process* ACCOUNT NO.

Date		Item	Post. Ref.	Debit	Credit	Balance Debit	Balance Credit
Dec.	1	Balance				3,000	
	31	Direct materials		13,000		16,000	
	31	Direct labor		11,000		27,000	
	31	Factory overhead		4,250		31,250	
	31	Jobs completed			10,250	21,000	

In this example, Job 71 was started in November and completed in December. The beginning December balance for Job 71 represents the costs carried over from the end of November. Job 72 was started in December but was not yet completed at the end of the month. Thus, the balance of the incomplete Job 72, or $21,000, will be shown on the balance sheet on December 31 as work in process inventory.

When Job 71 was completed, the direct materials costs, the direct labor costs, and the factory overhead costs were totaled and divided by the number of units produced to determine the cost per unit. If we assume that 1,000 units of a textbook titled *American History* were produced for Job 71, then the unit cost would be $10.25 ($10,250 ÷ 1,000).

Upon completing Job 71, the job cost sheet was removed from the cost ledger and filed for future reference. At the end of the accounting period (December), the total costs for all completed jobs during the period are determined, and the following entry is made:

g.	Finished Goods	10 2 5 0 00	
	Work in Process		10 2 5 0 00
	Job 71 completed in December.		

Finished Goods and Cost of Goods Sold

The finished goods account is a controlling account. Its related subsidiary ledger, which has an account for each product, is called the **finished goods ledger** or **stock ledger**. Each account in the finished goods ledger contains cost data for the units manufactured, units sold, and units on hand. Exhibit 10 illustrates an account in the finished goods ledger.

EXHIBIT 10
Finished Goods Ledger Account

ITEM: ***American History***

Manufactured			Shipped			Balance			
Job Order No.	Quantity	Amount	Ship Order No.	Quantity	Amount	Date	Quantity	Amount	Unit Cost
						Dec. 1	2,000	$20,000	$10.00
			643	2,000	$20,000	9	—	—	—
71	1,000	$10,250				31	1,000	10,250	10.25

Q&A *Boxer Company completed 80,000 units at a cost of $680,000. The beginning finished goods inventory was 10,000 units at $80,000. What is the cost of goods sold for 60,000 units, assuming a FIFO cost flow?*

$505,000 [$80,000 + (50,000 × $8.50)]

Just as there are various methods of costing materials entering into production, there are various methods of determining the cost of the finished goods sold. In Exhibit 10, the first-in, first-out method is used. A summary of the cost data for the units shipped ($20,000) becomes the basis for the following entry:

h.	Cost of Goods Sold	20 0 0 0 00	
	Finished Goods		20 0 0 0 00
	Cost of 2,000 *American History* textbooks sold.		

Sales

The selling price of the goods sold is recorded by debiting Accounts Receivable (or Cash) and crediting Sales. To illustrate, assume that Goodwell Printers sold the 2,000 *American History* textbooks during December for $14 per unit.[4] The entry to the accounts receivable controlling account would be:

[4] The price of the textbook is the amount paid by the textbook publisher for printing the book. Printing is one small part of the total cost of the textbook. The publisher must also pay royalties, development and production costs, and selling expenses. Thus, the price of the textbook to the final user will be higher than $14.

	i.	Accounts Receivable		28 000 00	
		Sales			28 000 00
		Revenue received from textbooks sold.			

Period Costs

In addition to product costs, businesses also have period costs. **Period costs** are expenses that are used in generating revenue during the current period and are not involved in the manufacturing process. Period costs are generally classified into two categories: selling and administrative. **Selling expenses** are incurred in marketing the product and delivering the sold product to customers. **Administrative expenses** are incurred in the administration of the business and are not related to the manufacturing or selling functions.

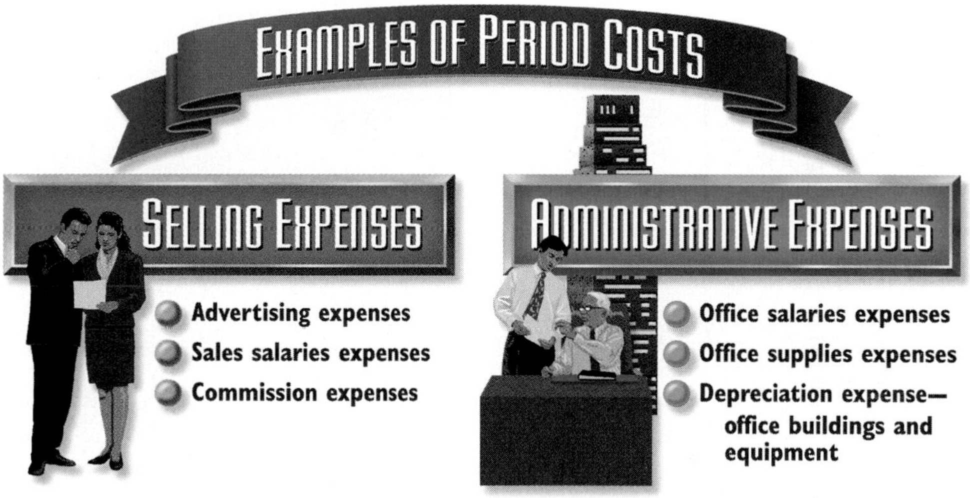

EXAMPLES OF PERIOD COSTS
SELLING EXPENSES
Advertising expenses
Sales salaries expenses
Commission expenses
ADMINISTRATIVE EXPENSES
Office salaries expenses
Office supplies expenses
Depreciation expense—office buildings and equipment

For Goodwell Printers, the following period expenses were recorded for December:

	j.	Sales Salaries Expense		2 000 00	
		Office Salaries Expense		1 500 00	
		Accounts Payable			3 500 00
		Recorded December period costs.			

Summary of Cost Flows for Goodwell Printers

Exhibit 11 shows the cost flow through the manufacturing accounts, together with summary details of the subsidiary ledgers for Goodwell Printers. Entries in the accounts are identified by letters that refer to the summary journal entries introduced in the preceding section.

The balances of the general ledger controlling accounts are supported by their respective subsidiary ledgers. The balances of the three inventory accounts—Finished Goods,

REAL WORLD

Service companies, such as telecommunications, insurance, banking, broadcasting, and hospitality, typically have a large portion of their total costs as period costs. This is because most service companies do not have products that can be inventoried, and hence, they do not have product costs.

EXHIBIT 11
Flow of Manufacturing Costs for Goodwell Printers

Materials

Dec. 1	6,500	(b)	13,000
(a)	10,500	(d)	500

Factory Overhead

(d)	500	Dec. 1	200
(d)	900		
(d)	1,200	(e)	4,250
(d)	2,000	(f)	150

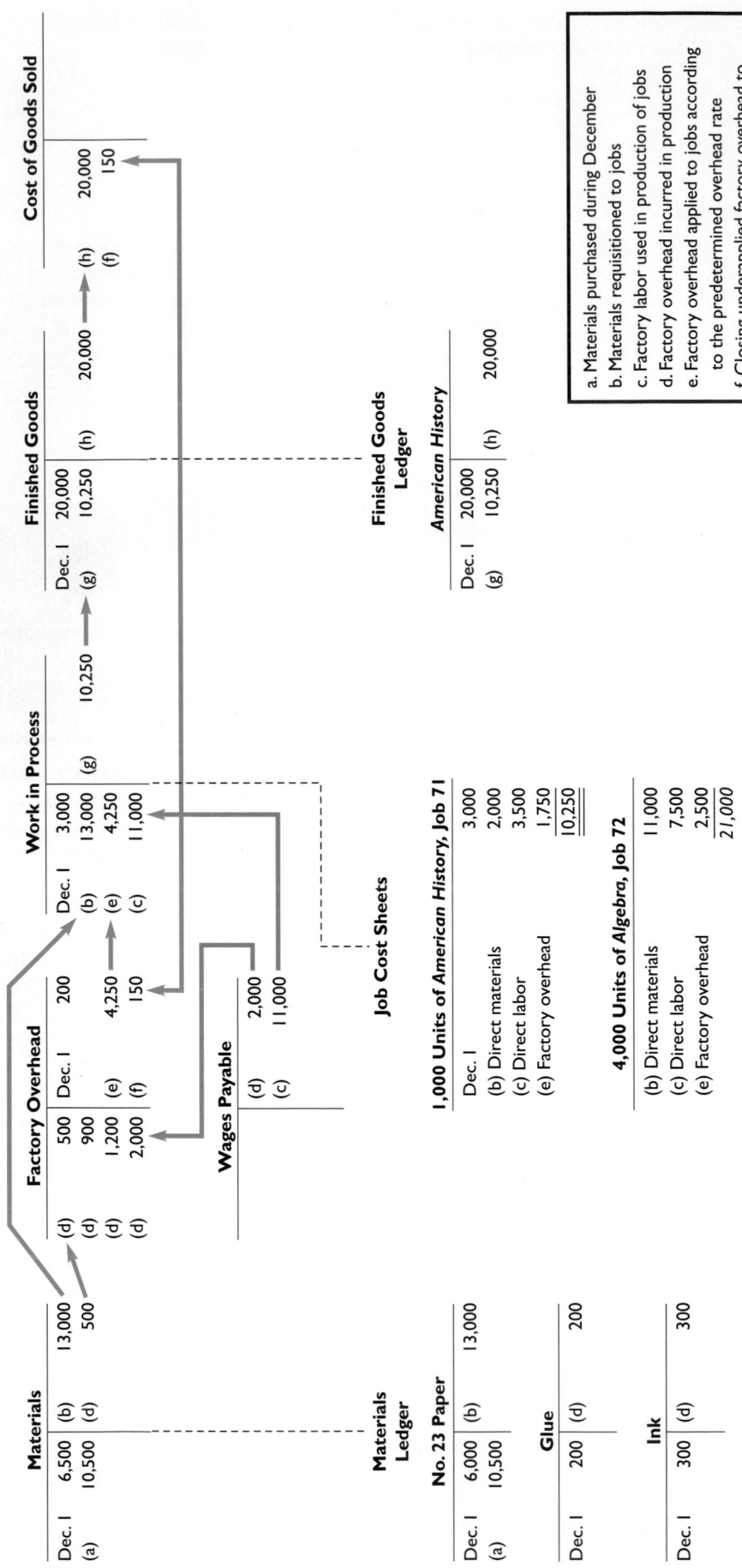

Work in Process

Dec. 1	3,000	(g)	10,250
(b)	13,000		
(e)	4,250		
(c)	11,000		

Finished Goods

Dec. 1	20,000	(h)	20,000
(g)	10,250		

Cost of Goods Sold

(h)	20,000		
(f)	150		

Wages Payable

		(d)	2,000
		(c)	11,000

Materials Ledger

No. 23 Paper

Dec. 1	6,000	(b)	13,000
(a)	10,500		

Glue

Dec. 1	200	(d)	200

Ink

Dec. 1	300	(d)	300

Job Cost Sheets

1,000 Units of *American History*, Job 71

Dec. 1	3,000
(b) Direct materials	2,000
(c) Direct labor	3,500
(e) Factory overhead	1,750
	10,250

4,000 Units of *Algebra*, Job 72

(b) Direct materials	11,000
(c) Direct labor	7,500
(e) Factory overhead	2,500
	21,000

Finished Goods Ledger

American History

Dec. 1	20,000	(h)	20,000
(g)	10,250		

a. Materials purchased during December
b. Materials requisitioned to jobs
c. Factory labor used in production of jobs
d. Factory overhead incurred in production
e. Factory overhead applied to jobs according to the predetermined overhead rate
f. Closing underapplied factory overhead to cost of goods sold
g. Job 71 completed in December
h. Cost of 2,000 *American History* textbooks sold

Work in Process, and Materials—represent the respective ending inventories of December 31 on the balance sheet. These balances are as follows:

Materials	$ 3,500
Work in process	21,000
Finished goods	10,250

The income statement for Goodwell Printers would be as shown in Exhibit 12.

EXHIBIT 12
Income Statement of Goodwell Printers

Goodwell Printers
Income Statement
For the Month Ended December 31, 2000

Sales		$28,000
Cost of goods sold		20,150
Gross profit		$ 7,850
Selling and administrative expenses:		
Sales salaries expense	$2,000	
Office salaries expense	1,500	
Total selling and administrative expenses		3,500
Income from operations		$ 4,350

Job Order Costing for Decision Making

OBJECTIVE 6

Use job order cost information for decision making.

The job order cost system that we developed in the previous sections can be used to evaluate an organization's cost performance. The unit costs for similar jobs can be compared over time to determine if costs are staying within expected ranges. If costs increase for some unexpected reason, the details in the job cost sheets can help discover the reasons.

To illustrate, consider the direct materials from the job cost sheets for Jobs 144 and 163 in Exhibit 13. Since both job cost sheets refer to the same type and number of chairs, the direct materials cost per unit should be about the same. However, the materials cost per chair for Job 144 is $28, while for Job 163 it is $35. For some reason, materials costs have increased since the folding chairs were produced for Job 144.

EXHIBIT 13
Comparing Data from Job Cost Sheets

Job 144
Item: 200 folding chairs

	Materials Quantity (board feet)	Materials Price	Materials Amount
Direct materials:			
Wood	1,600	$3.50	$5,600
Direct materials per chair			$28

Job 163
Item: 200 folding chairs

	Materials Quantity (board feet)	Materials Price	Materials Amount
Direct materials:			
Wood	2,000	$3.50	$7,000
Direct materials per chair			$35

Major electric utilities such as **Tennessee Valley Authority**, **Consolidated Edison**, and **Pacific Gas and Electric** use job order accounting to control the costs associated with major repairs and overhauls that occur during forced or planned outages. A forced outage is an unexpected shutdown of a power plant, whereas a planned outage is a scheduled shutdown. During an outage, the power plant stops generating electricity while maintenance crews perform extensive repairs. Accumulating these costs controls the materials, labor, and overhead costs of these repairs by the various tasks that make up a repair job. Typically, such jobs can last several months. Management maintains records of all repair jobs by type of repair. In this way, management can develop trend data and cost experience that can support cost planning and control in future projects.

We can use the job cost sheets to investigate possible reasons for the increased cost. First, we should note that the rates for direct materials did not change. Thus, the cost increase is not related to increasing prices. What about the wood consumption? This tells us a different story. The quantity of wood used to produce 200 chairs in Job 144 is 1,600 board feet. However, Job 163 required 2,000 board feet. How can this be explained? Any one of the following explanations is possible and could be investigated further:

1. There was a new employee that was not adequately trained for cutting the wood for chairs. As a result, the employee improperly cut and scrapped many pieces.
2. The lumber was of poor quality. As a result, the cutting operator ended up using and scrapping additional pieces of lumber.
3. The cutting tools were in need of repair. As a result, the cutting operators miscut and scrapped many pieces of wood.
4. The operator was careless. As a result of poor work, many pieces of cut wood had to be scrapped.
5. The instructions attached to the job were incorrect. The operator cut wood according to the instructions but discovered that the pieces would not fit. As a result, many pieces had to be scrapped.

You should note that many of these explanations are not necessarily related to operator error. Poor cost performance may be the result of root causes that are outside the control of the operator.

Job Order Cost Systems for Service Businesses

OBJECTIVE 7

Diagram the flow of costs for a service business that uses a job order cost accounting system.

A job order cost accounting system may be useful to the management of a service business in planning and controlling operations. For example, an advertising agency, an attorney, and a physician all share the common characteristic of providing services to individual customers, clients, or patients. In such cases, the customer, client, or patient can be viewed as an individual job for which costs are accumulated.

Since the "product" of a service business is service, management's focus is on direct labor and overhead costs. The cost of any materials or supplies used in rendering services for a client is usually small and is normally included as part of the overhead.

The direct labor and overhead costs of rendering services to clients are accumulated in a work in process account. This account is supported by a cost ledger. A job cost sheet is used to accumulate the costs for each client's job. When a job is completed and the client is billed, the costs are transferred to a cost of services account. This account is similar to the cost of merchandise sold account for a merchandising business or the cost of goods sold account for a manufacturing business. A finished goods account and related finished goods ledger are not necessary, since the revenues associated with the services are recorded after the services have been provided. The flow of costs through a service business using a job order cost accounting system is shown in Exhibit 14.

In practice, additional accounting considerations unique to service businesses may need to be considered. For example, a service business may bill clients on a

EXHIBIT 14
Flow of Costs Through a Service Business

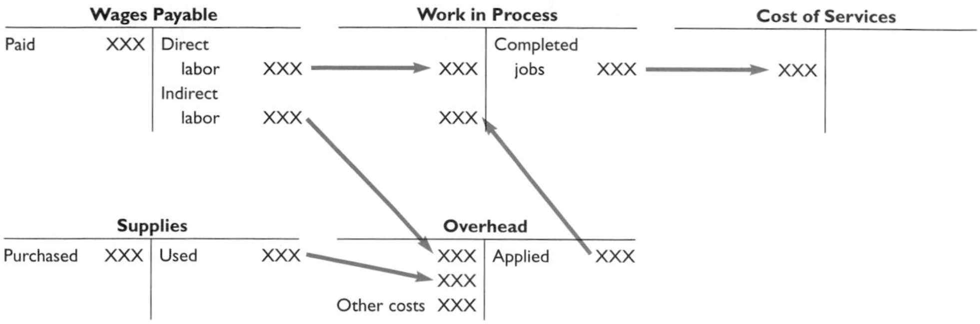

weekly or monthly basis rather than waiting until a job is completed. In these situations, a portion of the costs related to each billing should be transferred from the work in process account to the cost of services account. A service business may also have advance billings that would be accounted for as deferred revenue until the services have been completed.

ENCORE

Life Becomes a Box of Chocolates for Author of *Forrest Gump*

Winston Groom, the author of *Forrest Gump*, was promised $350,000 and 3% of the net profits of the *Forrest Gump* movie. We would think that Winston Groom was a lucky man. After all, *Forrest Gump* grossed $670 million in worldwide ticket sales, ranking its revenues as one of the highest in movie history. Unfortunately, Groom has yet to see any money from participating in the profits, because the movie has yet to make a profit. Instead, **Paramount Studios** estimated that the movie had a loss of $62 million! This can be explained by the unique form of job order costing used in Hollywood, termed *contract accounting.* Under contract accounting, all the costs associated with the movie are accumulated by each movie project, including overhead allocations. Many are critical of some of the overhead allocation practices. For example, it is common to add in a distribution fee to the cost of the movie. This fee compensates the studio for maintaining its distribution arm. In the case of *Forrest Gump,* Paramount included a distribution fee equal to 32% of the gross revenues. Critics argue that the actual cost of distribution is closer to 10% of the gross revenue. For example, in *Coming To America,* the distribution fee for this one film ($42 million) more than covered Paramount's entire distribution costs for the whole year. All this raises an interesting question: Is it possible under contract accounting for a hit movie to ever show a profit?

It looks as if Groom has wised up to the ways of Hollywood accounting. Groom has made a new seven-figure deal with Paramount for *Gump & Co.,* the sequel to *Forrest Gump.* In this deal, Groom takes a percentage of the gross revenues, *before expenses.* Under this contract, Groom won't care about "distribution fees" and other cost allocations. ■

APPENDIX: COMPUTERIZED JOB ORDER COSTING

We will illustrate computerized job order costing for direct materials for Campus Graphics & Copies (CG&C), using QuickBooks® accounting software.[5] CG&C purchases 20-lb. bond paper and uses the "Enter Bills" electronic form as shown in Exhibit 15. At the bottom of this form, you can see that CG&C purchased 10,000 sheets of 20-lb. bond paper for $200 ($0.02 per sheet) from American Paper Co.

EXHIBIT 15
Enter Bill Form

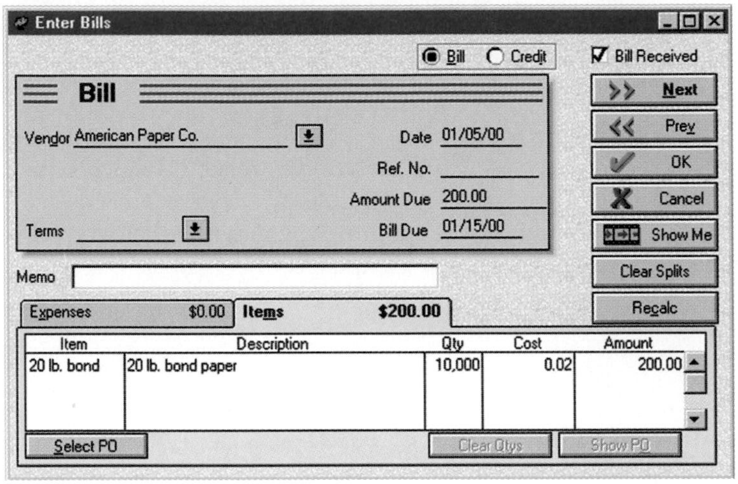

Once this form is completed, 10,000 pages of 20-lb. bond will be added to the inventory. Exhibit 16 is an invoice for Job No. 64, a copying job for the Business School requiring 3,450 sheets of paper. The invoice form records the revenue from the service at $0.06 per page, or $207. The form also shows the use of 3,450 sheets of 20-lb. bond. Although there is no price charged for the paper, the cost of the paper ($0.02 per page) is automatically removed from inventory and applied to Job No. 64 when this form is completed. In this way, the invoice form serves the same function as the materials requisition form discussed in the chapter.

EXHIBIT 16
Create Invoice Form

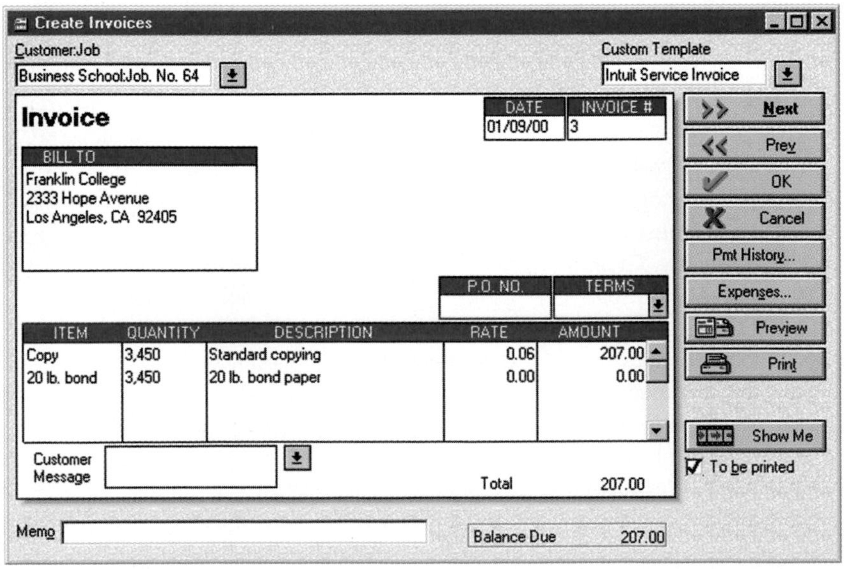

[5] Although not illustrated here, you can also apply direct labor to jobs, using the payroll feature of QuickBooks®.

QuickBooks can provide a report showing the inventory balance for 20-lb. bond after these two transactions have been completed, as shown in Exhibit 17.

EXHIBIT 17   Inventory Valuation Detail Report

Inventory Valuation Detail

Customize... | Filters.. | Format... | Header/Footer... | Hide Header | Print... | Memorize... | Show Me...

Dates [Custom]   From [01/01/00] To [01/31/00]

Campus Graphics & Copies
Inventory Valuation Detail
January 2000

Type	Date	Name	Num	Qty	Cost	On Hand	Avg Cost	Asset Value
20 lb. bond								
Bill	01/05/00	American ...		10,000	200.00	10,000	0.02	200.00
Invoice	01/09/00	Business ...	3	-3,450		6,550	0.02	131.00
Total 20 lb. bond						6,550		131.00
TOTAL						**6,550**		**131.00**

The profitability of a job can be determined by comparing the revenues with the costs. Exhibit 18 shows the Profit and Loss by Job Report for CG&C's Job No. 64. As you can see, Job No. 64 earned CG&C a $138 gross profit.

EXHIBIT 18
Profit and Loss by Job
Report

Profit and Loss by Job

Customize... | Filters.. | Format... | Header/Footer... | Hide Header | Collapse | Print... | Memorize...

Dates [Custom]   From [01/01/00] To [01/31/00] Columns [Customer:Job]

Campus Graphics & Copies
Profit and Loss by Job
January 2000
Job. No. 64

	(Business School)	Total Business School	TOTAL
Ordinary Income/Expense			
Income			
Copy Service Revenue	207.00	207.00	207.00
Total Income	207.00	207.00	207.00
Cost of Goods Sold			
Cost of Goods Sold	69.00	69.00	69.00
Total COGS	69.00	69.00	69.00
Gross Profit	138.00	138.00	138.00
Net Ordinary Income	138.00	138.00	138.00
Net Income	**138.00**	**138.00**	**138.00**

KEY POINTS

1 Describe the differences between managerial and financial accounting.

Managerial accounting and financial accounting serve different needs and, as such, have different characteristics. Managerial accounting serves the reporting needs of managers in meeting strategic and operational goals. Managerial accounting is not bound by a set of generally accepted accounting principles, as is financial accounting. As a result, the practice of managerial accounting is as diverse as are organizations. This additional complexity in understanding the structure of managerial accounting is offset by the degree of creativity that can be applied to managerial information needs.

2 Evaluate the organizational role of management accountants.

The financial function is generally a staff function of the organization. The chief accountant is often called the controller. The controller's function includes providing a variety of reports to support management decision making.

3 Define and illustrate materials, factory labor, and factory overhead costs.

A manufacturer converts materials into a finished product by using machinery and labor. The cost of materials that are an integral part of the manufactured product is direct materials cost. The cost of wages of employees who are involved in converting materials into the manufactured product is direct labor cost. Costs other than direct materials and direct labor costs are factory overhead costs, including indirect materials and labor. Direct labor and factory overhead are termed conversion costs. Direct materials, direct labor, and factory overhead costs are associated with products and are called product costs.

4 Describe accounting systems used by manufacturing businesses.

A cost accounting system accumulates product costs. The cost accounting system is used by management to determine the proper product cost for inventory valuation on the financial statements, to support product pricing decisions, and to identify opportunities for cost reduction and improved production efficiency. The two primary cost accounting systems are job order and process cost systems.

5 Describe and prepare summary journal entries for a job order cost accounting system.

A job order cost system provides for a separate record of the cost of each particular quantity of product that passes through the factory. Direct materials, direct labor, and factory overhead costs are accumulated in a subsidiary cost ledger, in which each account is represented by a job cost sheet. Work in Process is the controlling account for the cost ledger. As a job is finished, its costs are transferred to the finished goods ledger, for which Finished Goods is the controlling account.

6 Use job order cost information for decision making.

Job order cost information can support pricing and cost analysis. Managers can use job cost information to identify unusual trends and areas for cost improvement.

7 Diagram the flow of costs for a service business that uses a job order cost accounting system.

A cost flow diagram for a service business using a job order cost accounting system is shown in Exhibit 14. For a service business, the cost of materials or supplies used is normally included as part of the overhead. The direct labor and overhead costs of rendering services are accumulated in a work in process account. When a job is completed and the client is billed, the costs are transferred to a cost of services account.

ILLUSTRATIVE PROBLEM

Derby Music Company specializes in producing and packaging compact discs (CDs) for the music recording industry. Derby uses a job order cost system. The following data summarize the operations related to production for March, the first month of operations:

a. Materials purchased on account, $15,500.
b. Materials requisitioned and labor used:

	Materials	Factory Labor
Job No. 100	$2,650	$1,770
Job No. 101	1,240	650
Job No. 102	980	420
Job No. 103	3,420	1,900
Job No. 104	1,000	500
Job No. 105	2,100	1,760
For general factory use	450	650

c. Factory overhead costs incurred on account, $2,700.
d. Depreciation of machinery, $1,750.
e. Factory overhead is applied at a rate of 70% of direct labor cost.
f. Jobs completed: Nos. 100, 101, 102, 104.
g. Jobs 100, 101, and 102 were shipped, and customers were billed for $8,100, $3,800, and $3,500, respectively.

Instructions

1. Journalize the entries to record the transactions identified above.
2. Determine the account balances for Work in Process and Finished Goods.
3. Prepare a schedule of unfinished jobs to support the balance in the work in process account.
4. Prepare a schedule of completed jobs on hand to support the balance in the finished goods account.

Solution

1.	a.	Materials	15,500	
		Accounts Payable		15,500
	b.	Work in Process	11,390	
		Materials		11,390
		Work in Process	7,000	
		Wages Payable		7,000
		Factory Overhead	1,100	
		Materials		450
		Wages Payable		650
	c.	Factory Overhead	2,700	
		Accounts Payable		2,700
	d.	Factory Overhead	1,750	
		Accumulated Depreciation—Machinery		1,750
	e.	Work in Process	4,900	
		Factory Overhead (70% of $7,000)		4,900
	f.	Finished Goods	11,548	
		Work in Process		11,548

Computation of the cost of jobs finished:

Job	Direct Materials	Direct Labor	Factory Overhead	Total
Job No. 100	$2,650	$1,770	$1,239	$ 5,659
Job No. 101	1,240	650	455	2,345
Job No. 102	980	420	294	1,694
Job No. 104	1,000	500	350	1,850
				$11,548

g.	Accounts Receivable	15,400	
	Sales		15,400
	Cost of Goods Sold	9,698	
	Finished Goods		9,698

Cost of jobs sold computation:

Job No. 100	$5,659
Job No. 101	2,345
Job No. 102	1,694
	$9,698

2. Work in Process: $11,742 ($11,390 + $7,000 + $4,900 − $11,548)
Finished Goods: $1,850 ($11,548 − $9,698)

3.

Schedule of Unfinished Jobs

Job	Direct Materials	Direct Labor	Factory Overhead	Total
Job No. 103	$3,420	$1,900	$1,330	$ 6,650
Job No. 105	2,100	1,760	1,232	5,092
Balance of Work in Process, March 31				$11,742

4.

Schedule of Completed Jobs

Job No. 104:	
Direct materials	$1,000
Direct labor	500
Factory overhead	350
Balance of Finished Goods, March 31	$1,850

SELF-EXAMINATION QUESTIONS

Answers at End of Chapter

Matching

Match each of the following statements with its proper term. Some terms may not be used.

- **A.** **activity base**
- **B.** **activity-based costing**
- **C.** **controller**
- **D.** **conversion costs**
- **E.** **cost**
- **F.** **cost accounting system**
- **G.** **cost allocation**
- **H.** **cost of goods sold**
- **I.** **direct labor cost**
- **J.** **direct materials cost**
- **K.** **factory overhead cost**
- **L.** **financial accounting**
- **M.** **finished goods inventory**

C 1. The chief management accountant of a division or other segment of a business.

L 2. The branch of accounting that is concerned with the recording of transactions using generally accepted accounting principles (GAAP) for a business or other economic unit and with a periodic preparation of various statements from such records.

Q 3. The branch of accounting that uses both historical and estimated data in providing information that management uses in conducting daily operations, in planning future operations, and in developing overall business strategies.

E 4. A payment of cash (or a commitment to pay cash in the future) for the purpose of generating revenues.

F 5. A system used to accumulate manufacturing costs for decision-making and financial reporting purposes.

P 6. A type of cost accounting system that provides for a separate record of the cost of each particular quantity of product that passes through the factory.

K 7. All of the costs of operating the factory except for direct materials and direct labor.

J 8. The cost of materials that are an integral part of the finished product.

I 9. Wages of factory workers who are directly involved in converting materials into a finished product.

N. finished goods ledger
O. job cost sheet
P. job order cost system
Q. managerial accounting
R. materials inventory
S. materials ledger
T. materials requisitions
U. overapplied factory overhead
V. period costs
W. predetermined factory overhead rate
X. product costs
Y. receiving report
Z. time tickets
AA. underapplied factory overhead
BB. work in process inventory

D 10. The combination of direct labor and factory overhead costs.

X 11. The three components of manufacturing cost: direct materials, direct labor, and factory overhead costs.

BB 12. The direct materials costs, the direct labor costs, and the factory overhead costs that have entered into the manufacturing process, but are associated with products that have not been finished.

O 13. An account in the work in process subsidiary ledger in which the costs charged to a particular job order are recorded.

T 14. The form or electronic transmission used by a manufacturing department to authorize the issuance of materials from the storeroom.

R 15. The cost of materials that have not yet entered into the manufacturing process.

H 16. The cost of the manufactured product sold.

S 17. The subsidiary ledger containing the individual accounts for each type of material.

Y 18. The form or electronic transmission used by the receiving personnel to indicate that materials have been received and inspected.

Z 19. The form on which the amount of time spent by each employee and the labor cost incurred for each individual job, or for factory overhead, are recorded.

G 20. The process of assigning indirect costs to a cost object, such as a job.

A 21. A measure of activity that is related to changes in cost and is used in the denominator in calculating the predetermined factory overhead rate to assign factory overhead costs to cost objects.

W 22. The rate used to apply factory overhead costs to the goods manufactured. The rate is determined from budgeted overhead cost and estimated activity usage data at the beginning of the fiscal period.

U 23. The amount of factory overhead applied in excess of the actual factory overhead costs incurred for production during a period.

B 24. An accounting framework based on determining the cost of activities.

N 25. The subsidiary ledger that contains the individual accounts for each kind of commodity or product produced.

M 26. The cost of finished products on hand that have not been sold.

V 27. Those costs that are used up in generating revenue during the current period and that are not involved in the manufacturing process.

Multiple Choice

1. Which of the following best describes the difference between financial and managerial accounting?
   A. Managerial accounting provides information to support decisions, while financial accounting does not.
   B. Managerial accounting is not restricted to generally accepted accounting principles (GAAP), while financial accounting is restricted to GAAP.
   C. Managerial accounting does not result in financial reports, while financial accounting does result in financial reports.
   D. Managerial accounting is concerned solely with the future and does not record events from the past, while financial accounting records only events from past transactions.

2. Which of the following is *not* considered a cost of manufacturing a product?
   A. Direct materials cost
   B. Factory overhead cost
   C. Sales salaries
   D. Direct labor cost

3. Which of the following costs would be included as part of the factory overhead costs of a microcomputer manufacturer?
   A. The cost of memory chips
   B. Depreciation of testing equipment
   C. Wages of computer assemblers
   D. The cost of disk drives

4. For which of the following would the job order cost system be appropriate?
   A. Antique furniture repair shop
   B. Rubber manufacturer
   C. Coal mining
   D. All of the above

5. If the factory overhead account has a credit balance, factory overhead is said to be:
   A. underapplied
   B. overapplied
   C. underabsorbed
   D. in error

6. Debit balance means under applied

CLASS DISCUSSION QUESTIONS

1. What are the major differences between managerial accounting and financial accounting?
2. a. Differentiate between a department with line responsibility and a department with staff responsibility.
   b. In an organization that has a Sales Department and a Personnel Department, among others, which of the two departments has (1) line responsibility and (2) staff responsibility?
3. a. What is the role of the controller in a business organization?
   b. Does the controller have a line or staff responsibility?
4. For a company that produces microcomputers, would memory chips be considered a direct or an indirect materials cost of each microcomputer produced?
5. What three costs make up the cost of manufacturing a product?
6. If the cost of wages paid to employees who are directly involved in converting raw materials into a manufactured end product is not a significant portion of the total product cost, how would the wages cost be classified as to type of manufacturing cost?
7. Name the three inventory accounts for a manufacturing business, and describe what each balance represents at the end of an accounting period.
8. For a manufacturer, what is comparable to a merchandising business's cost of merchandise sold?
9. How is product cost information used by managers?
10. a. Name two principal types of cost accounting systems.
    b. Which system provides for a separate record of each particular quantity of product that passes through the factory?
    c. Which system accumulates the costs for each department or process within the factory?
11. What kind of firm would use a job order cost system?
12. **Hewlett-Packard Company** assembles printed circuit boards in which a high volume of standardized units are assembled and tested. Is the job order cost system appropriate in this situation?
13. Which account is used in a job order cost system to accumulate direct materials, direct labor, and factory overhead applied to production costs for individual jobs?
14. What is the job cost sheet?
15. How does the use of the materials requisition help control the issuance of materials from the storeroom?
16. a. Differentiate between the clock card and the time ticket.
    b. Why should the total time reported on an employee's time tickets for a payroll period be compared with the time reported on the employee's clock cards for the same period?
17. What document serves as the basis for posting to (a) the direct materials section of the job cost sheet and (b) the direct labor section of the job cost sheet?
18. Describe the source of the data for debiting Work in Process for (a) direct materials, (b) direct labor, and (c) factory overhead.
19. Discuss how the predetermined factory overhead rate can be used in job order cost accounting to assist management in pricing jobs.
20. a. How is a predetermined factory overhead rate calculated?
    b. Name three common bases used in calculating the rate.
21. a. What is (1) overapplied factory overhead and (2) underapplied factory overhead?
    b. If the factory overhead account has a debit balance, was factory overhead underapplied or overapplied?
    c. If the factory overhead account has a credit balance at the end of the first month of the fiscal year, where will the amount of this balance be reported on the interim balance sheet?
22. At the end of the fiscal year, there was a relatively minor balance in the factory overhead account. What procedure can be used for disposing of the balance in the account?
23. What account is the controlling account for (a) the materials ledger, (b) the job cost sheets, and (c) the finished goods ledger or stock ledger?

24. What is the difference between a product cost and a period cost?
25. How can job cost information be used to identify cost improvement opportunities?
26. What account is debited for completed service jobs?

Warren Reeve Fess

Resources for Your Success On-Line at warren.swcollege.com

Remember! If you need additional help, visit South-Western's Web site. See page 26 for a description of the online and printed materials that are available.

EXERCISES

Exercise 17–1
Classify costs as materials, labor, or factory overhead
Objective 3

Indicate whether each of the following costs of a furniture manufacturer would be classified as direct materials cost, direct labor cost, or factory overhead cost:

a. Furniture hardware
b. Saw blades
c. Supervisor salaries
d. Assembly wages
e. Wood
f. Wages of wood cutters
g. Inspector salaries
h. Depreciation on woodworking machinery

Exercise 17–2
Classify costs as materials, labor, or factory overhead
Objective 3

Indicate whether each of the following costs of the **Procter & Gamble Company** would be classified as direct materials cost, direct labor cost, or factory overhead cost:

a. Depreciation on the St. Bernard (Cincinnati) soap plant
b. Wages paid to Packing Department employees
c. Maintenance supplies
d. Packaging materials
e. Plant manager salary of the Lima, Ohio, liquid soap plant
f. Pulp
g. Wages of Making Department employees
h. Scents and fragrances
i. Depreciation on disposable diaper converting machines
j. Salary of process engineers

Exercise 17–3
Classify costs as product or period costs
Objectives 3, 5

Classify the following costs for **Ford Motor Company** as either a product cost or a period cost.

a. Advertising
b. Tires
c. Assembly employee wages
d. Salary of marketing executive
e. Depreciation of Dearborn, Michigan, executive building
f. CEO's salary
g. Plant manager's salary
h. Depreciation on Atlanta, Georgia, assembly plant
i. Maintenance supplies
j. Glass

k. Property taxes on Kansas City, Missouri, assembly plant
l. Shipping costs
m. New product design costs
n. Travel costs used by sales personnel
o. Utility costs used in executive building
p. Stamping Department employee wages
q. Steel

Exercise 17–4
Classify factory overhead costs

Objective 3

Which of the following items are properly classified as part of factory overhead?

a. Property taxes on factory buildings
b. Plant manager's salary
c. Chief Financial Officer's salary
d. Direct materials
e. Sales commissions
f. Amortization of patents on factory processes
g. Interest expense
h. Consultant's fees for surveying production employee morale
i. Factory supplies used

Exercise 17–5
Concepts and terminology

Objectives 3, 5

From the choices presented in the parentheses, choose the appropriate term for completing each of the following sentences:

a. Advertising expenses are usually viewed as (period, product) costs.
b. The balance sheet of a manufacturer would include an account for (cost of goods sold, work in process inventory).
c. Materials that are an integral part of the manufactured product are classified as (direct materials, materials inventory).
d. An example of factory overhead is (plant depreciation, sales office depreciation).
e. The wages of an assembly worker are normally considered a (period, product) cost.
f. Direct labor costs combined with factory overhead costs are called (product, conversion) costs.
g. Implementing automatic factory robotics equipment normally (increases, decreases) the factory overhead component of product costs.
h. Payments of cash or its equivalent or the commitment to pay cash in the future for the purpose of generating revenues are (costs, expenses).

Exercise 17–6
Transactions in a job order cost system

Objective 5

Five selected transactions for the current month are indicated by letters in the following T accounts in a job order cost accounting system:

Materials

	(a)

Work in Process

(a)	(d)
(b)	
(c)	

Wages Payable

	(b)

Finished Goods

(d)	(e)

Factory Overhead

(a)	(c)
(b)	

Cost of Goods Sold

(e)	

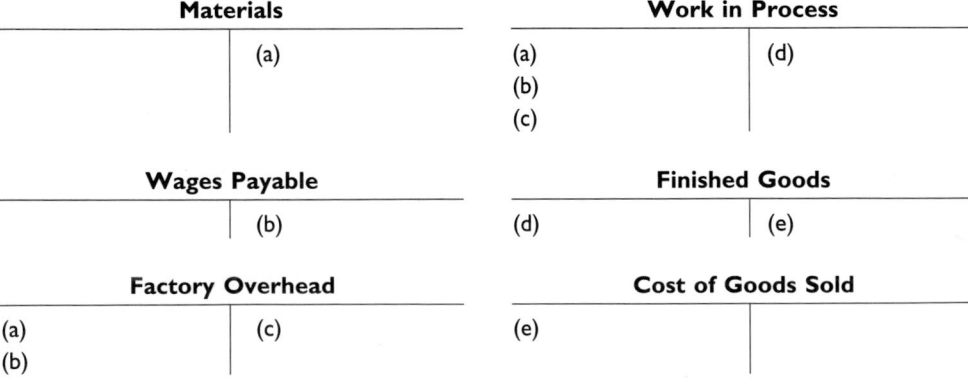

Describe each of the five transactions.

Exercise 17–7
Cost flow relationships

Objective 5

✓ c. $508,000

The following information is available for the first month of operations of Royal Crystal Company, a manufacturer of glassware:

Sales	$850,000
Gross profit	210,000
Indirect labor	12,000

Indirect materials	$ 30,000
Other factory overhead	15,000
Materials purchased	250,000
Total manufacturing costs for the period	760,000
Materials inventory, end of period	25,000

Using the above information, determine the following missing amounts:

a. Cost of goods sold
b. Direct materials cost
c. Direct labor cost

Exercise 17–8
Cost of materials issuances by FIFO method
Objective 5

✓ b. $5,440

An incomplete subsidiary ledger of wire cable for May is as follows:

RECEIVED			ISSUED			BALANCE			
Receiving Report Number	Quantity	Unit Price	Materials Requisition Number	Quantity	Amount	Date	Quantity	Amount	Unit Price
						May 1	320	$8,960	$28.00
23	370	$30.00				May 3			
			104	550		May 5			
29	280	32.00				May 19			
			117	250		May 25			

a. Complete the materials issuances and balances for the wire cable subsidiary ledger under FIFO.
b. Determine the balance of wire cable at the end of May.
c. Journalize the summary entry to transfer materials to work in process.
d. Explain how the materials ledger might be used as an aid in maintaining inventory quantities on hand.

Exercise 17–9
Entry for issuing materials
Objective 5

Materials issued for the current month are as follows:

Requisition No.	Material	Job No.	Amount
711	Steel	511	$ 6,800
712	Copper	514	12,300
713	Plastic	526	2,400
714	Abrasives	Indirect	400
715	Titanium alloy	533	27,600

Journalize the entry to record the issuance of materials.

Exercise 17–10
Entries for materials
Objective 5

✓ c. fabric, $86,500

Reclining Comfort Furniture Company (RCFC) manufactures furniture. RCFC uses a job order cost system. Balances on June 1 from the materials ledger are as follows:

Fabric	$38,000
Polyester filling	12,700
Lumber	64,600
Glue	2,400

The materials purchased during June are summarized from the receiving reports as follows:

Fabric	$412,400
Polyester filling	146,800
Lumber	742,100
Glue	17,300

Materials were requisitioned to individual jobs as follows:

	Fabric	Polyester Filling	Lumber	Total
Job 11	$124,300	$ 36,700	$203,600	$ 364,600
Job 12	86,400	15,300	124,600	226,300
Job 13	153,200	52,300	335,000	540,500
Factory overhead—indirect materials				14,300
Total	$363,900	$104,300	$663,200	$1,145,700

The glue is not a significant cost, so it is treated as indirect materials (factory overhead).

a. Journalize the entry to record the purchase of materials in June.
b. Journalize the entry to record the requisition of materials in June.
c. Determine the June 30 balances that would be shown in the materials ledger accounts.

Exercise 17–11
Entry for factory labor costs
Objective 5

A summary of the time tickets for the current month follows:

Job No.	Amount	Job No.	Amount
101	$1,240	141	$1,540
122	2,360	Indirect labor	8,570
133	870	143	3,240
139	4,230	147	1,950

Journalize the entry to record the factory labor costs.

Exercise 17–12
Entries for direct labor and factory overhead
Objective 5

Lincoln Homes Inc. manufactures log homes. Lincoln uses a job order cost system. The time tickets from September jobs are summarized below.

Job 502	$ 890
Job 503	1,750
Job 504	3,650
Job 505	2,310
Factory supervision	1,850

Factory overhead is applied to jobs on the basis of a predetermined overhead rate of $18 per direct labor hour. The direct labor rate is $10 per hour.

a. Journalize the entry to record the factory labor costs.
b. Journalize the entry to apply factory overhead to production for September.

Exercise 17–13
Factory overhead rates, entries, and account balance
Objective 5

✓ b. $22 per direct labor hour

High Definition Images Inc. operates two consumer appliance factories. The company applies factory overhead to jobs on the basis of machine hours in Factory 1 and on the basis of direct labor hours in Factory 2. Estimated factory overhead costs, direct labor hours, and machine hours are as follows:

	Factory 1	Factory 2
Estimated factory overhead cost for fiscal year beginning April 1	$516,000	$184,800
Estimated direct labor hours for year		8,400
Estimated machine hours for year	17,200	
Actual factory overhead costs for April	$ 45,000	$ 14,000
Actual direct labor hours for April		650
Actual machine hours for April	1,400	

a. Determine the factory overhead rate for Factory 1.
b. Determine the factory overhead rate for Factory 2.
c. Journalize the entries to apply factory overhead to production in each factory for April.

d. Determine the balances of the factory accounts for each factory as of April 30, and indicate whether the amounts represent overapplied or underapplied factory overhead.

Exercise 17–14
Entry for jobs completed; cost of unfinished jobs

Objective 5

✓ b. $12,200

The following account appears in the ledger after only part of the postings have been completed for March:

Work in Process

Balance, March 1	$24,300
Direct materials	94,300
Direct labor	45,700
Factory overhead	63,200

Jobs finished during March are summarized as follows:

Job 320	$45,700	Job 327	$32,700
Job 326	61,200	Job 350	75,700

a. Journalize the entry to record the jobs completed.
b. Determine the cost of the unfinished jobs at March 31.

Exercise 17–15
Entries for factory costs and jobs completed

Objective 5

✓ d. $45,400

Partner Printing Company began manufacturing operations on May 1. Jobs 1 and 2 were completed during the month, and all costs applicable to them were recorded on the related cost sheets. Jobs 3 and 4 are still in process at the end of the month, and all applicable costs except factory overhead have been recorded on the related cost sheets. In addition to the materials and labor charged directly to the jobs, $3,200 of indirect materials and $8,700 of indirect labor were used during the month. The cost sheets for the four jobs entering production during the month are as follows, in summary form:

Job 1		Job 2	
Direct materials	7,600	Direct materials	12,300
Direct labor	5,400	Direct labor	9,600
Factory overhead	3,780	Factory overhead	6,720
Total	16,780	Total	28,620

Job 3		Job 4	
Direct materials	5,600	Direct materials	16,500
Direct labor	4,100	Direct labor	12,600
Factory overhead		Factory overhead	

Journalize the summary entry to record each of the following operations for May (one entry for each operation):

a. Direct and indirect materials used.
b. Direct and indirect labor used.
c. Factory overhead applied (a single overhead rate is used based on direct labor *cost*).
d. Completion of Jobs 1 and 2.

Exercise 17–16
Financial statements of a manufacturing firm

Objective 5

✓ a. Income from operations, $74,000

The following events took place for Glow Bright Company during May, the first month of operations as a producer of lighting fixtures:

- Purchased $95,000 of materials.
- Used $75,000 of direct materials in production.
- Incurred $120,000 of direct labor wages.
- Applied factory overhead at a rate of 70% of direct labor cost.
- Transferred $251,000 of work in process to finished goods.
- Sold goods with a cost of $236,000.
- Sold goods for $400,000.
- Incurred $54,000 of selling expenses.
- Incurred $36,000 of administrative expenses.

a. Prepare the May income statement from Glow Bright Company. Assume that Glow Bright uses the perpetual inventory method.
b. Determine the inventory balances at the end of the first month of operations.

Exercise 17–17

Decision making with job order costs

Objective 6

Nomura Manufacturing Company is a job shop. The management of Nomura uses the cost information from the job sheets to assess their cost performance. Information on the total cost, product type, and quantity of items produced is as follows:

Date	Job No.	Quantity	Product Type	Amount
Jan. 1	1	400	XXY	$14,000
Jan. 29	26	1200	AAB	48,000
Feb. 15	43	600	AAB	24,600
Mar. 10	64	450	XXY	14,400
Mar. 31	75	900	MM	14,400
May 10	91	1000	MM	20,000
June 20	104	400	XXY	11,200
Aug. 2	112	1500	MM	34,500
Sept. 20	114	400	AAB	16,000
Nov. 1	126	600	XXY	13,800
Dec. 3	133	850	MM	22,950

a. Develop a graph for *each* product, with Job No. (in date order) on the horizontal axis and unit cost on the vertical axis. Use this information to determine Nomura's cost performance over time for the three products.
b. What additional information would you require to investigate Nomura's cost performance more precisely?

Exercise 17–18

Job order cost accounting entries for a service business

Objective 7

✓ d. Dr. Cost of Services, $660,000

New Era Advertising provides media services for clients across the nation. New Era is presently working on four projects, each for a different client. New Era accumulates costs for each account (client) on the basis of both direct costs and allocated indirect costs. The direct costs include the charged time of professional personnel and media purchases (air time and ad space). Overhead is allocated to each project as a percentage of media purchases. The predetermined overhead rate is 30% of media purchases.

On March 1, the four advertising projects had the following accumulated costs:

	March 1 Balances
Stone Beverage	$110,000
Hampshire Bank	155,000
All-Right Rentals	65,000
SleepEzz Hotel	15,000

During March, New Era incurred the following personnel and media purchase costs related to preparing advertising for each of the four accounts:

	Personnel Salaries	Media Purchases
Stone Beverage	$ 45,000	$160,000
Hampshire Bank	25,000	90,000
All-Right Rentals	65,000	105,000
SleepEzz Hotel	70,000	165,000
Total	$205,000	$520,000

At the end of March, both the Stone Beverage and Hampshire Bank campaigns were completed. The cost of completed campaigns are debited to the cost of services account.

Journalize the summary entry to record each of the following for the month:

a. Direct personnel costs
b. Media purchases
c. Overhead applied
d. Completion of Stone Beverage and Hampshire Bank campaigns

PROBLEMS SERIES A

Problem 17–1A
Classify costs

Objectives 3, 5

The following is a list of costs that were incurred in the production and sale of lawn mowers.

a. Salary of quality control supervisor who inspects each lawn mower before it is shipped.
b. Plastic for outside housing of lawn mowers.
c. Cost of advertising in a national magazine.
d. Tires for lawn mowers.
e. Salary of factory supervisor.
f. Gasoline engines used for lawn mowers.
g. Premiums on insurance policy for factory buildings.
h. Cost of boxes used in storing and shipping lawn mowers.
i. Filter for spray gun used to paint the lawn mowers.
j. Payroll taxes on hourly assembly-line employees.
k. Rivets, bolts, and other fasteners used in lawn mowers.
l. Cash paid to outside firm for janitorial services for factory.
m. Engine oil used in mower engines prior to shipment.
n. Attorney fees for drafting a new lease for headquarters offices.
o. Maintenance costs for new factory robotics equipment, based upon hours of usage.
p. Straight-line depreciation on the robotics machinery used to manufacture the lawn mowers.
q. License fees for use of patent for lawn mower blade, based upon the number of lawn mowers produced.
r. Hourly wages of operators of robotics machinery used in production.
s. Salary of vice-president of marketing.
t. Property taxes on the factory building and equipment.
u. Factory cafeteria cashier's wages.
v. Electricity used to run the robotics machinery.
w. Commissions paid to sales representatives, based upon the number of lawn mowers sold.
x. Steel used in producing the lawn mowers.
y. Paint used to paint the lawn mowers.
z. Telephone charges for controller's office.

Instructions

Classify each cost as either a product cost or a period cost. Indicate whether each product cost is a direct materials cost, a direct labor cost, or a factory overhead cost. Indicate whether each period cost is a selling expense or an administrative expense. Use the following tabular headings for your answer, placing an "X" in the appropriate column.

Product Costs			Period Costs	
Direct Materials Cost	Direct Labor Cost	Factory Overhead	Selling Expense	Admin. Expense

Problem 17–2A
Entries for costs in a job order cost system

Objective 5

Towson Industries Inc. uses a job order cost system. The following data summarize the operations related to production for June:

a. Materials purchased on account, $85,600.
b. Materials requisitioned, $75,650, of which $2,400 was for general factory use.
c. Factory labor used, $180,000, of which $24,500 was factory overhead.
d. Other costs incurred on account were for factory overhead, $34,600; selling expenses, $17,500; and administrative expenses, $15,000.
e. Prepaid expenses expired for factory overhead were $1,250; for selling expenses, $350; and for administrative expenses, $250.
f. Depreciation of factory equipment was $6,500; of office equipment, $1,400; and of store equipment, $1,750.
g. Factory overhead costs applied to jobs, $68,000.

h. Jobs completed, $289,500.
i. Cost of goods sold, $295,700.

Instructions

Journalize the entries to record the summarized operations.

Problem 17–3A

Entries and schedules for unfinished jobs and completed jobs

Objective 5

GENERAL LEDGER

✓ 3. Work in Process balance, $32,905

New Media Printing Company uses a job order cost system. The following data summarize the operations related to production for April, the first month of operations:

a. Materials purchased on account, $41,300.
b. Materials requisitioned and factory labor used:

Job	Materials	Factory Labor
No. 101	$5,740	$2,500
No. 102	4,250	1,940
No. 103	8,410	5,300
No. 104	2,460	1,140
No. 105	4,000	2,480
No. 106	5,570	3,250
For general factory use	2,400	1,580

c. Factory overhead costs incurred on account, $14,600.
d. Depreciation of machinery and equipment, $4,100.
e. The factory overhead rate is $25 per machine hour. Machine hours used:

Job	Machine Hours
No. 101	120
No. 102	105
No. 103	250
No. 104	70
No. 105	140
No. 106	165
Total	850

f. Jobs completed: 101, 102, 104, and 105.
g. Jobs were shipped and customers were billed as follows: Job 101, $15,100; Job 102, $10,200; Job 104, $6,500.

Instructions

1. Journalize the entries to record the summarized operations.
2. Post the appropriate entries to T accounts for Work in Process and Finished Goods, using the identifying letters as dates. Insert memorandum account balances as of the end of the month.
3. Prepare a schedule of unfinished jobs to support the balance in the work in process account.
4. Prepare a schedule of completed jobs on hand to support the balance in the finished goods account.

If the working papers correlating with the textbook are not used, omit Problem 17–4A.

Problem 17–4A

Job order cost sheet

Objectives 5, 6

SPREADSHEET

Franklin Furniture Company refinishes and reupholsters furniture. Franklin uses a job order cost system. When a prospective customer asks for a price quote on a job, the estimated cost data are inserted on an unnumbered job cost sheet. If the offer is accepted, a number is assigned to the job, and the costs incurred are recorded in the usual manner on the job cost sheet. After the job is completed, reasons for the variances between the estimated and actual costs are noted on the sheet. The data are then available to management in evaluating the efficiency of operations and in preparing quotes on future jobs. On June 10, an estimate of $452.40 for reupholstering a chair and couch was given to Jamal Evans. The estimate was based on the following data:

Estimated direct materials:	
12 meters at $15 per meter	$180.00
Estimated direct labor:	
10 hours at $12 per hour	120.00
Estimated factory overhead (40% of direct labor cost)	48.00
Total estimated costs	$348.00
Markup (30% of production costs)	104.40
Total estimate	$452.40

On June 16, the chair and couch were picked up from the residence of Jamal Evans, 1900 Peachtree, Atlanta, with a commitment to return it on July 16. The job was completed on July 11.

The related materials requisitions and time tickets are summarized as follows:

Materials Requisition No.	Description	Amount
U642	8 meters at $15	$120
U651	6 meters at $15	90

Time Ticket No.	Description	Amount
1519	9 hours at $12	$108
1520	3 hours at $12	36

Instructions

1. Complete that portion of the job order cost sheet that would be prepared when the estimate is given to the customer.
2. Assign number 00-8-38 to the job, record the costs incurred, and complete the job order cost sheet. Comment on the reasons for the variances between actual costs and estimated costs. For this purpose, assume that two meters of materials were spoiled, the factory overhead rate has been proved to be satisfactory, and an inexperienced employee performed the work.

Problem 17–5A
Analyzing manufacturing cost accounts
Objective 5
✓ G. $366,350

Kay-Two Company manufactures snow skis in a wide variety of lengths and styles. The following incomplete ledger accounts refer to transactions that are summarized for January:

Materials

Jan. 1	Balance	10,000	Jan. 31	Requisitions	(A)
Jan. 31	Purchases	256,000			

Work in Process

Jan. 1	Balance	(B)	Jan. 31	Completed jobs	(F)
Jan. 31	Materials	(C)			
Jan. 31	Direct labor	(D)			
Jan. 31	Factory overhead applied	(E)			

Finished Goods

Jan. 1	Balance	0	Jan. 31	Cost of goods sold	(G)
Jan. 31	Completed jobs	(F)			

Wages Payable

			Jan. 31	Wages incurred	100,000

Factory Overhead

Jan. 1	Balance	4,000	Jan. 31	Factory overhead applied	(E)
Jan. 31	Indirect labor	(H)			
Jan. 31	Indirect materials	3,000			
Jan. 31	Other overhead	125,000			

In addition, the following information is available:

a. Materials and direct labor were applied to six jobs in January:

Job No.	Style	Quantity	Direct Materials	Direct Labor
Job 51	V-100	240	$ 40,000	$18,000
Job 52	V-200	200	30,000	15,000
Job 53	V-500	160	25,000	12,000
Job 54	A-200	300	50,400	19,000
Job 55	V-400	350	88,100	26,000
Job 56	A-100	100	12,000	6,000
Total		1,350	$245,500	$96,000

b. Factory overhead is applied to each job at a rate of 140% of direct labor cost.

c. The January 1 Work in Process balance consisted of two jobs, as follows:

Job No.	Style	Work in Process, Jan. 1
Job 51	V-100	$ 8,000
Job 52	V-200	12,000
Total		$20,000

d. Customer jobs completed and units sold in January were as follows:

Job No.	Style	Completed in January	Units Sold in January
Job 51	V-100	X	200
Job 52	V-200	X	170
Job 53	V-500		0
Job 54	A-200	X	250
Job 55	V-400	X	335
Job 56	A-100		0

Instructions

1. Determine the missing amounts associated with each letter. Provide supporting calculations by completing a table with the following headings:

Job	Quantity	Jan. 1 Work in Process	Direct Materials	Direct Labor	Factory Overhead	Total Cost	Unit Cost	Units Sold	Cost of Goods Sold

2. Determine the January 31 balances for each of the inventory accounts and factory overhead.

Problem 17–6A

Flow of costs and income statement

Objective 5

HAT

✓ 1. Income from operations, $1,597,500

Olympus Records is in the business of developing, promoting, and selling musical talent on compact disc (CD). The company signed a new musical act, called *Critical Mass,* on January 1, 2000. For the first six months of 2000, the company spent $1,400,000 on a media campaign for *Critical Mass* and $350,000 in legal costs and royalties. The CD production began on February 22, 2000.

Olympus uses a job order cost system to accumulate costs associated with a CD title. The unit direct materials cost for the CD is:

Blank CD	$4.00
Plastic package	0.50
Song lyric insert	0.25

The production process is straightforward. First, the blank CDs are brought to a production area, where the digital soundtrack is copied on to the CD. The copying machine requires one hour per 1,000 CDs.

After the CDs are copied, they are brought to an assembly area where an employee packs the CD with a plastic package and song lyric insert. The direct labor cost is $0.40 per unit.

The CDs are sold to record stores. Each record store is given promotional materials, such as posters and aisle displays. Promotional materials cost $30 per record store. In addition, shipping costs average $0.25 per CD.

Total completed production was 900,000 units during the year. Other information is as follows:

Number of customers (record stores)	40,000
Number of CDs sold	850,000
Wholesale price (to record store) per CD	$11

Factory overhead cost is applied to jobs at the rate of $250 per copy machine hour. There were an additional 10,000 CDs waiting to be assembled on December 31, 2000.

Instructions

1. Prepare an income statement for the *Critical Mass* CD, including supporting calculations, from the information above.
2. Determine the balances in the work in process and finished goods inventory for the *Critical Mass* CD on December 31, 2000.

PROBLEMS SERIES B

Problem 17–1B
Classify costs
Objectives 3, 5

The following is a list of costs that were incurred in the production and sale of boats:

a. Cost of metal hardware for boats, such as ornaments and tie-down grasps.
b. Power used by sanding equipment.
c. Yearly cost of maintenance contract for robotics equipment.
d. Premiums on business interruption insurance in case of a natural disaster.
e. Cost of normal scrap from defective hulls.
f. Masks for use by sanders in smoothing boat hulls.
g. Cost of paving the employee parking lot.
h. Hourly wages of assembly-line workers.
i. Oil to lubricate factory equipment.
j. Straight-line depreciation on factory equipment.
k. Wood paneling for use in interior boat trim.
l. Commissions to sales representatives, based upon the number of boats sold.
m. Steering wheels.
n. Special advertising campaign in *Bass World*.
o. Cost of boat for "grand prize" promotion in local bass tournament.
p. Memberships for key executives in the Bass World Association.
q. Navigation and fishing instruments for boats.
r. Cost of electrical wiring for boats.
s. Executive end-of-year bonuses.
t. Salary of shop supervisor.
u. Decals for boat hulls.
v. Annual fee for Jim Bo Wilks, a famous fisherman, to promote the boats.
w. Legal department costs for the year.
x. Paint for boats.
y. Salary of president of company.
z. Fiberglass for producing the boat hull.

Instructions

Classify each cost as either a product cost or a period cost. Indicate whether each product cost is a direct materials cost, a direct labor cost, or a factory overhead cost. Indicate whether each period cost is a selling expense or an administrative expense. Use the following tabular headings for your answer, placing an "X" in the appropriate column.

Product Costs			Period Costs	
Direct Materials Cost	Direct Labor Cost	Factory Overhead Cost	Selling Expense	Admin. Expense

Problem 17–2B

Entries for costs in a job order cost system

Objective 5

Jack and Jill Apparel Company uses a job order cost system. The following data summarize the operations related to production for June:

a. Materials purchased on account, $145,700.
b. Materials requisitioned, $136,800, of which $4,700 was for general factory use.
c. Factory labor used, $121,400, of which $16,400 was factory overhead.
d. Other costs incurred on account were for factory overhead, $53,400; selling expenses, $45,700; and administrative expenses, $27,000.
e. Prepaid expenses expired for factory overhead were $2,100; for selling expenses, $900; and for administrative expenses, $1,100.
f. Depreciation of factory equipment was $17,600; of office equipment, $9,200; and of store equipment, $3,200.
g. Factory overhead costs applied to jobs, $97,000.
h. Jobs completed, $336,700.
i. Cost of goods sold, $330,100.

Instructions

Journalize the entries to record the summarized operations.

Problem 17–3B

Entries and schedules for unfinished jobs and completed jobs

Objective 5

GENERAL LEDGER

✓ 3. Work in Process balance, $15,510

Hi Gloss Printing Company uses a job order cost system. The following data summarize the operations related to production for June, the first month of operations:

a. Materials purchased on account, $39,700.
b. Materials requisitioned and factory labor used:

Job	Materials	Factory Labor
No. 601	$9,470	$5,300
No. 602	3,260	1,890
No. 603	5,790	3,050
No. 604	2,450	1,240
No. 605	8,450	4,160
No. 606	4,380	2,540
For general factory use	2,500	1,600

c. Factory overhead costs incurred on account, $12,800.
d. Depreciation of machinery and equipment, $3,200.
e. The factory overhead rate is $20 per machine hour. Machine hours used:

Job	Machine Hours
No. 601	250
No. 602	105
No. 603	185
No. 604	85
No. 605	230
No. 606	160
Total	1,015

f. Jobs completed: 601, 602, 603, and 605.
g. Jobs were shipped and customers were billed as follows: Job 601, $25,000; Job 602, $11,400; Job 605, $19,800.

Instructions

1. Journalize the entries to record the summarized operations.
2. Post the appropriate entries to T accounts for Work in Process and Finished Goods, using the identifying letters as dates. Insert memorandum account balances as of the end of the month.
3. Prepare a schedule of unfinished jobs to support the balance in the work in process account.
4. Prepare a schedule of completed jobs on hand to support the balance in the finished goods account.

If the working papers correlating with the textbook are not used, omit Problem 17–4B.

Problem 17–4B
Job order cost sheet

Objectives 5, 6

SPREADSHEET

Royal Oak Furniture Company refinishes and reupholsters furniture. Royal Oak uses a job order cost system. When a prospective customer asks for a price quote on a job, the estimated cost data are inserted on an unnumbered job cost sheet. If the offer is accepted, a number is assigned to the job, and the costs incurred are recorded in the usual manner on the job cost sheet. After the job is completed, reasons for the variances between the estimated and actual costs are noted on the sheet. The data are then available to management in evaluating the efficiency of operations and in preparing quotes on future jobs. On September 1, an estimate of $1,071.20 for reupholstering two chairs and a couch was given to Kendra Bowen. The estimate was based on the following data:

Estimated direct materials:	
16 meters at $20 per meter	$ 320.00
Estimated direct labor:	
24 hours at $15 per hour	360.00
Estimated factory overhead (40% of direct labor cost)	144.00
Total estimated costs	$ 824.00
Markup (30% of production costs)	247.20
Total estimate	$1,071.20

On September 4, the chairs and couch were picked up from the residence of Kendra Bowen, 1244 Merchants Drive, Columbus, with a commitment to return them on October 13. The job was completed on October 10.

The related materials requisitions and time tickets are summarized as follows:

Materials Requisition No.	Description	Amount
3480	12 meters at $20	$240
3492	7 meters at $20	140

Time Ticket No.	Description	Amount
H143	15 hours at $15	$225
H151	12 hours at $15	180

Instructions

1. Complete that portion of the job order cost sheet that would be prepared when the estimate is given to the customer.
2. Assign number 00-10-23 to the job, record the costs incurred, and complete the job order cost sheet. Comment on the reasons for the variances between actual costs and estimated costs. For this purpose, assume that 3 meters of materials were spoiled, the factory overhead rate has been proved to be satisfactory, and an inexperienced employee performed the work.

Problem 17–5B
Analyzing manufacturing cost accounts

Objective 5

✓ G. $265,020

Mongoose Golf Equipment Company manufactures golf club sets in a wide variety of lengths and weights. The following incomplete ledger accounts refer to transactions that are summarized for August:

Materials

Aug. 1	Balance	8,000	Aug. 31	Requisitions	(A)
Aug. 31	Purchases	125,000			

Work in Process

Aug. 1	Balance	(B)	Aug. 31	Completed jobs	(F)
Aug. 31	Materials	(C)			
Aug. 31	Direct labor	(D)			
Aug. 31	Factory overhead applied	(E)			

Finished Goods

Aug. 1	Balance	0	Aug. 31	Cost of goods sold	(G)
Aug. 31	Completed jobs	(F)			

Wages Payable

			Aug. 31	Wages incurred	106,000

Factory Overhead

Aug. 1	Balance	2,000	Aug. 31	Factory overhead applied	(E)
Aug. 31	Indirect labor	(H)			
Aug. 31	Indirect materials	2,500			
Aug. 31	Other overhead	60,000			

In addition, the following information is available:

a. Materials and direct labor were applied to six jobs in January:

Job No.	Style	Quantity	Direct Materials	Direct Labor
Job 111	DL-8	100	$ 24,500	$ 19,000
Job 112	DL-18	120	33,550	24,500
Job 113	DL-11	60	17,750	18,500
Job 114	SL-101	150	12,900	8,000
Job 115	SL-110	70	29,400	28,000
Job 116	DL-14	75	4,200	3,000
Total		575	$122,300	$101,000

b. Factory overhead is applied to each job at a rate of 70% of direct labor cost.
c. The August 1 Work in Process balance consisted of two jobs, as follows:

Job No.	Style	Work in Process, Aug. 1
Job 111	DL-8	$22,000
Job 112	DL-18	40,000
Total		$62,000

d. Customer jobs completed and units sold in August were as follows:

Job No.	Style	Completed in August	Units Sold in August
Job 111	DL-8	X	90
Job 112	DL-18	X	105
Job 113	DL-11	X	40
Job 114	SL-101		0
Job 115	SL-110	X	55
Job 116	DL-14		0

Instructions

1. Determine the missing amounts associated with each letter. Provide supporting calculations by completing a table with the following headings:

Job	Quantity	Aug. 1 Work in Process	Direct Materials	Direct Labor	Factory Overhead	Total Cost	Unit Cost	Units Sold	Cost of Goods Sold

2. Determine the August 31 balances for each of the inventory accounts and factory overhead.

Problem 17–6B
Flow of costs and income statement

Objective 5

✓ 1. Income from operations, $1,410,750

Productivity Tools Inc. (PT) is a designer, manufacturer, and distributor of software for microcomputers. A new product, *Wordsmith 2000,* was released for production and distribution in early 2000. In January, $450,000 was spent to design print advertisement. For the first six months of 2000, the company spent $1,800,000 promoting *Wordsmith 2000* in computer trade magazines. The product was ready for manufacture on January 21, 2000.

PT uses a job order cost system to accumulate costs associated with each software title. Direct materials unit costs are:

Blank disk	$ 6.00
Packaging	8.70
Manual	12.00
Total	$26.70

The actual production process for the software product is fairly straightforward. First, blank disks are brought to a disk-copying machine. The copying machine requires 1 hour per 1,000 disks.

After the program is copied onto the disk, the disk is brought to assembly, where assembly personnel pack the disk and manual for shipping. The direct labor cost for this work is $0.80 per unit.

The completed packages are then sold to retail outlets through a sales force. The sales force is compensated by a 15% commission on the wholesale price for all sales. In addition, salespersons are trained at a cost of $1,500 per individual.

Total completed production was 25,000 units during the year. Other information is as follows:

Number of salespersons	450
Number of software units sold in 2000	23,500
Wholesale price per unit	$250

Factory overhead cost is applied to jobs at the rate of $500 per copy machine hour. There were an additional 800 CDs waiting to be assembled on December 31, 2000.

Instructions

1. Prepare an income statement for the *Wordsmith 2000* product, including supporting calculations, from the information above.
2. Determine the balances in the work in process and finished goods inventory for the *Wordsmith 2000* product on December 31, 2000.

QUICKBOOKS® APPENDIX PROBLEM

Job Order Cost System

This case uses the Larry's Landscaping sample company provided with QuickBooks® 5.0. Begin by first copying *sample.qbw* into another file name, **joborder.qbw,** so that the original sample.qbw file will not be changed. You must copy the file using the copy and paste commands in your operating system. This is an important step, since we will be using the unchanged sample.qbw file later in the text. If you do not first copy sample.qbw into another file name, then you will automatically change sample.qbw. We will be assuming that you have an unchanged version in future exercises throughout this text.

Larry's Landscaping is going to perform a landscaping job for Ashmi Desai. In the process, Larry will purchase 30 garden lighting fixtures from Denk's Nursery. Ten of these fixtures will be invoiced to the Desai Job.

Instructions

1. Open the "Enter Bills" form. Select "Denk's Nursery" as the vendor. Clear the line for the expenses at the bottom of the form (use the edit menu to delete the line). Under the items tab, enter "Lighting" and a quantity of 30 at a cost of $14.75 per fixture.
2. Open the "Create Invoices" form and select Ashmi Desai as the customer. At the bottom of the invoice select "Lighting" for a quantity of ten and price of $50.
3. Print a profit and loss report for the Ashmi Desai job. Set the dates for the report from December 1 to December 15. Use the "filters" button to report only Ashmi Desai (use "name" in the drop down list). What is the gross profit on this job?

SPECIAL ACTIVITIES

Activity 17–1 Sequoia Fabrication Enterprises
Ethics and professional conduct in business

Sequoia Fabrication Enterprises allows employees to purchase, at cost, manufacturing materials, such as metal and lumber, for personal use. To purchase materials for personal use, an employee must complete a materials requisition form, which must then be approved by the employee's immediate supervisor. Cheryl Long, an assistant cost accountant, charges the employee an amount based on Sequoia's net purchase cost.

Cheryl Long is in the process of replacing a deck on her home and has requisitioned lumber for personal use, which has been approved in accordance with company policy. In computing the cost of the lumber, Long reviewed all the purchase invoices for the past year. She then used the lowest price to compute the amount due the company for the lumber.

Discuss whether Cheryl behaved in an ethical manner.

Activity 17–2 Blind Flight Aerospace Company
Financial vs. managerial accounting

The following statement was made by the vice-president of finance of Blind Flight Aerospace Company: "The managers of a company should use the same information as the shareholders of the firm. When managers use the same information in guiding their internal operations as shareholders use in evaluating their investments, the managers will be aligned with the stockholders' profit objectives."

Respond to the vice-president's statement.

Activity 17–3 Speedy TV Repairs
Classifying costs

Speedy TV Repairs provides TV repair services for the community. Gail Song's TV was not working, and she called Speedy for a home repair visit. The Speedy technician arrived at 2:00 P.M. to begin work. By 4:00 P.M. the problem was diagnosed as a failed circuit board. Unfortunately, the technician did not have a new circuit board in the truck, since the technician's previous customer had the same problem, and a board was used on that visit. Replacement boards were available back at the Speedy shop. Therefore, the technician drove back to the shop to retrieve a replacement board. From 4:00 to 5:00 P.M., the Speedy technician drove the round trip to retrieve the replacement board from the shop.

At 5:00 P.M. the technician was back on the job at Song's home. The replacement procedure is somewhat complex, since a variety of tests must be performed once the board is installed. The job was completed at 6:00 P.M.

Gail Song's repair bill showed the following:

Circuit board	$ 50
Labor charges	140
Total	$190

Gail Song was surprised at the size of the bill and asked for some greater detail supporting the calculations. Speedy responded with the following explanations.

Cost of materials:	
Purchase price of circuit board	$40
Markup on purchase price to cover storage and handling	10
Total materials charge	$50

The labor charge per hour is detailed as follows:

2:00–3:00 P.M.	$ 30
3:00–4:00 P.M.	25
4:00–5:00 P.M.	35
5:00–6:00 P.M.	50
Total labor charge	$140

Further explanations in the differences in the hourly rates are as follows:

First hour:	
Base labor rate	$15
Fringe benefits	5
Overhead (other than storage and handling)	5
Total base labor rate	$25
Additional charge for first hour of any job to cover the cost of vehicle depreciation, fuel, and employee time in transit. A 30-minute transit time is assumed.	5
	$30
Third hour:	
Base labor rate	$25
The trip back to the shop includes vehicle depreciation and fuel; therefore, a charge was added to the hourly rate to cover these costs. The round trip took an hour.	10
	$35
Fourth hour:	
Base labor rate	$25
Overtime premium for time worked in excess of an eight-hour day (starting at 5:00 P.M.) is equal to the base rate.	25
	$50

1. If you were in Gail Song's position, how would you respond to the bill? Are there parts of the bill that appear incorrect to you? If so, what argument would you employ to convince Speedy that the bill is too high?
2. Use the headings below to construct a table. Fill in the table by first listing the costs identified in the activity in the left-hand column. For each cost, place a check mark in the appropriate column identifying the correct cost classification. Assume that each service call is a job.

Cost	Direct Materials	Direct Labor	Overhead

Activity 17–4 Ohio Molding Company

Managerial analysis

The controller of the plant of Ohio Molding Company prepared a graph of the unit costs from the job cost reports for Product XD. The graph appeared as follows:

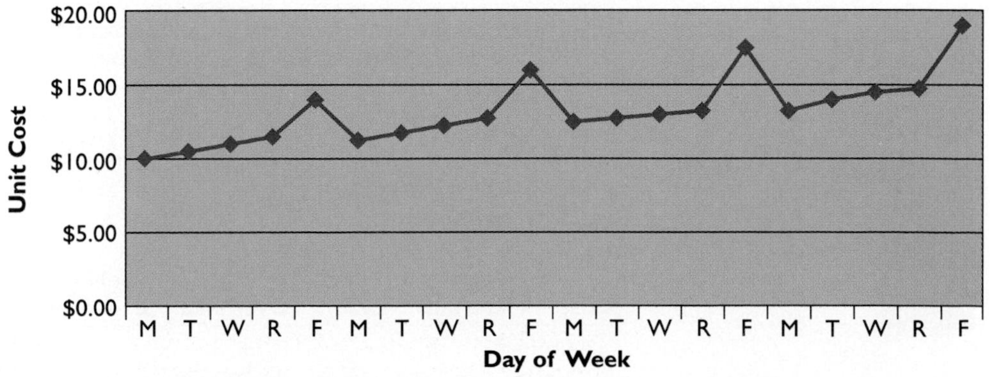

How would you interpret this information? What further information would you request?

Activity 17–5 Pacific Instruments Inc.

Factory overhead rate

What do you THINK?

Pacific Instruments Inc., an electronics instrument manufacturer, uses a job order costing system. The overhead is allocated to jobs on the basis of direct labor hours. The overhead rate is now $1,000 per direct labor hour. The design engineer thinks that this is illogical. The design engineer has stated the following:

Our accounting system doesn't make any sense to me. It tells me that every labor hour carries an additional burden of $1,000. This means that direct labor makes up only 5% of our total product cost, yet it drives all our costs. In addition, these rates give my design engineers incentives to "design out" direct labor by using machine technology. Yet, over the past years as we have had less and less direct labor, the overhead rate keeps going up and up. I won't be surprised if next year the rate is $1,200 per direct labor hour. I'm also concerned because small errors in our estimates of the direct labor content can have a large impact on our estimated costs. Just a 30-minute error in our estimate of assembly time is worth $500. Small mistakes in our direct labor time estimates really swing our bids around. I think this puts us at a disadvantage when we are going after business.

1. What is the engineer's concern about the overhead rate going "up and up?"
2. What did the engineer mean about the large overhead rate being a disadvantage when placing bids and seeking new business?
3. What do you think is a possible solution?

Activity 17–6 Holiday Delights Inc.

Recording manufacturing costs

What's Wrong WITH THIS?

Jeff Flowers just began working as a cost accountant for Holiday Delights Inc. Holiday Delights manufactures gift items. Flowers is preparing to record summary journal entries for the month. Flowers begins by recording the factory wages as follows:

Wages Expense	15,000	
Wages Payable		15,000

Then the factory depreciation:

Depreciation Expense—Factory Machinery	4,000	
Accumulated Depreciation—Factory Machinery		4,000

Flowers' supervisor, Hanna Tully, walks by and notices the entries. The following conversation takes place.

Hanna: That's a very unusual way to record our factory wages and depreciation for the month.

Jeff: What do you mean? This is exactly the way we were taught to record wages and depreciation in school. You know, debit an expense and credit Cash or payables, or in the case of depreciation, credit Accumulated Depreciation.

Hanna: Well, it's not the credits I'm concerned about. It's the debits—I don't think you've recorded the debits correctly. I wouldn't mind if you were recording the administrative wages or office equipment depreciation this way, but I've got real questions about recording factory wages and factory machinery depreciation this way.

Jeff: Now I'm really confused. You mean this is correct for administrative costs, but not for factory costs? Well, what am I supposed to do—and why?

1. Play the role of Hanna and answer Jeff's questions.
2. Why would Hanna accept the journal entries if they were for administrative costs?

Activity 17–7 Into the Real World

Classifying costs

GROUP ACTIVITY

With a group of students, visit a local copy and graphics shop or a pizza restaurant. As you observe the operation, consider the costs associated with running the business. As a group, identify as many costs as you can and classify them according to the following table headings:

Cost	Direct Materials	Direct Labor	Overhead	Selling Expenses

ANSWERS TO SELF-EXAMINATION QUESTIONS

Matching

1. C	5. F	9. I	13. O	16. H	19. Z	22. W	25. N
2. L	6. P	10. D	14. T	17. S	20. G	23. U	26. M
3. Q	7. K	11. X	15. R	18. Y	21. A	24. B	27. V
4. E	8. J	12. BB					

Multiple Choice

1. **B** Both financial and managerial accounting support decision making (answer A). Financial accounting is mostly concerned with the decision making of external users, while managerial accounting supports decision making of management. Both financial and managerial accounting can result in financial reports (answer C). Managerial accounting reports are developed for internal use by managers at various levels in the organization. Both managerial and financial accounting record events from the past (answer D); however, managerial accounting can also include information about the future in the form of budgets and cash flow projections. It is true that managerial accounting is not restricted to generally accepted accounting principles, as is financial accounting (answer B).
2. **C** Sales salaries (answer C) is a selling expense and is not considered a cost of manufacturing a product. Direct materials cost (answer A), factory overhead cost (answer B), and direct labor cost (answer D) are costs of manufacturing a product.
3. **B** Depreciation of testing equipment (answer B) is included as part of the factory overhead costs of the microcomputer manufacturer. The cost of memory chips (answer A) and the cost of disk drives (answer D) are both considered a part of direct materials cost. The wages of microcomputer assemblers (answer C) are part of direct labor costs.
4. **A** Job order cost systems are best suited to businesses manufacturing for special orders from customers, such as would be the case for a repair shop for antique furniture (answer A). A process cost system is best suited for manufacturers of homogeneous units of product, such as rubber (answer B) and coal (answer C).
5. **B** If the amount of factory overhead applied during a particular period exceeds the actual overhead costs, the factory overhead account will have a credit balance and is said to be overapplied (answer B) or overabsorbed. If the amount applied is less than the actual costs, the account will have a debit balance and is said to be underapplied (answer A) or underabsorbed (answer C). Since an "estimated" predetermined overhead rate is used to apply overhead, a credit balance does not necessarily represent an error (answer D).

18

Process Cost Systems

Setting the STAGE

If you bake cookies, the ingredients would include flour, sugar, and water. These ingredients would all be added at the beginning of the baking process by mixing them in a bowl. After mixing, do you have cookies? No. Why? Because they aren't baked (converted). But are they 100% complete with respect to materials? Yes, all the materials have been added to the baking process. When will they be cookies? When they are 100% complete with respect to materials *and* baking.

Now, assume that you ask the question, "How much cost have I incurred in baking cookies after 15 minutes (out of 30 minutes) of baking time?" The answer would require that you separate the ingredients and the electricity costs. These two costs are incurred in the baking process at different rates, and so it is convenient to identify them separately. The ingredient costs have all been incurred, since they were all introduced at the beginning of the process. The electricity costs, however, are a different story. Since the baking is only 50% complete, only 50% of the electricity costs (for the oven) have been incurred in the baking process. Therefore, the answer to the question is that all the materials costs and half the electricity costs have been incurred in the baking process after 15 minutes of baking.

In this chapter, we apply these concepts to manufacturers that use a process cost system. After introducing process costing, we discuss decision making with process cost system reports. We conclude the chapter with a brief discussion of just-in-time cost systems.

objectives

After studying this chapter, you should be able to:

1. Distinguish between job order costing and process costing systems.
2. Explain and illustrate the physical flows and cost flows for a process manufacturer.
3. Calculate and interpret the accounting for completed and partially completed units under the fifo method.
4. Prepare a cost of production report.
5. Prepare journal entries for transactions of a process manufacturer.
6. Use cost of production reports for decision making.
7. Contrast just-in-time processing with conventional manufacturing practices.

Comparing Job Order Costing and Process Costing

OBJECTIVE 1

Distinguish between job order costing and process costing systems.

As we discussed in the previous chapter, the job order cost system is best suited to industries that make special orders for customers or manufacture different products in groups. Industries that may use job order cost systems include special-order printing, custom-made tailoring, furniture manufacturing, shipbuilding, aircraft building, and construction. Process manufacturing is different from job-order manufacturing. **Process manufacturers** typically use large machines to process a flow of raw materials into a finished state. For example, a petro-chemical business processes crude oil through numerous refining steps to produce higher grades of oil until gasoline is produced. The cost accounting system used by process manufacturers is called the **process cost system**.

Industries and examples of companies that may use process cost systems are:

Industry	Example Company
Automobile	**General Motors**
Beverages	**Coca-Cola**
Chemicals	**Dow Chemical**
Food	**H.J. Heinz**
Forest and paper products	**Georgia Pacific**
Metals	**Alcoa**
Petroleum refining	**Exxon**
Pharmaceuticals	**Eli Lilly**
Soap and cosmetics	**Procter & Gamble**

In some ways, the process cost and job order cost systems are similar. Both systems accumulate product costs—direct materials, direct labor, and factory overhead—and allocate these costs to the units produced. Both systems maintain perpetual inventory accounts with subsidiary ledgers for materials, work in process, and finished goods. Both systems also provide product cost data to management for planning, directing, improving, controlling, and decision making. The main difference between the two systems is the form in which the product costs are accumulated and reported.

Exhibit 1 illustrates the main differences between the job order and process cost systems. In a job order cost system, product costs are accumulated by job and are summarized on job cost sheets. The job cost sheets provide unit cost information and can be used by management for product pricing, cost control, and inventory valuation. The process manufacturer does not manufacture according to "jobs." Thus, costs are accumulated by department. Each unit of product that passes through the department is similar. Thus, the production costs reported by each department provide unit cost information that can be used by management for cost control. In a job or-

EXHIBIT 1
Job Order and Process Cost Systems Compared

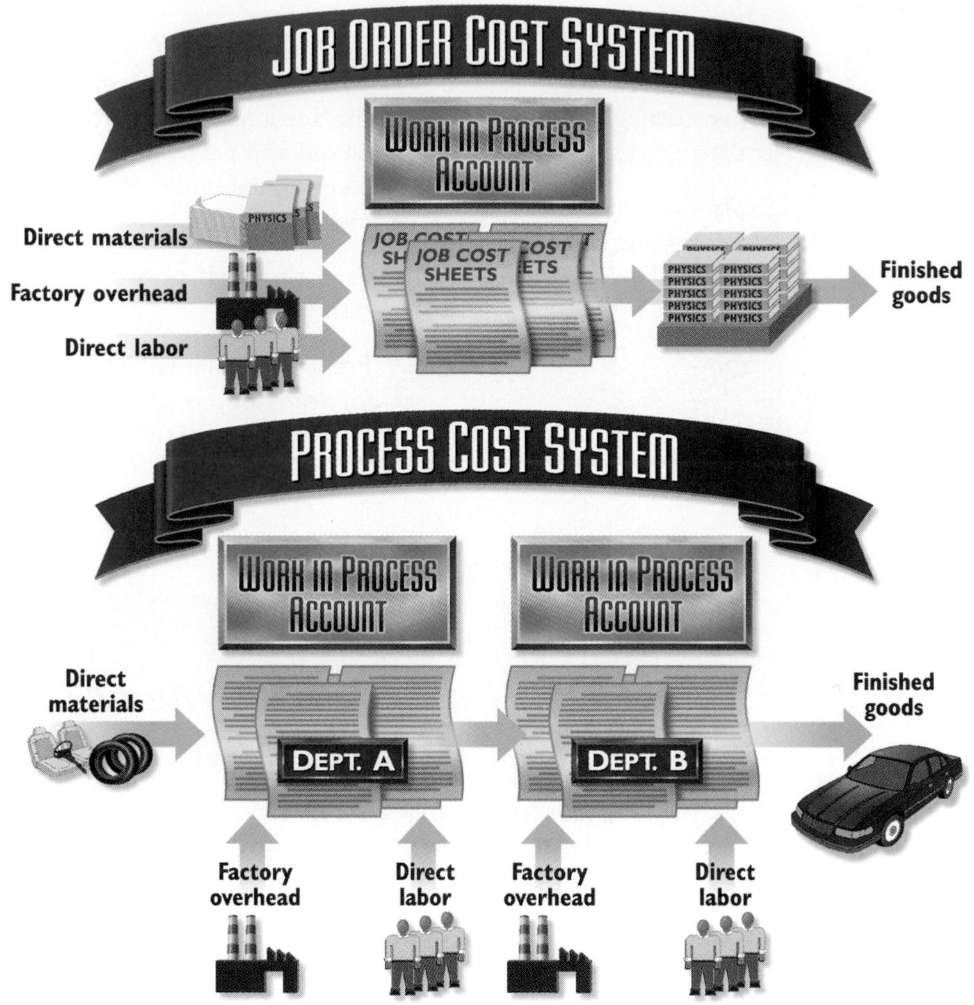

der cost system, the work in process inventory at the end of the accounting period is the sum of the job cost sheets for partially completed jobs. In a process cost system, the amount of work in process inventory is determined by allocating costs between completed and partially completed units within a department.

Process manufacturers accumulate costs by department.

Physical Flows and Cost Flows for a Process Manufacturer

OBJECTIVE 2

Explain and illustrate the physical flows and cost flows for a process manufacturer.

Materials costs are a large portion of the costs for most process manufacturers. Often, the materials costs can be as high as 70% of the total manufacturing costs. Thus, accounting for materials costs is very important for process operations.

Exhibit 2 illustrates the physical flow of materials for a steel processor. Direct materials in the form of scrap metal are placed into a furnace in the Melting Department. The Melting Department uses conversion costs (direct labor and factory overhead) during the melting process. The molten metal is then transferred to the Casting Department, where it is poured into an ingot casting. The Casting Depart-

EXHIBIT 2 Physical Flows for a Process Manufacturer

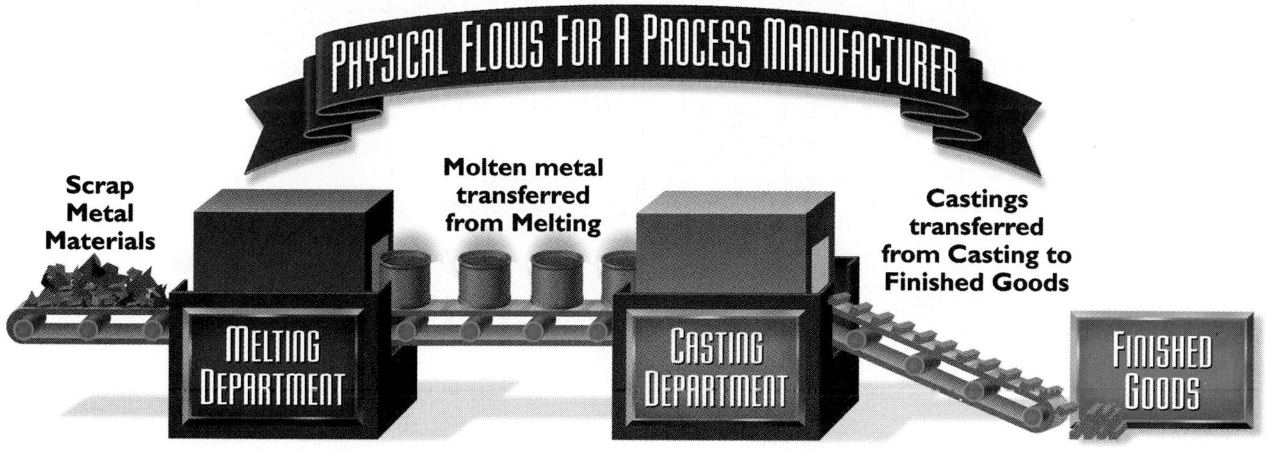

ment also uses conversion costs during the casting process. The ingot castings are transferred to the finished goods inventory for shipment to customers.

The cost flows in a process cost system reflect the physical materials flows and are illustrated in Exhibit 3. Purchased materials are debited to Materials (a) and credited to Accounts Payable (not shown). Direct materials (scrap metal) used by the Melting Department are debited to Work in Process—Melting and credited to Materials (b). In addition, indirect materials and other overhead incurred are debited to department factory overhead accounts and credited to Materials (d) and other accounts. Direct labor in the Melting Department is debited to the department's work in process account (c) and credited to Wages Payable (not shown). Applied factory overhead is debited to Work in Process—Melting, using a predetermined overhead rate (e). The cost of completed production from the Melting Department is transferred to the Casting Department by debiting Work in Process—Casting and crediting Work in Process—Melting (f). The transferred costs include the direct materials and conversion costs for completed production of the Melting Department. The direct labor and applied factory overhead costs in the Casting Department are debited to Work in Process—Casting (g and h). The cost of the finished ingots is transferred out of the Casting Department by debiting Finished Goods and credit-

EXHIBIT 3 Cost Flows for a Process Manufacturer

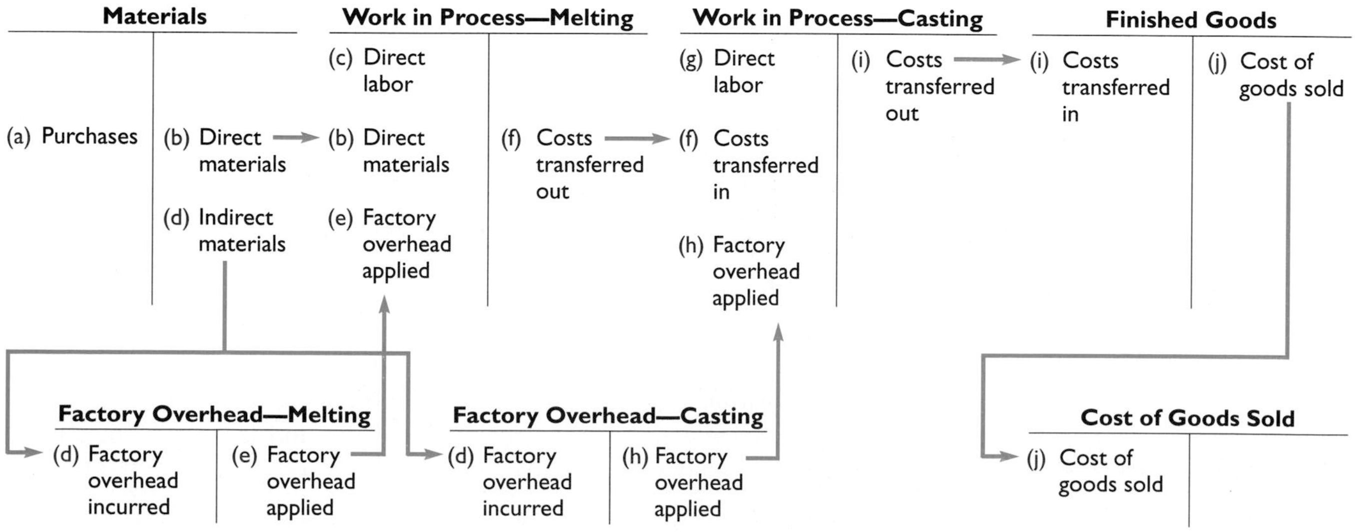

BUSINESS ON STAGE

In manufacturing, inputs are processed into a product with physical attributes. In business, however, a product is often thought of in terms other than just its physical attributes. For example, why a customer buys a product usually impacts how a business markets the product. Other considerations, such as warranty needs, servicing needs, and perceived quality, also affect business strategies.

Four types of products are (1) convenience products, (2) shopping products, (3) specialty products, and (4) unsought products. To illustrate, consider the following four products:

1. Convenience product: Snickers candy bar
2. Shopping product: Sony television
3. Specialty product: Diamond ring
4. Unsought product: Prearranged funeral

For each of these products, the frequency of purchase, the profit per unit, and the number of retailers differ. As a result, the sales and marketing approach for each product differs as shown below. ■

Product	Frequency of Purchase	Profit per Unit	Number of Retailers	Sales/Marketing Approach
Snickers	often	low	many	mass advertising
Sony TV	occasional	moderate	many	mass advertising; personal selling
Diamond ring	seldom	high	few	personal selling
Prearranged funeral	rare	high	few	aggressive personal selling

ing Work in Process—Casting (i). The cost of ingots sold to customers is transferred out of finished goods with a debit to Cost of Goods Sold and a credit to Finished Goods (j).

The First-In, First-Out (Fifo) Method

OBJECTIVE 3

Calculate and interpret the accounting for completed and partially completed units under the fifo method.

In a process cost system, the accountant determines the cost transferred out and thus the amount remaining in inventory for each department. For many manufacturing processes, materials are added at the beginning of production, and the units are moved through the production processes in a **first-in, first-out (fifo) flow**. That is, the first units entering the production process are the first to be completed.[1]

Most process manufacturers have more than one department. In the illustrations that follow, McDermott Steel Inc. has two departments, Melting and Casting. McDermott melts scrap metal and then pours the molten metal into an ingot casting.

To illustrate the first-in, first-out method, we will simplify by using only the Melting Department of McDermott Steel Inc. The following data for the Melting Department are for July of the current year:

Inventory in process, July 1, 500 tons:		
Direct materials cost, for 500 tons	$24,550	
Conversion costs, for 500 tons, 70% completed	3,600	
Total inventory in process, July 1		$28,150
Direct materials cost for July, 1,000 tons		50,000
Conversion costs for July		9,690
Goods finished in July (includes units in process on July 1), 1,100 tons		?
Inventory in process, July 31, 400 tons, 25% completed as to conversion costs		?

We assume that all materials used in the department are added at the beginning of the process, and conversion costs (direct labor and factory overhead) are incurred evenly throughout the melting process. The objective is to determine the

[1] An alternative method—the average cost method—is discussed in advanced textbooks.

cost of goods completed and the ending inventory valuation, which are represented by the question marks. We determine these amounts by using the following four steps:

1. Determine the units to be assigned costs.
2. Calculate equivalent units of production.
3. Determine the cost per equivalent unit.
4. Allocate costs to transferred and partially completed units.

Step 1: Determine the Units To Be Assigned Costs

The first step in our illustration is to determine the units to be assigned costs. A unit can be any measure of completed production, such as tons, gallons, pounds, barrels, or cases. We use tons as the definition for units in McDermott Steel.

McDermott Steel had 1,500 tons of direct materials charged to production in the Melting Department for July, as shown below.

Total tons charged to production:	
In process, July 1	500 tons
Received from materials storeroom	1,000
Total units accounted for by the Melting Department	1,500 tons

There are three categories of units to be assigned costs for an accounting period: **(A)** units in beginning in-process inventory, **(B)** units started and completed during the period, and **(C)** units in ending in-process inventory. Exhibit 4 illustrates these categories in the Melting Department for July. The 500-ton beginning inventory **(A)** was completed and transferred to the Casting Department. McDermott Steel started another 1,000 tons of material into the process during July. Of the 1,000 tons introduced in July, 400 tons were left incomplete at the end of the month **(C)**. Thus, only 600 of the 1,000 tons were actually started and completed in July **(B)**.

EXHIBIT 4
July Units To Be Costed—Melting Department

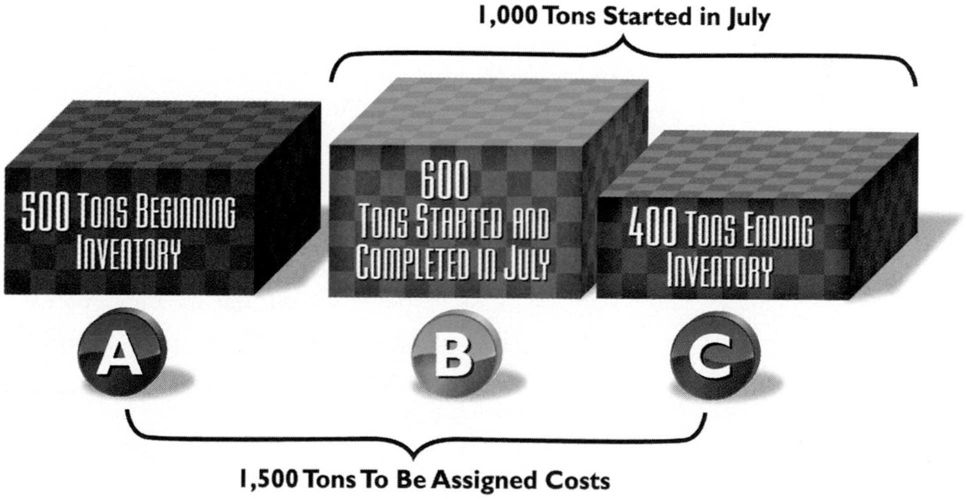

The total units (tons) to be assigned costs for McDermott Steel can be summarized as shown below.

(A) Inventory in process, July 1, completed in July	500 tons
(B) Started and completed in July	600
Transferred out to the Casting Department in July	1,100
(C) Inventory in process, July 31	400
Total tons to be assigned costs	1,500 tons

Q&A

Department 2 received 2,400 tons from Department 1. During the period, Department 2 completed 2,600 tons and had 600 tons of work in process at the beginning of the period. The ending work in process inventory was 400 tons. How many tons were started and completed during the period?

2,000 tons (2,400 − 400, or 2,600 − 600)

Note that the total tons to be assigned costs equals the total tons accounted for by the department. The three unit categories (**A**, **B**, and **C**) are used in the remaining steps to determine the cost transferred to the Casting Department and the cost remaining in work in process inventory at the end of the period.

Step 2: Calculate Equivalent Units of Production

Process manufacturers often have some partially processed materials remaining in production at the end of a period. In these cases, the costs of production must be allocated between the units that have been completed and transferred to the next process (or finished goods) and those that are only partially completed and remain within the department. This allocation can be determined by using the equivalent units of production.

The **equivalent units of production** are the number of units that *could have been* completed within a given accounting period. In contrast, **whole units** are the number of units in production during a period, whether or not completed. For example, assume that 800 whole units are in work in process at the end of a period. If the units are 60% complete, the number of equivalent units in process is 480 (800 × 60%).

Equivalent units for materials and conversion costs are usually determined separately because they are often introduced at different times or at different rates in the production process. In contrast, direct labor and factory overhead are combined together as conversion costs because they are often incurred in production at the same time and rate.

Point of INTEREST

Some process manufacturers try to avoid "turning off" their processes. Thus, work in process never stands still. In fact, in some processes, such as petroleum refining, the material can't even be seen. Materials processes are run this way because they are very expensive to shut down, clean, and then start again.

The equivalent units of production are the number of units that could have been completed during a period.

Materials Equivalent Units

To allocate materials costs between the completed and partially completed units, it is necessary to determine how materials are added during the manufacturing process. In the case of McDermott Steel, the materials are added at the beginning of the melting process. In other words, the melting process cannot begin without the scrap metal. The equivalent unit computation for materials in July is as follows:

	Direct Materials Equivalent Units in July		
	Total Whole Units	**Percent Materials Added in July**	**Equivalent Units for Direct Materials**
Inventory in process, July 1	500	0%	0
Started and completed in July (1,100 − 500)	600	100%	600
Transferred out to Casting Dept. in July	1,100	—	600
Inventory in process, July 31	400	100%	400
Total tons to be assigned cost	1,500		1,000

The whole units from Step 1 are multiplied by the percentage of materials that are added in July for the in-process inventories and units started and completed. The equivalent units for direct materials are illustrated in Exhibit 5.

EXHIBIT 5
Direct Materials Equivalent Units

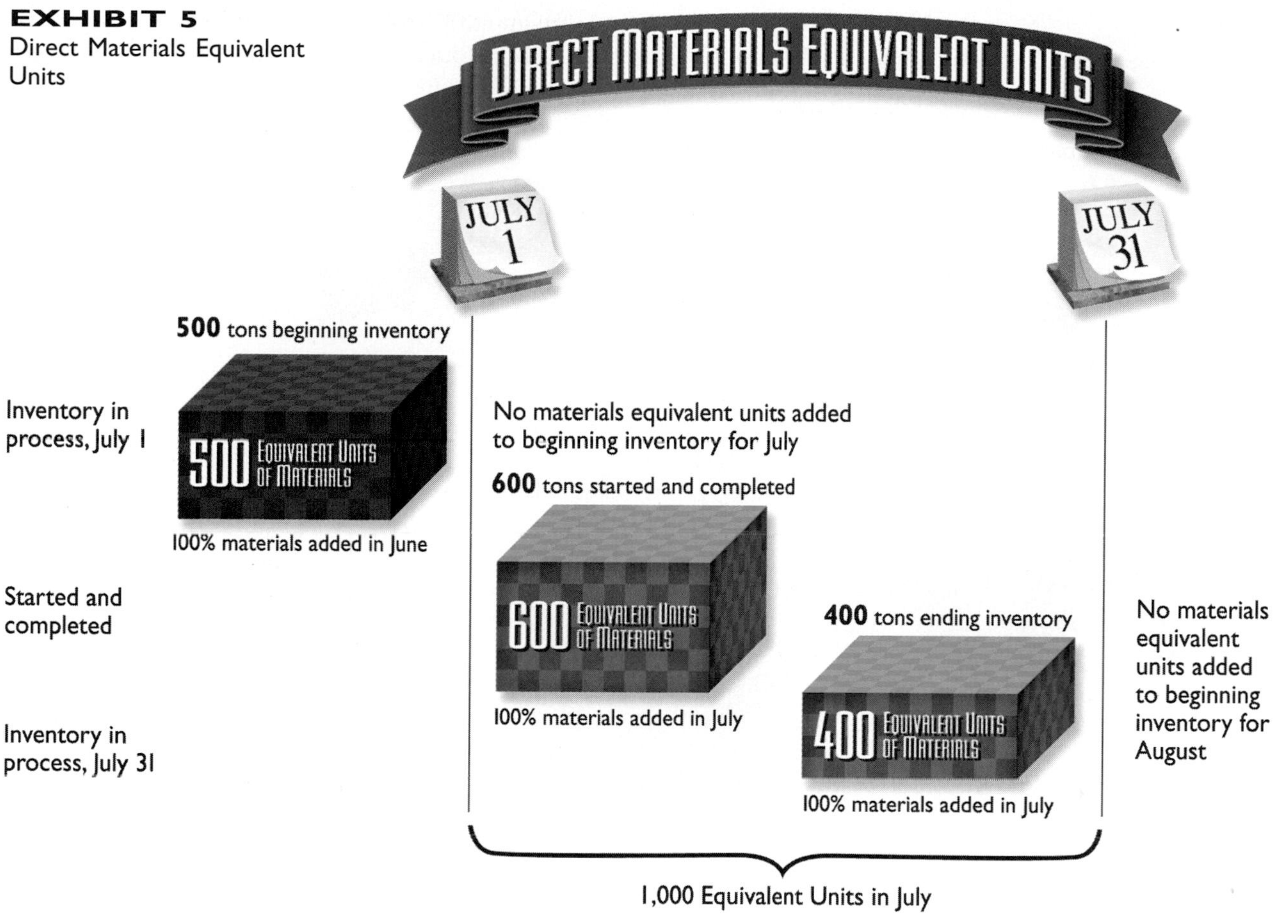

Q&A

Department 3 had 400 tons in beginning work in process inventory (30% complete). During the period, 5,800 tons were completed. The ending work in process inventory was 600 tons (60% complete). What are the equivalent units for direct materials, if materials are added at the beginning of the process?

6,000 tons (5,800 − 400 + 600)

The direct materials for the 500 tons of July 1 in-process inventory were introduced in June. Thus, no materials units were added in July for the inventory in process on July 1. All of the 600 tons started and completed in July were 100% complete with respect to materials. Thus, 600 equivalent units of materials were added in July. All the materials for the July 31 in-process inventory were introduced at the beginning of the process. Thus, 400 equivalent units of material for the July 31 in-process inventory were added in July.

Conversion Equivalent Units

The conversion costs are usually incurred evenly throughout a process. For example, direct labor, utilities, and machine depreciation are usually used uniformly during processing. Thus, the conversion equivalent units are added in July in direct relation to the percentage of processing completed in July. The computations for July are as follows:

	Conversion Equivalent Units in July		
	Total Whole Units	Percent Conversion Completed in July	Equivalent Units for Conversion
Inventory in process, July 1	500	30%	150
Started and completed in July (1,100 − 500)	600	100%	600
Transferred out to Casting Dept. in July	1,100	—	750
Inventory in process, July 31	400	25%	100
Total tons to be assigned cost	1,500		850

The whole units from Step 1 are multiplied by the percentage of conversion completed in July for the in-process inventories and units started and completed. The equivalent units for conversion are illustrated in Exhibit 6.

EXHIBIT 6
Conversion Equivalent Units

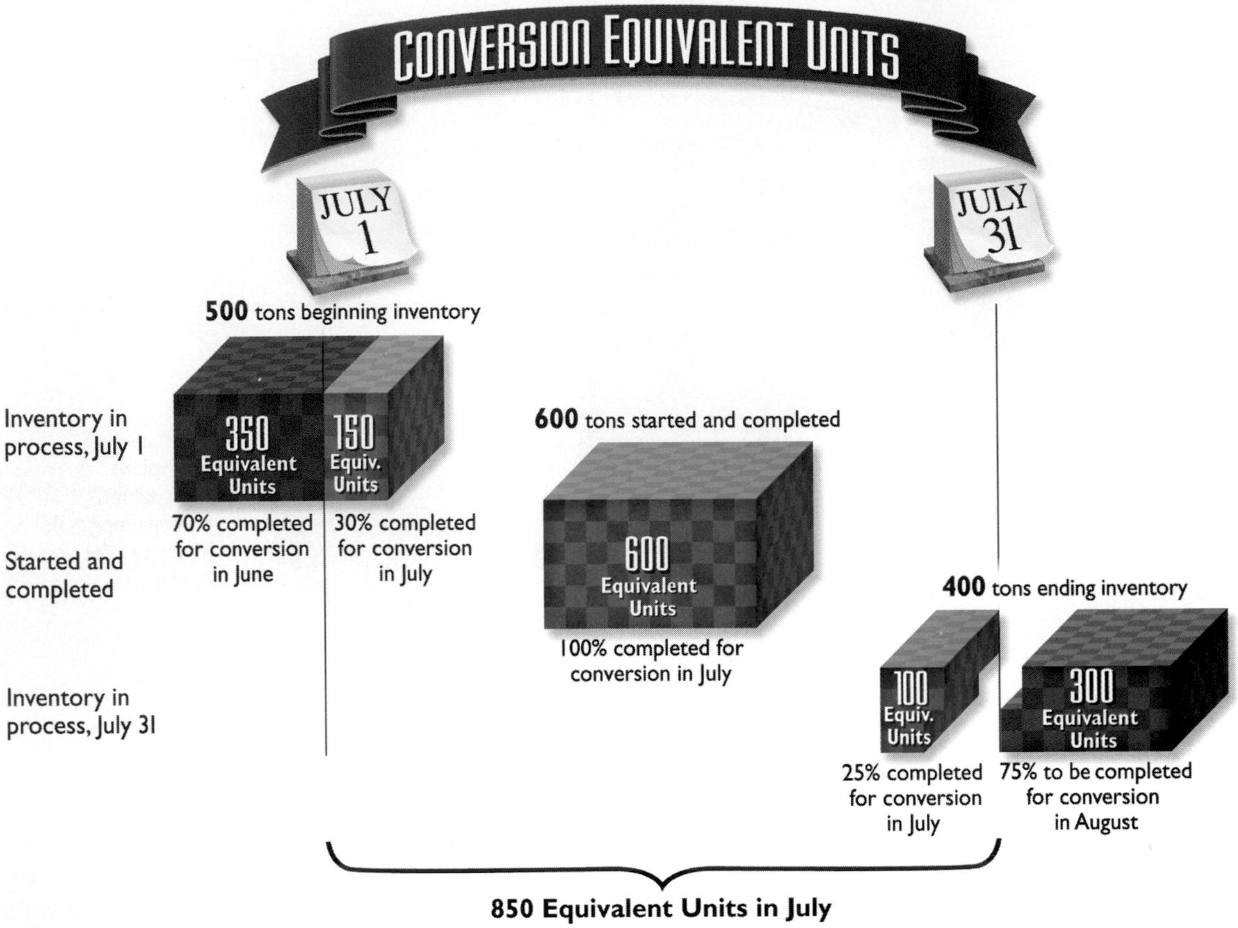

Department 3 had 400 tons in beginning work in process inventory (30% complete). During the period, 5,800 tons were completed. The ending work in process inventory was 600 tons (60% complete). What are the equivalent units for conversion costs?

6,040 tons [(70% × 400) + (5,800 − 400) + (60% × 600)]

The conversion equivalent units of the July 1 in-process inventory are 30% of the 500 tons, or 150 equivalent units. Since 70% of the conversion had been completed on July 1, only 30% of the conversion effort for these tons was incurred in July. All the units started and completed used converting effort in July. Thus, conversion equivalent units are 100% of these tons. The equivalent units for the July 31 in-process inventory are 25% of the 400 tons because only 25% of the converting has been completed with respect to these tons in July.

Step 3: Determine the Cost per Equivalent Unit

In Step 3, we calculate the cost per equivalent unit. The July equivalent unit totals for McDermott Steel's Melting Department are reproduced from Step 2 as follows:

	Equivalent Units	
	Direct Materials	Conversion
Inventory in process, July 1	0	150
Started and completed in July (1,100 − 500)	600	600
Transferred out to Casting Dept. in July	600	750
Inventory in process, July 31	400	100
Total tons to be assigned cost	1,000	850

The **cost per equivalent unit** is determined by dividing the direct materials and conversion costs incurred in July by the respective total equivalent units for direct materials and conversion costs. The direct materials and conversion costs were given at the beginning of this illustration. These calculations are as follows:

Equivalent unit cost for direct materials:

$$\frac{\$50{,}000 \text{ direct materials cost}}{1{,}000 \text{ direct materials equivalent units}} = \begin{array}{l}\$50.00 \text{ per equivalent} \\ \text{unit of direct materials}\end{array}$$

Equivalent unit cost for conversion:

$$\frac{\$9{,}690 \text{ conversion cost}}{850 \text{ conversion equivalent units}} = \begin{array}{l}\$11.40 \text{ per equivalent} \\ \text{unit of conversion}\end{array}$$

We will use these rates in Step 4 to allocate the direct materials and conversion costs to the completed and partially completed units.

Step 4: Allocate Costs to Transferred and Partially Completed Units

In Step 4, we multiply the equivalent unit rates by their respective equivalent units of production in order to determine the cost of transferred and partially completed units. The cost of the July 1 in-process inventory, completed and transferred out to the Casting Department, is determined as follows:

Q&A

What costs are included in the $28,150 beginning work in process inventory for McDermott Steel?

70% of the conversion cost and all of the materials costs for 500 tons.

	Direct Materials Costs	Conversion Costs	Total Costs
Inventory in process, July 1 balance			$28,150
Equivalent units for completing the July 1 in-process inventory	0	150	
Equivalent unit cost	×$50.00	×$11.40	
Cost of completed July 1 in-process inventory	0	$1,710	1,710
Cost of July 1 in-process inventory transferred to Casting Department			$29,860

The July 1 in-process inventory cost of $28,150 is carried over from June and will be transferred to Casting. The cost required to finish the July 1 in-process inventory is $1,710, which consists of conversion costs required to complete the remaining 30% of the processing. This total does not include direct materials costs, since these costs were added at the beginning of the process in June. The conversion costs required to complete the beginning inventory are added to the balance carried over from the previous month to yield a total cost of the completed July 1 in-process inventory of $29,860.

The 600 units started and completed in July receive 100% of their direct materials and conversion costs in July. The costs associated with the units started and completed are determined by multiplying the equivalent units in Step 2 by the unit costs in Step 3, as follows:

	Direct Materials Costs	Conversion Costs	Total Costs
Units started and completed in July	600	600	
Equivalent unit cost	×$50.00	×$11.40	
Cost to complete the units started and completed in July	$ 30,000	$ 6,840	$36,840

The total cost transferred to the Casting Department is the sum of the beginning inventory cost from the previous period ($28,150), the additional costs incurred in July to complete the beginning inventory ($1,710), and the costs incurred for the units started and completed in July ($36,840). Thus, the total cost transferred to Casting is $66,700.

The units of ending inventory have not been transferred, so they must be valued at July 31. The costs associated with the partially completed units in the ending inventory are determined by multiplying the equivalent units in Step 2 by the unit costs in Step 3, as follows:

	Direct Materials Costs	Conversion Costs	Total Costs
Equivalent units in ending inventory	400	100	
Equivalent unit cost	×$50.00	×$11.40	
Cost of ending inventory	$ 20,000	$ 1,140	$21,140

The units in the ending inventory have received 100% of their materials in July. Thus, the materials cost incurred in July for the ending inventory is $20,000, or 400 equivalent units of materials multiplied by $50. The conversion cost incurred in July for the ending inventory is $1,140, which is 100 equivalent units of conversion (400 units, 25% complete) for the ending inventory multiplied by $11.40. Summing the conversion and materials costs, the total ending inventory cost is $21,140.

GPP's Gencorp Polymer Products designed its process cost accounting system not only to provide cost of goods sold information for financial reporting, but also to help managers improve operating costs. They discovered that the primary drivers influencing the cost of packaging materials included poor use of machine capacities, complex material formulas, long processing times, machine cleaning time, and the frequency of cleaning. These insights led management to simplify product formulations, to reduce cleaning time, and to change pricing strategies to reflect the cost of using machine capacity.

Bringing It All Together: The Cost of Production Report

OBJECTIVE 4

Prepare a cost of production report.

A **cost of production report** is normally prepared for each processing department at periodic intervals. This report summarizes the four previous steps by providing the following production quantity and cost data:

1. The units for which the department is accountable and the disposition of those units.
2. The production costs incurred by the department and the allocation of those costs between completed and partially completed units.

The cost of production report is also used to control costs. Each department manager is responsible for the units entering production and the costs incurred in the department. Any failure to account for all costs and any significant differences in unit product costs from one month to another should be investigated.

The July cost of production report for McDermott Steel's Melting Department is shown in Exhibit 7.

EXHIBIT 7 Cost of Production Report for McDermott Steel's Melting Department—FIFO

McDermott Steel Inc.
Cost of Production Report—Melting Department
For the Month Ended July 31, 20—

UNITS	**Whole Units (Step 1)**	**Equivalent Units (Step 2) Direct Materials**	**Equivalent Units (Step 2) Conversion**	
Units charged to production:				
Inventory in process, July 1	500			
Received from materials storeroom	1,000			
Total units accounted for by the Melting Dept.	1,500			
Units to be assigned costs:				
Inventory in process, July 1 (70% completed)	500	0	150	
Started and completed in July	600	600	600	
Transferred to Casting Department in July	1,100	600	750	
Inventory in process, July 31 (25% complete)	400	400	100	
Total units to be assigned cost	1,500	1,000	850	
COSTS		**Costs Direct Materials**	**Costs Conversion**	**Total Costs**
Unit costs (Step 3):				
Total costs for July in Melting Dept.		$50,000	$9,690	
Total equivalent units (from Step 2 above)		÷ 1,000	÷ 850	
Cost per equivalent unit		$ 50.00	$11.40	
Costs charged to production:				
Inventory in process, July 1				$28,150
Costs incurred in July				59,690
Total costs accounted for by the Melting Dept.				$87,840
Costs allocated to completed and partially completed units (Step 4):				
Inventory in process, July 1—balance				$28,150
To complete inventory in process, July 1		$ 0	$1,710[a]	1,710
Started and completed in July		30,000[b]	6,840[c]	36,840
Transferred to Casting Dept. in July				$66,700
Inventory in process, July 31		$20,000[d]	$1,140[e]	21,140
Total costs assigned by the Melting Dept.				$87,840

[a]150 units × $11.40 = $1,710 [c]600 units × $11.40 = $6,840 [e]100 units × $11.40 = $1,140
[b]600 units × $50.00 = $30,000 [d]400 units × $50.00 = $20,000

OBJECTIVE 5

Prepare journal entries for transactions of a process manufacturer.

Journal Entries for a Process Cost System

To illustrate the journal entries to record the cost flows in a process costing system, we will use the July transactions for McDermott Steel. The entries in summary form for these transactions are shown on the following page. In practice, transactions would be recorded daily.

JOURNAL

Date	Description	Post. Ref.	Debit	Credit
a.	Materials		62000 00	
	Accounts Payable			62000 00
	Materials purchased on account.			
b.	Work in Process—Melting		50000 00	
	Factory Overhead—Melting		4000 00	
	Factory Overhead—Casting		3000 00	
	Materials			57000 00
	Materials requisitioned.			
c.	Work in Process—Melting		5000 00	
	Work in Process—Casting		4500 00	
	Wages Payable			9500 00
	Direct labor used.			
d.	Factory Overhead—Melting		1000 00	
	Factory Overhead—Casting		7000 00	
	Accumulated Depreciation			8000 00
	Depreciation expenses.			
e.	Work in Process—Melting		4690 00	
	Work in Process—Casting		9640 00	
	Factory Overhead—Melting			4690 00
	Factory Overhead—Casting			9640 00
	Factory overhead applied.			
f.	Work in Process—Casting		66700 00	
	Work in Process—Melting			66700 00
	Melting Department transferred $66,700 to Casting Department (from Exhibit 7).			
g.	Finished Goods		78600 00	
	Work in Process—Casting			78600 00
	Casting Department transferred $78,600 to Finished Goods.			
h.	Cost of Goods Sold		73700 00	
	Finished Goods			73700 00
	Goods sold.			

Exhibit 8 shows the flow of costs for each transaction. Note that the highlighted amounts in Exhibit 8 were determined from assigning the costs charged to production in the Melting Department. These amounts were computed in the prior section and are shown at the bottom of the cost of production report for the Melting Department in Exhibit 7. Likewise, the amount transferred out of the Casting Department to Finished Goods would have also been determined from a cost of production report for the Casting Department.

EXHIBIT 8 McDermott Steel's Cost Flows

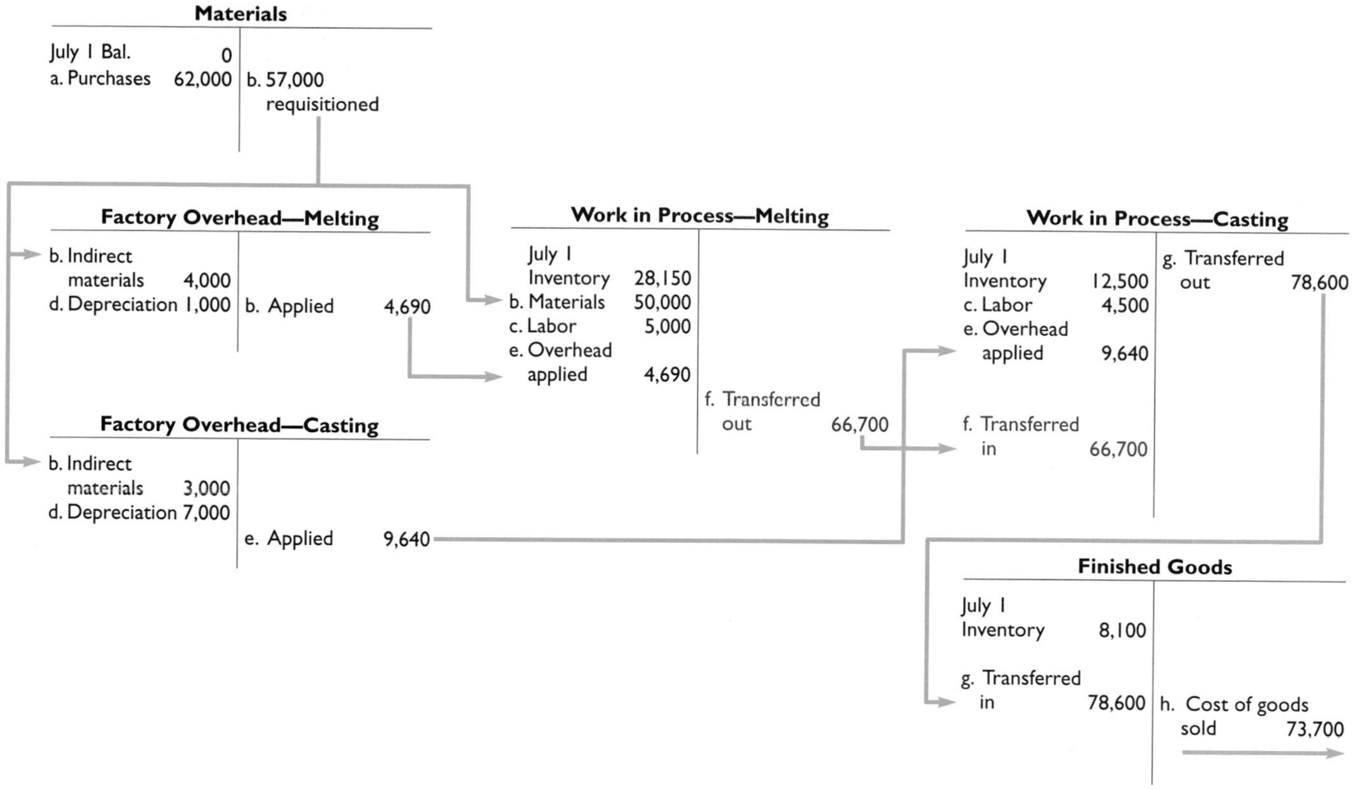

Using the Cost of Production Report for Decision Making

OBJECTIVE 6

Use cost of production reports for decision making.

The cost of production report is one source of information that may be used by managers to control and improve operations. A cost of production report will normally list costs in greater detail than in Exhibit 7. This greater detail helps management isolate problems and opportunities. To illustrate, assume that the Blending Department of Holland Beverage Company prepared cost of production reports for April and May. In addition, assume that the Blending Department had no beginning or ending work in process inventory either month. Thus, in this simple case, there is no need to determine equivalent units of production for allocating costs between completed and partially completed units. The cost of production report for April and May in the Blending Department is as follows:

Cost of Production Reports
Holland Beverage Company—Blending Department
For the Months Ended April 30 and May 31, 2000

	April	May
Direct materials	$ 20,000	$ 40,600
Direct labor	15,000	29,400
Energy	8,000	20,000
Repairs	4,000	8,000
Tank cleaning	3,000	8,000
Total	$ 50,000	$ 106,000
Units completed	÷100,000	÷200,000
Cost per unit	$ 0.50	$ 0.53

Note that the preceding reports provide more cost detail than simply reporting direct materials and conversion costs. The May results indicate that total unit costs have increased from $0.50 to $0.53, or 6% from the previous month. What caused this increase? To determine the possible causes for this increase, the cost of production report may be restated in per-unit terms, as shown below.

Middle Tennessee Lumber Company produces cabinet and furniture panels from various hardwoods. The company purchased new computer and sawing technology that improved the cutting yield by approximately 10%. The cutting yield is the ratio of finished panel board feet to the number of board feet input to the sawing operation. The new equipment scans the rough-cut lumber with a laser beam. The scanned information is input to a software program that calculates the optimum cutting pattern for minimizing trim waste. The wood is then sent to a computer-controlled saw, which proceeds to cut the board according to the calculations from the laser scan.

Blending Department Per-Unit Expense Comparisons

	April	May	% Change
Direct materials	$0.200	$0.203	1.50%
Direct labor	0.150	0.147	−2.00%
Energy	0.080	0.100	25.00%
Repairs	0.040	0.040	0.00%
Tank cleaning	0.030	0.040	33.33%
Total	$0.500	$0.530	6.00%

Both energy and tank cleaning per-unit costs have increased dramatically in May. Further investigation should focus on these costs. For example, an increasing trend in energy may indicate that the machines are losing fuel efficiency, thereby requiring the company to purchase an increasing amount of fuel. This unfavorable trend could motivate management to repair the machines. The tank cleaning costs could be investigated in a similar fashion.

In addition to unit production cost trends, managers of process manufacturers are also concerned about yield trends. **Yield** is the ratio of the materials output quantity to the input quantity. A yield less than one occurs when the output quantity is less than the input quantity due to materials losses during the process. For example, if 1,000 pounds of sugar entered the packing operation, and only 980 pounds of sugar were packed, the yield would be 98%. Two percent or 20 pounds of sugar were lost or spilled during the packing process.

Just-in-Time Processing

OBJECTIVE 7

Contrast just-in-time processing with conventional manufacturing practices.

The objective of many companies is to produce products with high quality, low cost, and instant availability. One approach to achieving this objective is to implement just-in-time processing. **Just-in-time processing (JIT)** is a new philosophy that focuses on reducing time and cost and eliminating poor quality. A JIT system achieves production efficiencies and flexibility by reorganizing the traditional production process.

In a traditional production process (illustrated in Exhibit 9), a product moves from process to process as each function or step is completed. Each worker is as-

EXHIBIT 9
Traditional Production Line—Furniture Manufacturer

INTERMISSION

American Standard manufactures commodes in Thailand to be sold in China, where it competes with a Japanese company, called **Toto Corporation**. American Standard has about 40% of the Chinese bathroom fixture market, while Toto has only about 15%. How has American Standard achieved this success in Toto's own backyard? Part of the answer lies in American Standard's manufacturing processes. American Standard uses a JIT production process that is flexible enough to fill most orders by making new commodes, rather than selling from inventory. This process allows it to stock only 14 days of inventory, while Toto stocks a two-month supply. In a typical case, an order is received for Cadet® commodes with custom-built outlet ports to line up with the existing sewage pipes. Toto would be unable to build this order. Thus, the JIT process gives American Standard a distinct competitive advantage in the marketplace. ■

Source: Steve Glain, "Top Toilet Makers From U.S. and Japan Vie for Chinese Market," *The Wall Street Journal,* December 19, 1996, p. 1.

signed a specific job, which is performed repeatedly as unfinished products are received from the preceding department. For example, a furniture manufacturer might use seven production departments to perform the operating functions necessary to manufacture furniture, as shown in the diagram in Exhibit 9.

For the furniture maker in the illustration, manufacturing would begin in the Cutting Department, where the wood would be cut to design specifications. Next, the Drilling Department would perform the drilling function, after which the Sanding Department would sand the wood, the Staining Department would stain the furniture, and the Varnishing Department would apply varnish and other protective coatings. Then, the Upholstery Department would add fabric and other materials. Finally, the Assembly Department would assemble the furniture to complete the process.

In the traditional production process, production supervisors attempt to enter enough materials into the process to keep all the manufacturing departments operating. Some departments, however, may process materials more rapidly than others. In addition, if one department stops production because of machine breakdowns, for example, the preceding departments usually continue production in order to avoid idle time. This may result in a build-up of work in some departments. Furthermore, if bottlenecks occur, the entire production line slows or stops because the unfinished product is not passed on to the next department.

In a just-in-time system, processing functions are combined into work centers, sometimes called **manufacturing cells**. For example, the seven departments illustrated above for the furniture manufacturer might be reorganized into three work centers. As shown in the diagram in Exhibit 10, Work Center One would perform the cutting, drilling, and sanding functions, Work Center Two would perform the staining and varnishing functions, and Work Center Three would perform the upholstery and assembly functions.

In the traditional production line, a worker typically performs only one function. However, in a work center in which several functions take place, the workers are often cross-trained to perform more than one function. Research has indicated that workers who perform several manufacturing functions identify better with the end product. This creates pride in the product and improves quality and productivity.

EXHIBIT 10
Just-in-Time Production Line—Furniture Manufacturer

Implementing JIT may also result in a reorganization of activities involving services. Specifically, the service activities may be assigned to individual work centers, rather than to centralized service departments. For example, each work center may be assigned the responsibility for the repair and maintenance of its machinery and equipment. Accepting this responsibility creates an environment in which workers gain a better understanding of the production process and the machinery. In turn, workers tend to take better care of the machinery, which decreases repairs and maintenance costs, reduces machine downtime, and improves product quality.

In a JIT system, wasted motion from moving the product and materials is reduced. The product is often placed on a movable carrier that is centrally located in the work center. After the workers in a work center have completed their activities with the product, the entire carrier and any additional materials are moved just in time to satisfy the demand or need of the next work center. In this sense, the product is said to be "pulled through." Each work center is connected to other work centers through information contained on Kanbans, which is a Japanese term for cards.

The experience of **Caterpillar Inc.** illustrates the impact of JIT. Before implementing JIT, an average transmission would travel 10 miles through the factory and require 1,000 pieces of paper for materials, labor, and movement transactions. After implementing JIT, Caterpillar improved manufacturing so that an average transmission traveled only 200 feet and required only 10 pieces of paper.

In summary, the primary benefit of JIT systems is the increased efficiency of operations, which is achieved by eliminating waste and simplifying the production process. At the same time, JIT systems emphasize continuous improvement in the manufacturing process and the improvement of product quality.

ENCORE

P & G's "Pit Stops"

What do **Procter & Gamble** and Formula One racing have in common? The answer begins with P&G's Packing Department, which is where detergents and other products are filled on a "pack line." Containers move down the pack line and are filled with products from a multihead packing machine. When it was time to change from a 36-oz. to a 54-oz. *Tide* box, for example, the changeover involved stopping the line, adjusting guide rails, retrieving items from the tool room, placing items back in the tool room, changing and cleaning the pack heads, and performing routine maintenance. Changing the pack line could be a very difficult process and typically took up to eight hours. Management realized that it was important to reduce this time significantly in order to become more flexible and cost efficient in packing products. Where could they learn how to do changeovers faster? They turned to Formula One racing, reasoning that a pit stop was much like a changeover. As a result, P&G videotaped actual Formula One pit stops. These videos were used to form the following principles for conducting a fast changeover:

- Position the tools near their point of use on the line prior to stopping the line, to reduce time going back and forth to the tool room.
- Arrange the tools in the exact order of work, so that no time is wasted looking for a tool.
- Have each employee perform a very specific task during the changeover.
- Design the workflow so that employees don't interfere with each other.
- Have each employee in position at the moment the line is stopped.
- Train each employee, and practice, practice, practice.
- Put a stop watch on the changeover process.
- Plot improvements over time on a visible chart.

As a result of these changes, P&G was able to reduce pack-line changeover time from eight hours to 20 minutes. This allowed them to produce a much larger variety of products every day and to improve the cost performance of the Packing Department. ■

KEY POINTS

1 Distinguish between job order costing and process costing systems.

The process cost system is best suited for industries that mass-produce identical units of a product that often have passed through a sequence of processes on a continuous basis. In process cost accounting, costs are charged to processing departments, and the cost of the finished unit is determined by dividing the total cost incurred in each process by the number of units produced.

2 Explain and illustrate the physical flows and cost flows for a process manufacturer.

Materials are introduced, converted, and passed from one department to the next department or to finished goods. The accumulated costs transferred from preceding departments and the costs of direct materials and direct labor incurred in each processing department are debited to the related work in process account in a process cost system. Each work in process account is also debited for the factory overhead applied.

3 Calculate and interpret the accounting for completed and partially completed units under the fifo method.

Frequently, partially processed materials remain in various stages of production in a department at the end of a period. In this case, the manufacturing costs must be allocated between the units that have been completed and those that are only partially completed and remain within the department. To allocate processing costs between the output completed and the inventory of goods within the department under fifo, it is necessary to determine the number of equivalent units of production during the period for the beginning inventory, units started and completed currently, and the ending inventory.

4 Prepare a cost of production report.

A cost of production report is prepared periodically for each processing department. It summarizes (1) the units for which the department is accountable and the disposition of those units and (2) the production costs incurred by the department and the allocation of those costs. The report is used to control costs and improve the process.

5 Prepare journal entries for transactions of a process manufacturer.

Summary journal entries for common process manufacturer transactions are illustrated for McDermott Steel in the text. Basic entries include debiting the processing department work in process account for direct materials, direct labor, and applied factory overhead costs incurred in production. Costs for completed units are credited to the transferring department's work in process account and debited to the receiving department's work in process account.

6 Use cost of production reports for decision making.

The cost of production report provides information for controlling and improving operations. Most cost of production reports include the detailed manufacturing costs incurred for completing production during the period. Analyzing trends in each of these costs over time can provide insights about process performance.

7 Contrast just-in-time processing with conventional manufacturing practices.

The just-in-time processing philosophy focuses on reducing time, cost, and poor quality within the process. This is accomplished by combining process functions into work centers, assigning overhead services directly to the cells, involving the employees in process improvement efforts, eliminating wasteful activities, and reducing the amount of work in process inventory required to fulfill production targets.

ILLUSTRATIVE PROBLEM

Southern Aggregate Company manufactures concrete by a series of four processes. All materials are introduced in Crushing. From Crushing, the materials pass through Sifting, Baking, and Mixing, emerging as finished concrete. All inventories are costed by the first-in, first-out method.

The balances in the accounts Work in Process—Mixing and Finished Goods were as follows on May 1:

Work in Process—Mixing (2,000 units, 1/4 completed)	$13,700
Finished Goods (1,800 units at $8.00 a unit)	14,400

The following costs were charged to Work in Process—Mixing during May:

Direct materials transferred from Baking:	
15,200 units at $6.50 a unit	$98,800
Direct labor	17,200
Factory overhead	11,780

During May, 16,000 units of concrete were completed, and 15,800 units were sold. Inventories on May 31 were as follows:

Work in Process—Mixing: 1,200 units, 1/2 completed
Finished Goods: 2,000 units

Instructions

1. Prepare a cost of production report for the Mixing Department.
2. Determine the cost of goods sold (indicate number of units and unit costs).
3. Determine the finished goods inventory, May 31.

Solution

1.

Southern Aggregate Company
Cost of Production Report—Mixing Department
For the Month Ended May 31, 20—

		Equivalent Units	
UNITS	**Whole Units**	**Direct Materials**	**Conversion**
Units charged to production:			
Inventory in process, May 1	2,000		
Received from Baking	15,200		
Total units accounted for by the Mixing Dept.	17,200		
Units to be assigned costs:			
Inventory in process, May 1 (25% completed)	2,000	0	1,500
Started and completed in May	14,000	14,000	14,000
Transferred to finished goods in May	16,000	14,000	15,500
Inventory in process, May 31 (50% complete)	1,200	1,200	600
Total units to be assigned cost	17,200	15,200	16,100

	Costs		
COSTS	**Direct Materials**	**Conversion**	**Total Costs**
Unit costs:			
Total cost for May in Mixing	$ 98,800	$28,980	
Total equivalent units (from above)	÷15,200	÷16,100	
Cost per equivalent unit	$ 6.50	$ 1.80	
Costs charged to production:			
Inventory in process, May 1			$ 13,700
Costs incurred in May			127,780
Total costs accounted for by the Mixing Dept.			$141,480

	Direct Materials	Conversion	Total Costs
Costs allocated to completed and partially completed units:			
Inventory in process, May 1—balance			$ 13,700
To complete inventory in process, May 1	$ 0	$ 2,700 (a)	2,700
Started and completed in May	91,000 (b)	25,200 (c)	116,200
Transferred to finished goods in May			$132,600
Inventory in process, May 31	$ 7,800 (d)	$ 1,080 (e)	8,880
Total costs assigned by the Mixing Department			$141,480

(a) 1,500 × $1.80 = $2,700 (c) 14,000 × $1.80 = $25,200 (e) 600 × $1.80 = $1,080
(b) 14,000 × $6.50 = $91,000 (d) 1,200 × $6.50 = $7,800

2. Cost of goods sold:

1,800 units at $8.00	$ 14,400	(from finished goods beginning inventory)
2,000 units at $8.20*	16,400	(from work in process beginning inventory)
12,000 units at $8.30**	99,600	(from May production started and completed)
15,800 units	$130,400	

*($13,700 + $2,700) ÷ 2,000
**$116,200 ÷ 14,000

3. Finished goods inventory, May 31:

2,000 units at $8.30 $16,600

SELF-EXAMINATION QUESTIONS

Answers at End of Chapter

Matching

Match each of the following statements with its proper term. Some terms may not be used.

A. cost of production report
B. cost per equivalent unit
C. equivalent units of production
D. first-in, first-out (FIFO) cost method
E. just-in-time processing
F. manufacturing cells
G. oil refinery
H. process cost system
I. process manufacturers
J. transferred-out costs
K. yield

H 1. A type of cost system that accumulates costs for each of the various departments within a manufacturing facility.

I 2. Manufacturers that use large machines to process a continuous flow of raw materials through various stages of completion into a finished state.

C 3. The number of production units that could have been completed within a given accounting period, given the resources consumed.

D 4. A method of inventory costing that assumes the unit product costs should be determined separately for each period in the order in which the costs were incurred.

B 5. The rate used to allocate costs between completed and partially completed production.

A 6. A report prepared periodically by a processing department, summarizing the costs incurred by the department and the allocation of those costs between completed and incomplete production.

K 7. A measure of materials usage efficiency.

F 8. A grouping of processes where employees are cross-trained to perform more than one function.

E 9. A processing approach that focuses on eliminating time, cost, and poor quality within manufacturing and nonmanufacturing processes.

Multiple Choice

1. For which of the following businesses would the process cost system be most appropriate?
   A. Custom furniture manufacturer
   B. Commercial building contractor
   C. Crude oil refinery
   D. Automobile repair shop

2. There were 2,000 pounds in process at the beginning of the period in the Packing Department. Packing received 24,000 pounds from the Blending Department during the month, of which 3,000 pounds were in process at the end of the month. How many pounds were completed and transferred to finished goods from the Packing Department?
   A. 23,000 C. 26,000
   B. 21,000 D. 29,000

3. Information relating to production in Department A for May is as follows:

May	1	Balance, 1,000 units, ¾ completed	$22,150
	31	Direct materials, 5,000 units	75,000
	31	Direct labor	32,500
	31	Factory overhead	16,250

If 500 units were one-fourth completed at May 31, 5,500 units were completed during May, and inventories are costed by the first-in, first-out method, what was the number of equivalent units of production with respect to conversion costs for May?
   A. 4,500 C. 5,500
   B. 4,875 D. 6,000

4. Based on the data presented in Question 3, what is the conversion cost per equivalent unit?
   A. $10 C. $25
   B. $15 D. $32

5. Information from the accounting system revealed the following:

	Day 1	Day 2	Day 3	Day 4	Day 5
Materials	$20,000	$18,000	$22,000	$20,000	$20,000
Electricity	2,500	3,000	3,500	4,000	4,700
Maintenance	4,000	3,800	3,400	3,000	2,800
Total costs	$26,500	$24,800	$28,900	$27,000	$27,500
Pounds produced	÷10,000	÷9,000	÷11,000	÷10,000	÷10,000
Cost per unit	$ 2.65	$ 2.75	$ 2.63	$ 2.70	$ 2.75

Which of the following statements best interprets this information?
   A. The total costs are out of control.
   B. The product costs have steadily increased because of higher electricity costs.
   C. Electricity costs have steadily increased because of lack of maintenance.
   D. The unit costs reveal a significant operating problem.

CLASS DISCUSSION QUESTIONS

1. Which type of cost system, process or job order, would be best suited for each of the following: (a) custom jewelry manufacturer, (b) paper manufacturer, (c) automobile repair shop, (d) building contractor, (e) TV assembler? Give reasons for your answers.
2. Are perpetual inventory accounts for materials, work in process, and finished goods generally used for (a) job order and (b) process cost systems?
3. In job order cost accounting, the three elements of manufacturing cost are charged directly to job orders. Why is it not necessary to charge manufacturing costs in process cost accounting to job orders?
4. In a job order cost system, direct labor and factory overhead applied are debited to individual jobs. How are these items treated in a process cost system and why?
5. What two groups of manufacturing costs are referred to as conversion costs?
6. What are transferred-out materials?
7. What account for a production department receives the debit for "transferred-in materials"?
8. What are the four steps for determining the cost of goods completed and the ending inventory?
9. What is meant by the term *equivalent units*?
10. Why is the cost per equivalent unit often determined separately for direct materials and conversion costs?
11. What is the purpose for determining the cost per equivalent unit?

12. Domingo Company is a process manufacturer with two production departments, Departments A and B. All direct materials are introduced in Department A from the materials store area. What is included in the cost transferred to Department B?
13. How is actual factory overhead accounted for in a process manufacturer?
14. What data are summarized in the two principal sections of the cost of production report?
15. What is the most important purpose of the cost of production report?
16. How are cost of production reports used for controlling and improving operations?
17. How is "yield" determined for a process manufacturer?
18. What is just-in-time processing?
19. How does just-in-time processing differ from the conventional manufacturing process?

Warren Reeve Fess

Resources for Your Success On-Line at warren.swcollege.com

Remember! If you need additional help, visit South-Western's Web site. See page 26 for a description of the online and printed materials that are available.

EXERCISES

Exercise 18–1
Flowchart of accounts related to service and processing departments
Objective 2

Rigid Panels Inc. manufactures metal sheet products. The entire output of the Shearing Department is transferred to the Slitting Department. Part of the fully processed goods from the Slitting Department are sold as uncoated sheet, and the remainder of the goods are transferred to the Coating Department for further processing into coated sheet.

Prepare a chart of the flow of costs from the processing department accounts into the finished goods accounts and then into the cost of goods sold account. The relevant accounts are as follows:

Cost of Goods Sold	Finished Goods—Uncoated Sheet
Materials	Finished Goods—Coated Sheet
Factory Overhead—Shearing Department	Work in Process—Shearing Department
Factory Overhead—Slitting Department	Work in Process—Slitting Department
Factory Overhead—Coating Department	Work in Process—Coating Department

Exercise 18–2
Entries for flow of factory costs for process cost system
Objectives 2, 5

Juniper Company manufactures a sugar product by a continuous process, involving three production departments. The records indicate that direct materials, direct labor, and applied factory overhead for the first department, Refining, were \$145,000, \$96,000, and \$31,600, respectively. Also, work in process in the Refining Department at the beginning of the period totaled \$22,000, and work in process at the end of the period totaled \$67,000.

Journalize the entries to record (a) the flow of costs into the Refining Department during the period for (1) direct materials, (2) direct labor, and (3) factory overhead, and (b) the transfer of production costs to the second department, Sifting.

Exercise 18–3
Factory overhead rate, entry for applying factory overhead, and factory overhead account balance
Objectives 2, 5

✓ a. 70%

The chief cost accountant for Glacier Beverage Co. estimated that total factory overhead cost for the Blending Department for the coming fiscal year beginning April 1 would be \$315,000, and total direct labor costs would be \$450,000. During April, the actual direct labor cost totaled \$28,500, and factory overhead cost incurred totaled \$20,000.

a. What is the predetermined factory overhead rate based on direct labor cost?
b. Journalize the entry to apply factory overhead to production for April.
c. What is the April 30 balance of the account Factory Overhead—Blending Department?
d. Does the balance in (c) represent overapplied or underapplied factory overhead?

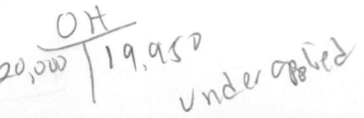

WIP 28,500 | 19,950

OH 20,000 | 19,950 Underapplied

Exercise 18–4
Equivalent units of production

Objective 3

✓ Direct materials, 9,400 units

The Converting Department of Chou Napkin Company had 900 units in work in process at the beginning of the period, which were 60% complete. During the period, 9,900 units were completed and transferred to the Packing Department. There were 400 units in process at the end of the period, which were 30% complete. Direct materials are placed into the process at the beginning of production. Determine the number of equivalent units of production with respect to direct materials and conversion costs.

Exercise 18–5
Equivalent units of production

Objective 3

✓ a. Conversion, 72,400 units

Units of production data for the two departments of Structural Forms Inc. for August of the current fiscal year are as follows:

	Stamping Department	Forming Department
Work in process, August 1	8,000 units, 55% completed	4,500 units, 70% completed
Completed and transferred to next processing department during August	66,000 units	68,500 units
Work in process, August 31	12,000 units, 90% completed	2,000 units, 20% completed

If all direct materials are placed in process at the beginning of production, determine the direct materials and conversion equivalent units of production for August for (a) the Stamping Department and (b) the Forming Department.

Exercise 18–6
Equivalent units of production

Objectives 2, 3

✓ b. Direct materials, 72,000

The following information concerns production in the Painting Department for March. All direct materials are placed in process at the beginning of production.

ACCOUNT ***Work in Process—Painting Department*** **ACCOUNT NO.**

Date		Item	Debit	Credit	Balance Debit	Balance Credit
Mar.	1	Bal., 18,000 units, 1/5 completed			24,300	
	31	Direct materials, 72,000 units	54,000		78,300	
	31	Direct labor	24,200		102,500	
	31	Factory overhead	17,000		119,500	
	31	Goods finished, 66,500 units		96,518	22,982	
	31	Bal.—units, 2/5 completed			22,982	

a. Determine the number of units in work in process inventory at the end of the month.
b. Determine the equivalent units of production for direct materials and conversion costs in March.

Exercise 18–7
Costs per equivalent unit

Objective 3

✓ c. $3.00

Pressure Form Manufacturing Company completed and transferred 24,000 units of production from the Pressing Department. There was no beginning inventory in process in the department. The ending in-process inventory was 1,200 units, which were 75% complete as to conversion cost. All materials are added at the beginning of the process. Direct materials cost incurred was $75,600, direct labor cost incurred was $20,000, and factory overhead applied was $22,330.

Determine the following for the Pressing Department:

a. Total conversion cost
b. Conversion cost per equivalent unit
c. Direct materials cost per equivalent unit

Exercise 18–8
Equivalent units of production and related costs

Objective 3

The charges to Work in Process—Baking Department for a period, together with information concerning production, are as follows. All direct materials are placed in process at the beginning of production.

SPREADSHEET

✓ b. Direct materials, $4.50

Work in Process—Baking Department

Bal., 12,000 units, 60% completed	75,000	To Finished Goods, 44,600 units	303,980
Direct materials, 32,600 units @ $4.50	146,700		
Direct labor	40,000		
Factory overhead	42,280		

Determine the following:

a. Equivalent units of production for direct materials and conversion.
b. Costs per equivalent unit for direct materials and conversion.

Exercise 18–9

Errors in equivalent unit computation

Objective 3

What's Wrong WITH THIS?

Tri-State Oil Refining Company processes gasoline. At May 1 of the current year, 3,000 units were ⅕ completed in the Blending Department. During May, 16,500 units entered the Blending Department from the Refining Department. During May, the units in process at the beginning of the month were completed. Of the 16,500 units entering the department, all were completed except 3,900 units that were ⅓ completed. The equivalent units for conversion costs for May for the Blending Department were computed as follows:

Equivalent units of production in May:	
To process units in inventory on May 1:	
3,000 × ⅕	600
To process units started and completed in May:	
16,500 − 3,000	13,500
To process units in inventory on May 31:	
3,900 × ⅓	1,300
Equivalent units of production	15,400

List the errors in the computation of equivalent units for conversion costs for the Blending Department for May.

Exercise 18–10

Cost per equivalent unit

Objectives 2, 3

✓ Conversion, $7.80

The following information concerns production in the Forging Department for April. All direct materials are placed into the process at the beginning of production, and conversion costs are incurred evenly throughout the process. The beginning inventory consists of $70,000 of direct materials and $13,000 of conversion costs.

ACCOUNT ***Work in Process—Forging Department*** **ACCOUNT NO.**

Date		Item	Debit	Credit	Balance Debit	Balance Credit
April	1	Bal., 5,500 units, 30% completed			83,000	
	30	Direct materials, 22,000 units	286,000		369,000	
	30	Direct labor	84,435		453,435	
	30	Factory overhead	84,435		537,870	
	30	Goods transferred, 20,500 units		425,030	112,840	
	30	Bal., 7,000 units, 40% completed			112,840	

Determine the cost per equivalent unit of direct materials and conversion.

Exercise 18–11

Cost of production report

Objective 4

✓ d. $40,370

The debits to Work in Process—Melting Department for Atlas Steel Company for January 2000, together with information concerning production, are as follows:

Work in process, January 1, 7,500 units, 30% complete	$ 48,000
Materials added during January, 54,000 units	318,600
Conversion costs during January	136,920
Work in process, January 31, 5,500 units, 60% completed	—
Goods finished during January, 56,000 units	—

All direct materials are placed in process at the beginning of production.

Prepare a cost of production report, presenting the following computations:

a. Direct materials and conversion equivalent units of production for the period.
b. Direct materials and conversion cost per equivalent unit for the period.
c. Cost of goods finished during the period.
d. Cost of work in process at the end of the period.

Exercise 18–12
Cost of production report
Objective 4

SPREADSHEET

✓ Conversion rate, $2.30

Prepare a cost of production report for the Finishing Department of Victoria Molding Company for May 2001, using the following data and assuming that all materials are added at the beginning of the process:

Work in process, May 1, 12,000 units, 70% complete	$ 70,000
Materials added during May from Sanding Dept., 89,000 units	440,550
Direct labor for May	151,940
Factory overhead for May	50,000
Goods finished during May (includes goods in process, May 1), 95,000 units	—
Work in process, May 31, 6,000 units, 20% completed	—

Exercise 18–13
Decision making
Objective 6

Western Bottling Company bottles popular beverages. The beverages are produced by blending concentrate with water and sugar. The concentrate is purchased from a concentrate producer. The concentrate producer sets higher prices for the more popular concentrate flavors. Below is a simplified cost of production report separating the cost of bottling the four flavors.

	Orange	Cola	Lemon-Lime	Root Beer
Concentrate	$ 2,000	$31,200	$20,000	$ 4,000
Water	500	6,000	4,000	1,000
Sugar	1,200	14,400	9,600	2,400
Bottles	2,400	28,800	19,200	4,800
Flavor changeover	5,000	1,560	1,040	2,500
Conversion cost	800	6,000	4,000	1,600
Total cost	$11,900	$87,960	$57,840	$16,300
Number of cases	1,000	12,000	8,000	2,000

Beginning and ending work in process inventories are negligible, so are omitted from the cost of production report. The flavor changeover cost represents the cost of cleaning the bottling machines between production runs of different flavors.

Prepare a memo to the production manager analyzing this cost of production report. In your memo, provide recommendations for further action, along with supporting schedules.

Exercise 18–14
Decision making
Objective 6

Westman Kodiac Company produces film products for cameras. One of the processes for this operation is a coating (solvent spreading) operation, where chemicals are coated on to film stock. There has been some concern about the cost performance of this operation. As a result, you have begun an investigation. You first discover that all input prices have not changed for the last six months. If there is a problem, it is related to the quantity of input. You have discovered three possible problems from some of the operating personnel whose quotes follow:

Operator 1: "I've been keeping an eye on my operating room instruments. I feel as though our energy consumption is becoming less efficient."

Operator 2: "Every time the coating machine goes down, we produce waste on shutdown and subsequent startup. It seems like during the last half year we have had more unscheduled machine shutdowns than in the past. Thus, I feel as though our yields must be dropping."

Operator 3: "My sense is that our coating costs are going up. It seems to me like we are spreading a thicker coating than we should. Perhaps the coating machine needs to be recalibrated."

The Coating Department had no beginning or ending inventories for any month during the study period. The following data from the cost of production report is made available:

	January	February	March	April	May	June
Transferred-in materials	$39,900	$37,050	$42,750	$45,600	$51,300	$57,000
Coating cost	9,975	9,880	12,825	15,200	18,810	23,750
Conversion cost (incl. energy)	26,600	24,700	28,500	30,400	34,200	38,000
Pounds input to the process	70,000	65,000	75,000	80,000	90,000	100,000
Pounds transferred out	66,500	61,750	71,250	76,000	85,500	95,000

Use the preceding information to discover the problem in the operation.

Exercise 18–15

Just-in-time manufacturing

Objective 7

The following are some quotes provided by a number of managers at Western Sprocket Company regarding the company's planned move toward a just-in-time manufacturing system:

Director of Purchasing: *I'm very concerned about moving to a just-in-time system for materials. What would happen if one of our suppliers were unable to make a shipment? A supplier could fall behind in production or have a quality problem. Without some safety stock in our materials, our whole plant would shut down.*

Director of Manufacturing: *If we go to just-in-time, I think our factory output will drop. We need in-process inventory in order to "smooth out" the inevitable problems that occur during manufacturing. For example, if a machine that is used to process a product breaks down, I would starve the next machine if I don't have in-process inventory between the two machines. If I have in-process inventory, then I can keep the next operation busy while I fix the broken machine. Thus, the in-process inventories give me a safety valve that I can use to keep things running when things go wrong.*

Director of Sales: *I'm afraid we'll miss some sales if we don't keep a large stock of items on hand just in case demand increases. It only makes sense to me to keep large inventories in order to assure product availability for our customers.*

How would you respond to these managers?

PROBLEMS SERIES A

Problem 18–1A

Entries for process cost system

Objectives 2, 5

HAT

✓ 2. Materials July 31 balance, $13,370

Tidy Soap Company manufactures powdered detergent. Phosphate is placed in process in the Making Department, where it is turned into granulars. The output of Making is transferred to the Packing Department, where packaging is added at the beginning of the process. On July 1, Tidy Soap Company had the following inventories:

Finished Goods	$16,400
Work in Process—Making	2,460
Work in Process—Packing	6,350
Materials	4,700

Departmental accounts are maintained for factory overhead, which both have zero balances on July 1.

Manufacturing operations for July are summarized as follows:

a. Materials purchased on account	$63,400
b. Materials requisitioned for use:	
Phosphate—Making Department	$38,700
Packaging—Packing Department	12,450
Indirect materials—Making Department	2,450
Indirect materials—Packing Department	1,130

c. Labor used:	
Direct labor—Making Department	$45,700
Direct labor—Packing Department	67,900
Indirect labor—Making Department	4,600
Indirect labor—Packing Department	4,200
d. Depreciation charged on fixed assets:	
Making Department	$43,700
Packing Department	12,600
e. Expired prepaid insurance:	
Making Department	$2,300
Packing Department	900
f. Applied factory overhead:	
Making Department	$54,000
Packing Department	18,300
g. Production costs transferred from Making Dept. to Packing Dept.	$137,500
h. Production costs transferred from Packing Dept. to finished goods	$241,200
i. Cost of goods sold during the period	$250,100

See page 726 for example

Look at Extra

Instructions

1. Journalize the entries to record the operations, identifying each entry by letter.
2. Compute the July 31 balances of the inventory accounts.
3. Compute the July 31 balances of the factory overhead accounts.

Problem 18–2A
Entries for process cost system
Objectives 2, 5

HAT
GENERAL LEDGER

Thompson Container Company manufactures aluminum cans. Materials are placed in production in the Blanking Department and after processing are transferred to the Forming Department, where more materials (coatings) are added. The finished product emerges from the Forming Department.

There were no inventories of work in process at the beginning or at the end of July. Finished goods inventory at July 1 was 5,000 cases of aluminum cans at a total cost of $125,000.

Transactions related to manufacturing operations for July are summarized as follows:

a. Materials purchased on account, $134,000.
b. Materials requisitioned for use: Blanking, $98,300 ($93,400 entered directly into the product); Forming, $32,800 ($28,600 entered directly into the product).
c. Labor costs incurred: Blanking, $76,450 ($71,200 entered directly into the product); Forming, $102,700 ($92,300 entered directly into the product).
d. Miscellaneous costs and expenses incurred on account: Blanking, $11,400; Forming, $19,900.
e. Expiration of various prepaid expenses: Blanking, $3,600; Forming, $2,800.
f. Depreciation charged on fixed assets: Blanking, $32,000; Forming, $22,500.
g. Factory overhead applied to production, based on machine hours: $58,000 for Blanking and $60,000 for Forming.
h. Output of Blanking: 15,000 cases.
i. Output of Forming: 15,000 cases of aluminum cans.
j. Sales on account: 18,000 cases of aluminum cans at $40. Credits to the finished goods account are to be made according to the first-in, first-out method.

Instructions

Journalize the entries to record the transactions, identifying each by letter. Include as an explanation for entry (j) the number of cases and the cost per case of cans sold.

Problem 18–3A
Cost of production report
Objectives 3, 4

✓ Conversion rate per equivalent unit, $3.20

Venus Chocolate Company processes chocolate into candy bars. The process begins by placing direct materials (raw chocolate, milk, and sugar) into the Blending Department. All materials are placed into production at the beginning of the blending process. After blending, the milk chocolate is then transferred to the Molding Department, where the milk chocolate is formed into candy bars. The following is a partial work in process account of the Blending Department at December 31:

ACCOUNT *Work in Process—Blending Department* ACCOUNT NO.

Date		Item	Debit	Credit	Balance Debit	Balance Credit
Dec.	1	Bal., 12,000 units, 40% completed			91,500	
	31	Direct materials, 95,600 units	745,680		837,180	
	31	Direct labor	142,760		979,940	
	31	Factory overhead	175,000		1,154,940	
	31	Goods finished, 102,600 units		?		
	31	Bal. _?_ units, 30% completed			?	

Instructions

Prepare a cost of production report and identify the missing amounts for the Work in Process—Blending Department account.

Problem 18–4A

Equivalent units and related costs; cost of production report; entries

Objectives 3, 4, 5

SPREADSHEET

✓ Transferred to finished goods, $883,680

Union Chemical Company manufactures specialty chemicals by a series of three processes, all materials being introduced in the Blending Department. From the Blending Department, the materials pass through the Reaction and Filling Departments, emerging as finished chemicals.

The balance in the account Work in Process—Filling was as follows on March 1:

Work in Process—Filling Department (8,000 units, 60% completed)	$124,000

The following costs were charged to Work in Process—Filling during March:

Direct materials transferred from Reaction Department: 64,300 units at $8.20 a unit	$527,260
Direct labor	58,276
Factory overhead	241,000

During March, 66,200 units of specialty chemicals were completed. Work in Process—Filling Department on March 31 was 6,100 units, 60% completed.

Instructions

1. Prepare a cost of production report for the Filling Department for March.
2. Journalize the entries for costs transferred from Reaction to Filling and the cost of goods transferred to finished goods.
3. Discuss the uses of the cost of production report.

Problem 18–5A

Work in process account data for two months; cost of production reports

Objectives 2, 3, 4, 5

✓ 1. c. $157,550

National Aluminum Company uses a process cost system to record the costs of manufacturing rolled aluminum, which requires a series of five processes. The inventory of Work in Process—Rolling on September 1, 2000, and debits to the account during September were as follows:

Bal., 12,500 units, 10% completed	$12,400
From Smelting Dept., 82,000 units	77,900
Direct labor	29,892
Factory overhead	43,700

During September, 12,500 units in process on September 1 were completed, and of the 82,000 units entering the department, all were completed except 4,200 units that were 70% completed.

Charges to Work in Process—Rolling for October were as follows:

From Smelting Department, 104,000 units	$106,080
Direct labor	36,417
Factory overhead	52,000

During October, the units in process at the beginning of the month were completed, and of the 104,000 units entering the department, all were completed except 6,200 units that were 80% completed.

Instructions

1. Enter the balance as of September 1 in a four-column account for Work in Process—Rolling. Record the debits and the credits in the account for September. Construct a cost of production report and present computations for determining (a) equivalent units of production for materials and conversion, (b) equivalent costs per unit, (c) cost of goods finished, differentiating between units started in the prior period and units started and finished in September, and (d) work in process inventory.
2. Provide the same information for October by recording the October transactions in the four-column work in process account. Construct a cost of production report, and present the October computations (a through d) listed in (1).

PROBLEMS SERIES B

Problem 18–1B
Entries for process cost system
Objectives 2, 5

✓ Materials Oct. 31 balance, $33,340

Aladdin Company manufactures carpets. Cotton is placed in process in the Spinning Department, where it is spun into yarn. The output of the Spinning Department is transferred to the Tufting Department, where carpet backing is added at the beginning of the process and the process is completed. On October 1, Aladdin Company had the following inventories:

Finished Goods	$56,000
Work in Process—Spinning Department	0
Work in Process—Tufting Department	34,500
Materials	21,600

Departmental accounts are maintained for factory overhead, and both have zero balances on October 1.

Manufacturing operations for October are summarized as follows:

a. Materials purchased on account	$78,000
b. Materials requisitioned for use:	
Cotton—Spinning Department	$47,800
Carpet backing—Tufting Department	13,500
Indirect materials—Spinning Department	4,210
Indirect materials—Tufting Department	750
c. Labor used:	
Direct labor—Spinning Department	$87,000
Direct labor—Tufting Department	58,800
Indirect labor—Spinning Department	7,800
Indirect labor—Tufting Department	6,250
d. Depreciation charged on fixed assets:	
Spinning Department	$38,900
Tufting Department	42,350
e. Expired prepaid insurance:	
Spinning Department	$1,400
Tufting Department	1,200
f. Applied factory overhead:	
Spinning Department	$50,760
Tufting Department	51,500
g. Production costs transferred from Spinning Dept. to Tufting Dept.	$173,400
h. Production costs transferred from Tufting Dept. to finished goods	$321,300
i. Cost of goods sold during the period	$326,400

Instructions

1. Journalize the entries to record the operations, identifying each entry by letter.
2. Compute the October 31 balances of the inventory accounts.
3. Compute the October 31 balances of the factory overhead accounts.

Problem 18–2B
Entries for process cost system

Objectives 2, 5

GENERAL LEDGER

Elf Bakery Inc. manufactures cookies. Materials are placed in production in the Baking Department and after processing are transferred to the Packing Department, where more materials are added. The finished products emerge from the Packing Department.

There were no inventories of work in process at the beginning or at the end of March. Finished goods inventory at March 1 was 20,000 cases of cookies at a total cost of $300,000.

Transactions related to manufacturing operations for March are summarized as follows:

a. Materials purchased on account, $245,000.
b. Materials requisitioned for use: Baking Department, $191,500 ($185,000 entered directly into the product); Packing Department, $40,100 ($36,000 entered directly into the product).
c. Labor costs incurred: Baking Department, $81,200 ($78,000 entered directly into the product); Packing Department, $67,100 ($65,000 entered directly into the product).
d. Miscellaneous costs and expenses incurred on account: Baking Department, $16,800; Packing Department, $12,400.
e. Depreciation charged on fixed assets: Baking Department, $45,200; Packing Department, $12,400.
f. Expiration of various prepaid expenses: Baking Department, $4,300; Packing Department, $800.
g. Factory overhead applied to production, based on machine hours: $75,000 for Baking and $32,000 for Packing.
h. Output of Baking Department: 30,000 cases.
i. Output of Packing Department: 30,000 cases of cookies.
j. Sales on account: 40,000 cases of cookies at $25. Credits to the finished goods account are to be made according to the first-in, first-out method.

Instructions
Journalize the entries to record the transactions, identifying each by letter. Include as an explanation for entry (j) the number of cases and the cost per case of cookies sold.

Problem 18–3B
Cost of production report

Objectives 3, 4

✓ Conversion cost per equivalent unit, $3.40

Rise N' Shine Inc. roasts and packs coffee beans. The process begins by placing coffee beans into the Roasting Department. From the Roasting Department, coffee beans are then transferred to the Packing Department. The following is a partial work in process account of the Roasting Department at March 31:

ACCOUNT ***Work in Process—Roasting Department*** **ACCOUNT NO.**

Date		Item	Debit	Credit	Balance Debit	Balance Credit
Mar.	1	Bal., 10,000 units, 4/5 completed			123,000	
	31	Direct materials, 69,800 units	614,240		737,240	
	31	Direct labor	128,860		866,100	
	31	Factory overhead	100,300		966,400	
	31	Goods finished, 74,300 units		?		
	31	Bal. ? units, 1/5 completed			?	

Instructions
Prepare a cost of production report, and identify the missing amounts for the Work in Process—Roasting Department account.

Problem 18–4B
Equivalent units and related costs; cost of production report; entries

Objectives 3, 4, 5

SPREADSHEET

Daily Times Inc. manufactures newsprint by a series of four processes, all materials being introduced in the Chipping Department. From the Chipping Department, the materials pass through the Pulping, Papermaking, and Converting Departments, emerging as finished newsprint.

The balance in the account Work in Process—Converting Department was as follows on July 1:

Work in Process—Converting Department (120,000 units, 3/4 completed) $63,000

The following costs were charged to Work in Process—Converting Department during July:

✓ Transferred to finished goods, $568,700

Direct materials transferred from Papermaking Department: 750,000 units at $0.37 a unit	$277,500
Direct labor	143,150
Factory overhead	94,000

During July, 850,000 units of newsprint were completed. Work in Process—Converting Department on July 31 was 20,000 units, $\frac{1}{4}$ completed.

Instructions

1. Prepare a cost of production report for the Converting Department for July.
2. Journalize the entries for costs transferred from Papermaking to Converting and the cost of goods transferred to finished goods.
3. Discuss the uses of the cost of production report.

Problem 18–5B
Work in process account data for two months; cost of production reports

Objectives 2, 3, 4, 5

✓ 1. c. $333,256

Hearty N' Healthy Soups Inc. uses a process cost system to record the costs of processing soup, which requires a series of three processes. The inventory of Work in Process—Filling on July 1 and debits to the account during July 2000 were as follows:

Bal., 120 units, 35% completed	$ 6,300
From Cooking Dept., 7,000 units	175,000
Direct labor	95,908
Factory overhead	58,400

During July, 120 units in process on July 1 were completed, and of the 7,000 units entering the department, all were completed except 80 units that were 20% completed.

Charges to Work in Process—Filling for August were as follows:

From Cooking Dept., 7,600 units	$205,200
Direct labor	100,720
Factory overhead	52,000

During August, the units in process at the beginning of the month were completed, and of the 7,600 units entering the department, all were completed except 140 units that were $\frac{4}{5}$ completed.

Instructions

1. Enter the balance as of July 1, 2000, in a four-column account for Work in Process—Filling. Record the debits and the credits in the account for July. Construct a cost of production report, and present computations for determining (a) equivalent units of production for materials and conversion, (b) equivalent costs per unit, (c) cost of goods finished, differentiating between units started in the prior period and units started and finished in July, and (d) work in process inventory.
2. Provide the same information for August by recording the August transactions in the four-column work in process account. Construct a cost of production report, and present the August computations (a through d) listed in (1).

SPECIAL ACTIVITIES

Activity 18–1 Crunchy Cookie Company
Ethics and professional conduct in business

You are the division controller for Crunchy Cookie Company. Crunchy has introduced a new chocolate chip cookie called Chock Full of Chips, and it is a success. As a result, the product manager responsible for the launch of this new cookie was promoted to division vice-president and became your boss. A new product manager, Davis, has been brought in to replace the promoted manager. Davis notices that the Chock Full of Chips cookie uses a lot of chips, which increases the cost of the cookie. As a result, Davis has ordered that the amount of chips used in the cookies be reduced by 5%. The manager believes that a 5% reduction in chips will not adversely affect sales, but will reduce costs, and hence improve margins. The increased margins would help Davis meet profit targets for the period.

You are looking over some cost of production reports segmented by cookie line. You notice that there is a drop in the materials costs for Chock Full of Chips. On further investigation, you discover why the chip costs have declined (fewer chips). Both you and Davis report to the division vice-president, who was the original product manager for Chock Full of Chips. You are trying to decide what to do, if anything.

Discuss the options you might consider.

Activity 18–2 International Paper, Inc.

Accounting for materials costs

In papermaking operations for companies such as **International Paper, Inc.**, wet pulp is fed into paper machines, which press and dry pulp into a continuous sheet of paper. The paper is formed at very high speeds (60 mph). Once the paper is formed, the paper is rolled onto a reel at the back end of the paper machine. One of the characteristics of paper making is the creation of "broke" paper. Broke is paper that fails to satisfy quality standards and is therefore rejected for final shipment to customers. Broke is recycled back to the beginning of the process by combining the recycled paper with virgin (new) pulp material. The combination of virgin pulp and recycled broke is sent to the paper machine for papermaking. Broke is fed into this recycle process continuously from all over the facility.

In this industry it is typical to charge the papermaking operation with the cost of direct materials, which is a mixture of virgin materials and broke. Broke has a much lower cost than does virgin pulp. Therefore, the more broke in the mixture, the lower the average cost of direct materials to the department. Papermaking managers will frequently comment on the importance of broke for keeping their direct materials costs down.

a. How do you react to this accounting procedure?
b. What "hidden costs" are not considered when accounting for broke as described above?

Activity 18–3 Forever Fresh Can Company

Analyzing unit costs

Forever Fresh Can Company manufactures cans for the canned food industry. The operations manager of a can manufacturing operation wants to conduct a cost study investigating the relationship of tin content in the material (can stock) to the energy cost for enameling the cans. The enameling was necessary to prepare the cans for labeling. A higher percentage of tin content in the can stock increases the cost of material. The operations manager believed there was a relationship between the tin content and energy costs for enameling. During the analysis period the amount of tin content in the steel can stock was increased for every week, from week 1 to week 6. The following operating reports were available from the controller:

	Week 1	Week 2	Week 3	Week 4	Week 5	Week 6
Energy	$ 1,300	$ 2,880	$ 2,420	$ 1,400	$ 1,620	$ 1,500
Materials	1,200	3,000	2,860	1,890	2,520	2,900
Total cost	$ 2,500	$ 5,880	$ 5,280	$ 3,290	$ 4,140	$ 4,400
Units produced	÷10,000	÷24,000	÷22,000	÷14,000	÷18,000	÷20,000
Cost per unit	$ 0.250	$ 0.245	$ 0.240	$ 0.235	$ 0.230	$ 0.220

Differences in materials unit costs were entirely related to the amount of tin content.

Interpret this information and report to the operations manager your recommendations with respect to tin content.

Activity 18–4 Winner Paper Company

Decision making

Alex Greenbar, plant manager of Winner Paper Company's papermaking mill, was looking over the cost of production reports for October and November for the Papermaking Department. The reports revealed the following:

	October	November
Pulp and chemicals	$300,000	$307,000
Conversion cost	150,000	153,000
Total cost	$450,000	$460,000
Number of tons	÷ 625	÷ 575
Cost per ton	$ 720	$ 800

Alex was concerned about the growth in the cost per ton from the output of the department. As a result, he asked the plant controller to perform a study to help explain these results. The controller, Alicia Bond, began the analysis by performing some interviews of key plant personnel in order to understand what the problem might be. Excerpts from an interview with Niles Gilbert, a paper machine operator, follow:

Niles: We have two papermaking machines in the department. I have no data, but I think paper machine 1 is applying too much pulp, and thus is wasting both conversion and materials resources. We haven't had repairs on paper machine 1 in a while. Maybe this is the problem.

Alicia: How does too much pulp result in wasted resources?

Niles: Well, you see, if too much pulp is applied, then we will waste pulp material. The customer will not pay for the extra weight. Thus, we just lose that amount of material. Also, when there is too much pulp, the machine must be slowed down in order to complete the drying process. This results in a waste of conversion costs.

Alicia: Do you have any other suspicions?

Niles: Well, as you know, we have two products—red paper and blue paper. They are identical except for the color. The color is added to the paper-making process in the paper machine. I think that during November these two color papers have been behaving very differently. I don't have any data, but it just seems as though the amount of waste associated with the red paper has increased.

Alicia: Why is this?

Niles: I understand that there has been a change in specifications for the red paper near the beginning of November. This change could be causing the machines to run poorly when making red paper. If this is the case, the cost per ton would increase for red paper.

Alicia also asked for a computer printout providing greater detail on November's operating results.

Computer run: 42
December 4
Requested by: Alicia Bond

Papermaking Department—November detail

Paper Machine	Color	Materials Costs	Conversion Costs	Tons
1	Red	35,800	17,400	60
1	Blue	41,700	21,200	70
1	Red	44,600	22,500	75
1	Blue	36,100	18,100	60
2	Red	38,300	18,800	80
2	Blue	41,300	19,900	85
2	Red	35,600	18,100	75
2	Blue	33,600	17,000	70
Total		307,000	153,000	575

Assuming that you're Alicia Bond, write a memo to Alex Greenbar with a recommendation to management. You should analyze the November data to determine whether the paper machine or the paper color explains the increase in the unit cost from October. Include any supporting schedules that are appropriate.

Activity 18–5
Into the Real World
Process costing companies

GROUP ACTIVITY

The following categories represent typical process manufacturing industries.

Beverages	Metals
Chemicals	Petroleum refining
Food	Pharmaceuticals
Forest and paper products	Soap and cosmetics

In each category, identify one company (following your instructor's specific instructions) and determine the following:

1. Typical products manufactured by the selected company, including brand names.
2. Typical raw materials used by the selected company.
3. Types of processes used by the selected company.

Use annual reports, the Internet, or library resources in doing this activity.

ANSWERS TO SELF-EXAMINATION QUESTIONS

Matching

1. H 2. I 3. C 4. D 5. B 6. A 7. K 8. F 9. E

Multiple Choice

1. **C** The process cost system is most appropriate for a business where manufacturing is conducted by continuous operations and involves a series of uniform production processes, such as the processing of crude oil (answer C). The job order cost system is most appropriate for a business where the product is made to customer's specifications, such as custom furniture manufacturing (answer A), commercial building construction (answer B), or automobile repair shop (answer D).
2. **A** The total pounds transferred to finished goods (23,000) are the 2,000 in-process pounds at the beginning of the period plus the number of pounds started and completed during the month, 21,000 (24,000 − 3,000). Answer B incorrectly assumes that the beginning inventory is not transferred during the month. Answer C assumes that all 24,000 pounds started during the month are transferred to finished goods, instead of only the portion started and completed. Answer D incorrectly adds all the numbers together.
3. **B** The number of units that could have been produced from start to finish during a period is termed equivalent units. The 4,875 equivalent units (answer B) is determined as follows:

To process units in inventory on May 1 (1,000 × ¼)	250
To process units started and completed in May (5,500 units − 1,000 units)	4,500
To process units in inventory on May 31 (500 units × ¼)	125
Equivalent units of production in May	4,875

4. **A** The conversion costs (direct labor and factory overhead) totaling $48,750 are divided by the number of equivalent units (4,875) to determine the unit conversion cost of $10 (answer A).
5. **C** The electricity costs have increased, and maintenance costs have decreased. Answer C would be a reasonable explanation for these results. The total costs, materials costs, and costs per unit do not reveal any type of pattern over the time period. In fact, the materials costs have stayed at exactly $2.00 per pound over the time period. This demonstrates that aggregated numbers can sometimes hide underlying information that can be used to improve the process.

19

Cost Behavior and Cost-Volume-Profit Analysis

Setting *the* STAGE

What are the costs of operating your car? You will normally pay a license plate (tag) fee once a year. This cost does not change, regardless of the number of miles you drive. On the other hand, the total amount you spend on gasoline during the year changes on a day-to-day basis as you drive. The more you drive, the more you spend on gasoline.

How does such operating cost information affect you? Information on how your car's operating costs behave could be relevant in planning a summer vacation. For example, you might be trying to decide between taking an airline flight or driving your car to your vacation destination. In this case, your license plate fee and annual car insurance costs will not change, regardless of whether you drive your car or fly. Thus, these costs would not affect your decision. However, the estimated cost of gasoline and routine maintenance would affect your decision.

As in operating your car, all of the costs of operating a business do not behave in the same way. In this chapter, we discuss commonly used methods for classifying costs according to how they change. We also discuss how management uses cost-volume-profit analysis as a tool in making decisions.

objectives

After studying this chapter, you should be able to:

1. Classify costs by their behavior as variable costs, fixed costs, or mixed costs.
2. Compute the contribution margin, the contribution margin ratio, and the unit contribution margin, and explain how they may be useful to managers.
3. Using the unit contribution margin, determine the break-even point and the volume necessary to achieve a target profit.
4. Using a cost-volume-profit chart and a profit-volume chart, determine the break-even point and the volume necessary to achieve a target profit.
5. Calculate the break-even point for a business selling more than one product.
6. Compute the margin of safety and the operating leverage, and explain how managers use these concepts.
7. List the assumptions underlying cost-volume-profit analysis.

Cost Behavior

OBJECTIVE 1

Classify costs by their behavior as variable costs, fixed costs, or mixed costs.

Knowing how costs behave is useful to management for a variety of purposes. For example, knowing how costs behave allows managers to predict profits as sales and production volumes change. Knowing how costs behave is also useful for estimating costs. Estimated costs, in turn, affect a variety of management decisions, such as whether to use excess machine capacity to produce and sell a product at a reduced price.

Cost behavior refers to the manner in which a cost changes as a related activity changes. To understand cost behavior, two factors must be considered. First, we must identify the activities that are thought to cause the cost to be incurred. Such activities are called **activity bases** (or **activity drivers**). Second, we must specify the range of activity over which the changes in the cost are of interest. This range of activity is called the **relevant range**.

To illustrate, hospital administrators must plan and control hospital food costs. To fully understand why food costs change, the activity that causes cost to be incurred must be identified. In the case of food costs, the feeding of patients is a major cause of these costs. The number of patients *treated* by the hospital would not be a good activity base, since some patients are outpatients who do not stay in the hospital. The number of patients who *stay* in the hospital, however, is a good activity base for studying food costs. Once the proper activity base is identified, food costs can then be analyzed over the range of the number of patients who normally stay in the hospital (the relevant range).

Three of the most common classifications of cost behavior are variable costs, fixed costs, and mixed costs. We discuss each of these cost classifications next.

Variable Costs

When the level of activity is measured in units produced, direct materials and direct labor costs are generally classified as variable costs. **Variable costs** are costs that vary in total in proportion to changes in the level of activity. For example, assume that Jason Inc. produces stereo sound systems under the brand name of J-Sound. The parts for the stereo systems are purchased from outside suppliers for $10 per unit and are assembled in Jason Inc.'s Waterloo plant. The direct materials costs for Model JS-12 for the relevant range of 5,000 to 30,000 units of production are shown below.

Number of Units of Model JS-12 Produced	Direct Materials Cost per Unit	Total Direct Materials Cost
5,000 units	$10	$ 50,000
10,000	10	100,000
15,000	10	150,000
20,000	10	200,000
25,000	10	250,000
30,000	10	300,000

Variable costs are the same per unit, while the total variable cost changes in proportion to changes in the activity base. For Model JS-12, for example, the direct materials cost for 10,000 units ($100,000) is twice the direct materials cost for 5,000 units ($50,000). The total direct materials cost varies in proportion to the number of units produced because the direct materials cost per unit ($10) is the same for all levels of production. Thus, producing 20,000 additional units of JS-12 will increase the direct materials cost by $200,000 (20,000 × $10), producing 25,000 additional units will increase the materials cost by $250,000, and so on.

Exhibit 1 illustrates how the variable costs for direct materials for Model JS-12 behave in total and on a per-unit basis as production changes.

EXHIBIT 1 Variable Cost Graphs

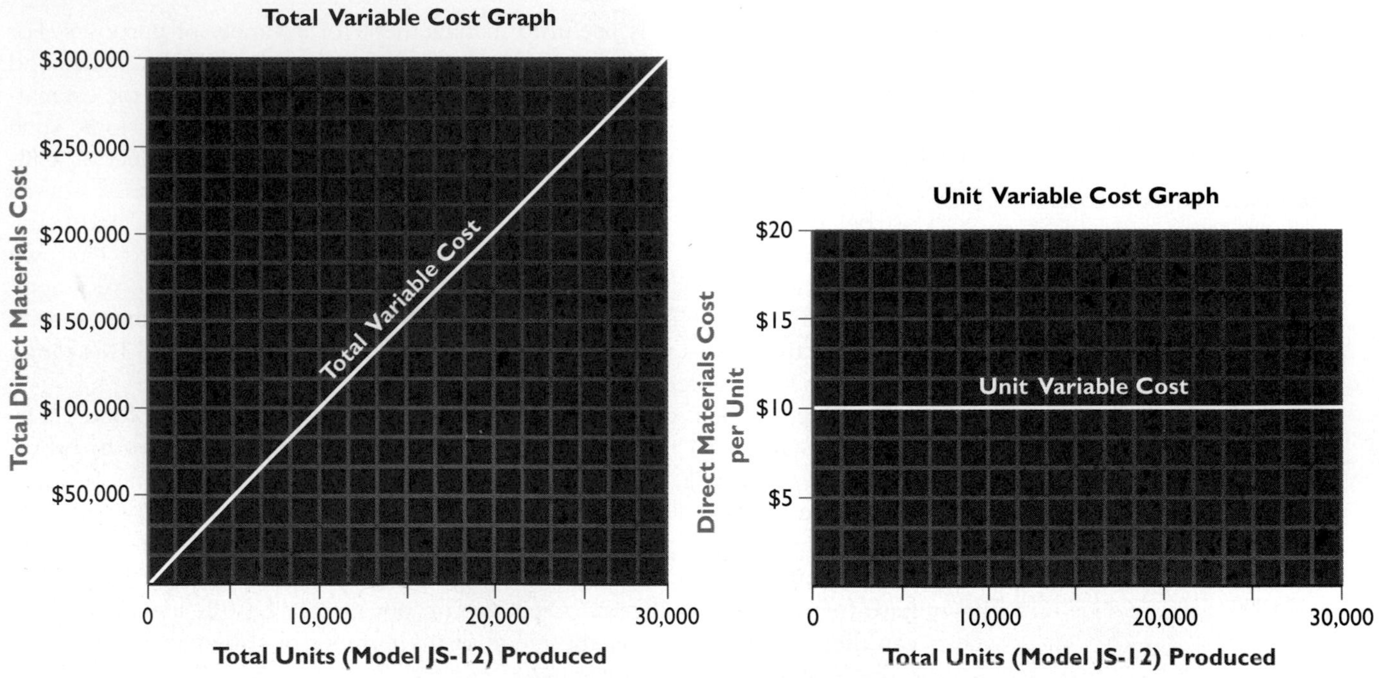

There are a variety of activity bases used by managers for evaluating cost behavior. The list below provides some examples, along with their related cost categories for various types of businesses.

Type of Business	Cost Category	Activity Base
University	Faculty salaries	Number of classes
Passenger airline	Fuel	Number of miles flown
Manufacturing	Direct materials	Number of units produced
Hospital	Nurse wages	Number of patients
Hotel	Maid wages	Number of guests
Bank	Teller wages	Number of banking transactions
Insurance	Claim processing salaries	Number of claims

Fixed Costs

When units produced is the measure of activity, examples of fixed costs include straight-line depreciation of factory equipment, insurance on factory plant and equipment, and salaries of factory supervisors. **Fixed costs** are costs that remain the same in total dollar amount as the level of activity changes.

To illustrate, assume that Minton Inc. manufactures, bottles, and distributes La Fleur Perfume at its Los Angeles plant. The production supervisor at the Los Angeles plant is Jane Sovissi, who is paid a salary of $75,000 per year. The relevant range of activity for a year is 50,000 to 300,000 bottles of perfume. Sovissi's salary is a fixed cost that does not vary with the number of units produced. Regardless of the number of bottles produced within the range of 50,000 to 300,000 bottles, Sovissi receives a salary of $75,000.

Although the total fixed cost remains the same as the number of bottles produced changes, the fixed cost per bottle changes. As more bottles are produced, the total fixed costs are spread over a larger number of bottles, and thus the fixed cost per bottle decreases. This relationship is shown below for Jane Sovissi's $75,000 salary.

Number of Bottles of Perfume Produced	Total Salary for Jane Sovissi	Salary per Bottle of Perfume Produced
50,000 bottles	$75,000	$1.500
100,000	75,000	0.750
150,000	75,000	0.500
200,000	75,000	0.375
250,000	75,000	0.300
300,000	75,000	0.250

Exhibit 2 illustrates how the fixed cost of Jane Sovissi's salary behaves in total and on a per-unit basis as production changes.

EXHIBIT 2 Fixed Cost Graphs

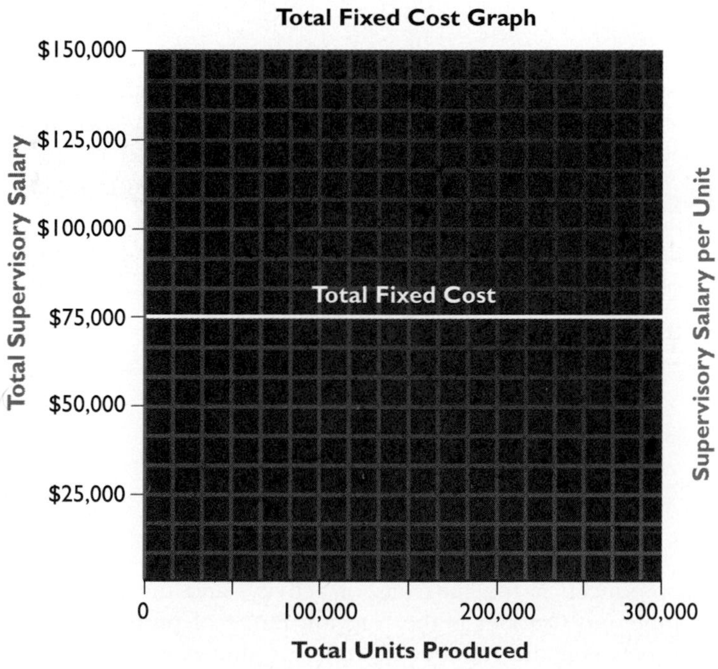

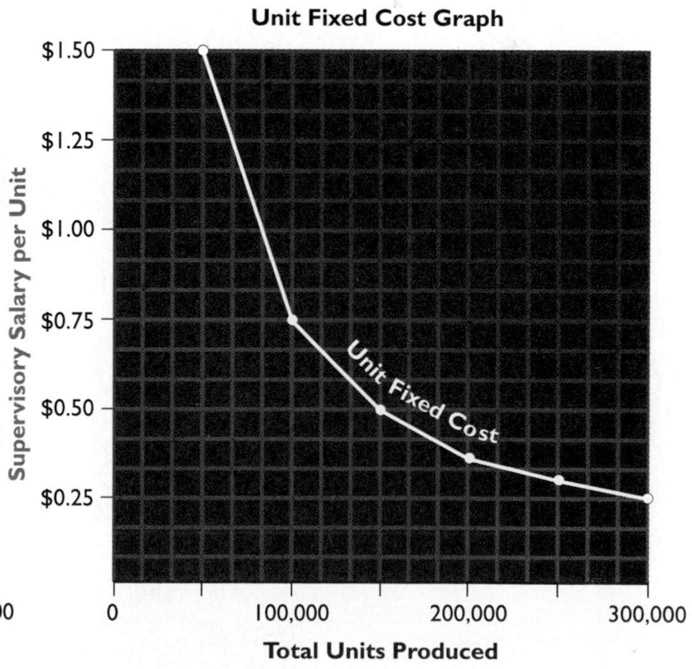

Mixed Costs

A **mixed cost** has characteristics of both a variable and a fixed cost. For example, over one range of activity, the total mixed cost may remain the same. It thus behaves as a fixed cost. Over another range of activity, the mixed cost may change in proportion to changes in the level of activity. It thus behaves as a variable cost. Mixed costs are sometimes called *semivariable* or *semifixed costs.*

To illustrate, assume that Simpson Inc. manufactures sails, using rented machinery. The rental charges are $15,000 per year, plus $1 for each machine hour used over 10,000 hours. If the machinery is used 8,000 hours, the total rental charge is $15,000. If the machinery is used 20,000 hours, the total rental charge is $25,000 [$15,000 + (10,000 hours × $1)], and so on. Thus, if the level of activity is measured in machine hours and the relevant range is 0 to 40,000 hours, the rental charges are a fixed cost up to 10,000 hours and a variable cost thereafter. This mixed cost behavior is shown graphically in Exhibit 3.

EXHIBIT 3
Mixed Costs

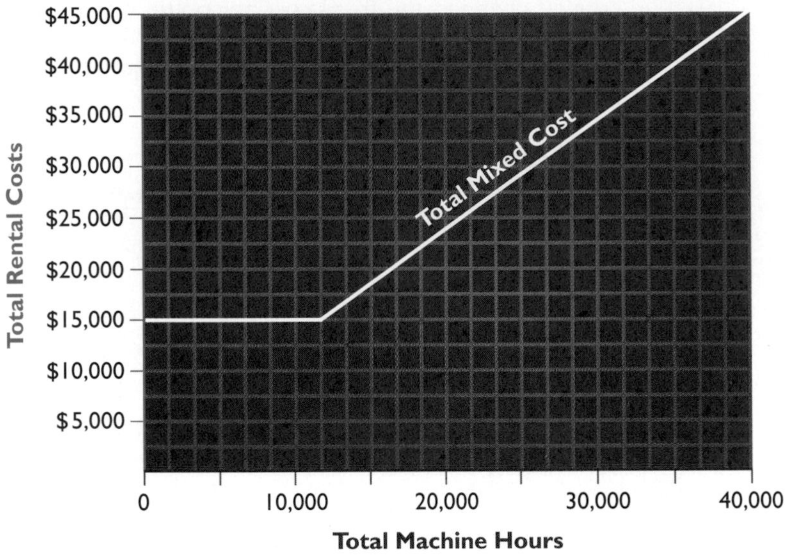

In analyses, mixed costs are usually separated into their fixed and variable components. The **high-low method** is a cost estimation technique that may be used for this purpose.[1] The high-low method uses the highest and lowest activity levels and their related costs to estimate the variable cost per unit and the fixed cost component of mixed costs.

To illustrate, assume that the Equipment Maintenance Department of Kason Inc. incurred the following costs during the past five months:

	Production	Total Cost
June	1,000 units	$45,550
July	1,500	52,000
August	2,100	61,500
September	1,800	57,500
October	750	41,250

The number of units produced is the measure of activity, and the number of units produced between June and October is the relevant range of production. For Kason Inc., the difference between the number of units produced and the differ-

[1] Other methods of estimating costs, such as the scattergraph method and the least squares method, are discussed in cost accounting textbooks.

ence between the total cost at the highest and lowest levels of production are as follows:

	Production	Total Cost
Highest level	2,100 units	$61,500
Lowest level	750	41,250
Difference	1,350 units	$20,250

Since the total fixed cost does not change with changes in volume of production, the $20,250 difference in the total cost is the change in the total variable cost. Hence, dividing the difference in the total cost by the difference in production provides an estimate of the variable cost per unit. For Kason Inc., this estimate is $15, as shown below.

$$\textbf{Variable cost per unit} = \frac{\textbf{Difference in total cost}}{\textbf{Difference in production}}$$

$$\text{Variable cost per unit} = \frac{\$20{,}250}{1{,}350 \text{ units}} = \$15$$

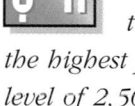

The manufacturing cost at the highest production level of 2,500 units is $125,000. The manufacturing cost at the lowest production level of 1,000 units is $80,000. Using the high-low method, what are (a) the variable cost per unit and (b) the total fixed cost?

(a) $30 per unit [($125,000 − $80,000) ÷ (2,500 − 1,000)]; (b) $50,000 [$125,000 − ($30 × 2,500)]

The fixed cost will be the same at both the highest and the lowest levels of production. Thus, the fixed cost can be estimated at either of these levels. This is done by subtracting the estimated total variable cost from the total cost, using the following total cost equation:

Total cost = (Variable cost per unit × Units of production) + Fixed cost

Highest level:

$61,500 = ($15 × 2,100 units) + Fixed cost
$61,500 = $31,500 + Fixed cost
$30,000 = Fixed cost

Lowest level:

$41,250 = ($15 × 750 units) + Fixed cost
$41,250 = $11,250 + Fixed cost
$30,000 = Fixed cost

The total equipment maintenance cost for Kason Inc. can thus be analyzed as a $30,000 fixed cost and a $15-per-unit variable cost. Using these amounts in the total cost equation above, the total equipment maintenance cost at other levels of production can be estimated.

Summary of Cost Behavior Concepts

Examples of common variable, fixed, and mixed costs when the number of units produced is the activity base are:

Variable Cost	Fixed Cost	Mixed Cost
Direct materials	Depreciation expense	Quality Control Department salaries
Direct labor	Property taxes	Purchasing Department salaries
Electricity expense	Officer salaries	Maintenance expenses
Sales commissions	Insurance expense	Warehouse expenses

Mixed costs contain a fixed cost component that is incurred even if nothing is produced. For analyses, the fixed and variable cost components of mixed costs should be separated.

The following table summarizes the cost behavior attributes of variable costs and fixed costs:

	Effect of Changing Activity Level	
Cost	**Total Amount**	**Per-Unit Amount**
Variable	Increases and decreases proportionately with activity level.	Remains the same regardless of activity level.
Fixed	Remains the same regardless of activity level.	Increases and decreases inversely with activity level.

Reporting Variable and Fixed Costs

Separating costs into their variable and fixed components for reporting purposes can be useful for decision making. One method of reporting variable and fixed costs is called **variable costing** or **direct costing.** Under variable costing, only the variable manufacturing costs (direct materials, direct labor, and variable factory overhead) are included in the product cost. The fixed factory overhead is an expense of the period in which it is incurred.[2]

Cost-Volume-Profit Relationships

OBJECTIVE 2

Compute the contribution margin, the contribution margin ratio, and the unit contribution margin, and explain how they may be useful to managers.

After costs have been classified as fixed and variable, their effect on revenues, volume, and profits can be studied by using cost-volume-profit analysis. **Cost-volume-profit analysis** is the systematic examination of the relationships among selling prices, sales and production volume, costs, expenses, and profits.

Cost-volume-profit analysis provides management with useful information for decision making. For example, cost-volume-profit analysis may be used in setting selling prices, selecting the mix of products to sell, choosing among marketing strategies, and analyzing the effects of changes in costs on profits. In today's business environment, management must make such decisions quickly and accurately. As a result, the importance of cost-volume-profit analysis has increased in recent years.

Contribution Margin Concept

One relationship among cost, volume, and profit is the contribution margin. The **contribution margin** is the excess of sales revenues over variable costs. The contribution margin concept is especially useful in business planning because it gives insight into the profit potential of

BUSINESS ON STAGE

Cost Behavior and Employee Compensation

There are several methods for compensating employees, each of which has a different cost behavior. The most common form is a *wage* based on the number of hours worked. This type of compensation causes wages to be variable to the number of hours worked. Alternatively, some industries, such as the garment industry, use a *piecework* system to pay their employees. Under this type of plan, the employee is paid a given amount for each unit completed. The compensation is variable to the number of units produced. In contrast, many staff employees are paid a weekly or monthly *salary.* A salaried employee's compensation does not depend on the number of hours worked or the actual number of units produced or sold. Thus, a salary is fixed to the underlying level of production or sales. In between these two extremes are several plans that have both fixed and variable elements and, as such, are mixed costs. Examples include pay for salespeople based on a straight salary plus a *commission* based on sales. In manufacturing settings, *gain-sharing* plans are becoming very popular. Under these plans, employees receive a straight wage plus a bonus for achieving production targets or other efficiency gains. In a *profit-sharing* plan, employees receive a wage or salary plus a periodic bonus based on the profits earned by the business. Compensation plans that use variable compensation are attempting to provide employees incentives for achieving specific goals. ■

[2] The variable costing concept is discussed more fully in the appendix at the end of this chapter.

a firm. To illustrate, the income statement of Lambert Inc. in Exhibit 4 has been prepared in a contribution margin format.

EXHIBIT 4
Contribution Margin Income Statement

Sales	$1,000,000
Variable costs	600,000
Contribution margin	$ 400,000
Fixed costs	300,000
Income from operations	$ 100,000

The contribution margin of $400,000 is available to cover the fixed costs of $300,000. Once the fixed costs are covered, any remaining amount adds directly to the operating income of the company. Think of the fixed costs as a bucket and the contribution margin as water filling the bucket. Once the bucket is filled, the overflow represents operating income (income from operations). Up until the point of overflow, however, the contribution margin contributes to fixed costs (filling the bucket).

Contribution Margin Ratio

The contribution margin can also be expressed as a percentage. The **contribution margin ratio**, sometimes called the **profit-volume ratio**, indicates the percentage of each sales dollar available to cover the fixed costs and to provide operating income. For Lambert Inc., the contribution margin ratio is 40%, as computed below.

$$\text{Contribution margin ratio} = \frac{\text{Sales} - \text{Variable costs}}{\text{Sales}}$$

$$\text{Contribution margin ratio} = \frac{\$1{,}000{,}000 - \$600{,}000}{\$1{,}000{,}000} = 40\%$$

The contribution margin ratio measures the effect on operating income of an increase or a decrease in sales volume. For example, assume that the management of Lambert Inc. is studying the effect of adding $80,000 in sales orders. Multiplying the contribution margin ratio (40%) by the change in sales volume ($80,000) indicates that operating income will increase $32,000 if the additional orders are obtained. The validity of this analysis is illustrated by the following contribution margin income statement of Lambert Inc.:

Sales	$1,080,000
Variable costs ($1,080,000 × 60%)	648,000
Contribution margin ($1,080,000 × 40%)	$ 432,000
Fixed costs	300,000
Income from operations	$ 132,000

Variable costs as a percentage of sales are equal to 100% minus the contribution margin ratio. Thus, in the above income statement, the variable costs are 60% (100% − 40%) of sales, or $648,000 ($1,080,000 × 60%). The total contribution margin, $432,000, can also be computed directly by multiplying the sales by the contribution margin ratio ($1,080,000 × 40%).

In using the contribution margin ratio in analysis, factors other than sales volume, such as variable cost per unit and sales price, are assumed to remain constant. If such factors change, their effect must be considered.

The contribution margin ratio is also useful in setting business policy. For example, if the contribution margin ratio of a firm is large and production is at a level below 100% capacity, a large increase in operating income can be expected from an increase in sales volume. A firm in such a position might decide to devote more effort to sales promotion because of the large change in operating income that will result from changes in sales volume. In contrast, a firm with a small contribution margin ratio will probably want to give more attention to reducing costs before attempting to promote sales.

Unit Contribution Margin

The unit contribution margin is also useful for analyzing the profit potential of proposed projects. The **unit contribution margin** is the dollars from each unit of sales available to cover fixed costs and provide operating profits. For example, if Lambert Inc.'s unit selling price is $20 and its unit variable cost is $12, the unit contribution margin is $8 ($20 − $12).

The *contribution margin ratio* is most useful when the increase or decrease in sales volume is measured in sales dollars. The *unit contribution margin* is most useful when the increase or decrease in sales volume is measured in sales units (quantities). To illustrate, assume that Lambert Inc. sold 50,000 units. Its operating income (income from operations) is $100,000, as shown in the following contribution margin income statement:

Q&A *Sales are 20,000 units at $12 per unit, variable costs are $9 per unit, and fixed costs are $25,000. What are (a) the contribution margin ratio, (b) the unit contribution margin, and (c) the operating income?*

(a) 25% [($240,000 − $180,000) ÷ $240,000];
(b) $3 per unit ($12 − $9);
(c) $35,000 ($240,000 − $180,000 − $25,000)

Sales (50,000 units × $20)	$1,000,000
Variable costs (50,000 units × $12)	600,000
Contribution margin (50,000 units × $8)	$ 400,000
Fixed costs	300,000
Income from operations	$ 100,000

If Lambert Inc.'s sales could be increased by 15,000 units, from 50,000 units to 65,000 units, its operating income would increase by $120,000 (15,000 units × $8), as shown below.

Sales (65,000 units × $20)	$1,300,000
Variable costs (65,000 units × $12)	780,000
Contribution margin (65,000 units × $8)	$ 520,000
Fixed costs	300,000
Income from operations	$ 220,000

Unit contribution margin analyses can provide useful information for managers. The preceding illustration indicates, for example, that Lambert could spend up to $120,000 for special advertising or other product promotions to increase sales by 15,000 units.

REAL WORLD A $200-per-night room at the **Ritz Carlton** may have a variable cost, including maids' salaries, linens, towels, soap, and utilities, of only $25 per night and thus a high contribution margin per room. Likewise, the contribution margin per unit for **Microsoft** software will also be very high. The variable costs per unit include packaging, CDs, and copying costs. These costs are small relative to the price. In both these cases, the high contribution margin per unit is necessary to cover other costs. In the case of the hotel, the fixed costs for the hotel must be covered by the high contribution margin per unit, while for Microsoft, the high contribution margin is necessary to fund software development expenditures.

Mathematical Approach to Cost-Volume-Profit Analysis

OBJECTIVE 3

Using the unit contribution margin, determine the break-even point and the volume necessary to achieve a target profit.

Accountants use various approaches for expressing the relationship of costs, sales (volume), and operating income (profit). The mathematical approach is one approach that is used often in practice.

The mathematical approach to cost-volume-profit analysis uses equations (1) to determine the units of sales necessary to achieve the break-even point in operations or (2) to determine the units of sales necessary to achieve a target or desired profit. We will next describe and illustrate these equations and their use by management in profit planning.

Break-Even Point

The **break-even point** is the level of operations at which a business's revenues and expired costs are exactly equal. At break-even, a business will neither realize an operating income nor incur an operating loss. The break-even point is useful in business planning, especially when expanding or decreasing operations.

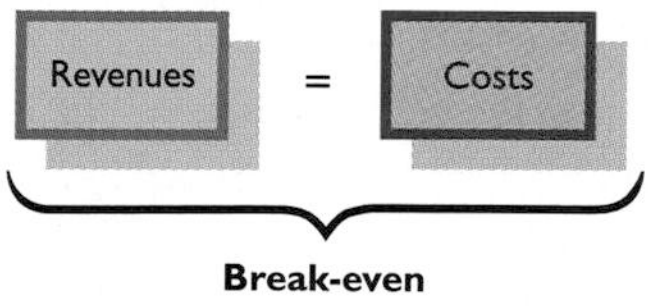

To illustrate the computation of the break-even point, assume that the fixed costs for Barker Corporation are estimated to be $90,000. The unit selling price, unit variable cost, and unit contribution margin for Barker Corporation are as follows:

Unit selling price	$25
Unit variable cost	15
Unit contribution margin	$10

The break-even point is 9,000 units, which can be computed by using the following equation:

$$\text{Break-even sales (units)} = \frac{\text{Fixed costs}}{\text{Unit contribution margin}}$$

$$\text{Break-even sales (units)} = \frac{\$90{,}000}{\$10} = 9{,}000 \text{ units}$$

The following income statement verifies the preceding computation:

Sales (9,000 units × $25)	$225,000
Variable costs (9,000 units × $15)	135,000
Contribution margin	$ 90,000
Fixed costs	90,000
Income from operations	$ 0

The break-even point is affected by changes in the fixed costs, unit variable costs, and the unit selling price. Next, we will briefly describe the effect of each of these factors on the break-even point.

Point of INTEREST

When the owner of a shopping center was asked how he was doing, he said, "My properties are *almost* fully rented." The questioner commented, "That must be pretty good." The shopping center owner responded, "Maybe so. But as you know, the profit is in the *almost*." This exchange reveals an important business principle: profit is earned only after the break-even point is reached.

Effect of Changes in Fixed Costs

Although fixed costs do not change in total with changes in the level of activity, they may

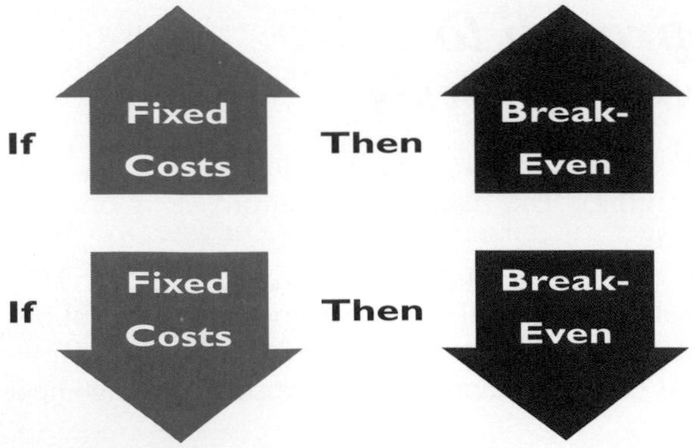

change because of other factors. For example, changes in property tax rates or factory supervisors' salaries change fixed costs. Increases in fixed costs will raise the break-even point. Likewise, decreases in fixed costs will lower the break-even point. For example, **General Motors** closed 21 plants and eliminated 74,000 jobs to lower its break-even from approximately 7 million to 5 million automobiles through the mid-1990s.

To illustrate, assume that Bishop Co. is evaluating a proposal to budget an additional $100,000 for advertising. Fixed costs before the additional advertising are estimated at $600,000, and the unit contribution margin is $20. The break-even point before the additional expense is 30,000 units, computed as follows:

$$\text{Break-even sales (units)} = \frac{\text{Fixed costs}}{\text{Unit contribution margin}}$$

$$\text{Break-even sales (units)} = \frac{\$600,000}{\$20} = 30,000 \text{ units}$$

If the additional amount is spent, the fixed costs will increase by $100,000 and the break-even point will increase to 35,000 units, computed as follows:

$$\text{Break-even sales (units)} = \frac{\text{Fixed costs}}{\text{Unit contribution margin}}$$

$$\text{Break-even sales (units)} = \frac{\$700,000}{\$20} = 35,000 \text{ units}$$

The $100,000 increase in the fixed costs requires an additional 5,000 units ($100,000 ÷ $20) of sales to break even. In other words, an increase in sales of 5,000 units is required in order to generate an additional $100,000 of total contribution margin (5,000 units × $20) to cover the increased fixed costs.

REAL WORLD

Reducing the break-even point by decreasing fixed costs is the idea behind low earth-orbiting satellite (LEOS) networks. These networks are now being developed for worldwide wireless voice and data communications by companies such as **Iridium** and **Teledesic**. LEOS are 95-pound satellites that can be launched for about one-twentieth the cost of a conventional multi-ton satellite. As a result, the number of new cellular subscribers required to break even for such a network has been estimated at one million worldwide, which is much less than would be required for a conventional satellite network.

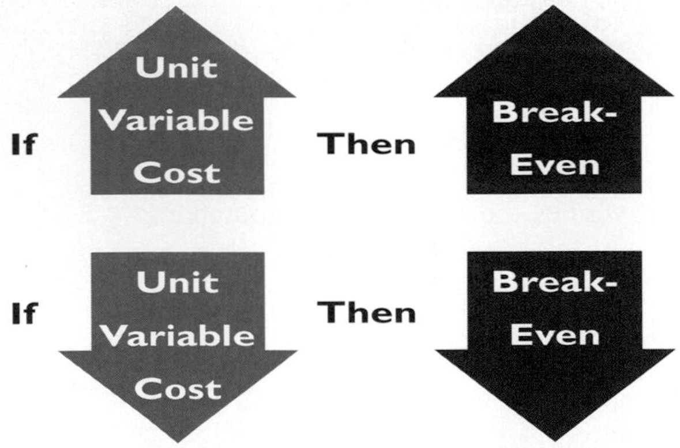

Effect of Changes in Unit Variable Costs

Although unit variable costs are not affected by changes in volume of activity, they may be affected by other factors. For example, changes in the price of direct materials and the wages for factory workers providing direct labor change unit variable costs. Increases in unit variable costs will raise the break-even point. Likewise, decreases in unit variable costs will lower the break-even point. For example, when fuel prices rise or decline, there is a direct impact on the break-even passenger load for **American Airlines**.

To illustrate, assume that Park Co. is evaluating a proposal to pay an additional 2% commission to its sales representatives as an incentive to increase sales. Fixed costs are estimated at $840,000, and the unit selling price, unit variable cost, and unit contribution margin before the additional 2% commission are as follows:

Unit selling price	$250
Unit variable cost	145
Unit contribution margin	$105

The break-even point is 8,000 units, computed as follows:

Basic cable TV services, such as **CNN**, **E!**, and **A&E**, receive over 80% of their revenues from subscriber fees, rather than advertising. The fees earned per month per subscriber will have an impact on the number of subscribers required to break even. For example, CNN earns approximately 25 cents per subscriber per month, while Entertainment TV (E!) earns only 11 cents per subscriber per month. If all else were equal, CNN would have a lower break-even number of subscribers than would E! due to this difference.

$$\text{Break-even sales (units)} = \frac{\text{Fixed costs}}{\text{Unit contribution margin}}$$

$$\text{Break-even sales (units)} = \frac{\$840{,}000}{\$105} = 8{,}000 \text{ units}$$

If the sales commission proposal is adopted, variable costs will increase by $5 per unit ($250 × 2%). This increase in the variable costs will decrease the unit contribution margin by $5 (from $105 to $100). Thus, the break-even point is raised to 8,400 units, computed as follows:

$$\text{Break-even sales (units)} = \frac{\text{Fixed costs}}{\text{Unit contribution margin}}$$

$$\text{Break-even sales (units)} = \frac{\$840{,}000}{\$100} = 8{,}400 \text{ units}$$

At the original break-even point of 8,000 units, the new unit contribution margin of $100 would provide only $800,000 to cover fixed costs of $840,000. Thus, an additional 400 units of sales will be required in order to provide the additional $40,000 (400 units × $100) contribution margin necessary to break even.

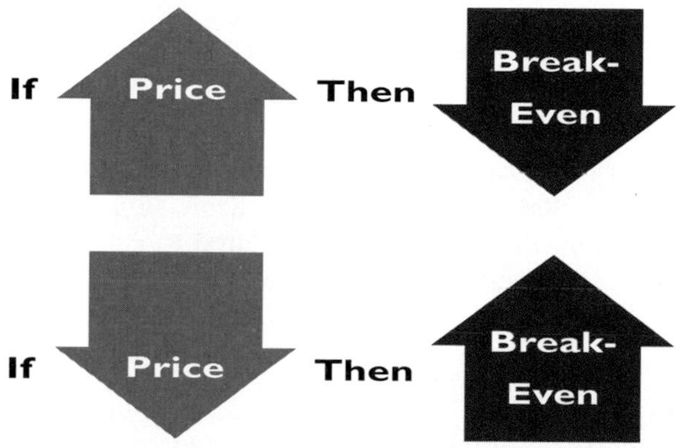

Effect of Changes in the Unit Selling Price

Increases in the unit selling price will lower the break-even point, while decreases in the unit selling price will raise the break-even point. Thus, for example, computer price reductions for **Apple Computers** increased its break-even point.

To illustrate, assume that Graham Co. is evaluating a proposal to increase the unit selling price of its product from $50 to $60. The following data have been gathered:

	Current	Proposed
Unit selling price	$50	$60
Unit variable cost	30	30
Unit contribution margin	$20	$30
Total fixed costs	$600,000	$600,000

The selling price for a product is $60 per unit. The variable cost is $35 per unit, while fixed costs are $80,000. What are the following amounts: (a) the break-even point in sales units and (b) the break-even point if the selling price were increased to $67 per unit?

(a) 3,200 units [$80,000 ÷ ($60 − $35)]; (b) 2,500 units [$80,000 ÷ ($67 − $35)]

The break-even point based on the current selling price is 30,000 units, computed as follows:

$$\text{Break-even sales (units)} = \frac{\text{Fixed costs}}{\text{Unit contribution margin}}$$

$$\text{Break-even sales (units)} = \frac{\$600{,}000}{\$20} = 30{,}000 \text{ units}$$

If the selling price is increased by $10 per unit, the break-even point is decreased to 20,000 units, computed as follows:

$$\text{Break-even sales (units)} = \frac{\text{Fixed costs}}{\text{Unit contribution margin}}$$

$$\text{Break-even sales (units)} = \frac{\$600{,}000}{\$30} = 20{,}000 \text{ units}$$

The airline and hotel portions of the travel industry use break-even analysis extensively. In the hotel industry, individual hotels determine break-even occupancy over a span of time. Occupancy is the percentage of available room space that has been used by guests. Depending on room rates, a typical hotel will need to exceed 60% occupancy to remain profitable. Airlines also determine the break-even passenger load for particular routes. Thus, for example, an airline may determine how many seats must be sold in order for a flight from New York to Chicago to be profitable. In the highly competitive airline industry, break-even passenger loads are approaching 70%–80% on some routes.

The increase of $10 per unit in the selling price increases the unit contribution margin by $10. Thus, the break-even point decreases by 10,000 units (from 30,000 units to 20,000 units).

Summary of Effects of Changes on Break-Even Point

The break-even point in sales (units) moves in the same direction as changes in the variable cost per unit and fixed costs. In contrast, the break-even point in sales (units) moves in the opposite direction to changes in the sales price per unit. A summary of the impact of these changes on the break-even point in sales (units) is shown below.

Type of Change	Direction of Change	Effect of Change on Break-Even Sales (Units)
Fixed cost	Increase	Increase
	Decrease	Decrease
Variable cost per unit	Increase	Increase
	Decrease	Decrease
Unit sales price	Increase	Decrease
	Decrease	Increase

Target Profit

At the break-even point, sales and costs are exactly equal. However, the break-even point is not the goal of most businesses. Rather, managers seek to maximize profits. By modifying the break-even equation, the sales volume required to earn a target or desired amount of profit may be estimated. For this purpose, a factor for target profit is added to the break-even equation as shown below.

$$\text{Sales (units)} = \frac{\text{Fixed costs} + \text{Target profit}}{\text{Unit contribution margin}}$$

To illustrate, assume that fixed costs are estimated at $200,000, and the desired profit is $100,000. The unit selling price, unit variable cost, and unit contribution margin are as follows:

Unit selling price	$75
Unit variable cost	45
Unit contribution margin	$30

The sales volume necessary to earn the target profit of $100,000 is 10,000 units, computed as follows:

$$\text{Sales (units)} = \frac{\text{Fixed costs} + \text{Target profit}}{\text{Unit contribution margin}}$$

$$\text{Sales (units)} = \frac{\$200{,}000 + \$100{,}000}{\$30} = 10{,}000 \text{ units}$$

The following income statement verifies this computation:

Sales (10,000 units × $75)	$750,000	
Variable costs (10,000 units × $45)	450,000	
Contribution margin (10,000 units × $30)	$300,000	
Fixed costs	200,000	
Income from operations	$100,000	← Target profit

The sales price is $140 per unit, variable costs are $60 per unit, and fixed costs are $240,000. What would be (a) the break-even point in sales units and (b) the break-even point in sales units if a target profit of $50,000 is desired?

(a) 3,000 units [$240,000 ÷ ($140 − $60)]; (b) 3,625 units [($240,000 + $50,000) ÷ ($140 − $60)]

Graphic Approach to Cost-Volume-Profit Analysis

OBJECTIVE 4

Using a cost-volume-profit chart and a profit-volume chart, determine the break-even point and the volume necessary to achieve a target profit.

Cost-volume-profit analysis can be presented graphically as well as in equation form. Many managers prefer the graphic format because the operating profit or loss for different levels of sales can readily be determined. Next, we describe two graphic approaches that managers find useful.

Cost-Volume-Profit (Break-Even) Chart

A **cost-volume-profit chart**, sometimes called a **break-even chart**, may assist management in understanding relationships among costs, sales, and operating profit or loss. To illustrate, the cost-volume-profit chart in Exhibit 5 is based on the following data:

Unit selling price	$50
Unit variable cost	30
Unit contribution margin	$20
Total fixed costs	$100,000

EXHIBIT 5
Cost-Volume-Profit Chart

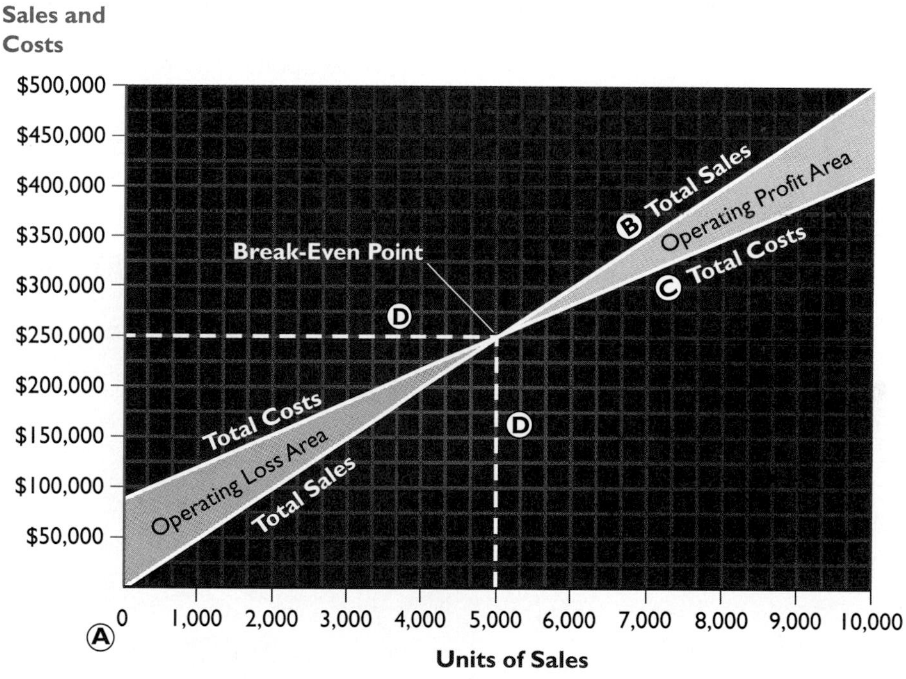

We constructed the cost-volume-profit chart in Exhibit 5 as follows:

A. Volume expressed in units of sales is indicated along the horizontal axis. The range of volume shown on the horizontal axis should reflect the *relevant range* in which the business expects to operate. Dollar amounts representing total sales and costs are indicated along the vertical axis.

B. A sales line is plotted by beginning at zero on the left corner of the graph. A second point is determined by multiplying any units of sales on the horizontal axis by the unit sales price of $50. For example, for 10,000 units of sales, the total sales would be $500,000 (10,000 units × $50). The sales line is drawn upward to the right from zero through the $500,000 point.

C. A cost line is plotted by beginning with total fixed costs, $100,000, on the vertical axis. A second point is determined by multiplying any units of sales on the horizontal axis by the unit variable costs and adding the fixed costs. For example, for 10,000 units of sales, the total estimated costs would be $400,000 [(10,000 units × $30) + $100,000]. The cost line is drawn upward to the right from $100,000 on the vertical axis through the $400,000 point.

D. Horizontal and vertical lines are drawn at the point of intersection of the sales and cost lines, which is the break-even point, and the areas representing operating profit and operating loss are identified.

In Exhibit 5, the dotted lines drawn from the point of intersection of the total sales line and the total cost line identify the break-even point in total sales dollars and units. The break-even point is $250,000 of sales, which represents a sales volume of 5,000 units. Operating profits will be earned when sales levels are to the right of the break-even point (operating profit area). Operating losses will be incurred when sales levels are to the left of the break-even point (operating loss area).

Changes in the unit selling price, total fixed costs, and unit variable costs can be analyzed by using a cost-volume-profit chart. Using the data in Exhibit 5, assume that a proposal to reduce fixed costs by $20,000 is to be evaluated. In this case, the total fixed costs would be $80,000 ($100,000 − $20,000). As shown in Exhibit 6, the total cost line should be redrawn, starting at the $80,000 point (total fixed costs) on the vertical axis. A second point is determined by multiplying any units of sales on the horizontal axis by the unit variable costs and adding the fixed costs. For example, for 10,000 units of sales, the total estimated costs would be $380,000 [(10,000 units × $30) + $80,000]. The cost line is drawn upward to the right from $80,000 on the vertical axis through the $380,000 point. The revised cost-volume-profit chart in Exhibit 6 indicates that the break-even point decreases to $200,000 or 4,000 units of sales.

EXHIBIT 6
Revised Cost-Volume-Profit Chart

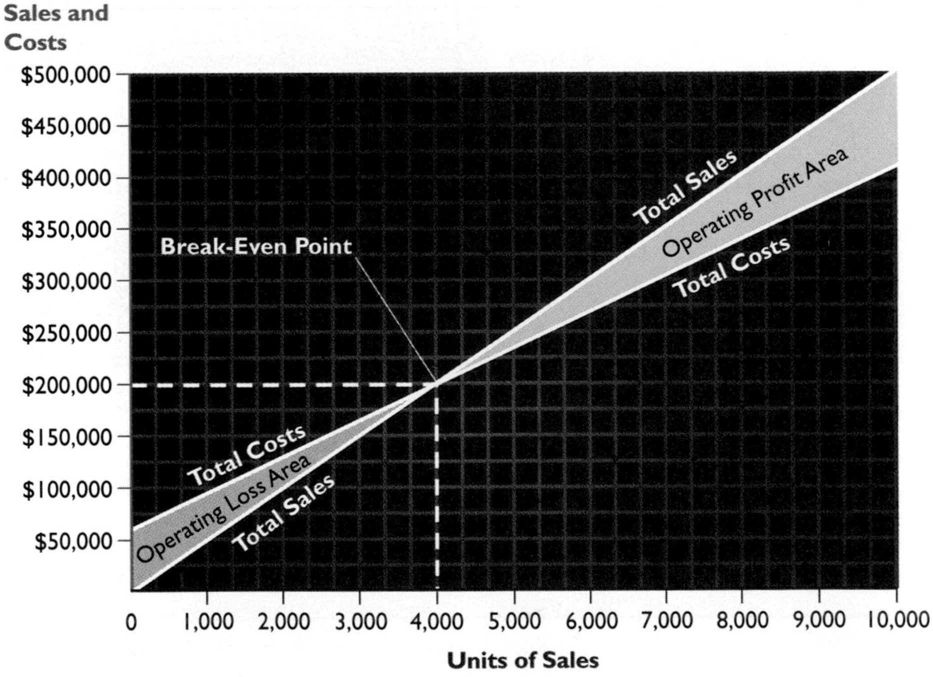

Profit-Volume Chart

Another graphic approach to cost-volume-profit analysis, the **profit-volume chart**, focuses on profits. This is in contrast to the cost-volume-profit chart, which focuses on sales and costs. The profit-volume chart plots only the difference between total sales and total costs (or profits). In this way, the profit-volume chart allows managers to determine the operating profit (or loss) for various levels of operations.

To illustrate, assume that the profit-volume chart in Exhibit 7 is based on the same data as used in Exhibit 5. These data are as follows:

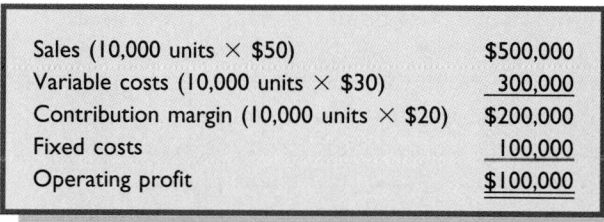

Unit selling price	$50
Unit variable cost	30
Unit contribution margin	$20
Total fixed costs	$100,000

The maximum operating loss is equal to the fixed costs of $100,000. Assuming that the maximum unit sales within the relevant range is 10,000 units, the maximum operating profit is $100,000, computed as follows:

Sales (10,000 units × $50)	$500,000
Variable costs (10,000 units × $30)	300,000
Contribution margin (10,000 units × $20)	$200,000
Fixed costs	100,000
Operating profit	$100,000

EXHIBIT 7
Profit-Volume Chart

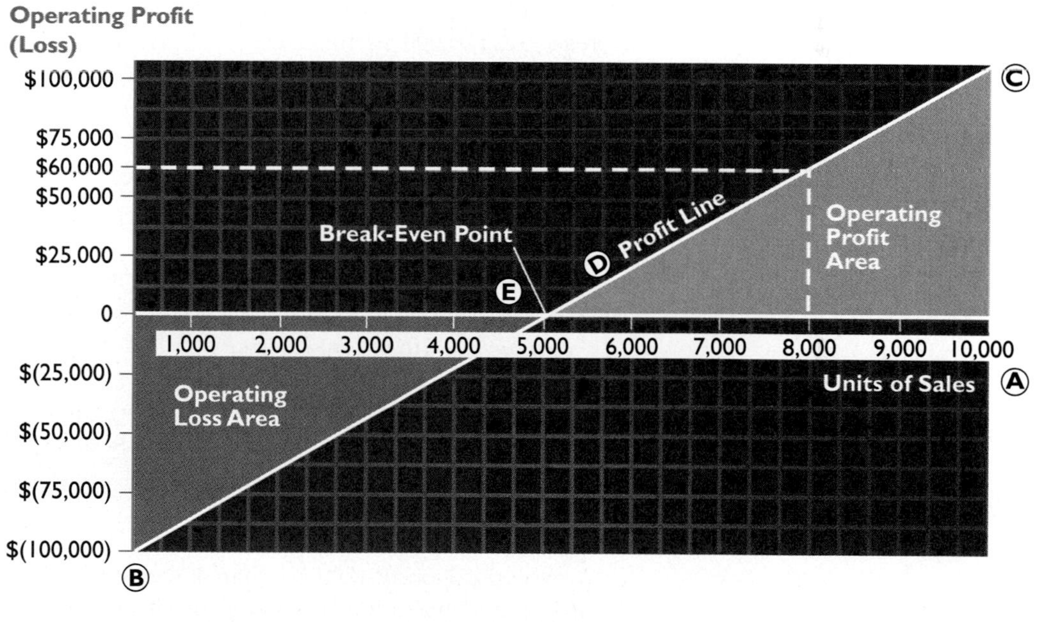

We constructed the profit-volume chart in Exhibit 7 as follows:

A. Volume expressed in units of sales is indicated along the horizontal axis. The range of volume shown on the horizontal axis should reflect the *relevant range* in which the business expects to operate. In this illustration, the maximum number of sales units within the relevant range is assumed to be 10,000 units. Dollar amounts indicating operating profits and losses are shown along the vertical axis.

B. A point representing the maximum operating loss is plotted on the vertical axis at the left. This loss is equal to the total fixed costs at the zero level of sales.

C. A point representing the maximum operating profit within the relevant range is plotted on the right.

D. A diagonal profit line is drawn connecting the maximum operating loss point with the maximum operating profit point.

E. The profit line intersects the horizontal axis at the break-even point expressed in units of sales, and the areas indicating operating profit and loss are identified.

In Exhibit 7, the break-even point is 5,000 units of sales, which is equal to total sales of $250,000 (5,000 units × $50). Operating profit will be earned when sales levels are to the right of the break-even point (operating profit area). Operating losses will be incurred when sales levels are to the left of the break-even point (operating loss area). For example, at sales of 8,000 units, an operating profit of $60,000 will be earned, as shown in Exhibit 7.

The effect of changes in the unit selling price, total fixed costs, and unit variable costs on profit can be analyzed using a profit-volume chart. To illustrate, using the data in Exhibit 7, we will evaluate the effect on profit of an increase of $20,000 in fixed costs. In this case, the total fixed costs would be $120,000 ($100,000 + $20,000), and the maximum operating loss would also be $120,000. If the maximum sales within the relevant range is 10,000 units, the maximum operating profit would be $80,000, computed as follows:

REAL WORLD

The break-even point for some NBA basketball franchises is the number of tickets sold during the regular season. The owner of the **Los Angeles Lakers** has stated that the financial goal of the organization is to break even for the regular season and to make their profit during the playoffs. The playoffs provide additional sold-out home games at higher ticket prices as well as additional TV revenues. The deeper the team goes into the playoffs, the more profit earned. The **San Antonio Spurs** lost $2.58 million during the regular 1995–1996 season, but managed to break even due to ticket sales for playoffs. They earned a profit of $4.9 million the year before because they went deeper into the playoffs and earned $4.36 million in playoff income.

Sales (10,000 units × $50)	$500,000	
Variable costs (10,000 units × $30)	300,000	
Contribution margin (10,000 units × $20)	$200,000	
Fixed costs	120,000	
Operating profit	$ 80,000	← Maximum profit

A revised profit-volume chart is constructed by plotting the maximum operating loss and maximum operating profit points and drawing the revised profit line. The original and the revised profit-volume charts are shown in Exhibit 8.

The revised profit-volume chart indicates that the break-even point is 6,000 units of sales. This is equal to total sales of $300,000 (6,000 units × $50). The operating loss area of the chart has increased, while the operating profit area has decreased under the proposed change in fixed costs.

Use of Computers in Cost-Volume-Profit Analysis

With computers, the graphic approach as well as the mathematical approach to cost-volume-profit analysis are becoming increasingly easy to use. Managers can vary assumptions regarding selling prices, costs, and volume and can immediately see the effects of each change on the break-even point and profit. Such an analysis is called a **"what if" analysis** or **sensitivity analysis**.

EXHIBIT 8
Original Profit-Volume Chart and Revised Profit-Volume Chart

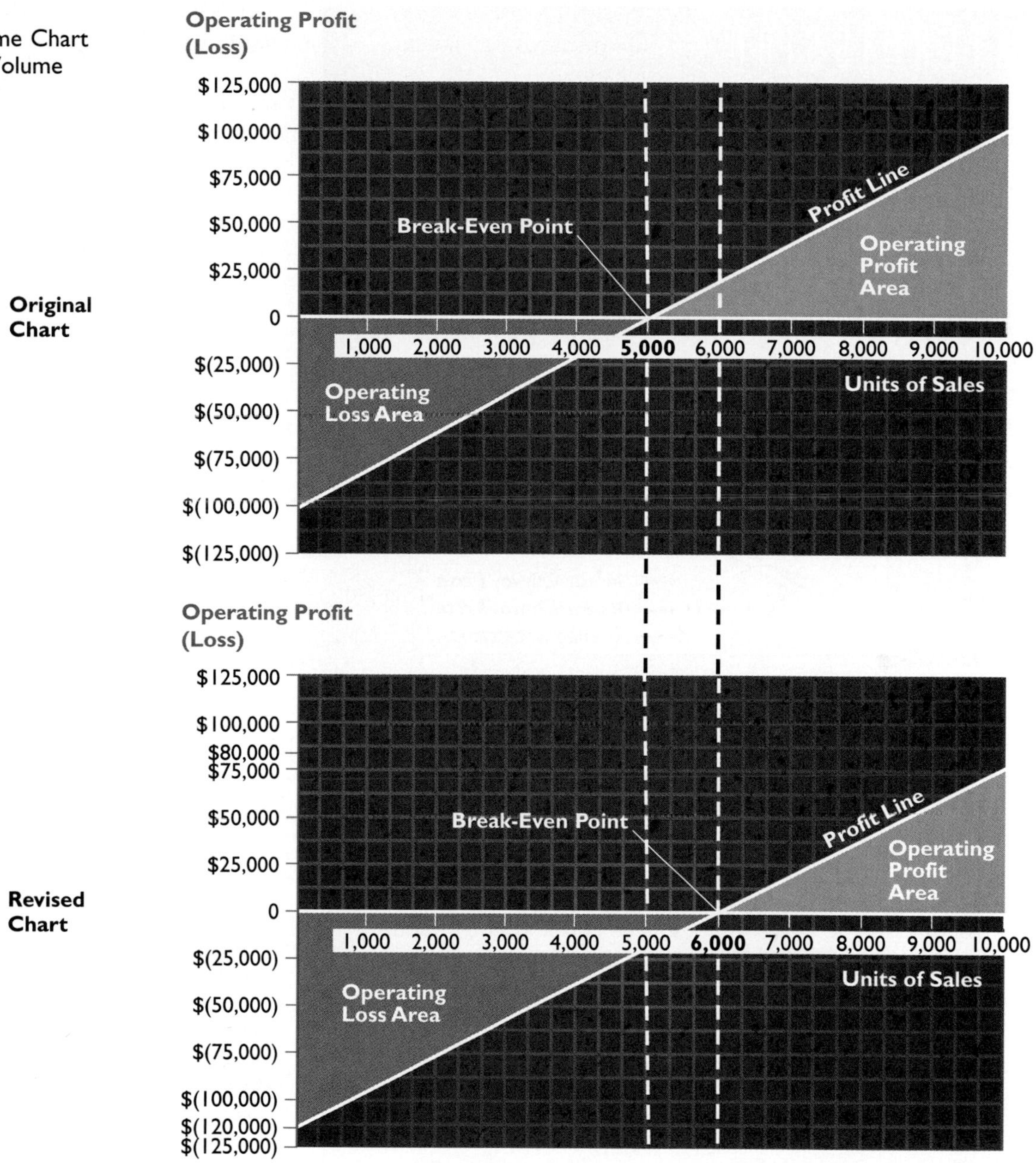

Sales Mix Considerations

OBJECTIVE 5

Calculate the break-even point for a business selling more than one product.

In most businesses, more than one product is sold at varying selling prices. In addition, the products often have different unit variable costs, and each product makes a different contribution to profits. Thus, the sales volume necessary to break even or to earn a target profit for a business selling two or more products depends upon the sales mix. The **sales mix** is the relative distribution of sales among the various products sold by a business.

To illustrate the calculation of the break-even point for a company that sells more than one product, assume that Cascade Company sold 8,000 units of Product A

INTERMISSION

Using Break-Even Analysis to Guide Strategy

The Motor Convoy Inc. (now known as **Allied Systems**) is a Georgia-based common carrier operating primarily in the southeastern United States. The Motor Convoy Inc.'s chief financial officer prepared the break-even chart below.

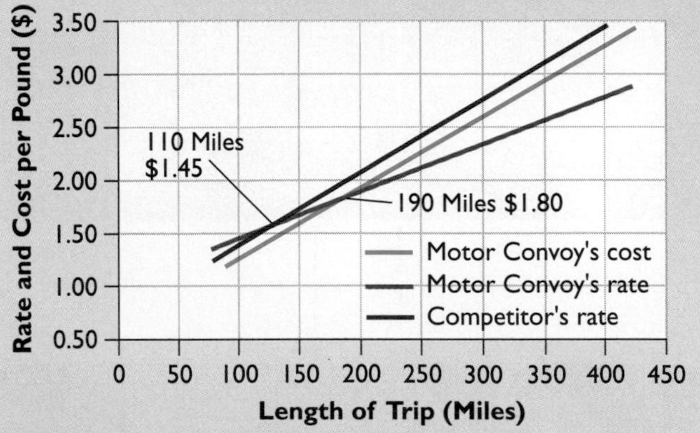

The chart illustrates a typical break-even analysis at The Motor Convoy for a normal load of 2,000 pounds over a relevant range of trips—from about 100 miles to 450 miles. The rate and cost per pound are plotted along the vertical axis, while the length of the trip (in miles) is plotted along the horizontal axis. The rate charged by The Motor Convoy's primary competitor is also graphed, so that the company can assess the effect of competition on developing its operating strategy.

In the above chart, the rate and cost curves are drawn only in the relevant range. The competitor's rate curve is parallel to The Motor Convoy's cost curve, and both rate curves cross at 110 miles. At this volume, The Motor Convoy's business should be concentrated on trips between 110 miles and 190 miles. On shorter trips, the competition is cheaper than The Motor Convoy. On longer trips, The Motor Convoy is losing money. ■

Source: "Multidimensional Break-even Analysis," *The Journal of Accountancy,* January 1987, pp. 132–133.

and 2,000 units of Product B during the past year. The sales mix for products A and B can be expressed as percentages (80% and 20%) or as a ratio (80:20).

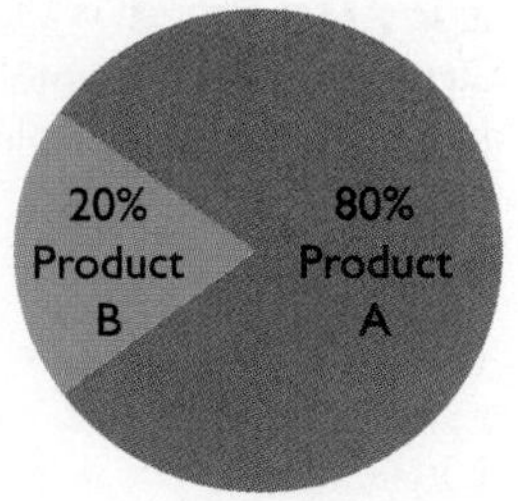

Sales Mix

Cascade Company's fixed costs are $200,000. The unit selling prices, unit variable costs, and unit contribution margins for products A and B are as follows:

Product	Unit Selling Price	Unit Variable Cost	Unit Contribution Margin
A	$ 90	$70	$20
B	140	95	45

In computing the break-even point, it is useful to think of the individual products as components of one overall enterprise product. For Cascade Company, this overall enterprise product is called E. We can think of the unit selling price of E as equal to the total of the unit selling prices of products A and B, multiplied by their sales mix percentages. Likewise, we can think of the unit variable cost and unit contribution margin of E as equal to the total of the unit variable costs and unit contribution margins of products A and B, multiplied by the sales mix percentages. These computations are as follows:

Unit selling price of E:	($90 × 0.8) + ($140 × 0.2) = $100
Unit variable cost of E:	($70 × 0.8) + ($ 95 × 0.2) = $ 75
Unit contribution margin of E:	($20 × 0.8) + ($ 45 × 0.2) = $ 25

The break-even point of 8,000 units of E can be determined in the normal manner as follows:

$$\text{Break-even sales (units)} = \frac{\text{Fixed costs}}{\text{Unit contribution margin}}$$

$$\text{Break-even sales (units)} = \frac{\$200{,}000}{\$25} = 8{,}000 \text{ units}$$

Since the sales mix for products A and B is 80% and 20%, the break-even quantity of A is 6,400 units (8,000 units × 80%) and B is 1,600 units (8,000 units × 20%). This analysis can be verified in the following income statement:

REAL WORLD

The daily break-even attendance at **Universal Studios** theme areas depends on how many tickets were sold at an advance purchase discount rate vs. the full gate rate. Likewise, the break-even point for an overseas flight of **Delta Air Lines** will be influenced by the number of first class, business class, and tourist class tickets sold for the flight. The weekly break-even number of long distance minutes for **AT&T** depends on the number of minutes called during day, evening, and weekend rates.

	Product A	Product B	Total
Sales:			
6,400 units × $90	$576,000		$576,000
1,600 units × $140		$224,000	224,000
Total sales	$576,000	$224,000	$800,000
Variable costs:			
6,400 units × $70	$448,000		$448,000
1,600 units × $95		$152,000	152,000
Total variable costs	$448,000	$152,000	$600,000
Contribution margin	$128,000	$ 72,000	$200,000
Fixed costs			200,000
Operating profit			$ 0 ← Break-even point

The effects of changes in the sales mix on the break-even point can be determined by repeating this analysis, assuming a different sales mix.

Special Cost-Volume-Profit Relationships

OBJECTIVE 6

Compute the margin of safety and the operating leverage, and explain how managers use these concepts.

Some additional relationships useful to managers can be developed from cost-volume-profit data. Two of these relationships are the margin of safety and operating leverage.

Margin of Safety

The difference between the current sales revenue and the sales at the break-even point is called the **margin of safety**. It indicates the possible decrease in sales that may occur before an operating loss results. For example, if the margin of safety is low, even a small decline in sales revenue may result in an operating loss.

If sales are $250,000, the unit selling price is $25, and sales at the break-even point are $200,000, the margin of safety is 20%, computed as follows:

$$\text{Margin of safety} = \frac{\text{Sales} - \text{Sales at break-even point}}{\text{Sales}}$$

$$\text{Margin of safety} = \frac{\$250{,}000 - \$200{,}000}{\$250{,}000} = 20\%$$

The margin of safety may also be stated in terms of units. In this illustration, for example, the margin of safety of 20% is equivalent to $50,000 ($250,000 × 20%). In units, the margin of safety is 2,000 units ($50,000 ÷ $25). Thus, the current sales of $250,000 may decline $50,000 or 2,000 units before an operating loss occurs.

Operating Leverage

The relative mix of a business's variable costs and fixed costs is measured by the **operating leverage**. It is computed as follows:

$$\text{Operating leverage} = \frac{\text{Contribution margin}}{\text{Operating income}}$$

Since the difference between contribution margin and operating income is fixed costs, companies with large amounts of fixed costs will generally have a high operating leverage. Thus, companies in capital-intensive industries, such as the airline and automotive industries, will generally have a high operating leverage. A low operating leverage is normal for companies in industries that are labor-intensive, such as professional services.

REAL WORLD

One type of business that has high operating leverage is what is called a "network" business—one in which service is provided over a network that moves either goods or information. Examples of network businesses include **United Airlines, USWEST, America Online,** and **Union Pacific.**

Managers can use operating leverage to measure the impact of changes in sales on operating income. A high operating leverage indicates that a small increase in sales will yield a large percentage increase in operating income. In contrast, a low operating leverage indicates that a large increase in sales is necessary to significantly increase operating income. To illustrate, assume the following operating data for Jones Inc. and Wilson Inc.:

	Jones Inc.	Wilson Inc.
Sales	$400,000	$400,000
Variable costs	300,000	300,000
Contribution margin	$100,000	$100,000
Fixed costs	80,000	50,000
Income from operations	$ 20,000	$ 50,000

Both companies have the same sales, the same variable costs, and the same contribution margin. Jones Inc. has larger fixed costs than Wilson Inc. and, as a result, a lower operating income and a higher operating leverage. The operating leverage for each company is computed as follows:

Jones Inc.

$$\text{Operating leverage} = \frac{\$100{,}000}{\$20{,}000} = 5$$

Wilson Inc.

$$\text{Operating leverage} = \frac{\$100{,}000}{\$50{,}000} = 2$$

Q&A

What is the operating leverage for a company with sales of $410,000, variable costs of $250,000, and fixed costs of $80,000?

2.0 [($410,000 − $250,000) ÷ ($410,000 − $250,000 − $80,000)]

Jones Inc.'s operating leverage indicates that, for each percentage point change in sales, operating income will change five times that percentage. In contrast, for each percentage point change in sales, the operating income of Wilson Inc. will only change two times that percentage. For example, if sales increased by 10% ($40,000) for each company, operating income will increase by 50% (10% × 5), or $10,000 (50% × $20,000), for Jones Inc. The sales increase of $40,000 will increase operating income by only 20% (10% × 2), or $10,000 (20% × $50,000), for Wilson Inc. The validity of this analysis is shown as follows:

	Jones Inc.	Wilson Inc.
Sales	$440,000	$440,000
Variable costs	330,000	330,000
Contribution margin	$110,000	$110,000
Fixed costs	80,000	50,000
Income from operations	$ 30,000	$ 60,000

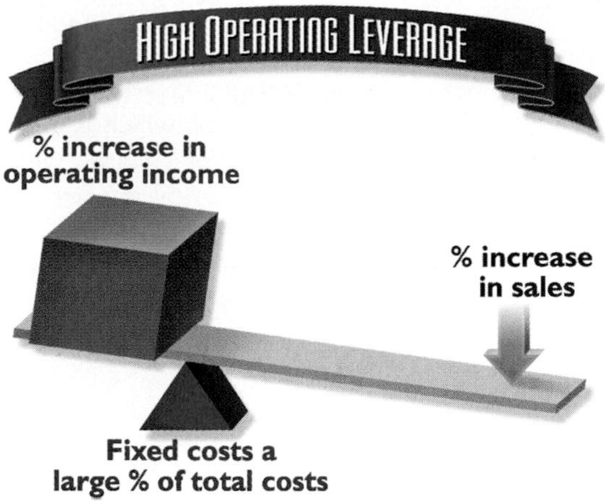

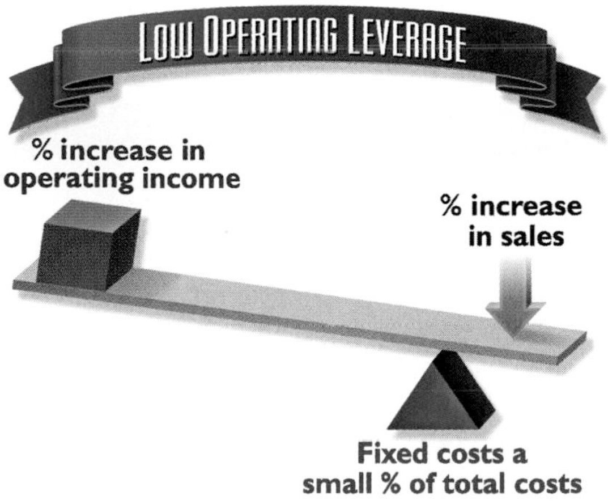

For Jones Inc., even a small increase in sales will generate a large percentage increase in operating income. Thus, Jones's managers may be motivated to think of ways to increase sales. In contrast, Wilson's managers might attempt to increase operating leverage by reducing variable costs and thereby change the cost structure.

Assumptions of Cost-Volume-Profit Analysis

OBJECTIVE 7

List the assumptions underlying cost-volume-profit analysis.

The reliability of cost-volume-profit analysis depends upon the validity of several assumptions. The primary assumptions are as follows:

1. Total sales and total costs can be represented by straight lines.
2. Within the relevant range of operating activity, the efficiency of operations does not change.
3. Costs can be accurately divided into fixed and variable components.
4. The sales mix is constant.
5. There is no change in the inventory quantities during the period.

These assumptions simplify cost-volume-profit analysis. Since they are often valid for the relevant range of operations, cost-volume-profit analysis is useful to decision making.[3]

[3] The impact of violating these assumptions is discussed in advanced accounting texts.

ENCORE

Broken Arrow Tour Isn't Broken

The veteran rocker Neil Young completed his 40-date "Broken Arrow" North American tour. The summer and fall tour averaged 9,000 sold seats per date, or 360,000 seats for the total tour. Ticket prices averaged $25 to $35 per seat. Did the tour exceed the break-even point? The answer depends on the mix between low- and high-price tickets and the total cost for conducting the tour.

The total tour revenues were estimated at $10,000,000, which would suggest an average ticket price of approximately $27.78 ($10,000,000/360,000 seats). The total costs for the tour (which are fixed with respect to the number of tickets sold) include:

- Labor for the set-up crew, technicians, and musicians

- Leases for three trucks and two tour buses
- A 2,150-square-foot "portable" stage and lighting
- Fuel
- Fees for backup artists such as Patti Smith, Jewel, *Gin Blossoms,* and *Afghan Whigs*
- Fees for the venue (arena or amphitheater)
- Promotional fees

The tour was considered a financial success, suggesting that the total revenues exceeded the break-even point.

One of the tour highlights was the sold-out two-day Bridge School Benefit at the 20,000-seat Shoreline Amphitheater in Mountain View, California. The annual Bridge School Benefit features Young and other popular artists, such as *Pearl Jam* and Bonnie Raitt. The concert profits are used to fund The Bridge School, which is an educational program for children with severe speech and physical impairments. The school was founded in 1986 by several individuals, including Neil Young's wife, Pegi Young. ■

APPENDIX: VARIABLE COSTING

For financial reporting to external users, the cost of manufactured products normally consists of direct materials, direct labor, and factory overhead. The reporting of all these costs as product costs, called **absorption costing**, is required under generally accepted accounting principles. However, **variable costing** or **direct costing** reporting may be used in decision making.

In variable costing, the cost of goods manufactured is composed only of variable costs. For units produced, variable costs normally include direct materials, direct labor, and variable factory overhead. Fixed factory overhead costs are related to the productive capacity of the manufacturing plant and are normally not affected by the number of units produced. In a variable costing income statement, fixed factory overhead costs do not become a part of the cost of goods manufactured. Instead, fixed factory overhead costs are treated as an expense of the period.

To illustrate preparing a variable costing income statement, assume that 15,000 units were manufactured and sold at a price of $50 and the costs were as follows:

	Total Cost	Number of Units	Unit Cost
Manufacturing costs:			
Variable	$375,000	15,000	$25
Fixed	150,000	15,000	10
Total	$525,000		$35
Selling and administrative expenses:			
Variable ($5 per unit sold)	$ 75,000		
Fixed	50,000		
Total	$125,000		

Exhibit 9 shows the variable costing income statement prepared from these data. The computations are shown in parentheses.

EXHIBIT 9
Variable Costing Income Statement

Sales (15,000 × $50)		$750,000
Variable cost of goods sold (15,000 × $25)		375,000
Manufacturing margin		$375,000
Variable selling and administrative expenses		75,000
Contribution margin		$300,000
Fixed costs:		
Fixed manufacturing costs	$150,000	
Fixed selling and administrative expenses	50,000	200,000
Income from operations		$100,000

In a variable costing income statement, the **manufacturing margin** is the excess of sales over the variable cost of goods sold. In Exhibit 9, the manufacturing margin is **$375,000** ($750,000 sales − $375,000 variable cost of goods sold). The variable selling and administrative expenses of $75,000 are deducted from the manufacturing margin to yield the contribution margin of **$300,000**. Income from operations of **$100,000** is then determined by deducting fixed costs from the contribution margin.

Exhibit 10 shows the absorption costing income statement prepared from the same data. The absorption costing income statement does not distinguish between variable and fixed costs. All manufacturing costs are included in the cost of goods sold. Deducting the cost of goods sold from sales yields the gross profit. Deducting the selling and administrative expenses from gross profit yields the income from operations.

EXHIBIT 10
Absorption Costing Income Statement

Sales (15,000 × $50)	$750,000
Cost of goods sold (15,000 × $35)	525,000
Gross profit	$225,000
Selling and administrative expenses ($75,000 + $50,000)	125,000
Income from operations	$100,000

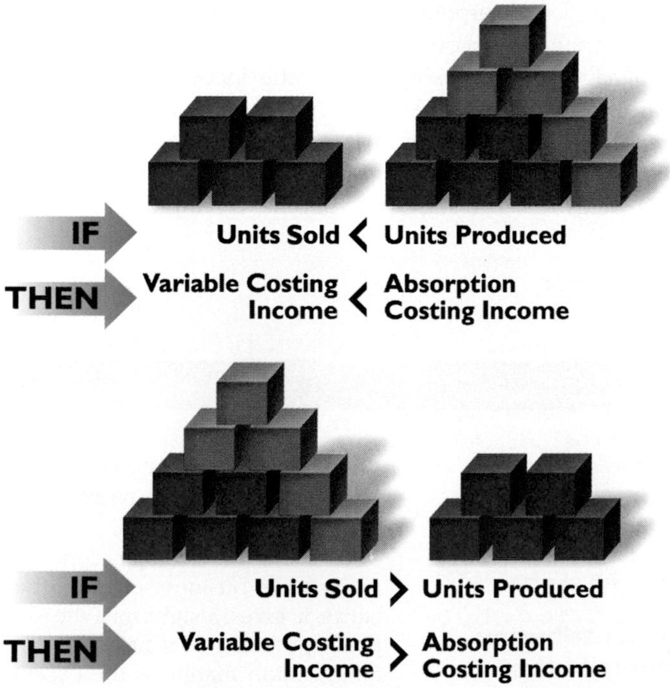

In Exhibits 9 and 10, 15,000 units were manufactured and sold. Both the absorption and the variable costing income statements reported the same income from operations of $100,000. Thus, when the number of units manufactured equals the number of units sold, operating income will be the same under both methods.

When the number of units manufactured is less than the number of units sold, the variable costing operating income will be greater than the absorption costing operating income. When the number of units manufactured exceeds the number of units sold, variable costing operating income will be less than absorption costing operating income. To illustrate this latter case, assume that in the preceding example only 12,000 units of the 15,000 units manufactured were sold. Exhibit 11 shows the two income statements that result.

The $30,000 difference in the amount of income from operations ($70,000 − $40,000) is due to the different treatment of the fixed manufacturing costs. The entire amount of the $150,000 of fixed manufacturing

EXHIBIT 11
Units Manufactured Exceed Units Sold

Variable Costing Income Statement

Sales (12,000 × $50)		$600,000
Variable cost of goods sold:		
Variable cost of goods manufactured (15,000 × $25)	$375,000	
Less ending inventory (3,000 × $25)	75,000	
Variable cost of goods sold		300,000
Manufacturing margin		$300,000
Variable selling and administrative expenses		60,000
Contribution margin		$240,000
Fixed costs:		
Fixed manufacturing costs	$150,000	
Fixed selling and administrative expenses	50,000	200,000
Income from operations		$ 40,000

Absorption Costing Income Statement

Sales (12,000 × $50)		$600,000
Cost of goods sold:		
Cost of goods manufactured (15,000 × $35)	$525,000	
Less ending inventory (3,000 × $35)	105,000	
Cost of goods sold		420,000
Gross profit		$180,000
Selling and administrative expenses [(12,000 × $5) + $50,000]		110,000
Income from operations		$ 70,000

costs is included as an expense of the period in the variable costing statement. The ending inventory in the absorption costing statement includes $30,000 (3,000 × $10) of fixed manufacturing costs. This $30,000, by being included in inventory, is thus excluded from the current cost of goods sold and deferred to another period.

A similar analysis verifies that operating income under variable costing is greater than operating income under absorption costing when the units manufactured are less than the units sold. In both cases where sales and production differ, finished goods inventory will also be different under absorption costing and variable costing. As a result, increases or decreases in operating income due to changes in inventory levels could be misinterpreted by managers using absorption costing income statements as operating efficiencies or inefficiencies. This is one of the reasons that variable costing rather than absorption costing is used by managers for decision-making purposes.

Variable costing is especially useful to managers for cost control, product pricing, and production planning purposes. Such uses of variable costing are discussed in advanced accounting texts.

KEY POINTS

1 **Classify costs by their behavior as variable costs, fixed costs, or mixed costs.**
Cost behavior refers to the manner in which a cost changes as a related activity changes. Variable costs are costs that vary in total in proportion to changes in the level of activity. Fixed costs are costs that remain the same in total dollar amount as the level of activity changes. A mixed cost has attributes of both a variable and a fixed cost.

2 **Compute the contribution margin, the contribution margin ratio, and the unit contribution margin, and explain how they may be useful to managers.**
The contribution margin concept is useful in business planning because it gives insight into the profit potential of a firm. The contribution margin is the excess of sales revenues over variable

costs. The contribution margin ratio is computed as follows:

Contribution margin ratio =

$$\frac{\textbf{Sales} - \textbf{Variable costs}}{\textbf{Sales}}$$

The unit contribution margin is the excess of the unit selling price over the unit variable cost.

3 Using the unit contribution margin, determine the break-even point and the volume necessary to achieve a target profit.

The mathematical approach to cost-volume-profit analysis uses the unit contribution margin concept and the following equations to determine the break-even point and the volume necessary to achieve a target profit for a business:

Break-even sales (units) =

$$\frac{\textbf{Fixed costs}}{\textbf{Unit contribution margin}}$$

Sales (units) =

$$\frac{\textbf{Fixed costs} + \textbf{Target profit}}{\textbf{Unit contribution margin}}$$

4 Using a cost-volume-profit chart and a profit-volume chart, determine the break-even point and the volume necessary to achieve a target profit.

A cost-volume-profit chart focuses on the relationships among costs, sales, and operating profit or loss. Preparing and using a cost-volume-profit chart to determine the break-even point and the volume necessary to achieve a target profit are illustrated in this chapter.

The profit-volume chart focuses on profits rather than on revenues and costs. Preparing and using a profit-volume chart to determine the break-even point and the volume necessary to achieve a target profit are illustrated in this chapter.

5 Calculate the break-even point for a business selling more than one product.

Calculating the break-even point for a business selling two or more products is based upon a specified sales mix. Given the sales mix, the break-even point can be computed, using the methods illustrated for Cascade Company in this chapter.

6 Compute the margin of safety and the operating leverage, and explain how managers use these concepts.

The margin of safety as a percentage of current sales is computed as follows:

Margin of safety =

$$\frac{\textbf{Sales} - \textbf{Sales at break-even point}}{\textbf{Sales}}$$

The margin of safety is useful in evaluating past operations and in planning future operations. For example, if the margin of safety is low, even a small decline in sales revenue will result in an operating loss.

Operating leverage is computed as follows:

Operating leverage =

$$\frac{\textbf{Contribution margin}}{\textbf{Operating income}}$$

Operating leverage is useful in measuring the impact of changes in sales on operating income without preparing formal income statements. For example, a high operating leverage indicates that a small increase in sales will yield a large percentage increase in operating income.

7 List the assumptions underlying cost-volume-profit analysis.

The primary assumptions underlying cost-volume-profit analysis are as follows:

1. Total sales and total costs can be represented by straight lines.
2. Within the relevant range of operating activity, the efficiency of operations does not change.
3. Costs can be accurately divided into fixed and variable components.
4. The sales mix is constant.
5. There is no change in the inventory quantities during the period.

ILLUSTRATIVE PROBLEM

Wyatt Inc. expects to maintain the same inventories at the end of the year as at the beginning of the year. The estimated fixed costs for the year are $288,000, and the estimated variable costs per unit are $14. It is expected that 60,000 units will be sold at a price of $20 per unit. Maximum sales within the relevant range are 70,000 units.

Instructions

1. What is (a) the contribution margin ratio and (b) the unit contribution margin?
2. Determine the break-even point in units.
3. Construct a cost-volume-profit chart, indicating the break-even point.
4. Construct a profit-volume chart, indicating the break-even point.
5. What is the margin of safety?

Solution

1\. a. $$\text{Contribution margin ratio} = \frac{\text{Sales} - \text{Variable costs}}{\text{Sales}}$$

$$\text{Contribution margin ratio} = \frac{(60{,}000 \text{ units} \times \$20) - (60{,}000 \text{ units} \times \$14)}{(60{,}000 \text{ units} \times \$20)}$$

$$\text{Contribution margin ratio} = \frac{\$1{,}200{,}000 - \$840{,}000}{\$1{,}200{,}000} = \frac{\$360{,}000}{\$1{,}200{,}000}$$

Contribution margin ratio = 30%

b. Unit contribution margin = Unit selling price − Unit variable costs
Unit contribution margin = \$20 − \$14 = \$6

2\. $$\text{Break-even sales (units)} = \frac{\text{Fixed costs}}{\text{Unit contribution margin}}$$

$$\text{Break-even sales (units)} = \frac{\$288{,}000}{\$6} = 48{,}000 \text{ units}$$

3\.

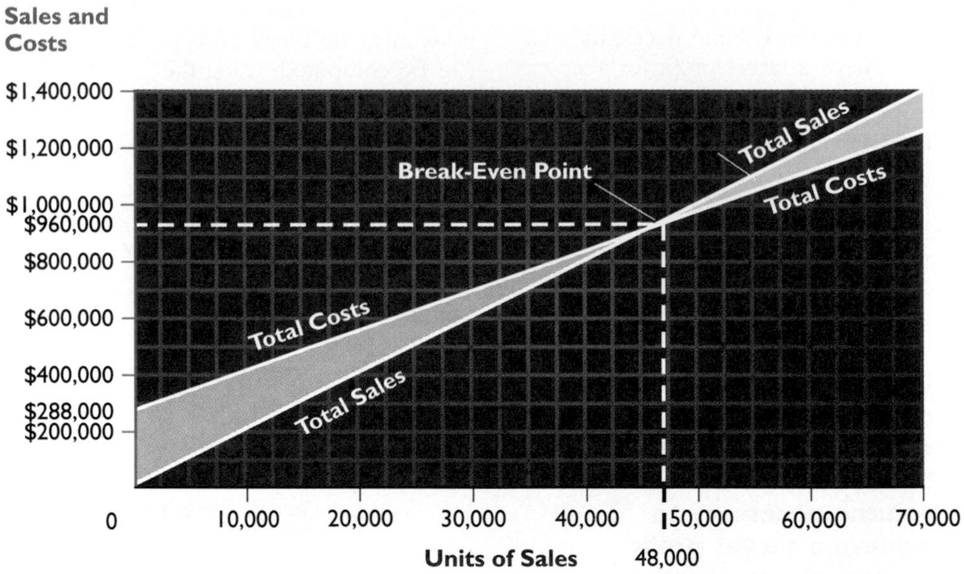

4\.

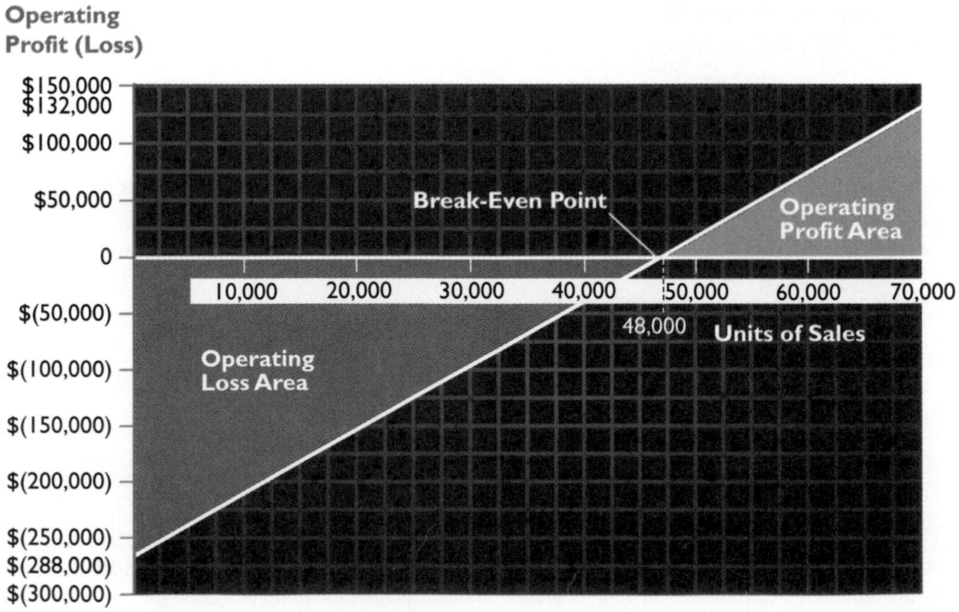

5. Margin of safety:

Expected sales (60,000 units × $20)	$1,200,000
Break-even point (48,000 units × $20)	960,000
Margin of safety	$ 240,000

or

$$\text{Margin of safety} = \frac{\text{Sales} - \text{Sales at break-even point}}{\text{Sales}}$$

$$\text{Margin of safety} = \frac{\$240{,}000}{\$1{,}200{,}000} = 20\%$$

SELF-EXAMINATION QUESTIONS

Answers at End of Chapter

Matching

Match each of the following statements with its proper term. Some terms may not be used.

A. activity bases (drivers)
B. break-even point
C. contribution margin
D. contribution margin ratio
E. cost behavior
F. cost-volume-profit analysis
G. cost-volume-profit chart
H. fixed costs
I. high-low method
J. margin of safety
K. mixed cost
L. operating leverage
M. operating profit
N. profit-volume chart
O. relevant range
P. sales mix
Q. unit contribution margin
R. variable costing
S. variable costs

S 1. Costs that vary in total dollar amount as the level of activity changes.

C 2. Sales less variable cost of goods sold and variable selling and administrative expenses.

A 3. A measure of activity that is thought to cause a cost; used in analyzing and classifying cost behavior.

D 4. The percentage of each sales dollar that is available to cover the fixed costs and provide an operating income.

H 5. Costs that tend to remain the same in amount, regardless of variations in the level of activity.

O 6. The range of activity over which changes in cost are of interest to management.

I 7. A technique that uses the highest and lowest total cost as a basis for estimating the variable cost per unit and the fixed cost component of a mixed cost.

B 8. The level of business operations at which revenues and expired costs are equal.

F 9. The systematic examination of the relationships among costs, expenses, sales, and operating profit or loss.

E 10. The manner in which a cost changes in relation to its activity base (driver).

G 11. A chart used to assist management in understanding the relationships among costs, expenses, sales, and operating profit or loss.

Q 12. The dollars available from each unit of sales to cover fixed costs and provide operating profits.

N 13. A chart used to assist management in understanding the relationship between profit and volume.

K 14. A cost with both variable and fixed characteristics.

J 15. The difference between current sales revenue and the sales at the break-even point.

P 16. The relative distribution of sales among the various products available for sale.

L 17. A measure of the relative mix of a business's variable costs and fixed costs, computed as contribution margin divided by operating income.

R 18. A method of reporting variable and fixed costs that includes only the variable manufacturing costs in the cost of the product.

Multiple Choice

1. Which of the following statements describes variable costs?
   A. Costs that vary on a per-unit basis as the level of activity changes.
   B. Costs that vary in total in direct proportion to changes in the level of activity.
   C. Costs that remain the same in total dollar amount as the level of activity changes.
   D. Costs that vary on a per-unit basis, but remain the same in total as the level of activity changes.

2. If sales are $500,000, variable costs are $200,000, and fixed costs are $240,000, what is the contribution margin ratio?
   A. 40%
   B. 48%
   C. 52%
   D. 60%

3. If the unit selling price is $16, the unit variable cost is $12, and fixed costs are $160,000, what are the break-even sales (units)?
   A. 5,714 units
   B. 10,000 units
   C. 13,333 units
   D. 40,000 units

4. Based on the data presented in Question 3, how many units of sales would be required to realize an operating profit of $20,000?
   A. 11,250 units
   B. 35,000 units
   C. 40,000 units
   D. 45,000 units

5. Based on the following operating data, what is the operating leverage?

Sales	$600,000
Variable costs	240,000
Contribution margin	$360,000
Fixed costs	160,000
Operating income	$200,000

   A. 0.8
   B. 1.2
   C. 1.8
   D. 4.0

CLASS DISCUSSION QUESTIONS

1. What are the three most common classifications of cost behavior?
2. Describe how total variable costs and unit variable costs behave with changes in the level of activity.
3. How would each of the following costs be classified if units produced is the activity base?
   a. Direct labor costs
   b. Direct materials cost
   c. Electricity costs of $0.20 per kilowatt-hour
4. Describe the behavior of (a) total fixed costs and (b) unit fixed costs as the level of activity increases.
5. How would each of the following costs be classified if units produced is the activity base?
   a. Straight-line depreciation of plant and equipment
   b. Salary of factory supervisor ($80,000 per year)
   c. Property insurance premiums of $5,000 per month on plant and equipment
6. In cost analyses, how are mixed costs treated?
7. Which of the following graphs illustrates how total variable costs behave with changes in total units produced?

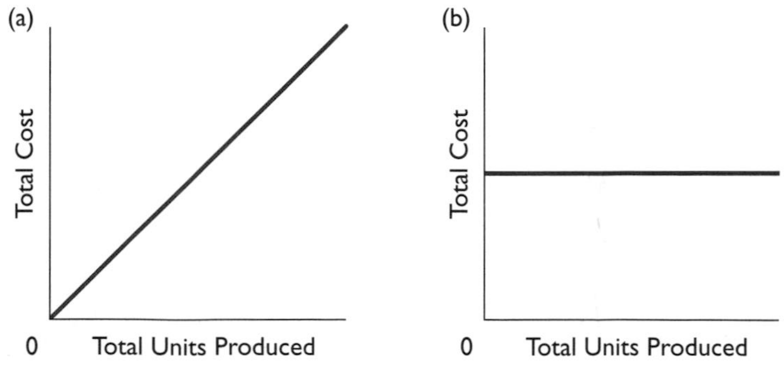

8. Which of the following graphs illustrates how unit variable costs behave with changes in total units produced?

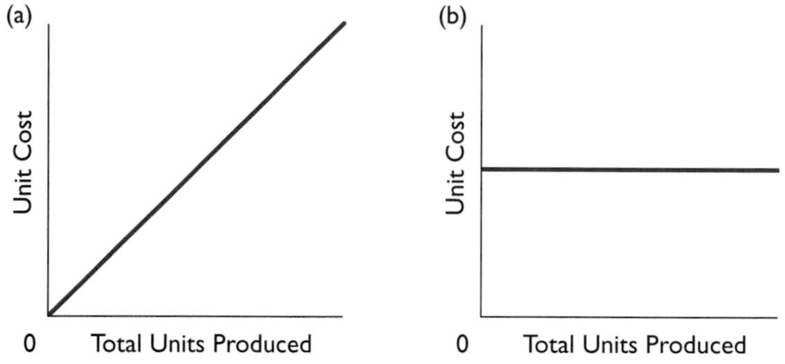

9. Which of the following graphs best illustrates fixed costs per unit as the activity base changes?

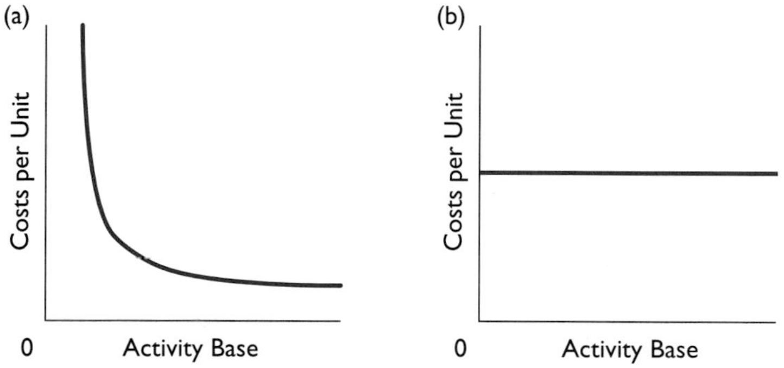

10. In applying the high-low method of cost estimation, how is the total fixed cost estimated?
11. How is contribution margin calculated?
12. If fixed costs increase, what would be the impact on the (a) contribution margin? (b) operating profit?
13. An examination of the accounting records of Hudson Company disclosed a high contribution margin ratio and production at a level below maximum capacity. Based on this information, suggest a likely means of improving operating profit. Explain.
14. What equation is used to determine the break-even point in sales units?
15. If the unit cost of direct materials is decreased, what effect will this change have on the break-even point?
16. If insurance rates are increased, what effect will this change in fixed costs have on the break-even point?
17. Both Simmons Company and Pate Company had the same sales, total costs, and operating profit for the current fiscal year; yet Simmons Company had a lower break-even point than Pate Company. Explain the reason for this difference in break-even points.
18. How does the sales mix affect the calculation of the break-even point?
19. How is the margin of safety calculated?
20. a. How is operating leverage computed?
    b. What does operating leverage measure?

EXERCISES

Exercise 19–1
Classify costs
Objective 1

Following is a list of various costs incurred in producing frozen pizzas. With respect to the production and sale of frozen pizzas, classify each cost as either variable, fixed, or mixed.

1. Dough
2. Hourly wages of machine operators
3. Janitorial costs, $3,000 per month
4. Rent on warehouse, $5,000 per month plus $5 per square foot of storage used
5. Tomato paste
6. Electricity costs, $0.08 per kilowatt-hour
7. Salary of plant manager
8. Pepperoni
9. Refrigerant used in refrigeration equipment
10. Straight-line depreciation on the production equipment
11. Packaging
12. Property insurance premiums, $1,500 per month plus $0.005 for each dollar of property over $3,000,000
13. Property taxes, $50,000 per year on factory building and equipment
14. Pension cost, $0.50 per employee hour on the job
15. Hourly wages of inspectors

Exercise 19–2
Identify cost graphs
Objective 1

The following cost graphs illustrate various types of cost behavior:

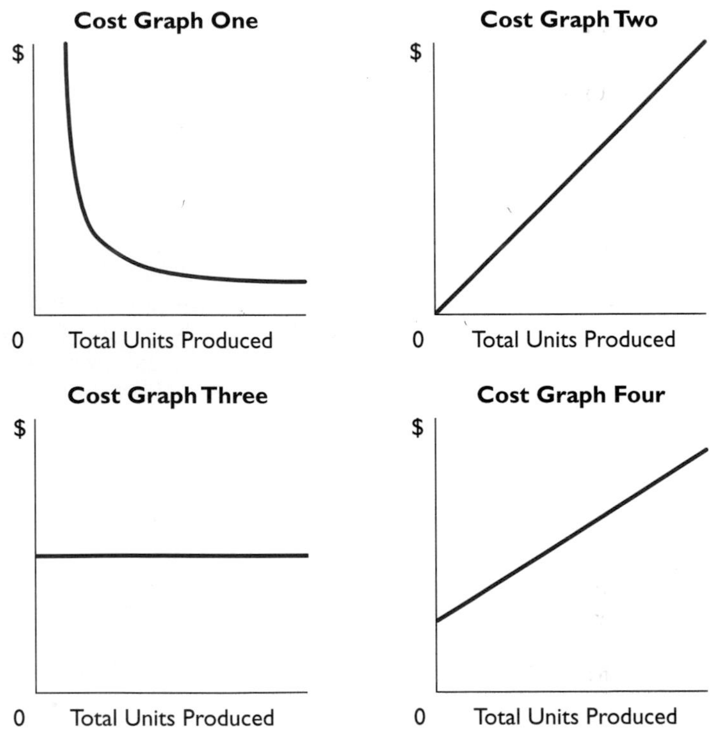

For each of the following costs, identify the cost graph that best illustrates its cost behavior as the number of units produced increases.

a. Total direct materials cost
b. Salary of quality control supervisor, $4,000 per month
c. Electricity costs of $2,000 per month plus $0.02 per kilowatt-hour
d. Per-unit direct labor cost
e. Per-unit cost of straight-line depreciation on factory equipment

Exercise 19–3
Identify activity bases

Objective 1

For Westchase University, match each cost in the following table with the activity base most appropriate to it. An activity base may be used more than once, or not used at all.

Cost:
1. Instructor salaries
2. Financial aid office salaries
3. Housing personnel wages
4. Supplies
5. Admissions office salaries
6. Record office salaries

Activity Base:
a. Number of enrollment applications
b. Number of financial aid applications
c. Student credit hours
d. Number of enrolled students and alumni
e. Number of students living on campus
f. Number of student/athletes

Exercise 19–4
Identify activity bases

Objective 1

From the following list of activity bases for an automobile dealership, select the base that would be most appropriate for each of these costs: (1) preparation costs (cleaning, oil, and gasoline costs) for each car received, (2) salespersons' commission of 3% for each car sold, and (3) property taxes at the end of the year.

a. Number of cars ordered
b. Number of cars sold
c. Number of cars received
d. Number of cars on hand
e. Dollar amount of cars received
f. Dollar amount of cars ordered
g. Dollar amount of cars sold
h. Dollar amount of cars on hand

Exercise 19–5
Identify fixed and variable costs

Objective 1

REAL WORLD

Intuit Inc. develops and sells software products for the personal finance market, including popular titles such as Quicken® and TurboTax®. Classify each of the following costs and expenses for this company as either variable or fixed to the number of units produced and sold:

a. Packaging costs
b. Salaries of software developers
c. Salaries of customer support personnel
d. Disks
e. Sales salaries
f. Advertising
g. Depreciation of computer equipment
h. Shipping expenses
i. Wages of telephone order assistants
j. Property taxes on general offices
k. User's guides
l. President's salary

Exercise 19–6
Relevant range and fixed and variable costs

Objective 1

✓ a. $15

Tender Toes Inc. manufactures children's shoes within a relevant range of 400,000 to 600,000 shoes per year. Within this range, the following partially completed manufacturing cost schedule has been prepared:

Shoes produced	400,000	500,000	600,000
Total costs:			
Total variable costs	$6,000,000	(d)	(j)
Total fixed costs	2,400,000	(e)	(k)
Total costs	$8,400,000	(f)	(l)
Cost per unit:			
Variable cost per unit	(a)	(g)	(m)
Fixed cost per unit	(b)	(h)	(n)
Total cost per unit	(c)	(i)	(o)

Complete the cost schedule, identifying each cost by the appropriate letter (a) through (o).

Exercise 19–7

High-low method

Objective 1

✓ a. $6.50 per unit

Good Earth Map Company has decided to use the high-low method to estimate the total cost and the fixed and variable cost components of the total cost. The data for the highest and lowest levels of production are as follows:

	Units Produced	Total Costs
Highest level	40,000	$485,000
Lowest level	15,000	$322,500

a. Determine the variable cost per unit and the fixed cost.
b. Based on (a), estimate the total cost for 30,000 units of production.

Exercise 19–8

High-low method for service company

Objective 1

✓ Fixed cost, $180,000

Mercy Hospital decided to use the high-low method and operating data from the past six months to estimate the fixed and variable components of total occupancy-related costs. The activity base used by Mercy Hospital is a measure of hospital occupancy, termed "patient-days," which is the total number of days used by patients in the hospital.

	Total Occupancy Costs	Patient-Days
January	$342,000	2,500
February	332,000	2,800
March	288,000	1,800
April	385,000	3,200
May	396,000	3,600
June	305,000	2,200

Determine the variable cost per patient-day and the fixed cost.

Exercise 19–9

Contribution margin ratio

Objective 2

SPREADSHEET

✓ a. 36%

(a) Connor Company budgets sales of $1,800,000, fixed costs of $320,000, and variable costs of $1,152,000. What is the contribution margin ratio for Connor Company?
(b) If the contribution margin ratio for Jacob Company is 28%, sales were $1,400,000, and fixed costs were $325,000, what was the operating income?

Exercise 19–10

Contribution margin and contribution margin ratio

Objective 2

REAL WORLD

✓ b. 50.88%

For the year ended December 31, 1996, **McDonald's Corporation** had the following sales and expenses (in millions):

Sales		$10,687
Food	$ 2,547	
Payroll	1,910	
Occupancy (rent, etc.)	2,227	
General, selling, and administrative expenses	1,321	
		$ 8,005
Operating income		$ 2,682

Assume that the variable costs consist of food, payroll, and 60% of the general, selling, and administrative expenses.

a. What is McDonald's contribution margin?
b. What is McDonald's contribution margin ratio?
c. How much would operating income increase if same-store sales increased by $313 million for 1997, with no change in the contribution margin ratio or fixed costs?

Exercise 19–11
Break-even sales and sales to realize operating profit
Objective 3

✓ b. 14,250 units

For the current year ending March 31, Baxter Company expects fixed costs of $388,600, a unit variable cost of $36, and a unit selling price of $65.

a. Compute the anticipated break-even sales (units).
b. Compute the sales (units) required to realize an operating income of $24,650.

Exercise 19–12
Break-even sales
Objective 3

SPREADSHEET

REAL WORLD

✓ a. 54,732,896 barrels

The **Anheuser Busch Corporation** reported the following operating information for the year ended 1996 (in millions):

Net sales	$ 10,900
Cost of production	$ 7,000
Marketing and distribution	1,900
Other	60
	$ 8,960
Operating income	$ 1,940

In addition, Anheuser Busch sold 91.1 million barrels of beer during 1996. Assume that variable costs were 70% of the cost of production and 60% of marketing and distribution expenses. Assume that the remaining costs are fixed. For 1997, assume that Anheuser Busch expects all revenue and costs to remain constant, except that a new computer system and general office facility is expected to increase fixed costs by $30 million.

a. Compute the break-even sales (barrels) for 1996.
b. Compute the anticipated break-even (barrels) for 1997.

Exercise 19–13
Break-even sales
Objective 3

✓ a. 8,500 units

Currently, the unit selling price of a product is $360, the unit variable cost is $250, and the total fixed costs are $935,000. A proposal is being evaluated to increase the unit selling price to $375.

a. Compute the current break-even sales (units).
b. Compute the anticipated break-even sales (units), assuming that the unit selling price is increased and all costs remain constant.

Exercise 19–14
Cost-volume-profit chart
Objective 4

✓ b. $1,000,000

For the coming year, Tamko Inc. anticipates fixed costs of $400,000, a unit variable cost of $30, and a unit selling price of $50. The maximum sales within the relevant range are $2,000,000.

a. Construct a cost-volume-profit chart.
b. Estimate the break-even sales (dollars) by using the cost-volume-profit chart constructed in (a).
c. What is the main advantage of presenting the cost-volume-profit analysis in graphic form rather than equation form?

Exercise 19–15
Profit-volume chart
Objective 4

✓ b. $400,000

Using the data for Tamko Inc. in Exercise 19–14, (a) determine the maximum possible operating loss, (b) compute the maximum possible operating income, (c) construct a profit-volume chart, and (d) estimate the break-even sales (units) by using the profit-volume chart constructed in (c).

Exercise 19–16
Break-even chart

Objective 4

Name the following chart, and identify the items represented by the letters (a) through (f).

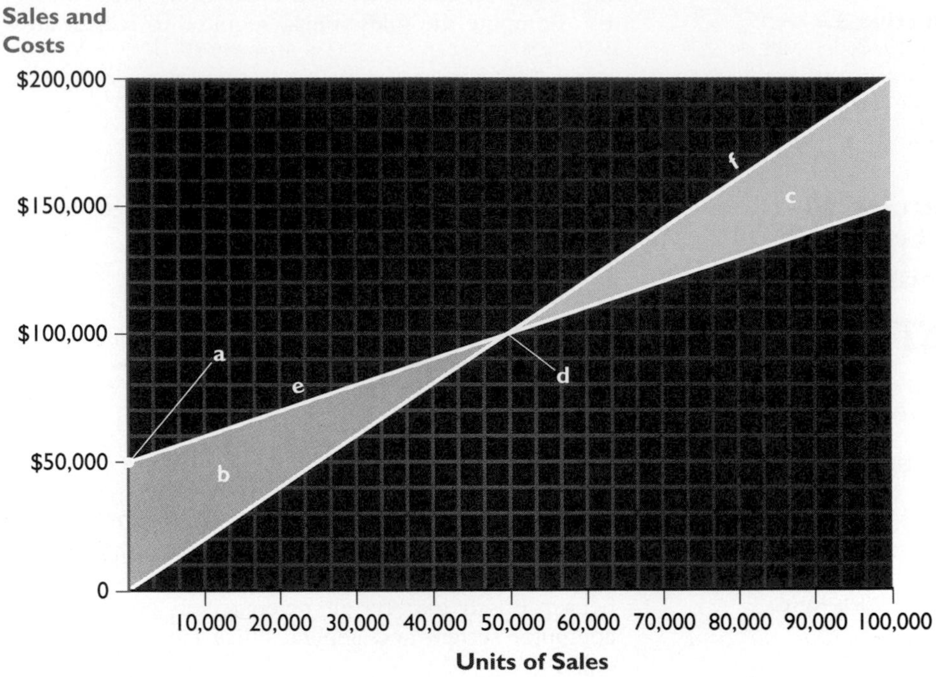

Exercise 19–17
Break-even chart

Objective 4

Name the following chart, and identify the items represented by the letters (a) through (f).

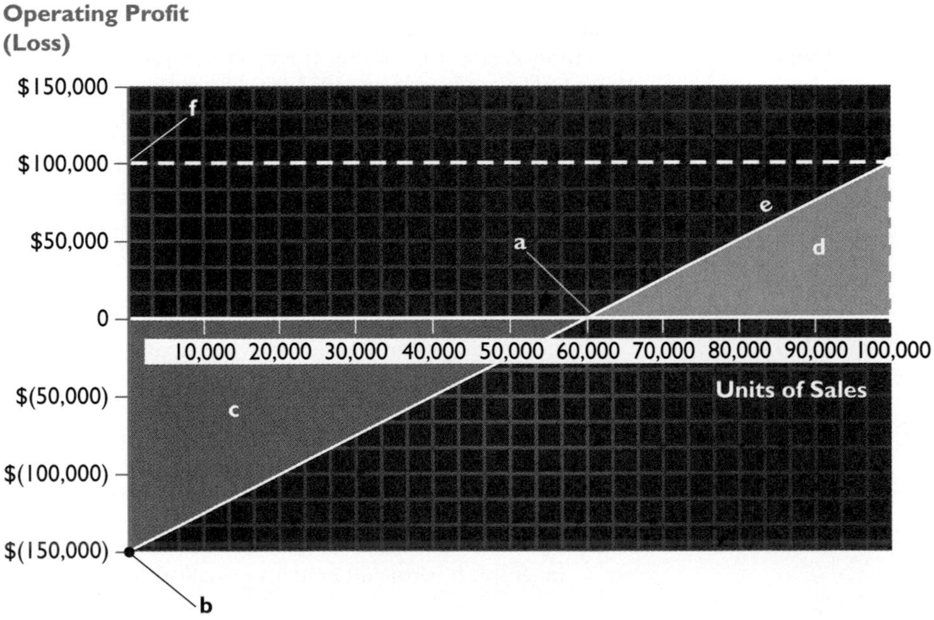

Exercise 19–18
Sales mix and break-even sales

Objective 5

✓ a. 400,000 units

Crispy Snacks Inc. manufactures and sells two products, potato chips and pretzels. The fixed costs are $292,000, and the sales mix is 65% potato chips and 35% pretzels. The unit selling price and the unit variable cost for each product are as follows:

Products	Unit Selling Price	Unit Variable Cost
Potato Chips	$1.80	$1.00
Pretzels	1.50	0.90

a. Compute the break-even sales (units) for the overall product, E.
b. How many units of each product, potato chips and pretzels, would be sold at the break-even point?

Exercise 19–19
Break-even sales and sales mix for a service company

Objective 5

✓ a. 92 seats

Blue Sky Airways provides air transportation services between New York and Miami. A single New York to Miami round-trip flight has the following operating statistics:

Fuel	$14,600
Flight crew salaries	10,280
Airplane depreciation	6,400
Variable cost per passenger—business class	58
Variable cost per passenger—tourist class	34
One-way ticket price—business class	500
One-way ticket price—tourist class	340

It is assumed that the fuel, airplane depreciation, and crew salaries are fixed, regardless of the number of seats sold for the round-trip flight.

a. Compute the break-even number of seats sold on a single round-trip flight for the overall product. Assume that the overall product is 25% business class and 75% tourist class tickets.
b. How many business class and tourist class seats would be sold at the break-even point?

Exercise 19–20
Margin of safety

Objective 6

✓ a. 1. $65,000

a. If Dover Company, with a break-even point at $435,000 of sales, has actual sales of $500,000, what is the margin of safety expressed (1) in dollars and (2) as a percentage of sales?
b. If the margin of safety for Jackson Company was 20%, fixed costs were $600,000, and variable costs were 70% of sales, what was the amount of actual sales (dollars)?

Exercise 19–21
Break-even and margin of safety relationships

Objectives 4, 6

What's Wrong WITH THIS?

At a recent staff meeting, the question of discontinuing Product Q from the product line was being discussed. The chief financial analyst reported the following current monthly data for Product Q:

Units of sales	20,000
Break-even units	23,000
Margin of safety in units	3,000

For what reason would you question the validity of these data?

Exercise 19–22
Operating leverage

Objective 6

✓ a. Banner, 5.75

Banner Inc. and Xu Inc. have the following operating data:

	Banner	Xu
Sales	$460,000	$600,000
Variable costs	276,000	390,000
Contribution margin	$184,000	$210,000
Fixed costs	152,000	70,000
Operating income	$ 32,000	$140,000

a. Compute the operating leverage for Banner Inc. and Xu Inc.
b. How much would operating income increase for each company if the sales of each increased by 20%?
c. Why is there a difference in the increase in operating income for the two companies? Explain.

Appendix Exercise 19–23
Items on variable costing income statement

In the following equations, based on the variable costing income statement, identify the items designated by "X":

a. Net sales − X = Manufacturing margin
b. Manufacturing margin − X = Contribution margin
c. Contribution margin − X = Income from operations

Appendix Exercise 19–24
Variable costing income statement

✓ Contribution margin, $172,250

On July 31, the end of the first month of operations, Noir Ink Company prepared the following income statement, based on the absorption costing concept:

Sales (6,500 units)		$546,000
Cost of goods sold:		
Cost of goods manufactured	$301,000	
Less ending inventory (500 units)	21,500	
Cost of goods sold		279,500
Gross profit		$266,500
Selling and administrative expenses		165,700
Income from operations		$100,800

Prepare a variable costing income statement, assuming that the fixed manufacturing costs were $24,500 and the variable selling and administrative expenses were $117,000.

Appendix Exercise 19–25
Absorption costing income statement

✓ Gross profit, $96,000

On June 30, the end of the first month of operations, Athens Electric Company prepared the following income statement, based on the variable costing concept:

Sales (800 units)		$272,000
Variable cost of goods sold:		
Variable cost of goods manufactured (850 units × $180 per unit)	$153,000	
Less ending inventory (50 units × $180 per unit)	9,000	
Variable cost of goods sold		144,000
Manufacturing margin		$128,000
Variable selling and administrative expenses		20,000
Contribution margin		$108,000
Fixed costs:		
Fixed manufacturing costs	$ 34,000	
Fixed selling and administrative expenses	60,000	94,000
Income from operations		$ 14,000

Prepare an absorption costing income statement.

Appendix Exercise 19–26
Income statements under absorption costing and variable costing

✓ a. Operating income, $17,900

Fast Fit Components Company began operations on July 1 and operated at 100% of capacity during the first month. The following data summarize the results for July:

Sales (25,000 units)		$412,500
Production costs (27,000 units):		
Direct materials	$137,700	
Direct labor	99,900	
Variable factory overhead	32,400	
Fixed factory overhead	48,600	318,600
Selling and administrative expenses:		
Variable selling and administrative expenses	$ 60,000	
Fixed selling and administrative expenses	39,600	99,600

a. Prepare an absorption costing income statement.
b. Prepare a variable costing income statement.
c. What is the reason for the difference in the amount of operating income reported in (a) and (b)?

PROBLEMS SERIES A

Problem 19–1A
Classify costs
Objective 1

Timber Denim Company manufactures blue jeans for distribution to several major retail chains. The following costs are incurred in the production and sale of blue jeans:

a. Janitorial supplies, $2,000 per month
b. Salary of production vice-president

c. Straight-line depreciation on sewing machines
d. Leather for patches identifying each jean style
e. Rent on experimental equipment, $25,000 per year
f. Shipping boxes used to ship orders
g. Sewing supplies
h. Property taxes on property, plant, and equipment
i. Thread
j. Blue dye
k. Insurance premiums on property, plant, and equipment, $10,000 per year plus $3 per $10,000 of insured value over $5,000,000
l. Salary of designers
m. Salesperson's salary, $12,000 plus 3% of the total sales
n. Rental costs of warehouse, $2,000 per month plus $1 per square foot of storage used
o. Brass buttons
p. Consulting fee of $50,000 paid to industry specialist for marketing advice
q. Legal fees paid to attorneys in defense of the company in a patent infringement suit, $20,000 plus $100 per hour
r. Electricity costs of $0.07 per kilowatt-hour
s. Blue denim fabric
t. Hourly wages of sewing machine operators

Instructions

Classify the preceding costs as either fixed, variable, or mixed. Use the following tabular headings and place an "X" in the appropriate column. Identify each cost by letter in the cost column.

Cost	Fixed Cost	Variable Cost	Mixed Cost

Problem 19–2A

Break-even sales under present and proposed conditions

Objectives 2, 3

✓ 2. a. $48

Radiance Lamp Company, operating at full capacity, sold 100,000 units at a price of $80 per unit during 2000. Its income statement for 2000 is as follows:

Sales		$8,000,000
Cost of goods sold		4,000,000
Gross profit		$4,000,000
Operating expenses:		
Selling expenses	$2,500,000	
Administrative expenses	500,000	
Total operating expenses		3,000,000
Operating income		$1,000,000

The division of costs between fixed and variable is as follows:

	Fixed	Variable
Cost of sales	35%	65%
Selling expenses	20%	80%
Administrative expenses	60%	40%

Management is considering a plant expansion program that will permit an increase of $1,150,000 in yearly sales. The expansion will increase fixed costs by $300,000, but will not affect the relationship between sales and variable costs.

Instructions

1. Determine for 2000 the total fixed costs and the total variable costs.
2. Determine for 2000 (a) the unit variable cost and (b) the unit contribution margin.
3. Compute the break-even sales (units) for 2000.
4. Compute the break-even sales (units) under the proposed program.
5. Determine the amount of sales (units) that would be necessary under the proposed program to realize the $1,000,000 of operating income that was earned in 2000.
6. Determine the maximum operating income possible with the expanded plant.

(continues)

7. If the proposal is accepted and sales remain at the 2000 level, what will the operating income or loss be for 2001?
8. Based on the data given, would you recommend accepting the proposal? Explain.

Problem 19–3A
Break-even sales and cost-volume-profit chart
Objectives 3, 4

✓ 1. 11,000 units

For the coming year, Life-Line Medical Company anticipates a unit selling price of $360, a unit variable cost of $300, and fixed costs of $660,000.

Instructions

1. Compute the anticipated break-even sales (units).
2. Compute the sales (units) required to realize an operating income of $120,000.
3. Construct a cost-volume-profit chart, assuming maximum sales of 16,000 units within the relevant range.
4. Determine the probable operating income (loss) if sales total 11,500 units.

Problem 19–4A
Break-even sales and cost-volume-profit chart
Objectives 3, 4

✓ 1. 7,000 units

Last year, Nair Company had sales of $304,000, based on a unit selling price of $40. The variable cost per unit was $28, and fixed costs were $84,000. The maximum sales within Nair Company's relevant range are 10,000 units. Nair Company is considering a proposal to spend an additional $12,000 on billboard advertising during the current year in an attempt to increase sales and utilize unused capacity.

Instructions

1. Construct a cost-volume-profit chart indicating the break-even sales for last year.
2. Using the cost-volume-profit chart prepared in (1), determine (a) the operating income for last year and (b) the maximum operating income that could have been realized during the year.
3. Construct a cost-volume-profit chart indicating the break-even sales for the current year, assuming that a noncancelable contract is signed for the additional billboard advertising. No changes are expected in the unit selling price or other costs.
4. Using the cost-volume-profit chart prepared in (3), determine (a) the operating income if sales total 9,000 units and (b) the maximum operating income that could be realized during the year.

Problem 19–5A
Sales mix and break-even sales
Objective 5

✓ 1. 100,000 units

Data related to the expected sales of golf balls and tennis balls for Outdoor Recreation Inc. for the current year, which is typical of recent years, are as follows:

Products	Unit Selling Price	Unit Variable Cost	Sales Mix
Golf balls	$19.00	$14.00	40%
Tennis balls	4.50	2.00	60%

The estimated fixed costs for the current year are $350,000.

Instructions

1. Determine the estimated units of sales of the overall product necessary to reach the break-even point for the current year.
2. Based on the break-even sales (units) in (1), determine the unit sales of both golf balls and tennis balls for the current year.
3. Assume that the sales mix was 60% golf balls and 40% tennis balls. Compare the break-even point with that in (1). Why is it so different?

Problem 19–6A
Contribution margin, break-even sales, cost-volume-profit chart, margin of safety, and operating leverage
Objectives 2, 3, 4, 6

Venus Products Inc. expects to maintain the same inventories at the end of 2000 as at the beginning of the year. The total of all production costs for the year is therefore assumed to be equal to the cost of goods sold. With this in mind, the various department heads were asked to submit estimates of the costs for their departments during 2000. A summary report of these estimates is as follows:

SPREADSHEET

✓ 2. 37.5%

	Estimated Fixed Cost	Estimated Variable Cost (per unit sold)
Production costs:		
Direct materials	—	$114.00
Direct labor	—	94.50
Factory overhead	$185,000	25.80
Selling expenses:		
Sales salaries and commissions	156,000	8.30
Advertising	62,000	—
Travel	46,000	—
Miscellaneous selling expense	32,000	4.30
Administrative expenses:		
Office and officers' salaries	80,000	—
Supplies	25,000	1.80
Miscellaneous administrative expense	14,000	1.30
Total	$600,000	$250.00

It is expected that 5,000 units will be sold at a price of $400 a unit. Maximum sales within the relevant range are 10,000 units.

Instructions

1. Prepare an estimated income statement for 2000.
2. What is the expected contribution margin ratio?
3. Determine the break-even sales in units.
4. Construct a cost-volume-profit chart indicating the break-even sales.
5. What is the expected margin of safety?
6. Determine the operating leverage.

PROBLEMS SERIES B

Problem 19–1B
Classify costs

Objective 1

Day-Rest Sofas Inc. manufactures sofas for distribution to several major retail chains. The following costs are incurred in the production and sale of sofas:

a. Straight-line depreciation on factory equipment
b. Cartons used to ship sofas
c. Fabric for sofa coverings
d. Salary of production vice-president
e. Insurance premiums on property, plant, and equipment, $5,000 per year plus $20 per $10,000 of insured value over $8,000,000
f. Employer's FICA taxes on controller's salary of $75,000
g. Springs
h. Rent on experimental equipment, $25 for every sofa produced
i. Consulting fee of $15,000 paid to efficiency specialists
j. Janitorial supplies, $10 for each sofa produced
k. Salesperson's salary, $12,000 plus 5% of the selling price of each sofa sold
l. Legal fees paid to attorneys in defense of the company in a patent infringement suit, $10,000 plus $75 per hour
m. Rental costs of warehouse, $10,000 per month
n. Wood for framing the sofas
o. Salary of designers
p. Foam rubber for cushion fillings
q. Sewing supplies
r. Hourly wages of sewing machine operators
s. Property taxes on property, plant, and equipment
t. Electricity costs of $0.02 per kilowatt-hour

Instructions

Classify the preceding costs as either fixed, variable, or mixed. Use the following tabular headings and place an "X" in the appropriate column. Identify each cost by letter in the Cost column.

Cost	Fixed Cost	Variable Cost	Mixed Cost

Problem 19–2B

Break-even sales under present and proposed conditions

Objectives 2, 3

✓ 3. 100,000 units

Home Harvest Garden Tools Inc., operating at full capacity, sold 350,000 units at a price of $50 per unit during 2000. Its income statement for 2000 is as follows:

Sales		$17,500,000
Cost of goods sold		8,000,000
Gross profit		$ 9,500,000
Operating expenses:		
Selling expenses	$ 800,000	
Administrative expenses	1,200,000	
Total operating expenses		2,000,000
Operating income		$ 7,500,000

The division of costs between fixed and variable is as follows:

	Fixed	Variable
Cost of sales	25%	75%
Selling expenses	20%	80%
Administrative expenses	70%	30%

Management is considering a plant expansion program that will permit an increase of $2,500,000 in yearly sales. The expansion will increase fixed costs by $600,000, but will not affect the relationship between sales and variable costs.

Instructions

1. Determine for 2000 the total fixed costs and the total variable costs.
2. Determine for 2000 (a) the unit variable cost and (b) the unit contribution margin.
3. Compute the break-even sales (units) for 2000.
4. Compute the break-even sales (units) under the proposed program.
5. Determine the amount of sales (units) that would be necessary under the proposed program to realize the $7,500,000 of operating income that was earned in 2000.
6. Determine the maximum operating income possible with the expanded plant.
7. If the proposal is accepted and sales remain at the 2000 level, what will the operating income or loss be for 2001?
8. Based on the data given, would you recommend accepting the proposal? Explain.

Problem 19–3B

Break-even sales and cost-volume-profit chart

Objectives 3, 4

✓ 1. 21,000 units

For the coming year, Horizon Paint Company anticipates a unit selling price of $65, a unit variable cost of $45, and fixed costs of $420,000.

Instructions

1. Compute the anticipated break-even sales (units).
2. Compute the sales (units) required to realize an operating income of $84,000.
3. Construct a cost-volume-profit chart, assuming maximum sales of 40,000 units within the relevant range.
4. Determine the probable operating income (loss) if sales total 23,000 units.

Problem 19–4B

Break-even sales and cost-volume-profit chart

Objectives 3, 4

✓ 1. 1,750 units

Last year, Korr Company had sales of $156,000, based on a unit selling price of $120. The variable cost per unit was $72, and fixed costs were $84,000. The maximum sales within Korr Company's relevant range are 3,000 units. Korr Company is considering a proposal to spend an additional $18,000 on billboard advertising during the current year in an attempt to increase sales and utilize unused capacity.

Instructions

1. Construct a cost-volume-profit chart indicating the break-even sales for last year.
2. Using the cost-volume-profit chart prepared in (1), determine (a) the operating in-

come for last year and (b) the maximum operating income that could have been realized during the year.

3. Construct a cost-volume-profit chart indicating the break-even sales for the current year, assuming that a noncancelable contract is signed for the additional billboard advertising. No changes are expected in the selling price or other costs.
4. Using the cost-volume-profit chart prepared in (3), determine (a) the operating income if sales total 2,300 units and (b) the maximum operating income that could be realized during the year.

Problem 19–5B

Sales mix and break-even sales

Objective 5

✓ 1. 180,000 units

Data related to the expected sales of CDs and cassette tapes for Encore Music Inc. for the current year, which is typical of recent years, are as follows:

Products	Unit Selling Price	Unit Variable Cost	Sales Mix
CDs	$16.00	$10.00	75%
Cassette tape	10.00	6.00	25%

The estimated fixed costs for the current year are $990,000.

Instructions

1. Determine the estimated units of sales of the overall product necessary to reach the break-even point for the current year.
2. Based on the break-even sales (units) in (1), determine the unit sales of both CDs and cassette tapes for the current year.
3. Assume that the sales mix was 25% CDs and 75% cassette tapes. Compare the break-even point with that in (1). Why is it so different?

Problem 19–6B

Contribution margin, break-even sales, cost-volume-profit chart, margin of safety, and operating leverage

SPREADSHEET

✓ 2. 31.25%

Ellis Inc. expects to maintain the same inventories at the end of 2000 as at the beginning of the year. The total of all production costs for the year is therefore assumed to be equal to the cost of goods sold. With this in mind, the various department heads were asked to submit estimates of the costs for their departments during 2000. A summary report of these estimates is as follows:

	Estimated Fixed Cost	Estimated Variable Cost (per unit sold)
Production costs:		
Direct materials	—	$24.30
Direct labor	—	14.60
Factory overhead	$104,000	8.20
Selling expenses:		
Sales salaries and commissions	79,000	2.40
Advertising	44,000	—
Travel	14,000	—
Miscellaneous selling expense	23,000	1.60
Administrative expenses:		
Office and officers' salaries	120,000	—
Supplies	11,000	1.80
Miscellaneous administrative expense	5,000	2.10
Total	$400,000	$55.00

It is expected that 20,000 units will be sold at a price of $80 a unit. Maximum sales within the relevant range are 30,000 units.

Instructions

1. Prepare an estimated income statement for 2000.
2. What is the expected contribution margin ratio?
3. Determine the break-even sales in units.
4. Construct a cost-volume-profit chart indicating the break-even sales.
5. What is the expected margin of safety?
6. Determine the operating leverage.

SPECIAL ACTIVITIES

Activity 19–1
Real Assets Inc.
Ethics and professional conduct in business

Howard Skinner is a financial consultant to Real Assets Inc., a real estate syndicate. Real Assets Inc. finances and develops commercial real estate (office buildings). The completed projects are then sold as limited partnership interests to individual investors. The syndicate makes a profit on the sale of these partnership interests. Howard provides financial information for the offering prospectus, which is a document that provides the financial and legal details of the limited partnership offerings. In one of the projects, the bank has financed the construction of a commercial office building at a rate of 6% for the first four years, after which time the rate jumps to 10% for the remaining 26 years of the mortgage. The interest costs are one of the major ongoing costs of a real estate project. Howard has reported prominently in the prospectus that the break-even occupancy for the first four years is 60%. This is the amount of office space that must be leased to cover the interest and general upkeep costs over the first four years. The 60% break-even is very low and thus communicates a low risk to potential investors. Howard uses the 60% break-even rate as a major marketing tool in selling the limited partnership interests. Buried in the fine print of the prospectus is additional information that would allow an astute investor to determine that the break-even occupancy will jump to 85% after the fourth year because of the contracted increase in the mortgage interest rate. Howard believes prospective investors are adequately informed as to the risk of the investment.

Comment on the ethical considerations of this situation.

Activity 19–2
U.S. Airlines
Break-even sales, contribution margin

What do you THINK? REAL WORLD

"For a student, a grade of 65 percent is nothing to write home about. But for the airline . . . [industry], filling 65 percent of the seats . . . is the difference between profit and loss. For [this] hard-pressed [industry], simply breaking even this year would seem like a moral victory. . . .

The [economy] might be just strong enough to sustain all the carriers on a cash basis, but not strong enough to bring any significant profitability to the industry. . . . For the airlines . . . , the emphasis will be on trying to consolidate routes and raise ticket prices. . . ."

The airline industry is notorious for boom and bust cycles. Why is airline profitability very sensitive to these cycles? Do you think that during a down cycle the strategy to consolidate routes and raise ticket prices is reasonable? What would make this strategy succeed or fail? Why?

Source: Edwin McDowell, "Empty Seats, Empty Beds, Empty Pockets," *New York Times,* January 6, 1992, p. C3.

Activity 19–3
Creative Arts Company
Break-even analysis

Creative Arts Company has finished a new VCR movie offering, *Keeping in Balance.* Management is now considering its marketing strategies. The following information is available:

Anticipated sales price per unit	$25
Variable cost per unit*	$5
Anticipated volume	750,000
Movie production costs	$10,000,000
Anticipated advertising	$5,000,000

*The cost of the VCR tape, packaging, and copying costs.

Two managers, Ann Wilson and John Harris, had the following discussion of ways to increase the profitability of this new offering.

Ann: I think we need to think of some way to increase our profitability. Do you have any ideas?
John: Well, I think the best strategy would be to become aggressive on price.
Ann: How aggressive?
John: If we drop the price to $20 per unit and maintain our advertising budget at $5,000,000, I think we will generate sales of 1,600,000 units.
Ann: I think that's the wrong way to go. You're giving too much up on price. Instead, I think we need to follow an aggressive advertising strategy.
John: How aggressive?

Ann: If we increase our advertising to a total of $8,000,000, we should be able to increase sales volume to 1,500,000 units without any change in price.

John: I don't think that's reasonable. We'll never cover the increased advertising costs.

Which strategy is best: Do nothing? Follow the advice of Ann Wilson? Or follow John Harris's strategy?

Activity 19–4
Personal Images Inc.
Variable costs and activity bases in decision making

What do you THINK?

The owner of Personal Images Inc., a T-shirt printing company, is planning direct labor needs for the upcoming year. The owner has provided you with the following information for next year's plans:

	One Color	Two Color	Three Color	Four Color	Total
Number of T-shirts	300	800	900	1,000	3,000

Each color on the T-shirt must be printed one at a time. Thus, for example, a four-color T-shirt will need to be run through the silk screen operation four separate times. The total production volume last year was 2,000 T-shirts, as shown below.

	One Color	Two Color	Three Color	Total
Number of T-shirts	300	800	900	2,000

As you can see, the four-color T-shirt is a new product offering for the upcoming year. The owner believes that the expected 1,000-unit increase in volume from last year means that direct labor expenses should increase by 50% (1,000/2,000). What do you think?

Activity 19–5
Long Company
Variable costs and activity bases in decision making

Sales volume has been dropping at Long Company. During this time, however, the Shipping Department manager has been under severe financial constraints. The manager knows that most of the Shipping Department's effort is related to pulling inventory from the warehouse for each order and performing the paperwork. The paperwork involves preparing shipping documents for each order. Thus, the pulling and paperwork effort associated with each sales order is essentially the same, regardless of the size of the order. The Shipping Department manager has discussed the financial situation with senior management. Senior management has responded by pointing out that sales volume has been dropping, so that the amount of work in the Shipping Department should be dropping. Thus, senior management told the Shipping Department manager that costs should be decreasing in the department.

The Shipping Department manager prepared the following information:

Month	Sales Volume	Number of Customer Orders	Sales Volume per Order
January	$95,000	500	$190
February	93,600	520	180
March	90,100	530	170
April	90,000	600	150
May	89,900	620	145
June	85,000	625	136
July	81,900	630	130
August	80,000	640	125

Given this information, how would you respond to senior management?

Activity 19–6
Into the Real World
Break-even analysis

GROUP ACTIVITY

Break-even analysis is one of the most fundamental tools for managing any kind of business unit. Consider the management of your school. In a group, brainstorm some applications of break-even analysis at your school. Identify three areas where break-even analysis might be used. For each area, identify the revenues, variable costs, and fixed costs that would be used in the calculation.

Activity 19–7
Into the Real World
Cost-volume-profit analysis

Internet ACTIVITY

Access the portion of **Microsoft's** Web site at **www.microsoft.com/msft** that deals with stockholder information. There are a number of features accessible from this contents page. Go to the annual report section and find the online analysis tools. One of these tools is a Microsoft Excel® "what-if" model. Download this model, and use Excel® (or the Excel Viewer if you don't have Excel) to open the model.

a. Use the model to project next year's net income, based on the following assumptions:*

Revenue to change by	0.12
Cost of revenue to be	9% of revenue
Sales and marketing to change by	0.10
Research and development to change by	0.14
General and administrative expenses to change by	0.12
Interest revenue to be	$700 million
Noncontinuing items to be	$0
Other expenses to be	$400 million
Tax rate to be	0.35
Average number of shares to be	1,300 million

*If the model has changed since this text was written, complete the projection by filling in your own assumptions required by the model.

b. Why did your net income increase a different percentage than did sales?

ANSWERS TO SELF-EXAMINATION QUESTIONS

Matching

1. S
2. C
3. A
4. D
5. H
6. O
7. I
8. B
9. F
10. E
11. G
12. Q
13. N
14. K
15. J
16. P
17. L
18. R

Multiple Choice

1. **B** Variable costs vary in total in direct proportion to changes in the level of activity (answer B). Costs that vary on a per-unit basis as the level of activity changes (answer A) or remain constant in total dollar amount as the level of activity changes (answer C), or both (answer D), are fixed costs.
2. **D** The contribution margin ratio indicates the percentage of each sales dollar available to cover the fixed costs and provide operating income and is determined as follows:

$$\text{Contribution margin ratio} = \frac{\text{Sales} - \text{Variable costs}}{\text{Sales}}$$

$$\text{Contribution margin ratio} = \frac{\$500{,}000 - \$200{,}000}{\$500{,}000}$$

$$= 60\%$$

3. **D** The break-even sales of 40,000 units (answer D) is computed as follows:

$$\text{Break-even sales (units)} = \frac{\text{Fixed costs}}{\text{Unit contribution margin}}$$

$$\text{Break-even sales (units)} = \frac{\$160{,}000}{\$4} = 40{,}000 \text{ units}$$

4. **D** Sales of 45,000 units are required to realize an operating income of $20,000, computed as follows:

$$\text{Sales (units)} = \frac{\text{Fixed costs} + \text{Target profit}}{\text{Unit contribution margin}}$$

$$\text{Sales (units)} = \frac{\$160{,}000 + \$20{,}000}{\$4} = 45{,}000 \text{ units}$$

5. **C** The operating leverage is 1.8, computed as follows:

$$\text{Operating leverage} = \frac{\text{Contribution margin}}{\text{Operating income}}$$

$$\text{Operating leverage} = \frac{\$360{,}000}{\$200{,}000} = 1.8$$

20

Budgeting

Setting the STAGE

You may have financial goals for your life. To achieve these goals, it is necessary to plan for future expenses. For example, you may consider taking a part-time job to save money for school expenses for the coming school year. How much money would you need to earn and save in order to pay these expenses? One way to answer this question would be to prepare a budget. For example, a budget would show an estimate of your expenses associated with school, such as tuition, fees, and books. In addition, you would have expenses for day-to-day living, such as rent, food, and clothing. You might also have expenses for travel and entertainment. Once the school year begins, you can use the budget as a tool for guiding your spending priorities during the year.

The budget is used in businesses in much the same way as it can be used in personal life. For example, Chrysler Corporation uses budgeting to determine the number of cars to be produced, number of shifts to operate, number of people to be employed, and amount of material to be purchased. The budget provides the company a "game plan" for the year. In this chapter, you will see how budgets can be used for financial planning and control.

objectives

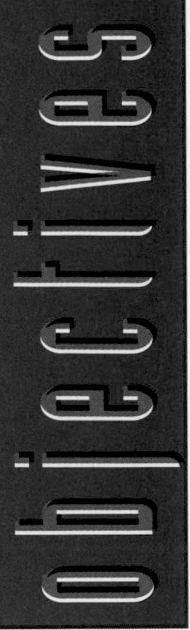

After studying this chapter, you should be able to:

1. Describe budgeting, its objectives, and its impact on human behavior.
2. Describe the basic elements of the budget process, the two major types of budgeting, and the use of computers in budgeting.
3. Describe the master budget for a manufacturing business.
4. Prepare the basic income statement budgets for a manufacturing business.
5. Prepare balance sheet budgets for a manufacturing business.

Nature and Objectives of Budgeting

OBJECTIVE 1

Describe budgeting, its objectives, and its impact on human behavior.

If you were driving across the country, you might plan your trip with the aid of a road map. The road map would lay out your route across the country, identify stopovers, and reduce your chances of getting lost. In the same way, a **budget** charts a course for a business by outlining the plans of the business in financial terms. Like the road map, the budget can help a company navigate through the year and reduce negative outcomes.

Although budgets are normally associated with profit-making businesses, they also play an important role in operating most units of government. For example, budgets are important in managing rural school districts and small villages as well as agencies of the federal government. Budgets are also important for managing the operations of churches, hospitals, and other nonprofit institutions. Individuals and families also use budgeting techniques in managing their financial affairs. In this chapter, we discuss the principles of budgeting in the context of a business organized for profit.

REAL WORLD

By January 1, 1999, the **U.S. Treasury** is planning to eliminate the use of paper checks in favor of electronic funds transfer. It is estimated to cost 42 cents to issue and mail a paper check, compared to only 2 cents to process an electronic payment. Thus, the Treasury is planning on saving $423 million over five years.

Point of INTEREST

The chart below shows the estimated portion of your total monthly income that should be budgeted for various living expenses.

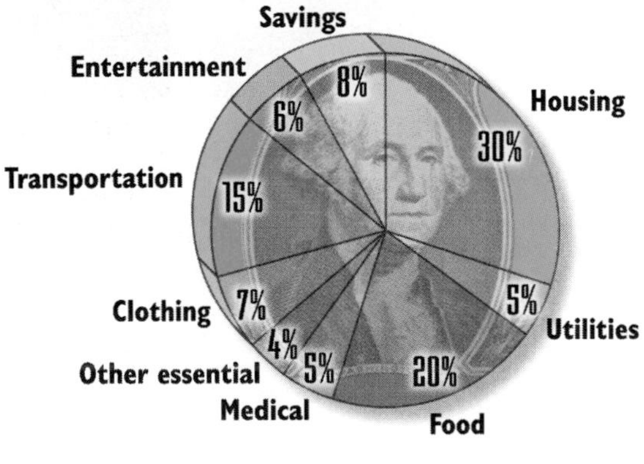

Source: Consumer Credit Counseling Service

Objectives of Budgeting

Budgeting involves (1) establishing specific goals, (2) executing plans to achieve the goals, and (3) periodically comparing actual results with the goals. These goals include both the overall business goals as well as the specific goals for the individual units within the business. Establishing specific goals for future operations is part of the *planning* function of management, while executing actions to meet the goals is the *directing* function of management. Periodically comparing actual results with these goals and taking appropriate action is the *control* function of management. The relationships of these functions are illustrated in Exhibit 1.

EXHIBIT 1
Planning, Directing, and Controlling

Planning

A set of goals is often necessary to guide and focus individual and group actions. For example, students set academic goals, athletes set athletic goals, employees set career goals, and businesses set financial goals. These goals, in turn, motivate individuals and groups to perform at high levels. In the same way, budgeting supports the planning process by requiring all organizational units to establish their goals for the upcoming period. The process is similar to a football team establishing team goals at the beginning of the season. The process of establishing goals through the budget increases the motivation of managers and employees by providing an agreed-upon set of expectations. For example, **Florida Power and Light (FP&L)**, an electric utility, announced plans to reduce costs by 8% of their total budget in order to maintain their target profitability. Using the budget to communicate these expectations throughout the organization helped FP&L to reach its target. Without the budget establishing this clear expectation, these results would have been very difficult to achieve.

Planning not only motivates employees to attain goals, but also improves overall decision making. During the planning phase of the budget process, all viewpoints are considered, options identified, and cost reduction opportunities assessed. This effort leads to better decision making for the organization. As a result, the budget process may reveal opportunities or threats that were not known prior to the budget planning process. For example, the financial planning process helped **General Motors** identify the high costs associated with its far-flung parts operations. As a result, GM decided to sell over 45 lines of businesses (radiator caps, vacuum pumps, electric motors, etc.) in order to focus on its core auto-making business.

Point of INTEREST

Planning is also an important part of personal finances. The **Toronto Dominion Bank** offers a student budget planner and budget worksheet on the Internet at **www.tdbank.ca/tdbank/pers/student/stbud.html**. Visit this site if you would like to prepare a budget or download helpful budgeting tips.

Directing

Once the budget plans are in place, they can be used to direct and coordinate operations in order to achieve the stated goals. For example, your goal to receive an "A" in a course would result in certain activities, such as reading the book, completing assignments, participating in class, and studying for exams. Such actions are fairly easy to direct and coordinate. A business, however, is much more complex and requires more formal direction and coordination. The budget is one way to di-

BUSINESS ON STAGE

Strategic planning is essential for successful business. The strategic plan, which is the starting point for developing operating budgets, involves five steps:

1. Define the company's purpose, vision, and mission. The purpose of the company is the reason it exists. For most companies, this purpose is to maximize shareholder value by maximizing profits. The vision of a company is how it plans to achieve its purpose. The mission of a company represents the specific manner in which the company plans to achieve its purpose and vision.
2. Set specific performance goals that are consistent with the company's purpose, vision, and mission. For example, a specific performance goal might be to earn an 18% rate of return on stockholders' equity for the coming year.
3. Formulate a strategic plan by analyzing the company's strengths, weaknesses, opportunities, and threats. For example, a proven management team is a strength; obsolete machinery is a weakness; demand for a new product or service is an opportunity; and the entry of new competitors into the market is a threat. The analysis of strengths, weaknesses, opportunities, and threats should provide the company with alternative strategies to achieve its purpose, vision, and mission.
4. Implement the strategic plan. This implementation should be reflected in the company's operating budgets.
5. Continually reevaluate the strategic plan and make any necessary changes. For example, new legislation might create new opportunities for services or products. ■

rect and coordinate business activities and units to achieve stated goals. The budgetary units of an organization are called **responsibility centers**. Each responsibility center is led by a manager who has the authority over and responsibility for the unit's performance.

If there is a change in the external environment, the budget process can also be used by unit managers to readjust the operations. For example, **SKI Ltd.** uses weather information to plan expenditures at its Killington and Mt. Snow ski resorts in Vermont. When the weather is forecasted to turn cold and dry, the company increases expenditures in snow-making activities and adds to the staff in order to serve a greater number of skiers.

Controlling

As time passes, the actual performance of an operation can be compared against the planned goals. This provides prompt feedback to employees about their performance. If necessary, employees can use such **feedback** to adjust their activities in the future. For example, a salesperson may be given a quota to achieve $100,000 in sales for the period. If the actual sales are only $75,000, the salesperson can use this feedback about underperformance to change sales tactics and improve future sales. Feedback is not only helpful to individuals, but it can also redirect a complete organization. For example, **Euro Disney**, the company that operates Euro Disneyland theme park outside of Paris, France, estimated 11 million visitors per year when it first opened, but drew only 9.6 million the first year. As a result, the theme park lost money. Management responded to this feedback with new budget plans that reflected lower ticket prices (from $38 to $30), lower hotel prices, 900 fewer jobs, and six new attractions. As a result of implementing these plans, Euro Disney began earning an operating profit.

Comparing actual results to the plan also helps prevent unplanned expenditures. The budget encourages employees to establish their spending priorities. For example, departments in universities have budgets to support faculty travel to conferences and meetings. The travel budget communicates to the faculty the upper limit on travel. Often, desired travel exceeds the budget. Thus, the budget requires the faculty to prioritize travel-related opportunities. In the next chapter, we will discuss comparing actual costs with budgeted costs in greater detail.

Human Behavior and Budgeting

In the budgeting process, business, team, and individual goals are established. Human behavior problems can arise if (1) the budget goal is unachievable (too tight), (2) the budget goal is very easy to achieve (too loose), or (3) the budget goals of the business conflict with the objectives of employees (goal conflict).

INTERMISSION

Georgia Tech introduced what it terms a "responsibility center approach" (RCA) to financial management in its athletic department. The approach requires each sport to be responsible for its own budgeted revenues and outlays. Thus, for example, budgeted outlays for operating costs, scholarships, staff salaries, and recruiting were compared to budgeted revenues to determine anticipated surplus and deficits in each sport. This new approach provides coaches with incentives to control costs and seek revenue possibilities. For example, the baseball program took advantage of revenue-growing opportunities by developing the "Grand Slam Club," leasing scoreboard advertising, and increasing baseball yearbook advertising. These extra revenues could be used by the baseball program to support additional expenditures for promotions, recruiting, and operating costs. ■

Source: C. David Strupeck, Ken Milani, and James E. Murphy, "Financial Management at Georgia Tech," *Management Accounting*, February 1993, pp. 58–63.

Setting Budget Goals Too Tightly

People can become discouraged if performance expectations are set too high. For example, would you be inspired or discouraged by a guitar instructor expecting you to play like Eric Clapton after only a few lessons? You'd probably be discouraged. This same kind of problem can occur in businesses if employees view budget goals as unrealistic or unachievable. In such a case, the budget discourages employees from achieving the goals. On the other hand, aggressive but attainable goals are likely to inspire employees to achieve the goals. Therefore, it is important that employees (managers and nonmanagers) be involved in establishing reasonable budget estimates.

Involving all employees encourages cooperation both within and among departments. It also increases awareness of each department's importance to the overall objectives of the company. Employees view budgeting more positively when they have an opportunity to participate in the budget-setting process. This is because employees with a greater sense of control over the budget process will have a greater commitment to achieving its goals. In such cases, budgets are valuable planning tools that increase the possibility of achieving business goals.

Setting Budget Goals Too Loosely

Although it is desirable to establish attainable goals, it is undesirable to plan lower goals than may be possible. Such budget "padding" is termed **budgetary slack**. An example of budgetary slack is including spare employees in the plan. Managers may plan slack in the budget in order to provide a "cushion" for unexpected events or improve the appearance of operations. Budgetary slack can be avoided if lower- and mid-level managers are required to support their spending requirements with operational plans.

REAL WORLD There is strong evidence that loose budgets may be appropriate in settings involving high uncertainty, such as research and development. The loose budget acts as a sort of "shock absorber," giving managers maneuvering room to minimize work disruptions.

Slack budgets can cause employees to develop a "spend it or lose it" mentality. This often occurs at the end of the budget period when actual spending is much less than the budget. Employees may attempt to spend the remaining budget (purchase equipment, hire consultants, purchase supplies) in order to avoid having the budget cut next period.

Setting Conflicting Budget Goals

Goal conflict occurs when individual self-interest differs from business objectives. To illustrate, the manager of the Transportation Department of one company was instructed to stay within the department's budget. To meet the budget goal, the manager stopped transporting all shipments for the last two weeks of the period. Though the Transportation Department budget was met, customers were upset because they did not receive their orders. As a result, many customers stopped doing business with the company or demanded price discounts that far exceeded the additional transportation costs that should have been spent. In this example, the budget pressure caused the Transportation Department manager to make a decision that appeared correct from the department's view, but was harmful to the business. Goal conflict can be avoided if budget goals are carefully designed for consistency across all areas of the organization.

Budgeting Systems

OBJECTIVE 2

Describe the basic elements of the budget process, the two major types of budgeting, and the use of computers in budgeting.

Budgeting systems vary among businesses because of such factors as organizational structure, complexity of operations, and management philosophy. Differences in budget systems are even more significant among different types of businesses, such as manufacturers and service businesses. The details of a budgeting system used by an automobile manufacturer such as **Ford** would obviously differ from a service company such as **American Airlines**. However, the basic budgeting concepts illustrated in the following paragraphs apply to all types of businesses and organizations.

The budgetary period for operating activities normally includes the fiscal year of a business. A year is short enough that future operations can be estimated fairly accurately, yet long enough that the future can be viewed in a broad context. However, to achieve effective control, the annual budgets are usually subdivided into shorter time periods, such as quarters of the year, months, or weeks.

A variation of fiscal-year budgeting, called **continuous budgeting**, maintains a twelve-month projection into the future. The twelve-month budget is continually revised by removing the data for the period just ended and adding estimated budget data for the same period next year, as shown in Exhibit 2.

REAL WORLD

Sprint Corporation was spending twice as many resources producing budgets as it was analyzing them. As a result, Sprint reengineered its budget process by replacing its annual budget with quarterly reviews of six-quarter rolling forecasts of key business drivers, coupled with exception-based monitoring. The new process shortened the budget process from 137 days to less than two months, and gave Sprint the ability to respond faster to changes in business conditions.

EXHIBIT 2 Continuous Budgeting

Developing budgets for the next fiscal year usually begins several months prior to the end of the current year. This responsibility is normally assigned to a budget committee. Such a committee often consists of the budget director and such high-level executives as the controller, the treasurer, the production manager, and the sales manager. Once the budget has been approved, the budget process is monitored and summarized by the Accounting Department, which reports to the committee.

Lockheed Martin Corporation used a zero-based budgeting approach, called risk-based budgeting, to identify cost savings during the downsizing of some of its military and weapons programs. Lockheed Martin divided its operations into core and supplemental activities. Core activities were spared from deep budget cuts, but supplemental activities were evaluated for possible budget reductions.

There are several methods of developing budget estimates. One method, termed **zero-based budgeting**, requires managers to estimate sales, production, and other operating data as though operations are being started for the first time. This approach has the benefit of taking a fresh view of operations each year. A more common approach is to start with last year's budget and revise it for actual results and expected changes for the coming year. Two major budgets using this approach are the static budget and the flexible budget.

Static Budget

A **static budget** shows the expected results of a responsibility center for only one activity level. Once the budget has been determined, it is not changed, even if the activity changes. Static budgeting is used by many service companies and for some administrative functions of manufacturing companies, such as purchasing, engineering, and accounting. For example, the Assembly Department manager for Colter Manufacturing Company prepared the static budget for the upcoming year, shown in Exhibit 3.

EXHIBIT 3
Static Budget

Colter Manufacturing Company
Assembly Department Budget
For the Year Ending July 31, 2000

Direct labor	$40,000
Electric power	5,000
Supervisor salaries	15,000
Total department costs	$60,000

A disadvantage of static budgets is that they do not adjust for changes in activity levels. For example, assume that the actual amounts spent by the Assembly Department of Colter Manufacturing totaled $72,000, which is $12,000 or 20% ($12,000 ÷ $60,000) more than budgeted. Is this good news or bad news? At first you might think that this is a bad result. However, this conclusion may not be valid, since static budget results may be difficult to interpret. To illustrate, assume that the assembly manager constructed the budget based on plans to assemble *8,000* units during the year. However, *10,000* units were actually produced, which represents 25% (2,000 ÷ 8,000) more work than expected. Should the additional $12,000 in spending in excess of the budget be considered "bad news"? Maybe not. The Assembly Department provided 25% more output for only 20% additional cost.

Flexible Budget

Flexible budgets show expected results for several activity levels.

Unlike static budgets, **flexible budgets** show the expected results of a responsibility center for several activity levels. You can think of a flexible budget as a series of static budgets for different levels of activity. Such budgets are especially useful in estimating and controlling factory costs and operating expenses.

Exhibit 4 is a flexible budget for the annual manufacturing expense in the Assembly Department of Colter Manufacturing Company.

EXHIBIT 4
Flexible Budget

Colter Manufacturing Company
Assembly Department Budget
For the Year Ending July 31, 2000

Units of production	8,000	9,000	10,000
Variable cost:			
Direct labor ($5 per unit)	$40,000	$45,000	$50,000
Electric power ($0.50 per unit)	4,000	4,500	5,000
Total variable cost	$44,000	$49,500	$55,000
Fixed cost:			
Electric power	$ 1,000	$ 1,000	$ 1,000
Supervisor salaries	15,000	15,000	15,000
Total fixed cost	$16,000	$16,000	$16,000
Total department costs	$60,000	$65,500	$71,000

When constructing a flexible budget, we first identify the relevant activity levels. In Exhibit 4, there are 8,000, 9,000, and 10,000 units of production. Alternative activity bases, such as machine hours or direct labor hours, may be used in measuring the volume of activity. Second, we identify the fixed and variable cost components of the costs being budgeted. For example, in Exhibit 4, the electric power cost is separated into its fixed cost ($1,000 per month) and variable cost ($0.50 per unit). Lastly, we prepare the budget for each activity level by multiplying the variable cost per unit by the activity level and then adding the monthly fixed cost.

With a flexible budget, the department manager can be evaluated by comparing actual expenses to the budgeted amount for actual activity. For example, if Colter Manufacturing Company's Assembly Department actually spent $72,000 to produce 10,000 units, the manager would be considered over budget by $1,000 ($72,000 − $71,000). Under the static budget in Exhibit 3, the department was $12,000 over budget. This comparison is illustrated in Exhibit 5. The flexible budget for the Assembly Department is much more accurate than the static budget, because budget amounts adjust for changes in activity.

Q&A

At the beginning of the period, the Assembly Department budgeted direct labor of $45,000 and supervisor salaries of $30,000 for 5,000 hours of production. The department actually completed 6,000 hours of production. What is the appropriate total budget for the department, assuming that it uses flexible budgeting?

$84,000 [($9 × 6,000) + $30,000]

Computerized Budgeting Systems

In developing budgets, many firms use computerized budgeting systems. Such systems speed up and reduce the cost of preparing the budget. This is especially true

EXHIBIT 5 Static and Flexible Budgets

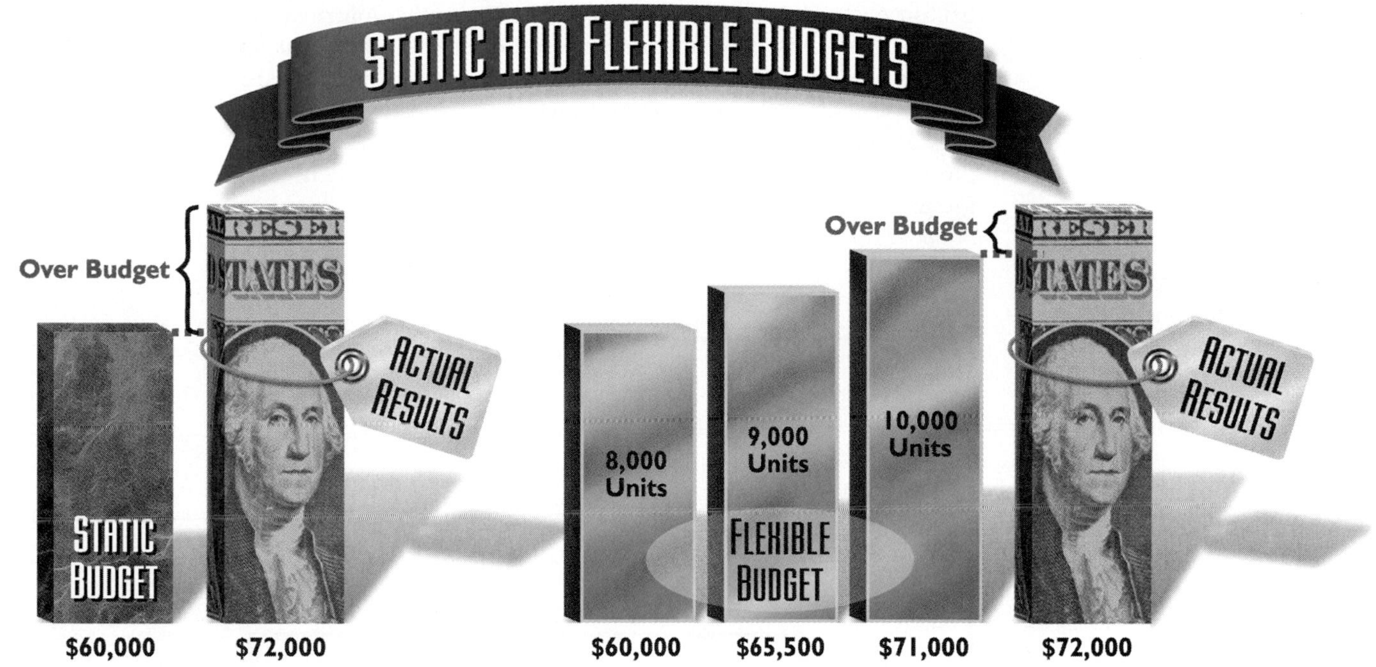

REAL WORLD

Many hospitals use budget models to plan the number of nurses for patient floors. These models use a measure termed "relative value units." A relative value unit is a measure of effort related to a nursing activity, such as feeding the patient or verifying vital signs. The total relative value units for a floor can be determined from a computer simulation, based on the number of patients on the floor and the type of illnesses. Naturally, the more patients and the more severe their illnesses, the higher the total relative value units. The total relative units can then be translated into the number of nurses required to support the patients.

when large quantities of data need to be processed. Computers are also useful in continuous budgeting. Reports that compare actual results with amounts budgeted can also be prepared on a timely basis through the use of computerized systems.

Managers often use computer spreadsheets or simulation models to represent the operating and budget relationships. By using computer simulation models, the impact of various operating alternatives on the budget can be assessed. For example, the budget can be revised to show the impact of a proposed change in indirect labor wage rates. Likewise, the budgetary effect of a proposed product line can be determined.

A common objective of using computer-based budgeting is to tie all the budgets of the organization together. In the next section, we will illustrate how a company ties its budgets together to develop a complete plan.

Master Budget

OBJECTIVE 3

Describe the master budget for a manufacturing business.

Manufacturing operations require a series of budgets that are linked together in a **master budget**. The major parts of the master budget are as follows:

Budgeted Income Statement	Budgeted Balance Sheet
Sales budget	Cash budget
Cost of goods sold budget:	Capital expenditures budget
Production budget	
Direct materials purchases budget	
Direct labor cost budget	
Factory overhead cost budget	
Selling and administrative expenses budget	

Exhibit 6 shows the relationship among the income statement budgets. The budget process begins by estimating sales. The sales information is then provided to the various units for estimating the production and selling and administrative expenses budgets. The production budgets are used to prepare the direct materials purchases, direct labor cost, and factory overhead cost budgets. These three budgets are used to develop the cost of goods sold budget. Once these budgets and the selling and administrative expenses budget have been completed, the budgeted income statement can be prepared.

EXHIBIT 6
Income Statement Budgets

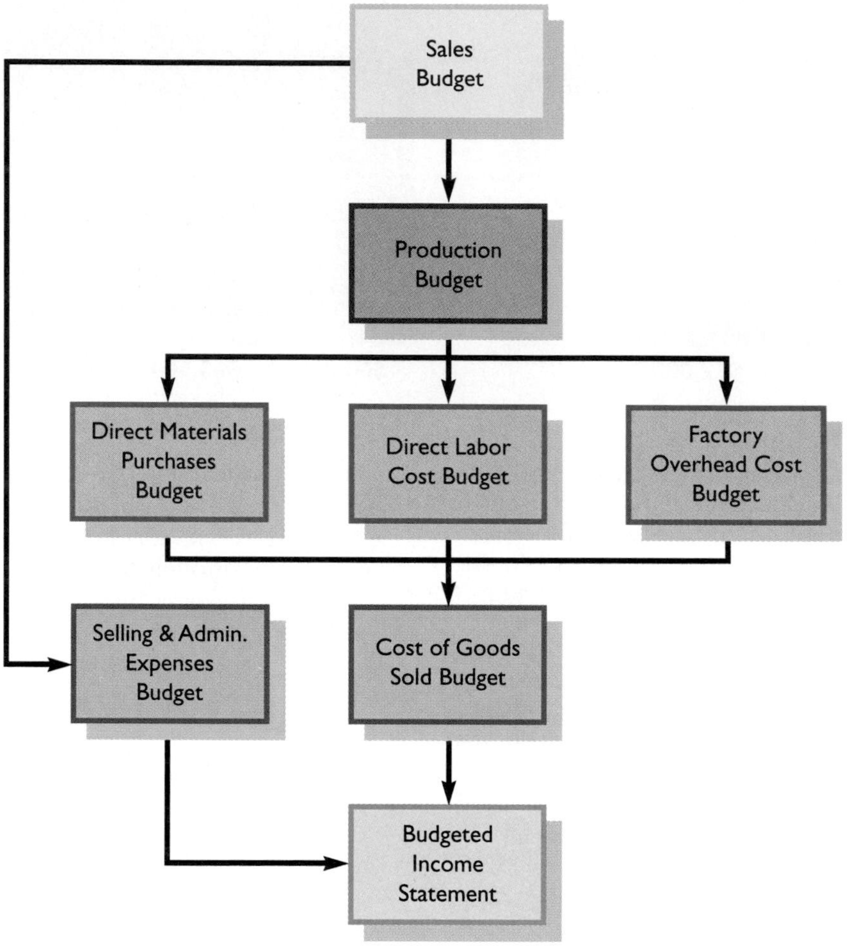

After the budgeted income statement has been developed, the budgeted balance sheet can be prepared. Two major budgets comprising the budgeted balance sheet are the cash budget and the capital expenditures budget.

Income Statement Budgets

OBJECTIVE 4

Prepare the basic income statement budgets for a manufacturing business.

In the following sections, we will illustrate the major elements of the income statement budget. We will use a small manufacturing business, Elite Accessories Inc., as the basis for our illustration.

Sales Budget

The **sales budget** normally indicates for each product (1) the quantity of estimated sales and (2) the expected unit selling price. These data are often reported by regions or by sales representatives.

In estimating the quantity of sales for each product, past sales volumes are often used as a starting point. These amounts are revised for factors that are expected to affect future sales, such as the factors listed below.

- backlog of unfilled sales orders
- planned advertising and promotion
- expected industry and general economic conditions
- productive capacity
- projected pricing policy
- findings of market research studies

Once an estimate of the sales volume is obtained, the expected sales revenue can be determined by multiplying the volume by the expected unit sales price. Exhibit 7 is the sales budget for Elite Accessories Inc.

EXHIBIT 7
Sales Budget

Elite Accessories Inc.
Sales Budget
For the Year Ending December 31, 2000

Product and Region	Unit Sales Volume	Unit Selling Price	Total Sales
Wallet:			
East	287,000	$12.00	$ 3,444,000
West	241,000	12.00	2,892,000
Total	528,000		$ 6,336,000
Handbag:			
East	156,400	$25.00	$ 3,910,000
West	123,600	25.00	3,090,000
Total	280,000		$ 7,000,000
Total revenue from sales			$13,336,000

For control purposes, management can compare actual sales and budgeted sales by product, region, or sales representative. Management would investigate any significant differences and take possible corrective actions.

Production Budget

Production should be carefully coordinated with the sales budget to ensure that production and sales are kept in balance during the period. The number of units to be manufactured to meet budgeted sales and inventory needs for each product is set forth in the **production budget**. The budgeted volume of production is determined as follows:

Expected units sold
\+ Desired units in ending inventory
− Estimated units in beginning inventory
Total units to be produced

Exhibit 8 is the production budget for Elite Accessories Inc.

Q&A

Sales of 45,000 units are budgeted for the period. The estimated beginning inventory is 3,000 units, and the desired ending inventory is 5,000 units. What is the budgeted production (in units) for the period?

47,000 units (45,000 units + 5,000 units − 3,000 units)

EXHIBIT 8
Production Budget

Elite Accessories Inc. Production Budget For the Year Ending December 31, 2000	Units	
	Wallet	Handbag
Sales (from Exhibit 7)	528,000	280,000
Plus desired ending inventory, December 31, 2000	80,000	60,000
Total	608,000	340,000
Less estimated beginning inventory, January 1, 2000	88,000	48,000
Total production	520,000	292,000

Direct Materials Purchases Budget

The production budget is the starting point for determining the estimated quantities of direct materials to be purchased. Multiplying these quantities by the expected unit purchase price determines the total cost of direct materials to be purchased.

Materials needed for production
\+ Desired ending materials inventory
− Estimated beginning materials inventory
Direct materials to be purchased

In Elite Accessories Inc.'s production operations, leather and lining are required for wallets and handbags. The quantity of direct materials expected to be used for each unit of product is as follows:

Wallet:
Leather: 0.30 square yard per unit
Lining: 0.10 square yard per unit

Handbag:
Leather: 1.25 square yards per unit
Lining: 0.50 square yard per unit

Based on these data and the production budget, the **direct materials purchases budget** is prepared. As shown in the budget in Exhibit 9, for Elite Accessories Inc. to produce 520,000 wallets, 156,000 square yards (520,000 units × 0.30 square yard per unit) of leather are needed. Likewise, to produce 292,000 handbags, 365,000 square yards (292,000 units × 1.25 square yards per unit) of leather are needed. We can compute the needs for lining in a similar manner. Then adding the desired ending inventory for each material and deducting the estimated beginning inventory determines the amount of each material to be purchased. Multiplying these amounts by the estimated cost per square yard yields the total materials purchase cost.

The direct materials purchases budget helps management maintain inventory levels within reasonable limits. For this purpose, the timing of the direct materials purchases should be coordinated between the purchasing and production departments.

Direct Labor Cost Budget

The production budget also provides the starting point for preparing the direct labor cost budget. For Elite Accessories Inc., the labor requirements for each unit of product are estimated as follows:

Wallet:
Cutting Department: 0.10 hour per unit
Sewing Department: 0.25 hour per unit

Handbag:
Cutting Department: 0.15 hour per unit
Sewing Department: 0.40 hour per unit

EXHIBIT 9
Direct Materials Purchases Budget

Elite Accessories Inc.
Direct Materials Purchases Budget
For the Year Ending December 31, 2000

	Direct Materials		
	Leather	**Lining**	**Total**
Square yards required for production:			
Wallet (Note A)	156,000	52,000	
Handbag (Note B)	365,000	146,000	
Plus desired inventory, December 31, 2000	20,000	12,000	
Total	541,000	210,000	
Less estimated inventory, January 1, 2000	18,000	15,000	
Total square yards to be purchased	523,000	195,000	
Unit price (per square yard)	× $4.50	× $1.20	
Total direct materials purchases	$2,353,500	$234,000	$2,587,500

Note A: Leather: 520,000 units × 0.30 sq. yd. per unit = 156,000 sq. yds.
Lining: 520,000 units × 0.10 sq. yd. per unit = 52,000 sq. yds.

Note B: Leather: 292,000 units × 1.25 sq. yds. per unit = 365,000 sq. yds.
Lining: 292,000 units × 0.50 sq. yd. per unit = 146,000 sq. yds.

Based on these data and the production budget, Elite Accessories Inc. prepares the direct labor budget. As shown in the budget in Exhibit 10, for Elite Accessories Inc. to produce 520,000 wallets, 52,000 hours (520,000 units × 0.10 hour per unit) of labor in the Cutting Department are required. Likewise, to produce 292,000 handbags, 43,800 hours (292,000 units × 0.15 hour per unit) of labor in the Cutting De-

EXHIBIT 10
Direct Labor Cost Budget

Elite Accessories Inc.
Direct Labor Cost Budget
For the Year Ending December 31, 2000

	Cutting	**Sewing**	**Total**
Hours required for production:			
Wallet (Note A)	52,000	130,000	
Handbag (Note B)	43,800	116,800	
Total	95,800	246,800	
Hourly rate	× $12.00	× $15.00	
Total direct labor cost	$1,149,600	$3,702,000	$4,851,600

Note A: Cutting Department: 520,000 units × 0.10 hour per unit = 52,000 hours
Sewing Department: 520,000 units × 0.25 hour per unit = 130,000 hours

Note B: Cutting Department: 292,000 units × 0.15 hour per unit = 43,800 hours
Sewing Department: 292,000 units × 0.40 hour per unit = 116,800 hours

partment are required. In a similar manner, we can determine the direct labor hours needed in the Sewing Department to meet the budgeted production. Multiplying the direct labor hours for each department by the estimated department hourly rate yields the total direct labor cost for each department.

The direct labor needs should be coordinated between the production and personnel departments. This ensures that there will be enough labor available for production.

Q&A

Budgeted production is 22,000 units. Each unit requires 0.70 pound of steel and 0.20 direct labor hour. Steel is purchased for $45 per pound, and direct labor is $18 per hour. Steel has an estimated beginning inventory of 700 units and a desired ending inventory of 200 units. For the period, what is the budgeted (a) direct materials purchases and (b) direct labor cost?

(a) $670,500 {[(22,000 units × 0.70 lb.) + 200 lbs. − 700 lbs.] × $45}; (b) $79,200 (22,000 units × 0.20 hr. × $18)

Factory Overhead Cost Budget

The estimated factory overhead costs necessary for production make up the factory overhead cost budget. This budget usually includes the total estimated cost for each item of factory overhead, as shown in Exhibit 11.

EXHIBIT 11
Factory Overhead Cost Budget

Elite Accessories Inc.
Factory Overhead Cost Budget
For the Year Ending December 31, 2000

Indirect factory wages	$ 732,800
Supervisor salaries	360,000
Power and light	306,000
Depreciation of plant and equipment	288,000
Indirect materials	182,800
Maintenance	140,280
Insurance and property taxes	79,200
Total factory overhead cost	$2,089,080

A business may prepare supporting departmental schedules, in which the factory overhead costs are separated into their fixed and variable cost elements. Such schedules enable department managers to direct their attention to those costs for which they are responsible and to evaluate performance.

Cost of Goods Sold Budget

The direct materials purchases budget, direct labor cost budget, and factory overhead cost budget are the starting point for preparing the **cost of goods sold budget**. The desired ending inventory and the estimated beginning inventory data are combined with these data to determine the budgeted cost of goods sold.

To illustrate, the cost of goods sold budget shown in Exhibit 12 is based on the following work in process and finished goods inventories for Elite Accessories Inc.:

Estimated inventories on January 1, 2000:		Desired inventories on December 31, 2000:	
Finished goods	$1,095,600	Finished goods	$1,565,000
Work in process	214,400	Work in process	220,000

EXHIBIT 12 Cost of Goods Sold Budget

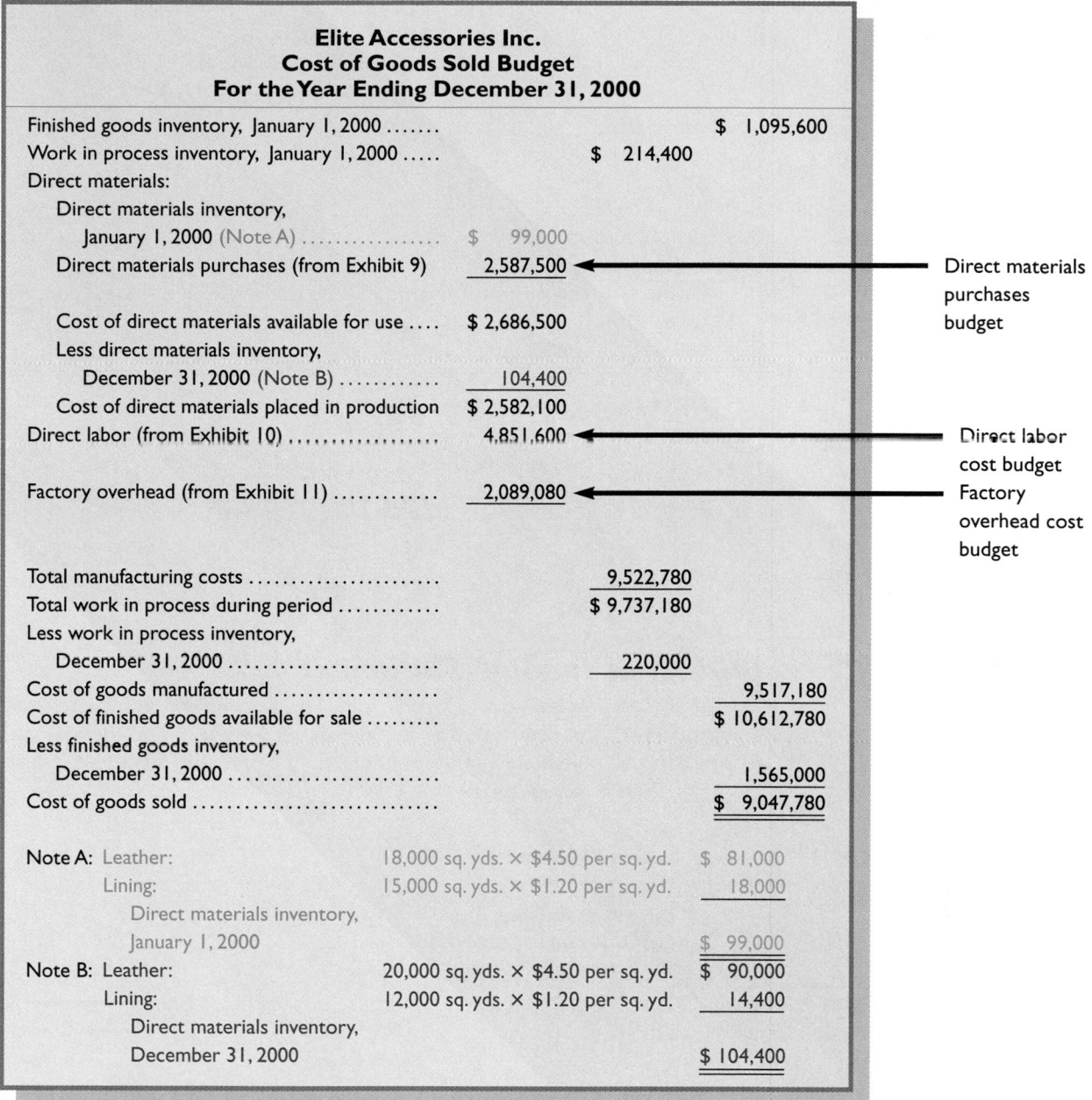

Elite Accessories Inc.
Cost of Goods Sold Budget
For the Year Ending December 31, 2000

Finished goods inventory, January 1, 2000			$ 1,095,600
Work in process inventory, January 1, 2000		$ 214,400	
Direct materials:			
Direct materials inventory, January 1, 2000 (Note A)	$ 99,000		
Direct materials purchases (from Exhibit 9)	2,587,500		
Cost of direct materials available for use	$ 2,686,500		
Less direct materials inventory, December 31, 2000 (Note B)	104,400		
Cost of direct materials placed in production	$ 2,582,100		
Direct labor (from Exhibit 10)	4,851,600		
Factory overhead (from Exhibit 11)	2,089,080		
Total manufacturing costs		9,522,780	
Total work in process during period		$ 9,737,180	
Less work in process inventory, December 31, 2000		220,000	
Cost of goods manufactured			9,517,180
Cost of finished goods available for sale			$ 10,612,780
Less finished goods inventory, December 31, 2000			1,565,000
Cost of goods sold			$ 9,047,780

Note A:	Leather:	18,000 sq. yds. × $4.50 per sq. yd.	$ 81,000
	Lining:	15,000 sq. yds. × $1.20 per sq. yd.	18,000
	Direct materials inventory, January 1, 2000		$ 99,000
Note B:	Leather:	20,000 sq. yds. × $4.50 per sq. yd.	$ 90,000
	Lining:	12,000 sq. yds. × $1.20 per sq. yd.	14,400
	Direct materials inventory, December 31, 2000		$ 104,400

Direct materials purchases budget

Direct labor cost budget

Factory overhead cost budget

Selling and Administrative Expenses Budget

The sales budget is often used as the starting point for estimating the selling and administrative expenses. For example, a budgeted increase in sales may require more advertising. Exhibit 13 is a selling and administrative expenses budget for Elite Accessories Inc.

Detailed supporting schedules are often prepared for major items in the selling and administrative expenses budget. For example, an advertising expense schedule for the Marketing Department should include the advertising media to be used (newspaper, direct mail, television), quantities (column inches, number of pieces, minutes), and the cost per unit. Attention to such details results in realistic budgets.

The **U.S. Post Office** had a 16% growth rate for its Priority Mail service as the result of its very successful advertising campaign comparing the $3 Priority Mail rate to **FedEx's** $12 and **UPS's** $6 rate. Unfortunately, the $140 million advertising budget was overspent by $85 million. The Post Office's top advertising executive used monies budgeted for other marketing efforts to subsidize the additional advertising expenditures. The Post Office's board of governors was critical of the budget overrun, even though the program's success more than covered the added cost. Soon after this, the top advertising executive left his position with the service.

EXHIBIT 13 Selling and Administrative Expenses Budget

Elite Accessories Inc.
Selling and Administrative Expenses Budget
For the Year Ending December 31, 2000

Selling expenses:		
Sales salaries expense	$715,000	
Advertising expense	360,000	
Travel expense	115,000	
Total selling expenses		$1,190,000
Administrative expenses:		
Officers' salaries expense	$360,000	
Office salaries expense	258,000	
Office rent expense	34,500	
Office supplies expense	17,500	
Miscellaneous administrative expenses	25,000	
Total administrative expenses		695,000
Total selling and administrative expenses		$1,885,000

Effective control results from assigning responsibility for achieving the budget to department supervisors.

Budgeted Income Statement

The budgets for sales, cost of goods sold, and selling and administrative expenses, combined with the data on other income, other expense, and income tax, are used to prepare the budgeted income statement. Exhibit 14 is a budgeted income statement for Elite Accessories Inc.

EXHIBIT 14 Budgeted Income Statement

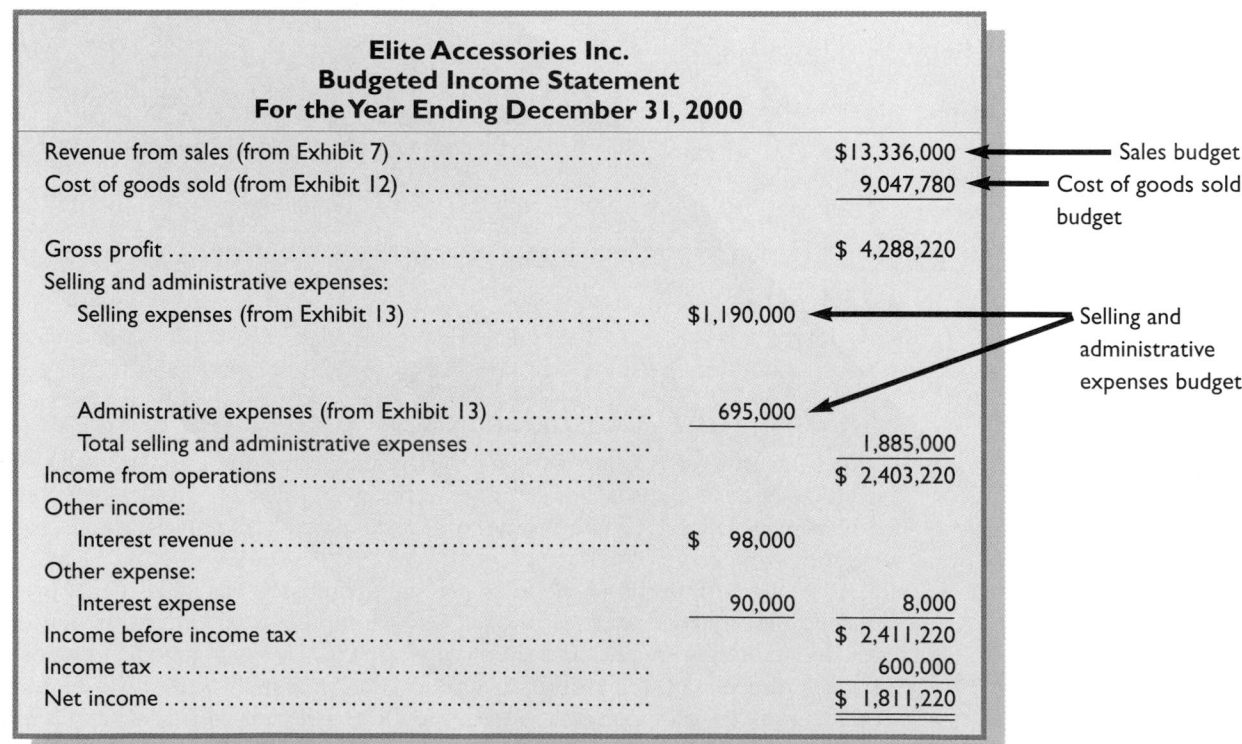

Elite Accessories Inc.
Budgeted Income Statement
For the Year Ending December 31, 2000

Revenue from sales (from Exhibit 7)		$13,336,000
Cost of goods sold (from Exhibit 12)		9,047,780
Gross profit		$ 4,288,220
Selling and administrative expenses:		
Selling expenses (from Exhibit 13)	$1,190,000	
Administrative expenses (from Exhibit 13)	695,000	
Total selling and administrative expenses		1,885,000
Income from operations		$ 2,403,220
Other income:		
Interest revenue	$ 98,000	
Other expense:		
Interest expense	90,000	8,000
Income before income tax		$ 2,411,220
Income tax		600,000
Net income		$ 1,811,220

Sales budget
Cost of goods sold budget
Selling and administrative expenses budget

The budgeted income statement summarizes the estimates of all phases of operations. This allows management to assess the effects of the individual budgets on profits for the year. If the budgeted net income is too low, management could review and revise operating plans in an attempt to improve income.

REAL WORLD **Emerson Electric** is known for its state-of-the-art financial planning. The CEO at Emerson, Charles F. Knight, uses at least 50% of his time for planning activities. One tool used by Emerson Electric is the "5-back-by-5-forward" income statement. This statement reports both five years of Emerson's history and five years of projected operating results. The rigorous planning practiced at Emerson fosters teamwork, communication, and improved skills among its managers. As Knight states, "We want proof that a division is stretching to reach its goals, and we want to see the details of the actions division management believes will yield improved results."

Source: Charles F. Knight, "Emerson Electric: Consistent Profits, Consistently," *Harvard Business Review* (January–February 1992), pp. 57–70.

Balance Sheet Budgets

OBJECTIVE 5

Prepare balance sheet budgets for a manufacturing business.

Balance sheet budgets are used by managers to plan financing, investing, and cash objectives for the firm. The balance sheet budgets illustrated for Elite Accessories Inc. in the following sections are the cash budget and the capital expenditures budget.

Cash Budget

The **cash budget** is one of the most important elements of the budgeted balance sheet. The cash budget presents the expected receipts (inflows) and payments (outflows) of cash for a period of time.

Information from the various operating budgets, such as the sales budget, the direct materials purchases budget, and the selling and administrative expenses budget, affects the cash budget. In addition, the capital expenditures budget, dividend policies, and plans for equity or long-term debt financing also affect the cash budget.

We illustrate the monthly cash budget for January, February, and March 2000, for Elite Accessories Inc. We begin by developing the estimated cash receipts and estimated cash payments portion of the cash budget.

The cash budget presents the expected receipts and payments of cash for a period of time.

Estimated Cash Receipts

Estimated cash receipts are planned additions to cash from sales and other sources, such as issuing securities or collecting interest. A supporting schedule can be used in determining the collections from sales. To illustrate this schedule, assume the following information for Elite Accessories Inc.:

Accounts receivable, January 1, 2000 . . . . $370,000

	January	February	March
Budgeted sales	$1,080,000	$1,240,000	$970,000

Elite Accessories Inc. expects to sell 10% of its merchandise for cash. Of the remaining 90% of the sales on account, 60% are expected to be collected in the month of the sale and the remainder in the next month.

Using this information, we prepare the schedule of collections from sales, shown in Exhibit 15. The cash receipts from sales on account are determined by adding the amounts collected from credit sales earned in the current period (60%) and the amounts accrued from sales in the previous period as accounts receivable (40%).

EXHIBIT 15
Schedule of Collections from Sales

Elite Accessories Inc.
Schedule of Collections from Sales
For the Three Months Ending March 31, 2000

	January	February	March
Receipts from cash sales:			
Cash sales (10% × current month's sales—Note A)	$108,000	$ 124,000	$ 97,000
Receipts from sales on account:			
Collections from prior month's sales (40% of previous month's credit sales—Note B)	$370,000	$ 388,800	$446,400
Collections from current month's sales (60% of current month's credit sales—Note C)	583,200	669,600	523,800
Total receipts from sales on account	$953,200	$1,058,400	$970,200

Note A: $108,000 = $1,080,000 × 10%
$124,000 = $1,240,000 × 10%
$ 97,000 = $ 970,000 × 10%

Note B: $370,000, given as January 1, 2000 Accounts Receivable balance
$388,800 = $1,080,000 × 90% × 40%
$446,400 = $1,240,000 × 90% × 40%

Note C: $583,200 = $1,080,000 × 90% × 60%
$669,600 = $1,240,000 × 90% × 60%
$523,800 = $ 970,000 × 90% × 60%

Q&A

A company collects 25% of its sales in the month of the sale and 75% in the month following the sale. If sales are budgeted to be $750,000 for March and $900,000 for April, what are the budgeted cash receipts for April?

$787,500 [($750,000 × 0.75) + ($900,000 × 0.25)]

Estimated Cash Payments

Estimated cash payments are planned reductions in cash from manufacturing costs, selling and administrative expenses, capital expenditures, and other sources, such as buying securities or paying interest or dividends. A supporting schedule can be used in estimating the cash payments for manufacturing costs. To illustrate, assume the following information for Elite Accessories Inc.:

Accounts payable, January 1, 2000 . . . . $190,000

	January	February	March
Manufacturing costs	$840,000	$780,000	$812,000

Depreciation expense on machines is estimated to be $24,000 per month and is included in the manufacturing costs. The accounts payable were incurred for manufacturing costs. Elite Accessories Inc. expects to pay 75% of the manufacturing costs in the month in which they are incurred and the balance in the next month.

Using this information, we can prepare the schedule of payments for manufacturing costs, as shown in Exhibit 16.

EXHIBIT 16
Schedule of Payments for Manufacturing Costs

Elite Accessories Inc.
Schedule of Payments for Manufacturing Costs
For the Three Months Ending March 31, 2000

	January	February	March
Payments of prior month's manufacturing costs {[25% × previous month's manufacturing costs (less depreciation)]—Note A}	$190,000	$204,000	$189,000
Payments of current month's manufacturing costs {[75% × current month's manufacturing costs (less depreciation)]—Note B}	612,000	567,000	591,000
Total payments	$802,000	$771,000	$780,000

Note A: $190,000, given as January 1, 2000 Accounts Payable balance
$204,000 = ($840,000 − $24,000) × 25%
$189,000 = ($780,000 − $24,000) × 25%

Note B: $612,000 = ($840,000 − $24,000) × 75%
$567,000 = ($780,000 − $24,000) × 75%
$591,000 = ($812,000 − $24,000) × 75%

In Exhibit 16, the cash payments are determined by adding the amounts paid from costs incurred in the current period (75%) and the amounts accrued as a liability from costs in the previous period (25%). The $24,000 of depreciation must be excluded from all calculations, since depreciation is a noncash expense that should not be included in the cash budget.

Completing the Cash Budget

To complete the cash budget for Elite Accessories Inc., as shown in Exhibit 17, assume that Elite Accessories Inc. is expecting the following:

Cash balance on January 1	$280,000
Quarterly taxes paid on March 31	150,000
Quarterly interest expense paid on January 10	22,500
Quarterly interest revenue received on March 21	24,500
Sewing equipment purchased in February	274,000

In addition, monthly selling and administrative expenses, which are paid in the month incurred, are estimated as follows:

	January	February	March
Selling and administrative expenses	$160,000	$165,000	$145,000

We can compare the estimated cash balance at the end of the period with the minimum balance required by operations. Assuming that the minimum cash balance for Elite Accessories Inc. is $340,000, we can determine any expected excess or deficiency.

The minimum cash balance protects against variations in estimates and for unexpected cash emergencies. For effective cash management, much of the minimum cash balance should be deposited in income-producing securities that can be readily converted to cash. U.S. Treasury Bills or Notes are examples of such securities.

EXHIBIT 17 Cash Budget

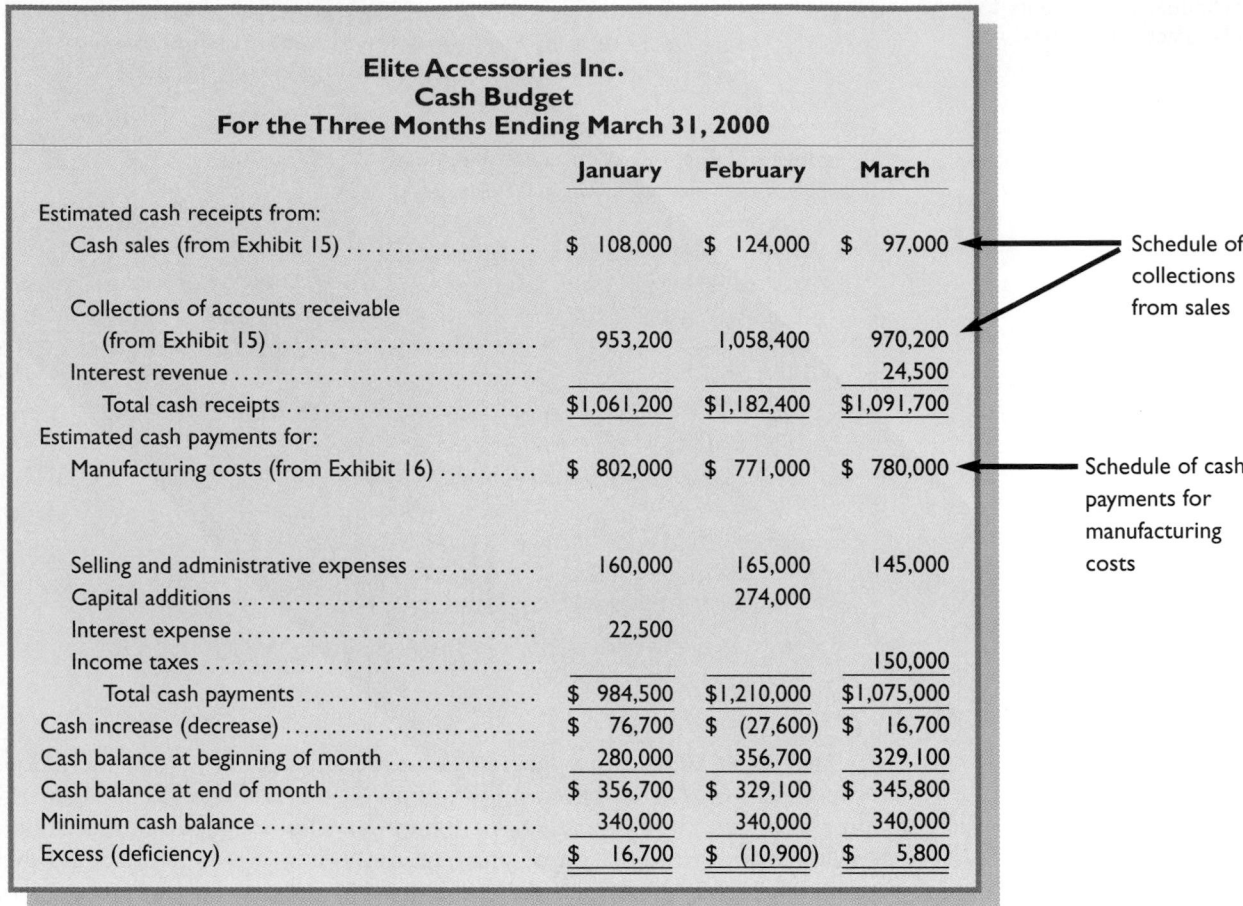

Elite Accessories Inc.
Cash Budget
For the Three Months Ending March 31, 2000

	January	February	March
Estimated cash receipts from:			
Cash sales (from Exhibit 15)	$ 108,000	$ 124,000	$ 97,000
Collections of accounts receivable (from Exhibit 15)	953,200	1,058,400	970,200
Interest revenue			24,500
Total cash receipts	$1,061,200	$1,182,400	$1,091,700
Estimated cash payments for:			
Manufacturing costs (from Exhibit 16)	$ 802,000	$ 771,000	$ 780,000
Selling and administrative expenses	160,000	165,000	145,000
Capital additions		274,000	
Interest expense	22,500		
Income taxes			150,000
Total cash payments	$ 984,500	$1,210,000	$1,075,000
Cash increase (decrease)	$ 76,700	$ (27,600)	$ 16,700
Cash balance at beginning of month	280,000	356,700	329,100
Cash balance at end of month	$ 356,700	$ 329,100	$ 345,800
Minimum cash balance	340,000	340,000	340,000
Excess (deficiency)	$ 16,700	$ (10,900)	$ 5,800

Schedule of collections from sales

Schedule of cash payments for manufacturing costs

Capital Expenditures Budget

The **capital expenditures budget** summarizes plans for acquiring fixed assets. Such expenditures are necessary as machinery and other fixed assets wear out, become obsolete, or for other reasons need to be replaced. In addition, expanding plant facilities may be necessary to meet increasing demand for a company's product.

The useful life of many fixed assets extends over long periods of time. In addition, the amount of the expenditures for such assets may vary from year to year. It is normal to project the plans for a number of periods into the future in preparing the capital expenditures budget. Exhibit 18 is a five-year capital expenditures budget for Elite Accessories Inc.

EXHIBIT 18
Capital Expenditures Budget

Elite Accessories Inc.
Capital Expenditures Budget
For the Five Years Ending December 31, 2004

Item	2000	2001	2002	2003	2004
Machinery—Cutting Department	$400,000			$280,000	$360,000
Machinery—Sewing Department	274,000	$260,000	$560,000	200,000	
Office equipment		90,000			60,000
Total	$674,000	$350,000	$560,000	$480,000	$420,000

The capital expenditures budget should be considered in preparing the other operating budgets. For example, the estimated depreciation of new equipment affects the factory overhead cost budget and the selling and administrative expenses budget. The plans for financing the capital expenditures may also affect the cash budget.

Budgeted Balance Sheet

The budgeted balance sheet estimates the financial condition at the end of a budget period. The budgeted balance sheet assumes that all operating budgets and financing plans are met. It is similar to a balance sheet based on actual data in the accounts. For this reason, we do not illustrate a budgeted balance sheet for Elite Accessories Inc. If the budgeted balance sheet indicates a weakness in financial position, revising the financing plans or other plans may be necessary. For example, a large amount of long-term debt in relation to stockholders' equity might require revising financing plans for capital expenditures. Such revisions might include issuing equity rather than debt.

ENCORE

The Anatomy of a Budget Overrun: The Case of *Waterworld*

How does a film budgeted for $100 million turn into one of the most expensive films ever made at an actual cost of $175 million? In the case of *Waterworld,* it comes from poor planning, bad luck, and underestimating the difficulty of filming under and around water.

The film was originally planned for a 96-day shoot, which eventually ballooned to over 150 days. Trouble dogged the project from the very beginning when filming began without a completed script and without an actor cast for the main villain, the Deacon. One month into the shoot, Dennis Hopper was eventually cast to play the villain. This caused delays, refilmed scenes, and script rewrites.

Scenes on the water were very difficult to shoot. Makeup artists and other technical crew had to be ferried everywhere by boat, adding to costs and causing film disruptions. One 10-minute scene involving the attack of the atoll by 50 villains on jet skis took a complete month to finish. These types of complicated and dangerous stunts required even more spending for additional safety.

At one point late in the shooting, the "slave colony" set sank 100 feet into a Hawaiian harbor. As the film came to a close, scenes were simplified or eliminated to save costs. The production moved from Hawaii to an outdoor tank in Los Angeles. A stunt scene having the Deacon (Hopper) land an airplane on "the Deez" (the rusted Exxon Valdez) was eliminated.

The film ended up grossing $88 million in the United States, and performed much better than expected overseas and in the videotape market. As a result, *Waterworld* broke even

and would have made money if it had stayed to its original budget.

Casey Silver, president of **Universal Pictures**, stated, "I won't be disingenuous and say that the movie didn't get away from us a bit. But it sold a lot of tickets. This movie was no *Ishtar, Howard the Duck,* or *Heaven's Gate. . . .* It just cost too much to make." ■

KEY POINTS

1 Describe budgeting, its objectives, and its impact on human behavior.

Budgeting involves (1) establishing specific goals, (2) executing plans to achieve the goals, and (3) periodically comparing actual results with these goals. In addition, budget goals should be established to avoid problems in human behavior. Thus, budgets should not be set too tightly, too loosely, or with goal conflict.

2 Describe the basic elements of the budget process, the two major types of budgeting, and the use of computers in budgeting.

The budget process is initiated by a budget committee. The annual estimates received by the budget committee should be carefully studied, analyzed, revised, and finally integrated together into the budget. Two major types of budgets are the static budget and the flexible budget. The static budget does not adjust with changes in activity, while the flexible budget does adjust with changes in activity. Computers can be useful in speeding up the budgetary process and in preparing timely budget performance reports. In addition, simulation models can be used to determine the impact of operating alternatives on various budgets.

3 Describe the master budget for a manufacturing business.

The master budget consists of the budgeted income statement and budgeted balance sheet. These two budgets are developed from detailed budgets that are described in the next two objectives.

4 Prepare the basic income statement budgets for a manufacturing business.

The basic income statement budgets are the sales budget, production budget, direct materials purchases budget, direct labor cost budget, factory overhead cost budget, cost of goods sold budget, and selling and administrative expenses budget.

5 Prepare balance sheet budgets for a manufacturing business.

Both the cash budget and the capital expenditures budget can be used in preparing the budgeted balance sheet. The cash budget consists of budgeted cash receipts and budgeted cash payments. The capital expenditures budget is an important tool for planning expenditures for fixed assets.

ILLUSTRATIVE PROBLEM

Selected information concerning sales and production for Cabot Co. for July of the current year are summarized as follows:

a. Estimated sales:

Product K: 40,000 units at $30.00 per unit
Product L: 20,000 units at $65.00 per unit

b. Estimated inventories, July 1, 20—:

Material A: 4,000 lbs.	Product K: 3,000 units at $17 per unit	$ 51,000
Material B: 3,500 lbs.	Product L: 2,700 units at $35 per unit	94,500
	Total	$145,500

There were no work in process inventories estimated for July 1, 20—.

c. Desired inventories at July 31, 20—:

Material A: 3,000 lbs.	Product K: 2,500 units at $17 per unit	$ 42,500
Material B: 2,500 lbs.	Product L: 2,000 units at $35 per unit	70,000
	Total	$112,500

There were no work in process inventories desired for July 31, 20—.

d. Direct materials used in production:

	Product K	Product L
Material A:	0.7 lb. per unit	3.5 lbs. per unit
Material B:	1.2 lbs. per unit	1.8 lbs. per unit

e. Unit costs for direct materials:

Material A:	$4.00 per lb.
Material B:	$2.00 per lb.

f. Direct labor requirements:

	Department 1	Department 2
Product K	0.4 hour per unit	0.15 hour per unit
Product L	0.6 hour per unit	0.25 hour per unit

g.

	Department 1	Department 2
Direct labor rate	$12.00 per hour	$16.00 per hour

h. Estimated factory overhead costs for July:

Indirect factory wages	$200,000
Depreciation of plant and equipment	40,000
Power and light	25,000
Indirect materials	34,000
Total	$299,000

Instructions

1. Prepare a sales budget for July.
2. Prepare a production budget for July.
3. Prepare a direct materials purchases budget for July.
4. Prepare a direct labor cost budget for July.
5. Prepare a cost of goods sold budget for July.

Solution

1.

Cabot Co.
Sales Budget
For the Month Ending July 31, 20—

Product	Unit Sales Volume	Unit Selling Price	Total Sales
Product K	40,000	$30.00	$1,200,000
Product L	20,000	65.00	1,300,000
Total revenue from sales . .			$2,500,000

2.

Cabot Co.
Production Budget
For the Month Ending July 31, 20—

	Units	
	Product K	**Product L**
Sales	40,000	20,000
Plus desired inventories at July 31, 20—	2,500	2,000
Total	42,500	22,000
Less estimated inventories, July 1, 20—	3,000	2,700
Total production	39,500	19,300

3.

Cabot Co.
Direct Materials Purchases Budget
For the Month Ending July 31, 20—

	Direct Materials		
	Material A	**Material B**	**Total**
Units required for production:			
Product K (39,500 × lbs. per unit)	27,650 lbs.*	47,400 lbs.*	
Product L (19,300 × lbs. per unit)	67,550**	34,740**	
Plus desired units of inventory, July 31, 20—	3,000	2,500	
Total	98,200 lbs.	84,640 lbs.	
Less estimated units of inventory, July 1, 20—	4,000	3,500	
Total units to be purchased	94,200 lbs.	81,140 lbs.	
Unit price	× $4.00	× $2.00	
Total direct materials purchases	$376,800	$162,280	$539,080

*27,650 = 39,500 × 0.7 47,400 = 39,500 × 1.2
**67,550 = 19,300 × 3.5 34,740 = 19,300 × 1.8

4.

Cabot Co.
Direct Labor Cost Budget
For the Month Ending July 31, 20—

	Department 1	**Department 2**	**Total**
Hours required for production:			
Product K (39,500 × hours per unit)	15,800*	5,925*	
Product L (19,300 × hours per unit)	11,580**	4,825**	
Total	27,380	10,750	
Hourly rate	×$12.00	×$16.00	
Total direct labor cost	$328,560	$172,000	$500,560

*15,800 = 39,500 × 0.4 5,925 = 39,500 × 0.15
**11,580 = 19,300 × 0.6 4,825 = 19,300 × 0.25

5.

Cabot Co.
Cost of Goods Sold Budget
For the Month Ending July 31, 20—

Finished goods inventory, July 1, 20—		$ 145,500
Direct materials:		
Direct materials inventory, July 1, 20— (Note A)	$ 23,000	
Direct materials purchases	539,080	
Cost of direct materials available for use	$562,080	
Less direct materials inventory, July 31, 20— (Note B)	17,000	
Cost of direct materials placed in production	$545,080	
Direct labor	500,560	
Factory overhead	299,000	
Cost of goods manufactured		1,344,640
Cost of finished goods available for sale		$1,490,140
Less finished goods inventory, July 31, 20—		112,500
Cost of goods sold		$1,377,640

Note A:

Material A	4,000 lbs.	at $4.00 per lb.	$16,000
Material B	3,500 lbs.	at $2.00 per lb.	7,000
Direct materials inventory, July 1, 20—			$23,000

Note B:

Material A	3,000 lbs.	at $4.00 per lb.	$12,000
Material B	2,500 lbs.	at $2.00 per lb.	5,000
Direct materials inventory, July 31, 20—			$17,000

SELF-EXAMINATION QUESTIONS

Answers at End of Chapter

Matching

Match each of the following statements with its proper term. Some terms may not be used.

- **A.** **budget**
- **B.** **capital expenditures budget**
- **C.** **cash budget**
- **D.** **continuous budgeting**
- **E.** **cost of goods sold budget**
- **F.** **direct materials purchases budget**
- **G.** **flexible budget**
- **H.** **goal conflict**
- **I.** **master budget**
- **J.** **production budget**
- **K.** **responsibility center**
- **L.** **sales budget**
- **M.** **static budget**
- **N.** **zero-based budgeting**

I 1. The comprehensive budget plan linking all the individual budgets related to sales, cost of goods sold, operating expenses, projects, capital expenditures, and cash.

D 2. A method of budgeting that provides for maintaining a twelve-month projection into the future.

N 3. A concept of budgeting that requires all levels of management to start from zero and estimate budget data as if there had been no previous activities in their units.

A 4. An accounting device used to plan and control resources of operational departments and divisions.

F 5. A budget that uses the production budget as a starting point.

B 6. The budget summarizing future plans for acquiring plant facilities and equipment.

E 7. A budget of the estimated direct materials, direct labor, and factory overhead consumed by sold products.

J 8. A budget of estimated unit production.

M 9. A budget that does not adjust to changes in activity levels.

G 10. A budget that adjusts for varying rates of activity.

C 11. A budget of estimated cash receipts and payments.

K 12. An organizational unit for which a manager is assigned responsibility over costs, revenues, or assets.

Multiple Choice

1. A tight budget may create:
   A. budgetary slack
   B. discouragement
   C. a flexible budget
   D. a "spend it or lose it" mentality

2. The first step of the budget process is:
   A. plan
   B. direct
   C. control
   D. feedback

3. Static budgets are often used by:
   A. production departments
   B. administrative departments
   C. responsibility centers
   D. capital projects

4. The total estimated sales for the coming year is 250,000 units. The estimated inventory at the beginning of the year is 22,500 units, and the desired inventory at the end of the year is 30,000 units. The total production indicated in the production budget is:
   A. 242,500 units
   B. 257,500 units
   C. 280,000 units
   D. 302,500 units

5. Dixon Company expects $650,000 of credit sales in March and $800,000 of credit sales in April. Dixon historically collects 70% of its sales in the month of sale and 30% in the following month. How much cash does Dixon expect to collect in April?
   A. $800,000
   B. $560,000
   C. $755,000
   D. $1,015,000

CLASS DISCUSSION QUESTIONS

1. What are the three major objectives of budgeting?
2. What is the manager's role in a responsibility center?
3. Briefly describe the type of human behavior problems that might arise if budget goals are set too tightly.
4. Why should all levels of management and all departments participate in preparing and submitting budget estimates?
5. Give an example of budgetary slack.
6. What behavioral problems are associated with setting a budget too loosely?
7. What behavioral problems are associated with establishing conflicting goals within the budget?
8. When would a company use zero-based budgeting?
9. Under what circumstances would a static budget be appropriate?
10. How do computerized budgeting systems aid firms in the budgeting process?
11. What is the first step in preparing a master budget?
12. Why should the production requirements set forth in the production budget be carefully coordinated with the sales budget?
13. Why should the timing of direct materials purchases be closely coordinated with the production budget?
14. In preparing the budget for the cost of goods sold, what are the three budgets from which data on relevant estimates of quantities and costs are combined with data on estimated inventories?
15. a. Discuss the purpose of the cash budget.
    b. If the cash for the first quarter of the fiscal year indicates excess cash at the end of each of the first two months, how might the excess cash be used?
16. How does a schedule of collections from sales assist in preparing the cash budget?
17. Give an example of how the capital expenditures budget affects other operating budgets.

Resources for Your Success On-Line at warren.swcollege.com
Remember! If you need additional help, visit South-Western's Web site. See page 26 for a description of the online and printed materials that are available.

EXERCISES

Exercise 20–1
Personal cash budget

Objectives 2, 5

✓ December 31 cash balance, $380

At the beginning of the 2000 school year, David Kerr decided to prepare a cash budget for the months of September, October, November, and December. The following information relates to the budget:

Cash balance, September 1	$5,000
Purchase season football tickets in September	180
Additional entertainment for each month	200
Pay semester tuition on September 3	4,000
Pay rent at the beginning of each month	460
Pay for food each month	250
Pay apartment deposit on September 2 (to be returned December 15)	500
Part-time job earnings each month	800

a. Prepare a cash budget for September, October, November, and December.
b. Are the budgets prepared as static budgets or flexible budgets?
c. What are the budget implications for David Kerr?

Exercise 20–2
Flexible budget for selling and administrative expenses

Objectives 2, 4

✓ Total selling and administrative expenses at $200,000 sales, $46,300

Nordic Furniture Company uses flexible budgets that are based on the following data:

Sales commissions	6% of sales
Advertising expense	10% of sales
Miscellaneous selling expense	$1,000 plus 2% of sales
Office salaries expense	$5,000 per month
Office supplies expense	1½% of sales
Miscellaneous administrative expense	$300 per month plus ½% of sales

Prepare a flexible selling and administrative expenses budget for May of the current year for sales volumes of $120,000, $160,000, and $200,000. (Use Exhibit 4 as a model.)

Exercise 20–3
Static budget vs. flexible budget

Objectives 2, 4

GENERAL LEDGER (Windows only)

✓ b. Excess of actual over budget for March, $28,000

The production supervisor of the Welding Department for Baxter Company agreed to the following monthly static budget for the upcoming year:

Baxter Company
Welding Department
Monthly Production Budget

Wages	$300,000
Utilities	160,000
Depreciation	50,000
Total	$510,000

The actual amount spent for the first three months of the year 2000 in the Welding Department was as follows:

January	$475,000
February	435,000
March	400,000

The Welding Department supervisor has been very pleased with this performance, since actual expenditures have been less than the monthly budget. However, the plant manager believes that the budget should not remain fixed for every month, but should "flex" or adjust to the volume of work that is produced in the Welding Department. Additional budget information for the Welding Department is as follows:

Wages per hour	$15.00
Utility cost per direct labor hour	$8.00
Direct labor hours per unit	0.40
Planned unit production	50,000

The actual units produced in the Welding Department were as follows:

January	45,000 units
February	40,000
March	35,000

a. Prepare a flexible budget for the actual units produced for January, February, and March in the Welding Department.
b. Compare the flexible budget with the actual expenditures for the first three months. What does this comparison suggest?

Exercise 20–4
Sales and production budgets
Objective 4

SPREADSHEET

✓ b. Model R4 total production, 144,500 units

Wave Electronics Company manufactures two models of clock radios, R4 and R8. Based on the following production and sales data for September 2001, prepare (a) a sales budget and (b) a production budget.

	R4	R8
Estimated inventory (units), September 1 . .	10,000	8,000
Desired inventory (units), September 30 . .	12,500	6,600
Expected sales volume (units):		
East Region	54,000	34,500
West Region	88,000	43,400
Unit sales price	$32.00	$45.00

Exercise 20–5
Professional fees budget
Objective 4

✓ Total professional fees, $13,238,000

Leno and Letterman, CPAs, offer three types of services to clients: auditing, tax, and computer consulting. Based on experience and projected growth, the following billable hours have been estimated for the year ending December 31, 2000:

	Billable Hours
Audit Department:	
Staff	42,000
Partners	6,700
Tax Department:	
Staff	37,500
Partners	8,400
Computer Consulting Department:	
Staff	21,400
Partners	9,500

The average billing rate for staff is $80 per hour, and the average billing rate for partners is $210 per hour. Prepare a professional fees budget for Leno and Letterman, CPAs, for the year ending December 31, 2000, using the following column headings and showing the estimated professional fees by type of service rendered:

Billable Hours	Hourly Rate	Total Revenue

Exercise 20–6
Professional labor cost budget
Objective 4

✓ Staff total labor cost, $3,027,000

Based on the data in Exercise 20–5 and assuming that the average compensation per hour for staff is $30 and for partners is $110, prepare a labor cost budget for Leno and Letterman, CPAs, for the year ending December 31, 2000. Use the following column headings:

Billable Hours Required	
Staff	Partners

Exercise 20–7
Direct materials purchases budget
Objective 4

✓ Total cheese purchases, $201,411

Mama Leona's Frozen Pizza Inc. has determined from its production budget the following estimated production volumes for 12″ and 16″ frozen pizzas for August:

	Units	
	12″ Pizza	16″ Pizza
Budgeted production volume	36,100	56,700

There are three direct materials used in producing the two types of pizza. The quantities of direct materials expected to be used for each pizza are as follows:

	12″ Pizza	16″ Pizza
Direct materials:		
Dough	1.00 lb. per unit	1.50 lbs. per unit
Tomato	0.50	0.80
Cheese	0.70	1.10

In addition, Mama Leona's has determined the following information about each material:

	Dough	Tomato	Cheese
Estimated inventory, August 1, 2000	500 lbs.	200 lbs.	450 lbs.
Desired inventory, August 31, 2000	600 lbs.	280 lbs.	380 lbs.
Price per pound	$1.20	$1.80	$2.30

Prepare a direct materials purchases budget for Mama Leona's Frozen Pizza Inc.

Exercise 20–8
Direct materials purchases budget

Objective 4

What's Wrong WITH THIS?

✓ Total steel belt purchases, $425,000

Anticipated sales for SureTread Tire Company were 30,000 passenger car tires and 10,000 truck tires. There were no anticipated beginning finished goods inventories for either product. The planned ending finished goods inventories were 2,000 units for each product. Rubber and steel belts are used in producing passenger car and truck tires according to the following table:

	Passenger Car	Truck
Rubber	20 lbs. per unit	50 lbs. per unit
Steel belts	2 lbs. per unit	5 lbs. per unit

The purchase prices of rubber and steel are $2.20 and $3.40 per pound, respectively. The desired ending inventories of rubber and steel belts are 40,000 and 6,000 pounds, respectively. The estimated beginning inventories for rubber and steel belts are 70,000 and 5,000 pounds, respectively.

The following materials purchases budget was prepared for SureTread Tire Company:

SureTread Tire Company
Direct Materials Purchases Budget
For the Year Ending December 31, 2000

	Rubber	Steel Belts	Total
Units required for production:			
Passenger tires	600,000 lbs.	60,000 lbs.	
Truck tires	500,000	50,000	
Total	1,100,000 lbs.	110,000 lbs.	
Unit price	× $2.20	× $3.40	
Total direct materials purchases	$2,420,000	$374,000	$2,794,000

Correct the direct materials purchases budget for SureTread Tire Company.

Exercise 20–9
Direct labor cost budget

Objective 4

✓ Total direct labor cost, Finishing, $1,275,040

Sampras Sporting Goods Company manufactures two types of tennis rackets, the Junior and Pro-Striker models. The production budget for November for the two rackets is as follows:

	Junior	Pro-Striker
Production budget	24,500 units	84,300 units

Both rackets are produced in two departments, Molding and Finishing. The direct labor hours required for each racket are estimated as follows:

	Molding Department	Finishing Department
Junior	0.20 hour per unit	0.50 hour per unit
Pro-Striker	0.40 hour per unit	0.80 hour per unit

The direct labor rate for each department is as follows:

Molding Department	$14.00 per hour
Finishing Department	$16.00 per hour

Prepare the direct labor cost budget for November 2000.

Exercise 20–10
Factory overhead cost budget
Objective 4

✓ Total variable factory overhead costs, $196,000

Ambassador Watch Company budgeted the following costs for anticipated production for April 2000:

Advertising expenses	$350,000
Manufacturing supplies	10,000
Power and light	45,000
Sales commissions	280,000
Factory insurance	24,000
Supervisor wages	95,000
Production control salaries	32,000
Executive officer salaries	210,000
Materials management salaries	14,000
Factory depreciation	28,000

Prepare a factory overhead cost budget, separating variable and fixed costs. Assume that all indirect factory labor costs are variable.

Exercise 20–11
Cost of goods sold budget
Objective 4

✓ Cost of goods sold, $336,960

The controller of Danish Charm Ceramic Company wishes to prepare a cost of goods sold budget for June. The controller assembled the following information for constructing the cost of goods sold budget:

Direct materials:

	Enamel	Paint	Porcelain	Total
Total direct material purchases budgeted for June	$23,600	$14,300	$78,900	$116,800
Estimated inventory, June 1, 2000	2,450	1,600	4,250	8,300
Desired inventory, June 30, 2000	2,000	1,850	3,900	7,750

Direct labor cost:

	Kiln Department	Decorating Department	Total
Total direct labor cost budgeted for June	$42,400	$94,900	$137,300

Finished goods inventories:

	Dish	Bowl	Figurine	Total
Estimated inventory, June 1, 2000	$3,260	$2,570	$4,140	$9,970
Desired inventory, June 30, 2000	2,960	3,260	2,670	8,890

Work in process inventories:

Estimated inventory, June 1, 2000	$2,900
Desired inventory, June 30, 2000	3,740

Budgeted factory overhead costs for June:

Indirect factory wages	$37,590
Depreciation of plant and equipment	24,300
Power and light	11,600
Indirect materials	8,580
Total	$82,070

Use the preceding information to prepare a cost of goods sold budget for June 2000.

Exercise 20–12
Schedule of cash collections of accounts receivable

Objective 5

SPREADSHEET

✓ Total cash collected in May, $815,200

Mann Company was organized on March 1 of the current year. Projected sales for each of the first three months of operations are as follows:

March	$640,000
April	720,000
May	900,000

The company expects to sell 20% of its merchandise for cash. Of sales on account, 50% are expected to be collected in the month of the sale, 30% in the month following the sale, and the remainder in the following month.

Prepare a schedule indicating cash collections from sales for March, April, and May.

Exercise 20–13
Schedule of cash payments

Objective 5

✓ Total cash payments in August, $137,000

Vision Systems Inc. was organized on May 31, 2000. Projected selling and administrative expenses for each of the first three months of operations are as follows:

June	$128,000
July	172,000
August	152,000

Depreciation, insurance, and property taxes represent $20,000 of the estimated monthly expenses. The annual insurance premium was paid on May 31, and property taxes for the year will be paid in December. Three-fourths of the remainder of the expenses are expected to be paid in the month in which they are incurred, with the balance to be paid in the following month.

Prepare a schedule indicating cash payments for selling and administrative expenses for June, July, and August.

Exercise 20–14
Schedule of cash payments

Objective 5

✓ Total cash payments in December, $441,730

The Oasis Hotel is planning its cash payments for operations for the fourth quarter (October–December), 2001. The Accrued Expenses Payable balance on October 1 is $136,000. The budgeted expenses for the next three months are as follows:

	October	November	December
Salaries	$365,000	$403,400	$326,000
Utilities	21,000	24,000	20,000
Other operating expenses	123,400	132,500	100,800
Total	$509,400	$559,900	$446,800

Other operating expenses include $36,000 of monthly depreciation expense and $3,000 of monthly insurance expense that was prepaid for the year on March 1 of the current year. Of the remaining expenses, 70% are paid in the month in which they are incurred, with the remainder paid in the following month. The Accrued Expenses Payable balance on October 1 relates to the expenses incurred in September.

Prepare a schedule of cash payments for operations for October, November, and December.

Exercise 20–15
Capital expenditures budget

Objective 5

✓ Total capital expenditures in 2002, $5,800,000

On January 1, 1999, the controller of Tan Manufacturing Company is planning capital expenditures for the years 1999–2002. The following interviews helped the controller collect the necessary information for the capital expenditures budget.

Director of Facilities: A construction contract was signed in late 1998 for the construction of a new factory building at a contract cost of $12,000,000. The construction is scheduled to begin in 1999 and be completed in 2000.

Vice-President of Manufacturing: Once the new factory building is finished in late 2000, we plan to purchase $1.8 million in equipment. I expect that an additional $400,000 will be needed early in the following year to test and install the equipment before we can begin production. If sales continue to grow, I expect we'll need to invest another million in equipment in 2002.

Vice-President of Marketing: We have really been growing lately. I wouldn't be surprised if we need to expand the size of our new factory building in 2002 by at least 40%. Fortunately, we expect inflation to have minimal impact on construction costs over the next four years.

Director of Information Systems: We need to upgrade our information systems to local area network (LAN) technology. It doesn't make sense to do this until after the new factory building is completed and producing product. Once the factory is up and running, we should equip the whole facility with LAN technology. I think it would cost us $1,800,000 today to install the technology. However, prices have been dropping by 20% per year, so it should be less expensive at a later date.

President: I am excited about our long-term prospects. My only short-term concern is financing the $7,000,000 of construction costs on the portion of the new factory building scheduled to be completed in 1999.

Use the interview information above to prepare a capital expenditures budget for Tan Manufacturing Company for the years 1999–2002.

PROBLEMS SERIES A

Problem 20–1A
Forecast sales volume and sales budget
Objective 4

✓ 3. Total revenue from sales, $32,329,080

Paul Revere Security Alarm Company prepared the following sales budget for the current year:

Paul Revere Security Alarm Company
Sales Budget
For the Year Ending December 31, 2000

Product and Area	Unit Sales Volume	Unit Selling Price	Total Sales
Home Alert System:			
United States	18,000	$240	$ 4,320,000
Europe	15,000	240	3,600,000
Asia	36,000	240	8,640,000
Total	69,000		$16,560,000
Business Alert System:			
United States	4,500	$850	$ 3,825,000
Europe	3,200	850	2,720,000
Asia	5,800	850	4,930,000
Total	13,500		$11,475,000
Total revenue from sales			$28,035,000

At the end of December 2000, the following unit sales data were reported for the year:

	Unit Sales	
	Home Alert System	Business Alert System
United States	19,800	4,590
Europe	14,250	3,392
Asia	37,440	5,626

For the year ending December 31, 2001, unit sales are expected to follow the patterns established during the year ending December 31, 2000. The unit selling price for the Home Alert System is expected to increase to $280, and the unit selling price for the Business Alert System is expected to be reduced to $840, effective January 1, 2001.

Instructions

1. Compute the increase or decrease of actual unit sales for the year ended December 31, 2000, over budget. (Round percent changes to the nearest whole percent.) Place your answers in a columnar table with the following format:

	Unit Sales, Year Ended 2000		Increase (Decrease) Actual Over Budget	
	Budget	Actual Sales	Amount	Percent
Home Alert System:				
United States				
Europe				
Asia				
Business Alert System:				
United States				
Europe				
Asia				

2. Assuming that the trend of sales indicated in (1) is to continue in 2001, compute the unit sales volume to be used for preparing the sales budget for the year ending December 31, 2001. Place your answers in a columnar table with the following format:

	2000 Actual Units	Percentage Increase (Decrease)	2001 Budgeted Units
Home Alert System:			
United States			
Europe			
Asia			
Business Alert System:			
United States			
Europe			
Asia			

3. Prepare a sales budget for the year ending December 31, 2001.

Problem 20–2A

Sales, production, direct materials, and direct labor budgets

Objective 4

✓ 3. Total direct materials purchases, $12,542,236

The budget director of Monarch Chair Company requests estimates of sales, production, and other operating data from the various administrative units every month. Selected information concerning sales and production for July 2000 is summarized as follows:

a. Estimated sales of King and Prince chairs for July by sales territory:

Northern Domestic:	
King	22,500 units at $400 per unit
Prince	35,200 units at $320 per unit
Southern Domestic:	
King	18,300 units at $380 per unit
Prince	24,800 units at $310 per unit
International:	
King	6,500 units at $440 per unit
Prince	9,100 units at $350 per unit

b. Estimated inventories at July 1:

Direct materials:	
Fabric	10,800 sq. yds.
Wood	6,300 lineal ft.
Filler	4,000 cu. ft.
Springs	13,900 units
Finished products:	
King	840 units
Prince	280 units

c. Desired inventories at July 31:

Direct materials:	
Fabric	9,500 sq. yds.
Wood	5,700 lineal ft.
Filler	4,300 cu. ft.
Springs	15,300 units
Finished products:	
King	700 units
Prince	300 units

d. Direct materials used in production:

In manufacture of King:	
Fabric	4 sq. yds. per unit of product
Wood	28 lineal ft. per unit of product
Filler	3.5 cu. ft. per unit of product
Springs	12 units per unit of product
In manufacture of Prince:	
Fabric	3.2 sq. yds. per unit of product
Wood	22 lineal ft. per unit of product
Filler	3.0 cu. ft. per unit of product
Springs	10 units per unit of product

e. Anticipated purchase price for direct materials:

Fabric	$8.00 per square yard
Wood	2.10 per lineal foot
Filler	2.80 per cubic foot
Springs	1.80 per unit

f. Direct labor requirements:

King:	
Framing Department	1.5 hours at $10 per hour
Cutting Department	0.5 hour at $11 per hour
Upholstery Department	2.5 hours at $15 per hour
Prince:	
Framing Department	1.2 hours at $10 per hour
Cutting Department	0.4 hour at $11 per hour
Upholstery Department	1.8 hours at $15 per hour

Instructions

1. Prepare a sales budget for July.
2. Prepare a production budget for July.
3. Prepare a direct materials purchases budget for July.
4. Prepare a direct labor cost budget for July.

Problem 20–3A

Budgeted income statement and supporting budgets

Objective 4

✓ 4. Total direct labor cost in Assembly Dept., $321,060

The budget director of Impact Helmet Company, with the assistance of the controller, treasurer, production manager, and sales manager, has gathered the following data for use in developing the budgeted income statement for August 2000:

a. Estimated sales for August:

Batting helmet	19,400 units at $38 per unit
Football helmet	42,300 units at $65 per unit

b. Estimated inventories at August 1:

Direct materials:		Finished products:	
Plastic	9,500 lbs.	Batting helmet	2,450 units at $21 per unit
Foam lining	4,700 lbs.	Football helmet	3,900 units at $40 per unit

c. Desired inventories at August 31:

Direct materials:		Finished products:	
Plastic	11,400 lbs.	Batting helmet	2,400 units at $21 per unit
Foam lining	4,500 lbs.	Football helmet	3,500 units at $40 per unit

d. Direct materials used in production:

In manufacture of batting helmet:	
Plastic	1.50 lbs. per unit of product
Foam lining	0.50 lb. per unit of product
In manufacture of football helmet:	
Plastic	3.50 lbs. per unit of product
Foam lining	1.00 lb. per unit of product

e. Anticipated cost of purchases and beginning and ending inventory of direct materials:

Plastic	$6.00 per lb.
Foam lining	$3.50 per lb.

f. Direct labor requirements:

Batting helmet:	
Molding Department	0.15 hour at $15 per hour
Assembly Department	0.30 hour at $12 per hour
Football helmet:	
Molding Department	0.20 hour at $15 per hour
Assembly Department	0.50 hour at $12 per hour

g. Estimated factory overhead costs for August:

Indirect factory wages	$265,000
Depreciation of plant and equipment	63,000
Power and light	24,000
Insurance and property tax	9,700

h. Estimated operating expenses for August:

Sales salaries expense	$295,700
Advertising expense	183,200
Office salaries expense	145,800
Depreciation expense—office equipment	6,200
Telephone expense—selling	4,700
Telephone expense—administrative	900
Travel expense—selling	42,100
Office supplies expense	4,000
Miscellaneous administrative expense	5,000

i. Estimated other income and expense for August:

Interest revenue	$12,500
Interest expense	15,700

j. Estimated tax rate: 35%

Instructions

1. Prepare a sales budget for August.
2. Prepare a production budget for August.
3. Prepare a direct materials purchases budget for August.
4. Prepare a direct labor cost budget for August.
5. Prepare a factory overhead cost budget for August.
6. Prepare a cost of goods sold budget for August. Work in process at the beginning of August is estimated to be $43,600, and work in process at the end of August is estimated to be $37,800.
7. Prepare a selling and administrative expenses budget for August.
8. Prepare a budgeted income statement for August.

Problem 20–4A

Cash budget

Objective 5

SPREADSHEET

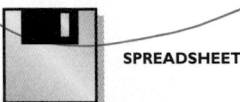

✓ 1. June deficiency, $12,900

The treasurer of Edison Lighting Company instructs you to prepare a monthly cash budget for the next three months. You are presented with the following budget information:

	April	May	June
Sales	$260,000	$340,000	$280,000
Manufacturing costs	130,000	170,000	150,000
Selling and administrative expenses	80,000	105,000	100,000
Capital expenditures	—	—	125,000

The company expects to sell about 10% of its merchandise for cash. Of sales on account, 70% are expected to be collected in full in the month following the sale and the remainder the following month. Depreciation, insurance, and property tax expense represent $15,000 of the estimated monthly manufacturing costs. The annual insurance premium is paid in July, and the annual property taxes are paid in November. Of the remainder of the manufacturing costs, 80% are expected to be paid in the month in which they are incurred and the balance in the following month.

Current assets as of April 1 include cash of $40,000, marketable securities of $65,000, and accounts receivable of $370,000 ($280,000 from March sales and $90,000 from February sales). Current liabilities as of April 1 include a $70,000, 12%, 90-day note payable due June 20 and $25,000 of accounts payable incurred in March for manufacturing costs. All selling and administrative expenses are paid in cash in the period they are incurred. It is expected that $3,000 in dividends will be received in April. An estimated income tax payment of $32,000 will be made in May. Edison's regular quarterly dividend of $10,000 is expected to be declared in May and paid in June. Management desires to maintain a minimum cash balance of $35,000.

Instructions

1. Prepare a monthly cash budget and supporting schedules for April, May, and June.
2. On the basis of the cash budget prepared in (1), what recommendation should be made to the treasurer?

Problem 20–5A

Budgeted income statement and balance sheet

Objectives 4, 5

✓ 1. Net income, $395,100

As a preliminary to requesting budget estimates of sales, costs, and expenses for the fiscal year beginning January 1, 2001, the following tentative trial balance as of December 31, 2000, is prepared by the Accounting Department of Patton Pulp and Paper Company:

Cash	$ 142,500	
Accounts Receivable	246,700	
Finished Goods	157,800	
Work in Process	37,800	
Materials	57,800	
Prepaid Expenses	4,500	
Plant and Equipment	620,000	
Accumulated Depreciation—Plant and Equipment		$ 267,000
Accounts Payable		184,500
Common Stock, $15 par		450,000
Retained Earnings		365,600
	$1,267,100	$1,267,100

Factory output and sales for 2001 are expected to total 24,000 units of product, which are to be sold at $150 per unit. The quantities and costs of the inventories (lifo method) at December 31, 2001, are expected to remain unchanged from the balances at the beginning of the year.

Budget estimates of manufacturing costs and operating expenses for the year are summarized as follows:

	Estimated Costs and Expenses	
	Fixed (Total for Year)	Variable (Per Unit Sold)
Cost of goods manufactured and sold:		
Direct materials	—	$68.00
Direct labor	—	8.50
Factory overhead:		
Depreciation of plant and equipment	$145,000	—
Other factory overhead	21,000	4.80
Selling expenses:		
Sales salaries and commissions	96,000	12.80
Advertising	121,000	—
Miscellaneous selling expense	13,500	3.20
Administrative expenses:		
Office and officers salaries	62,700	7.30
Supplies	4,200	1.50
Miscellaneous administrative expense	2,000	1.20

Balances of accounts receivable, prepaid expenses, and accounts payable at the end of the year are not expected to differ significantly from the beginning balances. Federal income tax of $164,300 on 2001 taxable income will be paid during 2001. Regular quarterly cash dividends of $2.00 a share are expected to be declared and paid in March, June, September, and December. It is anticipated that fixed assets will be purchased for $150,000 cash in May.

Instructions

1. Prepare a budgeted income statement for 2001.
2. Prepare a budgeted balance sheet as of December 31, 2001, with supporting calculations.

PROBLEMS SERIES B

Problem 20–1B

Forecast sales volume and sales budget

Objective 4

✓ 3. Total revenue from sales, $3,521,476

Rembrandt Frame Company prepared the following sales budget for the current year:

Rembrandt Frame Company
Sales Budget
For the Year Ending December 31, 2000

Product and Area	Unit Sales Volume	Unit Selling Price	Total Sales
8″ × 10″ Frame:			
East	30,000	$15.00	$ 450,000
Central	25,000	15.00	375,000
West	15,000	15.00	225,000
Total	70,000		$1,050,000
12″ × 16″ Frame:			
East	36,000	$20.00	$ 720,000
Central	18,000	20.00	360,000
West	32,000	20.00	640,000
Total	86,000		$1,720,000
Total revenue from sales			$2,770,000

At the end of December 2000, the following unit sales data were reported for the year:

	Unit Sales	
	8″ × 10″ Frame	12″ × 16″ Frame
East	32,400	34,200
Central	24,000	19,080
West	16,500	32,640

For the year ending December 31, 2001, unit sales are expected to follow the patterns established during the year ending December 31, 2000. The unit selling price for the 8″ × 10″ frame is expected to change to $18, and the unit selling price for the 12″ × 16″ frame is expected to be increased to $25, effective January 1, 2001.

Instructions

1. Compute the increase or decrease of actual unit sales for the year ended December 31, 2000, over budget. (Round percent changes to the nearest whole percent.) Place your answers in a columnar table with the following format:

	Unit Sales, Year Ended 2000		Increase (Decrease) Actual Over Budget	
	Budget	Actual Sales	Amount	Percent
8″ × 10″ Frame:				
East				
Central				
West				
12″ × 16″ Frame:				
East				
Central				
West				

2. Assuming that the trend of sales indicated in (1) is to continue in 2001, compute the unit sales volume to be used for preparing the sales budget for the year ending December 31, 2001. Place your answers in a columnar table with the following format:

	2000 Actual Units	Percentage Increase (Decrease)	2001 Budgeted Units
8″ × 10″ Frame:			
East			
Central			
West			
12″ × 16″ Frame:			
East			
Central			
West			

3. Prepare a sales budget for the year ending December 31, 2001.

Problem 20–2B

Sales, production, direct materials, and direct labor budgets

Objective 4

The budget director of New England Outdoor Grill Company requests estimates of sales, production, and other operating data from the various administrative units every month. Selected information concerning sales and production for May 2000 is summarized as follows:

✓ 3. Total direct materials purchases, $10,245,560

a. Estimated sales for May by sales territory:

Maine:	
Backyard Chef	9,000 units at $550 per unit
Master Chef	3,500 units at $1,300 per unit
Vermont:	
Backyard Chef	12,000 units at $500 per unit
Master Chef	4,000 units at $1,200 per unit
New Hampshire:	
Backyard Chef	6,000 units at $600 per unit
Master Chef	1,000 units at $1,500 per unit

b. Estimated inventories at May 1:

Direct materials:	
Grates	1,000 units
Stainless steel	2,500 lbs.
Burner subassemblies	600 units
Shelves	400 units
Finished products:	
Backyard Chef	1,500 units
Master Chef	400 units

c. Desired inventories at May 31:

Direct materials:	
Grates	800 units
Stainless steel	1,900 lbs.
Burner subassemblies	800 units
Shelves	480 units
Finished products:	
Backyard Chef	1,200 units
Master Chef	500 units

d. Direct materials used in production:

In manufacture of Backyard Chef:	
Grates	2 units per unit of product
Stainless steel	28 lbs. per unit of product
Burner subassemblies	1 unit per unit of product
Shelves	2 units per unit of product
In manufacture of Master Chef:	
Grates	6 units per unit of product
Stainless steel	71 lbs. per unit of product
Burner subassemblies	4 units per unit of product
Shelves	3 units per unit of product

e. Anticipated purchase price for direct materials:

Grates	$15 per unit
Stainless steel	$3 per lb.
Burner subassemblies	$66 per unit
Shelves	$7 per unit

f. Direct labor requirements:

Backyard Chef:	
Stamping Department	0.50 hour at $12 per hour
Forming Department	0.75 hour at $10 per hour
Assembly Department	1.20 hours at $9 per hour
Master Chef:	
Stamping Department	0.60 hour at $12 per hour
Forming Department	1.50 hours at $10 per hour
Assembly Department	2.20 hours at $9 per hour

Instructions

1. Prepare a sales budget for May.
2. Prepare a production budget for May.
3. Prepare a direct materials purchases budget for May.
4. Prepare a direct labor cost budget for May.

Problem 20–3B

Budgeted income statement and supporting budgets

Objective 4

✓ 4. Total direct labor cost in Slitting Dept., $257,600

The budget director of Lasting Image Film Company, with the assistance of the controller, treasurer, production manager, and sales manager, has gathered the following data for use in developing the budgeted income statement for October 2000:

a. Estimated sales for October:

Instant Image	35,000 units at $62 per unit
Pro Image	24,500 units at $91 per unit

b. Estimated inventories at October 1:

Direct materials:		Finished products:	
Celluloid	2,700 lbs.	Instant Image	4,800 units at $35 per unit
Silver	3,000 ozs.	Pro Image	2,400 units at $55 per unit

c. Desired inventories at October 31:

Direct materials:		Finished products:	
Celluloid	3,400 lbs.	Instant Image	5,400 units at $35 per unit
Silver	2,900 ozs.	Pro Image	1,900 units at $55 per unit

d. Direct materials used in production:

In manufacture of Instant Image:	
Celluloid	0.50 lb. per unit of product
Silver	3.00 ozs. per unit of product
In manufacture of Pro Image:	
Celluloid	0.70 lb. per unit of product
Silver	4.50 ozs. per unit of product

e. Anticipated cost of purchases and beginning and ending inventory of direct materials:

Celluloid	$1.30 per lb.	Silver	$6 per oz.

f. Direct labor requirements:

Instant Image:	
Coating Department	0.20 hour at $14 per hour
Slitting Department	0.25 hour at $16 per hour
Pro Image:	
Coating Department	0.50 hour at $14 per hour
Slitting Department	0.30 hour at $16 per hour

g. Estimated factory overhead costs for October:

Indirect factory wages	$545,000
Depreciation of plant and equipment	145,000
Power and light	46,000
Insurance and property tax	18,400

h. Estimated operating expenses for October:

Sales salaries expense	$245,000
Advertising expense	146,500
Office salaries expense	112,400
Depreciation expense—office equipment	5,300
Telephone expense—selling	5,000
Telephone expense—administrative	1,900
Travel expense—selling	38,500
Office supplies expense	3,000
Miscellaneous administrative expense	4,200

i. Estimated other income and expense for October:

Interest revenue	$16,700
Interest expense	12,300

j. Estimated tax rate: 40%

Instructions

1. Prepare a sales budget for October.
2. Prepare a production budget for October.
3. Prepare a direct materials purchases budget for October.
4. Prepare a direct labor cost budget for October.
5. Prepare a factory overhead cost budget for October.
6. Prepare a cost of goods sold budget for October. Work in process at the beginning of October is estimated to be $28,500, and work in process at the end of October is estimated to be $34,200.
7. Prepare a selling and administrative expenses budget for October.
8. Prepare a budgeted income statement for October.

In Class Example

Problem 20–4B

Cash budget

Objective 5

SPREADSHEET

✓ 1. October deficiency, $26,700

The treasurer of Lindy Lawn Equipment Company instructs you to prepare a monthly cash budget for the next three months. You are presented with the following budget information:

	August	September	October
Sales	$470,000	$420,000	$590,000
Manufacturing costs	280,000	260,000	320,000
Selling and administrative expenses	~~120,000~~	~~105,000~~	~~160,000~~
Capital expenditures	—	—	120,000

Forgot to include

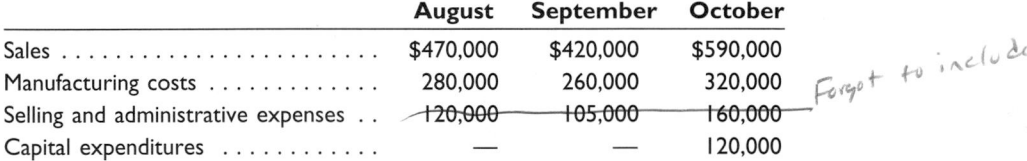

The company expects to sell about 10% of its merchandise for cash. Of sales on account, 60% are expected to be collected in full in the month following the sale and the remainder the following month. Depreciation, insurance, and property tax expense represent $25,000 of the estimated monthly manufacturing costs. The annual insurance premium is paid in July, and the annual property taxes are paid in November. Of the remainder of the manufacturing costs, 80% are expected to be paid in the month in which they are incurred and the balance in the following month.

Current assets as of August 1 include cash of $55,000, marketable securities of $85,000, and accounts receivable of $594,000 ($442,000 from July sales and $152,000 from June sales). Current liabilities as of August 1 include an $80,000, 10%, 90-day note payable due October 20 and $60,000 of accounts payable incurred in July for manufacturing costs. All selling and administrative expenses are paid in cash in the period they are incurred. It is expected that $1,500 in dividends will be received in August. An estimated income tax payment of $42,000 will be made in September. Lindy's regular quarterly dividend of $15,000 is expected to be declared in September and paid in October. Management desires to maintain a minimum cash balance of $45,000.

Instructions

1. Prepare a monthly cash budget and supporting schedules for August, September, and October.
2. On the basis of the cash budget prepared in (1), what recommendation should be made to the treasurer?

Problem 20–5B

Budgeted income statement and balance sheet

Objectives 4, 5

✓ 1. Net income, $236,600

As a preliminary to requesting budget estimates of sales, costs, and expenses for the fiscal year beginning January 1, 2001, the following tentative trial balance as of December 31, 2000, is prepared by the Accounting Department of Stanley Steel Company:

Cash	$ 64,000	
Accounts Receivable	104,700	
Finished Goods	74,800	
Work in Process	25,600	
Materials	46,700	
Prepaid Expenses	2,400	
Plant and Equipment	340,000	
Accumulated Depreciation—Plant and Equipment		$135,200
Accounts Payable		59,000
Common Stock, $10 par		200,000
Retained Earnings		264,000
	$658,200	$658,200

Factory output and sales for 2001 are expected to total 90,000 units of product, which are to be sold at $32 per unit. The quantities and costs of the inventories (lifo method) at December 31, 2001, are expected to remain unchanged from the balances at the beginning of the year.

Budget estimates of manufacturing costs and operating expenses for the year are summarized as follows:

	Estimated Costs and Expenses	
	Fixed (Total for Year)	Variable (Per Unit Sold)
Cost of goods manufactured and sold:		
Direct materials	—	$11.80
Direct labor	—	4.80
Factory overhead:		
Depreciation of plant and equipment	$35,000	—
Other factory overhead	5,000	1.50
Selling expenses:		
Sales salaries and commissions	54,000	3.50
Advertising	36,000	—
Miscellaneous selling expense	6,800	1.20
Administrative expenses:		
Office and officers salaries	34,500	1.80
Supplies	3,500	0.80
Miscellaneous administrative expense	1,800	0.50

Balances of accounts receivable, prepaid expenses, and accounts payable at the end of the year are not expected to differ significantly from the beginning balances. Federal income tax of $135,800 on 2001 taxable income will be paid during 2001. Regular quarterly cash dividends of $0.75 a share are expected to be declared and paid in March, June, September, and December. It is anticipated that fixed assets will be purchased for $110,000 cash in May.

Instructions

1. Prepare a budgeted income statement for 2001.
2. Prepare a budgeted balance sheet as of December 31, 2001, with supporting calculations.

QUICKBOOKS PROBLEM

Cash Flow Forecast

A simple cash flow forecast can be developed in QuickBooks by projecting expected cash inflows from accounts receivable collections against expected cash outflows from accounts payable payments.

Open the **sample.qbw** file (Larry's Landscaping) in QuickBooks. Select the "Reports" menu and select "Other reports" from the drop-down list. Select the "cash flow forecast" option.

1. Print the "Cash Flow Forecast" report from Larry's Landscaping.
2. What does the $8,051.41 for the first projected week under the "Accounts Receivable" column mean?
3. How did QuickBooks determine the $8,051.41?
4. Why is the Larry's Landscaping cash balance projected to increase by $14,290.66 for the next four weeks?

SPECIAL ACTIVITIES

Activity 20–1 Sage Software Company

Ethics and professional conduct in business

The director of marketing for Sage Software Company, Ron Keller, had the following discussion with the company controller, Jo Johnson, on July 26 of the current year:

Ron: Jo, it looks like I'm going to spend much less than my July budget.
Jo: I'm glad to hear it.
Ron: Well, I'm not so sure it's good news. I'm concerned that the president will see that I'm under budget and reduce my budget in the future. The only reason that I look good is that we've delayed an advertising campaign. Once the campaign hits in September, I'm sure my actual figures will go up. You see, we are also having our sales convention in September. Having the advertising campaign and the convention at the same time is going to kill my September numbers.
Jo: I don't think that's anything to worry about. We all expect some variation in actual spending month to month. What's really important is staying within the budgeted targets for the year. Does that look like it's going to be a problem?
Ron: I don't think so, but just the same, I'd like to be on the safe side.
Jo: What do you mean?
Ron: Well, this is what I'd like to do. I want to pay the convention-related costs in advance this month. I'll pay the hotel for room and convention space and purchase the airline tickets in advance. In this way, I can charge all these expenditures to July's budget. This would cause my actual expenses to come close to budget for July. Moreover, when the big advertising campaign hits in September, I won't have to worry about expenditures for the convention on my September budget as well. The convention costs will already be paid. Thus, my September expenses should be pretty close to budget.
Jo: I can't tell you when to make your convention purchases, but I'm not too sure that it should be expensed on July's budget.
Ron: What's the problem? It looks like "no harm, no foul" to me. I can't see that there's anything wrong with this—it's just smart management.

How should Jo Johnson respond to Ron Keller's request to expense the advanced payments for convention-related costs against July's budget?

Activity 20–2 Elgin Sweeper Company

Evaluating budgeting systems

What do you THINK?

REAL WORLD

Elgin Sweeper Company began an overhaul of its planning and control system. This overhaul is described in the following excerpt from an article in *Management Accounting*:

How could we bring responsibility for and management of costs to the individual department managers? For two years before we began our efforts, the annual budget had been prepared substantially by the accounting department with little ownership for results felt by persons outside top management.

Our first step was to modify the budget responsibility reports to reflect only those costs controllable by the department manager. . . . The next step was the actual budget preparation. . . . [Expense] accounts did not segregate variable and fixed costs. When volume-adjusted numbers were required for either budget preparation or budget-to-actual comparison, we merely would use an "executive judgment" percentage to adjust the appropriate expenses. Needless to say, this system resulted in some unusual variations, which sometimes required "innovative" explanations.

Source: J. P. Callan, W. N. Tredup, and R. S. Wisinger, "Elgin Sweeper Company's Journey Toward Cost Management," *Management Accounting,* July 1991, pp. 24–27.

What are the behavioral ramifications of including expenses within a responsibility center for which a manager has no control? Did Elgin previously use static budgeting or flexible budgeting? What type of budgeting will Elgin use in the future?

Activity 20–3 Evergreen Bancorp

Service company static decision making

A bank manager of Evergreen Bancorp uses the managerial accounting system to track the costs of operating the various departments within the bank. The departments include Cash Management, Trust Commercial Loans, Mortgage Loans, Operations, Credit Card, and Branch Services. The budget and actual results for the Operations Department are as follows:

Resources	Budget	Actual
Salaries	$150,000	$150,000
Benefits	30,000	30,000
Supplies	45,000	42,000
Travel	20,000	30,000
Training	25,000	30,000
Overtime	25,000	20,000
Total	$295,000	$302,000
Excess of actual over budget	$ 7,000	

a. What information is provided by the budget? Specifically, what questions can the bank manager ask of the Operations Department manager?
b. What information does the budget fail to provide? Specifically, could the budget information be presented differently to provide even more insight for the bank manager?

Activity 20–4 Dell Computer Company

Objectives of the master budget

REAL WORLD

Dell Computer Company has been a fast growing company throughout the decade. However, many analysts were concerned that its internal business systems would not keep up with its growth. Indeed, Michael S. Dell, chairman and chief executive officer, said, "The systems and processes in the company didn't grow as fast as the business." As a result, one Dell official stated, "This is like building a high-performance car while going around the racetrack." Some analysts were concerned that the lack of internal systems could harm Dell's future growth. Mr. Dell stated, "I believe the issues the company faces are quite serious."

How would a master budget support planning, directing, and control in Dell Computer Company?

Activity 20–5 SRC

Behavioral aspects of financial goals

REAL WORLD

One aspect of motivating line employees is to provide them financial improvement targets. The following excerpt describes this approach:

*For managers and line workers to be similarly focused on bottom-line issues, it's critical that all employees are first well-trained in understanding the financials. . . . While training is important, what makes Bottom Line Powered Management so powerful is that financial and performance data are presented to employees to be used as direct, practical feedback for operations. At **SRC**, for example, financial and performance data become critical to individual performance when the profit-and-loss statement is broken down for all operations—that is, for all employee teams and work groups. Each employee team then knows if it is on target and can make the appropriate corrections. If sales to a particular customer are off track, that is immediately investigated. If the team's overhead is above the projection, that is attacked. Moreover, this information is provided weekly, letting the* *employees quickly pounce on any problem. . . . To ensure that financial data are actually used, [they are given] numbers the employees can understand and influence.*

Source: Willard I. Zangwill, "Focusing All Eyes on the Bottom Line," *Wall Street Journal,* March 21, 1994, p. A12.

Identify the critical characteristics of the Bottom Line Powered Management (BLPM) approach and explain how they appear to affect human behavior.

Activity 20–6 Carol Greer

Objectives of budgeting

At the beginning of the year, Carol Greer decided to prepare a cash budget for the year, based upon anticipated cash receipts and payments. The estimates in the budget represent a "best guess." The budget is as follows:

Expected annual cash receipts:		
Salary from part-time job	$10,000	
Salary from summer job	4,000	
Total receipts		$14,000
Expected annual cash payments:		
Tuition	$ 4,500	
Books	400	
Rent	3,500	
Food	2,500	
Utilities	800	
Entertainment	4,000	
Total payments		15,700
Net change in cash		$(1,700)

1. What does this budget suggest? In what ways is this information useful to Carol?
2. a. Some items in the budget are more certain than are others. Which items are the most certain? Which items are the most uncertain? What are the implications of these different levels of certainty to Carol's planning?
   b. Some payment items are more controllable than others. Assuming that Carol plans to go to school, classify the items as controllable, partially controllable, or not controllable. What are the implications of controllable items to planning?
3. What actions could Carol take in order to avoid having the anticipated shortfall of $1,700 at the end of the year?
4. What does this budget fail to consider, and what are the implications of these omissions to Carol's planning?

Activity 20–7 Into the Real World

Budget for a state government

Internet ACTIVITY GROUP ACTIVITY

In a group, find the home page of the state in which you presently live. The state's home page, if it has one, will be in the form: **www.state.*stateabbreviation*.us/**. At the home page site, search for annual budget information. If you are unable to find the budget of your state, then go to the state of Ohio's budget page at **www.state.oh.us/obm/** to complete this activity.

1. What are the budgeted sources of revenue and their percentage breakdown?
2. What are the major categories of budgeted expenditures (or appropriations) and their percentage breakdown?
3. Is the projected budget in balance?

ANSWERS TO SELF-EXAMINATION QUESTIONS

Matching

1. I
2. D
3. N
4. A
5. F
6. B
7. E
8. J
9. M
10. G
11. C
12. K

Multiple Choice

1. **B** Individuals can be discouraged with budgets that appear too tight or unobtainable. Flexible budgeting (answer C) provides a series of budgets for varying rates of activity and thereby builds into the budgeting system the effect of fluctuations in the level of activity. Budgetary slack (answer A) comes from a loose budget, not a tight budget. A "spend it or lose it" mentality (answer D) is often associated with loose budgets.
2. **A** The first step of the budget process is to develop a plan. Once plans are established, management may direct actions (answer B). The results of actions can be controlled (answer C) by comparing them to the plan. This feedback (answer D) can be used by management to change plans or redirect actions.
3. **B** Administrative departments (answer B), such as Purchasing or Human Resources, will often use static budgeting. Production departments (answer A) frequently use flexible budgets. Responsibility centers (answer C) can use either static or flexible budgeting. Capital expenditure budgets are used to plan capital projects (answer D).
4. **B** The total production indicated in the production budget is 257,500 units (answer B), which is computed as follows:

Sales	250,000 units
Plus desired ending inventory	30,000 units
Total	280,000 units
Less estimated beginning inventory	22,500 units
Total production	257,500 units

5. **C** Dixon expects to collect 70% of April sales ($560,000) plus 30% of the March sales ($195,000) in April, for a total of $755,000 (answer C). Answer A is 100% of April sales. Answer B is 70% of April sales. Answer D adds 70% of both March and April sales.

21

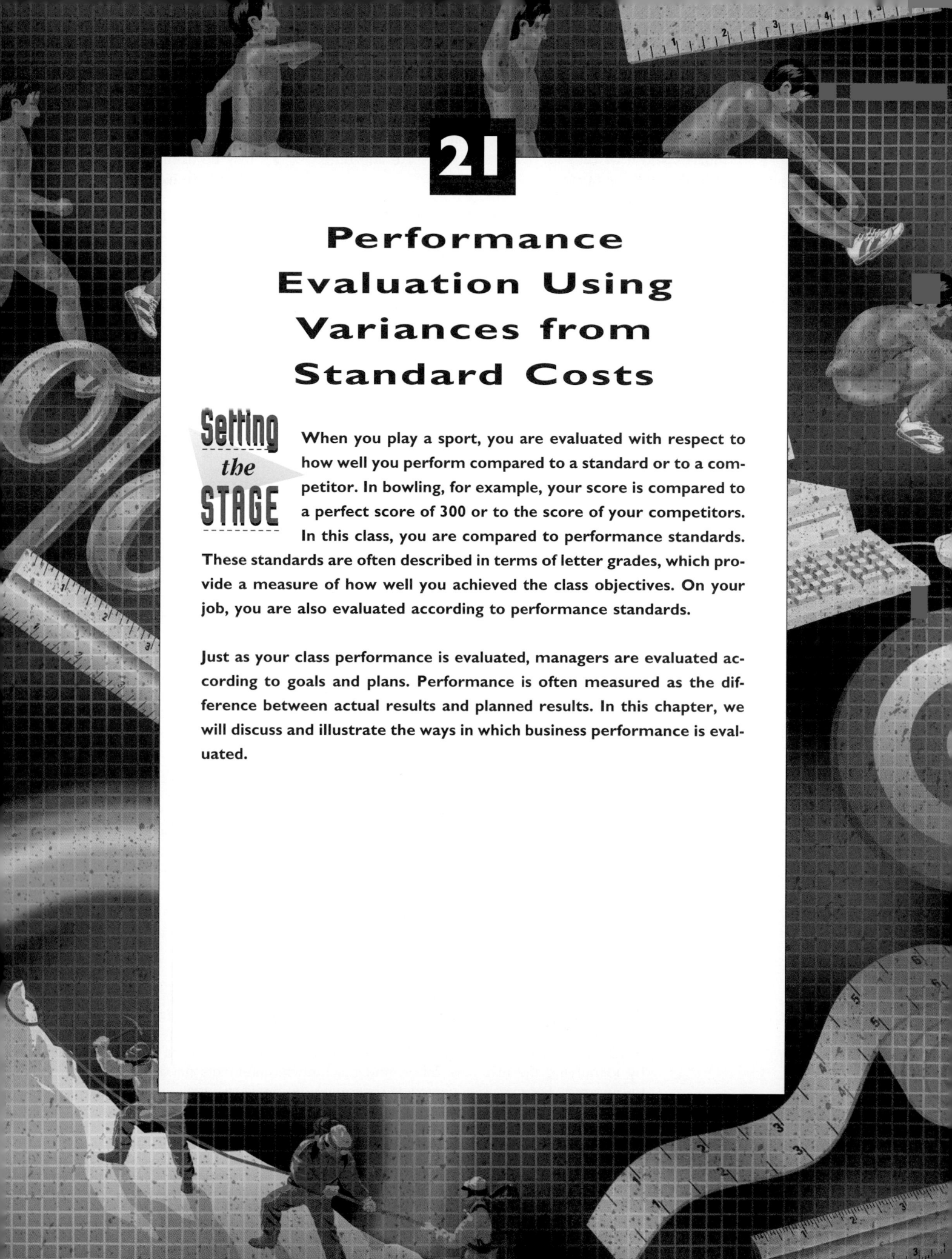

Performance Evaluation Using Variances from Standard Costs

Setting the STAGE

When you play a sport, you are evaluated with respect to how well you perform compared to a standard or to a competitor. In bowling, for example, your score is compared to a perfect score of 300 or to the score of your competitors. In this class, you are compared to performance standards. These standards are often described in terms of letter grades, which provide a measure of how well you achieved the class objectives. On your job, you are also evaluated according to performance standards.

Just as your class performance is evaluated, managers are evaluated according to goals and plans. Performance is often measured as the difference between actual results and planned results. In this chapter, we will discuss and illustrate the ways in which business performance is evaluated.

objectives

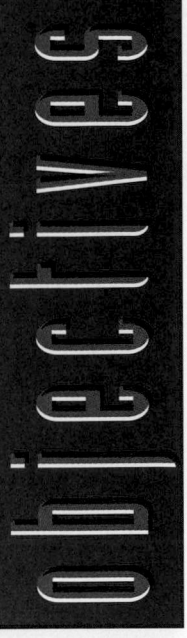

After studying this chapter, you should be able to:

1 Describe the types of standards and how they are established for businesses.

2 Explain and illustrate how standards are used in budgeting.

3 Calculate and interpret direct materials price and quantity variances.

4 Calculate and interpret direct labor rate and time variances.

5 Calculate and interpret factory overhead controllable and volume variances.

6 Journalize the entries for recording standards in the accounts and prepare an income statement that includes variances from standard.

7 Explain how standards may be used for nonmanufacturing expenses.

8 Explain and provide examples of nonfinancial performance measures.

Standards

OBJECTIVE 1

Describe the types of standards and how they are established for businesses.

What are standards? **Standards** are performance goals. Service, merchandising, and manufacturing businesses may all use standards to evaluate and control operations. For example, long-haul drivers for **United Parcel Service** are expected to drive a standard distance per day. Salespersons for **The Limited** are expected to meet sales standards.

Manufacturers normally use standard costs for each of the three manufacturing costs: direct materials, direct labor, and factory overhead. Accounting systems that use standards for these costs are called **standard cost systems**. These systems enable management to determine how much a product should cost (**standard cost**), how much it does cost (actual cost), and the causes of any difference (**cost variances**). When actual costs are compared with standard costs, only the exceptions or variances are reported for cost control. This reporting by the *principle of exceptions* allows management to focus on correcting the variances. Thus, using standard costs assists management in controlling costs and in motivating employees to focus on costs.

Standard cost systems are commonly used with job order and process systems. One survey of manufacturing firms reported that 87% of the firms use some form of standard costing.[1] Automated manufacturing operations may also integrate standard cost data with the computerized system that directs operations. Such systems detect and report variances automatically and make adjustments to operations in progress.

Setting Standards

Setting standards is both an art and a science. The standard-setting process normally requires the joint efforts of accountants, engineers, and other management personnel. The accountant plays an essential role by expressing in dollars and cents the results of judgments and studies. Engineers contribute to the standard-setting process by identifying the materials, labor, and machine requirements needed to produce the product. For example, engineers determine the direct materials requirements by studying the materials specifications for products and estimating normal spoilage in

[1] B. R. Gaumnitz and F. P. Kollaritsch, "Manufacturing Variances: Current Trends and Practice," *Journal of Cost Management,* Spring 1991, pp. 58–63.

production. Time and motion studies may be used to determine the length of time required for each manufacturing operation. Engineering studies may also be used to determine standards for factory overhead, such as the amount of power needed to operate machinery.

Setting standards often begins with analyzing past operations. However, standards are not just an extension of past costs, and caution must be used in relying on past cost data. For example, inefficiencies may be contained within past costs. In addition, changes in technology, machinery, or production methods may make past costs irrelevant for future operations.

Types of Standards

Standards imply an acceptable level of production efficiency. One of the major objectives in setting standards is to motivate workers to achieve efficient operations.

Like the budgets we discussed earlier, tight, unrealistic standards may have a negative impact on performance. This is because workers may become frustrated with an inability to meet the standards and may give up trying to do their best. Such standards can be achieved only under perfect operating conditions, such as no idle time, no machine breakdowns, and no materials spoilage. These standards, often called **theoretical standards** or **ideal standards**, are not widely used.

REAL WORLD Some firms use standards as a cost improvement target. Under this approach, the standard is beyond what is currently attainable, but it could be obtained with changes and improvement. This approach has been termed "Kaizen Costing." "Kaizen" is a Japanese term meaning "continuous improvement."

Standards that are too loose might not motivate employees to perform at their best. This is because the standard level of performance can be reached too easily. As a result, operating performance may be lower than what could be achieved.

Most companies use **currently attainable standards** (sometimes called **normal standards**). These standards can be attained with reasonable effort. Such standards allow for normal production difficulties and mistakes, such as materials spoilage and machine breakdowns. When reasonable standards are used, employees become more focused on cost and are more likely to put forth their best efforts.

An example from the game of golf illustrates the distinction between ideal and normal standards. In golf, "par" is an *ideal* standard for most players. Each player's **USGA** (United States Golf Association) handicap is the player's *normal* standard. The motivation of average players is to beat their handicaps because they may view beating par as unrealistic. Normal and ideal standards are illustrated as follows:

Reviewing and Revising Standards

Standard costs should be continuously reviewed and should be revised when they no longer reflect operating conditions. Inaccurate standards may distort management decision making and may weaken management's ability to plan and control operations.

Standards should not be revised, however, just because they differ from actual costs. They should be revised only when they no longer reflect the operating conditions that they were intended to measure. For example, the direct labor standard would not be revised simply because workers were unable to meet properly determined standards. On the other hand, standards should be revised when prices, product designs, labor rates, or manufacturing methods change. For example, when aluminum beverage cans were redesigned to taper slightly at the top of the can, manufacturers reduced the standard amount of aluminum per can because less aluminum was required for the top piece of the tapered can.

Support and Criticism of Standards

Standards are used to value inventory and to plan and control costs. As evidence of the increasing importance of standards, one survey indicates that companies are now using standards to assess performance at lower levels of the organization, for shorter accounting periods, and for an increasing number of costs.[2]

Using standards for performance evaluation has been criticized by some. For example, critics assert that standards limit improvement of operations by discouraging improvement beyond the standard. Regardless of this criticism, standards are widely used. One survey reports that managers strongly support standard cost systems and that they regard standards as critical for running large businesses efficiently.[3]

Budgetary Performance Evaluation

OBJECTIVE 2

Explain and illustrate how standards are used in budgeting.

As we discussed in the previous chapter, the master budget assists a company in planning, directing, and controlling performance. In the remainder of this chapter, we will discuss using the master budget for control purposes. The control function, or budgetary performance evaluation, compares the actual performance against the budget.

We illustrate budget performance evaluation using Western Rider Inc., a manufacturer of blue jeans. Western Rider Inc. uses standard manufacturing costs in its budgets. The standards for direct materials, direct labor, and factory overhead are separated into two components: (1) a price standard and (2) a quantity standard. Multiplying these two elements together yields the standard cost per unit for a given manufacturing cost category, as shown for style XL jeans in Exhibit 1.

EXHIBIT 1
Standard Cost for XL Jeans

Manufacturing Costs	Standard Price	×	Standard Quantity per Pair	=	Standard Cost per Pair of XL Jeans
Direct materials	$5.00 per square yard		1.5 square yards		$ 7.50
Direct labor	$9.00 per hour		0.80 hour per pair		7.20
Factory overhead	$6.00 per hour		0.80 hour per pair		4.80
Total standard cost per pair					$19.50

[2] *Ibid.*

[3] C. Graham, D. Lydall, and A. G. Puxty, "Cost Control: The Manager's Perspective," *Management Accounting*, UK, October 1992, pp. 26–27.

INTERMISSION

SCM Corporation identified its business units as either "harvest" or "build." Harvest business units contain mature products. Build business units develop and grow new product markets. The budget system reflects the differences between these two types of business units. Harvest business units are concerned about competing with low costs. Thus, performance against budget is the primary control tool. Unfavorable cost variances direct the company to areas where improvements must be made. Build business units are concerned about developing successful new products. In these business units, low cost is not as important as is innovative new products. Thus, performance against budget is a minor control tool. Instead, nonfinancial performance measures, such as number of new product introductions, are used to control the business. ■

The standard price and quantity are separated because the means of controlling them are normally different. For example, the direct materials price per square yard is controlled by the Purchasing Department, and the direct materials quantity per pair is controlled by the Production Department.

As we illustrated in the previous chapter, the budgeted costs at planned volumes are included in the master budget at the beginning of the period. The standard amounts budgeted for materials purchases, direct labor, and factory overhead are determined by multiplying the standard costs per unit by the *planned* level of production. At the end of the month, the standard costs per unit are multiplied by the *actual* production and compared to the actual costs. To illustrate, assume that Western Rider produced and sold 5,000 pairs of XL jeans. It incurred direct materials costs of $40,150, direct labor costs of $38,500, and factory overhead costs of $22,400. The **budget performance report** shown in Exhibit 2 summarizes the actual costs, the standard amounts for the actual level of production achieved, and the differences between the two amounts. These differences are called **cost variances**. A *favorable* cost variance occurs when the actual cost is less than the standard cost (at actual volumes). An *unfavorable* variance occurs when the actual cost exceeds the standard cost (at actual volumes).

Based on the information in the budget performance report, management can investigate major differences and take corrective action. In Exhibit 2, for example, the direct materials cost variance is an unfavorable $2,650. There are two possible explanations for this variance: (1) the amount of blue denim used per pair of blue jeans was different than expected, and/or (2) the purchase price of blue denim was

Q&A

What is the amount of standard cost per unit of a product that has 3 standard pounds of material at a standard cost of $12 per pound, 4.5 standard direct labor hours at a standard cost of $11 per direct labor hour, and standard factory overhead of $7 per direct labor hour?

$117 [($12 × 3 pounds) + ($11 × 4.5 hours) + ($7 × 4.5 hours)]

EXHIBIT 2
Budget Performance Report

Western Rider Inc.
Budget Performance Report
For the Month Ended June 30, 2000

Manufacturing Costs	Actual Costs	Standard Cost at Actual Volume (5,000 pairs of XL Jeans)*	Cost Variance—(Favorable) Unfavorable
Direct materials	$ 40,150	$37,500	$2,650
Direct labor	38,500	36,000	2,500
Factory overhead	22,400	24,000	(1,600)
Total manufacturing costs	$101,050	$97,500	$3,550

*5,000 pairs × $7.50 per pair = $37,500
5,000 pairs × $7.20 per pair = $36,000
5,000 pairs × $4.80 per pair = $24,000

Actual cost < Standard cost at actual volumes: Favorable cost variance

Actual cost > Standard cost at actual volumes: Unfavorable cost variance

different than expected. In the next sections, we will illustrate how to separate the price and quantity variances for direct materials, the rate and time variances for direct labor, and the controllable and volume variances for factory overhead.

The relationship of these variances to the total manufacturing cost variance is shown below.

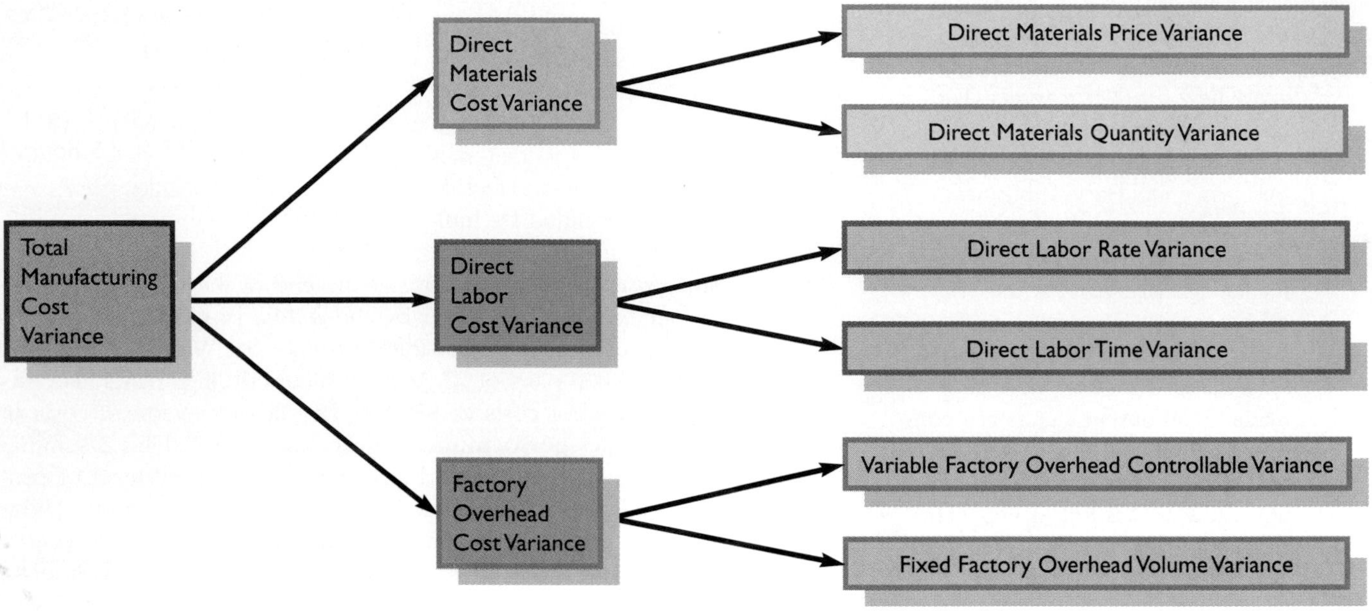

Direct Materials Variances

OBJECTIVE 3

Calculate and interpret direct materials price and quantity variances.

What caused Western Rider Inc.'s unfavorable materials variance of $2,650? Recall that the direct materials standards from Exhibit 1 are as follows:

Price standard: $5.00 per square yard
Quantity standard: 1.5 square yards per pair of XL jeans

To determine the number of standard square yards of denim budgeted, multiply the actual production for June 2000 (5,000 pairs) by the quantity standard (1.5 square yards per pair). Then multiply the standard square yards by the standard price per square yard ($5.00) to determine the *standard* budgeted cost at the actual volume. The calculation is shown as follows:

Standard square yards per pair of jeans	1.5 sq. yards
Actual units produced	× 5,000 pairs of jeans
Standard square yards of denim budgeted for actual production	7,500 sq. yards
Standard price per square yard	× $5.00
Standard direct materials cost at actual production (same as Exhibit 2)	$37,500

This calculation assumes that there is no change in the beginning and ending materials inventories. Thus, the amount of materials budgeted for production equals the amount purchased.

Assume that the *actual* total cost for denim used during June 2000 was as follows:

Actual quantity of denim used in production	7,300 sq. yards
Actual price per square yard	× $5.50
Total actual direct materials cost (same as Exhibit 2)	$40,150

Most restaurants use standards to control the amount of food served to customers. For example, **Darden Restaurants Inc.**, the operator of the **Red Lobster** chain, establishes standards for the number of shrimp, scallops, or clams on a seafood plate. In the same way, **Keystone Foods, Inc.**, a major food supplier to **McDonald's**, uses standards to carefully control the size and weight of chicken nuggets.

The total unfavorable cost variance of $2,650 ($40,150 − $37,500) results from an excess price per square yard of $0.50 and using 200 fewer square yards of denim. These two reasons can be reported as two separate variances, as shown in the next sections.

Direct Materials Price Variance

The **direct materials price variance** is the difference between the actual price per unit ($5.50) and the standard price per unit ($5.00), multiplied by the actual quantity used (7,300 square yards). If the actual price per unit exceeds the standard price per unit, the variance is unfavorable, as shown for Western Rider Inc. If the actual price per unit is less than the standard price per unit, the variance is favorable. The calculation for Western Rider Inc. is as follows:

Price variance:	
Actual price per unit	$5.50 per square yard
Standard price per unit	5.00 per square yard
Price variance—unfavorable	$0.50 per square yard × actual qty., 7,300 sq. yds. = $3,650 U

Direct Materials Quantity Variance

The **direct materials quantity variance** is the difference between the actual quantity used (7,300 square yards) and the standard quantity at actual production (7,500 square yards), multiplied by the standard price per unit ($5.00). If the actual quantity of materials used exceeds the standard quantity budgeted, the variance is unfavorable. If the actual quantity of materials used is less than the standard quantity, the variance is favorable, as shown for Western Rider Inc.:

A product requires 6 standard pounds per unit. The standard price is $4.50 per pound. If 3,000 units required 18,500 pounds, which were purchased at $4.35 per pound, what is the direct materials (1) price variance and (2) quantity variance?

(1) $2,775 favorable [($4.35 − $4.50) × 18,500 lbs.];
(2) $2,250 unfavorable [(18,500 lbs. − 18,000 lbs.) × $4.50]

Quantity variance:	
Actual quantity	7,300 square yards
Standard quantity at actual production	7,500
Quantity variance—favorable	(200) square yards × standard price, $5.00 = ($1,000) F

Direct Materials Variance Relationships

The direct materials variances can be illustrated by making the three calculations shown in Exhibit 3.

EXHIBIT 3
Direct Materials Variance Relationships

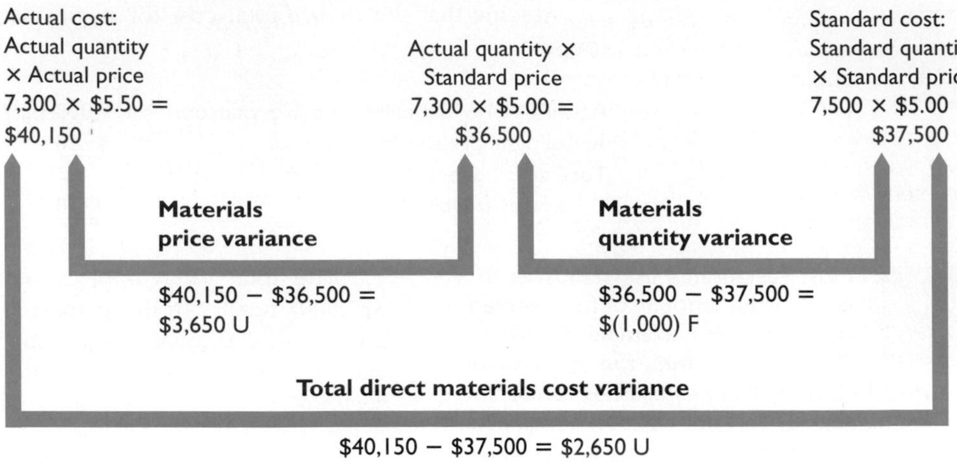

Reporting Direct Materials Variances

The direct materials quantity variance should be reported to the proper operating management level for corrective action. For example, an unfavorable quantity variance might have been caused by malfunctioning equipment that has not been properly maintained or operated. However, unfavorable materials quantity variances are not always caused by operating departments. For example, the excess materials usage may be caused by purchasing inferior raw materials. In this case, the Purchasing Department should be held responsible for the variance.

The materials price variance should normally be reported to the Purchasing Department, which may or may not be able to control this variance. If materials of the same quality could have been purchased from another supplier at the standard price, the variance was controllable. On the other hand, if the variance resulted from a marketwide price increase, the variance may not be controllable.

Direct Labor Variances

OBJECTIVE 4

Calculate and interpret direct labor rate and time variances.

Western Rider Inc.'s direct labor cost variance can also be separated into two parts. Recall that the direct labor standards from Exhibit 1 are as follows:

Rate standard: $9.00 per hour
Time standard: 0.80 hour per pair of XL jeans

The actual production (5,000 pairs) is multiplied by the time standard (0.80 hour per pair) to determine the number of standard direct labor hours budgeted. The standard direct labor hours are then multiplied by the standard rate per hour ($9.00) to determine the *standard* direct labor cost at actual volumes. These calculations are shown below.

Standard direct labor hours per pair of XL jeans	0.80 direct labor hours
Actual units produced	× 5,000 pairs of jeans
Standard direct labor hours budgeted for actual production	4,000 direct labor hours
Standard rate per direct labor hour	× $9.00
Standard direct labor cost at actual production (same as Exhibit 2)	$36,000

Hospitals are now developing cost standards for various categories of procedures. Variances from standard cost can be accumulated by procedure, by patient, or by doctor. Doctor variances occur when a doctor consistently prescribes treatment that varies from the standard. Doctors who have consistent unfavorable variances may be asked to review their treatment decisions.

Assume that the *actual* total cost for direct labor during June 2000 was as follows:

Actual direct labor hours used in production	3,850 direct labor hours
Actual rate per direct labor hour	× $10.00
Total actual direct labor cost (same as Exhibit 2)	$ 38,500

The total unfavorable cost variance $2,500 ($38,500 − $36,000) results from an excess rate of $1.00 per direct labor hour and using 150 fewer direct labor hours. These two reasons can be reported as two separate variances, as we discuss next.

Direct Labor Rate Variance

The **direct labor rate variance** is the difference between the actual rate per hour ($10.00) and the standard rate per hour ($9.00), multiplied by the actual hours worked (3,850 hours). If the actual rate per hour is less than the standard rate per hour, the variance is favorable. If the actual rate per hour exceeds the standard rate per hour, the variance is unfavorable, as shown below for Western Rider Inc.

A product requires 2.5 standard hours per unit at a standard hourly rate of $12 per hour. If 800 units required 1,920 hours at an hourly rate of $12.30 per hour, what is the direct labor (1) rate variance and (2) time variance?

(1) $576 unfavorable [($12.30 − $12.00) × 1,920 hours]; (2) $960 favorable [(1,920 hrs. − 2,000 hrs.) × $12.00]

Rate variance:

Actual rate	$10.00 per hour
Standard rate	9.00
Rate variance—unfavorable	$ 1.00 per hour × actual time, 3,850 hours = $3,850 U

Direct Labor Time Variance

The **direct labor time variance** is the difference between the actual hours worked (3,850 hours) and the standard hours at actual production (4,000 hours), multiplied by the standard rate per hour ($9.00). If the actual hours worked exceed the standard hours, the variance is unfavorable. If the actual hours worked are less than the standard hours, the variance is favorable, as shown below for Western Rider Inc.

Time variance:

Actual hours	3,850 direct labor hours
Standard hours at actual production	4,000
Time variance—favorable	(150) direct labor hours × standard rate, $9.00 = ($1,350) F

Direct Labor Variance Relationships

The direct labor variances can be illustrated by making the three calculations shown in Exhibit 4.

EXHIBIT 4
Direct Labor Variance Relationships

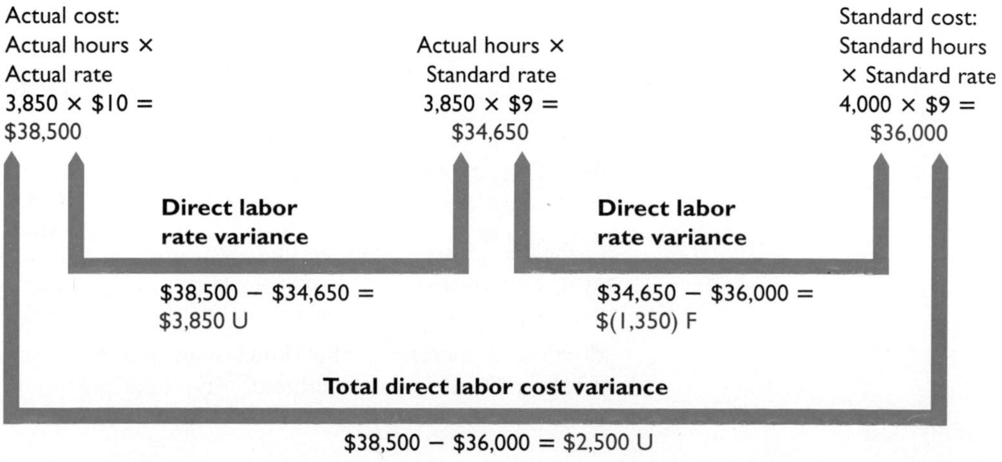

Business on Stage

Measuring the Performance of Teams

Many organizations are using cross-functional teams in order to foster higher cooperation in achieving objectives. For example, **Procter & Gamble** has a "Wal-Mart" team that is designed to support its largest customer by integrating the sales, logistical, and customer service functions. Manufacturing companies such as **Northern Telecom** and **Harley-Davidson** have created self-directed work teams on the manufacturing floor to reduce waste and improve cost. When a company uses teams, how should performance be measured?

The following three concepts are relevant to team measurement:

1. Identify team performance targets and standards.
2. Identify individual contributions required to achieve team targets.
3. Establish the relative weights between individual and team goals.

If a company has developed a manufacturing cell that uses a team of individuals from a variety of functional areas, the team goals should address performance of the complete team. Examples include overall quality goals, productivity standards, and cost targets. To illustrate, a team goal would be to achieve 100% of standard output of the cell per day.

Because a team is made up of individuals, individual goals should be established to support the team goals. In this way, individuals will be less likely to "free ride" on the team's performance. Individual goals focus more on what an individual can directly control. To illustrate, an individual objective for a machinist would be to scrap less than 1% of the machined parts. This individual goal contributes to the team's overall quality and cost targets.

Once the team and individual goals are determined, weights should be established between the various goals in determining an individual's performance. For example, a team member may have 60% of his or her evaluation based on achieving team goals and the remaining 40% on achieving individual goals. The actual weighting depends on how much management wishes to reward team versus individual performance.

Once the performance system is in place, the measures should be used to provide feedback to the team. Such feedback can be used to monitor and adjust team and individual performance relative to expectations. ■

Reporting Direct Labor Variances

Controlling direct labor cost is normally the responsibility of the production supervisors. To aid them, reports analyzing the cause of any direct labor variance may be prepared. Differences between standard direct labor hours and actual direct labor hours can be investigated. For example, a time variance may be incurred because of the shortage of skilled workers. Such variances may be uncontrollable unless they are related to high turnover rates among employees, in which case the cause of the high turnover should be investigated.

REAL WORLD **In highly automated industries, such as chemical, metal, food, and paper processing, direct labor variances are rarely used. This is because factory employees run and maintain equipment, and thus the cost of their labor is part of factory overhead.**

Likewise, differences between the rates paid for direct labor and the standard rates can be investigated. For example, unfavorable rate variances may be caused by the improper scheduling and use of workers. In such cases, skilled, highly paid workers may be used in jobs that are normally performed by unskilled, lower paid workers. In this case, the unfavorable rate variance should be reported for corrective action to the managers who schedule work assignments.

Factory Overhead Variances

OBJECTIVE 5

Calculate and interpret factory overhead controllable and volume variances.

Factory overhead costs are more difficult to manage than are direct labor and materials costs. This is because the relationship between production volume and indirect costs is not easy to determine. For example, when production is increased, the direct materials will increase. But what about the Engineering Department overhead? The relationship between production volume and cost is less clear for the Engineering Department. Companies normally respond to this difficulty by separating factory overhead into variable and fixed costs. For example, manufacturing supplies are considered variable to production volume, whereas straight-line plant depreciation is considered fixed. In the following sections, we discuss the approaches used to budget and control factory overhead by separating overhead into fixed and variable components.

The Factory Overhead Flexible Budget

A flexible budget may be used to determine the impact of changing production on fixed and variable factory overhead costs. The standard overhead rate is determined by dividing the budgeted factory overhead costs by the standard amount of productive activity, such as direct labor hours. Exhibit 5 is a flexible factory overhead budget for Western Rider Inc.

EXHIBIT 5
Factory Overhead Cost Budget Indicating Standard Factory Overhead Rate

Western Rider Inc.
Factory Overhead Cost Budget
For the Month Ending June 30, 2000

Percent of normal capacity	80%	90%	100%	110%
Units produced	5,000	5,625	6,250	6,875
Direct labor hours (0.80 hour per unit)	4,000	4,500	5,000	5,500
Budgeted factory overhead:				
Variable costs:				
Indirect factory wages	$ 8,000	$ 9,000	$10,000	$11,000
Power and light	4,000	4,500	5,000	5,500
Indirect materials	2,400	2,700	3,000	3,300
Total variable cost	$14,400	$16,200	$18,000	$19,800
Fixed costs:				
Supervisory salaries	$ 5,500	$ 5,500	$ 5,500	$ 5,500
Depreciation of plant and equipment	4,500	4,500	4,500	4,500
Insurance and property taxes	2,000	2,000	2,000	2,000
Total fixed cost	$12,000	$12,000	$12,000	$12,000
Total factory overhead cost	$26,400	$28,200	$30,000	$31,800

Factory overhead rate per direct labor hour, $30,000 ÷ 5,000 = $6.00

In Exhibit 5, the standard factory overhead cost rate is $6.00. It is determined on the basis of the currently attainable standard for activity at 100% of normal capacity, or 5,000 direct labor hours. This rate can be subdivided into $3.60 per hour for variable factory overhead ($18,000 ÷ 5,000 hours) and $2.40 per hour for fixed factory overhead ($12,000 ÷ 5,000 hours).

Variances from standard for factory overhead cost result from:

1. Actual variable factory overhead cost greater or less than budgeted variable factory overhead for actual production.
2. Actual production at a level above or below 100% of normal capacity.

The first factor results in the controllable variance for variable overhead costs. The second factor results in a volume variance for fixed overhead costs. We will discuss each of these variances next.

Variable Factory Overhead Controllable Variance

The variable factory overhead **controllable variance** is the difference between the actual variable overhead incurred and the budgeted variable overhead for actual production. The controllable variance measures the *efficiency* of using variable overhead resources. Thus, if the actual variable overhead is less than the budgeted variable overhead, the variance is favorable. If the actual variable overhead exceeds the budgeted variable overhead, the variance is unfavorable.

To illustrate, recall that Western Rider Inc. produced 5,000 pairs of XL jeans in June. Each pair requires 0.80 standard labor hour for production. As a result, Western Rider Inc. had 4,000 standard hours at actual production (5,000 × 0.80). This represents 80% of normal productive capacity. The standard variable overhead at 4,000 hours worked, according to the budget in Exhibit 5, was $14,400 (4,000 direct labor hours × $3.60). The following actual factory overhead costs were incurred in June:

Actual costs:	
Variable factory overhead	$10,400
Fixed factory overhead	12,000
Total actual factory overhead	$22,400

The controllable variance can be calculated as follows:

Controllable variance:		
Actual variable factory overhead	$10,400	
Budgeted variable factory overhead for actual amount produced (4,000 hrs. × $3.60)	14,400	
Variance—favorable	$ (4,000)	F

The variable factory overhead controllable variance indicates management's ability to keep the factory overhead costs within the budget limits. Since variable factory overhead costs are normally controllable at the department level, responsibility for controlling this variance usually rests with department supervisors.

Fixed Factory Overhead Volume Variance

The variance related to fixed factory overhead is measured by focusing on the difference between normal capacity and actual production. Using currently attainable standards, Western Rider Inc. set its budgeted normal capacity at 5,000 direct labor hours. This is the amount of expected capacity that management believes will be used under normal business conditions. You should note that this amount may be much less than the total available capacity if management believes demand will be low.

The fixed factory overhead **volume variance** is the difference between the budgeted fixed overhead at 100% of normal capacity and the standard fixed overhead for the actual production achieved during the period. The volume variance measures the use of fixed overhead resources. If the standard fixed overhead exceeds the budgeted overhead at 100% of normal capacity, the variance is favorable. Thus, the firm used its plant and equipment more than would be expected under normal operating conditions. If the standard fixed overhead is less than the budgeted overhead at 100% of normal capacity, the variance is unfavorable. Thus, the company used its plant and equipment less than would be expected under normal operating conditions.

The volume variance for Western Rider Inc. is shown in the following calculation:

Q&A

A company produced 1,500 units of product that required 3.5 standard hours per unit. The standard variable and fixed overhead cost is $2.20 and $0.90 per hour, respectively, at 5,500 hours, which is 100% of normal capacity. The actual variable overhead was $12,000. What are (1) the variable factory overhead controllable variance and (2) the fixed factory overhead volume variance?

(1) $450 unfavorable [$12,000 − ($2.20 × 5,250 hrs.)]; (2) $225 unfavorable [$0.90 × (5,500 hrs. − 5,250 hrs.)]

100% of normal capacity	5,000 direct labor hours
Standard hours at actual production	4,000
Capacity not used	1,000 direct labor hours
Standard fixed overhead rate	× $2.40
Volume variance—unfavorable	$ 2,400 U

Exhibit 6 illustrates the volume variance graphically. For Western Rider Inc., the budgeted fixed overhead is $12,000 at all levels. The standard fixed overhead at 5,000 hours is also $12,000. This is the point at which the standard fixed overhead line intersects the budgeted fixed cost line. For actual volume greater than 100% of normal capacity, the volume variance is favorable. For volume at less than 100% of normal volume, the volume variance is unfavorable. For Western Rider Inc., the volume variance is unfavorable because the actual production is 4,000 standard hours, or 80% of normal volume. The amount of the volume variance, $2,400, can be viewed as the cost of the unused capacity (1,000 hours).

EXHIBIT 6
Graph of Fixed Overhead Volume Variance

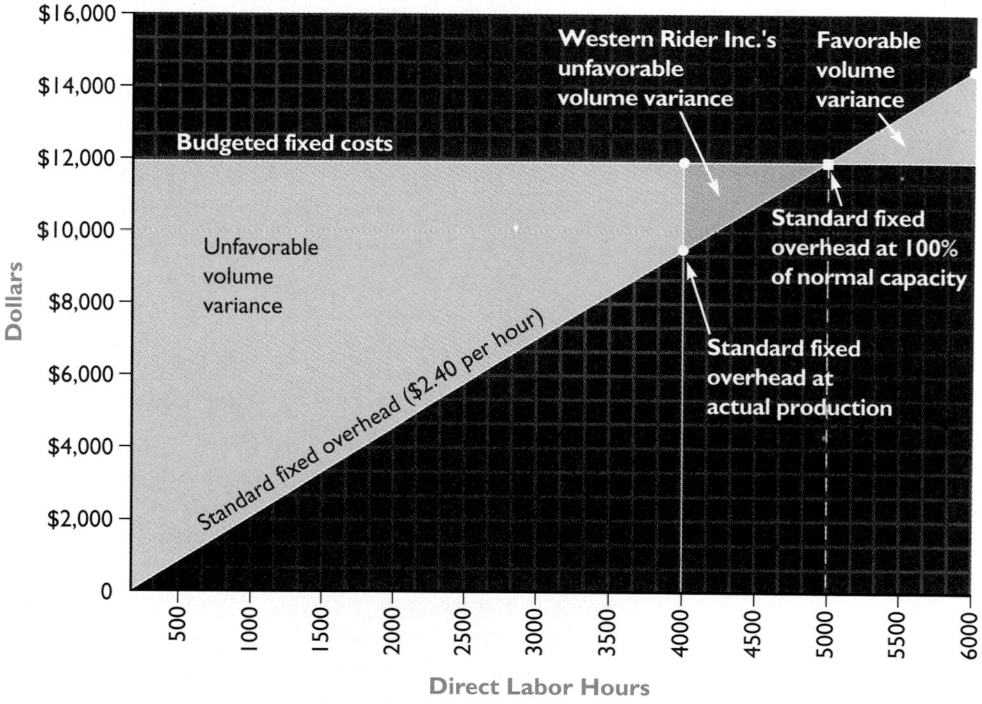

An unfavorable volume variance may be due to such factors as failure to maintain an even flow of work, machine breakdowns, repairs causing work stoppages, and failure to obtain enough sales orders to keep the factory operating at normal capacity. Management should determine the causes of the unfavorable variance and consider taking corrective action. A volume variance caused by an uneven flow of work, for example, can be remedied by changing operating procedures. Volume variances caused by lack of sales orders may be corrected through increased advertising or other sales effort.

Volume variances tend to encourage manufacturing managers to run the factory above the normal capacity. This is favorable when the additional production can be sold. However, if the additional production cannot be sold and must be stored as inventory, favorable volume variances may actually be harmful. For example, one paper company ran paper machines above normal volume in order to create favorable volume variances. Unfortunately, this created a six months' supply of finished goods inventory that had to be stored in public warehouses. The "savings" from the favorable volume variances were exceeded by the additional inventory carrying costs. By creating incentives for manufacturing managers to over produce, the volume variances produced *goal conflicts*, as we described in a preceding chapter.

Reporting Factory Overhead Variances

The total factory overhead cost variance is the difference between the actual factory overhead and the total overhead applied to production. This calculation is as follows:

Total actual factory overhead	$22,400
Factory overhead applied (4,000 hours × $6.00 per hour)	24,000
Total factory overhead cost variance—favorable	$(1,600) F

The factory overhead cost variance may be broken down by each variable factory overhead cost and fixed factory overhead cost element in a **factory overhead cost variance report**. Such a report, which is useful to management in controlling costs, is shown in Exhibit 7. The report indicates both the controllable variance and the volume variance.

EXHIBIT 7
Factory Overhead Cost Variance Report

Western Rider Inc.
Factory Overhead Cost Variance Report
For the Month Ended June 30, 2000

Productive capacity for the month (100% of normal)	5,000 hours			
Actual production for the month	4,000 hours			

	Budget (at Actual Production)	Actual	Variances: Favorable	Variances: Unfavorable
Variable factory overhead costs:				
Indirect factory wages	$ 8,000	$ 5,100	$2,900	
Power and light	4,000	4,200		$ 200
Indirect materials	2,400	1,100	1,300	
Total variable factory overhead cost	$14,400	$10,400		
Fixed factory overhead costs:				
Supervisory salaries	$ 5,500	$ 5,500		
Depreciation of plant and equipment	4,500	4,500		
Insurance and property taxes	2,000	2,000		
Total fixed factory overhead cost	$12,000	$12,000		
Total factory overhead cost	$26,400	$22,400		
Total controllable variances			$4,200	$ 200
Net controllable variance—favorable				$4,000
Volume variance—unfavorable:				
Capacity not used at the standard rate for fixed factory overhead—1,000 × $2.40				2,400
Total factory overhead cost variance—favorable				$1,600

It is also possible to break down many of the individual factory overhead cost variances into quantity and price variances, similar to direct materials and direct labor. For example, the indirect factory wages variance may include both time and rate variances. Likewise, the indirect materials variance may include both a quantity variance and a price variance. Such variances are illustrated in advanced textbooks.

Recording and Reporting Variances from Standards

OBJECTIVE 6

Journalize the entries for recording standards in the accounts and prepare an income statement that includes variances from standard.

Standard costs can be used solely as a management tool separate from the accounts in the general ledger. However, many companies include both standard costs and variances, in addition to actual costs, in their accounts. In doing so, one approach is to record the standard costs and variances at the same time the actual manufacturing costs are recorded in the accounts. To illustrate, assume that Western Rider Inc. purchased, on account, the 7,300 square yards of blue denim used at $5.50 per square yard. The standard price for direct materials is $5.00 per square yard. The entry to record the purchase and the unfavorable direct materials price variance is as follows:

	Debit	Credit
Materials (7,300 sq. yds. × $5.00)	36 5 0 0 00	
Direct Materials Price Variance	3 6 5 0 00	
Accounts Payable (7,300 sq. yds. × $5.50)		40 1 5 0 00

The materials account is debited for the actual quantity purchased at the standard price, $36,500 (7,300 square yards × $5.00). Accounts Payable is credited for the $40,150 actual cost. The unfavorable direct materials price variance is $3,650 [($5.50 actual price per square yard − $5.00 standard price per square yard) × 7,300 square yards purchased]. It is recorded by debiting Direct Materials Price Variance. If the variance had been favorable, Direct Materials Price Variance would have been credited for the amount of the variance.

The direct materials quantity variance is recorded in a similar manner. For example, Western Rider Inc. used 7,300 square yards of blue denim to produce 5,000 pairs of XL jeans, compared to a standard of 7,500 square yards. The entry to record the materials used is as follows:

	Debit	Credit
Work in Process (7,500 sq. yds. × $5.00)	37 5 0 0 00	
Direct Materials Quantity Variance		1 0 0 0 00
Materials (7,300 sq. yds. × $5.00)		36 5 0 0 00

Q&A

A company produces 2,300 units that require 2.4 standard hours per unit. The standard direct labor cost is $9 per hour. The actual direct labor cost totaled $50,670. What is the amount of direct labor debited to Work in Process?

$49,680 (2,300 units × 2.4 hrs. × $9 per hr.)

The work in process account is debited for the standard price of the standard amount of direct materials required, $37,500 (7,500 square yards × $5.00). Materials is credited for the actual amount of materials used at the standard price, $36,500 (7,300 square yards × $5.00). The favorable direct materials quantity variance of $1,000 [(7,500 standard square yards − 7,300 actual square yards) × $5.00 standard price per square yard] is credited to Direct Materials Quantity Variance. If the variance had been unfavorable, Direct Materials Quantity Variance would have been debited for the amount of the variance.

The entries for direct labor are recorded in a manner similar to direct materials. Thus, the work in process account is debited for the standard cost of direct labor and direct materials, as well as factory overhead. Likewise, the work in process account is credited for the standard cost of the product completed and transferred to the finished goods account.

In a given period, it is possible to have both favorable and unfavorable variances. At the end of the period, the balances of the variance accounts will indicate the net favorable or unfavorable variance for the period.

Variances from standard costs are usually not reported to stockholders and others outside the business. If standards are recorded in the accounts, however, the variances may be reported in income statements prepared for management's use. Exhibit 8 is an example of such an income statement prepared for Western Rider Inc.'s internal use. In this exhibit, we assume a sales price of $28 per pair of jeans, selling expenses of $14,500, and administrative expenses of $11,225.

EXHIBIT 8
Variances from Standards in Income Statement

Western Rider Inc.
Income Statement
For the Month Ended June 30, 2000

Sales			$140,000[1]
Cost of goods sold—at standard			97,500[2]
Gross profit—at standard			$ 42,500
	Favorable	**Unfavorable**	
Less variances from standard cost:			
Direct materials price		$ 3,650	
Direct materials quantity	$1,000		
Direct labor rate		3,850	
Direct labor time	1,350		
Factory overhead controllable	4,000		
Factory overhead volume		2,400	3,550
Gross profit			$ 38,950
Operating expenses:			
Selling expenses		$14,500	
Administrative expenses		11,225	25,725
Income before income tax			$ 13,225

[1]5,000 × $28
[2]$37,500 + $36,000 + $24,000 (from Exhibit 2), or 5,000 × $19.50 (from Exhibit 1)

At the end of the fiscal year, the variances from standard are usually transferred to the cost of goods sold account. However, if the variances are significant or if many of the products manufactured are still in inventory, the variances should be allocated to the work in process, finished goods, and cost of goods sold accounts. Such an allocation converts these account balances from standard cost to actual cost.

Standards for Nonmanufacturing Expenses

OBJECTIVE 7

Explain how standards may be used for nonmanufacturing expenses.

The use of standards for selling and administrative expenses is not as common as the use of standards for manufacturing costs. This is due in large part to the fact that many selling and administrative expenses are often not directly related to a unit of product or other measure of activity. For example, the administrative expenses associated with the work of the office manager are not easily related to a product.

When selling and administrative activities are repetitive and produce a common output, standards can be applied. In these cases, the use of standards is similar to that described for a manufactured product. For example, standards can be applied to the work of office personnel who process sales orders. A standard cost for processing a sales order could be developed. The variance between the actual cost of processing a sales order and the standard cost could then be used to control sales order processing costs.

In practice, using standards for selling and administrative expenses is becoming more common. This is because managers have begun to direct more attention to controlling such expenses. When standards are not used, selling and administrative expenses are normally controlled by using budgets.

Nonfinancial Performance Measures

OBJECTIVE 8

Explain and provide examples of nonfinancial performance measures.

Many managers believe that financial performance measures, such as variances from standard, should be supplemented with nonfinancial measures of performance. Measuring both financial and nonfinancial performance helps employees consider multiple, and sometimes conflicting, performance objectives. For example, one company had a machining operation that was measured according to a direct labor time standard. Employees did their work quickly in order to create favorable direct labor time variances. Unfortunately, the fast work resulted in poor quality that, in turn, created difficulty in the assembly operation. The company decided to use both a labor time standard *and* a quality standard in order to encourage employees to consider both the speed and quality of their work.

REAL WORLD

U.S. airlines use a variety of nonfinancial measures, such as on-time performance, lost baggage, and customer complaints. These nonfinancial measures are used to balance customer satisfaction with cost reduction. Many airlines have admitted going too far in cutting costs. For example, **Northwest Airlines** recently increased the frequency of steam-cleaning its planes' lavatories from every 14 days to every 9 days. **America West** has upgraded food and installed in-flight phones. **Delta Air Lines** has added baggage handlers and gate agents to reduce waiting time during arrivals and departures.

In another company, 1–800 customer service phone representatives were placed on labor time standards that required completing a given number of phone calls per hour. This caused representatives to become more concerned with completing phone calls than delivering customer service. As a result, the company added a performance measure, customer satisfaction. Both the efficiency and the quality of the response were then considered in controlling the 1–800 customer service operation.

In the preceding examples, nonfinancial performance measures brought additional perspectives, such as quality of work, to evaluating performance. Some additional examples of nonfinancial performance measures are as follows:

Nonfinancial Performance Measures[4]
Inventory turnover (82%)
On-time delivery (41%)
Elapsed time between a customer order and product delivery (35%)
Customer preference rankings compared to competitors
Response time to a service call
Time to develop new products
Employee satisfaction
Number of customer complaints

[4] The first three examples indicate the percentage of firms using the nonfinancial performance measure, taken from a survey by Forrest B. Green and Felix E. Amenkhienan, "Accounting Innovations: A Cross-Sectional Survey of Manufacturing Firms," *Journal of Cost Management,* Spring 1992, pp. 58–64.

ENCORE

Frederick Taylor and "Scientific Management"

The use of standards has its roots in the work of Frederick Taylor, who in the late 1800s proposed what he termed scientific management. *Scientific management* is, in part, a philosophy of improving operations by breaking work down into its components, measuring the work content of the components, and then making improvements. Taylor illustrated his concept with a pig-iron loading operation. In this operation, workers were to move 92-lb. ingots 36 feet up an incline and drop the load into a railcar. By studying, measuring, and standardizing the work elements of this operation, Taylor was able to improve the daily loading rate from 12.5 tons to 47.5 tons per man.

Many criticize scientific management for dehumanizing work and treating workers as if they were mere machines. This criticism resulted from the apparent focus by these early engineers on specializing and measuring labor for repetitive tasks, such as grasping, positioning, and moving. However, a closer reading of Taylor's original work suggests a man who was ahead of his time. The four principles of scientific management as described by Taylor are:

1. Develop a science for each element of a person's work.
2. Select, train, and develop each worker.
3. Encourage a close cooperation between workers and management.
4. Share responsibility and rewards for success between workers and management.

The first principle was widely embraced in the early part of the twentieth century and is often considered the sum and substance of scientific management. However, Taylor considered the last three principles as equally important. Unfortunately, it has taken nearly one hundred years before these latter principles have taken root in business. Today, these latter principles go by such names as *just-in-time, quality circles, team-based management, total quality management,* and *gainsharing.* ■

KEY POINTS

1 Describe the types of standards and how they are established for businesses.
Standards represent performance benchmarks that can be compared to actual results in evaluating performance. Standards are developed, reviewed, and revised by accountants and engineers, based upon studies of operations. Standards are established so that they are neither too high nor too low, but are attainable.

2 Explain and illustrate how standards are used in budgeting.
Budgets are prepared by multiplying the standard cost per unit by the planned production. To measure performance, the standard cost per unit is multiplied by the actual number of units produced, and the actual results are compared with the standard cost at actual volumes (cost variance).

3 Calculate and interpret direct materials price and quantity variances.
The direct materials cost variance can be separated into a direct materials price and quantity variance. The direct materials price variance is calculated by multiplying the actual quantity by the difference between the actual and standard price. The direct materials quantity variance is calculated by multiplying the standard price by the difference between the actual materials used and the standard materials at actual volumes.

4 Calculate and interpret direct labor rate and time variances.
The direct labor cost variance can be separated into a direct labor rate and time variance. The direct labor rate variance is calculated by multiplying the actual hours worked by the difference between the actual labor rate and the standard labor rate. The

direct labor time variance is calculated by multiplying the standard labor rate by the difference between the actual labor hours worked and the standard labor hours at actual volumes.

5 Calculate and interpret factory overhead controllable and volume variances.
The factory overhead cost variance can be separated into a variable factory overhead controllable variance and a fixed factory overhead volume variance. The controllable variance is calculated by subtracting the actual variable factory overhead from the budgeted variable factory overhead at actual volumes. The volume variance is determined by multiplying the fixed factory overhead rate by the difference between the budgeted hours at 100% of normal capacity and the standard hours used at actual production.

6 Journalize the entries for recording standards in the accounts and prepare an income statement that includes variances from standard.
Standard costs and variances can be recorded in the accounts at the same time the manufacturing costs are recorded in the accounts. For example, the purchase of direct materials on account is recorded as a debit to Materials for the standard cost of materials and a credit to Accounts Payable for the actual cost. Any difference is debited or credited to the direct materials price variance account.

The entries for direct labor, factory overhead, and other variances are recorded in a manner similar to the entries for direct materials. The work in process account is debited for the standard costs of direct labor and factory overhead as well as direct materials. Likewise, the work in process account is credited for the standard cost of the product completed and transferred to the finished goods account.

Under a standard cost system, the cost of goods sold will be reported at standard cost. Manufacturing variances can be disclosed on the income statement to adjust the gross profit at standard to the actual gross profit. Such a disclosure is generally limited for use by management. At the end of the year, the variances from standard are usually transferred to the cost of goods sold account.

7 Explain how standards may be used for nonmanufacturing expenses.
Standards may be used for nonmanufacturing expenses when nonmanufacturing activities are repetitive and related to an activity base. Such standards may be useful to managers in planning, directing, and controlling nonmanufacturing expenses.

8 Explain and provide examples of nonfinancial performance measures.
Many companies use a combination of financial and nonfinancial measures in order for multiple perspectives to be incorporated in evaluating performance. Com bining financial and nonfinancial measures helps employees balance cost efficiency with quality and customer service performance.

ILLUSTRATIVE PROBLEM

Hawley Inc. manufactures Product S for national distribution. The standard costs for the manufacture of Product S were as follows:

	Standard Costs	Actual Costs
Direct materials	1,500 pounds at $35	1,600 pounds at $32
Direct labor	4,800 hours at $11	4,500 hours at $11.80
Factory overhead	Rates per labor hour, based on 100% of normal capacity of 5,500 labor hours:	
	Variable cost, $2.40	$12,300 variable cost
	Fixed cost, $3.50	$19,250 fixed cost

Instructions

1. Determine the quantity variance, price variance, and total direct materials cost variance for Product S.
2. Determine the time variance, rate variance, and total direct labor cost variance for Product S.
3. Determine the controllable variance, volume variance, and total factory overhead cost variance for Product S.

Solution

1. Direct Materials Cost Variance

Quantity variance:		
Actual quantity	1,600 pounds	
Standard quantity	1,500	
Variance—unfavorable	100 pounds × standard price, $35	$3,500
Price variance:		
Actual price	$32.00 per pound	
Standard price	35.00	
Variance—favorable	$(3.00) per pound × actual quantity, 1,600	(4,800)
Total direct materials cost variance—favorable		$(1,300)

2. Direct Labor Cost Variance

Time variance:		
Actual time	4,500 hours	
Standard time	4,800 hours	
Variance—favorable	(300) hours × standard rate, $11	$(3,300)
Rate variance:		
Actual rate	$11.80	
Standard rate	11.00	
Variance—unfavorable	$ 0.80 per hour × actual time, 4,500 hrs.	3,600
Total direct labor cost variance—unfavorable		$ 300

3. Factory Overhead Cost Variance

Variable factory overhead—controllable variance:		
Actual variable factory overhead cost incurred	$12,300	
Budgeted variable factory overhead for 4,800 hours	11,520*	
Variance—unfavorable		$ 780
Fixed factory overhead—volume variance:		
Budgeted hours at 100% of normal capacity	5,500 hours	
Standard hours for actual production	4,800	
Productive capacity not used	700 hours	
Standard fixed factory overhead cost rate	× $3.50	
Variance—unfavorable		2,450
Total factory overhead cost variance—unfavorable		$ 3,230

*4,800 hrs. × $2.40 = $11,520

SELF-EXAMINATION QUESTIONS

Answers at End of Chapter

Matching

Match each of the following statements with its proper term. Some terms may not be used.

- **A.** **budget performance report**
- **B.** **controllable variance**
- **C.** **cost variance**
- **D.** **currently attainable standards**
- **E.** **direct labor rate variance**

D 1. Standards that represent levels of operation that can be obtained with reasonable effort.

H 2. The cost associated with the difference between the standard quantity and the actual quantity of direct materials used in producing a commodity.

A 3. A report comparing actual results with budget figures.

L 4. Standards that represent levels of performance that can be achieved only under perfect operating conditions.

J 5. A detailed estimate of what a product should cost.

F. **direct labor time variance**
G. **direct materials price variance**
H. **direct materials quantity variance**
I. **nonfinancial performance measures**
J. **standard cost**
K. **standard cost systems**
L. **theoretical standards**
M. **volume variance**

M 6. The difference between the budgeted fixed overhead at 100% of normal capacity and the standard fixed overhead for the actual production achieved during the period.

F 7. The cost associated with the difference between the standard hours and the actual hours of direct labor spent producing a commodity.

B 8. The difference between the actual amount of variable factory overhead cost incurred and the amount of variable factory overhead budgeted for actual production.

G 9. The cost associated with the difference between the standard price and the actual price of direct materials used in producing a commodity.

C 10. The difference between the actual cost and the standard cost at actual volumes.

E 11. The cost associated with the difference between the standard rate and the actual rate paid for direct labor used in producing a commodity.

K 12. Accounting systems that use standards for each manufacturing cost entering into the finished product.

Multiple Choice

1. The actual and standard direct materials costs for producing a specified quantity of product are as follows:

Actual:	51,000 pounds at $5.05	$257,550
Standard:	50,000 pounds at $5.00	$250,000

The direct materials price variance is:
A. $50 unfavorable (C.) $2,550 unfavorable
B. $2,500 unfavorable D. $7,550 unfavorable

2. Bower Company produced 4,000 units of product. Each unit requires 0.5 standard hour. The standard labor rate is $12 per hour. Actual direct labor for the period was $22,000 (2,200 hours × $10 per hour). The direct labor time variance is:
A. 200 hours unfavorable C. $4,000 favorable
B. $2,000 unfavorable (D.) $2,400 unfavorable

3. The actual and standard factory overhead costs for producing a specified quantity of product are as follows:

Actual:	Variable factory overhead	$72,500	
	Fixed factory overhead	40,000	$112,500
Standard:	19,000 hours at $6 ($4 variable and $2 fixed)		114,000

If 1,000 hours were unused, the fixed factory overhead volume variance would be:
A. $1,500 favorable C. $4,000 unfavorable
(B.) $2,000 unfavorable D. $6,000 unfavorable

4. Ramathan Company produced 6,000 units of product Y, which is 80% of capacity. Each unit required 0.25 standard machine hour for production. The standard variable factory overhead rate is $5.00 per machine hour. The actual variable factory overhead incurred during the period was $8,000. The variable factory overhead controllable variance is:
A. $500 favorable C. $1,875 favorable
(B.) $500 unfavorable D. $1,875 unfavorable

5. Applegate Company has a normal budgeted capacity of 200 machine hours. Applegate produced 600 units. Each unit requires a standard 0.2 machine hour to complete. The standard fixed factory overhead is $12.00 per hour, determined at normal capacity. The fixed factory overhead volume variance is:
A. $4,800 unfavorable C. $960 favorable
B. $4,800 favorable (D.) $960 unfavorable

CLASS DISCUSSION QUESTIONS

1. What are the basic objectives in the use of standard costs?
2. How can standards be used by management to help control costs?
3. What is meant by reporting by the "principle of exceptions," as the term is used in reference to cost control?
4. How often should standards be revised?
5. How are standards used in budgetary performance evaluation?
6. a. What are the two variances between the actual cost and the standard cost for direct materials?
   b. Discuss some possible causes of these variances.
7. The materials cost variance report for Nickols Inc. indicates a large favorable materials price variance and a significant unfavorable materials quantity variance. What might have caused these offsetting variances?

8. a. What are the two variances between the actual cost and the standard cost for direct labor?
   b. Who generally has control over the direct labor cost?
9. A new assistant controller recently was heard to remark: "All the assembly workers in this plant are covered by union contracts, so there should be no labor variances." Was the controller's remark correct? Discuss.
10. a. Describe the two variances between the actual costs and the standards costs for factory overhead.
    b. What is a factory overhead cost variance report?
11. What are budgeted fixed costs at normal volume?
12. If variances are recorded in the accounts at the time the manufacturing costs are incurred, what does a debit balance in Direct Materials Price Variance represent?
13. If variances are recorded in the accounts at the time the manufacturing costs are incurred, what does a credit balance in Direct Materials Quantity Variance represent?
14. Are variances from standard costs usually reported in financial statements issued to stockholders and others outside the firm?
15. Assuming that the variances from standards are not significant at the end of the period, to what account are they transferred?
16. Would the use of standards be appropriate in a nonmanufacturing setting, such as a fast food restaurant?
17. Briefly explain why firms might use nonfinancial performance measures.
18. REAL WORLD During the ten-year period 1986–1996, the ratio of cost of products sold to sales for **Hershey Foods Corporation** decreased from 63% to 57%. During this same period, the sales of Hershey Foods Corporation increased by almost 244%. As sales increase, why would management normally expect the ratio of cost of products sold to sales to decrease?

Warren Reeve Fess

Resources for Your Success On-Line at warren.swcollege.com

Remember! If you need additional help, visit South-Western's Web site. See page 26 for a description of the online and printed materials that are available.

EXERCISES

Exercise 21–1
Standard direct materials cost per unit
Objective 2

Venus Chocolate Company produces chocolate bars. The primary materials used in producing chocolate bars are cocoa, sugar, and milk. The standard costs for a batch of chocolate (700 bars) are as follows:

Ingredient	Quantity	Price
Cocoa	200 pounds	$0.20 per pound
Sugar	150 pounds	$0.30 per pound
Milk	50 gallons	$1.80 per gallon

Determine the standard direct materials cost per bar of chocolate.

Exercise 21–2
Standard product cost
Objective 2

Old Hickory Furniture Company manufactures unfinished oak furniture. Old Hickory uses a standard cost system. The direct labor, direct materials, and factory overhead standards for an unfinished dining room table are as follows:

Direct labor:	standard rate	$14.00 per hour
	standard time per unit	4.2 hours
Direct materials (oak):	standard price	$18.00 per board foot
	standard quantity	25 board feet
Variable factory overhead:	standard rate	$4.50 per hour
Fixed factory overhead:	standard rate	$2.00 per hour

Determine the standard cost per dining room table.

Exercise 21–3
Budget performance report

Objective 2

✓ b. Direct labor cost variance, $200 U

Curtis Container Company (CCC) manufactures plastic 2-liter bottles for the beverage industry. The cost standards per 100 2-liter bottles are as follows:

Cost Category	Standard Cost per 100 2-Liter Bottles
Direct labor	$1.50
Direct materials	6.80
Factory overhead	0.80
Total	$9.10

At the beginning of May, CCC management planned to produce 400,000 bottles. The actual number of bottles produced for May was 420,000 bottles. The actual costs for May of the current year were as follows:

Cost Category	Actual Cost for the Month Ended May 31, 20—
Direct labor	$ 6,500
Direct materials	27,420
Factory overhead	3,700
Total	$37,620

a. Prepare the May manufacturing standard cost budget (direct labor, direct materials, and factory overhead) for CCC, assuming planned production.
b. Prepare a budget performance report for manufacturing costs, showing the total cost variances for direct materials, direct labor, and factory overhead for May.
c. Interpret the budget performance report.

Exercise 21–4
Direct materials variances

Objective 3

✓ a. Price variance, $12,250 F

The following data relate to the direct materials cost for the production of 4,000 automobile tires:

Actual:	122,500 pounds at $1.70	$208,250
Standard:	120,000 pounds at $1.80	$216,000

a. Determine the price variance, quantity variance, and total direct materials cost variance.
b. To whom should the variances be reported for analysis and control?

Exercise 21–5
Standard direct materials cost per unit from variance data

Objectives 2, 3

The following data relating to direct materials cost for August of the current year are taken from the records of PlayTime Inc., a manufacturer of plastic toys:

Quantity of direct materials used	36,000 pounds
Actual unit price of direct materials	$1.20 per pound
Units of finished product manufactured	5,500 units
Standard direct materials per unit of finished product	6 pounds
Direct materials quantity variance—unfavorable	$3,360
Direct materials price variance—unfavorable	$2,880

Determine the standard direct materials cost per unit of finished product, assuming that there was no inventory of work in process at either the beginning or the end of the month.

Exercise 21–6
Direct labor variances
Objective 4

✓ a. Rate variance, $26,840 U

The following data relate to labor cost for production of 8,000 cellular telephones:

Actual:	12,200 hours at $18.20	$222,040
Standard:	12,500 hours at $16.00	$200,000

a. Determine the rate variance, time variance, and total direct labor cost variance.
b. Discuss what might have caused these variances.

Exercise 21–7
Direct labor variances
Objective 4

✓ a. Time variance, $1,820 U

Rough Trails Bicycle Company manufactures mountain bikes. The following data for March of the current year are available:

Quantity of direct labor used	1,740 hours
Actual price of direct labor	$12.50 per hour
Bicycles completed in March	200
Standard direct labor per bicycle	8 hours
Standard price of direct labor	$13.00 per hour
Planned bicycles for March	180

a. Determine the direct labor rate and time variance.
b. How much direct labor should be debited to Work in Process?

Exercise 21–8
Direct materials and direct labor variances
Objectives 2, 3, 4

✓ Direct materials quantity variance, $2,500 F

At the beginning of September, Franklin Printers Company budgeted 18,000 books to be printed in September at standard direct materials and direct labor costs as follows:

Direct materials	$28,800
Direct labor	21,600
Total	$50,400

The standard materials price is $0.40 per pound. The standard direct labor rate is $12 per hour. At the end of September, the actual direct materials and direct labor costs were as follows:

Actual direct materials	$29,500
Actual direct labor	20,200
Total	$49,700

There were no direct materials price or direct labor rate variances for September. In addition, assume no changes in the direct materials inventory balances in September. Franklin Printers Company actually produced 20,000 units during September.

Determine the direct materials quantity and direct labor time variances.

Exercise 21–9
Flexible overhead budget
Objective 5

✓ Total factory overhead, 8,000 hrs: $91,600

Cherokee Wood Products Company prepared the following factory overhead cost budget for the Press Department for August of the current year, during which it expected to require 6,000 hours of productive capacity in the department:

Variable overhead cost:		
Indirect factory labor	$19,200	
Power and light	2,100	
Indirect materials	15,000	
Total variable cost		$36,300
Fixed overhead cost:		
Supervisory salaries	$16,800	
Depreciation of plant and equipment	24,000	
Insurance and property taxes	2,400	
Total fixed cost		43,200
Total factory overhead cost		$79,500

Assuming that the estimated costs for September are the same as for August, prepare a flexible factory overhead cost budget for the Press Department for September for 4,000, 6,000, and 8,000 hours of production.

Exercise 21–10

Factory overhead cost variances

Objective 5

✓ Volume variance, $12,000 U

The following data relate to factory overhead cost for the production of 20,000 microcomputers:

Actual:	Variable factory overhead	$326,000
	Fixed factory overhead	48,000
Standard:	60,000 hours at $5.80	348,000

If productive capacity of 100% was 80,000 hours and the factory overhead cost applied at the level of 60,000 standard hours was $348,000, determine the variable factory overhead controllable variance, fixed factory overhead volume variance, and total factory overhead cost variance. The fixed factory overhead rate was $0.60 per hour.

Exercise 21–11

Factory overhead cost variances

Objective 5

✓ a. $5,800 F

Amber Fabrics Corporation began March with a budget for 30,000 hours of production in the Weaving Department. The department has a full capacity of 36,000 hours under normal business conditions. The budgeted overhead at the planned volumes at the beginning of March was as follows:

Variable overhead	$186,000
Fixed overhead	126,000
Total	$312,000

The actual factory overhead was $331,000 for March. The actual fixed factory overhead was as budgeted. During March, the Weaving Department had standard hours at actual production volume of 34,000 hours.

a. Determine the variable factory overhead controllable variance.
b. Determine the fixed factory overhead volume variance.

Exercise 21–12

Factory overhead cost variance report

Objective 5

✓ Net controllable variance, $0

Titanium Bearing Company prepared the following factory overhead cost budget for the Finishing Department for May of the current year, during which it expected to use 25,000 hours for production:

Variable overhead cost:		
Indirect factory labor	$60,000	
Power and light	5,000	
Indirect materials	37,500	
Total variable cost		$102,500
Fixed overhead cost:		
Supervisory salaries	$93,900	
Depreciation of plant and equipment	37,400	
Insurance and property taxes	6,300	
Total fixed cost		137,600
Total factory overhead cost		$240,100

Titanium Bearing Company has available 40,000 hours of monthly productive capacity in the Finishing Department under normal business conditions. During May, the Finishing Department actually used 30,000 hours for production. The actual fixed costs were as budgeted. The actual variable overhead for May was as follows:

Actual variable factory overhead cost:	
Indirect factory labor	$ 73,400
Power and light	6,400
Indirect materials	43,200
Total variable cost	$123,000

Construct a factory overhead cost variance report for the Finishing Department for May.

Exercise 21–13
Recording standards in accounts
Objective 6

Concord Manufacturing Company incorporates standards in the accounts and identifies variances at the time the manufacturing costs are incurred. Journalize the entries to record the following transactions:

a. Purchased 500 units of copper tubing on account at $36.50 per unit. The standard price is $38.00 per unit.
b. Used 380 units of copper tubing in the process of manufacturing 80 air conditioners. Five units of copper tubing are required, at standard, to produce one air conditioner.

Exercise 21–14
Income statement indicating standard cost variance
Objective 6

✓ Income before income tax, $89,600

The following data were taken from the records of Hazemount Company for January of the current year:

Administrative expenses	$ 44,000
Cost of goods sold (at standard)	745,000
Direct materials price variance—favorable	800
Direct materials quantity variance—favorable	2,200
Direct labor rate variance—unfavorable	1,800
Direct labor time variance—unfavorable	3,000
Variable factory overhead controllable variance—favorable	3,800
Fixed factory overhead volume variance—unfavorable	10,000
Interest expense	1,900
Sales	960,000
Selling expenses	71,500

Prepare an income statement for presentation to management.

Exercise 21–15
Variance calculations
Objectives 3, 4, 5

What's Wrong WITH THIS?

The data related to Reel 'N Line Sporting Goods Company's factory overhead cost for the production of 75,000 units of product are as follows:

Actual:	Variable factory overhead	$382,300
	Fixed factory overhead	270,000
Standard:	50,000 hours at $12 ($7.50 for variable factory overhead)	600,000

Productive capacity at 100% of normal was 60,000 hours, and the factory overhead cost budgeted at the level of 50,000 standard hours was $645,000. Based upon these data, the chief cost accountant prepared the following variance analysis:

Variable factory overhead controllable variance:		
Actual variable factory overhead cost incurred	$382,300	
Budgeted variable factory overhead for 50,000 hours	375,000	
Variance—unfavorable		$ 7,300
Fixed factory overhead volume variance:		
Normal productive capacity at 100%	60,000 hours	
Standard for amount produced	50,000	
Productive capacity not used	10,000 hours	
Standard variable factory overhead rate	× $7.50	
Variance—unfavorable		75,000
Total factory overhead cost variance—unfavorable		$82,300

Identify the errors in the factory overhead cost variance analysis.

Exercise 21–16
Standards for nonmanufacturing expenses
Objective 7

✓ a. $1,440

Hope Hospital began using standards to evaluate its Admissions Department. The standard was broken into two types of admissions as follows:

Type of Admission	Standard Time to Complete Admission Record
Unscheduled admission	42 minutes
Scheduled admission	24 minutes

The unscheduled admission took longer, since name, address, and insurance information needed to be determined at the time of admission. Information was collected on scheduled admissions prior to the admissions, which was less time consuming.

The Admissions Department employs three full-time people (40 productive hours per week) at $12 per hour. For the most recent week, the department handled 60 unscheduled and 210 scheduled admissions.

a. How much was actually spent on labor for the week?
b. What are the standard hours for the actual volume for the week?
c. Calculate a time variance, and report how well the department performed for the week.

Exercise 21–17

Standards for nonmanufacturing operations

Objectives 2, 4, 7

✓ b. $7,200 U

One of the operations in the **U.S. Post Office** is a mechanical mail sorting operation. In this operation, letter mail is sorted at a rate of one letter per second. The letter is mechanically sorted from a three-digit code input by an operator sitting at a keyboard. The manager of the mechanical sorting operation wishes to determine the number of temporary employees to hire for December. The manager estimates that there will be an additional 25.92 million pieces of mail in December, due to the upcoming holiday season.

Assume that the sorting operators are temporary employees. The union contract requires that temporary employees be hired for one month at a time. A temporary employee is hired for 180 hours in the month.

a. How many temporary employees should the manager hire for December?
b. If each employee earns a standard $16 per hour, what would be the labor time variance if there were only 24.3 million additional letters sorted in December?

PROBLEMS SERIES A

Problem 21–1A

Direct materials and direct labor variance analysis

Objectives 2, 3, 4

✓ c. Direct labor time variance, $260 F

Xanadu Fixtures Company manufactures faucets in a small manufacturing facility. The faucets are made from zinc. Manufacturing consists of 10 employees, who are paid $14 per hour. Each employee presently provides 40 hours of labor per week. Information about a production week is as follows:

Standard wage per hour	$13.00
Standard labor time per faucet	9 minutes
Standard number of pounds of zinc	2 pounds
Standard price per pound of zinc	$7.90
Actual price per pound of zinc	$7.60
Actual pounds of zinc used during the week	5,750 lbs.
Number of faucets produced during the week	2,800

Instructions

Determine (a) the standard cost per unit for direct materials and direct labor, (b) the price variance, quantity variance, and total direct materials cost variance, and (c) the rate variance, time variance, and total direct labor cost variance.

Problem 21–2A

Flexible budgeting and variance analysis

Objectives 2, 3, 4

✓ 1. b. ~~Time variance~~, $220 F

Frost Guard Company makes women's and men's coats. Both products require leather and lining material. The following planning information has been made available:

	Standard Quantity		
	Women's Coats	Men's Coats	Standard Price per Unit
Leather	3 yds.	5 yds.	$30.00
Liner	4 yds.	3 yds.	$ 8.00
Standard labor time	0.15 hr.	0.25 hr.	
Planned production	2,500 units	3,600 units	
Standard labor rate	$13.00 per hour	$12.00 per hour	

Frost Guard does not expect there to be any beginning or ending inventories of leather and lining material.

At the end of the budget year, Frost Guard experienced the following actual results:

	Women's Coats	Men's Coats
Actual production	3,000	4,000

	Actual Price	Actual Quantity Purchased and Used
Leather	$28.00	30,000
Liner	9.00	22,000

	Actual Labor Rate	Actual Labor Hours Used
Woman's Coat	$13.50	470
Man's Coat	13.00	960

The expected beginning inventory and desired ending inventory were realized.

Instructions

1. Prepare the following variance analyses, based on the actual results and production levels at the end of the budget year:
   a. Direct materials price, quantity, and total variance.
   b. Direct labor rate, time, and total variance.
2. Why are the standard amounts in (1) based on the actual production at the end of the year instead of the planned production at the beginning of the year?

Problem 21–3A

Direct materials, direct labor, and factory overhead cost variance analysis

Objectives 3, 4, 5

SPREADSHEET

✓ a. Price variance, $44,000 F

Golden Glide Tire Co. manufacturers automobile tires. Standard costs and actual costs for direct materials, direct labor, and factory overhead incurred for the manufacture of 20,000 tires were as follows:

	Standard Costs	Actual Costs
Direct materials	200,000 pounds at $4.20	220,000 pounds at $4.00
Direct labor	6,000 hours at $18.00	6,200 hours at $19.00
Factory overhead	Rates per direct labor hour, based on 100% of normal capacity of 10,000 direct labor hours:	
	Variable cost, $2.80	$16,000 variable cost
	Fixed cost, $4.00	$40,000 fixed cost

Each tire requires 0.30 hour of direct labor.

Instructions

Determine (a) the price variance, quantity variance, and total direct materials cost variance, (b) the rate variance, time variance, and total direct labor cost variance, and (c) variable factory overhead controllable variance, the fixed factory overhead volume variance, and total factory overhead cost variance.

Problem 21–4A

Standard factory overhead variance report

Objective 5

GENERAL LEDGER

✓ Net controllable variance, $190 F

Health-Tex Company, a manufacturer of disposable medical supplies, prepared the following factory overhead cost budget for the Assembly Department for July of the current year. The company expected to operate the department at 100% of normal capacity of 6,000 hours.

Variable costs:		
Indirect factory wages	$15,000	
Power and light	4,800	
Indirect materials	6,600	
Total variable cost		$26,400
Fixed costs:		
Supervisory salaries	$24,400	
Depreciation of plant and equipment	6,400	
Insurance and property taxes	2,200	
Total fixed cost		33,000
Total factory overhead cost		$59,400

During July, the department operated at 4,500 hours, and the factory overhead costs incurred were: indirect factory wages, $10,990; power and light, $3,710; indirect materials, $4,910; supervisory salaries, $24,400; depreciation of plant and equipment, $6,400; and insurance and property taxes, $2,200.

Instructions

Prepare a factory overhead cost variance report for July. To be useful for cost control, the budgeted amounts should be based on 4,500 hours.

Problem 21–5A

Standards for nonmanufacturing expenses

Objectives 4, 7, 8

✓ 2. $60 F

TestRite Company provides quality testing services for the mining industry. One important activity in quality testing is transcribing tape-recorded analyses of mineral samples into a written report. The manager of the Transcription Department determined that the average transcriptionist could type 400 lines of a report in an hour. The plan for the first week in May called for 42,400 typed lines to be written. The Transcription Department has three transcriptionists. Each transcriptionist is hired from an employment firm that requires that temporary employees be hired for a minimum of a 40-hour week. Transcriptionists are paid $12.00 per hour. The manager offered a bonus if the department could type more than 45,000 lines for the week, without overtime. Due to high customer testing service demands, the transcriptionists typed more lines in the first week of May than planned. The actual amount of lines typed in the first week of May was 50,000 lines, without overtime. As a result, the bonus caused the average transcriptionist hourly rate to increase to $16.00 per hour during the first week in May.

Instructions

1. If the department typed 42,400 lines according to the original plan, what would have been the labor time variance?
2. What was the actual labor time variance as a result of typing 50,000 lines?
3. What was the labor rate variance as a result of the bonus?
4. The manager is trying to determine if a better decision would have been to hire a temporary transcriptionist to meet the higher typing demands in the first week of May, rather than paying out the bonus. If another employee was hired from the employment firm, what would have been the labor time variance in the first week?
5. Which decision is better, paying the bonus or hiring another transcriptionist?
6. Are there any performance-related issues that the labor time and rate variances fail to consider? Explain.

PROBLEMS SERIES B

Problem 21–1B

Direct materials and direct labor variance analysis

Objectives 2, 3, 4

✓ c. Rate variance, $432 F

Summer Breeze, Inc. manufactures silk dresses in a small manufacturing facility. Manufacturing consists of 24 employees, who are paid $10.50 per hour. Each employee presently provides 36 hours of productive labor per week. Information about a production week is as follows:

Standard wage per hour	$11.00
Standard labor time per dress	24 minutes
Standard number of yards of silk per dress	3.5 yards
Standard price per yard of silk	$5.50
Actual price per yard of silk	$6.00
Actual yards of silk used during the week	7,900 yards
Number of dresses produced during the week	2,300

Instructions

Determine (a) the standard cost per dress for direct materials and direct labor, (b) the price variance, quantity variance, and total direct materials cost variance, and (c) the rate variance, time variance, and total direct labor cost variance.

Problem 21–2B
Flexible budgeting and variance analysis
Objectives 2, 3, 4

✓ 1. a. Direct materials quantity variance, $1,000 U

Belgium Delight Company makes dark chocolate and light chocolate. Both products require cocoa and sugar. The following planning information has been made available:

	Standard Quantity		
	Dark Chocolate	Light Chocolate	Standard Price
Cocoa	6 lbs.	10 lbs.	$10.00
Sugar	12 lbs.	16 lbs.	$ 3.00
Standard labor time	0.30 hr.	0.40 hr.	
Planned production	2,550 units	3,600 units	
Standard labor rate	$10.00 per hour	$11.00 per hour	

Belgium Delight does not expect there to be any beginning or ending inventories of cocoa or sugar.

At the end of the budget year, Belgium Delight had the following actual results:

	Dark Chocolate	Light Chocolate
Actual production	4,000	5,000

	Actual Price	Actual Quantity Purchased and Used
Cocoa	$9.50	73,500
Sugar	3.20	130,000

	Actual Labor Rate	Actual Labor Hours Used
Dark chocolate	$10.50	1,150
Light chocolate	10.50	2,100

Instructions

1. Prepare the following variance analyses, based on the actual results and production levels at the end of the budget year:
   a. Direct materials price, quantity, and total variance.
   b. Direct labor rate, time, and total variance.
2. Why are the standard amounts in (1) based on the actual production for the year instead of the planned production for the year?

Problem 21–3B
Direct materials, direct labor, and factory overhead cost variance analysis
Objectives 3, 4, 5

SPREADSHEET

✓ c. Controllable variance, $500 F

Ivory Polymer Company processes a base chemical into plastic. Standard costs and actual costs for direct materials, direct labor, and factory overhead incurred for the manufacture of 500 units of product were as follows:

	Standard Costs	Actual Costs
Direct materials	70,000 pounds at $2.80	72,000 pounds at $3.00
Direct labor	2,000 hours at $20.00	1,920 hours at $22.00
Factory overhead	Rates per direct labor hour, based on 100% of normal capacity of 2,500 direct labor hours:	
	Variable cost, $4.80	$9,100 variable cost
	Fixed cost, $12.00	$30,000 fixed cost

Each unit requires 4 hours of direct labor.

Instructions

Determine (a) the price variance, quantity variance, and total direct materials cost variance, (b) the rate variance, time variance, and total direct labor cost variance, and (c) variable factory overhead controllable variance, the fixed factory overhead volume variance, and total factory overhead cost variance.

Problem 21–4B

Standard factory overhead variance report

Objective 5

GENERAL LEDGER (Windows only)

✓ Volume variance, $9,900 U

Centipede, Inc., a manufacturer of construction equipment, prepared the following factory overhead cost budget for the Welding Department for May of the current year. The company expected to operate the department at 100% of normal capacity of 9,000 hours.

Variable costs:		
Indirect factory wages	$76,500	
Power and light	21,600	
Indirect materials	25,200	
Total variable cost		$123,300
Fixed costs:		
Supervisory salaries	$67,500	
Depreciation of plant and equipment	26,400	
Insurance and property taxes	5,100	
Total fixed cost		99,000
Total factory overhead cost		$222,300

During May, the department operated at 8,100 hours, and the factory overhead costs incurred were: indirect factory wages, $68,100; power and light, $19,950; indirect materials, $23,020; supervisory salaries, $67,500; depreciation of plant and equipment, $26,400; and insurance and property taxes, $5,100.

Instructions

Prepare a factory overhead cost variance report for May. To be useful for cost control, the budgeted amounts should be based on 8,100 hours.

Problem 21–5B

Standards for nonmanufacturing expenses

Objectives 4, 7, 8

✓ 3. $800 U

QuickSoft Company does software development. One important activity in software development is writing software code. The manager of the Venus Development Team determined that the average software programmer could write 25 lines of code in an hour. The plan for the first week in July called for 3,600 lines of code to be written on the Venus product. The Venus Team has four programmers. Each programmer is hired from an employment firm that requires that temporary employees be hired for a minimum of a 40-hour week. Programmers are paid $20.00 per hour. The manager offered a bonus if the team could generate more than 3,375 lines for the week, without overtime. Due to a project emergency, the programmers wrote more code in the first week, of July than planned. The actual amount of code written in the first week of July was 4,400 lines, without overtime. As a result, the bonus caused the average programmer's hourly rate to increase to $25.00 per hour during the first week in July.

Instructions

1. If the team generated 3,600 lines of code according to the original plan, what would have been the labor time variance?
2. What was the actual labor time variance as a result of generating 4,400 lines of code?
3. What was the labor rate variance as a result of the bonus?
4. The manager is trying to determine if a better decision would have been to hire a temporary programmer to meet the higher programming demand in the first week of July, rather than paying out the bonus. If another employee was hired from the employment firm, what would have been the labor time variance in the first week?
5. Which decision is better, paying the bonus or hiring another programmer?
6. Are there any performance-related issues that the labor time and rate variances fail to consider? Explain.

SPECIAL ACTIVITIES

Activity 21–1 Pinnacle Insurance Company

Ethics and professional conduct in business

Dan Hendrix is a cost analyst with Pinnacle Insurance Company. Pinnacle is applying standards to its claims payment operation. Claims payment is a repetitive operation that could be evaluated with standards. Dan used time and motion studies to identify a theoretical standard of 25 claims processed per hour. The Claims Processing Department manager, Angie Street, has rejected this standard and has argued that the standard should be 20 claims processed per hour. Angie and Dan were unable to agree, so they decided to discuss this matter openly at a joint meeting with the vice-president of operations, who would arbitrate a final decision. Prior to the meeting, Dan wrote the following memo to the VP.

Discuss the ethical and professional issues in this situation.

To: Kim Jan, Vice-President of Operations
From: Dan Hendrix
Re: Standards in the Claims Processing Department

As you know, Angie and I are scheduled to meet with you to discuss our disagreement with respect to the appropriate standards for the Claims Processing Department. I have conducted time and motion studies and have determined that the theoretical standard is 25 claims processed per hour. Angie argues that 20 claims processed per hour would be more appropriate. I believe she is trying to "pad" the budget with some slack. I'm not sure what she is trying to get away with, but I believe a tight standard will drive efficiency up in her area. I hope you will agree when we meet with you next week.

Activity 21–2
Conway Company
Nonfinancial performance measures

The senior management of Conway Company has proposed the following three performance measures for the company:

1. Net income as a percent of stockholders' equity
2. Revenue growth
3. Employee satisfaction

Management believes these three measures combine both financial and nonfinancial measures and are thus superior to using just financial measures.

What advice would you give Conway Company for improving on its performance measurement system?

Activity 21–3
Rogers Corporation
Nonfinancial performance measures

At the Soladyne Division of **Rogers Corporation**, the controller used a number of measures to provide managers information about the performance of a just-in-time (JIT) manufacturing operation. Three measures used by the company are:

Orders Past Due: Sales dollar value of orders that were scheduled for shipment, but were not shipped during the period.

Buyer Misery Index: Number of different customers that have orders that are late (scheduled for shipment, but not shipped).

Scrap Index: The sales dollar value of scrap for the period.

1. How is the "orders past due" measure different from the "buyer's misery index," or are the two measures just measuring the same thing?
2. Why do you think the scrap index is measured at sales dollar value, rather than at cost?

Source: John W. Schmitthenner, "Metrics," *Management Accounting,* May 1993, pp. 27–30.

Activity 21–4
Kass Co.
Variance interpretation

You have been asked to investigate some cost problems in the Assembly Department of Kass Co., a consumer electronics company. To begin your investigation, you have obtained the following budget performance report for the department for the last quarter:

Kass Co.—Assembly Department
Quarterly Budget Performance Report

	Standard Quantity at Standard Rates	Actual Quantity at Standard Rates	Quantity Variances
Direct labor	$ 45,000	$ 65,000	$20,000 U
Direct materials	85,000	110,000	25,000 U
Total	$130,000	$175,000	$45,000 U

The following reports were also obtained:

Kass Co.—Purchasing Department
Quarterly Budget Performance Report

	Actual Quantity at Standard Rates	Actual Quantity at Actual Rates	Price Variance
Direct materials	$125,000	$110,000	$15,000 F

Kass Co.—Fabrication Department
Quarterly Budget Performance Report

	Standard Quantity at Standard Rates	Actual Quantity at Standard Rates	Quantity Variances
Direct labor	$ 70,000	$ 58,000	$12,000 F
Direct materials	40,000	40,000	0
Total	$110,000	$ 98,000	$12,000 F

You also interviewed the Assembly Department supervisor. Excerpts from the interview follow.

Q: *What explains the poor performance in your department?*
A: *Listen, you've got to understand what it's been like in this department recently. Lately, it seems no matter how hard we try, we can't seem to make the standards. I'm not sure what is going on, but we've been having a lot of problems lately.*
Q: *What kind of problems?*
A: *Well, for instance, all this quarter we've been requisitioning purchased parts from the material storeroom, and the parts just didn't fit together very well. I'm not sure what is going on, but during most of this quarter we've had to scrap and sort purchased parts—just to get our assemblies put together. Naturally, all this takes time and material. And that's not all.*
Q: *Go on.*
A: *All this quarter, the work that we've been receiving from the Fabrication Department has been shoddy. I mean, maybe around 20% of the stuff that comes in from Fabrication just can't be assembled. The fabrication is all wrong. As a result, we've had to scrap and rework a lot of the stuff. Naturally, this has just shot our quantity variances.*

Interpret the variance reports in light of the comments by the Assembly Department supervisor.

Activity 21–5 Juniper Company
Variance interpretation

Juniper Company is a small manufacturer of electronic musical instruments. The plant manager received the following variable factory overhead report for the period:

	Actual	Budgeted Variable Factory Overhead at Actual Production
Supplies	$21,000	$20,000
Power and light	9,000	8,000
Indirect factory wages	50,000	40,000
Total	$80,000	$68,000

Actual units produced: 4,000 (90% of practical capacity)

The plant manager is not pleased with the $12,000 unfavorable variable factory overhead controllable variance and has come to discuss the matter with the controller. The following discussion occurred:

Plant Manager: I just received this factory report for the latest month of operation. I'm not very pleased with these figures. Before these numbers go to headquarters, you and I will need to reach an understanding.

Controller: Go ahead, what's the problem?

Plant Manager: What's the problem? Well, everything. Look at the variance. It's too large. If I understand the accounting approach being used here, you are assuming that my costs are variable to the units produced. Thus, as the production volume declines, so should these costs. Well, I don't believe that these costs are variable at all. I think they are fixed costs. As a result, when we operate below capacity, the costs really don't go down at all. I'm being penalized for costs I have no control over at all. I need this report to be redone to reflect this fact. If anything, the difference between actual and budget is essentially a volume variance. Listen, I know that you're a team player. You really need to reconsider your assumptions on this one.

If you were in the controller's position, how would you respond to the plant manager?

Activity 21–6 Into the Real World

Government performance review

Internet ACTIVITY

GROUP ACTIVITY

One U.S. government initiative is the National Performance Review (NPR), which is an effort to improve the performance of the government. The NPR has a wide variety of performance measurement and benchmark reports regarding the U.S. government, including a June 1997 report entitled, "Serving the American Public: Best Practices in Performance Measurement." Find an online executive summary of this report within NPR's Web pages at **www.npr.gov**. Briefly summarize in your own words this report's conclusions regarding best practices in performance measurement. If you are in a group, have different members of the group summarize different elements of best practice and prepare a group report.

ANSWERS TO SELF-EXAMINATION QUESTIONS

Matching

1. D
2. H
3. A
4. L
5. J
6. M
7. F
8. B
9. G
10. C
11. E
12. K

Multiple Choice

1. **C** The unfavorable direct materials price variance of $2,550 is determined as follows:

Actual price	$5.05 per pound
Standard price	5.00
Price variance—unfavorable	$0.05 per pound

$0.05 × 51,000 actual pounds = $2,550

2. **D** The unfavorable direct labor time variance of $2,400 is determined as follows:

Actual direct labor time	2,200
Standard direct labor time	2,000
Direct labor time variance—unfavorable	200 × $12 standard rate = $2,400

3. **B** The unfavorable factory overhead volume variance of $2,000 is determined as follows:

Productive capacity not used	1,000 hours
Standard fixed factory overhead cost rate	× $2
Factory overhead volume variance—unfavorable	$2,000

4. **B** The controllable variable factory overhead variance is determined as follows:

6,000 units × 0.25 hour = 1,500 hours

1,500 hours × $5.00 per hour = $7,500

Actual variable overhead:	$8,000
Less: Budgeted variable overhead at actual volume	7,500
Unfavorable controllable variance	$ 500

5. **D** The fixed factory overhead volume variance can be determined as follows:

Actual production in standard hours:
600 units × 0.2 machine hour = 120 machine hours

Practical capacity	200 machine hours
Standard hours at actual production	120
Idle capacity	80 machine hours

80 hours × $12.00 = $960 unfavorable volume variance

22

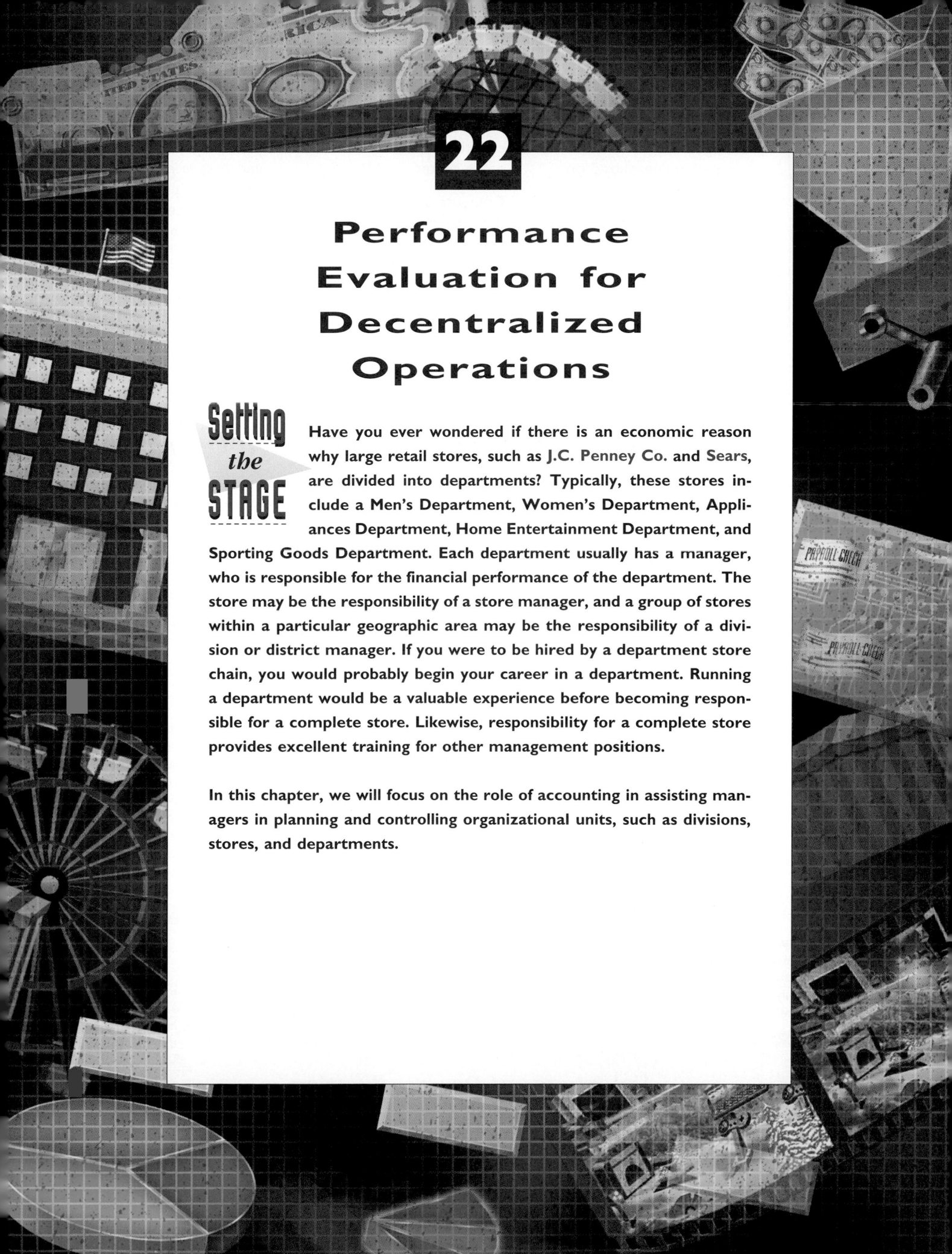

Performance Evaluation for Decentralized Operations

Setting *the* STAGE

Have you ever wondered if there is an economic reason why large retail stores, such as J.C. Penney Co. and Sears, are divided into departments? Typically, these stores include a Men's Department, Women's Department, Appliances Department, Home Entertainment Department, and Sporting Goods Department. Each department usually has a manager, who is responsible for the financial performance of the department. The store may be the responsibility of a store manager, and a group of stores within a particular geographic area may be the responsibility of a division or district manager. If you were to be hired by a department store chain, you would probably begin your career in a department. Running a department would be a valuable experience before becoming responsible for a complete store. Likewise, responsibility for a complete store provides excellent training for other management positions.

In this chapter, we will focus on the role of accounting in assisting managers in planning and controlling organizational units, such as divisions, stores, and departments.

objectives

After studying this chapter, you should be able to:

1. List and explain the advantages and disadvantages of decentralized operations.
2. Prepare a responsibility accounting report for a cost center.
3. Prepare responsibility accounting reports for a profit center.
4. Compute and interpret the rate of return on investment and the residual income for an investment center.
5. Explain how the market price, negotiated price, and cost price approaches to transfer pricing may be used by decentralized segments of a business.

Centralized and Decentralized Operations

OBJECTIVE 1

List and explain the advantages and disadvantages of decentralized operations.

A **centralized** business is one in which all major planning and operating decisions are made by top management. For example, a one-person, owner/manager-operated business is centralized because all plans and decisions are made by one person. In a small owner/manager-operated business, centralization may be desirable. This is because the owner/manager's close supervision ensures that the business will be operated in the way the owner/manager wishes.

REAL WORLD

A trend among large international companies is to decentralize into smaller customer-focused units, while maintaining the advantage of a big company. For example, **Siemens**, the giant $45 billion German electronics company, divided responsibility into 16 minicorporations, each with its own CEO and board of directors. To streamline decision making and enhance financial accountability, **Aluminum Company of America (Alcoa)** restructured its centrally managed divisions into 22 autonomous business units.

Separating a business into **divisions** or operating units and delegating responsibility to unit managers is called **decentralization**. In a decentralized business, the unit managers are responsible for planning and controlling the operations of their units.

Divisions are often structured around common functions, products, customers, or regions. For example, **Delta Air Lines** is organized around *functions,* such as the Flight Operations Division. The **Procter & Gamble Company** is organized around common *products,* such as the Soap Division, which sells a wide array of cleaning products.

There is no one best amount of decentralization for all businesses. In some companies, division managers have authority over all operations, including fixed asset acquisitions and retirements. In other companies, division managers have authority over profits, but not fixed asset acquisitions and retirements. The proper amount of decentralization for a company depends on its advantages and disadvantages for the company's unique circumstances.

REAL WORLD

Nucor Corporation, a $4 billion steel company, practices a highly decentralized form of management, with only 21 people on its headquarters staff.

Advantages of Decentralization

As a business grows, it becomes more difficult for top management to maintain close daily contact with all operations. In such cases, delegating authority to managers closest to the operations usually results in better decisions. These managers often

REAL WORLD

Time Warner Inc. is a major media and entertainment empire that is decentralized into publishing, broadcasting, music, and movie production units. The publishing division produces a number of popular magazines, including *Time, People, Sports Illustrated,* and *Money*. The broadcasting division consists of Turner Broadcasting, which produces CNN. The music division records and distributes music for such artists as Hootie & The Blowfish, Leann Rimes, and Alanis Morissette. The movie production division produces Warner Brothers films, such as *Space Jam*. These divisions are treated as separate units, with their own financial performance targets.

BUSINESS ON STAGE

Generating Creativity in Business

One of the advantages of decentralized operations is that it brings a wide variety of managers' ideas and insights together to solve business problems and issues. Several methods often used in business to generate creative solutions to problems and issues are described below.

- **Brainstorming** involves bringing a small group of people together in a room, presenting them with a problem or issue, and directing them to follow four rules. First, no ideas can be criticized. Second, any idea, no matter how wild or unconventional, is acceptable. Third, the more ideas the better. Fourth, each participant should try to improve on others' ideas and thus create a chain of inspiration. Many businesses use brainstorming to come up with new products and customer service opportunities. For example, the fuel-efficient engine for the *Honda Civic* was developed through brainstorming.
- **Retroduction** challenges the assumptions about the way things are and thus forces managers to look at problems and issues from a different perspective. For example, some **Citibank** managers challenged the widespread assumption that customers prefer to bank with human tellers. This led to the use of automatic teller machines by Citibank.
- **Listing** involves identifying alternative ways a business might use something it already has. Often, a checklist of idea-spurring questions is used, such as SCAMPER, which stands for *Substitute, Combine, Adapt, Modify* or *Magnify, Put to other uses, Eliminate* or *reduce, Reverse* or *rearrange*. For example, Kiichiro Toyoda, the founder of **Toyota**, sought ways to eliminate large inventories and the need for warehouses. He was fascinated by how American supermarkets sold vast amounts of food that might spoil if large inventories were kept at each store. He adapted this observation into the just-in-time approach to manufacturing automobiles. ■

anticipate and react to operating data more quickly than could top management. In addition, as a company expands into a wide range of products and services, it becomes more difficult for top management to maintain operating expertise in all product lines and services. Decentralization allows managers to focus on acquiring expertise in their areas of responsibility. For example, in a company that maintains operations in insurance, banking, and health care, managers could become "experts" in their area of operation and responsibility.

Decentralized decision making also provides excellent training for managers. This may be a factor in helping a company retain quality managers. Since the art of management is best acquired through experience, delegating responsibility allows managers to acquire and develop managerial expertise early in their careers.

Businesses that work closely with customers, such as hotels, are often decentralized. This helps managers create good customer relations by responding quickly to customers' needs. In addition, because managers of decentralized operations tend to identify with customers and with operations, they are often more creative in suggesting operating and product improvements.

Disadvantages of Decentralization

A primary disadvantage of decentralized operations is that decisions made by one manager may negatively affect the profitability of the entire company. For example, the *Coke* manager may engage in price cutting to win customers. However, this may cause *Diet Coke* to lose customers, which may prompt the *Diet Coke* manager to cut prices. As a result, the overall company profit may be less than if the price cutting had not occurred.

Another potential disadvantage of decentralized operations is duplicating assets and costs in operating divisions. For example, each manager of a product line might have a separate sales force and administrative office staff. Centralizing these personnel could save money.

Responsibility Accounting

In a decentralized business, an important function of accounting is to assist unit managers in evaluating and controlling their areas of responsibility, called **responsibility centers**. Responsibility accounting is the process of measuring and reporting operating data by responsibility center. Three common types of responsibility centers are cost centers, profit centers, and investment centers. These three responsibility centers differ in their scope of responsibility, as shown below.

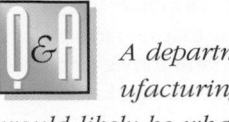

Q&A *A department in a manufacturing facility would likely be what type of performance center?*

Cost center

Cost Center	Profit Center	Investment Center
	Revenue	Revenue
Cost	− Cost	− Cost
	Profit	Profit
		Investment in assets

Responsibility Accounting for Cost Centers

OBJECTIVE 2

Prepare a responsibility accounting report for a cost center.

In a cost center, the unit manager has responsibility and authority for controlling the costs incurred. For example, the supervisor of the Power Department has responsibility for the costs incurred in providing power. A cost center manager does not make decisions concerning sales or the amount of fixed assets invested in the center. Cost centers may vary in size from a small department to an entire manufacturing plant. In addition, cost centers may exist within other cost centers. For example, we could view an entire university as a cost center, and each college and department within the university could also be a cost center, as shown in Exhibit 1.

EXHIBIT 1 Cost Centers in a University

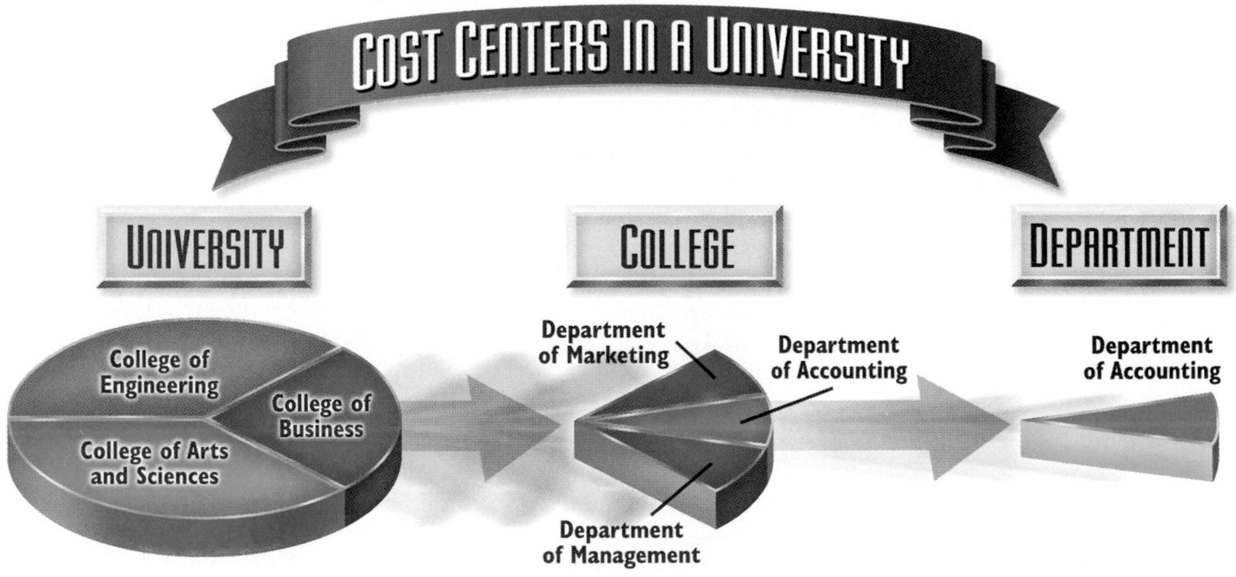

Since managers of cost centers have responsibility and authority over costs, responsibility accounting for cost centers focuses on costs. To illustrate, the budget performance reports in Exhibit 2 are part of a responsibility accounting system. These reports aid the managers in controlling costs.

EXHIBIT 2
Responsibility Accounting Reports for Cost Centers

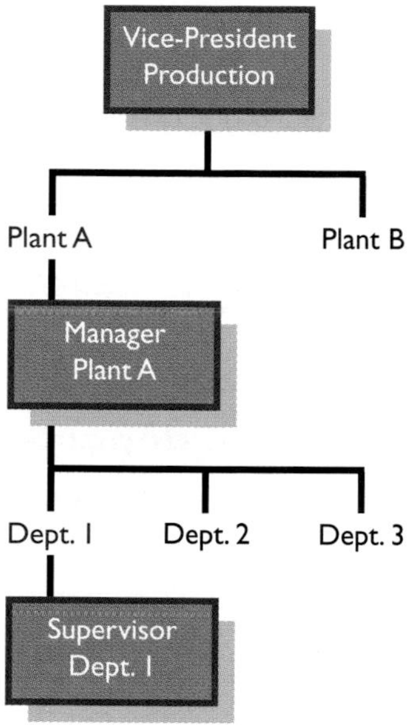

Budget Performance Report
Vice-President, Production
For the Month Ended October 31, 2000

	Budget	Actual	Over Budget	Under Budget
Administration	$ 19,500	$ 19,700	$ 200	
Plant A	467,475	470,330	2,855	
Plant B	395,225	394,300		$925
	$882,200	$884,330	$3,055	$925

Budget Performance Report
Manager, Plant A
For the Month Ended October 31, 2000

	Budget	Actual	Over Budget	Under Budget
Administration	$ 17,500	$ 17,350		$150
Department 1	109,725	111,280	$1,555	
Department 2	190,500	192,600	2,100	
Department 3	149,750	149,100		650
	$467,475	$470,330	$3,655	$800

Budget Performance Report
Supervisor, Department 1—Plant A
For the Month Ended October 31, 2000

	Budget	Actual	Over Budget	Under Budget
Factory wages	$ 58,100	$ 58,000		$100
Materials	32,500	34,225	$1,725	
Supervisory salaries	6,400	6,400		
Power and light	5,750	5,690		60
Depreciation of plant and equipment	4,000	4,000		
Maintenance	2,000	1,990		10
Insurance and property taxes	975	975		
	$109,725	$111,280	$1,725	$170

In Exhibit 2, the reports prepared for the department supervisors show the budgeted and actual manufacturing costs for their departments. The supervisors can use these reports to focus on areas of significant difference, such as the difference between the budgeted and actual materials cost. The supervisor of Department 1 in Plant A may use additional information from a scrap report to determine why materials are over budget. Such a report might show that materials were scrapped as a result of machine malfunctions, improper use of machines by employees, or low quality materials.

For higher levels of management, responsibility accounting reports are usually more summarized than for lower levels of management. In Exhibit 2, for example, the budget performance report for the plant manager summarizes budget and actual cost data for the departments under the manager's supervision. This report enables the plant manager to identify the department supervisors responsible for major differences. Likewise, the report for the vice-president of production summarizes the cost data for each plant. The plant managers can thus be held responsible for major differences in budgeted and actual costs in their plants.

Responsibility Accounting for Profit Centers

OBJECTIVE 3

Prepare responsibility accounting reports for a profit center.

In a **profit center**, the unit manager has the responsibility and the authority to make decisions that affect both costs and revenues (and thus profits). Profit centers may be divisions, departments, or products. For example, a consumer products company might organize its brands (product lines) as divisional profit centers. The manager of each brand could have responsibility for product manufacturing cost and decisions regarding revenues, such as setting sales prices. The manager of a profit center does not make decisions concerning the fixed assets invested in the center. For example, the brand manager of a consumer products company does not make the decision to expand the plant capacity for the brand.

Profit centers may be divisions, departments, or products.

Profit centers are often viewed as an excellent training assignment for new managers. For example, Lester B. Korn, Chairman and Chief Executive Officer of **Korn/Ferry International**, offered the following strategy for young executives en route to top management positions:

Get Profit-Center Responsibility—Obtain a position where you can prove yourself as both a specialist with particular expertise and a generalist who can exercise leadership, authority, and inspire enthusiasm among colleagues and subordinates.

Responsibility accounting reports usually show the revenues, expenses, and income from operations for the profit center. The profit center income statement should include only revenues and expenses that are controlled by the manager. **Controllable revenues** are revenues earned by the profit center. **Controllable expenses** are costs that can be influenced (controlled) by the decisions of profit center managers. For example, the manager of the Sporting Goods Department at **Sears** most likely controls the salaries of department personnel, but does not control the property taxes of the store.

Service Department Charges

We will illustrate profit center income reporting for the Nova Entertainment Group (NEG). Assume that NEG is a diversified entertainment company with two operating divisions organized as profit centers: the Theme Park Division and the Movie Production Division. The revenues and operating expenses for the two divisions are shown below. The operating expenses consist of the direct expenses, such as the wages and salaries of a division's employees.

	Theme Park Division	Movie Production Division
Revenues	$6,000,000	$2,500,000
Operating expenses	2,495,000	405,000

In addition to direct expenses, divisions may also have expenses for services provided by internal centralized **service departments**. Examples of such service departments, which may be more efficient than outside service providers, include the following:

- Research and Development
- Government Relations
- Telecommunications
- Publications and Graphics
- Facilities Management
- Purchasing
- Information Systems
- Payroll Accounting
- Transportation
- Personnel Administration

Q&A

Which of the following departments—Legal Department, Fabrication Department, MIS Department, Maintenance Department—are examples of service departments?

Legal Department, MIS Department, and Maintenance Department

A division's income from operations should reflect the cost of any internal services used by the division. To illustrate, assume that NEG established a Payroll Accounting Department. The costs of the payroll services, called **service department charges**, are charged to NEG's profit center, as shown in Exhibit 3.

EXHIBIT 3
Payroll Accounting Department Charges to NEG's Theme Park and Movie Production Divisions

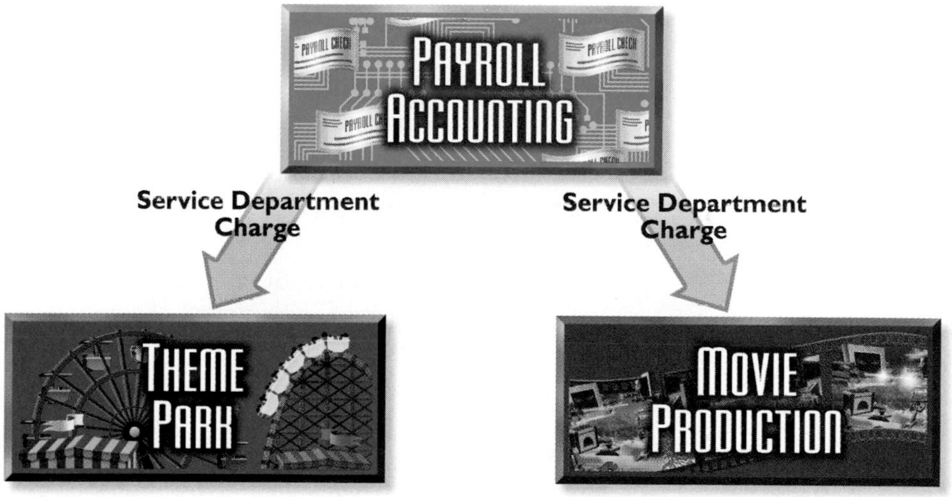

Employees of **IBM** speak of "green money" and "blue money." Green money comes from customers. Blue money comes from providing services to other IBM departments via service department charges. IBM employees note that blue money is easier to earn than green money; yet from the stockholders' perspective, green money is the only money that counts.

Service department charges are *indirect expenses* to a profit center. They are similar to the expenses that would be incurred if the profit center had purchased the services from a source outside the company. A profit center manager has control over such expenses if the manager is free to choose *how much* service is used from the service department.

To illustrate service department charges, assume that NEG has two other service departments—Purchasing and Legal, in addition to Payroll Accounting. The expenses for the year ended December 31, 2000, for each department are as follows:

Purchasing	$400,000
Payroll Accounting	255,000
Legal	250,000
Total	$905,000

The **activity base** of the service departments is used to charge service expenses to the Theme Park and Movie Production Divisions. The activity base for each service department is a measure of the services performed. For NEG, the service department activity bases are as follows:

Department	Activity Base
Purchasing	Number of purchase requisitions
Payroll Accounting	Number of payroll checks
Legal	Number of billed hours

The usage of services by the Theme Park and Movie Production Divisions is as follows:

	Service Usage		
	Purchasing	Payroll Accounting	Legal
Theme Park Division	25,000 purchase requisitions	12,000 payroll checks	100 billed hours
Movie Production Division	15,000	3,000	900
Total	40,000 purchase requisitions	15,000 payroll checks	1,000 billed hours

The rates at which services are charged to each division are called **service department charge rates**. These rates are determined by dividing each service department's expenses by the total service usage as follows:

$$\text{Purchasing: } \frac{\$400{,}000}{40{,}000 \text{ purchase requisitions}} = \$10 \text{ per purchase requisition}$$

$$\text{Payroll Accounting: } \frac{\$255{,}000}{15{,}000 \text{ payroll checks}} = \$17 \text{ per payroll check}$$

$$\text{Legal: } \frac{\$250{,}000}{1{,}000 \text{ hours}} = \$250 \text{ per hour}$$

The usage of services by the Theme Park and Movie Production Divisions is multiplied by the service department charge rates to determine the charges to each division, as shown in Exhibit 4.

Q&A *The centralized payroll department has expenses of $120,000. The department processed a total of 25,000 payroll checks for the period. If the Eastern Division has 6,000 payroll checks for the period, how much should it be charged for payroll services?*

$28,800 [($120,000/25,000) × 6,000]

EXHIBIT 4 Service Department Charges to NEG Divisions

Nova Entertainment Group
Service Department Charges to NEG Divisions
For the Year Ended December 31, 2000

Service Department	Theme Park Division	Movie Production Division
Purchasing (Note A)	$250,000	$150,000
Payroll Accounting (Note B)	204,000	51,000
Legal (Note C)	25,000	225,000
Total service department charges	$479,000	$426,000

Note A:
25,000 purchase requisitions × $10 per purchase requisition = $250,000
15,000 purchase requisitions × $10 per purchase requisition = $150,000
Note B:
12,000 payroll checks × $17 per check = $204,000
3,000 payroll checks × $17 per check = $51,000
Note C:
100 hours × $250 per hour = $25,000
900 hours × $250 per hour = $225,000

REAL WORLD

Some companies require service departments to measure the quality of their service. For example, the **Weyerhaeuser** human resource, accounting, and quality control service departments must measure the quality of their services to line departments, such as sales, marketing, and production. So while the internal line departments "pay" for service in the form of service department charges, they also provide feedback on the service quality. In this way, the line departments are treated like customers.

The Theme Park Division employs many temporary and part-time employees who are paid weekly. This is in contrast to the Movie Production Division, which has a more permanent payroll that is paid on a monthly basis. As a result, the Theme Park Division requires 12,000 payroll checks. This results in a large service charge from Payroll Accounting to the Theme Park Division. In contrast, the Movie Production Division uses many legal services for contract negotiations. Thus, there is a large service charge from Legal to the Movie Production Division.

Profit Center Reporting

The divisional income statements for NEG are presented in Exhibit 5. These statements show the service department charges to the divisions.

EXHIBIT 5
Divisional Income Statements—NEG

Nova Entertainment Group
Divisional Income Statements
For the Year Ended December 31, 2000

	Theme Park Division	Movie Production Division
Revenues*	$6,000,000	$2,500,000
Operating expenses	2,495,000	405,000
Income from operations before service department charges	$3,505,000	$2,095,000
Less service department charges:		
Purchasing	$ 250,000	$ 150,000
Payroll Accounting	204,000	51,000
Legal	25,000	225,000
Total service department charges	$ 479,000	$ 426,000
Income from operations	$3,026,000	$1,669,000

*For a profit center that sells products, the income statement would show: Net sales − Cost of goods sold = Gross profit. The operating expenses would be deducted from the gross profit.

Q&A

If sales are $500,000, the cost of goods sold is $285,000, selling expenses are $85,000, and service department charges are $53,000, what is the income from operations?

$77,000 ($500,000 − $285,000 − $85,000 − $53,000)

The income from operations is a measure of a manager's performance. In evaluating the profit center manager, the income from operations should be compared over time to a budget. It should not be compared across profit centers, since the profit centers are usually different in terms of size, products, and customers.

Responsibility Accounting for Investment Centers

OBJECTIVE 4

Compute and interpret the rate of return on investment and the residual income for an investment center.

In an **investment center**, the unit manager has the responsibility and the authority to make decisions that affect not only costs and revenues but also the assets invested in the center. Investment centers are widely used in highly diversified companies organized by divisions.

The manager of an investment center has more authority and responsibility than the manager of a cost center or a profit center. The manager of an investment center occupies a position similar to that of a chief operating officer or president of a company and is evaluated in much the same way.

Since investment center managers have responsibility for revenues and expenses, income from operations is an important part of investment center reporting. In addition, because the manager has responsibility for the assets invested in the center, two additional measures of performance are often used. These measures are the rate of return on investment and residual income. Top management often compares these measures across investment centers to reward performance and assess investment in the centers.

To illustrate, assume that Baldwin Company is a cellular phone company that has three regional divisions, Northern, Central, and Southern. Condensed divisional income statements for the investment centers are shown in Exhibit 6.

EXHIBIT 6
Divisional Income Statements—Baldwin Company

Baldwin Company
Divisional Income Statements
For the Year Ended December 31, 2000

	Northern Division	Central Division	Southern Division
Revenues	$560,000	$672,000	$750,000
Operating expenses	336,000	470,400	562,500
Income from operations before service department charges	$224,000	$201,600	$187,500
Service department charges	154,000	117,600	112,500
Income from operations	$ 70,000	$ 84,000	$ 75,000

Using only income from operations, the Central Division is the most profitable division. However, income from operations does not reflect the amount of assets invested in each center. For example, if the amount of assets invested in the Central Division is twice that of the other divisions, then the Central Division would be the least profitable in terms of the rate of return on these assets.

Rate of Return on Investment

Since investment center managers also control the amount of assets invested in their centers, they should be held accountable for the use of these assets. One measure that considers the amount of assets invested is the rate of **return on investment** (ROI) or **rate of return on assets**. It is one of the most widely used measures for investment centers and is computed as follows:

$$\textbf{Rate of return on investment (ROI)} = \frac{\textbf{Income from operations}}{\textbf{Invested assets}}$$

The rate of return on investment is useful because the three factors subject to control by divisional managers (revenues, expenses, and invested assets) are used in its computation. By measuring profitability relative to the amount of assets invested in each division, the rate of return on investment can be used to compare divisions. The higher the rate of return on investment, the better the division is utilizing its assets to generate income. To illustrate, the rate of return on investment for each division of Baldwin Company, based on the book value of invested assets, is as follows:

	Northern Division	Central Division	Southern Division
Income from operations	$ 70,000	$ 84,000	$ 75,000
Invested assets	$350,000	$700,000	$500,000
Rate of return on investment	20%	12%	15%

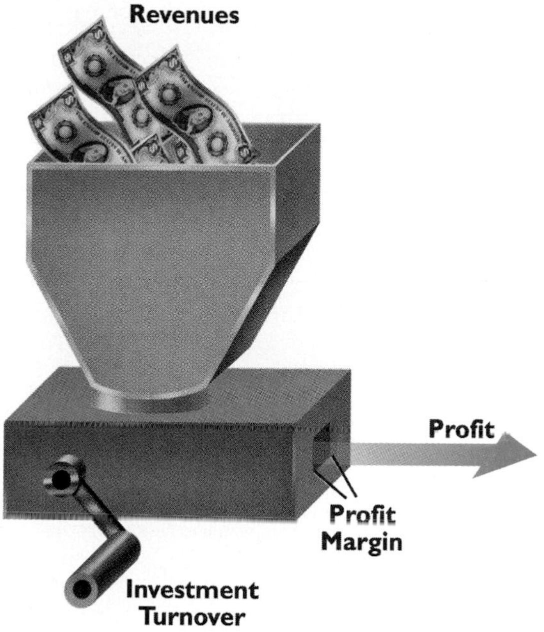

Although the Central Division generated the largest income from operations, its rate of return on investment (12%) is the lowest. Hence, relative to the assets invested, the Central Division is the least profitable division. In comparison, the rate of return on investment of the Northern Division is 20% and the Southern Division is 15%. These differences in the rates of return on investment can be further analyzed using an expanded formula for the rate of return on investment.

In the expanded formula, the rate of return on investment is the product of two factors. The first factor is the ratio of income from operations to sales, often called the **profit margin**. The second factor is the ratio of sales to invested assets, often called the **investment turnover**. In the illustration at the left, profits can be earned by either increasing the investment turnover (turning the crank faster), by increasing the profit margin (increasing the size of the opening), or both.

Using the expanded expression yields the same rate of return on investment for the Northern Division, 20%, as computed previously.

Rate of return on investment (ROI) = Profit margin × Investment turnover

$$\text{Rate of return on investment (ROI)} = \frac{\text{Income from operations}}{\text{Sales}} \times \frac{\text{Sales}}{\text{Invested assets}}$$

$$\text{ROI} = \frac{\$\ 70{,}000}{\$560{,}000} \times \frac{\$560{,}000}{\$350{,}000}$$

$$\text{ROI} = 12.5\% \times 1.6$$

$$\text{ROI} = 20\%$$

The expanded expression for the rate of return on investment is useful in evaluating and controlling divisions. This is because the profit margin and the investment turnover focus on the underlying operating relationships of each division.

The profit margin component focuses on profitability by indicating the rate of profit earned on each sales dollar. If a division's profit margin increases, and all other factors remain the same, the division's rate of return on investment will increase. For example, a division might add more profitable products to its sales mix and thereby increase its overall profit margin and rate of return on investment.

The investment turnover component focuses on efficiency in using assets and indicates the rate at which sales are generated for each dollar of invested assets. The more sales per dollar invested, the greater the efficiency in using the assets. If a division's investment turnover increases, and all other factors remain the same, the division's rate of return on investment will increase. For example, a division might attempt to increase sales through special sales promotions or reduce inventory assets by using just-in-time principles, either of which would increase investment turnover.

The profit margin indicates the rate of profit on each sales dollar, while the investment turnover indicates the rate of sales on each dollar of invested assets.

The rate of return on investment, using the expanded expression for each division of Baldwin Company, is summarized as follows:

$$\text{Rate of return on investment (ROI)} = \frac{\text{Income from operations}}{\text{Sales}} \times \frac{\text{Sales}}{\text{Invested assets}}$$

$$\text{Northern Division (ROI)} = \frac{\$70{,}000}{\$560{,}000} \times \frac{\$560{,}000}{\$350{,}000}$$

$$\text{ROI} = 12.5\% \times 1.6$$
$$\text{ROI} = 20\%$$

$$\text{Central Division (ROI)} = \frac{\$84{,}000}{\$672{,}000} \times \frac{\$672{,}000}{\$700{,}000}$$

$$\text{ROI} = 12.5\% \times 0.96$$
$$\text{ROI} = 12\%$$

$$\text{Southern Division (ROI)} = \frac{\$75{,}000}{\$750{,}000} \times \frac{\$750{,}000}{\$500{,}000}$$

$$\text{ROI} = 10\% \times 1.5$$
$$\text{ROI} = 15\%$$

Q&A *Income from operations is $35,000, invested assets are $140,000, and sales are $437,500. What is the (a) profit margin, (b) investment turnover, and (c) rate of return on investment?*

(a) 8% ($35,000/$437,500); (b) 3.125 ($437,500/$140,000); (c) 25% (8% × 3.125, or $35,000/$140,000)

Although the Northern and Central Divisions have the same profit margins, the Northern Division investment turnover (1.6) is larger than that of the Central Division (0.96). Thus, by more efficiently utilizing its invested assets, the Northern Division's rate of return on investment is higher than the Central Division's. The Southern Division's profit margin of 10% and investment turnover of 1.5 are lower than those of the Northern Division. The product of these factors results in a return on investment of 15% for the Southern Division, compared to 20% for the Northern Division.

To determine possible ways of increasing the rate of return on investment, the profit margin and investment turnover for a division may be analyzed. For example, if the Northern Division is in a highly competitive industry where the profit margin cannot be easily increased, the division manager might focus on increasing the investment turnover. To illustrate, assume that the revenues of the Northern Division could be increased by $56,000 through increasing operating expenses to $385,000. The Northern Division's income from operations will increase from $70,000 to $77,000, as shown below.

Revenues ($560,000 + $56,000)	$616,000
Operating expenses	385,000
Income from operations before service department charges	$231,000
Service department charges	154,000
Income from operations	$ 77,000

The rate of return on investment for the Northern Division, using the expanded expression, is recomputed as follows:

$$\text{Rate of return on investment (ROI)} = \frac{\text{Income from operations}}{\text{Sales}} \times \frac{\text{Sales}}{\text{Invested assets}}$$

$$\text{Northern Division revised ROI} = \frac{\$77{,}000}{\$616{,}000} \times \frac{\$616{,}000}{\$350{,}000}$$

$$\text{ROI} = 12.5\% \times 1.76$$
$$\text{ROI} = 22\%$$

Although the Northern Division's profit margin remains the same (12.5%), the investment turnover has increased from 1.6 to 1.76, an increase of 10% (0.16 ÷ 1.6).

The 10% increase in investment turnover also increases the rate of return on investment by 10% (from 20% to 22%).

In addition to using it as a performance measure, the rate of return on investment may assist management in other ways. For example, in considering a decision to expand the operations of Baldwin Company, management might consider giving priority to the Northern Division because it earns the highest rate of return on investment. If the current rates of return on investment are maintained in the future, an investment in the Northern Division will return 20 cents (20%) on each dollar invested. In contrast, investments in the Central Division will earn only 12 cents per dollar invested, and investments in the Southern Division will return only 15 cents per dollar.

A disadvantage of the rate of return on investment as a performance measure is that it may lead divisional managers to reject new investments that could be profitable for the company as a whole. For example, the Northern Division of Baldwin Company has an overall rate of return on investment of 20%. The average rate of return on investment for Baldwin Company, with all divisions considered, is 14.8% ($229,000/$1,550,000). The manager of the Northern Division has the opportunity of investing in a new project that is estimated will earn a 17% rate of return. If the manager of the Northern Division invests in the project, however, the Northern Division's overall rate of return will decrease from 20%. Thus, the division manager might decide to reject the project, even though the investment would increase Baldwin Company's overall rate of return of 14.8%.

REAL WORLD

Mars, Inc., candy company uses ROI as a measure of responsibility center performance. In its equation, total assets are measured at replacement cost instead of book value. As a result, it believes that its ROI gives management an incentive to replace equipment with the latest technology. In other words, adding new equipment does not penalize the ROI with a larger denominator, since the denominator already is expressed at replacement cost. Using the latest technology provides the company with highly efficient production processes that are able to adjust quickly to changes in product demand.

Residual Income

An additional measure of evaluating divisional performance—residual income—is useful in overcoming some of the disadvantages associated with the rate of return on investment. **Residual income** is the excess of income from operations over a minimum amount of *desired* income from operations, as illustrated below.

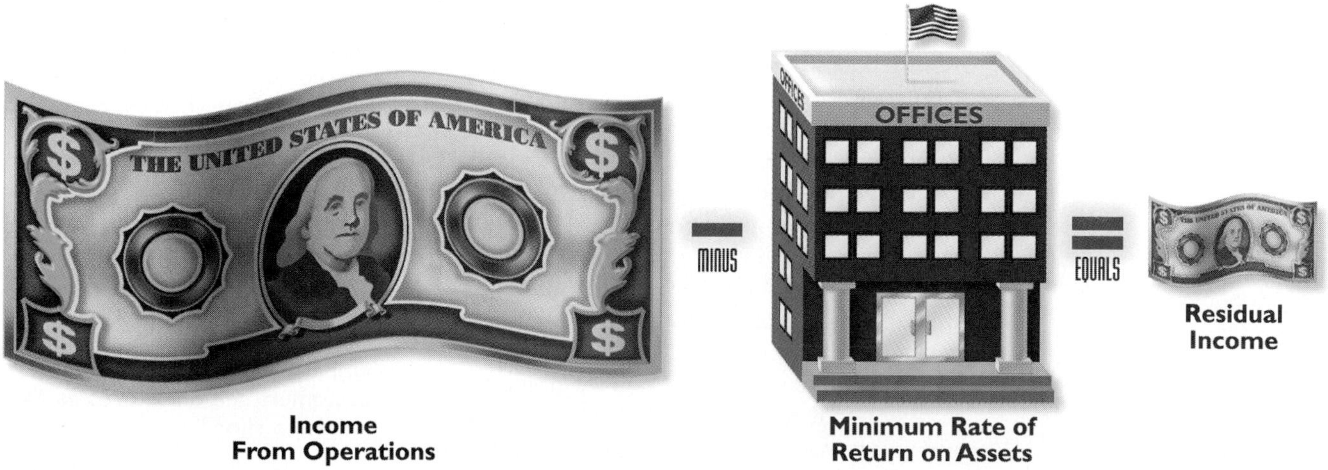

The minimum amount of desired income from operations is set by top management, based on such factors as the cost of financing the business operations. It is normally computed by multiplying a minimum rate of return for the invested assets by the amount of divisional assets. To illustrate, assume that Baldwin Company has established 10% as the minimum rate of return on divisional assets. The residual incomes for the three divisions are as follows:

	Northern Division	Central Division	Southern Division
Income from operations	$70,000	$84,000	$75,000
Minimum amount of income from operations as a percent of assets:			
$350,000 × 10%	35,000		
$700,000 × 10%		70,000	
$500,000 × 10%			50,000
Residual income	$35,000	$14,000	$25,000

The Northern Division has more residual income than the other divisions, even though it has the least amount of income from operations. This is because the assets on which to earn a minimum rate of return are less for the Northern Division than for the other divisions.

The International Division has income from operations of $87,000 and assets of $240,000. The minimum expected rate of return on assets is 12%. What is the residual income for the division?

$58,200 [$87,000 − ($240,000 × 12%)]

The major advantage of residual income as a performance measure is that it considers both the minimum rate of return and the total amount of the income from operations earned by each division. Residual income encourages division managers to maximize income from operations in excess of the minimum. This provides an incentive to accept any project that is expected to have a rate of return in excess of the minimum. Thus, the residual income number supports both divisional and overall company objectives.

Companies such as **Quaker Oats Company** and **Coca-Cola Company** are using residual income (sometimes called "economic value added") to guide their investment decisions and to measure managers' abilities to return profits from the assets entrusted to them.

Nonfinancial Divisional Performance Measurement

In practice, most companies use a variety of divisional performance measures. For example, a survey of manufacturers found that 70% of the respondents used operating income as a percent of sales, 62% used rate of return on investment, and 13% used residual income as performance measures in setting company goals.[1] In addition, some companies are relying on nonfinancial measures to take into account customer perspectives and innovativeness. Examples include measures of product quality, customer complaints, warranty experience, customer retention rates, product availability, on-time performance, customer satisfaction, new product time to market, and market share. These nonfinancial measures combined with conventional financial measures can provide a company with a balanced performance perspective.

A new trend in business is to use a variety of financial and nonfinancial measures to guide the organization's strategy. Using measures in this way is called a "balanced scorecard." **Sears** designed its balanced scorecard using measures targeted to three themes: Sears as a compelling place to work, a compelling place to shop, and a compelling place to invest. A Sears senior executive stated that ". . . there are some leading indicators that predict what financial performance will be. In our case they turn out to be things like employee attitudes and whether customers see our stores as fun places to shop."

[1] Robert A. Howell, James D. Brown, Stephen R. Soucy, and Allen H. Seed, *Management Accounting in the New Manufacturing Environment,* National Association of Accountants, Montvale, New Jersey, 1987.

Transfer Pricing

OBJECTIVE 5

Explain how the market price, negotiated price, and cost price approaches to transfer pricing may be used by decentralized segments of a business.

When divisions transfer products or render services to each other, a **transfer price** is used to charge for the products or services. Since transfer prices affect the goals for both divisions, setting these prices is a sensitive matter for division managers.

Transfer prices should be set so that overall company income is increased when goods are transferred between divisions. As we will illustrate, however, transfer prices may be misused in such a way that overall company income suffers.

In the following paragraphs, we discuss various approaches to setting transfer prices. Exhibit 7 shows the range of prices that results from common approaches to setting transfer prices.[2] Transfer prices can be set as low as the variable cost per unit or as high as the market price. Often, transfer prices are negotiated at some point between variable cost per unit and market price.

EXHIBIT 7
Commonly Used Transfer Prices

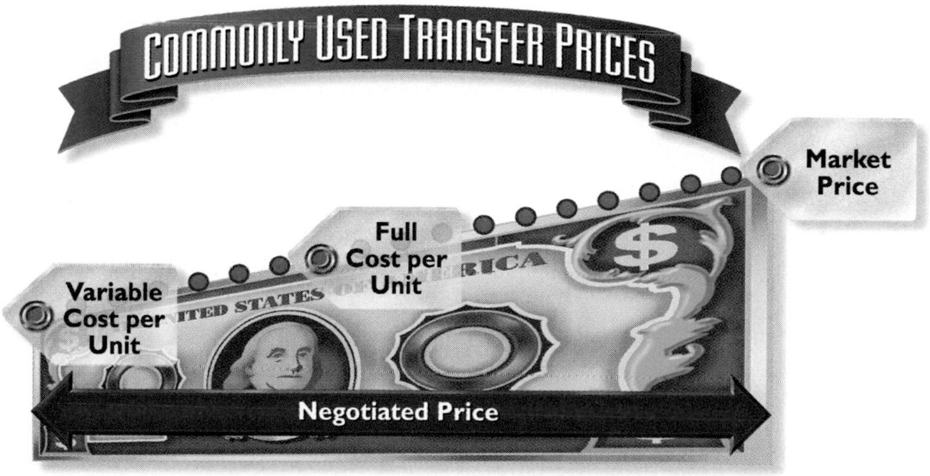

A survey of transfer pricing practices has reported the following usage:

Cost price (variable or full)	46%
Negotiated price	17
Market price	37

Source: Roger Y. W. Tang, "Transfer Pricing in the 1990's," *Management Accounting,* February 1992, pp. 22–26.

Transfer prices may be used when decentralized units are organized as cost, profit, or investment centers. To illustrate, we will use a packaged snack food company (Wilson Company) with no service departments and two operating divisions (Eastern and Western) organized as investment centers. Condensed divisional income statements for Wilson Company, assuming no transfers between divisions, are shown in Exhibit 8.

Market Price Approach

Using the **market price approach**, the transfer price is the price at which the product or service transferred could be sold to outside buyers. If an outside market exists for the product or service transferred, the current market price may be a proper transfer price.

[2] The discussion in this chapter highlights the essential concepts of transfer pricing. In-depth discussion of transfer pricing can be found in advanced texts.

EXHIBIT 8
Income Statement—No Transfers Between Divisions

Wilson Company
Divisional Income Statements
For the Year Ended December 31, 2000

	Eastern Division	Western Division	Total
Sales:			
50,000 units × $20 per unit . . .	$1,000,000		$1,000,000
20,000 units × $40 per unit . . .		$800,000	800,000
			$1,800,000
Expenses:			
Variable:			
50,000 units × $10 per unit	$ 500,000		$ 500,000
20,000 units × $30* per unit		$600,000	600,000
Fixed	300,000	100,000	400,000
Total expenses	$ 800,000	$700,000	$1,500,000
Income from operations	$ 200,000	$100,000	$ 300,000

*$20 of the $30 per unit represents materials costs, and the remaining $10 per unit represents other expenses incurred within the Western Division.

To illustrate, assume that materials used by Wilson Company in producing snack food in the Western Division are currently purchased from an outside supplier at $20 per unit. The same materials are produced by the Eastern Division. The Eastern Division is operating at full capacity of 50,000 units and can sell all it produces to either the Western Division or to outside buyers. A transfer price of $20 per unit (the market price) has no effect on the Eastern Division's income or total company income. The Eastern Division will earn revenues of $20 per unit on all its production and sales, regardless of who buys its product. Likewise, the Western Division will pay $20 per unit for materials (the market price). Thus, the use of the market price as the transfer price has no effect on the Eastern Division's income or total company income. In this situation, the use of the market price as the transfer price is proper. The condensed divisional income statements for Wilson Company in this case are also shown in Exhibit 8.

INTERMISSION

Transfer prices can be used by multinational corporations to shift tax burdens across different countries. For example, assume that a multinational corporation has one division in the United States and another division outside the U.S. The two divisions sell goods to each other. If the tax rate is lower outside the U.S., the corporation may want to shift income to the division outside the U.S. This can be done by setting the U.S. division's purchase transfer prices high and selling transfer prices low. For example, a recent Government Accounting Office (GAO) report found some American subsidiaries bought safety pins at $29 apiece and toothbrushes at $8 each and sold pianos for $50 each and tractor tires for $7.89 each. To change this behavior, the tax codes in the United States and most other countries require transfer prices to be set at "Basic Arm's-Length Standard" (BALS), which is often interpreted as market price. Due to their subjectivity, transfer pricing practices are frequently audited by the Internal Revenue Service (IRS). ■

Negotiated Price Approach

If unused or excess capacity exists in the supplying division (the Eastern Division), and the transfer price is equal to the market price, total company profit may not be maximized. This is because the manager of the Western Division will be indifferent toward purchasing materials from the Eastern Division or from outside suppliers. Thus, the Western Division may purchase the materials from outside suppliers. If, however, the Western Division purchases the materials from the Eastern Division, the difference between the market price of $20 and the variable costs of the Eastern Division can cover fixed costs and contribute to company profits. When the negotiated price approach is used in this situation, the manager of the Western Division is encouraged to purchase the materials from the Eastern Division.

The **negotiated price approach** allows the managers of decentralized units to agree (negotiate) among themselves as to the transfer price. The only constraint on the negotiations is that the transfer price be less than the market price but greater than the supplying division's variable costs per unit.

To illustrate the use of the negotiated price approach, assume that instead of a capacity of 50,000 units, the Eastern Division's capacity is 70,000 units. In addition, assume that the Eastern Division can continue to sell only 50,000 units to outside buyers. A transfer price less than $20 would encourage the manager of the Western Division to purchase from the Eastern Division. This is because the Western Division's materials cost per unit would decrease, and its income from operations would increase. At the same time, a transfer price above the Eastern Division's variable costs per unit of $10 (from Exhibit 8) would encourage the manager of the Eastern Division to use the excess capacity to supply materials to the Western Division. In doing so, the Eastern Division's income from operations would increase.

We continue the illustration with the aid of Exhibit 9, assuming that Wilson Company's division managers agree to a transfer price of $15 for the Eastern Division's product. By purchasing from the Eastern Division, the Western Division's materials cost would be $5 per unit less. At the same time, the Eastern Division would increase its sales by $300,000 (20,000 units × $15 per unit) and increase its income by $100,000 ($300,000 sales − $200,000 variable costs). The effect of reducing the Western Division's materials cost by $100,000 (20,000 units × $5 per unit) is to increase its income by $100,000. Therefore, Wilson Company's income is increased by $200,000 ($100,000 reported by the Eastern Division and $100,000 reported by the Western Division), as shown in the condensed income statements in Exhibit 9.

Point of INTEREST

An important business skill is negotiation. In the popular book on negotiation, *Getting To Yes,* the authors suggest a philosophy of negotiation based on *principles,* rather than *positions.* The authors advise.

- Separating the people from the problem.
- Focusing on interests, not positions.
- Inventing options for mutual gain.
- Insisting on using objective criteria.

Source: Roger Fisher and William Ury, *Getting To Yes* (Penguin Books, 1981).

EXHIBIT 9
Income Statements—Negotiated Transfer Price

Wilson Company
Divisional Income Statements
For the Year Ended December 31, 2000

	Eastern Division	Western Division	Total
Sales:			
50,000 units × $20 per unit . . .	$1,000,000		$1,000,000
20,000 units × $15 per unit . . .	300,000		300,000
20,000 units × $40 per unit . . .		$800,000	800,000
	$1,300,000	$800,000	$2,100,000
Expenses:			
Variable:			
70,000 units × $10 per unit	$ 700,000		$ 700,000
20,000 units × $25* per unit		$500,000	500,000
Fixed	300,000	100,000	400,000
Total expenses	$1,000,000	$600,000	$1,600,000
Income from operations	$ 300,000	$200,000	$ 500,000

*$10 of the $25 is incurred solely within the Western Division, and $15 per unit represents the transfer price per unit from the Eastern Division.

In this illustration, any transfer price less than the market price of $20 but greater than the Eastern Division's unit variable costs of $10 would increase each division's income. In addition, overall company profit would increase by $200,000. By establishing a range of $20 to $10 for the transfer price, each division manager has an incentive to negotiate the transfer of the materials.

Cost Price Approach

Under the **cost price approach**, cost is used to set transfer prices. With this approach, a variety of cost concepts may be used. For example, cost may refer to either total product cost per unit or variable product cost per unit. If total product cost per unit is used, direct materials, direct labor, and factory overhead are included in the transfer price. If variable product cost per unit is used, the fixed factory overhead component of total product cost is excluded from the transfer price.

Either actual costs or standard (budgeted) costs may be used in applying the cost price approach. If actual costs are used, inefficiencies of the producing division are transferred to the purchasing division. Thus, there is little incentive for the producing division to control costs carefully. For this reason, most companies use standard costs in the cost price approach. In this way, differences between actual and standard costs remain with the producing division for cost control purposes.

When division managers have responsibility for cost centers, the cost price approach to transfer pricing is proper and is often used. The cost price approach may not be proper, however, for decentralized operations organized as profit or investment centers. In profit and investment centers, division managers have responsibility for both revenues and expenses. The use of cost as a transfer price ignores the supplying division manager's responsibility for revenues. When a supplying division's sales are all intracompany transfers, for example, using the cost price approach prevents the supplying division from reporting any income from operations. A cost-based transfer price may therefore not motivate the division manager to make intracompany transfers, even though they are in the best interests of the company.

ENCORE

Turning a Cost Center Into a Profit Center

Over the last 20 years, Richard Sasso has turned the production department at *Scientific American* into a profit center. Under Sasso's leadership, the production department (normally a boring "nuts and bolts" operation) has been a constant source of innovation and experimentation.

In 1975, Sasso began to use computers to typeset the magazine electronically. As the computer revolution advanced through the 1980s, so did Sasso's production department. The department purchased Apple McIntoshes and QuarkXPress software. This allowed Sasso to convert the entire production process to computers, using what is termed "direct to plate" technologies. This marked the turning point, because now the magazine's content became available in digital form. Once in digital form, it could be made available through media other than print form. Sasso says, "We want to be in position to take all of our products and make the information available on a variety of platforms."

The first product developed by Sasso was *Scidex,* an electronic index of *Scientific American,* which sold 6,500 copies at nearly $50 a piece, more than paying for itself. Next, in 1993, *Scientific American* became the first magazine to publish simultaneously a print and CD version of the "Ancient Cities" issue. A recent Sasso success was the "Computer in the 21st Century" issue. In this issue, **Apple Computer** became the sole advertiser. All advertising was submitted electronically, so that the complete magazine was printed without using any advertising "film" in the production process. This was the first complete electronic print run of a major magazine. The issue was a public relations and financial bonanza. Sasso is looking now to launch new electronic magazines, such as *The Cancer Journal* and *Science & Medicine*, which are planned for **America Online**.

For all this hard work and creativity, Sasso was recently named "associate publisher," an unprecedented title for someone coming from the production side. The publisher, John Moeling, states, "The role of the production director may be changing. It certainly has at *Scientific American*." ■

Source: Hanna Rubin, "Ink in His Veins," *Folio: The Magazine for Magazine Management*, June 15, 1995.

KEY POINTS

1 List and explain the advantages and disadvantages of decentralized operations.

The advantages of decentralization may include better decisions by the managers closest to the operations, more time for top management to focus on strategic planning, training for managers, improved ability to serve customers and respond to their needs, and improved manager morale. The disadvantages of decentralization may include failure of the company to maximize profits because decisions made by one manager may affect other managers in such a way that the profitability of the entire company may suffer.

2 Prepare a responsibility accounting report for a cost center.

Since managers of cost centers have responsibility and authority to make decisions regarding costs, responsibility accounting for cost centers focuses on costs. The primary accounting tools for planning and controlling costs for a cost center are budgets and budget performance reports. An example of a budget performance report is shown in Exhibit 2.

3 Prepare responsibility accounting reports for a profit center.

In preparing a profitability report for a profit center, operating expenses are subtracted from revenues in order to determine the income from operations before service department charges. Service department charges are then subtracted in order to determine the income from operations of the profit center. An example of a divisional income statement is shown in Exhibit 5.

4 Compute and interpret the rate of return on investment and the residual income for an investment center.

The rate of return on investment for an investment center is the income from operations divided by invested assets. The rate of return on investment may also be computed as the product of (1) the profit margin and (2) the investment turnover. Residual income for an investment center is the excess of income from operations over a minimum amount of desired income from operations.

5 Explain how the market price, negotiated price, and cost price approaches to transfer pricing may be used by decentralized segments of a business.

Under the market price approach, the transfer price is the price at which the product or service transferred could be sold to outside buyers. Market price should be used when the supplier division is able to sell to outsiders and is operating at capacity.

Under the negotiated price approach, the managers of decentralized units agree (negotiate) among themselves as to the transfer price. Negotiated prices should be used when the supplier division is operating below capacity.

Under the cost price approach, cost is used as the basis for setting transfer prices. A variety of cost concepts may be used, such as total product cost per unit or variable product cost per unit. In addition, actual costs or standard (budgeted) costs may be used. The cost price approach should be used for supplier divisions that are organized as cost centers.

ILLUSTRATIVE PROBLEM

Quinn Company has two divisions, Domestic and International. Invested assets and condensed income statement data for each division for the past year ended December 31 are as follows:

	Domestic Division	International Division
Revenues	$675,000	$480,000
Operating expenses	450,000	372,400
Service department charges	90,000	50,000
Invested assets	600,000	384,000

Instructions

1. Prepare condensed income statements for the past year for each division.
2. Using the expanded expression, determine the profit margin, investment turnover, and rate of return on investment for each division.
3. If management desires a minimum rate of return of 10%, determine the residual income for each division.

Solution

1.

Quinn Company
Divisional Income Statements
For the Year Ended December 31, 20—

	Domestic Division	International Division
Revenues	$675,000	$480,000
Operating expenses	450,000	372,400
Income from operations before service department charges	$225,000	$107,600
Service department charges	90,000	50,000
Income from operations	$135,000	$ 57,600

2.

$$\text{Rate of return on investment (ROI)} = \text{Profit margin} \times \text{Investment turnover}$$

$$\text{Rate of return on investment (ROI)} = \frac{\text{Income from operations}}{\text{Sales}} \times \frac{\text{Sales}}{\text{Invested assets}}$$

$$\text{Domestic Division: ROI} = \frac{\$135{,}000}{\$675{,}000} \times \frac{\$675{,}000}{\$600{,}000}$$

$$\text{ROI} = 20\% \times 1.125$$

$$\text{ROI} = 22.5\%$$

$$\text{International Division: ROI} = \frac{\$\ 57{,}600}{\$480{,}000} \times \frac{\$480{,}000}{\$384{,}000}$$

$$\text{ROI} = 12\% \times 1.25$$

$$\text{ROI} = 15\%$$

3. Domestic Division: $75,000 [$135,000 − (10% × $600,000)]
International Division: $19,200 [$57,600 − (10% × $384,000)]

SELF-EXAMINATION QUESTIONS

Answers at End of Chapter

Matching

Match each of the following statements with its proper term. Some terms may not be used.

A. **controllable expenses**
B. **cost center**
C. **cost price approach**

___ 1. A measure of managerial efficiency in the use of investments in assets, computed as income from operations divided by invested assets.

___ 2. An approach to transfer pricing that uses the price at which the product or service transferred could be sold to outside buyers as the transfer price.

D. cost variance
E. decentralization
F. division
G. income from operations
H. investment center
I. investment turnover
J. market price approach
K. negotiated price approach
L. profit center
M. profit margin
N. rate of return on investment
O. residual income
P. responsibility accounting
Q. service department charges
R. transfer price

___ 3. Revenues less operating expenses and service department charges for a profit or investment center.

___ 4. The costs of services provided by an internal service department and transferred to a responsibility center.

___ 5. An approach to transfer pricing that uses cost as the basis for setting the transfer price.

___ 6. A decentralized unit in which the manager has the responsibility and authority to make decisions that affect not only costs and revenues but also the fixed assets available to the center.

___ 7. Costs that can be influenced by the decisions of a manager.

___ 8. An approach to transfer pricing that allows managers of decentralized units to agree (negotiate) among themselves as to the transfer price.

___ 9. A component of the rate of return on investment, computed as the ratio of income from operations to sales.

___ 10. The price charged one decentralized unit by another for the goods or services provided.

___ 11. The separation of a business into more manageable operating units.

___ 12. The excess of divisional income from operations over a "minimum" amount of desired income from operations.

___ 13. A decentralized unit in which the manager has the responsibility and the authority to make decisions that affect both costs and revenues (and thus profits).

___ 14. A decentralized unit that is structured around a common function, product, customer, or geographical territory.

___ 15. The process of measuring and reporting operating data by areas of responsibility.

___ 16. A decentralized unit in which the department or division manager has responsibility for the control of costs incurred and the authority to make decisions that affect these costs.

___ 17. A component of the rate of return on investment, computed as the ratio of sales to invested assets.

Multiple Choice

1. When the manager has the responsibility and authority to make decisions that affect costs and revenues, but no responsibility for or authority over assets invested in the department, the department is called:
   A. a cost center
   B. a profit center
   C. an investment center
   D. a service department

2. The Accounts Payable Department has expenses of $600,000 and makes 150,000 payments to the various vendors who provide products and services to the divisions. Division A has income from operations of $900,000, before service department charges, and requires 60,000 payments to vendors. If the Accounts Payable Department is treated as a service department, what is Division A's income from operations?
   A. $300,000
   B. $900,000
   C. $660,000
   D. $540,000

3. Division A of Kern Co. has sales of $350,000, cost of goods sold of $200,000, operating expenses of $30,000, and invested assets of $600,000. What is the rate of return on investment for Division A?
   A. 20%
   B. 25%
   C. 33%
   D. 40%

4. Division L of Liddy Co. has a rate of return on investment of 24% and an investment turnover of 1.6. What is the profit margin?
   A. 6%
   B. 15%
   C. 24%
   D. 38%

5. Which approach to transfer pricing uses the price at which the product or service transferred could be sold to outside buyers?
   A. Cost price approach
   B. Negotiated price approach
   C. Market price approach
   D. Standard cost approach

CLASS DISCUSSION QUESTIONS

1. Name three common types of responsibility centers for decentralized operations.
2. Differentiate between a cost center and a profit center.
3. Differentiate between a profit center and an investment center.

4. In what major respect would budget performance reports prepared for the use of plant managers of a manufacturing business with cost centers differ from those prepared for the use of the various department supervisors who report to the plant managers?
5. For what decisions is the manager of a cost center *not* responsible?
6. How are service department costs charged to responsibility centers?
7. How is a service department charge rate determined?
8. **Weyerhaeuser Company** developed a system that assigns service department expenses to user divisions on the basis of actual services consumed by the division. Here are a number of Weyerhaeuser's activities in its central financial services department:

   - Payroll
   - Accounts payable
   - Accounts receivable
   - Database administration—report preparation

   For each activity, identify an output measure that could be used to charge user divisions for service.
9. Name two performance measures useful in evaluating investment centers.
10. What is the major shortcoming of using income from operations as a performance measure for investment centers?
11. Why should the factors under the control of the investment center manager (revenues, expenses, and invested assets) be considered in computing the rate of return on investment?
12. What are two ways of expressing the rate of return on investment?
13. In evaluating investment centers, what does multiplying the profit margin by the investment turnover equal?
14. In a decentralized company in which the divisions are organized as investment centers, how could a division be considered the least profitable even though it earned the largest amount of income from operations?
15. Which component of the rate of return on investment (profit margin or investment turnover) focuses on efficiency in the use of assets and indicates the rate at which sales are generated for each dollar of invested assets?
16. How does using the rate of return on investment facilitate comparability between divisions of decentralized companies?
17. The rates of return on investment for Harmon Co.'s three divisions, A, B, and C, are 20%, 17%, and 15%, respectively. In expanding operations, which of Harmon Co.'s divisions should be given priority? Explain.
18. Why would a firm use nonfinancial measures in evaluating divisional performance?
19. What is the objective of transfer pricing?
20. When is the negotiated price approach preferred over the market price approach in setting transfer prices?
21. If division managers cannot agree among themselves on a transfer price when using the negotiated price approach, how is the transfer price established?
22. When using the negotiated price approach to transfer pricing, within what range should the transfer price be established?

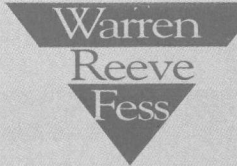

Warren Reeve Fess

Resources for Your Success On-Line at warren.swcollege.com

Remember! If you need additional help, visit South-Western's Web site. See page 26 for a description of the online and printed materials that are available.

EXERCISES

Exercise 22–1

Budget performance reports for cost centers

Objective 2

✓ c. $2,400

Partially completed budget performance reports of Klondike Company, a manufacturer of air conditioners, are provided below.

Klondike Company
Budget Performance Report—Vice-President, Production
For the Month Ended April 30, 2000

Plant	Budget	Actual	Over Budget	Under Budget
St. Louis Plant	$678,000	$665,000		$13,000
Tempe Plant	810,000	800,000		10,000
Cupertino Plant	(g)	(h)	$ (i)	
	$ (j)	$ (k)	$ (l)	$23,000

Klondike Company
Budget Performance Report—Manager, Cupertino Plant
For the Month Ended April 30, 2000

Department	Budget	Actual	Over Budget	Under Budget
Compressor Assembly	$ (a)	$ (b)	$ (c)	
Electronic Assembly	189,000	189,500	500	
Final Assembly	345,000	344,400		$600
	$ (d)	$ (e)	$ (f)	$600

Klondike Company
Budget Performance Report—Supervisor, Compressor Assembly
For the Month Ended April 30, 2000

Costs	Budget	Actual	Over Budget	Under Budget
Factory wages	$ 85,600	$ 87,900	$2,300	
Materials	112,400	109,700		$2,700
Power and light	18,700	19,400	700	
Maintenance	24,300	26,400	2,100	
	$241,000	$243,400	$5,100	$2,700

a. Complete the budget performance reports by determining the correct amounts for the lettered spaces.

b. Compose a memo to Harold Poling, vice-president of production for Klondike Company, explaining the performance of the production division for April.

Exercise 22–2

Divisional income statements

Objective 3

SPREADSHEET

✓ Consumer Division income from operations, $68,700

The following data were summarized from the accounting records for Polymer Plastics Company for the current year ended June 30:

Cost of goods sold:	
Consumer Division	$397,000
Industrial Division	490,000
Administrative expenses:	
Consumer Division	134,000
Industrial Division	187,000
Service department charges:	
Consumer Division	45,300
Industrial Division	65,700
Net sales:	
Consumer Division	645,000
Industrial Division	876,000

Prepare divisional income statements for Polymer Plastics Company.

Exercise 22–3
Service department charges
Objective 4

✓ a. Commercial payroll, $58,000

In divisional income statements prepared for Anchor Cement Company, the Payroll Department costs are charged back to user divisions on the basis of the number of payroll checks, and the Purchasing Department costs are charged back on the basis of the number of purchase requisitions. The Payroll Department had expenses of $180,000, and the Purchasing Department had expenses of $154,000 for the year. The following annual data for Residential, Commercial, and Highway Divisions were obtained from corporate records:

	Residential	Commercial	Highway
Sales	$2,400,000	$2,600,000	$3,000,000
Number of employees:			
Weekly payroll (52 weeks per year)	150	100	50
Monthly payroll	80	50	70
Number of purchase requisitions per year	500	400	200

a. Determine the amount of payroll and purchasing costs charged back to the Residential, Commercial, and Highway Divisions from payroll and purchasing services.
b. Why does the Residential Division have a larger service department charge than the other two divisions even though its sales are lower?

Exercise 22–4
Service department charges and activity bases
Objective 3

For each of the following service departments, identify an activity base that could be used for charging the expense to the profit center.

a. Electronic data processing
b. Duplication services
c. Accounts receivable
d. Telecommunications
e. Central purchasing
f. Legal

Exercise 22–5
Activity bases for service department charges
Objective 3

For each of the following service departments, select the activity base listed that is most appropriate for charging service expenses to responsible units.

	Service Department		Activity Base
a.	Conferences	1.	Number of purchase requisitions
b.	Accounts Receivable	2.	Number of travel claims
c.	Telecommunications	3.	Number of conference attendees
d.	Payroll Accounting	4.	Number of payroll checks
e.	Computer Support	5.	Number of telephone lines
f.	Employee Travel	6.	Number of computers
g.	Central Purchasing	7.	Number of employees trained
h.	Training	8.	Number of sales invoices

Exercise 22–6
Divisional income statements with service department charges
Objective 3

✓ Audio income from operations, $521,500

Cascade Electronics Company has two divisions, Video and Audio, and two corporate service departments, Computer Support and Accounts Payable. The corporate expenses for the year ended December 31 are as follows:

Computer Support Department	$ 460,000
Accounts Payable Department	260,000
Other corporate administrative expenses	400,000
Total corporate expense	$1,120,000

The other corporate administrative expenses include officers' salaries and other expenses required by the corporation. The Computer Support Department charges the divisions for services rendered, based on the number of computers in the department, and the Accounts Payable Department charges divisions for services, based on the number of checks issued. The usage of service by the two divisions is as follows:

Video Division	400 computers	3,200 checks
Audio Division	240	4,800
Total	640 computers	8,000 checks

The service department charges of the Computer Support Department and the Accounts Payable Department are considered controllable by the divisions. Corporate administrative expenses are not considered controllable by the divisions. The revenues, cost of goods sold, and operating expenses for the two divisions are as follows:

	Video	Audio
Revenues	$4,400,000	$3,250,000
Cost of goods sold	1,450,000	1,300,000
Operating expenses	1,200,000	1,100,000

Prepare the divisional income statements for the two divisions.

Exercise 22–7

Corrections to service department charges

Objective 3

What's Wrong WITH THIS?

✓ b. Income from operations, Cargo Division, $2,610,000

Pegasus Airlines Inc. has two divisions organized as profit centers, the Passenger Division and the Cargo Division. The following divisional income statements were prepared:

Pegasus Airlines Inc.
Divisional Income Statements
For the Year Ended October 31, 2001

	Passenger Division		Cargo Division	
Revenues		$8,000,000		$8,000,000
Operating expenses		5,500,000		5,000,000
Income from operations before service department charges		$2,500,000		$3,000,000
Less service department charges:				
Training	$225,000		$225,000	
Flight scheduling	250,000		250,000	
Reservations	450,000	925,000	450,000	925,000
Income from operations		$1,575,000		$2,075,000

The service department charge rate for the service department costs was based on revenues. Since the revenues of the two divisions were the same, the service department charges to each division were also the same.

The following additional information is available:

	Passenger Division	Cargo Division	Total
Number of flight personnel trained	240	60	300
Number of flights	160	240	400
Number of reservations requested	30,000	—	30,000

a. Does the income from operations for the two divisions accurately measure performance?
b. Correct the divisional income statements, using the activity bases provided above in revising the service department charges.

Exercise 22–8

Profit center responsibility reporting

Objectives 3, 5

SPREADSHEET

✓ Income from operations, Camping Equipment Division, $51,035

Fresh Air Sporting Goods Co. operates two divisions—the Camping Equipment Division and the Ski Equipment Division. The following income and expense accounts were provided from the trial balance as of June 30, the end of the current fiscal year, after all adjustments, including those for inventories, were recorded and posted:

Sales—Camping Equipment Division	$800,000
Sales—Ski Equipment Division	645,000
Cost of Goods Sold—Camping Equipment Division	548,000
Cost of Goods Sold—Ski Equipment Division	395,000
Sales Expense—Camping Equipment Division	80,000
Sales Expense—Ski Equipment Division	76,800
Administrative Expense—Camping Equipment Division	65,400
Administrative Expense—Ski Equipment Division	76,700
Advertising Expense	17,200
Transportation Expense	25,090
Accounts Receivable Collection Expense	4,465
Warehouse Expense	45,000

The bases to be used in allocating expenses, together with other essential information, are as follows:

a. Advertising expense—incurred at headquarters, charged back to divisions on the basis of usage: Camping Equipment Division, $9,800; Ski Equipment Division, $7,400.
b. Transportation expense—charged back to divisions at a transfer price of $5.20 per bill of lading: Camping Equipment Division, 2,575 bills of lading; Ski Equipment Division, 2,250 bills of lading.
c. Accounts receivable collection expense—incurred at headquarters, charged back to divisions at a transfer price of $1.90 per invoice: Camping Equipment Division, 1,250 sales invoices; Ski Equipment Division, 1,100 sales invoices.
d. Warehouse expense—charged back to divisions on the basis of floor space used in storing division products: Camping Equipment Division, 10,000 square feet; Ski Equipment Division, 5,000 square feet.

Prepare a divisional income statement with two column headings: Camping Equipment Division and Ski Equipment Division. Provide supporting schedules for determining service department charges.

Exercise 22–9

Rate of return on investment

Objective 4

✓ a. Milk Division, 16%

The income from operations and the amount of invested assets in each division of Wisconsin Dairy Company are as follows:

	Income from Operations	Invested Assets
Cheese Division	$1,408,000	$ 6,400,000
Milk Division	1,696,000	10,600,000
Butter Division	1,840,000	9,200,000

a. Compute the rate of return on investment for each division.
b. Which division is the most profitable per dollar invested?

Exercise 22–10

Residual income

Objective 4

✓ a. Cheese Division, $512,000

Based on the data in Exercise 22–9, assume that management has established a 14% minimum rate of return for invested assets.

a. Determine the residual income for each division.
b. Based on residual income, which of the divisions is the most profitable?

Exercise 22–11

Determining missing items in rate of return computation

Objective 4

✓ d. 2.0

One item is omitted from each of the following computations of the rate of return on investment:

Rate of return on investment	=	Profit margin	×	Investment turnover
20%	=	25%	×	(a)
(b)	=	20%	×	1.3
24%	=	(c)	×	1.5
16%	=	8%	×	(d)
(e)	=	15%	×	0.6

Determine the missing items, identifying each by the appropriate letter.

Exercise 22–12

Profit margin, investment turnover, and rate of return on investment

Objective 4

✓ a. ROI, 18.75%

The condensed income statement for the Southern Division of OmniVision Cinemas Inc. is as follows (assuming no service department charges):

Sales	$720,000
Cost of goods sold	450,000
Gross profit	$270,000
Administrative expenses	90,000
Income from operations	$180,000

The manager of the Southern Division is considering ways to increase the rate of return on investment.

a. Using the expanded expression for rate of return on investment, determine the profit margin, investment turnover, and rate of return on investment of the Southern Division, assuming that $960,000 of assets have been invested in the Southern Division.
b. If expenses could be reduced by $36,000 without decreasing sales, what would be the impact on the profit margin, investment turnover, and rate of return on investment for the Southern Division?

Exercise 22–13
Determining missing items in rate of return and residual income computations

SPREADSHEET

✓ c. $18,600

Data for Texas Tea Drilling Company is presented in the following table of rates of return on investment and residual incomes:

Invested Assets	Income from Operations	Rate of Return on Investment	Minimum Rate of Return	Minimum Amount of Income from Operations	Residual Income
$620,000	$93,000	(a)	12%	(b)	(c)
180,000	(d)	22%	(e)	$27,000	$12,600
940,000	(f)	(g)	(h)	$131,600	$(18,800)
550,000	$101,750	(i)	10%	(j)	(k)

Determine the missing items, identifying each item by the appropriate letter.

Exercise 22–14
Determining missing items from computations

Objective 4

✓ a. (e) 16%

Data for the North, East, South, and West Divisions of Valley Power and Light Company are as follows:

	Sales	Income from Operations	Invested Assets	Rate of Return on Investment	Profit Margin	Investment Turnover
North	$464,000	$55,680	$348,000	(a)	(b)	(c)
East	$326,000	(d)	$260,800	20%	(e)	(f)
South	(g)	$119,000	(h)	(i)	14%	1.25
West	$960,000	(j)	(k)	15%	10%	(l)

a. Determine the missing items, identifying each by the letters (a) through (l).
b. Determine the residual income for each division, assuming that the minimum rate of return established by management is 15%.
c. Which division is the most profitable in terms of (a) return on investment and (b) residual income?

Exercise 22–15
Decision on transfer pricing

Objective 5

✓ a. $3,500,000

Materials used by the Truck Division of Carriage Motors are currently purchased from outside suppliers at a cost of $260 per unit. However, the same materials are available from the Component Division. The Component Division has unused capacity and can produce the materials needed by the Truck Division at a variable cost of $190 per unit.

a. If a transfer price of $220 per unit is established and 50,000 units of materials are transferred, with no reduction in the Component Division's current sales, how much would Carriage Motors' total income from operations increase?
b. How much would the Truck Division's income from operations increase?
c. How much would the Component Division's income from operations increase?

Exercise 22–16
Decision on transfer pricing

Objective 5

✓ b. $500,000

Based on the Carriage Motors data in Exercise 22–15, assume that a transfer price of $250 has been established and that 50,000 units of materials are transferred, with no reduction in the Component Division's current sales.

a. How much would Carriage Motors' total income from operations increase?
b. How much would the Truck Division's income from operations increase?
c. How much would the Component Division's income from operations increase?
d. If the negotiated price approach is used, what would be the range of acceptable transfer prices and why?

PROBLEMS SERIES A

Problem 22–1A
Budget performance report for a cost center

Objective 2

GENERAL LEDGER (Windows only)

The Reaction Department of the Gulf River Plant is organized as a cost center. The budget for the Reaction Department of the Gulf River Plant for the current month ended March 31 is as follows:

Factory wages	$245,000
Materials	346,000
Power and light	46,000
Supervisory salaries	54,000
Depreciation of plant and equipment	28,700
Maintenance	19,600
Insurance and property taxes	14,000
Total	$753,300

During March, the costs incurred in the Reaction Department were as follows:

Factory wages	$244,400
Materials	357,500
Power and light	47,700
Supervisory salaries	54,000
Depreciation of plant and equipment	28,700
Maintenance	19,300
Insurance and property taxes	14,000
Total	$765,600

Instructions

1. Prepare a budget performance report for the supervisor of the Reaction Department of the Gulf River Plant for the month of March.
2. For which costs might the supervisor be expected to request supplemental reports?

Problem 22–2A
Profit center responsibility reporting

Objective 3

✓ 1. Income from operations, Coastal Division, $100,950

Clean Comfort Gas Company has three regional divisions organized as profit centers. The CEO evaluates divisional performance, using income from operations as a percent of revenues. The following quarterly income and expense accounts were provided from the trial balance as of December 31, 2001:

Revenues—Central Division	$620,000
Revenues—Coastal Division	670,000
Revenues—Metro Division	890,000
Operating Expenses—Central Division	420,000
Operating Expenses—Coastal Division	500,000
Operating Expenses—Metro Division	540,000
Corporate Expenses—Shareholder Relations	46,000
Corporate Expenses—Customer Support	63,000
Corporate Expenses—Central Accounting	120,000
General Corporate Officers' Salaries	240,000

The company operates three service departments, Shareholder Relations, Customer Support, and Central Accounting. The Shareholder Relations Department conducts a variety of services for shareholders of the company. The Customer Support Department is the company's telephone point of contact for new service, complaints, and requests for repair. The department believes that the number of customer calls drives its work. The Central Accounting Department provides reports for division management. The department believes that the number of reports drives its work. The following additional information has been gathered:

	Central	Coastal	Metro
Number of customer calls	3,000	4,500	6,500
Number of accounting reports	10,300	12,200	7,500

Instructions

1. Prepare quarterly income statements showing income from operations for the three divisions. Use three column headings: Central, Coastal, and Metro.
2. Which division would the CEO identify as the most successful?
3. Provide a recommendation to the CEO for a better method for evaluating the performance of the divisions. In your recommendation, identify the major weakness of the present method.

Problem 22–3A

Divisional income statements and rate of return on investment analysis

Objective 4

SPREADSHEET

✓ 2. Cereal Division, ROI, 16%

Healthy Start Company is a diversified food products company with three operating divisions organized as investment centers. Condensed data taken from the records of the three divisions for the year ended June 30, 2001, are as follows:

	Cereal Division	Fruit Juice Division	Bread Division
Sales	$775,000	$1,400,000	$970,000
Cost of goods sold	540,000	850,000	740,000
Operating expenses	80,000	340,000	113,600
Invested assets	968,750	1,000,000	606,250

The management of Healthy Start Company is evaluating each division as a basis for planning a future expansion of operations.

Instructions

1. Prepare condensed divisional income statements for the three divisions, assuming that there were no service department charges.
2. Using the expanded expression for rate of return on investment, compute the profit margin, investment turnover, and rate of return on investment for each division.
3. If available funds permit the expansion of operations of only one division, which of the divisions would you recommend for expansion, based on (1) and (2)? Explain.

Problem 22–4A

Effect of proposals on divisional performance

Objective 4

✓ 1. ROI, 18.75%

A condensed income statement for the Music Division of Platinum Entertainment Inc. for the year ended December 31, 2000, is as follows:

Sales	$1,280,000
Cost of goods sold	440,000
Gross profit	$ 840,000
Operating expenses	360,000
Income from operations	$ 480,000

Assume that the Music Division received no charges from service departments. The president of Platinum Entertainment is concerned with the Music Division's rate of return on invested assets of $2,560,000 and has indicated that the division's rate of return on investment must be increased to at least 20% by the end of the next year if operations are to continue. The division manager is considering the following three proposals:

Proposal 1: Reduce invested assets by discontinuing a product line. This action would eliminate sales of $160,000, cost of goods sold of $92,000, and operating expenses of $13,600. Assets of $320,000 would be transferred to other divisions at no gain or loss.

Proposal 2: Transfer equipment with a book value of $960,000 to other divisions at no gain or loss and lease similar equipment. The annual lease payments would exceed the amount of depreciation expense on the old equipment by $96,000. This increase in expense would be included as part of the cost of goods sold. Sales would remain unchanged.

Proposal 3: Purchase new and more efficient machinery and thereby reduce the cost of goods sold by $128,000. Sales would remain unchanged, and the old machinery, which has no remaining book value, would be scrapped at no gain or loss. The new machinery would increase invested assets by $640,000 for the year.

Instructions

1. Using the expanded expression for rate of return on investment, determine the profit margin, investment turnover, and rate of return on investment for the Music Division for the past year.
2. Prepare condensed estimated income statements and calculate the invested assets for each proposal.
3. Using the expanded expression for rate of return on investment, determine the profit margin, investment turnover, and rate of return on investment for each proposal.
4. Which of the three proposals would meet the required 20% rate of return on investment?
5. If the Music Division were in an industry where the profit margin could not be increased, how much would the investment turnover have to increase to meet the president's required 20% rate of return on investment?

Problem 22–5A

Divisional performance analysis and evaluation

Objective 4

SPREADSHEET

✓ 2. Men's Division ROI, 17.6%

The vice-president of operations of Mercury Shoe Company is evaluating the performance of two divisions organized as investment centers. Invested assets and condensed income statement data for the past year for each division are as follows:

	Men's Division	Women's Division
Sales	$3,400,000	$2,600,000
Cost of goods sold	2,250,000	1,388,000
Operating expenses	402,000	640,000
Invested assets	4,250,000	2,080,000

Instructions

1. Prepare condensed divisional income statements for the year ended December 31, 2000, assuming that there were no service department charges.
2. Using the expanded expression for rate of return on investment, determine the profit margin, investment turnover, and rate of return on investment for each division.
3. If management desires a minimum rate of return of 15%, determine the residual income for each division.
4. Discuss the evaluation of the two divisions, using the performance measures determined in (1), (2), and (3).

Problem 22–6A

Transfer pricing

Objective 5

✓ 3. Total income from operations, $1,693,000

No-Crush Container Company manufactures cardboard and container products, with two operating divisions, the Cardboard and Box Divisions. Condensed divisional income statements, which involve no intracompany transfers and which include a breakdown of expenses into variable and fixed components, are as follows:

No-Crush Container Company
Divisional Income Statements
For the Year Ended December 31, 2000

	Cardboard Division	Box Division	Total
Sales:			
30,000 units × $86 per unit	$2,580,000		$2,580,000
45,000 units × $164 per unit		$7,380,000	7,380,000
			$9,960,000
Expenses:			
Variable:			
30,000 units × $60 per unit	$1,800,000		$1,800,000
45,000 units × $128* per unit		$5,760,000	5,760,000
Fixed	255,000	660,000	915,000
Total expenses	$2,055,000	$6,420,000	$8,475,000
Income from operations	$ 525,000	$ 960,000	$1,485,000

*$86 of the $128 per unit represents materials costs, and the remaining $42 per unit represents other expenses incurred within the Box Division.

The Cardboard Division is presently producing 30,000 units out of a total capacity of 38,000 units. Materials used in producing the Box Division's product are currently purchased from outside suppliers at a price of $86 per unit. The Cardboard Division is able to produce the materials used by the Box Division. Except for the possible transfer of materials between divisions, no changes are expected in sales and expenses.

Instructions

1. Would the market price of $86 per unit be an appropriate transfer price for No-Crush Container Company? Explain.
2. If the Box Division purchases 8,000 units from the Cardboard Division at a negotiated transfer price of $70 per unit, how much would the income from operations of each division and the total company income from operations increase?
3. Prepare condensed divisional income statements for No-Crush Container Company, based on the data in (2).
4. If a transfer price of $65 per unit is negotiated, how much would the income from operations of each division and the total company income from operations increase?
5. a. What is the range of possible negotiated transfer prices that would be acceptable for No-Crush Container Company?
   b. Assuming that the managers of the two divisions cannot agree on a transfer price, what price would you suggest as the transfer price?

PROBLEMS SERIES B

Problem 22–1B

Budget performance report for a cost center

Objective 2

GENERAL LEDGER (Windows only)

The Eastern District of Mobile Communications Inc. is organized as a cost center. The budget for the Eastern District of Mobile Communications Inc. for the current month ended September 30 is as follows:

Sales salaries	$ 735,000
Network administration salaries	410,000
Customer service salaries	145,000
Billing salaries	74,600
Maintenance	205,000
Depreciation of plant and equipment	174,600
Insurance and property taxes	24,200
Total	$1,768,400

During September, the costs incurred in the Eastern District were as follows:

Sales salaries	$ 747,900
Network administration salaries	408,300
Customer service salaries	163,600
Billing salaries	73,000
Maintenance	201,400
Depreciation of plant and equipment	174,600
Insurance and property taxes	24,200
Total	$1,793,000

Instructions

1. Prepare a budget performance report for the manager of the Eastern District of Mobile Communications Inc. for the month of September.
2. For which costs might the supervisor be expected to request supplemental reports?

Problem 22–2B
Profit center responsibility reporting

Objective 3

✓ 1. Income from operations, Northern Division, $520,000

Trans Coast Railroad organizes its three divisions, the Northwest, Northern, and Western Regions, as profit centers. The CEO evaluates divisional performance, using income from operations as a percent of revenues. The following quarterly income and expense accounts were provided from the trial balance as of December 31, 2001:

Revenues—NW Region	$1,600,000
Revenues—W Region	2,400,000
Revenues—N Region	2,200,000
Operating Expenses—NW Region	1,000,000
Operating Expenses—W Region	1,800,000
Operating Expenses—N Region	1,200,000
Corporate Expenses—Internal Auditing	400,000
Corporate Expenses—Dispatching	360,000
Corporate Expenses—Equipment	650,000
Corporate Expenses—Officers' Salaries	560,000

The company operates three service departments: the Dispatching Department, the Equipment Department, and the Internal Auditing Department. The Dispatching Department manages the scheduling and releasing of complete trains. The Equipment Department manages the railroad car inventories. It makes sure the right freight cars are at the right place at the right time. The Internal Auditing Department conducts a variety of services for the company as a whole. The following additional information has been gathered:

	Northwest	Western	Northern
Number of scheduled trains	640	760	1,000
Number of railroad cars in inventory	8,600	4,200	13,200

Instructions

1. Prepare quarterly income statements showing income from operations for the three divisions. Use three column headings: Northwest, Western, and Northern.
2. Which division would the CEO identify as the most successful?
3. Provide a recommendation to the CEO for a better method for evaluating the performance of the divisions. In your recommendation, identify the major weakness of the present method.

Problem 22–3B
Divisional income statements and rate of return on investment analysis

Objective 4

SPREADSHEET

✓ 2. Brake Division ROI, 16%

MasterWrench Company is a diversified automotive components company with three operating divisions organized as investment centers. Condensed data taken from the records of the three divisions for the year ended December 31, 2000, are as follows:

	Brake Division	Starter Division	Seat Division
Sales	$550,000	$820,000	$695,000
Cost of goods sold	360,000	610,000	505,000
Operating expenses	80,000	111,600	78,800
Invested assets	687,500	410,000	868,750

The management of MasterWrench Company is evaluating each division as a basis for planning a future expansion of operations.

Instructions

1. Prepare condensed divisional income statements for the three divisions, assuming that there were no service department charges.
2. Using the expanded expression for rate of return on investment, compute the profit margin, investment turnover, and rate of return on investment for each division.

3. If available funds permit the expansion of operations of only one division, which of the divisions would you recommend for expansion, based on (1) and (2)? Explain.

Problem 22–4B
Effect of proposals on divisional performance

Objective 4

✓ 3. Proposal 3 ROI, 15%

A condensed income statement for the Golf Equipment Division of Augusta Inc. for the year ended January 31, 2000, is as follows:

Sales	$6,750,000
Cost of goods sold	4,875,000
Gross profit	$1,875,000
Operating expenses	1,200,000
Income from operations	$ 675,000

Assume that the Golf Equipment Division received no charges from service departments.

The president of Augusta Inc. is concerned with the Golf Equipment Division's rate of return on invested assets of $4,500,000 and has indicated that the division's rate of return on investment must be increased to at least 18% by the end of the next year if operations are to continue. The division manager is considering the following three proposals:

Proposal 1: Reduce invested assets by discontinuing a product line. This action would eliminate sales of $450,000, cost of goods sold of $390,000, and operating expenses of $78,000. Assets of $900,000 would be transferred to other divisions at no gain or loss.

Proposal 2: Transfer equipment with a book value of $750,000 to other divisions at no gain or loss and lease similar equipment. The annual lease payments would exceed the amount of depreciation expense on the old equipment by $33,750. This increase in expense would be included as part of the cost of goods sold. Sales would remain unchanged.

Proposal 3: Purchase new and more efficient machinery and thereby reduce the cost of goods sold by $168,750. Sales would remain unchanged, and the old machinery, which has no remaining book value, would be scrapped at no gain or loss. The new machinery would increase invested assets by $1,125,000 for the year.

Instructions

1. Using the expanded expression for rate of return on investment, determine the profit margin, investment turnover, and rate of return on investment for the Golf Equipment Division for the past year.
2. Prepare condensed estimated income statements and calculate the invested assets for each proposal.
3. Using the expanded expression for rate of return on investment, determine the profit margin, investment turnover, and rate of return on investment for each proposal.
4. Which of the three proposals would meet the required 18% rate of return on investment?
5. If the Golf Equipment Division were in an industry where the profit margin could not be increased, how much would the investment turnover have to increase to meet the president's required 18% rate of return on investment?

Problem 22–5B
Divisional performance analysis and evaluation

Objective 4

SPREADSHEET

✓ 2. Office Division ROI, 20.4%

The vice-president of operations of Heritage Commercial Furniture Company is evaluating the performance of two divisions organized as investment centers. Invested assets and condensed income statement data for the past year for each division are as follows:

	Office Division	Hotel Division
Sales	$ 8,500,000	$4,000,000
Cost of goods sold	5,350,000	2,600,000
Operating expenses	600,000	160,000
Invested assets	12,500,000	3,200,000

Instructions

1. Prepare condensed divisional income statements for the year ended July 31, 2000, assuming that there were no service department charges.
2. Using the expanded expression for rate of return on investment, determine the profit margin, investment turnover, and rate of return on investment for each division.
3. If management desires a minimum rate of return of 12%, determine the residual income for each division.
4. Discuss the evaluation of the two divisions, using the performance measures determined in (1), (2), and (3).

Problem 22–6B

Transfer pricing

Objective 5

✓ 4. Instruments Division, $210,000

Highflight Company is a diversified aerospace company, with two operating divisions, Electronics and Instruments Divisions. Condensed divisional income statements, which involve no intracompany transfers and which include a breakdown of expenses into variable and fixed components, are as follows:

Highflight Company
Divisional Income Statements
For the Year Ended December 31, 2000

	Electronics Division	Instruments Division	Total
Sales:			
1,200 units × $2,500 per unit	$3,000,000		$ 3,000,000
1,800 units × $5,500 per unit		$9,900,000	9,900,000
			$12,900,000
Expenses:			
Variable:			
1,200 units × $1,570 per unit	$1,884,000		$ 1,884,000
1,800 units × $4,200* per unit		$7,560,000	7,560,000
Fixed	530,000	1,145,000	1,675,000
Total expenses	$2,414,000	$8,705,000	$11,119,000
Income from operations	$ 586,000	$1,195,000	$ 1,781,000

*$2,500 of the $4,200 per unit represents materials costs, and the remaining $1,700 per unit represents other expenses incurred within the Instruments Division.

The Electronics Division is presently producing 1,200 units out of a total capacity of 1,500 units. Materials used in producing the Instruments Division's product are currently purchased from outside suppliers at a price of $2,500 per unit. The Electronics Division is able to produce the materials used by the Instruments Division. Except for the possible transfer of materials between divisions, no changes are expected in sales and expenses.

Instructions

1. Would the market price of $2,500 per unit be an appropriate transfer price for Highflight Company? Explain.
2. If the Instruments Division purchases 300 units from the Electronics Division at a negotiated transfer price of $2,000 per unit, how much would the income from operations of each division and total company income from operations increase?
3. Prepare condensed divisional income statements for Highflight Company, based on the data in (2).
4. If a transfer price of $1,800 per unit is negotiated, how much would the income from operations of each division and total company income from operations increase?
5. a. What is the range of possible negotiated transfer prices that would be acceptable for Highflight Company?
   b. Assuming that the managers of the two divisions cannot agree on a transfer price, what price would you suggest as the transfer price?

SPECIAL ACTIVITIES

Activity 22–1 Forever Fresh Food Company

Ethics and professional conduct in business

Forever Fresh Food Company has two divisions, the Can Division and the Food Division. The Food Division may purchase cans from the Can Division or from outside suppliers. The Can Division sells can products both internally and externally. The market price for cans is $100 per 1,000 cans. Lee Tazwell is the controller of the Food Division, and Tracy Ford is the controller of the Can Division. The following conversation took place between Lee and Tracy:

Lee: I hear you are having problems selling cans out of your division. Maybe I can help.

Tracy: You've got that right. We're only producing and selling at 70% of our capacity to outsiders. Last year we were selling all we could make. It would help a great deal if your division would divert some of your purchases to our division so we could use up our capacity. After all, we are part of the same company.

Lee: What kind of price could you give me?

Tracy: Well, you know as well as I that we are under strict profit responsibility in our divisions, so I would expect to get market price, $100 for 1,000 cans.

Lee: I'm not so sure we can swing that. I was expecting a price break from a "sister" division.

Tracy: Hey, I can only take this "sister" stuff so far. If I give you a price break, our profits will fall from last year's levels. I don't think I could explain that. I'm sorry, but I must remain firm—market price. After all, it's only fair—that's what you would have to pay from an external supplier.

Lee: Fair or not, I think we'll pass. Sorry we couldn't have helped.

Was Lee behaving ethically by trying to force the Can Division into a price break? Comment on Tracy's reactions.

Activity 22–2 Farnsworth University

Service department charges

The Accounting Department of Farnsworth University asked the Publications Department to prepare a brochure for the Masters of Accountancy program. The Publications Department delivered the brochures and charged the Accounting Department a rate that was 20% higher than could be obtained from an outside printing company. The policy of the university required the Accounting Department to use the internal publications group for brochures. The Publications Department claimed that they had a drop in demand for their services during the fiscal year, so they had to charge higher prices in order to recover their payroll and fixed costs.

Should the cost of the brochure be transferred to the Accounting Department in order to hold the department head accountable for the cost of the brochure? What changes in policy would you recommend?

Activity 22–3 Wonder Media Enterprises

Evaluating divisional performance

The three divisions of Wonder Media Enterprises are Publications, Broadcasting, and Music. The divisions are structured as investment centers. The following responsibility reports were prepared for the three divisions for the prior year:

	Publications	Broadcasting	Music
Revenues	$ 600,000	$1,400,000	$500,000
Operating expenses	240,000	800,000	100,000
Income from operations before service department charges	$ 360,000	$ 600,000	$400,000
Service department charges:			
Promotion	$ 100,000	$ 200,000	$200,000
Legal	50,000	40,000	80,000
	$ 150,000	$ 240,000	$280,000
Income from operations	$ 210,000	$ 360,000	$120,000
Invested assets	$1,500,000	$3,000,000	$800,000

1. Which division is making the best use of invested assets and thus should be given priority for future capital investments?

2. Assuming that the expected rate of return on new projects is 10%, would all investments that produce a return in excess of 10% be accepted by the divisions?
3. Can you identify opportunities for improving the company's financial performance?

Activity 22–4 Gleason Foods Inc.

Evaluating division performance over time

The Snack Foods Division of Gleason Foods Inc. has been experiencing revenue and profit growth during the years 1999–2001. The divisional income statements are provided below.

Gleason Foods Inc.
Divisional Income Statements, Snack Foods Division
For the Years Ended December 31, 1999–2001

	1999	2000	2001
Sales	$420,000	$540,000	$650,000
Cost of goods sold	264,000	310,000	342,500
Gross profit	$156,000	$230,000	$307,500
Operating expenses	93,000	116,600	145,000
Income from operations	$ 63,000	$113,400	$162,500

Assume that there are no charges from service departments. The vice-president of the division, Harlan Tyson, is proud of his division's performance over the last three years. The president of Gleason Foods, Janice Gleason, is discussing the division's performance with Harlan, as follows:

Harlan: As you can see, we've had a successful three years in the Snack Foods Division.
Janice: I'm not too sure.
Harlan: What do you mean? Look at our results. Our income from operations has nearly tripled, while our profit margins are improving.
Janice: I am looking at your results. However, your income statements fail to include one very important piece of information; namely, the invested assets. You have been investing a great deal of assets into the division. You had $210,000 in invested assets in 1999, $540,000 in 2000, and $1,000,000 in 2001.
Harlan: You are right. I've needed the assets in order to upgrade our technologies and expand our operations. The additional assets are one reason we have been able to grow and improve our profit margins. I don't see that this is a problem.
Janice: The problem is that we must maintain a 20% rate of return on invested assets.

1. Determine the profit margins for the Snack Foods Division for 1999–2001.
2. Calculate the investment turnover for the Snack Foods Division for 1999–2001.
3. Calculate the rate of return on investment for the Snack Foods Division for 1999–2001.
4. Evaluate the division's performance over the 1999–2001 time period. Why was Janice concerned about the performance?

Activity 22–5 Ontario Company

Evaluating division performance

Your father is president of Ontario Company, a privately held diversified company with five separate divisions organized as investment centers. A condensed income statement for the Sporting Goods Division for the past year, assuming no service department charges, is as follows:

Ontario Company—Sporting Goods Division
Income Statement
For the Year Ended December 31, 20—

Sales	$16,000,000
Cost of goods sold	10,100,000
Gross profit	$ 5,900,000
Operating expenses	1,900,000
Income from operations	$ 4,000,000

The manager of the Sporting Goods Division was recently presented with the opportunity to add an additional product line, which would require invested assets of $12,000,000. A projected income statement for the new product line is as follows:

New Product Line
Projected Income Statement
For the Year Ended December 31, 20—

Sales	$7,500,000
Cost of goods sold	4,200,000
Gross profit	$3,300,000
Operating expenses	2,100,000
Income from operations	$1,200,000

The Sporting Goods Division currently has $20,000,000 in invested assets, and Ontario Company's overall rate of return on investment, including all divisions, is 8%. Each division manager is evaluated on the basis of divisional rate of return on investment, and a bonus equal to $5,000 for each percentage point by which the division's rate of return on investment exceeds the company average is awarded each year.

Your father is concerned that the manager of the Sporting Goods Division rejected the addition of the new product line, when all estimates indicated that the product line would be profitable and would increase overall company income. You have been asked to analyze the possible reasons why the Sporting Goods Division manager rejected the new product line.

1. Determine the rate of return on investment for the Sporting Goods Division for the past year.
2. Determine the Sporting Goods Division manager's bonus for the past year.
3. Determine the estimated rate of return on investment for the new product line.
4. Why might the manager of the Sporting Goods Division decide to reject the new product line?
5. Can you suggest an alternative performance measure for motivating division managers to accept new investment opportunities that would increase the overall company income and rate of return on investment?

Activity 22–6 Into the Real World
The balanced scoreboard and EVA

GROUP ACTIVITY   Internet ACTIVITY

Divide responsibilities between two groups, with one group going to the home page of **Renaissance Solutions, Inc.**, at **www.rens.com**, and the second group going to the home page of **Stern Stewart & Co.** at **www.eva.com**. Renaissance Solutions, Inc., is a consulting firm that developed the concept of the "balanced scorecard," which is a method of measuring corporate and divisional performance. Stern Stewart & Co. is a consulting firm that developed the concept of "economic value added" (EVA), another method of measuring corporate and divisional performance.

In the Renaissance group, use links in the home page of Renaissance Solutions, Inc., to learn about the balanced scorecard. After reading about the balanced scorecard, prepare a brief report describing the balanced scorecard and its claimed advantages. In the Stern group, use links in the home page of Stern Stewart & Co. to learn about EVA. After reading about EVA, prepare a brief report describing EVA and its claimed advantages. After preparing these reports, both groups should discuss their research and prepare a brief analysis comparing and contrasting these two approaches to corporate and divisional performance measurement.

ANSWERS TO SELF-EXAMINATION QUESTIONS

Matching

1. N	4. Q	6. H	8. K	10. R	12. O	14. F	16. B
2. J	5. C	7. A	9. M	11. E	13. L	15. P	17. I
3. G							

Multiple Choice

1. **B** The manager of a profit center (answer B) has responsibility for and authority over costs and revenues. If the manager has responsibility for only costs, the department is called a cost center (answer A). If the responsibility and authority extend to the investment in assets as well as costs and revenues, it is called an investment center (answer C). A service department (answer D) provides services to other departments. A service department could be a cost center, profit center, or investment center.
2. **C** \$600,000/150,000 = \$4 per payment. Division A anticipates 60,000 payments or \$240,000 (60,000 × \$4) in service department charges from the Accounts Payable Department. Income from operations is thus \$900,000 − \$240,000, or \$660,000. Answer A assumes that all of the service department overhead is assigned to Division A, which would be incorrect, since Division A does not use all of the accounts payable service. Answer B incorrectly assumes that there are no service department charges from Accounts Payable. Answer D incorrectly determines the accounts payable transfer rate from Division A's income from operations.
3. **A** The rate of return on investment for Division A is 20% (answer A), computed as follows:

$$\text{Rate of return on investment (ROI)} = \frac{\text{Income from operations}}{\text{Invested assets}}$$

$$\text{ROI} = \frac{\$350{,}000 - \$200{,}000 - \$30{,}000}{\$600{,}000} = 20\%$$

4. **B** The profit margin for Division L of Liddy Co. is 15% (answer B), computed as follows:

$$\text{Rate of return on investment (ROI)} = \text{Profit margin} \times \text{Investment turnover}$$

$$24\% = \text{Profit margin} \times 1.6$$

$$15\% = \text{Profit margin}$$

5. **C** The market price approach (answer C) to transfer pricing uses the price at which the product or service transferred could be sold to outside buyers. The cost price approach (answer A) uses cost as the basis for setting transfer prices. The negotiated price approach (answer B) allows managers of decentralized units to agree (negotiate) among themselves as to the proper transfer price. The standard cost approach (answer D) is a version of the cost price approach that uses standard costs in setting transfer prices.

23

Differential Analysis and Product Pricing

Setting the STAGE

Most of you will buy an automobile at some time in the future. But rather than buying a car, would it be better to lease one?

To answer this question, you need to consider the costs of owning the car versus the costs of leasing the car. For example, if you own the car, you will need to pay the license fees, insurance, and maintenance and repair costs. How many of these costs you need to pay to lease the car depends on the lease contract. For example, the lease contract may require you to purchase a minimum amount of liability insurance. The lease contract will also require a monthly payment. In addition, if you drive the car more than a maximum number of miles (for example, 15,000 miles per year), you may be charged an additional cost per mile. Finally, whether you intend to keep the car or trade it in after three or four years may affect your decision.

The decision to buy or lease a car depends on comparing the estimated costs of each alternative. Likewise, managers must consider the effects of alternative decisions on their business.

In this chapter, we discuss differential analysis, which reports the effects of alternative decisions on total revenues and costs. We also describe and illustrate practical approaches to setting product prices. Finally, we discuss how production bottlenecks influence product mix and pricing decisions.

objectives

After studying this chapter, you should be able to:

1. Prepare a differential analysis report for decisions involving:
   - Leasing or selling equipment.
   - Discontinuing an unprofitable segment.
   - Manufacturing or purchasing a needed part.
   - Replacing usable fixed assets.
   - Processing further or selling an intermediate product.
   - Accepting additional business at a special price.
2. Determine the selling price of a product, using the total cost, product cost, and variable cost concepts.
3. Calculate the relative profitability of products in bottleneck production environments.

Differential Analysis

OBJECTIVE 1

Prepare a differential analysis report for decisions involving:

- Leasing or selling equipment.
- Discontinuing an unprofitable segment.
- Manufacturing or purchasing a needed part.
- Replacing usable fixed assets.
- Processing further or selling an intermediate product.
- Accepting additional business at a special price.

Planning for future operations involves decision making. For some decisions, revenue and cost data from the accounting records may be useful. However, the revenue and cost data for use in evaluating courses of future operations or choosing among competing alternatives are often not available in the accounting records and often must be estimated.

Consider:

- The decision by **Chrysler** to purchase oil filters from **Allied Signal Corp.** instead of making them internally.
- The decision by **Mercedes** to expand manufacturing operations into the United States (Alabama).
- The decision by **Sears** to sell its **Allstate Insurance** unit.

In each of these decisions, the estimated revenues and costs were **relevant**. The relevant revenues and costs focus on the differences between each alternative. Costs that have been incurred in the past are not relevant to the decision. These costs are called **sunk costs**.

Differential revenue is the amount of increase or decrease in revenue expected from a course of action as compared with an alternative. To illustrate, assume that certain equipment is being used to manufacture calculators, which are expected to generate revenue of $150,000. If the equipment could be used to make digital clocks, which would generate revenue of $175,000, the differential revenue from making and selling digital clocks is $25,000.

Differential cost is the amount of increase or decrease in cost that is expected from a course of action as compared with an alternative. For example, if an increase in advertising expenditures from $100,000 to $150,000 is being considered, the differential cost of the action is $50,000.

Differential income or loss is the difference between the differential revenue and the differential costs. Differential income indicates that a particular decision is expected to be profitable, while a differential loss indicates the opposite.

Decision	Differential Analysis
Alternative A	
	Differential revenue
or	− Differential costs
	Differential income or loss
Alternative B	

INTERMISSION

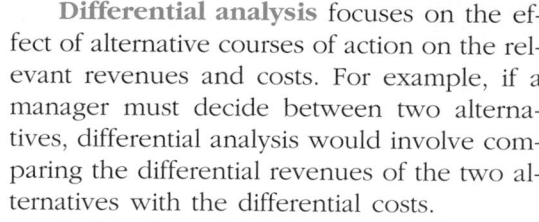

The following excerpt discusses using differential analysis in individual life decisions:

Cost-benefit analysis pays off in everyday living, a University of Michigan team concludes.

Richard Nisbett and two colleagues quizzed Michigan faculty members and university seniors on such questions as how often they walk out on a bad movie, refuse to finish a bad meal, start over on a weak term paper or abandon a research project that no longer looks promising. They believe that people who cut their losses this way are following sound economic rules: calculating the net benefits of alternative courses of action, writing off past costs that can't be recovered and weighing the opportunity to use future time and effort more profitably elsewhere.

They find that among faculty members, those who use cost-benefit reasoning in this fashion—being more likely to give up on research that isn't getting anywhere or using labor-saving devices as often as possible—have higher salaries relative to their age and departments. Not surprisingly, economists are more likely to apply the approach than professors of humanities or biology.

Among students, those who have learned to use cost-benefit analysis frequently are apt to have far better grades than their Scholastic Aptitude Test scores would have predicted. Again, the more economics courses the students have, the more likely they are to apply cost-benefit analysis outside the classroom.

Dr. Nisbett concedes that for many Americans, cost-benefit rules often appear to conflict with such traditional principles as "never give up" and "waste not, want not." ■

Source: Alan L. Otten, "Economic Perspective Produces Steady Yields" from People Patterns, *The Wall Street Journal,* March 31, 1992, p. B1.

Differential analysis focuses on the effect of alternative courses of action on the relevant revenues and costs. For example, if a manager must decide between two alternatives, differential analysis would involve comparing the differential revenues of the two alternatives with the differential costs.

In this chapter, we will discuss the use of differential analysis in analyzing the following alternatives:

1. Leasing or selling equipment.
2. Discontinuing an unprofitable segment.
3. Manufacturing or purchasing a needed part.
4. Replacing usable fixed assets.
5. Processing further or selling an intermediate product.
6. Accepting additional business at a special price.

Lease or Sell

Management may have a choice between leasing or selling a piece of equipment that is no longer needed in the business. In deciding which option is best, management may use differential analysis. To illustrate, assume that Marcus Company is considering disposing of equipment that cost $200,000 and has $120,000 of accumulated depreciation to date. Marcus Company can sell the equipment through a broker for $100,000 less a 6% commission. Alternatively, Potamkin Company (the lessee) has offered to lease the equipment for five years for a total of $160,000. At the end of the fifth year of the lease, the equipment is expected to have no residual value. During the period of the lease, Marcus Company (the lessor) will incur repair, insurance, and property tax expenses estimated at $35,000. Exhibit 1 shows Marcus Company's analysis of whether to lease or sell the equipment.

EXHIBIT 1 Differential Analysis Report—Lease or Sell

Proposal to Lease or Sell Equipment June 22, 2000		
Differential revenue from alternatives:		
Revenue from lease	$160,000	
Revenue from sales	100,000	
Differential revenue from lease		$60,000
Differential cost of alternatives:		
Repair, insurance, and property tax expenses	$ 35,000	
Commission expense on sale	6,000	
Differential cost of lease		29,000
Net differential income from the lease alternative		**$31,000**

Note that in Exhibit 1, the $80,000 book value ($200,000 − $120,000) of the equipment is a sunk cost and is not considered in the analysis. The $80,000 is a cost that resulted from a previous decision. It is not affected by the alternatives now being considered in leasing or selling the equipment. The relevant factors to be considered are the differential revenues and differential costs associated with the lease or sell decision. This analysis is verified by the traditional analysis in Exhibit 2.

EXHIBIT 2
Traditional Analysis

Lease or Sell			
Lease alternative:			
Revenue from lease		$160,000	
Depreciation expense for remaining five years	$80,000		
Repair, insurance, and property tax expenses	35,000	115,000	
Net gain			$45,000
Sell alternative:			
Sales price		$100,000	
Book value of equipment	$80,000		
Commission expense	6,000	86,000	
Net gain			14,000
Net differential income from the lease alternative			**$31,000**

The alternatives presented in Exhibits 1 and 2 were relatively simple. However, regardless of the complexity, the approach to differential analysis is basically the same. Two additional factors that often need to be considered are (1) differential revenue from investing the funds generated by the alternatives and (2) any income tax differential. In Exhibit 1, there could be differential interest revenue related to investing the cash flows from the two alternatives. Any income tax differential would be related to the differences in the timing of the income from the alternatives and the differences in the amount of investment income.

REAL WORLD

Many companies that manufacture expensive equipment give customers the choice of leasing the equipment. For example, construction equipment from **Caterpillar Inc.** can either be purchased outright or leased through Caterpillar's financial services subsidiary. **IBM** makes its large mainframe computers available by lease, as does **Xerox** with its copy machines.

Discontinue a Segment or Product

When a product or a department, branch, territory, or other segment of a business is generating losses, management may consider eliminating the product or segment.

It is often assumed, sometimes in error, that the total income from operations of a business would be increased if the operating loss could be eliminated. Discontinuing the product or segment usually eliminates all of the product or segment's variable costs (direct materials, direct labor, sales commissions, and so on). However, if the product or segment is a relatively small part of the business, the fixed costs (depreciation, insurance, property taxes, and so on) may not be decreased by discontinuing it. It is possible in this case for the total operating income of a company to decrease rather than increase by eliminating the product or segment. To illustrate, the income statement for Battle Creek Cereal Co. presented in Exhibit 3 is for a normal year ending August 31, 2000.

EXHIBIT 3
Income (Loss) by Product

Battle Creek Cereal Co.
Condensed Income Statement
For the Year Ended August 31, 2000

	Corn Flakes	Toasted Oats	Bran Flakes	Total
Sales	$500,000	$400,000	$100,000	$1,000,000
Cost of goods sold:				
Variable costs	$220,000	$200,000	$ 60,000	$ 480,000
Fixed costs	120,000	80,000	20,000	220,000
Total cost of goods sold	$340,000	$280,000	$ 80,000	$ 700,000
Gross profit	$160,000	$120,000	$ 20,000	$ 300,000
Operating expenses:				
Variable expenses	$ 95,000	$ 60,000	$ 25,000	$ 180,000
Fixed expenses	25,000	20,000	6,000	51,000
Total operating expenses	$120,000	$ 80,000	$ 31,000	$ 231,000
Income (loss) from operations	$ 40,000	$ 40,000	$(11,000)	$ 69,000

Because Bran Flakes incurs annual losses, management is considering discontinuing them. Total annual operating income of $80,000 ($40,000 Toasted Oats + $40,000 Corn Flakes) might seem to be indicated by the income statement in Exhibit 3 if Bran Flakes are discontinued.

Discontinuing Bran Flakes, however, would actually decrease operating income by $15,000, to $54,000 ($69,000 − $15,000). This is shown by the differential analysis report in Exhibit 4, in which we assume that discontinuing Bran Flakes would have no effect on fixed costs and expenses.

EXHIBIT 4 Differential Analysis Report—Discontinue an Unprofitable Segment

Proposal to Discontinue Bran Flakes
September 29, 2000

Differential revenue from annual sales of Bran Flakes:		
Revenue from sales		$100,000
Differential cost of annual sales of Bran Flakes:		
Variable cost of goods sold	$60,000	
Variable operating expenses	25,000	85,000
Annual differential income from sales of Bran Flakes		**$ 15,000**

Q&A *Product A has a loss from operations of $18,000 and fixed costs of $25,000. Product B has a loss from operations of $12,000 and fixed costs of $8,000. All remaining products have income from operations of $75,000 and fixed costs of $30,000. (1) Which product(s) should be discontinued, and (2) what would be the estimated income from operations if the action in (1) is taken?*

(1) Product B; (2) $79,000 ($75,000 + $4,000)

The traditional analysis in Exhibit 5 verifies the preceding differential analysis. In Exhibit 5, only the short-term (one year) effects of discontinuing Bran Flakes are considered. When eliminating a product or segment, management may also consider the long-term effects. For example, the plant capacity made available by discontinuing Bran Flakes might be eliminated. This could reduce fixed costs. Some employees may have to be laid off, and others may have to be relocated and retrained. Further, there may be a related decrease in sales of more profitable products to those customers who were attracted by the discontinued product.

REAL WORLD **Chrysler Corporation** discontinued selling the *Eagle* in 1998. One of Chrysler's executive vice-presidents stated, "*Eagle* sales have declined to a point at which the volume no longer justifies the expense of maintaining the brand."

EXHIBIT 5 Traditional Analysis

Proposal to Discontinue Bran Flakes
September 29, 2000

	Bran Flakes, Toasted Oats, and Corn Flakes	Discontinue Bran Flakes*	Toasted Oats and Corn Flakes
Sales	$1,000,000	$100,000	$900,000
Cost of goods sold:			
Variable costs	$ 480,000	$ 60,000	$420,000
Fixed costs	220,000	—	220,000
Total cost of goods sold	$ 700,000	$ 60,000	$640,000
Gross profit	$ 300,000	$ 40,000	$260,000
Operating expenses:			
Variable expenses	$ 180,000	$ 25,000	$155,000
Fixed expenses	51,000	—	51,000
Total operating expenses	$ 231,000	$ 25,000	$206,000
Income (loss) from operations	**$ 69,000**	**$ 15,000**	**$ 54,000**

*Fixed costs do not decline with the discontinuance of Bran Flakes.

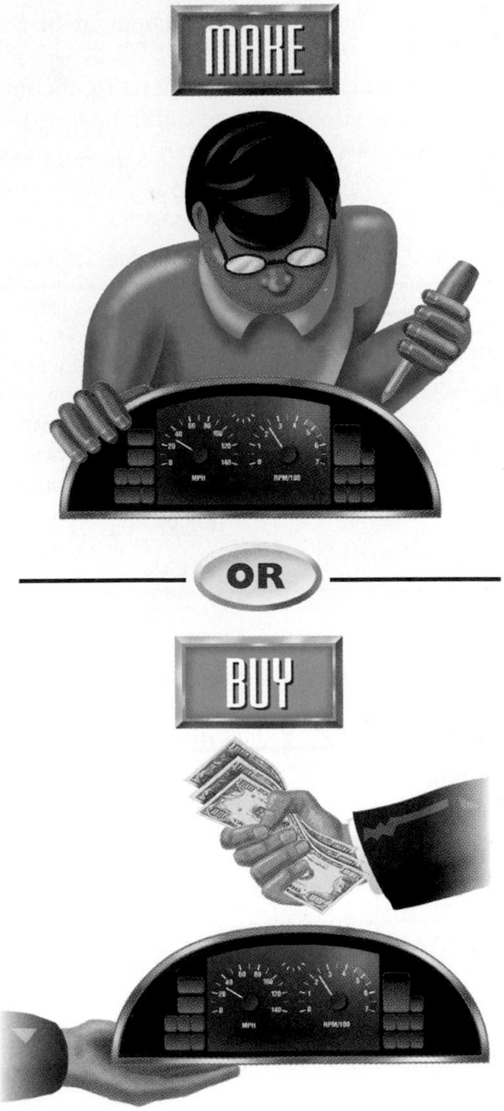

Make or Buy

The assembly of many parts is often a major element in manufacturing some products, such as automobiles. These parts may be made by the product's manufacturer, or they may be purchased. For example, some of the parts for an automobile, such as the motor, may be produced by the automobile manufacturer. Other parts, such as tires, may be purchased from other manufacturers. In addition, in manufacturing motors, such items as spark plugs and nuts and bolts may be acquired from suppliers.

Management uses differential costs to decide whether to make or buy a part. For example, if a part is purchased, management has concluded that it is less costly to buy the part than to manufacture it. Make or buy options often arise when a manufacturer has excess productive capacity in the form of unused equipment, space, and labor.

Nike, Inc., does not make shoes, but buys 100% of its shoe manufacturing from outside suppliers. Nike, Inc., believes that its strengths are in designing, marketing, distributing, and selling athletic shoes. Thus, Nike focuses on the parts of the business where it believes that it adds the greatest value to the customer, and thus the greatest profitability to the company.

The differential analysis is similar, whether management is considering making a part that is currently being purchased or purchasing a part that is currently being made. To illustrate, assume that an automobile manufacturer has been purchasing instrument panels, for $60 a unit. The factory is currently operating at 80% of capacity, and no major increase in production is expected in the near future. The cost per unit of manufacturing an instrument panel, including fixed costs, is estimated as follows:

Direct materials	$20
Direct labor	20
Factory overhead (150% of direct labor cost)	30
Total cost per unit	$70

Part K can be purchased for $30 per unit. Part K can be manufactured internally using $7.50 of direct materials and 0.75 hours of direct labor at $12 per direct labor hour (dlh). Factory overhead is applied at a rate of $20 per direct labor hour. ($7 per dlh is fixed.) What is the cost savings or penalty from manufacturing the part internally?

$3.75 cost savings {$30 − [$7.50 + (0.75 × $12) + (0.75 × $13)]}

If the *make* price of $70 is simply compared with the *buy* price of $60, the decision is to buy the instrument panel. However, if unused capacity could be used in manufacturing the part, there would be no increase in the total amount of fixed factory overhead costs. Thus, only the variable factory overhead costs need to be considered. Assume that variable factory overhead costs, such as power and maintenance, are estimated at $13 per unit. The relevant costs are summarized in the differential report in Exhibit 6.

EXHIBIT 6 Differential Analysis Report—Make or Buy

Proposal to Manufacture Instrument Panels
February 15, 2000

Purchase price of an instrument panel		$60.00
Differential cost to manufacture:		
Direct materials	$20.00	
Direct labor	20.00	
Variable factory overhead	13.00	53.00
Cost savings from manufacturing an instrument panel		**$ 7.00**

Other possible effects of a decision to manufacture the instrument panel should also be considered. For example, increasing production in the future might require using the currently idle capacity. This decision may affect employees. It may also affect future business relations with the instrument panel supplier, who may provide other essential parts. The company's decision to manufacture instrument panels might jeopardize the timely delivery of these other parts.

REAL WORLD

Some companies develop unique skills and capabilities, called *core competencies*. For example, **Honda Motor's** core competency is designing and producing small engines; **3M's** core competency is developing and producing adhesives; and **Canon's** core competencies are a combination of precision mechanics and optics. Core competencies are strategic capabilities that should be developed internally—not handed over to a supplier to be purchased externally.

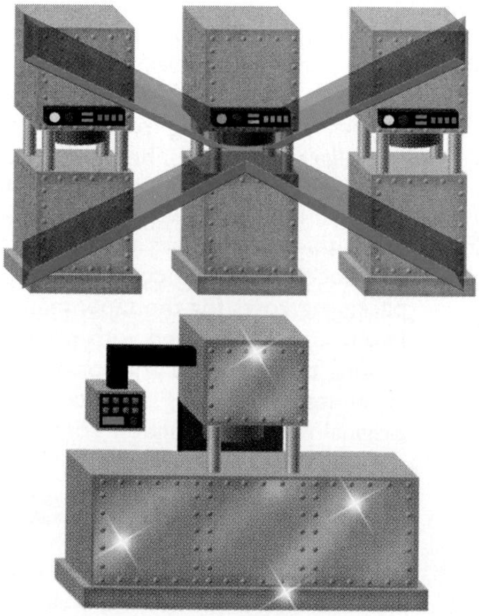

Replace Equipment

The usefulness of fixed assets may be reduced long before they are considered to be worn out. For example, equipment may no longer be efficient for the purpose for which it is used. On the other hand, the equipment may not have reached the point of complete inadequacy. Decisions to replace usable fixed assets should be based on relevant costs. The relevant costs are the future costs of continuing to use the equipment versus replacement. The book values of the fixed assets being replaced are sunk costs and are irrelevant.

To illustrate, assume that a business is considering disposing of several identical machines having a total book value of $100,000 and an estimated remaining life of five years. The old machines can be sold for $25,000. They can be replaced by a single high-speed machine at a cost of $250,000. The new machine has an estimated useful life of five years and no residual value. Analyses indicate an estimated annual reduction in variable manufacturing costs from $225,000 with the old machine to

$150,000 with the new machine. No other changes in the manufacturing costs or the operating expenses are expected. The relevant costs are summarized in the differential report in Exhibit 7.

EXHIBIT 7
Differential Analysis Report—Replace Equipment

Proposal to Replace Equipment November 28, 2000		
Annual variable costs—present equipment	$225,000	
Annual variable costs—new equipment	150,000	
Annual differential decrease in cost	$ 75,000	
Number of years applicable	× 5	
Total differential decrease in cost	$375,000	
Proceeds from sale of present equipment	25,000	$400,000
Cost of new equipment		250,000
Net differential decrease in cost, 5-year total		$150,000
Annual net differential decrease in cost—new equipment		**$ 30,000**

Other factors are often important in equipment replacement decisions. For example, differences between the remaining useful life of the old equipment and the estimated life of the new equipment could exist. In addition, the new equipment might improve the overall quality of the product, resulting in an increase in sales volume. Additional factors could include the time value of money and other uses for the cash needed to purchase the new equipment.[1]

The amount of income that is forgone from an alternative use of cash is called **opportunity cost**. Although the opportunity cost does not appear as a part of historical accounting data, it is useful in analyzing alternative courses of action. To illustrate, assume that the cash outlay of $250,000 for the new equipment, less the $25,000 proceeds from the sale of the present equipment, could be invested to yield a 10% return. Thus, the annual opportunity cost related to the purchase of the new equipment is $22,500 (10% × $225,000).

Process or Sell

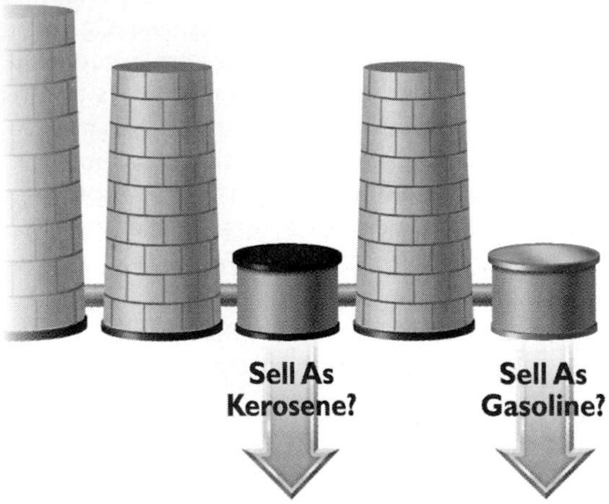

When a product is manufactured, it progresses through various stages of production. Often a product can be sold at an intermediate stage of production, or it can be processed further and then sold. In deciding whether to sell a product at an intermediate stage or to process it further, differential analysis is useful. The differential revenues from further processing are compared to the differential costs of further processing. The costs of producing the intermediate product do not change, regardless of whether the intermediate product is sold or processed further. Thus, these costs are not differential costs and are irrelevant to the decision to process further.

REAL WORLD

Film studios "process" movies and release them in VHS format for the home VCR market. Items that are relevant to making this decision are the copying and packaging costs for the tape, marketing costs associated with promoting the tape, and anticipated revenues from selling the tape. The original movie production costs are not relevant to the decision.

To illustrate, assume that a business produces kerosene in batches of 4,000 gallons.

[1] The importance of the time value of money in equipment replacement decisions is discussed in a later chapter.

Standard quantities of 4,000 gallons of direct materials are processed, which cost $0.60 per gallon. Kerosene can be sold without further processing for $0.80 per gallon. It can be processed further to yield gasoline, which can be sold for $1.25 per gallon. Gasoline requires additional processing costs of $650 per batch, and 20% of the gallons of kerosene will evaporate during production. Exhibit 8 summarizes the differential revenues and costs in deciding whether to process kerosene to produce gasoline.

Q&A

Product T is produced for $2.50 per gallon ($1.00 fixed cost) and can be sold without additional processing for $3.50 per gallon. Product T can be processed further into Product V at a cost of $1.60 per gallon ($0.90 fixed). Product V can be sold for $4.00 per gallon. What is the differential income or loss per gallon from processing Product T into Product V?

$0.20 loss [$4.00 − $3.50 − $1.60 + $0.90]

EXHIBIT 8 Differential Analysis Report—Process or Sell

Proposal to Process Kerosene Further
October 1, 2000

Differential revenue from further processing per batch:		
Revenue from sale of gasoline [(4,000 gallons − 800 gallons evaporation) × $1.25]	$4,000	
Revenue from sale of kerosene (4,000 gallons × $0.80)	3,200	
Differential revenue		$800
Differential cost per batch:		
Additional cost of producing gasoline		650
Differential income from further processing gasoline per batch		**$150**

The differential income from further processing kerosene into gasoline is $150 per batch. The initial cost of producing the intermediate kerosene, $2,400 (4,000 gallons × $0.60), is not considered in deciding whether to process kerosene further. This initial cost will be incurred, regardless of whether gasoline is produced.

REAL WORLD

The **Coca-Cola Company** manufactures concentrate for its carbonated and noncarbonated beverages. The concentrate is shipped to bottling plants, where it is mixed with water to create the consumer beverage. Why does Coca-Cola manufacture through these two stages? Ralph Cooper, chairman of Coca-Cola Foods, states that this policy was "highly economic" because shipping concentrate to local bottlers meant that water was not being transported at high cost. Apparently, bottling the final product close to the consumer's point of use saves the company from spending large differential transportation costs that would be associated with a centralized single-stage process.

Accept Business at a Special Price

Differential analysis is also useful in deciding whether to accept additional business at a special price. The differential revenue that would be provided from the additional business is compared to the differential costs of producing and delivering the product to the customer. If the company is operating at full capacity, any additional production will increase both fixed and variable production costs. If, however, the normal production of the company is below full capacity, additional business may be undertaken without increasing fixed production costs. In this case, the differential costs of the additional production are the variable manufacturing costs. If operating expenses increase because of the additional business, these expenses should also be considered.

REAL WORLD

The airline industry has offered special discount summer fares when it was difficult to fill seats at the regular price. In the short term, filling seats with discount fare customers added differential income. However, airline passengers begin to expect the special discount pricing. As a result, airlines sometimes have to continue offering special discounts throughout the year. Thus, the special discount periods can become a normal part of operations and a revenue drain for the industry.

To illustrate, assume that the monthly capacity of a sporting goods business is 12,500 basketballs. Current sales and production are averaging 10,000 basketballs

per month. The current manufacturing cost of $20 per unit consists of variable costs of $12.50 and fixed costs of $7.50. The normal selling price of the product in the domestic market is $30. The manufacturer receives from an exporter an offer for 5,000 basketballs at $18 each. Production can be spread over a three-month period without interfering with normal production or incurring overtime costs. Pricing policies in the domestic market will not be affected. Simply comparing the sales price of $18 with the present unit manufacturing cost of $20 indicates that the offer should be rejected. However, by focusing only on the differential cost, which in this case is the variable cost, the decision is different. Exhibit 9 shows the differential analysis report for this decision.

Q&A

Product D is normally sold for $4.40 per unit. A special price of $3.60 is offered for the export market. The variable production cost is $3.00 per unit. An additional export tariff of 10% of revenue will be required for all export products. What is the differential income or loss per unit from selling Product D for export?

$0.24 income [$3.60 − $3.00 − (0.10 × $3.60)]

EXHIBIT 9 Differential Analysis Report—Sell at Special Price

Proposal to Sell Basketballs to Exporter
March 10, 2000

Differential revenue from accepting offer:	
Revenue from sale of 5,000 additional units at $18	$90,000
Differential cost of accepting offer:	
Variable costs of 5,000 additional units at $12.50	62,500
Differential income from accepting offer	**$27,500**

Proposals to sell a product in the domestic market at prices lower than the normal price may require additional considerations. For example, it may be unwise to increase sales volume in one territory by price reductions if sales volume is lost in other areas. Manufacturers must also conform to the Robinson-Patman Act, which prohibits price discrimination within the United States unless differences in prices can be justified by different costs of serving different customers.

Setting Normal Product Selling Prices

OBJECTIVE 2

Determine the selling price of a product, using the total cost, product cost, and variable cost concepts.

Differential analysis may be useful in deciding to lower selling prices for special short-run decisions, such as whether to accept business at a price lower than the normal price. In such cases, the minimum short-run price is set high enough to cover all variable costs. Any price above this minimum price will improve profits in the short run. In the long run, however, the normal selling price must be set high enough to cover all costs and expenses (both fixed and variable) and provide a reasonable profit. Otherwise, the business may not survive.

The normal selling price can be viewed as the target selling price to be achieved in the long run. The basic approaches to setting this price are as follows:

Market Methods	Cost-Plus Methods
1. Demand-based methods	1. Total cost concept
2. Competition-based methods	2. Product cost concept
	3. Variable cost concept

Managers using the market methods refer to the external market to determine the price. Demand-based methods set the price according to the demand for the product. If there is high demand for the product, then the price may be set high, while lower demand may require the price to be set low. An example of setting different prices according to the demand for the product is found in the telecommunications industry, with low weekend rates and high business day rates for long-distance telephone calls.

Competition-based methods set the price according to the price offered by competitors. For example, if a competitor reduces the price, then management may be required to adjust the price to meet the competition. The market-based pricing approaches are discussed in greater detail in marketing courses, so we will not expand upon them here.

Managers using the cost-plus methods price the product in order to achieve a target profit. Managers add to the cost an amount called a **markup**, so that all costs plus a profit are included in the selling price. In the following paragraphs, we describe and illustrate the three cost concepts often used in applying the cost-plus approach: (1) total cost, (2) product cost, and (3) variable cost.

REAL WORLD

McDonald's Corporation evaluated the *Extra Value Meals* concept and determined that combination meals priced at a discount would create additional revenue from customer "trade-ups" from a la carte purchases. The concept was so successful that it has become an industry standard.

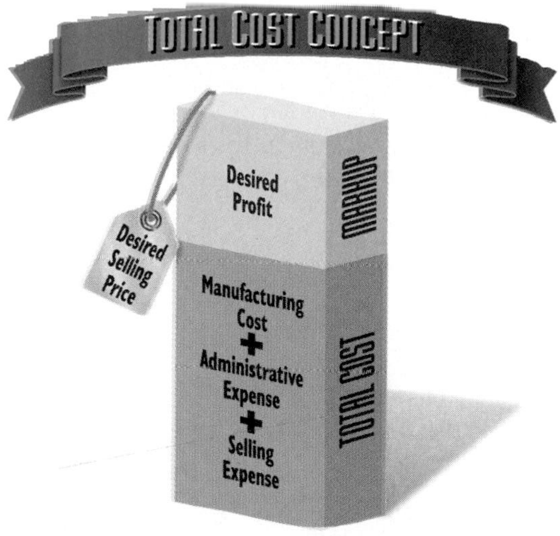

Total Cost Concept

Using the **total cost concept**, all costs of manufacturing a product plus the selling and administrative expenses are included in the cost amount to which the markup is added. Since all costs and expenses are included in the cost amount, the dollar amount of the markup equals the desired profit.

The first step in applying the total cost concept is to determine the total cost of manufacturing the product. This cost includes the costs of direct materials, direct labor, and factory overhead and should be available from the accounting records. The next step is to add the estimated selling and administrative expenses to the total cost of manufacturing the product. The cost amount per unit is then computed by dividing the total costs by the total units expected to be produced and sold.

After the cost amount per unit has been determined, the dollar amount of the markup is determined. For this purpose, the markup is expressed as a percentage of cost. This percentage is then multiplied by the cost amount per unit. The dollar amount of the markup is then added to the cost amount per unit to arrive at the selling price.

The markup percentage for the total cost concept is determined by applying the following formula:

$$\textbf{Markup percentage} = \frac{\textbf{Desired profit}}{\textbf{Total costs}}$$

The numerator of the formula is only the desired profit. This is because all costs and expenses are included in the cost amount to which the markup is added. The denominator of the formula is the total costs.

To illustrate, assume that the costs for calculators of Digital Solutions Inc. are as follows:

Variable costs:	
Direct materials	$ 3.00 per unit
Direct labor	10.00
Factory overhead	1.50
Selling and administrative expenses	1.50
Total	$ 16.00 per unit
Fixed costs:	
Factory overhead	$50,000
Selling and administrative expenses	20,000

REAL WORLD

The microcomputer industry is developing products that can be sold to consumers for under $1,000. By using the total cost concept, the following price can be determined:

Motherboard	$140
Memory	50
Processor	90
Disk drive	198
Peripherals	265
Factory overhead and assembly	48
Product cost	$791
Administrative expenses	26
Total cost	$817
Manufacturer markup	91
Manufacturer's price to retailer	$908
Retailer markup	91
Retail price to final consumer	$999

Notice that there are two markups included in the final price—one for the manufacturer and one for the retailer.

Digital Solutions Inc. desires a profit equal to a 20% rate of return on assets, $800,000 of assets are devoted to producing calculators, and 100,000 units are expected to be produced and sold. The calculators' total cost is $1,670,000, or $16.70 per unit, computed as follows:

Variable costs ($16.00 × 100,000 units)		$1,600,000
Fixed costs:		
Factory overhead	$50,000	
Selling and administrative expenses	20,000	70,000
Total costs		$1,670,000
Total cost per calculator ($1,670,000 ÷ 100,000 units)		$16.70

The desired profit is $160,000 (20% × $800,000), and the markup percentage for a calculator is 9.6%, computed as follows:

$$\textbf{Markup percentage} = \frac{\textbf{Desired profit}}{\textbf{Total costs}}$$

$$\text{Markup percentage} = \frac{\$160,000}{\$1,670,000} = 9.6\%$$

Based on the total cost per unit and the markup percentage for a calculator, Digital Solutions Inc. would price each calculator at $18.30 per unit, as shown below.

Total cost per calculator	$16.70
Markup ($16.70 × 9.6%)	1.60
Selling price	$18.30

The ability of the selling price of $18.30 to generate the desired profit of $160,000 is shown by the following income statement:

Digital Solutions Inc.
Income Statement
For the Year Ended December 31, 2000

Sales (100,000 units × $18.30)		$1,830,000
Expenses:		
Variable (100,000 units × $16.00)	$1,600,000	
Fixed ($50,000 + $20,000)	70,000	1,670,000
Income from operations		$ 160,000

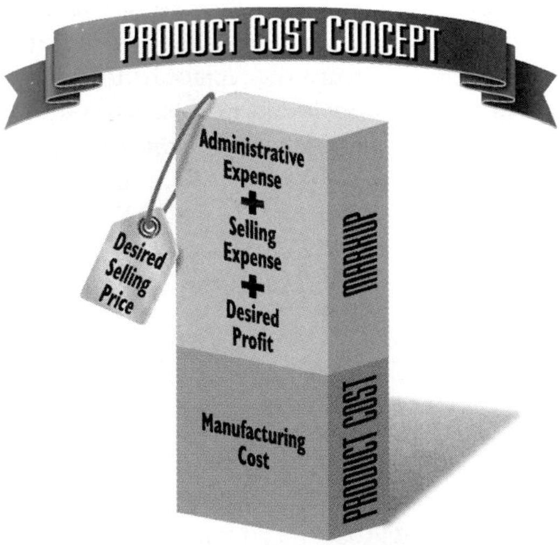

The total cost concept of applying the cost-plus approach to product pricing is often used by contractors who sell products to government agencies. In many cases, government contractors are required by law to be reimbursed for their products on a total-cost-plus-profit basis.

Product Cost Concept

Using the **product cost concept**, only the costs of manufacturing the product, termed the product cost, are included in the cost amount to which the markup is added. Estimated selling expenses, administrative expenses, and profit are included in the markup. The markup percentage is determined by applying the following formula:

$$\text{Markup percentage} = \frac{\textbf{Desired profit + Total selling and administrative expenses}}{\textbf{Total manufacturing costs}}$$

The numerator of the markup percentage formula is the desired profit plus the total selling and administrative expenses. These expenses must be included in the markup, since they are not included in the cost amount to which the markup is added. The denominator of the formula includes the costs of direct materials, direct labor, and factory overhead.

To illustrate, assume the same data used in the preceding illustration. The manufacturing cost for Digital Solutions Inc.'s calculator is $1,500,000, or $15 per unit, computed as follows:

Direct materials ($3 × 100,000 units)		$ 300,000
Direct labor ($10 × 100,000 units)		1,000,000
Factory overhead:		
Variable ($1.50 × 100,000 units)	$150,000	
Fixed	50,000	200,000
Total manufacturing costs		$1,500,000
Manufacturing cost per calculator ($1,500,000 ÷ 100,000 units)		$15

Federal Express Corporation decided to abandon its flat price strategy in favor of setting the price based on the distance a parcel travels. As a result, prices decreased on many short-distance parcels, while prices increased on long-distance shipments. This decision was made because FedEx could no longer ignore the different costs associated with shipping short and long distances.

The desired profit is $160,000 (20% × $800,000), and the total selling and administrative expenses are $170,000 [(100,000 units × $1.50 per unit) + $20,000]. The markup percentage for a calculator is 22%, computed as follows:

$$\text{Markup percentage} = \frac{\textbf{Desired profit + Total selling and administrative expenses}}{\textbf{Total manufacturing costs}}$$

$$\text{Markup percentage} = \frac{\$160{,}000 + \$170{,}000}{\$1{,}500{,}000}$$

$$\text{Markup percentage} = \frac{\$330{,}000}{\$1{,}500{,}000} = 22\%$$

Based on the manufacturing cost per calculator and the markup percentage, Digital Solutions Inc. would price each calculator at $18.30 per unit, as shown below.

Manufacturing cost per calculator	$15.00
Markup ($15 × 22%)	3.30
Selling price	$18.30

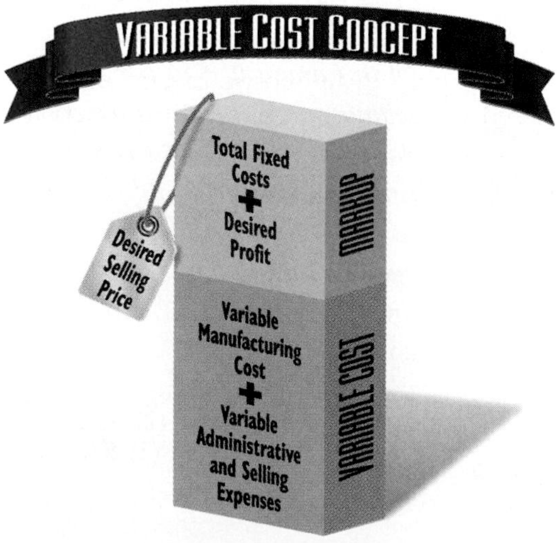

Variable Cost Concept

The **variable cost concept** emphasizes the distinction between variable and fixed costs in product pricing. Using the variable cost concept, only variable costs are included in the cost amount to which the markup is added. All variable manufacturing costs, as well as variable selling and administrative expenses, are included in the cost amount. Fixed manufacturing costs, fixed selling and administrative expenses, and profit are included in the markup.

The markup percentage is determined by applying the following formula:

$$\textbf{Markup percentage} = \frac{\textbf{Desired profit + Total fixed costs}}{\textbf{Total variable costs}}$$

The numerator of the markup percentage formula is the desired profit plus the total fixed manufacturing costs and the total fixed selling and administrative expenses. These costs and expenses must be included in the markup, since they are not included in the cost amount to which the markup is added. The denominator of the formula includes the total variable costs.

To illustrate, assume the same data used in the two preceding illustrations. The calculator variable cost is \$1,600,000, or \$16.00 per unit, computed as follows:

Variable costs:	
Direct materials (\$3 × 100,000 units)	\$ 300,000
Direct labor (\$10 × 100,000 units)	1,000,000
Factory overhead (\$1.50 × 100,000 units)	150,000
Selling and administrative expenses (\$1.50 × 100,000 units)	150,000
Total variable costs	\$1,600,000
Variable cost per calculator (\$1,600,000 ÷ 100,000 units)	\$16.00

The desired profit is \$160,000 (20% × \$800,000), the total fixed manufacturing costs are \$50,000, and the total fixed selling and administrative expenses are \$20,000. The markup percentage for a calculator is 14.4%, computed as follows:

$$\textbf{Markup percentage} = \frac{\textbf{Desired profit + Total fixed costs}}{\textbf{Total variable costs}}$$

$$\text{Markup percentage} = \frac{\$160{,}000 + \$50{,}000 + \$20{,}000}{\$1{,}600{,}000}$$

$$\text{Markup percentage} = \frac{\$230{,}000}{\$1{,}600{,}000} = 14.4\%$$

Based on the variable cost per calculator and the markup percentage, Digital Solutions Inc. would price each calculator at \$18.30 per unit, as shown below.

Variable cost per calculator	\$16.00
Markup (\$16.00 × 14.4%)	2.30
Selling price	\$18.30

Choosing a Cost-Plus Approach Cost Concept

All three cost concepts produced the same selling price (\$18.30) for Digital Solutions Inc. In practice, however, the three cost concepts are usually not viewed as alternatives. Each cost concept requires different estimates of costs and expenses. This difficulty and the complexity of the manufacturing operations should be considered in choosing a cost concept.

To reduce the costs of gathering data, estimated (standard) costs rather than actual costs may be used with any of the three cost concepts. However, management should exercise caution when using estimated costs in applying the cost-plus approach. The estimates should be based on normal (attainable) operating levels and not theoretical (ideal) levels of performance. In product pricing, the use of estimates based on ideal- or maximum-capacity operating levels might lead to setting product prices too low. In this case, the costs of such factors as normal spoilage or normal periods of idle time might not be considered.

The decision-making needs of management are also an important factor in selecting a cost concept for product pricing. For example, managers who often make special pricing decisions

Q&A

Product Z has a total cost of \$30 per unit. Of this amount, \$10 per unit is selling and administrative costs. The total variable cost is \$18 per unit. The desired profit is \$3 per unit. Determine the markup percentage on (1) total cost, (2) product cost, and (3) variable cost.

(1) 10% (\$3 ÷ \$30); (2) 65% [(\$10 + \$3) ÷ \$20]; (3) 83.3% [(\$12 + \$3) ÷ \$18]

are more likely to use the variable cost concept. In contrast, a government defense contractor would be more likely to use the total cost concept.

BUSINESS ON STAGE

Alternative Pricing Approaches

At various times, a business may use alternative pricing approaches, often as a supplement to the traditional cost-plus pricing of products. Some of these alternative approaches are described below.

- **Price skimming** is normally short-term in nature and is used when a business has a new product that is unique in the marketplace. Because of the lack of competing products, the business sets the price at an artificially high level. It anticipates that it will have to lower the price once competitors enter the market. In the meantime, however, it will be able to earn high profits that can be used to cover the costs of developing the product. For example, **Hewlett-Packard (HP)** initially set the price of its laser printer for personal computers at around $4,000. Eventually, as competitors entered the market, HP lowered the price. Today, an HP laser printer can be purchased for less than $1,000.
- **Psychological pricing** is based on two behavioral tendencies of customers. First, customers often assume that the higher the price of a product, the higher the quality. Thus, for a special occasion, a novice wine buyer might be more inclined to purchase a higher-priced bottle of wine than a lower-priced bottle. Second, consumers are more likely to purchase a product priced just below the next whole number. For example, retailers often price products at $899 or $895, rather than $900. This type of pricing, called *odd-even pricing,* is used to imply bargains, even though the price difference between the odd and even number is insignificant.
- **Bundle pricing** involves grouping two related products together and pricing them as a single product. For example, appliance retailers often bundle a clothes washer and dryer together at a price that is less than the sum of the price of the washer and dryer separately. Other examples of bundle pricing include "value meals" in fast food restaurants and software bundled with PCs. Bundling products at a slightly reduced total price is intended to generate additional sales that otherwise might not have been made. ■

REAL WORLD

The following survey results show the pricing strategies used by manufacturers and service companies. As you can see, cost-plus approaches to pricing dominate practice, and the product (or total) cost approach dominates the cost-plus approaches. In addition, there is little difference between manufacturing and service companies in their pricing approaches.

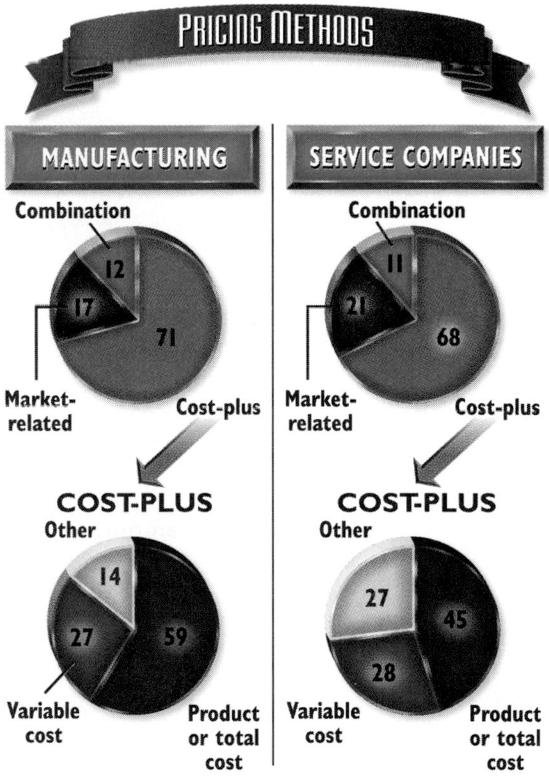

Source: R. W. Mills, and C. Sweeting, *Pricing Decisions in Practice,* London: CIMA, 1988.

A variation of the cost concepts discussed in the preceding paragraphs is the **target cost concept**. Under this concept, which was first used by the Japanese, the selling price is assumed to be set by the marketplace. The target cost is determined by *subtracting* a desired profit from the selling price. Thus, managers must design and manufacture the product to achieve its target cost. In contrast, the three cost concepts discussed previously start with a given product cost and *add* a markup to determine the selling price. Some argue that the target cost concept may be better than the cost-plus approaches in highly competitive markets that require continual product cost reductions to remain competitive.

Activity-Based Costing

As illustrated in the preceding paragraphs, costs are an important consideration in setting product prices. To more accurately measure the costs of producing and selling products, some companies use activity-based costing. **Activity-based costing** (ABC) identifies and traces activities to specific products.

Activity-based costing may be useful in making product pricing decisions where manufacturing operations involve large amounts of factory overhead. In such cases, traditional overhead allocation using activity bases such as units produced or machine hours may yield inaccurate cost allocations. This, in turn, may result in distorted product costs and product prices. By providing more accurate product cost allocations, activity-based costing aids in setting product prices that will cover costs and expenses.[2]

REAL WORLD **Guardian Industries** uses both target costing and activity-based costing to determine actual and expected costs for its auto glass products.

OBJECTIVE 3

Calculate the relative profitability of products in bottleneck production environments.

Product Profitability and Pricing Under Production Bottlenecks

An important consideration influencing production volumes and prices is production bottlenecks. A **production bottleneck** (or **constraint**) occurs at the point in the process where the demand for the company's product exceeds the ability to produce the product. The **theory of constraints** (TOC) is a manufacturing strategy that focuses on reducing the influence of bottlenecks on a process.

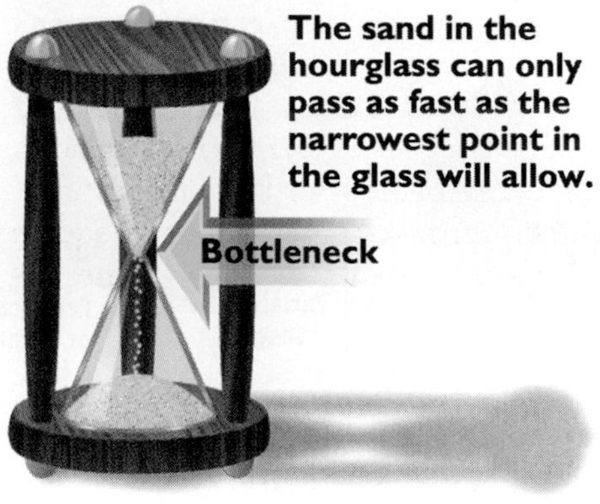

The sand in the hourglass can only pass as fast as the narrowest point in the glass will allow.

Product Profitability Under Production Bottlenecks

When a company has a bottleneck in its production process, it should attempt to maximize its profitability, subject to the influence of the bottleneck. To illustrate, assume that Snapp-Off Tool Company makes three types of wrenches: small, medium, and large. All three products are processed through a heat treatment operation, which hardens the steel tools. Snapp-Off Tool's heat treatment process is operating at full capacity and is a production bottleneck. The product contribution margin per unit and the number of hours of heat treatment used by each type of wrench are as follows:

	Small Wrench	Medium Wrench	Large Wrench
Sales price per unit	$130	$140	$160
Variable cost per unit	40	40	40
Contribution margin per unit	$ 90	$100	$120
Heat treatment hours per unit	1	4	8

The large wrench appears to be the most profitable product because its contribution margin per unit is the greatest. However, the contribution margin per unit can be a misleading indicator of profitability in a bottleneck operation. The correct measure of performance is the value of each bottleneck hour, or the contribution

[2] Activity-based costing is further discussed and illustrated in the appendix at the end of this chapter.

Q&A *Product A has a contribution margin of $15 per unit. Product B has a contribution margin of $20 per unit. Product A requires 3 furnace hours, while Product B requires 5 furnace hours. Determine the most profitable product, assuming that the furnace is a bottleneck.*

Product A ($15 ÷ 3 hours = $5 per hour, which is greater than $20 ÷ 5 hours, or $4 per hour)

margin per bottleneck hour. Using this measure, each product has a much different profitability than compared to the contribution margin per unit information, as shown in Exhibit 10.

EXHIBIT 10 Contribution Margin per Bottleneck Hour

	Small Wrench	Medium Wrench	Large Wrench
Sales price	$130	$140	$160
Variable cost per unit	40	40	40
Contribution margin per unit	$ 90	$100	$120
Bottleneck (heat treatment) hours per unit	÷ 1	÷ 4	÷ 8
Contribution margin per bottleneck hour	$ 90	$ 25	$ 15

The small wrench produces the most contribution margin per bottleneck (heat treatment) hour used, while the large wrench produces the smallest profit per bottleneck hour. Thus, the small wrench is the most profitable product. This information is the opposite of that implied by the unit contribution margin profit.

REAL WORLD Latrobe Steel Division of **Timken Company** originally used total cost plus a markup to price its steel products. However, Latrobe discovered that one of its machines was a bottleneck in its operation. It recalculated the profitability of its products, based on the contribution margin per hour of constraint. The results showed that some products that had appeared only marginally profitable had, in fact, a high contribution margin per bottleneck hour. This analysis caused Latrobe management to change the product mix in favor of products with high contribution margins per constraint hour. Management estimated that these changes improved income from operations by 20%.

Product Pricing Under Production Bottlenecks

Each hour of a bottleneck delivers profit to the company. When a company has a production bottleneck, the contribution margin per hour of bottleneck provides a measure of the product's relative profitability. This information can also be used to adjust the product price to better reflect the value of the product's use of a bottleneck. Products that use a large number of bottleneck hours per unit require more contribution margin than products that use few bottleneck hours per unit. For example, Snapp-Off Tool Company should increase the price of the large wrench in order to deliver more contribution margin per bottleneck hour.

To determine the price of the large wrench that would equate its profitability to the small wrench, we need to solve the following equation:

$$\textbf{Contribution margin per bottleneck hour per small wrench} = \frac{\textbf{Revised price of large wrench} - \textbf{Variable cost per large wrench}}{\textbf{Bottleneck hours per large wrench}}$$

$$\$90 = \frac{\text{Revised price of large wrench} - \$40}{8}$$

$$\$720 = \text{Revised price of large wrench} - \$40$$
$$\$760 = \text{Revised price of large wrench}$$

The large wrench's price would need to be increased to $760 in order to deliver the same contribution margin per bottleneck hour as does the small wrench, as verified below.

Revised price of large wrench	$760
Less: Variable cost per unit of large wrench	40
Contribution margin per unit of large wrench	$720
Bottleneck hours per unit of large wrench	÷ 8
Revised contribution margin per bottleneck hour	$ 90

At a price of $760, the company would be indifferent between producing and selling the small wrench or the large wrench, all else being equal. This analysis assumes that there is unlimited demand for the products. If the market were unwilling to purchase the large wrench at this price, then the company should produce the small wrench.

ENCORE

A "Fat Handle" Yields Fat Profits for Nypro

The male executives of **Gillette Company** thought that women's shaving needs were the same as men's. All you had to do was take a disposable razor and give it a pink handle, and you had a product for the women's market! Then along came Gillette's only female designer, Jill Shurleff, who asked a simple question—how do women shave? The answer: not at all like men. Women shave over 412 square inches of the surface area (compared to 48 square inches for men), but only a couple of times each week (compared to daily for men). They change blades about 10 times per year (compared to 30 times per year for men). Women shave in the shower, a poorly lit and slippery environment, while men shave in front of a lighted mirror. Women shave areas that are difficult to reach and see, such as the back of the legs. Men, on the other hand, require fine motor control to shave across the multiple angles of the face and, therefore, need a long narrow handle. All of these insights led Shurleff to invent *Sensor for Women. Sensor for Women* is unlike any other shaving system in that it has a broad flat handle, especially designed for women. The stout handle provides women the control they need to maintain a constant shaving angle and avoid nicks and cuts. After two weeks of use, women in the initial Chicago focus group begged to keep the product.

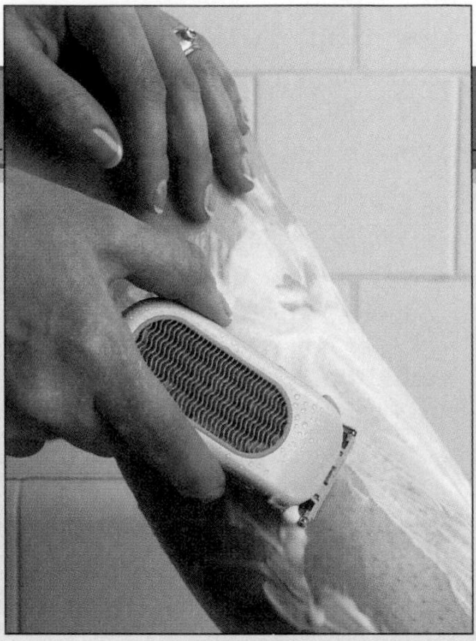

When the all-male executive team first saw the new design, they were skeptical. After all, prior to the early 1990s, women rarely used permanent shaving systems, but instead relied more on disposable razors. As a result of this skepticism, the advertising and product development budget was kept small. To save money, Gillette asked a plastic molding company called **Nypro** to co-develop and manufacture the razor. This would be one of the few times that Gillette would call on an outside supplier to manufacture a razor product.

The rest, as they say, is history. *Sensor for Women* grabbed over 40% of the women's razor market in six months. Unit volume exploded beyond everyone's expectations. All the while, Nypro invested in new methods and machines to satisfy the demands. As a result, Nypro has become a very valuable supplier to Gillette. ■

APPENDIX: ACTIVITY-BASED COSTING

As discussed in this chapter, activity-based costing may more accurately identify and trace factory overhead costs to products. The following paragraphs further discuss and illustrate how activity-based costing may provide more accurate and useful product cost data.

Exhibit 11 illustrates the activity-based costing framework for Ruiz Company. In the exhibit, five activities are used in manufacturing snowmobiles and lawnmowers: fabrication, assembly, setup, quality control inspection, and engineering changes.

EXHIBIT 11 Activity-Based Costing—Ruiz Company

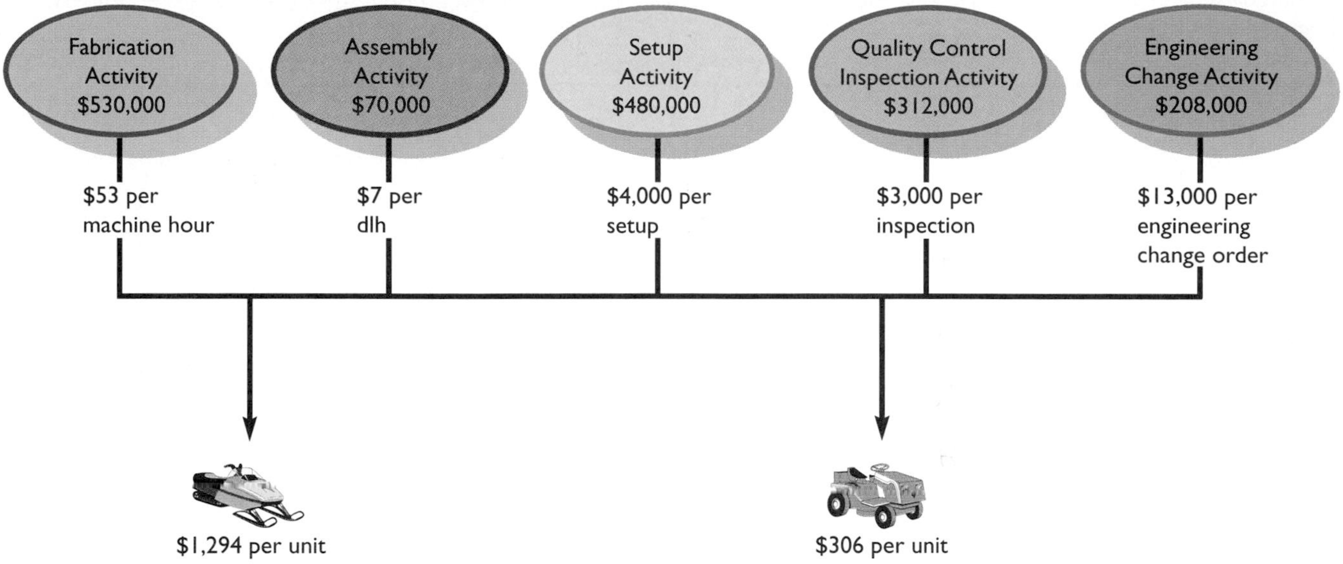

These activities can be defined as follows:

- **Fabrication**—The activity of cutting excess metal in order to properly shape a product. This activity is machine-intensive and, for this reason, costs more than does assembly.
- **Assembly**—The activity of manually assembling machined pieces into a final product. This activity is labor-intensive.
- **Setup**—The activity of changing tooling in a machine to prepare for making a new product. Thus, each production run requires a setup.
- **Quality control inspections**—The activity of inspecting the product for conformance to specifications.
- **Engineering changes**—The activity of processing changes in design or process specifications of a product. The document that initiates the administrative process to change the requirements of a product or process is called **the engineering change order (ECO)**.

Assume the following additional information about the two products for Ruiz Company:

- **Snowmobiles:** Ruiz Company estimates that the total production for snowmobiles will be 1,000 units. Snowmobiles are a new product, and the engineers are still tinkering with design changes. Thus, there are 12 engineering change orders estimated for the period. In addition, the snowmobile production run is expected to be set up 100 times during the period, or 10 units per production run (1,000 units ÷ 100 setups). Due to quality problems, 100 snowmobiles (10% of total production) will be quality-control inspected.
- **Lawnmowers:** Ruiz Company estimates that the total production for lawnmowers will also be 1,000 units. Lawnmowers are a mature and stable product that has been produced by Ruiz Company for many years. Thus, Ruiz Company expects the lawnmower to have only four engineering changes for the period. Due to fewer quality problems, only four lawnmowers (0.4% of production) will be quality-control inspected. In addition, the lawnmower production run is expected to be set up 20 times during the period, or 50 units per production run (1,000 units total production ÷ 20 setups).

The estimated activity base quantities associated with each product reflect differences with respect to using setup, quality control inspection, and engineering change activities, as we noted in the previous paragraphs. In addition, each product uses different amounts of direct labor hours in the fabrication and assembly activities. The estimated activity base usage quantities are shown in Exhibit 12.

EXHIBIT 12
Estimated Activity Base Usage Quantities—Ruiz Company

Products	Activities: Fabrication	Assembly	Setup	Quality Control Inspections	Engineering Changes
Snowmobile	8,000 mh	2,000 dlh	100 setups	100 inspections	12 ECOs
Lawnmower	2,000	8,000	20	4	4
Total activity base	10,000 mh	10,000 dlh	120 setups	104 inspections	16 ECOs

The activity rates for each activity can now be determined by dividing the budgeted activity cost pool by the total estimated activity base from Exhibit 12, as shown for Ruiz Company in Exhibit 13.

EXHIBIT 13
Activity Rates—Ruiz Company

Activity	Budgeted Activity Cost Pool	÷	Estimated Activity Base	=	Activity Rate
Fabrication	$530,000		10,000 direct labor hours		$53 per machine hour
Assembly	$ 70,000		10,000 direct labor hours		$7 per direct labor hour
Setup	$480,000		120 setups		$4,000 per setup
Quality control inspections	$312,000		104 inspections		$3,000 per inspection
Engineering changes	$208,000		16 engineering changes		$13,000 per engineering change order

The product costs for the snowmobile and lawnmower are calculated by multiplying the activity rate by the associated activity base quantity for each product. The total of these costs for each product is the total factory overhead cost for that product. This amount is divided by the total number of units of that product budgeted for manufacture in the period. This result, as shown in Exhibit 14, is the factory overhead cost per unit.

EXHIBIT 14
Activity Base Product Cost Calculations

	Snowmobile			Lawnmower		
Activity	Activity Base Usage ×	Activity Rate =	Activity Cost	Activity Base Usage ×	Activity Rate =	Activity Cost
Fabrication	8,000 mh	$ 53	$ 424,000	2,000 mh	$ 53	$106,000
Assembly	2,000 dlh	7	14,000	8,000 dlh	7	56,000
Setup	100 setups	4,000	400,000	20 setups	4,000	80,000
Quality control inspections	100 inspections	3,000	300,000	4 inspections	3,000	12,000
Engineering changes	12 ECOs	13,000	156,000	4 ECOs	13,000	52,000
Total factory overhead cost			$1,294,000			$306,000
Budgeted units of production			÷ 1,000			÷ 1,000
Factory overhead cost per unit			$ 1,294			$ 306

Under the activity-based approach, each product consumed factory overhead activities in different proportions. Namely, snowmobiles consumed a large majority of the machine, machine setup, quality control inspections, and engineering change activities, while lawnmowers consumed lesser quantities of these activities. Only under the activity-based approach are these differences between the products reflected in the product cost.

When differences in products are not reflected in the product costs, management's strategies may be flawed. To illustrate, **Rockwell International** conducted a special activity-based costing study after one of its best-selling axles had begun losing market share. The study found that incorrect factory overhead cost allocations had "overcosted" its highest-volume axle by roughly 20%, while underestimating the cost of low-volume axles by as much as 40%. Since sales prices were based on these estimated costs, Rockwell had underpriced its low-volume axles and overpriced its high-volume axles. Meanwhile, competitors had been attracting customers away from Rockwell's best-selling, high-volume axles. Mispricing the products was not a strategy that management had chosen, but was the result of a lack of accurate product cost information. Without the special study, Rockwell might well have discovered that they were gradually being squeezed out of the high-volume axle business because of poor product costing.

KEY POINTS

1 Prepare a differential analysis report for decisions involving:

- **Leasing or selling equipment.**
- **Discontinuing an unprofitable segment.**
- **Manufacturing or purchasing a needed part.**
- **Replacing usable fixed assets.**
- **Processing further or selling an intermediate product.**
- **Accepting additional business at a special price.**

Differential analysis reports for leasing or selling, discontinuing a segment or product, making or buying, replacing equipment, processing or selling, and accepting business at a special price are illustrated in the text. Each analysis focuses on the differential revenues and/or costs of the alternative courses of action.

2 Determine the selling price of a product, using the total cost, product cost, and variable cost concepts.

The three cost concepts commonly used in applying the cost-plus approach to product pricing are summarized below:

Cost Concept	Covered in Cost Amount	Covered in Markup
Total cost	Total costs	Desired profit
Product cost	Total manufacturing costs	Desired profit + Total selling and administrative expenses
Variable cost	Total variable costs	Desired profit + Total fixed costs

The markup percentages used in applying each cost concept are as follows:

Total cost concept:

$$\textbf{Markup percentage} = \frac{\textbf{Desired profit}}{\textbf{Total costs}}$$

Product cost concept:

$$\textbf{Markup percentage} = \frac{\textbf{Desired profit} + \textbf{Total selling and administrative expenses}}{\textbf{Total manufacturing costs}}$$

Variable cost concept:

$$\textbf{Markup percentage} = \frac{\textbf{Desired profit} + \textbf{Total fixed costs}}{\textbf{Total variable costs}}$$

3 Calculate the relative profitability of products in bottleneck production environments.

The profitability of a product in a bottleneck production environment may not be accurately shown in the contribution margin product report. Instead, the best measure of profitability is determined by dividing the contribution margin per unit by the bottleneck hours per unit. The resulting measure indicates the product's profitability per hour of bottleneck use. This information can be used to support product pricing decisions.

ILLUSTRATIVE PROBLEM

Inez Company recently began production of a new product, M, which required the investment of $1,600,000 in assets. The costs of producing and selling 80,000 units of Product M are estimated as follows:

Variable costs:	
Direct materials	$ 10.00 per unit
Direct labor	6.00
Factory overhead	4.00
Selling and administrative expenses	5.00
Total	$ 25.00 per unit
Fixed costs:	
Factory overhead	$800,000
Selling and administrative expenses	400,000

Inez Company is currently considering establishing a selling price for Product M. The president of Inez Company has decided to use the cost-plus approach to product pricing and has indicated that Product M must earn a 10% rate of return on invested assets.

Instructions

1. Determine the amount of desired profit from the production and sale of Product M.
2. Assuming that the total cost concept is used, determine (a) the cost amount per unit, (b) the markup percentage, and (c) the selling price of Product M.
3. Assuming that the product cost concept is used, determine (a) the cost amount per unit, (b) the markup percentage, and (c) the selling price of Product M.
4. Assuming that the variable cost concept is used, determine (a) the cost amount per unit, (b) the markup percentage, and (c) the selling price of Product M.
5. Assume that for the current year, the selling price of Product M was $42 per unit. To date, 60,000 units have been produced and sold, and analysis of the domestic market indicates that 15,000 additional units are expected to be sold during the remainder of the year. Recently, Inez Company received an offer from Wong Inc. for 4,000 units of Product M at $28 each. Wong Inc. will market the units in Korea under its own brand name, and no additional selling and administrative expenses associated with the sale will be incurred by Inez Company. The additional business is not expected to affect the domestic sales of Product M, and the additional units could be produced during the current year, using existing capacity. (a) Prepare a differential analysis report of the proposed sale to Wong Inc. (b) Based upon the differential analysis report in (a), should the proposal be accepted?

Solution

1. $160,000 ($1,600,000 × 10%)

2. a. Total costs:

Variable ($25 × 80,000 units)	$2,000,000
Fixed ($800,000 + $400,000)	1,200,000
Total	$3,200,000

Cost amount per unit: $3,200,000 ÷ 80,000 units = $40.00

b. $$\text{Markup percentage} = \frac{\text{Desired profit}}{\text{Total costs}}$$

$$\text{Markup percentage} = \frac{\$160,000}{\$3,200,000} = 5\%$$

c.

Cost amount per unit	$40.00
Markup ($40 × 5%)	2.00
Selling price	$42.00

3. a. Total manufacturing costs:

Variable ($20 × 80,000 units)	$1,600,000
Fixed factory overhead	800,000
Total	$2,400,000

Cost amount per unit: $2,400,000 ÷ 80,000 units = $30.00

b.
$$\text{Markup percentage} = \frac{\text{Desired profit} + \text{Total selling and administrative expenses}}{\text{Total manufacturing costs}}$$

$$\text{Markup percentage} = \frac{\$160{,}000 + \$400{,}000 + (\$5 \times 80{,}000 \text{ units})}{\$2{,}400{,}000}$$

$$\text{Markup percentage} = \frac{\$160{,}000 + \$400{,}000 + \$400{,}000}{\$2{,}400{,}000}$$

$$\text{Markup percentage} = \frac{\$960{,}000}{\$2{,}400{,}000} = 40\%$$

c.

Cost amount per unit	$30.00
Markup ($30 × 40%)	12.00
Selling price	$42.00

4. a. Variable cost amount per unit: $25
Total variable costs: $25 × 80,000 units = $2,000,000

b.
$$\text{Markup percentage} = \frac{\text{Desired profit} + \text{Total fixed costs}}{\text{Total variable costs}}$$

$$\text{Markup percentage} = \frac{\$160{,}000 + \$800{,}000 + \$400{,}000}{\$2{,}000{,}000}$$

$$\text{Markup percentage} = \frac{\$1{,}360{,}000}{\$2{,}000{,}000} = 68\%$$

c.

Cost amount per unit	$25.00
Markup ($25 × 68%)	17.00
Selling price	$42.00

5. a.

Proposal to Sell to Wong Inc.	
Differential revenue from accepting offer:	
Revenue from sale of 4,000 additional units at $28	$112,000
Differential cost from accepting offer:	
Variable production costs of 4,000 additional units at $20	80,000
Differential income from accepting offer	$ 32,000

b. The proposal should be accepted.

SELF-EXAMINATION QUESTIONS

Answers at End of Chapter

Matching

Match each of the following statements with its proper term. Some terms may not be used.

A. **activity-based costing**
B. **bottleneck**
C. **differential analysis**

G 1. The amount of income forgone from an alternative to a proposed use of cash or its equivalent.

B 2. A condition that occurs when product demand exceeds production capacity.

L 3. A concept used in applying the cost-plus approach to product pricing, in which all

D. **differential cost**
E. **differential revenue**
F. **markup**
G. **opportunity cost**
H. **product cost concept**
I. **sunk cost**
J. **target cost concept**
K. **theory of constraints (TOC)**
L. **total cost concept**
M. **variable cost concept**

the costs of manufacturing the product plus the selling and administrative expenses are included in the cost amount to which the markup is added.

I 4. A cost that is not affected by subsequent decisions.

C 5. The area of accounting concerned with the effect of alternative courses of action on revenues and costs.

M 6. A concept used in applying the cost-plus approach to product pricing, in which only the variable costs are included in the cost amount to which the markup is added.

E 7. The amount of increase or decrease in revenue expected from a particular course of action as compared with an alternative.

A 8. A cost allocation method that identifies activities causing the incurrence of costs and allocates these costs to products (or other cost objects), based upon activity drivers (bases).

D 9. The amount of increase or decrease in cost expected from a particular course of action compared with an alternative.

K 10. A manufacturing strategy that attempts to remove the influence of bottlenecks (constraints) on a process.

H 11. A concept used in applying the cost-plus approach to product pricing, in which only the costs of manufacturing the product, termed the product cost, are included in the cost amount to which the markup is added.

J 12. A concept used to design and manufacture a product at a cost that will deliver a target profit for a given market-determined price.

F 13. An amount that is added to a "cost" amount to determine product price.

Multiple Choice

1. Marlo Company is considering discontinuing a product. The costs of the product consist of $20,000 fixed costs and $15,000 variable costs. The variable operating expenses related to the product total $4,000. What is the differential cost?
   A. $19,000 C. $35,000
   B. $15,000 D. $39,000

2. Victor Company is considering disposing of equipment that was originally purchased for $200,000 and has $150,000 of accumulated depreciation to date. The same equipment would cost $310,000 to replace. What is the sunk cost?
   A. $50,000 C. $200,000
   B. $150,000 D. $310,000

3. Henry Company is considering spending $100,000 for a new grinding machine. This amount could be invested to yield a 12% return. What is the opportunity cost?
   A. $112,000 C. $12,000
   B. $88,000 D. $100,000

4. For which cost concept used in applying the cost-plus approach to product pricing are fixed manufacturing costs, fixed selling and administrative expenses, and desired profit allowed for in determining the markup?
   A. Total cost C. Variable cost
   B. Product cost D. Standard cost

5. Mendosa Company produces three products. All the products use a furnace operation, which is a production bottleneck. The following information is available:

	Product 1	Product 2	Product 3
Unit volume—March	1,000	1,500	1,000
Per unit information:			
Sales price	$35	$33	$29
Variable cost	15	15	15
Contribution margin	$20	$18	$14
Furnace hours	4	3	2

From a profitability perspective, which product should be emphasized in April's advertising campaign?
   A. Product 1 C. Product 3
   B. Product 2 D. All three

CLASS DISCUSSION QUESTIONS

1. Explain the meaning of (a) differential revenue, (b) differential cost, and (c) differential income.
2. It was recently reported that **Exabyte**, a fast growing (100-fold in four years) Colorado marketer of tape drives, has decided to purchase key components of its product from others. For example, **Sony** provides Exabyte with mechanical decks, and **Solectron** provides circuit boards. Exabyte's chief executive officer, Peter Behrendt, states, "If we'd tried to build our own plants, we could never have grown that fast

or maybe survived." The decision to purchase key product components is an example of what type of decision illustrated in this chapter?
3. In the long run, the normal selling price must be set high enough to cover what factors?
4. What are the two primary methods of setting prices?
5. What are three cost concepts commonly used in applying the cost-plus approach to product pricing?
6. In using the product cost concept of applying the cost-plus approach to product pricing, what factors are included in the markup?
7. The variable cost concept used in applying the cost-plus approach to product pricing includes what costs in the cost amount to which the markup is added?
8. In determining the markup percentage for the product cost concept of applying the cost-plus approach, what is included in the denominator?
9. Why might the use of ideal standards in applying the cost-plus approach to product pricing lead to setting product prices that are too low?
10. Although the cost-plus approach to product pricing may be used by management as a general guideline, what are some examples of other factors that managers should also consider in setting product prices?
11. What method of determining product cost may be appropriate in settings where the manufacturing process is complex?
12. How does the target cost concept differ from cost-plus approaches?
13. What is a production bottleneck?
14. What is the appropriate measure of a product's value when a firm is operating under production bottlenecks?

Resources for Your Success On-Line at warren.swcollege.com

Remember! If you need additional help, visit South-Western's Web site. See page 26 for a description of the online and printed materials that are available.

EXERCISES

Exercise 23–1
Lease or sell decision

Objective 1

✓ a. Differential revenue from lease, $20,000

Fowler Construction Company is considering selling excess machinery with a book value of $200,000 (original cost of $325,000 less accumulated depreciation of $125,000) for $160,000 less a 10% brokerage commission. Alternatively, the machinery can be leased for a total of $180,000 for five years, after which it is expected to have no residual value. During the period of the lease, Fowler Construction Company's costs of repairs, insurance, and property tax expenses are expected to be $33,000.

a. Prepare a differential analysis report, dated January 3 of the current year, for the lease or sell decision.
b. On the basis of the data presented, would it be advisable to lease or sell the machinery? Explain.

Exercise 23–2
Differential analysis report for a discontinued product

Objective 1

✓ a. Differential cost of annual sales, $204,000

A condensed income statement by product line for Kold Kola Co. indicated the following for Diet Kola for the past year:

Sales	$260,000
Cost of goods sold	160,000
Gross profit	$100,000
Operating expenses	120,000
Loss from operations	$ (20,000)

It is estimated that 25% of the cost of goods sold represents fixed factory overhead costs and that 30% of the operating expenses are fixed. Since Diet Kola is only one of many products, the fixed costs will not be materially affected if the product is discontinued.

a. Prepare a differential analysis report, dated January 3 of the current year, for the proposed discontinuance of Diet Kola.
b. Should Diet Kola be retained? Explain.

Exercise 23–3
Differential analysis report for a discontinued product
Objective 1

✓ a. Differential income: cups, $14,000

The condensed product-line income statement for Contemporary Ceramics Company for the current year is as follows:

Contemporary Ceramics Company
Product-Line Income Statement
For the Year Ended December 31, 20—

	Bowls	Plates	Cups
Sales	$200,000	$160,000	$ 80,000
Cost of goods sold	110,000	90,000	50,000
Gross profit	$ 90,000	$ 70,000	$ 30,000
Selling and administrative expenses	35,000	50,000	45,000
Income from operations	$ 55,000	$ 20,000	$(15,000)

Fixed costs are 40% of the cost of goods sold and 20% of the selling and administrative expenses. Contemporary Ceramics assumes that fixed costs would not be materially affected if the Cups line were discontinued.

a. Prepare a differential analysis report for all three products for the current year.
b. Should the Cups line be retained? Explain.

Exercise 23–4
Decision to discontinue a product
Objective 1

What's Wrong WITH THIS?

On the basis of the following data, the general manager of Sole Mates Inc. decided to discontinue Children's Shoes because it reduced income from operations by $22,000. What is the flaw in this decision?

Soul Mates Inc.
Product-Line Income Statement
For the Year Ended August 31, 20—

	Children's Shoes	Men's Shoes	Women's Shoes	Total
Sales	$105,000	$300,000	$500,000	$905,000
Costs of goods sold:				
Variable costs	$ 70,000	$150,000	$220,000	$440,000
Fixed costs	20,000	60,000	120,000	200,000
Total cost of goods sold	$ 90,000	$210,000	$340,000	$640,000
Gross profit	$ 15,000	$ 90,000	$160,000	$265,000
Operating expenses:				
Variable expenses	$ 30,000	$ 45,000	$ 95,000	$170,000
Fixed expenses	7,000	20,000	25,000	52,000
Total operating expenses	$ 37,000	$ 65,000	$120,000	$222,000
Income (loss) from operations	$ (22,000)	$ 25,000	$ 40,000	$ 43,000

Exercise 23–5
Make or buy decision
Objective 1

✓ a. Cost savings from making, $4.20 per case

Mobile Computer Company has been purchasing carrying cases for its portable computers at a delivered cost of $30 per unit. The company, which is currently operating below full capacity, charges factory overhead to production at the rate of 40% of direct materials cost. The costs to produce comparable carrying cases are expected to be $14 per unit for direct materials and $9 per unit for direct labor. If Mobile Computer Company manufactures the carrying cases, fixed factory overhead costs will not increase and variable factory overhead costs associated with the cases are expected to be 20% of the direct materials costs.

a. Prepare a differential analysis report, dated June 5 of the current year, for the make or buy decision.

b. On the basis of the data presented, would it be advisable to make or to continue buying the carrying cases? Explain.

Exercise 23–6
Machine replacement decision
Objective 1

✓ a. Annual differential income, $10,000

A company is considering replacing an old piece of machinery, which cost $500,000 and has $390,000 of accumulated depreciation to date, with a new machine that costs $405,000. The old equipment could be sold for $165,000. The variable production costs associated with the old machine are estimated to be $120,000 for six years. The variable production costs for the new machine are estimated to be $70,000 for six years.

a. Determine the differential annual income or loss from replacing the old machine.
b. What is the sunk cost in this situation?

Exercise 23–7
Differential analysis report for machine replacement
Objective 1

SPREADSHEET

✓ a. Annual differential decrease in costs, $23,000

Hoover Company produces wood chips by using a manually operated machine to cut logs (direct materials). The original cost of the machine is $150,000, the accumulated depreciation is $110,000, its remaining useful life is 10 years, and its salvage value is negligible. On January 20, a proposal was made to replace the present manufacturing procedure with a fully automatic machine that will cost $200,000. The automatic machine has an estimated useful life of 10 years and no significant salvage value. For use in evaluating the proposal, the accountant accumulated the following annual data on present and proposed operations:

	Present Operations	Proposed Operations
Sales	$480,000	$480,000
Direct materials	195,000	195,000
Direct labor	72,300	—
Power and maintenance	17,500	31,000
Taxes, insurance, etc.	9,200	25,000
Selling and administrative expenses	45,000	45,000

a. Prepare a differential analysis report for the proposal to replace the machine. Include in the analysis both the net differential decrease in costs anticipated over the 10 years and the net annual differential decrease in costs anticipated.
b. Based only on the data presented, should the proposal be accepted?
c. What are some of the other factors that should be considered before a final decision is made?

Exercise 23–8
Decision on accepting additional business
Objective 1

✓ a. Differential income, $30,000

Residential Glass Company has a plant capacity of 60,000 units, and current production is 45,000 units. Monthly fixed costs are $200,000, and variable costs are $27 per unit. The present selling price is $40 per unit. On May 18, the company received an offer from Barker Company for 10,000 units of the product at $30 each. The Barker Company will market the units in a foreign country under its own brand name. The additional business is not expected to affect the regular selling price or quantity of sales of Residential Glass Company.

a. Prepare a differential analysis report for the proposed sale to Barker Company.
b. Briefly explain the reason why accepting this additional business will increase operating income.
c. What is the minimum price per unit that would produce a contribution margin?

Exercise 23–9
Sell or process further
Objective 1

✓ a. $250

Lakeside Lumber Company incurs a cost of $450 per hundred board feet in processing certain "rough-cut" lumber, which it sells for $600 per hundred board feet. An alternative is to produce a "finished-cut" at a total processing cost of $560 per hundred board feet, which can be sold for $850 per hundred board feet. For these alternatives, what is the amount of (a) the differential revenue, (b) differential cost, and (c) differential income?

Exercise 23–10
Sell or process further
Objective 1

✓ c. $10.60

Sunrise Coffee Company produces Columbian coffee in batches of 6,000 pounds. The standard quantity of materials required in the process are 6,000 pounds, which cost $4.20 per pound. Columbian coffee can be sold without further processing for $8 per pound. Columbian coffee can also be processed further to yield Decaf Columbian, which can be sold for $10 per pound. The processing into Decaf Columbian requires additional processing costs of $12,420 per batch. The additional processing will also cause a 5% loss of product due to evaporation.

a. Prepare a differential analysis report for the decision to sell or process further.
b. Should Sunrise sell Columbian coffee or process further and sell Decaf Columbian?
c. Determine the price of Decaf Columbian that would cause neither an advantage or disadvantage for processing further and selling Decaf Columbian.

Exercise 23–11
Accepting business at a special price

Objective 1

Forever Ready Company expects to operate at 90% of productive capacity during May. The total manufacturing costs for May for the production of 15,000 batteries are budgeted as follows:

Direct materials	$146,000
Direct labor	65,000
Variable factory overhead	29,000
Fixed factory overhead	40,000
Total manufacturing costs	$280,000

The company has an opportunity to submit a bid for 1,000 batteries to be delivered by May 31 to a government agency. If the contract is obtained, it is anticipated that the additional activity will not interfere with normal production during May or increase the selling or administrative expenses. What is the unit cost below which Forever Ready Company should not go in bidding on the government contract?

Exercise 23–12
Total cost concept of product costing

Objective 2

✓ c. 10%

Cardinal Company uses the total cost concept of applying the cost-plus approach to product pricing. The costs of producing and selling 3,000 units of mobile phones are as follows:

Variable costs:		Fixed costs:	
Direct materials	$140.00 per unit	Factory overhead	$150,000
Direct labor	60.00	Selling and adm. exp.	90,000
Factory overhead	15.00		
Selling and adm. exp.	25.00		
Total	$240.00 per unit		

Cardinal Company desires a profit equal to a 24% rate of return on invested assets of $400,000.

a. Determine the amount of desired profit from the production and sale of mobile phones.
b. Determine the total costs and the cost amount per unit for the production and sale of 3,000 units of mobile phones.
c. Determine the markup percentage for mobile phones.
d. Determine the selling price of mobile phones.

Exercise 23–13
Product cost concept of product pricing

Objective 2

✓ c. $352

Based on the data presented in Exercise 23–12, assume that Cardinal Company uses the product cost concept of applying the cost-plus approach to product pricing.

a. Determine the total manufacturing costs and the cost amount per unit for the production and sale of 3,000 units of mobile phones.
b. Determine the markup percentage (rounded to two decimals) for mobile phones.
c. Determine the selling price of mobile phones.

Exercise 23–14
Variable cost concept of product pricing

Objective 2

✓ b. 46.67%

Based on the data presented in Exercise 23–12, assume that Cardinal Company uses the variable cost concept of applying the cost-plus approach to product pricing.

a. Determine the variable costs and the cost amount per unit for the production and sale of 3,000 units of mobile phones.
b. Determine the markup percentage for mobile phones.
c. Determine the selling price of mobile phones.

Exercise 23–15
Product decisions under bottlenecked operations

Objective 3

✓ a. Total income from operations, $215,000

Penn Glass Company manufactures three types of safety plate glass: large, medium, and small. All three products have high demand. Thus, Penn is able to sell all the safety glass that it can make. The production process includes an autoclave operation, which is an oil spray heat treatment. The autoclave is a production bottleneck. Fixed costs are $250,000. In addition, the following information is available about the three products:

	Large	Medium	Small
Sales price per unit	$ 230	$ 190	$ 120
Variable cost per unit	110	70	50
Contribution margin per unit	$ 120	$ 120	$ 70
Autoclave hours per unit	12	15	10
Total process hours per unit	30	25	22
Budgeted units of production	1,500	1,500	1,500

a. Determine the contribution margin by glass type and the total company income from operations for the budgeted units of production.
b. Prepare an analysis showing which product is the most profitable per bottleneck hour.

Exercise 23–16
Product pricing under bottlenecked operations

Objective 3

✓ Medium, $220

Based on the data presented in Exercise 23–15, assume that Penn wanted to price all products so that they produced the same profit potential as the highest profit product. What would be the prices of all three products that would produce the largest profit?

Appendix Exercise 23–17
Activity-based costing

✓ Cost per stationary bicycle, $209.80

Samson Company manufactures stationary bicycles and rowing machines. The products are produced in the Fabrication and Assembly production departments. The production and other activities and their associated activity rates are as follows:

Activity	Activity Rate
Fabrication	$45 per machine hour
Assembly	$15 per direct labor hour
Setup	$120 per setup
Inspecting	$30 per inspection
Production scheduling	$15 per production order
Purchasing	$5 per purchase order

The activity base usage quantities used by each product and units produced for each product were as follows:

	Stationary Bicycle	Rowing Machine
Machine hours	4,000	2,500
Direct labor hours	1,000	1,500
Setups	20	40
Inspections	400	1,000
Production orders	10	20
Purchase orders	50	80
Units produced	1,000	1,000

Use the activity rate and usage information to calculate the total activity costs and the activity costs per unit for each product.

Appendix Exercise 23–18
Activity-based costing

✓ b. Custom, $46 per unit

Mohawk Industries manufactures two types of electrical power units, custom and standard, which involve four overhead activities—production setup, procurement, quality control, and materials management. An activity analysis of the overhead revealed the following estimated costs for these activities:

Production setup	$ 44,000
Procurement	160,000
Quality control	175,000
Materials management	150,000
Total	$529,000

The appropriate activity drivers and the amount of each activity driver for the two products are as follows:

Activity	Activity Driver
Production setup	Number of setups
Procurement	Number of purchase orders
Quality control	Number of inspections
Materials management	Number of components

	Setups	Purchase Orders	Inspections	Components	Unit Volume
Custom	1,000	3,000	6,000	80	10,000
Standard	100	200	1,000	20	10,000
Total	1,100	3,200	7,000	100	20,000

a. Determine an activity rate for each activity.
b. Assign activity costs to each product, and determine the unit activity cost, using the activity rates from (a).
c. Determine the total and unit activity cost if overhead is allocated on the basis of production volume.
d. Explain why the answers in (b) and (c) are different.

PROBLEMS SERIES A

Problem 23–1A
Differential analysis report involving opportunity costs
Objective 1

SPREADSHEET

✓ 3. $860,000

On December 1, Safe-Passage Distribution Company is considering leasing a building and buying the necessary equipment to operate a public warehouse. The project would be financed by selling $500,000 of 8% U.S. Treasury bonds that mature in 16 years. The bonds were purchased at face value and are currently selling at face value. The following data have been assembled:

Cost of equipment	$500,000
Life of equipment	16 years
Estimated residual value of equipment	$ 80,000
Yearly costs to operate the warehouse, in addition to depreciation of equipment	$ 65,000
Yearly expected revenues—years 1–8	$160,000
Yearly expected revenues—years 9–16	$130,000

Instructions

1. Prepare a report presenting a differential analysis of the proposed operation of the warehouse for the 16 years as compared with present conditions.
2. Based on the results disclosed by the differential analysis, should the proposal be accepted?
3. If the proposal is accepted, what is the total estimated income from operation of the warehouse for the 16 years?

Problem 23–2A

Differential analysis report for machine replacement proposal

Objective 1

Dawson Tooling Company is considering replacing a machine that has been used in its factory for three years. Relevant data associated with the operations of the old machine and the new machine, neither of which has any estimated residual value, are as follows:

Old Machine	
Cost of machine, 9-year life	$270,000
Annual depreciation (straight-line)	30,000
Annual manufacturing costs, exclusive of depreciation	95,000
Annual nonmanufacturing operating expenses	45,000
Annual revenue	205,000
Current estimated selling price	175,000

New Machine	
Cost of machine, 6-year life	$420,000
Annual depreciation (straight-line)	70,000
Estimated annual manufacturing costs, exclusive of depreciation	35,000

Annual nonmanufacturing operating expenses and revenue are not expected to be affected by purchase of the new machine.

Instructions

1. Prepare a differential analysis report as of March 22 of the current year, comparing operations utilizing the new machine with operations using the present equipment. The analysis should indicate the differential income that would result over the 6-year period if the new machine is acquired.
2. List other factors that should be considered before a final decision is reached.

Problem 23–3A

Differential analysis report for sales promotion proposal

Objective 1

✓ 1. Differential income, tennis shoe, $78,000

Jordan Athletic Shoe Company is planning a one-month campaign for April to promote sales of one of its two shoe products. A total of $24,000 has been budgeted for advertising, contests, redeemable coupons, and other promotional activities. The following data have been assembled for their possible usefulness in deciding which of the products to select for the campaign.

	Tennis Shoe	Walking Shoe
Unit selling price	$57	$68
Unit production costs:		
Direct materials	$18	$20
Direct labor	12	18
Variable factory overhead	4	7
Fixed factory overhead	6	2
Total unit production costs	$40	$47
Unit variable selling expenses	6	10
Unit fixed selling expenses	5	2
Total unit costs	$51	$59
Operating income per unit	$ 6	$ 9

No increase in facilities would be necessary to produce and sell the increased output. It is anticipated that 6,000 additional units of tennis shoes or 7,000 additional units of walking shoes could be sold without changing the unit selling price of either product.

Instructions

1. Prepare a differential analysis report as of March 3 of the current year, presenting the additional revenue and additional costs anticipated from the promotion of tennis shoes and walking shoes.

2. The sales manager had tentatively decided to promote walking shoes, estimating that operating income would be increased by $39,000 ($9 operating income per unit for 7,000 units, less promotion expenses of $24,000). The manager also believed that the selection of tennis shoes would increase operating income by only $12,000 ($6 operating income per unit for 6,000 units, less promotion expenses of $24,000). State briefly your reasons for supporting or opposing the tentative decision.

Problem 23–4A
Differential analysis report for further processing
Objective 1

✓ Differential revenue, $15,500

The management of Brazil Aluminum Company is considering whether to process further aluminum ingot into rolled aluminum. Rolled aluminum can be sold for $14 per pound, and ingot can be sold without further processing for $9 per pound. Ingot is produced in batches of 4,500 pounds by smelting 5,000 pounds of bauxite, which costs $4 per pound. Rolled aluminum will require additional processing costs of $3.50 per pound of ingot, and 1.125 pounds of ingot will produce 1 pound of rolled aluminum.

Instructions

1. Prepare a report as of February 20, presenting a differential analysis associated with the further processing of aluminum ingot to produce rolled aluminum.
2. Briefly report your recommendations.

Problem 23–5A
Product pricing using the cost-plus approach concepts; differential analysis report for accepting additional business
Objectives 1, 2

✓ 2. b. Markup percentage, 20%

Neon Company recently began production of a new product, the halogen light, which required the investment of $2,000,000 in assets. The costs of producing and selling 30,000 halogen lights are estimated as follows:

Variable costs per unit:	
Direct materials	$ 24.00
Direct labor	10.40
Factory overhead	2.60
Selling and administrative expenses	3.00
Total	$ 40.00
Fixed costs:	
Factory overhead	$180,000
Selling and administrative expenses	120,000

Neon Company is currently considering establishing a selling price for the halogen light. The president of Neon Company has decided to use the cost-plus approach to product pricing and has indicated that the halogen light must earn a 15% rate of return on invested assets.

Instructions

1. Determine the amount of desired profit from the production and sale of the halogen light.
2. Assuming that the total cost concept is used, determine (a) the cost amount per unit, (b) the markup percentage, and (c) the selling price of the halogen light.
3. Assuming that the product cost concept is used, determine (a) the cost amount per unit, (b) the markup percentage, and (c) the selling price of the halogen light. Round to the nearest cent.
4. Assuming that the variable cost concept is used, determine (a) the cost amount per unit, (b) the markup percentage, and (c) the selling price of the halogen light.
5. Comment on any additional considerations that could influence establishing the selling price for the halogen light.
6. Assume that as of May 1, 6,500 units of halogen light have been produced and sold during the current year. Analysis of the domestic market indicates that 20,500 additional units of the halogen light are expected to be sold during the remainder of the year at the normal product price determined under the total cost concept. On May 5, Neon Company received an offer from Yee Inc. for 2,000 units of the halogen light at $39 each. Yee Inc. will market the units in Japan under its own brand name, and no additional selling and administrative expenses associated with the sale will be incurred by Neon Company. The additional business is not expected to af-

fect the domestic sales of the halogen light, and the additional units could be produced using existing capacity.

a. Prepare a differential analysis report of the proposed sale to Yee Inc.
b. Based upon the differential analysis report in (a), should the proposal be accepted?

Problem 23–6A

Product pricing and profit analysis with bottleneck operations

Objectives 1, 3

✓ 3. Butane price, $285

Delaware Chemical Company produces three products: ethylene, butane, and ester. Each of these products has high demand in the market, and Delaware Chemical is able to sell as much as it can produce of all three. The reaction operation is a bottleneck in the process and is running at 100% of capacity. Delaware Chemical is attempting to determine how to improve profitability for the chemical operations. The variable conversion cost is $4 per process hour. The fixed cost is $1,050,000. In addition, the cost analyst was able to determine the following information about the three products:

	Ethylene	Butane	Ester
Budgeted units produced	5,000	5,000	5,000
Total process hours per unit	12	15	15
Reactor hours per unit	4	5	8
Price per unit	$240	$280	$300
Direct materials cost per unit	$100	$110	$120

The reaction operation is part of the total process for each of these three products. So, for example, 4 of the 12 hours required to process Ethylene are associated with the reactor.

Instructions

1. Determine the contribution margin per unit for each product.
2. Provide an analysis to determine the relative product profitabilities.
3. Assume that management wishes to improve profitability by increasing prices on selected products. At what price would Butane and Ester need to be offered in order to produce the same relative profitability as Ethylene?

PROBLEMS SERIES B

Problem 23–1B

Differential analysis report involving opportunity costs

Objective 1

SPREADSHEET

✓ 3. $1,580,000

On July 1, Neptune Storage Company is considering leasing a building and purchasing the necessary equipment to operate a public warehouse. The project would be financed by selling $700,000 of 12% U.S. Treasury bonds that mature in 20 years. The bonds were purchased at face value and are currently selling at face value. The following data have been assembled:

Cost of equipment	$700,000
Life of equipment	20 years
Estimated residual value of equipment	$180,000
Yearly costs to operate the warehouse, in addition to depreciation of equipment	$ 80,000
Yearly expected revenues—years 1–10	$200,000
Yearly expected revenues—years 11–20	$170,000

Instructions

1. Prepare a report presenting a differential analysis of the proposed operation of the warehouse for the 20 years as compared with present conditions.
2. Based on the results disclosed by the differential analysis, should the proposal be accepted?
3. If the proposal was accepted, what would be the total estimated income from operation of the warehouse for the 20 years?

Problem 23–2B

Differential analysis report for machine replacement decision

Objective 1

Ohio Printing Company is considering replacing a machine that has been used in its factory for two years. Relevant data associated with the operations of the old machine and the new machine, neither of which has any estimated residual value, are as follows:

Old Machine	
Cost of machine, 10-year life	$350,000
Annual depreciation (straight-line)	35,000
Annual manufacturing costs, exclusive of depreciation	425,000
Annual nonmanufacturing operating expenses	274,000
Annual revenue	890,000
Current estimated selling price	240,000

New Machine	
Cost of machine, 8-year life	$720,000
Annual depreciation (straight-line)	90,000
Estimated annual manufacturing costs, exclusive of depreciation	325,000

Annual nonmanufacturing operating expenses and revenue are not expected to be affected by purchase of the new machine.

Instructions

1. Prepare a differential analysis report as of August 11 of the current year, comparing operations utilizing the new machine with operations using the present equipment. The analysis should indicate the total differential income that would result over the 8-year period if the new machine is acquired.
2. List other factors that should be considered before a final decision is reached.

Problem 23–3B

Differential analysis report for sales promotion proposal

Objective 1

✓ 1. Cologne differential income, $85,000

Lilac Cosmetics Company is planning a one-month campaign for May to promote sales of one of its two cosmetics products. A total of $45,000 has been budgeted for advertising, contests, redeemable coupons, and other promotional activities. The following data have been assembled for their possible usefulness in deciding which of the products to select for the campaign:

	Cologne	Perfume
Unit selling price	$47	$68
Unit production costs:		
Direct materials	$12	$18
Direct labor	7	12
Variable factory overhead	3	5
Fixed factory overhead	4	2
Total unit production costs	$26	$37
Unit variable selling expenses	12	21
Unit fixed selling expenses	3	1
Total unit costs	$41	$59
Operating income per unit	$ 6	$ 9

No increase in facilities would be necessary to produce and sell the increased output. It is anticipated that 10,000 additional units of cologne or 10,500 additional units of perfume could be sold without changing the unit selling price of either product.

Instructions

1. Prepare a differential analysis report as of April 5 of the current year, presenting the additional revenue and additional costs anticipated from the promotion of cologne and perfume.
2. The sales manager had tentatively decided to promote perfume, estimating that operating income would be increased by $49,500 ($9 operating income per unit for 10,500 units, less promotion expenses of $45,000). The manager also believed

that the selection of cologne would increase operating income by only $15,000 ($6 operating income per unit for 10,000 units, less promotion expenses of $45,000). State briefly your reasons for supporting or opposing the tentative decision.

Problem 23–4B

Differential analysis report for further processing

Objective 1

✓ Differential revenue, $3,480

The management of Hawaiian Sugar Company is considering whether to process further raw sugar into refined sugar. Refined sugar can be sold for $1.30 per pound, and raw sugar can be sold without further processing for $0.75 per pound. Raw sugar is produced in batches of 12,000 pounds by processing 18,000 pounds of sugar cane, which costs $0.20 per pound. Refined sugar will require additional processing costs of $0.25 per pound of raw sugar, and 1.25 pounds of raw sugar will produce 1 pound of refined sugar.

Instructions

1. Prepare a report as of May 30, presenting a differential analysis of the further processing of raw sugar to produce refined sugar.
2. Briefly report your recommendations.

Problem 23–5B

Product pricing using the cost-plus approach concepts; differential analysis report for accepting additional business

Objectives 1, 2

✓ 2. b. Markup percentage, 15%

Video Labs Inc. recently began production of a new product, instrument LCD's, which required the investment of $1,200,000 in assets. The costs of producing and selling 25,000 units of instrument LCD's are estimated as follows:

Variable costs per unit:	
Direct materials	$ 15.90
Direct labor	8.90
Factory overhead	5.20
Selling and administrative expenses	2.00
Total	$ 32.00
Fixed costs:	
Factory overhead	$150,000
Selling and administrative expenses	50,000

Video Labs Inc. is currently considering establishing a selling price for instrument LCD's. The president of Video Labs has decided to use the cost-plus approach to product pricing and has indicated that the LCD's must earn a 12.5% rate of return on invested assets.

Instructions

1. Determine the amount of desired profit from the production and sale of instrument LCD's.
2. Assuming that the total cost concept is used, determine (a) the cost amount per unit, (b) the markup percentage, and (c) the selling price of instrument LCD's.
3. Assuming that the product cost concept is used, determine (a) the cost amount per unit, (b) the markup percentage, and (c) the selling price of instrument LCD's.
4. Assuming that the variable cost concept is used, determine (a) the cost amount per unit, (b) the markup percentage, and (c) the selling price of instrument LCD's.
5. Comment on any additional considerations that could influence establishing the selling price for instrument LCD's.
6. Assume that as of September 1, 20,000 units of instrument LCD's have been produced and sold during the current year. Analysis of the domestic market indicates that 2,000 additional units are expected to be sold during the remainder of the year at the normal product price determined under the total cost concept. On September 3, Video Labs Inc. received an offer from Kimble Company for 3,000 units of instrument LCD's at $27 each. Kimble Company will market the units in Canada under its own brand name, and no additional selling and administrative expenses associated with the sale will be incurred by Video Labs Inc. The additional business is not expected to affect the domestic sales of instrument LCD's, and the additional units could be produced using existing capacity.
   a. Prepare a differential analysis report of the proposed sale to Kimble Company.
   b. Based upon the differential analysis report in (a), should the proposal be accepted?

Problem 23–6B
Product pricing and profit analysis with bottleneck operations
Objectives 1, 3

✓ 3. High Grade price, $830

Ohio Valley Steel Company produces three grades of steel: high, good, and regular grade. Each of these products (grades) has high demand in the market, and Ohio Valley is able to sell as much as it can produce of all three. The furnace operation is a bottleneck in the process and is running at 100% of capacity. Ohio Valley is attempting to determine how to improve profitability for the steel operations. The variable conversion cost is $5 per process hour. The fixed cost is $1,560,000. In addition, the cost analyst was able to determine the following information about the three products:

	High Grade	Good Grade	Regular Grade
Budgeted units produced	4,000	4,000	4,000
Total process hours per unit	40	40	35
Furnace hours per unit	20	15	10
Price per unit	$640	$590	$550
Direct materials cost per unit	$160	$150	$140

The furnace operation is part of the total process for each of these three products. So, for example, 20 of the 40 hours required to process High Grade steel are associated with the furnace.

Instructions

1. Determine the contribution margin per unit for each product.
2. Provide an analysis to determine the relative product profitabilities.
3. Assume that management wishes to improve profitability by increasing prices on selected products. At what price would High and Good Grades need to be offered in order to produce the same relative profitability as Regular Grade steel?

SPECIAL ACTIVITIES

Activity 23–1
Morton Enterprises
Product pricing

Lee Davis is a cost accountant for Morton Enterprises. Ann Yeager, vice-president of marketing, has asked Lee to meet with representatives of Morton's major competitor to discuss product cost data. Yeager indicates that the sharing of these data will enable Morton to determine a fair and equitable price for its products.

Would it be ethical for Davis to attend the meeting and share the relevant cost data?

Activity 23–2
Ralley Sporting Goods Company
Decision on accepting additional business

A manager of Ralley Sporting Goods Company is considering accepting an order from an overseas customer. This customer has requested an order for 20,000 dozen golf balls at a price of $10.00 per dozen. The variable cost to manufacture a dozen golf balls is $8.00 per dozen. The full cost is $12.00 per dozen. Ralley has a normal selling price of $18.00 per dozen. Ralley's plant has just enough excess capacity on the second shift to make the overseas order.

What are some considerations in accepting or rejecting this order?

Activity 23–3
Almont Hotel
Business decisions with contribution margin

The management of the Almont Hotel is evaluating a proposal for a 100-person convention in the hotel. The professional society sponsoring the convention insists on a $50 per night room rate. The variable cost per guest is $15 per night. However, the full operating cost of the hotel per guest is $60 per night, including fixed costs such as hotel depreciation and management salaries. The convention is scheduled for a weekend, when the hotel will be empty.

Should Almont management accept the business? Discuss.

Activity 23–4
Owens Company
Product profitability with production constraints

Owens Company produces glass products for the automobile industry. The company produces three types of products: small, medium, and large windows. One of the process steps in glass making involves a furnace operation. Presently, the furnace runs 24 hours per day, seven days per week. The following per-unit information is available about the three major product lines:

	Small Window	Medium Window	Large Window
Sales price	$14.00	$24.00	$32.00
Variable cost	6.00	14.00	18.00
Contribution margin	$ 8.00	$10.00	$14.00
Furnace hours	2	4	5

The product manager of Owens Company believes that the company should increase incremental sales effort on the large window, since the contribution margin per unit is the highest.

Respond to this suggestion. What recommendations would you suggest to improve profitability?

Activity 23–5
Hull Company
Make or buy decision

The president of Hull Company, Jason Sheppard, asked the controller, Gil Adkins, to provide an analysis of a make vs. buy decision for material TS-101. The material is presently processed in Hull Company's Roanoke facility. TS-101 is used in processing of final products in the facility. Adkins determined the following unit production costs for the material as of March 15, 2000:

Unit production costs:	
Direct materials	$ 6.70
Direct labor	2.50
Variable factory overhead	1.20
Fixed factory overhead	2.00
Total production costs per unit	$12.40

In addition, material TS-101 requires special hazardous material handling. This special handling adds an additional cost of $1.40 for each unit produced.

Material TS-101 can be purchased from an overseas supplier. The supplier does not presently do business with Hull Company. This supplier promises monthly delivery of the material at a price of $9.00 per unit, plus transportation cost of $0.40 per unit. In addition, Hull would need to incur additional administrative costs to satisfy import regulations for hazardous material. This additional administrative cost is estimated to be $0.80 per purchased unit. Each purchased unit would also require special hazardous material handling of $1.40 per unit.

a. Prepare a differential analysis report to support Adkins recommendation on whether to continue making material TS-101 or whether to purchase the material from the overseas supplier.

b. What additional considerations should Adkins address in the recommendation?

Activity 23–6
Apex Computer Company
Cost-plus and target costing concepts

The following conversation took place between Alex Myers, vice-president of marketing, and Jill Jacoby, controller of Apex Computer Company:

Alex: I am really excited about our new computer coming out. I think it will be a real market success.

Jill: I'm really glad you think so. I know that our price is one variable that will determine if it's a success. If our price is too high, our competitors will be the ones with the market success.

Alex: Don't worry about it. We'll just mark our product cost up by 25% and it will all work out. I know we'll make money at those markups. By the way, what does the estimated product cost look like?

Jill: Well, there's the rub. The product cost looks like its going to come in at around $2,400. With a 25% markup, that will give us a selling price of $3,000.

Alex: I see your concern. That's a little high. Our research indicates that computer prices are dropping by about 20% per year, and that this type of computer should be selling for around $2,500 when we release it to the market.

Jill: I'm not sure what to do.

Alex: Let me see if I can help. How much of the $2,400 is fixed cost?

Jill: About $400.

Alex: There you go. The fixed cost is sunk. We don't need to consider it in our pricing decision. If we reduce the product cost by $400, the new price with a 25% markup would be right at $2,500. Boy, I was really worried for a minute there. I knew something wasn't right.

a. If you were Jill, how would you respond to Alex's solution to the pricing problem?

b. How might target costing be used to help solve this pricing dilemma?

Activity 23–7 Into the Real World

Internet marketing

Internet ACTIVITY GROUP ACTIVITY

Many businesses are offering their products and services over the Internet. Some of these companies and their Internet addresses are listed below.

Company Name	Internet Address (URL)	Product
Delta Air Lines	**www.delta-air.com**	airline tickets
Amazon.com, Inc.	**www.amazon.com**	books
Dell Computer Company	**www.dell.com**	personal computers

a. In groups of three, assign each person in your group to one of the Internet sites listed above. For each site, determine the following:
   1. A product (or service) description.
   2. A product price.
   3. A list of costs that are required to produce and sell the product selected in (1).
   4. Whether the costs identified in (3) are fixed costs or variable costs.

b. Which of the three products do you believe has the largest markup on variable cost?

ANSWERS TO SELF-EXAMINATION QUESTIONS

Matching

1. G	3. L	5. C	7. E	9. D	11. H	12. J	13. F
2. B	4. I	6. M	8. A	10. K			

Multiple Choice

1. **A** Differential cost is the amount of increase or decrease in cost that is expected from a particular course of action compared with an alternative. For Marlo Company, the differential cost is $19,000 (answer A). This is the total of the variable product costs ($15,000) and the variable operating expenses ($4,000), which would not be incurred if the product is discontinued.
2. **A** A sunk cost is not affected by later decisions. For Victor Company, the sunk cost is the $50,000 (answer A) book value of the equipment, which is equal to the original cost of $200,000 (answer C) less the accumulated depreciation of $150,000 (answer B).
3. **C** The amount of income that could have been earned from the best available alternative to a proposed use of cash is the opportunity cost. For Henry Company, the opportunity cost is 12% of $100,000, or $12,000 (answer C).
4. **C** Under the variable cost concept of product pricing (answer C), fixed manufacturing costs, fixed administrative and selling expenses, and desired profit are allowed for in determining the markup. Only desired profit is allowed for in the markup under the total cost concept (answer A). Under the product cost concept (answer B), total selling and administrative expenses and desired profit are allowed for in determining the markup. Standard cost (answer D) can be used under any of the cost-plus approaches to product pricing.
5. **C** Product 3 has the highest unit contribution margin per bottleneck hour ($14/2 = $7). Product 1 (answer A) has the largest contribution margin per unit, but the lowest unit contribution per bottleneck hour ($20/4 = $5), so it is the least profitable product in the constrained environment. Product 2 (answer B) has the highest total profitability in March (1,500 units × $18), but this does not suggest that it has the highest profit potential. Product 2's unit contribution per bottleneck hour ($18/3 = $6) is between Products 1 and 3. Answer D is not true, since the products all have different profit potential in terms of unit contribution margin per bottleneck hour.

24

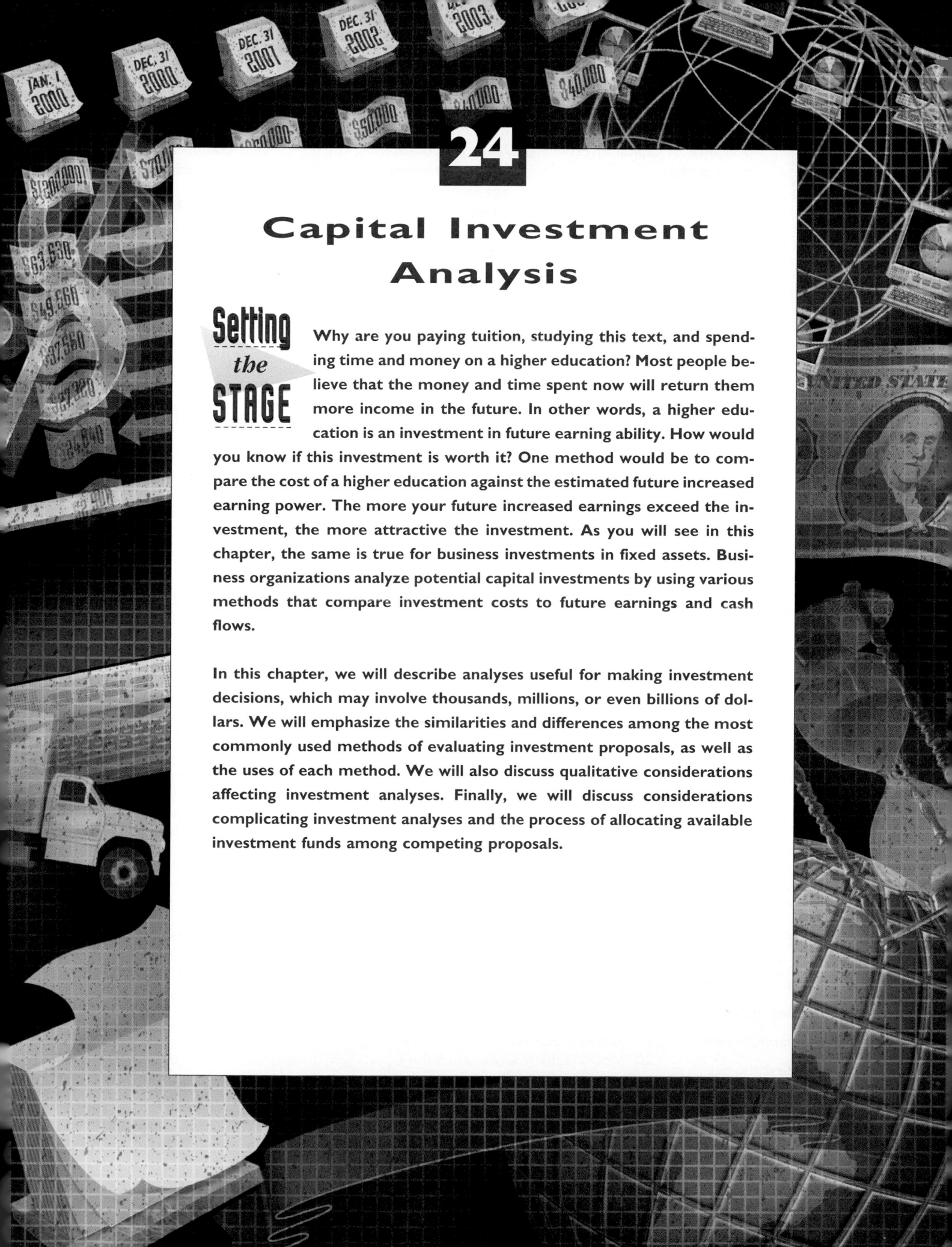

Capital Investment Analysis

Setting *the* STAGE

Why are you paying tuition, studying this text, and spending time and money on a higher education? Most people believe that the money and time spent now will return them more income in the future. In other words, a higher education is an investment in future earning ability. How would you know if this investment is worth it? One method would be to compare the cost of a higher education against the estimated future increased earning power. The more your future increased earnings exceed the investment, the more attractive the investment. As you will see in this chapter, the same is true for business investments in fixed assets. Business organizations analyze potential capital investments by using various methods that compare investment costs to future earnings and cash flows.

In this chapter, we will describe analyses useful for making investment decisions, which may involve thousands, millions, or even billions of dollars. We will emphasize the similarities and differences among the most commonly used methods of evaluating investment proposals, as well as the uses of each method. We will also discuss qualitative considerations affecting investment analyses. Finally, we will discuss considerations complicating investment analyses and the process of allocating available investment funds among competing proposals.

objectives

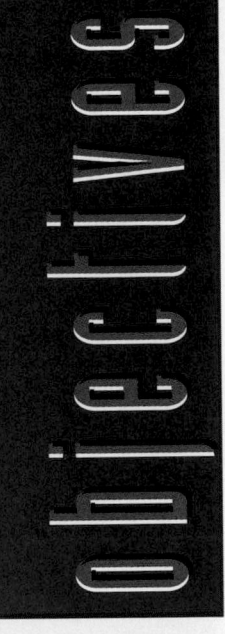

After studying this chapter, you should be able to:

1. Explain the nature and importance of capital investment analysis.
2. Evaluate capital investment proposals, using the following methods: average rate of return, cash payback, net present value, and internal rate of return.
3. List and describe factors that complicate capital investment analysis.
4. Diagram the capital rationing process.

Nature of Capital Investment Analysis

OBJECTIVE 1

Explain the nature and importance of capital investment analysis.

How do companies decide to make significant investments such as the following?

- **Toyota Motor Company** doubles its annual production capacity to 400,000 cars at its Georgetown, Kentucky assembly plant.
- **General Electric** invests over $1 billion in plant and equipment to build new kitchen appliance products.
- **Hilton Hotels** builds a new 3,642-room hotel/casino at the site of the old Flamingo hotel in Las Vegas, Nevada.

Companies use capital investment analysis to help evaluate long-term investments. **Capital investment analysis** (or **capital budgeting**) is the process by which management plans, evaluates, and controls investments in fixed assets. Capital investments involve the long-term commitment of funds and affect operations for many years. Thus, these investments must earn a reasonable rate of return, so that the business can meet its obligations to creditors and provide dividends to stockholders. Because capital investment decisions are some of the most important decisions that management makes, capital investment analysis must be carefully developed and implemented.

A capital investment program should encourage employees to submit proposals for capital investments. It should communicate to employees the long-range goals of the business, so that useful proposals are submitted. All reasonable proposals should be considered and evaluated with respect to economic costs and benefits. The program may reward employees whose proposals are accepted.

Methods of Evaluating Capital Investment Proposals

OBJECTIVE 2

Evaluate capital investment proposals, using the following methods: average rate of return, cash payback, net present value, and internal rate of return.

Capital investment evaluation methods can be grouped into the following two categories:

1. Methods that do not use present values
2. Methods that use present values

Two methods that do not use present values are (1) the average rate of return method and (2) the cash payback method. Two methods that use present values are (1) the net present value method and (2) the internal rate of return method.

A survey of business practices in a variety of industries reported the following use of capital investment analysis methods:

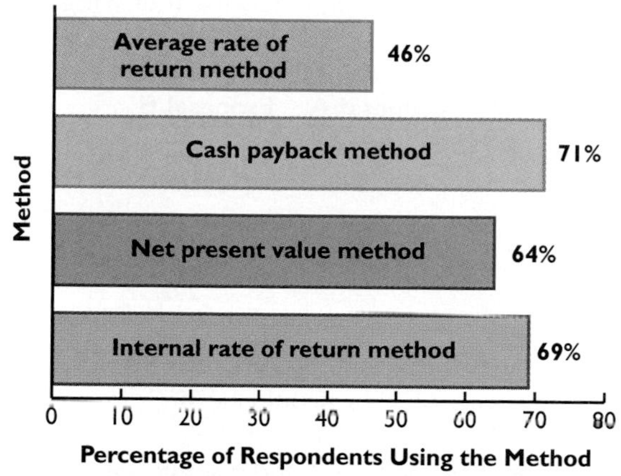

Source: Robert A. Howell, James D. Brown, Stephen R. Soucy, and Allen H. Seed, *Management Accounting in the New Manufacturing Environment,* National Association of Accountants and Computer Aided Manufacturing International, Montvale, New Jersey, 1987.

These methods consider the time value of money. The **time value of money concept** recognizes that an amount of cash invested today will earn income and therefore has value over time.

Management often uses a combination of methods in evaluating capital investment proposals. Each method has advantages and disadvantages. In addition, some of the computations are complex. Computers, however, can perform the computations quickly and easily. Computers can also be used to analyze the impact of changes in key estimates in evaluating capital investment proposals.

Methods that Ignore Present Value

The average rate of return and the cash payback methods are easy to use. These methods are often initially used to screen proposals. Management normally sets minimum standards for accepting proposals, and those not meeting these standards are dropped from further consideration. If a proposal meets the minimum standards, it is often subject to further analysis.

The methods that ignore present value are often useful in evaluating capital investment proposals that have relatively short useful lives. In such cases, the timing of the cash flows is less important.

Average Rate of Return Method

The **average rate of return**, sometimes called the **accounting rate of return**, is a measure of the average income as a percent of the average investment in fixed assets. The average rate of return is determined by using the following equation:

$$\textbf{Average rate of return} = \frac{\textbf{Estimated average annual income}}{\textbf{Average investment}}$$

The numerator is the average of the annual income expected to be earned from the investment over the investment life. The denominator is the average book value over the investment life. Thus, if straight-line depreciation and no residual value are assumed, the average investment over the useful life is equal to one-half of the original cost.[1]

To illustrate, assume that management is considering the purchase of a machine at a cost of \$500,000. The machine is expected to have a useful life of 4 years, with no residual value, and to yield total income of \$200,000. The estimated average annual income is therefore \$50,000 (\$200,000 ÷ 4), and the average investment is \$250,000 [(\$500,000 + \$0 residual value) ÷ 2]. Thus, the average rate of return on the average investment is 20%, computed as follows:

$$\text{Average rate of return} = \frac{\text{Estimated average annual income}}{\text{Average investment}}$$

$$\text{Average rate of return} = \frac{\$200{,}000 \div 4}{(\$500{,}000 + \$0) \div 2} = 20\%$$

The average rate of return of 20% should be compared with the minimum rate for such investments. If the average rate of return equals or exceeds the minimum rate, the machine should be purchased.

[1] The average investment is the midpoint of the depreciable cost of the asset. Since a fixed asset is never depreciated below its residual value, this midpoint is determined by adding the original cost of the asset to the estimated residual value and dividing by 2.

Q&A *What is the average rate of return for a project that is estimated to yield total income of $273,600 over three years, cost $690,000, and has a $70,000 residual value?*

24% [($273,600 ÷ 3)/($690,000 + $70,000) ÷ 2]

When several capital investment proposals are considered, the proposals can be ranked by their average rates of return. The higher the average rate of return, the more desirable the proposal. For example, assume that management is considering two capital investment proposals and has computed the following average rates of return:

	Proposal A	Proposal B
Estimated average annual income	$ 30,000	$ 36,000
Average investment	$120,000	$180,000
Average rate of return:		
$30,000 ÷ $120,000	25%	
$36,000 ÷ $180,000		20%

If only the average rate of return is considered, Proposal A, with an average rate of return of 25%, would be preferred over Proposal B.

The average rate of return method considers the amount of income earned over the life of a proposal.

In addition to being easy to compute, the average rate of return method has several advantages. One advantage is that it includes the amount of income earned over the entire life of the proposal. In addition, it emphasizes accounting income, which is often used by investors and creditors in evaluating management performance. Its main disadvantage is that it does not directly consider the expected cash flows from the proposal and the timing of these cash flows.

Cash Payback Method

Cash flows are important because cash can be reinvested. Very simply, the capital investment uses cash, and must therefore return cash in the future in order to be successful.

The expected period of time that will pass between the date of an investment and the complete recovery in cash (or equivalent) of the amount invested is the **cash payback period**. To simplify the analysis, the revenues and expenses other than depreciation related to operating fixed assets are assumed to be all in the form of cash. The excess of the cash flowing in from revenue over the cash flowing out for expenses is termed **net cash flow**. The time required for the net cash flow to equal the initial outlay for the fixed asset is the payback period.

To illustrate, assume that the proposed investment in a fixed asset with an 8-year life is $200,000. The annual cash revenues from the investment are $50,000, and the annual cash expenses are $10,000. Thus, the annual net cash flow is expected to be $40,000 ($50,000 − $10,000). The estimated cash payback period for the investment is 5 years, computed as follows:

$$\frac{\$200,000}{\$\ 40,000} = \text{5-year cash payback period}$$

In this illustration, the annual net cash flows are equal ($40,000 per year). If these annual net cash flows are *not* equal, the cash payback period is determined by adding the annual net cash flows until the cumulative sum equals the amount of the proposed investment. To illustrate, assume that for a proposed investment of $400,000, the annual net cash flows and the cumulative net cash flows over the proposal's 6-year life are as follows:

Q&A *A project has estimated annual net cash flows of $30,000. It is estimated to cost $105,000. What is the cash payback period?*

3½ years ($105,000 ÷ $30,000)

Year	Net Cash Flow	Cumulative Net Cash Flow
1	$ 60,000	$ 60,000
2	80,000	140,000
3	105,000	245,000
4	155,000	400,000
5	100,000	500,000
6	90,000	590,000

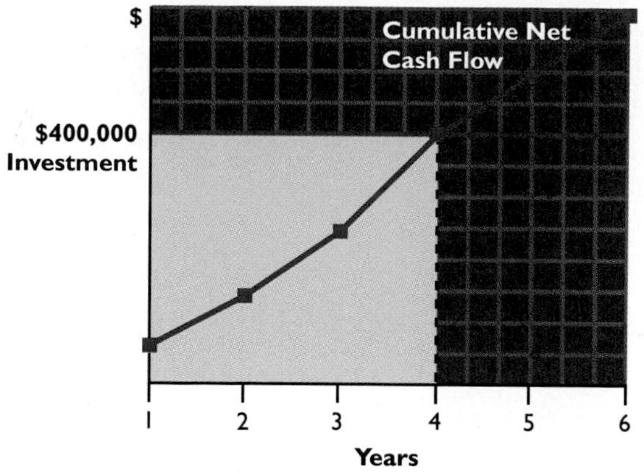

The cumulative net cash flow at the end of the fourth year equals the amount of the investment, $400,000. Thus, the payback period is 4 years. If the amount of the proposed investment had been $450,000, the cash payback period would occur during the fifth year. If the net cash flows are uniform during the period, the cash payback period would be 4½ years.

The cash payback method is widely used in evaluating proposals for investments in new projects. A short payback period is desirable, because the sooner the cash is recovered, the sooner it becomes available for reinvestment in other projects. In addition, there is less possibility of losses from economic conditions, out-of-date assets, and other unavoidable risks when the payback period is short. The cash payback period is also important to bankers and other creditors who may be depending upon net cash flow for repaying debt related to the capital investment. The sooner the cash is recovered, the sooner the debt or other liabilities can be paid. Thus, the cash payback method is especially useful to managers whose primary concern is liquidity.

REAL WORLD

General Electric Corporation has invested over $1.5 billion in research and development for the Boeing 777 jet engine. Due to intense competition from **Pratt & Whitney** and **Rolls Royce**, the prices for 777 jet engines are at about 75% below list prices, or about half of their full cost. As a result, GE now estimates the program's payback period will be at least 10 years. However, management believes that there will be significant profitability from jet engine repairs and overhauls in the long term.

One of the disadvantages of the cash payback method is that it ignores cash flows occurring after the payback period. In addition, the cash payback method does not use present value concepts in valuing cash flows occurring in different periods. In the next section, we will review present value concepts and introduce capital investment methods that use present value.

Present Value Methods

An investment in fixed assets may be viewed as acquiring a series of net cash flows over a period of time. The period of time over which these net cash flows will be received may be an important factor in determining the value of an investment. Present value methods use both the amount and the timing of net cash flows in evaluating an investment. Before illustrating how these methods are used in capital investment analysis, we will review basic present value concepts.[2]

[2] Present value calculations were introduced in accounting for bond liabilities. Present value concepts are developed again here in order to reinforce that introduction.

Point of INTEREST

Present value concepts can also be used to evaluate personal finances. For example, one analyst compared the present value of social security contributions of an average earner (making $24,444) born in 1953 with the present value of social security benefits. Using an interest rate of 6%, the present value of the social security benefits is $268,000 less than the present value of the contributions. For a younger worker or a higher-salary earner, the difference is even greater.

Present Value Concepts

Present value concepts can be divided into the *present value of an amount* and the *present value of an annuity*. We describe and illustrate these two concepts next.

Present Value of an Amount. If you were given the choice, would you prefer to receive $1 now or $1 three years from now? You should prefer to receive $1 now, because you could invest the $1 and earn interest for three years. As a result, the amount you would have after three years would be greater than $1.

To illustrate, assume that on January 1, 2000, you invest $1 in an account that earns 12% interest compounded annually. After one year, the $1 will grow to $1.12 ($1 × 1.12), because interest of 12¢ is added to the investment. The $1.12 earns 12% interest for the second year. Interest earning interest is called **compounding**. By the end of the second year, the investment has grown to $1.254 ($1.12 × 1.12). By the end of the third year, the investment has grown to $1.404 ($1.254 × 1.12). Thus, if money is worth 12%, you would be equally satisfied with $1 on January 1, 2000, or $1.404 three years later.

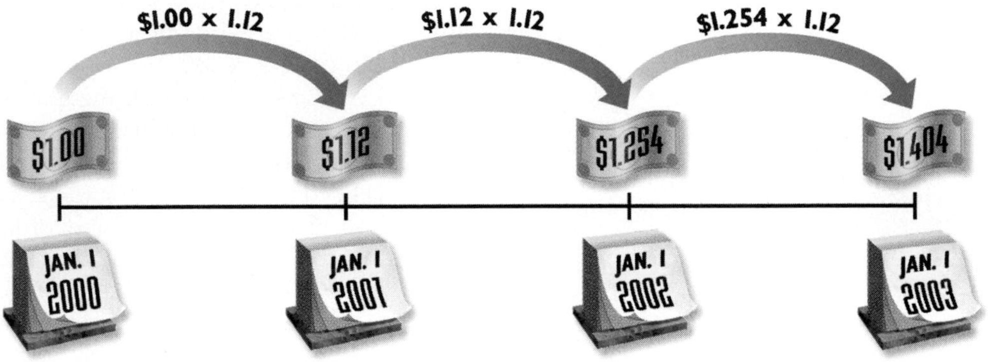

On January 1, 2000, what is the present value of $1.404 to be received on January 1, 2003? This is a present value question. The answer can be determined with the aid of a present value of $1 table. For example, the partial table in Exhibit 1 indicates that the present value of $1 to be received three years hence, with earnings compounded at the rate of 12% a year, is 0.712. Multiplying 0.712 by $1.404 yields $1, which is the present value that started the compounding process.[3]

EXHIBIT 1
Partial Present Value of $1 Table

Present Value of $1 at Compound Interest					
Year	**6%**	**10%**	**12%**	**15%**	**20%**
1	0.943	0.909	0.893	0.870	0.833
2	0.890	0.826	0.797	0.756	0.694
3	0.840	0.751	**0.712**	0.658	0.579
4	0.792	0.683	0.636	0.572	0.482
5	0.747	0.621	0.567	0.497	0.402
6	0.705	0.564	0.507	0.432	0.335
7	0.665	0.513	0.452	0.376	0.279
8	0.627	0.467	0.404	0.327	0.233
9	0.592	0.424	0.361	0.284	0.194
10	0.558	0.386	0.322	0.247	0.162

[3] The present value factors in the table are rounded to three decimal places. More complete tables of both present values and future values are in Appendix A.

Present Value of an Annuity. An **annuity** is a series of equal net cash flows at fixed time intervals. Annuities are very common in business. For example, monthly rental, salary, and bond interest cash flows are all examples of annuities. The **present value of an annuity** is the sum of the present values of each cash flow. In other words, the present value of an annuity is the amount of cash that is needed today to yield a series of equal net cash flows at fixed time intervals in the future.

To illustrate, the present value of a $100 annuity for five periods at 12% could be determined by using the present value factors in Exhibit 1. Each $100 net cash flow could be multiplied by the present value of $1 at 12% factor for the appropriate period and summed to determine a present value of $360.50, as shown in the following timeline:

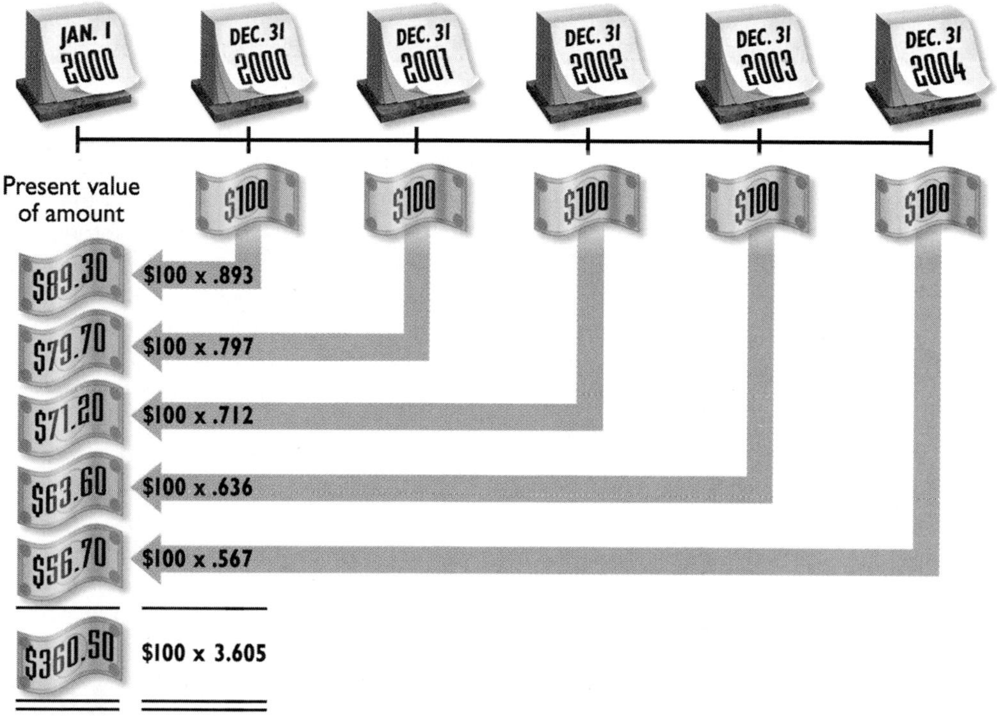

Using a present value of an annuity table is a simpler approach. Exhibit 2 is a partial table of present value of annuity factors.[4] These factors are merely the sum

EXHIBIT 2
Partial Present Value of an Annuity Table

Present Value of an Annuity of $1 at Compound Interest

Year	6%	10%	12%	15%	20%
1	0.943	0.909	0.893	0.870	0.833
2	1.833	1.736	1.690	1.626	1.528
3	2.673	2.487	2.402	2.283	2.106
4	3.465	3.170	3.037	2.855	2.589
5	4.212	3.791	**3.605**	3.353	2.991
6	4.917	4.355	4.111	3.785	3.326
7	5.582	4.868	4.564	4.160	3.605
8	6.210	5.335	4.968	4.487	3.837
9	6.802	5.759	5.328	4.772	4.031
10	7.360	6.145	5.650	5.019	4.192

[4] Expanded tables for the present value of an annuity are in Appendix A.

of the present value of $1 factors in Exhibit 1 for the number of annuity periods. Thus, 3.605 in the annuity table (Exhibit 2) is the sum of the five individual present value of $1 factors at 12%. Multiplying $100 by 3.605 yields the same amount ($360.50) that was determined in the preceding illustration by five successive multiplications.

Net Present Value Method

REAL WORLD A 55-year-old bank janitor won a $5 million lottery jackpot, payable in 21 annual installments of $240,245. Unfortunately, the bank janitor died after collecting only one payment. What happens to the remaining unclaimed payments? In this case, the lottery winnings were auctioned off for the benefit of the janitor's estate. The winning bid approximated the present value of the remaining cash flows, or about $2.1 million.

The **net present value method** analyzes capital investment proposals by comparing the initial cash investment with the present value of the net cash flows. It is sometimes called the **discounted cash flow method**. The interest rate (return) used in net present value analysis is set by management. This rate is often based upon such factors as the nature of the business, the purpose of the investment, the cost of securing funds for the investment, and the minimum desired rate of return. If the net present value of the cash flows expected from a proposed investment equals or exceeds the amount of the initial investment, the proposal is desirable.

The net present value method compares an investment's initial cash outflow with the present value of its cash inflows.

To illustrate, assume a proposal to acquire $200,000 of equipment with an expected useful life of five years (no residual value) and a minimum desired rate of return of 10%. The present value of the net cash flow for each year is computed by multiplying the net cash flow for the year by the present value factor of $1 for that year. For example, the $70,000 net cash flow to be received on December 31, 2000, is multiplied by the present value of $1 for one year at 10% (0.909). Thus, the present value of the $70,000 is $63,630. Likewise, the $60,000 net cash flow on December 31, 2001, is multiplied by the present value of $1 for two years at 10% (0.826) to yield $49,560, and so on. The amount to be invested, $200,000, is then subtracted from the total present value of the net cash flows $202,900, to determine the net present value, $2,900, as shown below. The

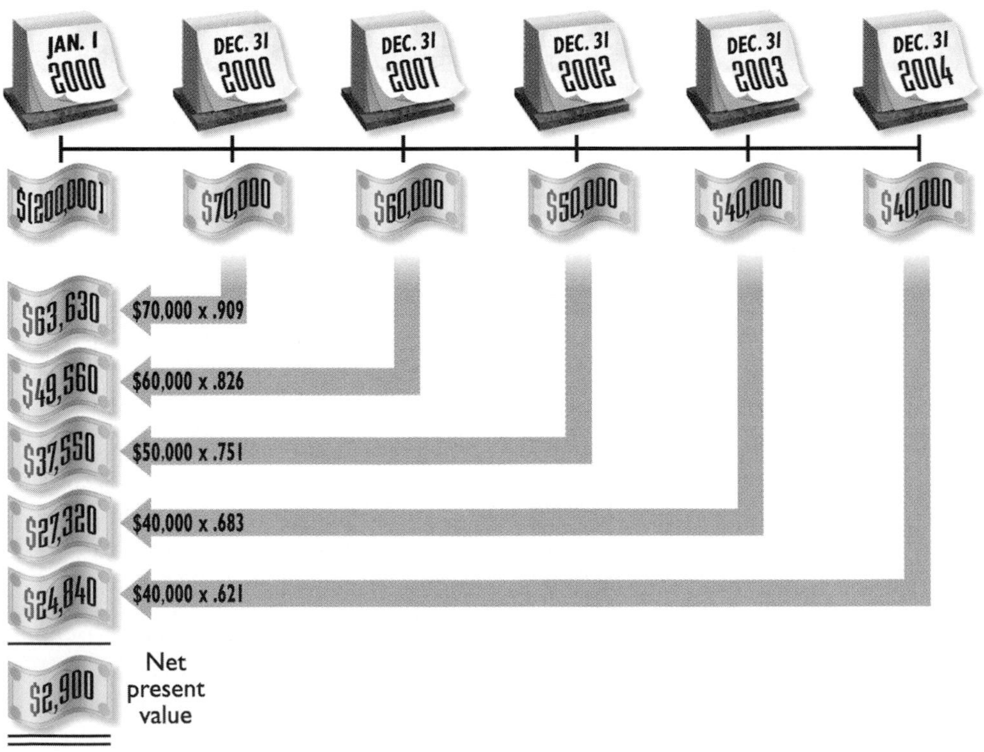

net present value indicates that the proposal is expected to recover the investment and provide more than the minimum rate of return of 10%.

When capital investment funds are limited and the alternative proposals involve different amounts of investment, it is useful to prepare a ranking of the proposals by using a present value index. The **present value index** is calculated by dividing the total present value of the net cash flow by the amount to be invested. The present value index for the investment in the previous illustration is calculated as follows:

$$\textbf{Present value index} = \frac{\textbf{Total present value of net cash flow}}{\textbf{Amount to be invested}}$$

$$= \frac{\$202{,}900}{\$200{,}000} = \mathbf{1.0145}$$

If a business is considering three alternative proposals and has determined their net present values, the present value index for each proposal is as follows:

	Proposal A	**Proposal B**	**Proposal C**
Total present value of net cash flow	$107,000	$86,400	$93,600
Amount to be invested.	100,000	80,000	90,000
Net present value.	$ 7,000	$ 6,400	$ 3,600
Present value index	**1.07** ($107,000 ÷ $100,000)	**1.08** ($86,400 ÷ $80,000)	**1.04** ($93,600 ÷ $90,000)

Although Proposal A has the largest net present value, the present value indices indicate that it is not as desirable as Proposal B. In other words, Proposal B returns $1.08 present value per dollar invested, whereas Proposal A returns only $1.07. Proposal B requires an investment of $80,000, compared to an investment of $100,000 for Proposal A. Management should consider the possible use of the $20,000 difference between Proposal A and Proposal B investments before making a final decision.

An advantage of the net present value method is that it considers the time value of money. A disadvantage is that the computations are more complex than those for the methods that ignore present value. In addition, the net present value method assumes that the cash received from the proposal during its useful life can be reinvested at the rate of return used in computing the present value of the proposal. Because of changing economic conditions, this assumption may not always be reasonable.

A project has estimated annual net cash flows of $50,000 for seven years and is estimated to cost $240,000. Assume a minimum rate of return of 12%. For this project, what is the (1) net present value and (2) present value index? (3) Should the project be accepted, based on this analysis?

(1) ($11,800) [($50,000 × 4.564) − $240,000]; (2) 0.95 (rounded) ($228,200 ÷ $240,000); (3) No.

How does a company like **Marriott Corporation** determine when and where to build a new hotel? Marriott will first identify a likely site for the hotel. The site is evaluated with respect to the estimated cash flows from the hotel rooms. In addition, Marriott considers the cash flows of building the hotel. For example, Marriott built a "western" style hotel in Warsaw, Poland at a modest cost, due to favorable land and construction costs. As eastern Europe's business opportunities grow, this hotel is often booked to capacity, providing a positive net present value on Marriott's investment.

Internal Rate of Return Method

The **internal rate of return method** uses present value concepts to compute the rate of return from the net cash flows expected from capital investment proposals. This method is sometimes called the **time-adjusted rate of return method**. It is similar to the net present value method, in that it focuses on the present value of the net cash flows. However, the internal rate of return method starts with the net cash flows and, in a sense, works backwards to determine the rate of return expected from the proposal.

To illustrate, assume that management is evaluating a proposal to acquire equipment costing $33,530. The equipment is expected to provide annual net cash flows of $10,000 per year for five years. If we assume a rate of return of 12%, we can calculate the present value of the net cash flows, using the present value of an annuity table in Exhibit 2. These calculations are shown in Exhibit 3.

EXHIBIT 3
Net Present Value Analysis at 12%

Annual net cash flow (at the end of each of five years)	$10,000
Present value of an annuity of $1 at 12% for 5 years (Exhibit 2)	× 3.605
Present value of annual net cash flows	$36,050
Less amount to be invested	33,530
Net present value	$ 2,520

In Exhibit 3, the $36,050 present value of the cash inflows, based on a 12% rate of return, is greater than the $33,530 to be invested. Therefore, the internal rate of return must be greater than 12%. Through trial-and-error procedures, the rate of return that equates the $33,530 cost of the investment with the present value of the net cash flows is determined to be 15%, as shown below.

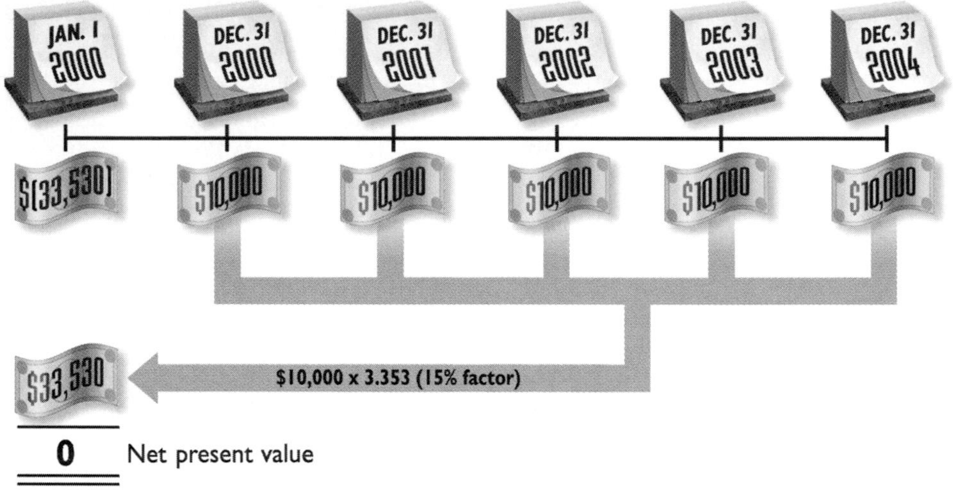

Such trial-and-error procedures are time-consuming. However, when equal annual net cash flows are expected from a proposal, as in the illustration, the calculations are simplified by using the following procedures:[5]

1. Determine a present value factor for an annuity of $1 by dividing the amount to be invested by the equal annual net cash flows, as follows:

$$\textbf{Present value factor for an annuity of \$1} = \frac{\textbf{Amount to be invested}}{\textbf{Equal annual net cash flows}}$$

2. In the present value of an annuity of $1 table, locate the present value factor determined in (1). First locate the number of years of expected useful life of the investment in the Year column, and then proceed horizontally across the table until you find the present value factor computed in (1).
3. Identify the internal rate of return by the heading of the column in which the present value factor in (2) is located.

[5] Equal annual net cash flows are assumed in order to simplify the illustration. If the annual net cash flows are not equal, the calculations are more complex, but the basic concepts are the same.

To illustrate, assume that management is considering a proposal to acquire equipment costing $97,360. The equipment is expected to provide equal annual net cash flows of $20,000 for seven years. The present value factor for an annuity of $1 is **4.868**, calculated as follows:

Present value factor for an annuity of $1

$$= \frac{\text{Amount to be invested}}{\text{Equal annual net cash flows}}$$

$$= \frac{\$97{,}360}{\$20{,}000} = \mathbf{4.868}$$

Q&A

What is the internal rate of return for a project estimated to cost $208,175 and provide annual net cash flows of $55,000 for six years?

15% ($208,175 ÷ $55,000 = 3.785, the present value of an annuity factor for six periods at 15%)

For a period of seven years, the partial present value of an annuity of $1 table indicates that the factor **4.868** is related to a percentage of **10%**, as shown below. Thus, 10% is the internal rate of return for this proposal.

Present Value of an Annuity of $1 at Compound Interest

Year	6%	10%	12%
1	0.943	0.909	0.893
2	1.833	1.736	1.690
3	2.673	2.487	2.402
4	3.465	3.170	3.037
5	4.212	3.791	3.605
6	4.917	4.355	4.111
7	5.582	**4.868**	4.564
8	6.210	5.335	4.968
9	6.802	5.759	5.328
10	7.360	6.145	5.650

If the minimum acceptable rate of return for similar proposals is 10% or less, then the proposed investment should be considered acceptable. When several proposals are considered, management often ranks the proposals by their internal rates of return. The proposal with the highest rate is considered the most desirable.

REAL WORLD

The minimum acceptable rate of return (often termed the *hurdle rate*) for **Owens-Corning Fiberglass** is 18%; for **General Electric**, it is 20%. David Devonshire, CFO of Owens-Corning, states, "I'm here to challenge anyone—even the CEO—who gets emotionally attached to a project that doesn't reach our benchmark."

The primary advantage of the internal rate of return method is that the present values of the net cash flows over the entire useful life of the proposal are considered. In addition, by determining a rate of return for each proposal, all proposals are compared on a common basis. The primary disadvantage of the internal rate of return method is that the computations are more complex than for some of the other methods. However, spreadsheet software programs have internal rate of return functions that simplify the calculation. Also, like the net present value method, this method assumes that the cash received from a proposal during its useful life will be reinvested at the internal rate of return. Because of changing economic conditions, this assumption may not always be reasonable.

Business on Stage

Capital investment analysis often requires managers to assess whether a proposed investment meets a minimum rate of return. This minimum rate of return is often the cost of capital of the business. Investments that provide rates of return less than the cost of capital should normally be rejected.

The **cost of capital** for a business is the cost of financing its long-term operations. If a business financed all its operations by issuing common stock, its cost of capital would be the rate of return that the common stockholders demanded from their investments. Most businesses, however, use a combination of financing that includes common stock, preferred stock, and various types of debt. The costs of these common components are briefly described below.

- The cost of various types of debt is expressed in terms of its after-tax interest rate. For example, if debt has an interest rate of 10% and the business's tax rate is 40%, the after-tax interest rate is 6% [10% × (1 − 40%)]. The cost of debt financing is expressed after tax because interest is tax deductible in determining tax expense.
- The cost of preferred stock is expressed as the preferred dividends divided by the issuing price (proceeds) of the preferred stock. Since preferred dividends are not tax deductible, no after-tax adjustments are necessary.
- The cost of common stock and retained earnings is expressed as the rate of return that stockholders demand from their investments. This return reflects what stockholders could earn from other comparable investments.

The overall cost of capital for a business is determined by weighting the costs of each of the financing components. Once determined, the overall cost of capital is used in deciding which capital investment alternatives to implement. ■

Factors That Complicate Capital Investment Analysis

OBJECTIVE 3

List and describe factors that complicate capital investment analysis.

In the preceding discussion, we described four widely used methods of evaluating capital investment proposals. In practice, additional factors may have an impact on the outcome of a capital investment decision. In the following paragraphs, we discuss some of the most important of these factors: the federal income tax, unequal lives of alternative proposals, leasing, uncertainty, changes in price levels, and qualitative factors.

Income Tax

In many cases, the impact of the federal income tax on capital investment decisions can be material. For example, in determining depreciation for federal income tax purposes, useful lives that are much shorter than the actual useful lives are often used. Also, depreciation can be calculated by methods that approximate the 200-percent declining-balance method. Thus, depreciation for tax purposes often exceeds the depreciation for financial statement purposes in the early years of an asset's use. The tax reduction in these early years is offset by higher taxes in the later years, so that accelerated depreciation does not result in a long-run saving in taxes. However, the timing of the cash outflows for income taxes can have a significant impact on capital investment analysis.[6]

Unequal Proposal Lives

In the preceding discussion, the illustrations of the methods of analyzing capital investment proposals were based on the assumption that alternative proposals had the same useful lives. In practice, however, alternative proposals may have unequal lives.

[6] The impact of income taxes on capital investment analysis is described and illustrated in advanced textbooks.

To illustrate, assume that alternative investments, a truck and computers, are being compared. The truck has a useful life of 8 years, and the computer network has a useful life of 5 years. Each proposal requires an initial investment of $100,000, and the company desires a rate of return of 10%. The expected cash flows and net present value of each alternative are shown in Exhibit 4. Because of the unequal useful lives of the two proposals, however, the net present values in Exhibit 4 are not comparable.

To make the proposals comparable for the analysis, they can be adjusted to end at the same time. This can be done by assuming that the truck is to be sold at the end of 5 years. The residual value of the truck must be estimated at the end of 5 years, and this value must then be included as a cash flow at that date. Both proposals will then cover 5 years, and net present value analysis can be used to compare the two proposals over the same 5-year period. If the truck's estimated residual value is $40,000 at the end of year 5, the net present value for the truck exceeds the net present value for the computers by $1,835 ($18,640 − $16,805), as shown in Exhibit 5. Therefore, the truck may be viewed as the more attractive of the two proposals.

EXHIBIT 4 Net Present Value Analysis

Truck

Year	Present Value of $1 at 10%	Net Cash Flow	Present Value of Net Cash Flow
1	0.909	$ 30,000	$ 27,270
2	0.826	30,000	24,780
3	0.751	25,000	18,775
4	0.683	20,000	13,660
5	0.621	15,000	9,315
6	0.564	15,000	8,460
7	0.513	10,000	5,130
8	0.467	10,000	4,670
Total		$155,000	$112,060
Amount to be invested			100,000
Net present value			$ 12,060

Computers

Year	Present Value of $1 at 10%	Net Cash Flow	Present Value of Net Cash Flow
1	0.909	$ 30,000	$ 27,270
2	0.826	30,000	24,780
3	0.751	30,000	22,530
4	0.683	30,000	20,490
5	0.621	35,000	21,735
Total		$155,000	$116,805
Amount to be invested			100,000
Net present value			$ 16,805

EXHIBIT 5
Net Present Value Analysis

Truck—Revised to 5-Year Life

Year	Present Value of $1 at 10%	Net Cash Flow	Present Value of Net Cash Flow
1	0.909	$ 30,000	$ 27,270
2	0.826	30,000	24,780
3	0.751	25,000	18,775
4	0.683	20,000	13,660
5	0.621	15,000	9,315
5 (Residual value)	0.621	40,000	24,840
Total		$160,000	$118,640
Amount to be invested			100,000
Net present value			$ 18,640

Truck NPV > Computers NPV

Lease Versus Capital Investment

Leasing fixed assets has become common in many industries. For example, hospitals often lease diagnostic and other medical equipment. Leasing allows a business to use fixed assets without spending large amounts of cash to purchase them. In addition, management may believe that a fixed asset has a high risk of becoming obsolete. This risk may be reduced by leasing rather than purchasing the asset. Also, the *Internal Revenue Code* allows the lessor (the owner of the asset) to pass tax deductions on to the lessee (the party leasing the asset). These provisions of the tax law have made leasing assets more attractive. For example, a company that pays $50,000 per year for leasing a $200,000 fixed asset with a life of 8 years is permitted to deduct from taxable income the annual lease payments.

In many cases, before a final decision is made, management should consider leasing assets instead of purchasing them. Normally, leasing assets is more costly than purchasing because the lessor must include in the rental price not only the costs associated with owning the assets but also a profit. Nevertheless, using the methods of evaluating capital investment proposals, management should consider whether it is more profitable to lease rather than purchase an asset.

Uncertainty

All capital investment analyses rely on factors that are uncertain. For example, the estimates related to revenues, expenses, and cash flows are uncertain. The long-term nature of capital investments suggests that some estimates are likely to involve uncertainty. Errors in one or more of the estimates could lead to incorrect decisions.

REAL WORLD

Merck, a major pharmaceutical company, at one time questioned whether developing new drugs was good business. New drugs in the research and development pipeline seemed to barely earn the minimum acceptable rate of return. However, Judy Lewent, Merck's CFO, insisted on using uncertainty in analyzing drugs under research and development. She understood that a single hit would pay for the investment costs of many failures. She used a technique in probability theory, called *Monte Carlo analysis,* which showed that the drugs under development were actually very profitable.

Changes in Price Levels

Periods of increasing price levels are described as periods of **inflation**. In recent years, the rates of inflation have varied widely, making the estimation of future revenues, expenses, and cash flows even more difficult. Management should, however, attempt to anticipate future price levels and consider their effects on the estimates used in capital investment analyses. Changes in anticipated price levels could significantly affect the analyses.

Qualitative Considerations

Some benefits of capital investments are qualitative in nature and cannot be easily estimated in dollar terms. If management does not consider these qualitative considerations, the quantitative analyses may suggest rejecting a worthy investment.

Qualitative considerations in capital investment analysis are most appropriate for strategic investments. Strategic investments are those that are designed to affect a company's long-term ability to generate profits. Strategic investments often have many uncertainties and intangible benefits. Unlike capital investments that are designed to cut costs, strategic investments have very few "hard" savings. Instead, they may affect future revenues, which are difficult to estimate. An example of a strategic investment is **Nucor's** decision to be the first to invest in a new continuous cast-

INTERMISSION

Capital investment analysis may not be useful in evaluating all investments. Such investments are usually strategic decisions involving a high degree of uncertainty. Often the investments have no historical precedent, so benefits are very difficult to estimate. An example would be **Matsushita's** (JVC and Panasonic brand names) fifteen-year quest to develop the video cassette recorder and VHS tape. Such a long-term decision was probably not evaluated using traditional capital investment analysis. The product and market didn't even exist when Matsushita began its investments. Thus, the size of the potential market could not be accurately estimated. Indeed, Matsushita states that this investment was based on its *belief* that customers would value "time shifting." In other words, customers would value a product that would allow viewing times for their favorite movies or TV shows to be shifted to times that would suit them. As it turns out, this strategic investment eventually paid off well for Matsushita.

The importance of considering qualitative aspects of capital investments is best summarized by John H. McConnell, Chairman of **Worthington Industries**, who stated, "We try to find the best technology, stay ahead of the competition, and serve the customer . . . We'll make any investment that will pay back quickly . . . but if it is something that we really see as a must down the road, payback is not going to be that important." ■

Source: Joseph Morone and Albert Paulson, "Cost of Capital: The Managerial Perspective," *California Management Review*, Summer 1991, pp. 9–32.

ing technology that had the potential to make thin gauge sheet steel and thus open new product markets. Nucor's new investment was justified more on the strategic importance of the investment than on the economic analysis. As it turned out, the investment was very successful.

Qualitative considerations that may influence capital investment analysis include product quality, manufacturing flexibility, employee morale, manufacturing productivity, and manufacturing control. Many of these qualitative factors may be as important, if not more important, than the results of quantitative analysis.

REAL WORLD

Intel Corporation makes the processor chip that goes into laptop and desktop computers. In 1996, Intel spent $5 billion on capital projects and research and development. Each chip fabrication plant costs around $2 billion—and Intel has been building one every year or so. How does Intel justify these investments? Intel's president, Craig Barrett, states, "We build factories two years in advance of needing them, before we have the product to run in them, and before we know the industry's going to grow." Andy Grove, CEO of Intel, adds, "Our fabs are fields of dreams. We build them and hope people will come." So far, Intel has been right. At $5.2 billion in profits, Intel ranks as the fifth most profitable company in the United States.

Capital Rationing

OBJECTIVE 4

Diagram the capital rationing process.

Funding for capital projects may be obtained from issuing bonds or stock or from operating cash. **Capital rationing** is the process by which management allocates these funds among competing capital investment proposals. In this process, management often uses a combination of the methods described in this chapter.

In capital rationing, alternative proposals are initially screened by establishing minimum standards for the cash payback and the average rate of return. The proposals that survive this screening are further analyzed, using the net present value and internal rate of return methods. Throughout the capital rationing process, qualitative factors related to each proposal should also be considered. For example, the acquisition of new, more efficient equipment that eliminates several jobs could lower employee morale to a level that could decrease overall plant productivity. Alternatively, new equipment might improve the quality of the product and thus increase consumer satisfaction and sales.

The final steps in the capital rationing process are ranking the proposals according to management's criteria, comparing the proposals with the funds available, and selecting the proposals to be funded. Funded proposals are included in the **capital expenditures budget** to aid the planning and financing of operations. Unfunded proposals may be reconsidered if funds later become available. Exhibit 6 portrays the capital rationing decision process.

EXHIBIT 6
Capital Rationing Decision Process

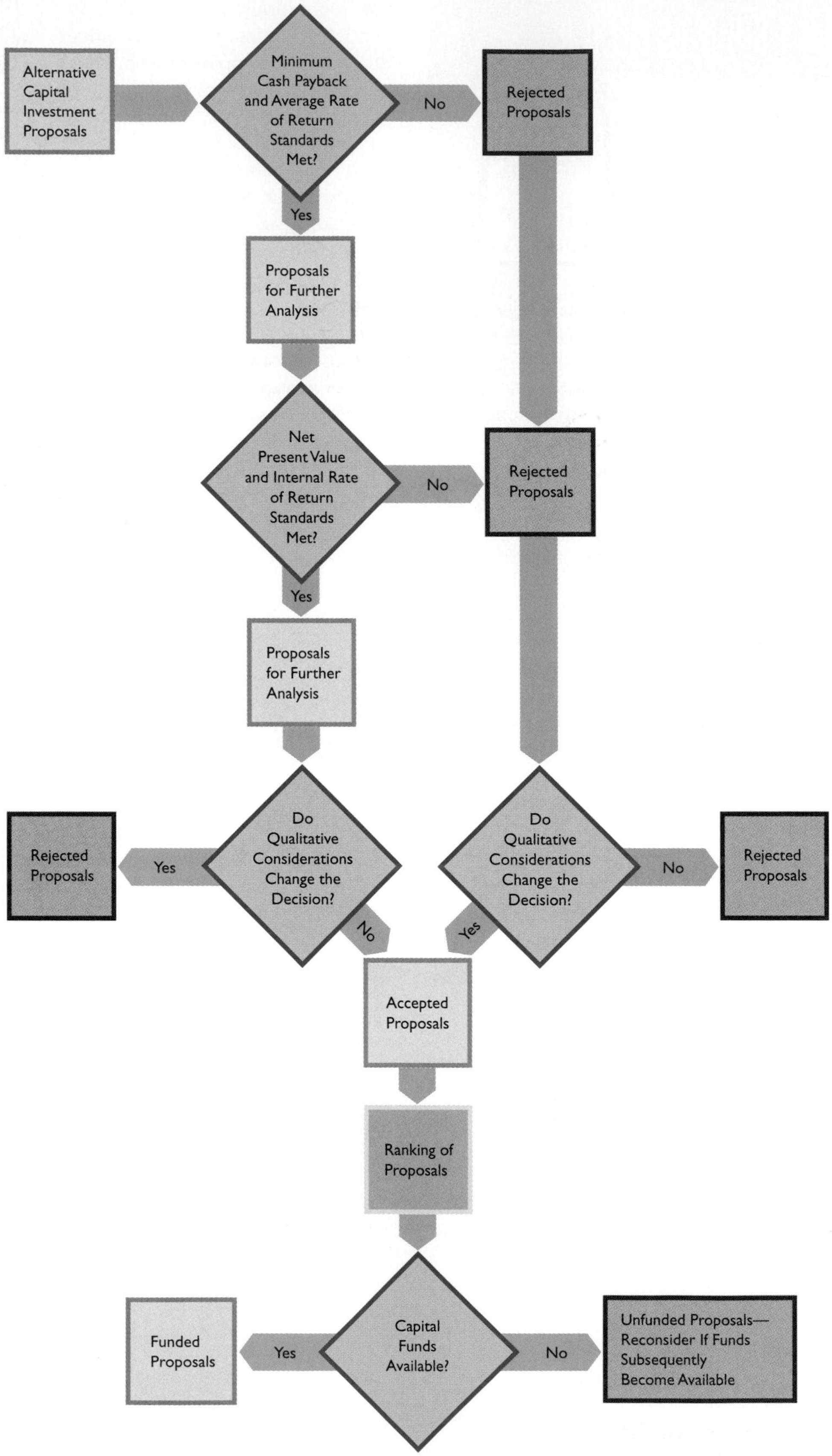

ENCORE

The $120 Million Man

In 1996, Shaq O'Neal signed a seven-year contract with the **LA Lakers** for $120 million. How can the Lakers afford such huge sums? As owner Jerry Buss states, "We certainly hope it'll pay for itself. There's a lot of ingredients that go into it." To begin, the Lakers have already experienced benefits from the deal. Prior to Shaq joining the team, the average attendance at the Forum was 15,845 fans. Now the 17,506-seat Forum sells out regularly. In addition, ticket prices were increased from $9.50 to $21 for regular seats, and from $500 to $600 for courtside seats. However, Shaq's contract begins at $10.6 million for the 1996 season, but escalates upward during the contract's life. By the 2003 season Shaq will be earning over twice this amount, so the deal has to have some big payoffs down the road.

In 1999, the Lakers expect to move into a new arena with 2,500 more seats, luxury boxes, and club seating. Ratings on basketball broadcasts are already climbing, due to Shaq. Ratings translate into dollars, so that the Lakers expect broadcast income to climb significantly during Shaq's contract period. Lastly, the real money is made on basketball's second season (the playoffs). Buss hopes that Shaq will propel the Lakers into the playoffs, where additional sellout games will translate into hefty cash flows.

There has, however, been one small casualty. **Coca-Cola** has declined to renew its contract with the Lakers, thus removing Coke as the Laker's official soft drink. This is because Shaq has a major sponsorship agreement with **PepsiCo**. No matter, since Pepsi has stepped in and is now poured as the Forum's official soft drink.

How will this all work out for Jerry Buss and the Lakers? Only time will tell. As Buss says, "If this were a one-shot deal, if you were thinking about signing the guy and thinking you'd have him only for a year, that's a deal that wouldn't work, . . . you wouldn't get your investment back. . . . You've got to have that special guy, and Shaq is that special guy." ■

KEY POINTS

1 Explain the nature and importance of capital investment analysis.

Capital investment analysis is the process by which management plans, evaluates, and controls investments involving fixed assets. Capital investment analysis is important to a business because such investments affect profitability for a long period of time.

2 Evaluate capit... ment prop... following... rate of ... back, net present value, and internal rate of return.

The average rate of return method measures the expected profitability of an investment in fixed assets. It is calculated using the following formula:

$$\text{Average rate of return} = \frac{\text{Estimated average annual income}}{\text{Average investment}}$$

...cted period of time ...n the date ...he complete recovery in cash (or equivalent) of the amount invested is the cash payback period. Investment proposals with the shortest cash payback are considered the most desirable.

The net present value method uses present values to compute the net present value of the cash flows expected from a proposal. The net present value of the cash flows are then compared across proposals. The present value of a cash flow is computed by looking up the present value of $1 from a table of present values and multiplying it by the amount of the future cash flow, as shown in the text.

The internal rate of return method uses present values to compute the rate of return from the net cash flows expected from capital investment proposals. When equal annual net cash flows are expected from a proposal, the computations are simplified by using a table of the present value of an annuity, as shown in the text.

3 List and describe factors that complicate capital investment analysis.
Factors that may complicate capital investment analysis include the impact of the federal income tax, unequal lives of alternative proposals, leasing, uncertainty, changes in price levels, and qualitative considerations. A brief description of the effect of each of these factors appears in the text.

4 Diagram the capital rationing process.
Capital rationing refers to the process by which management allocates available investment funds among competing capital investment proposals. A diagram of the capital rationing process appears in Exhibit 6.

ILLUSTRATIVE PROBLEM

The capital investment committee of Hopewell Company is currently considering two projects. The estimated income from operations and net cash flows expected from each project are as follows:

	Project A		Project B	
Year	Income from Operations	Net Cash Flow	Income from Operations	Net Cash Flow
1	$ 6,000	$ 22,000	$13,000	$ 29,000
2	9,000	25,000	10,000	26,000
3	10,000	26,000	8,000	24,000
4	8,000	24,000	8,000	24,000
5	11,000	27,000	3,000	19,000
	$44,000	$124,000	$42,000	$122,000

Each project requires an investment of $80,000. Straight-line depreciation will be used, and no residual value is expected. The committee has selected a rate of 15% for purposes of the net present value analysis.

Instructions

1. Compute the following:
   a. The average rate of return for each project, giving effect to depreciation on the investment.
   b. The net present value for each project. Use the present value of $1 table appearing in this chapter.
2. Why is the net present value of Project B greater than Project A, even though its average rate of return is less?
3. Prepare a summary for the capital investment committee, advising it on the relative merits of the two projects.

Solution

1. a. Average rate of return for Project A:

$$\frac{\$44{,}000 \div 5}{(\$80{,}000 + \$0) \div 2} = 22\%$$

Average rate of return for Project

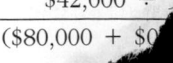

$$\frac{\$42{,}000 \div 5}{(\$80{,}000 + \$0}$$

b. Net present value analysis:

Year	Present Value of $1 at 15%	Net Cash Flow Project A	Net Cash Flow Project B	Present Value of Net Cash Flow Project A	Present Value of Net Cash Flow Project B
1	0.870	$ 22,000	$ 29,000	$19,140	$25,230
2	0.756	25,000	26,000	18,900	19,656
3	0.658	26,000	24,000	17,108	15,792
4	0.572	24,000	24,000	13,728	13,728
5	0.497	27,000	19,000	13,419	9,443
Total		$124,000	$122,000	$82,295	$83,849
Amount to be invested				80,000	80,000
Net present value				$ 2,295	$ 3,849

2. Project B has a lower average rate of return than Project A because Project B's total income from operations for the five years is $42,000, which is $2,000 less than Project A's. Even so, the net present value of Project B is greater than that of Project A, because Project B has higher cash flows in the early years.

3. Both projects exceed the selected rate established for the net present value analysis. Project A has a higher average rate of return, but Project B offers a larger net present value. Thus, if only one of the two projects can be accepted, Project B would be the more attractive.

SELF-EXAMINATION QUESTIONS

Answers at End of Chapter

Matching

Match each of the following statements with its proper term. Some terms may not be used.

- **A.** **annuity**
- **B.** **average rate of return**
- **C.** **capital investment analysis**
- **D.** **capital rationing**
- **E.** **cash payback period**
- **F.** **deflation**
- **G.** **inflation**
- **H.** **internal rate of return method**
- **I.** **net present value method**
- **J.** **present value concept**
- **K.** **present value index**
- **L.** **present value of an annuity**
- **M.** **time value of money concept**

H 1. A method of analysis of proposed capital investments that focuses on using present value concepts to compute the rate of return from the net cash flows expected from the investment.

K 2. An index computed by dividing the total present value of the net cash flow to be received from a proposed capital investment by the amount to be invested.

A 3. A series of equal cash flows at fixed intervals.

E 4. The expected period of time that will elapse between the date of a capital expenditure and the complete recovery in cash (or equivalent) of the amount invested.

M 5. The concept that an amount of money invested today will earn interest.

I 6. A method of analysis of proposed capital investments that focuses on the present value of the cash flows expected from the investments.

L 7. The sum of the present values of a series of equal cash flows to be received at fixed intervals.

C 8. The process by which management plans, evaluates, and controls long-term capital investments involving fixed assets.

G 9. A period when prices in general are rising and the purchasing power of money is declining.

J 10. Cash today is not the equivalent of the same amount of money to be received in the future.

D 11. The process by which management allocates available investment funds among competing capital investment proposals.

B 12. A method of evaluating capital investment proposals that focuses on the expected profitability of the investment.

Multiple Choice

1. Methods of evaluating capital investment proposals that ignore present value include:
   A. average rate of return
   B. cash payback
   C. both A and B
   D. neither A nor B

2. Management is considering a $100,000 investment in a project with a 5-year life and no residual value. If the total income from the project is expected to be $60,000 and recognition is given to the effect of straight-line depreciation on the investment, the average rate of return is:
   A. 12%
   B. 24%
   C. 60%
   D. 75%

3. The expected period of time that will elapse between the date of a capital investment and the complete recovery of the amount of cash invested is called:
   A. the average rate of return period
   B. the cash payback period
   C. the net present value period
   D. the internal rate of return period

4. A project that will cost $120,000 is estimated to generate cash flows of $25,000 per year for eight years. What is the net present value of the project, assuming an 11% required rate of return? (Use the present value tables in Appendix A.)
   A. $(38,214)
   B. $8,653
   C. $55,180
   D. $75,000

5. A project is estimated to generate cash flows of $40,000 per year for 10 years. The cost of the project is $226,009. What is the internal rate of return for this project?
   A. 8%
   B. 10%
   C. 12%
   D. 14%

CLASS DISCUSSION QUESTIONS

1. Which two methods of capital investment analysis ignore present value?
2. Which two methods of capital investment analysis can be described as present value methods?
3. How is the average rate of return computed for capital investment analysis, assuming that the effect of straight-line depreciation on the amount of the investment is considered?
4. What are the principal objections to the use of the average rate of return method in evaluating capital investment proposals?
5. Discuss the principal limitations of the cash payback method for evaluating capital investment proposals.
6. Which method of evaluating capital investment proposals reduces their expected future net cash flows to present values and compares the total present values to the amount of the investment?
7. A net present value analysis used to evaluate a proposed equipment acquisition indicated a $9,750 net present value. What is the meaning of the $9,750 as it relates to the desirability of the proposal?
8. How is the present value index for a proposal determined?
9. What are the major disadvantages of the use of the net present value method of analyzing capital investment proposals?
10. What are the major disadvantages of the use of the internal rate of return method of analyzing capital investment proposals?
11. What provision of the Internal Revenue Code is especially important to consider in analyzing capital investment proposals?
12. What method can be used to place two capital investment proposals with unequal useful lives on a comparable basis?
13. What are the major advantages of leasing a fixed asset rather than purchasing it?
14. Give an example of a qualitative factor that should be considered in a capital investment analysis related to acquiring automated factory equipment.
15. **Monsanto**, a large chemical and fibers company, invested $37 million in state-of-the-art systems to improve process control, laboratory automation, and local area network (LAN) communications. The investment was not justified merely on cost savings, but was also justified on the basis of qualitative considerations. Monsanto

management viewed the investment as a critical element toward achieving its vision of the future. What qualitative and quantitative considerations do you believe Monsanto would have considered in its strategic evaluation of these investments?

Warren Reeve Fess

Resources for Your Success On-Line at warren.swcollege.com

Remember! If you need additional help, visit South-Western's Web site. See page 26 for a description of the online and printed materials that are available.

EXERCISES

Exercise 24–1
Average rate of return

Objective 2

✓ Turning machine, 18%

The following data are accumulated by Miska Machining Company in evaluating two competing capital investment proposals:

	Turning Machine	Milling Machine
Amount of investment	$650,000	$760,000
Useful life	8 years	5 years
Estimated residual value	-0-	-0-
Estimated total income	$468,000	$380,000

Determine the expected average rate of return for each proposal, giving effect to straight-line depreciation on each investment.

Exercise 24–2
Average rate of return—cost savings

Objective 2

✓ 21%

Sprouse Company is considering an investment in equipment that will replace direct labor. The equipment has a cost of $64,000, with a $6,000 residual value and an 8-year life. The equipment will replace one employee who has an average wage of $24,000 per year. In addition, the equipment will have operating and energy costs of $9,400 per year.

Determine the average rate of return on the equipment.

Exercise 24–3
Average rate of return—new product

Objective 2

✓ 16%

Glow Right Lighting Company is considering an investment in new equipment that will be used to manufacture a desk lamp. The desk lamp is expected to generate additional annual sales of 3,000 units at $72 per unit. The equipment has a cost of $290,000, residual value of $10,000, and a 10-year life. The equipment can only be used to manufacture the desk lamp. The cost to manufacture the lamp is shown below.

Cost per unit:	
Direct labor	$20.00
Direct materials	32.00
Factory overhead (including depreciation)	12.00
Total cost per unit	$64.00

Determine the average rate of return on the equipment.

Exercise 24–4
Calculate cash flows

Objective 2

Spring Colours Inc. is planning to invest $230,000 in a new garden product that is expected to generate additional sales of 12,500 units at $16 each. The $230,000 investment includes $55,000 for initial launch-related expenses and $175,000 for equipment that has a 15-year life and a $25,000 residual value. Selling expenses related to the new product are expected to be 4% of sales revenue. The cost to manufacture the product includes the following per unit costs:

Direct labor	$ 4.00
Direct materials	6.50
Fixed factory overhead—depreciation	0.80
Variable factory overhead	1.50
Total	$12.80

Determine the net cash flows for the first year of the project, years 2–14, and for the last year of the project.

Exercise 24–5
Cash payback period
Objective 2

✓ Proposal 1: 4 years

Security Atlantic Bank Corporation is evaluating two capital investment proposals for a drive-up ATM, each requiring an investment of $200,000 and each with an 8-year life and expected total net cash flows of $400,000. Location 1 is expected to provide equal annual net cash flows of $50,000, and Location 2 is expected to have the following unequal annual net cash flows:

Year 1	$90,000	Year 5	$40,000
Year 2	60,000	Year 6	40,000
Year 3	50,000	Year 7	40,000
Year 4	40,000	Year 8	40,000

Determine the cash payback period for both proposals.

Exercise 24–6
Cash payback method
Objective 2

✓ a. Product 2: 4 years

Kim-Klark Consumer Products Company is considering an investment in one of two new product offerings. The investment required for either product is $420,000. The net cash flows associated with each product are as follows:

	Product 1	Product 2
Year 1	$ 70,000	$105,000
2	80,000	105,000
3	90,000	105,000
4	90,000	105,000
5	90,000	105,000
6	120,000	105,000
7	140,000	105,000
8	160,000	105,000
Total	$840,000	$840,000

a. Recommend a product offering to Kim-Klark Consumer Products Company, based on the cash payback period for each product.
b. Why is one product offering preferred over the other, even though they both have the same total net cash flows through eight periods?

Exercise 24–7
Net present value method
Objective 2

✓ a. NPV $40,370

The following data are accumulated by Snap-Top Container Company in evaluating the purchase of $240,000 of equipment, having a 4-year useful life:

	Net Income	Net Cash Flow
Year 1	$60,000	$120,000
Year 2	30,000	90,000
Year 3	20,000	80,000
Year 4	10,000	70,000

a. Assuming that the desired rate of return is 12%, determine the net present value for the proposal. Use the table of the present value of $1 appearing in this chapter.
b. Would management be likely to look with favor on the proposal? Explain.

Exercise 24–8
Net present value method—annuity
Objective 2

Pyramid Construction Company is planning an investment of $174,000 for a bulldozer. The bulldozer is expected to operate for 1,400 hours per year for five years. Customers will be charged $80 per hour for bulldozer work. The bulldozer operator is paid an hourly wage of $26 per hour. The bulldozer is expected to require annual maintenance

✓ a. $42,600

costing $5,000. The bulldozer uses fuel that is expected to cost $20 per hour of bulldozer operation.

a. Determine the equal annual net cash flows from operating the bulldozer.
b. Determine the net present value of the investment, assuming that the desired rate of return is 10%. Use the table of present values of an annuity of $1 in the chapter. Round to the nearest dollar.
c. Should Pyramid invest in the bulldozer, based on this analysis?

Exercise 24–9
Net present value—unequal lives

Objective 2

✓ Net present value, Proposal A, $9,434

Eden Development Company has two competing investments, Proposal A and Proposal B. Proposals A and B have an initial investment of $175,000. The net cash flows estimated for the two investments are as follows:

	Net Cash Flow	
Year	Proposal A	Proposal B
1	$62,000	$65,000
2	54,000	60,000
3	45,000	60,000
4	35,000	55,000
5	22,000	
6	20,000	
7	20,000	
8	18,000	

The estimated residual value of Proposal A at the end of year 4 is $70,000.

Determine which proposal should be favored, comparing the net present values of the two investments and assuming a minimum rate of return of 15%. Use the table of present values in the chapter.

Exercise 24–10
Present value index

Objective 2

✓ Proposal A, 0.96

Clear Sight Glass Company has computed the net present value for capital expenditure proposals A and B, using the net present value method. Relevant data related to the computation are as follows:

	Proposal A	Proposal B
Total present value of net cash flow	$576,000	$244,800
Amount to be invested	600,000	240,000
Net present value	$(24,000)	$ 4,800

Determine the present value index for each proposal.

Exercise 24–11
Net present value method and present value index

Objective 2

✓ b. Packing Machine, 1.10

Olympic Sporting Goods Company is considering an investment in one of two machines. The sewing machine will increase productivity from sewing 120 baseballs per hour to sewing 160 per hour. The contribution margin is $0.60 per baseball. Assume that any increased production of baseballs can be sold. The second machine is an automatic packaging machine for the golf ball line. The packaging machine will reduce packing labor cost. The labor cost saved is equivalent to $20 per hour. The sewing machine will cost $200,000, have an 8-year life, and will operate for 2,000 hours per year. The packing machine will cost $130,000, have an 8-year life, and will operate for 1,600 hours per year. Olympic seeks a minimum rate of return of 15% on its investments.

a. Determine the net present value for the two machines. Use the table of present values of an annuity of $1 in the chapter.
b. Determine the present value index for the two machines. Round to 2 decimal places.
c. If Olympic only has sufficient funds for one of the machines, and qualitative factors are equal between the two machines, in which machine should it invest?

Exercise 24–12
Average rate of return, cash payback period, net present value method

Objective 2

Tru-Cast Forging Company is considering acquiring equipment at a cost of $846,000. The equipment has an estimated life of 10 years and no residual value. It is expected to provide yearly net cash flows of $211,500. The company's minimum desired rate of return for net present value analysis is 12%.

SPREADSHEET

✓ b. 4 years

Compute the following:

a. The average rate of return, giving effect to straight-line depreciation on the investment.
b. The cash payback period.
c. The net present value. Use the table of the present value of an annuity of $1 appearing in this chapter.

Exercise 24–13
Internal rate of return method
Objective 2

✓ a. 3.837

The internal rate of return method is used by Hernandez Storage and Moving Company in analyzing a capital expenditure proposal that involves an investment of $57,555 and annual net cash flows of $15,000 for each of the 8 years of its useful life.

a. Determine a present value factor for an annuity of $1 which can be used in determining the internal rate of return.
b. Using the factor determined in (a) and the present value of an annuity of $1 table appearing in this chapter, determine the internal rate of return for the proposal.

Exercise 24–14
Internal rate of return method—two projects
Objective 2

✓ a. Delivery truck, 10%

The County Fair Popcorn Company is considering two possible investments: a delivery truck or a bagging machine. The delivery truck would cost $23,517 and could be used to deliver an additional 30,000 bags of popcorn per year. Each bag of popcorn can be sold for a contribution margin of $0.25. The delivery truck operating expenses, excluding depreciation, are $0.15 per mile for 14,000 miles per year. The bagging machine would replace an old bagging machine, and its net investment cost would be $32,066. The new machine would require 2.5 fewer hours of direct labor per day. Direct labor is $12 per hour. There are 260 operating days in the year. Both the truck and the bagging machine are estimated to have 6-year lives. The minimum rate of return is 9%. However, County Fair has funds to invest in only *one* of the projects.

a. Compute the internal rate of return for each investment. Use the table of present values of an annuity of $1 in the chapter.
b. Provide a memo to management with a recommendation.

Exercise 24–15
Net present value method and internal rate of return method
Objective 2

✓ a. ($12,543)

Kwik Klean Supply Co. is proposing to spend $94,016 on a 7-year project whose estimated net cash flows are $22,600 for each of the seven years.

a. Compute the net present value, using a rate of return of 20%. Use the table of present values of an annuity of $1 in the chapter.
b. Based on the analysis prepared in (a), is the rate of return (1) more than 20%, (2) 20%, or (3) less than 20%? Explain.
c. Determine the internal rate of return by computing a present value factor for an annuity of $1 and using the table of the present value of an annuity of $1 presented in the text.

Exercise 24–16
Identify error in capital investment analysis calculations
Objective 2

What's Wrong WITH THIS?

Quantum Computer Company is considering the purchase of automated machinery that is expected to have a useful life of 4 years and no residual value. The average rate of return on the average investment has been computed to be 25%, and the cash payback period was computed to be 4.5 years.

Do you see any reason to question the validity of the data presented? Explain.

PROBLEMS SERIES A

Problem 24–1A
Average rate of return method, net present value method, and analysis
Objective 2

The capital investment committee of Road Runner Trucking Inc. is considering two projects. The estimated income from operations and net cash flows from each project are as follows:

SPREADSHEET

✓ 1. a. 24%

	Project P		Project Q	
Year	Income from Operations	Net Cash Flow	Income from Operations	Net Cash Flow
1	$ 60,000	$160,000	$ 40,000	$140,000
2	60,000	160,000	50,000	150,000
3	60,000	160,000	60,000	160,000
4	60,000	160,000	70,000	170,000
5	60,000	160,000	80,000	180,000
Total	$300,000	$800,000	$300,000	$800,000

Each project requires an investment of $500,000. Straight-line depreciation will be used, and no residual value is expected. The committee has selected a rate of 12% for purposes of the net present value analysis.

Instructions

1. Compute the following:
   a. The average rate of return for each project, giving effect to depreciation on the investment.
   b. The net present value for each project. Use the present value of $1 table appearing in this chapter.
2. Prepare a brief report for the capital investment committee, advising it on the relative merits of the two projects.

Problem 24–2A

Cash payback period, net present value method, and analysis

Objective 2

✓ 1. b. Project A, $31,215

ClearView Television Company is considering two projects. The estimated net cash flows from each project are as follows:

Year	Project A	Project B
1	$100,000	$ 70,000
2	80,000	110,000
3	40,000	80,000
4	35,000	15,000
5	35,000	15,000
Total	$290,000	$290,000

Each project requires an investment of $180,000, with no residual value expected. A rate of 15% has been selected for the net present value analysis.

Instructions

1. Compute the following for each project:
   a. Cash payback period.
   b. The net present value. Use the present value of $1 table appearing in this chapter.
2. Prepare a brief report advising management on the relative merits of each of the two projects.

Problem 24–3A

Net present value method, present value index, and analysis

Objective 2

✓ 2. Project C, 0.97

Homestead Financial Company wishes to evaluate three capital investment projects by using the net present value method. Relevant data related to the projects are summarized as follows:

	Project C	Project D	Project E
Amount to be invested	$200,000	$150,000	$120,000
Annual net cash flows:			
Year 1	110,000	80,000	70,000
Year 2	90,000	80,000	70,000
Year 3	70,000	77,000	50,000

Instructions

1. Assuming that the desired rate of return is 20%, prepare a net present value analysis for each project. Use the present value of $1 table appearing in this chapter.
2. Determine a present value index for each project. Round to 2 decimal places.
3. Which project offers the largest amount of present value per dollar of investment? Explain.

Problem 24–4A

Net present value method, internal rate of return method, and analysis

Objective 2

✓ 1. a. Project I, $15,680

The management of Zenith Entertainment Group is considering two capital investment projects. The estimated net cash flows from each project are as follows:

Year	Project I	Project II
1	$35,000	$100,000
2	35,000	100,000
3	35,000	100,000
4	35,000	100,000

Project I requires an investment of $90,615, while Project II requires an investment of $285,500. No residual value is expected from either project.

Instructions

1. Compute the following for each project:
   a. The net present value. Use a rate of 12% and the present value of an annuity of $1 table appearing in this chapter.
   b. A present value index. Round to 2 decimal places.
2. Determine the internal rate of return for each project by (a) computing a present value factor for an annuity of $1 and (b) using the present value of an annuity of $1 table appearing in this chapter.
3. What advantage does the internal rate of return method have over the net present value method in comparing projects?

Problem 24–5A

Evaluate alternative capital investment decisions

Objectives 2, 3

✓ 1. Project B, $32,750

The investment committee of Cajun Delight Restaurants Inc. is evaluating two projects. The projects have different useful lives, but each requires an investment of $110,000. The estimated net cash flows from each project are as follows:

	Net Cash Flows	
Year	Project A	Project B
1	$35,000	$50,000
2	35,000	50,000
3	35,000	50,000
4	35,000	50,000
5	35,000	
6	35,000	

The committee has selected a rate of 15% for purposes of net present value analysis. It also estimates that the residual value at the end of each project's useful life is $0, but at the end of the fourth year, Project A's residual value would be $90,000.

Instructions

1. For each project, compute the net present value. Use the present value of an annuity of $1 table appearing in this chapter. (Ignore the unequal lives of the projects.)
2. For each project, compute the net present value, assuming that Project A is adjusted to a 4-year life for purposes of analysis. Use the present value of $1 table appearing in this chapter.
3. Prepare a report to the investment committee, providing your advice on the relative merits of the two projects.

Problem 24–6A

Capital rationing decision involving four proposals

Objectives 2, 4

✓ 1. Proposal A, 3 years

Star Broadcasting Company is considering allocating a limited amount of capital investment funds among four proposals. The amount of proposed investment, estimated income from operations, and net cash flow for each proposal are as follows:

	Investment	Year	Income from Operations	Net Cash Flow
Proposal A:	$84,000	1	$11,200	$28,000
		2	11,200	28,000
		3	11,200	28,000
		4	8,500	25,300
		5	6,200	23,000
Proposal B:	$120,000	1	$ 6,000	$30,000
		2	6,000	30,000
		3	6,000	30,000
		4	6,000	30,000
		5	(9,000)	15,000
Proposal C:	$48,000	1	$10,400	$20,000
		2	18,400	28,000
		3	400	10,000
		4	400	10,000
		5	400	10,000
Proposal D:	$400,000	1	$40,000	$120,000
		2	40,000	120,000
		3	40,000	120,000
		4	40,000	120,000
		5	20,000	100,000

The company's capital rationing policy requires a maximum cash payback period of three years. In addition, a minimum average rate of return of 10% is required on all projects. If the preceding standards are met, the net present value method and present value indexes are used to rank the remaining proposals.

Instructions

1. Compute the cash payback period for each of the four proposals.
2. Giving effect to straight-line depreciation on the investments and assuming no estimated residual value, compute the average rate of return for each of the four proposals. Round to 1 decimal place.
3. Using the following format, summarize the results of your computations in (1) and (2). By placing a check mark in the appropriate column at the right, indicate which proposals should be accepted for further analysis and which should be rejected.

Proposal	Cash Payback Period	Average Rate of Return	Accept for Further Analysis	Reject
A				
B				
C				
D				

4. For the proposals accepted for further analysis in (3), compute the net present value. Use a rate of 10% and the present value of $1 table appearing in this chapter.
5. Compute the present value index for each of the proposals in (4). Round to 2 decimal places.
6. Rank the proposals from most attractive to least attractive, based on the present values of net cash flows computed in (4).
7. Rank the proposals from most attractive to least attractive, based on the present value indexes computed in (5). Round to 2 decimal places.
8. Based upon the analyses, comment on the relative attractiveness of the proposals ranked in (6) and (7).

PROBLEMS SERIES B

Problem 24–1B
Average rate of return method, net present value method, and analysis

Objective 2

SPREADSHEET

✓ 1. a. 22.5%

The capital investment committee of Nature's Way Landscaping Company is considering two projects. The estimated income from operations and net cash flows from each project are as follows:

	Project A		Project X	
Year	Income from Operations	Net Cash Flow	Income from Operations	Net Cash Flow
1	$ 7,200	$ 20,000	$17,200	$ 30,000
2	7,200	20,000	12,200	25,000
3	7,200	20,000	7,200	20,000
4	7,200	20,000	2,200	15,000
5	7,200	20,000	(2,800)	10,000
	$36,000	$100,000	$36,000	$100,000

Each project requires an investment of $64,000. Straight-line depreciation will be used, and no residual value is expected. The committee has selected a rate of 10% for purposes of the net present value analysis.

Instructions

1. Compute the following:
   a. The average rate of return for each project, giving effect to depreciation on the investment.
   b. The net present value for each project. Use the present value of $1 table appearing in this chapter.
2. Prepare a brief report for the capital investment committee, advising it on the relative merits of the two projects.

Problem 24–2B
Cash payback period, net present value method, and analysis

Objective 2

✓ 1. b. Project E, $30,000

Safe-Case Luggage Company is considering two projects. The estimated net cash flows from each project are as follows:

Year	Project E	Project F
1	$100,000	$150,000
2	150,000	150,000
3	200,000	150,000
4	200,000	100,000
5	200,000	300,000
Total	$850,000	$850,000

Each project requires an investment of $450,000, with no residual value expected. A rate of 20% has been selected for the net present value analysis.

Instructions

1. Compute the following for each project:
   a. Cash payback period.
   b. The net present value. Use the present value of $1 table appearing in this chapter.
2. Prepare a brief report advising management on the relative merits of each of the two projects.

Problem 24–3B
Net present value method, present value index, and analysis

Objective 2

Great Plains Railroad Company wishes to evaluate three capital investment proposals by using the net present value method. Relevant data related to the proposals are summarized as follows:

✓ 2. Proposal P, 0.91

	Proposal O	Proposal P	Proposal Q
Amount to be invested	$150,000	$360,000	$285,000
Annual net cash flows:			
Year 1	120,000	180,000	190,000
Year 2	70,000	140,000	140,000
Year 3	30,000	100,000	90,000

Instructions

1. Assuming that the desired rate of return is 15%, prepare a net present value analysis for each proposal. Use the present value of $1 table appearing in this chapter.
2. Determine a present value index for each proposal.
3. Which proposal offers the largest amount of present value per dollar of investment? Explain.

Problem 24–4B

Net present value method, rate of return method, and analysis

Objective 2

✓ 1. a. Project S, $7,980

The management of Northern Utilities Inc. is considering two capital investment projects. The estimated net cash flows from each project are as follows:

Year	Project S	Project T
1	$60,000	$22,000
2	60,000	22,000
3	60,000	22,000
4	60,000	22,000

Project S requires an investment of $182,220, while Project T requires an investment of $62,810. No residual value is expected from either project.

Instructions

1. Compute the following for each project:
   a. The net present value. Use a rate of 10% and the present value of an annuity of $1 table appearing in this chapter.
   b. A present value index. Round to 2 decimal places.
2. Determine the internal rate of return for each project by (a) computing a present value factor for an annuity of $1 and (b) using the present value of an annuity of $1 table appearing in this chapter.
3. What advantage does the internal rate of return method have over the net present value method in comparing projects?

Problem 24–5B

Evaluate alternative capital investment decisions

Objectives 2, 3

✓ 2. Project II, $79,840

The investment committee of Clydesdale Brewery Inc. is evaluating two projects. The projects have different useful lives, but each requires an investment of $320,000. The estimated net cash flows from each project are as follows:

	Net Cash Flows	
Year	Project I	Project II
1	$100,000	$140,000
2	100,000	140,000
3	100,000	140,000
4	100,000	140,000
5	100,000	
6	100,000	

The committee has selected a rate of 15% for purposes of net present value analysis. It also estimates that the residual value at the end of each project's useful life is $0, but at the end of the fourth year, Project I's residual value would be $230,000.

Instructions

1. For each project, compute the net present value. Use the present value of an annuity of $1 table appearing in this chapter. (Ignore the unequal lives of the projects.)

2. For each project, compute the net present value, assuming that Project I is adjusted to a 4-year life for purposes of analysis. Use the present value of $1 table appearing in this chapter.
3. Prepare a report to the investment committee, providing your advice on the relative merits of the two projects.

Problem 24–6B

Capital rationing decision involving four proposals

Objectives 2, 4

✓ 5. Proposal C, 1.23

Golden Egg Capital Group is considering allocating a limited amount of capital investment funds among four proposals. The amount of proposed investment, estimated income from operations, and net cash flow for each proposal are as follows:

	Investment	Year	Income from Operations	Net Cash Flow
Proposal A:	$125,000	1	$25,000	$ 50,000
		2	25,000	50,000
		3	(5,000)	20,000
		4	(5,000)	20,000
		5	(5,000)	20,000
Proposal B:	$90,000	1	$22,000	$ 40,000
		2	12,000	30,000
		3	12,000	30,000
		4	12,000	30,000
		5	11,250	29,250
Proposal C:	$260,000	1	$48,000	$100,000
		2	28,000	80,000
		3	28,000	80,000
		4	28,000	80,000
		5	24,000	76,000
Proposal D:	$300,000	1	$20,000	$ 80,000
		2	20,000	80,000
		3	20,000	80,000
		4	0	60,000
		5	0	60,000

The company's capital rationing policy requires a maximum cash payback period of three years. In addition, a minimum average rate of return of 10% is required on all projects. If the preceding standards are met, the net present value method and present value indexes are used to rank the remaining proposals.

Instructions

1. Compute the cash payback period for each of the four proposals.
2. Giving effect to straight-line depreciation on the investments and assuming no estimated residual value, compute the average rate of return for each of the four proposals. Round to 1 decimal place.
3. Using the following format, summarize the results of your computations in (1) and (2). By placing a check mark in the appropriate column at the right, indicate which proposals should be accepted for further analysis and which should be rejected.

Proposal	Cash Payback Period	Average Rate of Return	Accept for Further Analysis	Reject
A				
B				
C				
D				

4. For the proposals accepted for further analysis in (3), compute the net present value. Use a rate of 10% and the present value of $1 table appearing in this chapter.

5. Compute the present value index for each of the proposals in (4). Round to 2 decimal places.
6. Rank the proposals from most attractive to least attractive, based on the present values of net cash flows computed in (4).
7. Rank the proposals from most attractive to least attractive, based on the present value indexes computed in (5).
8. Based upon the analyses, comment on the relative attractiveness of the proposals ranked in (6) and (7).

SPECIAL ACTIVITIES

Activity 24–1 HiPro Products Company

Ethics and professional conduct in business

Roland Dale was recently hired as a cost analyst by HiPro Products Company. One of Roland's first assignments was to perform a net present value analysis for a new warehouse. Roland performed the analysis and calculated a present value index of 0.75. The plant manager, I. M. Madd, is very intent on purchasing the warehouse because he believes that more storage space is needed. I. M. Madd asks Roland into his office and the following conversation takes place.

I. M.: Dale, you're new here, aren't you?

Roland: Yes, sir.

I. M.: Well, Dale, let me tell you something. I'm not at all pleased with the capital investment analysis that you performed on this new warehouse. I need that warehouse for my production. If I don't get it, where am I going to place our output?

Roland: Hopefully with the customer, sir.

I. M.: Now don't get smart with me, young man.

Roland: No, really, I was being serious. My analysis does not support constructing a new warehouse. There is no way that I can get the numbers to make this a favorable investment. In fact, it seems to me that purchasing a warehouse does not add much value to the business. We need to be producing product to satisfy customer orders, not to fill a warehouse.

I. M.: Listen, you need to understand something. The headquarters people will not allow me to build the warehouse if the numbers don't add up. I know as well as you that many assumptions go into your net present value analysis. Why don't you relax some of your assumptions so that the financial savings will offset the cost?

Roland: I'm willing to discuss my assumptions with you. Maybe I overlooked something.

I. M.: Good. Here's what I want you to do. I see in your analysis that you don't project greater sales as a result of the warehouse. It seems to me, if we can store more goods, then we will have more to sell. Thus, logically, a larger warehouse translates into more sales. If you incorporate this into your analysis, I think you'll see that the numbers will work out. Why don't you work it through and come back with a new analysis. I'm really counting on you on this one. Let's get off to a good start together and see if we can get this project accepted.

What is your advice to Roland?

Activity 24–2 Federal Mogul

Qualitative considerations

What do you THINK? REAL WORLD

Some companies have attempted to respond to competitive pressure by relying solely on automation. For example, **Federal Mogul**, a parts supplier to the automotive industry, invested in robots, production line computers, and automated materials movement systems in order to regain a cost advantage that it lost to Japanese competitors. Unfortunately, this automation not only failed to lower costs, but caused the plant to become much less flexible than required by its customers. The high technology could not be "changed over" quickly from one product to another. In addition, Federal Mogul found that the new automation reduced employee motivation. As indicated by one of the managers, "Very clearly, we made some poor decisions. One of them was that high-tech was the answer."

Why might relying solely on automation lead to lower profits?

Activity 24–3 Roadmaster Motorcycle Company
Investment analysis and qualitative considerations

The plant manager of Roadmaster Motorcycle Company is considering the purchase of a new robotic assembly plant. The new robotic line will cost $1,000,000. The manager believes that the new investment will result in direct labor savings of $250,000 per year for ten years.

1. What is the payback period on this project?
2. What is the net present value, assuming a 10% rate of return?
3. What else should the manager consider in the analysis?

Activity 24–4 Worthington Industries, Amgen, and Merck & Co.
Qualitative issues in investment analysis

REAL WORLD

The following are some selected quotes from senior executives:

John H. McConnel, CEO, **Worthington Industries** (a high technology steel company): *"We try to find the best technology, stay ahead of the competition, and serve the customer. . . . We'll make any investment that will pay back quickly . . . but if it is something that we really see as a must down the road, payback is not going to be that important."*

George Rathmann, Chairman Emeritus of **Amgen** (a biotech company): *"You cannot really run the numbers, do net present value calculations, because the uncertainties are really gigantic . . . You decide on a project you want to run, and then you run the numbers [as a reality check on your assumptions]. Success in a business like this is much more dependent on tracking rather than on predicting, much more dependent on seeing results over time, tracking and adjusting and readjusting, much more dynamic, much more flexible."*

Judy Lewent, Chief Financial Officer of **Merck & Co.** (a pharmaceutical company): *". . . at the individual product level—the development of a successful new product requires on the order of $230 million in R&D, spread over more than a decade—discounted cash flow style analysis does not become a factor until development is near the point of manufacturing scale-up effort. Prior to that point, given the uncertainties associated with new product development, it would be lunacy in our business to decide that we know exactly what's going to happen to a product once it gets out."*

Explain the role of capital investment analysis for these companies.

Activity 24–5 Fantasy Studies Inc.
Analyze cash flows

You are considering an investment of $360,000 in either Project K or Project L for Fantasy Studios Inc. In discussing the two projects with an advisor, you decided that, for the risk involved, a return of 12% on the cash investment would be required. For this purpose, you estimated the following economic factors for the projects:

	Project K	Project L
Useful life	4 years	4 years
Residual value	-0-	-0-
Net income:		
Year 1	$ 65,000	$ 25,000
2	50,000	40,000
3	40,000	58,000
4	25,000	64,200
Net cash flows:		
Year 1	$155,000	$115,000
2	140,000	130,000
3	130,000	148,000
4	115,000	154,200

Although the average rate of return exceeded 12% on both projects, you have tentatively decided to invest in Project L because the rate was higher for Project L. You noted that the total net cash flow from Project L is $547,200, which exceeds that of Project K by $7,200.

1. Determine the average rate of return for both projects.
2. Why is the timing of cash flows important in evaluating capital investments? Calculate the net present value of the two projects at a minimum rate of return of 12% to demonstrate the importance of net cash flows and their timing to these two projects. Round to the nearest dollar.

Activity 24–6
Into the Real World
Capital investment analysis

GROUP ACTIVITY

Internet ACTIVITY

In one group, find a local business, such as a copy shop, that rents time on microcomputers for an hourly rate. Determine the hourly rate. In the other group, determine the price of a mid-range microcomputer at **www.micron.com.** Combine this information from the two groups and perform a capital budgeting analysis. Assume that a computer will be used 35 hours per semester for the next three years. Also assume that the minimum rate of return is 10%. Use the interest tables in Appendix A in performing your analysis. (*Hint:* Use the appropriate present value factor for 5% compounded for six semiannual periods.)

Does your analysis support purchasing the computer?

ANSWERS TO SELF-EXAMINATION QUESTIONS

Matching

1. H	3. A	5. M	7. L	9. G	10. J	11. D	12. B
2. K	4. E	6. I	8. C				

Multiple Choice

1. **C** Methods of evaluating capital investment proposals that ignore the time value of money are categorized as methods that ignore present value. This category includes the average rate of return method (answer A) and the cash payback method (answer B).
2. **B** The average rate of return is 24% (answer B), determined by dividing the expected average annual earnings by the average investment, as follows:

$$\frac{\$60{,}000 \div 5}{(\$100{,}000 - \$0) \div 2} = 24\%$$

3. **B** Of the four methods of analyzing proposals for capital investments, the cash payback period (answer B) refers to the expected period of time required to recover the amount of cash to be invested. The average rate of return (answer A) is a measure of the anticipated profitability of a proposal. The net present value method (answer C) reduces the expected future net cash flows originating from a proposal to their present values. The internal rate of return method (answer D) uses present value concepts to compute the rate of return from the net cash flows expected from the investment.
4. **B** The net present value is determined as follows:

Present value of $25,000 for 8 years at 11% ($25,000 × 5.14612)	$128,653
Less: Project cost	120,000
Net present value	$ 8,653

5. **C** The internal rate of return of this project is determined by solving for the present value of an annuity factor that when multiplied by $40,000 will equal $226,009. By division, the factor is:

$$\frac{\$226{,}009}{\$40{,}000} = 5.65022$$

In Appendix A on pp. A-4 and A-5, scan along the n = 10 years row until finding the 5.65022 factor. The column for this factor is 12%.

Appendices

A. Interest Tables

B. Codes of Professional Ethics

C. Alternative Methods of Recording Deferrals

D. Periodic Inventory Systems for Merchandising Businesses

E. Foreign Currency Transactions

F. Partnerships

G. Hershey Foods Corporation Annual Report

Appendix A: Interest Tables

Present Value of $1 at Compound Interest Due in *n* Periods: $p_{\overline{n}\backslash i} = \frac{1}{(1+i)^n}$

n \ i	5%	5.5%	6%	6.5%	7%	8%
1	0.95238	0.94787	0.94334	0.93897	0.93458	0.92593
2	0.90703	0.89845	0.89000	0.88166	0.87344	0.85734
3	0.86384	0.85161	0.83962	0.82785	0.81630	0.79383
4	0.82270	0.80722	0.79209	0.77732	0.76290	0.73503
5	0.78353	0.76513	0.74726	0.72988	0.71290	0.68058
6	0.74622	0.72525	0.70496	0.68533	0.66634	0.63017
7	0.71068	0.68744	0.66506	0.64351	0.62275	0.58349
8	0.67684	0.65160	0.62741	0.60423	0.58201	0.54027
9	0.64461	0.61763	0.59190	0.56735	0.54393	0.50025
10	0.61391	0.58543	0.55840	0.53273	0.50835	0.46319
11	0.58468	0.55491	0.52679	0.50021	0.47509	0.42888
12	0.55684	0.52598	0.49697	0.46968	0.44401	0.39711
13	0.53032	0.49856	0.46884	0.44102	0.41496	0.36770
14	0.50507	0.47257	0.44230	0.41410	0.38782	0.34046
15	0.48102	0.44793	0.41726	0.38883	0.36245	0.31524
16	0.45811	0.42458	0.39365	0.36510	0.33874	0.29189
17	0.43630	0.40245	0.37136	0.34281	0.31657	0.27027
18	0.41552	0.38147	0.35034	0.32189	0.29586	0.25025
19	0.39573	0.36158	0.33051	0.30224	0.27651	0.23171
20	0.37689	0.34273	0.31180	0.28380	0.25842	0.21455
21	0.35894	0.32486	0.29416	0.26648	0.24151	0.19866
22	0.34185	0.30793	0.27750	0.25021	0.22571	0.18394
23	0.32557	0.29187	0.26180	0.23494	0.21095	0.17032
24	0.31007	0.27666	0.24698	0.22060	0.19715	0.15770
25	0.29530	0.26223	0.23300	0.20714	0.18425	0.14602
26	0.28124	0.24856	0.21981	0.19450	0.17211	0.13520
27	0.26785	0.23560	0.20737	0.18263	0.16093	0.12519
28	0.25509	0.22332	0.19563	0.17148	0.15040	0.11591
29	0.24295	0.21168	0.18456	0.16101	0.14056	0.10733
30	0.23138	0.20064	0.17411	0.15119	0.13137	0.09938
31	0.22036	0.19018	0.16426	0.14196	0.12277	0.09202
32	0.20987	0.18027	0.15496	0.13329	0.11474	0.08520
33	0.19987	0.17087	0.14619	0.12516	0.10724	0.07889
34	0.19036	0.16196	0.13791	0.11752	0.10022	0.07304
35	0.18129	0.15352	0.13010	0.11035	0.09366	0.06764
40	0.14205	0.11746	0.09722	0.08054	0.06678	0.04603
45	0.11130	0.08988	0.07265	0.05879	0.04761	0.03133
50	0.08720	0.06877	0.05429	0.04291	0.03395	0.02132

Present Value of $1 at Compound Interest Due in n Periods: $p_{\overline{n}\backslash i} = \frac{1}{(1 + i)^n}$

$n \backslash i$	9%	10%	11%	12%	13%	14%
1	0.91743	0.90909	0.90090	0.89286	0.88496	0.87719
2	0.84168	0.82645	0.81162	0.79719	0.78315	0.76947
3	0.77218	0.75132	0.73119	0.71178	0.69305	0.67497
4	0.70842	0.68301	0.65873	0.63552	0.61332	0.59208
5	0.64993	0.62092	0.59345	0.56743	0.54276	0.51937
6	0.59627	0.56447	0.53464	0.50663	0.48032	0.45559
7	0.54703	0.51316	0.48166	0.45235	0.42506	0.39964
8	0.50187	0.46651	0.43393	0.40388	0.37616	0.35056
9	0.46043	0.42410	0.39092	0.36061	0.33288	0.30751
10	0.42241	0.38554	0.35218	0.32197	0.29459	0.26974
11	0.38753	0.35049	0.31728	0.28748	0.26070	0.23662
12	0.35554	0.31863	0.28584	0.25668	0.23071	0.20756
13	0.32618	0.28966	0.25751	0.22917	0.20416	0.18207
14	0.29925	0.26333	0.23199	0.20462	0.18068	0.15971
15	0.27454	0.23939	0.20900	0.18270	0.15989	0.14010
16	0.25187	0.21763	0.18829	0.16312	0.14150	0.12289
17	0.23107	0.19784	0.16963	0.14564	0.12522	0.10780
18	0.21199	0.17986	0.15282	0.13004	0.11081	0.09456
19	0.19449	0.16351	0.13768	0.11611	0.09806	0.08295
20	0.17843	0.14864	0.12403	0.10367	0.08678	0.07276
21	0.16370	0.13513	0.11174	0.09256	0.07680	0.06383
22	0.15018	0.12285	0.10067	0.08264	0.06796	0.05599
23	0.13778	0.11168	0.09069	0.07379	0.06014	0.04911
24	0.12640	0.10153	0.08170	0.06588	0.05323	0.04308
25	0.11597	0.09230	0.07361	0.05882	0.04710	0.03779
26	0.10639	0.08390	0.06631	0.05252	0.04168	0.03315
27	0.09761	0.07628	0.05974	0.04689	0.03689	0.02908
28	0.08955	0.06934	0.05382	0.04187	0.03264	0.02551
29	0.08216	0.06304	0.04849	0.03738	0.02889	0.02237
30	0.07537	0.05731	0.04368	0.03338	0.02557	0.01963
31	0.06915	0.05210	0.03935	0.02980	0.02262	0.01722
32	0.06344	0.04736	0.03545	0.02661	0.02002	0.01510
33	0.05820	0.04306	0.03194	0.02376	0.01772	0.01325
34	0.05331	0.03914	0.02878	0.02121	0.01568	0.01162
35	0.04899	0.03558	0.02592	0.01894	0.01388	0.01019
40	0.03184	0.02210	0.01538	0.01075	0.00753	0.00529
45	0.02069	0.01372	0.00913	0.00610	0.00409	0.00275
50	0.01345	0.00852	0.00542	0.00346	0.00222	0.00143

Present Value of Ordinary Annuity of $1 per Period: $p_{\overline{n}\backslash i} = \dfrac{1 - \dfrac{1}{(1+i)^n}}{i}$

n \ i	5%	5.5%	6%	6.5%	7%	8%
1	0.95238	0.94787	0.94340	0.93897	0.93458	0.92593
2	1.85941	1.84632	1.83339	1.82063	1.80802	1.78326
3	2.72325	2.69793	2.67301	2.64848	2.62432	2.57710
4	3.54595	3.50515	3.46511	3.42580	3.38721	3.31213
5	4.32948	4.27028	4.21236	4.15568	4.10020	3.99271
6	5.07569	4.99553	4.91732	4.84101	4.76654	4.62288
7	5.78637	5.68297	5.58238	5.48452	5.38923	5.20637
8	6.46321	6.33457	6.20979	6.08875	5.97130	5.74664
9	7.10782	6.95220	6.80169	6.65610	6.51523	6.24689
10	7.72174	7.53763	7.36009	7.18883	7.02358	6.71008
11	8.30641	8.09254	7.88688	7.68904	7.49867	7.13896
12	8.86325	8.61852	8.38384	8.15873	7.94269	7.53608
13	9.39357	9.11708	8.85268	8.59974	8.35765	7.90378
14	9.89864	9.58965	9.29498	9.01384	8.74547	8.22424
15	10.37966	10.03758	9.71225	9.40267	9.10791	8.55948
16	10.83777	10.46216	10.10590	9.76776	9.44665	8.85137
17	11.27407	10.86461	10.47726	10.11058	9.76322	9.12164
18	11.68959	11.24607	10.82760	10.43247	10.05909	9.37189
19	12.08532	11.60765	11.15812	10.73471	10.33560	9.60360
20	12.46221	11.95038	11.46992	11.01851	10.59401	9.81815
21	12.82115	12.27524	11.76408	11.28498	10.83553	10.01680
22	13.16300	12.58317	12.04158	11.53520	11.06124	10.20074
23	13.48857	12.87504	12.30338	11.77014	11.27219	10.37106
24	13.79864	13.15170	12.55036	11.99074	11.46933	10.52876
25	14.09394	13.41393	12.78336	12.19788	11.65358	10.67478
26	14.37518	13.66250	13.00317	12.39237	11.82578	10.80998
27	14.64303	13.89810	13.21053	12.57500	11.98671	10.93516
28	14.89813	14.12142	13.40616	12.74648	12.13711	11.05108
29	15.14107	14.33310	13.59072	12.90749	12.27767	11.15841
30	15.37245	14.53375	13.76483	13.05868	12.40904	11.25778
31	15.59281	14.72393	13.92909	13.20063	12.53181	11.34980
32	15.80268	14.90420	14.08404	13.33393	12.64656	11.43500
33	16.00255	15.07507	14.23023	13.45909	12.75379	11.51389
34	16.19290	15.23703	14.36814	13.57661	12.85401	11.58693
35	16.37420	15.39055	14.49825	13.68696	12.94767	11.65457
40	17.15909	16.04612	15.04630	14.14553	13.33171	11.92461
45	17.77407	16.54773	15.45583	14.48023	13.60552	12.10840
50	18.25592	16.93152	15.76186	14.72452	13.80075	12.23348

Present Value of Ordinary Annuity of $1 per Period: $p_{\overline{n}\rceil i} = \dfrac{1 - \dfrac{1}{(1+i)^n}}{i}$

n \ i	9%	10%	11%	12%	13%	14%
1	0.91743	0.90909	0.90090	0.89286	0.88496	0.87719
2	1.75911	1.73554	1.71252	1.69005	1.66810	1.64666
3	2.53130	2.48685	2.44371	2.40183	2.36115	2.32163
4	3.23972	3.16986	3.10245	3.03735	2.97447	2.91371
5	3.88965	3.79079	3.69590	3.60478	3.51723	3.43308
6	4.48592	4.35526	4.23054	4.11141	3.99755	3.88867
7	5.03295	4.86842	4.71220	4.56376	4.42261	4.28830
8	5.53482	5.33493	5.14612	4.96764	4.79677	4.63886
9	5.99525	5.75902	5.53705	5.32825	5.13166	4.94637
10	6.41766	6.14457	5.88923	5.65022	5.42624	5.21612
11	6.80519	6.49506	6.20652	5.93770	5.68694	5.45273
12	7.16072	6.81369	6.49236	6.19437	5.91765	5.66029
13	7.48690	7.10336	6.74987	6.42355	6.12181	5.84236
14	7.78615	7.36669	6.96187	6.62817	6.30249	6.00207
15	8.06069	7.60608	7.19087	6.81086	6.46238	6.14217
16	8.31256	7.82371	7.37916	6.97399	6.60388	6.26506
17	8.54363	8.02155	7.54879	7.11963	6.72909	6.37286
18	8.75562	8.20141	7.70162	7.24967	6.83991	6.46742
19	8.95012	8.36492	7.83929	7.36578	6.93797	6.55037
20	9.12855	8.51356	7.96333	7.46944	7.02475	6.62313
21	9.29224	8.64869	8.07507	7.56200	7.10155	6.68696
22	9.44242	8.77154	8.17574	7.64465	7.16951	6.74294
23	9.58021	8.88322	8.26643	7.71843	7.22966	6.79206
24	9.70661	8.98474	8.34814	7.78432	7.28288	6.83514
25	9.82258	9.07704	8.42174	7.84314	7.32998	6.87293
26	9.92897	9.16094	8.48806	7.89566	7.37167	6.90608
27	10.02658	9.23722	8.54780	7.94255	7.40856	6.93515
28	10.11613	9.30657	8.60162	7.98442	7.44120	6.96066
29	10.19828	9.36961	8.65011	8.02181	7.47009	6.98304
30	10.27365	9.42691	8.69379	8.05518	7.49565	7.00266
31	10.34280	9.47901	8.73315	8.08499	7.51828	7.01988
32	10.40624	9.52638	8.76860	8.11159	7.53830	7.03498
33	10.46444	9.56943	8.80054	8.13535	7.55602	7.04823
34	10.51784	9.60858	8.82932	8.15656	7.57170	7.05985
35	10.56682	9.64416	8.85524	8.17550	7.58557	7.07005
40	10.75736	9.77905	8.95105	8.24378	7.63438	7.10504
45	10.88118	9.86281	9.00791	8.28252	7.66086	7.12322
50	10.96168	9.91481	9.04165	8.30450	7.67524	7.13266

Future Amount of $1 at Compound Interest Due in *n* Periods: $A_{\overline{n}|i} = (1 + i)^n$

n \ i	5%	5.5%	6%	6.5%	7%	8%
1	1.05000	1.05500	1.06000	1.06500	1.07000	1.08000
2	1.10250	1.11303	1.12360	1.13423	1.14490	1.16640
3	1.15762	1.17424	1.19102	1.20795	1.22504	1.25971
4	1.21551	1.23882	1.26248	1.28647	1.31080	1.36049
5	1.27628	1.30696	1.33823	1.37009	1.40255	1.46933
6	1.34100	1.37884	1.41852	1.45914	1.50073	1.58687
7	1.40710	1.45468	1.50363	1.55399	1.60578	1.71382
8	1.54347	1.53469	1.59385	1.65500	1.71819	1.85093
9	1.55133	1.61909	1.68948	1.76257	1.83846	1.99900
10	1.62890	1.70814	1.79085	1.87714	1.96715	2.15892
11	1.71034	1.80209	1.89830	1.99915	2.10485	2.33164
12	1.79586	1.90121	2.01220	2.12910	2.25219	2.51817
13	1.88565	2.00577	2.13293	2.26749	2.40984	2.71962
14	1.97993	2.11609	2.26091	2.41487	2.57853	2.93719
15	2.07893	2.23248	2.39656	2.57184	2.75903	3.17217
16	2.18288	2.35526	2.54035	2.73901	2.95216	3.42594
17	2.29202	2.48480	2.69277	2.91705	3.15882	3.70002
18	2.40662	2.62147	2.85434	3.10665	3.37993	3.99602
19	2.52695	2.76565	3.02560	3.30859	3.61653	4.31570
20	2.65330	2.91776	3.20714	3.52365	3.86968	4.66096
21	2.78596	3.07823	3.39956	3.75268	4.14056	5.03383
22	2.92526	3.24754	3.60354	3.99661	4.43040	5.43654
23	3.07152	3.42615	3.81975	4.25639	4.74053	5.87146
24	3.22510	3.61459	4.04894	4.53305	5.07237	6.34118
25	3.38636	3.81339	4.29187	4.82770	5.42743	6.84848
26	3.55567	4.02313	4.54938	5.14150	5.80735	7.39635
27	3.73346	4.24440	4.82235	5.47570	6.21387	7.98806
28	3.92013	4.47784	5.11169	5.83162	6.64884	8.62711
29	4.11614	4.72412	5.41839	6.21067	7.11426	9.31728
30	4.32194	4.98395	5.74349	6.61437	7.61226	10.06266
31	4.53804	5.25807	6.08810	7.04430	8.14511	10.86767
32	4.76494	5.54726	6.45339	7.50218	8.71527	11.73708
33	5.00319	5.85236	6.84059	7.98982	9.32534	12.67605
34	5.25335	6.17424	7.25102	8.50916	9.97811	13.69013
35	5.51602	6.51383	7.68609	9.06225	10.67658	14.78534
40	7.03999	8.51331	10.28572	12.41607	14.97446	21.72452
45	8.98501	11.12655	13.76461	17.01110	21.00245	31.92045
50	11.46740	14.54196	18.42015	23.30668	29.45702	46.90161

Future Amount of $1 at Compound Interest Due in *n* Periods: $A_{\overline{n}\backslash i} = (1 + i)^n$

n \ i	9%	10%	11%	12%	13%	14%
1	1.09000	1.10000	1.11000	1.12000	1.13000	1.14000
2	1.18810	1.21000	1.23210	1.25440	1.27690	1.29960
3	1.29503	1.33100	1.36763	1.40493	1.44290	1.48154
4	1.41158	1.46410	1.51807	1.57352	1.63047	1.68896
5	1.53862	1.61051	1.68506	1.76234	1.84244	1.92541
6	1.67710	1.77156	1.87041	1.97382	2.08195	2.19497
7	1.82804	1.94872	2.07616	2.21068	2.35261	2.50227
8	1.99256	2.14359	2.30454	2.47596	2.65844	2.85259
9	2.17189	2.35795	2.55804	2.77308	3.00404	3.25195
10	2.36736	2.59374	2.83942	3.10585	3.39457	3.70722
11	2.58043	2.85312	3.15176	3.47855	3.83586	4.22623
12	2.81266	3.13843	3.49845	3.89598	4.33452	4.81790
13	3.06580	3.45227	3.88328	4.36349	4.89801	5.49241
14	3.34173	3.79750	4.31044	4.88711	5.53475	6.26135
15	3.64248	4.17725	4.78459	5.47357	6.25427	7.13794
16	3.97031	4.59497	5.31089	6.13039	7.06733	8.13725
17	4.32763	5.05447	5.89509	6.86604	7.98608	9.27646
18	4.71712	5.55992	6.54355	7.68997	9.02427	10.57517
19	5.14166	6.11591	7.26334	8.61276	10.19742	12.05569
20	5.60441	6.72750	8.06231	9.64629	11.52309	13.74349
21	6.10881	7.40025	8.94917	10.80385	13.02109	15.66758
22	6.65860	8.14028	9.93357	12.10031	14.71383	17.86104
23	7.25787	8.95430	11.02627	13.55235	16.62663	20.36158
24	7.91108	9.84973	12.23916	15.17863	18.78809	23.21221
25	8.62308	10.83471	13.58546	17.00006	21.23054	26.46192
26	9.39916	11.91818	15.07986	19.04007	23.99051	30.16658
27	10.24508	13.10999	16.73865	21.32488	27.10928	34.38991
28	11.16714	14.42099	18.57990	23.88387	30.63349	39.20449
29	12.17218	15.86309	20.62369	26.74993	34.61584	44.69312
30	13.26768	17.44940	22.89230	29.95992	39.11590	50.95016
31	14.46177	19.19434	25.41045	33.55511	44.20096	58.08318
32	15.76333	21.11378	28.20560	37.58173	49.94709	66.21483
33	17.18203	23.22515	31.30821	42.09153	56.44021	75.48490
34	18.72841	25.54767	34.75212	47.14252	63.77744	86.05279
35	20.41397	28.10244	38.57485	52.79962	72.06851	98.10018
40	31.40942	45.25926	65.00087	93.05097	132.78155	188.88351
45	48.32729	72.89048	109.53024	163.98760	244.64140	363.67907
50	74.35752	117.39085	184.56483	289.00219	450.73593	700.23299

Future Amount of Ordinary Annuity of $1 per Period: $A_{\overline{n}\backslash i} = (1 + i)^n - 1/i$						
$n \backslash i$	5%	5.5%	6%	6.5%	7%	8%
1	1.00000	1.00000	1.00000	1.00000	1.00000	1.00000
2	2.05000	2.05500	2.06000	2.06500	2.07000	2.08000
3	3.15250	3.16802	3.18360	3.19922	3.21490	3.24640
4	4.31012	4.34227	4.37462	4.40717	4.43994	4.50611
5	5.52563	5.58109	5.63709	5.69364	5.75074	5.86660
6	6.80191	6.88805	6.97532	7.06373	7.15329	7.33593
7	8.14201	8.26689	8.39384	8.52287	8.65402	8.92280
8	9.54911	9.72157	9.89747	10.07688	10.25980	10.63663
9	11.02656	11.25626	11.49132	11.73185	11.97799	12.48756
10	12.57789	12.87535	13.18080	13.49442	13.81645	14.48656
11	14.20679	14.58350	14.97184	15.37156	15.78360	16.64549
12	15.91713	16.38559	16.86994	17.37071	17.88845	18.97713
13	17.71298	18.28680	18.88214	19.49981	20.14064	21.49530
14	19.59863	20.29257	21.01505	21.76730	22.55049	24.21492
15	21.57856	22.40866	23.27597	24.18217	25.12902	27.15211
16	23.65749	24.64114	25.67253	26.75401	27.88805	30.32428
17	25.84037	28.99640	28.21288	29.49302	30.84022	33.75023
18	28.13238	29.48120	30.90565	32.41007	33.99903	37.45024
19	30.53900	32.10267	33.75999	35.51672	37.37896	41.44626
20	33.06595	34.86832	36.78559	38.82531	40.99549	45.76196
21	35.71925	37.78608	39.99273	42.34895	44.86518	50.42292
22	38.50521	40.86431	43.39229	46.10164	49.00574	55.45676
23	41.43048	44.11185	46.99583	50.09824	53.43614	60.89330
24	44.50200	47.53800	50.81558	54.35463	58.17667	66.76476
25	47.72710	51.15259	54.86451	58.88768	63.24904	73.10594
26	51.11345	54.96598	59.15638	63.71538	68.67647	79.95442
27	54.66913	58.98911	63.70577	68.85688	74.48382	87.35077
28	58.40258	63.23351	68.52811	74.33257	80.69769	95.33883
29	62.32271	67.71135	73.62980	80.16419	87.34653	103.96594
30	66.43885	72.43548	79.05819	86.37486	94.46079	113.28321
31	70.76079	77.41943	84.80168	92.98923	102.07304	123.34587
32	75.29883	82.67750	90.88978	100.03353	110.21815	134.21354
33	80.06377	88.22476	97.34316	107.53571	118.93342	145.95062
34	85.06696	94.07712	104.18376	115.52553	128.25876	158.62667
35	90.32031	100.25136	111.43478	124.03469	138.23688	172.31680
40	120.79977	136.60561	154.76197	175.63192	199.63511	259.05652
45	159.70016	184.11917	212.74351	246.32459	285.74931	386.50562
50	209.34800	246.21748	290.33591	343.17967	406.52893	573.77016

Future Amount of Ordinary Annuity of $1 per Period: $A_{\overline{n}\backslash i} = (1 + i)^n - 1/i$						
n \ i	9%	10%	11%	12%	13%	14%
1	1.00000	1.00000	1.00000	1.00000	1.00000	1.00000
2	2.09000	2.10000	2.11000	2.12000	2.13000	2.14000
3	3.27810	3.31000	3.34210	3.37440	3.40690	3.43960
4	4.57313	4.64100	4.70973	4.77933	4.84980	4.92114
5	5.98471	6.10510	6.22780	6.35285	6.48027	6.61010
6	7.52334	7.71561	7.91286	8.11519	8.32271	8.53552
7	9.20044	9.48717	9.78327	10.08901	10.40466	10.73049
8	11.02847	11.43589	11.85943	12.29969	12.75726	13.23276
9	13.02104	13.57948	14.16397	14.77566	15.41571	16.08535
10	15.19293	15.93742	16.72201	17.54874	18.41975	19.33730
11	17.56029	18.53117	19.56143	20.65458	21.81432	23.04452
12	20.14072	21.38428	22.71319	24.13313	25.65018	27.27075
13	22.95338	24.52271	26.21164	28.02911	29.98470	32.08865
14	26.01919	27.97498	30.09492	32.39260	34.88271	37.58107
15	29.36092	31.77248	34.40536	37.27972	40.41746	43.84241
16	33.00340	35.94973	39.18995	42.75328	46.67173	50.98035
17	36.97370	40.54470	44.50084	48.88367	53.73906	59.11760
18	41.30134	45.59917	50.39594	55.74972	61.72514	68.39407
19	46.01846	51.15909	56.93949	63.43968	70.74941	78.96923
20	51.16012	57.27500	64.20283	72.05244	80.94683	91.02493
21	56.76453	64.00250	72.26514	81.69874	92.46992	104.76842
22	62.87334	71.40275	81.21431	92.50258	105.49101	120.43600
23	69.53194	79.54302	91.14788	104.60289	120.20484	138.29704
24	76.78981	88.49733	102.17415	118.15524	136.83147	158.65862
25	84.70090	98.34706	114.41331	133.33387	155.61956	181.87083
26	93.32398	109.18176	127.99877	150.33393	176.85010	208.33274
27	102.72314	121.09994	143.07864	169.37401	200.84061	238.49933
28	112.96822	134.20994	159.81729	190.69889	227.94989	272.88923
29	124.13536	148.63093	178.39719	214.58275	258.58338	312.09373
30	136.30754	164.49402	199.02088	241.33268	293.19922	356.78685
31	149.57522	181.94342	221.91317	271.29261	332.31511	407.73701
32	164.03699	201.13777	247.32362	304.84772	376.51608	465.82019
33	179.80032	222.25154	275.52922	342.42945	426.46317	532.03501
34	196.98234	245.47670	306.83744	384.52098	482.90338	607.51991
35	215.71076	271.02437	341.58955	431.66350	546.68082	693.57270
40	337.88244	442.59256	581.82607	767.09142	1013.70424	1342.02510
45	525.85873	718.90484	986.63856	1358.23003	1874.16463	2590.56480
50	815.08356	1163.90853	1668.77115	2400.01825	3459.50712	4994.52135

Appendix B: Codes of Professional Ethics for Accountants

In recent years, governments, businesses, and the public have given increased attention to ethical conduct. They have insisted upon a level of human behavior that goes beyond that required by laws and regulations. Thus many businesses, as well as professional groups (such as accountants) and governmental organizations, have established standards of ethical conduct. This text emphasizes the ethical conduct of accountants, who serve various business interests as well as the public.

This appendix sets forth the standards of professional conduct expected of accountants in public accounting and private accounting. For accountants employed in public accounting, the American Institute of Certified Public Accountants' *Code of Professional Conduct* is presented.[1] For accountants employed in private accounting, the Institute of Management Accountants' *Standards of Ethical Conduct for Management Accountants* is presented as a guide to professional conduct.[2]

Supplementing the codes of professional ethics are ethics discussion cases that appear at the end of each chapter. These cases represent "real world" examples of ethical issues facing accountants. It should be noted that codes of professional ethics are general guides to good behavior and their application to specific situations often requires the exercise of professional judgment. In some cases, the line between right and wrong may be quite fine, and reasonable people may disagree. In addition, business is dynamic and everchanging, and what society considers to be acceptable behavior changes from time to time.

Code of Professional Conduct

Composition, Applicability, and Compliance

The Code of Professional Conduct of the American Institute of Certified Public Accountants consists of two sections—(1) the Principles and (2) the Rules. The Principles provide the framework for the Rules, which govern the performance of professional services by members. The Council of the American Institute of Certified Public Accountants is authorized to designate bodies to promulgate technical standards under the Rules, and the bylaws require adherence to those Rules and standards.

The Code of Professional Conduct was adopted by the membership to provide guidance and rules to all members—those in public practice, in industry, in government, and in education—in the performance of their professional responsibilities.

Compliance with the Code of Professional Conduct, as with all standards in an open society, depends primarily on members' understanding and voluntary actions, secondarily on reinforcement by peers and public opinion, and ultimately on disciplinary proceedings, when necessary, against members who fail to comply with the Rules.

Other Guidance

The Principles and Rules as set forth herein are further amplified by interpretations and rulings contained in *AICPA Professional Standards* (Volume 2).

Interpretations of Rules of Conduct consists of interpretations which have been adopted, after exposure to state societies, state boards, practice units, and other interested parties, by the professional ethics division's executive committee to provide guidelines as to the scope and application of the Rules but are not intended to limit

[1] *Code of Professional Conduct* (New York: American Institute of Certified Public Accountants, 1994), pp. 3–8.
[2] *Standards of Ethical Conduct for Management Accountants,* Institute of Management Accountants, Montvale, New Jersey, 1994, pp. 1–2.

such scope or application. A member who departs from such guidelines shall have the burden of justifying such departure in any disciplinary hearing.

Ethics Rulings consist of formal rulings made by the professional ethics division's executive committee after exposure to state societies, state boards, practice units, and other interested parties. These rulings summarize the application of Rules of Conduct and interpretations to a particular set of factual circumstances. Members who depart from such rulings in similar circumstances will be requested to justify such departures.

Publication of an interpretation or ethics ruling in the *Journal of Accountancy* constitutes notice to members. Hence, the effective date of the pronouncement is the last day of the month in which the pronouncement is published in the *Journal of Accountancy*. The professional ethics division will take into consideration the time that would have been reasonable for the member to comply with the pronouncement.

Members should also consult, if applicable, the ethical standards of their state CPA society, state board of accountancy, the Securities and Exchange Commission, and any other governmental agency which may regulate their client's business or use their reports to evaluate the client's compliance with applicable laws and related regulations.

Section I—Principles

Preamble

Membership in the American Institute of Certified Public Accountants is voluntary. By accepting membership, a certified public accountant assumes an obligation of self-discipline above and beyond the requirements of laws and regulations.

These Principles of the Code of Professional Conduct of the American Institute of Certified Public Accountants express the profession's recognition of its responsibilities to the public, to clients, and to colleagues. They guide members in the performance of their professional responsibilities and express the basic tenets of ethical and professional conduct. The Principles call for an unswerving commitment to honorable behavior, even at the sacrifice of personal advantage.

Article I—Responsibilities

In carrying out their responsibilities as professionals, members should exercise sensitive professional and moral judgments in all their activities.

As professionals, certified public accountants perform an essential role in society. Consistent with that role, members of the American Institute of Certified Public Accountants have responsibilities to all those who use their professional services. Members also have a continuing responsibility to cooperate with each other to improve the art of accounting, maintain the public's confidence, and carry out the profession's special responsibilities for self-governance. The collective efforts of all members are required to maintain and enhance the traditions of the profession.

Article II—The Public Interest

Members should accept the obligation to act in a way that will serve the public interest, honor the public trust, and demonstrate commitment to professionalism.

A distinguishing mark of a profession is acceptance of its responsibility to the public. The accounting profession's public consists of clients, credit grantors, governments, employers, investors, the business and financial community, and others who rely on the objectivity and integrity of certified public accountants to maintain the orderly functioning of commerce. This reliance imposes a public interest responsibility on certified public accountants. The public interest is defined as the collective well-being of the community of people and institutions the profession serves.

In discharging their professional responsibilities, members may encounter conflicting pressures from among each of those groups. In resolving those conflicts, members should act with integrity, guided by the precept that when members fulfill their responsibility to the public, clients' and employers' interests are best served.

Those who rely on certified public accountants expect them to discharge their responsibilities with integrity, objectivity, due professional care, and a genuine interest in serving the public. They are expected to provide quality services, enter into fee arrangements, and offer a range of services—all in a manner that demonstrates a level of professionalism consistent with these Principles of the Code of Professional Conduct.

All who accept membership in the American Institute of Certified Public Accountants commit themselves to honor the public trust. In return for the faith that the public reposes in them, members should seek continually to demonstrate their dedication to professional excellence.

Article III—Integrity

To maintain and broaden public confidence, members should perform all professional responsibilities with the highest sense of integrity.

Integrity is an element of character fundamental to professional recognition. It is the quality from which the public trust derives and the benchmark against which a member must ultimately test all decisions.

Integrity requires a member to be, among other things, honest and candid within the constraints of client confidentiality. Service and the public trust should not be subordinated to personal gain and advantage. Integrity can accommodate the inadvertent error and the honest difference of opinion; it cannot accommodate deceit or subordination of principle.

Integrity is measured in terms of what is right and just. In the absence of specific rules, standards, or guidance, or in the face of conflicting opinions, a member should test decisions and deeds by asking: "Am I doing what a person of integrity would do? Have I retained my integrity?" Integrity requires a member to observe both the form and the spirit of technical and ethical standards; circumvention of those standards constitutes subordination of judgment.

Integrity also requires a member to observe the principles of objectivity and independence and of due care.

Article IV—Objectivity and Independence

A member should maintain objectivity and be free of conflicts of interest in discharging professional responsibilities. A member in public practice should be independent in fact and appearance when providing auditing and other attestation services.

Objectivity is a state of mind, a quality that lends value to a member's services. It is a distinguishing feature of the profession. The principle of objectivity imposes the obligation to be impartial, intellectually honest, and free of conflicts of interest. Independence precludes relationships that may appear to impair a member's objectivity in rendering attestation services.

Members often serve multiple interests in many different capacities and must demonstrate their objectivity in varying circumstances. Members in public practice render attest, tax, and management advisory services. Other members prepare financial statements in the employment of others, perform internal auditing services, and serve in financial and management capacities in industry, education, and government. They also educate and train those who aspire to admission into the profession. Regardless of service or capacity, members should protect the integrity of their work, maintain objectivity, and avoid any subordination of their judgment.

For a member in public practice, the maintenance of objectivity and independence requires a continuing assessment of client relationships and public responsibility. Such a member who provides auditing and other attestation services should be independent in fact and appearance. In providing all other services, a member should maintain objectivity and avoid conflicts of interest.

Although members not in public practice cannot maintain the appearance of independence, they nevertheless have the responsibility to maintain objectivity in rendering professional services. Members employed by others to prepare financial statements or to perform auditing, tax, or consulting services are charged with the same responsibility for objectivity as members in public practice and must be scrupulous in their application of generally accepted accounting principles and candid in all their dealings with members in public practice.

Activity V—Due Care

A member should observe the profession's technical and ethical standards, strive continually to improve competence and the quality of services, and discharge professional responsibility to the best of the member's ability.

The quest for excellence is the essence of due care. Due care requires a member to discharge professional responsibilities with competence and diligence. It imposes the obligation to perform professional services to the best of a member's ability with concern for the best interest of those for whom the services are performed and consistent with the profession's responsibility to the public.

Competence is derived from a synthesis of education and experience. It begins with a mastery of the common body of knowledge required for designation as a certified public accountant. The maintenance of competence requires a commitment to learning and professional improvement that must continue throughout a member's professional life. It is a member's individual responsibility. In all engagements and in all responsibilities, each member should undertake to achieve a level of competence that will assure that the quality of the member's services meets the high level of professionalism required by these Principles.

Competence represents the attainment and maintenance of a level of understanding and knowledge that enables a member to render services with facility and acumen. It also establishes the limitations of a member's capabilities by dictating that consultation or referral may be required when a professional engagement exceeds the personal competence of a member or a member's firm. Each member is responsible for assessing his or her own competence—of evaluating whether education, experience, and judgment are adequate for the responsibility to be assumed.

Members should be diligent in discharging responsibilities to clients, employers, and the public. Diligence imposes the responsibility to render services promptly and carefully, to be thorough, and to observe applicable technical and ethical standards.

Due care requires a member to plan and supervise adequately any professional activity for which he or she is responsible.

Article VI—Scope and Nature of Services

A member in public practice should observe the Principles of the Code of Professional Conduct in determining the scope and nature of services to be provided.

The public interest aspect of certified public accountants' services requires that such services be consistent with acceptable professional behavior for certified public accountants. Integrity requires that service and the public trust not be subordinated to personal gain and advantage. Objectivity and independence require that members be free from conflicts of interest in discharging professional responsibilities. Due care requires that services be provided with competence and diligence.

Each of these Principles should be considered by members in determining whether or not to provide specific services in individual circumstances. In some instances, they may represent an overall constraint on the nonaudit services that might be offered to a specific client. No hard-and-fast rules can be developed to help members reach these judgments, but they must be satisfied that they are meeting the spirit of the Principles in this regard.

In order to accomplish this, members should:

- Practice in firms that have in place internal quality-control procedures to ensure that services are competently delivered and adequately supervised.

- Determine, in their individual judgments, whether the scope and nature of other services provided to an audit client would create a conflict of interest in the performance of the audit function for that client.
- Assess, in their individual judgments, whether an activity is consistent with their role as professionals (for example, Is such activity a reasonable extension or variation of existing services offered by the member or others in the profession?).

Standards of Ethical Conduct for Management Accountants

Management accountants have an obligation to the organizations they serve, their profession, the public, and themselves to maintain the highest standards of ethical conduct. In recognition of this obligation, the Institute of Management Accountants has promulgated the following standards of ethical conduct for management accountants. Adherence to these standards is integral to achieving the *Objectives of Management Accounting.*[3] Management accountants shall not commit acts contrary to these standards nor shall they condone the commission of such acts by others within their organizations.

Competence

Management accountants have a responsibility to:

- Maintain an appropriate level of professional competence by ongoing development of their knowledge and skills.
- Perform their professional duties in accordance with relevant laws, regulations, and technical standards.
- Prepare complete and clear reports and recommendations after appropriate analyses of relevant and reliable information.

Confidentiality

Management accountants have a responsibility to:

- Refrain from disclosing confidential information acquired in the course of their work except when authorized, unless legally obligated to do so.
- Inform subordinates as appropriate regarding the confidentiality of information acquired in the course of their work and monitor their activities to assure the maintenance of that confidentiality.
- Refrain from using or appearing to use confidential information acquired in the course of their work for unethical or illegal advantage either personally or through third parties.

Integrity

Management accountants have a responsibility to:

- Avoid actual or apparent conflicts of interest and advise all appropriate parties of any potential conflict.
- Refrain from engaging in any activity that would prejudice their ability to carry out their duties ethically.
- Refuse any gift, favor, or hospitality that would influence or would appear to influence their actions.
- Refrain from either actively or passively subverting the attainment of the organization's legitimate and ethical objectives.
- Recognize and communicate professional limitations or other constraints that would preclude responsible judgment or successful performance of an activity.

[3] National Association of Accountants, *Statements on Management Accounting: Objectives of Management Accounting,* Statement No. 1B, New York, N.Y., June 17, 1982.

- Communicate unfavorable as well as favorable information and professional judgments or opinions.
- Refrain from engaging in or supporting any activity that would discredit the profession.

Objectivity

Management accountants have a responsibility to:

- Communicate information fairly and objectively.
- Disclose fully all relevant information that could reasonably be expected to influence an intended user's understanding of the reports, comments, and recommendations presented.

Appendix C: Alternative Methods of Recording Deferrals

As discussed in Chapter 3, deferrals are created by recording a transaction in a way that delays or defers the recognition of an expense or a revenue. Deferrals may be either deferred expenses (prepaid expenses) or deferred revenues (unearned revenues).

In Chapter 2, deferred expenses (prepaid expenses) were debited to an *asset* account at the time of payment. As an alternative, deferred expenses may be debited to an *expense* account at the time of payment. In Chapter 2, deferred revenues (unearned revenues) were credited to a *liability* account at the time of receipt. As an alternative, deferred revenues may be credited to a *revenue* account at the time of receipt. This appendix describes and illustrates these alternative methods of recording deferred expenses and deferred revenues.

Deferred Expenses (Prepaid Expenses)

As a basis for illustrating the alternative methods of recording deferred expenses, the insurance premium paid by Computer King in Chapter 2 is used. The amounts related to this insurance are as follows:

Prepayment of insurance for 24 months, starting December 1	$2,400
Insurance premium expired during December	100
Unexpired insurance premium at the end of December	$2,300

Based on the above data, the entries to account for the deferred expense (prepaid insurance) recorded initially as an *asset* are shown in the journal and T accounts in Exhibit 1. The adjusting entry in Exhibit 1 was shown in Chapter 3. The entries to account for the prepaid insurance recorded initially as an *expense* are shown in the journal and T accounts in Exhibit 2.

EXHIBIT 1

Prepaid Expense Recorded Initially as Asset

Initial entry (to record initial payment):

Dec. 1	Prepaid Insurance	2,400	
	Cash		2,400

Adjusting entry (to transfer amount *used* to proper *expense* account):

Dec. 31	Insurance Expense	100	
	Prepaid Insurance		100

Closing entry (to close income statement accounts with debit balances):

Income Summary	XXXX	
Supplies Expense		XXXX
Insurance Expense		100

Prepaid Insurance

Dec. 1		2,400	Dec. 31	Adjusting	100

Insurance Expense

Dec. 31	Adjusting	100	Dec. 31	Closing	100

EXHIBIT 2

Prepaid Expense Recorded Initially as Expense

Initial entry (to record initial payment):

Dec. 1	Insurance Expense	2,400	
	Cash		2,400

Adjusting entry (to transfer amount *unused* to the proper *asset* account):

Dec. 31	Prepaid Insurance	2,300	
	Insurance Expense		2,300

Closing entry (to close income statement accounts with debit balances):

Income Summary	XXXX	
Supplies Expense		XXXX
Insurance Expense		100

Prepaid Insurance

Dec. 31	Adjusting	2,300			

Insurance Expense

Dec. 1		2,400	Dec. 31	Adjusting	2,300
			31	Closing	100

Either of the two methods of recording deferred expenses (prepaid expenses) may be used. As illustrated in Exhibits 1 and 2, both methods result in the same account balances after the adjusting entries have been recorded. Therefore, the amounts reported as expenses in the income statement and as assets on the balance sheet will not be affected by the method used. To avoid confusion, the method used by a business for each kind of prepaid expense should be followed consistently from year to year.

Some businesses record all deferred expenses using one method. Other businesses use one method to record the prepayment of some expenses and the other method for other expenses. Initial debits to the asset account are logical for prepayments of insurance, which are usually for periods of one to three years. On the other hand, rent on a building may be prepaid on the first of each month. The prepaid rent will expire by the end of the month. In this case, it is logical to record the payment of rent by initially debiting an expense account rather than an asset account.

Deferred Revenues (Unearned Revenues)

As a basis for illustrating the alternative methods of recording deferred revenues, the rent received by Computer King in Chapter 2 is used. Computer King rented land on December 1 to a local retailer for use as a parking lot for three months and received $360 for the entire three months. On December 31, $120 (1/3 × $360) of the rent has been earned, and $240 (2/3 × $360) of the rent is still unearned.

Based on the above data, the entries to account for the deferred revenue (unearned rent) recorded initially as a liability are shown in the journal and ledger in Exhibit 3. The adjusting entry in Exhibit 3 was shown in Chapter 3. The entries to account for the unearned rent recorded initially as revenue are shown in the journal and ledger in Exhibit 4.

EXHIBIT 3

Unearned Revenue Recorded Initially as Liability

Initial entry (to record initial receipt):

Dec. 1	Cash	360	
	Unearned Rent		360

Adjusting entry (to transfer amount *earned* to proper *revenue* account):

Dec. 31	Unearned Rent	120	
	Rent Revenue		120

Closing entry (to close income statement accounts with credit balances):

Dec. 31	Fees Earned	XXXX	
	~		
	Rent Revenue	120	
	Income Summary		XXXX

Unearned Rent

Dec. 31	Adjusting	120	Dec. 1		360

Rent Revenue

Dec. 31	Closing	120	Dec. 31	Adjusting	120

EXHIBIT 4

Unearned Revenue Recorded Initially as Revenue

Initial entry (to record initial receipt):

Dec. 1	Cash	360	
	Rent Revenue		360

Adjusting entry (to transfer amount *unearned* to proper *liability* account):

Dec. 31	Rent Revenue	240	
	Unearned Rent		240

Closing entry (to close income statement accounts with credit balances):

Dec. 31	Fees Earned	XXXX	
	~		
	Rent Revenue	120	
	Income Summary		XXXX

Unearned Rent

			Dec. 31	Adjusting	240

Rent Revenue

Dec. 31	Adjusting	240	Dec. 1		360
31	Closing	120			

As illustrated in Exhibits 3 and 4, both methods result in the same account balances after the adjusting entries have been recorded. Therefore, the amounts reported as revenues in the income statement and as liabilities on the balance sheet will not be affected by the method used. Either of the methods may be used for all revenues received in advance. Alternatively, the first method may be used for advance receipts of some kinds of revenue and the second method for other kinds. To avoid confusion, the method used by a business for each kind of unearned revenue should be followed consistently from year to year.

Reversing Entries for Deferrals

As discussed in the appendix at the end of Chapter 4, the use of reversing entries is optional. However, the use of reversing entries generally simplifies the analysis of transactions and reduces the likelihood of errors in the subsequent recording of transactions. Normally, reversing entries are prepared for deferrals in the following two cases:

1. When a deferred expense (prepaid expense) is initially recorded as an expense.
2. When a deferred revenue (unearned revenue) is initially recorded as a revenue.

The entry to reverse the adjustment to record the prepaid insurance in Exhibit 2 is as follows:

Jan.	1	Insurance Expense	2,300	
		Prepaid Insurance		2,300

The entry to reverse the adjustment to record the unearned rent in Exhibit 4 is as follows:

Jan.	1	Unearned Rent	240	
		Rent Revenue		240

EXERCISES

Exercise C–1
Adjusting entries for office supplies

The office supplies purchased during the year total $1,980, and the amount of office supplies on hand at the end of the year is $235.

a. Record the following transactions directly in T accounts for Office Supplies and Office Supplies Expense, using the system of initially recording supplies as an asset: (1) purchases for the period; (2) adjusting entry at the end of the period. Identify each entry by number.
b. Record the following transactions directly in T accounts for Office Supplies and Office Supplies Expense, using the system of initially recording supplies as an expense: (1) purchases for the period; (2) adjusting entry at the end of the period. Identify each entry by number.

Exercise C–2
Adjusting entries for prepaid insurance

During the first year of operations, insurance premiums of $6,750 were paid. At the end of the year, unexpired premiums totaled $4,050. Journalize the adjusting entry at the end of the year, assuming that (a) prepaid expenses were initially recorded as assets and (b) prepaid expenses were initially recorded as expenses.

Exercise C–3
Adjusting entries for advertising revenue

The advertising revenues received during the year total $210,000, and the unearned advertising revenue at the end of the year is $35,900.

a. Record the following transactions directly in T accounts for Unearned Advertising Revenue and Advertising Revenue, using the system of initially recording advertising fees as a liability: (1) revenues received during the period; (2) adjusting entry at the end of the period. Identify each entry by number.

b. Record the following transactions directly in T accounts for Unearned Advertising Revenue and Advertising Revenue, using the system of initially recording advertising fees as revenue: (1) revenues received during the period; (2) adjusting entry at the end of the period. Identify each entry by number.

Exercise C–4
Year-end entries for deferred revenues

In their first year of operation, Snyder Publishing Co. received $1,275,000 from advertising contracts and $3,195,000 from magazine subscriptions, crediting the two amounts to Unearned Advertising Revenue and Circulation Revenue, respectively. At the end of the year, the unearned advertising revenue amounts to $300,000, and the unearned circulation revenue amounts to $542,000. Journalize the adjusting entries that should be made at the end of the year.

Appendix D: Periodic Inventory Systems for Merchandising Businesses

In this text, we emphasize the perpetual inventory system of accounting for purchases and sales of merchandise. Not all merchandise businesses, however, use perpetual inventory systems. For example, some managers/owners of small merchandise businesses, such as locally owned hardware stores, may feel more comfortable using manually kept records. Because a manual perpetual inventory system is time-consuming and costly to maintain, the periodic inventory system is often used in these cases.

Merchandise Transactions in a Periodic Inventory System

In a periodic inventory system, the revenues from sales are recorded when sales are made in the same manner as in a perpetual inventory system. However, no attempt is made on the date of sale to record the cost of the merchandise sold. Instead, the merchandise inventory on hand at the end of the period is counted. This physical inventory is then used to determine (1) the cost of merchandise sold during the period and (2) the cost of merchandise on hand at the end of the period.

In a periodic inventory system, purchases of inventory are recorded in a purchases account rather than in a merchandise inventory account. No attempt is made to keep a detailed record of the amount of inventory on hand at any given time.

The purchases account is normally debited for the amount of the invoice before considering any purchases discounts. Purchases discounts are normally recorded in a separate purchases discounts account.[1] The balance of this account is reported as a deduction from the amount initially recorded in Purchases for the period. Thus, the purchases discounts account is viewed as a contra (or offsetting) account to Purchases.

Purchases returns and allowances are recorded in a similar manner as purchases discounts. A separate account is used to keep a record of the amount of purchases returns and allowances during a period. Purchases returns and allowances are reported as a deduction from the amount initially recorded as Purchases. Like Purchases Discounts, the purchases returns and allowances account is a contra (or offsetting) account to Purchases.

When merchandise is purchased FOB shipping point, the buyer is responsible for paying the freight charges. In a periodic inventory system, freight charges paid when purchasing merchandise FOB shipping point are debited to Transportation In, Freight In, or a similarly titled account.

To illustrate the recording of merchandise transactions in a periodic system, we will use the following selected transactions for Taylor Co. We will also explain how the transaction would have been recorded under a perpetual system.

June 5. Purchased $30,000 of merchandise on account from Owen Clothing, terms 2/10, n/30.

Purchases	30,000	
Accounts Payable—Owen Clothing		30,000

Under the perpetual inventory system, such purchases would be recorded in the merchandise inventory account at their cost, $30,000.

June 8. Returned merchandise purchased on account from Owen Clothing on June 5, $500.

Accounts Payable—Owen Clothing	500	
Purchases Returns and Allowances		500

[1] Some businesses prefer to credit the purchases account. If this alternative is used, the balance of the purchases account will be a net amount—the total purchases less the total purchases discounts for the period.

Under the perpetual inventory system, returns would be recorded as a credit to the merchandise inventory account at their cost of $500.

June 15. Paid Owen Clothing for purchase of June 5, less return of $500 and discount of $590 [($30,000 − $500) × 2%].

Accounts Payable—Owen Clothing	29,500	
Cash		28,910
Purchases Discounts		590

Under a perpetual inventory system, a purchases discount account is not used. Instead the merchandise inventory account is credited for the amount of the discount, $590.

June 18. Sold merchandise on account to Jones Co., $12,500, 1/10, n/30. The cost of the merchandise sold was $9,000.

Accounts Receivable—Jones Co.	12,500	
Sales		12,500

The entry to record the sale is the same under both systems. Under the perpetual inventory system, the cost of merchandise sold and the reduction in merchandise inventory would also be recorded on the date of sale.

June 21. Received merchandise returned on account from Jones Co., $4,000. The cost of the merchandise returned was $2,800.

Sales Returns and Allowances	4,000	
Accounts Receivable—Jones Co.		4,000

The entry to record the sales return is the same under both systems. In addition, the cost of the merchandise returned would be debited to the merchandise inventory account and credited to the cost of merchandise sold account under the perpetual inventory system.

June 22. Purchased merchandise from Norcross Clothiers, $15,000, terms FOB shipping point, 2/15, n/30, with prepaid transportation charges of $750 added to the invoice.

Purchases	15,000	
Transportation In	750	
Accounts Payable—Norcross Clothiers		15,750

This entry is similar to the June 5 entry for the purchase of merchandise. Since the transportation terms were FOB shipping point, the prepaid freight charges of $750 must be added to the invoice cost of $15,000. Under the perpetual inventory system, the purchase is recorded in the merchandise inventory account at the cost of $15,750 (invoice price plus transportation).

June 28. Received $8,415 as payment on account from Jones Co., less return of June 21 and less discount of $85 [($12,500 − $4,000) × 1%].

Cash	8,415	
Sales Discounts	85	
Accounts Receivable—Jones Co.		8,500

This entry is the same under the perpetual inventory system.

June 29. Received $19,600 from cash sales. The cost of the merchandise sold was $13,800.

Cash	19,600	
Sales		19,600

The entry to record the sale is the same under both systems. Under the perpetual inventory system, the cost of merchandise sold and the reduction in merchandise inventory would also be recorded on the date of sale.

Cost of Merchandise Sold

Under the periodic inventory system, the cost of merchandise sold during a period is reported in a separate section in the income statement. To illustrate, assume that on January 3, 2000, Computer King opened a merchandising outlet selling microcomputers and software. During 2000, Computer King purchased $340,000 of merchandise. The inventory on December 31, 2000, is $59,700. The cost of merchandise sold during 2000 is reported as follows:

Cost of merchandise sold:	
Purchases	$340,000
Less merchandise inventory, December 31, 2000	59,700
Cost of merchandise sold	$280,300

To continue the example, assume that during 2001 Computer King purchased additional merchandise of $521,980. Computer King also received credit for purchases returns and allowances of $9,100, took purchases discounts of $2,525, and paid transportation costs of $17,400. The purchases returns and allowances and the purchases discounts are deducted from the total purchases to yield the net purchases. The transportation costs are then added to the net purchases to yield the cost of merchandise purchased. These amounts are reported in the cost of merchandise sold section of the Computer King income statement for 2001 as follows:

Purchases		$521,980	
Less: Purchases returns and allowances	$9,100		
Purchases discounts	2,525	11,625	
Net purchases		$510,355	
Add transportation in		17,400	
Cost of merchandise purchased			$527,755

The ending inventory of Computer King on December 31, 2000, $59,700, becomes the beginning inventory for 2001. In the cost of merchandise sold section of the income statement for 2001, this beginning inventory is added to the cost of merchandise purchased to yield the merchandise available for sale. The ending inventory on December 31, 2001, $62,150, is then subtracted from the merchandise available for sale to yield the cost of merchandise sold. Exhibit 1 shows the cost of merchandise sold during 2001.

EXHIBIT 1
Cost of Merchandise Sold—Periodic Inventory System

Cost of merchandise sold:				
Merchandise inventory, January 1, 2001			$ 59,700	
Purchases		$521,980		
Less: Purchases returns and allowances	$9,100			
Purchases discounts	2,525	11,625		
Net purchases		$510,355		
Add transportation in		17,400		
Cost of merchandise purchased			527,755	
Merchandise available for sale			$587,455	
Less merchandise inventory, December 31, 2001			62,150	
Cost of merchandise sold				$525,305

The multiple-step income statement under the periodic inventory system is illustrated in Exhibit 2. The multiple-step income statement under a perpetual inventory system is similar, except that the cost of merchandise sold is reported as a single amount.

EXHIBIT 2
Multiple-Step Income Statement—Periodic Inventory System

Computer King
Income Statement
For the Year Ended December 31, 2001

Revenue from sales:				
Sales			$720,185	
Less: Sales returns and allowances		$ 6,140		
Sales discounts		5,790	11,930	
Net sales				$708,255
Cost of merchandise sold:				
Merchandise inventory, January 1, 2001			$ 59,700	
Purchases		$521,980		
Less: Purchases returns and allowances	$9,100			
Purchases discounts	2,525	11,625		
Net purchases		$510,355		
Add transportation in		17,400		
Cost of merchandise purchased			527,755	
Merchandise available for sale			$587,455	
Less merchandise inventory, December 31, 2001			62,150	
Cost of merchandise sold				525,305
Gross profit				$182,950
Operating expenses:				
Selling expenses:				
Sales salaries expense		$ 60,030		
Advertising expense		10,860		
Depreciation expense—store equipment		3,100		
Miscellaneous selling expense		630		
Total selling expenses			$ 74,620	
Administrative expenses:				
Office salaries expense		$ 21,020		
Rent expense		8,100		
Depreciation expense—office equipment		2,490		
Insurance expense		1,910		
Office supplies expense		610		
Miscellaneous administrative expense		760		
Total administrative expenses			34,890	
Total operating expenses				109,510
Income from operations				$ 73,440
Other income:				
Interest revenue		$ 3,800		
Rent revenue		600		
Total other income			$ 4,400	
Other expense:				
Interest expense			2,440	1,960
Net income				$ 75,400

Chart of Accounts for a Periodic Inventory System

Exhibit 3 is the chart of accounts for Computer King when a periodic inventory system is used. The periodic inventory accounts related to merchandising transactions are shown in color.

EXHIBIT 3
Chart of Accounts—Periodic Inventory System

Balance Sheet Accounts		Income Statement Accounts	
	100 Assets		400 Revenues
110	Cash	410	Sales
111	Notes Receivable	411	Sales Returns and Allowances
112	Accounts Receivable	412	Sales Discounts
113	Interest Receivable		500 Costs and Expenses
115	Merchandise Inventory	510	Purchases
116	Office Supplies	511	Purchases Returns and Allowances
117	Prepaid Insurance	512	Purchases Discounts
120	Land	513	Transportation In
123	Store Equipment	520	Sales Salaries Expenses
124	Accumulated Depreciation—Store Equipment	521	Advertising Expense
125	Office Equipment	522	Depreciation Expense—Store Equipment
126	Accumulated Depreciation—Office Equipment	523	Transportation Out
	200 Liabilities	529	Miscellaneous Selling Expense
210	Accounts Payable	530	Office Salaries Expense
211	Salaries Payable	531	Rent Expense
212	Unearned Rent	532	Depreciation Expense—Office Equipment
215	Notes Payable	533	Insurance Expense
	300 Owner's Equity	534	Office Supplies Expense
310	Pat King, Capital	539	Misc. Administrative Expense
311	Pat King, Drawing		600 Other Income
312	Income Summary	610	Rent Revenue
		611	Interest Revenue
			700 Other Expense
		710	Interest Expense

End-of-Period Procedures in a Periodic Inventory System

The end-of-period procedures are generally the same for the periodic and perpetual inventory systems. In the remainder of this appendix, we will discuss the differences in procedures for the two systems which affect the work sheet, the adjusting entries, and the closing entries. As the basis for illustrations, we will use the data for Computer King, presented in Chapter 6.

Work Sheet

The differences in the work sheet for a merchandising business that uses the periodic inventory system are highlighted in the work sheet for Computer King in Exhibit 4. As we illustrated earlier, accounts for purchases, purchases returns and allowances, purchases discounts, and transportation in are used in a periodic inventory system.

Under the periodic inventory system, the merchandise inventory account, throughout the accounting period, shows the inventory at the beginning of the period. As shown in Exhibit 1, the merchandise inventory on January 1, 2001, \$59,700, is a part of the merchandise available for sale. At the end of the period, the beginning inventory amount in the ledger is replaced with the ending inventory amount. To update the inventory account, two adjusting entries are used.[2] The first adjust-

[2] Another method of updating the merchandise inventory account at the end of the period is called the *closing method*. This method adjusts the merchandise inventory through the use of closing entries. This method may not be appropriate for use in computerized accounting systems. Since the financial statements are the same under both methods and since computerized accounting systems are used by most businesses, the closing method is not illustrated.

ing entry transfers the beginning inventory balance to Income Summary. This entry, shown below, has the effect of increasing the cost of merchandise sold and decreasing net income.

Dec. 31	Income Summary	59,700	
	Merchandise Inventory		59,700

After the first adjusting entry has been recorded and posted, the balance of the merchandise inventory account is zero. The second adjusting entry records the cost of the merchandise on hand at the end of the period by debiting Merchandise Inventory. Since the merchandise inventory at December 31, 2001, $62,150, is subtracted from the cost of merchandise available for sale in determining the cost of merchandise sold, Income Summary is credited. This credit has the effect of decreasing the cost of merchandise available for sale during the period, $587,455, by the cost of the unsold merchandise. The second adjusting entry is shown below.

Dec. 31	Merchandise Inventory	62,150	
	Income Summary		62,150

After the second adjusting entry has been recorded and posted, the balance of the merchandise inventory account is the amount of the ending inventory. The accounts for Merchandise Inventory and Income Summary after both entries have been posted would appear in T account form as follows:

Merchandise Inventory

2001					
Jan. 1	Beginning inventory	59,700	Dec. 31	Beginning inventory	59,700
Dec. 31	Ending inventory	62,150			

Income Summary

Dec. 31	Beginning inventory	59,700	Dec. 31	Ending inventory	62,150

No separate adjusting entry can be made for merchandise inventory shrinkage in a periodic inventory system. This is because no perpetual inventory records are available to show what inventory should be on hand at the end of the period. One disadvantage of the periodic inventory system is that inventory shrinkage cannot be measured.[3]

Completing the Work Sheet

After all of the necessary adjustments have been entered on the work sheet, the work sheet is completed in the normal manner. An exception to the usual practice of extending only account balances is Income Summary. Both the debit and credit amounts for Income Summary are extended to the Adjusted Trial Balance columns. Extending both amounts aids in the preparation of the income statement because the debit adjustment (the beginning inventory of $59,700) and the credit adjustment (the ending inventory of $62,150) are reported as part of the cost of merchandise sold.

The purchases, purchases discounts, purchases returns and allowances, and transportation in accounts are extended to the Income Statement Columns of the work sheet, since they are used in computing the cost of merchandise sold. You should note that the two merchandise inventory amounts in Income Summary are extended to the Income Statement columns. After all of the items have been extended to the statement columns, the four columns are totaled and the net income or net loss is determined.

[3] Any inventory shrinkage that does exist is part of the cost of merchandise sold and is reported on the income statement, since a smaller ending inventory is deducted from other merchandise available for sale.

EXHIBIT 4
Work Sheet—Periodic Inventory System

Computer King
Work Sheet
For the Year Ended December 31, 2001

	Trial Balance		Adjustments		Adjusted Trial Balance		Income Statement		Balance Sheet	
Account Title	**Dr.**	**Cr.**	**Dr.**	**Cr.**	**Dr.**	**Cr.**	**Dr.**	**Cr.**	**Dr.**	**Cr.**
Cash	52,950				52,950				52,950	
Notes Receivable	40,000				40,000				40,000	
Accounts Receivable	60,880				60,880				60,880	
Interest Receivable			(a) 200		200				200	
Merchandise Inventory	59,700		(c)62,150	(b)59,700	62,150				62,150	
Office Supplies	1,090			(d) 610	480				480	
Prepaid Insurance	4,560			(e) 1,910	2,650				2,650	
Land	10,000				10,000				10,000	
Store Equipment	27,100				27,100				27,100	
Accum. Depr.—Store Equipment		2,600		(f) 3,100		5,700				5,700
Office Equipment	15,570				15,570				15,570	
Accum. Depr.—Office Equipment		2,230		(g) 2,490		4,720				4,720
Accounts Payable		22,420				22,420				22,420
Salaries Payable				(h) 1,140		1,140				1,140
Unearned Rent		2,400	(i) 600			1,800				1,800
Notes Payable (final payment, 2008)		25,000				25,000				25,000
Pat King, Capital		153,800				153,800				153,800
Pat King, Drawing	18,000				18,000				18,000	
Income Summary			(b)59,700	(c)62,150	59,700	62,150	59,700	62,150		
Sales		720,185				720,185		720,185		
Sales Returns and Allowances	6,140				6,140		6,140			
Sales Discounts	5,790				5,790		5,790			
Purchases	521,980				521,980		521,980			
Purchases Returns & Allowances		9,100				9,100		9,100		
Purchases Discounts		2,525				2,525		2,525		
Transportation In	17,400				17,400		17,400			
Sales Salaries Expense	59,250		(h) 780		60,030		60,030			
Advertising Expense	10,860				10,860		10,860			
Depr. Expense—Store Equipment			(f) 3,100		3,100		3,100			
Miscellaneous Selling Expense	630				630		630			
Office Salaries Expense	20,660		(h) 360		21,020		21,020			
Rent Expense	8,100				8,100		8,100			
Depr. Expense—Office Equipment			(g) 2,490		2,490		2,490			
Insurance Expense			(e) 1,910		1,910		1,910			
Office Supplies Expense			(d) 610		610		610			
Misc. Administrative Expense	760				760		760			
Rent Revenue				(i) 600		600		600		
Interest Revenue		3,600		(a) 200		3,800		3,800		
Interest Expense	2,440				2,440		2,440			
	943,860	943,860	131,900	131,900	1,012,940	1,012,940	722,960	798,360	289,980	214,580
Net income							75,400			75,400
							798,360	798,360	289,980	289,980

(a) Interest earned but not received on notes receivable, $200.
(b) Beginning merchandise inventory, $59,700.
(c) Ending merchandise inventory, $62,150.
(d) Office supplies used, $610 ($1,090 – $480).
(e) Insurance expired, $1,910.
(f) Depreciation of store equipment, $3,100.
(g) Depreciation of office equipment, $2,490.
(h) Salaries accrued but not paid (sales salaries, $780; office salaries, $360), $1,140.
(i) Rent earned from amount received in advance, $600.

Financial Statements

The financial statements for Computer King are essentially the same under both the perpetual and periodic inventory systems. The main difference is that the cost of goods is reported as a single amount under the perpetual system. Exhibit 2 illustrates the manner in which cost of merchandise sold is reported in a multiple-step income statement when the periodic inventory system is used.[4]

Adjusting and Closing Entries

The adjusting entries are the same under both inventory systems, except for merchandise inventory. As indicated previously, two adjusting entries for beginning and ending merchandise inventory are necessary in a periodic inventory system.

The closing entries differ in the periodic inventory system in that there is no cost of merchandise sold account to be closed to Income Summary. Instead, the purchases, purchases discounts, purchases returns and allowances, and transportation in accounts are closed to Income Summary.[5] To illustrate, the adjusting and closing entries under a periodic inventory system for Computer King are shown below.

JOURNAL **PAGE 16**

Date		Description	Post. Ref.	Debit	Credit
		Adjusting Entries			
2001 Dec.	31	Interest Receivable	113	200.00	
		Interest Revenue	611		200.00
	31	Income Summary	312	59,700.00	
		Merchandise Inventory	115		59,700.00
	31	Merchandise Inventory	115	62,150.00	
		Income Summary	312		62,150.00
	31	Office Supplies Expense	534	610.00	
		Office Supplies	116		610.00
	31	Insurance Expense	533	1,910.00	
		Prepaid Insurance	117		1,910.00
	31	Depreciation Expense—Store Equip.	522	3,100.00	
		Accumulated Depr.—Store Equip.	124		3,100.00
	31	Depreciation Expense—Office Equip.	532	2,490.00	
		Accumulated Depr.—Office Equip.	126		2,490.00
	31	Sales Salaries Expense	520	780.00	
		Office Salaries Expense	530	360.00	
		Salaries Payable	211		1,140.00
	31	Unearned Rent	212	600.00	
		Rent Revenue	610		600.00

[4] The single-step income statement would be the same for both the perpetual and the periodic inventory systems.

[5] The balance of Income Summary, after the merchandise inventory adjustments and the first two closing entries have been posted, is the net income or net loss for the period.

JOURNAL					PAGE 17
Date		Description	Post. Ref.	Debit	Credit
		Closing Entries			
2001 Dec.	31	Sales	410	720,185.00	
		Purchases Returns and Allowances	511	9,100.00	
		Purchases Discounts	512	2,525.00	
		Rent Revenue	610	600.00	
		Interest Revenue	611	3,800.00	
		Income Summary	312		736,210.00
	31	Income Summary	312	663,260.00	
		Sales Returns and Allowances	411		6,140.00
		Sales Discounts	412		5,790.00
		Purchases	510		521,980.00
		Transportation In	513		17,400.00
		Sales Salaries Expense	520		60,030.00
		Advertising Expense	521		10,860.00
		Depreciation Exp.—Store Equip.	522		3,100.00
		Miscellaneous Selling Expense	529		630.00
		Office Salaries Expense	530		21,020.00
		Rent Expense	531		8,100.00
		Depreciation Exp.—Office Equip.	532		2,490.00
		Insurance Expense	533		1,910.00
		Office Supplies Expense	534		610.00
		Miscellaneous Administrative Exp.	539		760.00
		Interest Expense	710		2,440.00
	31	Income Summary	312	75,400.00	
		Pat King, Capital	310		75,400.00
	31	Pat King, Capital	310	18,000.00	
		Pat King, Drawing	311		18,000.00

EXERCISES

Exercise D–1
Purchases-related transactions—periodic inventory system

Journalize entries for the following related transactions, assuming that Golf "R" Us Co. uses the periodic inventory system.

a. Purchased $8,000 of merchandise from Cobra Co. on account, terms 2/10, n/30.
b. Discovered that some of the merchandise was defective and returned items with an invoice price of $1,000, receiving credit.
c. Paid the amount owed on the invoice within the discount period.
d. Purchased $5,000 of merchandise from Callaway Co. on account, terms 1/10, n/30.
e. Paid the amount owed on the invoice within the discount period.

Exercise D–2
Sales-related transactions—periodic inventory system

Journalize entries for the following related transactions, assuming that Tedder Company uses the periodic inventory system.

Mar. 8 Sold merchandise to a customer for $7,500, terms FOB shipping point, 2/10, n/30.
8 Paid the transportation charges of $230, debiting the amounts to Accounts Receivable.

Mar. 12 Issued a credit memorandum for $1,800 to a customer for merchandise returned.
18 Received a check for the amount due from the sale.

Exercise D–3
Adjusting entries for merchandise inventory—periodic inventory system

Data assembled for preparing the work sheet for Givens Co. for the fiscal year ended December 31, 1999, included the following:

Merchandise inventory as of January 1, 1999	$205,000
Merchandise inventory as of December 31, 1999	$237,200

Journalize the two adjusting entries for merchandise inventory that would appear on the work sheet, assuming that the periodic inventory system is used.

Exercise D–4
Identification of missing items from income statement—periodic inventory system

For (a) through (i), identify the items designated by "X".

a. Sales − (X + X) = Net sales
b. Purchases − (X + X) = Net purchases
c. Net purchases + X = Cost of merchandise purchased
d. Merchandise inventory (beginning) + cost of merchandise purchased = X
e. Merchandise available for sale − X = Cost of merchandise sold
f. Net sales − cost of merchandise sold = X
g. X + X = Operating expenses
h. Gross profit − operating expenses = X
i. Income from operations + X − X = Net income

Exercise D–5
Multiple-step income statement—periodic inventory system

✓ Gross profit: $145,000

Selected data for Plantstar Company for the current year ended December 31 are as follows:

Merchandise inventory, January 1	$ 51,300
Merchandise inventory, December 31	67,500
Purchases	662,000
Purchases discounts	8,000
Purchases returns and allowances	15,500
Sales	805,000
Sales discounts	6,500
Sales returns and allowances	8,700
Transportation in	22,500

Prepare a multiple-step income statement through gross profit for Plantstar Company for the current year ended December 31.

Exercise D–6
Adjusting and closing entries—periodic inventory system

Selected account titles and related amounts appearing in the Income Statement and Balance Sheet columns of the work sheet of Delia Company for the year ended December 31 are listed in alphabetical order as follows:

Administrative Expenses	$ 69,500
Building	312,500
Cash	58,500
Delia Williams, Capital	472,580
Delia Williams, Drawing	45,000
Interest Expense	2,500
Merchandise Inventory (1/1)	300,000
Merchandise Inventory (12/31)	315,000
Notes Payable	25,000
Office Supplies	10,600
Purchases	750,000
Purchases Discounts	6,000
Purchases Returns and Allowances	7,000
Salaries Payable	4,220
Sales	1,375,000
Sales Discounts	10,200
Sales Returns and Allowances	44,300
Selling Expenses	232,700
Store Supplies	7,700
Transportation In	21,300

All selling expenses have been recorded in the account entitled Selling Expenses, and all administrative expenses have been recorded in the account entitled Administrative Expenses. Assuming that Delia Company uses the periodic inventory system, journalize (a) the adjusting entries for merchandise inventory and (b) the closing entries.

PROBLEMS

Problem D–1

Sales-related and purchase-related transactions—periodic inventory system

The following were selected from among the transactions completed by The Document Company during April of the current year:

Apr. 4. Purchased merchandise on account from Vela Co., list price $20,000, trade discount 40%, terms FOB destination, 2/10, n/30.
5. Sold merchandise for cash, $4,100.
7. Purchased merchandise on account from Summit Co., $7,500, terms FOB shipping point, 2/10, n/30, with prepaid transportation costs of $200 added to the invoice.
7. Returned $2,500 of merchandise purchased on April 4 from Vela Co.
11. Sold merchandise on account to Bowles Co., list price $2,250, trade discount 20%, terms 1/10, n/30.
14. Paid Vela Co. on account for purchase of April 4, less return of April 7 and discount.
15. Sold merchandise on nonbank credit cards and reported accounts to the card company, American Express, $5,850.
17. Paid Summit Co. on account for purchase of April 7, less discount.
21. Received cash on account from sale of April 11 to Bowles Co., less discount.
25. Sold merchandise on account to Clemons Co., $3,200, terms 1/10, n/30.
28. Received cash from American Express for nonbank credit card sales of April 15, less $280 service fee.
30. Received merchandise returned by Clemons Co. from sale on April 25, $1,700.

Instructions

Journalize the transactions for The Document Co. in a two-column general journal.

Problem D–2

Sales-related and purchase-related transactions—periodic inventory system

The following were selected from among the transactions completed by Taxel Company during March of the current year:

Mar. 2. Purchased merchandise on account from Queen Co., list price $25,000, trade discount 30%, terms FOB shipping point, 2/10, n/30, with prepaid transportation costs of $720 added to the invoice.
4. Purchased merchandise on account from Rossi Co., $6,000, terms FOB destination, 1/10, n/30.
6. Sold merchandise on account to C. F. Howell Co., list price $7,500, trade discount 40%, terms 2/10, n/30.
9. Returned merchandise purchased on March 4 from Rossi Co., $1,300.
12. Paid Queen Co. on account for purchase of March 2, less discount.
14. Paid Rossi Co. on account for purchase of March 4, less return of March 9 and discount.
16. Received cash on account from sale of March 6 to C. F. Howell Co., less discount.
19. Sold merchandise on nonbank credit cards and reported accounts to the card company, American Express, $4,450.
22. Sold merchandise on account to Vantage Co., $3,480, terms 2/10, n/30.
24. Sold merchandise for cash, $4,350.
25. Received merchandise returned by Vantage Co. from sale on March 22, $1,480.
31. Received cash from American Express for nonbank credit card sales of March 19, less $290 service fee.

Instructions

Journalize the transactions for Taxel Co. in a two-column general journal.

Problem D–3

Sales-related and purchase-related transactions for seller and buyer—periodic inventory system

The following selected transactions were completed during July between Servco Company and Barkey Co.:

July 3. Servco Company sold merchandise on account to Barkey Co., $10,500, terms FOB destination, 2/15, n/eom.
3. Servco Company paid transportation costs of $450 for delivery of merchandise sold to Barkey Co. on July 3.
10. Servco Company sold merchandise on account to Barkey Co., $12,000, terms FOB shipping point, n/eom.
11. Barkey Co. returned merchandise purchased on account on July 3 from Servco Company, $2,000.
14. Barkey Co. paid transportation charges of $200 on July 10 purchase from Servco Company.
17. Servco Company sold merchandise on account to Barkey Co., $20,000, terms FOB shipping point, 1/10, n/30. Servco prepaid transportation costs of $1,750, which were added to the invoice.
18. Barkey Co. paid Servco Company for purchase of July 3, less discount and less return of July 11.
27. Barkey Co. paid Servco Company on account for purchase of July 17, less discount.
31. Barkey Co. paid Servco Company on account for purchase of July 10.

Instructions

Journalize the July transactions for (1) Servco Company and for (2) Barkey Co.

Problem D–4

Preparation of work sheet, financial statements, and adjusting and closing entries—periodic inventory system

✓ 1. Net income: $169,250

The accounts and their balances in the ledger of The Shoe Co. on December 31 of the current year are as follows:

Cash	$ 38,000
Accounts Receivable	112,500
Merchandise Inventory	180,000
Prepaid Insurance	9,700
Store Supplies	4,250
Office Supplies	2,100
Store Equipment	132,000
Accumulated Depreciation—Store Equipment	40,300
Office Equipment	50,000
Accumulated Depreciation—Office Equipment	17,200
Accounts Payable	66,700
Salaries Payable	—
Unearned Rent	1,200
Note Payable (final payment, 2010)	105,000
J. Oxford, Capital	174,600
J. Oxford, Drawing	40,000
Income Summary	—
Sales	895,000
Sales Returns and Allowances	11,900
Sales Discounts	7,100
Purchases	535,000
Purchases Returns and Allowances	10,100
Purchases Discounts	4,900
Transportation In	6,200
Sales Salaries Expense	76,400
Advertising Expense	25,000
Depreciation Expense—Store Equipment	—
Store Supplies Expense	—
Miscellaneous Selling Expense	1,600
Office Salaries Expense	44,000
Rent Expense	26,000

Insurance Expense	—
Depreciation Expense—Office Equipment	—
Office Supplies Expense	—
Miscellaneous Administrative Expense	$ 1,650
Rent Revenue	—
Interest Expense	11,600

The data needed for year-end adjustments on December 31 are as follows:

Merchandise inventory on December 31		$212,000
Insurance expired during the year		6,500
Supplies on hand on December 31:		
Store supplies		1,300
Office supplies		750
Depreciation for the year:		
Store equipment		7,500
Office equipment		3,800
Salaries payable on December 31:		
Sales salaries	$3,850	
Office salaries	1,150	5,000
Unearned rent on December 31		400

Instructions

1. Prepare a work sheet for the fiscal year ended December 31, listing all accounts in the order given.
2. Prepare a multiple-step income statement.
3. Prepare a statement of owner's equity.
4. Prepare a report form of balance sheet, assuming that the current portion of the note payable is $15,000.
5. Journalize the adjusting entries.
6. Journalize the closing entries.

Appendix E: Foreign Currency Transactions

In this appendix, we describe and illustrate the accounting for transactions in which a U.S. company sells products or services to foreign companies or buys foreign products or services. If transactions with foreign companies require payment or receipt in U.S. dollars, no special accounting problems arise.[1] Such transactions are recorded as we described and illustrated earlier in this text. For example, the sale of merchandise to a Japanese company that is billed in and paid for in dollars would be recorded by the U.S. company in the normal manner. However, if the transaction is billed and payment is to be received in Japanese yen, the U.S. company may incur an exchange gain or loss. Some foreign manufacturers have begun building manufacturing plants in the United States, which avoids such gains and losses. For example, **BMW** has constructed its first U.S. plant.

Realized Currency Exchange Gains and Losses

When a U.S. company receives foreign currency, the amount must be converted to its equivalent in U.S. dollars for recording in the accounts. When payment is to be made in a foreign currency, U.S. dollars must be exchanged for the foreign currency for payment. To illustrate, assume that a U.S. company purchases merchandise from a British company that requires payment in British pounds. In this case, U.S. dollars ($) must be exchanged for British pounds (£) to pay for the merchandise. This exchange of one currency for another involves using an exchange rate. The **exchange rate** is the rate at which one unit of currency (the dollar, for example) can be converted into another currency (the British pound, for example).

To continue the example, assume that the U.S. company had purchased merchandise for £1,000 from a British company on June 1, when the exchange rate was $1.40 per British pound. Thus, $1,400 must be exchanged for £1,000 to make the purchase.[2] The U.S. company records the transaction in dollars, as follows:

June	1	Merchandise Inventory	1 400 00	
		Cash		1 400 00
		Payment of Invoice No. 1725 from		
		W. A. Sterling Co., £1,000; exchange		
		rate, $1.40 per British pound.		

Instead of a cash purchase, the purchase may be made on account. In this case, the exchange rate may change between the date of purchase and the date of payment of the account payable in the foreign currency. In practice, exchange rates vary daily.

To illustrate, assume that the preceding purchase was made on account. The entry to record it is as follows:

June	1	Merchandise Inventory	1 400 00	
		Accounts Payable—W. A. Sterling Co.		1 400 00
		Purchase on account; Invoice		
		No. 1725 from W. A. Sterling Co.,		
		£1,000; exchange rate, $1.40 per		
		British pound.		

[1] This discussion is from the point of view of a U.S. company. Unless otherwise indicated, the reference to the dollar refers to the U.S. dollar rather than a dollar of another country, such as Canada.

[2] Foreign exchange rates are quoted in major financial reporting services. Because the exchange rates are quite volatile, those used in this chapter are assumed rates.

Assume that on the date of payment, June 15, the exchange rate was $1.45 per pound. The £1,000 account payable must be settled by exchanging $1,450 (£1,000 × $1.45) for £1,000. In this case, the U.S. company incurs an exchange loss of $50 because $1,450 was needed to settle a $1,400 account payable. The cash payment is recorded as follows:

June	15	Accounts Payable—W. A. Sterling Co.		1 400 00	
		Exchange Loss		50 00	
		Cash			1 450 00
		Cash paid on Invoice No. 1725, for			
		£1,000, or $1,400, when exchange			
		rate was $1.45 per pound.			

We can analyze all transactions with foreign companies in the manner described. For example, assume that a sale on account for $1,000 to a Swiss company on May 1 was billed in Swiss francs. The cost of the merchandise sold was $600, and the selling company uses a perpetual inventory system. If the exchange rate was $0.25 per Swiss franc (F) on May 1, the transaction is recorded as follows:

May	1	Accounts Receivable—D. W. Robinson Co.		1 000 00	
		Sales			1 000 00
		Invoice No. 9772, F4,000; exchange			
		rate, $0.25 per Swiss franc.			
	1	Cost of Merchandise Sold		600 00	
		Merchandise Inventory			600 00

Assume that the exchange rate increases to $0.30 per Swiss franc on May 31 when cash is received. In this case, the U.S. company realizes an exchange gain of $200. This gain is realized because the F4,000, which had a value of $1,000 on the date of sale, has increased in value to $1,200 (F4,000 × $0.30) on May 31 when the payment is received. The receipt of the cash is recorded as follows:

May	31	Cash		1 200 00	
		Accounts Receivable—D. W. Robinson Co.			1 000 00
		Exchange Gain			200 00
		Cash received on Invoice No. 9772,			
		for F4,000, $1,000, when exchange			
		rate was $0.30 per Swiss franc.			

Unrealized Currency Exchange Gains and Losses

In the previous examples, the transactions were completed by either the receipt or the payment of cash. On the date the cash was received or paid, any related exchange gain or loss was realized and was recorded in the accounts. However, financial statements may be prepared between the date of the sale or purchase on account and the date the cash is received or paid. In this case, any exchange gain or loss created by a change in exchange rates between the date of the original transaction and the balance sheet date must be recorded. Such an exchange gain or loss is reported in the financial statements as an unrealized exchange gain or loss.

To illustrate, assume that a sale on account for $1,000 had been made to a German company on December 20 and had been billed in deutsche marks (DM). The cost of merchandise sold was $700. On this date, the exchange rate was $0.50 per deutsche mark. The transaction is recorded as follows:

Dec.	20	Accounts Receivable—T. A. Mueller Inc.	1,000 00	
		Sales		1,000 00
		Invoice No. 1793, DM2,000; exchange rate, $0.50 per deutsche mark.		
	20	Cost of Merchandise Sold	700 00	
		Merchandise Inventory		700 00

Assume that the exchange rate decreases to $0.45 per deutsche mark on December 31, the date of the balance sheet. Thus, the $1,000 account receivable on December 31 has a value of only $900 (DM2,000 × $0.45). This unrealized loss of $100 ($1,000 − $900) is recorded as follows:

Dec.	31	Exchange Loss	100 00	
		Accounts Receivable—T. A. Mueller Inc.		100 00
		Invoice No. 1793, DM2,000 × $0.05 decrease in exchange rate.		

Any additional change in the exchange rate during the following period is recorded when the cash is received. To continue the illustration, assume that the exchange rate declines from $0.45 to $0.42 per deutsche mark by January 19, when the DM2,000 is received. The receipt of the cash on January 19 is recorded as follows:

Jan.	19	Cash (DM2,000 × $0.42)	840 00	
		Exchange Loss (DM2,000 × $0.03)	60 00	
		Accounts Receivable—T. A. Mueller Inc.		900 00
		Cash received on Invoice No. 1793, for DM2,000, or $900, when exchange rate was $0.42 per deutsche mark.		

In contrast, assume that in the preceding example the exchange rate increases between December 31 and January 19. In this case, an exchange gain would be recorded on January 19. For example, if the exchange rate increases from $0.45 to $0.47 per deutsche mark during this period, Exchange Gain would be credited for $40 (DM2,000 × $0.02).

A balance in the exchange loss account at the end of the fiscal period is reported in the Other Expense section of the income statement. A balance in the exchange gain account is reported in the Other Income section.

EXERCISES

Exercise E–1
Entries for sales made in foreign currency

The Electric Toy Company makes sales on account to several Swedish companies that it bills in kronas. Journalize the entries for the following selected transactions completed during the current year, assuming that Electric uses the perpetual inventory system:

June 2. Sold merchandise on account, 12,000 kronas; exchange rate, $0.13 per krona. The cost of merchandise sold was $1,100.

July 3. Received cash from sale of June 2, 12,000 kronas; exchange rate, $0.14 per krona.

Aug. 30. Sold merchandise on account, 20,000 kronas; exchange rate, $0.14 per krona. The cost of merchandise sold was $1,550.
Sept. 30. Received cash from sale of August 30, 20,000 kronas; exchange rate, $0.12 per krona.

Exercise E–2
Entries for purchases made in foreign currency

Custom Care Inc. sells artificial arms and legs to hospitals and physicians. It purchases merchandise from a German company that requires payment in deutsche marks. Journalize the entries for the following selected transactions completed during the current year, assuming that Custom Care Inc. uses the perpetual inventory system:

Feb. 10. Purchased merchandise on account, net 30, 7,500 deutsche marks; exchange rate, $0.58 per deutsche mark.
Mar. 9. Paid invoice of Feb. 10; exchange rate, $0.59 per deutsche mark.
Apr. 1. Purchased merchandise on account, net 30, 4,000 deutsche marks; exchange rate, $0.59 per deutsche mark.
May 1. Paid invoice of April 1; exchange rate, $0.57 per deutsche mark.

PROBLEMS

Problem E–1
Foreign currency transactions

GENERAL LEDGER
HAT

Global Inc. is a wholesaler of sports equipment, including golf clubs and gym sets. It sells to and purchases from companies in Canada and the Philippines. These transactions are settled in the foreign currency. The following selected transactions were completed during the current fiscal year:

June 10. Sold merchandise on account to Marco Company, net 30, 250,000 pesos; exchange rate, $0.030 per Philippines peso. The cost of merchandise sold was $5,500.
July 10. Received cash from Marco Company; exchange rate, $0.029 per Philippines peso.
15. Purchased merchandise on account from LeRa Inc., net 30, $5,000 Canadian; exchange rate, $0.76 per Canadian dollar.
Aug. 14. Issued check for amount owed to LeRa Inc.; exchange rate, $0.75 per Canadian dollar.
31. Sold merchandise on account to Ramon Company, net 30, 100,000 pesos; exchange rate, $0.031 per Philippines peso. The cost of merchandise sold was $1,200.
Sept. 30. Received cash from Ramon Company; exchange rate, $0.032 per Phillipines peso.
Oct. 8. Purchased merchandise on account from Chevalier Company, net 30, $50,000 Canadian; exchange rate, $0.73 per Canadian dollar.
Nov. 7. Issued check for amount owed to Chevalier Company; exchange rate, $0.74 per Canadian dollar.
Dec. 15. Sold merchandise on account to Jason Company, net 30, $80,000 Canadian; exchange rate, $0.75 per Canadian dollar. The cost of merchandise sold was $32,500.
16. Purchased merchandise on account from Juan Company, net 30, 500,000 pesos; exchange rate, $0.033 per Philippines peso.
31. Recorded unrealized currency exchange gain and/or loss on transactions of December 15 and 16. Exchange rates on December 31: $0.76 per Canadian dollar; $0.034 per Philippines peso.

Instructions

1. Journalize the entries to record the transactions and adjusting entries for the year, assuming that Global uses the perpetual inventory system.
2. Journalize the entries to record the payment of the December 16 purchase, on January 15, when the exchange rate was $0.031 per Philippines peso, and the receipt of cash from the December 15 sale, on January 17, when the exchange rate was $0.77 per Canadian dollar.

Appendix F: Partnerships

The partnership form of business organization allows two or more persons to combine capital, managerial talent, and experience with a minimum of effort. This form is widely used by small businesses. In many cases, the only alternative form of organization for multiple owners is the corporate form. Some states, however, do not permit the corporate form for certain types of businesses. For example, physicians, attorneys, and certified public accountants often organize as partnerships.

Characteristics of Partnerships

A **partnership** is "an association of two or more persons to carry on as co-owners a business for profit."[1] Partnerships have several characteristics with accounting implications.

A partnership has a **limited life**. A partnership dissolves whenever a partner ceases to be a member of the firm. For example, a partnership is dissolved if a partner withdraws due to bankruptcy, incapacity, or death. Likewise, admitting a new partner dissolves the old partnership. When a partnership is dissolved, a new partnership must be formed if operations of the business are to continue.

In most partnerships, the partners have **unlimited liability**. Each partner is individually liable to creditors for debts incurred by the partnership. Thus, if a partnership becomes insolvent, the partners must contribute sufficient personal assets to settle the debts of the partnership.

Partners have **co-ownership of partnership property**. The property invested in a partnership by a partner becomes the property of all the partners jointly. When a partnership is dissolved, the partners' claims against the assets are measured by the amount of the balances in their capital accounts.

Another characteristic of a partnership is **mutual agency**. This means that each partner is an agent of the partnership. Thus, each partner has the authority to enter into contracts for the partnership. The acts of each partner bind the entire partnership and become the obligations of all partners.

An important right of partners is **participation in income** of the partnership. Net income and net loss are distributed among the partners according to their agreement.

A partnership, like a sole proprietorship, is a **nontaxable entity** and thus does not pay federal income taxes. However, revenue and expense and other results of partnership operations must be reported annually to the Internal Revenue Service. The partners must, in turn, report their share of partnership income on their personal tax returns.

A partnership is created by a contract, known as the **partnership agreement** or **articles of partnership**. It should include statements regarding such matters as amounts to be invested, limits on withdrawals, distributions of income and losses, and admission and withdrawal of partners.

Advantages and Disadvantages of Partnerships

The partnership form of business organization is less widely used than are the proprietorship and corporate forms. For many business purposes, however, the advantages of the partnership form are greater than its disadvantages.

A partnership is relatively easy and inexpensive to organize, requiring only an agreement between two or more persons. A partnership has the advantage of bringing together more capital, managerial skills, and experience than does a proprietorship. Since a partnership is a nontaxable entity, the combined income taxes paid by the individual partners may be lower than the income taxes that would be paid by a corporation, which is a taxable entity.

[1] This definition of a partnership is included in the Uniform Partnership Act, which has been adopted by over ninety percent of the states.

A major disadvantage of the partnership form of business organization is the unlimited liability feature for partners. Other disadvantages of a partnership are that its life is limited, and one partner can bind the partnership to contracts. Also, raising large amounts of capital is more difficult for a partnership than for a corporation.

Accounting for Partnerships

Most of the day-to-day accounting for a partnership is the same as the accounting for any other form of business organization. The accounting system described in this text may, with little change, be used by a partnership. However, the formation, income distribution, dissolution, and liquidation of partnerships give rise to unique transactions. In the remainder of this appendix, we discuss accounting principles related to these areas.

Forming a Partnership

A separate entry is made for the investment of each partner in a partnership. The assets contributed by a partner are debited to the partnership asset accounts. If liabilities are assumed by the partnership, the partnership liability accounts are credited. The partner's capital account is credited for the net amount.

To illustrate, assume that Joseph A. Stevens and Earl S. Foster, sole owners of competing hardware stores, agree to combine their businesses in a partnership. Each is to contribute certain amounts of cash and other assets. It is also agreed that the partnership is to assume the liabilities of the separate businesses. The entry to record the assets contributed and the liabilities transferred by Stevens is as follows:

Apr.	1	Cash	7 200 00	
		Accounts Receivable	16 300 00	
		Merchandise Inventory	28 700 00	
		Store Equipment	5 400 00	
		Office Equipment	1 500 00	
		Allowance for Doubtful Accounts		1 500 00
		Accounts Payable		2 600 00
		Joseph A. Stevens, Capital		55 000 00

A similar entry would record the assets contributed and the liabilities transferred by Foster. In each entry, the noncash assets are recorded at values agreed upon by the partners. These values normally represent current market values and therefore usually differ from the book values of the assets in the records of the separate businesses. For example, the store equipment recorded at $5,400 in the preceding entry may have had a book value of $3,500 in Stevens's ledger (cost of $10,000 less accumulated depreciation of $6,500).

Dividing Net Income or Net Loss

Many partnerships have been dissolved because partners could not agree on an equitable distribution of income. Therefore, the method of dividing partnership income should be stated in the partnership agreement. In the absence of an agreement or if the agreement is silent on dividing net income or net losses, all partners share equally. However, if one partner contributes a larger portion of capital than the others, then net income should be divided to reflect the unequal capital contributions. Likewise, if the services rendered by one partner are more important than those of the others, net income should be divided to reflect the unequal service contributions. In the following paragraphs, we illustrate partnership agreements that recognize these differences.

Income Division—Services of Partners

One method of recognizing differences in partners' abilities and in amount of time devoted to the business provides for salary allowances to partners. Since partners are legally not employees of the partnership, such allowances are treated as divisions of the net income and are credited to the partners' capital accounts.

To illustrate, assume that the partnership agreement of Jennifer L. Stone and Crystal R. Mills provides for monthly salary allowances. Jennifer Stone is to receive a monthly allowance of $2,500 ($30,000 annually), and Crystal Mills is to receive $2,000 a month ($24,000 annually). Any net income remaining after the salary allowances is to be divided equally. Assume also that the net income for the year is $75,000.

A report of the division of net income may be presented as a separate statement to accompany the balance sheet and the income statement. Another format is to add the division to the bottom of the income statement. If the latter format is used, the lower part of the income statement would appear as follows:

Net income $75,000

Division of net income:

	J. L. Stone	C. R. Mills	Total
Annual salary allowance	$30,000	$24,000	$54,000
Remaining income	10,500	10,500	21,000
Net income	$40,500	$34,500	$75,000

Net income division is recorded as a closing entry, even if the partners do not actually withdraw the amounts of their salary allowances. The entry for dividing net income is as follows:

Dec.	31	Income Summary		75 000 00	
		Jennifer L. Stone, Capital			40 500 00
		Crystal R. Mills, Capital			34 500 00

If Stone and Mills had withdrawn their salary allowances monthly, the withdrawals would have been debited to their drawing accounts during the year. At the end of the year, the debit balances of $30,000 and $24,000 in their drawing accounts would be transferred as reductions to their capital accounts.

Accountants should be careful to distinguish between salary allowances and partner withdrawals. The amount of net income distributed to each partner's capital account at the end of the year may differ from the amount the partner withdraws during the year. In some cases, the partnership agreement may limit the amount of withdrawals a partner may make during a period.

Income Division—Services of Partners and Investment

Partners may agree that the most equitable plan of dividing income is to provide for (1) salary allowances and (2) interest on capital investments. Any remaining net income is then divided as agreed. For example, assume that the partnership agreement for Stone and Mills divides income as follows:

1. Monthly salary allowances of $2,500 for Stone and $2,000 for Mills.
2. Interest of 12% on each partner's capital balance on January 1.
3. Any remaining net income divided equally between the partners.

Stone had a credit balance of $80,000 in her capital account on January 1 of the current fiscal year, and Mills had a credit balance of $60,000 in her capital account. The $75,000 net income for the year is divided in the following schedule:

Net income			$75,000

Division of net income:

	J. L. Stone	C. R. Mills	Total
Annual salary allowance	$30,000	$24,000	$54,000
Interest allowance	9,600[1]	7,200[2]	16,800
Remaining income	2,100	2,100	4,200
Net income	$41,700	$33,300	$75,000

[1]0.12 × $80,000 [2]0.12 × $60,000

For the above example, the entry to close the income summary account is shown below.

Dec.	31	Income Summary	75 000 00	
		Jennifer L. Stone, Capital		41 700 00
		Crystal R. Mills, Capital		33 300 00

Income Division—Allowances Exceed Net Income

In the examples so far, the net income has exceeded the total of the salary and interest allowances. If the net income is less than the total of the allowances, the **remaining balance** will be a negative amount. This amount must be divided among the partners as though it were a net loss.

To illustrate, assume the same salary and interest allowances as in the above example, but assume that the net income is $50,000. The salary and interest allowances total $39,600 for Stone and $31,200 for Mills. The sum of these amounts, $70,800, exceeds the net income of $50,000 by $20,800. It is necessary to divide the $20,800 excess between Stone and Mills. Under the partnership agreement, any net income or net loss remaining after deducting the allowances is divided equally between Stone and Mills. Thus, each partner is allocated one-half of the $20,800, and $10,400 is deducted from each partner's share of the allowances. The final division of net income between Stone and Mills is shown below.

Net income			$50,000

Division of net income:

	J. L. Stone	C. R. Mills	Total
Annual salary allowance	$30,000	$24,000	$54,000
Interest allowance	9,600	7,200	16,800
Total	$39,600	$31,200	$70,800
Excess of allowances over income	10,400	10,400	20,800
Net income	$29,200	$20,800	$50,000

In closing Income Summary at the end of the year, $29,200 would be credited to Jennifer L. Stone, Capital, and $20,800 would be credited to Crystal R. Mills, Capital.

Partnership Dissolution

When a partnership dissolves, its affairs are not necessarily wound up. For example, a partnership of two partners may admit a third partner. Or if one of the partners in a business withdraws, the remaining partners may continue to operate the business. In such cases a new partnership is formed and a new partnership agreement should be prepared. Many partnerships provide for the admission of new partners and partner withdrawals in the partnership agreement so that the partnership may continue operations without executing a new agreement.

Admission of a Partner

A person may be admitted to a partnership only with the consent of all the current partners, through either of two methods:[2]

1. Purchasing an interest from one or more of the current partners.
2. Contributing assets to the partnership.

When the first method is used, the capital interest of the incoming partner is obtained from current partners, and *neither the total assets nor the total owner's equity of the business is affected.* When the second method is used, *both the total assets and the total owner's equity of the business are increased.* In the following paragraphs, we discuss each of these methods.

Purchasing an Interest in a Partnership. A person may be admitted to a partnership by buying an interest from one or more of the existing partners. The purchase and sale of the partnership interest occurs between the new partner and the existing partners acting as individuals. The only entry needed is to transfer owner's equity amounts from the capital accounts of the selling partners to the capital account established for the incoming partner.

As an example, assume that partners Tom Andrews and Nathan Bell have capital balances of $50,000 each. On June 1, each sells one-fifth of his equity to Joe Canter for $10,000 in cash. The exchange of cash is not a partnership transaction and thus is not recorded by the partnership. The only entry required in the partnership accounts is as follows:

June	1	Tom Andrews, Capital	10 0 0 0 00	
		Nathan Bell, Capital	10 0 0 0 00	
		Joe Canter, Capital		20 0 0 0 00

The effect of the transaction on the partnership accounts is presented in the following diagram:

Partnership Accounts

The preceding entry is not affected by the amount paid by Canter for the one-fifth interest. Any gain or loss on the sale of the partnership interest accrues to the selling partners as individuals, and not to the partnership. Thus, in either case, the entry to transfer the capital interests is the same as shown above.

After Canter is admitted to the partnership, the total owner's equity of the firm is still $100,000. Canter now has a one-fifth interest, or a $20,000 capital balance. However, Canter may not be entitled to a one-fifth share of the partnership net in-

[2] Although an individual cannot become a partner without the consent of the other partners, the rights of a partner, such as the right to share in the income of a partnership, may be assigned to others without the consent of the other partners. Such issues are discussed in business law textbooks.

come. Division of net income or net loss will be made according to the new partnership agreement.

Contributing Assets to a Partnership. Instead of buying an interest from the current partners, the incoming partner may contribute assets to the partnership. In this case, both the assets and the owner's equity of the firm increase. For example, assume that Donald Lewis and Gerald Morton are partners with capital accounts of $35,000 and $25,000. On June 1, Sharon Nelson invests $20,000 cash in the business for an ownership equity of $20,000. The entry to record this transaction is as follows:

June	1	Cash		20,000 00	
		Sharon Nelson, Capital			20,000 00

The major difference between the admission of Nelson and the admission of Canter in the preceding examples may be observed by comparing the following diagram with the preceding diagram.

Partnership Accounts

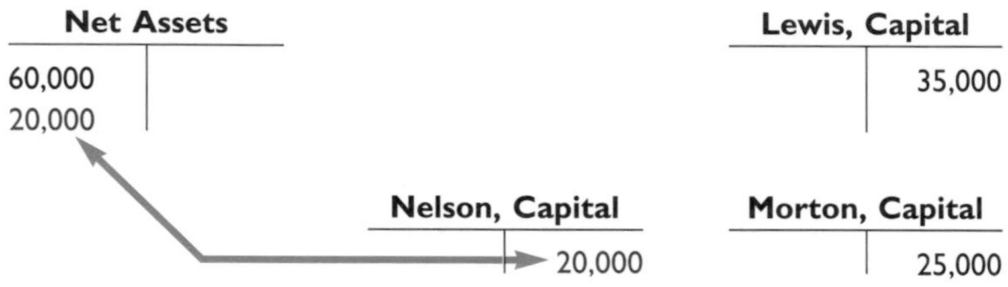

By admitting Nelson, the total owners' equity of the new partnership becomes $80,000, of which Nelson has a one-fourth interest, or $20,000. The extent of Nelson's share in partnership net income will be determined by the partnership agreement.

Revaluation of Assets. A partnership's asset account balances should be stated at current values when a new partner is admitted. If the accounts do not approximate current market values, the accounts should be adjusted. The net adjustment (increase or decrease) in asset values is divided among the capital accounts of the existing partners according to their income-sharing ratio. Failure to adjust the accounts for current values may result in the new partner sharing in asset gains or losses that arose in prior periods.

To illustrate, assume that in the preceding example for the Lewis and Morton partnership, the balance of the merchandise inventory account is $14,000 and the current replacement value is $17,000. Assuming that Lewis and Morton share net income equally, the revaluation is recorded as follows:

June	1	Merchandise Inventory		3,000 00	
		Donald Lewis, Capital			1,500 00
		Gerald Morton, Capital			1,500 00

Partner Bonuses. When a new partner is admitted to a partnership, the incoming partner may pay a bonus to the existing partners for the privilege of joining the partnership. Such a bonus is usually paid in expectation of high partnership profits in the future due to the contributions of the existing partners. Alternatively, the existing partners may pay the incoming partner a bonus to join the partnership. In this case, the bonus is usually paid in recognition of special qualities or skills that the incoming partner is bringing to the partnership. For example, celebrities such as actors, musicians, or sports figures often provide name recognition that is expected to increase partnership profits in the future. The amount of any bonus paid to the partnership is distributed among the partner capital accounts.[3]

To illustrate, assume that on March 1 the partnership of Marsha Jenkins and Helen Kramer is considering admitting a new partner, William Larson. After the assets of the partnership have been adjusted to current market values, the capital balance of Jenkins is $20,000 and the capital balance of Kramer is $24,000. Jenkins and Kramer agree to admit Larson to the partnership for $31,000. In return, Larson will receive a one-third equity in the partnership and will share equally with Jenkins and Kramer in partnership income or losses.

In this case Larson is paying Jenkins and Kramer a $6,000 bonus to join the partnership. This bonus is computed as follows:

Equity of Jenkins	$20,000
Equity of Kramer	24,000
Contribution of Larson	31,000
Total equity after admission of Larson	$75,000
Larson's equity interest after admission	× 1/3
Larson's equity after admission	$25,000
Contribution of Larson	$31,000
Larson's equity after admission	25,000
Bonus paid to Jenkins and Kramer	$ 6,000

The bonus is distributed to Jenkins and Kramer according to their income-sharing ratio. Assuming that Jenkins and Kramer share profits and losses equally, the entry to record the admission of Larson to the partnership is as follows:

Mar.	1	Cash	31 000 00	
		William Larson, Capital		25 000 00
		Marsha Jenkins, Capital		3 000 00
		Helen Kramer, Capital		3 000 00

If a new partner possesses unique qualities or skills, the existing partners may agree to pay the new partner a bonus to join the partnership. To illustrate, assume that after adjusting assets to market values the capital balance of Janice Cowen is $80,000 and the capital balance of Steve Dodd is $40,000. Cowen and Dodd agree to admit Sandra Ellis to the partnership on June 1 for an investment of $30,000. In return, Ellis will receive a one-fourth equity interest in the partnership and will share in one-fourth of the profits and losses.

In this case Cowen and Dodd are paying Ellis a $7,500 bonus to join the partnership. This bonus is computed as follows:

Equity of Cowen	$ 80,000
Equity of Dodd	40,000
Contribution of Ellis	30,000
Total equity after admission of Ellis	$150,000
Ellis's equity interest after admission	× 25%
Ellis's equity after admission	$ 37,500
Contribution of Ellis	30,000
Bonus paid to Ellis	$ 7,500

[3] Another method is sometimes used to record the admission of partners in situations such as that described in this paragraph. This method attributes goodwill rather than a bonus to the partners. This method is discussed in advanced accounting textbooks.

Assuming that the income-sharing ratio of Cowen and Dodd was 2:1 before the admission of Ellis, the entry to record the bonus and admission of Ellis to the partnership is as follows:

June	1	Cash	30 000 00	
		Janice Cowen, Capital	5 000 00	
		Steve Dodd, Capital	2 500 00	
		Sandra Ellis, Capital		37 500 00

Withdrawal of a Partner

When a partner retires or withdraws from a partnership, one or more of the remaining partners may buy the withdrawing partner's interest. The firm may then continue its operations uninterrupted. In such cases the purchase and sale of the partnership interest is between the partners as individuals. The only entry on the partnership's records is to debit the capital account of the partner withdrawing and to credit the capital account of the partner or partners buying the additional interest.

If the withdrawing partner sells the interest directly to the partnership, both the assets and the owner's equity of the partnership are reduced. Before the sale, the asset accounts should be adjusted to current values, so that the withdrawing partner's equity may be accurately determined. The net amount of the adjustment should be divided among the capital accounts of the partners according to their income-sharing ratio. If not enough partnership cash or other assets are available to pay the withdrawing partner, a liability may be created (credited) for the amount owed the withdrawing partner.

Death of a Partner

When a partner dies, the accounts should be closed as of the date of death. The net income for the current year should be determined and divided among the partners' capital accounts. The balance in the capital account of the deceased partner is then transferred to a liability account with the deceased's estate. The remaining partner or partners may continue the business, or the affairs may be terminated. If the partnership continues in business, the procedures for settling with the estate are the same as those discussed for the withdrawal of a partner.

Liquidating Partnerships

When a partnership goes out of business, it usually sells the assets, pays the creditors, and distributes the remaining cash or other assets to the partners. This winding-up process is called the **liquidation** of the partnership. Although liquidating refers to the payment of liabilities, it is often used to include the entire winding-up process.

When the partnership goes out of business and the normal operations are discontinued, the accounts should be adjusted and closed. The only accounts remaining open will be the asset, contra asset, liability, and owner's equity accounts.

The sale of the assets is called **realization**. As cash is realized, it is used to pay the claims of creditors. After all liabilities have been paid, the remaining cash is distributed to the partners based on the balances in their capital accounts.

The liquidating process may extend over a long period of time as individual assets are sold. This delays the distribution of cash to partners, but does not affect the amount each partner will receive.

To illustrate, assume that Farley, Greene, and Hall share income and losses in a ratio of 5:3:2 (5/10, 3/10, 2/10). On April 9, after discontinuing business operations of the partnership and closing the accounts, the following trial balance in summary form was prepared:

Cash	11,000	
Noncash Assets	64,000	
Liabilities		9,000
Jean Farley, Capital		22,000
Brad Greene, Capital		22,000
Alice Hall, Capital		22,000
Total	75,000	75,000

Based on these facts, we will show the accounting for liquidating the partnership by using three different selling prices for the noncash assets. To simplify, we assume that all noncash assets are sold in a single transaction and that all liabilities are paid at one time. In addition, Noncash Assets and Liabilities will be used as account titles in place of the various asset, contra asset, and liability accounts.

Gain on Realization

Between April 10 and April 30 of the current year, Farley, Greene, and Hall sell all noncash assets for $72,000. Thus, a gain of $8,000 ($72,000 − $64,000) is realized. The gain is divided among the capital accounts in the income-sharing ratio of 5:3:2. The liabilities are paid, and the remaining cash is distributed to the partners. *The cash is distributed to the partners based on the balances in their capital accounts.* A statement of partnership liquidation, which summarizes the liquidation process, is shown in Exhibit 1.

EXHIBIT 1 Gain on Realization

Farley, Greene, and Hall
Statement of Partnership Liquidation
For Period April 10–30, 20—

								Capital				
	Cash	**+**	**Noncash Assets**	**=**	**Liabilities**	**+**	**Farley (50%)**	**+**	**Greene (30%)**	**+**	**Hall (20%)**
Balances before realization	$11,000		$64,000		$9,000		$22,000		$22,000		$22,000
Sale of assets and division of gain	+72,000		−64,000		—		+ 4,000		+ 2,400		+ 1,600
Balances after realization	$83,000		$ 0		$9,000		$26,000		$24,400		$23,600
Payment of liabilities	− 9,000		—		−9,000		—		—		—
Balances after payment of liabilities	$74,000		$ 0		$ 0		$26,000		$24,400		$23,600
Cash distributed to partners	−74,000		—		—		−26,000		−24,400		−23,600
Final balances	$ 0		$ 0		$ 0		$ 0		$ 0		$ 0

The entries to record the steps in the liquidating process are as follows:

	Cash	72,000.00	
	Noncash Assets		64,000.00
	Gain on Realization		8,000.00
	Sold assets.		
	Gain on Realization	8,000.00	
	Jean Farley, Capital		4,000.00
	Brad Greene, Capital		2,400.00
	Alice Hall, Capital		1,600.00
	Divided gain from sale of assets.		

Liabilities	9,000.00	
Cash		9,000.00
Paid liabilities.		
Jean Farley, Capital	26,000.00	
Brad Greene, Capital	24,400.00	
Alice Hall, Capital	23,600.00	
Cash		74,000.00
Distributed cash to partners.		

As shown in Exhibit 1, the cash is distributed to the partners based on the balances of their capital accounts. These balances are determined after the gain on realization has been divided among the partners. *The income-sharing ratio should not be used as a basis for distributing the cash to partners.*

Loss on Realization

Assume that in the preceding example, Farley, Greene, and Hall dispose of all noncash assets for $44,000. A loss of $20,000 ($64,000 − $44,000) is realized. The steps in liquidating the partnership are summarized in Exhibit 2.

EXHIBIT 2 Loss on Realization

Farley, Greene, and Hall
Statement of Partnership Liquidation
For Period April 10–30, 20—

							Capital				
	Cash	+	Noncash Assets	=	Liabilities	+	Farley (50%)	+	Greene (30%)	+	Hall (20%)
Balances before realization	$11,000		$64,000		$9,000		$22,000		$22,000		$22,000
Sale of assets and division of loss	+44,000		−64,000		—		−10,000		− 6,000		− 4,000
Balances after realization	$55,000		$ 0		$9,000		$12,000		$16,000		$18,000
Payment of liabilities	− 9,000		—		−9,000		—		—		—
Balances after payment of liabilities	$46,000		$ 0		$ 0		$12,000		$16,000		$18,000
Cash distributed to partners	−46,000		—		—		−12,000		−16,000		−18,000
Final balances	$ 0		$ 0		$ 0		$ 0		$ 0		$ 0

The entries to liquidate the partnership are as follows:

Cash	44,000.00	
Loss on Realization	20,000.00	
Noncash Assets		64,000.00
Sold assets.		
Jean Farley, Capital	10,000.00	
Brad Greene, Capital	6,000.00	
Alice Hall, Capital	4,000.00	
Loss on Realization		20,000.00
Divided loss from sale of assets.		

Liabilities		9,000.00	
Cash			9,000.00
Paid liabilities.			
Jean Farley, Capital		12,000.00	
Brad Greene, Capital		16,000.00	
Alice Hall, Capital		18,000.00	
Cash			46,000.00
Distributed cash to partners.			

Loss on Realization—Capital Deficiency

In the preceding example, the capital account of each partner was large enough to absorb the partner's share of the loss from realization. The partners received cash to the extent of the remaining balances in their capital accounts. The share of loss on realization may exceed, however, the balance in the partner's capital account. The resulting debit balance in the capital account is called a **deficiency**. It represents a claim of the partnership against the partner.

To illustrate, assume that Farley, Greene, and Hall sell all of the noncash assets for $10,000. A loss of $54,000 ($64,000 − $10,000) is realized. The share of the loss allocated to Farley, $27,000 (50% of $54,000), exceeds the $22,000 balance in her capital account. This $5,000 deficiency represents an amount that Farley owes the partnership. Assuming that Farley pays the entire deficiency to the partnership, sufficient cash is available to distribute to the remaining partners according to their capital balances. The steps in liquidating the partnership in this case are summarized in Exhibit 3.

EXHIBIT 3 Loss on Realization—Capital Deficiency

Farley, Greene, and Hall
Statement of Partnership Liquidation
For Period April 10–30, 20—

							Capital				
	Cash	+	Noncash Assets	=	Liabilities	+	Farley (50%)	+	Greene (30%)	+	Hall (20%)
Balances before realization	$11,000		$64,000		$9,000		$22,000		$22,000		$22,000
Sale of assets and division of loss	+10,000		−64,000		—		−27,000		−16,200		−10,800
Balances after realization	$21,000		$ 0		$9,000		$ 5,000(Dr.)		$ 5,800		$11,200
Payment of liabilities	− 9,000		—		−9,000		—		—		—
Balances after payment of liabilities	$12,000		$ 0		$ 0		$ 5,000(Dr.)		$ 5,800		$11,200
Receipt of deficiency	+ 5,000		—		—		+ 5,000		—		—
Balances	$17,000		$ 0		$ 0		$ 0		$ 5,800		$11,200
Cash distributed to partners	−17,000		—		—		—		− 5,800		−11,200
Final balances	$ 0		$ 0		$ 0		$ 0		$ 0		$ 0

The entries to record the liquidation are as follows:

Cash		10,000.00	
Loss on Realization		54,000.00	
Noncash Assets			64,000.00
Sold assets.			

Jean Farley, Capital	27,000 00	
Brad Greene, Capital	16,200 00	
Alice Hall, Capital	10,800 00	
Loss on Realization		54,000 00
Divided loss from sale of assets.		
Liabilities	9,000 00	
Cash		9,000 00
Paid liabilities.		
Cash	5,000 00	
Jean Farley, Capital		5,000 00
Received cash from deficient partner.		
Brad Greene, Capital	5,800 00	
Alice Hall, Capital	11,200 00	
Cash		17,000 00
Distributed cash to partners.		

If cash is not collected from a deficient partner, the partnership cash will not be large enough to pay the other partners in full. Any uncollected deficiency becomes a loss to the partnership and is divided among the remaining partners' capital balances, based on their income-sharing ratio. The cash balance will then equal the sum of the capital account balances. Cash is then distributed to the remaining partners, based on the balances of their capital accounts.[4]

EXERCISES

Exercise F–1

Entry for partner's original investment

Todd Jost and D. Caldwell decide to form a partnership by combining the assets of their separate businesses. Jost contributes the following assets to the partnership: cash, $11,000; accounts receivable with a face amount of $96,000 and an allowance for doubtful accounts of $6,600; merchandise inventory with a cost of $85,000; and equipment with a cost of $140,000 and accumulated depreciation of $90,000.

The partners agree that $7,000 of the accounts receivable are completely worthless and are not to be accepted by the partnership, that $9,000 is a reasonable allowance for the uncollectibility of the remaining accounts, that the merchandise inventory is to be recorded at the current market price of $79,400, and that the equipment is to be valued at $67,600.

Journalize the partnership's entry to record Jost's investment.

Exercise F–2

Dividing partnership income

SPREADSHEET

✓ e. Moore net income, $91,500

Dan Moore and T. J. Knell formed a partnership, investing $300,000 and $150,000 respectively. Determine their participation in the year's net income of $180,000 under each of the following independent assumptions: (a) no agreement concerning division of net income; (b) divided in the ratio of original capital investment; (c) interest at the rate of 12% allowed on original investments and the remainder divided in the ratio of 2:3; (d) salary allowances of $60,000 and $75,000 respectively, and the balance divided equally; (e) allowance of interest at the rate of 12% on original investments, salary allowances of $60,000 and $75,000 respectively, and the remainder divided equally.

[4] The accounting for uncollectible deficiencies of partners is discussed and illustrated in advanced accounting texts.

Exercise F–3
Dividing partnership income

✓ d. Knell net income, $127,500

Determine the participation of Moore and Knell in the year's net income of $240,000, according to each of the five assumptions as to income division listed in Exercise F–2.

Exercise F–4
Admitting new partners

Jenny Kirk and Harold Spock are partners who share in the income equally and have capital balances of $120,000 and $62,500, respectively. Kirk, with the consent of Spock, sells one-third of her interest to Benjamin McCoy. What entry is required by the partnership if the sale price is (a) $30,000? (b) $50,000?

Exercise F–5
Admitting new partners who buy an interest and contribute assets

✓ b. Wood, Capital, $100,000

The capital accounts of Susan Laurel and Ben Hardy have balances of $120,000 and $100,000, respectively. Ken Mahl and Jeff Wood are to be admitted to the partnership. Mahl buys one-fourth of Laurel's interest for $32,000 and one-fifth of Hardy's interest for $24,000. Wood contributes $110,000 cash to the partnership, for which he is to receive an ownership equity of $100,000. All partners share equally in income.

a. Journalize the entries to record the admission of (1) Mahl and (2) Wood. Mahl is not credited with any of Wood's bonus.
b. What are the capital balances of each partner after the admission of the new partners?

Exercise F–6
Withdrawal of partner

Glenn Holmes is to retire from the partnership of Holmes and Associates as of March 31, the end of the current fiscal year. After closing the accounts, the capital balances of the partners are as follows: Glenn Holmes, $200,000; Jenny Watson, $125,000; and Pierre Periot, $140,000. They have shared net income and net losses in the ratio of 4:3:3. The partners agree that the merchandise inventory should be increased by $20,000, and the allowance for doubtful accounts should be increased by $2,000. Holmes agrees to accept a note for $130,000 in partial settlement of his ownership equity. The remainder of his claim is to be paid in cash. Watson and Periot are to share equally in the net income or net loss of the new partnership.

Journalize the entries to record (a) the adjustment of the assets to bring them into agreement with current market prices and (b) the withdrawal of Holmes from the partnership.

Exercise F–7
Distribution of cash upon liquidation

✓ a. $8,000 loss

Seinfeld and Kramer are partners, sharing gains and losses equally. At the time they decide to terminate their partnership, their capital balances are $12,000 and $50,000, respectively. After all noncash assets are sold and all liabilities are paid, there is a cash balance of $54,000.

a. What is the amount of a gain or loss on realization?
b. How should the gain or loss be divided between Seinfeld and Kramer?
c. How should the cash be divided between Seinfeld and Kramer?

Exercise F–8
Liquidating partnerships—capital deficiency

✓ b. $51,000

Douglas, Diaz, and Pitt share equally in net income and net losses. After the partnership sells all assets for cash, divides the losses on realization, and pays the liabilities, the balances in the capital accounts are as follows: Douglas, $20,000 Cr.; Diaz, $45,500 Cr.; and Pitt, $14,500 Dr.

a. What term is applied to the debit balance in Pitt's capital account?
b. What is the amount of cash on hand?
c. Journalize the transaction that must take place for Douglas and Diaz to receive cash in the liquidation process equal to their capital account balances.

Exercise F–9
Distribution of cash upon liquidation

✓ a. Grant net income, $100

Allyn Ashton, Jim Card, and Laura Grant arranged to import and sell orchid corsages for a university dance. They agreed to share equally the net income or net loss of the venture. Ashton and Card advanced $260 and $140 of their own respective funds to pay for advertising and other expenses. After collecting for all sales and paying creditors, the partnership has $700 in cash.

a. How should the money be distributed?
b. Assuming that the partnership has only $280 cash instead of $700, do any of the three partners have a capital deficiency? If so, how much?

Exercise F–10
Statement of partnership liquidation

✓ Cash distributed to Chow, $13,500

After closing the accounts on July 1, prior to liquidating the partnership, the capital account balances of Gibbs, Hill, and Chow are $40,000, $29,000, and $18,000, respectively. Cash, noncash assets, and liabilities total $22,000, $105,000, and $40,000, respectively. Between July 1 and July 29, the noncash assets are sold for $78,000, the liabilities are paid, and the remaining cash is distributed to the partners. The partners share net income and loss in the ratio of 3:2:1. Prepare a statement of partnership liquidation for the period July 1–29.

PROBLEMS

Problem F–1
Dividing partnership income

✓ 1. f. Dunn, $140,500

Phil Dunn and Russ Randall have decided to form a partnership. They have agreed that Dunn is to invest $140,000 and that Randall is to invest $210,000. Dunn is to devote full time to the business, and Randall is to devote one-half time. The following plans for the division of income are being considered:

a. Equal division.
b. In the ratio of original investments.
c. In the ratio of time devoted to the business.
d. Interest of 10% on original investments and the remainder in the ratio of 5:3.
e. Interest of 10% on original investments, salary allowances of $90,000 to Dunn and $45,000 to Randall, and the remainder equally.
f. Plan (e), except that Dunn is also to be allowed a bonus equal to 20% of the amount by which net income exceeds the salary allowances.

Instructions

For each plan, determine the division of the net income under each of the following assumptions: (1) net income of $225,000 and (2) net income of $150,000. Present the data in tabular form, using the following columnar headings:

	$225,000		$150,000	
Plan	**Dunn**	**Randall**	**Dunn**	**Randall**

Problem F–2
Statement of partnership liquidation

SPREADSHEET

✓ 1. d. Langley, $20,000

After the accounts are closed on May 10, prior to liquidating the partnership, the capital accounts of Mark Hernandez, Donna Collins, and Janice Langley are $56,800, $12,400, and $35,600, respectively. Cash and noncash assets total $18,900 and $142,400, respectively. Amounts owed to creditors total $56,500. The partners share income and losses in the ratio of 2:1:1. Between May 10 and May 30, the noncash assets are sold for $80,000, the partner with the capital deficiency pays his or her deficiency to the partnership, and the liabilities are paid.

Instructions

1. Prepare a statement of partnership liquidation, indicating (a) the sale of assets and division of loss, (b) the receipt of the deficiency (from the appropriate partner), and (c) the payment of liabilities.
2. If the partner with the capital deficiency declares bankruptcy and is unable to pay the deficiency, explain how the deficiency would be divided between the partners.

Hershey Foods Corporation

1996 Consolidated Financial Statements

and

Management's Discussion and Analysis

Consolidated Financial Statements and Management's Discussion and Analysis

HERSHEY FOODS CORPORATION

MANAGEMENT'S DISCUSSION AND ANALYSIS

OPERATING RESULTS

The Corporation achieved record sales levels in 1996 and 1995. Net sales during this two-year period increased at a compound annual rate of 5%, primarily reflecting volume growth from the introduction of new confectionery and grocery products and significant volume increases from seasonal packaged candy items. Sales increases also resulted from selected confectionery selling price increases in the United States partially offset by related sales volume declines, increased confectionery sales volume in various international markets and incremental sales from the acquisition of Henry Heide, Incorporated (Henry Heide). These increases were partially offset by lower sales resulting from the divestitures of Hershey Canada, Inc.'s *Planters* nut (Planters) and *Life Savers* and *Breath Savers* hard candy, and *Beech-Nut* cough drops (Life Savers) businesses in January 1996 and Overspecht B.V. (OZF Jamin) in the second quarter of 1995. The discontinuance of the Corporation's refrigerated pudding line in late 1994 also reduced sales during the two-year period.

Hershey Chocolate U.S.A. increased the wholesale price of its standard bar line and king size bars by approximately eleven percent in December 1995. These products represented approximately 25% of the Corporation's 1995 sales. Price increases were intended to offset higher costs for raw materials and packaging, together with the cumulative impact of inflation on other costs since the last standard bar price increase in early 1991. Hershey Pasta Group implemented selected price increases in late 1993, early 1994 and late 1995 in an effort to recover substantial increases in semolina costs. The price increases have not been sufficient to recover the full impact of the higher semolina costs, partly due to competition from subsidized pasta imports shipped into the United States.

The following acquisitions and divestitures occurred during the period:

- December 1996—The acquisition from an affiliate of Huhtamäki Oy (Huhtamaki), the international foods company based in Finland, of Huhtamaki's Leaf North America (Leaf) confectionery operations for $437.2 million, plus the assumption of $17.0 million in debt. In addition, the parties entered into a trademark and technology license agreement under which the Corporation will manufacture and/or market and distribute in North, Central and South America Huhtamaki's confectionery brands including *Good & Plenty*, *Heath*, *Jolly Rancher*, *Milk Duds*, *PayDay* and *Whoppers*.
- December 1996—The sale to Huhtamaki of the outstanding shares of Gubor Holding GmbH (Gubor) and Sperlari, S.r.l. (Sperlari). Gubor manufactures and markets high-quality assorted pralines and seasonal chocolate products in Germany and Sperlari manufactures and markets various confectionery and grocery products in Italy. The sale resulted in an after-tax loss of $35.4 million, since no tax benefit associated with the transaction was recorded. Combined net sales for Gubor and Sperlari were $216.6 million, $222.0 million and $186.6 million in 1996, 1995 and 1994, respectively.
- January 1996—The sale of the assets of Hershey Canada, Inc.'s Planters and Life Savers businesses to Johnvince Foods Group and Beta Brands Inc., respectively. Both transactions were part of a restructuring program announced by the Corporation in late 1994.
- December 1995—The acquisition of Henry Heide, a confectionery company which manufactures a variety of non-chocolate confectionery products including *Jujyfruits* candy and *Wunderbeans* jellybeans.
- June 1995—The sale of the outstanding shares of OZF Jamin to a management buyout group at OZF Jamin also as part of the restructuring program.

Income, excluding the loss on disposal of businesses in 1996 and the net after-tax effect of restructuring activities recorded in 1994, increased at a compound annual rate of 8% during the two-year period. This increase was a result of the growth in sales, partially offset by a slightly lower gross profit margin and higher selling, marketing and administrative expenses.

The Corporation's net sales, net income and cash flows are affected by the timing of business acquisitions and divestitures, new product introductions, promotional activities, price increases, and a seasonal sales bias toward the second half of the year. These factors, from time to time, cause fluctuations in net sales and net income versus the comparable quarterly periods of prior years.

Net Sales

Net sales rose $298.6 million or 8% in 1996 and $84.4 million or 2% in 1995. The increase in 1996 was primarily due to incremental sales from new confectionery and grocery products, increased confectionery sales volume in the North American seasonal packaged candy line and in various international markets, selected confectionery selling price increases in the United States partially offset by related sales volume declines, and incremental sales from the acquisition of Henry Heide. The increase in 1995 was due to incremental sales from new confectionery and grocery products, volume growth from existing domestic and foreign confectionery brands and pasta products, and selected selling price increases, principally in the Corporation's foreign businesses. These increases were partially offset by lower sales resulting from the divestiture of OZF Jamin in the second quarter of 1995 and the discontinuance of the Corporation's refrigerated pudding line in late 1994.

Costs and Expenses

Cost of sales as a percent of net sales declined from 58.2% in 1994 to 57.6% in 1995, but increased slightly to 57.7% in 1996. The decrease in gross margin in 1996 was principally the result of higher costs for certain major raw materials, primarily cocoa beans, milk, almonds and durum semolina and increased manufacturing labor and overhead rates, substantially offset by selected confectionery price increases, manufacturing efficiency improvements and the favorable impact of the OZF Jamin divestiture. The increase in gross margin in 1995 was primarily the result of manufacturing efficiency improvements, selling price increases in the Corporation's foreign businesses, and the favorable impact of the OZF Jamin divestiture. These increases were partially offset by higher costs for certain major raw materials and packaging, along with inflation in labor and overhead costs.

Selling, marketing and administrative costs increased by 7% in 1996 primarily due to a net increase in advertising and promotion expenses associated with the introduction of new products and higher selling expenses primarily related to international sales volume increases and new product introductions. Selling, marketing and administrative costs increased by 2% in 1995 primarily due to increased advertising for existing confectionery brands and the introduction of new products, partially offset by reduced promotion and administrative expenses.

Restructuring Activities

In the fourth quarter of 1994, the Corporation recorded a pre-tax restructuring charge of $106.1 million ($80.2 million after tax or $.46 per share) following a comprehensive review of domestic and foreign operations designed to enhance performance of operating assets by lowering operating and administrative costs, eliminating underperforming assets and streamlining the overall decision-making process. As of December 31, 1995, $81.8 million of restructuring reserves had been utilized and $16.7 million had been reversed to reflect revisions and changes in estimates to the original restructuring program.

During the third quarter of 1995, a pre-tax restructuring charge of $16.6 million was recorded in connection with a voluntary retirement program announced by the Corporation in August 1995. The charge was primarily related to the funding of retirement benefits for eligible employees who elected early retirement. The impact of this charge was more than offset by the partial reversal of 1994 accrued restructuring reserves, resulting in an increase to income before income taxes of $.2 million and an increase to net income of $2.0 million as the tax benefit associated with the 1995 charge more than offset the tax provision associated with the reversal of 1994 restructuring reserves.

The remaining $7.6 million of accrued restructuring reserves were utilized during 1996 as the restructuring program was completed. A portion of the restructuring reserves were used for severance and relocation benefits related to the consolidation of the pasta and grocery field sales organizations.

Interest Expense, Net

Net interest expense increased $3.2 million in 1996 as higher fixed interest expense was only partially offset by reduced short-term interest expense. Increased fixed interest expense resulted from the issuance of $200 million of 6.7% Notes due 2005 (Notes) in the fourth quarter of 1995. Lower short-term interest expense resulted from lower average borrowing balances and reduced interest rates as compared to 1995.

Net interest expense increased $9.5 million in 1995 primarily as a result of higher short-term interest expense. Short-term interest expense increased due to higher borrowing rates and increased borrowings associated with the purchase of approximately 9.0 million shares, on a pre-split basis, of the Corporation's Common Stock from the Hershey Trust Company, as Trustee for the benefit of Milton Hershey School (Milton Hershey School Trust).

Provision for Income Taxes

The Corporation's effective income tax rate was 43.1%, 39.5%, and 44.7% in 1996, 1995 and 1994, respectively. The higher 1996 rate compared to 1995 was due primarily to the lack of any tax benefit associated with the loss on disposal of businesses. The lower rate in 1995 compared to 1994 was principally due to the impact of restructuring activities.

Net Income

Net income decreased by 3% in 1996. Excluding the loss on the disposal of the Gubor and Sperlari businesses in 1996 and the net after-tax effects of the 1995 restructuring activities, income increased $28.6 million or 10%. Net income increased $15.5 million or 6% in 1995, excluding the net after-tax effects of the 1995 and 1994 restructuring activities. Income as a percent of net sales, after excluding the loss on the sale of the Gubor and Sperlari businesses in 1996 and the net after-tax effects of restructuring activities in 1995 and 1994 was 7.7% in 1996, 7.6% in 1995 and 7.3% in 1994.

FINANCIAL POSITION

The Corporation's financial position remained strong during 1996. The capitalization ratio (total short-term and long-term debt as a percent of stockholders' equity, short-term and long-term debt) was 46% as of December 31, 1996, and 42% as of December 31, 1995. The higher capitalization ratio in 1996 primarily reflected increased borrowings for business acquisitions and share repurchases. The ratio of current assets to current liabilities was 1.2:1 as of December 31, 1996, and 1.1:1 as of December 31, 1995.

Assets

Total assets increased $354.2 million or 13% as of December 31, 1996, primarily as a result of increases in inventories, property, plant and equipment and intangibles resulting from the Leaf acquisition, offset somewhat by decreases associated with the divestitures of Gubor and Sperlari.

Current assets increased by $63.9 million or 7% reflecting increased cash and cash equivalents and higher inventories in existing businesses, partly to support the introduction of new products, and current assets resulting from the Leaf acquisition, substantially offset by decreases associated with the business divestitures.

The $165.9 million net increase in property, plant and equipment principally reflected the Leaf acquisition and capital additions of $159.4 million, partly offset by the divestiture of the Gubor and Sperlari businesses, and depreciation expense of $119.4 million.

The increase in intangibles resulting from business acquisitions primarily reflected preliminary goodwill associated with the acquisition of the Leaf confectionery operations, partially offset by a decrease related to the divestiture of the Gubor and Sperlari businesses and the amortization of intangibles. The decrease in other assets was primarily associated with employee retirement plans.

Liabilities

Total liabilities increased by $276.1 million or 16% as of December 31, 1996, primarily due to an increase in long-term debt. The increase in long-term debt of $298.3 million reflected an increase in commercial paper borrowings associated with the acquisition of Leaf, net of proceeds received from the sale of the Gubor, Sperlari, Planters and Life Savers businesses. As of December 31, 1996, $300.0 million of commercial paper borrowings were reclassified as long-term debt in accordance with the Corporation's intent and ability to refinance such obligations on a long-term basis.

Stockholders' Equity

Total stockholders' equity rose by 7% in 1996, as net income exceeded dividends paid and the repurchase of Common Stock. Total stockholders' equity has increased at a compound annual rate of 5% over the past ten years.

Capital Structure

The Corporation has two classes of stock outstanding, Common Stock and Class B Common Stock (Class B Stock). Holders of the Common Stock and the Class B Stock generally vote together without regard to class on matters submitted to stockholders, including the election of directors, with the Common Stock having one vote per share and the Class B Stock having ten votes per share. However, the Common Stock, voting separately as a class, is entitled to elect one-sixth of the Board of Directors. With respect to dividend rights, the Common Stock is entitled to cash dividends 10% higher than those declared and paid on the Class B Stock.

LIQUIDITY

Historically, the Corporation's major source of financing has been cash generated from operations. The Corporation's income and, consequently, cash provided from operations during the year are affected by seasonal sales patterns, the timing of new product introductions, business acquisitions and divestitures, and price increases. Chocolate, confectionery and grocery seasonal and holiday-related sales have typically been highest during the third and fourth quarters of the year, representing the principal seasonal effect. Generally, seasonal working capital needs peak during the summer months and have been met by issuing commercial paper.

Over the past three years, cash requirements for share repurchases, business acquisitions, capital additions, and dividend payments exceeded cash provided from operating activities and proceeds from business divestitures by $404.6 million. Total debt, including debt assumed, increased during the period by $453.9 million. Cash and cash equivalents increased by $45.5 million during the period.

The Corporation anticipates that capital expenditures will be in the range of $175 million to $225 million per annum during the next several years as a result of continued modernization of existing facilities and capacity expansion to support new products and line extensions. As of December 31, 1996, the Corporation's principal capital commitments included manufacturing capacity expansion and modernization.

In August 1996, the Corporation's Board of Directors declared a two-for-one split of the Common Stock and Class B Common Stock effective September 13, 1996, to stockholders of record as of August 23, 1996. The split was effected as a stock dividend by distributing one additional share for each share held. Unless otherwise indicated, all shares and per share information have been restated to reflect the stock split.

A total of 9,437,770 shares of Common Stock have been repurchased for approximately $263.7 million under share repurchase programs which began in 1993. Of the shares repurchased, 528,000 shares were retired and the remaining 8,909,770 shares were held as Treasury Stock as of December 31, 1996.

In August 1995, the Corporation purchased an additional 18,099,546 shares (9,049,773 shares on a pre-split basis) of its Common Stock to be held as Treasury Stock from the Milton Hershey School Trust for $500.0 million. In connection with the share repurchase program begun in 1993, a total of 4,000,000 shares (2,000,000 shares on a pre-split basis) were also acquired from the Milton Hershey School Trust in 1993 for approximately $103.1 million. As of December 31, 1996, a total of 27,009,316 shares were held as Treasury Stock and $136.3 million remained available for repurchases of Common Stock under a program approved by the Corporation's Board of Directors in February 1996.

In October 1995, the Corporation issued $200 million of Notes under Form S-3 Registration Statements which were declared effective in June 1990 and November 1993. As of December 31, 1996, $300 million of debt securities remained available for issuance under the November 1993 Registration Statement. Proceeds from any offering of the $300 million of debt securities available under the shelf registration may be used for general corporate requirements including, reducing existing commercial paper borrowings, financing capital additions and funding future business acquisitions and working capital requirements.

In March 1997, the Corporation issued $150 million of 6.95% Notes due 2007 under the November 1993 Registration Statement. Proceeds from the debt issuance were used to repay a portion of the commercial paper borrowings associated with the Leaf acquisition.

In order to minimize its financing costs and to manage interest rate exposure, the Corporation, from time to time, enters into interest rate swap agreements to effectively convert a portion of its floating rate debt to fixed rate debt. As of December 31, 1996, the Corporation had agreements outstanding with an aggregate notional amount of $125.0 million, with maturities through October 1997. Any interest rate differential on interest rate swaps is recognized as an adjustment to interest expense over the term of each agreement. The Corporation's risk related to swap agreements is limited to the cost of replacing such agreements at current market rates.

In December 1995, the Corporation entered into committed credit facility agreements with a syndicate of banks under which it could borrow up to $600 million with options to increase borrowings by $1.0 billion with the concurrence of the banks. Lines of credit previously maintained by the Corporation were significantly reduced when the credit facility agreements became effective. Of the total committed credit facility, $200 million is for a renewable 364-day term and $400 million is effective for a five-year term. Both the short-term and long-term committed credit facility agreements were amended and renewed effective December 13, 1996. The credit facilities may be used to fund general corporate requirements, to support commercial paper borrowings and, in certain instances, to finance future business acquisitions.

Cash Flow Activities

Cash provided from operating activities totaled $1.3 billion during the past three years. Over this period, cash used by or provided from accounts receivable and inventories has tended to fluctuate as a result of sales during December and inventory management practices. The change in cash required for or provided from other assets and liabilities between the years was primarily related to variations in the funding status of pension plans, commodities transactions and the timing of payments for accrued liabilities, including income taxes, and in 1995 and 1994, restructuring expenses.

Investing activities included capital additions and business acquisitions and divestitures. Capital additions during the past three years included the purchase of manufacturing equipment, and expansion and modernization of existing facilities. Businesses acquired during the past three years included Leaf in 1996 and Henry Heide in 1995. The Gubor, Sperlari, Planters and Life Savers businesses were sold in 1996 and OZF Jamin was sold in 1995. Cash used for business acquisitions represented the purchase price paid and consisted of the current assets, property, plant and equipment, intangibles and other assets acquired, net of liabilities assumed.

Financing activities included debt borrowings and repayments, payment of dividends, the exercise of stock options, incentive plan transactions and the repurchase of Common Stock. During the past three years, short-term borrowings in the form of commercial paper or bank borrowings were used to fund seasonal working capital requirements, business acquisitions, a share repurchase program and the purchase of Common Stock from the Milton Hershey School Trust. The proceeds from the issuance of $200 million of Notes in October 1995 were used to reduce short-term borrowings. During the past three years, a total of 22,391,116 shares of Common Stock has been repurchased for approximately $631.9 million. Cash requirements for incentive plan transactions were $75.3 million during the past three years, partially offset by cash received from the exercise of stock options of $40.6 million.

Commodity Price Risk Management

The Corporation's most significant raw materials include cocoa, sugar, milk, peanuts, flour and almonds. The Corporation attempts to minimize the effect of price fluctuations related to the purchase of these raw materials primarily through forward purchasing to cover future manufacturing requirements, generally for periods from 3 to 24 months. With regard to cocoa, sugar and corn sweeteners, price risks are also managed by entering into futures and options contracts. At the present time, similar futures and options contracts are not available for use in pricing the Corporation's other major raw materials. Futures contracts are used in combination with forward purchasing of cocoa, sugar and corn sweetener requirements, principally to take advantage of market fluctuations which provide more favorable pricing opportunities and to increase diversity or flexibility in sourcing these raw materials. The Corporation's commodity procurement practices are intended to reduce the risk of future price increases, but also may potentially limit the ability to benefit from possible price decreases.

The cost of cocoa beans and the prices for the related commodity futures contracts historically have been subject to wide fluctuations attributable to a variety of factors, including the effect of weather on crop yield, other imbalances between supply and demand, currency exchange rates and speculative influences. Cocoa prices have been rising since 1992 due to cocoa demand exceeding production. During 1996, prices for cocoa futures were relatively stable as a result of record high cocoa production in West Africa. During 1997, any problems with the development of the West African crop to be harvested beginning in the fall, could result in demand exceeding production, leading to possible cocoa futures price increases. The Corporation's costs during 1997 will not necessarily reflect market price fluctuations because of its forward purchasing practices, premiums and discounts reflective of relative values, varying delivery times, and supply and demand for specific varieties and grades of cocoa beans.

The major raw material used in the manufacture of pasta products is semolina milled from durum wheat. The Corporation purchases semolina from commercial mills and is also engaged in custom milling agreements to obtain sufficient quantities of semolina. In the first half of 1996, the market price for durum semolina remained near historic highs. Durum wheat production during 1996 increased in almost every area of the world, resulting in some price declines in the last quarter of the year. However, prices remained well above long-term historical price levels.

Generally, the Corporation has been able to offset the effects of increases in the cost of its major raw materials, particularly cocoa beans, through selling price increases or reductions in product weights. Conversely, declines in the cost of major raw materials have served as a source of funds to enhance consumer value through increases in product weights, respond to competitive activity, develop new products and markets, and offset rising costs of other raw materials and expenses.

Market Prices and Dividends

Cash dividends paid on the Corporation's Common Stock and Class B Stock were $114.8 million in 1996 and $110.1 million in 1995. After adjustment for the two-for-one stock split, the annual dividend rate on the Common Stock was $.80 per share, an increase of 11% over the 1995 rate of $.72 per share. The 1996 dividend represented the 22nd consecutive year of Common Stock dividend increases.

On February 4, 1997, the Corporation's Board of Directors declared a quarterly dividend of $.20 per share of Common Stock payable on March 14, 1997, to stockholders of record as of February 24, 1997. It is the Corporation's 269th consecutive Common Stock dividend. A quarterly dividend of $.18 per share of Class B Stock also was declared.

Hershey Foods Corporation's Common Stock is listed and traded principally on the New York Stock Exchange (NYSE) under the ticker symbol "HSY." Approximately 47.0 million shares of the Corporation's Common Stock were traded during 1996. The Class B Stock is not publicly traded.

The closing price of the Common Stock on December 31, 1996, was $43¾. There were 42,483 stockholders of record of the Common Stock and the Class B Stock as of December 31, 1996.

The following table shows the dividends paid per share of Common Stock and Class B Stock and the price range of the Common Stock for each quarter of the past two years:

	Dividends Paid Per Share		Common Stock Price Range*	
	Common Stock	Class B Stock	High	Low
1996				
1st Quarter	**$ .180**	**$.1625**	**$40⅝**	**$31 15/16**
2nd Quarter	**.180**	**.1625**	**38 15/16**	**34⅞**
3rd Quarter	**.200**	**.1800**	**51¾**	**35**
4th Quarter	**.200**	**.1800**	**51¾**	**43½**
Total	**$ .760**	**$.6850**		
1995				
1st Quarter	$.1625	$ .1475	$26 3/16	$24
2nd Quarter	.1625	.1475	27 15/16	25 1/16
3rd Quarter	.1800	.1625	32 7/16	26 13/16
4th Quarter	.1800	.1625	33 15/16	29½
Total	$.6850	$ .6200		

* NYSE-Composite Quotations for Common Stock by calendar quarter.

RETURN MEASURES

Operating Return on Average Stockholders' Equity

The Corporation's operating return on average stockholders' equity was 27.5% in 1996. Over the most recent five-year period, the return has ranged from 17.3% in 1992 to 27.5% in 1996. For the purpose of calculating operating return on average stockholders' equity, earnings is defined as net income, excluding the catch-up adjustments for accounting changes and the after-tax gain on the sale of the investment in Freia Marabou a.s (Freia) in 1993, the after-tax restructuring activities in 1994 and 1995 and the after-tax loss on the disposal of businesses in 1996.

Operating Return on Average Invested Capital

The Corporation's operating return on average invested capital was 17.8% in 1996. Over the most recent five-year period, the return has ranged from 14.4% in 1992 to 17.8% in 1996. Average invested capital consists of the annual average of beginning and ending balances of long-term debt, deferred income taxes and stockholders' equity. For the purpose of calculating operating return on average invested capital, earnings is defined as net income, excluding the sale of the investment in Freia, the catch-up adjustments for accounting changes, the after-tax restructuring activities in 1994 and 1995, the after-tax loss on disposal of businesses in 1996, and the after-tax effect of interest on long-term debt.

HERSHEY FOODS CORPORATION

CONSOLIDATED STATEMENTS OF INCOME

For the years ended December 31, In thousands of dollars except per share amounts	1996	1995	1994
Net Sales	**$3,989,308**	$3,690,667	$3,606,271
Costs and Expenses:			
Cost of sales	**2,302,089**	2,126,274	2,097,556
Selling, marketing and administrative	**1,124,087**	1,053,758	1,034,115
Total costs and expenses	**3,426,176**	3,180,032	3,131,671
Restructuring Credit (Charge)	**—**	151	(106,105)
Loss on Disposal of Businesses	**(35,352)**	—	—
Income before Interest and Income Taxes	**527,780**	510,786	368,495
Interest expense, net	**48,043**	44,833	35,357
Income before Income Taxes	**479,737**	465,953	333,138
Provision for income taxes	**206,551**	184,034	148,919
Net Income	**$ 273,186**	$ 281,919	$ 184,219
Net Income Per Share	**$ 1.77**	$ 1.70	$ 1.06
Cash Dividends Paid Per Share:			
Common Stock	**$ .7600**	$ .6850	$ .6250
Class B Common Stock	**.6850**	.6200	.5675

The notes to consolidated financial statements are an integral part of these statements.

HERSHEY FOODS CORPORATION

CONSOLIDATED BALANCE SHEETS

December 31,	1996	1995
In thousands of dollars		
ASSETS		
Current Assets:		
Cash and cash equivalents	**$ 61,422**	$ 32,346
Accounts receivable—trade	**294,606**	326,024
Inventories	**474,978**	397,570
Deferred income taxes	**94,464**	84,785
Prepaid expenses and other	**60,759**	81,598
Total current assets	**986,229**	922,323
Property, Plant and Equipment, Net	**1,601,895**	1,436,009
Intangibles Resulting from Business Acquisitions	**565,962**	428,714
Other Assets	**30,710**	43,577
Total assets	**$3,184,796**	$2,830,623
LIABILITIES AND STOCKHOLDERS' EQUITY		
Current Liabilities:		
Accounts payable	**$ 134,213**	$ 127,067
Accrued liabilities	**357,828**	308,123
Accrued income taxes	**10,254**	15,514
Short-term debt	**299,469**	413,268
Current portion of long-term debt	**15,510**	383
Total current liabilities	**817,274**	864,355
Long-term Debt	**655,289**	357,034
Other Long-term Liabilities	**327,209**	333,814
Deferred Income Taxes	**224,003**	192,461
Total liabilities	**2,023,775**	1,747,664
Stockholders' Equity:		
Preferred Stock, shares issued: none in 1996 and 1995	**—**	—
Common Stock, shares issued: 149,471,964 in 1996 and 74,733,982 on a pre-split basis in 1995	**149,472**	74,734
Class B Common Stock, shares issued: 30,478,908 in 1996 and 15,241,454 on a pre-split basis in 1995	**30,478**	15,241
Additional paid-in capital	**42,432**	47,732
Cumulative foreign currency translation adjustments	**(32,875)**	(29,240)
Unearned ESOP compensation	**(31,935)**	(35,128)
Retained earnings	**1,763,144**	1,694,696
Treasury—Common Stock shares, at cost: 27,009,316 in 1996 and 12,709,553 on a pre-split basis in 1995	**(759,695)**	(685,076)
Total stockholders' equity	**1,161,021**	1,082,959
Total liabilities and stockholders' equity	**$3,184,796**	$2,830,623

The notes to consolidated financial statements are an integral part of these balance sheets.

HERSHEY FOODS CORPORATION

CONSOLIDATED STATEMENTS OF CASH FLOWS

For the years ended December 31,	1996	1995	1994
In thousands of dollars			
Cash Flows Provided from (Used by) Operating Activities			
Net income	**$ 273,186**	$ 281,919	$ 184,219
Adjustments to reconcile net income to net cash provided from operations:			
Depreciation and amortization	**133,476**	133,884	129,041
Deferred income taxes	**22,863**	26,380	(2,328)
Restructuring (credit) charge	**—**	(151)	106,105
Loss on disposal of businesses	**35,352**	—	—
Changes in assets and liabilities, net of effects from business acquisitions and divestitures:			
Accounts receivable—trade	**5,159**	1,666	(36,696)
Inventories	**(41,038)**	28,147	7,740
Accounts payable	**14,032**	14,767	(10,230)
Other assets and liabilities	**15,120**	(11,297)	(58,146)
Other, net	**5,593**	19,614	20,032
Net Cash Provided from Operating Activities	**463,743**	494,929	339,737
Cash Flows Provided from (Used by) Investing Activities			
Capital additions	**(159,433)**	(140,626)	(138,711)
Business acquisitions	**(437,195)**	(12,500)	—
Proceeds from divestitures	**149,222**	—	—
Other, net	**9,333**	8,720	(4,492)
Net Cash (Used by) Investing Activities	**(438,073)**	(144,406)	(143,203)
Cash Flows Provided from (Used by) Financing Activities			
Net change in short-term borrowings partially classified as long-term debt	**210,929**	103,530	(20,503)
Long-term borrowings	**—**	202,448	102
Repayment of long-term debt	**(3,103)**	(7,887)	(14,413)
Cash dividends paid	**(114,763)**	(110,090)	(106,961)
Exercise of stock options	**22,049**	15,106	3,494
Incentive plan transactions	**(45,634)**	(21,903)	(7,726)
Repurchase of Common Stock	**(66,072)**	(526,119)	(39,748)
Net Cash Provided from (Used by) Financing Activities	**3,406**	(344,915)	(185,755)
Increase in Cash and Cash Equivalents	**29,076**	5,608	10,779
Cash and Cash Equivalents as of January 1	**32,346**	26,738	15,959
Cash and Cash Equivalents as of December 31	**$ 61,422**	$ 32,346	$ 26,738
Interest Paid	**$ 52,143**	$ 43,731	$ 36,803
Income Taxes Paid	**180,347**	148,629	177,876

The notes to consolidated financial statements are an integral part of these statements.

HERSHEY FOODS CORPORATION

CONSOLIDATED STATEMENTS OF STOCKHOLDERS' EQUITY

In thousands of dollars	Preferred Stock	Common Stock	Class B Common Stock	Additional Paid-in Capital	Cumulative Foreign Currency Translation Adjustments	Unearned ESOP Compensation	Retained Earnings	Treasury Common Stock	Total Stockholders' Equity
Balance as of January 1, 1994	$ —	$ 74,669	$ 15,253	$ 51,196	$ (13,905)	$ (41,515)	$ 1,445,609	$ (118,963)	$ 1,412,344
Net income							184,219		184,219
Dividends:									
Common Stock, $.625 per share							(89,660)		(89,660)
Class B Common Stock, $.5675 per share							(17,301)		(17,301)
Foreign currency translation adjustments					(10,632)				(10,632)
Conversion of Class B Common Stock into Common Stock		10	(10)						—
Incentive plan transactions				(1,264)					(1,264)
Exercise of stock options				(548)					(548)
Employee stock ownership trust transactions				496		3,194			3,690
Repurchase of Common Stock								(39,748)	(39,748)
Balance as of December 31, 1994	—	74,679	15,243	49,880	(24,537)	(38,321)	1,522,867	(158,711)	1,441,100
Net income							281,919		281,919
Dividends:									
Common Stock, $.685 per share							(91,190)		(91,190)
Class B Common Stock, $.62 per share							(18,900)		(18,900)
Foreign currency translation adjustments					(4,703)				(4,703)
Conversion of Class B Common Stock into Common Stock		2	(2)						—
Incentive plan transactions				(180)					(180)
Exercise of stock options		53		(2,456)				(246)	(2,649)
Employee stock ownership trust transactions				488		3,193			3,681
Repurchase of Common Stock								(526,119)	(526,119)
Balance as of December 31, 1995	—	74,734	15,241	47,732	(29,240)	(35,128)	1,694,696	(685,076)	1,082,959
Net income							**273,186**		**273,186**
Dividends:									
Common Stock, $.76 per share							**(93,884)**		**(93,884)**
Class B Common Stock, $.685 per share							**(20,879)**		**(20,879)**
Foreign currency translation adjustments					**(3,635)**				**(3,635)**
Two-for-one stock split		**74,736**	**15,239**				**(89,975)**		**—**
Conversion of Class B Common Stock into Common Stock		**2**	**(2)**						**—**
Incentive plan transactions				**(426)**					**(426)**
Exercise of stock options				**(5,391)**				**(8,547)**	**(13,938)**
Employee stock ownership trust transactions				**517**		**3,193**			**3,710**
Repurchase of Common Stock								**(66,072)**	**(66,072)**
Balance as of December 31, 1996	**$ —**	**$149,472**	**$30,478**	**$42,432**	**$(32,875)**	**$(31,935)**	**$1,763,144**	**$(759,695)**	**$1,161,021**

The notes to consolidated financial statements are an integral part of these statements.

HERSHEY FOODS CORPORATION

NOTES TO CONSOLIDATED FINANCIAL STATEMENTS

1. SUMMARY OF SIGNIFICANT ACCOUNTING POLICIES

Significant accounting policies employed by the Corporation are discussed below and in other notes to the consolidated financial statements. Certain reclassifications have been made to prior year amounts to conform to the 1996 presentation. Unless otherwise indicated, all shares and per share information have been restated for the two-for-one stock split effective September 13, 1996.

Principles of Consolidation

The consolidated financial statements include the accounts of the Corporation and its subsidiaries after elimination of intercompany accounts and transactions.

Use of Estimates

The preparation of financial statements in conformity with generally accepted accounting principles requires management to make estimates and assumptions that affect the reported amounts of assets and liabilities, the disclosure of contingent assets and liabilities at the date of the financial statements and the reported amounts of revenues and expenses during the reporting period. Actual results could differ from those estimates, particularly for accounts receivable and certain current and long-term liabilities.

Cash Equivalents

All highly liquid debt instruments purchased with a maturity of three months or less are classified as cash equivalents.

Commodities Futures and Options Contracts

In connection with the purchasing of cocoa, sugar and corn sweeteners for anticipated manufacturing requirements, the Corporation enters into commodities futures and options contracts as deemed appropriate to reduce the effect of price fluctuations. In accordance with Statement of Financial Accounting Standards No. 80 "Accounting for Futures Contracts," these futures and options contracts meet the hedge criteria and are accounted for as hedges. Accordingly, gains and losses are deferred and recognized in cost of sales as part of the product cost.

Property, Plant and Equipment

Property, plant and equipment are stated at cost. Depreciation of buildings, machinery and equipment is computed using the straight-line method over the estimated useful lives.

Intangibles Resulting from Business Acquisitions

Intangible assets resulting from business acquisitions principally consist of the excess of the acquisition cost over the fair value of the net assets of businesses acquired (goodwill). Goodwill is amortized on a straight-line basis over 40 years. Other intangible assets are amortized on a straight-line basis over the estimated useful lives. The Corporation periodically evaluates whether events or circumstances have occurred indicating that the carrying amount of goodwill may not be recoverable. When factors indicate that goodwill should be evaluated for possible impairment, the Corporation uses an estimate of the acquired business' undiscounted future cash flows compared to the related carrying amount of net assets, including goodwill, to determine if an impairment loss should be recognized.

Accumulated amortization of intangible assets resulting from business acquisitions was $110.1 million and $101.5 million as of December 31, 1996 and 1995, respectively.

Foreign Currency Translation

Results of operations for foreign entities are translated using the average exchange rates during the period. For foreign entities, assets and liabilities are translated to U.S. dollars using the exchange rates in effect at the balance sheet date. Resulting translation adjustments are recorded in a separate component of stockholders' equity, "Cumulative Foreign Currency Translation Adjustments."

Foreign Exchange Contracts

The Corporation enters into foreign exchange forward and options contracts to hedge transactions primarily related to firm commitments to purchase equipment, certain raw materials and finished goods denominated in foreign currencies, and to hedge payment of intercompany transactions with its non-domestic subsidiaries. These contracts reduce currency risk from exchange rate movements.

Foreign exchange forward contracts are intended and effective as hedges of firm, identifiable, foreign currency commitments and foreign exchange options contracts meet required hedge criteria for anticipated transactions. Accordingly, gains and losses are deferred and accounted for as part of the underlying transactions. Gains and losses on terminated derivatives designated as hedges are accounted for as part of the originally hedged transaction. Gains and losses on derivatives designated as hedges of items which mature, are sold or terminated, or of anticipated transactions which are no longer likely to occur, are recorded currently in income. In entering into these contracts the Corporation has assumed the risk which might arise from the possible inability of counterparties to meet the terms of their contracts. The Corporation does not expect any losses as a result of counterparty defaults.

License Agreements

The Corporation has entered into license agreements under which it has access to certain trademarks and proprietary technology, and manufactures and/or markets and distributes certain products. The rights under these agreements are extendable on a long-term basis at the Corporation's option subject to certain conditions, including minimum sales levels, which the Corporation has met. License fees and royalties, payable under the terms of the agreements, are expensed as incurred.

Research and Development

The Corporation expenses research and development costs as incurred. Research and development expense was $26.1 million, $26.2 million and $26.3 million in 1996, 1995 and 1994, respectively.

Advertising

The Corporation expenses advertising costs as incurred. Advertising expense was $174.2 million, $159.2 million and $120.6 million in 1996, 1995 and 1994, respectively. Prepaid advertising as of December 31, 1996 and 1995, was $2.2 million and $3.0 million, respectively.

2. ACQUISITIONS AND DIVESTITURES

In December 1996, the Corporation acquired from an affiliate of Huhtamäki Oy (Huhtamaki), the international foods company based in Finland, Huhtamaki's Leaf North America (Leaf) confectionery operations for $437.2 million, plus the assumption of $17.0 million in debt. In addition, the parties entered into a trademark and technology license agreement under which the Corporation will manufacture and/or market and distribute in North, Central and South America Huhtamaki's confectionery brands including *Good & Plenty, Heath, Jolly Rancher, Milk Duds, PayDay* and *Whoppers*. Leaf's principal manufacturing facilities are located in Denver, Colorado; Memphis, Tennessee; and Robinson, Illinois.

In December 1995, the Corporation completed the acquisition of the outstanding shares of the confectionery company Henry Heide, Incorporated (Henry Heide), for approximately $12.5 million. Henry Heide's headquarters and manufacturing facility are located in New Brunswick, N.J., where it manufactures a variety of non-chocolate confectionery products including *Jujyfruits* candy and *Wunderbeans* jellybeans.

In accordance with the purchase method of accounting, the purchase prices of the acquisitions summarized above were allocated on a preliminary basis to the underlying assets and liabilities at the date of acquisition based on their estimated respective fair values, which may be revised at a later date. Total liabilities assumed, including debt, were $138.0 million in 1996 and $10.6 million in 1995. Results subsequent to the dates of acquisition are included in the consolidated financial statements. Had the results of the Henry Heide acquisition been included in consolidated results for the entire length of each period presented, the effect would not have been material.

Had the acquisition of Leaf occurred at the beginning of 1996, pro forma consolidated results would have been as follows:

For the year ended December 31,	**1996**
In thousands of dollars except per share amount	**(unaudited)**
Net sales	**$4,473,950**
Net income	**256,300**
Net income per share	**1.66**

The pro forma results are based on historical financial information provided by Huhtamaki, excluding a business restructuring charge recorded by Huhtamaki in 1996 and adjusted to give effect to certain costs and expenses, including fees under the trademark and technology license agreement, goodwill amortization, interest expense and income taxes which would have been incurred by the Corporation if it had owned and operated the Leaf confectionery business throughout 1996. These results are not necessarily reflective of the actual results which would have occurred if the acquisition had been completed at the beginning of the year, nor are they necessarily indicative of future combined financial results.

In December 1996, the Corporation completed the sale to Huhtamaki of the outstanding shares of Gubor Holding GmbH (Gubor) and Sperlari, S.r.l. (Sperlari). Gubor manufactures and markets high-quality assorted pralines and seasonal chocolate products in Germany and Sperlari manufactures and markets various confectionery and grocery products in Italy. The total proceeds from the sale of the Gubor and Sperlari businesses were $121.7 million. The transaction resulted in an after-tax loss of $35.4 million since no tax benefit associated with the transaction was recorded. Combined net sales for Gubor and Sperlari were $216.6 million, $222.0 million and $186.6 million in 1996, 1995 and 1994, respectively.

In January 1996, the Corporation completed the sale of the assets of Hershey Canada, Inc.'s *Planters* nut (Planters) and *Life Savers* and *Breath Savers* hard candy, and *Beech-Nut* cough drops (Life Savers) businesses to Johnvince Foods Group and Beta Brands Inc., respectively. Both transactions were part of a restructuring program announced by the Corporation in late 1994.

In June 1995, the Corporation completed the sale of the outstanding shares of Overspecht B.V. (OZF Jamin) to a management buyout group at OZF Jamin, as part of the Corporation's restructuring program. OZF Jamin manufactures chocolate and non-chocolate confectionery products, cookies, biscuits and ice cream for distribution primarily to customers in the Netherlands and Belgium.

3. RESTRUCTURING ACTIVITIES

In the fourth quarter of 1994, the Corporation recorded a pre-tax restructuring charge of $106.1 million, following a comprehensive review of domestic and foreign operations designed to enhance performance of operating assets by lowering operating and administrative costs, eliminating underperforming assets and streamlining the overall decision-making process. The charge of $106.1 million resulted in an after-tax charge of $80.2 million or $.46 per share in 1994.

The charge included $34.3 million of severance and termination benefits for the elimination of approximately 500 positions in the manufacturing, technical and administrative areas at both domestic and foreign operations. The charge also included anticipated losses on disposals of certain businesses of $39.1 million, product line discontinuations of $17.5 million and the consolidation of operations and disposal of machinery and equipment of $15.2 million.

As of December 31, 1995, $81.8 million of restructuring reserves had been utilized and $16.7 million had been reversed to reflect revisions and changes in estimates to the original restructuring program. Operating cash flows were used to fund cash requirements which represented approximately 25% of the total reserves utilized. The non-cash portion of restructuring reserve utilization was associated primarily with the divestiture of foreign businesses and the discontinuation of certain product lines.

During the third quarter of 1995, a pre-tax restructuring charge of $16.6 million was recorded in connection with a voluntary retirement program announced by the Corporation in August 1995. The charge was primarily related to the funding of retirement benefits for eligible employees who elected early retirement. This cash charge was funded from operating cash flows. The impact of this charge was more than offset by the partial reversal of 1994 accrued restructuring reserves in the fourth quarter of 1995 resulting in an increase to income before income taxes of $.2 million and an increase to net income of $2.0 million, as the tax benefit associated with the 1995 charge more than offset the tax provision associated with the reversal of 1994 restructuring reserves.

The remaining $7.6 million of accrued restructuring reserves as of December 31, 1995, were utilized during 1996 as the restructuring program was completed. A portion of the restructuring reserves were used for severance and relocation benefits related to the consolidation of the pasta and grocery field sales organizations.

4. RENTAL AND LEASE COMMITMENTS

Rent expense was $25.3 million, $24.9 million and $25.7 million for 1996, 1995 and 1994, respectively. Rent expense pertains to all operating leases, which were principally related to certain administrative buildings, distribution facilities and transportation equipment. Future minimum rental payments under non-cancelable operating leases with a remaining term in excess of one year as of December 31, 1996, were: 1997, $16.4 million; 1998, $15.1 million; 1999, $15.5 million; 2000, $15.1 million; 2001, $15.1 million; 2002 and beyond, $90.8 million.

5. FINANCIAL INSTRUMENTS

The carrying amounts of financial instruments including cash and cash equivalents, accounts receivable, accounts payable and short-term debt approximated fair value as of December 31, 1996 and 1995, because of the relatively short maturity of these instruments. The carrying value of long-term debt, including the current portion, approximated fair value as of December 31, 1996 and 1995, based upon quoted market prices for the same or similar debt issues.

As of December 31, 1996, the Corporation had foreign exchange forward contracts maturing in 1997 and 1998 to purchase $25.0 million in foreign currency, primarily British sterling and German marks, and to sell $24.6 million in foreign currency, primarily Canadian dollars and Japanese yen, at contracted forward rates.

As of December 31, 1995, the Corporation had foreign exchange forward contracts maturing in 1996 and 1997 to purchase $54.7 million in foreign currency, primarily Canadian dollars, British sterling and Swiss francs, and to sell $26.4 million in foreign currency, primarily Italian lira, Canadian dollars and Japanese yen, at contracted forward rates.

To hedge foreign currency exposure related to anticipated transactions associated with the purchase of certain raw materials and finished goods generally covering 3 to 24 months, the Corporation also purchases, from time to time, foreign exchange options which permit, but do not require, the Corporation to exchange foreign currencies at a future date with another party at a contracted exchange rate. To finance premiums paid on such options, the Corporation may also write offsetting options at exercise prices which limit but do not eliminate the effect of purchased options and forward contracts as a hedge. As of December 31, 1995, the Corporation had purchased foreign exchange options of $11.5 million and written foreign exchange options of $8.9 million, principally related to British sterling. Such options expired or were settled in the first quarter of 1996.

The fair value of foreign exchange forward contracts is estimated by obtaining quotes for future contracts with similar terms, adjusted where necessary for maturity differences, and the fair value of foreign exchange options is estimated using active market quotations. As of December 31, 1996 and 1995, the fair value of foreign exchange forward and options contracts approximated carrying value. The Corporation does not hold or issue financial instruments for trading purposes.

In order to minimize its financing costs and to manage interest rate exposure, the Corporation, from time to time, enters into interest rate swap agreements to effectively convert a portion of its floating rate debt to fixed rate debt. Agreements outstanding with an aggregate notional amount of $75.0 million matured during 1996. As of December 31, 1996, the Corporation had agreements outstanding with an aggregate notional amount of $125.0 million with maturities through October 1997. As of December 31, 1996 and 1995, interest rates payable were at weighted average fixed rates of 5.8% and 5.6%, respectively, and interest rates receivable were floating based on 30-day commercial paper composite rates. Any interest rate differential on interest rate swaps is recognized as an adjustment to interest expense over the term of each agreement. The Corporation's risk related to swap agreements is limited to the cost of replacing such agreements at current market rates.

6. INTEREST EXPENSE

Interest expense, net consisted of the following:

For the years ended December 31,	1996	1995	1994
In thousands of dollars			
Long-term debt and lease obligations	**$30,818**	$20,949	$19,103
Short-term debt	**22,752**	28,576	21,155
Capitalized interest	**(1,534)**	(1,957)	(3,009)
Interest expense, gross	**52,036**	47,568	37,249
Interest income	**(3,993)**	(2,735)	(1,892)
Interest expense, net	**$48,043**	$44,833	$35,357

7. SHORT-TERM DEBT

Generally, the Corporation's short-term borrowings are in the form of commercial paper or bank loans with an original maturity of three months or less. In December 1995, the Corporation entered into committed credit facility agreements with a syndicate of banks under which it could borrow up to $600 million as of December 31, 1996, with options to increase borrowings by $1.0 billion with the concurrence of the banks. Of the total committed credit facility, $200 million is for a renewable 364-day term and $400 million is effective for a five-year term. Both the short-term and long-term committed credit facility agreements were amended and renewed effective December 13, 1996. The credit facilities may be used to fund general corporate requirements, to support commercial paper borrowings and, in certain instances, to finance future business acquisitions. As of December 31, 1996, $300.0 million of commercial paper borrowings were reclassified as long-term debt in accordance with the Corporation's intent and ability to refinance such obligations on a long-term basis.

The Corporation also maintains lines of credit arrangements with domestic and international commercial banks, under which it could borrow in various currencies up to approximately $96.1 million and $97.7 million as of December 31, 1996 and 1995, respectively, at the lending banks' prime commercial interest rates or lower. The Corporation had combined domestic commercial paper borrowings, including the portion classified as long-term debt, and short-term foreign bank loans against its credit facilities and lines of credit of $599.5 million as of December 31, 1996, and $413.3 million as of December 31, 1995. The weighted average interest rates on short-term borrowings outstanding as of December 31, 1996 and 1995, were 5.5% and 5.7%, respectively.

The credit facilities and lines of credit were supported by commitment fee arrangements. The average fee during 1996 was approximately .05% per annum of the commitment. The Corporation is in compliance with all covenants included in the credit facility agreements. There were no significant compensating balance agreements which legally restricted these funds.

As a result of maintaining a consolidated cash management system, the Corporation maintains overdraft positions at certain banks. Such overdrafts, which were included in accounts payable, were $25.2 million and $24.8 million as of December 31, 1996 and 1995, respectively.

8. LONG-TERM DEBT

Long-term debt consisted of the following:

December 31,	1996	1995
In thousands of dollars		
Commercial Paper at interest rates ranging from 5.54% to 5.59%	**$300,000**	$ —
Medium-term Notes, 8.85% to 9.92%, due 1997-1998	**40,400**	40,400
6.7% Notes due 2005	**200,000**	200,000
8.8% Debentures due 2021	**100,000**	100,000
Other obligations, net of unamortized debt discount	**30,399**	17,017
Total long-term debt	**670,799**	357,417
Less—current portion	**15,510**	383
Long-term portion	**$655,289**	$357,034

As of December 31, 1996, $300.0 million of commercial paper borrowings were reclassified as long-term debt in accordance with the Corporation's intent and ability to refinance such obligations on a long-term basis.

Aggregate annual maturities during the next five years, excluding short-term borrowings reclassified, are: 1997, $15.5 million; 1998, $25.2 million; 1999, $.2 million; 2000, $2.2 million; and 2001, $.2 million. The Corporation's debt is principally unsecured and of equal priority. None of the debt is convertible into stock of the Corporation. The Corporation is in compliance with all covenants included in the related debt agreements.

9. INCOME TAXES

Income before income taxes was as follows:

For the years ended December 31, In thousands of dollars	1996	1995	1994
Domestic	**$499,607**	$452,084	$411,089
Foreign	**(19,870)**	13,869	(77,951)
Income before income taxes	**$479,737**	$465,953	$333,138

The provision for income taxes was as follows:

For the years ended December 31, In thousands of dollars	1996	1995	1994
Current:			
Federal	**$158,040**	$135,034	$126,234
State	**23,288**	22,620	24,712
Foreign	**2,360**	—	301
Current provision for income taxes	**183,688**	157,654	151,247
Deferred:			
Federal	**12,952**	12,455	6,221
State	**8,134**	8,198	2,652
Foreign	**1,777**	5,727	(11,201)
Deferred provision for income taxes	**22,863**	26,380	(2,328)
Total provision for income taxes	**$206,551**	$184,034	$148,919

The 1994 Foreign deferred income tax benefit was associated primarily with the restructuring charge recorded in the fourth quarter of that year.

The tax effects of the significant temporary differences which comprised the deferred tax assets and liabilities were as follows:

December 31, In thousands of dollars	1996	1995
Deferred tax assets:		
Post-retirement benefit obligations	**$ 88,885**	$ 85,907
Accrued expenses and other reserves	**91,675**	78,506
Net operating loss carryforwards, net of valuation allowances of $2,663 in 1996 and $25,544 in 1995	**2,663**	7,298
Accrued trade promotion reserves	**22,910**	16,389
Other	**18,013**	27,869
Total deferred tax assets	**224,146**	215,969
Deferred tax liabilities:		
Depreciation	**256,424**	239,389
Other	**97,261**	84,256
Total deferred tax liabilities	**353,685**	323,645
Net deferred tax liabilities	**$129,539**	$107,676
Included in:		
Current deferred tax assets, net	**$ 94,464**	$ 84,785
Non-current deferred tax liabilities, net	**224,003**	192,461
Net deferred tax liabilities	**$129,539**	$107,676

As of December 31, 1996, the Corporation had $15.7 million of operating loss carryforwards available to reduce the future taxable income of a foreign subsidiary. The loss carryforwards must be utilized within the next ten years.

The following table reconciles the Federal statutory income tax rate with the Corporation's effective income tax rate:

For the years ended December 31,	1996	1995	1994
Federal statutory income tax rate	**35.0%**	35.0%	35.0%
Increase (reduction) resulting from:			
State income taxes, net of Federal income tax benefits	**4.7**	4.6	6.0
Restructuring (credit) charge for which no tax benefit was provided	**—**	(.3)	4.5
Non-deductible acquisition costs	**.6**	.6	.8
Loss on disposal of businesses for which no tax benefit was provided	**2.6**	—	—
Other, net	**.2**	(.4)	(1.6)
Effective income tax rate	**43.1%**	39.5%	44.7%

10. RETIREMENT PLANS

The Corporation and its subsidiaries sponsor several defined benefit retirement plans covering substantially all employees. Plans covering most domestic salaried and hourly employees provide retirement benefits based on individual account balances which are increased annually by pay-related and interest credits. Plans covering certain non-domestic employees provide retirement benefits based on career average pay, final pay, or final average pay as defined within the provisions of the individual plans. The Corporation also participates in several multi-employer retirement plans which provide defined benefits to employees covered under certain collective bargaining agreements.

The Corporation's policy is to fund domestic pension liabilities in accordance with the minimum and maximum limits imposed by the Employee Retirement Income Security Act of 1974 and Federal income tax laws, respectively. Non-domestic pension liabilities are funded in accordance with applicable local laws and regulations. Plan assets are invested in a broadly diversified portfolio consisting primarily of domestic and international common stocks and fixed income securities.

Pension expense included the following components:

For the years ended December 31,	1996	1995	1994
In thousands of dollars			
Service cost	**$ 29,311**	$ 25,311	$ 30,077
Interest cost on projected benefit obligations	**35,374**	32,531	28,351
Investment (return) loss on plan assets	**(51,205)**	(71,578)	8,288
Net amortization and deferral	**14,844**	40,823	(40,550)
Corporate sponsored plans	**28,324**	27,087	26,166
Multi-employer plans	**571**	361	374
Other	**1,340**	615	622
Total pension expense	**$ 30,235**	$ 28,063	$ 27,162

The funded status and amounts recognized in the consolidated balance sheets for the retirement plans were as follows:

	December 31, 1996		December 31, 1995	
	Assets Exceeded Accumulated Benefits	Accumulated Benefits Exceeded Assets	Assets Exceeded Accumulated Benefits	Accumulated Benefits Exceeded Assets
In thousands of dollars				
Actuarial present value of:				
Vested benefit obligations	**$427,839**	**$27,316**	$17,241	$417,027
Accumulated benefit obligations	**$452,907**	**$32,422**	$17,833	$447,792
Actuarial present value of projected benefit obligations	**$502,371**	**$34,135**	$27,005	$476,439
Plan assets at fair value	**488,222**	**—**	19,765	389,064
Plan assets less than projected benefit obligations	**14,149**	**34,135**	7,240	87,375
Net gain (loss) unrecognized at date of transition	**906**	**(1,233)**	525	(818)
Prior service cost and amendments not yet recognized in earnings	**(26,885)**	**(2,305)**	(1,159)	(28,701)
Unrecognized net gain (loss) from past experience different than that assumed	**12,386**	**(2,502)**	(3,615)	(3,660)
Minimum liability adjustment	**—**	**4,494**	—	21,678
Pension liability	**$ 556**	**$32,589**	$ 2,991	$ 75,874

The projected benefit obligations for the plans were determined principally using discount rates of 7.50% as of December 31, 1996, and 7.25% as of December 31, 1995. For both 1996 and 1995 the assumed long-term rate of return on plan assets was 9.5%. The assumed long-term compensation increase rate for 1996 and 1995 was primarily 4.8%.

In the third quarter of 1995, the Corporation offered a voluntary retirement program to domestic eligible employees age 55 and over. The voluntary retirement program gave eligible salaried employees an opportunity to retire with enhanced retirement benefits. The pre-tax impact on pension expense of the 1995 charge was $13.0 million or $7.7 million after tax. This amount has not been included in the disclosure of pension expense by component.

11. POST-RETIREMENT BENEFITS

The Corporation and its subsidiaries provide certain health care and life insurance benefits for retired employees subject to pre-defined limits. Substantially all of the Corporation's domestic employees become eligible for these benefits at retirement with a pre-defined benefit being available at an early retirement date. The post-retirement medical benefit is contributory for pre-Medicare retirees and for most post-Medicare retirees retiring on or after February 1, 1993. Retiree contributions are based upon a combination of years of service and age at retirement. The post-retirement life insurance benefit is non-contributory.

Net post-retirement benefit costs consisted of the following components:

For the years ended December 31,	1996	1995	1994
In thousands of dollars			
Service cost	**$ 3,947**	$ 3,262	$ 3,642
Interest cost on projected benefit obligations	**10,853**	12,918	13,334
Amortization	**(2,986)**	(2,322)	(1,028)
Total	**$11,814**	$13,858	$15,948

Obligations are unfunded and the actuarial present values of accumulated post-retirement benefit obligations recognized in the consolidated balance sheets were as follows:

December 31,	1996	1995
In thousands of dollars		
Retirees	**$ 96,870**	$ 78,090
Fully eligible active plan participants	**22,096**	24,686
Other active plan participants	**58,578**	57,448
Total	**177,544**	160,224
Plan amendments	**28,903**	31,377
Unrecognized net gain from past experience different than that assumed	**12,127**	20,892
Accrued post-retirement benefits	**$218,574**	$212,493

The accumulated post-retirement benefit obligations were determined principally using discount rates of 7.50% and 7.25% as of December 31, 1996 and 1995, respectively. The assumed average health care cost trend rate used in measuring the accumulated post-retirement benefit obligation as of December 31, 1996 and 1995, was 6% which was also the ultimate trend rate. A one percentage point increase in the average health care cost trend rate for each year would increase the accumulated post-retirement benefit obligations as of December 31, 1996 and 1995, by $24.4 million and $22.2 million, respectively, and would increase the sum of the net service and interest cost components of net post-retirement benefit costs for 1996 and 1995 by $2.9 million and $2.4 million, respectively.

The pre-tax impact on post-retirement benefits expense and liabilities of the 1995 charge for the voluntary retirement program was $.4 million or $.2 million after tax. This amount has not been included in the disclosure of net post-retirement benefit costs by component.

As part of its long-range financing plans, the Corporation, in 1989, implemented a corporate-owned life insurance program covering most of its domestic employees. After paying employee death benefits, proceeds from this program were available for general corporate purposes and also could be used to offset future employee benefits costs, including retiree medical benefits. During 1996, Federal tax legislation sharply curtailed the financial viability of most corporate-owned life insurance programs. As a result, the Corporation began the phase-out of its corporate-owned life insurance program during 1996. The Corporation's investment in corporate-owned life insurance policies was recorded net of policy loans in other assets, and interest accrued on the policy loans was included in accrued liabilities as of December 31, 1996 and 1995. Net life insurance expense, including interest expense, was included in selling, marketing and administrative expenses.

12. EMPLOYEE STOCK OWNERSHIP TRUST

The Corporation's employee stock ownership trust (ESOP) serves as the primary vehicle for contributions to its existing employee savings and stock investment plan for participating domestic salaried and hourly employees. The ESOP was funded by a 15-year 7.75% loan of $47.9 million from the Corporation. During 1996 and 1995, the ESOP received a combination of dividends on unallocated shares and contributions from the Corporation equal to the amount required to meet its principal and interest payments under the loan. Simultaneously, the ESOP allocated to participants 159,176 shares of Common Stock each year. As of December 31, 1996, the ESOP held 687,610 allocated shares and 1,591,752 unallocated shares. All ESOP shares are considered outstanding for income per share computations.

The Corporation recognized net compensation expense equal to the shares allocated multiplied by the original cost of $20 1/16 per share less dividends received by the ESOP on unallocated shares. Compensation expense related to the ESOP for 1996, 1995 and 1994 was $1.8 million, $1.9 million and $1.7 million, respectively. Dividends paid on unallocated ESOP shares were $1.3 million in 1996 and $1.2 million in 1995 and 1994. The unearned ESOP compensation balance in stockholders' equity represented deferred compensation expense to be recognized by the Corporation in future years as additional shares are allocated to participants.

13. CAPITAL STOCK AND NET INCOME PER SHARE

As of December 31, 1996, the Corporation had 530,000,000 authorized shares of capital stock. Of this total, 450,000,000 shares were designated as Common Stock, 75,000,000 shares as Class B Common Stock (Class B Stock), and 5,000,000 shares as Preferred Stock, each class having a par value of one dollar per share. As of December 31, 1996, a combined total of 179,950,872 shares of both classes of common stock had been issued of which 152,941,556 shares were outstanding. No shares of the Preferred Stock were issued or outstanding during the three-year period ended December 31, 1996.

In August 1996, the Corporation's Board of Directors declared a two-for-one split of the Common Stock and Class B Common Stock effective September 13, 1996, to stockholders of record as of August 23, 1996. The split was effected as a stock dividend by distributing one additional share for each share held.

Holders of the Common Stock and the Class B Stock generally vote together without regard to class on matters submitted to stockholders, including the election of directors, with the Common Stock having one vote per share and the Class B Stock having ten votes per share. However, the Common Stock, voting separately as a class, is entitled to elect one-sixth of the Board of Directors. With respect to dividend rights, the Common Stock is entitled to cash dividends 10% higher than those declared and paid on the Class B Stock.

Class B Stock can be converted into Common Stock on a share-for-share basis at any time. On a pre-split basis during 1996, 1995 and 1994, a total of 2,000 shares, 1,525 shares and 10,300 shares, respectively, of Class B Stock were converted into Common Stock.

Hershey Trust Company, as Trustee for the benefit of Milton Hershey School (Milton Hershey School Trust), as institutional fiduciary for estates and trusts unrelated to Milton Hershey School, and as direct owner of investment shares, held a total of 24,587,025 shares of the Common Stock, and as Trustee for the benefit of Milton Hershey School, held 30,306,006 shares of the Class B Stock as of December 31, 1996, and was entitled to cast approximately 77% of the total votes of both classes of the Corporation's common stock. The Milton Hershey School Trust must approve the issuance of shares of Common Stock or any other action which would result in the Milton Hershey School Trust not continuing to have voting control of the Corporation.

A total of 9,437,770 shares of Common Stock have been repurchased for approximately $263.7 million under share repurchase programs which were approved by the Corporation's Board of Director's in 1993 and 1996. Of the shares repurchased, 528,000 shares were retired and the remaining 8,909,770 shares were held as Treasury Stock as of December 31, 1996. In August 1995, the Corporation purchased an additional 18,099,546 shares (9,049,773 shares on a pre-split basis) of its Common Stock to be held as Treasury Stock from the Milton Hershey School Trust for $500.0 million. A total of 27,009,316 shares were held as Treasury Stock as of December 31, 1996.

Net income per share has been computed based on the weighted average number of shares of the Common Stock and the Class B Stock outstanding during the year. Average shares outstanding were 153,995,307 for 1996, 165,687,082 for 1995 and 174,037,252 for 1994.

14. STOCK COMPENSATION PLAN

The long-term portion of the 1987 Key Employee Incentive Plan (Plan), provides for grants of stock-based compensation awards to senior executives and key employees of one or more of the following: non-qualified stock options (fixed stock options), performance stock units, stock appreciation rights and restricted stock units. The Plan also provides for the deferral of performance stock unit awards by participants. Under the long-term portion of the Plan, the Corporation may grant to its employees up to 6.5 million shares of Common Stock on a pre-split basis. The Corporation applies Accounting Principles Board Opinion No. 25 "Accounting for Stock Issued to Employees," and related Interpretations in accounting for its Plan.

Accordingly, no compensation cost has been recognized for its fixed stock option plan. Had compensation cost for the Corporation's stock-based compensation plan been determined based on the fair value at the grant dates for awards under the Plan consistent with the method of Statement of Financial Accounting Standards No. 123 "Accounting for Stock-Based Compensation," the Corporation's net income and net income per share would have been reduced to the pro forma amounts indicated below:

For the years ended December 31,		**1996**	**1995**
In thousands of dollars except per share amounts			
Net income	As reported	**$273,186**	$281,919
	Pro forma	**266,517**	281,015
Net income per share	As reported	**$1.77**	$1.70
	Pro forma	**1.73**	1.70

The fair value of each option grant is estimated on the date of grant using a Black-Scholes option-pricing model with the following weighted-average assumptions used for grants in 1996 and 1995, respectively: dividend yields of 2.4% and 2.7%, expected volatility of 20% and 21%, risk-free interest rates of 5.6% and 7.8%, and expected lives of 7½ and 7 years.

Fixed Stock Options

The exercise price of each option equals the market price of the Corporation's common stock on the date of grant and an option's maximum term is ten years. Options are granted in January and generally vest at the end of the second year.

A summary of the status of the Corporation's fixed stock options as of December 31, 1996, 1995, and 1994, and changes during the years ending on those dates is presented below:

	1996		1995		1994	
Fixed Options	**Shares**	**Weighted-Average Exercise Price**	**Shares**	**Weighted-Average Exercise Price**	**Shares**	**Weighted-Average Exercise Price**
Outstanding at beginning of year	**4,435,800**	**$22.54**	5,067,900	$21.62	3,460,850	$19.91
Granted	**2,619,200**	**$33.08**	237,400	$24.19	1,927,600	$24.50
Exercised	**(1,062,980)**	**$20.74**	(843,100)	$17.43	(209,950)	$18.58
Forfeited	**(89,800)**	**$31.92**	(26,400)	$24.24	(110,600)	$24.01
Outstanding at end of year	**5,902,220**	**$27.40**	4,435,800	$22.54	5,067,900	$21.62
Options exercisable at year-end	**3,670,020**		2,901,800		3,469,500	
Weighted-average fair value of options granted during the year (per share)	**$8.70**		$7.38			

The following table summarizes information about fixed stock options outstanding as of December 31, 1996:

	Options Outstanding			Options Exercisable	
Range of Exercise Prices	**Number Outstanding as of 12/31/96**	**Weighted-Average Remaining Contractual Life in Years**	**Weighted-Average Exercise Price**	**Number Exercisable as of 12/31/96**	**Weighted-Average Exercise Price**
$12 11/16-22 3/8	**1,370,820**	4.5	$21.22	**1,370,820**	$21.22
$23 1/2 -26 1/2	**1,990,000**	7.0	$24.40	**1,990,000**	$24.40
$33 1/16 -37 5/8	**2,541,400**	9.0	$33.08	**309,200**	$33.08
$12 11/16-37 5/8	**5,902,220**	7.3	$27.40	**3,670,020**	$23.94

Performance Stock Units

Under the long-term portion of the Plan, each January the Corporation grants selected executives and other key employees performance stock units whose vesting is contingent upon the achievement of certain performance objectives. If at the end of three-year performance cycles, targets for financial measures of earnings per share, return on net assets and free cash flow are met, the full number of shares are awarded to the participants. The performance scores can range from 0% to 150%. The compensation cost charged against income for the performance-based plan was $5.8 million, $3.6 million, and $1.8 million for 1996, 1995, and 1994, respectively.

As of December 31, 1996, a total of 259,730 contingent performance stock units and restricted stock units had been granted for potential future distribution, primarily related to three-year cycles ending December 31, 1996, 1997, and 1998. Deferred performance stock units and accumulated dividend amounts totaled 391,750 shares as of December 31, 1996.

No stock appreciation rights were outstanding as of December 31, 1996.

15. SUPPLEMENTAL BALANCE SHEET INFORMATION

Accounts Receivable—Trade

In the normal course of business, the Corporation extends credit to customers which satisfy pre-defined credit criteria. The Corporation believes that it has little concentration of credit risk due to the diversity of its customer base. Receivables, as shown on the consolidated balance sheets, were net of allowances and anticipated discounts of $14.1 million and $14.8 million as of December 31, 1996 and 1995, respectively.

Inventories

The Corporation values the majority of its inventories under the last-in, first-out (LIFO) method and the remaining inventories at the lower of first-in, first-out (FIFO) cost or market. LIFO cost of inventories valued using the LIFO method was $299.2 million and $282.0 million as of December 31, 1996 and 1995, respectively, and all inventories were stated at amounts that did not exceed realizable values. Total inventories were as follows:

December 31,	1996	1995
In thousands of dollars		
Raw materials	**$204,419**	$189,371
Goods in process	**31,444**	28,201
Finished goods	**316,726**	249,106
Inventories at FIFO	**552,589**	466,678
Adjustment to LIFO	**(77,611)**	(69,108)
Total inventories	**$474,978**	$397,570

Property, Plant and Equipment

Property, plant and equipment balances included construction in progress of $91.9 million and $119.5 million as of December 31, 1996 and 1995, respectively. Major classes of property, plant and equipment were as follows:

December 31,	1996	1995
In thousands of dollars		
Land	**$ 34,056**	$ 35,385
Buildings	**533,559**	471,663
Machinery and equipment	**1,855,087**	1,683,338
Property, plant and equipment, gross	**2,422,702**	2,190,386
Accumulated depreciation	**(820,807)**	(754,377)
Property, plant and equipment, net	**$1,601,895**	$1,436,009

Accrued Liabilities

Accrued liabilities were as follows:

December 31,	1996	1995
In thousands of dollars		
Payroll and other compensation	**$ 81,264**	$ 97,710
Advertising and promotion	**77,351**	87,368
Other	**199,213**	123,045
Total accrued liabilities	**$357,828**	$308,123

Other Long-term Liabilities

Other long-term liabilities were as follows:

December 31,	1996	1995
In thousands of dollars		
Accrued post-retirement benefits	**$207,881**	$204,044
Other	**119,328**	129,770
Total other long-term liabilities	**$327,209**	$333,814

16. SEGMENT INFORMATION

The Corporation operates in a single consumer foods line of business, encompassing the manufacture, distribution and sale of chocolate, confectionery, grocery and pasta products. The Corporation's principal operations and markets are located in North America. In December 1996, the Corporation sold its Gubor and Sperlari European businesses.

Net sales, income before interest and income taxes and identifiable assets of businesses outside of North America were not significant. Historically, transfers of product between geographic areas have not been significant. In 1996 and 1995, sales to Wal-Mart Stores, Inc. and Subsidiaries amounted to approximately 12% and 11% of total net sales, respectively.

17. QUARTERLY DATA (Unaudited)

Summary quarterly results were as follows:

Year 1996	First	Second	Third	Fourth
In thousands of dollars except per share amounts				
Net sales	**$931,514**	**$796,343**	**$1,072,336**	**$1,189,115**
Gross profit	**381,766**	**326,545**	**458,362**	**520,546**
Net income	**59,415**	**40,847**	**94,270**	**78,654**(a)
Net income per share(b)	**.38**	**.26**	**.61**	**.51**

Year 1995	First	Second	Third	Fourth
In thousands of dollars except per share amounts				
Net sales	$ 867,446	$ 722,269	$ 981,101	$ 1,119,851
Gross profit	364,085	298,506	408,658	493,144
Net income	60,633	33,323	82,127	105,836(c)
Net income per share(b)	.35	.19	.51	.68

(a) Net income for the fourth quarter and year 1996 included an after-tax loss on the sale of Gubor and Sperlari of $35.4 million. Net income per share was similarly impacted.

(b) Quarterly income per share amounts for 1996 and 1995 do not total to the annual amount due to the changes in weighted average shares outstanding during the year.

(c) Net income for the fourth quarter and year 1995 included a net after-tax credit of $2.0 million associated with adjustments to accrued restructuring reserves. Net income per share was similarly impacted.

RESPONSIBILITY FOR FINANCIAL STATEMENTS

Hershey Foods Corporation is responsible for the financial statements and other financial information contained in this report. The Corporation believes that the financial statements have been prepared in conformity with generally accepted accounting principles appropriate under the circumstances to reflect in all material respects the substance of applicable events and transactions. In preparing the financial statements, it is necessary that management make informed estimates and judgments. The other financial information in this annual report is consistent with the financial statements.

The Corporation maintains a system of internal accounting controls designed to provide reasonable assurance that financial records are reliable for purposes of preparing financial statements and that assets are properly accounted for and safeguarded. The concept of reasonable assurance is based on the recognition that the cost of the system must be related to the benefits to be derived. The Corporation believes its system provides an appropriate balance in this regard. The Corporation maintains an Internal Audit Department which reviews the adequacy and tests the application of internal accounting controls.

The financial statements have been audited by Arthur Andersen LLP, independent public accountants, whose appointment was ratified by stockholder vote at the stockholders' meeting held on April 30, 1996. Their report expresses an opinion that the Corporation's financial statements are fairly stated in conformity with generally accepted accounting principles, and they have indicated to us that their examination was performed in accordance with generally accepted auditing standards which are designed to obtain reasonable assurance about whether the financial statements are free of material misstatement.

The Audit Committee of the Board of Directors of the Corporation, consisting solely of non-management directors, meets regularly with the independent public accountants, internal auditors and management to discuss, among other things, the audit scopes and results. Arthur Andersen LLP and the internal auditors both have full and free access to the Audit Committee, with and without the presence of management.

REPORT OF INDEPENDENT PUBLIC ACCOUNTANTS

To the Stockholders and Board of Directors
of Hershey Foods Corporation:

We have audited the accompanying consolidated balance sheets of Hershey Foods Corporation (a Delaware Corporation) and subsidiaries as of December 31, 1996 and 1995, and the related consolidated statements of income, stockholders' equity and cash flows for each of the three years in the period ended December 31, 1996, appearing on pages B-9 through B-27. These financial statements are the responsibility of the Corporation's management. Our responsibility is to express an opinion on these financial statements based on our audits.

We conducted our audits in accordance with generally accepted auditing standards. Those standards require that we plan and perform the audit to obtain reasonable assurance about whether the financial statements are free of material misstatement. An audit includes examining, on a test basis, evidence supporting the amounts and disclosures in the financial statements. An audit also includes assessing the accounting principles used and significant estimates made by management, as well as evaluating the overall financial statement presentation. We believe that our audits provide a reasonable basis for our opinion.

In our opinion, the financial statements referred to above present fairly, in all material respects, the financial position of Hershey Foods Corporation and subsidiaries as of December 31, 1996 and 1995, and the results of their operations and their cash flows for each of the three years in the period ended December 31, 1996, in conformity with generally accepted accounting principles.

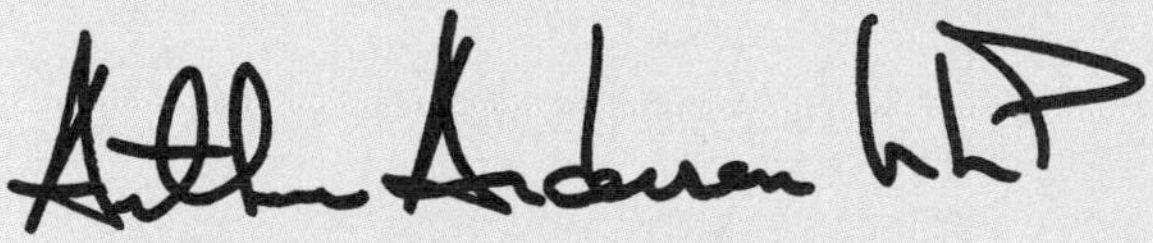

New York, New York
January 27, 1997

HERSHEY FOODS CORPORATION

ELEVEN-YEAR CONSOLIDATED FINANCIAL SUMMARY

All dollar and share amounts in thousands except market price and per share statistics

	10-Year Compound Growth Rate	1996	1995	1994
Summary of Operations(a)				
Net Sales	9.33%	$ **3,989,308**	3,690,667	3,606,271
Cost of Sales	8.35%	$ **2,302,089**	2,126,274	2,097,556
Selling, Marketing and Administrative	11.25%	$ **1,124,087**	1,053,758	1,034,115
Restructuring Credit, (Charge) and Gain, Net		$ **—**	151	(106,105)
(Loss)/Gain on Sale of Businesses and Investment Interest		$ **(35,352)**	—	—
Interest Expense, Net	19.54%	$ **48,043**	44,833	35,357
Income Taxes	7.42%	$ **206,551**	184,034	148,919
Income from Continuing Operations Before Accounting Changes	9.81%	$ **273,186**	281,919	184,219
Net Cumulative Effect of Accounting Changes		$ **—**	—	—
Discontinued Operations		$ **—**	—	—
Net Income	7.48%	$ **273,186**	281,919	184,219
Income Per Share:(b)				
From Continuing Operations Before Accounting Changes	12.00%	$ **1.77(h)**	1.70(i)	1.06(j)
Net Cumulative Effect of Accounting Changes		$ **—**	—	—
Net Income	9.56%	$ **1.77(h)**	1.70(i)	1.06(j)
Weighted Average Shares Outstanding(b)		**153,995**	165,687	174,037
Dividends Paid on Common Stock	8.66%	$ **93,884**	91,190	89,660
Per Share(b)	11.32%	$ **.760**	.685	.625
Dividends Paid on Class B Common Stock	11.21%	$ **20,879**	18,900	17,301
Per Share(b)	11.24%	$ **.685**	.620	.5675
Income from Continuing Operations Before Accounting Changes as a Percent of Net Sales		**7.7%(c)**	7.6%	7.3%(d)
Depreciation	14.35%	$ **119,443**	119,438	114,821
Advertising	7.62%	$ **174,199**	159,200	120,629
Promotion	13.36%	$ **429,208**	402,454	419,164
Payroll	7.49%	$ **491,677**	461,928	472,997
Year-end Position and Statistics(a)				
Capital Additions	7.91%	$ **159,433**	140,626	138,711
Total Assets	9.70%	$ **3,184,796**	2,830,623	2,890,981
Long-term Portion of Debt	13.44%	$ **655,289**	357,034	157,227
Stockholders' Equity	4.78%	$ **1,161,021**	1,082,959	1,441,100
Net Book Value Per Share(b)	6.51%	$ **7.59**	7.01	8.31
Operating Return on Average Stockholders' Equity		**27.5%**	22.2%	18.5%
Operating Return on Average Invested Capital		**17.8%**	17.1%	15.6%
Full-time Employees		**14,000**	13,300	14,000
Stockholders' Data(b)				
Outstanding Shares of Common Stock and Class B Common Stock at Year-end		**152,942**	154,532	173,470
Market Price of Common Stock at Year-end	13.52%	$ **43¾**	32½	24 3/16
Range During Year		**$51¾-31 15/16**	33 15/16-24	26¾-20 9/16

See Notes to the Eleven-Year Consolidated Financial Summary on page B-32.

1993	1992	1991	1990	1989	1988	1987	1986
3,488,249	3,219,805	2,899,165	2,715,609	2,420,988	2,168,048	1,863,816	1,635,486
1,995,502	1,833,388	1,694,404	1,588,360	1,455,612	1,326,458	1,149,663	1,032,061
1,035,519	958,189	814,459	776,668	655,040	575,515	468,062	387,227
—	—	—	35,540	—	—	—	—
80,642	—	—	—	—	—	—	—
26,995	27,240	26,845	24,603	20,414	29,954	22,413	8,061
213,642	158,390	143,929	145,636	118,868	91,615	99,604	100,931
297,233	242,598	219,528	215,882	171,054	144,506	124,074	107,206
(103,908)	—	—	—	—	—	—	—
—	—	—	—	—	69,443	24,097	25,558
193,325	242,598	219,528	215,882	171,054	213,949	148,171	132,764
1.66(k)	1.34	1.22	1.20(l)	.95	.80	.69	.57
(.58)	—	—	—	—	—	—	—
1.08(k)	1.34	1.22	1.20(l)	.95	1.19	.82	.71
179,514	180,373	180,373	180,373	180,373	180,373	180,373	187,017
84,711	77,174	70,426	74,161(f)	55,431	49,433	43,436	40,930
.570	.515	.470	.495(f)	.370	.330	.290	.260
15,788	14,270	12,975	13,596(f)	10,161	9,097	8,031	7,216
.5175	.4675	.425	.445(f)	.3325	.2975	.2625	.236
7.4%(e)	7.5%	7.6%	7.2%(g)	7.1%	6.7%	6.7%	6.6%
100,124	84,434	72,735	61,725	54,543	43,721	35,397	31,254
130,009	137,631	117,049	146,297	121,182	99,082	97,033	83,600
444,546	398,577	325,465	315,242	256,237	230,187	171,162	122,508
469,564	433,162	398,661	372,780	340,129	298,483	263,529	238,742
211,621	249,795	226,071	179,408	162,032	101,682	68,504	74,452
2,855,091	2,672,909	2,341,822	2,078,828	1,814,101	1,764,665	1,544,354	1,262,332
165,757	174,273	282,933	273,442	216,108	233,025	280,900	185,676
1,412,344	1,465,279	1,335,251	1,243,537	1,117,050	1,005,866	832,410	727,941
8.06	8.12	7.40	6.89	6.19	5.58	4.61	4.04
17.8%	17.3%	17.0%	16.6%	16.1%	17.5%	19.0%	18.2%
15.0%	14.4%	13.8%	13.4%	13.2%	13.3%	13.5%	13.5%
14,300	13,700	14,000	12,700	11,800	12,100	10,540	10,210
175,226	180,373	180,373	180,373	180,373	180,373	180,373	180,373
24½	23½	22 3/16	18¾	17 15/16	13	12¼	12 5/16
27 15/16-21¾	24 3/16-19⅛	22¼-17 9/16	19 13/16-14⅛	18 7/16-12⅜	14 5/16-10 15/16	18⅞-10⅜	15-7¾

Notes to the Eleven-Year Consolidated Financial Summary

(a) All amounts for years prior to 1988 have been restated for discontinued operations, where applicable. Operating Return on Average Stockholders' Equity and Operating Return on Average Invested Capital have been computed using Net Income, excluding the 1988 gain on disposal included in Discontinued Operations, the 1993 Net Cumulative Effect of Accounting Changes, and the after-tax impacts of the 1990 Restructuring Gain, Net, the 1993 Gain on Sale of the Investment Interest in Freia Marabou a.s (Freia), the 1994 Restructuring Charge, the net 1995 Restructuring Credit and the 1996 Loss on Sale of Businesses.

(b) All shares and per share amounts have been adjusted for the two-for-one stock split effective September 13, 1996.

(c) Calculated percent excludes the 1996 Loss on Sale of Businesses. Including the loss, Income from Continuing Operations Before Accounting Changes as a Percent of Net Sales was 6.8%.

(d) Calculated percent excludes the 1994 Restructuring Charge. Including the charge, Income from Continuing Operations Before Accounting Changes as a Percent of Net Sales was 5.1%.

(e) Calculated percent excludes the 1993 Gain on Sale of Investment Interest in Freia. Including the gain, Income from Continuing Operations Before Accounting Changes as a Percent of Net Sales was 8.5%.

(f) Amounts included a special dividend for 1990 of $11.2 million or $.075 per share of Common Stock and $2.1 million or $.0675 per share of Class B Common Stock.

(g) Calculated percent excludes the 1990 Restructuring Gain, Net. Including the gain, Income from Continuing Operations Before Accounting Changes as a Percent of Net Sales was 7.9%.

(h) Income Per Share from Continuing Operations Before Accounting Changes and Net Income Per Share for 1996 included a $.23 per share loss on the sale of the Gubor and Sperlari businesses. Excluding the impact of this loss, Income Per Share from Continuing Operations Before Accounting Changes and Net Income Per Share would have been $2.00.

(i) Income Per Share from Continuing Operations Before Accounting Changes and Net Income Per Share for 1995 included a net $.01 per share credit associated with adjustments to accrued restructuring reserves. Excluding the impact of this net credit, Income Per Share from Continuing Operations Before Accounting Changes and Net Income Per Share would have been $1.69.

(j) Income Per Share from Continuing Operations Before Accounting Changes and Net Income Per Share for 1994 included a $.46 per share restructuring charge. Excluding the impact of this charge, Income Per Share from Continuing Operations Before Accounting Changes and Net Income Per Share would have been $1.52.

(k) Income Per Share from Continuing Operations Before Accounting Changes and Net Income Per Share for 1993 included a $.23 per share gain on the sale of the investment interest in Freia. Excluding the impact of this gain, Income Per Share from Continuing Operations Before Accounting Changes would have been $1.43.

(l) Income Per Share from Continuing Operations Before Accounting Changes and Net Income Per Share for 1990 included an $.11 per share Restructuring Gain, Net. Excluding the impact of this gain, Income Per Share from Continuing Operations Before Accounting Changes and Net Income Per Share would have been $1.08.

Glossary

A

Accelerated depreciation method. A depreciation method that provides for a high depreciation expense in the first year of use of an asset and a gradually declining expense thereafter. (388)

Account. The form used to record additions and deductions for each individual asset, liability, owner's equity, revenue, and expense. (44)

Account form. The form of balance sheet with the assets section presented on the left-hand side and the liabilities and owner's equity sections presented on the right-hand side. (18, 243)

Account payable. A liability created by a purchase made on credit. (13)

Account receivable. A claim against a customer for services rendered or goods sold on credit. (13, 311)

Accounting. The process of identifying, measuring, and communicating economic information to permit informed judgments and decisions by users of the information. (5)

Accounting cycle. The sequence of basic accounting procedures during a fiscal period. (147)

Accounting equation. The expression of the relationship between assets, liabilities, and owner's equity; it is most commonly stated as Assets = Liabilities + Owner's Equity. (11)

Accounting period concept. An accounting principle that requires accounting reports be prepared at periodic intervals. (98)

Accounting system. The methods and procedures used by a business to record and report financial data for use by management and external users. (178)

Accounts payable subsidiary ledger. The subsidiary ledger containing the individual accounts with suppliers (creditors). (185)

Accounts receivable subsidiary ledger. The subsidiary ledger containing the individual accounts with customers (debtors). (185)

Accounts receivable turnover. The relationship between credit sales and accounts receivable. This ratio is computed by dividing net sales on account by the average net accounts receivable. (323, 634)

Accrual basis. A basis of accounting in which revenues are recognized in the period earned, and expenses are recognized in the period incurred in the process of generating revenues. (98)

Accrued expenses. Expenses that have been incurred but not paid. Sometimes called accrued liabilities. (100)

Accrued revenues. Revenues that have been earned but not collected. Sometimes called accrued assets. (100)

Accumulated depreciation account. The contra asset account used to accumulate the depreciation recognized to date on plant assets. (107)

Acid-test ratio. A ratio that measures the "instant" debt-paying ability of a company. Also known as quick ratio. (633)

Activity base. The measure used to allocate factory overhead. Also known as allocation base, or activity driver. (678)

Activity drivers. An activity that is thought to cause a cost to be incurred. Used in analyzing and classifying cost behavior. (749)

Activity-based costing. A cost allocation method that identifies activities causing the incurrence of costs and allocates these costs to products (or other cost objects) based upon activity bases (drivers). (679, 926)

Adjusted trial balance. The trial balance which is prepared after all the adjusting entries have been posted. Used to verify the equality of the total debit balances and total credit balances before preparing the financial statements. (111)

Adjusting entries. Entries required at the end of an accounting period to bring the ledger up to date. (99)

Adjusting process. The process of updating the accounts at the end of a period. (99)

Administrative expenses (general expenses). Expenses incurred in the administration or general operations of a business. (240)

Aging the receivables. The process of analyzing the accounts receivable and classifying them according to various age groupings, with the due date being the base point for determining age. (316)

Allowance method. A method of accounting for uncollectible receivables, whereby advance provision for the uncollectibles is made. (314)

Amortization. The periodic expense attributed to the decline in usefulness of an intangible asset. (398)

Annuity. A series of equal cash flows at fixed intervals. (542, 955)

Application software. Computer software that performs a particular task. (197)

Appropriation. The amount of a corporation's retained earnings that has been restricted and therefore is not available for distribution to shareholders as dividends. (506)

Assets. Physical items (tangible) or rights (intangible) that have value and that are owned by the business entity. (11, 44)

Available-for-sale security. A debt or equity security that is not classified as either a held-to-maturity or a trading security. (508)

Average cost method. The method of inventory costing that is based on the assumption that costs should be charged against revenue in accordance with the weighted average unit costs of the items sold. (348)

Average rate of return. A method of evaluating capital investment proposals that focuses on the expected profitability of the investment. (951)

B

Balance of the account. The amount of difference between the debits and the credits that have been entered into an account. (46)

Balance sheet. A financial statement listing the assets, liabilities, and owner's equity of a business entity as of a specific date. (16)

Bank reconciliation. The analysis that details the items responsible for the difference between the cash balance reported in the bank statement and the balance of the cash account in the ledger. (286)

Betterment. An expenditure that increases operating efficiency or capacity for the remaining useful life of a plant asset. (391)

Bond. A form of interest-bearing note employed by corporations to borrow on a long-term basis. (537)

Bond indenture. The contract between a corporation issuing bonds and the bondholders. (539)

Book value. The amount at which an asset or liability is reported on the balance sheet. Also called basis or carrying value. (387)

Book value of a fixed asset. The difference between the balance of a fixed asset account and its related accumulated depreciation account. (108)

Boot. The cash balance owed the seller when an old asset is traded for a new asset. (393)

Break-even point. The level of business operations at which revenues and expired costs are equal. (757)

Budget. An outline of a business's future plans, stated in financial terms. A budget is used to plan and control operational departments and divisions. (794)

Budget performance report. A report comparing actual results with budget figures. (843)

Business. An organization in which basic resources (inputs), such as materials and labor, are assembled and processed to provide goods or services (outputs) to customers. (2)

Business entity concept. The concept that accounting applies to individual economic units and that each unit is separate from the persons who supply its assets. (10)

Business stakeholder. A person or entity that has an interest in the economic performance of the business. (4)

Business transaction. The occurrence of an economic event or a condition that must be recorded in the accounting records. (11)

C

Capital expenditures. Costs that add to the usefulness of assets for more than one accounting period. (390)

Capital expenditures budget. The budget summarizing future plans for acquiring fixed assets. (812)

Capital investment analysis. The process by which management plans, evaluates, and controls long-term capital investments involving property, plant, and equipment. (950)

Capital leases. Leases that treat the leased assets as purchased assets in the accounts. (396)

Capital rationing. The process by which management allocates available investment funds among competing capital investment proposals. (963)

Carrying amount. The amount at which a long-term investment or a long-term liability is reported on the balance sheet. (548)

Cash. Coins, currency (paper money), checks, money orders, and money on deposit that is available for unrestricted withdrawal from banks or other financial institutions. (278)

Cash basis. A basis of accounting in which revenue is recognized in the period cash is received, and expenses are recognized in the period cash is paid. (98)

Cash budget. One of the most important elements of the budgeted balance sheet. It presents the expected receipts (inflows) and payments (outflows) of cash for a period of time. (809)

Cash dividend. A cash distribution of earnings by a corporation to its shareholders. (476)

Cash equivalents. Highly liquid investments that are usually reported on the balance sheet with cash. (291)

Cash flows from financing activities. The section of the statement of cash flows that reports cash flows from transactions affecting the equity and debt of the entity. (577)

Cash flows from investing activities. The section of the statement of cash flows that reports cash flows from transactions affecting investments in noncurrent assets. (577)

Cash flows from operating activities. The section of the statement of cash flows that reports the cash transactions affecting the determination of net income. (577)

Cash payback period. The expected period of time that will elapse between the date of a capital expenditure and the complete recovery in cash (or equivalent) of the amount invested. (952)

Cash payments journal. The special journal in which all cash payments are recorded. (192)

Cash receipts journal. The special journal in which all cash receipts are recorded. (190)

Cash short and over account. An account which has recorded errors in cash sales or errors in making change causing the amount of actual cash on hand to differ from the beginning amount of cash plus the cash sales for the day. (279)

Chart of accounts. The system of accounts that make up the ledger for a business. (44)

Closing entries. Entries necessary to eliminate the balances of temporary accounts in preparation for the following accounting period. (139)

Common-size statement. A financial statement in which all items are expressed only in relative terms. (630)

Common stock. The basic ownership class of corporate stock. (469)

Comprehensive income. All changes in stockholders' equity during a period, except those resulting from dividends and stockholders' investments. (507)

Consolidated financial statements. Financial statements resulting from combining parent and subsidiary company statements. (514)

Consolidation. The creation of a new corporation by the transfer of assets and liabilities from two or more existing corporations. (513)

Continuous budgeting. A method of budgeting that provides for maintaining a twelve-month projection into the future. (798)

Contra accounts. Accounts that are offset against other accounts. (107)

Contra asset. An account that affects an asset account, such as the allowance for uncollectible accounts receivable or accumulated depreciation. (314)

Contract rate. The interest rate specified on a bond; sometimes called the coupon rate of interest. (540)

Contribution margin. Sales less variable costs and variable selling and administrative expenses. (754)

Contribution margin ratio. The percentage of each sales dollar that is available to cover the fixed costs and provide an operating income. (755)

Controllable expenses. Costs that can be influenced by the decisions of a manager. (878)

Controllable variance. The difference between the actual amount of variable factory overhead cost incurred and the amount of variable factory overhead budgeted for the standard product. (850)

Controller. The chief management accountant of a business. (670)

Controlling account. The account in the general ledger that summarizes the balances of the accounts in a subsidiary ledger. (185)

Conversion costs. The combination of direct labor and factory overhead costs. (673)

Copyright. The exclusive right to publish and sell a literary, artistic, or musical composition. (398)

Corporation. A separate legal entity that is organized in accordance with state or federal statutes and in which ownership is divided into shares of stock. (3)

Cost. A disbursement of cash (or a commitment to pay cash in the future) for the purpose of generating revenues. (671)

Cost accounting system. A system used to accumulate manufacturing costs for financial reporting and decision-making purposes. (673)

Cost allocation. The process of assigning indirect cost to a cost object, such as a job. (678)

Cost behavior. The manner in which a cost changes in relation to its activity base (driver). (749)

Cost center. A decentralized unit in which the department or division manager has responsibility for the control of costs incurred and the authority to make decisions that affect these costs. (876)

Cost concept. The basis for entering the exchange price, or cost, into the accounting records. (10)

Cost method. A method of accounting for an investment in common stock, by which the investor recognizes as income its share of cash dividends of the investee. (511)

Cost of goods sold. The cost of the manufactured product sold. (675)

Cost of goods sold budget. A budget in which the desired ending inventory and the estimated beginning inventory data are combined with data from direct materials budget, direct labor budget, and factory overhead cost budget. (806)

Cost of merchandise sold. The cost of merchandise purchased by a merchandise business and sold. (225)

Cost of production report. A report prepared periodically by a processing department, summarizing (1) the units for which the department is accountable and the disposition of those units and (2) the costs incurred by the department and the allocation of those costs between completed and incomplete production. (724)

Cost per equivalent unit. The rate used to allocate costs between completed and partially completed production in a process costing system. (723)

Cost price approach. An approach to transfer pricing that uses cost as the basis for setting the transfer price. (890)

Cost variance. The difference between actual cost and the flexible budget at actual volumes. (840)

Cost-volume-profit analysis. The systematic examination of the relationships among selling prices, volume of sales and production, costs, expenses, and profits. (754)

Cost-volume-profit chart. A chart used to assist management in understanding the relationships among costs, expenses, sales, and operating profit or loss. (761)

Credit. (1) The right side of an account; (2) the amount entered on the right side of an account; (3) to enter an amount on the right side of an account. (46)

Credit memorandum. The form issued by a seller to inform a buyer that a credit has been posted to the buyer's account receivable. (232)

Cumulative preferred stock. Preferred stock that is entitled to current and past dividends before dividends may be paid on common stock. (470)

Current assets. Cash or other assets that are expected to be converted to cash or sold or used up, usually within a year or less, through the normal operations of a business. (137)

Current liabilities. Liabilities that will be due within a short time (usually one year or less) and that are to be paid out of current assets. (138)

Current ratio. A financial ratio that is computed by dividing current assets by current liabilities. (149, 632)

Currently attainable standards. Standards that represent levels of operation that can be attained with reasonable effort. (841)

D

Debit. (1) The left side of an account; (2) the amount entered on the left side of an account; (3) to enter an amount on the left side of an account. (46)

Debit memorandum. The form issued by a buyer to inform a seller that a debit has been posted to the seller's account payable. (229)

Decentralization. The separation of a business into more manageable operating units. (874)

Declining-balance depreciation method. A method of depreciation that provides declining periodic depreciation expense over the estimated life of an asset. (387)

Deferred expenses. Items that are initially recorded as assets but are expected to become expenses over time or through the normal operations of the business. Sometimes called prepaid expenses. (99)

Deferred revenues. Items that are initially recorded as liabilities but are expected to become revenues over time or through the normal operations of the business. Sometimes called unearned revenues. (100)

Deficit. A debit balance in the retained earnings account. (468)

Defined benefit plan. A pension plan that promises employees a fixed annual pension benefit at retirement, based on years of service and compensation levels. (439)

Defined contribution plan. A pension plan that requires a fixed amount of money to be invested for the employee's behalf during the employee's working years. (439)

Depletion. The cost of metal ores and other minerals removed from the earth. (397)

Depreciation. In a general sense, the decrease in usefulness of fixed assets other than land. In accounting, refers to the systematic allocation of a fixed asset's cost to expense. (107, 384)

Depreciation expense. The portion of the cost of a fixed asset that is recorded as an expense each year of its useful life. (107)

Differential analysis. The area of accounting concerned with the effect of alternative courses of action on revenues and costs. (913)

Differential cost. The amount of increase or decrease in cost expected from a particular course of action as compared with an alternative. (912)

Differential revenue. The amount of increase or decrease in revenue expected from a particular course of action as compared with an alternative. (912)

Direct labor cost. Wages of factory workers who are directly involved in converting materials into a finished product. (672)

Direct labor rate variance. The cost associated with the difference between the standard rate and the actual rate paid for direct labor used in producing a commodity. (847)

Direct labor time variance. The cost associated with the difference between the standard hours and the actual hours of direct labor spent producing a commodity. (847)

Direct materials cost. The cost of materials that are an integral part of the finished product. (672)

Direct materials price variance. The cost associated with the difference between the standard price and the actual price of direct materials used in producing a commodity. (845)

Direct materials purchases budget. A budget that uses the production budget as a starting point for determining the quantities of direct materials to purchase. (804)

Direct materials quantity variance. The cost associated with the difference between the standard quantity and the actual quantity of direct materials used in producing a commodity. (845)

Direct method. A method of reporting the cash flows from operating activities as the net income from operations adjusted for all deferrals of past cash receipts and payments and all accruals of expected future cash receipts and payments. (578)

Direct write-off method. A method of accounting for uncollectible receivables, whereby an expense is recognized only when specific accounts are judged to be uncollectible. (314)

Discontinued operations. The operations of a business segment that has been disposed of. (502)

Discount. The interest deducted from the maturity value of a note. (423); The excess of the face amount of bonds over their issue price. (540); The excess of par value of stock over its sales price. (472)

Discount rate. The rate used in computing the interest to be deducted from the maturity value of a note. (423)

Dishonored note receivable. A note that the maker fails to pay on its due date. (321)

Dividends per share. The cash dividends per common shares commonly used by investors in assessing alternative stock investments, computed by dividing dividends by the number of shares of stock outstanding. (641)

Dividend yield. The rate of return to stockholders in terms of cash dividend distributions. (479, 641)

Division. A decentralized organizational unit that is structured around a common function, product, customer, or geographical territory. Divisions can be cost, profit, or investment centers. (874)

Doomsday ratio. The ratio of cash and cash equivalents to current liabilities. (291)

Double-entry accounting. A system for recording transactions, based on recording increases and decreases in accounts so that debits always equal credits. (50)

Drawing. The account used to record amounts withdrawn by an owner of a proprietorship. (45)

E

Earnings per share (EPS) on common stock. The profitability ratio of net income available to common shareholders to the number of common shares outstanding. (503, 640)

Effective interest rate method. One method of amortizing a bond discount. Also known as the interest method. (545)

Effective rate. The market rate of interest when bonds are issued. (540)

Electronic funds transfer (EFT). A payment system that uses computerized information rather than paper (money, checks, etc.) to effect a cash transaction. (282)

Elements of internal control. The control environment, risk assessment, control activities, information and communication, and monitoring. (180)

Employee fraud. The intentional act of deceiving an employer for personal gain. (179)

Employee's earnings record. A detailed record of each employee's earnings. (433)

Equity method. A method of accounting for investments in common stock, by which the investment account is adjusted for the investor's share of periodic net income and dividends of the investee. (511)

Equity security. A security that represents ownership in a business, such as stock in a corporation. (508)

Equivalent units of production. The number of units that could have been completed within a given accounting period with respect to direct materials and conversion costs. Equivalent units are used to allocate departmental costs incurred during the period between completed units and in-process units at the end of the period. (720)

Ethics. The moral principles that guide the conduct of individuals. (7)

Expenses. Assets used up or services consumed in the process of generating revenues. (13, 45)

Extraordinary items. Events or transactions that are unusual and infrequent. (502)

Extraordinary repair. An expenditure that increases the useful life of an asset beyond the original estimate. (391)

F

Factory overhead cost. All of the costs of operating the factory except for direct materials and direct labor. (672)

FICA tax. Federal Insurance Contributions Act tax used to finance federal programs for old-age and disability benefits (social security) and health insurance for the aged (Medicare). (426)

Financial accounting. The branch of accounting that is concerned with the recording of transactions using generally accepted accounting principles (GAAP) for a business or other economic unit and with a periodic preparation of various statements from such records. (9, 669)

Financial Accounting Standards Board (FASB). An authoritative body for the development of accounting principles. (9)

Finished goods inventory. The cost of finished products on hand that have not been sold. (674)

Finished goods ledger. The subsidiary ledger that contains the individual accounts for each kind of commodity or product produced. (682)

First-in, first-out (FIFO) method. A method of inventory costing based on the assumption that the costs of merchandise sold should be charged against revenue in the order in which the costs were incurred. (348, 718)

Fiscal year. The annual accounting period adopted by a business. (147)

Fixed assets. Physical resources that are owned and used by a business and are permanent or have a long life. (107, 382)

Fixed costs. Costs that tend to remain the same in amount, regardless of variations in the level of activity. (751)

Flexible budget. A budget that adjusts for varying rates of activity. (799)

FOB (free on board) destination. Terms of agreement between buyer and seller whereby ownership passes when merchandise is received by the buyer, and the seller pays the transportation costs. (234)

FOB (free on board) shipping point. Terms of agreement between buyer and seller whereby ownership passes when merchandise is delivered to the freight carrier, and the buyer pays the transportation costs. (234)

Free cash flow. The amount of operating cash flow remaining after replacing current productive capacity and maintaining current dividends. (593)

Fringe benefits. A variety of employee benefits that may take many forms, including vacations, pension plans, and health, life, and disability insurance. (438)

Future value. The estimated worth in the future of an amount of cash on hand today invested at a fixed rate of interest. (541)

G

General journal. The two-column form used for entries that are otherwise not recorded in special journals. (187)

General ledger. The primary ledger, when used in conjunction with subsidiary ledgers, that contains all of the balance sheet and income statement accounts. (185)

Generally accepted accounting principles (GAAP). Generally accepted guidelines for the preparation of financial statements. (9)

Goal conflict. Occurs when an employee's self-interest differs from business objectives. (797)

Goodwill. An intangible asset of a business due to such favorable factors as location, product superiority, reputation, and managerial skill. (399)

Gross pay. The total earnings of an employee for a payroll period. (426)

Gross profit. The excess of net sales over the cost of merchandise sold. (225)

Gross profit method. A means of estimating inventory based on the relationship of gross profit to sales. (360)

H

Hardware. Computer equipment used for data input/output and internal data management and processing. (196)

Held-to-maturity securities. Investments in bonds or other debt securities that management intends to hold to their maturity. (554)

High-low method. A technique that uses the highest and lowest total costs as a basis for estimating the variable cost per unit and the fixed cost component of a mixed cost. (752)

Horizontal analysis. Financial analysis that compares an item in a current statement with the same item in prior statements. (67, 626)

I

Income from operations (operating income). The excess of gross profit over total operating expenses. (240, 881)

Income statement. A summary of the revenues and expenses of a business entity for a specific period of time. (16)

Income Summary. The account used in the closing process for transferring the revenue and expense account balances to the retained earnings account at the end of the period. (139)

Indirect method. A method of reporting the cash flows from operating activities as the net income from operations adjusted for all deferrals of past cash receipts and payments and all accruals of expected future cash receipts and payments. (579)

Inflation. A period when prices in general are rising and the purchasing power of money is declining. (962)

Intangible assets. Long-lived assets that are useful in the operations of a business, are not held for sale, and are without physical qualities. (398)

Internal controls. The detailed policies and procedures used to direct operations, ensure accurate reports, and ensure compliance with laws and regulations. (179)

Internal rate of return method. A method of analysis of proposed capital investments that focuses on using present value concepts to compute the rate of return from the net cash flows expected from the investment. (957)

Inventory shrinkage. Loss of inventory due to shoplifting, employee theft, or errors in recording or counting inventory. (242)

Inventory turnover. A ratio that measures the relationship between the volume of goods (merchandise) sold and the amount of inventory carried during the period. (361, 635)

Investment center. A decentralized unit in which the manager has the responsibility and authority to make decisions that affect not only costs and revenues but also the fixed assets available to the center. (881)

Investments. The balance sheet caption used to report long-term investments in stocks or bonds not intended as a source of cash in the normal operations of the business. (510)

Investment turnover. A component of the rate of return on investment, computed as the ratio of sales to invested assets. (883)

Invoice. The bill provided by the seller (who refers to it as a sales invoice) to a buyer (who refers to it as a purchase invoice) for items purchased. (227)

J

Job cost sheet. An account in the work in process subsidiary ledger in which the costs charged to a particular job order are recorded. (676)

Job order cost system. A type of cost accounting system that provides for a separate record of the cost of each particular quantity of product that passes through the factory. (673)

Journal. The initial record in which the effects of a transaction on accounts are recorded. (47)

Journal entry. The form of recording a transaction in a journal. (47)

Journalizing. The process of recording a transaction in a journal. (47)

Just-in-time processing. A processing approach that focuses on eliminating time, cost, and poor quality within manufacturing and nonmanufacturing processes. (728)

L

Last-in, first-out (LIFO) method. A method of inventory costing based on the assumption that the most recent merchandise costs incurred should be charged against revenue. (348)

Ledger. The group of accounts used by a business. (44)

Leverage. The tendency of the rate earned on stockholders' equity to vary from the rate earned on total assets because the amount earned on assets acquired through the use of funds provided by creditors varies from the interest paid to these creditors (639)

Liabilities. Debts owed to outsiders (creditors). (11, 44)

Long-term liabilities. Liabilities that are not due for a long time (usually more than one year). (138)

Loss from operations. The excess of operating expenses over gross profit. (240)

Lower-of-cost-or-market (LCM) method. A method of valuing inventory that reports the inventory at the lower of its cost or current market value (replacement cost). (358)

M

Managerial accounting. The branch of accounting that uses both historical and estimated data in providing information that management uses in conducting daily operations, in planning future operations, and in developing overall business strategies. (9, 669)

Managers. Individuals who the owners have authorized to operate the business. (4)

Manufacturing businesses. A type of business that changes basic inputs into products that are sold to individual customers. (2)

Manufacturing cells. A grouping of production processes where employees are cross-trained to perform more than one function. (729)

Margin of safety. The difference between current sales revenue and the sales at the break-even point. (767)

Market price approach. An approach to transfer pricing that uses the price at which the product or service transferred could be sold to outside buyers as the transfer price. (887)

Markup. An amount that is added to a "cost" amount to determine product price. (921)

Master budget. The comprehensive budget plan encompassing all the individual budgets related to sales, cost of goods sold, operating expenses, capital expenditures, and cash. (801)

Matching concept. The concept that expenses incurred in generating revenue should be matched against the revenue in determining the net income or net loss for the period. (16, 98)

Materiality concept. A concept of accounting that accounts for items that are deemed significant for a given size of operations. (65)

Materials inventory. The cost of materials that have not yet entered into the manufacturing process. (674)

Materials ledger. The subsidiary ledger containing the individual accounts for each type of material. (676)

Materials requisitions. The form or electronic transmission used by a manufacturing department to authorize materials issuances from the storeroom. (676)

Maturity value. The amount due (face value plus interest) at the maturity or due date of a note. (321)

Merchandise inventory. Merchandise on hand and available for sale to customers. (225)

Merchandising businesses. A type of business that purchases products from other businesses and sells them to customers. (3)

Merger. The combining of two corporations by the acquisition of the properties of one corporation by another, with the dissolution of one of the corporations. (513)

Minority interest. The portion of a subsidiary corporation's stock that is not owned by the parent corporation. (514)

Mixed cost. A cost with both variable and fixed characteristics, sometimes called a semivariable or semifixed cost. (751)

Multiple-step income statement. An income statement with several sections, subsections, and subtotals. (239)

N

Natural business year. A year that ends when a business's activities have reached the lowest point in its annual operating cycle. (147)

Negotiated price approach. An approach to transfer pricing that allows managers of decentralized units to agree (negotiate) among themselves as to the transfer price. (889)

Net income. The amount by which revenues exceed expenses. (16)

Net loss. The amount by which expenses exceed revenues. (16)

Net pay. Gross pay less payroll deductions; the amount the employer is obligated to pay the employee. (426)

Net present value method. A method of analysis of proposed capital investments that focuses on the present value of the cash flows expected from the investments. (956)

Net realizable value. The valuation of an asset at an amount equal to the estimated selling price less any direct cost of disposal. (358)

Nonparticipating preferred stock. Preferred stock with a limited dividend preference. (469)

Notes receivable. A written promise to pay by the maker, representing an amount to be received by the payee. (137, 311)

Number of days' sales in inventory. A measure of the length of time it takes to acquire, sell, and replace the inventory. (362)

Number of days' sales in receivables. An estimate of the length of time the accounts receivable have been outstanding. (324, 634)

Number of times the interest charges are earned. A ratio that measures the risk that interest payments to debtholders will continue to be made if earnings decrease. (554, 636)

O

Objectivity concept. Requires that the accounting records and reports be based upon objective evidence. (11)

Operating leases. Leases that do not meet the criteria for capital leases and thus are accounted for as operating expenses. (396)

Operating leverage. A measure of the relative mix of a business's variable costs and fixed costs, computed as contribution margin divided by operating income. (767)

Operating system. Computer software that provides the basic instructions to the computer and serves as the interface between the user and the computer. (197)

Opportunity cost. The amount of income forgone from an alternative use of cash or its equivalent. (918)

Other expense. An expense that cannot be traced directly to operations. (241)

Other income. Revenue from sources other than the primary operating activity of a business. (241)

Outstanding stock. The stock that is in the hands of stockholders. (468)

Overapplied factory overhead. The amount of factory overhead applied in excess of the actual factory overhead costs incurred for production during a period. (680)

Owner's equity. The owner's right to the assets of the business after the total liabilities are deducted. (11, 45)

P

Paid-in capital. The capital acquired from stockholders. (467)

Par. The monetary amount printed on a stock certificate. (468)

Parent company. The company owning a majority of the voting stock of another corporation. (513)

Partnership. An unincorporated business owned by two or more individuals. (3)

Patents. Exclusive rights to produce and sell goods with one or more unique features. (398)

Payroll. The total amount earned by employees for a certain period. (425)

Payroll register. A multicolumn form used to assemble and summarize payroll data at the end of each payroll period. (431)

Period costs. Those costs that are used up in generating revenue during the current period and that are not involved in the manufacturing process. These costs are recognized as expenses on the current period's income statement. (683)

Periodic inventory system. A system of inventory accounting in which only the revenue from sales is recorded each time a sale is made. The cost of merchandise on hand at the end of a period is determined by a detailed listing (physical inventory) of the merchandise on hand. (226)

Perpetual inventory system. A system of inventory accounting in which both the revenue from sales and the cost of merchandise sold are recorded each time a sale is made, so that the records continually disclose the amount of the inventory on hand. (226)

Petty cash fund. A special cash fund used to pay relatively small amounts. (289)

Physical inventory. The detailed listing of merchandise on hand. (226, 345)

Pooling-of-interests method. A method of accounting for an affiliation of two corporations resulting from an exchange of voting stock of one corporation for substantially all the voting stock of the other corporation. (513)

Post-closing trial balance. A trial balance prepared after all of the temporary accounts have been closed. (146)

Posting. The process of transferring debits and credits from a journal to the accounts. (52)

Postretirement benefits. Rights to benefits that employees earn during their term of employment for themselves and their dependents after they retire. (440)

Predetermined factory overhead rate. The rate used to apply factory overhead costs to the goods manufactured. The rate is determined by dividing the budgeted overhead cost by the estimated activity usage at the beginning of the fiscal period. (678)

Preferred stock. A class of stock with preferential rights over common stock. (469)

Premium. The excess of the issue price of bonds over the face amount. (405); The excess of the sales price of stock over its par amount. (472, 540)

Prepaid expenses. Purchased commodities or services that have not been used up at the end of an accounting period. (13)

Present value. The estimated worth today of an amount of cash to be received (or paid) in the future. (540)

Present value concept. A concept in which cash to be received (or paid) in the future is worth less than the same amount of money held today. (954)

Present value index. An index computed by dividing the total present value of the net cash flow to be received from a proposed capital investment by the amount to be invested. (957)

Present value of an annuity. The sum of the present values of a series of equal cash flows to be received at fixed intervals. (542, 955)

Price-earnings ratio. The ratio, often called the P/E ratio, computed by dividing the market price per share of common stock at a specific date by the company's earnings per share on common stock. (640)

Prior-period adjustments. Corrections of material errors related to a prior period or periods, excluded from the determination of net income. (507)

Proceeds. The net amount available from discounting a note. (423)

Process cost system. A type of cost accounting system that accumulates costs for each of the various departments or processes within a manufacturing facility. (673, 715)

Process manufacturers. Manufacturers that use machines to process a continuous flow of raw materials through various stages of completion into a finished state. (715)

Product cost concept. A concept used in applying the cost-plus approach to product pricing in which only the costs of manufacturing the product, termed the product cost, are included in the cost amount to which the markup is added. (922)

Product costs. The three components of manufacturing cost: direct materials, direct labor, and factory overhead costs. (673)

Production bottleneck. A condition that occurs when product demand exceeds production capacity. The bottleneck resource is a portion of the production process that is operating at 100% of capacity and is unable to meet product demand. (926)

Production budget. A budget of estimated production. (803)

Profitability. The ability of a firm to earn income. (631)

Profit center. A decentralized unit in which the manager has the responsibility and the authority to make decisions that affect both costs and revenues (and thus profits). (878)

Profit margin. A component of the rate of return on investment, computed as the ratio of income from operations to sales. (883)

Profit-volume chart. A chart used to assist management in understanding the relationship between profit and volume. (762)

Promissory note. A written promise to pay a sum in money on demand or at a definite time. (319)

Proprietorship. A business owned by one individual. (3)

Purchase method. The accounting method employed when a parent company acquires a controlling share of the voting stock of a subsidiary other than by the exchange of voting common stock. (513)

Purchases discounts. An available discount taken by a buyer for early payment of an invoice. (228)

Purchases journal. The special journal in which all items purchased on account are recorded. (192)

Purchases returns and allowances. Reductions in purchases, resulting from merchandise being returned to the seller or from the seller's reduction in the original purchase price. (229)

Q

Quick ratio. A financial ratio that measures the ability to pay current liabilities within a short period of time. (440)

Quick assets. The sum of cash, receivables, and marketable securities. (633)

R

Rate earned on common stockholders' equity. A measure of profitability computed by dividing net income, reduced by preferred dividend requirements, by common stockholders' equity. (639)

Rate earned on stockholders' equity. A measure of profitability computed by dividing net income by total stockholders' equity. (638)

Rate earned on total assets. A measure of the profitability of assets, computed as net income plus interest expense divided by total average assets. (638)

Rate of return on investment (ROI). A measure of managerial efficiency in the use of investments in assets, computed as income from operations divided by invested assets. (882)

Ratio of fixed assets to long-term liabilities. A financial ratio that provides a measure indicating the margin of safety to creditors. (400, 635)

Ratio of liabilities to stockholders'equity. The relationship between the total claims of the creditors and owners. (636)

Ratio of net sales to assets. A profitability measure that shows how effectively a firm utilizes its assets. (637)

Real accounts. Balance sheet accounts. (139)

Receivables. All money claims against other entities, including people, business firms, and other organizations. (311)

Receiving report. The form or electronic transmission used by the receiving personnel to indicate that materials have been received and inspected. (676)

Relevant range. The range of activity over which changes in cost are of interest to management. (749)

Report form. The form of balance sheet with the liabilities and owner's equity sections presented below the assets section. (18, 243)

Residual income. The excess of income from operations over a "minimum" amount of desired income from operations. (885)

Residual value. The estimated recoverable cost of a depreciable asset as of the time of its removal from service. (385)

Responsibility accounting. The process of measuring and reporting operating data by areas of responsibility. (876)

Responsibility center. An organizational unit for which a manager is assigned responsibility for the unit's performance. (796)

Retail inventory method. A means of estimating inventory based on the relationship of the cost and the retail price of merchandise. (359)

Retained earnings. Net income retained in a corporation. (467)

Revenue. The gross increase in owner's equity as a result of business and professional activities that earn income. (13, 45)

Revenue expenditures. Expenditures that benefit only the current period. (390)

Revenue journal. The special journal in which all sales of services on account are recorded. (187)

Revenue recognition concept. The principle by which revenues are recognized in the period in which they are earned. (98)

S

Sales budget. One of the major elements of the income statement budget that indicates the quantity of estimated sales and the expected unit selling price. (802)

Sales discounts. An available discount granted by a seller for early payment of an invoice; a contra account to Sales. (232)

Sales mix. The relative distribution of sales among the various products available for sale. (765)

Sales returns and allowances. Reductions in sales, resulting from merchandise being returned by customers or from the seller's reduction in the original sales price; a contra account to Sales. (232)

Selling expenses. Expenses incurred directly in the sale of merchandise. (240)

Services businesses. A business providing services rather than products to customers. (3)

Service department charges. The costs of services provided by an internal service department and transferred to a responsibility center. (879)

Single-step income statement. An income statement in which the total of all expenses is deducted in one step from the total of all revenues. (241)

Sinking fund. Assets set aside in a special fund to be used for a specific purpose. (547)

Slide. The erroneous movement of all digits in a number, one or more spaces to the right or the left, such as writing $542 as $5,420. (66)

Software. The programs that provide the computer with instructions. (197)

Solvency. The ability of a business to pay its debts. (148, 631)

Special journals. Journals designed to be used for recording a single type of transaction. (186)

Standard cost. A detailed estimate of what a product should cost. (840)

Standard cost systems. Accounting systems that use standards for each element of manufacturing cost entering into the finished product. (840)

Stated value. A value approved by the board of directors of a corporation for no-par stock. Similar to par value. (469)

Statement of cash flows. A summary of the major cash receipts and cash payments for a period. (16, 577)

Statement of owner's equity. A summary of the changes in the owner's equity of a business that have occurred during a specific period of time. (16)

Statement of stockholders' equity. A summary of the changes in the stockholders' equity of a corporation that have occurred during a specific period of time. (507)

Static budget. A budget that does not adjust to changes in activity levels. (799)

Stock. Shares of ownership of a corporation. (465)

Stock dividend. Distribution of a company's own stock to its shareholders. (478)

Stock split. A reduction in the par or stated value of a share of common stock and the issuance of a proportionate number of additional shares. (475)

Stockholders. The owners of a corporation. (465)

Stockholders' equity. The equity of the stockholders of a corporation. (467)

Straight-line depreciation method. A method of depreciation that provides for equal periodic depreciation expense over the estimated life of an asset. (386)

Subsidiary company. The corporation that is controlled by a parent company. (513)

Subsidiary ledger. A ledger containing individual accounts with a common characteristic. (185)

Sum-of-the-years-digits depreciation method. A method of depreciation that provides for declining periodic depreciation expense over the estimated life of an asset. (401)

Sunk cost. A cost that is not affected by subsequent decisions. (912)

T

T account. A form of account resembling the letter T, showing debits on the left and credits on the right. (46)

Target cost concept. A concept used to design and manufacture a product at a cost that will deliver a target profit for a given market-determined price. (925)

Taxable income. The base on which the amount of income tax is determined. (499)

Temporary accounts. Revenue, expense, or income summary accounts that are periodically closed; nominal accounts. (139)

Temporary differences. Differences between income before income tax and taxable income created by items that are recognized in one period for income statement purposes and in another period for tax purposes. Such differences reverse, or turn around, in later years. (499)

Temporary investments. Investments in securities that can be readily sold when cash is needed. (508)

Theoretical standards. Standards that represent levels of performance that can be achieved only under perfect operating conditions. (841)

Theory of constraints (TOC). A manufacturing strategy that attempts to remove the influence of bottlenecks (constraints) on a process. (926)

Time tickets. The form on which the amount of time spent by each employee and the labor cost incurred for each individual job, or for factory overhead, are recorded. (676)

Time value of money concept. The concept that an amount of money invested today will earn income. (951)

Total cost concept. A concept used in applying the cost-plus approach to product pricing in which all the costs of manufacturing the product plus the selling and administrative expenses are included in the cost amount to which the markup is added. (921)

Trade discounts. Special discounts from published list prices offered by sellers to certain classes of buyers. (234)

Trade-in allowance. The amount a seller grants a buyer for a fixed asset that is traded in for a similar asset. (393)

Trademark. A name, term, or symbol used to identify a business and its products. (399)

Trading security. A debt or equity security that management intends to actively trade for profit. (508)

Transfer price. The price charged one decentralized unit by another for the goods or services provided. (887)

Transposition. The erroneous arrangement of digits in a number, such as writing $542 as $524. (66)

Treasury stock. A corporation's issued stock that has been reacquired. (474)

Trial balance. A summary listing of the titles and balances of the accounts in the ledger. (64)

Two-column journal. An all-purpose general journal. (52)

U

Uncollectible accounts expense. The operating expense incurred because of the failure to collect receivables. (314)

Underapplied factory overhead. The amount of actual factory overhead in excess of the factory overhead applied to production during a period. (680)

Unearned revenue. The liability created by receiving cash in advance of providing goods or services. (54)

Unit contribution margin. The dollars available from each unit of sales to cover fixed costs and provide operating profits. (756)

Unit of measure concept. A concept of accounting that requires that economic data be recorded in dollars. (11)

Units-of-production depreciation method. A method of depreciation that provides for depreciation expense based on the expected productive capacity of an asset. (387)

Unrealized holding gain or loss. The difference between the fair market values of the securities and their cost. (509)

V

Variable cost concept. A concept used in applying the cost-plus approach to product pricing in which only the variable costs are included in the cost amount to which the markup is added. (923)

Variable costing. The concept that considers the cost of products manufactured to be composed only of those manufacturing costs that increase or decrease as the volume of production rises or falls (direct materials, direct labor, and variable factory overhead). (954)

Variable costs. Costs that vary in total dollar amount as the level of activity changes. (749)

Vertical analysis. An analysis that compares each item in a current statement witha total amount within the same statement. (112, 629)

Volume variance. The difference between the budgeted fixed overhead at 100% of normal capacity and the standard fixed overhead for the actual production achieved during the period. (850)

Voucher. A document that serves as evidence of authority to pay cash. (281)

Voucher system. Records, methods, and procedures used in verifying and recording liabilities and paying and recording cash payments. (281)

W

Working capital. The excess of the current assets of a business over its current liabilities. (148, 632)

Work in process inventory. The direct materials costs, the direct labor costs, and the applied factory overhead costs that have entered into the manufacturing process, but are associated with products that have not been finished. (674)

Work sheet. A working paper used to summarize adjusting entries and assist in the preparation of financial statements. (136)

Y

Yield. A measure of materials usage efficiency; it measures the ratio of the materials output quantity to the materials input quantity. Yields less than 1.0 are the result of materials losses in the process. (728)

Z

Zero-based budgeting. A concept of budgeting that requires all levels of management to start from zero and estimate budget data as if there had been no previous activities in their unit. (799)

Subject Index

A

B

C

F

G

H

I

J

N

O

Q

R

Company Index

Index of Web Site Addresses

Note: These Web site addresses may also be accessed at **warren.swcollege.com**.

Photo Credits

Page xv	Author photos © 1997, Olan Mills
Page 19	© Coco McCoy/Rainbow
Page 68	© 1996, PhotoDisc, Inc.
Page 113	© Tony Freeman/PhotoEdit
Page 149	© AP Wide World Photos
Page 200	© AP Wide World Photos
Page 245	© Jay Hamburger/Black Star Publishing Company
Page 292	© Jennifer Cogswell/The Picture Cube, Inc.
Page 324	© Terry Barner/Unicorn Stock Photos
Page 362	© 1988 Lucasfilm Ltd./Ralph Nelson Jr.
Page 401	© P. Perrin/Sygma
Page 480	© 1995 Ann and Carl Purcell/Words & Pictures
Page 516	© Brooks Kraft/Sygma
Page 555	© Sipa Press
Page 594	© James V. Biver
Page 645	© Tony Freeman/ PhotoEdit
Page 687	© Paramount Pictures Corp./Kobal Collection
Page 730	© Michael Cooper/AllSport USA
Page 769	© Ebet Roberts/Ebet Roberts Photography
Page 813	© Universal City/Kobal Collection
Page 856	© Gary J. Benson Photography
Page 890	© Jon Simon/Gamma Liaison International
Page 928	© Michael Newman/PhotoEdit
Page 965	© Elsa Hacch/Gamma Liaison International

Abbreviations and Acronyms Commonly Used in Business and Accounting

AAA	American Accounting Association
ABC	Activity-based costing
AICPA	American Institute of Certified Public Accountants
CIA	Certified Internal Auditor
CIM	Computer-integrated manufacturing
CMA	Certified Management Accountant
CPA	Certified Public Accountant
Cr.	Credit
Dr.	Debit
EFT	Electronic funds transfer
EPS	Earnings per share
FAF	Financial Accounting Foundation
FASB	Financial Accounting Standards Board
FEI	Financial Executives Institute
FICA tax	Federal Insurance Contributions Act tax
FIFO	First-in, first-out
FOB	Free on board
GAAP	Generally accepted accounting principles
GASB	Governmental Accounting Standards Board
GNP	Gross National Product
IMA	Institute of Management Accountants
IRC	Internal Revenue Code
IRS	Internal Revenue Service
JIT	Just-in-time
LIFO	Last-in, first-out
Lower of C or M	Lower of cost or market
MACRS	Modified Accelerated Cost Recovery System
n/30	Net 30
n/eom	Net, end-of-month
P/E Ratio	Price-earnings ratio
POS	Point of sale
ROI	Return on investment
SEC	Securities and Exchange Commission
TQC	Total quality control

Classification of Accounts

Account Title	*Account Classification*	*Normal Balance*	*Financial Statement*
Accounts Payable	Current liability	Credit	Balance sheet
Accounts Receivable	Current asset	Debit	Balance sheet
Accumulated Depreciation	Fixed asset	Credit	Balance sheet
Accumulated Depletion	Fixed asset	Credit	Balance sheet
Advertising Expense	Operating expense	Debit	Income statement
Allowance for Doubtful Accounts	Current asset	Credit	Balance sheet
Amortization Expense	Operating expense	Debit	Income statement
Bonds Payable	Long-term liability	Credit	Balance sheet
Building	Fixed asset	Debit	Balance sheet
__________ Capital	Owners' equity	Credit	Statement of owner's equity/ Balance sheet
Capital Stock	Stockholders' equity	Credit	Balance sheet
Cash	Current asset	Debit	Balance sheet
Cash Dividends	Stockholders' equity	Debit	Retained earnings statement
Cash Dividends Payable	Current liability	Credit	Balance sheet
Common Stock	Stockholders' equity	Credit	Balance sheet
Cost of Merchandise (Goods) Sold	Cost of merchandise (goods sold)	Debit	Income statement
Deferred Income Tax Payable	Current liability/Long-term liability	Credit	Balance sheet
Depletion Expense	Operating expense	Debit	Income statement
Discount on Bonds Payable	Long-term liability	Debit	Balance sheet
Dividend Revenue	Other income	Credit	Income statement
Dividends	Stockholders' equity	Debit	Retained earnings statement
Donated Capital	Stockholders' equity	Credit	Balance sheet
Employees Federal Income Tax Payable	Current liability	Credit	Balance sheet
Equipment	Fixed asset	Debit	Balance sheet
Exchange Gain	Other income	Credit	Income statement
Exchange Loss	Other expense	Debit	Income statement
Factory Overhead (Overapplied)	Deferred credit	Credit	Balance sheet (interim)
Factory Overhead (Underapplied)	Deferred debit	Debit	Balance sheet (interim)
Federal Income Tax Payable	Current liability	Credit	Balance sheet
Federal Unemployment Tax Payable	Current liability	Credit	Balance sheet
Finished Goods	Current asset	Debit	Balance sheet
Gain on Disposal of Fixed Assets	Other income	Credit	Income statement
Gain on Redemption of Bonds	Extraordinary item	Credit	Income statement
Gain on Sale of Investments	Other income	Credit	Income statement
Goodwill	Intangible asset	Debit	Balance sheet
Income Tax Expense	Income tax	Debit	Income statement
Income Tax Payable	Current liability	Credit	Balance sheet
Insurance Expense	Operating expense	Debit	Income statement
Interest Expense	Other expense	Debit	Income statement
Interest Receivable	Current asset	Debit	Balance sheet
Interest Revenue	Other income	Credit	Income statement
Investment in Bonds	Investment	Debit	Balance sheet
Investment in Stocks	Investment	Debit	Balance sheet
Investment in Subsidiary	Investment	Debit	Balance sheet
Land	Fixed asset	Debit	Balance sheet
Loss on Disposal of Fixed Assets	Other expense	Debit	Income statement
Loss on Redemption of Bonds	Extraordinary item	Debit	Income statement
Loss on Sale of Investments	Other expense	Debit	Income statement